International Documents and Analysis, Volume 1

THE CRISIS IN KOSOVO 1989-1999

BY

MARC WELLER

Centre of International Studies
University of Cambridge

Published by Documents & Analysis Publishing Ltd, 1999

Published by Documents & Analysis Publishing Ltd., PO Box 813, Cambridge, CB3 7GH, UK

www.docuanalysis.com

Distributed by:

Book Systems Plus, UK, e-mail: BSP2B@aol.com

Other titles to be available in the International Documents and Analysis Series:

Volume 2:   The Kosovo Conflict: Forced Displacement, the Conduct and Termination of Hostilities and the Renewed Search for a Settlement
Volume 3:   Coercive Disarmament: Iraq, UNSCOM and the Use of Force
Volume 4:   Armed Samaritans: Humanitarian Intervention Cases
Volume 5:   No Place to Hide: New Developments in the Exercise of International Criminal Jurisdiction
Volume 6:   Of Angels and Warlords: International Peace-enforcement in Somalia
Volume 7:   The Genie and the Bottle: International Attempts to Regulate Biotechnology
Volume 8:   Regulating Statehood: Innovative Attempts to Solve Self-Determination Conflicts
Volume 9:   Anatomy of Genocide: The Case of Bosnia and Herzegovina
Volume 10: The New European Security Architecture

100 205 1909

This volume is dedicated in gratitude to A. and W.P.G.

A catalogue record for this book is available from the British Library and the Library of Congress respectively.

ISBN 1 903033 00 4

Set in Garamond and Times Roman by Documents & Analysis Publishing Ltd. Printed in the United Kingdom by the University Printing Service, Cambridge University Press, for Documents & Analysis Publishing Ltd.

The International Documents & Analysis Series:
In Search of an International Constitutional Order

This *Series* presents the key materials necessary for an understanding of significant episodes or issues in international relations. Episodes which provide significant challenges for the international community are chosen for inclusion in the Series, with a view to illuminating new approaches that have been adopted in the international attempts to address them. Over time, it is hoped that a unique archive can be provided which will evidence the evolution of international institutions, standards and practices, especially in situations of crisis. The materials are supported by original analysis which explains and explores the measures taken by the principal actors involved and also considers the contribution of the respective episode as a whole to broader developments in the international system.

The *Series* also covers substantive issue areas demanding fresh international responses. Volumes will be devoted to problems such as international criminal responsibility, self-determination, humanitarian action, collective security, biotechnology, international environmental regulation, etc. Considerable space is devoted in these volumes to a critical assessment of these developments, once again investigating their contribution to the evolution of an international constitutional order at the turn of the millennium.

The *Series* is aimed at those who study international relations, or who are practitioners of or commentators on international affairs, as well as the wider public. The books have been specifically conceived so as to be accessible to the non-expert, while nevertheless contributing materials and critical ideas which will also be of interest to the specialist. Every effort is made to ensure the timely publication of particular volumes.

The *Series* is available in individual volumes, or by way of an annual subscription. The subscription covers at least 1,500 pages a year, in up to five volumes. Some volumes will be consolidated and also published on CD-ROM. The Series will also be available by way of an internet subscription in due course, at a significantly reduced rate to those subscribing to the hard copy edition.

Acknowledgement and Disclaimer

This book has benefited from the friendly support of Ms Caroline Soper of the Royal Institute of International Affairs, Dr Noel Malcolm, Professor Stefan Troebst, Dr Enver Hasani, T. M., Dr Stefan Wolff, Professor Paul Williams, Tim Judah, Mrs Wendy Cooke, Mrs Ann Kemp, Mrs Rachel Taft, Ms Wendy Slaninka and many others. Mr William Burke-White provided critical support for this project and wrote the Chronology. The cover photograph was kindly furnished by the United Nations Secretariat. The maps were drawn for this volume by Mr Ian Agnew of the University of Cambridge Department of Geography—the spelling of place-names on these maps is incidental and not intended to convey one particular view or another. A special thanks is due to Mr Andrew Harvey of Cambridge University Press who most ably guided this project through production and Dr Anne Dunbar, who was responsible for sub-editing of the analysis and proof-reading of the entire book. Of course, the views expressed in the analysis are those of the author alone. Responsibility for the contents of the documentary materials reprinted in this book lies with the originator, not the author/editor, publishers and/or distributors of this volume.

The author served as a legal advisor to the government of Kosovo and attended the London, Rambouillet and Paris peace conferences in that function. However, in keeping with the *International Documents & Analysis Series* as a whole, the presentation of the analysis and the selection of documentary materials conforms to standards of academic objectivity. The manuscript has been externally assessed to this end. In general, materials have been left unedited, to retain their authenticity, although document titles have on occasion been abbreviated. For the same reason, no effort has been made to impose a uniform style of writing or spelling on these materials, although some obvious typing errors have been corrected. The spelling of 'Kosovo' has been adopted throughout the book, merely because that remains, for the moment, the accepted usage. However, 'Kosova' is used in relation to materials emanating from the Kosova Government. The amount of materials reprinted in this volume has made it necessary to set the documents in rather small type. It is hoped that the reader will share the view that this is preferable to omitting a significant number of them altogether. Source references to official materials have been placed at the head of the relevant document.

Abbreviations

CSCE	Conference for Security and Cooperation in Europe
EC/EU	European Communities/European Union
ECMM	European Communities Monitoring Mission in the former Yugoslavia
FRY	Federal Republic of Yugoslavia, established in 1992, after the dissolution of the SFRY
IFOR/SFOR	NATO-led Implementation/Stabilizaton Force in Bosnia and Herzegovina established under the 1995 Dayton Accords for Bosnia and Herzegovina
KDOM	Kosovo Diplomatic Observer Mission
KLA	Kosovo Liberation Army (also known as UCK)
KVM	Kosovo Verification Mission
LDK	Moderate Kosovo Albanian party led by Dr Rugova
MUP	Serb special police
OSCE	Organization for Security and Cooperation in Europe
NATO	North Atlantic Treaty Organization
SFRY	Socialist Federal Republic of Yugoslavia, consisting of Bosnia and Herzegovina, Croatia, Macedonia, Montenegro, Serbia, Slovenia and the autonomous provinces of Kosovo and Vojvodina, dissolved in 1991/2
UNHCR	United Nations High Commissioner for Refugees
UNPROFOR	United Nations Protection Force in the Former Yugoslavia
UNPREDEP	United Nations Preventative Deployment in Macedonia, initially part of UNPROFOR
UNSC	United Nations Security Council
UNSG	United Nations Secretary-General
VJ	Yugoslav Army
WEU	Western European Union

Some Key Players

Fehmi Agani	Leader of the informal Kosovo negotiating team for the Hill shuttle mission, member of the Kosovo delegation of Rambouillet.
Madeleine Albright	US Secretary of State, reputed to maintain a hawkish stance on Kosovo and one of the principal driving forces behind the Rambouillet conference.
Kofi Annan	UN Secretary-General.
Bujar Bukoshi	Prime Minister of the Republic of Kosovo, based in Germany until the termination of hostilities in June 1999, when he returned to Prishtina.
Christopher Hill	US Ambassador to Macedonia, led the shuttle diplomacy aimed throughout 1998 at achieving a diplomatic settlement of the crisis and acted as one of three Contact Group Negotiators at Rambouillet.
Richard Holbrooke	US Special Envoy, negotiated the Dayton accords and an agreement with President Milosevic on Kosovo in October 1998.
Igor Ivanov	Russian Foreign Minister.
Zivadin Jovanovic	FRY Foreign Minister.
Ratko Markovic	Vice President of the Republic of Serbia, head of the FRY/Serb delegation at Rambouillet and other talks.
Boris Mayorski	Russian member of the Contact Group team of three negotiators at Rambouillet
Slobodan Milosevic	President of the Republic of Serbia until 1997, then President of the Federal Republic of Yugoslavia.
Milan Milotinovic	President of the Republic of Serbia.
Wolfgang Petritsch	EU Special Representative and one of the three Contact Group Negotiators at Rambouillet.
Rexhep Qosja	Leader of the Kosovo United Democratic Movement (LBD) and member of the Kosovo delegation at Rambouillet.
Ibrahim Rugova	Elected President of the Republic of Kosova in 1992, re-elected in March 1998, architect of a policy of moderation among ethnic Albanians in Kosovo and member of Kosovo delegation.
Javier Solana	Secretary-General of NATO.
Hashim Thaci	Member of the leadership of the KLA, Chairman of the Kosovo delegation at Rambouillet, later proclaimed by the KLA and some other Kosovo political parties head of an interim government.

CONTENTS

Source references are placed at the head of documents.

CHAPTER 1: CHRONOLOGY..**15**

CHAPTER 2: INTRODUCTION **24**

CHAPTER 3: THE POSITIONS OF THE PARTIES **34**
   A.   MEMORANDUM PREPARED BY THE FRY ON KOSOVO AND METOHIJA, PRESENTED ON 23 MARCH 1998............**38**
   B.   GOVERNMENT OF KOSOVA: A CASE FOR INDEPENDENCE, 31 SEPTEMBER 1998 ....**42**

CHAPTER 4: CONSTITUTIONAL ISSUES **45**
   A.   THE PERIOD 1943-1990 ....*50*
       *1. 1st Conference of the National Liberation Council for Kosovo & Dukagjin Plateau, 31 Dec. 1943—2 Jan. 1944...............*50
       *2. Constitution of the Federal People's Republic of Yugoslavia, 1946 ....*50
       *3. Constitution of the Federal People's Republic of Yugoslavia, 1953 ....*51
       *4. Constitution of the Socialist Federal Republic of Yugoslavia, 1963 ....*52
       *5. Constitution of the Socialist Republic of Serbia, 1963 ....*52
       *6. Constitution of the Socialist Federal Republic of Yugoslavia, 1974 ....*53
       *7. Constitution of the Socialist Republic of Serbia, 1974 ....*54
       *8. Constitution of the Socialist Autonomous Province of Kosovo, 1974 ....*56
   B.   THE DEVELOPMENTS OF 1989-1992 ....*58
       *1. Constitutional Amendments of the SR of Serbia, 1989 ....*59
       *2. Law on the Restriction of Real Property Transactions, 1989 ....*59
       *3. Law on the Amendment to the Law on the Restriction of Real Property Transactions, 1989 ....*60
       *4. Programme for Realization of Peace, Freedom, Equality, Democracy and Prosperity of SAP Kosovo, 30 March 1990 ...*60
       *5. Amendment of the University Law, 1990...*60
       *6. Law on the Actions of Republic Agencies under Special Circumstances, 26 June 1990 ....*60
       *7. Decision about the Existence of Special Circumstances on the Territory of the SAP of Kosovo, 26 June 1990 ...*60
       *8. SR Serbia, Law Terminating Work of SAP of Kosovo Assembly and the Executive Council, 5 July 1990 .....*61
       *9. Serb Assembly Regulation on Implementing Law Terminating Work of SAP Kosovo Assembly and Executive Council, 13 July 1990.*62
      *10. Constitution of the Socialist Republic of Serbia, 28 September 1990 ....*62
      *11. Law on Labour Relations under Special Circumstances, 1990 ....*62
      *12. Law on the Restriction of Real Property Transactions, 1991...*62
      *13. Elementary School Law, 1992 ....*63
      *14. Secondary School Law, 1992 ....*63
      *15. High School Law, 1992 ....*63
      *16. Declaration of Joint Session of the SFRY, Republic of Serbia and Republic of Montenegro Assemblies, 27 April 1992.......*63
      *17. Constitution of the Federal Republic of Yugoslavia, April 1992...*63
   C.   DECISIONS TAKEN IN KOSOVO *64
       *1. Declaration of the Albanian Political Parties of Kosova, 30 June 1990...*64
       *2. Assembly of Kosova, Constitutional Declaration, 2 July 1990...*64
       *3. Resolution of the Assembly of Kosova, 7 September 1990 ....*64
       *4. Constitution of the Republic of Kosova, 7 September 1990...*65
       *5. Resolution of the Assembly of the Republic of Kosova on Independence, 22 September 1991..............*65
       *6. Central Board of Kosova for the Conduct of the Referendum, Result, 7 October 1991 ....*72
       *7. Coordination Council of Albanian Political Parties in Yugoslavia, Political Declaration, 12 October 1991 .....*72
       *8. Kosova Report: 24 May Multiparty Elections for Parliament and President of Kosova, 15 June 1992...........*73

CHAPTER 5: INITIAL ATTEMPTS TO ADDRESS THE CRISIS: THE LONDON CONFERENCE AND THE OSCE MISSION OF LONG DURATION **74**
   A.   THE INTERNATIONAL CONFERENCE ON YUGOSLAVIA, 1991-1992 ....*80
       *1. Peace Conference on Yugoslavia, Carrington Draft Convention for a General Settlement, 18 October 1991.....*80
       *2. Peace Conference on Yugoslavia, Second Carrington Draft Provisions for a Convention, 1 November 1991......*80
       *3. EPC Guidelines on the Recognition of New States in Eastern Europe and in Soviet Union, 16 December 1991...*80
       *4. EPC Declaration on Yugoslavia, 16 December 1991 ....*81
       *5. Letter from Dr Rugova to Lord Carrington, Peace Conference on Yugoslavia, 22 December 1991 ....*81
       *6. Opinion No. 1 of the Arbitration Commission on the former Yugoslavia, 11 January 1992..................*81
       *7. Opinion No. 2 of the Arbitration Commission on the former Yugoslavia, 11 January 1992..................*82
       *8. Opinion No. 3 of the Arbitration Commission on the former Yugoslavia, 11 January 1992..................*82
       *9. Albanian Political Parties and Council for Defence of Human Rights in Prishtina, Memorandum, April 1992........*83
      *10. Letter from the Federal Republic of Yugoslavia to the President of the Security Council, 17 August 1992.........*85

11.   *Letter from Lord Carrington, Chairman, Conference on Yugoslavia, to Dr I. Rugova, 17 August 1992*...............86
12.   *Kosovo Memorandum to the International Conference on the former Yugoslavia, 26 August 1992*.....................86
13.   *London Conference, Statement by Mr Alfred Serreqi, Albanian Delegation, 26 August 1992*...........................88
14.   *London International Conference on the Former Yugoslavia, Work Programme, 27 August 1992*.......................89
15.   *London Conference, Co-Chairman's Paper on Serbia and Montenegro, 27 August 1992*...............................89
16.   *Security Council Resolution 777 (1992), 19 September 1992*..89

B.   THE FOLLOW-ON TALKS OF THE SPECIAL GROUP ON KOSOVO...89
1.   *Statement by the Republic of Kosovo to Conference on Yugoslavia, Geneva, 16 September 1992*.....................89
2.   *Report of the Secretary-General on the International Conference on the Former Yugoslavia, 11 November 1992*......89
3.   *Letter from Kosovo to the Special Group on Kosovo, Geneva Conference on the Former Yugoslavia, undated*.........90
4.   *Secretary-General Report: Recent Activities of the Working Groups, 30 March 1993*...............................91
5.   *Joint Action Programme of France, Spain, Russian Federation, the United Kingdom and the USA, 22 May 1993*.......92
6.   *Yugoslavia, Statement on Negotiations on Education Issues in Kosovo and Metohija, 29 August 1994*...............92
7.   *St Egidio [St Eugidio] Education Agreement, 1 September 1996*...93
8.   *Agreed Measures for the Implementation of the Agreement on Education, 23 March 1988.*.............................93

C.   INITIAL DECISIONS OF THE CSCE/OSCE...94
1.   *Decision of the Committee of Senior Officials of the CSCE, Prague, 22 October 1991*..............................94
2.   *CSO Decision on Human Rights Rapporteur Follow-up Mission to Yugoslavia, 12 May 1992*..........................94
3.   *CSO Statement on the former Yugoslavia, 20 May 1992*..94
4.   *Decisions of the Committee of Senior Officials, Helsinki, 8/10 June 1992*..94
5.   *Decision of the Committee of Senior Officials on the Suspension of Participation by the FRY, 7 July 1992*.........95
6.   *Decisions of the Committee of Senior Officials, Prague, 13-14 August 1992*...95
7.   *CSO Decision on Mission of Long Duration, 16/18 September 1992*...96
8.   *CSO Decision on Missions of Long Duration and Monitor Mission to Skopje, 5/6 November 1992*.....................96
9.   *Stockholm Meeting of the CSCE Council Decisions, 15 December 1992*...96
10.   *CSO Decision on Missions of Long Duration and the Spillover Mission, 26/28 April 1993*............................96
11.   *CSO Decision on the Former Yugoslavia, 29/30 June 1993*..96
12.   *Security Council Resolution 855, 9 August 1993*...97

D.   REPORTS OF THE CSCE MISSIONS AND RELATED COMMUNICATIONS...97
1.   *Report of the Human Rights Rapporteur Mission to Yugoslavia, 24 January 1992*....................................97
2.   *Republic of Serbia, Commentary Regarding the CSCE Mission on Human Rights in Yugoslavia, 6 March 1992*........100
3.   *Letter to CSCE from Kosovo Political Parties & Council for the Defence of Human Rights, 6 May 1992*..............100
4.   *Report of the Conflict Prevention Centre Fact-finding Mission to Kosovo, 5 June 1992*.............................102
5.   *Report of the Exploratory Mission to Kosovo, Vojvodina and Sandjak, 2-8 August 1992*.............................104
6.   *Interim Report from the Head of the Missions of Long Duration, 27 September 1992*................................106
7.   *CSCE Mission in Kosovo, Report on Kosovo Stalemate, 16 November 1992*...107
8.   *CSCE Missions to Kosovo, Sandzak and Vojvodina, Interim Report, 17 November 1992*..............................108
9.   *Interim Report of Head of Missions of Long Duration to Kosovo, Sandjak and Vojvodina, 6 December 1992*..........110
10.   *CSCE Mission in Kosova, Elections of 20 December 1992 in Kosovo, 23 December 1992*..............................112
11.   *CSCE Mission of Long Duration Report: Concern over Police Brutality in Kosovo, 23 December 1992*................112
12.   *7th Interim Report, Head of Missions to Kosovo, Sandjak & Vojvodina, 16 December 1992*...........................113
13.   *CSCE Mission in Kosovo, Fortnightly Report No. 1, 6 January 1993*...113
14.   *CSCE Mission Kosovo, Substantial Deduction of the Dakovica Hospital, 15 January 1993*............................114
15.   *CSCE Mission to Kosovo, Fortnightly Report No. 2, 18 January 1993*..115
16.   *CSCE Mission Kosovo, Fortnightly Report No. 4/93, 18 February 1993*..115
17.   *CSCE Kosovo, Fortnightly Report No. 5, 4 March 1993*..116
18.   *CSCE Mission in Kosovo, Special Report, 5 March 1993*...117
19.   *Special Report: Kosovo-Problems and Prospects, Tore Bogh, Head of Missions, 29 June 1993*........................117

CHAPTER 6: HUMAN RIGHTS ISSUES..**120**

A.   RESOLUTIONS OF THE UNITED NATIONS GENERAL ASSEMBLY..125
1.   *General Assembly Resolution 47/147, Situation of human rights, 18 December 1992*.................................125
2.   *United Nations General Assembly Resolution 48/153, Situation of human rights 20 December 1993*..................125
3.   *General Assembly Resolution 49/196, Situation of human rights, 23 December 1994*................................125
4.   *General Assembly Resolution 49/204, Situation of human rights in Kosovo, 23 December 1994*......................126
5.   *General Assembly Resolution 50/190, Situation of human rights in Kosovo, 22 December 1995*......................127
6.   *General Assembly Resolution 50/193, Situation of human rights, 22 December 1995*................................128
7.   *General Assembly Resolution 51/111, Situation of human rights in Kosovo, 12 December 1996*......................128
8.   *General Assembly Resolution 51/116, Situation of human rights, 12 December 1996*................................129
9.   *General Assembly Resolution 52/147, Situation of human rights, 12 December 1997*................................129
10.   *General Assembly Resolution 52/139, Situation of human rights in Kosovo, 1 December 1997*.......................129
11.   *General Assembly Resolution 53/163, Situation of human rights, 9 December 1998*.................................130
12.   *General Assembly Resolution 53/164, Situation of human rights in Kosovo, 9 December 1998*.......................131

B.   THE UN COMMISSION ON HUMAN RIGHTS AND ITS SUB-COMMISSION...133
1.   *Commission Resolution 1992/S-1/1, 14 August 1992*..133
2.   *Commission Resolution 1992/S-2, Human rights in the former Yugoslavia, 1 December 1992*........................133

Contents

3.   *Commission Resolution 1993/7, Human rights in the former Yugoslavia, 23 February 1993* *133*
4.   *Commission Resolution 1994/72, Human rights in the former Yugoslavia, 9 March 1994* *134*
5.   *Commission Resolution 1994/76, Human rights in Kosovo, 9 March 1994* *134*
6.   *Letter from the FRY to the Chairman of the Commission on Human Rights, 15 February 1995* *134*
7.   *Commission Resolution 1995/89, Human rights in the former Yugoslavia, 8 March 1995* *136*
8.   *Sub-Commission Resolution 1995/10, Human rights in Kosovo, 18 August 1995* *136*
9.   *Commission Resolution 1996/71, Human rights in the former Yugoslavia, 23 April 1996* *137*
10.   *Sub-Commission Resolution 1996/2, Human rights in Kosovo, 19 August 1996* *138*
11.   *Commission Resolution 1997/57, Human rights in the former Yugoslavia, 15 April 1997* *138*
12.   *Commission Resolution 1998/79, Human rights in the former Yugoslavia, 22 April 1998* *139*

C.   DECISIONS OF UNITED NATIONS TREATY-BASED HUMAN RIGHTS BODIES 141
1.   *Comments of the Human Rights Committee, FRY, 28 December 1992* *141*
2.   *Concluding Observations, the Committee on Elimination of Racial Discrimination: Yugoslavia, 15 September 1993* *141*
3.   *CERD, Supplementary Report of the FRY, 29 August 1994* *143*
4.   *Concluding Observations of CERD: Yugoslavia, 15/6 March 1995* *148*
5.   *CERD, Periodic Report, Yugoslavia, Addendum, 24 June 1997* *149*
6.   *Concluding Observations of CERD: Yugoslavia, 19 March 1998* *155*
7.   *CERD, Decision 3(53) on the Federal Republic of Yugoslavia 17 August 1998* *156*
8.   *Concluding Observations of Committee on Rights of the Child: Yugoslavia, 13 February 1996* *156*
9.   *Conclusions and Recommendations of Committee against Torture: Yugoslavia, 16 November 1998.* *157*

D.   SELECTED REPORTS OF THE UN COMMISSION ON HUMAN RIGHTS SPECIAL RAPPORTEUR FOR THE FORMER YUGOSLAVIA 158
1.   *Report on the Situation of Human Rights in the former Yugoslavia, 28 August 1992* *158*
2.   *Report on the Situation of Human Rights in the former Yugoslavia, 17 November 1992* *158*
3.   *Report on the Situation of Human Rights in the former Yugoslavia, 26 February 1993* *158*
4.   *Report on the Situation of Human Rights in the former Yugoslavia, 1 November 1993* *160*
5.   *Report on the Situation of Human Rights in the former Yugoslavia, 21 February 1994* *161*
6.   *Ninth Periodic Report on the Situation of Human Rights in the former Yugoslavia, 4 November 1994* *161*
7.   *Special Report on the Media of the Special Rapporteur, 13 December 1994* *162*
8.   *Tenth Periodic Report on Human Rights in the former Yugoslavia, 16 January 1995* *162*
9.   *Report by the Special Rapporteur of the Commission on Human Rights, 14 March 1996* *163*
10.   *Periodic Report by the Special Rapporteur, 22 October 1996* *164*
11.   *Special Report on Minorities by the Special Rapporteur, 25 October 1996* *164*
12.   *Report on the Situation of Human Rights in the former Yugoslavia, 4 November 1996* *169*
13.   *Periodic Report of the Special Rapporteur of the Commission on Human Rights, 29 January 1997* *169*
14.   *Special Report: Two Trials of Kosovo, 10 September 1997* *170*
15.   *Periodic Report on the Situation of Human Rights, 17 October 1997* *177*
16.   *Report on the Situation of Human Rights in the Federal Republic of Yugoslavia, 31 October 1997* *177*
17.   *Report on the Situation of Human Rights, 11 September 1998* *180*

E.   REPORTS OF THE UNITED NATIONS SECRETARY-GENERAL 181
1.   *Report of the Secretary-General, 20 November 1995* *181*
2.   *Report of the Secretary-General, 25 October 1996* *182*
3.   *Report of the Secretary-General, 17 October 1997* *183*
4.   *Report of the Secretary-General, 30 October 1998* *183*

CHAPTER 7: GENERAL RESOLUTIONS OF THE SECURITY COUNCIL **185**
1.   *Resolution 1160 (1998), 31 March 1998* *188*
2.   *Resolution 1186 (1998), 21 July 1998* *189*
3.   *Statement by the President of the Security Council, 24 August 1998* *189*
4.   *Resolution 1199 (1998), 23 September 1998* *190*
5.   *Resolution 1203 (1998), 24 October 1998* *191*

CHAPTER 8: INITIAL REPORTS OF THE UN SECRETARY-GENERAL, THE OSCE, NATO AND OTHERS **193**
1.   *Letter from the Secretary-General Addressed to the President of the Security Council, 8 April 1998* *195*
2.   *Report of the Secretary-General Prepared Pursuant to Security Council Resolution 1160, 30 April 1998* *195*
3.   *Report of the Secretary-General Prepared Pursuant to Security Council Resolution 1160, 4 June 1998* *198*
4.   *Report of the Secretary-General Prepared Pursuant to Security Council Resolution 1160, 2 July 1998* *202*
5.   *Report of the Secretary-General on the United Nations Preventative Deployment Force, 14 July 1998* *205*
6.   *Report of the Secretary-General Prepared Pursuant to Security Council Resolution 1160, 5 August 1998* *206*
7.   *Report of the Secretary-General Prepared Pursuant to Security Council Resolution 1160 (1998), 4 September 1998* *211*
8.   *Report of the Secretary-General, Annex, 21 September 1998* *214*
9.   *Report of the Secretary-General, 3 October 1998* *214*
10.   *Letter from the Secretary-General to the President of the Security Council, 14 October 1998* *218*

CHAPTER 9: SANCTIONS, POLITICAL ACTION OF THE EUROPEAN UNION AND CONTACT GROUP DECISIONS **219**
A.   EUROPEAN UNION SANCTIONS 222
1.   *Common Position on extension of suspension of restrictions on trade with FRY, 19 September 1995* *222*

2.   *Common Position on suspension of restrictions on trade with FRY and Bosnian Serbs, 4 December 1995* 222
3.   *Common Position on arms exports to the former Yugoslavia, 26 February 1996.* 222
4.   *Common Position on termination of restrictions on economic and financial relations, 9 December 1996.* 222
5.   *Common Position on restrictive measures against the FRY, 19 March 1998* 222
6.   *Council Regulation (EC) No. 926/98 on reduction of economic relations with FRY, 27 April 1998* 223
7.   *Common Position by the Council on freezing of funds held abroad by FRY and Serbian Governments, 7 May 1998.* 224
8.   *Common Position on the prohibition of new investment in Serbia, 8 June 1998.* 225
9.   *Council Regulation (EC) No. 1295/98 on freezing of funds held abroad of FRY and Republic of Serbia, 22 June 1998* 225
10.   *Council Common Position, Ban on flights by Yugoslav carriers between FRY and the EC, 29 June 1998* 226
11.   *Council Regulation (EC) No. 1607/98 on prohibition of new investment in Republic of Serbia, 24 July 1998.* 226
12.   *EC Council Regulation, No. 1901/98, ban on flights of Yugoslav carriers between FRY & EC, 7 September 1998.* 226
13.   *FRY Statement on the Suspension of Flights of Yugoslav Airlines, 10 October 1998* 227
14.   *Report of the Chairman of UN Committee pursuant to SC Resolution 1160 (1998), 26 February 1999* 227
B.   POLITICAL ACTION OF THE UNION 229
1.   *Council Conclusions on Kosovo, 31 March 1998* 229
2.   *Declaration by EU, associated countries of Central & Eastern Europe & Cyprus on Kosovo, 31 March 1998* 229
3.   *European Council Conclusions on Kosovo, 27 April 1998* 229
4.   *Joint Action on the nomination of an EU Special Representative for the FRY, 8 June 1998* 229
5.   *Declaration by the European Union on Kosovo, 11 June 1998* 230
6.   *Cardiff European Council Presidency Conclusions, Annex 2, Kosovo, 15/16 June 1998* 230
7.   *2111th Council Meeting, General Affairs, Luxembourg, 29 June 1998* 231
8.   *2113th Council Meeting, General Affairs, Brussels, 13 July 1998.* 232
9.   *Declaration by the Presidency on behalf of the European Union on recent fighting in Kosovo, 20 July 1998* 232
10.   *Declaration by the European Union on a comprehensive approach to Kosovo, 27 October 1998* 232
11.   *Vienna European Council, Presidency Conclusions, 11 & 12 December 1998* 233
C.   THE RESPONSE OF THE WESTERN EUROPEAN UNION 233
1.   *WEU Ministerial Council, Rhodes Declaration, 12 May 1998* 233
2.   *WEU Ministerial Council, Rome Declaration, 17 November 1998.* 234
D.   THE DECISIONS OF THE CONTACT GROUP 234
1.   *Statement of the Contact Group Foreign Ministers, New York, 24 September 1997.* 234
2.   *Contact Group Statement on Kosovo, 8 January 1998* 234
3.   *Statement by the Contact Group on Kosovo, Moscow, Russia, 25 February 1998* 235
4.   *Statement by the Contact Group, London, 9 March 1998* 235
5.   *Joint statement of Foreign Ministers of Countries of Southeastern Europe, Bonn, 25 March 1998* 236
6.   *Contact Group and the Foreign Ministers of Canada and Japan, Statement, London, UK, 12 June 1998* 236
7.   *Contact Group Statement, Bonn, 8 July 1998* 237
8.   *Chairman's Conclusions, Contact Group meeting on Kosovo in London, 2 October 1988.* 238
9.   *Contact Group Discussion on Kosovo, Statement by UK Foreign Secretary, 8 October 1998* 238

CHAPTER 10: THE INTERNATIONAL CRIMINAL TRIBUNAL FOR THE FORMER YUGOSLAVIA **239**
1.   *Security Council Resolution 808 (1993), 22 February 1993* 241
2.   *Security Council Resolution 827 (1993), 25 May 1993.* 241
3.   *Statute of the International Criminal Tribunal for the Former Yugoslavia, 25 May 1993* 242
4.   *Prosecutor's Statement Regarding the Tribunal's Jurisdiction over Kosovo, 10 March 1998* 243
5.   *Security Coucil Resolution 1166 (1998), 13 May 1998.* 243
6.   *Communication from the Prosecutor to the Contact Group, 7 July 1998* 243
7.   *ICTY President McDonald Statement to the Security Council, 2 October 1998* 243
8.   *Statement by the Office of the Prosecutor, 7 October 1998* 244
9.   *Statement by the President of the International Tribunal on the Agreements on Kosovo, 14 October 1998.* 245
10.   *Prosecutor seeks assurance from President Milosevic regarding Kosovo investigations, 15 October 1998* 245
11.   *Letter from President McDonald to the President of the Security Council, 22 October 1998* 245
12.   *Statement by Justice Louise Arbour, Prosecutor of the ICTY, 4 November 1998* 246
13.   *Statement by Judge McDonald, President of the ICTFY, 5 November 1998* 246
14.   *Statement by Justice Louise Arbour, Prosecutor of the ICTFY, 5 November 1998* 247
15.   *Letter from the President of the ICTFY to the President of the Security Council, 6 November 1998.* 247
16.   *Security Council Resolution 1207 (1998), 17 November 1998.* 248
17.   *Statement by the President of the ICTFY to the Security Council, 8 December 1998* 248
18.   *Statement by ICTFY Prosecutor Louise Arbour, 16 January 1999* 248
19.   *Letter from the ICTFY President to Foreign Ministers Vedrine and Cook, 22 February 1999* 249
20.   *Letter by the President of the ICTFY to the President of the Security Council, 16 March 1999* 249

CHAPTER 11: THE RESPONSE OF THE ICRC AND THE UNHCR **250**

A.   ICRC   252
1.   *Kosovo: ICRC at the ready, 4 March 1998* 252
2.   *Kosovo: ICRC concerned about escalating violence, 6 March 1998* 252
3.   *Update No. 98/01 on ICRC activities in the FRY: Special focus on Kosovo, 10 March 1998* 252

Contents

4.   Kosovo, Federal Republic of Yugoslavia: Latest developments, 11 March 1998 252
5.   Kosovo: ICRC position on invitation to head investigation, 20 March 1998 252
6.   Update No. 98/03 on activities in response to the crisis in Kosovo, 29 May 1998 252
7.   Kosovo: ICRC urgently requests access to affected area, 3 June 1998 253
8.   Kosovo: Humanitarian situation causing concern, 12 June 1998 253
9.   Update No. 98/04 on activities in response to the crisis in Kosovo, 15 June 1998 253
10.   Update No. 98/05 on activities of the Red Cross and Red Crescent Movement, 26 June 1998 254
11.   FRY: ICRC goes to Decane, 26 June 1998 254
12.   Federal Republic of Yugoslavia: ICRC reaches Kijevo, 2 July 1998 255
13.   Kosovo: ICRC calls for temporary halt to fighting in Orahovac on humanitarian grounds, 22 July 1998 255
14.   Federal Republic of Yugoslavia/Kosovo: ICRC aid for conflict victims, 29 July 1998 256
15.   Update No. 98/06 on the crisis in Kosovo, 30 July 1998 256
16.   Yugoslavia / Kosovo: Increasing alarm at scale of Kosovo crisis, 6 August 1998 256
17.   Update No. 98/07 on Kosovo, 12 August 1998 257
18.   Yugoslavia/Montenegro: Red Cross struggles to cope with influx of displaced from Kosovo, 19 August 1998 257
19.   Yugoslavia/Kosovo: ICRC brings surgical team to the wounded, 28 August 1998 258
20.   ICRC position on the crisis in Kosovo, 15 September 1998 258
21.   Kosovo crisis: ICRC stepping up activities, 14 October 1998 258
B.   THE UN HIGH COMMISSIONERS FOR HUMAN RIGHTS AND FOR REFUGEES 259
1.   UN High Commissioner for Human Rights, Field Operation in Former Yugoslavia, April 1998 259
2.   Human Rights Field Operation in the Former Yugoslavia, 30 April 1998 259
3.   UNHCR Briefing Notes, 12 May 1998 260
4.   Human Rights Field Operation in the Former Yugoslavia, 29 May 1998 262
5.   UN Inter-Agency Update on Kosovo, Friday 24 July 1998 262
6.   UN Inter-Agency Update on Kosovo, 27 July 1998 263
7.   UN Inter-Agency Update on Kosovo, 29 July 1998 264
8.   UNHCR Calls for immediate action to allow the return of the uprooted in Kosovo, 21 August 1998 264
9.   UN Inter-Agency Update on Kosovo, 24 August 1998 266
10.   UN Inter-Agency Update on Kosovo, 26 August 1998 266
11.   UN Inter-Agency Update on Kosovo Situation, 28 August 1998 267
12.   High Commissioner for Human Rights reiterates need for impartial investigation, 2 September 1998 268
13.   UN Inter-Agency Update on Kosovo Situation, 8 September 1998 268
14.   UNHCR Briefing Notes: Kosovo, 25 September 1998 269
15.   UN Inter-Agency Update on Kosovo Situation, 30 September 1998 270

CHAPTER 12: THE NATO THREAT OF FORCE AND THE HOLBROOKE AGREEMENT 272
1.   North Atlantic Council Statement on the Situation in Kosovo, 5 March 1998 275
2.   North Atlantic Council Statement on the Situation in Kosovo, 30 April 1998 275
3.   Statement of Ministerial Meeting, North Atlantic Council, Luxembourg, 28 May 1998 275
4.   Statement issued on behalf of the UN Secretary-General, 5 June 1998 276
5.   Statement issued at the Meeting of the North Atlantic Council in Defence Ministers Session, 11 June 1998 276
6.   Statement by NATO Secretary General on Exercise "Determined Falcon", 13 June 1998 276
7.   Press Release: Determined Falcon demonstrates NATO's resolve for peace, stability, 15 June 1998 277
8.   Exercise Cooperative Assembly 98, NATO Press Release, 6 August 1998 277
9.   NATO Exercise Cooperative Best Effort, NATO Press Release 3 September 1998 277
10.   Statement by NATO Secretary-General following ACTWARN Decision, Vilamoura, 24 September 1998 277
11.   Statement by the Government of the Russian Federation, 4 October 1998 277
12.   Remarks by US President on Kosovo, 8 October 1998 278
13.   Statement by Secretary of State Madeleine K. Albright, Situation in Kosovo, 8 October 1998 278
14.   Statement by the Secretary-General Following Decision on the ACTORD, 13 October 1998 278
15.   President Milosevic Announces Accord on Peaceful Solution, Belgrade, 13 October 1998 279
16.   Serbian Government Endorses Accord Reached by President Milosevic, Belgrade, 13 October 1998 279
17.   Statement of the Federal Government of the Federal Republic of Yugoslavia, 14 October 1998 279
18.   Press Conference, UK Foreign Secretary and Defence Secretary, 14 October 1998 280
19.   NATO/FRY Kosovo Verification Mission Agreement, FRY, 15 October 1998 281
20.   Press Points by the NATO Secretary-General, 15 October 1998 282
21.   NATO Statement on Kosovo following North Atlantic Council meeting, Brussels, 16 October, 1998 282
22.   Letter from the FRY to the Secretary-General of the United Nations, 23 October 1998 282
23.   Record of NATO-Serbia/FRY Meeting in Belgrade, 25 October 1998 283
24.   Understanding between KDOM and the Ministry of the Interior of the Republic of Serbia, 25 October 1999 284
25.   Statement by NATO Secretary General following Meeting of the North Atlantic Council, 27 October 1998 284
26.   Secretary of State Albright, Remarks on Kosovo, Washington, DC, 27 October 1996 284
27.   United Kingdom Parliamentary Testimony on the Threat or Use of Force, November 1998 & January 1999 285
28.   Press Statement by the North Atlantic Council on Kosovo, 19 November 1998 286
29.   NATO Press Statement on the Extraction Force, 5 December 1998 286
30.   NATO Statement on Kosovo, 8 December 1998 286

CHAPTER 13: THE OSCE VERIFICATION MISSION **287**

   A.   ESTABLISHMENT OF THE OSCE VERIFICATION MISSION 292
       1.   *OSCE Permanent Council Decision No. 218, 11 March 1998*...292
       2.   *Joint statement by President of Russian Federation and President of FRY, Moscow, 16 June 1998*........292
       3.   *Press Release by Professor Bronislaw Geremek, Chairman-in-Office the OSCE, Warsaw, 7 October 1998*.................292
       4.   *FRY Federal Government Statement, Extract, 14 October 1998*..293
       5.   *Press Release: US Special Envoy for Kosovo Addresses Permanent Council, Vienna, 15 October 1998*........293
       6.   *OSCE Permanent Council, Decision No. 259, 15 October 1998*.......................................293
       7.   *OSCE-FRY Kosovo Verification Mission Agreement, 16 October 1998*................................293
       8.   *OSCE Appoints Head of Kosovo Verification Mission, Warsaw, 17 October 1998*.................294
       9.   *Press Release, Foreign Ministers of the OSCE Troika Meet in Oslo, 21 October 1998*.........295
      10.   *OSCE Permanent Council Decision 263, 25 October 1998*...295
      11.   *Richard Holbrooke & William Walker, Press Conference, 28 October 1998*......................295
      12.   *Council of Europe, Final Communique, 103rd Session of the Committee of Ministers, Strasbourg, 3-4 November 1998*........299
      13.   *Organization for Security and Co-operation in Europe, Permanent Council Decision No. 266, 11 November 1998*.....299
      14.   *Organization for Security and Co-operation in Europe Ministerial Council Declaration, Oslo, 2 December 1998*.....299
      15.   *OSCE Ministerial Council Statement on Kosovo, Oslo, 2 December 1998*............................299
   B.   EVENTS FOLLOWING UPON THE ESTABLISHMENT OF THE VERIFICATION MISSION...................................300
       1.   *Letter from the UN Secretary-General to the President of the Security Council, 19 October 1998*........300
       2.   *UN Inter-Agency Update on Kosovo Situation, 21 October 1998*.....................................300
       3.   *UN Inter-Agency Update on Kosovo Situation, 28 October 1998*.....................................301
       4.   *Report of the Secretary-General, 12 November 1998*..302
       5.   *UN Inter-Agency Update on Kosovo Situation Report 72, 26 November 1998*.....................308
       6.   *Yugoslavia/Kosovo: ICRC steps up food distribution, 3 December 1998*...........................308
       7.   *Report of the Secretary-General, 4 December 1998*..309
       8.   *Press Release, OSCE Chairman-in-Office Condemns Kosovo Violence, Warsaw, 15 December 1998*........313
       9.   *ICRC Update on the Response to the Crisis in Kosovo, 22 December 1998*.........................313
      10.   *UN Inter-Agency Update on Kosovo Humanitarian Situation, 24 December 1998*................313
      11.   *Report of the Secretary-General, 24 December 1998*..314
      12.   *UN Inter-Agency Update on Kosovo Humanitarian Situation, 11 January 1999*.................319
      13.   *UN Secretary-General, Statement on the Racak massacre, New York City, 16 January 1999*........320
      14.   *Chairman's Concluding Statement, Special Meeting of Permanent Council, Vienna, 18 January 1999*........320
      15.   *U.S. Representative to OSCE, Statement at Extraordinary OSCE PC Meeting, Vienna, 18 January 1999*........320
      16.   *Kosovo: Ogata condemns atrocities, appeals for access, 18 January 1999*........................321
      17.   *Council of Europe condemns massacre in Kosovo, 18 January 1999*................................321
      18.   *Statement by James P. Rubin, US Spokesman, 18 January 1999*....................................321
      19.   *ICRC Takes action in Aftermath of Racak violence, 18 January 1999*............................321
      20.   *Statement by the President of the Security Council, 19 January 1999*.............................322
      21.   *Press Statement by James P. Rubin, US Spokesman, 23 January 1999*...........................322
      22.   *UN Inter-Agency Update on Kosovo Humanitarian Situation, 25 January 1999*.................322
      23.   *Statement by the President of the Security Council, 29 January 1999*.............................323
      24.   *Report of the Secretary-General, 31 January 1999*..323
      25.   *Report of the Secretary-General, 12 February 1999*..328
      26.   *UN Inter-Agency Update on Kosovo Humanitarian Situation, 22 February 1999*...............330
      27.   *Letter from the Secretary-General to the President of the Security Council, 26 February 1999*........330
      28.   *ICRC assists Civilians caught up in Clashes, 11 March 1999*.......................................333
      29.   *Report of the EU Forensic Team on the Racak Incident, 17 March 1999*.........................333
      30.   *Report of the Secretary-General, 17 March 1999*..335
      31.   *OSCE Chairman-in-Office Pulls out OSCE Personnel out of Kosovo, Oslo, 19 March 1999*........337
      32.   *Letter from the UN Secretary-General addressed to the President of the Security Council, 23 March 1999*........338
      33.   *Letter from the Secretary-General addressed to the President of the Security Council, 25 March 1999*........342

CHAPTER 14: THE HILL PROCESS..**347**

   A.   BILATERAL ATTEMPTS TO ACHIEVE A SETTLEMENT 351
       1.   *FRY statement: Serbia-Kosovo Methohija-Dialogue, 13 March 1998*..............................351
       2.   *FRY, Serbian Government again invites ethnic Albanians to Dialogue, 14 March 1998*........351
       3.   *FRY: Yugoslav President Milosevic calls for Referendum, 2 April 1998*..........................351
       4.   *Serbian President Milutinovic issues statement on President Milosevic's Letter, 2 April 1998*........352
       5.   *Serbian Government proposes calling of a Referendum, 2 April 1998*.............................352
       6.   *FRY, Letter of the Vice-President of Serbia to the President of the Democratic Alliance of Kosovo, 26 April 1998*........352
       7.   *FRY: Ethnic Albanian Representatives fail to appear at Talks once more, 28 April 1998*........352
       8.   *FRY: Serbian Vice Premier Markovic invites minorities to Talks on May 12, 5 May 1998*........353
       9.   *Statement on the talks of the FRY President S. Milosevic with Dr Ibrahim Rugova and his Delegation, 15 April 1998*........353
      10.   *FRY on talks in Pristina, including statement by Albanian side read by B. Salja, 22 May 1998*........353
      11.   *Press Release of the Ministry of the Interior of the Republic of Serbia, 5 June 1998*........354
   B.   THE HILL PROCESS 354

Contents

1. Venice Commission Outline for Main Elements for Agreement on Kosovo, undated 354
2. First [Hill] Draft Agreement for a Settlement of the Crisis in Kosovo, 1 October 1998 356
3. Draft Law Enforcement and Security Annex, 1 October 1998 359
4. Revised Hill Proposal, 1 November 1998 362
5. Kosovo Statement on Fundamental Principles for a Settlement, 3 November 1998 369
6. Press Release by the Yugoslav Federal Ministry of Foreign Affairs, 10 November 1998 370
7. Statement by Milan Milutinovic, President of Serb Republic, Pristina, 18 November 1998 370
8. Concluding Remarks by the President of the Republic of Serbia, Pristina, 18 November 1998 .. 371
9. Joint Proposal on Political Framework of Self-Governance in Kosovo and Metohija, Belgrade, 20 November 1998 .. 372
10. Declaration in Support of Joint Proposal for Agreement, Belgrade, 25 November 1998 375
11. Kosova Press Release: Hill draft plan should be further improved, 1 December 1998 375
12. 3rd Hill Draft Proposal for a Settlement of the Crisis in Kosovo, 2 December 1998 ... 376
13. Kosova Press Release: UCK won't settle for anything less than full independence, 5 December 1998 .. 382
14. Kosova Press Release: Demaci rejects Hill's Plan, 8 December 1998 382
15. Kosova Press Release: Kosovo Parliament's commissions discuss draft Plan, 11 December 1998 .. 382
16. Final Hill Proposal, 27 January 1999 383

CHAPTER 15: THE RAMBOUILLET CONFERENCE 392

A. THE SUMMONS TO THE CONFERENCE 414
1. Joint Statement by Secretary of State Albright and Russian Foreign Minister Ivanov, Moscow, 26 January 1999 .. 414
2. Statement by US Department of State Spokesman James P. Rubin, 27 January 1999 414
3. Statement to the Press by Dr Javier Solana, NATO Secretary General, Brussels, 28 January 1999 .. 414
4. Statement by UN Secretary General to North Atlantic Council, NATO HQ Brussels, 28 January 1999 .. 414
5. Statement to the Press by NATO Secretary General, Dr Javier Solana, 29 January 1999 414
6. Contact Group Statement, London, 29 January 1999 415
7. Security Council Presidential Statement, 29 January 1999 415
8. Statement by the North Atlantic Council on Kosovo, 30 January 1999 416
9. Statement to the Press by NATO Secretary General, Javier Solana, 30 January 1999 416
10. US Secretary of State Albright, Statement on NATO Final Warning on Kosovo, Washington, DC, January 30 .. 416
11. Contact Group Non-negotiable Principles/Basic Elements, 30 January 1999 417
12. Response of Kosova to Views Adopted by the Contact Group, 30 January 1999 417
13. Letter from Yugoslavia to the President of the Security Council, 1 February 1999 417

B. THE PROCEEDINGS OF THE RAMBOUILLET CONFERENCE 418
1. Address by Jacques Chirac, President of the Republic of France, 6 February 1999 419
2. Address by Mr Hubert Vedrine, French Foreign Minister, Rambouillet, 6 February 1999 419
3. Opening Remarks by Robin Cook, UK Secretary of State, Rambouillet, 6 February 1999 419
4. Joint Press Conference by Mr Vedrine and Mr Cook, Rambouillet, 6 February 1999 420
5. Interim Agreement for Peace and Self-Government in Kosovo, Initial Draft, 6 February 1999 .. 421
6. Statement of both Delegations on a Bomb Explosion in Pristina, 7 February 1999 428
7. Press Briefing by the three Negotiators, Rambouillet, 9 February, 1999 428
8. Annex 4, Economic Issues, dated 12 February 1999 430
9. Chairman's Conclusion, Contact Group Meeting, Paris, 14 February 1999 430
10. Secretary of State Albright, Briefing following Contact Group meeting, 14 February 1999 .. 431
11. Press Briefing by Spokesman for Contact Group Negotiators, Rambouillet, 16 February 1999 .. 432
12. Letter from Delegation of Kosova to Contact Group Negotiators, Rambouillet, 17 February 1999 .. 433
13. NATO-Russia Permanent Joint Council Meeting at Ambassadorial Level, NATO HQ, 17 February 1999 .. 433
14. Joint Press Briefing given by Messrs Vedrine & Cook, Paris, 17 February 1999 433
15. Interim Agreement for Peace and Self-Government in Kosovo, 2nd Draft, 18 February 1999 .. 433
16. Press Briefing by the Contact Group Negotiators, 18 February 1999 434
17. Kosova Delegation Statement on New Proposal for a Settlement, 18 February 1999 441
18. Draft Chapter 5, Implementation I, 19 February 1999 444
19. President Clinton and President Chirac, Joint press conference, Washington, DC, 19 February 1999 .. 445
20. Statement by the NATO Secretary General on behalf of the North Atlantic Council, 19 February 1999 .. 446
21. Department of State Spokesman Briefing on Kosovo peace talks, Rambouillet, 20 February 1999 .. 447
22. James Rubin, US Press Briefing, Rambouillet, 20 February 1999 447
23. Conclusions of the Contact Group, Rambouillet, 20 February 1999 448
24. Secretary of State Albright, Press conference on the Kosovo, France, 20 February 1999 ... 449
25. James Rubin, Press Briefing on the Kosovo peace talks, Rambouillet, France, 21 February 1999 .. 449
26. James Rubin, Press Briefing on the Kosovo peace talks, Rambouillet, France, 21 February 1999 .. 451
27. Draft for Chapter 8, Article 1 (3), 22 February 1999, 05.25 hrs, and proposed draft side-letter .. 451
28. James Rubin, Department of State Briefing, Rambouillet, 23 March 1999 452
29. James Rubin, Interview, Rambouillet, 23 February 1999 452
30. Interim Agreement for Peace and Self-Government in Kosovo, 23 February 1999 453
31. Letter from the FRY/Serb Delegation to the Negotiators, 23 February 1999 453
32. Letter from the FRY/Serb Delegation to the Negotiators, 23 February 1999 470
33. Letter from the FRY/Serb Delegation to the Negotiators, 23 February 1999, 16.00 hrs 470

34.   *Statement by the Delegation of Kosovo, 23 February 1999, 16.30hrs* 471
35.   *Letter from the Delegation of Kosovo to US Secretary of State Albright, 23 February 1999* 471
36.   *Co-chairmen's Conclusions on the Rambouillet Accords, 23 February 1999* 471
37.   *Joint Press Conference by the two Co-Chairmen, Rambouillet, 23 February 1999* 472
38.   *Secretary of State Albright, Press Conference, Rambouillet, 23 February 1999* 474
39.   *Press Statement by Members of the Security Council, 23 February 1999* 474
40.   *Statement by the Secretary General of NATO on the outcome of the Rambouillet talks, 23 February 1999* 474

CHAPTER 16: THE PARIS CONFERENCE AND THE OUTBREAK OF HOSTILITIES **475**

A.   PREPARATIONS FOR THE PARIS CONFERENCE 478
  1.   *Cook-Vedrine Statement on Kosovo, 5 March 1999* 478
  2.   *Press Statement by James P. Rubin, US Spokesman, 10 March 1999* 478
  3.   *US Envoy Senator Dole and Amb. Hill Press Conference, US Embassy London, 6 March 1999* 478
B.   THE PARIS FOLLOW-ON CONFERENCE 480
  1.   *Letter From Hashim Thaci, Chairman of the Presidency of the Kosova Delegation, 15 March 1999* 480
  2.   *FRY Revised Draft Agreement, 15 March 1999* 480
  3.   *Letter from the three Negotiators to Head of Republic of Serbia Delegation, 16 March 1999* 490
  4.   *NATO-Russia Permanent Joint Council Meeting at Ambassadorial Level, 17 March 1999* 490
  5.   *Declaration submitted by Kosovo to Negotiators upon Signature of the Rambouillet Accords, 18 March 1999* 490
  6.   *Kosovo Statement on Formal Signing of Interim Agreement for Peace and Self-government, 18 March 1999* 491
  7.   *Identical Letters from Kosova, 18 March 1999* 491
  8.   *Department of State Daily Press Briefing, Washington, DC, 18 March 1999* 491
  9.   *Secretary of State Albright, Remarks on Developments in Kosovo, Washington, DC, 18 March 1999* 493
  10. *Statement by the Co-Chairs of the Contact Group, France, 19 March 1999* 493
  11. *President Clinton, Excerpt from Press Conference, Washington, DC, 19 March 1999* 493
C.   THE INITIATION OF HOSTILITIES 495
  1.   *Statement by the North Atlantic Council on the Situation in Kosovo, 22 March 1999* 495
  2.   *Press Statement by Dr Javier Solana, Secretary General of NATO, 23 March 1999* 495
  3.   *Statement by the Prime Minister, Tony Blair, in the House of Commons, Tuesday, 23 March 1999* 495
  4.   *NATO Press Release: Political and Military Objectives of Action with Regard to in Kosovo, 23 March 1999* 496
  5.   *Ambassador Holbrooke, Interview on ABC's Nightline, March 24, 1999* 496
  6.   *Last Appeal to President Milosevic by the Chairman-in-Office of the OSCE, 24 March 1999* 497
  7.   *Press Statement by the NATO Secretary General following the Commencement of Air Operations, 24 March 1999* 497
  8.   *Statement made by the UN Secretary-General on NATO military action against Yugoslavia, 24 March 1999* 498
  9.   *President Clinton, Address to the Nation, Washington, DC, 24 March 1999* 498
  10. *Edited Transcript of Press Conference by Prime Minister Tony Blair, Berlin, 24 March 1999* 499
  11. *Security Council Provisional Record, 3988th Meeting, 24 March 1999, 5.35 p.m. (NY time), Extract* 499
  12. *Press Statement by Dr Javier Solana, NATO Secretary General, 25 March 1999* 501

SUMMARY INDEX **503**

Chapter 1: Chronology

1389	Serbs are defeated by advancing Ottomans at the battle of Kosovo Polje. This victory ultimately leads to Ottoman rule in the region.
1690	Patriarch of Pec Arsenije leads exodus of Serbs from Kosovo.
1781	Further displacement of Serbs follows upon Austro-Turkish war of 1788-1791.
1804	Nationalist risings in Serbia, also over the following decades, answered with significant repression.
1862	Ottoman withdraw last garrisons.
1878	Congress of Berlin; Montenegro and Serbia obtain formal recognition of impendence. Prizren League formed.
1882	Proclamation of Serb Kingdom.
1912/3	Balkan wars, Albania gains independence.
1914	Reports of genocide of ethnic Albanians in Kosovo, acts of revenge during World War I, repression and exodus of Kosovo Albanians at the conclusion of the War.
1939	In World War II, under Italian and then German tutelage, Serbs are persecuted in Kosovo. With the end of the conflict ethnic Albanians in turn face severe repression.
1943/4	At the turn of the year, Declaration of Bujan is adopted, envisaging union of Kosovo with Albania after the liberation. Document 4.A.1.
1945	On 3 September, Serbia creates autonomous region of Kosovo-Metohija as a constituent part of Serbia.
1946	New federal constitution confirms Kosovo's status as an autonomous region with limited self government. Document 4.A.2.
1953	New federal constitution preserves Kosovo's status. Document 4.A.3.
1963	Third constitution is adopted. Document 4.A.4.
1968	Riots at the University of Pristina in response to slow economic growth in Kosovo and other concerns.
1972	In June constitutional amendments create collective presidency of 23 members, including Marshal Tito and equal numbers from the six republics and two autonomous regions (Kosovo and Vojvodina) of Yugoslavia.
1974	New constitution provides for broad autonomy for Kosovo and equal status at federal level. Constitutional amendments also reduce collective presidency to 9 members: Tito + one representative from each republic and autonomous province. Document 4.A.8.
1980	Death of Marshal Tito, President of Yugoslavia on 4 May. Head of State passes to President of the Collective Presidency, Mr Lazar Kolisevski (Macedonia), on an annually rotating basis. In May 1981 the post passed again to Cvijetin Mijatovic (Bosnia-Herzegovina).
1981	
Mar-May	Riots in Kosovo due to high cost of living and privileges of party officials lead to declaration of a state of emergency (declared 3 April) and repressive measures against Albanian population. Deterioration of Yugoslav-Albanian relations due to accusations of Albanian involvement in Kosovo riots. Protesters demand full republic status for Kosovo.
5 May	Resignation of Mahmut Bakali, provincial (Kosovo) leader of League of Communists of Yugoslavia (LCY) as a result of rioting. Replaced by Veli Deva. Numerous other changes in local party apparatus.

Jun-Sep	Political changes in LCY in Kosovo. 14 of 19 members of Kosovo LCY Presidium removed from office.
Sep	Trials of those involved in Kosovo riots.
1982	
Mar-Sep	700 arrests in Kosovo for activities against the state. Heavy security presence stationed in Kosovo. Kosovo Albanians reiterate demands for full republic status.
Jul-Oct	Numerous convictions of Albanians in Kosovo involved in riots.
22 Oct	Execution by firing squad of ethnic Albanian in Kosovo for murdering a policeman.
1984	
9 June	Press reports that two policemen are shot and wounded in Pristina by Albanian nationalists.
Sep-Dec	Albanian nationalist activity continues in Kosovo. Bombs explode in Pristina on several occasions. Serbs and Montenegrins continue to leave Kosovo (7,000 leave in 1982-3). Economic difficulties continue, including 25% unemployment in Kosovo. Devaluation of Yugoslav dinar (June 1981 rate 35 dinar=1US$, May 1984 rate 134 dinar=1US$).
1985	Trials of ethnic Albanian in Kosovo continue. Official reports, however, note the stability of the province.
1986	
15 May	The collective presidency elects Sinan Hasani of Kosovo President of the Presidency for a one-year term to begin 16 May.
25 Jun	Speaking at the 13th Congress of the League of Communists, President Zarkovic reaffirms 'vigorous opposition' to 'all tendencies which ignore the fact . . . that republics and provinces have an irreplaceable role laid down by the constitution'. Zarkovic further condemns nationalism in Kosovo and calls for 'decisive action' in Kosovo to prevent Serbs from leaving the province due to Albanian intimidation. Economic difficulties are also discussed at the Congress, including inflation rates as high as 80%. Serb Academy memorandum calling for establishment of Greater Serbia published.
Jun	Federal and provincial leaders approve new methods for integrating Albanian and Serb groups in Kosovo, including restrictions on home sales, bilingual education, and housing incentives for the Serbs returning to the province.
19 Aug	71 ethnic Albanians sentenced in Kosovo for thefts from a silver refinery.
1987	
24 Apr	15,000 ethnic Albanians demonstrate in Kosovo Polje where Slobodan Milosevic, President of the Presidium of the Serbian League of Communists, was addressing a meeting of Serbs.
Sep	Rift in Serbian leadership as Belgrade Party Leader, Dragisa Pavlovic, and Belgrade Mayor, Zivana Olbinam, resign.
3 Sep	Ethnic Albanian Aziz Keljmendi shoots fellow conscripts at an army barracks in central Serbia. Government reports

declare him an 'Albanian chauvinist and separatist', leading to increased ethnic tensions.

12 Sep   Hamidja Pozderac, Yugoslav Federal Vice President, resigns amidst financial scandal. Milosevic proceeds with removal of Ivan Stambolic from Party leadership.

20 Oct   Fadilj Hodza, ethnic Albanian Kosovar leader expelled from League of Communists of Yugoslavia (LCY) after being accused of making ethnic slurs.

25 Oct   Tensions in the province mount as Serbs and Montenegrins claim they are being driven out of Kosovo. Special police units are dispatched to Kosovo to address continuing riots. Authority of provincial police is suspended.

Dec   Economic problems in Kosovo grow as unemployment reaches 50%.

14 Dec   Ivan Stambolic removed as President of the Presidency of Serbia in hard-line take over of Serbian leadership by Milosovic at the expense of those lenient on Albanians in Kosovo. The removal of Stambolic represents a significant rift in the Serbian leadership.

1988

11 Feb   Federal Chamber initiates proposal to amend Federal Constitution, increasing federal authority and reducing the autonomy of Kosovo and Vojvodina.

26 Feb   Economic difficulties continue with further currency devaluation (1,297 dinar = 1US$).

29-31 May   Emergency Conference of the (LCY) demands decisive reforms. Recovery program initiated at the conference leads to workers' strikes throughout the summer.

9-23 Jul   Protests by 1,000+ Kosovar Serbs in Novi Sad against Vojvodina's resistance to constitutional amendments which would reduce the autonomy of Kosovo and Vojvodina. Milosevic praises demonstrations.

28-30 Jul   LCY plenum on tensions in Kosovo.

6 Oct   Dispute over constitutional changes leads to resignation of the LCY Presidium of Vojvodina.

7-8 Oct   Protests by Serbs in Montenegro over lack of Montenegrin support for Serb actions in Kosovo.

17 Oct   LCY plenum to address growing unrest. Dispute between Milosevic and LCY president, Stipe Suvar, leads to resignations of Presidium members from Kosovo and Bosnia-Herzegovina.

25 Oct   Montenegrin government resigns.

17 Nov   Kosovo Communist Party asks Kacusa Jasari, party president, and Azem Vlasi, politburo member, to resign.

18 Nov   Kosovar Albanians (100,000) protest in Pristina, demanding the 1974 Constitution, which confirmed self-rule for Kosovo, be respected.

19 Nov   One million Serbs rally in Belgrade in support of constitutional changes.

23 Nov   Ethnic Albanian demonstration in Pristina leads to ban on demonstrations in Kosovo.

25 Nov   The Yugoslav Federal Assembly approves constitutional modifications that strengthen the federal government at the expense of regional autonomy. The constitutional changes also block the introduction of a market economy and change foreign investment laws in Yugoslavia. Constitutional changes are forwarded to regional and provincial assemblies for ratification.

1989

1 Feb   Azem Vlasi, Kosovar Albanian leader, dismissed from LCY central committee, resulting in strikes by ethnic Albanian miners in Kosovo from 4 February.

20 Feb   Miners' strikes continue in Kosovo with demands that proposed constitutional changes be rejected.

23 Feb   Serbian Republican Assembly approves constitutional changes. Amendments forwarded to provincial assemblies in Kosovo and Vojvodina for ratification.

27 Feb   General strike in Kosovo by ethnic Albanians causes pro-Serb Kosovo LC leadership, including Rahman Morina, Husamedin Azemi, and Ali Sukrija, to resign in apparent capitulation to strikers' demands.

28 Feb   Seven hundred thousand Serbs protest in Belgrade against Kosovar Albanian's separatist tendencies.

1 Mar   Emergency joint session of Kosovo Assembly hears claims that separatists in Kosovo are trying to stage a general revolt and form a 'Greater Albania.' Serb authorities strengthen ban on public protests in Kosovo. Serb demonstration in Belgrade against 27 February resignations of pro-Serb Kosovo LC leaders. Milosevic promises to arrest Azem Vlasi, Kosovar leader who may have organised miners' strikes.

2 Mar   Azem Vlasi arrested. Strikes in Kosovo follow to protest Vlasi's arrest.

23 Mar   Kosovo provincial assembly approves changes to Serbian constitution (approved by the Yugoslav Federal Assembly on 25 November 1988) granting Serbia control over internal affairs of Kosovo and Vojvodina.

27 Mar   Ensuing protests lead to death of two police officers in Kosovo and the introduction of a curfew in Kosovo.

28 Mar   Serbian Republican Assembly in Belgrade ratifies constitutional changes. Street violence continues in Kosovo. 18 demonstrators killed on 28 March alone. Total death toll in March approximately 30.

1 Apr   Kosovo LC meeting expels Vlasi and three other members for supporting strikes. Purge of Kosovo LC leadership follows.

9 Apr   Curfew (imposed 27 March) in Kosovo lifted.

Apr-May   Approximately 500 ethnic Albanians in Kosovo arrested and/or held in custody.

11 May   Ban on gatherings and demonstrations relaxed.

28 June   Six hundredth anniversary of Kosovo-Polje battle. One million Serbs commemorate the event with relative peace.

13 Sep   Economic protests in Belgrade. Annual inflation rate nears 1,000% (170,000 dinars = 1$US).

27 Sep   New constitution in Slovenia includes a right of secession from Yugoslavia.

30 Oct   Vlasi tried for 'counter-revolutionary activities'. Trial causes additional ethnic unrest. Youth gangs stone Pristina police.

10-12 Nov   Elections in Serbia are controlled by Milosevic supporters and increase his power base. Milosevic is re-elected as President of Serbia with 86% of the vote.

15 Nov   Ekrem Arifi, former member of presidium of Kosovo LC, is charged with instigating hate acts against Serbs.

Dec   Economic austerity package introduced.

1990

20 Jan LCY 14th Congress convenes in Belgrade. Congress plans to reform the nature of socialism in Yugoslavia to account for greater political changes in Eastern Europe. The proposed *New Outline for Democratic Socialism in Yugoslavia* includes a mixed economy and independent judiciary.

22 Jan Rift between Slovene delegation and Serb President Milosevic over the independence of republics in the reform process leads to walk-out by Slovene delegation. LCY Congress adjourns.

23 Jan New wave of violence in Kosovo in response to anti-Kosovo platform of Serb delegation at LCY Congress. Serb delegates seek to deny Kosovo the multiparty system that would give voice to ethnic Albanian groups. Clashes in last week of January between ethnic Albanians and security forces result in 27 deaths.

31 Jan Federal Collective State Presidency adopts special measures to end the violence in Kosovo and dispatches additional troops to the province. Serb protests in Belgrade demand full army occupation of Kosovo.

Apr-May First multi-party elections in republics of Slovenia and Croatia.

3 Apr Yusef Zehjnulahu, President of the Kosovo Executive Council, and other ethnic Albanian leaders in Kosovo resign over brutal Serb tactics toward Kosovar Albanians. The resignations are not accepted by the Kosovo provincial assembly.

17 Apr Milosevic, President of Serbia, declares that the Serb Internal Affairs Ministry has taken over control of Kosovo from federal organs.

18 Apr Special measures in Kosovo lifted by Federal Collective Presidency.

24 Apr Azem Vlasi acquitted and released from custody.

15 May Hard-liner Borisav Jovic (Serbia) takes over Yugoslav Collective State Presidency and attacks autonomy of republics.

16-30 May New non-communist governments formed in Slovenia and Croatia as result of April and May elections.

26 May LCY Party Congress (suspended since January) resumes.

26 Jun Serb authorities close Kosovo Assembly and take over its functions. Documents 4.B.6/7.

30 Jun New economic austerity package adopted. Inflation rates stabilise.

2 Jul Referendum in Serbia supports new constitutional proposals that would remove Kosovo's autonomous status. Only 25% voter turn-out in Kosovo after ethnic Albanians boycott the referendum. Ethnic Albanian delegates to Kosovo Assembly issue a declaration of sovereignty, claiming Kosovo is a full republic within Yugoslavia. Document 4.C.2. 114 of 118 delegates support the declaration, however Serb authorities had technically closed the Kosovo Assembly the previous week, invalidating the election. In Slovenia, Slovenian Assembly declares full sovereignty for the republics.

5 Jul Serbian Assembly votes to close Kosovo Assembly permanently. Responsibilities transferred to Serbian parliament.

6 Jul Protests begin in Pristina.

17 Jul League of Communists (LCY) changes name to Serbian Socialist Party.

23 Aug Hajrullah Gorani, president of Kosovo Independent Trade Union Organisation, sentenced to 60 days imprisonment for supporting strikes.

29 Aug US Senate Minority Leader, Bob Dole, visits Pristina and condemns treatment of ethnic Albanians, threatening potential withholding of US aid to Yugoslavia. Serb forces clash with Albanian demonstrators just prior to Dole's arrival.

3 Sep General strike (200,000 participants) in Kosovo as part of ongoing ethnic Albanian defiance of new constitution. Protests against the dismissal of 15,000 ethnic Albanians from state jobs since imposition of Serbian rule.

28 Sep New Serbian constitution enters into force removing elements of sovereignty Kosovo and Vojvodina that Kosovo had enjoyed under the 1974/8 Constitution. Authority of Serbian President increased.

23 Dec Slovenia holds referendum on secession from Yugoslavia (93.5% voter turn-out with 94.5% in favour).

1991

1 Jan Further devaluation of dinar by 22.2%

9 Mar Demonstrators (100,000+) in Belgrade led by Vuk Draskovic, chairman of the Serbian Renaissance Movement, protest Milosevic's confrontational policies. Draskovic is one of 636 arrested after riot police confront demonstrators. Demonstrations continue through 14 March.

16 Mar Milosevic calls for army intervention to hold the Yugoslav federation together.

19 Mar General staff of the army refuses to intervene in the 'political' dispute.

16 Apr 700,000 workers strike in Serbia demanding a minimum wage.

6 May US freezes aid to Yugoslavia due to human rights violations in the region.

6 June Meeting of six republic presidents to create new governmental structure for Yugoslavia.

13 June Protest in Kosovo to 'bury' the violence in the province. Demonstration leader, Veton Suroi, arrested for failing to register the protest.

25 June Slovenia and Croatia declare independence from Yugoslav federation. Fighting breaks out in Slovenia.

Aug Serbs take over rule of Kosovo towns formerly administered by Albanians and seize control of Kosovo television and media.

8 Aug Albanian Democratic Party proposes incorporation of Kosovo into Albania.

Sep Civil war continues in Croatia and other regions of Yugoslavia.

7 Sep Peace conference held at The Hague.

8 Sep Macedonian independence referendum held.

9 Sep Yugoslav National Army (JNA) shoots three Albanian border guards.

10 Sep Kosovo teachers protest against imposition of Serbian curriculum.

26-30 Sep Kosovo Assembly (closed by Serbia in 1990) holds referendum on sovereignty with 87.01% turnout and 99.87% support for a sovereign Kosovo. Document 4.C.6.

19 Oct Kosovo elects provisional coalition government under Bujar Bukoshi.

5 Nov US and EC sanctions imposed on Yugoslavia.

11 Nov 24 countries suspend all aid to Yugoslavia.

1992

8 Jan	UN Security Council resolution 737 approves deployment of 14,000 peace-keepers in Yugoslavia.
26 Jan	Further (80%) devaluation of dinar.
9-12 Mar	Protests in Belgrade call for resignation of Milosevic.
27 Apr	Federal Assembly of Yugoslavia accepts new constitution, forming the new state of the Federal Republic of Yugoslavia (FRY), consisting of Serbia and Montenegro along with Kosovo and Vojvodina. Documents 4.B. 16/17.
28 Apr	Bujar Bukoshi, Kosovo Provisional Government President, visits Albania and calls for separate Kosovar presence in the Conference on Security and Co-operation in Europe.
24 May	Democratic Alliance of Kosovo (DSK) wins elections held in Kosovo for 130-seat constituent republican assembly. Ibrahim Rugova, DSK leader, elected President of the Republic of Kosovo. Document 4.C.8.
31 May	Elections to bicameral FRY Assembly are held.
14 Jul	Rugova pays visit to Albania. US businessman Milan Panic elected Federal Prime Minister and appoints a 'government of experts' for the FRY.
15 June	Dobrica Cosic (nationalist writer) elected to FRY Presidency.
23 June	Serb forces surround Kosovo Assembly and arrest deputies.
1 Jul	Austerity measures in the FRY include a 40% reduction in public expenditures.
16-17 Jul	Rugova visits Greece for high-level meetings on the status of Kosovo.
20 Jul	EC refuses to accept FRY as 'sole successor state to Yugoslavia'. Lord Carrington, chair of the EC peace conference on Yugoslavia, calls for an international conference on Kosovo.
10 Aug	Panic lifts state of emergency in Kosovo but does not withdraw federal troops.
26 Aug	London Conference on Yugoslavia
4 Sep	Panic defeats no-confidence vote in Federal Assembly, moving more moderate politicians into government.
16 Sep	At Geneva meeting Rugova calls for Kosovo to be treated as a constituent part of Yugoslavia, not as a province of Serbia.
6 Oct	UN Security Council votes to establish war crimes commission for Yugoslavia.
11 Oct	Serbian government holds referendum on early elections. Panic hopes such elections will allow for early removal of President Milosevic. Low voter turnout (46%) invalidates referendum and early elections are not called.
12-13 Oct	Clashes between protesters and police in Pristina over right to education in Albanian language and at Albanian schools.
15 Oct	Panic visits Pristina and meets with Rugova. Joint working groups established to consider human rights violations.
29 Oct	Agreement reached for Albanian students to attend Albanian schools. Some discriminatory laws revoked.
2-3 Nov	Panic barely survives no-confidence vote. The resignations of the Economy Minister and a deputy prime minister follow.
5-6 Nov	CSCE calls for the creation of a criminal tribunal for Yugoslavia. CSCE further agrees to reinforce its monitoring missions in Kosovo.
11 Nov	Ethnic Albanians attack Serb headquarters in Pristina. Two Serb soldiers are wounded and one ethnic Albanian killed.
25 Nov	Istanbul meeting of foreign ministers from states in the region calls for deployment of UN forces on the borders of

	the Bosnia conflict to prevent the spread of violence into Kosovo and other threatened areas.
Nov	OSCE Mission of Long Duration deploys. *See* Chapters 5.C/D.
Dec	President Bush threatens US armed action in letter to Milosevic should force be used in Kosovo
29 Dec	Panic loses no-confidence vote and is replaced as Prime Minster by Radoje Kontic, a strong Milosevic supporter.

1993

28 Feb	US President Bill Clinton issues a statement to Milosevic, warning that if Serbs start a conflict in Kosovo, 'the USA is ready to send a military force against Serbs in Kosovo.'
Mar	Serbian troops mass on the Albania-Kosovo border. Serbian government announces its intention to hold elections in Serbia. Serb militias under Zeljko Raznjatovic increase terror aimed at Albanians, driving ethnic Albanians out of Kosovo.
8 Apr	International Court of Justice (ICJ) issues judgment in *Request for the Indication of Provisional Measures* (Bosnia v. FRY). ICJ calls on the FRY to 'take all necessary measures within its powers to prevent the commission of the crime of genocide.'
24 May	Hunger strikes in Kosovo by writers and journalists in protest of Serbian censorship and restrictions on Albanian publishing.
26 May	UN Security Council Resolution 827 establishes the International Criminal Tribunal for the Former Yugoslavia. *See* Chapter 10.
1 June	Dobrica Cosic, President of the FRY, removed from office as Milosevic consolidates power.
25 June	Zoran Lilic elected President of the FRY by Federal Assembly as replacement for Cosic.
9 Jul	Vuk Draskovic, opposition leader and head of Serbian Renewal Movement, released from prison following a hunger strike.
22 Jul	Further devaluation of dinar after July inflation reaches 366.7%.
28 Jul	CSCE observer mission (present in Kosovo since November 1992) withdraws from Kosovo after federal authorities refuse to renew its mandate to monitor human rights in Kosovo. *See* Chapter 5.C/D.
Aug	Hyperinflation reaches 1,800% in August as Yugoslav economy continues downward spiral. Beatings and arrests reported in Kosovo. Tensions with Albania increase after border incidents on 6 and 19 August.
9 Aug	UN Security Council Resolution 855 calls on the FRY to reconsider its 28 July expulsion of the CSCE mission. Document 5.C.12.
18 Aug	Rugova is temporarily detained by Serbian authorities in Pristina.
6-7 Sep	Further arrests in Kosovo, especially of those who had worked with the CSCE observer mission.
13 Sep	ICJ decision in the case of *Further Requests for the Indication of Provisional Measures* supports earlier decision calling on the FRY to prevent and punish acts of genocide.
16 Sep	Rugova meets with visiting CSCE delegation and subsequently calls for the internationalisation of the Kosovo situation due to Serb repression.
22 Sep	New Law of Defence centralises authority in the FRY Federal Assembly, further restricting the powers of republic and provincial assemblies.

20 Oct	Milosevic dissolves Serbian People's Assembly after attempts by the Assembly to call a no-confidence vote. General elections set for December 19.
28 Oct	Arrests of members of the People's Movement for the Republic of Kosovo and the National Movement for the Liberation of Kosovo after rumours of a planned uprising circulate.
17 Nov	International Criminal Tribunal for the Former Yugoslavia holds first official session at The Hague.
19 Dec	Elections result in victory for the Socialist Party of Serbia, further strengthening Milosevic's rule. Opposition parties, especially Draskovic's Serbian Renewal Party, shift toward nationalist platforms.

1994

24 Jan	New 'super dinar' introduced in attempt to check inflation.
3 Feb	Rugova meets with President Clinton during US visit. Clinton is reported to have shown 'concern and understanding' for the situation in Kosovo.
22 Feb	Milosevic appoints Mirko Marjanovic Prime Minister of Serbia with a national unity government controlled by Milosevic's Socialist Party of Serbia.
23 Feb	Serbian authorities close the Academy of Arts and Sciences of Kosovo.
28 Feb	First ever NATO combat action as four Serb attack aircraft shot down in no-fly zone over Bosnia.
28 Feb	Russian and Yugoslav Defence Ministers sign military cooperation pact.
15 Mar	Federal Statistics Institute claims that inflation has been halted.
17 Mar	New budget allocates 75% of spending to defence and other military uses.
21 Apr	Belgrade papers report statement by Montenegrin Foreign Minister Miodrag Lekic, calling for more autonomy for Kosovo in return for protection of historic Serb sites.
5 May	Douglas Hogg, Minister of State for the UK Foreign Office, attempts to cool situation in Kosovo, calling on the Serbs to grant Albanian 'political, cultural, and civil rights,' while simultaneously attempting to convince Albanian Kosovars that there 'was no need for an independent state of Kosovo.'
11 May	Serb administrator in Kosovo, Milos Simovic, calls for arrest of Rugova for 'four years of anti-constitutional and anti-Serb activities.'
1 June	Secret talks between ethnic Albanian leaders in Kosovo and Serb authorities take place in Belgrade.
15 Sep	New Yugoslav government, reduced to 14 ministers to increase efficiency, takes office.
16 Sep	Six Albanians convicted and sentenced to five years imprisonment for belonging to Kosovar separatist organisation.
18 Sep	Amnesty International Report warns of a 'dangerous escalation' of human rights abuses in Kosovo.
29 Sep	Uksin Hoti, leader of Albanian party in Kosovo, sentenced to five years' imprisonment for secessionist activity.
Nov	Largest wave of arrests since 1990 in Kosovo. Over 170 ethnic Albanians, mostly former police officers, arrested.
15 Dec	Yugoslav Internal Affairs Ministry describes Kosovo arrests as part of a plan to 'put a stop to illegal Albanian police' operations in Kosovo.
Dec	Serbian authorities take over main opposition newspaper, *Borba*.

1995

Jan 15	Up to 30,000 ethnic Albanians flee violence in Kosovo, according to reports by Albanian television.
7 Feb	Russian Deputy Prime Minister calls for free trade zone between Russia and Yugoslavia, despite international sanctions against Yugoslavia.
10 Feb	City Council of Belgrade claims ownership of opposition radio station Studio-B.
22 Feb	Russia objects to planned EU grants to Albanian publications in Kosovo.
28 Feb	Russia signs military co-operation agreement with Yugoslavia, set to enter into force after the lifting of international sanctions against Yugoslavia.
Apr	Former Serbian intelligence agent claims to have documents linking Milosevic to war crimes in Bosnia.
13 June	Milosevic intervenes to help end UN hostage crisis in Bosnia.
Aug	Serbia settles Serb refugees in Kosovo in the face of strong Albanian criticism.
8 Sep	Russian President Boris Yeltsin signs decree committing Russia to humanitarian assistance to Yugoslavia.
15 Sep	UN Security Council extends the suspension of sanctions against Yugoslavia (air travel, cultural contacts, etc.) until March 1996.
16 Sep	Albanian President Sali Berisha issues a statement upon return from Washington meetings with US President Bill Clinton, claiming that the US strongly supports autonomy for Kosovo.
1 Nov	Peace talks on Bosnia begin in Dayton.
9 Nov	Indictments against Serb officers of the Yugoslav National Army handed down by the ICTY.
21 Nov	Initialing of the Dayton Peace Accord brings peace to Bosnia-Hercegovina.
22 Nov	US and UN sanctions against Yugoslavia lifted in response to initialling of Dayton Accord. UN Security Council further votes to phase out arms embargo.
14 Dec	Presidents of Bosnia, Croatia, and Serbia formally sign Dayton Accords in Paris, leading the way for the deployment of a 60,000-member NATO implementation force.

1996

May	Dragoslav Avramovic, FRY Central Bank Governor, dismissed.
3 Nov	Opposition Zajedno coalition wins municipal elections in Belgrade, Nis, and other cities. However, the Milosevic regime fails to honour the election results and initiates a legal challenge. Daily anti-government demonstrations begin in Belgrade.
Dec	Large-scale demonstrations begin in response to the governments failure to recognize opposition victories in the November elections.
3 Dec	Independent radio station B92 closed for 2 days.
8 Dec	Serbian courts support government policy refusing to honour opposition victories in the November elections.
15 Dec	Mass demonstration of over 250,000 people in Belgrade.
17 Dec	In meetings with a student group Milosevic promises to investigate electoral improprieties.
27 Dec	OSCE election commission report calls on Serb government to recognize opposition victories.

1997

1 Jan	Students in Belgrade hold daily rallies against the Milosevic regime beginning on New Year's Day.
2 Jan	In a significant move, the Serbian Orthodox Church offers its support to the opposition. Church leaders accuse Milosevic of ballot stuffing, setting Serbs against Serbs, and undermining religious freedoms.
6 Jan	Student leaders meet with Yugoslav National Army Chief of Staff who pledges that soldiers will not be ordered onto the streets to break-up demonstrations. This move signals deteriorating relations between Milosevic and the Army, making him more and more reliant on the 120,000-strong police force. Protests continue.
7 Jan	Mass protests on Orthodox Christmas Day.
8 Jan	Serbian Ministry of Justice announces that the Zajedno party has won municipal elections in Nis, a further blow to Milosevic and his Socialist Party of Serbia.
12 Jan	Contact Group on the Former Yugoslavia (UK, USA, Russia, Germany, Italy, and France) meets to discuss the growing crisis in Serbia. The US issues a statement that it is considering a freeze on trade with Serbia.
14 Jan	Belgrade election commission reinstates Zajedno victory in the City Assembly.
27 Jan	Patriarch Pavle of the Orthodox Church leads protest in Belgrade.
2 Feb	Riot police turn water cannons and batons against protesters in Belgrade. The US State Department issues a statement condemning the crackdown and speaking of the further 'isolation' of Serbia.
3 Feb	Fighting between student protesters and police continues in Belgrade.
4 Feb	Milosevic recognizes opposition victories in the municipal elections, claiming that 'relations with the OSCE and the international community surpasses by far the importance of any number of council seats in several towns.' OSCE calls for 'further steps towards democratisation.'
16 Feb	Zajedno coalition announces end to daily demonstrations in Belgrade, but some student demonstrations continue, calling for the dismissal of the pro-Milosevic rector of Belgrade University.
20 Mar	Changes in Yugoslav government as cabinet is reshuffled to further strengthen Milosevic's hand.
11 Apr	Serbian Deputy Interior Minister shot by an unidentified gunman in Belgrade.
Apr	Informal talks held in New York City to help defuse the situation in Kosovo. Serb and ethnic Albanian officials are unable to reach an agreement.
May	US Secretary of State Madeleine Albright holds talks with Milosevic in Belgrade. The implementation of the Dayton Accords and the situation in Kosovo are on the agenda.
11 Jun	Steering Committee of the Socialist Party of Serbia nominates Milosevic to succeed Zoran Lilic as President of the Federal Republic of Yugoslavia.
24 Jun	Opposition Zajedno coalition breaks up due to internal disagreements.
15 July	Milosevic elected President of the Federal Republic of Yugoslavia by the Federal Assembly in an unopposed contest. Milosevic sought the Yugoslav Presidency due to a constitutional provision preventing him from serving a third term as Serb President.
23 Jul	Milosevic resigns as President of Serbia and is simultaneously sworn in as President of the FRY.
21 Sep	First round of presidential elections in Serbia results in no clear victor. A second round of balloting is scheduled for December.
1 Oct	Large demonstration by students in Pristina is broken up by violent police action.
13 Nov	Milosevic visits the People's Republic of China and signs cooperation agreement with President Jiang Zemin. China reportedly commits to US$100 million in aid in exchange for Yugoslav recognition of 'one China.'
7 Dec	Runoff elections in Serbia are inconclusive.
21 Dec	Second runoff held, in which Milan Milutinovic, former Yugoslav Foreign Minister, is elected President of Serbia.
30 Dec	Serb forces close all Albanian language schools in Pristina and other major cities in Kosovo.

1998

Jan	Kosovo Liberation Army (KLA), the ethnic-Albanian paramilitary force in Kosovo, clashes with Serb police leading to strong international criticism of Serb brutality.
4 Jan	KLA declares that it is the armed force of ethnic Albanians and that it will fight for the unification of Kosovo with Albania.
28 Jan	Council of Europe issues a resolution condemning 'Serbian repression' in Kosovo and blaming Serb policies for the 'armed resistance' in the region.
23 Feb	US makes concessions to Belgrade, easing some sanctions and allowing a Yugoslav consulate in New York. However, access to international financial institutions remains contingent upon improving the institutions of democracy and solving the problems in Kosovo.
28 Feb	Four Serb police officers shot in Likosane, central Kosovo. Serb police respond by killing 24 ethnic Albanians in villages in central Kosovo. Ethnic Albanians claim the killed were civilians, while Serbs argue that they were KLA members.
Mar	Crackdown against KLA in early March leads to 80 mainly civilian deaths. Recent unofficial census data shows a population of 2 million in Kosovo, of which approximately 90% are ethnic Albanians.
2 Mar	50,000 demonstrate in Pristina against Serb violence. US Statement condemns Serbian use of force in Kosovo and threatens to reimpose stricter sanctions against Yugoslavia. The UK government calls upon both sides to show 'restraint.'
5 Mar	US withdraws concessions of 23 February and reimposes strict sanctions due to Serb behaviour in Kosovo. US envoy to Yugoslavia Robert Gelbard reiterates President Bush's 1992 warning that the US might intervene militarily in Kosovo. UK Foreign Secretary Robin Cook holds talks with Milosevic in Belgrade, but the Yugoslav President refuses to discuss the Kosovo issue.
5-6 Mar	Serb offensives in Kosovo's Drenica region continue. Tank fire in Lausa indicates that the Yugoslav army has joined Serb police in Kosovo.
9 Mar	Serbs release bodies of 53 Albanians killed on 5-6 March, including those of 12 children and 13 women. Contact Group convenes at ministerial level in London to discuss Kosovo crisis and demands withdrawal of Serb forces from Kosovo by 19 March. The Contact Group statement calls upon Spanish Prime Minister Felipe Gonzalez Marquez to mediate the situation and opposes violent measures to achieve independence for Kosovo.
13 Mar	Trade unionists and students (50,000) demonstrate in Pristina.

17 Mar	Russian Foreign Minister Yevgeny Primakov visits Belgrade to urge Milosevic to accept Gonzalez's mediation mission.
18 Mar	Violence spreads to Pec in western Kosovo.
19 Mar	Serb and Albanian demonstrators clash in Pristina.
20 Mar	Foreign Ministers of Germany (Klaus Kinkel) and France (Hubert Vedrine) visit Belgrade in an effort to secure the withdrawal of Serb forces from Kosovo.
22 Mar	Elections held in Kosovo despite Serb claims of invalidity. New legislature is elected, controlled by Rugova's Democratic Alliance of Kosovo, which holds a platform of passive resistance.
23 Mar	Agreement signed between Serbs and ethnic Albanians allows for the reopening of Albanian language schools in Kosovo.
24 Mar	Coalition government created in Serbia includes the Socialist Party of Serbia, the Yugoslav United Left, and the Serbian Radical Party.
25 Mar	Contact Group meets again in Bonn. A statement issued by the Contact Group concedes that some progress had been made, but calls on Milosevic to implement an 'unconditional dialogue' and begin 'serious negotiations on Kosovo's status'.
31 Mar	UN Security Council Resolution 1160 imposes arms embargo against the FRY and urges Serb and ethnic Albanian leaders to enter into dialogue. Document 7.1.
2 Apr	Clashes between ethnic Albanians and Serb army forces intensify. Milosevic refuses call by the Contact Group to withdraw Interior Ministry Police from Kosovo.
4 Apr	First Albanian language school returns to ethnic Albanian control based on March education agreement.
7 Apr	Kosovar Albanians refuse offer of Serb President Milan Milutinovic to enter into discussions, noting that they will only negotiate with federal authorities in the presence of foreign mediators.
9 Apr	In Pristina, 30,000 ethnic Albanians march in support of an independent Kosovo. FRY Deputy Prime Minister Danko Djunic resigns, signalling Milosevic's shift away from meaningful economic reform. Economic chaos leads to further currency devaluations.
13 Apr	Montenegrin President Molo Djikanovic calls for the formation of a 'block of reformist forces' to 'bar the way for Milosevic.'
15 Apr	Rift forms in Rugova's Democratic Alliance of Kosovo as criticism of his policies of passive resistance mount and ethnic Albanians turn toward violent confrontation with Serb authorities.
17 Apr	Albania calls for the deployment of NATO troops to prevent the conflict from spreading across its borders.
22 Apr	UN Human Rights Commission condemns Serb repression in Kosovo.
23 Apr	Serb referendum on foreign involvement in Kosovo results in 94.73% vote against any foreign mediation. However, the Belgrade Centre for Free Elections and Democracy questions the validity of the elections, noting that ethnic minority political communities had boycotted the election.
24 Apr	JNA claims to have killed 23 members of the KLA near the Albanian border.
26 Apr	Albanian Prime Minister issues a public criticism of Serb leadership and military activities in Kosovo.
29 Apr	Contact Group members, except Russia, freeze international assets of the FRY and threaten to cut off all public investment.
1 May	Clashes between ethnic Albanians and Serb security forces continue.
9 May	Contact Group members tighten sanctions against Serbia with a ban on foreign investment, despite Russian opposition.
10 May	Ethnic Albanian demonstrators in Kosovo voice support for the KLA. Reports from Pristina indicate that the KLA has reached 12,000 members.
18 May	Milosevic dismisses Radoje Kontic, FRY Prime Minister, after reports that his support for Milosevic had wavered.
22 May	Milosevic and Rugova meet for the first time to discuss the future of Kosovo. Richard Holbooke, US architect of the Dayton Accords, and Robert Gelbard, US envoy to Yugoslavia, mediate the talks. Kosovo Albanians drop demands that meetings only occur with FRY, not Serb, authorities. They note, however, that this does not imply acceptance of Serb authority over Kosovo.
25 May	Large-scale operation against KLA initiated by Serb security forces.
8 Jun	Fighting in Kosovo continues. EU bans all foreign investment in Serbia in response to Milosevic's treatment of Kosovo.
13 Jun	Contact Group calls for immediate cease-fire and withdrawal of Serb security forces from Kosovo.
15 Jun	NATO exercise 'Determined Falcon' begins in Macedonia as a show of force for Milosevic.
16 Jun	Milosevic meets with Yeltsin and agrees to restart talks with Rugova. Milosevic refuses to allow KLA participation in the talks.
23 Jun	Holbrooke meets with Milosevic.
24 Jun	KLA seizes Belacevac coalmine, interrupting the Serbian power grid, in one of largest victories to date. British Prime Minister Tony Blair warns of possible NATO air strikes.
27 Jun	Splinter party (United Democratic League) from Rugova's Democratic League of Kosovo forms under the leadership of Rexhep Qosja.
29 Jun	Serb forces retake the mine, killing 10 KLA members.
1 Jul	Serb forces continue attacks against KLA. Nine Serb workers kidnapped by KLA and killed.
4-6 Jul	Holbrooke meets with Milosevic and Albanian leaders in attempt to broker peace deal. Holbrooke's efforts fail due to Milosevic's tough stance and the failure of the Kosovo delegation to form a united front.
6 Jul	Diplomatic observers from the USA, UK, Russia, Italy, and Germany begin patrols in Kosovo.
8 Jul	Contact Group meets in Bonn to work out peace proposal and makes first open admission that the KLA will have to be included in any eventual settlement.
12 Jul	Two Serb policemen killed by KLA at police checkpoint.
14 Jul	OSCE delegation meets with ethnic Albanian leaders in Kosovo.
15 Jul	Rugova's attempts to convene the Kosovo legislature that had been elected in March are thwarted by Serb police.
19 Jul	In significant turn of battle, Serb forces take control of town of the town of Orahavac, formerly under KLA control.
27 Jul	Serb police capture KLA base at Lapusnik and, after intense fighting, take Malisevo.
28 Jul	US Ambassador to Macedonia, Christopher Hall, meets with Kosovar Albanians to determine the constituency of a Kosovo delegation to participate in peace talks. Hall's efforts represent first major diplomatic break-through.

30 Jul	In talks with EU envoys in Belgrade, Milosevic commits to halt all military action in Kosovo.
31 Jul	Milosevic promises Christopher Hall that aid agencies will be given full access to Kosovo.
3 Aug	Despite Milosevic's commitment to halt fighting in Kosovo, three ethnic-Albanian villages in Kosovo are demolished. UNHCR estimates that up to 200,000 ethnic Albanians have been displaced by the fighting.
7-15 Aug	As Serb activities intensify, KLA strongholds of Likovac, Junik, and Glodjane fall.
9 Aug	Contact Group peace plan receives lukewarm welcome from both sides. The plan calls for autonomy for Kosovo as a 'special part' of Serbia, but does not back an independent Kosovo.
11 Aug	In the face of setbacks, KLA issues a statement claiming that Serb activities have 'strengthened our resolve to continue on the road to freedom'.
12 Aug	Montenegro refuses to provide reinforcements for Serb forces.
13 Aug	Rugova forms negotiating team composed of Fehmi Agani, Fatmir Sejdiu, Tadej Rodiqi, Edita Tahiri, and Ilaz Kurteshi. No KLA representatives are included in the negotiating team.
17 Aug	NATO show of force operation begins in Albania.
23 Aug	German Chancellor Helmut Kohl suggests the possibility of pre-emptive NATO action to avoid a humanitarian disaster.
24 Aug	UN Security Council calls for cease-fire in Kosovo, but fighting continues.
2 Sep	Christopher Hill secures agreement to postpone discussion of final status of Kosovo until after the fighting is stopped by an interim solution.
3 Sep	Serb forces begin shelling KLA bases in the mountains near Prizren.
4-8 Sep	600 ethnic-Albanians arrested for involvement with KLA.
8 Sep	Yugoslav airline JAT banned from flying to EU countries.
9 Sep	Shelling in Pec causes 25,000 civilians to flee.
16 Sep	Sixteen civilians, including infants and children, massacred in town of Gornje Obrinje.
20 Sep	Ethnic Albanian leaders present 16-point peace plan, which foresees Kosovo as 'temporarily part of Yugoslavia as an independent entity, equal to the other two republics in the federation.'
23 Sep	UN Security Council Resolution 1199 condemns 'all acts of violence' in Kosovo, especially 'indiscriminate use of force by Serb security forces.' Document 7.2.
24 Sep	NATO approves 'activation warning,' allowing the Supreme Allied Commander, General Wesley Clark, to seek forces from member states to carry out an intervention in Kosovo. Document 12.9.
26 Sep	14 civilians tortured and shot by Serb police in the village of Vraniq.
28 Sep	Serbian Prime Minister Mirko Marjanovic announces an end to the Serb offensive against the KLA.
29 Sep	US Defence Secretary William Cohen notes that despite Marjanovic's statement there is no evidence of a 'strategic drawback'. Cohen pressures Serbs to act on their commitments.
30 Sep	UK Foreign Secretary Robin Cook warns that NATO action will ensue if there are indications of non-compliance with Security Council Resolution 1199.
2 Oct	US Defense Secretary William Cohen announces that the US may begin strikes against Yugoslavia within two

weeks. Contact Group reiterates demands that Milosevic comply with UN Resolutions. Russian State Duma votes against any military action in Yugoslavia, toughening Russia's opposition to NATO strikes.

4 Oct	Milosevic gives assurances that forces will be withdrawn from Kosovo however no definitive actions are taken.
5 Oct	Holbrooke returns to Belgrade and presents Milosevic with a plan to avoid imminent NATO strikes. Terms include the withdrawal of Serb forces and open international monitoring in Kosovo.
6 Oct	Russia announces that it will veto any additional UN resolutions authorizing the use of force against Yugoslavia.
7 Oct	NATO commitment to military action in Kosovo begins to falter as Germany and Italy cite domestic considerations in a call for postponement of strikes.
8 Oct	Contact Group meets again and announces a six-point ultimatum, which includes withdrawal of Serb troops, freedom of access for the ICTY, a pledge to end operations in Serbia, safe return of refugees, and negotiations on a final solution for Kosovo. KLA announces cease-fire in order to increase pressure on Milosevic to withdraw forces from Kosovo.
12 Oct	Milosevic agrees to UN demands for an international observer force of 2,000 unarmed civilians under OSCE leadership. Additionally, he authorizes NATO reconnaissance flights over Kosovo. In a telephone call with the UN Secretary General, Milosevic pledges to comply with UN resolutions. *See* Chapters 12-13.
13 Oct	NATO approves air strikes, but delays implementation by four days so Milosevic can sign accords to prevent such strikes. In Belgrade, Serb authorities crack down against independent media sources. Document 12.13.
16 Oct	Milosevic signs agreement to allow OSCE verifiers in Kosovo and allow NATO overflight. Under the agreement, 20,000 Serb security forces will be allowed to remain in Kosovo. Document 13.A.7.
19 Oct	First OSCE verifiers arrive in Kosovo amidst partial Serb withdrawal.
20 Oct	New legislation allows the Serb government to censor reporting that is considered dangerous to Yugoslavia.
24 Oct	NATO Commander General Clark visits Belgrade and warns Milosevic that air strikes will follow by 27 October if withdrawal does not occur. Security Council approves Holbrooke agreement in Resolution 1203 (1998), Document 7.5.
27 Oct	NATO bombing threat suspended after partial compliance with NATO demands is evidenced.
5 Nov	ICTY Prosecutors denied entry into Kosovo.
6 Nov	Ethnic Albanians and Serb police clash in Opterusa in first significant test of the cease-fire. International monitors are able to secure the release of Serbs and Albanians kidnapped in the confrontation. First significant contingent of OSCE verifiers arrives in Kosovo, backed by an 1,800-member military extraction force in Macedonia.
15 Nov	Serb President Milan Milutinovic offers to hold direct talks with Albanians, but the offer is rejected by Rugova's 'government'.
7 Dec	New US draft of peace plan rejected by Fehmi Agani, a senior advisor to Rugova.
15 Dec	31 ethnic Albanians killed as Serb forces and KLA clash near Prizren. Four Serbs killed in a bar near Pec.
17 Dec	Serb police kill two KLA members.
18 Dec	Serb mayor of Kosovo Polje found dead after being kidnapped by KLA. Albanian language newspaper, *Bujka*, closed as Serbs further censor the free press.

20 Dec	Only 600 of possible 2,000 OSCE verifiers have arrived in Kosovo to date.
24 Dec	Heavy fighting in northern Kosovo undermines OSCE mission.
27 Dec	Local truce called to bring end to fighting in northern Kosovo.

1999

5 Jan	Ethnic Albanians shot in the town of Vitinia.
6 Jan	NATO Commander General Wesley Clark warns that a full-scale civil war is imminent.
8 Jan	Eight Serb soldiers captured by KLA in northern Kosovo. The soldiers are released five days later as part of a prisoner exchange deal.
11 Jan	Murder of Enver Maloku, a top aid to Rugova, increases tensions still further.
15 Jan	Two OSCE observers are wounded by gunfire near Decane. Massacre of 45 ethnic Albanians in Racak, 30 km from Pristina. Despite Serb claims that the victims were members of the KLA, UK Foreign Secretary Robin Cook concludes that the Serb forces have murdered civilians. Subsequent documents released on 28 January link Racak massacre to the highest levels of the Serb government.
17 Jan	NATO Secretary General Solana condemns Racak massacre and holds Milosevic personally responsible. Supreme Allied Commander, General Clark, flies to Belgrade to confront Milosevic.
20 Jan	Contact Group meets in Brussels in attempt to find a solution. NATO warships moved closer to FRY as attack notice time is reduced from 96 to 48 hours.
21 Jan	William Walker, OSCE monitoring mission chief, ordered out of Kosvo by Serb authorities before 5pm. Walker defies the Serb order and remains in Kosovo.
22 Jan	Contact Group meets again in London and agrees to push Milosevic and Albanian leaders towards the negotiating table.
25-27 Jan	Fighting in Kosovo intensifies with 24 ethnic Albanians killed.
30 Jan	Contact Group meets in London and calls for a peace conference in Rambouillet to begin by 6 February. Cook travels to Belgrade to order Milosevic and ethnic Albanian leaders to attend the conference.
2 Feb	Ethnic Albanians formally agree to participate in Rambouillet negotiations.
4 Feb	Serbian National Assembly votes in favour of participation in the Rambouillet negotiations. NATO announces that 45,000 troops are being readied to act as peacekeepers in Kosovo if an agreement is reached.
6 Feb	Rambouillet talks formally open. February 19 set as target date for agreement on a 24-page peace deal prepared by the Contact Group. The plan will grant autonomy to Kosovo while keeping institutional ties to the FRY. *See* Chapter 15.
11 Feb	British Foreign Secretary Cook and French Foreign Minister Vedrine meet with Milutinovic and accuse the Serbs of not fully engaging in the peace process. Victims of the Racak massacre are buried almost one month after the killings.
14 Feb	US Secretary of State Madeleine Albright visits Rambouillet. The talks are extended for an additional week. EU foreign ministers meeting in Paris pledge US$800 million as part of a Kosovo reconstruction fund.
15 Feb	NATO commanders meeting in Mons, Belgium develop plans for the deployment of 35,000 peacekeepers.

16 Feb	US chief mediator, Christopher Hill, leaves the talks and travels to Belgrade to meet with Milosevic.
18 Feb	US deploys 51 bombers to Europe for potential use against the FRY, escalating tensions with Russia.
19 Feb	Milosevic announces that he would prefer to face air-strikes than allow NATO peacekeepers in Kosovo.
20 Feb	Deadline for a peace deal passes and talks again extended by three days.
21 Feb	Albright returns to Rambouillet but once again is unable to secure concessions from the Serbs or to get the Albanian delegation to sign the peace deal.
22 Feb	Renewed fighting in Kosovo leads to the displacement of 4,000 ethnic Albanians. Fighting in Pristina continues through the end of February.
23 Feb	Serb and ethnic Albanian delegations agree in principle on elements of the plan for Kosovo. Neither side, however, signs the plan and new talks are set for 15 March in Paris.
26 Feb	Serb troops (4,000+) mass on the Kosovo border with tanks and heavy artillery.
2 Mar	Adem Demaci, a hard-liner in the KLA leadership, resigns, making it more likely that the Kosovars will sign the deal. The position of Hasim Thaci, the chief Kosovo Albanian negotiator, is strengthened.
8 March	KLA authorizes the signing of the Rambouillet peace plan.
10 Mar	Holbrooke meets with Milosevic in Belgrade in an attempt to secure his agreement with the plan. Despite eight hours of intense negotiations, no progress is reported. Milosevic still refuses to allow foreign troops in Kosovo.
15 Mar	A second round of peace talks open in Paris. The Albanian delegation announces that it has approved the Rambouillet deal.
18 Mar	Kosovo Albanian delegation formally signs the peace plan.
19 Mar	Final negotiations with Serbs result in no significant developments and the talks are adjourned. OSCE mission withdrawal announced.
20 Mar	Serb security forces begin major offensive in Kosovo, burning villages and driving ethnic Albanians from their homes.
21 Mar	UN High Commissioner for Refugees announces that in the 24 hours since the OSCE observers left an estimated 15,000 Kosovars have been forced from their homes.
22 Mar	Holbrooke travels to Belgrade in a final attempt to get Milosevic to agree to the Rambouillet deal. NATO countries provide Secretary General Solana with the authority to launch air-strikes against Yugoslavia at will.
23 Mar	Holbrooke announces the failure of his negotiations with Milosevic. Yugoslav General Alexander Dimitrijevik, the only dissenting voice in the Yugoslav military elite, is dismissed. NATO Secretary General Solana announces that he has directed General Clark to begin air operations against Yugoslavia. An emergency session of the Serb legislature condemns NATO and the KLA. Russian Prime Minister Yevgeny Primakov cancels visit to Washington, turning his plane back to Moscow while en route to meet with Vice President Gore and IMF officials.
24 Mar	Solana makes assurances to Albania, Bulgaria, Macedonia, Romania, and Slovenia that NATO will ensure their safety in the fighting spreads. At 7pm GMT NATO begins operations against FRY with cruise missile attacks on Yugoslav air defences from US and UK warships based in the Adriatic. *See* Chapter 16.

Chapter 2: Introduction

Foreign policy is not architecture, no matter what Dr Brzinski and others like to compare it to. In architecture, you make a plan down to the last nut, the last bolt, the last stress beam, and then you build the thing. Foreign policy, in my view, is more like jazz; it's an improvisation on a theme, and you change as you go along. [1] This sentiment was expressed by Richard Holbrooke, one of the senior US policy-makers who shaped the international response to the crisis in Kosovo. In fact, Ambassador Holbrooke voiced this view shortly after he appeared to have delivered a settlement of this (for the moment) last remaining conflict arising from the dissolution of the former Yugoslavia—a settlement brought about by an unprecedented threat of force by NATO and highly dramatic negotiations with Slobodan Milosevic in Belgrade. It is a sobering assessment for those who have begun to see in the international response to the Kosovo crisis a new paradigm of international relations, or a blueprint for a new world order in either a positive or negative sense. For, if anything is striking about this episode, it is the casual way in which policy was made at the highest levels, ultimately to the point of going to war.[2]

Nevertheless, while each step on the purported accidental road to war involved a considerable measure of improvisation by the principal actors involved, the end result was, paradoxically, predetermined. The Kosovo conflict proceeded along a path which was laid out by the basic structure of the classical international system. It represented a clash of values for which that system provided no peaceful resolution. In other words, war was inevitable. Or, at least there existed a presumption in favour of violent resolution which could only be overcome by stepping outside the classical international system and acting in accordance with a new framework of international order which is only just being explored by international decision-makers at the turn of the millennium.

A challenge to the classical state system

The classical system is one of states. They are considered to be international persons, endowed with a full set of natural rights upon birth. Among these rights is the rule of non-intervention, which precludes international action in relation to matters that states consider to be internal. Effectively, the classical system assigns to the state the exclusive power to represent internationally that which occurs internally (external sovereignty). At the same time, the state claims a monopoly of public power internally (internal sovereignty).

Since 1945, as the defenders of the classical system must now admit, some important changes have taken place. All states must accept that their sovereign powers are subject to certain limitations. For example, no state can under any circumstance lawfully engage in a campaign of genocide. Where a state significantly violates these limitations, it can be internationally criticised. More vigorous countermeasures, such as sanctions or military action, can be taken through the application of the exceptional machinery of collective security contained in Chapter VII of the United Nations Charter. However, the application of that system requires the concurrence of some of the most powerful sovereigns, the states holding a permanent seat on the UN Security Council.

Of course, these changes merely place a thin veneer of modernity upon a system which remains based on the one crucial assumption: the state is a person endowed with a full set sovereign rights which can only be diminished or reduced if the state itself consents. It was a view made necessary by the competition of differing social systems during the Cold War. Whatever the rhetoric of the politicians at the time, they realized that peace could only be retained, at least among the central players, if one did not interfere in the domestic affairs of the other. Vigorous assertions of sovereignty, especially by the Eastern block states, but also by many newly independent, former colonial nations, supported this kind of coexistence.

With the termination of the Cold War, a more advanced view had become possible—a view which is at present struggling to establish itself in the reality of international life. This view observes the gradual evolution of an international constitution in the more fluid post-Cold War world. This world is constructed from the bottom up, rather than from the top down. The fiction that the state is a supreme kind of international person endowed with absolute and natural rights is abandoned. Only the person is a person, endowed with human dignity and basic fundamental rights. The state only exists to the extent that the people out of which it is composed have transferred to it the competence to exercise public powers on their behalf. In that sense, the state is not conceptually different to, say, the Cambridgeshire District Council, the European Commission in Brussels or the UN Security Council. All of these bodies represent layers of competence to exercise public powers.

The unmasking of the state as nothing but a bundle of competences freely transferred to it by its constituents is, of course, nothing new. But to apply this discovery at the international level is new. For it has to be admitted that this finding makes the international system vastly more complex than the classical model based on absolute sovereignty.

---

[1] Richard Holbrooke, Press Conference, 28 October 1998, Document 13.11.
[2] The term 'war' is not employed in a technical legal sense here.

Several areas of tension at this time of fundamental re-evaluation of the international system are illustrated with great clarity throughout the Kosovo episode. In a sense, the Kosovo crisis and conflict was not merely played out over an area of some 10,887 square kilometres, inhabited by a population of 2 million, mostly ethnic Albanians. Throughout the past decade, the actors in this episode have been engaged in a far larger conflict—a struggle for the re-definition of the international system, specifically:

- the struggle for ultimate authority within the state: sovereignty vs. human rights;
- the struggle about the definition of the state: territorial integrity vs. self-determination;
- the struggle about manifestations of international interest: non-intervention vs. international action;
- the struggle among international actors: collective action vs. unilateralism.

State sovereignty vs. human rights

The state can no longer claim omnipotence in relation to its own citizens. It can only exercise the powers that have been granted to state organs through a constitutional compact. Few national constitutions will invite a state to engage in the systematic torture of its citizens. If a state nevertheless engages in such practices, it exceeds it competence, whether or not it has contracted into a special human rights treaty prohibiting torture. Secondly, as the state represents only one of many layers of public authority, its existence is part of, and regulated by, the universal international constitutional system. That system would, for example, preclude the assumption of authority by any one state, even with the full support of its constituents, which violates the global interest expressed in substantive rules of the international constitution. Hence, if the majority in a state votes to exterminate a minority, this is not a valid public act and can be lawfully opposed at all other layers of public authority in the international system.

The Kosovo conflict was one of dominance over a social system. The rump-Yugoslavia, which had emerged after the dissolution of the Socialist Federal Republic of Yugoslavia and consisted of Serbia and Montenegro, boasts a population of approximately 10.3 million. Of these, 62 per cent are ethnic Serbs. Perhaps surprisingly, by far the next largest ethnic group in the FRY is made up of ethnic Albanians. Most ethnic Albanians are Muslims, while Serbs tend to profess allegiance to their own branch of Christian Orthodoxy.[3] According to a Yugoslav census of 1991, 1.7 million of the overall population (16.6 per cent) were ethnic Albanians—that is over half of the population of Albania itself (3.3 million). In fact, the 1991 census probably underestimates the number of ethnic Albanians who boycotted it. The number of ethnic Albanians relative to Serbs was set to rise further, given the significantly higher birth rate within that community.

In Kosovo itself, the number of Serbs had dropped from some 27 per cent in the 1950s to a mere 8 percent by the 1990s. Some 90 per cent of the population of just short of 2 million were estimated to be ethnic Albanian. In addition, there were small groups of Turks, Goranies, Roma (Gypsies) and others. However, around 350,000 ethnic Albanians left, even before the 1998 hostilities, as a result of economic deprivation and repression exercised by the Serb government since 1988.

Kosovo, along with Vojvodina, had obtained a strong federal status under the 1974 SFRY constitution. While it was still an autonomous province within Serbia, it was equally represented in the federal organs, including the Federal Presidency. Governance in Kosovo too was principally independent of Serbia, and the territory enjoyed the right to create its own constitutional structure. The failure of ethnic Serbs to prosper in the territory, and their declining numbers, were taken as a sign of discrimination directed against them by the ethnic Albanian authorities in Kosovo. Slobodan Milosevic rose to power in Serbia on a promise to reverse this situation. And towards the end of the 1980's, ethnic politics began to grip a hold on Serbia. Tito's doctrine of brotherhood and unity among all ethnic groups was progressively replaced by an attempt to re-create a Greater Serbia, initially through Serb dominance of the entire Socialist Federal Republic of Yugoslavia (SFRY). The move to restore Serb direct control over Kosovo lay at the heart of this policy. While Kosovo had been populated mainly by Albanians for several centuries, official doctrine promoted the view that the territory was in fact the heartland of Serbia, given the presence of important and ancient religious sites there.

Serbia then embarked upon a strategy of reducing Kosovo's independent powers, subordinating them to direct rule by Serbia. At the same time, it took control of key organs of the overall federation. This move was resisted by other republics in the federation, most strongly by Slovenia, and subsequently also by Croatia. When their attempts to renegotiate federal arrangements failed, they declared independence in June 1991. Armed conflict ensued, leading to the complete dissolution of the SFRY and also bringing independence for Macedonia and Bosnia and Herzegovina. The hostilities were dominated by the attempt of Serbia to ensure that areas mainly inhabited by ethnic Serbs, but lying outside the Serb republic, would be detached from the other republics seeking independence. This applied to Croatia, where a vigorous ethnic cleansing campaign was launched in the autumn of 1991, and Bosnia and Herzegovina, which was subjected to an even more drastic armed campaign, commencing in May 1992. In Bosnia alone, a quarter of a million non-Serbs (mainly Muslims) were killed and some 2.4 million displaced as a result of a campaign of well-organized an militarily-executed ethnic cleansing and probable genocide.

---

[3] In addition there are 5 per cent Hungarians, 3.3 per cent 'Yugoslavs' and 3.1 per cent 'Muslims'.

Ethnic politics in Kosovo were initially administered through formal legislation. While Kosovo nominally retained its autonomous status, a new Serb constitution, adopted in 1990, made permanent the abolition of Kosovo's independent powers which had commenced in 1988. This result was consolidated by a new constitution for the rump-Yugoslavia, adopted in 1992. In the meantime, a whole host of openly discriminatory legislative acts had been adopted, directed at the ethnic Albanian population in Kosovo. This new constitutional and legal system was then enforced with some vigour, including the adoption of systematic acts of repression. While demographic manipulation was employed to reduce the ethnic Albanian population numbers, a formal programme was introduced to encourage Serb settlement in the territory.

Serbia, and the new federal government dominated by it, could claim that the events in Kosovo were matters falling entirely within the internal domain of the rump-Yugoslavia. The quite open and undisguised nature of the programme of ethnic politics and repression, enshrined in Serb law, was a reflection of the belief that the armour of state sovereignty would protect Belgrade from significant international interest in relation to these practices. After all, all the relevant decisions had been adopted by what Serbia claimed were the appropriate constitutional procedures, and only Serbia would be in a position to judge the validity of her own actions. While the abolition of Kosovo's independent powers had, in fact, occurred under rather controversial circumstances, the protestations of the ethnic Albanian leadership were now being portrayed as manifestations of separatism which, in turn, could justify even fiercer repression.

The organized international community, however, did not accept this view. From the beginning, the substantive violations of the human rights of the ethnic Albanian majority population were quite strongly criticised. More than that, international objections to the change in the status of Kosovo itself were expressed. And such criticism was not voiced solely by the European human rights organs. Significant condemnation came also from the universal level, including the United Nations General Assembly. It was made clear that the FRY/Serbia, or those who dominated the state organs, could not claim the sovereign freedom to arrange for an ethnic politics within their area of territorial jurisdiction. The state existed within an international constitutional framework which contained essential rules limiting the power of governments to adopt an openly discriminatory system of governance, characterized by widespread repression and attacks upon an entire population which could be characterized as crimes against humanity. In addition, the new Yugoslavia remained a party to several international human rights conventions. These treaties, too, ruled out discrimination, official acts of torture and other repressive measures.

The early insistence on the restoration of self-governance for Kosovo by several international bodies is also interesting. There appeared to be consensus that its population, contained in a clearly defined territory and previously permitted wide-ranging autonomy under established constitutional provisions, had an international personality of its own. While international demands did not generally extend to the full restoration of Kosovo's previous status, its separate identity at the international level was confirmed, whatever the constitutional manoeuvres performed by Serbia, although there was a lack of decisive action in response

State sovereignty and the issue of secession

Another difficult implication of international constitutionalism lies at the heart of the Kosovo issue. If the state is indeed nothing more than the accumulation of public powers assigned to it by its constituents, why then should not some of these constituents be able freely to remove their consent to leave the existing state structure and create another? This is a problem with which the international system has grappled since time immemorial. The answer that was found to this difficulty in the classical system was simple: unilateral opposed secession is not possible. If it occurs, the state finding itself under threat can use violent means to defeat secession. However, the events in the former Yugoslavia especially have brought out that this simple rule may no longer be adequate to address increasingly complex struggles for identity and control of peoples, for self-determination and statehood. Such conflicts do not disappear by virtue of being ignored.

In line with the classical approach, the limited recognition of a separate identity of Kosovo was balanced by the consistent rejection of Kosovo's claim to outright independence. In fact, Kosovo had initially answered the virtual abolition of its federal status in the former Yugoslavia and the adoption of the 1990 Serb constitution by a rather modest declaration of sovereignty. That declaration was aimed at re-establishing the territory as an equal unit within the old Yugoslavia. Only when the SFRY started to dissolve, with the declarations of independence of 1991 by Croatia and Slovenia, did Kosovo declare itself independent, with some reluctance. It was known by Kosovo politicians that such a move would not be internationally supported for the right to statehood still remained heavily rationed within the international system.

The classical international system, and the rules which govern it, have been created by governments acting on the international plane for their own benefit. It comes as no great surprise that all existing governments share an interest in perpetuating the existence within the existing boundaries of the respective states they claim to represent. Such an attitude is also seen to bring with it the benefit of international stability. Such stability is achieved through the doctrine of territorial unity which is enshrined in numerous international instruments, including the Helsinki Final Act.

Of course, this doctrine is circumscribed by the right to self-determination. While self-determination has many layers of meaning, its scope of application in the context of unilateral opposed secession has been defined by governments very narrowly. Self-determination as a legal entitlement to independent statehood has been made available only to colonial non-self-governing territories and analogous circumstances (internal colonialism, alien occupation, racist regimes and secondary colonialism). It is not a right appertaining to a self-constituting people, but instead applies to territorial entities defined through colonial administration to which a population is attached in a more or less incidental way. And the right is to be exercised only once, at the point of decolonisation, within the colonial boundaries.

In this way, the rhetoric of self-determination could be safely embraced by governments, including those of newly independent states (former colonies) from the 1960s onwards, without at the same time endorsing a concept which might be invoked against them at some future stage. However, the attempt by the Baltic republics to re-establish statehood and obtain independence from the USSR in 1990 foreshadowed the pressure which was exerted on this restrictive view after the unfreezing of international relations upon the conclusion of the Cold War. The unilateral declarations of independence of, initially, Croatia and Slovenia which followed in 1991 were seen to pose a dangerous challenge to the doctrine of territorial unity. Hence, when it emerged that these actions could not be undone, governments set about limiting the effect of these precedents in favour of unilateral opposed secession and wider self-determination. This was achieved by combining two arguments. The SFRY, it was asserted, had not been subjected to secession, but had in fact dissolved entirely. Hence, there was no bar to statehood for the federal republics which emerged free and unencumbered by the doctrine of territorial unity. After all, the beneficiary of that doctrine, the overall Federation, had disappeared. In addition, the federal republics were entitled to claim statehood on the basis of a right to self-determination which was not located in general international law, but in SFRY constitutional law. For, the SFRY constitution of 1974 had in fact provided for the possibility of secession of its constituent units.

Oddly enough, a wider assertion of the right to self-determination had been made by the rump-Yugoslavia. It claimed that the mainly Serb inhabited areas of Croatia and Bosnia and Herzegovina should be entitled to secede from secession, as it were, and to constitute themselves as independent states. This argument was rejected by the Badinter Commission, established to advise the International Conference on the Former Yugoslavia on issues of recognition, statehood and succession. While self-determination also applied to Serbs and others who now found themselves as minorities in new states, this was a different kind of self-determination. It was not an entitlement to statehood, but instead self-determination in this context was reduced in content to human and minority rights, and to autonomous structures of governance in areas where Serbs constituted a local majority.[4]

It was partially in order to prevent a further extension of self-determination claims that the governments involved in the international administration of the collapse of the SRFY, acting through the EU, the OSCE, NATO and the United Nations Security Council, insisted on the maintenance of Bosnia and Herzegovina as a state within its former SFRY boundaries. Hence, in Dayton it was accepted that the mainly Serb entity of Srpska would administer itself with a high degree of autonomy, but within the continued territorial unity of Bosnia and Herzegovina. The legal management of the creation of new states from within the former SFRY thus managed to avoid a precedent in favour of a wider right of secession outside the colonial context. However, it also soon became clear that the concept of self-determination merely based in the constitutional status of a republic within a federation was not free of dangers. This was made evident by the example of Chechnya. Chechnya had been an autonomous territory within Russia while Russia was a federal unit of the USSR. With the disappearance of the USSR, Russia achieved statehood. The new Russian constitution in turn promoted Chechnya to the status of a republic within the Russian Federation. Would Chechnya now be able to claim constitutional self-determination and statehood on the basis of the Yugoslav precedent? The answer provided by other governments was an emphatic no. Chechnya found that it was not accorded the legal protection available under the doctrine of self-determination when it took on the Russian Federation and engaged in an armed struggle for independence. Instead of insisting on a cessation of repressive measures, a withdrawal of Russian troops and the maintenance of the territorial integrity of Chechnya, the international community merely insisted on the compliance by Russia with human rights and humanitarian law when re-establishing effective control over the territory. Chechnya's status was only consolidated after Russia effectively lost the armed conflict and after it had to accept the possibility of Chechen independence in an interim agreement it voluntarily concluded in 1996.

The case of Kosovo was seen to fall squarely on the borderline between the precedent set by the Yugoslav republics and that set by Chechnya. Under the 1974 SFRY constitution, Kosovo was defined as a part of the Republic of Serbia, but it also had its own separate Federal status. It was represented separately on the Collective Presidency of the SFRY, had its own structures of governance (including a national bank) and its own territorial identity. The hesitations of the international community in view of the fact that Kosovo might constitute an unhelpful precedent for other cases made less of an impression on the people of Kosovo, who could not see why a population of 90 per cent Albanians should be left under

---

[4] Opinion No. 2 of the Badinter Arbitration Commission.

what they saw as the despotic and arbitrary rule of a small elite of ethnic Serbs in the territory. Nevertheless, a cautious attitude was adopted. Before declaring independence, the Kosovo leadership had obtained quite realistic legal advice, which indicated:

> Within the present international system, Kosova's claim to self-determination will not be heeded. Even a carefully crafted argument which would not necessary broaden the application of the doctrine of self-determination and would not give rise to a precedent which might threaten other governments is likely to be ignored. Kosova will have to decide whether it can survive in a state of limbo, seeking to consolidate its de-facto rule over time in the face of Serb repression. In this position, it would consistently remain under the threat of a forcible restoration of effective control by Serbia. The only alternative is an armed campaign which will bring with it untold suffering for the civilian population of Kosova and which it would not be likely to win. Instead, a gradual strategy of aligning the interests of the international community with those of Kosova, given the dangers to the stability to the region, might be pursued. On balance, however, a rapid resolution of the issue is unlikely.

The moderate Rogova government, which had been elected in 1992, was unwilling to risk the lives of those it purported to represent. Instead, it attempted to circumvent internal Serb repression by establishing parallel state structures in Kosovo. At the international level, arguments were put which were based not on a broad definition of self-determination, based on the fact that a population inhabiting a defined territory was being unlawfully suppressed and should, in consequence, be permitted to secede. Such argument, while politically persuasive to some, could also have applied to a wide range of other circumstances, be it the Kurds in Turkey, Iraq and Iran, the Basques in France and Spain, the Kashmiris in India or the Tamils in Sri Lanka. They would have been immediately rejected.

Proposals that Kosovo should consider itself a 'colonized' territory were also not taken up. While the Kosovars felt as if they were being colonized and subjected to a veritable apartheid regime, governments have developed an understanding which once again limits the application of this doctrine very significantly. The definition of a 'colonial territory' is very much restricted to classical colonialism, that is the occupation of a distant territory by an alien and racially different metropolitan state for the purposes of economic exploitation during the time of imperialism. To escape from this dilemma, Kosovo defined itself as a constitutional self-determination entity whose rights to statehood flowed directly from the situation which had obtained under the 1974 constitution, and from the dissolution of the state which had been supported by this constitution. Its case for independence was unique, and the acceptance of independence in this instance would pose no threat to other governments. Kosovo also pledged to respect the territorial integrity of neighbouring states and renounce all territorial claims, for example in relation to Macedonia. It ruled out a pan-Albanian agenda, indicating that it was indeed seeking independence, rather than union with Albania. And it indicated a willingness to accept all conceivable human and minority rights standards, and to subject itself to intrusive human rights monitoring, especially in relation to ethnic Serbs and others.

The governments and international organizations involved in responding to this claim opted for the restrictive view of constitutional self-determination and did not accept a right to statehood for Kosovo. In view of Serbia's position, and the fear of confrontation with the Milosevic government, it was held that Kosovo had not had republic status within the Socialist Federal Republic of Yugoslavia, and was thus barred from the entitlement to statehood claimed by republics. Instead, human rights should be respected in relation to the territory, and there should be meaningful self-administration. The clear expression of will in favour of independence by the Kosovo population in a referendum of September 1991 and the declaration of independence were ignored. Of course, there was no improvement in the human rights situation and no move towards the establishment of meaningful self-government. Instead, by the end of 1995, the issue of Kosovo appeared to have dropped from the international agenda altogether, with the exception of exhortations in relation to Serbia's human rights performance. With the Dayton settlement, the FRY/Serbia was relieved of all United Nations sanctions, despite earlier pledges that this would only occur once the Kosovo issue had also been addressed. All that was retained was an informal 'outer wall of sanctions' concerning access of Yugoslavia to international financial institutions. Given the need to rely on Serbia to keep the Dayton settlement afloat, this, too, was not pursued with the greatest of vigour. In the meantime, Serbia continued to insist that the issue of Kosovo was entirely an internal affair, not suited to international involvement. The evident lack of any perspective of change on the part of the FRY/Serb government, and the lack of decisive international involvement in addressing this simmering crisis, did not serve to strengthen the position of the Rugova government, despite the fact that it was overwhelmingly re-elected in March 1998, even after repression had escalated yet further.

State sovereignty vs. international action

According to the international constitutional view, a state can no longer claim exclusive control over, or representation of, its constituents. As public functions have also been transferred to international or supranational bodies, these can take a direct interest in the individuals whose fate falls into their competence, in parallel with the competence of state organs. A human rights body does therefore not commit an act of intervention if it criticises the systematic violation of the rights of a particular population by a particular state. Instead, it exercises its international constitutional function if it does so. Some states will now also claim such an entitlement to act on behalf of disenfranchised populations in other states.

International bodies were swift and uncharacteristically undiplomatic in their condemnations of FRY/Serb actions. But there was no significant action taken to enforce these demands. In fact, if one considers the clarity of the findings of a whole host of international bodies, adopted year after year throughout the 1990s and determining that the situation in Kosovo was entirely intolerable and would need to be remedied rapidly, the disjuncture between human rights monitoring and international action is very pronounced indeed.

The reluctance of the international community to address a crisis with a strong self-determination element lying at its heart was evident from the earliest attempts to seek a resolution of the Yugoslav crisis. The 1991 Carrington process treated the issue of Kosovo very much as an afterthought—despite the fact that political analysts were uniformly of the opinion that Kosovo represented the most dangerous aspect of the Balkan crisis for the region as a whole. The 1992 London conference, which also attempted to obtain an overall settlement of the Yugoslav crisis, was much overshadowed by the hostilities in Bosnia. The treatment of the Kosovo delegation on that occasion was perhaps symbolic of the way in which the Kosovo issue was to be addressed until it was too late. Kosovo was not permitted to participate, but was allowed to enter a room separate from the conference chamber and observe proceedings from there. In the follow-on process of the conference, the Kosovo issue was shunted into a 'Special Group', where little or no substantive negotiations took place. The group was kept alive for some time, giving the illusion of a diplomatic process in relation to Kosovo, but it silently disappeared without any progress whatever having been made.

The Conference for Security and Cooperation in Europe (CSCE, now OSCE) yielded a short-lived but not unimpressive success when Yugoslavia permitted the deployment of a long-term monitoring mission whose mandate also extended to Kosovo. That mission did introduce some stability to the region, although there was no progress in seeking to resolve the issue of Serb repression itself. The refusal to extend the mission was answered with a 1993 Security Council resolution requesting Belgrade to reconsider its decision. This was the only Council resolution on the Kosovo issue throughout the crisis, until the outbreak of wide-scale violence in 1998.

After 1993, international action on the Kosovo issue was focused mainly on praising the moderation of the Rugova government and requesting the Belgrade authorities to engage in meaningful dialogue. In the absence of any significant international pressure, there was little incentive for the Milosevic government to change its attitude to Kosovo and to negotiate. Politicians were unwilling to utilize international mechanisms to address the core problem of the crisis and to adopt measures to ensure that these would be employed constructively by the parties. A means towards this end would have existed in the shape of the Security Council, backed by economic pressure from the European Union. However, by the end of 1997, the Kosovo Liberation Army (KLA) had taken matters into its own hands. Initially, this had been quite a small group, launching very limited operations, mainly against Serb security installations, starting in 1996. Dr Rugova had dissociated himself publicly from these activities and he refused the support of his government to its activities. Towards the end of 1987, the KLA managed to establish itself in the Drenica region, from which some FRY/Serb forces had been withdrawn. When the security forces sought to establish their authority over the region again early in 1998, fighting erupted. The principal victims were ethnic Albanian civilians. In an application of the technique of ethnic cleansing exhibited earlier in Croatia and Bosnia and Herzegovina, Yugoslav Army forces (VJ) and Serb special police (MUP) would surround villages, shell and destroy them and drive out the local population. There were also the first reports of massacres of entire clans. The death of Adem Jashari, a regional KLA commander, added a sense of martyrdom on the part of the ethnic Albanians. There was a significant increase in the ranks of the KLA and a spread of hostilities.

The Security Council responded with the adoption of an arms embargo under Chapter VII of the UN Charter. It also started to lay down the principal elements which would need to be achieved to prevent an escalation: termination of violence and the excessive use of force again civilian populations, withdrawals of troops and special police, cessation of 'terrorist' acts and the initiation of meaningful dialogue. None of these conditions was met, however. Instead, the FRY/Serb security operations generated a massive displacement crisis, with some 300,000 ethnic Albanians driven from their homes over the summer of 1988. These actions were not countered by the imposition of economic sanctions by the Security Council, which was blocked by Russia, or by any other measures. The Contact Group, comprising France, Germany, Italy, Russia, the United Kingdom and the United States, was similarly hamstrung. On the one hand, it was found essential to keep Russia involved in the international administration of the escalating crisis. On the other hand, Russia precluded the adoption of measures which could have impressed upon the FRY/Serb leadership the need to moderate its policy. Instead, the EU/EC adopted rather limited sanctions which were not implemented by all of its members with equal vigour outside of the Contact Group or UN framework. In the meantime, the Contact Group attempted to establish dialogue among the parties with a view to achieving an interim political settlement which would stabilize the situation. This effort, led by US Ambassador Hill who engaged in shuttle diplomacy between the parties, progressed hesitantly, while the number of the displaced rose steadily. With the onset of winter, it was feared that a humanitarian catastrophe would become inevitable. There were also border incidents involving FRY/Serb forces and Albania, and a destabilization of

Macedonia, which has an ethnic Albanian population of around 30 per cent mainly inhabiting the regions adjacent to Kosovo, was feared. The UN Security Council adopted a further resolution, expressing its demands with greater force, but failing to add enforcement measures. NATO, however, issued a formal threat of the use of air strikes, or even a phased air campaign, against Yugoslavia, unless there was rapid compliance. There had been talk about possible NATO action throughout the summer. But a number of NATO states appeared unwilling to support the use of force, lessening the persuasiveness of threats uttered by politicians, especially in the United States and the United Kingdom. The Holbrooke mission of early October relieved NATO of having to carry out its uncomfortable threat. However, when inspected in the cold light of day, it emerged that the Holbrooke deal appeared to suffer from a number of shortcomings. Its military elements, providing for a cessation of offensive operations, a partial withdrawal of forces and the cantonment in Kosovo of others, were contained in unilateral FRY Serb commitments, which were not made public. Implementation was to be assured by a 2,000 strong OSCE verification mission which was unarmed and would need to rely on FRY/Serb cooperation. And the unilateral agreement by the Serb government to accept a political settlement within the space of a few weeks was permitted to dissipate in the further attempts of the Hill mission to achieve a settlement. Moreover, neither the political leadership of Kosovo nor the KLA had been involved in these arrangements. Nevertheless, the Holbrooke agreement was endorsed by the Security Council in a formal resolution.

Hostilities re-ignited in December 1998, when FRY/Serb forces commenced an offensive against ethnic Albanian villages in response to what it termed ethnic Albanian terrorism. The Racak massacre of January 1999 highlighted the brutality of such operations and a new stream of refugees emerged, this time under the harsh conditions of mid winter. In view of this situation, the Contact Group demanded that the parties assemble at Rambouillet near Paris to achieve a settlement based on the Hill proposals within a period of less than two weeks. This demand was backed by the threat of force by NATO. At Rambouillet, the Kosovar leadership moved with some difficulty towards the acceptance of an interim settlement, which was intended to bring with it NATO implementation according to the Dayton model for Bosnia and Herzegovina. However, neither side was initially willing to sign up to the interim agreement which emerged from the talks. After a period of consultation, the Kosovo delegation then signed. The FRY/Yugoslavia, which had appeared to be willing to endorse the political part of the text at Rambouillet, adopted a posture of total non-cooperation. It had in the meantime doubled its troop strength in Kosovo, and commenced an amazingly rapid and efficient strategy of forced deportation two days after the Kosovo delegates affixed their signatures to the text. This development led to the removal of the OSCE verifiers from the territory, and to the initiation of hostilities by NATO after a further attempt by Contact Group negotiators to achieve last minute agreement from Belgrade.

Whether it would have been possible at any stage in the period of relative inaction between 1990 and 1998 to obtain a settlement is of course open to question. Kosovo had taken a moderate position throughout. While not abandoning its claim to independence, it was willing to entertain other forms of settlement at least for the interim. However, no real attempt to address the crisis, rather than its symptoms, was made throughout those eight years. In the absence of significant outside pressure, Belgrade saw no reason to seek compromise and instead continued its policy of repression. Kosovo's own position became more difficult with the ascendancy of the KLA in 1998. However, by November of that year, the KLA had also declared that it might support at least an interim settlement. But Serbia's undertaking in the context of the Holbrooke agreement to accept an interim settlement was simply ignored. Instead, a situation was permitted to emerge whereby Serbia felt emboldened to test the decisiveness of NATO's threat of the use of force and to unmask the OSCE verifiers as impotent observers in the offensive that followed in December.

The inability or unwillingness of the key international actors to tackle the Kosovo issue head-on for nearly a decade could not even been undone by the Rambouillet process. This attempt to achieve a settlement at Rambouillet within the space of two weeks, backed by the threat of force, was clearly unique in modern history. However, it was not a genuine manifestation of a consensus by all actors that decisive action was now necessary, in the interest of humanity and of European stability. It was a desperate act launched by disparate actors. The prospects of Rambouillet were undermined by two factors. First, the negotiations were being conducted in a way which jeopardized Kosovo's acceptance of the outcome. This effectively nullified NATO's threat of force. In addition, the sponsors of the conference, the Contact Group, could not speak with one voice. Russia acted within the Contact Group, and within Chateau Rambouillet, as the openly declared champion of the FRY/Serbia, displaying division and disunity in the Contact Group. Again, the pressure which was believed to be brought to bear on Belgrade was dissipated in this way. A final opportunity to arrest the conflict was lost.

Competences of and hierarchies among international agencies

Another difficulty in the new constitutional system relates to the lack of institutional hierarchy in the formal assignment of public functions to international organs. While it is now accepted that states and international organizations can exercise international constitutional functions, for example when criticising the human rights performance of another state, or when acting together to reverse an act of aggression, it is not always clear which organs can exercise what competence and to what extent. The dispute about the legitimacy of action by a military alliance, NATO, to vindicate the humanitarian interests of a threatened population illustrates the sharp end of this dilemma.

The post-Cold War crisis of the former Yugoslavia occurred at a time when collective security institutions were seeking to adapt to a changing world. There emerged a the struggle for pre-eminence of conflict management agencies, a struggle which masked, to some extent, the conflict about the realignment of global power with the termination of the Cold War. The early episodes in the Yugoslav crisis had demonstrated that the much vaunted new European Security Architecture was more myth than reality. The attempt to achieve a settlement for Kosovo once again reopened the competition for pre-eminence between the OSCE, which Russia considers to be the principal focus of authority in relation to peace and security in Europe, the European Union and its as yet hesitant attempts to establish a Security Identity. Moreover, the United States and United Kingdom were fighting hard to preserve the dominant role of NATO.

Through the decade-long crisis in Kosovo, the CSCE/OSCE had undergone an important transformation, from a Cold War mechanism of confidence-building to a conflict-management structure of quite incredible complexity. The early CSCE mission to Kosovo highlighted the progress that had been made in this respect. The subsequent inactivity of the CSCE/OSCE, however, after Yugoslavia froze cooperation in view of the fact that her own participation in the organs of the CSCE had been suspended, also indicated the limitations of a mechanism still principally reliant on the cooperation of the target states of its diplomatic and other missions.

The European Union on the other hand was desperately attempting to inject new impetus into the establishment of its security and defence identity. A first attempt to use the EU as a crisis mechanism had failed in relation to Bosnia and Herzegovina. To the embarrassment of the Europeans, who had observed genocide take place unopposed, the crisis was finally resolved through the application of mainly US airpower under a NATO umbrella in a matter of days. While some attempts at mediation was made, the EU was unable to assert its position early in the Kosovo crisis. In the later stages, the EU adopted sanctions outside the United Nations Security Council, but with great hesitation. The EU also took a leading role in the Contact Group and its attempts to achieve a peaceful settlement and through its energetic Special Envoy, Austrian diplomat Wolfgang Petritsch. The economic muscle of the Union was also brought to bear in the context of the Rambouillet talks, where considerable resources were promised for reconstruction and development of the region. The choice of a French chateau for the talks, rather than a US airbase in Ohio, was intended to symbolize the ability of the Europeans to address matters in their own region. The strong role of the United States in the talks did, however, somewhat strain this illusion.

The Western European Union (WEU) had also attempted to change with the times. It saw itself as the military arm of European security cooperation. However, the United Kingdom and United States were not always fully enthusiastic about the development of structures which might devalue NATO. Hence, the WEU continued to develop on paper, ostensibly with the cooperation of NATO and its members, who promised to make available assets for its operations. In reality, however, the WEU was sidelined in most important instances, often reduced to minor support roles for NATO or other actors. It was not permitted to play any significant role in relation to Kosovo.

NATO itself was also in the process of transformation from a purely defensive alliance to a security organization with a broader remit. This had been powerfully demonstrated by the use of force under the aegis of NATO in relation to Bosnia and Herzegovina, and by the subsequent deployment of IFOR/SFOR, the NATO-led peace-enforcement mission in that territory. There remained, however, significant transatlantic differences as to NATO operations which might take place outside of a UN Security Council mandate.

The contest about the relationship between regional security and the universal system of collective security administered by the United Nations Security Council became, of course, particularly pronounced towards the final phase of the crisis. The provisions of Chapter VIII of the United Nations Charter which require prior Security Council authorization for enforcement action by regional organizations or arrangements had already been undermined by recent practice of ECOWAS in relation to Liberia and Sierra Leone, of SADC in relation to Lesotho, and, to a lesser extent, by NATO in relation to Bosnia and Herzegovina, the latter being covered by a measure of Security Council authority. But when NATO started to consider the threat of the use of force in the light of the displacement crisis of the summer 1998, Russia threatened a "new Cold War" over Kosovo.[5] It actively undermined the likelihood of such a threat emerging, by producing an apparent settlement of its own in direct talks with Belgrade in the middle of the ongoing hostilities, which failed to subside. When NATO finally moved towards the formal threat of the use of force, Russia formally protested. This attitude was evidence of an attempt to prevent the emergence of a unipolar system dominated by the United States and NATO. Hence, Russia continued to oppose the very concept of a settlement which might enforced by NATO. Should that turn out to be impossible, Russia at least sought to preserve a controlling role for itself in the further administration of the crisis. This was to be achieved by retaining the involvement in the crisis of collective bodies in which it was represented, and where it could block decisions requiring consensus. These bodies were the Contact Group itself, and the OSCE, which also mostly acts under the consensus principle, despite its membership of 55. Finally, there was the United Nations Security Council, where Russia enjoys veto powers.

---

[5] Russian General Warns of a 'New Cold War' over Kosovo, International Herald Tribune, 20-21 June 1998, p. 4.

The Security Council disenfranchised itself from exercising a leading role in the crisis. Initially, member states were unwilling to involve the body in a dispute which seemed to have strong internal dimensions. Subsequently, more decisive action in the Council was blocked by Russia. In an odd episode, China too made its ability to determine Council decisions felt. At a crucial phase in the crisis, shortly before the outbreak of hostilities involving NATO, China vetoed the routine extension of the United Nations preventative deployment mission in Macedonia. This action was really unrelated to the merits of that UN operation, which had been one of the most celebrated successes of proactive peace-keeping. The Mission had had a considerable role in preventing the outbreak of ethnic strife in Macedonia itself, and the need for this role to be fulfilled was just about to increase significantly. China took this action in the pursuit of national interest, to penalize Macedonia for its decision to establish diplomatic relations with Taiwan.

The UN Security Council can only fulfil its pre-eminent role in relation to international peace and security if its members regard themselves, when voting in the Council, as agents of the international system as a whole, rather than as representatives of national interest. Of course, China and Russia are not the only states that on occasion fail to perform their function in the Council in this way. But Russia's determination to protect the FRY/Serbia from stronger Council action made a side-lining of the UN layer of collective security at the peak phase of the crisis almost inevitable. Belgrade could feel immune from the threat of tough economic sanctions and was even less inclined to accept the advice of Russian interlocutors and settle the conflict within a UN framework and with strong Russian involvement as Moscow had intended. With no prospect of decisive action from the Council, and given the threat both to humanitarian values and to the stability of the region, the only remaining option appeared to be the unilateral threat or use of force by NATO.

This circumstance placed the UN Secretary-General in rather an invidious position. He had observed the unhappy role of UN peace-keepers in Bosnia and Herzegovina, culminating in the massacre committed by Bosnian Serb forces at Srebrenica, a UN protected 'safe area'. In his reports over the summer of 1998, he darkly observed that a similar situation was now emerging in Kosovo, civilians once again becoming the principal targets of FRY/Serb forces. Before NATO issued its threat of force in support of the Rambouillet talks, he actually ventured to NATO headquarters and reminded NATO that a new Bosnian-style scenario could not be tolerated, effectively encouraging NATO action. However, he knew full well that such action could only come about outside of a mandate from the Security Council. The hope was, of course, that the threat would not need to be implemented, a settlement having been achieved at Rambouillet. In the same way, the Security Council had formally endorsed the Holbrooke agreement after the fact. The agreement had also been obtained through the unilateral threat of force by NATO. When NATO did act upon its threat after the failure of Rambouillet, he adopted a carefully balanced statement, indicating his understanding of the need for even military action under certain circumstance while emphasizing the need to preserve the pre-eminence of the United Nations in such matters.

The need felt by NATO to threaten and ultimately take forcible action taken outside of Security Council raised difficult questions in relation to the assignment of decision-making authority in the emerging constitutional system. In principle, only the Council can authorize the use of force in circumstances other than self-defence. No such power resided in regional organizations of collective security or alliances. And the attempt by the United Kingdom and the United States to arrogate to themselves the authority to implement forcibly the demands of the Security Council had been rejected by a significant number of states only a few months before. In December 1998, those two states had launched a three-day aerial bombardment of Iraq, purportedly to constrain Baghdad to comply with Security Council resolutions concerning restrictions and the monitoring of its weapons programmes. However, the Council itself had not mandated such an operation.

Rather than claiming a right to exercise authority instead of the Council, NATO took a different tack in relation to Kosovo. It argued that it was internationally entitled to act under the legal justification of humanitarian intervention. Just like self-defence, that doctrine constituted according to NATO an exception to the prohibition of the use of force. It permitted direct action by individual states, alliances or regional organizations in the face of grave and overwhelming humanitarian emergencies which cannot be tackled by less invasive measures.

However, NATO would have to admit that, up to 1990, it was widely accepted that there existed no exception to the prohibition of the use of force which would permit forcible humanitarian action in the absence of the consent of the government and/or effective authorities of the target state. Of course, since 1990, there have been some 15 instances of forcible humanitarian action. But most of these were conducted within the framework of Chapter VII mandates granted by the UN Security Council. Some more adventurous activities undertaken by regional arrangements had at least obtained a retroactive blessing from the Council. The administration of forcible humanitarian action without some justificatory link to the Security Council was a more difficult issue. True, forcible action had been taken by a self-selected coalition of the willing in relation to northern and southern Iraq without a formal Chapter VII mandate. However, this action was initiated when Iraq had just suffered a significant military defeat by the international coalition and was internationally entirely isolated. It was therefore doubted whether the absence of significant objections in that instance really confirmed a universal acceptance of a new right of humanitarian 'intervention'.

The Security Council was, of course, not entirely left out of NATO's equation. It was argued that NATO was only acting after the Council itself had confirmed the existence of an overwhelming emergency and had laid down the requirements Belgrade would have to meet in order to terminate that emergency. It was clear, therefore, that NATO was not unilaterally imposing its own conditions upon Yugoslavia. Instead, it was using a unilateral right of action in a limited and proportionate way, precisely aiming at the achievement of the collective goals the Council had established.

Of course, even for those who agree that there does exist a right of humanitarian action in international law, the threat of the use of force in relation to the Rambouillet conference posed certain problems. It assumed that a failure by Belgrade to accept a very detailed settlement of the Kosovo issue would constitute a circumstance triggering an overwhelming humanitarian emergency. In the event, the commencement of a massive and pre-planned campaign of forced deportation of what at one stage seemed to be almost the entire ethnic Albanian population of Kosovo just before the bombing campaign commenced relieved NATO of having to answer this point. Still, the NATO operation did give rise to an important debate in the Security Council and elsewhere about the existence or otherwise of a right to unilateral humanitarian action involving the use of force—an issue to be addressed more fully in Volume 2 of this *Series*.

Conclusion

The emerging international constitutional system functioned well at the level of identifying the grave and persistent violations of the human rights of the majority population of Kosovo. In fact, in many respects, this episode inaugurated an integrated human rights reporting mechanism, involving a variety of organs in an impressive way. However, no matter how vigorously human rights violations are reported upon and condemned, where the offending state fails to take notice, further action is required.

Such further international action taken in response to the Kosovo crisis was hesitant and in some respects schizophrenic. On the one hand, there was universal agreement that Kosovo constituted the real 'powder keg' of the Balkans. On the other hand, this realization seemed to be transformed into a hope that the situation would go away if ignored for a sufficiently long time. The reluctance to tackle the crisis head-on was not really rooted in an absence of appropriate institutions or mechanisms which could be brought to bear upon it. The failure was rather based in the reluctance to deploy the existing mechanisms of collective security in relation to a crisis claimed to be internal to a member state of the United Nations. Inaction was also fostered by the knowledge that the FRY/Serb authorities would not easily be persuaded to depart from the course they had chosen in relation to Kosovo—an attitude which in turn led Belgrade to believe that its actions, however vigorously condemned, would in the end remain unopposed.

Given the inability of international decision-makers to escape from the strictures of the classical international system, which is not geared towards the adoption of an integrated strategy of addressing self-determination conflicts, it was indeed inevitable that significant conflict would break out at some stage. The population of Kosovo could not live forever under the kind of oppression which had been so clearly reported upon at the international level. In the end, contrary to the expectation of some, it was not a widespread and suicidal rising of that population which triggered international action. Instead, it was Belgrade's own way of engaging an initially small insurgent movement which led to more decisive international action, including eventually the use of force by NATO. Instead of employing counter-insurgency techniques of a more limited nature, military actions were focused on civilian concentrations, leading to an internationally visible exodus of ethnic Albanians and a humanitarian crisis of some magnitude. The international administration of the climax of this crisis through the Rambouillet Conference and the events which followed do confirm Richard Holbrooke's sentiment of the accidental nature of foreign policy-making, even by the world's most powerful states, and even when such states engage their national interest to the extent of going to war. If the materials presented in this book demonstrate one thing, however, it must surely be that belated and haphazard approaches to inevitable crises are not sufficient. Uncomfortable though it may be, the international community will have to find more structured ways of addressing difficult issues such as unacceptable practices of ethnic politics and struggles for self-determination.

Chapter 3: The Positions of the Parties

History is a nightmare from which I am trying to awake. James Joyce's famous dictum, it seems, underpins the saga of Serbia and Kosovo. The story of the Serbs and Kosovo Albanians (and, indeed, the Albanians in general) is one of two peoples struggling against the tides of history that have swept over the Balkan region. And, if one listens to the official historians or the politicians of both sides, it is these forces of history which have conspired to deprive each of them of the imagined promise of national destiny—the unification of Serbs and Albanians respectively in one state. This is a promise which the national states of Western Europe could more or less fulfil, when feudal empires and kingdoms consolidated into national states as the complex medieval world gave way to a simpler system based on 'national' sovereignty. It is a vision of nationhood which the Serbs, too, appeared to be able to realize for a brief period, at the brink of modernity.

Slav peoples who may be considered the ancestors of the Serbs had established themselves in the Balkans when the dark ages which followed upon the collapse of the Roman Empire melted into the early middle ages. However, only towards the end of the twelfth century did the Serbs expand their influence in the region, stretching the boundaries of Rascia (later Serbia) at the expense of the crumbling Byzantine Empire also towards the territory now known as Kosovo. By the middle of the thirteenth century, under the reign of Dusan, Rascia had not only achieved territorial expansion, with Kosovo at its heart, but also established its separate religious identity through the granting of a Serb Patriarchate by the Greek Orthodox Church, based in Pec. A Serb 'state' encompassing most Serbs (and, of course, others) had come into existence.

However, almost as soon as this consolidation of the Serb nation into early statehood had been achieved, it came under severe pressure from the Ottomans—a process made worse by internal divisions. In June 1389, an Ottoman army defeated the assembled Serb forces, led by Prince Lazar who fell during the battle at Kosovo Polje (the field of Blackbirds), near Prishtina. Lazar's son, Prince Stephan, and his successors retained control over Kosovo for several decades, but by 1459 there had occurred the "final extinction of the medieval Serbian state".[1]

Of course, Serbs continued to live in the region under Ottoman rule, although there occurred a significant exodus in 1690, led by Orthodox Patriach of Pec Arsenije IV himself, in the wake of an ill-fated attempt by Austria to conquer the territory which had been supported by Serbs. Similar events followed upon the Austro-Turkish war of 1788-91.[2] In 1804, and frequently afterwards, with the failing attempts of the Ottoman Empire to modernize its structures of governance and to retain control over its territorial possessions, Serb nationalism manifested itself in rebellions often centred in Kosovo and often involving bloodshed. It was within the context of the international administration of the dismantling of the Ottoman Empire, the 'sick man of Europe', through the Concert of Europe system of congress diplomacy that Serbia regained statehood. The Congress of Berlin of 1878 set about the reordering of the Balkans, granting independence for Serbia and Montenegro respectively, after the Ottomans had withdrawn their last garrisons in 1862, and providing for a suzerain status for Albania within the Ottoman Empire.[3] In 1882, a Serb Kingdom was proclaimed. In the years which followed, Serbia agitated for territorial expansion, including a demand for the incorporation of Kosovo, still part of the Ottoman Empire, and access to the Adriatic. A movement for the establishment of a Greater Serbia culminated in the establishment of the secret association of the Black Hand or 'Union of Death' under Colonel Dimitrijevic Apis in 1911.

While Serbia enjoyed a period of medieval statehood principally encompassing all Serbs, the Albanians saw themselves as a people forever denied their national state. The ethnic origin of the mainly Muslim Albanians is somewhat mysterious,[4] although they consider themselves descendants of the Illyrians.[5] They divide into the Gegs of the northern region, including Kosovo, and the Tosks of southern Albania. With the crumbling of the Ottoman Empire, hopes for the establishment of an Albanian state were finally raised. However, there also emerged the prospect of the apportionment of mainly Albanian inhabited territories among the states seeking to profit from a dismemberment of the Ottoman Empire. In response to these pressures, in 1878, there was formed the Prizren League, an alliance of clans, in due course demanding the establishment of a unified Albanian Ottoman province under Albanian administration.[6] Demands for autonomy were converted into claims for virtual Albanian independence in the cause of the rising of 1912. The ensuing instability emboldened the regional states of Bulgaria, Serbia, Montenegro and Greece to launch the first Balkan war later that year. Serbia rapidly expelled the remaining Turkish forces from Kosovo, advancing on the Adriatic and bringing significant

---

[1] Noel Malcolm, *Kosovo: A Short History* (1998, 2nd ed.) [*Kosovo*, hereinafter] 92.
[2] Several historians see this exodus as the starting point of the change of the demographic character of the territory in favour of ethnic Albanians, e.g., Barbara Jelavich, *History of the Balkans* (1983) 93; Miranda Vickers, *The Albanians* (rev. ed. 1997) 13.
[3] Vickers, *supra* note 2, at 70.
[4] Malcolm, *Kosovo* pp. 22ff.
[5] Vickers, *supra* note 2, at 1.
[6] Barbara Jelavich, *History of the Balkans* (1983) 363.

destruction upon the Albanian population. Montenegro, too, established control over Albanian-inhabited territories. However, at the London Conference, the Great European Powers decreed that some of these successes were to be reversed, leading to the creation of the state of Albania.

Kosovo remained under Serb control, although it has been pointed out that it was not, in fact, formally and constitutionally incorporated into Serbia.[7] During this period, events in Kosovo were so shocking to the international community that an international commission of enquiry was established by the Carnegie Endowment in 1914. It reported that a veritable policy of ethnic cleansing was in operation: "Houses and whole villages reduced to ashes, unarmed and innocent populations massacred … such were the means which were employed and are still being employed by the Serb-Montenegrin soldiery, with a view to the entire transformation of the ethnic character of regions inhabited exclusively by Albanians."[8]

During World War I, some of the horrors visited upon the Albanians of Kosovo in the course of the Balkan wars were replayed, although there was also counter-violence when local Albanians temporarily exercised control. The end of the war left Kosovo within the new Yugoslav Kingdom of the Serbs, Croats and Slovenes. Serbia immediately engaged in a regime of repression of the Albanian population, which was also subjected to confiscation of land and other property. An attempt was made to introduce Serb settlers. A resistance movement failed, having been isolated from support from Albania, which initially developed friendly relations with Belgrade. In 1937, Vaso Cubrilovic, a leading member of the Serbian Academy opined: "At a time when Germany can expel tens of thousands of Jews and Russia can shift millions of people from one part of the continent to another, the shifting of a few hundred thousands Albanians will not lead to the outbreak of world war."[9] However, when war did break out the pendulum of historical injustice swung back the other way. Albania came under Italian tutelage during the first part of the war, which also included Kosovo. Now, the Serbs were prosecuted by Albanians.[10] The capitulation of Italy in 1943 brought little relief, as many Kosovo Albanians appeared to view the German presence which was substituted for the Italians as something of a liberation from Serb dominance. Throughout World War II, acts of revenge drove several tenths of thousands of Serbs from the territory. However, not all Kosovo Albanians were collaborators. Some joined in Marshall Tito's partisan movement and a small communist cadre of Albanians was established in Kosovo.

At the end of the Second World War, Kosovo found itself under Serb rule once more, although within the framework of the new Federal Yugoslavia, consisting of six republics (Bosnia and Herzegovina, Croatia, Macedonia, Montenegro, Serbia, Slovenia). Given its majority Albanian population and the somewhat ambiguous promises of self-determination made during the war by the National Liberation forces, the territory was given autonomous status within Serbia, along with Vojvodina which contains a sizeable minority of Hungarians. Serb repression in Kosovo was severe, the memories of the treatment of Serbs during the war being freshly in the mind of the new regime of the republic.[11] Tens of thousands of ethnic Albanians were persuaded to emigrate, mainly to Turkey.[12]

Yugoslavia underwent several constitutional changes in the years that followed.[13] The position of Kosovo and of its majority population improved in the 1960s, presaging the great constitutional reform of 1974.[14] This development had been induced by increasing restlessness among the Kosovo Albanians culminating in risings in 1968—a development which somewhat shocked the Communist establishment. After all, the official doctrine of brotherhood and unity of peoples, nations and nationalities was supposed to have overcome ethnic differences. By 1969, a more liberal statute for Kosovo had been issued and other reforms followed. The 1974 Constitution of the Socialist Federal Republic of Yugoslavia brought for the two autonomous provinces of Kosovo and Vojvodina republic status in all but name. Ethnic Albanian self-administration was effectively established and guaranteed at the federal level, where the province enjoyed equal representation with the republics in federal organs. Kosovo also established important cultural and educational institutions of its own, leading to a clearer expression of ethnic Albanian identity. This, in turn, fed growing resentment in Serbia. While the leading politicians at the time did not wish to attack openly Tito's policy, the effective loss of control over Kosovo by Serbia was increasingly bemoaned.[15] Demographic shifts in the province were also occurring. According to Yugoslav statistics, in 1953 27 per cent of the population in Kosovo were Serbs and Montenegrins, but by the time of the 1991 census, they made up only 10 per cent or less. According to Serbia's official view, this development was due to a new phase of driving ethnic Serbs out of the province. Others simply observed that some Serbs left due to the economic backwardness imposed upon the region by economic central planning, coupled with the fact that the birth-rate among the urban Serb middle classes fell below that of the ethnic Albanian majority.

---

[7] Malcolm, *Kosovo, p.* 264ff.
[8] Carnegie Endowment, *Report* (1914) 151, quoted in Malcolm, *Kosovo*, p. 254.
[9] Quoted in Tim Judah, *The Serbs* (1997) 149f.
[10] Stevan K. Pavlowitch, *A History of the Balkans*, 1804-1945 (1999) 321.
[11] Tim Judah, *The Serbs* (1997) 131f.
[12] Viktor Meir, *Yugoslavia: A History of its Demise* (1999) 27 {Meir hereinafter].
[13] *See* Chapter 4.
[14] John R. Lampe, *Yugoslavia as History* (1996) 296
[15] A Serbian *Blue Book* criticising the reforms was cautiously published in 1977.

On 11 March 1981, a little less than a year after Tito's death, student unrest broke out in the University of Prishtina, quickly spreading into wider protest generated by economic and other conditions which the new autonomy had failed to redress. Over the following year, some 2,000 'nationalists' were convicted and official rhetoric about the purported suffering of Serbs in Kosovo increased in vigour. This view was given formal expression in the famous memorandum penned by members of the Serb Academy of Sciences in 1985, and published in fragments a year later.

By 1987, a move within Serbia to 'unify' the republic through constitutional changes in relation to Kosovo gained momentum. In September of that year, Slobodan Milosevic, at the 8th Plenum of the Serb Party Central Committee, commenced the process which led in December to the displacement of his mentor, Serb Party Chairman Ivan Stambolic, largely on the basis of nationalist programmes directed primarily against Kosovo.[16] Serbia then secured for itself an increasing role in the Federal organs by establishing control over Montenegro, Vojvodina and finally, Kosovo. The leadership of the province was replaced by what many Kosovo Albanians perceived to be 'stooges' of Belgrade, and its federal status was abolished through controversial reforms of the Serb constitution.[17] When, in 1990, Serbia adopted an entirely new constitution which fully subordinated Kosovo to the republic, Kosovo declared sovereignty. There followed a referendum on independence, a declaration of independence in 1991 and the election of a new government led by President Ibrahim Rugova in 1992.[18]

The take-over of Vojvodina and Kosovo, and to some extent of Montenegro, had been observed with great concern, initially by Slovenia, and then also by Croatia. Croatia, in particular, had special concerns, given the large number of Serbs inhabiting its Krajina region. After all, it appeared as if the scheme outlined by the Serb Academy members was now being implemented. The memorandum had claimed: "Except for the time under the Independent State of Croatia, the Serbs in Croatia have never before been as jeopardized as they are today. A resolution of their national status is a question of overriding political importance. If solutions are not found, the consequences might well be disastrous, not only for Croatia, but for the whole of Yugoslavia".[19] Having observed Serbia's action in relation to Kosovo, Croatia sought to strengthen the Federation, with the support of Slovenia, by preparing a draft for a new federal constitution in December 1990. However, attempts to rescue the Federation by restructuring it failed. Serbia was in a dominant position and could see that any changes could only to have negative consequences for it. Hence, none occurred.

On 25-6 June 1991, Croatia and Slovenia both declared independence, resulting in a short armed confrontation with the latter, and a prolonged armed struggle with the former. The violent struggle, characterized by brutal attacks against Croat civilians, left about a third of Croatia, including the Krajina region, under Serb occupation. Despite the attempts of the United Nations to set up so-called UN protected areas, a campaign of what was now called 'ethnic cleansing' continued to be pursued, only to be replaced by an exodus of Serbs when Croatia forcibly took the territory again a few years later.

While initially pressing for the continued territorial integrity of Yugoslavia, the international community accepted towards the end of 1991 that the Socialist Federal Republic of Yugoslavia was in a process of dissolution.[20] Recognition of Croatia and Slovenia by European Union and other states in January 1992 was followed by independence of Bosnia and Herzegovina that spring. Once again, the army of the rump-Yugoslavia (now composed only of Serbia and Montenegro), occupied a significant part of Bosnia's territory. In the 70 per cent of Bosnian territory under the control of the FRY and its local ally, the self-proclaimed Srpska Republic, a hitherto unprecedented campaign of ethnic cleansing probably amounting to genocide was unleashed. Mainly Muslim inhabited areas were surrounded by military forces. Civilian concentrations were attacked, the inhabitants driven out, conveyed to concentration camps or massacred. Over a quarter of a million mainly Muslim Bosnians were killed, and some 2.4 million of Bosnia's pre-war inhabitants found themselves displaced.

While the international community attempted to address the Yugoslav crisis, Serbia had continued to consolidate her position vis-à-vis Kosovo, adopting a formal legislative programme based on ethnic distinction. Some 80,000 ethnic Albanians were removed from public office and from leading positions in industry (then still state-run). Legislation was adopted to encourage Serb settlement in the province and attempts were made to de-nationalize Kosovo Albanians living abroad. It was also argued that many of the ethnic Albanians in Kosovo were not Kosovars at all, but had illegally filtered into the province and would need to be removed. Repression was fierce in the province, although it did not reach the level of violence exhibited in occupied Croatia and Bosnia and Herzegovina.[21]

Initially, Kosovo responded with great moderation, under the leadership of literary criticist Dr Ibrahim Rugova. A parallel system of civil administration was established for the 90 per cent ethnic Albanians in the territory. However, by the end of 1997 the Kosovo Liberation Army commenced more widespread operations. This was answered by a military campaign,

---

[16] Misha Glenny, *The Fall of Yugoslavia* (1993) 32.
[17] *See* Chapter IV.B.
[18] *See* Chapter IV.C.
[19] Quoted in Tim Judah, *The Serbs* (1997) 159.
[20] *See* Chapter V.A.
[21] *See* Chapter VI.

which employed some of the techniques previously witnessed in Croatia and Bosnia and Herzegovina. Again, rather than searching for individual 'terrorists', entire villages were surrounded, shelled and then attacked. Houses were burned to the ground and massacres of entire extended families, or clans, of ethnic Albanians took place. Over the summer of 1998, this led to the displacement of 300,000 ethnic Albanians. After a lull in the hostilities brought about by the short-lived Holbrooke agreement of October 1998, fighting commenced again in December, causing a further exodus, this time in the harsh conditions of mid-winter.

With the outbreak of hostilities involving NATO in March 1999, Kosovo was subjected to a massive and extraordinarily rapid campaign of ethnic cleansing, moving over half of its ethnic Albanian population of about 1,7 million out of the territory in a matter of a few weeks, and transforming hundreds of thousands more into internally displaced people, seeking to survive in the forests and mountains of Kosovo. The reversal of this action after the conclusion of NATO military operations in June 1999 left Kosovo temporarily in the control of the Kosovo Liberation Army. The massive presence of NATO, and the hesitant arrival of United Nations civilian administrators and police forces, could not prevent revenge attacks against the Serbs of Kosovo, most of whom fled.

Overall, therefore, the attempt to recreate medieval Greater Serbia resulted in another catastrophe for the Serbian people, at least those living outside of the Serb republic. The Krajina Serbs had to flee their ancient homeland. Some of them were settled in Kosovo, but had to move out again in the wake of the defeat of Yugoslavia at the hands of NATO. The Bosnian Serbs remain trapped in a twilight existence under the Dayton accords, formally part of Bosnia and Herzegovina, but inhabiting the internationally isolated territory of Srpska. And the Serbs from Kosovo have become unwelcome refugees in Serbia proper.

When considering this brief gloss on the history of the region, and the two perspectives on it which follow, one might indeed be tempted to think that one is observing the inevitable brutality of the ebb and flow of Balkan nationalism in operation. However, history is not a force of nature and its events are man-made. The freezing of inter-ethnic relations in Tito's Yugoslavia had not resulted in a break in the chain of history which had brought untold sorrows to the region before World War II. But the awakening of the forces of nationalism was a conscious act, inspired, fostered and exploited by politicians, in particular the Milosevic government of Serbia and later the rump-Yugoslavia. Outbreaks of violence which followed were not events of historical necessity. They were planned by politicians and executed by a military machine according to carefully laid strategic plans. Nationalist ideology underpinned these actions, and made popular support for such acts of brutality possible. It also stifled dissent. Those who doubted the wisdom of a campaign of ethnic cleansing and probable genocide were branded as 'traitors' rather than regarded as concerned patriots.

The sense of righteousness of the nationalists in Serbia and to some extent also in Croatia, and the denial of what had occurred in Bosnia and Herzegovina, was not really opposed by the European states who took a lead in attempting to 'manage' the Yugoslav crisis. Instead of being confronted by the international community with responsibility for Europe's first post-war genocide, Serb politicians were being relied upon to cooperate with the new 'freezing' of inter-ethnic relations in Bosnia, through the means of the Dayton settlement for Bosnia. That settlement endorsed the results of ethnic cleansing, by turning Bosnia and Herzegovina into a divided state, held together by a heavy international military presence.

The violence unleashed in Kosovo seemed to reflect this experience. Despite the invention of the International Criminal Tribunal for the former Yugoslavia, no accountability had been established for the leadership in Serbia. The Kosovo conflict, it could now be claimed, was an internal affair of Serbia. Ethnic cleansing was pursued a bit more cautiously, aiming less at the destruction of a population and more at its displacement. But the assumption that disputes can be effectively settled through the disproportionate use of force and action directed against civilians, who can simply be removed from their native homes by the hundreds of thousands, had not really been effectively challenged.

Of course, contrary to the explanations of some, this type of action or violence is not inherent in the Balkans. Even at the conclusion of World War II, Western Europe itself witnessed and sanctioned the forced displacement of millions. In other areas of the world, ethnic cleansing is being pursued in ways not unlike Serb action in Kosovo. As the final touches are put to this book, events in Eastern Timor bear this out with depressing clarity. The difference is, of course, that Western Europe has engaged in a conscious strategy to try and overcome the mindset which makes such actions possible, and to create institutions of political integration to support this process. The shock of Germany's genocide in World War II made this possible.

Even after the conclusion of NATO's armed operations, the issue of Kosovo is by no means settled. Given their recent experiences, the people of Kosovo will not accept a re-incorporation into Serbia, even if autonomy and self-governance is restored. The challenge will now be to induce the peoples of the region to understand what was actually done in their name over the past decade and to recognize the realities which have obtained as a result of recent events. Europe will have a very significant part to play in persuading the peoples of the region that ethnic division can and must be overcome, if stability is to be established in the long term. Otherwise, NATO will find itself having to continue freezing the status quo in the area through a large military presence indefinitely.

A.   Memorandum Prepared by the FRY on Kosovo and Metohija, presented on 23 March 1998

... It is a historical fact that since the sixth century, and for 1,300 years already, Kosovo and Metohija has been the cradle of Serbian statehood and of its culture, which is attested by the greatest concentration of Serbian medieval monasteries and other cultural monuments. Until the Turks came to the Balkans and began their domination in this part of Serbia at the end of the fourteenth century, the Serbian capital (Prizren) and the seat of the Serbian patriarchate (Pec) were located there. That Kosovo and Metohija is part of Serbia had also been confirmed by the London Treaty of 1912. With the Turkish occupation, the Serbs were gradually pushed out of the region towards the North and West (towards Budapest and Vienna) Kosovo and Metohija was settled with islamized Albanians. Consequently, even in the fourteenth century the process of ethnic cleansing of Serbs from Kosovo and Metohija started and the regions's resettlement with Albanians began. However, that has never brought into question the fact that Kosovo and Metohija is an integral part of Serbia until the present day. The process of ethnic cleansing of the Serbs from Kosovo and Metohija has continued over the entire period of history, particularly during periods of occupation of Kosovo and Metohija by foreign conquerors. Between 250,000 and 300,000 Serbs and Montenegrins currently live in Kosovo and Metohija. During the seventies and the eighties under pressure and as a result of an aggressive ideology of Albanian separatism, almost 200,000 Serbs and Montenegrins left the region. Most of them now live in Belgrade, Kragujevac, Krusevac, Kraljevo and in other larger towns in Serbia. They have been expelled by various methods, ranging from threats, burning of homes, mass destruction of gravestones, blackmail, to murders and execution of entire Serb families. The cases of the Milacic, Martinovic and many other families whose many members were ambushed and killed, are well known. Attacks on historical and cultural monuments, their destruction or damage, was also part of the methods of Albanian separatists to arouse fear and to force Serbs out. Thus, the case of raging Albanian terrorists who gouged out the eyes of a fresco painting at the twelfth-century monastery of Devic has entered the European and international records of vandalism and terrorism. At the end of 1997, and particularly in 1998, terrorism broke out suddenly with an aim of destabilizing the situation and internationalizing the problem. In the activities of the State authorities of the Republic of Serbia, on 28 February and 5 March 1998, the bulk of terrorist forces in Kosovo and Metohija was crushed, and order and peace were restored. However, these activities were used in some foreign circles as a pretext to internationalize this issue and put new pressures on the Republic of Serbia and the FR of Yugoslavia. Contrary to all international norms and the usual practice, the question of Kosovo and Metohija is being placed on the agenda of some international organizations and bodies. Ultimatums and threats of sanctions loom over the Republic of Serbia and the FR of Yugoslavia. Liquidation of terrorists is being interpreted as State repression, which is de facto leading to tacit support not only of separatism but terrorism as well.

Legal status: Kosovo and Metohija is one of the two autonomous provinces within the Republic of Serbia. The legal status of the provinces is regulated in the Constitution of the Republic of Serbia and is equal for both provinces. In Vojvodina, the other autonomous province where 27 national minorities live, accounting for 44 per cent of Vojvodina's total population, there is no inter-ethnic tension. The members of the predominant Serb population and national minorities live in harmony and fully exercise their constitutional and legal rights, including human and civil rights and the rights granted to national minorities (schools in mother tongue, additional national programmes in the framework of the education programmes of the Republic of Serbia, public media in the languages of national minorities, fostering their own language and culture, etc.). In Kosovo and Metohija where the Albanian national minority is predominant, the situation is totally different. The members of the Albanian national minority deliberately refuse to exercise some of the rights they have been granted. Even when they do, they hide it in order to leave the impression with the international political structures and media that they have been allegedly stripped of their rights and that their existence has been threatened, in an attempt to justify foreign interference into internal affairs of the Republic of Serbia. Members of the Albanian ethnic minority do not use one of the basic political rights - the right of universal suffrage in the Republic of Serbia and the FRY. The reason for this, apart from boycotting the Federal Republic of Yugoslavia and its state organs and institutions, is a deliberate attempt at manipulating the international community, as well as their fear that by going to the poles an insight would be gained as to the true number of the Albanian ethnic minority in Kosovo and Metohija. In this way they are losing the possibility of influencing political life on the local, provincial, republican and federal level and participating in the decision-making process and adoption of laws which directly pertain to their status and interests. Such conduct mostly harms the members of the Albanian national minority, causing tensions and inter-ethnic conflicts and slows down the province's development. At the same time, this is contrary to articles 20 and 21 of the Framework Convention of the Council of Europe on the protection of national minorities which calls for the loyalty of the members of the national minority to the State they live in. The reason for such behaviour of a part of members of the Albanian national minority is fear caused by threats and blackmail by separatist and terrorist leaders. This is convincingly proven by the fact that more than half of the victims of terrorists in Kosovo and Metohija are members of the Albanian national minority. Their only "sin" was that they have demonstrated loyalty towards Serbia as their State. Republics of Serbia and Montenegro comprise the Federal Republic of Yugoslavia. By their Constitutions they have been defined as States of equal citizens. The rights of members of national minorities in the FRY have been guaranteed also in accordance with the international documents in this field, as well as with the Council of Europe Framework Convention for protection of national minorities, which the Governments of Serbia and the FRY fully accept and respect. The Governments of the FRY and of the Republic of Serbia cannot possibly be responsible for failure to exercise the rights guaranteed under the Constitution and the laws.

In peace and harmony: In its policy, the Government of Serbia makes a clear distinction between the overwhelming majority of the members of Albanian national minority who live and work normally, who wish to exercise their rights in peace and harmony with other citizens of Serbia and Yugoslavia on the one hand, and separatist leaders who offer false promises, backwardness, uncertainty and poverty. The Government of Serbia is ready for any dialogue with the members of any national minority on possible inconsistencies of the legal system of the Republic of Serbia regarding national minorities or some shortcomings in the exercise of human, civil or national rights of national minorities. Wishing to do the best it can to assist in their full exercise, the Government of the Republic of Serbia charged a Minister in the Government of the Republic of Serbia to deal exclusively with the problems related to human and minority rights. Nevertheless, nowhere in the world is there negotiation with secessionists and terrorists, since they attack the country's territorial integrity and peace and security of the citizens.

Separatism: For many years now, the separatist leadership has had secession of Kosovo as its political goal and platform. As of late, encouraged by certain outside support they even claim that publicly, which unfortunately does not meet with adequate reaction of the international factors that offer relatively lukewarm reactions to this flagrant violation of one of the basic foundations of the international relations - preservation of the State borders and territorial integrity of the States. In doing so, they ignore the positions of major international factors that there should be no support for separatism, that the territorial integrity and sovereignty of Serbia and the FRY have to be respected. That leadership refuses dialogue which would lead to solutions to concrete questions within Serbia - they insist on their position all or nothing! To the extent that the region of the former Yugoslavia is being stabilized, owing to the great contribution of the FRY, through the implementation of the Dayton/Paris peace agreement - the separatist leadership, supported by certain foreign circles - does its best to create the atmosphere of tension and instability. On that basis, they seek pressures on the FRY and the internationalization of the issue. In such conditions, a number of extremist leaders opted for terrorism as a means to an end, whereas others still have not distanced themselves from it. It should be pointed out that political representatives of the Albanian national minority have monopolized Kosovo and Metohija seeking to leave the impression that except for the Serbs, Montenegrins and Albanians there are no other national minorities. On the contrary, there are other national minorities and ethnic communities in Kosovo and Metohija who have been equally threatened by the Albanian separatism and terrorism. At the most recent population censuses, under the influence of separatist-oriented leaders, the majority of the Albanian ethnic minority did not take part. The last official census in 1981 was taken by the ethnically pure census commission which, by methods of pressure and falsification, practically registered all other national minorities and ethnic communities, in particular Roma, the Muslims, Turks, Goranies and others as Albanians. During the 1981 census, a large number of illegal immigrants from Albania, who have not as yet been able to prove that they were born in Kosovo and Metohija or that they have acquired the nationality of Serbia or to that end of the FRY, have been registered. There is today plenty of evidence to that effect. Since the pressures of separatist ideology are lasting for a long time, the estimates of an approximate number of the Albanian ethnic population were, naturally and as a rule, blown out of proportion so as to use these huge figures to manipulate the international public and factors. Therefore, estimates that there are some 800,000 ethnic Albanians living in Kosovo and Metohija are realistic. On the other hand, according to official statements by high European officials and representatives of a number of EU member States, as many as 400,000-500,000 Albanians now live and work in Western Europe. Judging by all known facts, they are firmly determined to settle there permanently, regardless of the pressure put on them to return home. These pressures are partly the result of increased unemployment in the countries of Western Europe and partly the result of the social, security and similar risks (the narco mafia, arms smuggling, organized crime, illegal border crossing, etc.).

Terrorism: Terrorism is not new in Kosovo and Metohija. It is a proven method of a number of generations of secessionists on Kosovo and Metohija. It has been stepped up every time when the international situation was right. The sharp increase of terrorism in Kosovo and Metohija in the past two years, particularly in 1998, proves that it has been well prepared by outside sponsors and financial support of organized crime (Albanian mafia). The separatists in Kosovo and Metohija believe that the right time for forcible secession has come. Their basic goal, in addition to intimidation of the population and causing instability, is to have the problem internationalized with a view to engaging foreign factors in its resolution, from which they expect assistance in achieving secession. However, it should not be forgotten that terrorism is one of the present day scourges and that it has been publicly condemned by most of the countries in the world, including the

most influential ones. Combating terrorism is a priority for many countries. The widespread character of terrorism necessitated close cooperation among the States in its combating. To illustrate the seriousness of the problem in Kosovo and Metohija one should consider the following facts: in the period from 1991 until 5 March 1998, 200 terrorist attacks have been carried out (in 1996 - 31, in 1997 - 55, in the first two and a half months in 1998 - 86). In the period since 1994, Albanian terrorists attacked members of Albanian national minority 44 times. In 1996, they killed 4, in 1997 - 1 and in 1998 - 5 police officers. At the same time they killed 6 civilians in 1996, 10 in 1997 and 8 in 1998. On 28 February they ambushed and killed 4 police officers. In the ensuing defensive activity, 16 terrorists were liquidated and 9 captured. On 5 March 1998, in the village of Donje Prekaze, a terrorist base was taken out along with 25 terrorists including their leader Adem Jashari. Before attacking the terrorist base, the police asked them to surrender and invited civilians, women and children to leave the base. Some 30 members of the Albanian national minority heeded the call and safely left the scene. It is evident that terrorism and terrorists have nothing in common with the interests of the members of Albanian minority, inflicting on them enormous harm, suffering and direct victims instead. The Government of the Republic of Serbia and of the FRY expect the representatives of the political parties of the Albanian national minority to publicly and unequivocally distance themselves from terrorism on Kosovo and Metohija which they have failed to do so far. Foreign countries are expected not only to clearly and unequivocally condemn the terrorism in Kosovo and Metohija but to offer assistance and cooperation in its suppression.

Organized crime in the service of secession: Separatist goals of a part of the Albanian national minority in Kosovo and Metohija are linked to tight family and social organization and tribal solidarity (similar to Sicily), contributing to a faster development of international organized crime among the members of the Albanian national minority in Kosovo and Metohija and the Albanians from Albania, Macedonia and Greece and the creation of the so-called Albanian mafia. Drug-trafficking in Europe and the USA, and to a certain extent prostitution, are controlled in most part by the "Albanian mafia". The criminal activity certainly includes the 3 per cent protection racquet on income, which the members of the Albanian national minority in Kosovo and Metohija and elsewhere have to "pay" to their leadership. From these substantial resources long-standing separatist and terrorist activities in Kosovo and Metohija have been financed. What is at stake is not only the purchase of arms and smuggling, financing of training of terrorist groups abroad, financing of long-standing "political" activities of entire parallel (illegal) political, education and economic structures in Kosovo and Metohija in the wake of the boycott of the legal institutions of the system of the Republic of Serbia and the FR Yugoslavia but the financing of intensive propaganda activity not only in Kosovo and Metohija, but in Europe and the USA. They are not engaging only prominent, very expensive PR agencies, various political and economic lobbies, but numerous non-governmental humanitarian or other organizations, associations, funds or professions (doctors, journalists, etc). Therefore numerous reports and articles, coverage or footage "proving" that human, civil or national rights of the Albanian national minority have been threatened in Kosovo and Metohija, are the best illustration of how much money is invested in the project of secession of Kosovo and Metohija from the Republic of Serbia and FR of Yugoslavia. At the same time, they illustrate the profits of the "Albanian mafia" criminal activities affecting the health of young people all over the world, Europe, USA and Canada in particular.

Demonstrations: Kosovo Albanians have a long history of demonstration. At first, they protested over certain problems which have arisen in the exercise of their minority rights. Later on, they demonstrated because of their dissatisfaction with the constitutional status of Kosovo and Metohija under the Constitution of 1974 (the same status which they now allegedly seek) to stage henceforth openly separatist demonstrations. More recently, there have been several such demonstrations in Kosovo and Metohija which the biased, in particular foreign, media have portrayed as "non-violent", although they have been anything but non-violent. Also, the demonstration of the second March in Pristina were not only violent, which TV footage (throwing of stones, smashing of windows) clearly shows, but they were not notified either, even though that was an obligation under the law (which was probably due to the boycott of the government institutions or was precisely aimed at provoking police reaction). However, what is particularly important insofar as demonstrations are concerned is that the demonstrations were in defence of terrorists and separatists and that the protestors acted precisely like that - they were destructive. Whether the police had acted properly in every respect is to be determined by the appropriate authorities and they will take appropriate measures if these allegations are proven right.

Dialogue: Secessionist Albanian leaders frequently accuse the government authorities of the Republic of Serbia and the FRY that they refuse dialogue. Such accusations are adopted by some foreign factors requesting the Government of Serbia to "open" a dialogue with the Albanian ethnic community. However, the Government of Serbia has always been in favour of dialogue and has on various occasions and in various ways initiated on its own discussions with the representatives of the Albanian ethnic community demonstrating readiness to talk about all problems related to the exercise of human, civil and minority rights. However, the leaders of the Albanian ethnic community do not want a dialogue because their goal is to secede from the Republic of Serbia and the FRY and not to address minority rights. The Government of the Republic of Serbia remains open to resolve all specific issues regarding the position and exercise of the rights of persons belonging to ethnic minorities in Kosovo and Metohija and in the Republic as a whole through dialogue and within Serbia and they are looking forward to any initiative coming from any minority living in the Republic of Serbia. That there is a lack of will for dialogue on the part of the leaders of the Albanian ethnic community is irrefutably proved by their rejection of the invitation for talks addressed by the Government of the Republic of Serbia on 11, 12 and 16 of March 1998. In spite of numerous pressures from all quarters including from abroad, ethnic Albanian leaders have not accepted an open, unconditional and public dialogue, while Ibrahim Rugova stated in public on 11 March 1998 that "they do not want to talk about any form of autonomy except for independence for Kosovo only". That this was not the first time is also evidenced by the fact that after a lot of effort put into the search for generally accepted solutions for the implementation of the Education Agreement of 1996, it took 6 months for Ibrahim Rugova, after the final signing of the Agreement, to appoint his three representatives on the 3+3 group.

Education: Elementary state schools in general and more than 90 per cent of secondary schools in the Albanian language normally work. As far as the Government of the Republic of Serbia is concerned, there are no obstacles for full normalization even of university education. The Government's attitude in this respect is a positive one. (About 1,200 ethnic Albanians continue to study at the University of Pristina even today.) What needs to be pointed out is that the fundamental disagreement with respect to education is not that the Serbian authorities prevent Albanian children from attending classes in state schools, as it is often portrayed in foreign media, but that the ethnic Albanians refuse to receive education according to the curricula of the Republic of Serbia with all specific programmes applied as in the case of the classes organized for members of the Hungarian, Slovak, Ruthenian or any other national minority. Insistence on such an approach is not only odd, but is doing a huge damage to those children who are prevented from attending school regularly.

Alleged violation of human and minority rights: The proposition that human, civil and minority rights of persons belonging to the Albanian ethnic minority in Kosovo and Metohija are violated is the most frequent accusation levelled at the Republic of Serbia and the FR of Yugoslavia. It is aimed at discrediting the Republic of Serbia and the FRY and at creating the impression of such a violation of these rights that no solution other than complete secession from the motherland can help the protection of their rights. That is why the alleged violation of these rights forms the cornerstone of their efforts to secede from the Republic of Serbia and the FRY. The best proof that their human and civil rights are not violated is the fact that many ethnic minorities live in the Republic of Serbia and the FRY without any problems and they enjoy all the advantages as well as equal treatment both as citizens and as members of their respective ethnic minorities. The Republic of Serbia and the FRY as multiethnic communities, in which 27 national minorities and ethnic groups constitute a third of the population, have elaborated in their constitutions an entire system of guarantees of minority rights to foster, develop and express their ethnic, linguistic and cultural specific characteristics through special advantages in schooling, information, freedom of religion and social and political organizations. They exercise all other rights as any other citizens. Drawing upon the rich experience of the former multiethnic and multi-confessional state (SFRY), the legislation in the field of minority rights goes beyond the international standards in the field. However, what is of even greater significance is that these are all fully exercised also in practice. Groundlessness of the allegation about the lack of minority rights including the Albanian ethnic minority who are only complaining about it, is testified to by the fact that at present there are 52 daily and weekly newspapers published in the Albanian language in Kosovo and Metohija, along with other periodicals having an annual circulation of over 2.5 million, a circulation higher than that in all of Albania. If the right to impart and receive information is one of the most basic "modern" rights of this age, then the Albanian ethnic minority in Kosovo and Metohija can be considered as an advantaged rather than disadvantaged group. Persons belonging to ethnic minorities are also guaranteed the right to a free elementary school education in their own language, the Albanians included.

Local self-government: A new law on local self-government has been drafted; it contains many new solutions including a bicameral assembly in Kosovo and Metohija, preventing overrule of any part of the population and guaranteeing equality in the decision-making on many issues relevant for the development and improvement of the quality of life of all the population regardless of their ethnic origin. It is a fact that a large number of persons belonging to the Albanian ethnic minority do not object to their status within Serbia and Yugoslavia, regardless of whether they live in Kosovo and Metohija or in other places (e.g. about 80,000 citizens of Albanian ethnic origin normally live and work in Belgrade). The right to foster one's own ethnic identity, language, culture and tradition is guaranteed to persons belonging to all ethnic minorities including the Albanian ethnic minority in Kosovo and Metohija. In Kosovo and Metohija as well as in the whole territory of Serbia and Yugoslavia, full equality of citizens employed in the public and private sectors is guaranteed: the right of ownership, equal opportunities in employment, equality in the exercise of the rights related to health, education, culture, religion and the media.

Current situation: The situation in Kosovo and Metohija is calm and under control. All economic, social and other activities including transport operate normally. There have been no exceptional movements of the military nor any military call-ups. Following the police actions of 28 February and 5 March 1998, which were exclusively aimed at neutralizing terrorist groups that have posed a threat to the population of Kosovo and Metohija by their activities, which interfered with the normal life and safety of citizens and impeded regular traffic around the village of Drenica, the situation has been brought back to normal and is controlled by the state authorities of the Republic of Serbia. Many foreign diplomats and journalists who visited Kosovo and Metohija including Drenica area on 8 March were able to see it for themselves. The police performed their regular duties of maintaining the peace and public order. It is absolutely untrue that the police have been revengeful in their actions, that they ill-treated and killed the civilians, that they raped women as well as many other similar falsehoods. The police have always acted in defence, respecting the law and the code of conduct for law enforcement officials. Statements to the effect that "conflicts in Kosovo and Metohija" threaten to spill over into the neighbouring countries and that they are a threat to the stability of the entire region, are totally without foundation, since there are no conflicts in Kosovo and Metohija. There are certain political tensions aimed at internationalizing the problem, as the most important political parties of the Albanian ethnic minority more or less publicly advocate separatism and none of them have openly and in public distanced themselves from terrorism. True to its policy of openness for any dialogue and determined to solve all issues affecting the exercise of human and civil rights of all the population of Kosovo and Metohija by political means as well as to achieve a more rapid economic and cultural development in accordance with the Constitution of the Republic of Serbia, with European and international standards, OSCE principles, the Paris Charter and the United Nations Charter as well as the principles embodied in the Council of Europe Framework Convention on the protection of national minorities, the Government of the Republic of Serbia invited through the media on 10 March 1998 representatives of the Albanian ethnic community for public and unconditional talks. Representatives of the Serbian Government and those of the political parties represented in the Parliament of Serbia came in vain to the talks scheduled for 11 March, because the Albanian political leaders did not show up on the pretext that they had not been personally invited. The same day, 11 March, the Government of Serbia renewed its invitation for the following day, 12 March, but this time inviting political leaders and respected public figures of Albanian ethnic origin in person. Nevertheless, representatives of the Albanian ethnic community did not show up either on 12 March, thus proving that they are not ready for an open and, in particular, not for a public dialogue. Obviously, the realization of human, civil and minority rights of the Albanian ethnic community in Kosovo and Metohija is not their political goal but rather the achievement of secession through the internationalization of a non-existent problem. The best illustration of this is Ibrahim Rugova's statement of 11 March (in response to the invitation by the Government of the Republic of Serbia for dialogue), which was reported by the entire international press, to the effect that for them (members of the Albanian ethnic minority in Kosovo and Metohija) "any autonomy short of independence for Kosovo is unacceptable". Regardless of the fact that the representatives of the Albanian ethnic community have not come to the offered public and unconditional discussions on two occasions already, the Government of the Republic of Serbia repeated, on 14 March, its personal invitation to the political leaders and eminent public figures of Albanian ethnic origin for discussions on 16 March. The representatives of the Albanian minority again did not accept the invitation for dialogue. However some other national minorities and ethnic communities living in Kosovo and Metohija such as the Turks, Roma and the Muslims have expressed their interest in these talks. In their requests for participation in the talks they pointed out their loyalty to the Republic of Serbia, respect to the institutions of the system and the desire to discuss with the relevant institutions and individuals the specific problems related to the exercise of their minority rights, which the Government of the Republic of Serbia accepted.

Misconceptions: On the basis of the foregoing, it is clear that the conceptions created in the international public and in political structures and spread by some media and lobbies that the rights of the Albanian ethnic community are violated in Kosovo and Metohija are absolutely without any foundation. Their sole objective is to encourage international factors to help them achieve secession. Unprecedented anti-Serb and anti-Yugoslav language used by individuals are yet another proof of bias towards this problem and the best illustration of a long-term engagement in support of separatism and terrorism in Kosovo and Metohija as well as of continued activities aimed at jeopardizing the territorial integrity of Serbia and the FRY. Political positions of the FRY and the Republic of Serbia vis-a-vis Kosovo and Metohija: As part of the Republic of Serbia, Kosovo and Metohija is an internal affair of this Republic and there is no basis in international law for considering it outside this framework. The FRY and the Republic of Serbia accept all the provisions of the Framework Convention on the protection of national minorities including the position that the rights of persons belonging to ethnic minorities are also subject to international cooperation. However, the FRY opposes attempts at internationalizing the problem of Kosovo and Metohija and imposing of solutions contrary to the constitutional system of the country and international standards. This is interference in the internal affairs of Serbia and it is therefore unacceptable. To use double standards in relation to terrorism is unacceptable if one wants to fight terrorism as an universal scourge effectively. Attempts to equate terrorist attacks and defence against terrorist attacks, i.e. legitimate police action aimed at suppressing terrorist actions, protecting the citizens against terror and maintaining peace and public order, create confusion and imply support to terrorism, which is impermissible and dangerous. To accept or minimize the danger of terrorism in Kosovo and Metohija by references to alleged police violence is leading nowhere. Equating terrorism with legitimate police action to suppress it deliberately sows confusion and covers up support for terrorism and separatism. What the FRY expects of other countries:

- Strong and unequivocal condemnation of terrorism;
- Pressure on the leaders of some members of the Albanian ethnic community to condemn terrorism in unequivocal terms and to abandon the publicly declared programme of secession;
- Support to the principled position that all specific problems concerning the enjoyment of minority rights must be resolved through dialogue within Serbia and in accordance with international standards, i.e. the Council of Europe Framework Convention for the protection of minorities which the Government of Serbia fully accepts and respects;
- Cooperation on issues related to the exercise of minority rights but not imposition of solutions from outside and interference in the sovereign affairs of Serbia and the FRY; Rejection of the method of disinformation, artificial heightening of tension, application of double standards, attempts at internationalization;
- Refusal to consider the problem in Kosovo and Metohija in international organizations or in any international fora since it concerns an internal problem of the Republic of Serbia;
- Support to the FRY as a constructive factor of the peace process, stability and development in the region, normalizing its status in international political, economic and financial organizations and institutions.

B.   **Government of Kosova: A Case for Independence, 31 September 1998**

The question of Kosova and the justification for the Kosovars' demand for independence must be considered from different angles, from which two have been singled out: the historical context of the collapse of the Ottoman Empire and the emergence of new Balkan nation states, and the immediate context of the problems of the former Yugoslavia. As the Otoman Empire was approaching its total collapse, the Albanians, lacking natural or other allies and for the fear that their territories would be dismembered by their neighbouring peoples hungry for expansion, who were either stronger or had strong allies, had opted for autonomy within the Empire as a first step towards independence. The empire collapsed sooner than expected and the Albanians had to try and establish their national state like the other Balkan peoples. Albania gained recognition in 1913 and is often cited as a state that was recognised before her borders were determined. Albania had proclaimed independence the year before. The state of Albania was supposed to include all Albanian territories, or rather, those territories where the Albanians constituted the majority. The problem of borders was settled later by the so called "power of disposition". This for the Albanians meant that the great powers of the time decided to legitimise Serbian conquests. Leaving aside the reasons leading the great powers to this decision, it did create a massive injustice for the Albanians of Kosova and what was later to become Macedonia. The Albanians were not the only people to endure this kind of injustice. However, all the other peoples forcibly included in this short-lived state, apart from the Hungarians of Vojvodina, were of Slav origin and shared either language and religion, or both. As far as the Albanians were concerned, it was not just a small portion of the population that was left outside the borders of their state; one half of the population, living on their own lands since times immemorial, was forced to remain within the experimental state of the southern Slavs. Apart from the fact of being divided, in itself sufficient reason for resistance, the Albanians who were left in an alien state had bitter memories of the atrocities committed against them by the Serbian Army, after 1913 and throughout World War I, when the Albanian lands became a cross-roads of different invading armies and subject to disputes among neighbouring peoples, who sought to divide these lands among themselves. It was perhaps this, alongside the insistence of some world leaders, for whom the act of self-determination had some meaning, and also the West's interests in blocking the pan-Slavic movement's total access to the Adriatic, which contributed to the survival of an Albanian state even if reduced to a narrow strip of land along the Adriatic.

The circumstances under which the Albanians found themselves incorporated within the state of the Southern Slavs constitute the first element justifying their demand to improve their situation by either uniting with Albania, where they naturally belong, by asking for independence, or by becoming an equal partner in another form of a state organisation. The fact is that Albanian territories in the former Yugoslavia were incorporated in this state by force. After 1913 and throughout World War I, the Albanians, and not only those left within what was to become Yugoslavia, saw entire villages razed to the ground by the Serbian Army, hundreds and thousands of people massacred, and hundreds of thousands driven away from their homeland. The Serbs undertook these actions with arms provided for them by Russia and Western countries.

Serbian intentions then differed very little from today. Then as now, the Serbs were only interested in expanding their territories expelling non-Serb populations. This gave the Albanians every reason to refuse to consent to remaining as part of the first 'Yugoslav' state. Throughout the twenties and thirties the Albanians attempted to resist their inclusion within this state. The majority were extremely determined to remain on their land despite repression exerted by Serbian authorities of the time. The persistent refusal by the Albanians to give full consent to remaining within the 'Yugoslav' state constitutes the second condition in support of their aspirations.

The next element concerns the behaviour of Serbian or 'Yugoslav' authorities towards the Albanians. Even according to the international agreements of the time, i. e. after World War I, the then 'Yugoslav' authorities were obliged to protect the rights of the Albanians, to allow them to preserve their cultural traditions, practice their religion, use their language and also receive education in their mother tongue. The authorities of the first 'Yugoslavia' not only failed to protect these rights, but produced a number of programs to uproot the Albanians from their lands. The memorandum for the colonisation of Kosova drafted by the notorious Serbian academician Vasa Cubrilovic in 1937 and approved by the 'Yugoslav' authorities bears striking similarities to present Serbian behaviour throughout the former Yugoslavia, with the sole difference that Serbia now has much more sophisticated means and greater force of arms at its disposal. If the Serbian authorities had had enough time to implement all their programs, they would certainly have succeeded in driving almost all the Albanians out of Kosova. They did indeed expel hundreds of thousands of them, mainly to Turkey, by playing the card of religious differences. Although they managed to change the ethnic structure of the Albanian territories by increasing the percentage of the Serbs in Kosova from about five percent after the collapse of the Ottoman Empire to about thirty percent at the end of the thirties, they failed to reach their goal of a Serbian majority in the region. Another element is therefore the serious failure of the 'Yugoslav" government to protect the basic rights of the Albanians and to ensure their security. It should be pointed out that all these elements are also present, if in milder form, in the period after World War II. This war found Yugoslavia on the point of disintegration. The Slovenes and Croats, who had voluntarily joined what was first called the Kingdom of Serbs, Croats and Slovenes, and subsequently Yugoslavia, had by now realised that this unification hid a sinister Serbian intention, that of Serbian domination. For the Albanians in 'Yugoslavia' the war simply meant the substitution of one occupier for another. Ironically, the Italian fascists united all the Albanians' ethnic territories and were the first ever to allow schools in Albanian for Kosovars and other Albanians that had been included in the Yugoslav state.

While it is no use in dwelling on the development of the Albanian situation during the war, it is worth stressing that the Albanians were invited to fight fascism, which they did, under the promise that after the liberation they would be allowed to exercise the act of self-determination and to choose freely whether they wished to remain in Yugoslavia or unite with Albania. All the other Yugoslav peoples were promised absolute equality. The promise made to the Albanians was however not kept. After the war they felt cheated, thus their agony was to be prolonged indefinitely. In Yugoslavia's restructuring after the war, both Bosnia and Montenegro were accorded republic status, while Macedonia became another communist-manufactured republic including large number of Albanians and their territories within its borders.

The status of Kosova after the the war was at first left undetermined, allowing the Serbian authorities to continue their colonial policy for a further twenty years. The position of Kosova was later improved; under the 1974 Constitution, Kosova became one of eight Yugoslav federal units. However, full republic status, a measure of true and fair equality, was never granted. The Albanians' dissatisfaction with their position continued during the entire post-war period. Ethnic Albanians consistently constituted the largest number of political prisoners in Yugoslavia. In 1981, the Albanians in Kosova expressed their demand for full Yugoslav republican status through peaceful demonstrations which were brutally crushed by the Serbian dominated Yugoslav police and army. It was at this point that Serbia's true aspirations gradually began to reveal themselves. Echoing history, the Serbian Academy of Arts and Sciences drafted a memorandum that portrayed the Serbs as victims of peace. Milosevic came to the forefront of the political stage by fuelling extreme Serbian ultra nationalism. This coincided with the democratic movement throughout Eastern Europe. Everything Albanian was attacked, in Kosova, Macedonia, and wherever Albanians lived in the former Yugoslavia. It was the Albanians who were the first victims in the former Yugoslavia, and the Serbian attempt to revoke Kosova's autonomy marked the start of the country's disintegration. Neither the other former Yugoslav republics nor the international community did much to stop the Serbs. The Serbian leadership carefully judged its moment. Knowing they could get away with anything, they continued on their path which was eventually to destroy the country. This brings us to yet another condition that the Former Yugoslav government failed to meet for the Albanians in general, and Kosovars in particular: that is, it failed to safeguard Kosova's legitimate political interests. Another important element justifying the Kosovars' aspirations concerns the region's economic interests. Kosova has often been cited as the poorest and most undeveloped region not only in former Yugoslavia but probably in the whole of Europe, while at the same time the richest in resources. In terms of development, the gulf between Kosova and the other Yugoslav regions was larger at the end of the eighties than immediately after the war. Whatever investments were made in Kosova were channelled into huge projects from which the Kosovars themselves were the last to benefit. The people of Kosova were outraged that their land and resources were being exploited for the benefit primarily of Serbia and other parts of Yugoslavia.

This concludes what was referred to at the beginning as the historical context of the problem. Considering that no modern nation can base its claims on centuries long past dark ages of history were deliberately ignored. Events in this century sufficiently prove that the Albanians in Yugoslavia are a community with a long history of injustice. In what follows, the present state of affairs will dealt with. The first expression of Serbian nationalism, in terms of an 'enhanced psychic income' for Serbian masses was over the issue of Kosova. Serbian nationalism in Kosova tested both other former Yugoslav republics as well as the international community, and the successful conduct of this test was a sign for Serbian authorities to move on elsewhere. Let down both by the former Yugoslav republics and the international community, the Albanians faced hard decisions. They were compelled to adopt a strategy: either to accept Serbian rule or to resist. An armed resistance was not possible for several reasons. Firstly, the Albanian population was totally unarmed. Secondly, such a resistance would have to confront not only the Serbs, but also other former Yugoslav nationalities, certainly Montenegro as well as Macedonia which had been the long hand of Serbia throughout the history of communist Yugoslavia. Albania was in no position to provide much support for the Albanians in Yugoslavia, as she herself was about to embark on the process of democratisation.

Kosovo opted for a strategy of non-violent resistance, responding with moderation and restraint to all Serbian attempts to undermine the status of Kosova. The Belgrade authorities, who had prepared detailed military plans, found themselves locked into an unexpected game. They attempted to revoke Kosova's autonomy, and to dissolve the Kosova parliament. In 1990, this same parliament, denied access to its building by the Serbian police, issued a declaration on the parliament's steps that proclaimed Kosova a republic in a federal or confederal Yugoslavia. In a step strongly reminiscent of the start of apartheid in South Africa, the Belgrade authorities segregated the schools and subsequently denied Albanian pupils and students access to school premises; the Albanians responded by setting up their own educational network in private homes. The Belgrade authorities dismissed on ethnic grounds all Albanians from all state run institutions and companies; in response the Albanians organised their own institutions and their own welfare network. When Albanian doctors were dismissed, they set up their own clinics, thus initiating a network of social care.

When the concept of Yugoslavia finally died with the Slovene and Croatian declarations of independence, and when Serbia embarked on her adventures by attacking first Slovenia and then Croatia, the only logical thing for the Albanians to do was to disassociate themselves from Serbia and to go their own way. In September 1991, the Albanians organised a referendum in Kosova, as the highest form of democratic declaration by a people. Of a turnout of 87 percent of those eligible to vote, 99.5 percent voted for an independent Kosova. When the Serbian authorities invited the Kosova Albanians to participate in Serbian elections, in other words inviting them to accept Serbian rule, the Albanians boycotted these elections and, in response, organised their own, electing a new parliament and the president of the Republic of Kosova in May 1992. Throughout this time, the Serbian police and army have been continuing their repression, which reached intolerable levels. Albanians have been subjected to house searches and beatings, have been shot or beaten to death, they have been beaten severely, and have been arbitrarily arrested, detained and sentenced to long-term imprisonment. Young Albanians have been conscripted in order to create a climate of fear, forcing others to flee abroad. Nevertheless, in the face of all this brutality, the Albanians remained calm and patient for almost a whole decade.

Internationally wanted Serbian war criminals such as Arkan and Seselj, having completed their crimes in Croatia and Bosnia, were sent with their paramilitaries to Kosova in order to keep the Albanians in constant fear; the Albanians responded by ignoring them. The only effect of this brutality and this repression has been to strengthen the determination of the Kosova Albanians never to have anything to do with Serbia beyond neighbourly relations. A consistent pattern of violations of the basic rights of the Albanians has been documented by a number of renowned human rights organisations, such as Amnesty International and Helsinki Watch, and in the reports of different fact-finding missions, of the long-term CSCE (now OSCE) mission before it was expelled by the Serbian authorities, and of other governmental and non-governmental organisations. The UN Human Rights Commission passed a number of resolutions calling on Serbia to end its repression against the Albanians, all to no avail. Serbia has remained defiant. This has been a great setback for the Albanians, who suffered greatly in both the first and second Yugoslavia, and only secured certain basic rights for about one decade, in the 1970s. No wonder that the vast majority of the Albanian population see the present situation as a reoccupation of Kosova by Serbia. Albanians today possess scarcely more rights than in 1920s.

The dissolution of the former Yugoslavia presents a good reason for the international community and the great powers of today to reconsider the decisions made concerning Kosova made both before and after World War I, as they have done in the cases of Slovenia, Croatia, Bosnia, and Macedonia. The idea of a state shared by southern Slavs has already failed twice. Apparently the southern Slavs still suffer from a sense of incomplete shared identity, and to prove their identity, are often compelled to stress irrelevant characteristics such as religious and dialectical linguistic differences. Alongside the Greeks, the Albanians are the only indigenous people in the region. They have no problems with their identity. They are united in their language and their three different religious confessions are not seen as something that can divide them. To force the Albanians into a competition of this kind in a language that is foreign to them is simply to ensure that they will be subjected to discrimination for ever.

It will now be clear that under the second Yugoslavia the Albanians voiced their dissatisfaction only in an attempt to improve their position within the Yugoslav federation. Now that the country has disintegrated, all these elements acquire an entirely different validity. The complexity of Yugoslavia's structure also provided or was supposed to provide some protection to its several units. Following Serbia's attempt to revoke Kosova's autonomy, even the communist leaders in Kosova at that time lodged a complaint with the Yugoslav Constitutional Court. However, Yugoslavia disintegrated and the court never met to hear the complaint. In many ways the Kosovars were pushed in their move towards independence. The role of the international community and of other powerful nations in the crisis of the former Yugoslavia also deserves attention. It has been proved time and again that the Balkan peoples have never been able to solve their problems in a civilised way. Even in the late eighties, ominous signs of war in what was then Yugoslavia were discernible over the Kosova issue. Appropriate action by the international community and a more positive role on the part of the other former Yugoslav republics could have changed the subsequent course of events. However, the international community chose to intervene after the Serbian military adventure had begun, and then inadequately.

Without wishing to judge the intervention of the international community, it must be said that all the measures taken by the outside world have failed to rein in the Serbian authorities down to earth. If every measure for Kosova either imposed or advocated by the international community has failed, then surely the only solution is independence. The leadership of Kosova, although dissatisfied with the status offered at a number of international conferences, such as the Hague, the London and the Geneva Follow-up Conference on the Former Yugoslavia, have nevertheless expressed willingness to engage in negotiations leading to a satisfactory solution of the problem. A special Group on Kosova was established at the London Conference, thus to some extent recognising the special status of Kosova as a self-determining unit. However, neither this Group nor any of the other initiatives of the international community have achieved anything. In many ways, the action of the international community has directly or indirectly merely complicated the situation in the former Yugoslavia, and has suggested to the Serbian leadership what it should undertake next.

Every dispute involves different claims and at least two parties, and I would now like to look at the other side of the Kosova problem. I shall refer only briefly to the Serbian claims on Kosova, as I think they may be easily rejected. The Serbian claims on Kosova are based solely on historical grounds and moreover on the darkest ages of history. It is true that some seven centuries ago Kosova was part of a short-lived Serbian Kingdom that also included part of present-day Albania, Northern Greece, the whole of modern 'Macedonia' and part of Bulgaria. Kosova lay at the centre of these territories, and the Serbs therefore abandoned Raska, the true cradle of Serbian civilisation, in an attempt to establish Kosova as their centre. They built a number of important religious monuments, very possibly on the ruins of Albanian religious monuments, which survived to this day thanks to the Albanians who have cared for them for centuries. Exactly six centuries ago, the Serbs, alongside all the other Balkan peoples, fought a battle against the Ottoman Turks in Kosova. The battle was lost, to a large degree due to the activities of Serbian traitors. However, this defeat, which sealed the fate of the Medieval Serbian kingdom and of a number of other Balkan peoples, was later to become the principle theme of Serbian literary myth or folklore. Of course, myths and reality are two different things; nevertheless, the outside world appears prone to accepting false propaganda

nourished by such myths. These claims are irrational to the point of mental aberration; if applied elsewhere in the globe, the world's appearance would change completely. The Serbian religious monuments can only have the value of Christian monuments in Istanbul or Muslim mosques in Spain. Religious or other historical monuments do not determine the borders of modern states. Also, in view of Serbian behaviour towards the religious monuments of other peoples, such as the Croatian Catholic churches and the mosques of the Bosnian Muslims, not to mention the bombardment of Dubrovnik, this Serbian concern over their religious and cultural monuments in Kosova is nothing but hypocrisy of the highest order.

What do the Serbs actually have in Kosova? They amount to six percent of the population of Kosova, which is one percent of the entire Serbian people. The Albanians account for over 90 percent of the population of Kosova, constituting over 30 percent of the Albanian people. Bearing in mind the illegal annexation of the Albanian territories, the constant resistance of the Albanians to the Yugoslav state, the lack of their full consent to remain within this state, the failure of the Yugoslav Government to safeguard the rights of the Albanians, their cultural, economic and political interests, the Albanians have in the past been entitled to seek to improve their position. From the moment Yugoslavia disintegrated, all these conditions acquired a new value, entitling the Albanians to choose for themselves whether they want to become independent, as in the case of Kosova; to become equal partners with another community, as in the case of Macedonia; or even to join Albania, an option which the Albanians have not chosen, in order to avoid complications that would arise in the region. The disintegration of Yugoslavia and the dissolution of a common sovereign power therefore justify the aspirations of the Albanians. The option they have chosen is only a compromise, which should be appreciated.

Kosova is a geographically identifiable region with an identifiable population and an identifiable language, culture and tradition. Last but not least, it possesses a democratically elected government. Kosova is a viable territory and as a sovereign state would be both in terms of territory and population equal or bigger than over forty different existing sovereign states. An independent Kosova can only help in the search for a solution to the whole former Yugoslav crisis. With regards to 'Macedonia', I sincerely hope that the 'Macedonians' will acknowledge the opportunity the Albanians have offered them for the creation of a sovereign state. However, the state of 'Macedonia 'is extremely vulnerable without a proper solution to the problem of Kosova. An independent Kosova can only strengthen a 'Macedonian' state provided the Albanians there are given the status of a constituent nation. The common cliche that an independent Kosova would destroy 'Macedonia' following the logic that the Albanians there would also demand secession is entirely wrong. The aspirations of Kosova for independence are based predominantly on the status Kosova enjoyed, as a federal unit, in the former Yugoslav state.

Chapter 4: Constitutional Issues

Through law a society organizes the power relationships which govern it. The struggle for dominance in social relations is therefore most clearly established in legal rules, especially constitutional ones. The development of the legal status of Kosovo within the framework of Federal Yugoslavia bears this out in a rather striking fashion. In a sense, the legal developments described in this chapter crystallize the history of the Kosovo issue since the conclusion of World War II.

Constitutional development up to 1990

By 1943, fascist Italy had withdrawn from the war and capitulated. Albania, then temporarily united with most of Kosovo, gained nominal independence, but was placed in effect under German control. While some Kosovo Albanians collaborated with them, to avert a restoration of Slav dominance in the region, others took up the resistance struggle. Some joined the National Liberation Army, or partisans, led by Marshall Tito, organized according to the model of communist cadres. The Anti-Fascist Council for the People's Liberation of Yugoslavia (AVNOF) had decided in November 1943 that Kosovo would be accorded autonomous status at the end of the war. However, a few weeks later there was held at Bujan the first conference of the National Liberation Council for Kosovo, attended mainly by ethnic Albanians. A formal resolution was adopted, establishing the modalities of Kosovo Albanian participation in the liberation struggle. For many Albanians the Bujan resolution remains, to this day, a focal point of their national aspirations. The resolution stated:[1]

> Kosova and the Dukajin Plateau is a region in which the majority of the inhabitants are Albanian who today wish to be united with Albania, as they have done. Therefore, we feel it our duty to indicate the right road which [is] the road which the Albanian people must follow to realize their aspirations. The only way for the Albanian people of Kosova and the Dukagjin Plateau to be united with Albania is through joint struggle with the other peoples of Yugoslavia against the blood-thirsty Nazi occupier and its paid lackeys, because this is the only way to win the freedom, in which all peoples, including the Albanian people, will be able to determine their own destiny through the right of self-determination up to secession. The guarantee of this is the National Liberation Army of Albania with which it is closely linked. …

This pan-Albanian platform was neither directly endorsed nor disowned by the Tito leadership, which instead cautiously pointed out that developments should not prejudice the expected close future relations with Albania.[2] At the conclusion of the war, the communist cadres in Kosovo, of whom less than a quarter were ethnic Albanian, expressed themselves in favour of "the annexation of Kosovo-Methohija" to federal Serbia. On 3 September 1945, the Serb People's Assembly created an autonomous region of Kosovo-Methoija as a constituent part of Serbia. Serbia argues that Kosovo was thus confirmed as an integral part of its territory before the Federation was created. Kosovo, on the other hand, asserts that the decision to join was expressly conditioned upon a "federal" Serbia, i.e., Serbia and hence also Kosovo being part of a federal structure. While the legitimacy of the decision to join has been disputed in view of the limited representativeness of the communist structures at the time,[3] Serbia's view that an annexation was necessary at all is interesting. The timing of this act is, at any rate, irrelevant. For, even if Serbia had constituted itself with Kosovo as a constituent part of it before it became part of the federation, this does not affect the status which obtained when it joined the post-war Yugoslav federal structure. In joining the Federation, Serbia formally accepted the constitutional status for Kosovo provided in the federal constitution of 31 January 1946.

Of course, in the first Yugoslav constitution, there was no evidence of a pledge of self-determination for Kosovo which the Kosovo Albanians had thought they had obtained through the Bujan declaration. Instead, the People's Republic of Yugoslavia was constructed as a federation of Serbia, Croatia, Slovenia, Bosnia and Herzegovina, Macedonia and Montenegro. Each of these republics was seen to be the repository of the sovereign rights of equal 'peoples'. These peoples, organized in the individual republics, retained their right to self-determination and even secession in the Federation.[4] That is to say, the source of sovereignty, as it were, resided separately in the individual republics, and not in the Federation itself, as opposed to a centralist federal constitution, where the federal authorities exercise all authority not expressly granted to the constituent units. The "sovereignty of the peoples republics composing the FPRY is limited only by the rights which by this Constitution are given to the Federal Peoples Republic of Yugoslavia".[5]

Not having been promoted to the status of a republic, Kosovo was indeed included as an 'autonomous region' in the Republic of Serbia, as had been anticipated in the act of 'annexation' and subsequent Serb legislation. Under the federal

---

[1] Resolution of the 1st Conference of the National Liberation Council for Kosovo and the Dukagjin Plateau, 31 December 1943-2 January 1944, Document 4.A.1.

[2] Viktor Meir, *Yugoslavia: A History of its Demise* (1999) 26.

[3] Malcolm, *Kosovo*, p. 317.

[4] Constitution of the Federal People's Republic of Yugoslavia, 31 January 1946, Document 4.A.2.

[5] Article 9. Subsequent Yugoslav scholarship has somewhat tortuously argued that this language in fact means the opposite, i.e., that only the Federation is sovereign, as the republics exist within its legal framework; e.g.: R. Lukic, The Sovereignty of the Republics under the Preliminary Draft of the Federal Constitution, 14 *New Yugoslav Law* (1963) 27.

constitution, the rights and scope of autonomy of autonomous provinces and regions were determined by the Constitution of the republic. The people's assembly of an autonomous province or territory could establish its own statute, but required the approval of the Republic for such a document, which falls somewhat short of a constitution. Despite these limitations, Kosovo nevertheless enjoyed a dual status. According to the federal constitution, Kosovo's legal personality was not only established within Serbia, but directly in Yugoslavia's founding document—in fact in the same article which consecrates the republics as the sources of sovereignty.[6] That the status of autonomous provinces or republics was not solely a matter for the republics is confirmed in Article 44 of the Constitution. That provision requires federal approval for the establishment of new autonomous provinces or territories.

The ambiguous status of Kosovo, and for that matter, the other autonomous entity within Serbia, Vojvodina, was rooted in two facts. First, it would not have been realistic to attempt to remove the two territories from the dominance of Serbia. Such reasoning of *realpolitik* was underpinned by the doctrine of peoples or nations on the one hand, and of nationalities and minorities on the other. The republics are of course not actually the ethnically pure home of the one or other ethnic 'people' or nation. In fact, the ethnic identity of all these peoples may not even have been fully established by 1946. But as the Serbs, Slovenes, Macedonians, Montenegrans, Croats and Bosnians do not have an external kin-state, 'their' republic is considered a sovereign home-territory, as it were. The Hungarians of Vojvodina and the Kosovo Albanians, on the other hand, share an ethnic appurtenance with the majority population of a neighbouring state and merely constitute a nationality accommodated in an autonomous province or region. Other groups have the even less pronounced status of minority, which is not identified with any particular territory or with any form of self-rule.

The 1953 constitution, too, reflected the basic idea of a federation of 'sovereign and equal peoples'.[7] Again, federal powers existed only to the extent granted by the federal constitution. Republic powers, on the other hand, remained self-constituting. Still, the federal constitution imposed an express provision, in Article 113, which declared that the "self-governance of the autonomous province of Vojvodina and of the autonomous region of Kosovo-Metohija is guaranteed".[8] This federal guarantee is, however, balanced by a further sentence in that provision, which derives these powers of self-governance from the constitution of Serbia. In 1963, the rather symbolic distinction between autonomous province (Vojvodina) and region (Kosovo) was removed. While some observers see the 1963 constitution as a significant advance in the status of Kosovo, others have identified it as a regression. The source of this dispute lies in the removal of the specific guarantee of self-governance at the level of the federal constitution. Instead of such a guarantee, Kosovo was now described as a "social-political community within the republic"—the significance of which is not clear in itself.[9] However, the federal constitution retained the federal status of autonomous provinces. While they could still be founded by republics, such a decision could, as before, only take effect when constitutionally approved by the Federation. And the character of Kosovo as an existing autonomous province remained directly established in the federal constitution. Moreover, the special representation of autonomous provinces along with the republics in the federal Chamber of Nationalities was retained. The Serb Constitution of 1963 nevertheless remained quite restrictive in terms of the powers of autonomous provinces. It does refer to social self-government of the province and assigns powers to make regulations concerning matters of general relevance to the province. However, throughout it is made clear that this authority is based in, and restricted by, the competences of the republic.[10]

The constitutional position of Kosovo was significantly improved towards the end of the 1960s, especially in the wake of riots and demonstrations in the province in 1968. The name was changed from Kosovo and Metohija to Kosovo, to placate the sensitivities of the ethnic Albanians, and significantly more power was devolved locally. These developments reached their zenith with the adoption of the SFRY constitution of 1974. An express right to self-determination, including the right to secession, remained the preserve of the 'nation'. However, both nations and nationalities are now "free and equal". The Constitution actually assigned 'sovereign rights' to nationalities, exercised through the Socialist Autonomous Provinces in conformity with their constitutional rights.[11] Moreover, it expressly provides for full equality of republics and autonomous provinces in their participation in the federation, determining that federal decision were to be made "according to the principles of agreement among the republics and autonomous provinces".[12] Hence, although Kosovo was still a constituent part of Serbia, the new status of Kosovo has been described by Serb and Albanian scholars alike as that of a 'quasi republic'.[13] It was fully represented in the federal Presidency, had distinct representation in the federal organs and, crucially, it had full freedom in determining its own constitution (no longer a mere statute). Its own organs and powers were state-

---

[6] Vojvodina obtained the original Federal status of an autonomous province, possibly a somewhat 'higher' status than that of a region.

[7] Constitution of the Federal People's Republic of Yugoslavia, 1953, Article 1, Document 4.A.3.

[8] Also included is a mechanism for separate representation of the autonomous provinces and regions in the Federal Assembly which, along with Assembly members nominated by the republics, form the Chamber of Nationalities.

[9] Constitution of the Socialist Federal Republic of Yugoslavia, 1963, Article 112, Document 4.A.4.

[10] Constitution of the Socialist Republic of Serbia, 1963, Document 4.A.5.

[11] Constitution of the Socialist Federal Republic of Yugoslavia, 1974, 'Basic Principles', Document 4.A.6.

[12] *Id.*

[13] Indeed, this argument is frequently used by Serbia to demonstrate that it was necessary to reverse the provisions of the 1974 constitution.

like, including even a national bank and the power to engage in foreign relations. Like all republics, its Assembly had the power to block the coming into force of changes to the federal constitution. Serbia's constitution of 1974 also confirmed the equal status of all nations and nationalities in Serbia, determining again that they each individually and all collectively enjoyed "sovereignty rights".[14] Kosovo's own constitution confirmed that its people had freely organized themselves in the form of the Socialist Autonomous Province on the basis of equality with the nations and nationalities of Yugoslavia.[15] The Kosovo Assembly was given express powers "directly and exclusively" to decide on amendments to the Kosovo constitution, and to "approve" amendments to the constitution of the Socialist Republic of Serbia.[16]

The purported removal of Kosovo's federal status

When pressure within Serbia increased to counter the perceived marginalization of Serbs in Kosovo, or even their persecution, many in the still communist leadership sought to argue the case for moderation. In fact, the 1985 memorandum of members of the Serb Academy which agitated for a Greater Serbia and the re-establishment of Serb dominance in Kosovo was initially denounced when its contents were published in 1986. "The physical, political, legal and cultural genocide of the Serbian population in Kosovo and Metohija is a worse historical defeat than any experienced in the liberation wars waged by Serbia from the First Serbian Uprising in 1804 to the uprising of 1941," the memorandum declared, causing something of a scandal at the time.[17] However, the events which followed saw the gradual isolation and removal of those who still held to Tito's vision of a Federation of equal peoples, nations and nationalities. Serb nationalism, as well as the cunning exploitation of party rules, and the anxiety of old style officials not to oppose that which appeared to be emerging as a dominant view, facilitated this process.

Slobodan Milosevic is said to have discovered the Kosovo issue on the occasion of his celebrated visit to the autonomous province, where, on 24 April 1987, he was met by agitated Serbs, demanding action from Belgrade to protect them against ethnic Albanian dominance in Kosovo. His famous shout "no one should dare to beat you" energized the local crowds as well as himself.[18] He used the purported fate of the Kosovo Serbs as the key argument in his purge of Serbia's party chairman Ivan Stambolic and his supporters, which commenced in September 1987 and was concluded in December of that year. From then onwards, the process of the re-integration of Kosovo was pursued in earnest. In 1988, some 50,000 Serbs in Kosovo signed a petition, demanding closer integration with Serbia and threatening direct action of "self-defence of our freedom, honour and dignity".[19] This demand was met when, on 11 June 1988 a draft for a new Serb constitution was put forward. To ensure the eventual adoption of reform proposals, the leadership of Vojvodina was removed first. Measures were taken to ensure that Montenegro, too, would not oppose Serb action at the Federal level. While Slovenia remained opposed and was locked in an increasingly bitter struggle with Serbia and the federal organs increasingly dominated by it, Milosevic also initially managed to persuade leaders in Croatia and Bosnia and Herzegovina to remain silent, on the understanding that Serbia would not subsequently seek to take action in relation to the Serbs inhabiting those two republics. Macedonia, with its very sizeable ethnic Albanian minority of between 20 and 30 per cent, was also persuaded not to oppose the removal of the Kosovo Albanians from political power. Of course, the position of Croatia would soon change, once it became clear that Serbia appeared to be reaching beyond the boundaries of Kosovo, seeking to dominate the Federation as a whole. After all, if Serbia controlled not only her own votes, but also those of Montenegro, Macedonia, Vojvodina and Kosovo, she could muster an automatic majority in federal decision-making.

Having ensured that opposition at the Federal level would be limited, the next step was to disenfranchise the leadership of Kosovo itself, an act which could be performed from above, given the communist party structure which existed in parallel with the republic/province executive structure. This action took place amid demonstrations of Serbs in Belgrade and Albanians in Prishtina in November 1998, and coincided with the completion of the installation of a new, more 'reliable' leadership in Montenegro.[20] On 24 February 1989, the Serb parliament unanimously adopted proposals for the amendment of Serbia's constitution, no representative from Kosovo having felt it appropriate to vote against. A last minute amendment to the amendments, which had been put before the plenary of the Assembly two days earlier by its constitutional drafting commission, removed from Kosovo the power to oppose any further changes of the constitution. Whereas previously, its positive assent had been required, it would now only need to be consulted. The relevance of these developments was quickly understood in Kosovo. A hunger strike of miners at Trepca in Kosovo and more widespread demonstrations followed. This was immediately answered by the imposition of a state of emergency by the Federal State Presidency, now dominated by Serbia, on 27 February. Federal armed forces and federal police, mostly Serb, were deployed into Kosovo. The provincial government of Kosovo, which had been installed through Serb political intervention, approved the

---

[14] Constitution of the Socialist Republic of Serbia, 1974, Basic Principles, paras 2 & 3, Document 4.8.7.

[15] Constitution of the Socialist Autonomous Province of Kosovo, 1974, Basic Principles., Document 4.A.8

[16] *Id. Article 300.*

[17] Tim Judah, *The Serbs* (1997) 159.

[18] Laura Silber & Allan Little, *The Death of Yugoslavia* 1995) 37ff.

[19] Quoted in Meir, p. 73.

[20] *Id*, pp. 80-100.

constitutional amendments on 22 March. Two days later, in an episode which remains controversial, the Kosovo Assembly, too, is said to have opted for its own disenfranchisement, with only ten opposing votes out of 187.

Kosovo representatives point to the fact that over 15,000 army personnel had been deployed in the province by then, and that the Assembly was surrounded by tanks. Non-members of the Assembly were present, it is alleged, and some of them may have voted. Others are said to have directly intimidated the ethnic Albanian representatives. Kosovo also subsequently claimed that the decision was never effective, not having been published in the official gazette.[21] The decision of the Assembly provoked widespread rioting and a tough response from the police and army, leading to numerous deaths. Serbia then adopted a somewhat Orwellian *Programme for the Realization of Peace, Freedom, Equality, Democracy and Prosperity of the SAP of Kosovo.* That legislative programme was expressly intended to lay the foundation for the re-introduction of ethnic Serbs into the republic. It also sought to ensure that the Albanian majority in Kosovo would be effectively politically powerless, inasmuch as its representation was to be equalized with that of tiny minorities in the territory, in addition to the Serbs in the province, so as to "exclude majority votes". [22]

The restoration of Serbia's constitutional dominance over Kosovo was famously and rather provocatively celebrated in Kosovo itself, when Milosevic addressed the 600-year celebrations of the Serb defeat at Kosovo Polje, staged on the ancient battlefield on 28 June 1989.[23] Already, the first examples of Serb direct legislation for Kosovo had been adopted, revealing openly a public programme of ethnic politics and discrimination directed against the Albanians.[24] The 1990 Law on Special Circumstances formalized the possible exercise of Republic powers in Kosovo.[25] It was activated with a decision of 26 June 1990, permitting officials of the Serb republic to administer the affairs of Kosovo directly and to nullify public decisions which had been taken in Kosovo itself. This included the removal of criminal prosecutions and other judicial functions from Kosovo courts, and also the appointment of Serbs to head commercial undertakings in Kosovo, which were at the time still state-enterprises. Then, on 5 July 1990, Serbia purported formally to terminate the functioning of the Kosovo Assembly and of its Executive Council[26] and on 28 September 1990, Serbia gave itself a new constitution.[27] Contrary to the writings of some, the autonomous status of Kosovo was not formally abolished altogether. But the Socialist Republic was now no longer a "state of the Serb nation and parts of other nations and nationalities, which live and exercise their sovereign rights in it."[28]Instead, it became a "democratic state of the Serbian people" only,[29] merely noting the rights of other "nations and national minorities". That is to say, the status of the Kosovo Albanians as at least a "nationality" was abolished, and the overwhelming majority of Kosovo Albanians were now reduced to being a "national minority" in their own territory. The powers of the province were entirely subordinated to those of Serbia. Its constitution was again reduced to a "statute" which would be enacted after prior "approval" of the National Assembly. Again, provisions were made for direct executive action of the republic in Kosovo. The unilateral changes to Kosovo's status would, of course, have required an amendment of the federal constitution of Yugoslavia. However, initially there was little resistance and soon the Federation itself was in a process of dissolution. Unsurprisingly, the new federal Yugoslavia, composed only of Serbia and Montenegro, hardly mentions Kosovo or the collective rights of the Kosovo Albanians in its 1992 constitution. Instead, the status of Kosovo and Vojvodina is degraded to one of "territorial autonomy".[30]

The response in Kosovo

Up to the summer of 1990, the elected members of the Kosovo Assembly, and Kosovo's representatives in the Serb and Federal Assemblies, had failed to resist these developments with any vigour. However, when the Serb Assembly purported to terminate the work of the Kosovo Assembly and its members were literally locked out of their Assembly building, the elected representatives adopted a declaration of sovereignty in response.[31] That declaration was rather a modest one, anticipating the continued existence of Kosovo within Yugoslavia as an equal constituent unit. It expressly states that Kosovo would continue to comply with the Yugoslav Federal constitution, but not with the changes brought about unilaterally by Serbia.

---

[21] For the Kosovo Albanian view, see Council for the Defence of the Human rights and Freedoms in Kosovo, *The Ruin of Kosova's Autonomy: Material Proof* (undated) 1ff. Arsim Bajrami, Normative Constitutional and Political Acts by which Kosova Statehood was determined, 1 *Kosova Law Review* (1996) 57.

[22] Document 4.B.4.

[23] Misha Glenny, *The Fall of Yugoslavia* (1993) 34.

[24] See Documents 4.B.2-5. Chapter VI.

[25] Document 4.B.6.

[26] Law Terminating the Work of the Assembly of the SAP of Kosovo and the Executive Council of the SAP of Kosovo, 5 July 1990, Document 4.B.8, also Document 4.B.9.

[27] *See* Stevan Lilic, Die Verfassung der Republic Serbien, in Joseph Mark & Tomislav Boric, eds., *Slowenien—Kroatien—Serbien, Die Neuen Verfassungen* (1991) 286.

[28] 1974 Constitution of the SR Serbia, Article 1., Document 4.A.7.

[29] Constitution of the SR Serbia, 28 September 1990, Preamble, Document 4.B.10.

[30] Constitution of the Federal Republic of Yugoslavia, April 1992, Article 6, Document 4.B.6.

[31] Assembly of Kosova, Constitutional Declaration, 2 July 1990, Document 4.C.2.

The Kosovo representatives also annulled the decision of March 1989 which had purportedly legitimised the virtual abolition of Kosovo's autonomous status. The situation which ensued has been described as one of 'sovereignties in collision'.[32] In the exercise of its (at least former) prerogative of creating its own constitution, the Assembly of Kosovo then drafted and adopted a new constitution for Kosovo. This constitution now in turn defined Kosovo as a democratic, sovereign and independent state of the Albanian people and members of others peoples and national minorities.[33] However, a formal declaration of independence only followed a year later, on 22 September 1991, after the declarations of independence of Slovenia and Croatia had started to bring about the dissolution of the Socialist Federation Republic. This decision was confirmed in a referendum (mainly boycotted by ethnic Serbs) in which 87 per cent of voters participated, with close to 100 per cent opting for independence.[34] This was followed, again a year later, by elections, resulting in the overwhelming victory of the Democratic League of Kosovo (76 per cent), led by Ibrahim Rugova. Dr Rugova was directly elected as President by an even larger margin. A government was formed, under the leadership of Dr Bujar Bukoshi. The Rugova government opposed a violent answer to the repression which was increased in the territory. This was as much a result of the personality of Dr Rugova as a reflection of a certain sense of realism on the part of the Kosovo Albanian leadership. A more vigorous campaign, it was thought, would lead to even more vigorous counter-measures. With the exception of Albania, very few states seemed to take an interest in the fate of the Kosovars, beyond the occasional verbal condemnation of FRY/Serb action. And as the fate of Bosnia and Herzegovina appeared to demonstrate, no decisive action was likely to be forthcoming, even if the Albanian population would be willingly exposed to the risks of military operations or even genocide by the FRY/Serbia.

Instead, the Rugova government established a system of parallel administration, funded by voluntary contributions by the ethnic Albanian population in Kosovo and its not insignificant Diaspora abroad. In this way, many of the former public sector workers could continue to provide educational, medical and other social service after they had been dismissed by the Serb authorities. In the application of lessons drawn from the anti-apartheid struggle, there also emerged a parallel economy, which avoided the discriminatory Serb restrictions placed on property transactions, the registration of commercial ventures and other restraints. The moderation of the Rugova government appeared to be rewarded when the then Conference for Security and Cooperation established a long-term monitoring mission in the territory. While the mission did not in itself lead to a cessation of repression and severe human rights violations, it did provide a sense of security for the local population. However, in the summer of 1993, Yugoslavia simply terminated the mission.

The attempts of Dr Rugova and his team to engage the international community in diplomatic efforts on behalf of the Kosovo Albanians were met with only hesitant success. Dr Rugova, and his highly effective Prime Minister, Dr Bukoshi, were politely received by several foreign governments, although often unofficially. In fact, the Prime Minster established himself in Germany, from where he could coordinate the external activities of the government. However, while the cautious policy of the government was praised throughout, little action followed to reward this attitude. Nevertheless, in March 1998, Dr Rugova and his party, the LDK, again overwhelmingly won elections that were held in Kosovo. By that time, the KLA had formed itself into a more significant force, challenging the legitimacy of the democratic mandate of the government and engaging in direct military operations. In this attitude, the KLA gained the support of other parties which had not obtained a significant electoral mandate. Some of these parties were led by former LDK members and associates of Dr Rugova. There appeared a real risk of factional splits among the Kosovo Albanian leaders. This prospect was increased when Rugova gave in to pressure, in particular from the US government, and engaged in direct negotiations with the Belgrade authorities in April 1998, when hostilities had commenced and the Kosovo Albanian population was experiencing the first episodes of sustained ethnic cleansing. While these talks came to nothing, the struggle for political influence among Kosovo politicians was fostered by the need to establish a negotiating team for the Hill process and subsequently the Rambouillet conference. In the team which was eventually formed, again under US influence, the elected government constituted the minority. Instead, the KLA and opposition forces close to it dominated it. A KLA representative assumed the Chairmanship of its Presidency. Attempts to replace Drs Rugova and Bukoshi and to form a KLA led-interim government based on the negotiating team were even occasionally carried into the conference chamber at Rambouillet, when other issues might have more profitably occupied the delegation. The struggle between Dr Rugova and those who felt better placed to represent Kosovo actually dominated the activities of the Kosovo delegation at the Paris follow-on talks and was only interrupted by the outbreak of hostilities. After the termination of hostilities, this struggle for political power continued unabated, with the formation of a KLA-led transitional government and competition for influence in the Advisory Council created to represent Kosovo in relation to the international administrative structures of the territory.

---

[32] Lenard, J. Cohen, Broken Bonds: *Yugoslavia's Disintegration and Balkan Politics in Transition* (1993) 121.
[33] Constitution of the Republic of Kosova, 7 September 1990, Articles 1 & 2, Document 4.C.4.
[34] Central Board of Kosova for the Conduct of the Referendum, 7 October 1991, Document 4.C.6.

A.   The Period 1943-1990

1.   1st Conference of the National Liberation Council for Kosovo & Dukagjin Plateau, 31 Dec. 1943—2 Jan. 1944

The representatives of all parts of Kosova and the Dukagkin Plateau, Albanian, Serbia and Montenegrins: nationalists, communists, anti-fascist youth, communist youth, anti-fascist women, representatives of the National liberation Army and others inspired by the lofty ideal of the unification of various political trends, for the development and union of the peoples of Kosova and the Dukagjin Plateau, and the strengthening of the organised armed struggle of our peoples against fascist invaders and their lackeys, gathered at the moment when the situation at home and abroad is clear, examined the work of the national liberation councils to date, and elected the Standing Committee of the National Liberation Council.

The Conference noted:

I. A. International events are developing very rapidly to the detriment of German fascism, the defeat of which is inevitable and imminent.

The Red Army, smashing the resistance of the Germans, is advancing steadily westwards and is now on the borders of Poland, Finland, Hungary and the Balkans, accelerating the liberation of enslaved peoples. The struggle and efforts of the Soviet Union, which has defeated this fascist beast, make this country he liberator of enslaved peoples.

The capitulation of Italy has resulted from its heavy losses of troops on the Eastern front, as well as from its losses of troops on the Eastern front, as well as from its losses in Africa, in Sicily, in the enslaved countries, and especially in Yugoslavia.

The Anglo-American army is advancing in Italy, assisted by the struggle of the freedom-loving section of the Italian people. The liberated part of Italy makes possible large-scale actions against fascist Germany. The allied airforce is ceaselessly striking lethal blows against the war industry of fascist Germany.

The recent Moscow Conference and the Teheran Meeting and its Declaration have strengthened the powerful and sincere alliance between the Soviet Union, Britain and America. The date and place have been set for the opening of the second front and the direct assault against the 'Hitlerite fortress' from the east, the south and the west.

The struggle of enslaved peoples is assuming more and more the character of a general armed popular uprising in France, Greece, Poland, Albania and other countries, accelerating the defeat of fascism.

Pride of place in the national liberation war of enslaved peoples is held by the peoples of Yugoslavia who, through super-human efforts and sacrifices, have created their invincible National Liberation Army which for two and a half years now has been waging an uninterrupted war against the fascist occupiers and their lackeys, liberating more than one third of Yugoslavia. With the war it has waged, the National Liberation Army of Yugoslavia has been recognised by the allies as an independent and equal ally. In the course of this war, the conditions have been created to enable the formation of the National Committee for Liberation, headed by the commander of the National Liberation Army, Marshal Tito. This committee is the guarantee for the liberation of all peoples of Yugoslavia, for their independence, their equal rights, and their right of self-determination up to secession.

B. The first imperialist war ended with the Treaty of Versaille which, besides other injustices, created Yugoslavia in order to satisfy the hegemonic clique of Great-Serbs, headed by King Alexander. This Yugoslavia, created without consulting the people and against the will of the people, was a unique example of national, political and economic oppression in Europe.

The Albanian people of Kosova and the Dukagjin Plateau were subject not only to political, national and economic oppression, but also to physical alienation. All their national rights were denied (they lacked schools in the mother tongue and their political and cultural development was obstructed. Their so-called representatives have been faithful agents of the hegemonic clique of the Great-Serbs for robbery and oppression.

The culmination of the economic exploitation was the Agrarian reform, the purpose of which was: to incite chauvinist hatred between Albanian, Serbian and Montenegrin peoples; to impoverish the Albanians to such a degree as to oblige them the emigrate and, under these conditions, to form a support for reaction with the reactionary minions in Kosova and the Dukagjn Plateau. After the defeat of Yugoslavia, the Albanian people of Kosova and the Dukagjin Plateau, as a people without adequate political consciousness and brought to the point of desperation, were ready to welcome as friend anyone who would radically overturn the situation. Even the blood-thirsty soldiers of fascism, who had stained their hands with the blood of Albanians in Albania, were presented to them as saviours. The chorus of traitors in Albania, were Verlaci, Kruja, Biba and others united with that of our traitors; Agushi, Draga, Deva, Khevat, Rifat and Sefedin Begolli and others, formed a joint orchestra to sing the dirge for the unification of the lands of Kosova with the enslaved motherland Albania, lying in the clutches of the Italian fascist imperialism. Taking advantage of the situation of the Albanian masses under the rule of Great Serb hegemonists, these traitor cliques misled the Albanian people here and did not allow them to hear the true voice of their own sons who said that fascism is the sworn enemy of every people, and, therefore of the Albanian people, too. But, it was not long before fascism began to reveal its ugly face as a regime of economic political and national oppression.

Kosova, the granary of the Balkans, became the prey of the rapacious Italian-Albanian companies. E.A.G.A. and S.A.S.T.E.B. and others. Fascism, with the aid of the fifth column, employed the 'divide and rule' policy in Kosova and the Dukkagjin Plateau. With the assistance of traitors it incited feuds between Albanians and Serbo-Montenegrins, and between Moslems and Catholic, with the aim of hindering the unity of these peoples and extinguishing the freedom-loving flame of our peoples.

Through their uninterrupted work and struggle against the occupier, the communists and other patriots helped people to begin to see the aim of fascism. In this way, the chauvinist hatred began to diminish and the armed struggle against the occupiers began, a struggle in which all our peoples are called on to take part, regardless of their political, national and social differences. The vengeful rifles of freedom fighters echoed through the mountains, villages and cities. The partisan ceta of volunteers, headed by Fadil Hoxha and other military leaders, (at Karadak of Shkup, Cernaleva, Shermiria, Gilan, Shar, Gjakova, Prizren, Peja, Ferizaj, Prishtina, Dibra, Peshkopia, Kercova, etc.)

When it saw that here, too, it came under attack, fascism, which considers the freedom of any people a danger, hurled itself like a savage beast upon our peoples, terrorising them in the most inhuman way (at Mitrovica, Peja, Prizren, Gjakova, Bellac, etc.) killing children before their parents and parents before their children, and throwing them still alive into flames (at Gjakova, Garbolla, Vrella, Vitomirica, etc.)

C. After the capitulation on Italy, Kosova and the Dukagjin Plateau were occupied by German fascism, skilled in demagogy and terror, a cunning invader, that knows how to throw the stone and hide its hand. With the coming of the German, occupier, the looting, imprisonment, mass beatings, conscription to the army and obligatory labour, the burning of villages and violent expulsions continued. The German occupier employed as its agents the most evil and blood-thirsty traitors of the type of Nedic's agent, Xhafer Deva, who engaged in beastly tortures, murders and looting from Ferizaj-Prishtina to Mitrovica, Peja, Prizren and elsewhere. All these things were done to prolong the life of Hitler and the internal traitors.

Today our peoples have understood clearly what kind of freedom the Italian-German fascism have brought them, and that the freedom means national and political oppression and economic exploitation. The Germans keep Kosova as an apple of discord, sometimes they dangle it before the Great-Serb hegemonists, sometimes before the Great-Albanian reactionaries (Balli Kombetar etc.), exploiting the antagonisms between them for their own military purposes against the National Liberation Movement.

Various enemies of the peoples have rallied around the German occupier in the war against National Liberation Army. The agents of the Bali Kometar play an important role in close connection with the agents of Draza Mihajlovic. According to the desire of the occupiers, they undertake to drive the Serbian and Montenegrin population en masse from Kosova and the Dukagjin Plateau to Serbia, in order to force them in this way into the ranks of Draza Mihajlovic, who, like the hand of Balli Kombatar, is fighting on the side of the Germans against the National Liberation Armu. They mobilise the Albanians and send them to fight against the National Liberation Army of the peoples of Yugoslavia and the National Liberation Army of Albania in the interests of the German occupiers. On behalf of Greater Albania, the Albanian ballists pursue the same policy as the Drazists on behalf of Greater Yugoslavia. The Albanian and Yugoslav reactionaries fear the peoples who have taken up arms to fight for their freedom and rights. Let the Balli Kombetar, the godfather of Draza Mihajlovic, bellow as loud as it likes against the Serbo, Montenegrin danger: the National Liberation War of the peoples of Yugoslavia, which is wiping out the cetnici, sworn enemies of the Albanian people, is exposing the falsity of this tale. In the mountains of Montenegro, Bosnia, Herzegovina, Dalmatia and elsewhere, the grave has been dug for the Yugoslav hegemonists, enemies of the freedom of the Albanian people and other peoples.

Kosova and the Dukagjin Plateau is a region in which the majority of the inhabitants are Albanian who today wish to be united with Albania, as they have always done. Therefore, we feel it our duty to indicate the right road which the road which the Albanian people must follow to realise their aspirations. The only way for the Albanian people of Kosova and the Dukagjin Plateau to be united with Albania is through joint struggle with the other peoples of Yugoslavia against the blood-thirsty Nazi occupier and its paid lackeys, because this is the only way to win the freedom, in which all the peoples, including the Albanian people, will be able to determine their own destiny through the right of self-determination up to secession. The guarantee of this is the National Liberation Army of Yugoslavia and the National Liberation Army of Albania with which it is closely linked. Apart from them, our great allies the Soviet Union, Britain, and America also guarantee this (the Atlantic Charter, the Moscow and Teheran Conferences).

II. We, the representatives of Kosova and the Dukagjin Plateau, send greetings to the National Committee for the Liberation of Yugoslavia, headed by Marshal Tito, and associate ourselves with its just protest against the traitor Yugoslav government in exile in London and the return of King Peer II. Likewise, we demand that they and all the blood-suckers be brought before the people's court to render account for all their crimes.

II. The National Liberation Council is not a party, but a joint organ in which all the political trends take part, and therefore, we call on all honest patriots without distinction as to nationality, religion, political tendency or social position to rally around the National Liberation Council in the fight against the occupiers and its lackeys as this decisive moment for winning true freedom.

MEMBERS OF THE COUNCIL

[signed/initialed] Mehmet Dermani, Tefik Canga, Qamil Brovina, Qamil Luzha, Gani S. Cavdarbashj, Xheladin Hana, Sul B. Alaj, Halil Haxhija, Shaban Kajtazi, Ismet Shaqiri, Ferid Perollo, Adam Miftari, Haxhi Morina, Ismail Isufi, Xhavid Sh. Nimani, Sabrije Vokshi, Reshat Isa, Velisha Mickovic, Mehmet Bajraktari , Ljubomir Canic, Velie Niman Doci, Abdil Kerim Ibrahimi, Rasim Cokli, Spira Velkovic, S. Bekteshi, Xhevat Tahiri, Jaho Bajraktari, Ymer Pula, Shaban Haxhija, Et'hem Zurnaxhio, Aluah Gashi, Engineer Neshat Basha , Begir Ndou, Ajdin Bajraktari, Xhafer Vokshi, Bejto Samanovic, Sima H. Vasilevic, Milan A. Mickovic, Enver Dajci, Zymer Halili, Maxhun Doci Nimani.

We also call on those who have been in the service of the occupiers and have not stained their hands with the people's blood.

IV. Our National Liberation Army and the partisan ranks are expanding from day to day. Every day their needs are greater; therefore it is necessary that our people work to assist our fighters.

V. The Conference elected its Standing Committee consisting of the Chairman, two Vice-Chairman and six members.

VI. After reports were delivered and discussed, the National Liberation Council was charged with the following:

TASKS

1. To explain that the National Liberation Councils, in the present conditions, are organs of the war against the occupier and the embryo of the organs of the future people's state power;

2. To popularise the National Liberation Army, to assist the war with every means, and to mobilise as many people as possible in this war;

3. To make contact with the councils which have been formed up to date, and set them to work;

4. To form National Liberation Council wherever they have not been formed hitherto;

5. To further strengthen the fraternal links of our peoples (Albanian, Serbian and Montenegrin), continuously struggling against chauvinism; to explain to the broad masses of the people that the chauvinist policy is a weapon in the hands of the occupier and the traitors of the peoples to hinder their fraternisation and the waging of the National Liberation War in our province and the winning of freedom;

6. To publish its own organ;

7. To popularise the National Liberation Army of the peoples of Yugoslavia;

8. To popularise the National Liberation Army of Albania;

9. To popularise the National Committee for the liberation Yugoslavia;

10. To popularise the National Liberation General Council of Albania.

11. To use every possible means to hinder the mobilisation of the peoples in war against the National Liberation Armies of Yugoslavia and Albania, by explaining to them that whoever fights against the National Liberation Armies is fighting against himself;

12. To gather documents and evidence of the crimes the fascist occupiers and the traitors have committed;

13. To expose and fight the occupier and reactionary cliques of every hue and not permit the mobilisation of the people in the service of the occupier;

14. To popularise the Red Army, led by Marshal Stalin;

15. To popularise the Anglo-Soviet-American anti-fascist bloc;

16. To popularise the fraternity and National Liberation struggle of all enslaved peoples.

17. To popularise the fraternity of the peoples of the Balkans;

18. To conduct a campaign of aid for the families of those have been imprisoned, interned, forcibly expelled, who have fallen in the war, for the families of those whose homes have been burned, and those who are fighting in the National Liberation Army. Death to fascism-Freedom to the people:

  The Standing Committee
1. Mehment Hoxha, Chairman of the Council
2. Pavle Jovicevic, Vice Chairman of the Council
3. Rifat Berisha, Vice Chairman of the Council
4. Xhevdet Doda
5. Fadil Hoxha
6. Hajdar Dushi
7. Zekerija Rexha

As can be seen from the proclamation, elected in the Standing Committee are Milan Becar from Retkovci, Nerodima region, and Ali Shukrija, student from Mitrovica, whose signatures are not attached because they were not able to attend the conference.

2. Constitution of the Federal People's Republic of Yugoslavia, 1946

Part One Fundamental Principles

Chapter I. The Federal Peoples Republic of Yugoslavia

Article 1. The Federal Peoples Republic of Yugoslavia is a federal people's state republican in form, a community of peoples equal in rights who, on the basis of the right to self-determination, including the right of separation, have expressed their will to live together in a federative state.

Article 2. The Federal Peoples Republic of Yugoslavia is composed of the Peoples Republic of Serbia, the Peoples Republic of Croatia, the

Peoples Republic of Slovenia, the Peoples Republic of Bosnia and Herzegovina, the Peoples Republic of Macedonia and the Peoples Republic of Montenegro.

The Peoples Republic of Serbia includes the Autonomous Province of Vojvodina and the Autonomous Kosovo-Metohijan Region. ...

Article 9. The sovereignty of the peoples republics composing the FPRY is limited only by the rights which by this Constitution are given to the Federal Peoples Republic of Yugoslavia.

The Federal Peoples Republic of Yugoslavia protects and defends the sovereign rights of the peoples republics.

The Federal Peoples Republic of Yugoslavia protects the security and defends the sovereign rights of the peoples republics.

Article 10. Any act directed against the sovereignty, equality and national freedom of the peoples of the Federal Peoples Republic of Yugoslavia and their peoples republics is contrary to the Constitution.

Article 11. Each peoples republic has its own Constitution.

The peoples republic makes its own Constitution independently.

The Constitution of the peoples republic reflects the special characteristics of the republic and must be in conformity with the Constitution of the Federal Peoples Republic of Yugoslavia.

Article 12. The Peoples Assembly of the FPRY determines the boundaries between the people's republics.

The boundaries of a peoples republic cannot be altered without its consent.

Article 13. National minorities in the FPRY enjoy the right to and protection of their own cultural development and the free use of their language. ...

Article 44. The Federal Peoples Republic of Yugoslavia exercises all the rights vested in it by the Constitution.

Under the jurisdiction of the Federal Peoples Republic of Yugoslavia as represented by the highest federal organs of state authority and the organs of state administration are included:

1. Amendments to the Constitution of the FPRY, control over the observance of the Constitution, and the ensuring of the conformity of the constitutions of the people's republics with the Constitution of the FPRY;

2. The admission of new republics and approval of the foundation of new autonomous provinces and autonomous regions;

3. The delimitaiton of boundaries between republics;

... Outside these matters the people's republics exercise their authority independently.

Article 45. The territory of the FPR of Yugoslavia consists of the territories of its republics and forms a single state and economic area.

... Chapter XI. Organs of State Authority of Autonomous Provinces and Autonomous Regions

Article 103. The rights and the scope of the autonomy of autonomous provinces and autonomous regions are determined by the Constitution of the republic.

Article 104. The statute of an autonomous province or of an autonomous region is drawn up in conformity with the Constitution of the FRY and the Constitution of the republic by the highest organ of state authority of the autonomous province or autonomous region, and is confirmed by the people's Assembly of the republic.

Article 105. The highest organ of state authority of an autonomous province in the people's assembly of the autonomous province, which is elected by the citizens of the autonomous province for a period of three years and meets in accordance with the provisions of the Constitution of the Republic.

The people's assembly of an autonomous province elects the principal executive committee of the autonomous province as its executive and administrative organ.

106. The highest organ of state authority of an autonomous region is the regional people's committee, which is elected by the citizens of the autonomous region for a period of three years and holds its assemblies in accordance with the provisions of the Constitution of the republic.

The regional people's committee elects the regional executive committee as its executive and administrative organ. ...

3. Constitution of the Federal People's Republic of Yugoslavia, 1953

I. The Federal People's Republic of Yugoslavia

Article 1. The Federal People's Republic of Yugoslavia is a socialist, democratic Federation of sovereign and equal peoples. ...

Article 3. ... Federation only exercises the rights assigned to it by the Federal Constitution; the People's Republics exercise the rights established in the Republic Constitutions. ...

Article 10. The Territory of the Federal People's Republic of Yugoslavia consists of the territories of the People's Republics and constitutes a unified state, economic and customs area. ...

Article 44. The Federal Assembly acts as one Chamber; however, its members representing the representative organs of the People's Republics, autonomous provinces or regions have special rights established in this Constitution.

Article 45. Members of the Federal Assembly elected by the representative organs of the Republics, autonomous provinces or regions form the Chamber of Nationalities and take decisions when the Federal Assembly considers motions for amemdments of this Constitution or the Federal economic plan. ...

Article 100. The People's Assembly of the Republic represents the national sovereignty of the Republic and is its highest organ of public power. ...

IV. General Provisions concerning the Public Organs of the Autonomous Province and Autonomous Region.

Article 113. The self-governance of the autonomous province Vojvodina and of the autonomous region of Kosovo-Metohija is guaranteed. The powers of self-governance of the autonomous province and the autonomous region are established in the Constitution of the People's Republic of Serbia. The highest organ of public power of the autonomous province is the Provincial People's Assembly. The highest organ of public power of the autonomous region is the Regional People's Committee. The Provincial People's Assembly consists of the Provincial Council and the Production Council, the Regional People's Committee consists of the Territorial Council and the Production Council.

Article 114. The Constitution of the People's Republic of Serbia regulates in accordance with the principles of this Constitution the powers of the public organs of the autonomous province Vojvodina and of the Autonomous Region of Kosovo-Metohija. The Autonomous Province and the Autonomous Region establish their own statutes, regulating in accordance with the Constitution of the People's Republic of Serbia the powers of their public organs.

4. Constitution of the Socialist Federal Republic of Yugoslavia, 1963

BASIC PRINCIPLES

I. The peoples of Yugoslavia, on the basis of the right of every people to self-determination, including the right to secession, on the basis of their common struggle and their will freely declared in the People's Liberation War and socialist revolution, and in accord with their historical aspirations, aware that the further consolidation of their brotherhood and unity is to their common interest, have united in a federal republic of free and equal peoples and nationalities and have founded a socialist federal community of working people, the Socialist Federal Republic of Yugoslia, in which, in the interests of each people and all of them together, they are achieving and developing:

Socialist social relations and the protection of the socialist system of society;

National freedom and independence; ...

The working people and the peoples of Yugoslavia exercise their sovereign rights in the Federation when the Constitution determines this to be in the common interest and exercise all other relations in the socialist republics. ...

Chapter I. Article 1. The Socialist Federal Republic of Yugoslavia is a federal state of voluntarily united and equal peoples and a socialist democratic community based on the powers of the working people and of self-government.

Article 2. The Socialist Federal Republic of Yugoslavia comprises the Socialist Republics of Bosnia and Herzegovina, Croatia, Macedonia, Montenegro, Serbia and Slovenia.

The territory of the Socialist Federal Republic of Yugoslavia is unified, consisting of the territories of the socialist republic. ...
Chapter V.

Article 111. A Republic may found autonomous provinces in accordance with the constitution in areas with distinctive national characteristics or in areas with other distinguishing features, on the basis of the express will of the population of these areas.

The foundation or dissolution of an autonomous province shall take effect when this is sanctioned by the Constitution of Yugoslavia.

In the Socialist Republic of Serbia there are the Autonomous Provinces of Vojvodina and Kosvovo and Meohija, established in 1945 by decision of the People's Assembly of the People's Republic of Serbia in accordance with the express will of the population of these areas.

Article 112. The autonomous provinces are social-political communities within the republic. The autonomous rights and duties and the basic principles of organization in the autonomous provinces shall be determined by the republic constitution. ...

Article 113. In the Socialist Federal Republic of Yugoslavia the peoples and the citizens shall realize and safeguard the sovereignty, territorial integrity, security and defence of Yugoslavia, the international relations of Yugoslavia, the unity of the social-economic and political system, the economic unity of the country, the course and coordination of general economic development, and the basic freedoms and rights of man and the citizen; and they shall coordinate their political, economic, cultural and other common interests. In order to realize these common interests, the Constitution determines the rights and the duties of the Federation. The citizens shall also realize their political, social-economic, cultural and other common interests by means of social-political and other organizations which are active on the whole territory of Yugoslavia. In exercising its rights and duties the Federation shall have the cooperation of the republics and other social-political communities, and social-political and other organizations.

Article 114. The Federation shall protect the sovereign rights and equality of the peoples and the socialist social and political organization of the republics. ...

Article 165. ... The members of the Federal Chamber elected by the republican assemblies and the assemblies of the autonomous provinces shall constitute the Chamber of Nationalities, which shall have certain rights and duties under the Constitution for safeguarding the equality of the peoples of Yugoslavia and the rights of the republics, as determined by the Constitution. ...

5. Constitution of the Socialist Republic of Serbia, 1963

Article 129. The rights and duties of the autonomous province shall be determined within the restrictions of the rights and duties of the Republic by the Constitution and by republican law.

The autonomous province shall attend to the development of the economy and other social activities and to development of social self-government and socialist social relations on its territory. To this end it shall have the following rights and duties: it shall organize the provincial authorities and adopt a provincial statute; pass the provincial budget; organize affairs of general interest for the province in the fields of economy, education, culture, national health, social welfare and in the communal housing field; decide about the utilization of provincial revenues; attend to the enforcement of law and of other federal and republican regulations, attend to the enforcement of law and other federal and replication regulations; attend to the maintenance of public peace and order; directly enforce law and the other regulations when it is expressly authorized by the regulations in question to do so; supervice the enforcement of law by the district and their organs; exercise social supervision on the provincial territory; found working organizations and other autonomous institutions, organs and services to discharge affairs within the rights and duties of the province; lend assistance to the communes and districts in the performance of their rights and duties; discharge other affairs determined by republican law.

Article 130. In order to perform its rights and duties the autonomous province shall have permanent sources of revenue, which shall be determined by republican law.

The revenues of the autonomous province shall accrue from a part of the sources accumulating on the territory of the autonomous province which belong to the Republic in accordance with the law to develop the economy and for other social activities and for the requirements of general social expenditure.

The communes and districts on the teritory of the autonomous province may agree to forgo part of their funds in favour of the autonomous province towards the fulfilment of tasks of common concern.

Article 131. The affairs of general concern to the province as a whole shall be determined by the regulations of the autonomous province. If a republican law has been passed after a provincial regulation, the provision of the provincial regulation pertaining to affairs regulated by the republican law shall cease to be valid when the republican law take effect, unless this has otherwise been determined by law. The autonomous province may be authorized by republican law to depart from the provison of the republican law and to regulate particular affairs otherwise, in conformity with the characteristics of the province. The autonomous province may regulate certain affairs in the fields regulated only by law in conformity with the Constitution if it is authorized by republican law to do so. The organs of the autonomous province may adopt regulations to enforce federal republican regulations if they are expressly authorized by republican law or decree to do so. The regulations of the autonomous province shall be directly enforced by the communal organs.

Article 132. The provincial administrative organs shall adopt administrative acts and undertake administrative action only when this is placed in their jurisdiciton by provincial regulations, and in affairs placed by republican regulations in the jurisdicitons of the republican administrative organs, with the exception of those affairs which are placed by republican law or decree in the exclusive jurisdiction of the republican administrative organs. The adoption of administrative acts and the undertaking of administrative action may be placed by provincial regulations in the jurisdiction of the provincial administrative organs only when this is in the interest of the province as a whole.

Article 133. The provincial organs shall have only the rights determined by the Constitution and by republican law in relaton to the district and communal organs. Rights of supervising the legality of work of the communcal and district organs and organs of the working organizations which appertain to the republican organs of the basis of the Constitution and law shall be exercised on the territory of the autonomous province by the provincial organs, with the exception of the rights which are the exclusive jurisdiction of the republican organs in accordance with republican law.

Article 134. The relations between the republican organs and the organs of the autonomous province shall be based on the rights and duties of these organs determined by the constitution and by republican law and on cooperation between them. Posititions of principle adopted by the Republican Executive Council in its jurisdiciton shall be binding also on the political executive organs of the autonomous province. The directives issued by the Republican Executive Council shall be binding also on the adminstrative organs of the autonomous province. The instructions issued by the republican adminstrative organs which they issue in accordance with powers based on law shall be binding also on the administrative organs of the autonomous province.

Article 135. The autonomous province shall have a statute. The statute of the province, in conformity with the Constitution and law, shall determine the functions of the province; the conditions according to which autonomous institutions and services of concern to the province as a whole may be founded; inter-relations between the provincial organs and the organs of social self-government in the province; reglations between the provincial organs and the district and communal organs on the territory of the province in the discharge of affairs of common concern, and other matters of concern to the autonomous province.

6.   Constitution of the Socialist Federal Republic of Yugoslavia, 1974

BASIC PRINCIPLES

The nations of Yugoslavia, proceeding from the right of every nation to self-determination, including the right to secession, on the basis of their will freely expressed in the common struggle of all nations and nationalities in the National Liberation War and Socialist Revolution, and in conformity with their historic aspirations, aware that further consolidation of their brotherhood and unity is in the common interest, have, together with the nationalities with which they live, have united in a federal republic of free and equal nations and nationalities and founded a socialist federal community of working people - the Socialist Federal Republic of Yugoslavia, in which, in the interest of each nation and nationality separately and of all of them together, they shall realise and ensure;

- socialist social relations based on self-management by working people and the protection of the socialist self-management system;
- national freedom and independence;
- the brotherhood and unity of the nations and nationalities;
- the uniform interests of the working class, and solidarity among workers and all working people;
- possibilities and freedoms for the all-round development of the human personality and for the rapprochement of the nations and nationalities, in conformity with their interests and aspirations on the road to the creation of an ever richer culture and civilisation in a socialist society;
- the unification and adjustment of efforts to develop the economic foundations of a socialist society and the prosperity of the people;
- a system of socio-economic relations and uniform foundations for a political system which will ensure the common interests of the working class and all working people and equality of the nations and nationalities;
- the linking of Yugoslavia's aspirations with the progressive strivings of mankind.

The working people and the nations and nationalities shall exercise their sovereign rights in the Socialist Republics, and in the Socialist Autonomous Provinces in conformity with their constitutional rights, and shall exercise these rights in the Socialist Federal Republic of Yugoslavia when in their common interests it is so specified by the present Constitution.

The working people, nations and nationalities shall make decisions in the Federation according to the principles of agreement among the Republics and Autonomous Provinces, solidarity and reciprocity, equal participation by the Republics and Autonomous Provinces in federal agencies, in line with the present Constitution, and according to the principle of responsibility of the Republics and Autonomous Provinces for their own development and for the development of the socialist community as a whole. ...

THE SOCIALIST FEDERAL REPUBLIC OF YUGOSLAVIA

Article 1. The Socialist Federal Republic of Yugoslavia is a federal state having the form of a state community of voluntarily united nations and their Socialist Republics, and of the Socialist Autonomous Provinces of Vojvodina and Kosovo, which are constituent parts of the Socialist Republic Serbia, based on the power of an self-management by the working class and all working people; it is at the same time a socialist self-management democratic community of working people and citizens and of nations and nationalities having equal rights.

Article 2. The Socialist Republics are states based on the consists of the Socialist Republic of Croatia, the Socialist Republic of Macedonia, the Socialist Republic of Montenegro, the Socialist Republic of Serbia, the Socialist Autonomous Province of Vojvodina and the Socialist Autonomous Province of Kosovo, which are constituent parts of the Socialist Republic of Slovenia.

Article 3. The Socialist Republics are states based on the sovereignty of the people and the power of an elf-management by the working class and all working people, and are socialist, self-managing democratic communities of the working people and citizens, and of nations and nationalities having equal rights.

Article 4. The Socialist Autonomous Province are autonomous socialist self-managing democratic socio-political communities based on the power of an self-management by the working class and all working people, in which the working people, nations and nationalities realise their sovereign rights, and when so specified by the Constitution of the Socialist Republic of Serbia in the common interests of the working people, nations and nationalities of that Republic as a whole, they do so also within the Republic.

Article 5. The territory of the Socialist Federal Republic of Yugoslavia is a single unified whole and consists of the territories of the Socialist Republics.

The territory of a Republic may not be altered without the consent of that Republic, and the territory of an Autonomous province - without the consent of that Autonomous Province.

The frontiers of the Socialist Federal Republic of Yugoslavia may not be altered without the consent of that Autonomous Province.

The frontiers of the Socialist Federal Republic of Yugoslavia may not be altered without the consent of all Republics and Autonomous Provinces.

Boundaries between the Republics may only be altered on the basis of mutual agreement, and if the boundary of an Autonomous province is involved - also on the basis of the latter's agreement. ...

Article 206. Republican constitutions and the provincial constitutions may not be contrary to the S.F.R.Y. Constitution.

All statutes and other regulations and enactments passed by agencies and organisations of the socio-political communities, and self-management enactments of organisations of associated labour and other self-managing organisations and communities, must be in conformity with the S.F.R.Y. Constitution.

Article 207. All regulations and other enactments passed by federal agencies must be in conformity with federal statute.

Republicans and provincial statutes and other regulations and enactments passed by agencies of the socio-political communities, and self-management enactments may not be contrary to federal statute.

If a republican or provincial statute is contrary to federal statute, it will be temporarily applied pending a decision by the constitutional court, and if federal agencies are responsible for their enforcement, the federal statute concerned shall apply.

If an agency which has jurisdiction over individual matters deems that a statute, other regulation or enactment of self-management enactment is not in accord with federal statute, or that it is contrary to federal statute, it shall be bound to institute proceedings before he constitutional court. ...

Article 245. The nations and nationalities of the Socialist Federal Republic of Yugoslavia shall have equal rights.

Article 246. The languages of the nations and nationalities and their alphabets shall be equal throughout the territory of Yugoslavia. In the Socialist Federal Republic of Yugoslavia the languages of the nations shall be officially used, and the languages of the nationalities shall be used in conformity with the present Constitution and federal statute.

The realisation of the equality of languages and alphabets of the nations and nationalities regarding their official use in areas populated by individual nationalities shall be ensured and the way of and conditions for its realisation regulated by statute, the by-laws of the socio-political communities, and by self-management enactments of organisations of associated labour and other self-managing organisations and communities.

Article 247. In order to ensure that its right to express its nationality and culture shall be realised, each nationality shall be guaranteed the right freely to use its language and alphabet, to develop its culture and for this purpose to set up organisations and enjoy other constitutionally-established rights. ...

Article 250. Decisions, documents and individual acts issued by state agencies and authorised organisations in one republic or autonomous province shall be equally valid in other Republics and Autonomous Provinces. ...

Article 262. The National Bank of Yugoslavia, the National Banks of the Republics and the National Banks of the Autonomous Provinces shall operate deposit accounts of the socio-political communities and shall be authorised, on behalf of the socio-political communities and on their account, to perform other banking affairs, if so specified by the constitution.

The National Bank of Yugoslavia shall act as a depository of federal resources, conduct credit and other banking business for the needs of the Yugoslav People's Army and for the needs of national defence, as laid down by the federal statute, and shall carry out other statutorily specified credit and banking operations on account of the Federation.

The National Bank of Yugoslavia, the National Banks of the Republics and the National Banks of the Autonomous Provinces shall not engage in other activities of commercial banks. ...

Article 263. The status of the National Bank of Yugoslavia and uniform monetary operations of the National Banks of the Republics and Autonomous Provinces shall be regulated by federal statute.

The operations of the National Bank of Yugoslavia concerning the execution of common currency issue, monetary-credit and foreign exchange policy shall be managed by the Board of Governors. In managing these operations the Board of Governors shall make decisions and take measures, and shall be responsible for their implementation.

The Board of Governors shall be composed of the Governor of the National Bank of Yugoslavia, the governors of the National Banks of the Republics and the governors of the National Banks of the Autonomous Provinces. ...

Article 265. The Republics and Autonomous Provinces shall co-operate in the pursuance of tax policy and shall through compacts adjust the basic principles of tax policy and the tax system whenever it is necessary to ensure the unity and stability of the Yugoslav market.

In order to prevent and eliminate disruptions on the market, federal agencies shall have the right and duty to propose to the Republics and Autonomous Provinces in conformity with mutual compacts to decrease or increase taxes and contributions fixed by the socio-political communities, temporarily to postpone the spending of part of the revenue of the socio-political communities, and to lay down common foundations of the tax policy of the Republics and/or Autonomous Provinces. Non-existence of compacts shall not prevent the Republics and Autonomous Provinces from passing regulations and other enactments in the sphere of tax policy and the tax system within the framework of their rights and obligations. ...

Article 268. In exercising the rights and duties laid down by the present Constitution, federal agencies shall formulate policy and pass federal statutes and other regulations and enactments.

In the sphere regulated by federal statutes, the Republics and Autonomous Provinces may pass statutes within the framework of their rights and duties.

If in areas to be regulated by Federal statute no such statute has been passed, the Republics and/or Autonomous Provinces may pass their own statutes if this is in the interests of the realisation of their rights and duties.

Article 269. Federal statutes and other regulations and enactments shall be promulgated in the Official Gazette of the Socialist Federal Republic of Yugoslavia in authentical texts in the languages of the nations of Yugoslavia specified by the republican constitutions.

Federal statutes and other regulations and enactments shall be promulgated in the Official Gazette of the Socialist Federal Republic of Yugoslavia as authentical texts in the languages of the Albanian and Hungarian nationalities also.

Article 270. Federal statutes and other regulations and enactments shall be binding throughout the entire territory of the Socialist Federal Republic of Yugoslavia, unless their application is restricted by these statutes, regulations or enactments to a narrower territory.

Article 271. International treaties which entail the enactment of new or amendments to existing republican and/or provincial statutes, or which entail special obligations for one or more Republics and/or Autonomous Provinces, shall be concluded in agreement with the competent republican and/or provincial agencies. The procedure for the conclusion of such international treaties shall be regulated by federal statute, in agreement with the republican and provincial assemblies.

In co-operating with agencies and organisations of other states and with international agencies and organisations, the Republics and Autonomous Provinces shall keep within the established foreign policy of the Socialist Federal Republic of Yugoslavia and international treaties.

In co-operating with appropriate foreign agencies and organisations, international organisations and territorial units of foreign states, Communes, organisations of associated labour and other organisations and communities shall keep within the established foreign policy of the Socialist Federal Republic of Yugoslavia and international treaties.

The principle of the equality of languages of the nations of Yugoslavia, and analogously the principle of the nations and nationalities, shall be applied in international communication.

When international treaties are drawn up in the languages of the signatory countries, the languages of the nations of Yugoslavia shall be equally used. ...

Article 280. The Socialist Federal Republic of Yugoslavia shall be represented by the federal agencies specified by the present Constitution.

Article 281. The Federation shall through its agencies:

...

(11) regulate matters concerning settlement of conflicts of law between republicans and/or provincial Autonomous Provinces (conflict rules), and jurisdictional disputes between republican and/or provincial agencies of difference Republics; regulate matters concerning conflicts between domestic laws and legal rules of other countries; ...

Article 284. The rights and duties of the S.F.R.Y. Assembly shall be exercised by the Federal Chamber and the Chamber of Republics and Provinces in accordance with the provisions of the present Constitution.

The Federal Chamber shall be composed of delegates of self-managing organisations and communities and socio-political organisations in the Republics and Autonomous Provinces.

The Chamber of Republics and Provinces shall be composed of delegations of the Assemblies of the Republics and the Assemblies of the Autonomous Provinces.

Article 291. The Federal Chamber shall be composed of thirty delegates of self-managing organisations and communities and socio-political organisations from each Republic, and of twenty delegates from each Autonomous Province.

The nominating procedure shall be carried out by the Socialist Alliance of the Working People. Candidates for delegates to the Federal Chamber shall be proposed by delegations of basic self-managing organisations and communities from among members of the delegations of these organisations and communities, and also by socio-political communities, within the framework of the Socialist Alliance of the Working People, from among members of their delegations.

The list of candidates for delegates to the Federal Chamber shall be drawn up by the nominating conference of the Socialist Alliance of the Working People of the Republics and Autonomous Provinces.

Delegates to the Federal Chamber shall be elected, on the basis of a list of candidates, by the Commune Assemblies on the territories of the Republics and the Autonomous Provinces, by secret ballot.

The election and recall of delegates of the Federal Chamber shall be regulated by federal statute.

The nominating procedure for the election of delegates of the Federal Chamber to posts of delegates whose tenure has ended before the expiry of their terms shall be regulated by federal statute.

Article 292. The Chamber of Republics and Provinces shall be composed of twelve delegates of each Republican Assembly and eight delegates of each Provincial Assembly.

The delegations to the Chamber of Republics and Provinces shall be elected and recalled by secret ballot by all Chambers of the Assemblies of the respective Republics and of the Assemblies of the respective Autonomous Provinces sitting in joint session.

Delegates elected to the Chamber of Republics and Provinces shall retain their tenure in the assemblies to which they have been elected. ...

Article 298. The right to introduce bills and other draft enactments falling within the province of work of the Chamber of Republics and Provinces which must be adopted in agreement with the Assemblies of the Republics and the Assemblies of the Autonomous Provinces shall be vested with every delegation to, and working body of, the Chamber, the Assemblies of the Republics and the Assemblies of the Autonomous Provinces, and in the Federal Executive council.

...

Article 313. The S.F.R.Y. Presidency shall represent the Socialist Federal Republic of Yugoslavia at home and abroad, and shall have other rights and duties as laid down by the present Constitution.

Within the framework of its rights and duties, and in order to realise the equality of the nations and nationalities, the S.F.R.Y. Presidency shall work to achieve adjustment of the common interests of the Republics and Autonomous Provinces, in conformity with their responsibility concerning the realisation of federal rights and duties.

The S.F.R.Y. Presidency is the supreme body in charge of the administration and command of the Armed Forces of the Socialist Federal Republic of Yugoslavia in war and peace.

The S.F.R.Y. Presidency shall consider foreign policy and the safeguard of the order established by the present Constitution (state security), and shall take stands to provide initiative for adopting measures and adjusting the activities of competent agencies in the execution of established policy in these spheres. ...

Article 321. The S.F.R.Y. Presidency shall be composed of a member from each Republic and Autonomous Province, elected by secret ballot by the Assemblies of the Republics and the Assemblies of the Autonomous Provinces, respectively, at a joint session of all Chambers of the Assemblies, and of the President of the League of Communities of Yugoslavia by virtue of his office. ...

THE CONSTITUTIONAL COURT OF YUGOSLAVIA

Article 375. The Constitutional Court of Yugoslavia shall:

(1) decide on the conformity of statutes to the Constitution of the Socialist Federal Republic of Yugoslavia;

(2) decide whether or not a republican or provincial statute is contrary to federal statute;

(3) decide disputes involving rights and duties between the Federation and the Republics and/or Autonomous Provinces, between the Republics, between the Republics and the Autonomous Provinces, and between other socio-political communities from the territories of different Republics, if no jurisdiction of another court has been provided by statute for the settlement of such disputes; ...

Article 396. The federal chamber will decide about the changes of the federal constitution with the consent of the assemblies of all republics and autonomous provinces. ...

Article 398. Amendments to the S.F.R.Y. Constitution shall be decided upon by the Federal Chamber of the S.F.R.Y. Assembly, in agreement with the Assemblies of all Republics and Autonomous Provinces; if an amendments to the S.F.R.Y. Constitution only concerns the status of the Republics and mutual relations between the Federation and the Republics, it shall be decided upon by the Federal Chamber of the S.F.R.Y. Assembly in agreement with the Assemblies of all Republics.

Article 399. A motion to initiate proceedings for amending the S.F.R.Y. Constitution may be introduced by at least thirty delegates to the Federal Chamber, the S.F.R.Y. Presidency, the Assembly of a Republic, the Assembly of an Autonomous Province, and the Federal Executive Council.

Article 400. A motion to initiate proceedings for amending the S.F.R.Y. Constitution shall be decided upon by the Federal Chamber of the S.F.R.Y. Assembly.

The Federal Chamber may decide to initiate proceedings for amending the S.F.R.Y. Constitution if the motion for the initiation of amendment proceedings has been agreed upon by the Assemblies of all Republics and Autonomous Provinces and the Assemblies of all Republics respectively.

Article 401. Draft amendments to the S.F.R.Y. Constitution shall be drawn up by the Federal Chamber of the S.F.R.Y. Assembly, which shall refer them to the Assemblies of all Republics and Autonomous Provinces for opinion, and shall submit them to public discussion.

Draft amendments to the S.F.R.Y. Constitution shall be debated upon by the Assemblies of all Republics and Autonomous Provinces, which shall give their opinions thereon.

When the opinions of the Assemblies of al Republics and Autonomous Provinces have been obtained and public discussion conducted, the Federal Chamber shall draw up a motion for the amendment of the S.F.R.Y. Constitution and take a vote thereon.

An amendment to the S.F.R.Y. Constitution shall be deemed passed in the Federal Chamber if it has received a two-thirds majority vote from all delegates to the Chamber.

If an amendment to the S.F.R.Y. Constitution has not been adopted in the Federal Chamber, a motion for the same amendment to the S.F.R.Y. Constitution may not be introduced again before the expiry of one year from the day the motion was rejected.

Article 402. An amendment to the S.F.R.Y. Constitution shall be deemed passed when the text adopted by the Federal Chamber of the S.F.R.Y. Assembly has agreed to by the Assemblies of all Republics and Autonomous Provinces and the Assemblies of all Republics respectively.

If the Assembly of one or more Republics or the Assembly of either of the Autonomous Provinces has not agreed with the text of the motion for the amendment of the S.F.R.Y. Constitution passed by the Federal Chamber, the motion for the amendment of the S.F.R.Y. Constitution on which no agreement has been reached may not be placed on the agenda before the expiry of one year from the day the Federal Chamber ruled that no agreement had been reached.

Amendment IV. 1. The SFRY Presidium shall consist of one member from each republic and autonomous province, elected by the assembly of the respective republic or autonomous province by secret ballot at a joint session of all chambers of the assembly, and of the president of the organ of the League of Communists of Yugoslavia specified by the By-Laws of the League of Communists of Yugoslavia, by virtue of his office ...

7. Constitution of the Socialist Republic of Serbia, 1974

INTRODUCTORY PART: BASIC PRINCIPLES

The Serb nation, together with other nations and nationalities of Yugoslavia, headed by the Communist Party of Yugoslavia in the struggle during the National Liberation War and socialist revolution, overthrew the old class order based on exploitation and national subjugation ...

Paragraph 2. Proceeding from the right of every nation to self-determination, including the right of secession, on the basis of the common struggle and will freely expressed in the National Liberation War and socialist revolution, and in conformity with their historic aspirations, aware that the further consolidation of brotherhood and unity is in the common interest of all nations and nationalities, the Serb nation has, together with nationalities with which it lives, united with other Yugoslav nations in a federal republic of free and equal nations and founded a socialist federal community of working people - the Socialist Federal Republic of Yugoslavia, in which, in the interests of each nation and nationality separately and all together, it shall realise and ensure:

• national freedom and independence;

• the brotherhood and unity of the nations and nationalities;

• the uniform interest of the working class and solidarity among worker and all working people;

• possibilities and freedoms for the all-round development of the human personality and for the rapprochement of the nations and nationalities, in conformity with their interests and aspirations on the road to the creation of an ever-richer culture and civilisation in a socialist society;

Paragraph 3. The working people and the nations and nationalities of Serbia shall exercise their sovereign rights in the Socialist Republic of Serbia and in the Socialist Autonomous Provinces in conformity with their constitutional rights, and in the S.F.R.Y. when in their common interest it is so specified by the Constitution of the Socialist Federal Republic of Yugoslavia.

Paragraph 4. The Socialist Republic of Serbia is a self-managing socialist democratic socio-political community of working people and citizens and of equal nations and nationalities.

As the state of the Serb nation, members of other nations of Yugoslavia and nationalities within Serbia, the Socialist Republic of Serbia is based on the sovereignty of the people and by the power of and self-management by the working class and all working people. ...

Paragraph 6. The Socialist Republic of Serbia comprises the Socialist Autonomous Province of Vojvodina and the Socialist Autonomous Province of Kosovo, which originated in the common struggle of nations and nationalities of Yugoslavia in the National Liberation War and socialist revolution and united, on the basis of the freely expressed will of the population, nations and nationalities of the provinces and Serbia, in the Socialist Republic of Serbia within the Socialist Federal Republic of Yugoslavia.

Paragraph 7. The provinces are autonomous socialist self-managing democratic socio-political communities with a special ethnic composition and other specificities, in which working people and citizens, nations and nationalities exercise their sovereign rights, exercising them also in the Republic as a whole when in the common interest of working people and citizens, nations and nationalities of the Republic it is so specified by the Constitution of the Socialist Republic of Serbia.

Paragraph 8. The working people, nations and nationalities of the Socialist Republic of Serbia shall make decisions on the federal level according to the principles of agreement among the Republics and Autonomous Provinces, solidarity and reciprocity, equal participation by the Republics and Autonomous Provinces in federal agencies consistent with the Constitution of the Socialist Federal Republic of Yugoslavia and the Constitution of the Socialist Republic of Serbia, and according to the principle of responsibility for their own development and for the development of the socialist community as a whole.

THE SOCIALIST REPUBLIC OF SERBIA

Article 1. The Socialist Republic of Serbia is a socialist democratic state based on the power of and self-management by the working class and all working people, and a socialist self-managing democratic community of working people and citizens, and equal nations and nationalities, based on the self-management by the working people in associated labour and in other forms of self-management association and free social organisation.

The Socialist Republic of Serbia is a state of the Serb nation and parts of other nations and nationalities, which live and exercise their sovereign rights in it.

The Socialist Autonomous Province of Vojvodina and the Socialist Autonomous Province of Kosovo are parts of the Socialist Republic of Serbia.

The Socialist Republic of Serbia is a part of the Socialist Federal Republic of Yugoslavia.

Article 2. Working people and citizens, nations and nationalities of Serbia shall exercise their sovereign rights in the Socialist Republic of Serbia and in the Socialist Autonomous Provinces consistent with their constitutional rights, and in the Socialist Federal Republic of Yugoslavia when it is so specified by the Constitution of the S.F.R.Y. in the common interest of working people, nations and nationalities of Yugoslavia. ...

Article 145. In the Socialist Republic of Serbia the nations and nationalities shall be equal.

Every nationality shall be guaranteed the freedom to use its language and alphabet, develop its culture and establish organisations, and enjoy other constitutional rights in the exercise of its right to express its nationality and culture.

Article 146. In the Socialist Republic of Serbia the languages of nations and nationalities and their alphabets shall be equal.

Members of nationalities shall, in conformity with the Constitution and statute, have the right to use their language and alphabet in the exercise of their rights and duties and in proceedings before state agencies and organisations exercising public powers.

The equality of languages and alphabets of nations and nationalities in official use in the areas where individual nationalities live, and the mode of and conditions for the exercise of this equality shall be ensured by law and statutes of the socio-political community and self-management enactments of organisations of associated labour and other self-managing organisations and communities.

Republican law shall lay down the mode of the exercise of the right of members of nationalities to use their language and alphabet in republican agencies and organisations exercising public powers.

Article 147. Members of other nations and nationalities shall have the right to instruction in their language in schools and other institutions of learning in conformity with law and the municipal statute.

In the areas where members of the Serb or other nations of Yugoslavia live together, schools or classes with bilingual instruction may be established. ...

Article 177. The freedoms and rights of man and citizen, spelled out by the Constitution, shall be realised through solidarity among people and through the fulfillment of duties and responsibilities of everyone towards all and all towards everyone.

The freedoms and rights of man and citizen shall only be restricted by the equal freedoms and rights of others and by the constitutionally specified interests of the socialist community.

Each shall be bound to respect the freedoms and rights of others and shall be responsible therefor.

Article 178. Citizens shall be equal in their rights and duties regardless of nationality, race, sex, language, religion, education, or social status. All shall be equal before the law. ...

Article 240. The state agencies and organisations exercising public powers shall conduct proceedings in the Serbo-Croatian language.

The state agencies and organisations exercising public powers shall also conduct proceedings in the language of the nationality specified by the municipal statute or the enactment of the organisation of associated labour on other self-managing organisation or community.

The languages in which the proceedings shall be conducted in state agencies and organisations in the territory of the Autonomous Provinces shall be specified by the provincial constitutions. ...

THE SOCIALIST AUTONOMOUS PROVINCE

Article 291. The Socialist Autonomous Provinces are autonomous, socialist, self-managing democratic sociopolitical communities based on the power of and self-management by the working class and all working people, in which the working people and the citizens, nations and nationalities exercise their sovereign rights, with the exception of those, which are, in the common interest of the working people, citizens, nations and nationalities of the Republic as a whole, exercised in the Republic.

Article 292. The territory of an autonomous province consists of the territories of the present municipalities as specified by statute.

The territory of an autonomous province may not be altered without the consent of the provincial assembly.

Article 293. In the exercise of their rights and duties the Autonomous Provinces shall regulate autonomously the social relations by statute and other regulations, with the exception of the relations which are by the present Constitution and on the basis thereof regulated uniformly for the whole territory of the Republic by republican statute.

Within the framework of the relations regulated uniformly for the whole territory of the Republic by republican statute, the Autonomous Provinces may regulate matters not regulated by Republican statute.

If a republican law on relations regulated uniformly for the whole territory of the Republic has not been adopted, the Autonomous Provinces may adopt their laws if this is of interest for the exercise of their rights and duties. After the adoption of a republican law on the regulation of these relations, the provisions of the provincial law relative to the matters regulated by the republican law shall be invalidated, unless specified otherwise by this law.

Article 294. Agencies in the Autonomous Provinces shall be responsible for the enforcement and implementation of republican laws and other republican regulations, applied throughout the territory of the Republic, in the territory of the Province.

The regulations for the enforcement of the republican laws applied throughout the territory of the republic, and other acts and measures for the enforcement and implementation of these laws when the Executive Council of the Assembly of the SR Serbia is authorised to pass such acts, shall be adopted by the Executive Council of the Socialist

Autonomous Province for the territory of the autonomous province unless otherwise specified by statute.

Provincial administrative agencies shall adopt regulations and other acts for the enforcement and implementation of republican laws and other republican regulations applicable throughout the territory of the Republic when the republican administrative agencies are responsible for the adoption of these acts unless otherwise specified by statute.

The regulations for the enforcement and implementation of laws adopted by consent by the Assembly of the Socialist Republic of Serbia and the Assembly of the Socialist Autonomous Province shall be adopted by provincial agencies.

Article 295. Consistent with the responsibility of the agencies in the Autonomous Provinces for the enforcement and application of republican laws and other republican acts valid throughout the territory of the Republic, the relations between republican agencies and agencies in the Autonomous Provinces bearing on the enforcement of these laws and other regulations shall be based on mutual co-operation, information and agreement, and on the rights and duties laid down by the present Constitution and republican statute.

If agencies in the Autonomous Provinces fail to enforce republican laws or other republican regulations, for the enforcement and application of which they are responsible, the Executive Council of the Assembly of the Socialist Republic of Serbia shall notify the competent agency of the Autonomous Province and take other measures within the framework of its rights and duties. ...

Article 415. If proceedings have been initiated for the assessment of constitutionality and legality of a regulation or other enactment of an agency of the socio-political community or a self-management enactment, found to be in simultaneous contravention with the Constitution of the Socialist Republic of Serbia or republican law of the provincial constitution or provincial law, the constitutionality and legality shall be assessed by the Constitutional Court of the Province, which shall only assess the conformity of this regulation of other enactment with the provincial constitution or provincial law.

If the Constitutional Court of the Province decides that a regulation or other enactment is in conformity with the provincial Constitution or provincial law, it shall submit the case to the Constitutional Court of Serbia, which shall assess the conformity of the regulation or other enactment with the Constitution of the Socialist Republic of Serbia and republican statute. ...

Article 423. The uniform implementation of the republican laws by supreme and higher courts in the Republic and settlement of the conflicts of competence between courts in the territory of the Supreme Courts of the Autonomous Provinces and the Supreme Court of Serbia shall be ensured in the Republic.

A special chamber consisting of an equal number of judges of the Supreme Court of Serbia and the Supreme Court of the Autonomous Provinces shall be established at the Supreme Court of Serbia for the discharge of these matters. ...

Article 427. The Assembly of the SR of Serbia decides about the changes in the constitution of the SR of Serbia. If the change of the constitution of the SR of Serbia is related to questions of interest for the republic as a whole, the Assembly of the SR of Serbia will decide the question with the consent of the Assemblies of the autonomous provinces.

8. Constitution of the Socialist Autonomous Province of Kosovo, 1974

INTRODUCTORY PART: BASIC PRINCIPLES
I. United in their past equally by common life and aspirations for freedom and social progress, the Albanians, Montenegrins, Muslims, Serbs, Turks and members of other nations and nationalities of Yugoslavia in the National Liberation War and socialist revolution, headed by the working class and the Communist Party of Yugoslavia, overthrew the old class system based on exploitation, political subjugation and national inequality, have found themselves free, equal and fraternised for the first time in the Socialist Autonomous Province of Kosovo, which has become the political and social form of their

close association and mutual equality and their equality with the nations and nationalities of Yugoslavia.

The Socialist Autonomous province of Kosovo emerged from the common struggle of the nations and nationalities in the National Liberation War and socialist revolution of Yugoslavia and, proceeding from the freely expressed will of the population - the nations and nationalities of Kosovo and the freely expressed will of the people of Serbia, has associated itself with the Socialist Republic of Serbia within the framework of the Socialist Federal Republic of Yugoslavia. ...

Paragraph 3. The working people and the nations and nationalities of Kosovo shall exercise their sovereign rights in the Socialist Autonomous Province of Kosovo and in the Republic when in the common interest of the working people, nations and nationalities of the Republic as a whole it is so specified by the Constitution of the Socialist Republic of Serbia, and in the Socialist Federal Republic of Yugoslavia when in the common interest it is so specified by the Constitution of the Socialist Federal Republic of Yugoslavia.

Paragraph 4. In the exercise of their common interests the working people, nations and nationalities of Kosovo shall make decisions on the federal level according to the principles of agreement among the Republics and Autonomous Provinces, solidarity and reciprocity, equal participation by the Republics and Autonomous Provinces in federal agencies, consistent with the Constitution of the S.F.R.Y. and the Constitution of the S.A.P. Kosovo, and according to the principle of responsibility of the Republics and Autonomous provinces for their own development and the development of the Yugoslav socialist community as a whole. ...

GENERAL PROVISIONS

Article 1. The Socialist Autonomous Province of Kosovo is an autonomous, socialist, democratic socio-political and self-managing community of working people and citizens, equal Albanians, Montenegrins, Muslims, Serbs, Turks, and members of other nations and nationalities and ethnic groups, based on the power of and self-management by the working class and all working people. The Socialist Autonomous province of Kosovo is a part of the Socialist Republic of Serbia and the Socialist Federal Republic of Yugoslavia.

Article 2. The working people and citizens, nations and nationalities of Kosovo shall exercise their sovereign rights in the SAP Kosovo and in the Republic when in the common interest of the working people, nations and nationalities in the Republic as a whole it is so specified by the Constitution of the SR Serbia, and in the S.F.R.Y. when in their common interest it is so specified by the Constitution of the S.F.R.Y.

Article 3. The territory of the Socialist Autonomous Province of Kosovo consists of the territory of the present municipalities.

The territory of the Socialist Autonomous Province of Kosovo may not be altered without the consent of the Provincial Assembly.

Article 4. The nations and nationalities in the Socialist Autonomous Province of Kosovo shall be equal in their rights and duties.

To ensure the equality of the nations and nationalities, their right to the free development and expression of national specificities, language, culture, history and other attributes shall be guaranteed.

Article 5. In the Socialist Autonomous Province of Kosovo the equality of the Albanian, Serbo-Croatian and Turkish languages and their alphabets shall be ensured.

The implementation of this principle shall be regulated and ensured by the present Constitution and by provincial statute.

Article 6. Members of all nations and nationalities in the Socialist Autonomous Province of Kosovo shall have the right to use their national flag.

The conditions and manner of the use of the national flag shall be regulated by statute. ...

THE FREEDOMS, RIGHTS AND DUTIES OF MAN AND CITIZEN
Article 187. Citizens shall be guaranteed the freedom to express their affiliation with a nation or nationality, the freedom to express their national culture and the freedom to use their language and alphabet.

No citizen shall be obliged to state to which nation or nationality he belongs nor to opt for any one nation or nationality.

Citizens shall be guaranteed the freedom to express their affiliation with an ethnic group, the freedom to develop their culture and the freedom to use their language and alphabet.

Propagating or practicing national inequality and any incitement of national, racial or religious hatred and intolerance shall be unconstitutional and punishable. ...

THE EQUALITY OF LANGUAGES AND ALPHABETS

Article 217. The Albanian and Serbo-Croatian languages and their alphabets shall be equally used in the Socialist Autonomous Province of Kosovo.

The Turkish language and alphabet shall be equally used in the territories where the Turks also live.

Agencies, institutions, work and other organisations in the Province shall be bound to comply in their work with the principle of equality of the languages and alphabets of the nations and nationalities in the Socialist Autonomous Province of Kosovo.

Article 218. In elementary, secondary, high and higher schools of learning, and in their classes conditions shall be ensured for instruction in mother language, that is the Albanian Serbo-Croatian and Turkish languages, in conformity with statute.

Members of other nations and nationalities of Yugoslavia shall have the right to instruction in their languages, in conformity with provincial statute.

Article 292. The National Bank of Kosovo is an establishment of the integral monetary system. The National Bank of Kosovo shall, together with the National Bank of Yugoslavia and the National Banks of the Republics and the Province of Vojvodina, pursue the common policy of issue.

The national Bank of Kosovo, consistent with the Constitution and statue and within the framework of the common policy of issue, shall spell out the conditions and mode of utilisation of monetary resources in the Province and take other measures necessary to implement the credit policy of the Province. ...

ORGANS OF THE S.A.P. KOSOVO, THE ASSEMBLY OF THE S.A.P. KOSOVO; 1. STATUS AND COMPETENCE

Article 300. The Assembly of the Socialist Autonomous Province of Kosovo is a body of social self-management and the supreme organ of power within the framework of provincial rights and duties.

The Assembly shall exercise the duties within its competence and on the basis of and within the framework of the Constitution and statute.

Article 301. As the principal subject of the rights and duties of the Province, the Assembly shall directly and exclusively:

1. decide on amendments to the Constitution of the S.A.P. Kosovo and approve the amendments to the Constitution of the S.F.R.Y. and the Constitution of the SR Serbia;
2. lay down the policy and decide on other basic issues of importance for the political, economic, social and cultural life, national defence and social development of the Province;
3. adopt provincial laws and provide authentic interpretation of provincial laws;
4. adopt the social plan, budget and the annual balance sheet of the Province;
5. adopt the regional plan and the plan of the spatial development of the Province;
6. discuss issues of the foreign policy and international relations; consent to the conclusion of international treaties in cases specified by the Constitution of the S.F.R.Y.; ratify agreements concluded by the Province with agencies and organisations of foreign states and international agencies and organisations, within the framework of the specified foreign policy of the S.F.R.Y.; ...
18. consent to the alteration of the territory of the S.A.P. Kosovo;
19. elect and relieve of office the delegation of the Assembly of the S.A.P. Kosovo to the Chamber of Republics and Provinces of the Assembly of the S.F.R.Y.;
20. elect and relieve of office the member of the Presidency of the S.F.R.Y. from the S.A.P. Kosovo;
21. elect and relieve of office the members of the Presidency of the S.A.P. Kosovo ...

THE PRESIDENCY OF THE S.A.P. KOSOVO

Article 339. The Presidency of the S.A.P. Kosovo shall represent the S.A.P. Kosovo and shall exercise other rights and duties as laid down by the Constitution.

THE EXECUTIVE COUNCIL OF THE S.A.P. KOSOVO

Article 349. The Executive Council shall be the executive body of the S.A.P. Kosovo. The Executive Council shall exercise its rights and duties on the basis of and within the framework of the present Constitution and statute.

THE PROVINCIAL ADMINISTRATION

Article 362. Provincial secretariats and other provincial administrative agencies shall be established to perform administrative duties within the framework of the rights and duties of the Province.

THE CONSTITUTIONAL COURT OF KOSOVO

Article 372. The Constitutional Court of Kosovo shall:

1. decide on the conformity of provincial statues to the Constitution of the S.A.P. Kosovo;
2. decide on the conformity of municipal statues to the Constitution of the S.A.P. Kosovo and provincial statutes; ...

THE SUPREME COURT OF KOSOVO, THE OFFICE OF PROVINCIAL PUBLIC PROSECUTOR, THE OFFICE OF PROVINCIAL SOCIAL ATTORNEY OF SELF-MANAGEMENT

Article 390. The Supreme Court of Kosovo shall:

1. decide on appeals against judgments and other rulings of regular courts, within the framework of its competence as laid down by statute;
2. decide in first instance when so specified by statute;
3. decide on extraordinary legal remedies against valid sentences of regular courts in conformity with statute; ...

Article 391. The functions of the Office of Public Prosecutor shall be discharged by the Provincial Public Prosecutor within the framework of the rights and duties of the Province.

Article 393. The provincial Social Attorney of Self-Management within the framework of the rights and duties of the Province shall discharge the function of the social attorney of self-management.

The provincial Social Attorney of Self-Management shall be designated and relieved of office by the Assembly of the S.A.P. Kosovo.

B.   The Developments of 1989-1992

Official Gazette of the SR Serbia, No. 11/89

1.   Constitutional Amendments of the SR of Serbia, 1989

AMENDMENT XXCI: 3. Members of the nations and nationalities shall have the right to instruction in their language in schools and other educational institutions in conformity with the Constitution and statute. Item 3 replaces Article 147, paragraph 1 of the Constitution of the SR Serbia.

AMENDMENT XXVII: In the official and public use in the SR Serbia shall be the Serbo-Croatian language and its alphabets - Cyrillic and Latin. In the SR Serbia, in the territories inhabited by individual nationalities, the Serbo-Croatian language and its alphabets and the languages of these nationalities and their alphabets shall be in equal official and public use consistent with the Constitution and statute. The official and public use of the Cyrillic alphabet shall be prescribed by republican statute. State agencies and organisations exercising public powers in the SR Serbia shall use the Cyrillic alphabet unless specified otherwise by republican statute in individual cases. The provincial Constitutions shall specify, consistent with the present Constitution that the languages of nationalities shall be in equal official and public use in the territories of the Autonomous Provinces. The Autonomous Provinces shall ensure the equality of the languages and alphabets of the nationalities and the Serbo-Croatian language and its alphabets. This amendment supplements Article 146 and replaces Article 240, paragraphs 1-3 of the Constitution of the SR Serbia.

AMENDMENT XLVII: The Assembly of the SR of Serbia decides about changes of the Constitution. ... The Assembly of Serbia, before deciding upon a proposal to adopt changes in the Constitution of Serbia, presents the proposal for consideration to the assemblies of the autonomous provinces, taking into account the opinion of the assemblies of the autonomous provinces, and takes decisions upon these opinions.

Official Gazette of the SR Serbia, No. 30/89

2. Law on the Restriction of Real Property Transactions, 1989

Article 1. Real property transactions between physical persons, and between physical and civil legal persons in the territory covering a part of the territory of the SR Serbia, without the territory of the S.A.P. Vojvodina, shall be restricted for a period of 10 years since the day of the entry of the present law into force.

Article 2. The real property transactions, within the meaning of the present Law, is the transfer of property rights and other rights in rem. to real property, lease and other forms of entry into possession.

Article 3. The commission formed by the Assembly of the SR Serbia shall authorise a real property transaction specified in Article 1 of the present Law, upon satisfying itself that the said transaction will not result in a change of the national structure of the population or the emigration of members of a certain nation or nationality and that this transaction shall not provoke anxiety or insecurity or inequality among citizens of another nation or nationality.

If the Commission does not approve the real property transaction, the Assembly of the SR Serbia at a session of the Chamber of Municipalities shall rule upon the appeal of the person concerned, filed within 30 days of the receipt of the notification.

Administrative suit may not be brought against the act, whereby the Assembly of the SR Serbia rules upon the appeal.

Technical and administrative affairs for the Commission, specified in this Article, paragraph 1, shall be discharged by the republican administrative agency responsible for property law issues.

Article 4. The competent municipal agency shall be bound, immediately after learning about the entry into possession of the real property without a contract concluded on the basis of the authorisation within the meaning of the present Law, Article 3, paragraph 1, to take measures to prevent such further possession.

Article 5. The contract on the real property transaction concluded in contravention of the present Law, Article 1 and Article 3, paragraph 1, shall be null and void.

Article 6. A person who enters into possession of real property without a contract concluded on the basis of authorisation as specified by the present Law, Article 3, paragraph 1, shall be punished for the transgression by imprisonment of not more than 60 days or by a fine of not more than 420,000 dinars.

Article 7. The entry of the present Law into force shall invalidate the Law on Real Property Transactions, Article 3, paragraphs 4 and 5 (Off. Gazette of the Socialist Republic of Serbia, No. 43/81; 24/85; 28/87 and 6/89).

Official Gazette of the Socialist Republic of Serbia No. 42/89

3. Law on the Amendment to the Law on the Restriction of Real Property Transactions, 1989

Article 3 of the Law on the Restriction of Real Property Transactions shall be amended to read: "The Republican Secretariat of Finance - Administration for Property Law Affairs shall authorise the real property transactions as specified in the present Law, Article 1 when it satisfies itself that it will not result in the emigration of members of a nation or nationality and that the transaction will not cause anxiety or insecurity or inequality among citizens of another nation or nationality".

If the Republican Secretariat of Finance - Administration for Property Law Affairs does not authorise the real property transaction, the appeal of the person concerned, filed within 30 days of the receipt of the decision, shall be ruled upon by the Commission appointed by the Assembly of the Socialist Republic of Serbia. Administrative suit may not be brought against the ruling of the Commission specified in this Article, paragraph 2.

Official Gazette of the Socialist Republic of Serbia No. 15/90

4. Programme for Realization of Peace, Freedom, Equality, Democracy and Prosperity of SAP Kosovo, 30 March 1990

[Extracts] 6. ... In ensuring the rule of law in Kosovo, one must proceed from the fact that it cannot be a state; it is a part of the republic—state and therefore, in an adequate manner, of the federal state of Yugoslavia. The autonomy of Kosovo may not serve as an excuse or reason for the malfunctioning of the rule of law and possible repetition of nationalistic and separatist unrest and persistent inter-ethnic tension. It may not be misused in pursuit of unacceptable and unfeasible gaols: prevention of the return of Serbs and Montenegrins, displaced under pressure, and all the others who wish to come and live in Kosovo, and especially for any further emigration of Serbs and Montenegrins and secession of a part of the territory of the Republic—the state of Serbia so as to constitute a new state within or outside of Yugoslavia. If the rule of law is to operate efficiently and fully realize the policy spelled out in this programme, in the light of the autonomy and decentralization of some state functions to Kosovo agencies, there msut exist efficient means to ensure that this may happen. Under the conditions of a multi-party system an adequate national representation of Serbs, Montenegrins, Turks, Muslims and others needs to be ensure in the Assembly of the multi-ethnic Kosovo so as to exclude majority votes. The Assembly of Serbia will be able to annul the laws and decisions adopted by the Assembly or Kosovo if they contravene the Constitution of Serbia and realisation of the policy of peace, freedom, equality and democracy. Inadequate functioning of the executive state administrative bodies, the office of the public prosecutor and judiciary may not call into question the implementation of the Constutitoin, peace, freedom, equality and democracy, that is the efficient functioning of the rule of law. If this happens, relevant state agencies of Serbia will take over some state administrative, prosecutor's and judicial functions.

Official Gazette Socialist Republic of Serbia, No. 5/90

5. Amendment of the University Law, 1990

Article 43. The language of instruction shall be Serbo-Croatian.

Paragraph 2. In the Socialist Autonomous Provinces the syllabi shall also be followed in the language of another nation and nationality when not less than 30 students of the same year of study so opt.

Paragraph 3. The faculty shall also ensure the instruction in the language of another nation or nationality for the whole course or for individual subjects for a lesser number of students if the need for it is established by the republican or provincial administrative agency responsible for educational affairs. The post-graduate studies and special forms of studies may be in a foreign language. ...

Article 126. Provisions under Article 43, paragraphs 2 and 3 shall not be applied in the territory of the S.A.P. Kosovo.

Official Gazette of the SR Serbia No. 30/90

6. Law on the Actions of Republic Agencies under Special Circumstances, 26 June 1990

Article 1. To ensure constitutionality and legality, democratic freedoms and rights, duties and responsibilities of citizens and their equality throughout the territory of the SR Serbia, the republican agencies, the Supreme Court of Serbia, the Office of Public Attorney of Serbia, the Republican Public Prosecutor, the Republican Social Attorney of Self-Management, the Court of Associated Labour of Serbia and the Higher Business Court (hereinafter: republican agencies) shall have the right and the duty to act in conformity with the provisions of the present Law when so necessitated by reasons of security (special circumstances) in a part of the territory of the SR Serbia.

Article 2. The special circumstances specified in the present Law, Article 1, shall be deemed to have arisen in a part of the territory of the

SR Serbia (hereinafter: part of the territory of the Republic) when there are organised:

1. activities directed at overthrowing the constitutional order and the territorial integrity;
2. failures to comply with laws and by-laws;
3. acts which may be hazardous for human life and health;
4. exercise of rights and duties spelled out by the Constitution and by statute in a manner severely damaging public interests and their use in pursuit of unconstitutional objectives.

Article 3. The objectives specified in Article 1 and the removal of causes specified in Article 2 of the present Law shall be ensured by:

1. administrative supervision and other forms of enforcement of laws and other regulations;
2. delegation of competence of the courts and other agencies;
3. decisions on certain matters under the jurisdiction of agencies in that part of the territory;
4. provisional restriction of the exercise of individual self-management rights and implementation of other provisional measures by the Assembly of the SR Serbia in enterprises and establishment;
5. abolition, invalidation or suspension of regulations and other enactments and actions of agencies and socio-political communities, organs of enterprises and establishments; and
6. assumption of control of the enforcement of decisions and other individual acts.

The Assembly of the SR Serbia shall establish, upon the proposal of the Executive Council of the Assembly of the SR Serbia, that special circumstances in a part of the Republic have arisen or ceased.

Article 4. The organs of the Republic will take action according to Article 2 according to the provictions which provide for their administration of a part of the territory of the Republic where special circumstances prevail.

Article 5. The exercise of administrative supervision and other forms of implementation of laws and other regulations the part of the territory where special circumstances prevail will be ensured by the organs of the Republic or other organs nominated by them within their sphere of competence.

Article 6. The High Court of Serbia will determine in cases under Article 2 another appropriate court or other organ in individual crimial, civil, ... administrative cases or misdemeanours. ... Article 11. In the case of special circumstances as spelled out by this Law, Article 2, item 4 and in other cases of severe damage to public interests or in the case of non-compliance with statutory duties or serious disruption of self-management relations, the Assembly of the SR Serbia may temporarily restrict the exercise of certain self-management rights and undertake other provisional measures in individual socially-owned enterprises and establishments in the part of the territory of the Republic where such circumstances have arisen.

Reasons for provisional measures shall be established by the agency or body authorised by the Assembly of the SR Serbia.

The implementation of provisional measures in enterprises and establishments specified in this Article, paragraph 1 may be initiated by a republican administrative agency, workers of the enterprise or establishment where the measures are to be implemented, and other interested persons.

The Republican Social Attorney of Self-Management shall submit to the Assembly of the SR Serbia the proposal to launch the proceedings for the adoption of provisional measures.

As an exception to this Article, paragraph 2, if the postponement of provisional measures could produce particularly severe disruptions of self-management relations or damages to public interest, the Assembly of the SR Serbia may decide to establish the presence of reasons for the adoption of provisional measures directly at its session. ...

Article 13. The Assembly of the SR Serbia may, consistent with its rights and duties, determine the responsibility of agencies and bearers of state and other public functions in a part of the territory of the Republic, where special circumstances have arisen if the latter have failed to take measures within the framework of their rights and duties as specified by the Constitution and by statute.

When in determining the responsibility of the bearers of functions specified in this Article, paragraph 1, the Assembly of the SR Serbia pronounces the measure of dismissal or relief of the bearers of these functions of their office, it shall at the same time elect or appoint new bearers of these functions.

Article 14. The Assembly of the SR Serbia may abolish or invalidate an unconstitutional or unlawful regulation or other enactment of an executive and administrative body of the socio-political community in the part of the territory of the Republic where the special circumstances have arisen. ...

Article 16. The Assembly of the SR Serbia may make decisions on matters falling under the jurisdiction of the assembly of the socio-political community in the part of the territory of the Republic where the special circumstances have arisen if the failure to make such a decision could case significant damage to the Republic, endanger the interest of the people and the exercise of democratic freedoms and rights of citizens in the Republic.

The Assembly of the SR Serbia shall have the right and the duty to suspend the enforcement of a decision of the assembly of the socio-political community in the part of the territory of the Republic where the special circumstances have arisen if such a decision could cause consequences specified in this Article, paragraph 1.

7. Decision about the Existence of Special Circumstances on the Territory of the SAP of Kosovo, 26 June 1990

Article 1. It is hereby determined that the special circumstances as defined in Article 2 (1) of the Law on the Action of Republican Agencies under Special Circumstances (Official Gazette (30/90) are present on the territory of the SAP of Kosovo.

Article 2. This decision will enter into force on the day of its publication in the Official Gazette.

Official Gazette of SSRS, 33/90

8. SR Serbia, Law Terminating Work of SAP of Kosovo Assembly and the Executive Council, 5 July 1990

According to the Amendment 39, paragraph 7, of the Constitution of the Socialist Republic of Serbia, I make the following

DECREE ON PROCLAIMING THE LAW TERMINATING THE WORK OF THE ASSEMBLY OF THE SOCIALIST AUTONOMOUS PROVINCE OF KOSOVA AND EXECUTIVE COUNCIL OF THE SOCIALIST AUTONOMOUS PROVINCE OF KOSOVA

The Law Terminating the work of the Assembly of the Socialist Autonomous Province of Kosova and Executive Council of the Socialist Autonomous Province of Kosova is being proclaimed as decided by the Assembly of the Socialist Republic of Serbia in the meetings of the Chamber of Associated Labour and in the meeting of Social-Political Chamber, both held on 5 July 1990. RS number 343, Belgrade, 5 July 1990, Chairman of the Assembly of Serbia - Zoran Sokolovic

THE LAW TERMINATING THE WORK OF THE ASSEMBLY OF THE SAP KOSOVA AND EXECUTIVE COUNCIL OF THE SAP OF KOSOVA

Article 1. Based on the facts that for a long period of time the Assembly of SAP Kosova is not functioning and acting in accordance with the Constitution and that the majority of the delegates to the Assembly of SAP Kosova and most of the members of the Executive Council of the Assembly of SAP Kosova, with their work endanger sovereignty, territorial integrity and constitutional order of the Socialist Republic of Serbia, the Assembly of SAP Kosova and the Executive Council of the Assembly of SAP Kosova cease to work.

Article 2. The rights and duties of the Assembly of SAP Kosova are undertaken by the Assembly of Serbia, and those of the Executive Council of the Assembly of SAP Kosova by the Executive Council of SR Serbia, until the constitution of the new Assembly of SAP Kosova and the Executive Council of SAP Kosova.

Article 3. All acts ratified by the Assembly of SAP Kosova and the Executive Council of the Assembly of SAP Kosova after this law comes into force - are invalid.

Article 4. The Executive Council of the Assembly of SR of Serbia will outline the way of taking over the duties of the Executive Council of the Assembly of SAP Kosova and will undertake other necessary measures for realisation of this law.

Article 5. From the day this Law comes into force, officials in the Assembly of SAP Kosova, members of the Executive Council of the Assembly of SAP Kosova, and officials heading provincial organs or administration, administering organisations, and professional services, the secretary of the Executive Council of the Assembly of SAP Kosova, and their deputies are discharged from office.

Officials heading republican organs of administration, republican organs, and professional services, will head respective provincial organisations and services until the Assembly of Serbia makes the election, or appointment of those officials, respectively.

The decision discharging the officials, who had been elected or appointed by the Assembly of SAP Kosova, will be passed by the Administration Commission of the Assembly of SR Serbia.

Article 6. This law comes into force on the day it is published in the 'Official Gazette of Socialist Republic of Serbia'.

9. Serb Assembly Regulation on Implementing Law Terminating Work of SAP Kosovo Assembly and Executive Council, 13 July 1990

Article 1. This Regulation governs the assumption of the functions of the Executive Council of the Assembly of the SAP of Kosovo, the functions of the provincial organs of administration and institutions, as well as other matters of importance for the implementaiton of the Law Terminating the Work of the Assembly of the Socialist Autonomous Province of Kosova and Executive Council of the Socialist Autonomous Province of Kosovo (law on termination hereinafter).

Article 2. ... Public officials who have taken over the direction of organs, organizations and services according to Article 1 of this Regulation can draw on officials from other organs of the Republic in the exercise of their functions in the respective organs, organizations and services.

Article 3. The Republic public officials having taken over the direction of the provincial organs of administration, exercise all the functions and powers of their predecessors, ...

Article 5. Public officials having taken office according to Article 3 of this Regulation are obliged to report regularly and in a timely manner to the Executive Council of the Assembly of the SR of Serbia about state of affairs in the areas of comptence of the administrative organs organizations and services which they have taken over, as well as about the implementation of the policy, laws and regulations and decisions in their area of responsibility and also the decisions of the Executive Council of the Assembly of the SR of Serbia and other tasks they may have been charged to fullfil. ...

Article 7. The Executive Council of the SR of Serbia will establish one or more working groups to take decisions about matters of adminstration and other issues arising from the former competence of the Executive Council of the SAP of Kosovo.

10. Constitution of the Socialist Republic of Serbia, 28 September 1990

The Assembly of the Socialist Republic of Serbia, at the joint session of all chambers, on September 28, 1990, has passed THE DECISION ON THE PROMULGATION OF THE CONSTITUTION OF THE REPUBLIC OF SERBIA. The Constitution of the Republic of Serbia which is adopted by the Assembly of the Socialist Republic of Serbia at the joint session of all chambers, on September 28, 1990, is hereby promulgated.

Mindful of the centuries-long struggle of the Serbian people for freedom, their freedom-loving, democratic and nation-building

traditions, and the historical development and life in common of all the peoples and national minorities in Serbia;

Determined to create a democratic State of the Serbian people in which members of other nations and national minorities will be able to exercise their national rights, based upon observance of the freedoms and rights of man and citizen, sovereignty vested in all citizens, the rule of law, social justice and equal opportunities for the advancement of the individual and society; ...

The Autonomous Province of Vojvodina and the Autonomous Province of Kosovo and Metohia

Article 108. The autonomous provinces have been formed in accordance with the particular national, historical, cultural, and other characteristics of their areas. Citizens within the autonomous province shall autonomously realize the rights and fulfill the duties established by the Constitution and law. The territory of an autonomous province shall be determined by law

Article 109. The autonomous province shall, through its own agencies:

1) enact the program of economic, scientific. technological, demographic, regional and social development, development of agriculture and rural areas, in accordance with the development plan of the Republic of Serbia, and shall lay down measures for their implementation;

2) adopt a budget and annual balance sheet;

3) enact decisions and general enactments in accordance with the Constitution and law, to regulate matters affecting the citizens in the autonomous province in the areas of: culture; education; official use of the' language and alphabet of the national minority; public information; health and social welfare; child welfare; protection and advancement of environment; urban and country planning; and in other areas established by law;

4) enforce laws, other regulations and general enactments of the Republic of Serbia, whose enforcement has been entrusted to the agencies of the autonomous province, and pass regulations necessary for their enforcement if so provided by the law; see to the execution of provincial decisions and general enactments;

5) establish agencies, organisations and services of the autonomous province, and regulate their organisation and work;

6) attend to other business laid down under the Constitution and law, as well as by the statute of the autonomous province. The Republic of Serbia may entrust by a law an autonomous province with the performance of specific affairs within its own competencies and transfer to it the necessary funds for this purpose. The autonomous province shall collect revenues as laid down by, law.

Article 110. The statute is the highest legal act of the autonomous province which, on the ground of the Constitution, shall lay down the competencies of the autonomous province, election, organisation and work of its agencies, and other questions pertaining to the autonomous province. The statute of the autonomous province shall be enacted by its assembly, subject to prior approval of the National Assembly. Deputies in the assembly of an autonomous province shall not be held responsible for an opinion expressed or for casting a vote in the assembly of the autonomous province. The same immunity shall be enjoyed by the members of the executive council.

Article 111. The agencies of the autonomous province shall be its assembly, executive council, and agencies of administration. The assembly of an autonomous province shall be composed of deputies elected in direct election by secret ballot.

Article 112. If an agency of an autonomous province, despite a warning of the corresponding republic agency, fails to execute a decision or a general enactment of the autonomous province, the republic agency may provide for its direct execution. ...

Official Gazette Socialist Republic of Serbia, No. 40/90

11. Law on Labour Relations under Special Circumstances, 1990

Article 1. In the part of the territory of the SR Serbia where, in conformity with statute, special circumstances have arisen, the provisions of laws and other regulations regulating the labour relations shall be applied to labour relations in work communities in administrative agencies, administrative organisations of technical services and other state agencies subject to regulations on the state administration (hereinafter: organ), and in enterprises, organisations of non-production activities and other organisations and communities, in which provisional measures are enforced for the social protection of self-managing rights and social property (hereinafter: organisations), for the duration of such circumstances, unless individual matters and relations are regulated otherwise by the present Law.

Article 6. The official or manager shall decide on the disciplinary responsibility of the workers and pronounce all disciplinary measures as specified by statute.

Official Gazette of the Republic of Serbia, No. 22/91

12. Law on the Restriction of Real Property Transactions, 1991

Article 1. The title of the Law on the Restriction of Real Property Transactions shall be altered and read: The Law on Special Conditions of Real Property Transactions.

Article 2. Article 1 shall be amended to read:

"The real property transactions between physical persons and between physical and legal persons in the area covering a part of the territory of the Republic of Serbia, with the exception of the AP Vojvodina, shall be performed under special conditions laid down by the present Law, for a period of 10 years since the entry of the present Law into force. Legal persons within the meaning of the present Law, paragraph 1, shall be, in addition to civil legal persons, co-operatives, privately-owned enterprises and socially-owned enterprises engaging in the marketable production of residential and business premises."

Article 3. A new paragraph 2 shall be added to Article 2, which will read:

"As an exception to this Article, paragraph 1, a gift between relatives belonging to the first class of entitled heirs, shall not be treated as a property transaction".

Article 4. In Article 3, paragraphs 1 and 2 the words "The Republican Secretariat of Finance" shall be replaced by the works "the Ministry of Finance". In paragraph 2 the words "the Assembly of the SR Serbia" shall be replaced by the words "The National Assembly".

Official Gazette of the Republic of Serbia, No. 50/92

13. Elementary School Law, 1992

Article 4. The language of instruction shall be Serbian.

Article 5. The instruction for members of nationalities shall also be provided in the mother tongue or bilingually if not less than 15 pupils enroll the first grade, subject to the consent of the Minister of Education.

The Minister of Education shall prescribe the mode of the bilingual instruction. When the instruction is in the languages of nationalities, the pupils shall follow the syllabus of the Serbian language.

When the language of instruction is Serbian, the pupils who are members of nationalities shall be ensured the instruction in the mother tongue with elements of the national culture.

Officaial Gazette of the Republic of Serbia, No. 50/92

14. Secondary School Law, 1992

Article 5. The school shall conduct the instruction in the Serbian language. The school shall follow the syllabus in the language of nationalities or bilingually when not less than 15 pupils of the same grade opt for it when enrolling the first grade.

The syllabus specified in this Article, paragraph 2 may be provided even for a lesser number of pupils if there is a social need for it.

Pupils specified in this Article, paragraphs 2 and 3 shall follow the syllabus of the Serbian language.

Official Gazette of the Republic of Serbia, No. 50/92

15. High School Law, 1992

Article 4. High education shall be acquired in the Serbian language. Instruction at a high school may be in the languages of nationalities or national minorities and in one of the world languages as decided by the founder.

16. Declaration of Joint Session of the SFRY, Republic of Serbia and Republic of Montenegro Assemblies, 27 April 1992

The representatives of the people of the Republic of Serbia and the Republic of Montenegro, expressing the will of the citizens of their respective republics to stay in the common state of Yugoslavia; accepting all basic principles of the charter of the United Nations and the CSCE Helsinki and Paris charters, and particularly the principles of parliamentary democracy, market economy and respect for human rights and the rights of national minorities; remaining strictly committed to a peaceful resolution of the Yugoslav crisis, wish to state in this declaration their views on the basic, immediate and lasting objectives of the policy of their common state, and on its relations with the former Yugoslav Republics.

In that regard, the representatives of the people of the Republic of Serbia and the Republic of Montenegro declare:

1. The federal Republic of Yugoslavia, continuing the state, international, legal and political personality of the socialist federal Republic of Yugoslavia, shall strictly abide by all the commitments that the SFR of Yugoslavia assumed internationally in the past.

2. At the same time, it shall be ready to fully respect the rights and interests of the Yugoslav republics which declared independence. The recognition of the newly-formed states will follow after all the outstanding questions negotiated on within the conference on Yugoslavia have been regulated.

3. Remaining bound by all obligations to international organisations and institution whose member it is, the federal republic of Yugoslavia shall not obstruct the newly formed states to join these organisations and institutions, particularly the United Nations and its specialised agencies.

4. The Federal Republic of Yugoslavia shall respect and fulfil the rights and obligations the SFR of Yugoslavia assumed vis-à-vis the territories of Krajina which have been placed, within the framework of the United Nations peace-keeping operation, under the protection of the world organisation.

5. The Federal Republic of Yugoslavia also remains ready to negotiate, within the conference on Yugoslavia, on all problems related to the division of assets, which means both to assets and debts acquired jointly, in case of a dispute regarding these issues, the Federal Republic of Yugoslavia shall be ready to accept the arbitration of the permanent court of arbitration in the Hague.

6. The diplomatic and consular missions of the Federal Republic of Yugoslavia shall continue without interruption to perform their functions of representing and protecting the interests of Yugoslavia.

7. Until further notice they shall continue to take care of all the assets of Yugoslavia abroad.

8. They shall also extend consular protection to all nationals of the SFR of Yugoslavia whenever they request them to do so until a final regulation of their nationality status.

9. The Federal Republic of Yugoslavia recognised, at the same time, the full continuity of the representation of foreign states by their diplomatic and consular missions in its territory.

10. The FR of Yugoslavia is interested in the reconstruction of economic, transport, energy and other flows and ties in the territory of the SFR of Yugoslavia, it is ready to make its full contribution to that end.

11. The FR of Yugoslavia has no territorial aspiration against anybody in its surroundings. Respecting the objectives and principles of the United Nations charter and CSCE documents, it remains strictly

committed to the principle of non-use of force in settling and outstanding issues.

12. The FR of Yugoslavia shall ensure the highest standard of the protection of human rights and the rights of national minorities provided for in international legal instrument and CSCE documents.

13. In addition, the FR of Yugoslavia shall be ready to additionally recognise to the national minorities in its territory all those rights which would be recognised to and practised by the national minorities in other CSCE participating states.

14. In its foreign relations, the FR of Yugoslavia shall be guided by the principles of the Unites Nations chapter, as well as the principles of CSCE documents, particularly the Paris charter for new Europe.

15. As the founding member of the movement of non-aligned countries, it shall remain committed to the principles and objectives of the policy of non-alignment.

16. It shall build relations of confidence and understanding towards its neighbours proceeding from the principle of goodneighbourliness.

17. The Federal Republic of Yugoslavia shall, as a state of free citizens, be guided in its democratic development by the standards and achievements of the Council of Europe, the European Community and other European Institutions, with an orientation to join them itself in the foreseeable future.

The participants of the joint session of the SFRY Assembly, The National Assembly of the Republic of Serbia and the Assembly of the Republic of Montenegro.

17.   Constitution of the Federal Republic of Yugoslavia, April 1992

Mindful of the freedom-loving, democratic and nation-building traditions, historical ties and shared interests of the state of Serbia and the state of Montenegro.

Arising from the unbroken continuity of Yugoslavia and voluntary association between Serbia and Montenegro.

The Federal Chamber of the Assembly of the Socialist Federal Republic of Yugoslavia, following upon the proposals and consent of the National Assembly of the Republic of Serbia and the Assembly of the Republic of Montenegro.

Hereby adopts and promulgates:
THE CONSTITUTION OF THE FEDERAL REPUBLIC OF YUGOSLAVIA
SECTION I
BASIC PROVISIONS
Article 1. The Federal Republic of Yugoslavia shall be a sovereign federal state, founded on the equality of citizens and the equality of its member republics.
Article 2. The Federal Republic of Yugoslavia shall be composed of the Republic of Serbia and the Republic of Montenegro. The Federal Republic of Yugoslavia may be joined by other member republics, in accordance with the present Constitution.
Article 3. The territory of the Federal Republic of Yugoslavia shall be a single entity comprising the territories of the member republics. The frontiers of the Federal Republic of Yugoslavia shall be inviolable. The boundaries between member republics may be changed only subject to their agreement, in accordance with the constitutions of the member republics. ...
Article 6. The Republic of Serbia includes the Autonomous Province of Vojvodina and the Autonomous Province of Kosovo and Metohia, these being the forms of territorial autonomy. ...
CONSTITUTIONALITY AND LEGALITY
Article 115. The constitutions of the member republics, federal statutes, the legislation of member republics and all other laws and general enactments must be in conformity with the Constitution of the Federal Republic of Yugoslavia. Statutes, other laws and general enactments in a member republic must be in conformity with federal law. Regulations and other general enactments adopted by federal agencies must be in conformity with federal law.

C.   Decisions Taken in Kosovo

1.   Declaration of the Albanian Political Parties of Kosova, 30 June 1990

The actual political circumstances in Yugoslavia have been aggravated to the extent of a disastrous war with unpredictable consequences for all Yugoslav national as well as for the Balkans and Europe. As we have made it known many times until now, this situation is a direct consequence of the hegemonistic, unitary and militaristic policy of Serbia and its leadership guided by Milosevic. The Albanian political parties of Kosova express their regret for the victims of the military intervention in Slovenia. As we have previously announced, the Albanian political parties of Kosova strongly support the peaceful solution of all political disagreements excluding any use of force in order to impose certain political aims. Concerning the actual situation, the Albanian political parties declare that:
- every nation should decide for its own fate;
- the announcement of the sovereignty of Slovenia and Croatia is an irrefutable right to express the free political will of their citizens;
- the intervention of the Yugoslav army is an action of violence, resulting from the militaristic logic in solving political problems in direct contradiction to the principles of the CSCE and of the Charter of the United Nations.

We support the international arbitration as the only solution for the present conditions and circumstances created in Yugoslavia. The Albanian political parties of Kosova, considering the escalation of crisis, and in particular considering within this context the position of the ethnic Albanians who might be drawn into this crisis against their will, warn the authorities of the Yugoslav army not to use ethnic Albanian conscripts against the political will of the Slovenian and any other peoples. The Albanian political parties in Kosova call upon Albanian conscripts and officers not to raise arms against the Slovenian and other peoples. Within present conditions and circumstances, Albanian reservists have the right to refuse the call for mobilisation, as these troops may be used to solve political problems through violence. As there is a possibility of the escalation of this crisis to Kosova, the Albanian political parties in Kosova call upon all its citizens not to respond to provocation, to avoid conflict, and at the same time to remain vigilant observe events closely. The Albanian political parties in Kosova, in view of the fact that Albanians in Yugoslavia are an unprotected people, call upon all international organisations and the governments of the member states of the CSCE to urgently activate adequate mechanisms to halt the further escalation of terror against Albanians.

If the moratorium proposed by the European Community is adopted by the Yugoslav Federal Executive Council, then it should be applied to decisions issued by Serbia which have suspended the political and juridical institutions of Albanians in Kosova, enabling Albanians to be included in future dialogues and negotiations.

Dr Ibrahim Rugova, Democratic League of Kosova; Kivzi Islami, Peasants' Party of Kosova; Shkelzen Maliqi, Social Democratic Party of Kosova; Shkelzen Maliqi; Lazar Krasniqi, Demochristian Party of Kosova; Veton Surroi, Parliamentary Party of Kosova; Reshat Hurboja, Republican Party of Kosova

2.   Assembly of Kosova, Constitutional Declaration, 2 July 1990

Following the expressed will of the majority of the population and approved by the Declaration of the science and Art Academy of Kosova; following the role of Kosova's Assembly as the highest organ as representative and constituent maker of power and self-administration, the Assembly of Kosova declares THE CONSTITUTIONAL DECLARATION on Kosova as an independent and equal constituent unit within the framework of the Federation (Confederation) of Yugoslavia entitled to the same constitutional denomination as other constituent units.
1. This declaration expresses and distinctly states the fundamental attitude held by the people of Kosova and by the Assembly towards the

constitution and considers it an act of political self-determination within the framework of Yugoslavia.

2. This Assembly, on its own and with its standing, in declaring Kosova an equal constituent unit within Yugoslavia, according to the principles of genuine democracy and respect they expressed will of the individual, social groups and national collectives, expects to obtain the confirmation of their constitutional act in the (forthcoming) Constitution of Yugoslavia and the full support of the democratic voices in Yugoslavia and of the international opinion as well.

3. This Assembly confirms that Kosova, in its constitutional position, is a political-constitutional community of people, its political-constitutional position being shared by all its citizens and by the national groups of Kosova on an equal basis. Also, Albanians being the overwhelming majority in Kosova and one of the largest groups of people in Yugoslavia consider themselves to be worthy of a nation as Serbians and others do - and no longer a national minority.

4. In the meantime, while waiting for the juridical and definite fulfilment of this constitutional declaration, the Assembly and the organs of Kosova in their relations within the constitutional order or Yugoslavia will respect the existing constitution of Yugoslavia and not the amendments to the constitution by the Republic of Serbia in the year 1989. This statement also voids the decision of the Assembly of Kosova on March 23, 1989 which approved those amendments at the time.

5. From now and until the promulgation of the New Constitution of Kosova, the Assembly of Kosova will communicate publicly with this name. As a representative body, it will simultaneously refer to the socio-ploitical community simply as Kosova.

3.   Resolution of the Assembly of Kosova, 7 September 1990

In a joint meeting of all three councils (Council of Associated Labour; Council of Boroughts and the Social-Political Council) of the Parliament of Kosova, held on the 7th of September 1990, according to article 301, paragraph 2 of the Constitution of the Socialist Autonomous Province of Kosova the following resolution was passed:

On the basis of the right to self-determination in respect to the overwhelming sovereign will of the Albanian people expressed by a plebiscite all over Kosova, on the basis of political-juridical subjectivism and way of implementation of the subjectivity expressed in the Constitutional Declaration of the assembly of Kosova on July 2nd 1990, The Assembly of Kosova passed the constitution of the Republic of Kosova in the joint meeting of all its three councils on the 7th September 1990 in Kosova. It proclaimed all of the following documents and passed the law on formation of political and other civic associations, the law on elections as well as made required decisions for the work of the Assembly of Kosova and its representation in the Federal Assembly of Yugoslavia.

These decisions made by the legitimate representatives of the sovereign people of Kosova are in agreement with the Federal Presidency position expressed publicly in all the Republics during the talks on the future of Yugoslavia. Yet, though the use of anti-constitutional measures by the Republic of Serbia, the people of Kosova and particularly the Albanian people were expelled from the talks on the future of Yugoslavia where Albanians together with other peoples (nations) would have decided on their equal position as a pre-condition for co-existence, but in an unprecedented way for civilised societies to behave they were exposed to an inhuman terror of national, political, economical and human discrimination extending even to physical threats.

This is just one part of what Albanian people in Kosova have been suffering because of its unsolved status and the status of Kosova within the Yugoslavian Community despite their commitment to Yugoslavia. Therefore, the solution of its status is its constitution as a sovereign state with other peoples and national minorities in the Republic of Kosova as an equal member within the Yugoslav Peoples community. Like other people of Yugoslavia this way allows the Albanian people the implementation to achieve their aims proclaimed in documents of historic events during its history for National Liberation.

Following the declared commitments of the Albanian people for co-existence with other people in Yugoslavia and its sovereignty and territorial integrity; following the democratic aim of other people of Yugoslavia and Europe of which Yugoslavia is a part of, the constitution of the republic of Kosova through the definition of Kosova as a sovereign state within the Yugoslavian Peoples Community guarantees the freedom of human rights of citizens according to the most civilised democratic societies as well as equality of all national communities in all domains. In such a way has been expressed the commitment of the Albanian people to prevent any application of any kind of discrimination against national or ethnic community in the Republic of Kosova.

Following the positive Constitutional solutions and experiences of other democratic countries in Europe and the rest of the World, the Constitution of the Republic of Kosova consists of forms of state rules relying on: the sovereignty of all the citizens; the pluralism of forms of property; the free market; the constitutional and legislation appropriate to a juridical state which provides democratic government and just protection for all its citizens regardless of their ethnic, political, racial faith or any other affiliation. This is a clear commitment towards democracy, equality, freedom of all citizens and all ethnic communities towards their prosperity and integrity within Yugoslavia, Europe and the Freedom-loving World as a whole.

This way, we, the legal representatives of the Kosovan people are contributing to the democratic process which have taken place in certain parts of Yugoslavia and the process of integrating Yugoslavia into the Democratic European Community. Therefore, we expect other Yugoslav Federal Units to recognise the sovereignty of Kosova as an equal member within the Yugoslav Community. Also, we expect sovereign countries of Europe and the World to support us on the recognition of the Republic of Kosova within the Yugoslav Community.

4.   Constitution of the Republic of Kosova, 7 September 1990

On the basis of the age-old democratic, progressive, and freedom-loving tradition of the Albanian people and the members of the other nationalities of the Republic of Kosova;

on the basis of the liberation struggles and the struggle for the defence of our existence and independence as a nation;

aiming to secure the general prosperity of the people and of humanity and the establishment of freedom, equality, and justice for ourselves and for generations to come;

aiming at a democratic society with continually growing wealth for the people, with education, science, progressive culture, and comprehensive development of the personality and the individual;

on the basis of the right of the people to freely determine, when and how they wish, their political position and identity and to freely exercise their right to their own independent economic, social, and cultural development; on the basis of the right of the people to dispose freely of their own natural resources, property, and means of subsistence and development;

aiming to create a law-governed democratic state on legal and social bases that guarantee the exercise of national rights, human and civil freedoms and rights, social justice, solidarity, prosperity, individual and social progress, and full human dignity;

while securing full rights to the members of other nationalities that live in the Republic of Kosova;

fulfilling by a free and independent decision the desire to continue on the path of democracy, social justice, peace, and friendship among peoples;

and on the basis of the principle that the will of the people is the foundation of state power, and that the people have expressed this will in a plebiscitary manner, determining their own political and legal identity, The Albanian people of the Republic of Kosova, in full accordance with the principles of democracy and equality and on the basis of the right to self-determination to the point of secession, guarantee full human and civil rights to all citizens, and on the basis of the Declaration of Independence of 2 July 1990,

THE ASSEMBLY OF THE REPUBLIC OF KOSOVA promulgates THE CONSTITUTION OF THE REPUBLIC OF KOSOVA.

I. General Dispositions

Article 1. The Republic of Kosova is a democratic state of the Albanian people and members of other peoples and national minorities that are its citizens: Serbs, Muslims, Montenegrins, Croats, Turks, Romanies, and others who live in Kosova.

Article 2. The Republic of Kosova is a sovereign and independent state. (Article Two has been changed by the First Amendment to the Constitution of the Republic of Kosova)

Article 3. The sovereignty of the Republic of Kosova derives from the people and belongs to the people. The will of the people is the basis of state power.

Article 4. The sovereignty of the people is exercised through their elected representatives in the organs of the state and by referendum.

Article 5. All members of the state's representative bodies are elected by adult citizens on the basis of the right to a general, equal, direct, and secret ballot, from among several candidates. The people's elected members on representative state bodies are answerable to their electors.

Article 6. As holders of power, citizens have the right to organise themselves in political parties and citizens' alliances, movements, and associations.

Article 7. Every person and citizen is guaranteed political, economic, social, national, and cultural freedoms and rights and other rights laid down in this constitution. Nobody can be denied the freedom and right to undertake an act, if this act is not explicitly forbidden by the constitution and the law.

Article 8. The territory of Kosova is single, inalienable, and indivisible. The borders of the republic can only be changed on the basis of a decision by the Assembly of the Republic of Kosova and in accordance with the expressed will of the people whom the change concerns.

Article 9. The citizens of the Republic of Kosova enjoy the rights of citizens of the Republic.

Article 10. The territorial organisation of the Republic of Kosova is defined by law. Communes and municipalities are the territorial units that conduct local self-administration.

Article 11. The Albanian language and its alphabet are in official use in the Republic of Kosova. In areas of the Republic where members of other nationalities also live, the Serbian, Croatian, and Turkish languages and their alphabets are also in equal official use, in accordance with the law.

Article 12. The Republic of Kosova exercises state power in a sovereign manner. The sovereign rights of the Republic of Kosova, its security, and its socio-economic and political order are defended by this constitution. Article 13. The power to make the constitution and the laws belongs to the Assembly of the Republic of Kosova, and is defined in this constitution.

Article 14. The president of the Republic of Kosova is the head of state. The rights and duties of the president of the Republic are defined in this constitution. (Article 14 has been changed by Sections One and Two of the Second Amendment to the Constitution of the Republic of Kosova.)

Article 15. The government is the highest organ of executive power. The rights and duties of the government are defined in this constitution.

Article 16. Independent courts exercise judicial authority. Courts work only on the basis of the constitution and the law.

Article 17. The Constitutional Court of Kosova, as an independent organ of the Republic of Kosova, protects constitutionality and legality.

Article 18. The work of the bodies of the state is public. The work of the bodies of the state may be kept from the public only in cases provided for by the law.

Article 19. The Republic has its own coat of arms. The shape and use of the coat of arms are defined by law.

Article 20. The Republic has its own flag. The shape and use of the flag are defined by law.

Article 21. The Republic has its own anthem. The character and use of the anthem are defined by law.

Article 22. In the Republic of Kosova the members of nations and national minorities have the right to use their own symbols. The conditions and use of their symbols are regulated by law.

Article 23. Prishtina is the capital city of the Republic of Kosova.

II. Economic and Social Order

Article 24. Economic and social life is organised in a manner that secures all citizens a standard of living in accordance with justice, based on their work as a whole as a source of prosperity, and in accordance with human dignity. It is a duty of the state, in accordance with democratic principles, to encourage and achieve economic, social, and cultural development, with the aim of increasing national earnings and the economic, social, and cultural prosperity of citizens. For this purpose, the state undertakes to make investments where the social interest demands it, especially in less-developed regions, and to prepare plans for the development and harmonious construction of the Republic. Within these limits and on this basis, a free market economy, freedom of enterprise and of association, the independence and equality of economic persons in the market, and the freedom of private economic initiative are guaranteed, enabling each person to secure himself an adequate livelihood through his own work.

Article 25. The law defines in greater detail that free economic activity cannot be conducted contrary to social interest, or in any way harmful to human safety, freedom, equality, or dignity. The law defines how public and private economic activities are managed and co-ordinated for the purposes of society.

Article 26. All forms of property are guaranteed. All forms of property are equal and enjoy the same protection. Physical and legal persons exercise property rights.

Article 27. The law may define the exploitation and management of property in accordance with the general interest. Expropriation is permitted only for social purposes on the basis of the law and solely against compensation corresponding to the market value of the property on the day of the announcement of the act of expropriation. Expropriation is only permitted if general social purposes cannot be achieved in other ways. Compensation is always defined by a civil court.

Article 28. Citizens are guaranteed the right of possession of agricultural land. The law defines conditions and restrictions on whose basis property rights of forest and forest land may be acquired.

Article 29. Natural resources and resources in common use, as well as resources of general interest, are social or state property. The law may define conditions for acquiring the right to exploit natural resources and resources in common use.

Article 30. It is the duty of the state, of economic and social organisations, and of all citizens to protect land, natural resources, water, and air from damage and pollution.

Article 31. Foreign persons may acquire property rights under conditions defined by law. Foreign persons are guaranteed the right to conduct and organise independent activity, to invest in the country's enterprises, or to form joint enterprises, according to conditions defined by law.

Article 32. Protection & development of trades are regulated by law.

Article 33. All cultural and historical treasures, regardless of whose property they may be, are the heritage of the people. They are under the protection of the state and the law prescribes measures for their preservation.

Article 34. The protection of intellectual labour and authors' rights, and the rights of inventions and innovations both in art and science are guaranteed. Science, scientific research, and the application of scientific knowledge are a vital foundation of society, to which the state and society are obliged to give comprehensive assistance.

Article 35. The right of inheritance is guaranteed and regulated by law.

Article 36. Citizens enjoy rights to security, pensions, and assistance in cases of their inability to work, sickness, accident, maternity, invalidity, age, or death, as well as for the upbringing of children, besides other forms of assistance in cases defined by law. The state secures citizens vital medical aid in health centres in the Republic.

Article 37. Every child, by virtue of his status as a minor, and regardless of race, sex, language, religion, national or social origin, wealth, or birth, has the right to the protection of the family, society, and the state.

Article 38. Under-age persons, persons unable to work, and the aged who have no relatives or have been left without the care of their relatives are under the state's particular protection.

Article 39. Every citizen enjoys the right to adequate housing. The law defines hygienic and economic standards through measures designed to assist the use and acquisition of property and to encourage private capital investment for this purpose.

Article 40. The budget secures means for citizens to exercise the rights guaranteed by this constitution and by law in the fields of health, social protection, the protection of children and other forms of social security, in education, science, culture, physical culture, and other areas defined by law. Employees and employers secure means for realizing employees' rights on the basis of social security contributions for health, pension, invalidity, and other benefits, in accordance with the law.

Article 41. The law may define activities that have the character of public services and defines how they are conducted.

III. Human and Civil Freedoms, Rights, and Duties.

Article 42. Human and civil freedoms and rights are restricted only by the equal freedoms and rights of others.

Article 43. Citizens are equal in rights and duties and enjoy the same protection before state bodies and other authorities, without distinction of nationality, race, sex, language, religion, political or other convictions, education, social origin, material position, or other personal characteristics.

Article 44. Human life is inviolable. The death sentence may be defined by law and pronounced exceptionally, only for the most serious forms of serious crimes.

Article 45. Human freedom is inviolable. Nobody can be deprived of their freedom, except in cases and following a procedure defined by law, on the basis of the decision of a competent court. Illegal deprivation of freedom is punishable.

Article 46. A person reasonably suspected of having committed a crime may be detained on remand and kept in custody only when this is necessary for the conduct of penal procedure of for people's security. Remand is determined by a court decision and, in exceptional cases, in accordance with conditions prescribed by law, and by a decision for another body authorised by law, may last up to a maximum of three days. A person kept in custody must be handed a written and reasoned warrant at the moment of detention. A person has the right to an appeal against this warrant, which the court decides within a period of 48 hours. Detention on remand must be reduced to as short a period as is necessary. Detention under an order of a primary court may be extended to up to three months from the date of detention. By decision of the Supreme Court, this period may be extended by a further three months, if no case is brought by the end of these periods, the suspect is released.

Article 47. Citizens are guaranteed the freedom of movement and place of residence, and the right to leave the country and to return to it.

Article 48. Personal dignity and privacy are inviolable.

Article 49. Citizens are guaranteed freedom of work, the free choice of their profession and work, and the right, under the same conditions, to every place of work and office.

Article 50. Workers have the right to working conditions that ensure their physical safety and moral integrity.

Article 51. Employees have the right to adequate remuneration for their labor, in a manner defined by law and by collective contract.

Article 52. Employees have the right to strike, according to a manner defined by law.

Article 53. In accordance with the law, employees have the right to a working week restricted to 42 hours, to daily and weekly rest, and to paid annual holiday.

Article 54. Citizens who are not fully able to work are guaranteed training for suitable work, and, in accordance with the law, conditions are created for their employment. Under conditions defined by law, the right to material security during a period of temporary unemployment is guaranteed.

Article 55. A citizen who has reached the age of eighteen has the right to vote and to be elected. Freely-formed and acting political parties, movements, alliances, associations, and groups of citizens take part in the elections. They must respect the principle of the people's sovereignty and of democracy, and confine themselves to the activities defined by the constitution and the law.

Article 56. Freedom of association, of assembly, and of public gatherings of citizens is guaranteed, as is the freedom of political and trade union organisation and activity, in ways defined by law. With the aim of protecting their rights and interests, employees may organise trade unions and become members of them at will. Political organisation and activities directed toward changing by force the order laid down in the constitution, violating the territorial integrity and independence of the republic, and inciting national, racial, and religious hatred and intolerance are forbidden. The manner of achieving freedom of the organisation of political and trade union activity is regulated by law.

Article 57. The privacy of letters and other means of communication is inviolable. The law may define exceptions to the principle of the inviolability of the privacy of letters and other means of communication only on the basis of a court decision, if this is necessary for the conduct of court procedure or for national security.

Article 58. The protection of personal data is guaranteed. The collection, processing, and use of personal data are regulated by law.

Article 59. The home is inviolable. The law may define when an official person, only on the basis of a court decision, may enter a home or other premises against the will of their occupiers and conduct searches. A search may be conducted only in the presence of two witnesses. In accordance with conditions defined by law, an official person may enter a home or other premises without a court decision, and conduct a search, if this is necessary to seize immediately the culprit of a criminal act or in order to rescue lives or property.

Article 60. Each person has the right to the equal defence of his rights in a court procedure, in front of state bodies and other authorities that decide on his rights, obligations, and interests. Each person is guaranteed the right to appeal and to further judicial recourse against the decisions of courts, state bodies and other authorities that decide on his legally-based rights or interests.

Article 61. Nobody can be convicted of a crime which, at the time it was committed, was not considered by law to be a punishable offence, or be sentenced to a punishment that was not provided for this offence. Crimes and penal sanctions can be defined only by law. Penal sanctions are considered by a competent court according to a procedure defined by law. Nobody can be considered guilty of a crime until this is proved by a final court verdict. A person who is unfairly convicted of a crime or who has been deprived of his freedom without grounds has the right to rehabilitation and compensation for his sentence from state funds, as well as other rights defined by law.

Article 62. Every person is guaranteed the right to defence before a court. Nobody can be brought before a court or other responsible authority for the conduct of a trial, or be convicted, if he has not been questioned according to the law and given the opportunity to defend himself. A defendant has the right to a defence counsel, who, in accordance with the law, is enabled to defend and secure the rights and interests of the defendant. The law defines in which cases a defendant must necessarily be represented by a defence counsel.

Article 63. In accordance with conditions defined by law, a citizen has the right to seek compensation from the state for a conviction caused by the unlawful behaviour of state bodies during the course of their duties, or of organisations acting on public authorisation.

Article 64. Respect for the human personality and human dignity in penal procedure, and in all other procedures connected with the deprivation or restriction of freedom, and during the period of the execution of the sentence, is guaranteed. The inviolability of human integrity and personality and of personal and family life and other personal rights is guaranteed. Any use of violence against a defendant to make him confess or to make a statement is forbidden and punishable. Nobody can be submitted to degrading treatment, punishment, or behaviour. It is in particular forbidden to conduct medical or other scientific experiments on a person without his permission.

Article 65. It is a person's right to decide the place of birth of their child.

Article 66. The family enjoys particular legal protection. Mothers and children enjoy particular protection. Marriage and legal relationships within marriage are regulated by law.

Article 67. Primary education lasting at least eight years is compulsory. The citizen has the right, under equal conditions defined by law, to acquire knowledge and professional training at all levels of education. Education is free of charge in schools financed by the public purse.

Article 68. Conditions for instruction in one's mother tongue of Albanian, Serbian, Croatian and Turkish are secured, in accordance with the law, in primary and secondary schools, colleges, and faculties. In areas where Romanies live, primary education in the Romany language is also secured, depending on conditions.

Article 69. The freedom of creativity, academic, professional, and literary publication and other forms of cultural creativity is guaranteed.

Article 70. Freedom of opinion and of the public expression of opinion is guaranteed.

Article 71. Freedom of the press and other public information media is guaranteed. Citizens have the right to publish their own opinions in the public information media. Citizens, state bodies, political parties, alliances, citizens' movements and associations, under conditions defined by law, may issue publications and disseminate information through the other media. Censorship and all other preventive measures violating the freedom of the press and other public information media are punished by law.

Article 72. The citizen has the right to publicly criticise the work of a state body, political party, alliance, citizens' movement or association, or a holder of public office, as well as to present to them submissions, petitions, proposals, and initiatives, and to receive an answer to them.

Article 73. A citizen of the Republic of Kosova when abroad enjoys the protection of his republic. A citizen of the Republic of Kosova cannot be deprived of his citizenship, banished from the country, or extradited. A citizen of the Republic of Kosova who is not within the country and who possesses another citizenship may be deprived of his citizenship only exceptionally and on the basis of the law, when by his activities he causes harm to international interests or other interests of the Republic of Kosova, or if he refuses to perform his civil duties.

Article 74. Foreign citizens and stateless persons who are persecuted because of their commitment to democratic views and to movements for democracy and social and national liberation, to human rights and freedoms, or to academic or artistic freedom are guaranteed the right to asylum.

Article 75. A citizen is guaranteed freedom of expression of his national identity, freedom to express his national culture, and freedom to use his language and its alphabet. A citizen is not obliged to declare a national allegiance, or to declare his membership of one of the peoples or national minorities. Any advocacy or implementation of national inequality and all sowing of national, racial, or religious hatred and intolerance, or the denial of history, or cultural and other national values, is punishable by law.

Article 76. Freedom of conscience, religious belief, and the practice of religion is guaranteed. Religious communities are separated from the state and are free to conduct their religious work and religious ceremonies. The religious communities may open religious schools and charitable institutions.

Article 77. The defence of the country is an inviolable and inalienable right, obligation, and duty for every citizen.

Article 78. It is everybody's duty to help each other in danger and to assist in averting a general danger.

Article 79. The freedoms and rights guaranteed by the constitution cannot be taken away or restricted. Freedoms and rights are exercised, and obligations fulfilled, on the basis of the constitution. The law may define only the manner in which some freedoms and rights are to be exercised, when this is defined by the constitution or when such definition is necessary for them to be exercised. Legal defence of the freedoms and rights guaranteed by the constitution is provided.

IV Constitutionality and Legality

Article 80. Attention to constitutionality and legality is the obligation of each and every person.

Article 81. Laws, dispositions, and other acts must be in accordance with the constitution. Dispositions and other acts of the republican organs must be in accordance with the laws. Other acts and dispositions cannot be in contravention of the law and other republican dispositions.

Article 82. The laws, dispositions, and other acts come into effect no earlier than eight days after their announcement, if their earlier implementation is not foreseen for particular reasons. Laws, dispositions, and other acts of the republican, communal, and municipal organs are published in the "Official Gazette of the Republic of Kosova."

Article 83. Laws, dispositions, and other acts cannot have a retroactive effect. If the general interest demands it, certain dispositions may be defined as retroactive only by law. Punishable acts are defined and sentences for these acts are pronounced according to the law or other disposition that was in effect at the time the act was committed, except where the new law or disposition is more lenient on the culprit.

Article 84 . State bodies and the organisations exercising public authority may in individual cases decide on rights or obligations, or, on the basis of the law, apply measures of coercion or detention only in accordance with the procedure defined by the law which gives each legal person the opportunity to defend his own interests and to raise an appeal against a measure that has been issued, or to have recourse to other judicial means provided for by the law.

Article 85. Appeals may be submitted to the competent authority against decisions and other individual acts of judicial and administrative authorities and other state organs, as well as against acts of organs and organisations that exercise primary public authority. In exceptional circumstances defined by law, appeals may be disallowed, if the defence of rights and legality is secured by other means. The court decides administrative disputes on the legality of individual final acts, in which state organs or organisations exercising public authority decide rights or obligations, if the law provides for no other legal defence for the relevant case. Administrative disputes on specific administrative matters may be disallowed only by law.

Article 86. Ignorance of the language in which a case is conducted cannot be an obstacle for the defence and exercise of citizens' rights and interests. Everybody is guaranteed the right to use his own language in court procedures, in front of other state organs and other organs and organisations that decide on the rights and duties of citizens, and has the right to be informed in his own language of the proceedings and materials of these procedures.

V. The Territorial Organisation of the Republic

The Commune and the City

Article 87. The commune is the territorial unit through which citizens administer themselves in accordance with the status of the commune. The republic may entrust the performance of certain tasks to the commune by law.

Article 88. In accordance with the Constitution and within the framework of the Constitution and the law, the commune, through its authorities:

- approves a development program, a town planning program, the budget, and the final accounts;
- ensures the performance of communal services and according to its own regulations controls general conditions for their completion;
- cares for the construction, maintenance, and use of local and minor roads and public facilities of communal concern;
- regulates the use of building land and commercial space;
- cares for meeting citizens' needs in the field of culture, education, health, social welfare, child care, sports, handicrafts, tourism, and catering, and protects and promotes the living environment, also meeting citizens' needs in other spheres of direct concern to themselves;
- ensures the enforcement of communal regulations and republican laws and other dispositions whose enforcement has been entrusted to the commune;
- creates communal authorities and organisations and performs communal services.

The commune is entitled to the revenues determined by law. Funds to meet citizens' needs may also be secured from personal contributions, in accordance with the law. Citizens decide by a referendum to levy personal contributions.

Article 89. The commune has a statute, which regulates the commune's functions, the organisation and work of the communal authorities, and other matters of concern to the commune. The communal assembly produces the statute.

Article 90. Citizens decide communal affairs by a referendum and through deputies to the communal assembly. The communal assembly is composed of deputies elected by a secret ballot at free and direct elections.

Article 91. The law may determine that a commune has the status of a city. The law defines the affairs that the republic entrusts to the city.

Article 92. The City of Prishtina is a separate territorial unit. The City has a statute regulating the functions of the city, the organisation and work of the city authorities, and other matters of concern to the City. The City Assembly produces the City Statute. The City Assembly is composed of deputies elected by a secret ballot at free and direct elections. The City of Prishtina performs the tasks of a commune as laid down in the Constitution, which are of concern for the City of Prishtina as a whole. Certain rights and duties of the republic may be delegated by law to the responsibility of the City.

VI. The rights and duties of the Republic

Article 93. The authorities defined by the Constitution exercise the rights and perform the duties of the republic. Human and civil rights and freedoms, equality before the law, and the independence and equality of all economic persons are the basis and framework of the authority and responsibility of the republican authorities.

Article 94. The republican authorities, within the framework of the republic's rights and duties as defined by law, determine policy, approve and enforce the law, regulations, and other acts, and protect constitutionality and legality according to constitutional law. Other authorities in the republic may be entrusted with the enforcement of laws and other dispositions from the framework of the rights and duties of the republic, on condition that the republican authorities are responsible for the performance of these duties.

Article 95. The republic embodies and ensures:

- the sovereignty, independence, and territorial integrity of the republic and the international position of the republic's relations with other states and different international organisations, and;
- human and civil rights and freedoms, constitutionality, and legality;
- the protection and security of citizens and the defence of the system defined by the Constitution;
- material rights and obligations, the judicial position of economic persons, the system of finance, foreign economic relations, the market, planning, employment relations, safety at work, social welfare, other forms of social security, and other matters of general concern in the sphere of social and economic relations;
- the health service and the system of social welfare, child care, education, science, culture, sports, and social and public information;
- the control of legality in connection with the disposal of the assets of legal persons, the financial inspection of public expenditure, and the way in which these matters are organised;
- the basic goals and directions of economic, demographic, regional, and social development, the organisation and use of land, the protection and promotion of the living environment, policies and measures for the guidance and encouragement of development, including the development of less-developed areas; reserves of goods;
- the financing of the functions of the republic as defined by the Constitution and the law;
- the organisation, competence, and work of state authorities;
- other matters defined by the Constitution.

VII. The Republican Authorities

1. The Republican Assembly

Article 96. The Republican Assembly is the organ of legislative power.

Article 97. The Republican Assembly:

- decides to promulgate and change the Republican Constitution;
- defines policy, and issues dispositions and other general acts;
- approves plans for development, land use, the budget, and the final accounts;
- decides on changes to the republic's borders;
- defines the republic's territorial organisation;

- decides on war and peace;
- ratifies international agreements;
- announces republican referendums;
- elects and dismisses: the chairman and deputy chairmen of the Republican Assembly; the chairman, deputy chairman, and ministers of the government of the republic; the chairman and judges of the Constitutional Court, the Supreme Court, and the republic's regular courts; the republican prosecutor and public prosecutors in the republic and other holders of public offices defined by law;
- controls the work of the government and other bodies and holders of public offices that are responsible to the Republican Assembly, in accordance with the Constitution and the Law;
- announces early elections for the communal and city assemblies in cases in which it observes that serious violations of the Constitution and the law have taken place and when the rights of citizens and nationalities have been infringed;
- amnesties the culprits of crimes;
- proclaims laws;
- provides conclusive interpretations of the law;
- performs other tasks defined by the Constitution.

(Point One of Item One of Article 97 has been changed by Point One of Item Three of the First Amendment of the Constitution of the Republic of Kosova)

Article 98. The Republican Assembly is composed of a single chamber and has 130 deputies. The deputies are elected by a secret ballot in free and direct elections. Political parties, movements, leagues, associations, and groups of citizens may nominate candidates for deputies. The manner of the election and recall of deputies and the formation of electoral constituencies are regulated by law.

Article 99. A deputy represents the citizens of the constituency for which he has been elected.

Article 100. A deputy enjoys immunity. A deputy cannot be held criminally responsible or be arrested or convicted because of a view he has expressed or because of a vote cast in the Republican Assembly. A deputy cannot be arrested without the permission of the Republican Assembly, and, if he is summoned while under immunity, criminal proceedings cannot be initiated against him without the permission of the Republican Asembly. A deputy may be arrested without the permission of the Republican Assembly only if he is caught in flagrant commission of an act for which a punishment of more than five years' imprisonment is prescribed. The Republican Assembly may decide to uphold the immunity of a deputy when he is summoned while under immunity, if this is necessary for him to perform his duty.

Article 101. Deputies are elected for four years. The chairman and deputy chairman of the Republican Assembly are elected for the same period. Deputies whose mandate expires cease to hold their seats on the day the mandates of the new deputies are verified. In case of immediate danger of war or in case of a state of war, the Republican Assembly decides to extend the mandates of republican deputies and of deputies in communal and city assemblies.

Article 102. The Republican Assembly holds regular meetings. An Assembly meeting with a predetermined agenda may also be convened on the demand of the president of the republic, the chairman of the republican government, or of no less than 30 deputies of the assembly. The Republican Assembly makes decisions at meetings at which a majority of the total number of deputies are present. The Assembly makes decisions by a majority of votes, if the Constitution does not prescribe a special majority. The government, every deputy, and at least 20,000 citizens possessing electoral rights have the right to propose laws and other dispositions.

Article 103. The chairman of the Republican Assembly, or in his absence the deputy chairman, represent the Assembly, convene meetings of the Assembly, sign acts issued by the Assembly, and proclaim by decree republican laws and elections.

Article 104. The Assembly can form permanent and temporary commissions in order to examine proposed laws and other acts and to follow through their enactment. The Assembly forms a Commission for Civil Rights and Freedoms and a Commission for National Equality.

Article 105. The Republican Assembly may decide that citizens should determine certain matters within its own competence by a republic-wide referendum.

Article 106. The work of the Republican Assembly and the commissions, their internal organisation, and the rights and duties of deputies are regulated by the Rule-Book of the Assembly's work.

2. The President of the Republic.

Article 107. The president of the Republic of Kosova represents the republic. (Article 107 was changed by Item Two, Line Two, of the Third Amendment to the Constitution of the Republic of Kosova.)

Article 108. The president of the republic represents the Republic of Kosova at home and abroad and is the supreme commander of its armed forces. He:

- decides matters in the field of defence, in accordance with the Constitution and the Law, and leads popular resistance in wartime;
- approves decrees with the force of law in the case of the immediate danger of war, during time of war, when national independence or territorial integrity is endangered, or if the republican authorities are unable to function normally
- if the Republican Assembly is unable to meet. Decrees with the force of law may suspend certain dispositions of the Constitution dealing with the freedoms and rights of citizens and with the organisation, composition, and authorities of certain republican bodies. The president of the republic presents decrees with the force of law to the Republican Assembly for verification as soon as it has the opportunity to meet;
- determines plans and measures for the country's protection; gives instructions for measures to prepare and mobilise resources and the country's defence forces and to co-ordination the plans and measures of other bodies; assesses the existence of an immediate danger of war; and orders general and partial mobilisation.
- determines the plan and use of the armed forces in case of war and orders the use of the armed forces in peacetime;
- decides issues in the sphere of foreign policy and international relations in accordance with the Constitution and the law; decides on the opening of diplomatic representatives and other representations in the world according to the proposal of the government;
- appoints and discharges by decree the diplomatic representatives of the Republic of Kosova, and accepts the letters of credential of diplomatic representatives from abroad.

The president of the republic is chairman of the Security Council of the Republic of Kosova. The Security Council of the Republic of Kosova is composed of: the president of the republic, the chairman of the Assembly, the chairman of the government, the ministers leading the organs of the state administration in the fields of security, defence, and foreign affairs, and three members nominated by the president of the republic. The Council examines security and defence issues of the republic and makes proposals to the Assembly and the government.

The president of the republic:

- in agreement with the leaders of the parliamentary groups proposes to the assembly the candidate for chairman of the government;
- proposes to the Republican Assembly candidates for the chairman and the judges of the Kosova Constitutional Court;
- appoints three members of the Security Council of the Republic of Kosova;
- proposes to the Republican Assembly and the government the examination of matters of general concern to the republic;
- pardons criminals serving sentences;
- awards decorations and legally-defined expressions of gratitude;
- also performs other tasks defined by the Constitution.

Election of the president of the republic:

The citizens of the republic elect the president of the republic by secret ballot in free and direct elections, in accordance with the law. The mandate of the president of the republic lasts for five years. The same person cannot be elected to this post more than twice. The president of the republic must necessarily be a citizen of the Republic of Kosova. A person who on election day is not less than 40 years old may be elected president of the republic. Registered political parties, at least 50,000

electors, or at least 30 deputies may propose a candidate for president of the republic. If the mandate of the president of the republic expires during time of war or during the period of an extension of a state of emergency, his mandate may be extended for six months after the end of the war or the state of emergency. The president of the republic is elected by a majority of the votes of electors who have voted. If none of the candidates wins a majority of votes, the election is repeated after 14 days. The two candidates who gained the largest numbers of votes in the first round of voting have the right to participate in the second round. If one of these withdraws his candidature, the following candidate according to the number of votes gained acquires the right to enter the poll again. If no candidate wins the necessary majority of votes in the second round of voting, the entire electoral procedure is repeated. If a candidate is proposed for president of the republic, but does not achieve the required majority of votes in the second round of voting, the entire electoral procedure is repeated. The election of a president of the republic takes place at the latest 15 days before the expiry date of the previous president's mandate. Before accepting his duties, the president of the republic takes an oath of loyalty to the Constitution before the Republican Assembly. The president of the republic cannot occupy any other public office as long as his mandate lasts. The president of the republic enjoys immunity, in the same way as the deputies. In the case of the president of the republic's death, resignation, or a permanent obstacle preventing him from performing his duties, the chairman of the Assembly of the Republic of Kosova temporarily assumes the duties of president of the republic, on the proposal of the republican government. The Kosova Constitutional Court determines the reasonableness and legality of the assembly chairman's assumption of the duties of the president of the republic. A new president of the republic must be elected without fail within 60 days following the day on which the previous president ceased to perform his duties.

The president of the republic presents to the Republican Assembly a report on the state of the republic no less than once a year. The president performs tasks within his prerogative on the basis of the Constitution and within its framework and that of the law, and is accountable to the citizens of the republic. The president of the republic is accountable for violations of the Constitution and the law. A minimum of two-thirds of the deputies of the Republican Assembly or the republic's Constitutional Court may initiate proceedings calling the president of the republic to account. The republic's Constitutional Court determines the responsibility of the president of the republic by a majority of two-thirds of the votes of all citizens. If the Kosova Constitutional Court proves his responsibility, the president of the republic surrenders his duties under the Constitution. (Article 109 was replaced by the subsection "Election of the president of the republic" and by Line One of the Fourth Amendment to the Constitution of the Republic of Kosova.)

The defence of the republic, a state of war, and a state of emergency:

Article 110. The armed forces of the Republic of Kosova defend the independence,sovereignty, and territorial integrity of the republic. The defence of the republic is regulated by a law issued by a majority of two-thirds of the votes of the total number of deputies. Nobody has the right to accept the occupation of the Republic of Kosova or any part of it. A state of war is considered if there exists an immediate danger of an attack against the Republic of Kosova, if the republic is attacked, or if war is declared against it.

The Assembly declares a state of war by a two-thirds majority of the votes of all the deputies, at the proposal of the president of the republic, the government, or at least 30 deputies. If the Assembly cannot meet, the president of the republic issues the decision for a state of war, and this decision is presented to the Assembly for its verification when conditions are created for the Assembly to meet. A state of emergency is considered when major natural disasters or epidemics occur. The Assembly determines the existence of a state of emergency in the territory of the Republic of Kosova or part of it at the proposal of the president of the republic, the government, or at least 30 deputies.

In cases where a state of war or a state of emergency exists, the government issues a decree with the force of law, in accordance with the Constitution and the law. The authorization of the government to issue decrees with the force of law lasts as long as the state of war or the state of emergency determined by the Assembly continues. During time of war, if the Assembly cannot meet, the president of the republic may appoint and discharge the government, and may also appoint and discharge officials whose election is the prerogative of the Assembly. The mandate of the president of the republic, the government, and the judges of the Constitutional Court continues for the duration of the war or state of emergency. (Article 110 supplemented by Lines 2-19 of the Fourth Amendment to the Constitution of the Republic of Kosova.)

Article 111. (incorporated in Article 110 under Items One to Seven of the Fourth Amendment to the Constitution of the Republic of Kosova.)

3. The Government of the Republic

Article 112. The government of the republic is the organ of executive power.

Article 113. [The government of the republic:]

- proposes and enacts the policy of the republic and applies the laws, dispositions, and other acts of the Republican Assembly, in accordance with the Constitution;
- approves decrees, resolutions, and other dispositions for the enforcement of the laws;
- proposes laws, the development plan, plan of land use, the budget, and the final accounts as well as other dispositions and general acts;
- guides the work of the ministries and other administrative authorities;
- supervises the work of the ministries, revokes or annuls their dispositions that are in contravention of the law or dispositions that it has approved, and determines the internal organisation of ministries;
- creates professional services and other services for its own needs, and appoints and discharges ministry officials;
- also carries out other tasks defined by the Constitution and the law.

Article 114. The government is composed of the chairman, the deputy chairmen, and the ministers. The organisation, manner of work, and seat of the government are regulated by law and in the working rule-book.

Article 115. The candidate for chairman of the government presents to the Republican Assembly his own program and proposes the composition of the government. The government is considered elected if the majority of the total number of deputies to the Assembly vote for it. The government is elected after the Republican Assembly is convened. The chairman, deputy chairmen, and members of the government enjoy immunity, in the same way as deputies.

Article 116. The government and each of its members are responsible to the Republican Assembly for their work. The government and each of its members may submit their resignation to the Republican Assembly. The resignation of the chairman of the government or his discharge from his post entails the resignation of the government. The chairman of the government may propose to the Republican Assembly the discharge of several members of the government. No less than 30 deputies may submit a proposal for a vote of no confidence in the government. A decision to dismiss the government may be considered approved, if the majority of the total number of Assembly deputies vote for it. The government which has not been granted a vote of confidence or has submitted its resignation remains in office until the new government is elected.

Article 117. The ministries enact administrative functions. The ministries enforce the laws, dispositions, and other acts of the Republican Assembly and the government and the acts of the president of the republic; they decide administrative matters, conduct administrative controls and inspections, and perform other administrative tasks, as defined by law. Ministries are independent in the exercise of responsibilities defined by the Constitution and the law. The minister heads the ministry's work. The minister answers to the Assembly and the government for the work of the ministry. The organisation and responsibilities of the ministries are defined by law. (Under Article 117, the words "Presidium of the Republic" have been replaced by the words "president of the republic," according to Line

One of the Fifth Amendment to the Constitution of the Republic of Kosova.)

4. Courts and Public Prosecutors

Article 118. Regular courts that are organs of the state exercise judicial functions. Other kinds of courts may be created for the settlement of relevant disputes.

Article 119. The regular courts are independent and judge solely on the basis of the Constitution and the law.

Article 120. Court hearings are public. The law determines from which hearings the public may be excluded in order to protect secrets, morality, the interests of minors, or other general interests. The work of the court is collegial. The law may decide that individual judges may decide certain cases.

Article 121. Judges and citizen judges take part in trials, according to the manner defined by law. The law may determine that only judges may participate in certain specific courts and in certain cases.

Article 122. The formation, organisation, competencies, and composition of courts, and also court procedure, are regulated by law.

Article 123. Judges and regular courts are elected and discharged according to the manner prescribed by law.

Article 124. Courts are formed as primary or secondary courts. The Supreme Court of the Republic of Kosova is the highest court in the republic.

Article 125. The public prosecutor is the independent state authority who prosecutes those who commit crimes and other acts punishable under the law and proposes judicial means for the defence of constitutionality and the law. The formation, organisation, and competencies of the public prosecutor are regulated by law.

Article 126. The function, manner of election, and discharge of the public prosecutor are regulated by law. The public prosecutor of the republic exercises the function of public prosecutor, within the framework of the rights and duties of the republic, in the manner prescribed by law.

5. The People's Bank

Article 127. The republic possesses a People's Bank The status, organisation, government, and activity of the People's Bank are regulated by law.

6. The Constitutional Court of the Republic

Article 128. The Constitutional Court of the Republic of Kosova:

- decides on the compatibility of laws, dispositions, other acts, and the statutes of communes and the City with the Constitution;
- decides on the compatibility of dispositions and other acts of republican authorities with the law;
- decides on the compatibility of all other dispositions and laws with the law and other republican dispositions;
- decides on the compatibility of statutes or other acts of political parties, movements, leagues, and associations with the Constitution or their irreconcilably with the law;
- decides on forbidding the activities of political parties, movements, leagues, and associations;
- decides on the responsibility for violations of the Constitution of the president of the republic, the prime minister, and the members of the government;
- settles disputes relating to elections, if these are not within the competence of the courts and other state organs;
- performs other tasks that the Constitution leaves to its responsibility.

The Constitutional Court assesses the constitutionality of law and the constitutionality and legality of dispositions and other acts if they have fallen into abeyance, if no more than one year has passed from their lapse into abeyance until the start of the procedure. (The words "and members of the Presidium" of Item Seven of Article 128 have been replaced by Line Two of the Fifth Amendment to the Constitution of the Republic of Kosova.)

Article 129. The Constitutional Court consists of seven judges. A judge who is a member of the Constitutional Court holds office for eight years, and may be re-elected to the same office. The chairman of the Constitutional Court is elected from among the judges for four years and may be re-elected for one further term of office. A judge of the

Constitutional Court cannot hold other posts of public authority or professional offices. A judge of the Constitutional Court enjoys immunity, in the same way as Assembly deputies.

Article 130. A judge of the Constitutional Court may be discharged at his own request, if he is sentenced to imprisonment following a crime, if he permanently loses the ability to exercise his function, or when he reaches pensionable age, as defined by law. The Constitutional Court informs the Assembly of the existence of reasons to discharge a judge of the Constitutional Court. The Constitutional Court may decide that the judge of the Constitutional Court against whom penal procedures have begun should not exercise his office as long as the procedure lasts..

Article 131. Any person may take the initiative to start procedures to assess constitutionality and legality. State authorities initiate the procedure before the Constitutional Court. The Constitutional Court may itself start procedures to assess constitutionality and legality.

Article 132. The Constitutional Court decides by a majority of votes in the Court. The verdicts of the Constitutional Court are binding and enforceable.

Article 133. When the Constitutional Court proves that a law, disposition, other act, or statute of a commune or the City is not in accordance with the Constitution, this law, disposition, other act, or statute of a commune or the City falls into abeyance.

Article 134. The procedure before the Constitutional Court and the judicial effect of its decisions are regulated by law. The Constitutional Court regulates its organisation through its rule-book.

VIII. Changing the Constitution

Article 135. No less than 50,000 electors, no less than 30 deputies of the Republican Assembly, the president of the republic, and the republican government may submit proposals to initiate changes to the Constitution. The Republican Assembly decides on a proposal to embark on constitutional change by a majority of votes of all the assembly deputies. The proposal for changing the Constitution may take the form of a constitutional amendment, a constitutional law, or a new constitution. (The words "Presidium of the republic" in Article 135 are replaced by the words "president of the republic" according to Item One of the Fifth Amendment to the Constitution of the Republic of Kosova.)

Article 136. The Republican Assembly drafts the bill for changing the Constitution and publishes it for public discussion. After public discussion, the Assembly draws up the bill on changing the Constitution and decides on it. Constitutional change is considered approved by the Assembly if the majority of the total number of assembly deputies vote for it. If the constitutional change is not approved, no proposal for changing the Constitution in the same way can be submitted before one year has elapsed following the rejection of the proposal for this change. If the Assembly does not approve the proposal to change the Constitution after one year has elapsed following the rejection of the proposal for this change, the proposal for changing the Constitution is decided by referendum.

Article 137. A bill for changing the Constitution is approved by referendum if more than one-half of the total number of electors vote in favour of it. If a bill for changing the Constitution is not approved even by referendum, no new proposal for changing the Constitution in the same way can be submitted before one year has elapsed following the day on which this bill has failed to meet approval. The Assembly of the Republic of Kosova announces approved changes to the Constitution.

Article 138. (Article 138 of the Constitution has been annulled.)

IX. Transitional and Final Dispositions

Article 139. A separate constitutional law will be issued on implementing this Constitution and ensuring its practical application. The Republican Assembly issues the constitutional law by a majority of votes of all the assembly deputies. The constitutional law on implementing the Constitution of the Republic of Kosova is announced and comes into effect at the same time as the Constitution of the Republic of Kosova.

Article 140. This Constitution comes into effect on the day it is announced.

5. Resolution of the Assembly of the Republic of Kosova on Independence, 22 September 1991

ASSEMBLY OF THE REPUBLIC OF KOSOVA

The Assembly of the Republic of Kosova, in its session of 22nd September, 1991, according to Article 97, paragraph 1, item 8 of the Constitution of the Republic of Kosova, has adopted and proclaimed the following RESOLUTION on the Republic of Kosova as a sovereign and independent state, with the right to participate as a constituent republic in Yugoslavia, on a basis of freedom and quality.

1. By this resolution, will be presented in accordance with the will of the people and the authorisation of the Assembly of the Republic of Kosova, provided for in the Constitutional Declaration of Kosova dated July 2nd, 1990 regarding the independence and equality of Kosova with other federal units and in conformity with the Constitution of the Republic of Kosova dated September 7th 1990, and on the basis of freedom and full equality, the Republic of Kosova as a sovereign and independent state has all constitutional rights in relation with other Yugoslav republics and has all freedoms as a republic or nation with all rights and guarantees.

2. This Resolution will be presented to seek appropriate recognition to: Republics of Yugoslavia; Parliaments and Governments of European States; Parliaments and Governments of the Permanent Member-States of the United Nations Security Council; Domestic and foreign opinion.

6. Central Board of Kosova for the Conduct of the Referendum, Result, 7 October 1991

… Out of the total number of the citizens of Kosova with the right to vote (estimated to be 1,051,357 citizens) 914,802 voted in the Referendum, i.e. 87.01%. Out of this number 913,705 voters, that is 99.87%, voted 'FOR', 'AGAINST' voted 164 citizens, whereas 933 ballots were 'INVALID'.

On diverse grounds and for diverse reasons 136,555 citizens, i.e. 12.99% of the citizens of Kosova with the right to vote, did not come out in the Referendum.

The Central Board of the Parliament of the Republic of Kosova for the Conducting of the Referendum, concludes that the Referendum on the Republic of Kosova as a sovereign and independent state, held during September 26-30, 1991, was successful. According to legal regulations of the Republic of Kosova, a referendum is (considered as) successful if two thirds of the total number of the citizens that participate in the referendum declare themselves 'for' 87.01% of the total number of the voters came out in the Referendum on the Republic of Kosova as a sovereign and independent state, 99.87 of whom declared themselves 'in favour'. …

7. Coordination Council of Albanian Political Parties in Yugoslavia, Political Declaration, 12 October 1991

1. The unsolved Albanian national issue in Yugoslavia is the result of the partition of Albanian ethnic territory when with the foundation of the Albanian state in 1913, more than half of the Albanian nation remained outside the state in compact ethnical territories where they have never realised their legitimate national rights neither under the monarchy of Yugoslavia nor the socialist state of Yugoslavia.

2. When drawing state borders the partitioning of Albanian territories was made ignoring ethnical principles and the will of the Albanian people. This also continued in Yugoslavia where Albanians were divided between the political and administrative borders of Kosova, Serbia, Macedonia and Montenegro. Albanians enjoyed certain political autonomy in Kosova guaranteed by the Constitution of 1974 which is still lawful and states that Kosova is a constituent element of the Yugoslav Federation.

3. In 1989 Serbia, contrary to Yugoslav Constitutional principles, abolished Kosova autonomy, all national rights and the right to sovereignty and subjectivity for the Albanian people, removed them from all state institutions, dissolved both the Assembly and Government of Kosova as well as all District Assemblies. Serbia has prohibited schooling in the Albanian language, declared the

Serbian language and the Cyrillic alphabet as the official medium in public communications, and has sacked more than 80,000 Albanians from their jobs.

4. As an expression of disagreement towards the situation the Albanian population have organised peaceful protests, workers strikes and general strikes in which half a million people have participated. Serbian authorities have reacted violently. They have killed more than one hundred Albanians, wounded three hundred and more than 12,000 have been jailed and given long term sentences. Over 600,000 have passed through police procedures.

5. Realising that Yugoslavia was an unsuccessful model of solving the national question in the Balkans, members of the Kosova Parliament on the 2nd of July declared Independence and on the 7th of September 1990 declared Kosova a Republic. This was a logical solution of state organisation of Kosova as a political and territorial unit where ninety percent of the entire population are Albanians and other nationalities comprise ten percent.

Albanian political parties in Yugoslavia, as the legal representatives of the political will of the Albanian people, and who are committed to the peaceful and democratic solution of all issues based on the people's right to self-determination in accordance with the CSCE Paris Conference, have committed themselves to these following options on solving the Albanian issue in Yugoslavia:

a) If external and internal borders of Yugoslavia are not to be changed then the Republic of Kosova should exist as a sovereign and independent state entitled to join the Commonwealth of the New Sovereign States of Yugoslavia. Those Albanian people remaining in the areas of Macedonia, Serbia and Montenegro should be entitled to the national statute with all relevant rights.

b) If the external borders of Yugoslavia remain unchanged but the internal borders are altered, then the demand is that the Albanian Republic of Yugoslavia be founded on both ethnic principles and other principles which apply to Serbs, Croats, Slovenes and other nations in Yugoslavia.

c) If external borders of Yugoslavia change then the Albanians in Yugoslavia through a general declaration with plebiscite will decide for territorial unification with Albania - so by creating an integral Albanian State in the Balkans with ethnic boundaries.

Albanian political parties declare that the political will of the Albanian people expressed in the referendum organised in Kosova on the 26th - 30th of September 1991, which declared Kosova as a sovereign and independent Republic, is a real force which cannot be ignored by anybody. The crisis in Yugoslavia began in Kosova with the expression of dissatisfaction shown by the Albanian people with regards to their plight and therefore will never end without the participation of more than three million Albanians in Yugoslavia. Albanians, about seven million of them, as an autochthonous nation with European tradition, were, are and will be a factor of great importance in the stability of the Balkans and Europe as a whole.

was supported also by other Albanian political parties, then the (Muslim) Party of Democratic Action, and the Turkish People's Party.

In Kosova, the electoral register comprised of 835,432 voters, of whom 762,257 participated in the elections, that is 89.32 per cent of registered voters. 80,791 voters did not come up in the elections, whereas 10,384 were invalid. In direct elections, the candidates of the Democratic League of Kosova received 574,755 votes, that is 76.44 per cent; the candidates of the Parliamentary of Kosova received 36,549 votes, that is 4.86 per cent' the candidates of the Peasants Party of Kosova received 23,682 votes, that is 3.15 per cent; the candidates of the Albanian Christian Democratic Party got 23,303, that is 3.10 per cent; independent (non-party) candidates received 24,702 votes, that is 3.29 per cent. Other electoral subjects that participated in these elections received less than 1.87 per cent of votes, therefore failing to secure the right of participation in the proportional distribution of seats in the Parliament. The Kosova Albanians, Muslims, Turks, Gypsies, Croats, and a minor number of Serbs and Montenegrins participated in the May 24th elections. The picture of seats in the Parliament is as follows:

- Democratic League of Kosova: 96 Deputies
- Parliamentary Party of Kosova: 13 Deputies
- Peasants Party of Kosova: 7 Deputies
- Albanian Christian Democratic Party: 7 Deputies
- Independent (non-party) candidates: 2 Deputies

People of Muslim ethnicity, according to the percentage of the population and proportional distribution, have 4 Deputies, whereas 1 candidate of Muslim ethnicity won in direct voting procedures. In the composition of the new Parliament of Kosova are 2 deputies of Turkish ethnicity who won seats in the elections as candidates of the Democratic League of Kosova. 14 seats in the Parliament of Kosova have remained vacant which, according to the percentage of the Kosova population and the proportional distribution of seats in the Parliament belong to people of Serbian and Montenegrin ethnicity. Election of the President of Kosova has been held both in Kosova and abroad in countries where Albanians from Kosova have been working as temporary job-holders. In Kosova, 762,257 voters voted for Dr. Ibrahim Rugova, the proposed candidate for President, (3,812 votes were 'against' and 'spoilt') whereas 105,300 voters outside Kosova. In sum, 867,557 voters voted in favour of the candidate for the President of the Republic of Kosova.

The Serbian police interfered in some polling stations in order to disrupt the election process. In two polling stations police removed part of the voting material. The entire polling material of the May 24th elections was handed over to the Parliament of the Republic of Kosova. Elections in Kosova were monitored by eight monitoring groups from the USA and European countries. The elections were covered by 82 journalist crews/news agencies from all over the world. Fairness of the elections were also confirmed by the political subjects that participated in the elections, but the Republican Election Board, by foreign monitoring groups, as well as many reports and articles of foreign and home journalists, in which a full picture of the election process was offered. ...

8. Kosova Report: 24 May Multiparty Elections for Parliament and President of Kosova, 15 June 1992

In its session of May 2nd, the Parliament of the Republic of Kosova announced the holding of free multiparty elections in Kosova for May 24, 1992, for the elections of members to the Parliament and the President of the Republic of Kosova. ... The elections were conducted according to a combined electoral system out of at least 130 seats in the Parliament, 100 of them were elected through direct voting, i.e. According to the majority system, whereas a further 30 seats were selected through the proportional representation system.

Elections were held on May 24, 1992. Polling stations were open from 07.00 hours to 19.00 hours. 22 electoral subjects filed candidacy of 490 candidates for deputies (100 of them) in the Parliament of Kosova. The Democratic League of Kosova announced the candidacy of Dr. Ibrahim Rugova for the Presidency. His candidacy however,

Chapter 5: Initial Attempts to Address the Crisis: The London Conference and the OSCE Mission of Long Duration

The crisis in Kosovo had been predicted by observers to constitute the most dangerous aspect of the dissolution of the former Yugoslavia. Particular worries had been expressed in relation to the potential threat to the stability of Macedonia, and a conflict involving Albania was also considered possible. But while the constitutional crisis concerning Kosovo had been festering since 1988, international attempts to address the issue of Kosovo only commenced when it became increasingly likely that Slovenia and Croatia would secede from the Socialist Federal Republic of Yugoslavia. And the events in Croatia, and subsequently in Bosnia and Herzegovina, were soon to dominate international attempts to address the Yugoslav problem. Kosovo was soon sidelined and removed from the list of issues which would need to be resolved, rather than just observed.

The Carrington Plan and the London Conference.

On 27 September 1990, Slovenia declared that it would no longer give effect to federal legislation. Attempts to re-negotiate the structure of the federation were blocked by Serbia in spring of the following year. Despite the urgings of the Conference for the Security and Cooperation in Europe (CSCE, now OSCE), the European Community/Union and diplomatic attempts by the United States government, Slovenia and also Croatia declared independence on 25-6 June 1991. The initial military confrontation in Slovenia triggered a very rapid response from both the CSCE and the European institutions. The CSCE was at that stage just about to reconstitute itself as a pan-European crisis management mechanism, after having served as a confidence building structure since its founding Helsinki Final Act of 1975. The European Union, too, was seeking to develop an identity as a leading player in the area of foreign and security policy. Both institutions saw the looming crisis in Yugoslavia as a first test of the emerging security structures in the New Europe.

By early July, some success seemed to have been achieved. According to the Brioni agreement, the republics would suspend their independence temporarily, to permit a peaceful resolution of the crisis. In reality, however, the Brioni accord masked a decision that had been reached in Belgrade. It had been agreed to accept Slovenian independence. Croatia, on the other hand, would not be able to leave the Federation unopposed, at least within her accepted boundaries, given the large number of ethnic Serbs in Croatia, many of whom inhabited the territorially identifiable Krajina region. Serbia, now in control of the federal organs of the rump-Yugoslavia, later declared that "The Serbian people ... demanded respect and protection of their legitimate national and civil rights. When Croatia decided to secede from Yugoslavia to form its own independent state, the Serb inhabiting their ethnical territories decided to break away from Croatia and remain within Yugoslavia. ... In such a situation it is essential to protect the Serbian people from extermination."[1] Essentially, the Yugoslav (Serb) authorities determined that secession could only occur if all mainly Serb-inhabited territories would remain within the rump Yugoslavia, finally constituting, as it were, the Greater Serbia of old. This vision seemed partially fulfilled when the Yugoslav national army, now controlled by Serbia, occupied the Krajina and other, in fact not mainly Serb-inhabited territories in Croatia a short time after signing the Brioni agreement.

The European Union condemned the use of force by Belgrade and confirmed the territorial integrity of Croatia. It also strongly opposed the brutal policy of ethnic cleansing, which had led to the exodus of thousands of Croats from occupied territories. The policy consisted of attacks on civilian concentrations and villages, the murder of civilians, and the expulsion of non-Serbs. At the same time, it urged the parties to accept the creation of a EU sponsored peace conference, supported by an arbitration procedure.[2] The Conference had its initial meeting at The Hague on 7 September 1991, under the chairmanship of Lord Carrington and with a mandate "to ensure peaceful accommodation of the conflicting aspirations of the Yugoslav peoples, on the basis of the following principles: no unilateral change of borders by force, protection for the rights of all in Yugoslavia and full account to be taken of all legitimate concerns and aspirations".[3]

While success eluded the Hague conference, it led to the development of a framework for the settlement of the Yugoslav crisis as a whole.[4] The plan was to provide for an overall settlement of all outstanding issues, based on the right for all republics that wished it to obtain independence. With this aim in mind, the initial Carrington proposal provided for the creation of autonomous regions or 'special status' areas, applying "in particular, to the Serbs living in areas in Croatia where they form a majority". Without mentioning Kosovo and Vojvodina, the draft added, in something of an afterthought, that

[1] Address of Dr Borislav Jociv in the SFRY Assembly, 19 March 1991, *Review of International Affairs*, Belgrade, 1 April 1991, at 11f.
[2] These developments are detailed in Weller, The International Response to the Dissolution of the Socialist Federal Republic of Yugoslavia, 86 *American Journal of International Law* (1992) 569.
[3] EPC Declaration on Yugoslavia, 3 September 1999.
[4] Carrington Draft for a Settlement, 18 October 1991, Document 5.A.1.

the republics would also apply "fully and in good faith established provisions for the benefit of ethnic and national groups, and for autonomous provinces which were given a special constitutional status."

This formulation was rather ambiguous, inasmuch as Serbia would undoubtedly argue that the "established provisions" were those contained in its own constitution of 1990 which had obliterated the effective autonomy for those two areas. A second draft of the Carrington plan strengthened the international involvement in the monitoring of the situation in the special status or autonomy areas. In addition, republics would need to apply fully and in good faith the "provisions existing prior to 1990 for autonomous provinces".[5]

Kosovo politicians had noted this rather incidental treatment of their cause with some concern. Even within the Socialist Federal Republic, Kosovo's status had been unilaterally abrogated and very severe discrimination and mistreatment had been applied by Serb authorities without any significant opposition. For Kosovo to remain within a rump-Yugoslavia, entirely dominated by Serbia, and having to rely on its "good faith" in the application of autonomy provisions, appeared unacceptable. Moreover, the crucial changes to its status had already taken place before 1990, when it lost the right to determine its own constitution and to influence changes in the constitution of the Serb republic. To Kosovo it appeared (with some justification) as if its case was getting lost, and that the international community was focusing principally on assuring Serbia in relation Serbs in Croatia and elsewhere. Clearly, the Carrington plan relied on the assumption that assurances of a minority and autonomy regime for these Serbs would render groundless Belgrade's opposition to independence for those republics that whished it. After all, they would enjoy international protection and far wider rights to autonomy than they had enjoyed under the 1974 constitutional system in the republics. While this appeared to be a reasonable compromise, it was of course not one which could satisfy the agenda of a Greater Serbia—the unification of the Serb people in one state, while at the same time retaining its strong direct rule over 'minorities' within her own borders. It failed, having been rejected by Serbia as unsuitable for discussion,[6] even after the EC threatened the adoption of sanctions in order to achieve Belgrade's acceptance.

To escape from the Serb veto of the peace plan for all of Yugoslavia, the EC then changed tack. It offered recognition to republics wishing independence, provided they committed themselves unilaterally to certain conditions, including especially the provisions on human and minority rights proposed in the Carrington draft.[7] While this opened the way for recognized statehood for Croatia and Slovenia, and also for Bosnia and Herzegovina and Macedonia, this decision spelt disaster for Kosovo. Effectively, the attempt to achieve a settlement of all questions arising from the dissolution of the Socialist Federal Republic, including the Kosovo issue, had now been abandoned.

The EC had invited the republics to state, by 23 December 1991, whether they wished to opt for independent statehood. After a period of consideration, decisions on recognition were supposed to be implemented on 15 January.[8] These decisions would be based on an evaluation of the commitments by the republics to the demands made by the European institutions. That evaluation would be performed by the EC arbitration commission headed by the French constitutional jurist Badinter and attached to the Peace Conference.

Kosovo formally applied for recognition in a letter to Lord Carrington, the Chair of the Peace Conference on Yugoslavia, a day before the deadline expired.[9] However, in contrast to the requests of the four republics seeking statehood, this request was not considered by the Badinter commission. The Commission itself, before addressing the four applications for recognition brought before it by Bosnia and Herzegovina, Croatia, Macedonia and Slovenia, also answered a number of general questions. It confirmed that the Socialist Federal Republic was in a process of total dissolution. Hence, there would not be one state continuing the legal personality of the SFRY, as Serbia had argued. Instead, the SFRY would cease to exist, and all the entities emerging from it would be treated as new states. In determining which entities could be states, the Commission followed the traditional international legal test of statehood, that is to say, to evaluate objectively whether or not an entity possessed the classical attributes of a state (territory, population and government). In a passage which sounded encouraging for Kosovo, the Commission ruled:[10]

> That in the case of a federal-type state, which embraces communities that possess a degree of autonomy and, moreover, participate in the exercise of political power with in the framework of institutions common to the Federation, the existence of the state implies that the federal organs represent the components of the Federation and wield effective power.

---

[5] Second Carrington Draft, 1 November 1991, Document 5.A.2.
[6] Report of the United Nations Secretary-General, S/23169, 25 October 1991, para 23.
[7] EPC *Guidelines on Recognition of New States*, and EPC *Declaration on Yugoslavia*, 16 December 1991, Documents 5.A.3/4.
[8] Controversially, Germany announced before that date, on 23 December, that it would recognize Croatia and Slovenia, although it suspended implementation of that decision in compliance with the EC decision.
[9] Letter from Dr Rugova to Lord Carrington, 22 December 1991, Document 5.A.5.
[10] Badinter Opinion No. 1, 11 January 1999, Document 5.A.6.

Under the 1974 constitution, Kosovo had been a federal entity, directly represented in the federal institutions, and possessing more than just a degree of autonomy. Hence, it argued, given the disappearance of the Federation, it, too, should emerge as an entity entitled to constitute itself as a state. On no account could it be left within Serbia, without the protection of its status by a strong Federation. After all, even under the provisions of the SFRY constitution, Serbia had managed unilaterally to attempt to alter its status considerably.[11] The pleadings of Kosovo were ignored and remained unanswered.[12]

A similar attitude was exhibited on the occasion of the second major international attempt to address the Yugoslav crisis. By the summer of 1992, the situation in Bosnia and Herzegovina dominated the agenda. Shortly before Bosnia and Herzegovina obtained recognition on 6 April, Yugoslav armed forces, now entirely under Serb control, had commenced hostilities in the republic and begun a strategy of ethnic cleansing, destruction and extermination of the mainly Muslim population which surpassed even the brutality of the operation in Croatia, probably amounting to genocide. The situation had been clearly identified by objective international agencies, from the UN Security Council to the General Assembly and special human rights bodies as one of abhorrent abuses which had to cease immediately, and the consequences of which had to be reversed.[13] But it had not been possible to take action beyond the adoption of sanctions and the half-hearted deployment of UN peace-keepers, who failed to pursue their mandates aggressively.[14]

In the absence of decisive action, a new diplomatic attempt was made in the shape of the London Conference on Yugoslavia of August 1992, especially as the rump-Yugoslavia was being led, for a brief period and ineffectively, as it turned out, by the moderate FRY Prime Minister Milan Panic. Before the conference, and in preparation for it, Milan Panic had officially declared to the UN Security Council that his government was "conducting its own investigation into human rights violations of its citizens, particularly in Kosovo". In relation to Kosovo, he promised a careful examination with particular urgency of all laws regulations and administrative practices to ensure that human rights abuses would cease.[15] There was no mention of the issue of the status of Kosovo, and the promise of an "investigation" into Serb practices in relation to that territory certainly struck the Kosovo delegation as a rather cynical exercise, given that the FRY/Serb leadership was itself directly responsible for them.

The letter addressed by Lord Carrington to the leader of Kosovo, Dr Rugova, before the Conference aptly symbolized the approach of the international community to the issue of Kosovo. Strictly speaking, Kosovo was not invited to attend. However, should Dr Rugova happen to plan "to be in London at the time of the Conference", he would be permitted to approach the conference building. While not permitted to enter the conference chamber, a Kosovo delegation would be allowed to occupy a separate room (known as the echo chamber), from which it could observe the proceedings via a specially installed video link.[16] Not having a voice at the conference table, it fell to the delegation of Albania to present the case of Kosovo.[17]

In the end, the entire London Conference proved a failure. Once again, the rump-Yugoslavia, and the Serb republic individually, committed themselves to pledges in relation to Bosnia and Herzegovina which were never fulfilled. The Kosovo issue itself was not really substantively addressed, although the Chairman indicated in an odd unilateral statement that Serbia and Montenegro had committed themselves to the restoration of "the full civil and constitutional rights of the inhabitants of Kosovo".[18]

The Special Group

The conference was to remain in place through a process of follow-on meetings, which would also address the issue of Kosovo. Serbia insisted that Kosovo could only be considered under the heading of "minority issues". This was strongly rejected by the Kosovo Albanians, who considered themselves a majority suffering repression at the hands of a minority. In the end a "Special Group" was set up to work on the Kosovo issue, which permitted both sides to retain their view as to status issues. The follow-on meetings of the Conference were convened that autumn in Geneva, and subsequent meetings were also held in Belgrade and Prishtina. The Kosovo Special Group, chaired by Ambassador Geert Ahrens of Germany, quickly determined to circumvent the difficult issues of status, and instead attempted to focus on practical improvements of

---

[11] On Kosovo's legal position, *see* Documents 5.A.12, 5.B.3, 5.C.3.

[12] Macedonia and Slovenia were found to have fulfilled the conditions for recognition, whereas Croatia and Bosnia and Herzegovina would have to take certain additional steps. However, in the first round of recognitions, Croatia and Slovenia were recognized, followed after some delay by the other two.

[13] E.g., Bethlehem & Weller, *The Crisis in Yugoslavia: General Issues* (1998), *passim*.

[14] Weller, Peace-keeping and Peace-enforcement in the Republic of Bosnia and Herzegovina, 56 *Heidelberg Journal of International Law [Zeitschrift fuer auslaendisches oeffentliches Recht und Voelkerrecht]* (1996) 70.

[15] Letter dated 17 August 1992, S/24452, Annex.

[16] Letter from Lord Carrington to Dr Rugova, 17 August 1992, Document 5.A.11.

[17] Statement by Alfred Serreqi, 26 August 1992. The Kosovo delegation was permitted to meet Lord Carrington, who on this occasion was not a man given to an overly welcoming or receptive attitude and conducted himself much in accordance with the tone of his letter.

[18] Co-Chairman's Paper on Serbia and Montenegro, 27 August 1992, Document 5.A.15.

life in the territory. The issue of education was picked as one area where progress might be possible.[19] In Kosovo, a Serb curriculum had been introduced and large numbers of ethnic Albanian teachers and professors had been dismissed. The Rugova Government had managed to establish the famous parallel school system. Teachers would continue to exercise their profession, often in private houses, and funded from voluntary contributions, or taxes, paid by the majority population. However, given the urgent need to avoid an entire generation of young people growing up without more regular schooling, it was felt that progress might be in the interest of both parties. The parallel school system, after all, also caused considerable embarrassment to Serbia, for it demonstrated, on the one hand, the effectiveness of the Rugova administration, while at the same time highlighting the effect of Serb repression internationally.

The talks in the Special Group quickly got bogged down.[20] Worse than the lack of progress on the education issue may have been that the mere existence of the Special Group gave the impression that the Kosovo problem was now being addressed in some way by an international forum. In the end, an education accord was reached some four years after the first meeting of the Special Group, but outside of it, through the mediation of an NGO.[21] However, that very brief agreement was never implemented. A final attempt to achieve progress in this limited sector was undertaken when fighting and displacement had already taken hold in Kosovo in spring 1998. Serbia, it seemed, wanted to demonstrate that it was, after all, willing to negotiate in good faith.[22] However, the process ceased in view of the parallel military action and the reports of massacres and displacement that were starting to emerge.

CSCE monitoring

While negotiations even on practical issues remained fruitless, another international attempt was made at least to stabilize the situation on the ground. This effort was spearheaded by the Conference on Security and Cooperation in Europe. When the Yugoslav crisis broke out, the CSCE had just begun to implement important changes to its founding documents, institutionalising international crisis management mechanisms and procedures for the reporting on human and minority rights issues. While these procedures may have appeared innovative, they constituted at the same time an odd regression in the history of European security. Under the post World War I system of the League of Nations, there had existed a permanent international organization, formally based on a treaty, equipped with international organs and quite tough collective security procedures. While these had of course been incapable of stopping aggressive fascism, they did have a number of notable successes before Hitler came to power, including the management of quite dangerous European crises.

Now, after the conclusion of the Cold War, Europe was attempting to generate a more modern system of security. However, the European Community or Union found it difficult to establish its security and defence identity and, at any rate, its membership was not all-inclusive. The CSCE, on the other hand, was rapidly growing in membership from the original 35 signatories of the Helsinki Final Act of 1975, to the present number of 55, stretching from the Atlantic (including the US and Canada) to Vladivostok. But it was a very odd creature, created during the Cold War. Its basis lay in a non-binding instrument, the Final Act. It was not an organization and it functioned under the consensus principle, which meant that every state could veto any proposed action.

In 1990, the first steps had been taken to add new functions and procedures, celebrated in the Paris Charter for a New Europe of 21 November 1990. Provision was made for more regular inter-governmental consultation, a Secretariat and a Conflict Prevention Centre. At the CSCE meetings in Vienna, Paris, Copenhagen, Moscow, Berlin, Prague, Helsinki and Stockholm, further crisis management mechanisms and dispute settlement arrangements were put into place, covering security directly (the military dimension and preventative crisis management) and indirectly (the human dimension). These included the capacity to take decisions in certain circumstances under the 'consensus minus one' rule, which would circumvent the veto of a state targeted by a proposed decision. There was also the possibility of activating rapporteur missions. However, in principle, it remained subject to consensus. The obligations on the basis of which the CSCE operated remained legally non-binding. And, although the CSCE converted itself into the Organization for Security and Cooperation in Europe at the Budapest summit of 5/6 December 1994, it was still not established by treaty—a very odd result for an 'organization' which was accorded the status of a regional organization or arrangement under Chapter VIII of the United Nations Charter. This meant that the OSCE could, in principle, have acted as a fully fledged collective security organization, including the taking of enforcement action under Security Council authority. But from the beginning, the CSCE/OSCE determined that it would only engage in consensual peace-keeping, and even that possibility has as yet not been fully developed.

Despite these drawbacks, the CSCE/OSCE displayed an important activism in relation to the Yugoslav crisis. It deployed many if not most elements of the plethora of new CSCE mechanisms from the moment of their inception, often in an

[19] Report of the Secretary-General, 11 November 1992, S/24795, paras 90ff, Document 5.B.2.

[20] Report of the Secretary-General, 30 March 1993, S/25490, Document 5.B.4.

[21] Education Agreement, 1 September 1996, Document 5.B.7.

[22] Agreed Measures of the Implementation of the Agreement on Education, 23 March 1998, Document 5.B.8.

imaginative and highly pro-active way. This included the Vienna and Moscow Human Dimension Mechanisms, the Berlin Emergency Mechanism for Consultation and Cooperation and the Mechanism for Consultation and Cooperation as Regards Unusual Military Activities. Action by the high profile High Commissioner on National Minorities, established in 1992 to respond at the earliest possible stage to ethnic tension with the potential to develop into a conflict in the CSCE/OSCE region was limited, in view of the fact that the situation in Kosovo was already threatening the stability of the region.

CSCE interest in the situation was legitimised by three factors. First, there was the danger of instability spreading from Kosovo into Macedonia, possibly leading to a wider confrontation also involving Greece and perhaps Turkey. This contingency was answered with the deployment of a CSCE 'spill-over' mission to Macedonia, in addition to the application of preventative diplomacy. Second, there was the risk of the overall conflict in Yugoslavia involving some of the other neighbouring states, hence the application of the emergency mechanism on unusual military activities. And, the developments in Croatia and Bosnia, but also in Kosovo, posed an obvious challenge to the 'human dimension', which from the beginning had constituted one of the principal pillars of CSCE concern. In fact, among the various actors involved in the Yugoslav crisis, the CSCE was the only one which focused directly, expressly and at an early stage on the crisis in Kosovo itself, rather than regarding it as a matter incidental to the rest of the turmoil in the former Yugoslavia.

The most significant early CSCE actions were the human dimension exploratory missions and the deployment of the Mission of Long Duration in Kosovo, Sandjak and Vojvodina in the exercise of the early warning and preventative action functions. The latter mission started on 8 September 1992 and remained in place until June 1993, when Belgrade withdrew its consent in response to the decision to suspend Yugoslavia from participation in the work of the CSCE. This action had been taken in view of Yugoslavia's grave and severe violation of CSCE principles, especially in Bosnia and Herzegovina, and had in fact already been in force by the time the mission was established.[23] Yugoslavia may have hoped that cooperation with the mission might assist in her campaign for the restoration of membership privileges. When the mission failed to fulfil this function, and instead brought an unwelcome transparency to Kosovo, it was terminated—highlighting the weakness in the constitutional structure of the CSCE which continued to require the consent of its member states for most types of operations.

The activities of the CSCE in many difficult and lingering crises in Central and Eastern Europe are generally ignored by observers and scholarship. The tremendous value of the work that has been done by this unestablished organization, which has fewer powers than even the League of Nations, which does not have a large secretariat and which often has to draw upon officers seconded by member government, is therefore not really appreciated. In the case of Kosovo, the breadth of action undertaken early on in the crisis is all the more difficult to appreciate, inasmuch as many of the key mission documents have been kept confidential. However, a review of these materials, reproduced along with previously available materials in the chapter which follows, provides a good indication of the perspicacity of the mission leaders, and of the actual activities of the mission.

The initial Human Rights Rapporteur Mission pointed out that while world attention was focused on Croatia, human rights were frequently and systematically being violated in other areas, in particular Kosovo and Sanjak. It rejected the Serb argument of ethnic differentiation, on the basis of according 'nationality' status to Serbs and treating the Kosovo Albanians according to a different legal regime.[24] The Conflict Prevention Centre Fact-finding mission found that military activities in the province were not unusual. However, in terms of the allegations of repression, the Mission found that there was often no clear distinction between the army and the militia, which was primarily employed for that purpose. The Mission also related the fear of the ethnic Albanians that there would eventually emerge an armed conflict, under the guise of which they would force the Albanians out of Kosovo altogether. "If it started, it would produce a massacre and vast numbers of refugees". [25]

The Mission of Long-Duration gradually established a significant presence in Yugoslavia, including field offices in Pec and Prizren. In addition to general reports on the situation, it investigated the removal of most ethnic Albanians from all public functions in the province, including the judiciary, the take-over of the infrastructure of organs of the media in the territory (by creating a new state concern regulating access to publishing technology and paper), the running down of ethnic Albanian health care and the exclusion of Albanians from the social security system, instances of intimidation and police brutality, etc. The mission also expressed its astonishment at the establishment of the parallel administrative structure and of a parallel economy by the ethnic Albanians.

The mission repeatedly attempted to persuade the majority population to try and exhaust the legal procedures available under the Serb administration of the territory. This was supposed to provide a better opportunity for the CSCE and human

[23] Decision by the CSO, 7 July 1992, Document 5.C.5
[24] Report of 24 January 1992, Document 5.D.1.
[25] Report of 5 June 1992, Document 5.D.4.

rights bodies to take up particular cases with the FRY/Serb government, but was not taken to be a realistic prospect by the local population, given their past experiences. Instead, the Mission consistently attempted to engage Serb and Albanian leaders in dialogue, and to arrange for small and practical improvements in the situation. Through its presence, it did manage to alleviate the lot of elements of the local population and on occasion it interceded on behalf of individuals who had been detained and were being mistreated.[26]

Hence, contrary to scholarly assessments thus far, the missions served far broader purposes than furnishing internal reports on the situation for CSCE decision-makers, or rather member governments taking decisions within the framework of the CSCE. Their presence in Kosovo, while it lasted, went beyond reporting, straying into mediation and the active protection of threatened individuals. Through direct contact with the Yugoslav/Serb governments, a modicum of accountability could also be introduced. However, as with the very detailed reports of the European Community/Union monitors who witnessed probable genocide in Croatia and Bosnia and Herzegovina, an even greater sense of accountability could have been introduced had the findings of the missions in the field been published by the CSCE.

The value of the mission was recognized in the international protest which followed the termination of its operation by Yugoslavia, including a call from the United Nations Security Council to readmit the CSCE operation.[27] This resolution was to remain the only action of the Council targeted specifically at the situation in Kosovo from the outbreak of the crisis in 1988 to 1998, when open hostilities erupted, highlighting once more the special value of CSCE involvement which remained unique among the political organs within the international constitutional system (human rights organs were, of course, very active, as will be related in Chapter VI).

Overall, the early efforts to address the crisis leave a somewhat mixed impression. The dangers of the situation in Kosovo, and the deplorable fate of its population, were identified and officially noted over and over again. However, given the nature of the dispute as one involving a claim to self-determination and possible secession, there was a reluctance to address it. Although Kosovo would have qualified under the definition provided by the Badinter commission as a candidate for statehood, its claims in this respect were simply ignored, as were the representations by Kosovo's leadership. In the Carrington process, the Kosovo issue was almost completely ignored, probably in view of the fact that it would only complicate efforts to tempt the FRY/Serbia into accepting an overall framework for a settlement. However, sacrificing Kosovo in this way was in vain. It soon emerged that the FRY/Serbia remained unwilling to compromise and accept an overall settlement which would ensure the rights of ethnic Serbs within the emerging new states. Instead, an armed campaign was waged to create a Greater Serbia containing Serb inhabited areas of Croatia and most of Bosnia and Herzegovina.

The London Conference, too, was plagued by the assumption that the FRY/Serbia might accept a reasonable settlement. Again, an overall attempt to settle the Yugoslav crisis was made and again the issue of Kosovo was excluded. The follow-on negotiations in the Special Group were not really pursued in earnest and soon turned into a fig-leaf exercise, silently abandoned after some years. In the meantime, the CSCE did manage to establish an effective international mission in the territory. However, no action was taken in response to the quite drastic findings of the mission. A similar situation obtained when the findings of the CSCE were mirrored by the efforts of the United Nations human rights machinery, addressed in the next chapter.

---

[26] *See* Documents 5.D.6-19.
[27] Resolution 855 (1993), 9 August 1993, Document 5.C.12.

A. The International Conference on Yugoslavia, 1991-1992

S/23169, Annex

1. Peace Conference on Yugoslavia, Carrington Draft Convention for a General Settlement, 18 October 1991

1.1. The arrangements for a general settlement of the Yugoslav crisis will comprise the following components:

a. Sovereign and independent republics with international personality for those that wish it;

b. A free association of the republics with an international personality as envisaged in these arrangements;

c. Comprehensive arrangements, including supervisory mechanisms for the protection of human rights and special status for certaion groups and areas

d. European involvement, where appropriate;

e. In the framework of a general settlement, recognition of the independence, within the existing borders, unless otherwise agreed, of those republics withing it. ...

b. Rights of national and ethnic groups

2.2. The Republics reaffirm their commitment ot the principles of human rights as particularly applied to national or thnic groups. These are, in particular, embodied in:

- The instruments of the United Nations, CSCE and the Council of Europe as set out in paragraph 1;
- The Conventions for the Elimination of Racial Discimination, the Convention against Genocide and the Convention on the Rights of the Child of the United Nations;
- The report of the CSCE meeting of experts on national minorities held in Geneva.

In working out these arrangements for a general settlement they will keep in mind:

- Proposals for a United Nations declaration on the rights of persons of national, ethnic and linguistic minorities;
- The proposal for a convention for the protection of minorities of the European Commission for democracy and law in the framework of the Euncil of Europe.

2.3. Persons belonging to a national or ethnic group, not forming a majority in the area where they live, will enjoy the following rights:

- The principle of non-discrimination as set out in the legal instruments mentioned in paragraph 2.1 [human rights instruments];
- All cultural rights as set out in the legal instruments mentioned in paragraph 2, in particular the right to identity, culture, religion, use of language and alphabet both in public and private, and education;
- Protection of equal participation in public affairs such as the exercise of political and economic freedoms, in the social sphere, in access to the media and in the field of education and cultrural affairs generally;
- The right to decide to which national or ethnic group he or she wishes to belong, and to exercise any rights pertaining to this choice as an individual or in association with others. This will particularly apply in the case of marriage between persons of different national or ethnic groups. Those persons of the same national or ethnic group living distant from others of the same origin, for example in isolated villages, shall be granted a practicable degree of self-administration.

The above principles shall also apply in areas where members of the main national or ethnic group are numerically inferior to one or more other national or ethnic groups in that area.

2.4 In respect of person belonging to a national or ethnic group forming a substantial part of the population in the area where they live but nor forming a majority: in addition to the principles set out in paragraph 2.3, a general right of participation of members of this group in public affairs must be granted. On the level of central government, they must be able to participate in decision-making by the central government concerning their affairs.

c. Special Status

2.5. In addition, areas in which persons belonging to a national or ethnic group form a majority, will enjoy a special status (autonomy). Such will provide for:

a. The right to have and show the national emblems of that group;

b. The right to a second nationality for members of that group in addition to the nationality of the republic;

c. An educational system which respects the values and needs of that group;

d. (i) a legislative body (ii) an administrative structure, including a regional police force (iii) and a judiciary responsible for matters concerning the area which reflects the composition of the population of the area;

e. Provisions for appropriate internatonal monitoring.

The status set out will apply, in particular, to the Serbs living in areas in Croatia where they form a majority.

d. General Provisions

2.6. It is recognized that persons belonging to a national or ethnic group, in exercising their rights, must respect the rights of the majority and of persons belonging to other groups.

2.7. Without prejudice to the implementation of the arrangements set forth in paragraph 2.5, the republics will apply fully and in good faith established provisions for the benefit of ethnic and national groups, and for autonomous provinces which were given a special constitutional status. ...

S/23169, Annex

2. Peace Conference on Yugoslavia, Second Carrington Draft Provisions for a Convention, 1 November 1991

[*The following provision additional to those listed above was proposed for 'Special Status' areas:*]

5.A. Such areas, unless they are defined in part by an international frontier with a State not party to this Convention, shall be permanently demilitarized and no military forces, exercises or activities on land or in the air shall be permitted in those areas.

5.B. (a) The republics shall provide for international monitoring of the implementation of the special status of autonomy. To this end, they shall conclude agreements which would provide for a permanent international body to monitor implementation of this paragraph.

(b) The monitoring missions thus established shall:

Report to the republics in question as well as to the other parties to the agreement, and

As appropriate formulate recommendations on the implementation of the special status.

(c) The republics shall give effect to such recommendations through legislation or otherwise. In case of dispute, the Court of Human Rights shall be requested to give its decision.

6. Without prejudice to the implemention of the arrangements set forth in this paragraph, the republics shall apply fully and in good faith the provisions existing prior to 1990 for autonomous provinces.

European Political Cooperation, Press release, P. 128/91

3. EPC Guidelines on the Recognition of New States in Eastern Europe and in Soviet Union, 16 December 1991

In compliance with the European Council's request, Ministers have assessed developments in Eastern Europe and in the Soviet Union with a view to elaborating an approach regarding relations with new States. In this connection they have adopted the following guidelines on the formal recognition of new states in Eastern Europe and in the Soviet Union:

"The Community and its member States confirm their attachment to the principles of the Helsinki Final Act and the Charter of Paris, in particular the principle of self-determination. They affirm their readiness to recognise, subject to the normal standards of international practice and the political realities in each case, those new States which, following the historic changes in the region, have constituted themselves on a democratic basis, have accepted the appropriate international obligations and have committed themselves in good faith to a peaceful process and to negotiations.

Therefore, they adopt a common position on the process of recognition of these new States, which requires:

- respect for the provisions of the Charter of the United Nations and the commitments subscribed to in the Final Act of Helsinki and in the Charter of Paris, especially with regard to the rule of law, democracy and human rights;
- guarantees for the rights of ethnic and national groups and minorities in accordance with the commitments subscribed to in the framework of the CSCE;
- respect for the inviolability of all frontiers which can only be changed by peaceful means and by common agreement;
- acceptance of all relevant commitments with regard to disarmament and nuclear non-proliferation as well as to security and regional stability;
- commitment to settle by agreement, including where appropriate by recourse to arbitration, all questions concerning State succession and regional disputes.

The Community and its member States will not recognise entities which are the result of aggression. They would take account of the effects of recognition on neighbouring States.

The commitment to these principles opens the way to recognition by the Community and its member States and to the establishment of diplomatic relations. It could be laid down in agreements."

4. EPC Declaration on Yugoslavia, 16 December 1991

The European Community and its member States discussed the situation in Yugoslavia in the light of their guidelines on the recognition of new states in Eastern Europe and in the Soviet Union. They adopted a common position with regard to the recognition of Yugoslav Republics. In this connection they concluded the following:

The Community and its member States agree to recognise the independence of all the Yugoslav Republics fulfilling all the conditions set out below. The implementation of this decision will take place on January 15, 1992.

They are therefore inviting all Yugoslav Republics to state by 23 December whether:

- they wish to be recognised as independent States;
- they accept the commitments contained in the above-mentioned guidelines;
- they accept the provisions laid down in the draft Convention - especially those in Chapter II on human rights and rights of national or ethnic groups - under consideration by the Conference on Yugoslavia;
- they continue to support the efforts of the Secretary General and the Security Council of the United Nations, and
- the continuation of the Conference on Yugoslavia.

The applications of those Republics which reply positively will be submitted through the Chair of the Conference to the Arbitration Commission for advice before the implementation date.

In the meantime, the Community and its member States request the UN Secretary General and the UN Security Council to continue their efforts to establish an effective cease-fire and promote a peaceful and negotiated outcome to the conflict. They continue to attach the greatest importance to the early deployment of a UN peace-keeping force referred to in UN Security Council Resolution 724.

The Community and its member States also require a Yugoslav Republic to commit itself, prior to recognition, to adopt constitutional and political guarantees ensuring that it has no territorial claims towards a neighbouring Community State and that it will conduct no hostile propaganda activities versus a neighbouring Community State, including the use of a denomination which implies territorial claims.

5. Letter from Dr Rugova to Lord Carrington, Peace Conference on Yugoslavia, 22 December 1991

Your Excellency,

In accordance with the Declaration on Yugoslavia adopted December 16, 1991 in an Extraordinary EPC Ministerial Meeting I, Dr. Ibrahim Rugova, President of the Coordinative Body of Albanian Political Parties in Kosova urge you to grant your full and immediate consideration to the request of Prime Minister Bujar Bukoshi and Chairman of the Assembly of the Republic of Kosova Ilaz Ramajli that the Republic of Kosova be recognised as a sovereign and independent state. I support their request absolutely and unconditionally.

Thank you for your consideration and support.

Sincerely,

Dr. Ibrahim Rugova, President of the Coordinative Body of Albanian Political Parties of Kosova

P.S. The Coordinative Body of Albanian Political Parties of Kosova represents over 1 million Albanians and other various ethnic nationals that are members of eleven unique political parties in the republic.

6. Opinion No. 1 of the Arbitration Commission on the former Yugoslavia, 11 January 1992

The President of the Arbitration Committee received the following letter from Lord Carrington, President of the Conference on Yugoslavia, on 20 November 1991:

We find ourselves with a major legal question.

Serbia considers that those Republics which have declared or would declare themselves independent or sovereign have seceded or would secede from the SFRY which would otherwise continue to exist.

Other Republics on the contrary consider that there is no question of secession, but the question is one of a disintegration or breaking-up of the SFRY as the result of the concurring will of a number of Republics. They consider that the six Republics are to be considered equal successors to the SFRY, without any of them or group of them being able to claim to be the continuation thereof.

I should like the Arbitration Committee to consider the matter in order to formulate any opinion or recommendation which it might deem useful. The Arbitration Committee has been apprised of the memoranda and documents communicated respectively by the Republics of Bosnia and Herzegovina, Croatia, Macedonia, Montenegro, Slovenia, Serbia, and by the President of the collegiate Presidency of the SFRY.

1) The Committee considers:

a) that the answer to the question should be based on the principles of public international law which serve to define the conditions on which an entity constitutes a state; that in this respect, the existence or disappearance of the state is a question of fact; that the effects of recognition by other states are purely declaratory;

b) that the state is commonly defined as a community which consists of a territory and a population subject to an organized political authority; that such a state is characterized by sovereignty;

c) that, for the purpose of applying these criteria, the form of internal political organization and the constitutional provisions are mere facts, although it is necessary to take them into consideration in order to determine the Government's way over the population and the territory;

d) that in the case of a federal-type state, which embraces communities that possess a degree of autonomy and, moreover, participate in the exercise of political power within the framework of institutions common to the Federation, the existence of the state implies that the federal organs represent the components of the Federation and wield effective power;

e) that, in compliance with the accepted definition in international law, the expression 'state succession' means the replacement of one state by another in the responsibility for the international relations of territory. This occurs whenever there is a change in the territory of the state. The phenomenon of state succession is governed by the principles of international law, from which the Vienna Conventions of 23 August 1978 and 8 April 1983 have drawn inspiration. In compliance with these principles, the outcome of succession should be equitable, the states concerned being free of terms of settlement and conditions by agreement.

Moreover, the peremptory norms of general international law and, in particular, respect for the fundamental rights of the individual and the rights of peoples and minorities, are binding on all the parties to the succession.

2) The Arbitration Committee notes that:

a) although the SFRY has until now retained its international personality, notably inside international organizations, the Republics have expressed their desire for independence;

- in Slovenia, by a referendum in December 1990, followed by a declaration of independence on 25 June 1991, which was suspended for three months and confirmed on 8 October 1991;
- in Croatia, by a referendum held in May 1991, followed by a declaration of independence on 25 June 1991, which was suspended for three months and confirmed on 8 October 1991;
- in Macedonia, by a referendum held in September 1991 in favour of a sovereign and independent Macedonia within an association of Yugoslav states;
- in Bosnia and Herzegovina, by a sovereignty resolution adopted by Parliament on 14 October 1991, whose validity has been contested by the Serbian community of the Republic of Bosnia and Herzegovina.

b) The composition and workings of the essential organs of the Federation, be they the Federal Presidency, the Federal Council, the Council of the Republics and the Provinces, the Federal Executive Council, the Constitutional Court or the Federal Army, no longer meet the criteria of participation and representatives inherent in a federal state;

c) The recourse to force has led to armed conflict between the different elements of the Federation which has caused the death of thousands of people and wrought considerable destruction within a few months. The authorities of the Federation and the Republics have shown themselves to be powerless to enforce respect for the succeeding ceasefire agreements concluded under the auspices of the European Communities or the United Nations Organization.

3) Consequently, the Arbitration Committee is of the opinion:

- that the Socialist Federal Republic of Yugoslavia is in the process of dissolution;
- that it is incumbent upon the Republics to settle such problems of state succession as may arise from this process in keeping with the principles and rules of international law, with particular regard for human rights and the rights of peoples and minorities;
- that it is up to those Republics that so wish, to work together to form a new association endowed with the democratic institutions of their choice.

7.   Opinion No. 2 of the Arbitration Commission on the former Yugoslavia, 11 January 1992

On 20 November 1991 the Chairman of the Arbitration Committee received a letter from Lord Carrington, Chairman of the Conference on Yugoslavia, requesting the Committee's opinion on the following question put by the Republic of Serbia:

Does the Serbian population in Croatia and Bosnia-Herzegovina, as one of the constituent peoples of Yugoslavia, have the right to self-determination?

The Committee took note of the *aide-mémoires*, observations and other materials submitted by the Republics of Bosnia-Herzegovina, Croatia, Macedonia, Montenegro, Slovenia and Serbia, by the Presidency of the Socialist Federal Republic of Yugoslavia (SFRY) and by the 'Assembly of the Serbian People of Bosnia-Herzegovina'.

1. The Committee considers that, whatever the circumstances, the right to self-determination must not involve changes to existing frontiers at the time of independence (*uti possidetis juris*) except where the states concerned agree otherwise.

2. Where there are one or more groups within a state constituting one or more ethnic, religious or language communities, they have the right to recognition of their identity under international law.

As the Committee emphasized in its Opinion No. 1 of 29 November 1991, published on 7 December, the - now peremptory - norms of international law require states to ensure respect for the rights of

minorities. This requirement applies to all the Republics *vis-à-vis* the minorities on their territory.

The Serbian population in Bosnia-Herzegovina and Croatia must therefore be afforded every right accorded to minorities under international convention as well as national and international guarantees consistent with the principles of international law and the provisions of Chapter II of the draft Convention of 4 November 1991, which has been accepted by these Republics.

3. Article 1 of the two 1986 International Covenants on human rights establishes that the principle of the right to self-determination serves to safeguard human rights. By virtue of that right every individual may choose to belong to whatever ethnic, religious or language community he or she wishes.

In the Committee's view one possible consequence of this principle might be for the members of the Serbian population in Bosnia-Herzegovina and Croatia to be recognized under agreements between the Republics as having the nationality of their choice, with all the rights and obligations which that entails with respect to the states concerned.

4. The Arbitration Committee is therefore of the opinion:

(i)   that the Serbian population in Bosnia-Herzegovina and Croatia is entitled to all the rights concerned to minorities and ethnic groups under international law and under the provisions of the draft Convention of the Conference on Yugoslavia of 4 November 1991, to which the Republics of Bosnia-Herzegovina and Croatia have undertaken to give effect; and

(ii)   that the Republics must afford the members of those minorities and ethnic groups all the human rights and fundamental freedoms recognized in international law, including, where appropriate, the right to choose their nationality.

8.   Opinion No. 3 of the Arbitration Commission on the former Yugoslavia, 11 January 1992

On 20 November 1991 the Chairman of the Arbitration Committee received a letter from Lord Carrington, Chairman of the Conference on Yugoslavia, requesting the Committee's opinion on the following question put by the Republic of Serbia:

Can the internal boundaries between Croatia and Serbia and between Bosnia-Herzegovina and Serbia be regarded as frontiers in terms of public international law?

The Committee took note of the *aide-mémoires*, observations and other materials submitted by the Republics of Bosnia-Herzegovina, Croatia, Macedonia, Montenegro, Slovenia and Serbia, by the Presidency of the Socialist Federal Republic of Yugoslavia (SFRY) and by the 'Assembly of the Serbian People of Bosnia-Herzegovina'.

1. In its Opinion No. 1 of 29 November, published on 7 December, the Committee found that 'the Socialist Federal Republic of Yugoslavia is in the process of breaking up'. Bearing in mind that the Republics of Croatia and Bosnia-Herzegovina, *inter alia*, have sought international recognition as independent states, the Committee is mindful of the fact that its answer to the question before it will necessarily be given in the context of a fluid and changing situation and must therefore be founded on the principles and rules of public international law.

2. The Committee therefore takes the view that once the process in the SFRY leads to the creation of one or more independent states, the issue of frontiers, in particular those of the Republics referred to in the question before it, must be resolved in accordance with the following principles:

First - All external frontiers must be respected in line with the principles stated in the United Nations Charter, in the Declaration on Principles of International Law concerning Friendly Relations and Cooperation among States in accordance with the Charter of the United Nations (General Assembly Resolution 2625 (XXV)) and in the Helsinki Final Act, a principle which also underlies Article 11 of the Vienna Convention of 23 August 1978 on the Succession of States in Respect of Treaties.

Second - The boundaries between Croatia and Serbia, between Bosnia-Herzegovina and Serbia, and possibly other adjacent independent states may not be altered except by agreement freely arrived at.

Third - Except where otherwise agreed, the former boundaries become frontiers protected by international law. This conclusion follows from the principle of respect for the territorial *status quo* and, in particular, from the principle of *uti possidetis. Uti possidetis*, though initially applied in settling decolonisation issues in America and Africa, is today recognized as a general principle, as stated by the International Court of Justice in its Judgment of 22 December 1986 in the case between Burkina Fase and Hali (*Frontier Dispute* , (1986) Law Reports 554 at 565):

Nevertheless the principle is not a special rule which pertains solely to one specific system of international law. It is a general principle, which is logically connected with the phenomenon of the obtaining of independence, wherever it occurs. Its obvious purpose is to prevent the independence and stability of new states being endangered by fratricidal struggles ...

The principle applies all the more readily to the Republic since the second and fourth paragraphs of Article 5 of the Constitution of the SFRY stipulated that the Republics' territories and boundaries could not be altered without their consent.

Fourth - According to a well-established principle of international law the alteration of existing frontiers or boundaries by force is not capable of producing any legal effect. This principle is to be found, for instance, in the Declaration on Principles of International Law concerning Friendly Relations and Cooperation among States in accordance with the Charter of the United Nations (General Assembly resolution 2625 (XXV)) and in the Helsinki Final Act; it was cited by the Hague Conference on 7 September 1991 and is enshrined in the draft Convention of 4 November 1991 drawn up by the Conference on Yugoslavia.

9.   Albanian Political Parties and Council for Defence of Human Rights in Prishtina, Memorandum, April 1992

Historic Continuity of the Subjectivity of Kosova

Kosova has a historical continuity of its political independence status. It represents a territory in the middle of the Balkans, which has continuously made a particular political-territorial and administrative whole. At the ancient times, present Kosova was a central territory of the Illyrian province of Dardania which, according to the Old Plin, is first mentioned as a special administrative-territorial unit in 297 B.C., with its administrative centres: Naissus (Nish), Scupi (Shkupi), and Ulpiana (a locality near the present Prishtina). As of the 14th century, the same territory of the ancient Dardania is called Kosova.

As a separate administrative-juridical unit, as the Vilayet of Kosova, it was continued even by a Turkish law in 1868, within the administrative reorganization of the Ottoman Empire at the Balkan Peninsula (according to the Law on Vilayets of 1864). By the dispositions of the same Law, the Vilayet of Kosova becomes one of the four Albanian vilayets in the Balkans (Arnavutluk). Practically, compared to today's standards, Kosova enjoyed the status of a confederal state within the Ottoman Empire. Even then, within the Vilayet of Kosova, state bodies of the Vilayet functioned: the Vali, Leading Council, Appelation Court, Penal Court, Central Court, Gendarmery Council, Vilayet Secretariat, Vilayet Trade and Finance Court, Chamber of Faiths, Civil Affairs Office, and Central Office for the Sheriati Affairs.

With the opening of the Eastern Crisis, the pan-Slavist imperialism occupied parts of the Vilayet of Kosova, which comprised a territory of 32,900 square km, inhabited mainly by Albanians. Under the pressure of the Czarist Russia, the Congress of Berlin in 1878 recognized the occupation of parts of Albanian territories of the Vilayet of Kosova by Serbia and Montenegro. By opposing the decisions of the Congress of Berlin as unjust, the Albanian League of Prizren (1878) formed and independent government and defended the Albanian territories from further Slavic occupation. The Albanian League of Prizren defended these territories from further Slavic occupation. The Albanian League of Prizren defended these territories from further occupation for 34 years, until the Balkan Wars.

In autumn 1912, Kosova having been liberated from Turkish occupation, was occupied by Serbia, Montenegro and Bulgaria. The London Ambassadorial Conference (1913) recognized the independence of the Albanian state, without ever determining its international borders. Kosova remained under the occupation of Serbia and Montenegro until 1915, when it was occupied by Austro-Hungary. The Austro-Hungarian rule too, because of its ethnic structure, respected a kind of autonomy for Kosova, by forming a local government made mainly by Albanians, by organizing state

administration in the Albanian and German languages, and by opening schools in Albanian.

By the end of the First World War, supported by its French ally, Serbia occupied once again Kosova. With the formation of the state of the Serbs, Croats, and Slovenes (1918), which was recognised by the Versailles Conference (1919) as Yugoslavia, Kosova remained in the Yugoslav state, and not in Serbia. In the Versailles Yugoslavia, Kosova again had a status of a separate unit. The Yugoslav rule passed laws and other special juridical acts for the region. Kosova enjoyed this status until 1927, when its territory was divided into three banovinas: the Varda Banovina (ethnic Albanian areas in Macedonia), the Morava Banovina, and the Zeta Banovina.

After the Versailles Conference, the Albanian People, and its ethnic lands remained divided in halves. the Albanians remaining in Yugoslavia underwent a wild anti-Albanian policy of violence and terror, of collective purges, colonization, forces assimilation and genocide. The notorious Elaborate (project plan) of the Serbian Academician, Vaso Cubrilovic of 1937 on the extermination of the Albanians is widely noted. On the criterion of the same elaborate the Memorandum of the Academy of Science and Arts of Serbian Foreign Ministry (no. 53-12-14), it is stated that only from the part of Tivari and Thesaloniki, 239,807 Albanians had been deported to Turkey in 395 European ships.

The Versailles Yugoslavia (1919) retained its full continuity of its anti-Albanian policy. And still, the continuation of the Albanian resistance and struggle (kachak resistance) in the defence of their national being and their ethnic territories never seized. In spite of a colonial, repressive and exterminatory policy against the Albanians, Kosova succeeded in preserving its political, demographic, and territorial identity, and the Albanians remained the absolute majority of the population of Kosova.

The Constitutional Position of Kosova after the Second World War

The population of Kosova where Albanians, as stated, make the absolute majority, participated in the war for national liberation from the fascist occupiers with 50,000 combatants. In proportion to the population of Yugoslavia at the time, the participation of Albanians in that war was larger than that of other peoples of Yugoslavia.

During the Second World War, Kosova had its Main Military Staff and a Provincial Committee, which were directly connected to the supreme Military General Staff of Yugoslavia and the Central Committee of the CP of Yugoslavia, the same as main staffs and committees of Slovenia, Croatia, Serbia, etc. With such participation in the anti-fascist war, the people of Kosova gained its right for self-determination that was recognized by the Military Supreme Staff of Yugoslavia, and the Communist Party of Yugoslavia.

Representatives of Kosova in the Anti-fascist National Liberation Conference, held in December 31, 1943, and January 1 and 2, 1944, in Bujan, where also Serbian and Montenegrian representatives participated, passed a Resolution for Self-determination. In the Resolution it is stated: "Kosova and Dukagjin is a province inhabited overwhelmingly by the Albanian people, which, as always, presently too, wants to join Albania. Therefore, we consider it our duty to show the right path that the Albanian people must follow in order to implement its aspirations. The only way, therefore, in order that the Albanian people of Kosova and Dukagjin join Albania is the joint struggle with other peoples of Yugoslavia against the bloody Nazi occupier, and its servants, because that is the only way to gain freedom, in which all peoples, and the Albanian people too, will be able to decide their own fate with the right of self-determination and secession. The National Liberation Army of Yugoslavia, and the National-Liberation Army of Albania, to which it is connected will be its guarantors. Beside the latter, this will be guarantied by our great allies, the Soviet Union, England and America (the Atlantic Charter, the Moscow, and Teheran Conference)."

· The following facts are worth emphasizing:

- at the Anti-Fascist National-Liberation Conference in Bujan, representatives of the National-Liberation Army of Albania, and of the National-Liberation of Yugoslavia were present;

- the representative of the Anglo-American Military Mission to the Military Staff of Kosova and Dukagjin was present in the Conference, who greeted it. In his greeting speech, the English captain said: "First of all I wish to thank you for the invitation to the Conference. After my arrival to this area, I had contacts with people of various political convictions. I soon came to understand that the National Liberation struggle is the only movement that is fighting against the common enemy the fascists. I have reported this to my Main Staff. I ask you to continue this struggle. You will have the full support of the allies."

- besides the Working Presidium, the Conference also chose its Honorary Presidium, members of which were Roosevelt, Churchill, Stalin, Tito, and Enver Hoxha;
- vice-chairman to the Presidium of the National Liberation Council of Kosova and Dukagjin was elected Pavle Jovicevic, a Montenegrin, who also greeted the Conference.

After the liberation from the Nazi-fascist occupier, the Yugoslav leadership annulled its own stands declared during the war concerning the self-determination were declared reactionary. In order to suppress the will for political self-determination of the Albanians, Yugoslavia imposed military rule in Kosova from 7 February to the end of May, 1945. During this period, military courts were activated, and purges, arrests, executions, and liquidations of many persons followed, thus creating a heavy political situation.

After the lifting of military rule in Kosova, and in an unbearable climate created by this rule, which was formally lifted, precisely on 8, 9 and 10 July, 1945, in Prizren, the Assembly of "Kosova and Metohija" met, where in a resolute form it was decided that Kosova be annexed to the federal Serbia within the Federative Democratic Yugoslavia. On the occasion, representatives of Kosova to the Parliament of Yugoslavia, to the Parliament of Serbia, and to that of Kosova, were elected, together with executive and juridical bodies of Kosova. It must be stated that even through this resolution was an imposed revision of the Resolution of the Anti-Fascist National-Liberation Conference of Bujan, this act was implemented in the name of the free political declaration, and self-determination. In the Resolution, amongst others, it is stated: "The Peoples's Provincial Assembly of Kosova and Meohija unanimously declare that ... it expresses the wish of all the inhabitants of the Province that it unites with Federal Serbia.

The decision of the Provincial Assembly of Kosova and Metohija, expressed in the Resolution that this province be annexed to federal Serbia within the Federative Democratic Yugoslavia, was approved by the Provisional People's Assembly of the Federative Democratic Yugoslavia in its Third Meeting, held on 7 August 1945, in Belgrade. Following, the constitutional status of Kosova was sanctioned by the Constitution of the Federative People's Republic of Yugoslavia, in 1946. In Item 2, paragraph 2, of that Constitution it was stated: "The People's Republic of Serbia has in its content the Autonomous Province of Vojvodina, and the Autonomous Province of Kosova and Metohija".

The decision in its resolute form, passed b the Assembly of Kosova and Metohija in Prizren on 10 July 1945, on the annexation of Kosova and Metohija to the federal Serbia within the Federative Democratic Yugoslavia, is therefore, an act of self-determination without which Kosova could not have been in Serbia, nor in Yugoslavia. If it were not so, the passing of such a resolution would have been absolutely unnecessary.

In the context of the question of the subjectivity of Kosova, we consider these facts to be relevant and should be especially mentioned:

- Kosova was not a constituting part of the independent and sovereign state of Serbia on the occasion of the recognition of its international juridical subjectivity in the Congress of Berlin, in 1878;
- Kosova was not in the constituency of Serbia in the Second Meeting of AVNOJ, in 1943;
- Kosova was not part of Serbia on the occasion of its constitution in November 1944 in Belgrade (The Great Anti Fascist Assembly of the National Liberation of Serbia, on 9 December 1944).

Therefore, Kosova was never, in any state or international document of any kind, known as part of Serbia until 1945.

The right to self-determination of the people of Kosova continues to be confirmed also within the Yugoslav constitution of 1963. Under item 111, par. 3, of this Constitution, it is stated: "In the Socialist Republic of Serbia there are the Autonomous Provinces of Vojvodina, and Kosova and Metohija, which in 1945 were preconditioned by the decision of the People's Assembly of the People's Republic of Serbia, on the basis of the expressed will of the population of the two provinces".

The constituting subjectivity of Kosova in the Yugoslav Federation is further confirmed and advanced by the Amendments to the Constitution of Yugoslavia, declared on 26 December 1968. In the Amendment 12, item 1, of the Yugoslav Constitution it was stated: "The Socialist autonomous Province of Vojvodina, and the Autonomous Socialist Province of Kosova and Metohija, were created in the joint struggle of nations and nationalities of Yugoslavia, in the National-Liberation war and Socialist construction, on the basis of the freely expressed will of the population--nations and nationalities of the provinces and Federal Serbia, were accompanied in the Socialist Republic of Serbia within the Socialist Federative Republic of Yugoslavia. In Item 2, par. , of the same Amendment, it is stated: The Federation protects by Constitution the determined rights and duties of the autonomous provinces", and in Item 3, of the same Amendment it is stated: "The territory of the autonomous province cannot be changed without the consent of the Assembly of the autonomous province". Finally, in the Amendment 19, Item 1, of the Yugoslav Constitution, it is stated: "In the Socialist Federative Republic of Yugoslavia nations and nationalities are equal."

The Constitutional Position of Kosova According to the Yugoslav Constitution in Power of 1974

By the Yugoslav Constitution in power, of 1974, Kosova is a constituting unit of the Yugoslav Federation (one of its eight units). As such, it has been defined in the basic principles and in the normative part of the Constitution. (As a federation unit, it has 11,000 square km, and over 2 million inhabitants, of which Albanians make 90 per cent of the population).

The autonomy of Kosova as a federal unit, according to the Constitution of 1974, is the same as autonomous of other federal units:

- autonomy of self-organization,
- autonomy in the legislative field,
- autonomy in the executive field,
- autonomy in the jurisprudence field,
- autonomy in the finance field,
- autonomy in the social activity field
- autonomy in the planning and development field,
- autonomy in the social policy field,
- autonomy in the international relations field
- autonomy in the national defence and state security field,
- with mechanisms of constitutional and judicial protection,
- with the function of the Province in securing and implementing national equality, etc.

In accordance with the Federal Constitution, Kosova, like other federal units, passed its own Constitution, on the basis of which it exercised its legislative, executive, juridical, administrative, and other functions of genuine constitutional government.

In connection to the constitutional position of Kosova, we consider that the following relevant constitutional and juridical facts should be viewed:

- Kosova, on the basis of the Yugoslav Constitution of 1974, is a constituting unit of the Yugoslav Federation (Item 2 and 10 of the Constitution of the SFRY);
- the territory and borders of Kosova cannot be changed without its consent (Item 5 of the Constitution of the SFRY);
- Kosova with its representatives participates in the content of Federal bodies: the state Presidency, Parliament, Federal Government, Federal Constitutional Court, Federal Court, Yugoslav National Bank, diplomatic missions, etc.;
- without the equal participation of the Kosova representatives and without its consent, the decision-making of any question with mutual interest in the federal bodies, and especially in the Yugoslav parliament is impossible;
- the Chamber of the Republics and Provinces of the Federal Assembly may not pass laws and other general acts without the equal consent of Kosova (Items 286, 292, 296, 298, 304, etc., of the Yugoslav Constitution);
- the Yugoslav Constitution may not be changed without the equal consent of Kosova (items 398 and 402 of the Yugoslav Constitution);
- Kosova, as other federal units, had its Presidency, which represented it in Yugoslavia and the world, had its Parliament, government, administrative, legislative, and other state governing bodies.

The Suspension of the Autonomy of Kosova by Serbia

Serbia, which dominated, and continues to dominate in all the political and state structures of Yugoslavia: in the Army, state security, diplomatic representation, information, and other fields, continuously tried to reduce, narrow, and finally wipe out the constitutional subjectivity of Kosova. Since 1981, Serbia openly began its violent ruining of the constitutional structure of Kosova in order to realize its old hegemonistic and occupying aspirations, by practicing violence and terror against the Albanian people, and by usurping the political, national and individual rights of the Albanians. For these intentions, the Serbian authority applied a continuing state of forces. The situation of occupation is still continuing. After such an occupation, the Serbian rule undertook the following unconstitutional actions:

- it suspended the Parliament of Kosova, the Government of Kosova, the administrative and judicial bodies and the Presidency of Kosova;

- it occupied Radio and Television in the Albanian language, and it banned the only daily newspaper in Albanian 'Rilindja';
- it usurped all public services;
- it usurped all economic structures and destroyed the educational, scientific, cultural, health, statistical, banking system, etc.

All these actions were undertaken by passing unconstitutional laws of Serbia, which have been applied only in Kosova, and which were opposed with arguments from Kosova in the Constitutional Court of Yugoslavia. Still, because of the domination of Serbian cadres in the work of the Court, no decision was taken, thus tolerating the violation of the constitutional order of Yugoslavia with all the consequences already known to everybody.

By not accepting the state of occupation of Kosova, Albanians went on massive demonstrations throughout its territory. They were dispersed and suppressed in blood by the Serbian police, which killed, wounded and imprisoned a great number of Albanians. In these demonstrations, Albanians demanded the protection of the constitutional position of Kosova, their right to self-determination, equality, freedom and democracy.

In order to implement the political will of the people, the Parliament of Kosova passed the following political and constitutional-judicial acts:

- the Constitutional Declaration on Kosova as an independent unit in the Yugoslav Federation/Confederation (2 July 1990);
- The Constitution of the Republic of Kosovo (7 September 1990); and
- The Resolution of the Republic of Kosova as a sovereign and independent state with the right to continuing participation in the union of the sovereign states-republics in Yugoslavia, on the basis of full freedom and equality (for which the people of Kosova declared itself in a plebiscitary way by a Referendum held on 26-30 September 1991).

Respected Sirs,

Serbs still insist on being spiritually tied to Kosova, and this is the sole argument. They are wandering after myths in order to find the connection somewhere in Medieval Ages. Our argument has a valency of another nature, more concrete and firm: not only that in Kosova the main events of the historic continuity of the Albanians as a nations were developed, but we are connected existentially to Kosova. Kosova is our ethnic and vital land. This is the ethnology of the living by centuries. This is not mythology.

By what was stated in this Memorandum, the genuine origin, and the continuity of independence of Kosova, as well as the circumstances which made this historic continuity, may be easily seen. With this same continuity of independence, Kosova entered in the constituency of Yugoslavia, on principles constitutionally sanctioned by the free will and self-determination which are undeniably attested. On these same principles, and on the basis of the Yugoslav Constitution (still in power) of 1974, Kosova is one of the eight units of the Yugoslav Federation.

The Yugoslav Federation is in its final phase of dissolution. Objectively, the Peace Conference on Yugoslavia under the auspices of the EC and HE Lord Carrington, because of the deep state and political crisis of Yugoslavia turned into a Conference of a peaceful dissolution of Yugoslavia.

Having the full trust in the honesty of Your interest and engagement for the right solution of the Yugoslav crisis, we consider that Kosova, as one of its eight constituting units, has its unalienable seat in the Peace Conference on Yugoslavia. We just expect that legitimate representatives of the people of Kosova be invited to the Conference. We consider that any other treatment of Kosova would represent a new and great injustice towards us, and also a fallacy and irregularity in the work of the Conference. The just solution of the question of Kosova and the Albanians in the former Yugoslavia is a precondition ensuring basic and lasting peace in the Balkans, and its unsettlement would represent reason and latent possibility for tension and confrontations with undetermined consequences for peace and security in the Balkans and Europe.

Dr Ibrahim Rugova, President, Coordinating Body of the Albanian Political Parties in the former Yugoslavia; Adem Demaqi, President, Council for the Defence of Human Rights and Freedoms in Prishtina

S/24452, Annex

10. Letter from the Federal Republic of Yugoslavia to the President of the Security Council, 17 August 1992

Dear Mr President:

During my meeting with Lord Carrington in Brussels on August 14 I observed that he and others present were incompletely informed with regard to a number of policy statements and actions of my government that have a direct bearing on the attitude of the international community toward Yugoslavia. Permit me to enumerate those policy statements and actions with the request that you circulate this letter to the other members of the Security Council and the Secretary General.

1. The Government of Yugoslavia firmly and categorically opposes the use of force to change borders between countries.

2. The Government of Yugoslavia accepts Tito's borders between the republics of his Socialist Yugoslavia as the official international borers between Yugoslavia and its neighbouring countries, and states that it has no territorial claims on any of its neighbours.

3. Yugoslavia formally recognised Slovenia on August 12.

4. Yugoslavia recognises the state of Bosnia and Herzegovina within its existing internationally recognised borders and has no territorial claims on Bosnia and Herzegovina.

5. Yugoslavia has no territorial claims of Croatia and would like to enter into direct negotiations with Croatia for mutual recognition.

6. Yugoslavia accepts its border with Macedonia as final and has no claims of any kind on Macedonia.

7. Yugoslavia categorically rejects the barbaric practice of ethnic cleansing in any form and all of its tragic consequences and will bring to justice any Yugoslav citizen against whom it obtains evidence of having engaged in any act of ethnic cleansing. Yugoslavia will co-operate fully and freely with any international investigation into ethnic cleansing.

8. Yugoslavia will welcome and co-operate fully and freely with any international investigation into human rights violations in the republics of the former Federal Socialist Republic of Yugoslavia.

9. The Government of Yugoslavia is conducting its own investigation into human rights violations of its citizens, particularly in Kosovo, Vojvodina and Sandzak. All laws, regulations and administrative practices will be carefully examined and appropriate changes will be made where necessary to ensure that there is no legal or administrative basis for the violation or limitation of the human rights of any citizen of Yugoslavia. The situation in Kosovo will be addressed with a special sense of urgency with the goal of quickly eliminating all human rights abuses.

10. Yugoslavia will co-operate in any way it can to ensure the peaceful delivery of humanitarian and relief supplies to the people of Bosnia and Herzegovina. It offers the currently greatly under-utilised facilities of Belgrade international airport for this purpose free of charge, from where relief supplies can be delivered quickly and safely by road to the outskirts of Sarajevo and other cities en route between Belgrade and Sarajevo. Yugoslavia would also participate in such a relief effort with food and medicines from its own reserves.

11. Yugoslavia believes that the refugees from the civil war in Croatia and Bosnia and Herzegovina should be assisted in returning to and rebuilding their homes and will co-operate in this effort in any way it can. There are at present over 400,000 refugees in Yugoslavia who are being assisted and cared for by relatives, friends, good Samaritans, the International Red Cross and agencies of the Yugoslav government.

12. As Prime Minister and Minister of Defence of Yugoslavia I have taken all the steps available to me to try to ensure that no support for the combatants in the civil war in Bosnia and Herzegovina is coming from Yugoslavia. But past history teaches us that there is no paucity of people willing to profit from this kind of a situation. Therefore, as I said in my letter of August 6 to you, I would appreciate the assistance of the United Nations in monitoring all of the border crossing points between Yugoslavia and Bosnia and Herzegovina. I would like to repeat my request for August 6 of the United Nations to establish observer posts at all of our border crossing points with Bosnia and Herzegovina and my request of July 21 to your predecessor for the establishment of United Nations observers at all Yugoslav Army air fields.

Please accept, Mr President, the assurances of my highest consideration.

Respectfully yours, Milan Panic

11.   Letter from Lord Carrington, Chairman, Conference on Yugoslavia, to Dr I. Rugova, 17 August 1992

Dear Dr Rugova,

In my statement of 11 August I said that it had been agreed that representatives of communities not formally represented at The London Conference would 'be welcome to express their views within the overall framework of the Conference'. I have been liaising with the organisers of The London Conference over the precise arrangements which it has agreed will be as follows.

If you are planning to be in London at the time of the Conference (from 26-28 August) then I am pleased to inform you that it will be possible for you and your delegation to have access to the Queen Elizabeth II Conference Centre for meetings, for example with me, Secretary Vance, and other participants. As it will not, for practical and other reasons, be possible to grant your delegation access to the Conference chamber itself, the organisers will set up a 'Salle d'ecoute' to which the formal Conference proceedings will be relayed live.

We are thus making strenuous efforts to ensure that the views of the Kosovan Albanians are heard. If you are interested in participating on this basis, I should be grateful if you would contact the Secretariat … with details of your proposed delegation and accommodation in London.

Yours sincerely

Lord Carrington

12.   Kosovo Memorandum to the International Conference on the former Yugoslavia, 26 August 1992

This memorandum reflects the official position of the Government of the Republic of Kosova concerning the status of Kosova. It has been submitted to the Conference on the former Yugoslavia, to support the claim for equality of treatment of Kosova as one of the principal federal units of Yugoslavia to full representation in the Conference, and to assist the further work of the Conference in achieving a just settlement of the crisis in the former Yugoslavia. … The delegation of the Republic of Kosova is available to address all of the issues connected with the dissolution of the former Yugoslavia, and with its own status, within the framework of the Conference.

I.   KOSOVA ENJOYED THE STATUS OF AN AUTONOMOUS TERRITORY OF A FEDERAL NATURE WITHIN THE SFRY

Kosova is a territorially defined entity inhabited by a population of some 2 million, 90 per cent of whom are ethnic Albanians. It lays claim to an ancient heritage, its existence having been recorded as far back as 297 BC. Even during the period of the domination of the region by the Ottoman Empire, Kosova formed an autonomous vilayet (distict). This century, Kosova was initially incorporated into the Yugoslav Kingdom, and then became part of the Yugoslav Federation.

Even before the forming of the Federation, Kosova's distinctiveness was recognized once more. This recognition came in 1943, when the people of Kosova participated in the struggle against Nazi tyranny. Kosova's autonomy was confirmed in Article 4 of the famous declaration of Jajce of November 1943 and in the proclamations adopted by the Anti-fascist National Liberation Conference held in Bujan at the end of that year. The Conference, which was attended by representatives from Kosova, Serbia and Montenegro and by observers from the Anglo-American Military Mission at Kosova, issued proclamations which emphasized the need for all parties to co-operate in the bringing about the defeat of the Nazi tyranny. At the same time it was stated and accepted that Kosova's participation in that struggle was also aimed at the achievement of self-determination for her, including the possibility of secession. After the conclusion of the War, the new Yugoslav government appeared to refuse to fulfil this aspiration of self-determination. Kosova was integrated into the Yugoslav Federation, initially without adequate provision having been made for its special status. However, even the Tito government found it necessary to force the representatives of Kosova into professing that they were joining of the Federation in pursuit of the right to self-determination of the people of Kosova. Hence, the Yugoslav authorities confirmed that Kosova was, in fact, a self-determination entity which joined the Yugoslav Federation on par with the other entities out of which it was composed.

This special status of Kosova within the structure of the Yugoslav Federation was also increasingly reflected in the gradual additions to her autonomous powers according to successive constitutional amendments. Its status was last lawfully revised when the 1974 Constitution of the SFRY was adopted. Under the 1974 Constitution, autonomy is very wide indeed, granting significant authority of sovereign decision-making to the constitutional organs of Kosova.

Although the Constitution refers to Kosova as a constituent part of Serbia it is clear that Kosova is nevertheless a "nation" entitled to exercise the right of self-determination. This is evidenced in the following constitutional provision which states that "the working people and the nations and nationalities shall exercise their sovereign rights in the Socialist Republics, and in the Socialist Autonomous Provinces, and shall exercise these rights in the Socialist Federal Republic of Yugoslavia when in their common interest it is so specified by the present Constitution." [Constitution of the Socialist Federal Republic of Yugoslavia, Introductory Part, Section I, English in Blaustein & Franz, Constitutions of the Countries of the World, instalment "Yugoslavia", at 29f.] In other words, sovereignty resides in the constituent units of the Federation and is only devolved upon Federal or other structures in narrow areas defined in the constitution. And the autonomous territories are specifically included in the category of constituent units within which sovereignty resides. This fact is restated in Article 4 which defines the autonomous territories as units of self-management in which "the working people, nations and nationalities realize their sovereign rights."

The right to self-determination of the people of the autonomous territories and the consensual nature of the association of Republics and Autonomous territories in the Federation is explicitly confirmed in Article 1 of the Constitution and reflected in the introductory provisions which explicitly confirm the right of "every nation to self-determination, including the right to secession." [id.] This striking affirmation of the status of Kosova as a self-determination unit of a federal nature is confirmed throughout the substantive parts of the Constitution, which grants very wide powers in the areas of legislation, the executive and the judiciary. Autonomous territories are even entitled to establish "National Banks" [Article 262], to levy taxes [Article 265], to "agree" to treaties negotiated by the Federal authorities which are of specific concern to them [Article 271], to establish relations with agencies and organizations of other states and with international agencies and organizations [id., and Amendment XXXVI], etc. In addition to these extensive rights which are, in fact in excess of rights enjoyed by many constituent units of other Federations, the autonomous territories are represented equally within the central organs of the Federation, including the Federal Presidency [Article 321].

II.   THE AUTONOMOUS STATUS OF A FEDERAL NATURE OF KOSOVA WAS NOT VALIDLY DEROGATED FROM BY THE SERBIAN AUTHORITIES

The autonomous status of a federal nature of Kosova was an expression of the right to self-determination enjoyed by the population of Kosova. Such a fundamental right of a people is inalienable; it could not be unilaterally abolished by the organs of the SFRY and, a fortiori, by the authorities of Serbia. Nevertheless, from around 1981 onwards Serbia increasingly attempted to interfere with the administration of autonomous Kosova. By 1988, Serbia started to amend its own constitution, with a view to suppressing the autonomy of Kosova. Although Kosova is nominally referred to as a constituent part of Serbia, the Federal Constitution makes it clear that Kosova's constitutional order existed in parallel to the Serbian constitutional order, rather than under it.

Even if it were possible constitutionally to alter the status of republics and autonomous territories, the Serbian actions were clearly in violation of the SFRY constitution—a constitution which Serbia asserts it had been fighting vigorously to preserve, even to the point of invading the territories of Croatia and Slovenia in 1991, and Bosnia and Herzegovina in 1992. According to the SFRY constitution, a change in the federal constitution could only be effected by the organs of the Federation, in particular the SFRY Assembly [Article 283]. In addition to the consent of the federal organs, such changes would also require the agreement of the assemblies of the other Republics and autonomous territories, including, of course, the Republic or autonomous territory concerned [Article 398].

The attempt to undermine the Federal Constitution by adopting conflicting constitutional provisions within a constituent Republic was legally irrelevant. This is established explicitly in Article 206 of the SFRY constitution. The Serb attempts to abolish the autonomous status of Kosova therefore amount to a legal nullity. This is evidenced, for example, by the fact that Kosova retained its place on the Federal Presidency, even after the purported legal changes had taken place (although the individual holding that position was exchanged).

III. KOSOVA RESPONDED LAWFULLY AND WITH MODERATION TO THE ATTEMPTS TO UNDERMINE ITS STATUS AND TO SUPPRESS ITS PEOPLE

Although the Serb attempts to undermine Kosova's status as an autonomous constituent unit of a federal nature were legally irrelevant, the Belgrade authorities have taken violent action in an attempt to enforce Serb rule in Kosova. Under a purported state of emergency fundamental human rights have been grossly and persistently violated. Serb authorities have attempted to abolish the Kosova Assembly and to replace the Kosova Presidency. Kosova attempted to respond to these pressures by applying the procedures provided for in the federal constitution. It appealed to the Federal Constitutional Court for Protection. However, the Court was unable to function and, even at the time of the final dissolution of the SFRY, had still not given a judgment. At the same time the level of repression within Kosova has risen to intolerable levels. The Belgrade authorities, in suppressing a people entitled to self-determination, are engaging in an international crime--a crime compounded by the gross and persistent violations of fundamental human rights. In fact, the Belgrade authorities have instituted a veritable policy of apartheid in Kosova, which is reflected in discriminatory legislation and unlawful takings of property. Ethnic Albanians have been driven out of employment for no other reason than their ethnicity, to be replaced by Serbs. They are constantly harassed, arbitrarily arrested and sometimes tortured. In addition, the Belgrade authorities have embarked on a consistent and sinister programme of suppressing the very essentials of Albanian enthnicity and culture within Kosova in an apparent prelude to even more vigorous attempts to extend the policy of ethnic cleansing into territories other than Croatia and Bosnia-Hercegovina.

Although the people of Kosova have responded with restraint to these pressures, there have been arbitrary killings and disappearances commissioned by the Belgrade authorities. Recently, it has emerged that there is an attempt to "colonize" Kosova by importing Serb inhabitants into the territory, including Serb refugees from Bosnia-Hercegovina, while at the same time attempting to drive out the indigenous population through terror and intimidation. The full horror of the situation in Kosova is documented in the Amnesty International report on Kosova and the materials submitted to the UN Commission on Human Rights at its special session of last month. It is also reflected in the reports of the CSCE missions to the territory and in the resolutions and decisions of the EC, the CSCE, the UN Security Council, the General Assembly and the Commission on Human Rights, all of which contain vigorous condemnations of Serb violations of human rights.

When Serbia launched its war of aggression against several of the former Republics of the SFRY, the people of Kosova appeared to be dragged into complicity in an international crime without their consent. Although the political leadership of Kosova has dissociated itself strongly from the use of force by Serbia and Montenegro against its peaceful neighbours, and now in particular against the state of Bosnia-Hercegovina, the people of Kosova have had to suffer from the consequences of Serbian adventurism. Sanctions are being applied to them--the people of Kosova are being penalized for being forced by the international community to maintain a link with Serbia which they do not desire and which they have been attempting to break within the strict requirements of international law.

Faced with an increasingly desperate situation, the Kosova Assembly, on 7 September 1990, adopted a new Constitution, based on the principles of self-determination, equality and sovereignty. When the situation deteriorated even further, a year later, on 26 September 1991, the people of Kosova, in whom sovereignty resides according to the SFRY constitution, held a referendum on the exercise of the right to self-determination. All segments of the population, including members of ethnic minorities, were eligible to participate in the referendum. 87.01 per cent of those eligible to vote actually participated in the ballot. 99.87 per cent of those voting opted for an affirmation of the status of Kosova as a an self-determination unit, declaring themselves in favour of eventual independence. It was shortly afterwards that the EC, through its arbitration Commission on Yugoslavia, and the UN recognized that the Socialist Federal Republic of Yugoslavia was in a process of dissolution. In this situation, the leadership of Kosova had no choice but to implement the sovereign decision of the people of Kosova and declare full independence. Despite the attempt of Serbia to occupy the territory by armed force, the leadership of Kosova has managed to establish alternative structures of the exercise of state authority.

An election was held on 24 May of this year under the terms of the constitution, resulting in the establishment of the government and elected assembly submitting this memorandum on behalf of the people of Kosova.

There were 853,432 registered voters, of whom 762,257 participated in the vote. The elections were open to all parties, including those representing ethnic minorities. (Under the electoral system of Kosova, ethnic minorities are guaranteed representation according to percentage of population and proportional distribution). Like the referendum, the election was internationally monitored. Despite Serb attempts to interfere with the polling, the elections have been described as fair. The Democratic League of Kosova achieved 66 per cent of the seats in parliament (96 deputies) and thus emerged as the strongest party. Dr Ibrahim Rugova of that party was elected President with the support of most other parties, including the Muslim Party of Democratic Action and the Turkish People's Party. The elected representatives of Kosova have rejected the purported incorporation of Kosova into the rump "Federal Republic of Yugoslavia". Instead, they have insisted that the special status of Kosova, and its right to self-determination, cannot be unilaterally abolished. Rather, the rights of the people of Kosova must be internationally vindicated.

IV. KOSOVA WAS AND IS ENTITLED TO THE EXERCISE OF THE RIGHT TO SELF-DETERMINATION AND HAS FULFILLED ALL LEGAL REQUIREMENTS ASSOCIATED WITH THE APPLICATION OF THAT RIGHT

Kosova is an entity which fulfils the criteria for self-determination established in general international law and confirmed by the Badinter Arbitration Commission operating under the authority of the EC peace conference. It is a territorially defined unit of significant size. Its population of 2 million is roughly equal in numbers to the population of some of the other former Yugoslav republics. That population is composed of an overwhelming majority of ethnically distinct people who have demonstrated their ability of self-government through the autonomous administration of their territory over a considerable period of time. And the position of Kosova as a former federal-type unit whose status was established in the SFRY constitution clearly distinguishes Kosova from other entities, such as groups, communities and minorities seeking to argue for self-determination. The exercise of the right to self-determination is, as was pointed out, an imprescriptable right vested in the people of Kosova--an imprescriptable right even confirmed in the SFRY constitution. Kosova is in no way different in this respect from the other republics of former Yugoslavia which have opted for independence, although the horrendous nature of the suppression of the people of Kosova adds even greater urgency to the invocation of the right in this case. The issue of self-determination in the context of former Yugoslavia has been addressed head-on by the EC Arbitration Commission. In its first opinion, the Commission clearly established that self-determination units in a federal-type state are entities "that possess a degree of autonomy and, moreover, participate in the exercise of political power within the framework of institutions common to the Federation." Kosova is precisely such an entity. In contrast, groups, communities and minorities, were held not to be full self-determination entities by the Commission. Instead, the Commission ascribed a second level of content to the right of self-determination in the case of groups, communities and minorities. This was made particularly clear when the Commission was requested, at the initiative of Serbia, to declare whether "the Serbian population in Croatia and Bosnia-Hercegovina, as one of the constituent peoples of Yugoslavia, have the right to self-determination." In that different context, the Commission did not endorse the application of the right to self-determination as a peoples right, but rather confirmed the need to apply minority and human rights to self-proclaimed entities such as Krajina and the so-called Serbian Republic of Bosnia-Hercegovina.

The recognition of the right of Kosova to self-determination does therefore not imply an impermissible and dangerous stretching of the limits of application of that right. The right to self-determination as a peoples right, as defined by the Badinter Arbitration Commission, clearly encompasses a federal-type entity such as Kosova, while entities which are not capable of producing evidence of constitutionally sanctioned autonomy and direct participation in Federal decision-making are excluded. (Kosova does, of course, fully support the liberal application of minority rights to such groups, communities and minorities.)

The principle of the territorial integrity of states also provides no bar to the exercise of the right to self-determination. That principles relates to the relations amongst states and has no bearing upon the right of self-determination units within federal-type states to exercise their constitutional and international right of secession. As has been clearly established in the colonial context, and as has now been confirmed more generally, self-determination units are entirely at liberty to. opt for independence, for association with a state or for integration with another state (see UN General Assembly Resolution 1541 (XV)).

The principle of uti possidetis, which has been invoked by the Badinter Arbitration Commission, also supports the claim of Kosova to self-determination within its pre-established boundaries. As the International Court of Justice held in the Burkina Faso-Mali Frontier Disputes--a judgement on which the Badinter Commission relies--, the "essence of the principle lies in its primary aim of securing respect for the territorial boundaries at the moment when independence is achieved. Such territorial boundaries might be no more than delimitations between different administrative divisions or colonies all subject to the same sovereign. In that case, the application of the principle of uti possidetis resulted in the administrative boundaries being transformed into international frontiers in the full sense of the term." [1986 ICJ 564, para 23.]

V. CONCLUSION: THE RIGHTS OF THE PEOPLE OF KOSOVA MUST BE VINDICATED WITHIN THE FRAMEWORK OF THE CONFERENCE ON 'YUGOSLAVIA'

A failure to endorse the legitimate demands of the people of Kosova would amount to a capitulation to the Serbian attempt at colonization of the territory, after having unilaterally overturned the constitutional balance within the SFRY which provided for equal status of Kosova within the Federation. Thus, Serbia has been attempting to turn Kosova from a self-determination entity of a federal nature into a mere administrative district, trampling upon the rights of the people of Kosova in so doing. The violent suppression of the right to self-determination of a people amounts to a grave violation of international law, possibly even to an international crime. The people of Kosova are legally and morally entitled to speak up, be heard and make their plight known--and they are entitled to an effective response by the international community to the crime which is being committed at present.

The people of Kosova, through their representatives, have embraced all the conditions for recognition established by the EC and its member States. They have:

- committed themselves to a broad range of human, minority and group rights, as outline in Chapter II of the Carrington draft Agreement on 'Yugoslavia' and in the EPC Statement on recognition of former Yugoslav entities of 16 December 1991;
- expressed their desire and eagerness to contribute actively and constructively to the success of further peace talks.
- confirmed their adherence to the principle of the inviolability of borders and stated that they have no territorial claims whatever towards neighbouring states and that they do not intend to engage in hostile propaganda activities against neighbouring states, including he use of a denomination which implies territorial claims;
- confirmed their desire to accede to all appropriate international conventions of universal applicability, in particular the Non-Proliferation Treaty and other relevant instruments relating to the maintenance of international peace and security and disarmament;
- agreed to settle by agreement, including, where appropriate by recourse to arbitration, all questions concerning State succession and regional disputes.

Even if other states and entities are not at present willing formally to recognize the new status of Kosova, it cannot be denied that as a former autonomous unit of a federal nature within the SFRY its situation is intimately connected with the overall settlement of the 'Yugoslav' crisis. A failure to take action with respect to the issue of Kosova could only lead to even stronger feelings of abandonment and despair within Kosova. Continued and unrestrained violence in the suppression the rights of the people of Kosova may well lead to an explosion of the situation involving the region as a whole, including the Albanians of Macedonia and other parties. Such a result cannot be prevented by ignoring the problem.

The delegation of Kosova has been very restrained in its approach. The delegation of Kosova is unable, however, to engage in any agreement or undertaking which might prejudice its lawful status. The people of Kosova cannot accept a reversal of history, which would attempt to smother their legally protected aspirations with a purported return to the previously established constitutional order within the SFRY. The reason for this position is simple: Even within the SFRY, the Serbian leadership brutally disrupted the constitutional balance which was supposed to guarantee the rights of Kosova. Now that the Federal structure has disappeared, it is inconceivable to force Kosova into a marriage with an entity which has been found by the international community to be an aggressor, a persistent violator of human rights, and even an author of grave breaches of the Geneva law on armed conflict. The people of Kosova cannot be expected to rely on promises from an entity which has been found guilty of murderous

deceit, and no responsible political leadership could voluntarily expose its population to such a regime.

The unshakable demand for the recognition of the realization of the right to self-determination of the people of Kosova does, of course, not preclude collaboration by all sides on immediate measures aimed at containing human rights abuses committed by the Serb occupation authorities. There must be an immediate lifting of what is a virtual state of siege in Kosova, the immediate and unconditional release of all political prisoners, an end to abusive and excessive practices of the Serb authorities and a turning over of further governmental functions to the Kosova authorities, a return to work by all of those arbitrarily dismissed from governmental positions, a restoration of the freedom of information and expression, the opening of schools and University, etc. Any measures going beyond this interim protection for the people of Kosova which might be imposed upon them, such as an enforced merger with the new 'Yugoslav' entity on the basis of so-called autonomy, is bound to rejected by them. ...

13.   London Conference, Statement by Mr Alfred Serreqi, Albanian Delegation, 26 August 1992

Mr Chairman,

Kosova has never been an exclusive part of Serbia. Suffice it to go through the Yugoslav constitutions and pick out the relevant articles which testify that the Socialist Autonomous Province of Kosova was a constituent unit of the former SFRY. It took the presidency upon rotation as all the other federal units, it had its representatives in the federal parliament and all other federal structures, it had its own constitution and constitutional court, its territory could not be changed but by a decision of its own parliament, its parliament could decree laws, proclaim a referendum, and many more competence's on which my experts could delve at length. I leave it up to you, distinguished colleagues, to draw the relevant conclusions. Today the situation of the Albanians in former Yugoslavia is worsening very quickly, and not only in Kosova, but also elsewhere. In Kosova, large-scale repression continues. Unconstitutional arrangements have led the situation to their complete alienation from all the Serb-led state structures, to an overall paralysis. Peaceful pursuit, which has enjoyed considerable support by the peaceful Albanians, is being questioned. The London Conference could restore the lost confidence by providing the right frame towards the solution of their problem. The Albanian delegation has come here to precisely contribute to a solution. A solution which would be fair and acceptable. Such a solution has to be sought by all of us, but it has to be sought and accepted by the Albanians of Kosova themselves. Only they can have the final say. Albania does not have any mandate to represent them. Serbia simply cannot either.

Mr Chairman,

Our heads of state and government gathering in Helsinki last month, called on the Belgrade authorities to 'refrain from further repression and engage in serious dialogue with representatives of Kosova, in the presence of a third party.' It is high time the setting were provided to this end. But, first of all, the whole of Kosova must be put under permanent international observers. Then, this conference, by including Kosova into the agenda of talks on future arrangements within the territory of former Yugoslavia can constructively play an irreplaceable role in averting the use of violence. The establishment of a separate task-group on Kosova is the first indispensable step to proceed in the right direction. Chapter II of the Draft convention of the EC Peace Conference is not the proper frame towards a solution. The Kosovars have made it clear that they will not accept a solution under those terms, and Albania, on its part, has also made it clear that it will only accept what is acceptable to them, and will only exercise its margin of discretion on the representatives of Kosova. The institutionalisation of dialogue will prove to be the only way to keep an already deteriorating situation under control. Kosova has mandated its representatives to conduct talks on their future. The will of the people, of which all international documents speak, has materialised peacefully and democratically. A referendum has been held on September 26-30, 1991, elections on May 24, 1992. The new parliament attempted to convene and constitute a government: it was not allowed to. All has gone in full accordance with the laws. What was against the laws, was the violation of the will of the people by Serbia, through illegal arrangements and open violence. In 1945, under martial law, unification with federal Serbia within Federal Yugoslavia took place. It was proclaimed as an act of the will of the people. In 1989, the will of the people decided to lead a new life. This time the act was nicknamed 'illegal'. Self-determination seemed to have lost the marvel of its doings, while the Helsinki Final Act does not say so. This delegation finds it difficult to understand double standards.

Document LC/C/4

14. London International Conference on the Former Yugoslavia, Work Programme, 27 August 1992

1. The International Conference on the former Yugoslavia will remain in being until a final settlement of the problems of the former Yugoslavia has been reached. It will build on the work already done by the EC Conference on Yugoslavia, especially the documents already produced, and will be guided by the provisions of the statement of principles agreed today. .....

4. There will be six Working Groups in continuous session at the Office of the United Nations in Geneva: ...

(d) Ethnic and National Communities and Minorities Working Group. The Group's task is to recommend initiatives for resolving ethnic questions in the former Yugoslavia. A special group on the former autonomous province of Kosovo will be set up; ...

15. London Conference, Co-Chairman's Paper on Serbia and Montenegro, 27 August 1992

We welcome the fact that all participants in the Conference have subscribed to the Statement on Bosnia and Herzegovina. All participants must fulfil the obligations to which they have agreed. In particular, Serbia and Montenegro face a clear choice. They have undertaken to:

- cease intervention across their border with Bosnia and Croatia;
- to the best of their ability restrain the Bosnian Serbs from taking territory by force and expelling the local population;
- restore in full the civil and constitutional rights of the inhabitants of the Kosovo and Vojvodina and also to ensure the civil rights of the inhabitants of the Sandjak;
- use their influence with the Bosnian Serbs to obtain the closure of their detention camps, to comply with their obligations under international humanitarian law and in particular the Geneva Conventions, and to permit the return of refugees to their homes. The Bosnian Croats and Muslims have given similar undertakings;
- fully observe the relevant resolutions of the UN Security Council;
- declare that they fully respect the integrity of present frontiers;
- guarantee the right of ethnic and national communities and minorities within the borders of Serbia and Montenegro in accordance with the UN Charter, the CSCE and the draft convention of the EC Conference on Yugoslavia;
- work for the normalization of the situation in Croatia, for implementation of the Vance plan and for acceptance by the Serbs in the Kajina of special status as forseen in the draft convention of the EC Conference on Yugoslavia;
- respect all relevant international treatis and agreements.

If, as suggested by Mr Panic's letter to the President of the Security Council of the UN, Serbia and Montenegro do intend to fulfil these obligations in deed as well as word they will resume a respected position in the international community. They will be eneabled to trade, to receive assistance and to enjoy the full cooperation of all members of the international community. If they do not comply the Security Council will be invited to apply stringent sanctions leading to their total international isolation.

16. Security Council Resolution 777 (1992), 19 September 1992

The Security Council,

Reaffirming its resolution 713 (1991) of 25 September 1991 and all subsequent relevant resolutions,

Considering that the State formerly known as the Socialist Federal Republic of Yugoslavia has ceased to exist,

Recalling in particular resolution 757 (1992) which notes that 'the claim by the Federal Republic of Yugoslavia (Serbia and Montenegro) to continue automatically the membership of the former Socialist Federal Republic of Yugoslavia in the United Nations has not been generally accepted',

1. *Considers* that the Federal Republic of Yugoslavia (Serbia and Montenegro) cannot continue automatically the membership of the former Socialist Federal Republic of Yugoslavia in the United Nations; and therefore *recommends* to the General Assembly that it decide that the Federal Republic of Yugoslavia (Serbia and Montenegro) should apply for membership in the United Nations and that it shall not participate in the work of the General Assembly;

2. *Decides* to consider the matter again before the end of the main part of the forty-seventh session of the General Assembly.

B. The Follow-on Talks of the Special Group on Kosovo

1. Statement by the Republic of Kosovo to Conference on Yugoslavia, Geneva, 16 September 1992

The Delegation of the Republic of Kosova, chaired by Dr Rugova, President, Dr Bukoshi, Prime Minister, academician Gezmend Zajmi, parliamentary member, on the opening day of the special Group on Kosova, in a meeting with the two co-chairman, Lord Owen and UN envoy Cyrus Vance, proposed the following measures to be undertaken immediately:

1. The urgent engagement of Mr Cyrus Vance and Lord Owen to allow the continuation of schooling in the Albanian language at all educational levels, including the University of Prishtina, and to allow the free functioning of the Academy of Science and Arts of Kosova;
2. Lifting of discriminatory laws, measures and actions, namely the removal of imposed coercive management from Kosova institutions and companies and the reinstatement of sacked Albanian workers;
3. The suspension of recent attempts by Serbian authorities to colonise Kosova, particularly through the use of Serbian and Montenegrin refugees from Croatia and Bosnia;
4. The deployment of permanent EC and CSCE monitors on the border between Serbia and Kosova;
5. Kosova to be excluded from current UN sanctions that have been applied to Serbia and Montenegro. Due to the fact that Kosova has in no way participated in, or condoned, the present 'Yugoslav' conflict, it is unreasonable to expect it to endure both Serbian repression and international sanctions.

Geneva, September 16th 1992

S/24795, 11 November 1992

2. Report of the Secretary-General on the International Conference on the Former Yugoslavia, 11 November 1992

...

82. This working Group is chaired by Ambassador Geert Ahrens. Its task is to recommend initiatives for resolving ethnic questions in the former Yugoslavia. A special group on the former autonomous province of Kosovo has been set up.

...

90. Intensive work was done in the Special Group on Kosovo. The basic approach agreed to by both sides is to try a pragmatic

breakthrough in one important sector—the ethnic Albanians chose education—in order to improve the political atmosphere for talks on more fundamental issues where positions are at present irreconcilable. After difficult and tedious preparations, in which the release of the Chairman of the Albanian Teachers Association from prison could be achieved, the first Conference-sponsored talks between the Federal and the Serbian Governments from Belgrade on one side and ethnic Albanian respresentatives from Kosovo on the other took place. On 14 October, all parties agreed to the following statement:

1. "Representatives of the Government of the FRY and Serbia led by the Federal Minister of Education, Mr Ivic, and representatives of the Albanians met in Pristina on 13 and 14 October with the participation of the Geneva Conference Special Groups on Kosovo, under the Chairmanship of Ambassador Ahrens. The representative of the CSCE mission was also present.

2. After detailed discussion of the problems of education in the Albanian language, the participants agreed that the present situation must be changed. They further agreed on the urgent desirability of the return to normal working conditions for schools and other educational institutions.

3. It was agreed that, to achieve this, it would be necessary to adopt a pragmatic approach requiring urgent resolution, without prejudice to the positions of the parties on broader political issues.

4. The Albanian representatives agreed to provide a list of schools and other educational institutions to be covered by the measures mentioned in (2); as well as a list of teaching plans and programmes.

5. The Group agreed to meet again in Belgrade on 22 October. At that meeting discussions will be held on all the issues mentioned above and on the equal working status of teaching and educational personnel with the aim of reaching the necessary decisions for immediate action."

91. These talks were continued accordingly on 22 October in Belgrade, after meetings with both President Cosic and Mr Rugova. The participants reaffirmed their commitment to the necessity of changing the existing situation in the field of education, and the urgent need for a return to normal conditions in schools and other educational institutions in Kosovo, as set out in their statement of 14 October. They agreed that this commitment refers to all four levels of education: pre-school, elementary school, secondary school and higher education. On Albanian insistence, there was agreement that all problems related to education in Albania at all levels are related and must be treated as a whole. The Serbian and Federal representatives made plain the material and financial constraints affecting their areas of responsibility. Within those constraints, there will be no discrimination as between the support which they will provide for instruction in both the Alabanian and the Serbian language. However, no agreement could be reached so far on conditions under which school buildings should be opened, teachers should be reinstated and entrance examinations should be handled. The Working Groups has done its best to arrange proper coordination with the CSCE efforts in the former Yugoslavia. ....

KOSOVA, VOJVODINA, SANDZAK
The next potential flashpoint concerns the minorities in Serbia - by far and away the most important of which is Kosova, where nearly 2 million Albanians live and 200,000 Serbs, or thereabouts. The Albanians living in Kosova have had an election of their own and declared their independence from Serbia. But this, as in the Krajina, is not a solution, since existing borders must be maintained, and it is certainly not one which the Serbs would ever accept, since Kosova is perceived as the birthplace of Serbian nationhood.

The Kosovans have recently shown willingness to negotiate without pre-judging the outcome but have, given the general antipathy between Kosovan and Serb, asked the Conference to mediate. Regrettably, the Serbs have so far refused to accept EC Conference participation. I believe it is essential for the Peace Conference to be involved in seeking a settlement between the Kosovans and the Serbian government. The dangers there are infinitely great and it is overwhelmingly in the interest of both sides to come to the negotiating table and hammer out a solution on the basis of real autonomy.

3.   Letter from Kosovo to the Special Group on Kosovo, Geneva Conference on the Former Yugoslavia, undated

We welcome the establishment, conception and the commencement of the work of the Special Group on Kosova and we, the delegation, wish to express our hopes and convictions that the Special Group on Kosova, operating within the framework of structures and mechanisms of the Geneva Peace Conference on the former Yugoslavia, will be an international democratic forum, effective and prolific over the issue of Kosova, dealing with the current situation and solving the international position of Kosova following the disintegration of former Yugoslavia.

It is right to hope that in this significant Group, within the structure of the Geneva Conference, parallelly, on two planes closely connected to each other, both the difficult and tense situation in Kosova as well as the urgent animation of international measures will be considered, including those of an international character for the elimination of such a situation. In addition to this, an international solution of the position of Kosova should be considered and a proposal given now that the Yugoslav Federation, in which Kosova was a constitutive element, has definitely disintegrated.

It is understandable that in the international democratic aspect which implies the application of the principle of self-determination in the case of the dissemination of federal links between federal units, for what necessary support can be found in the principles of the Badinter Commission, this solution has to be sought in the direction of democratic compliance with the political will of the people of Kosova expressed through the referendum on Kosova as a sovereign and independent state, a state which is laterally open to mutual, bilateral or multilateral links with other social subjects of the basis of the preliminary evaluations of usefulness of the links, while at the same time retaining the principles of self-determination, sovereignty and equality, as well as in the direction of respect, validation and the international guarantee for the results of the referendum's outcome reflecting such a political will which is deeply just and democratic.

There is an undeniable fact, which becomes even more so on the plane of historic and factual truth that the majority population of Kosova, through the referendum has proclaimed Kosova's independence, that is has proclaimed Kosova a sovereign and independent state with the demand for international recognition.

There is an undeniable fact, known to the international community, that on the basis of results of the Referendum in Kosova held in September 1991, in May of this year pluralist and democratic elections were held with international monitoring, in which the President and Parliament of the Republic of Kosova were elected, as there is also the undeniable historic fact that Kosova's position in the Yugoslav Federation of the 1974 constitution, where it had the position of a federal unit with an almost equal inter-federal and international subjectivity, even with a subjectivity more emphasised than many federal units in some other federations, was cruelly, one sidedly and in an arbitrary way, unknown to federal systems, destroyed by the government of the Republic of Serbia through the imposition of a state of emergency, violence, fraudulity in the procedure of constitutional changes, in direct and flagrant opposition to the Federal Constitution as well as with the police implementation of emergency measures. This fact is can be corroborated by conclusive evidence on the constitutional breach, violence and fraudulence of the procedures of constitutional and law changes by the Serbian regime. The majority of the population of Kosova not only did not accept such an undertaking of the Serbian regime but at the same time, through legitimate democratic procedure, involving the participation of the whole population, issued and approved through the referendum, the basic documents of Kosova's independence.

Riding above all these facts is the most firmly established social, political, demographic and ethnic fact: this is by all means the two million strong Albanian population, a non-Slav population which comprises nine tenths of the population of Kosova, a people with a articulated and institutionalised political will for the international subjectivity of Kosova.

Within all international circles, on the basis of numerous international inspections, it is known nowadays that Kosova a European region where human rights and freedoms are violated more than anywhere else and where human and national rights in general are violated. (It was for this reason that the Kosova Delegation earlier issued a five point plan listing proposals for measures to be undertaken to alleviate this situation). Therefore, instead of describing here the situation in Kosova, it should be pointed out that it would be groundless for Kosova, if Kosova's political individuality were to be percepted purely in terms of the violation of human rights and freedoms, and not first of all in terms of the ethnic and territorial individuality of Kosova as well as the democratic will of the majority population of Kosova for international institutionalisation of this individuality.

Regardless of some distinction within the framework of the organisational scheme of work of the Geneva Conference, it is exactly the formation of a special Group on Kosova as well as the one on Bosnia-Herzegovina, speaks about an important valuation start of the International community on the political individuality of Kosova which, following the disintegration of Yugoslavia (being originally a constitutional entity with residuum of sovereignty as a constituent element of the former Yugoslav federation) means that it is not anyone's internal affair, but rather an internal issue of its own self and a matter of the International resolution of the International crisis emerging from the space of a previously multinational state.

It is right to expect that the strength of facts and arguments offered, will further advance this valuation of the international political individuality of Kosova in accordance with real and essential demographic, ethnic, democratic and political dimensions which contain this individuality as a step that would at the same time contribute towards long term peace and stability in the Balkans and towards an opening of a sound perspective of friendship and mutual respect between the Albanian nation and Serbian nation in the Balkans.

It is also worth pointing out that Kosova, as an original political entity with its own Constitution, with individualised and constitutionally protected borders, as a constitutive unit with the equal right of participation in deciding on constitution and law making of the federation, as well as in its overall functioning and state presentation, where not a single square metre not only of Kosova's borders but also of the outside borders of the federation could not change without the consent of Kosova, was not a part of Serbia but was only structured in the complex constitutional structure of the Republic of Serbia on the basis of the presumption of Kosova's political will for as long there existed a common political contractual interest between Serbia and Kosova. Since the Constitutional Declaration of the Parliament of Kosova June 2nd (1990) on the independence on the equality of Kosova in the juridical constitutional and legitimate aspect this presumption does exist any longer likewise former multinational Yugoslavia in which Kosova was a federal constituent part.

Finally it should be pointed out by all means that the mere existence of a special Group on Kosova surpasses every eventual concept which would concentrate and confine in a formula of a special status for Kosova. Were this not so, the formation of a special Group for Kosova would not have its meaning the position of a special status for Kosova could then be settled within the framework of special statuses which would emerge from the general group on national and ethnic communities and minorities.

If special status is to be seriously considered for Kosova, then may complex questions would arise: what kind of special status is to be considered, will it be a special status within Serbia or within Yugoslavia; what will constitute this special status since the contents of a special status for Kosova could not be below the starting constitutional position that Kosova had according to the Constitution of 1974 within the now non-existent multinational Federation - Confederation; the question of international guarantees would have to be considered without which no special status would have any meaning, and since, when Kosova is at issue, not only how just would such a status be as opposed to the constitutional state position that Kosova had before and especially as opposed to the political will of the majority population of Kosova institutionalised through the referendum for the independence of Kosova and the election of the governing bodies of the Republic of Kosova, but also how stable would such a status be within a game of permanent centripetal and centrifugal forces,

a question that is suggested by the historical experience in connection with the individuality of Kosova, and the groundless possessive ethnic aspiration of Serbia toward Kosova, that during the occupying Balkans wars of 1912, not only partitioned into two the territorial ethnic body of the Albanian nation in the Balkans, but even today, at complete different times, without any grounds and in an anti-democratic and hegemonistic way fails to respect the will of the majority of the population in the territory of Kosova for an independent Kosova for all her citizens and nationalities. It is worth mentioning that Kosova is not an ethnic enclave but a territory on its own and wide not with an Serbian ethnic majority but with a predominantly ethnic Albanian majority.

From all this emerges the imminent necessity that the group on Kosova with its attitudes and proposals be permissive towards the essential arguments concerning international individuality of Kosova and the international positive valuation of Kosova, where as a sovereign and independent Republic would have open borders with all its neighbours and would be a demilitarised zone of the Balkans with the will itself of the people of Kosova followed if necessary with an international guarantee of just inter-ethnic relations in it as well as with an international guarantee of the free circulation of national values both of the Albanian nation and Serbian nation in the Balkans, as well as of all other nationalities no matter how small they may be demographically.

Following the great significance of the foundation of the special group on Kosova, as a matter of respect towards Kosova's political individuality with international importance, the Kosova Delegation, during the preliminary talks with the Special Group on Kosova held in Geneva, stated that it was willing to participate in activities of the Special Group on Kosova, but not in any other plenary or special meetings within the General Group on national communities and minorities. Such an attitude is understandable when the political, ethnic and territorial content of Kosova and the position it enjoyed according to the Constitution of 1974 are taken into consideration, a position that by all means must determine the equal position of Kosova with other federal units of former Yugoslavia in deciding about their individual political will as well as when deciding about general matters of what was Yugoslavia such as the question of succession and ways of overcoming conflictual situations etc.

Finally, we would like to remind you that all aspects raised in this letter of address have been treated and proved in detail in the political constitutional elaborate on Kosova which was earlier submitted to the International Conference on Yugoslavia through Ambassador Ahrens.
The Delegation
Dr. Bujar Bukoshi, The Prime Minister of the Republic of Kosova
Academician Gazmend Zajmi, Dr. Hivzi Islami

S/25490, 30 March 1993

4.   Secretary-General Report: Recent Activities of the Working Groups, 30 March 1993

...

17. The Special Group on Kosovo met at Geneva from 26 to 28 January and in Belgrade on 17 and 18 February. As in past meetings, the talks were limited to the subject of education, on which the Group still endeavours to reach pragmatic solutions in the hope of improving the overall climate between the parties, which continues to be far from positive.

18. The Kosovar Albanians presented their teaching plans. These were rejected by the Government on the ground that they contained an underlying assumption of independence for Kosovo. The Government made new proposals on the reinstatement of teachers and on the recognition of years spent in the parallel school system run by the Albanians. They were rejected by the Kosovar Albanian side, which insists on the 'unconditional' reopening of school premises before they would be ready to address other issues.

19. In the talks on Kosovo, fundamental issues are constantly hindering the pragmatic approach for solutions in the field of education. The Groups will pursue its efforts, but at the same time it is necessary to

address fundamental issues in the light of the principles agreed upon at the London Conference.

20. When in Belgrade on 10 March, the Chair emphasized to Mr Jovanovic, the Federal Minister for Foreign Affairs, the necessity of this double-track approach. While agreeing in principle, the Foreign Minister stressed the desirability for success on the educational issue as a first step before other issues were approached. On 17 March, Ambassador Ahrens had a discussion with Mr Bukoshi, who spoke on behalf of Albanians from Kosovo. There was agreement that everything should be tried to achieve progress in the ongoing talks. Mr Bukoshi informed Ambassador Ahrens that authorities in Kosovo had taken away the passport of Professor Statovci, a member of the Kosovar Albanian negotiating team since the beginning, on whose participation the Kosovar Albanians had to insist.

S/25829, Annex

5.   Joint Action Programme of France, Spain, Russian Federation, the United Kingdom and the USA, 22 May 1993

...

11. Kosovo. We favour an increase in the international monitoring presence in Kosovo. International standards of human rights should be strictly respected in the formerly autonomous region of Kosovo, although we do not support declarations of independence there.

...

We five members of the United Nations Security Council are firmly united and firmly committed to taking these immediate steps. We will work closely with the United Nations and the involved regional organizations as we carry out these efforts.

CERD/C/248/Add.1, 15 September 1994

6.   Yugoslavia, Statement on Negotiations on Education Issues in Kosovo and Metohija, 29 August 1994

1. The education of the Albanian ethnic community in Kosovo and Metohija was the subject-matter of year-long talks between the Federal and Republican education authorities, representatives of the Geneva Conference, headed by Mr. G. Ahrens, and the representatives of Kosovo and Metohija Albanians. The talks were conducted within the Subgroup for the Education Problems in Kosovo and Metohija of the Working Group on Ethnic and National Communities and Minorities of the International Conference on the Former Yugoslavia in the period between October 1992 and June 1993.

2. The programme of the Federal Government for the solution of the problems in the field of the education and culture of the Albanian minority in Kosovo and Metohija, adopted on 10 September 1992, provides for the following principal measures:

Solving urgent education problems, i.e. normalization of Albanian language instruction, reinstatement of teachers and the recognition of two previous years;

Respect for cultural specificities of Albanians in school programmes;

Improving the quality of education and the development of intercultural communication.

3. The first meeting of the Subgroup was held on 13 and 14 October 1992 in Pristina. In an atmosphere of cooperation-building, it was agreed that Albanians should submit to the Working Group elementary school programmes for the Albanian language instruction so that contentious issues could be considered.

4. The next meeting was held in Belgrade on 22 October 1992, when Albanian representatives requested revision of the previous agreement: they went back on the "step-by-step" method (solving problems first in elementary, then in secondary and finally in university education), demanding categorically that the education system they had under the 1974 Constitution be reintroduced and that the problems of all education levels be solved at the same time.

5. The failure of these negotiations brought about an impasse in further talks: first, Albanians refused to come to a meeting in Novi Sad on 11 November 1992 for political reasons. On that day Ambassador Ahrens had a meeting with members of other minorities, which Albanians refused to accept.

6. The next meeting, in Geneva on 17 November 1992, was not attended by the representatives of the Federal and Republican authorities, because of the position of the Government of the Republic of Serbia that the question of education in Kosovo and Metohija is an internal question and that going to Geneva would have meant the "internationalization of the problem of Kosovo and Metohija". The representatives of the Federal Government also failed to travel to Geneva in these circumstances since they could not take over the obligations which, according to the Constitution, can be implemented only by the Republican Ministry.

7. For the same reasons, the representatives of the Government of Serbia did not attend the next meeting in Geneva, on 3 December 1992, when a draft programme was finally handed over to the then Federal Minister for Education and Culture, Mr. I. Ivic.

8. The next meeting, in Pristina on 9 December 1992, failed to yield satisfactory results, too: Albanian representatives continued to insist on the reintroduction of the education system they had before the change of the Constitution of Serbia.

9. The subordination by the Albanians of the educational and pedagogical problems in Kosovo and Metohija to the question of the political and constitutional status of the Province lead to the failure of the Geneva meeting, held on 26 and 28 January 1993, to produce concrete results.

10. On 16 and 17 February, the representatives of the Government of the Federal Republic of Yugoslavia and the Republic of Serbia came out with proposals for an urgent solution of education problems and the normalization of the Albanian language instruction which also constituted the initial basis of the Platform prepared for the 8th meeting of the Subgroup (7 and 8 April 1993):

(a) Acceptance, as a point of departure, of the Albanian language instruction programmes from 1990 which were devised with the largest level of autonomy on the part of Albanians in the field of education;

(b) Reinstatement of Albanian language instruction teachers dismissed after the interruption of education in Kosovo and Metohija, bar the few who committed flagrant violations of the law and for whom the Government was required to proffer individual explanations of their unsuitability to participate in education;

(c) Recognition of the time spent by students in the "parallel" Albanian language education system;

(d) The same model of normalization of the Albanian language instruction would be applied to the secondary education as well;

(e) All proposed solutions were to be of a temporary nature until a final normalization of the situation in Kosovo and Metohija.

11. At the suggestion of the education representatives from Kosovo and Metohija, the Government side accepted that:

(i) The same model for the solution of problems be applied also to university education, with respect for the specificities of problems at this educational level; and

(ii) Agreements on the normalization of instruction at all levels be worked out successively, while the implementation of solutions made would begin simultaneously at all levels.

12. Albanians were go give their views about these proposals at the next meeting in Geneva, scheduled for 7 and 8 April 1993, which they boycotted because of the arrest of E. Statovci.

13. At a meeting with Mr. G. Ahrens on 21 April 1993 in Belgrade, the Federal Minister for Education and Culture, Dr. Slavko Gordic, informed him of the two principal positions of the Federal Government on the question of the Yugoslav side approach to further talks on the Albanian language instruction in Kosovo and Metohija:

(a) The negotiating framework is the Constitution of the Federal Republic of Yugoslavia, which defines Kosovo and Metohija as part of Serbia and Yugoslavia, which has been confirmed also by the London Conference on the Former Yugoslavia;

(b) Only educational and pedagogical problems can be considered within the Subgroup (the Working Group is not mandated to prejudge political solutions and constitutional and legal changes).

14. It was agreed that solutions brought by the Subgroup constituted proposals to be submitted to the Federal Government for adoption.

15. On 26 May 1993 a meeting was held between the representatives of the Federal, Republic and Provincial education authorities with Mr. G. Ahrens, who transmitted the information that the representatives of the Kosovo and Metohija Albanians had accepted in principle the proposals of the Federal and Republican Governments and suggested that compromise solutions were to be sought in future talks which would circumvent Albanian demands to have school facilities ceded unconditionally and the instruction at the university level normalized as a matter of priority.

16. However, Albanian representatives failed to appear at the planned trilateral meeting in Pristina on 9 June 1993, explaining that they allegedly had not understood that the meeting had been convened for that date and that they were not ready for it. Refusing to hold the meeting in the "Jedinstvo" building because of the cessation of the publication of "Rilindja" and the ongoing strike, they handed Ambassador Ahrens a document for Lord Owen and Mr. Stoltenberg with the "Albanian side's requests for the solution of the problem of the education of Albanians from Kosovo". Among other things, these requests re-include the unconditional ceding of school facilities and the insistence that the solution of the question of Albanian language education be left to Albanians alone.

17. On that occasion Ambassador Ahrens distanced himself from infringing upon questions of political autonomy, emphasizing that the consideration of ceding school facilities could only follow and not precede an agreement.

<u>Causes for the interruption of talks</u>

Refusal by the Albanians to recognize the competence of the Republic of Serbia in the question of Albanian language instruction;

Demands for a larger autonomy than is granted to other national minorities in the Federal Republic of Yugoslavia;

Attempts to relate educational and pedagogical questions to political ones; and

Avoidance by the Albanians of making their views known on the proposals of the Federal and Republican Governments and their presentation of ever new demands.

7. St Egidio [St Eugidio] Education Agreement, 1 September 1996

[The] educational system in Kosovo, from primary to university education, has not been functioning normally for several years.

By signifying their consent, the undersigned, President of Serbia Slobodan Milosevic and Dr Ibrahim Rugova, have reached agreement to start the normalization of education system for Albanian children and youth in Kosovo.

The agreement envisages the return of Albanian pupils and teachers to schools.

Because of its social and humanitarian importance, this agreement is beyond any political dispute. The mutual concern of the undersigned for the future of Albanian children and youth made them reach this agreement.

They would like to thank their mutual friends from the humanitarian community St Egidio for their help and support rendered in facilitating their dialogue.

The undersigned are convinced of the readiness of all those who are in charge of implementation of the education system to achieve normalization. For the implemention of this agreement a mixed group (3+3) will be established.

When young people seriously start their educational and cultural improvement, thus becoming responsible citizens, it will be a victory of civilization and not a victory of one over another.

Signed: Dr Ibrahim Rugova, President of the Republic of Serbia Slobodan Milosevic, 1 September 1996.

8. Agreed Measures for the Implementation of the Agreement on Education, 23 March 1988.

1. The following measures have been temporarily adopted to enable the implementation of the Agreement on Education signed on September 1 by President Slobodan Milosevic and Dr. Ibrahim Rugova [above].

2. The Institute for Albanology in Pristina will be open for its previous users on March 31.

3. By March 31, the St. Egidio Community will, in view of the proposals submitted by the two sides in the 3+3 Committee, determine the first three faculties of the Pristina University where the Albanian students and professors will be reintegrated by April 30, 1998.

In principle, the following is a condition for reintegration:

Students currently normally conducting their studies at the University and the Albanian students will use the University facilities and equipment alternately, through a system of double shifts which will change every semester. During the first semester of the application of these measures, students currently normally studying in the University facilities will use them in the morning (until 2 p.m.), and the Albanian students in the afternoon; in the second semester, the shifts will change and the Albanian students will be in the morning and the students now studying in the University facilities in the afternoon, and this order will change in the following semesters.

Apart from using facilities for holding classes, Albanian students and professors will also have at their disposal the corresponding space at each faculty for administrative functions and the teaching staff (if this is not possible, another solution will be found).

4. By April 30, 1998, the St. Egidio Community will, taking into consideration proposals submitted by the two sides in the 3+3 Committee, determine the next three faculties of the Pristina University where the Albanian students and professors will be reintegrated by May 31, 1998. The conditions for this will be the same as for the faculties in point 3.

5. Albanian students and professors of the remaining seven faculties will be able to re-enter the facilities of the Pristina University by June 30, 1998 according to the same conditions as the faculties in points 3 and 4.

By September 30, 1998, Albanian students and professors will be able to use University facilities (cafeterias, libraries, student dormitories, etc.) in the corresponding way. The St. Egidio Community will, after hearing the proposals of both sides, reach a solution for possible problems which could occur. In any case, the school year must start normally on October 1, 1998.

6. By June 30, 1998, Albanian students and professors will be able to use the facilities of seven schools of higher learning in Pristina and other cities in Kosovo which are specialized for teaching, economic and technical subjects. Their use will be regulated in keeping with the conditions for the renewed use of University facilities, as in point 3, if these schools are to be used.

7. The 3+3 Committee, with the support of St. Egidio, underlines the need for securing funds for the faster construction of new facilities in order to make more space for holding classes, research and administration, and which will be at the disposal of all. New University buildings, which can be built speedily, will be able to accommodate, under equal conditions, all structures of the University. This will be the subject of a special program, which will contain deadlines and the financing of its realization in keeping with real needs and material capabilities.

8. Similarly, by March 31, 1998, Albanian pupils of elementary and high schools will be able to return to elementary and high schools which are currently not is use, in keeping with a list to be prepared by the 3+3 Committee.

St. Egidio will find a solution for possible problems which could emerge.

Albanian pupils of elementary and high schools will return to those elementary and high school buildings which are partially in use by April 30, 1998. Their use will be regulated in keeping with the conditions for the renewed use of University facilities mentioned in point 3, or in another mutually acceptable way.

9. The 3+3 Committee, assisted by St. Egidio, will meet by March 30 at the latest to guarantee the implementation of the transitional normalization measures. The 3+3 Committee will immediately set up working groups for each faculty. The 3+3 Committee will examine the remaining problems which are concerned with the normalization of the education system (funding, administration, languages, programs, diplomas, status questions of employees).

  In Pristina, March 23, 1998
   Fehmi Agani Ratomir Vico
   Abdulj Rama Goran Percevic
   Redzep Osmani Dobrosav Bjeletic
  In the presence of the members of the St. Egidio Community
   Monsignor Vicenzo Paglia
   Prof. Roberto Moroco della Roca
   Dr. Mario Giro

C. Initial Decisions of the CSCE/OSCE

1. Decision of the Committee of Senior Officials of the CSCE, Prague, 22 October 1991

CSCE Human Rights Rapporteur Mission to Yugoslavia

 Recalling the Moscow Concluding Document, the CSCE Committee of Senior Officials agreed to form a human rights rapporteur mission. The mission will visit Bosnia-Hercegovina, Croatia, Macedonia, Montenegro, Serbia and Slovenia at a time to be agreed through consultation with Yugoslavia. It will inform itself of the situation with respect to human rights, including the rights of minorities, and will report to the Committee. Its report will be circulated by the CSCE Secretariat through the CSCE points of contact and will be considered by the Committee at a future meeting. The report will be made available to the Chairman of the Conference on Yugoslavia. The mission will be led by the designated representative of the Chairman of the CSCE Council of Ministers. A representative from the CSCE Office for Free Elections will serve as secretary for the mission. The mission will also include, inter alia, a representative from the European Community, and a representative of the Chairman of the Conference on Yugoslavia.

7-CSO/Journal No. 2, Annex 2

2. CSO Decision on Human Rights Rapporteur Follow-up Mission to Yugoslavia, 12 May 1992

Referring to the Summary of Conclusions of the Prague Meeting of the CSCE Council, the CSCE Committee of Senior Offficials examined the need for further action concerning the human rights situation in Yugoslavia. The Committee agreed that the human rights situation, including the situation of national minorities, requires further consideration and follow-up action by the CSCE. To that end, the Committee decided to send a follow-up mission to the Human Rights Rapporteur Mission to Yugoslavia, as established by decision of the Committee on October 22, 1991 in Prague. The follow-up mission will examine further the situation in the previously visited Republics and give particular attention to the subjects mentioned for consecutive action in the first report. The mission will not take place before the end of April and it will report to the Committee. The report will be circulated by the CSCE Secretariat through the CSCE points of contact and will be considered by the Committee at a future meeting. The report will be made available to the Chairman of the Conference on Yugoslavia.

11-CSO/Journal No. 3, Annex 2

3. CSO Statement on the former Yugoslavia, 20 May 1992

... The CSO also discussed reports of the grave situation of ethnic Albanians in Kosovo and the denial of fundamental freedoms to them and to Hungarian, Muslim and other ethnic minorities as well as reports that the preparations for elections on 31 May 1992 failed to provide the basis for free and fair elections, and stressed the responsibility of the authorities of Belgrade for these situations.

 In view of these developments the CSO decided that: ...
4. The Consultative Committee of the CSCE Conflict Prevention Centre is entrusted with the dispatch of a fact-finding mission as soon as possible with a view to determining the military situation in Kosovo. All parties should co-operate with the mission. The consultative Committee should submit the report of the fact-finding mission to the next Meeting of the Committee of Senior Officials.

 In view of the gravity of recent developments the Chairman-in-Office will convene the next Meeting of the Committee of Senior Officials, as appropriate, no later than 8 June 1992 to review the situation in the light of its decision and take whatever action may be necessary.

Interpretative statement by Yugoslavia:

The Yugoslav delegation would like to stress again the full support and readiness of the Yugoslav authorities to help within their possibilities and responsibilities the free access of humanitarian aid. The Yugoslav delegation us fully in favour of all efforts aimed at the lasting solution to the serious refugee problem, including the proposed international high-level meeting convened for 21 May. Having in mind the very serious problems, with over 500,000 refugees. Yugoslavia is ready to participate actively in any international meeting. Concerning the ongoing mission of the CSCE Office for Democratic Institutions and Human Rights and its expected report, Yugoslavia remains co-operative, open and ready for further deliberations on the preparation of elections scheduled for 31 May. The Yugoslav delegation cannot accept the *a priori* judgement that the preparations for the elections failed to provide the basis for free and fair elections, as indicated in the proposed text. The Yugoslav delegation is fully ready to respect all CSCE commitments, including those of the Vienna Document 1990 of the Negotiations on Confidence and Security-building Measures and the Prague Document 1992 on Further Development of CSCE Institutions and Structures, with regard to the right of the Consultative Committee of the CSCE Conflict Prevention Centre to dispatch a fact-finding mission. The Yugoslav delegation cannot agree with the one-sided and unacceptable approach on the so-called 'military situation in Kosovo' and deeply believes that it is only an artificially added new element to the complexity of the Yugoslav crisis. Otherwise, it is very well known that the Yugoslavia has never rejected any mission sent by the CSCE and has shown full and open co-operation with those missions. The general approach in the proposed text of the declaration is obviously one-sided, particularly in references to the use of force and violence and to the continued violation of CSCE commitments. The approach is neither just nor objective, and does not reflect at all the actual situation in Bosnia-Herzegovina; it is not a contribution to a peaceful settlement based on an equal and just solution. The Yugoslav delegation expresses its formal reservation to the declaration as well as to the Chairman's statement, and states that it cannot give its consent to the proposed text of the declaration on the Yugoslav crisis or to the Chairman's statement, but it cannot prevent their adoption owing to the application of paragraph 16 of the Prague Document on Further Development of CSCE Institutions and Structures.

12-CSO/Journal No. 3, Annex

4. Decisions of the Committee of Senior Officials, Helsinki, 8/10 June 1992

...
7. The Committee of Senior Officials also decided on the following specific steps:

 (a) In accordance with its decision of 12 May 1992, the CSO will decide on 29 June 1992 further action to be taken in the light of the information provided by the EC about the situation on the ground and about progress at the EC Peace Conference. To facilitate this decision, the Chairman-in-Office, after consultations with delegations, has invited representatives of Austria, Canada, the Czech and Slovak Federal Republic, Germany, Greece, Portugal-European Community, the Russian Federation, Sweden, Switzerland, Turkey and the United States of America to form a task force. This task force will commence its work by 22 June 1992 at the latest and will consider the assessment provided by the EC and the conclusions of the review to be conducted by the United Nations. The task force will present its recommendations for further action to the CSO by 29 June 1992, including those on the question of the participation of the delegation of Yugoslavia in the CSCE, particularly with a view to the arrangements for the forthcoming Helsinki Summit.

(b) The task force will also prepare recommendations, for consideration by the CSO at its Meeting on 29 June 1992, on the role that further CSCE missions, of either short or long duration, might play in promoting peace, averting violence and restoring respect for human rights and fundamental freedoms in Kosovo, Vojvodina and Sandjak and in support of the efforts of the EC Peace Conference. To help prepare such a recommendation the CSO has decided to send an exploratory mission to the above regions within the next two weeks.

'Following the adoption of the text entitled 'Decisions of the Committee of Senior Officials' the Chairman made the following announcement:
'The Chairman-in-Office will continue his efforts, outside this CSO Meeting, to create conditions enabling the fulfilment of the CSO decision on an exploratory mission. He also urges all the participating States to contribute to these efforts. In this connection, he would like to point out that in his view the Helsinki Follow-up Meeting should adopt appropriate decisions as far as practical modalities, including logistic support and the question of financing such missions as CSCE operations, are concerned'.
In connection with the adoption of the text entitled 'Decisions of the Committee of Senior Officials' statements were made by the following delegations with the request that they should be recorded in the Journal:
By the Russian Federation: The delegation of the Russian Federation understands that the missions referred to in paragraph 7(b) are being sent to the specified regions of the Federal Republic of Yugoslavia.
By Yugoslavia: Referring to the statement of the Chairman that he will contact the authorities of the regions mentioned in order to send missions, my delegation would like to say that those local authorities are not authorised to give consent to the proposed missions and under these circumstances Yugoslavia is not ready to receive them.

13-CSO/Journal No. 7, Annex

5. Decision of the Committee of Senior Officials on the Suspension of Participation by the FRY, 7 July 1992

1. With reference to the decision of the CSO of 12 May 1992, (Serbia and Montenegro) and in the light of the statement by the authorities of Yugoslavia (Serbia and Montenegro), it is decided that no representative of Yugoslavia will be present at the CSCE Summit in Helsinki or at any subsequent meetings of the CSCE until 14 October 1992.

2. This decision will be reviewed by the CSO at its meeting to be held not later than 13 October 1992, in the light of the compliance of Yugoslavia (Serbia and Montenegro) with the principles, commitments and provisions of the CSCE.

3. As a part of its review on compliance, the CSO will take into account the acceptance by, and co-operation of, Yugoslavia (Serbia and Montenegro) with CSCE missions to Kosova, Vojvodina and Sandjak as reflected in its decision of 10 June 1992, as well as any other missions to Yugoslavia (Serbia and Montenegro) that the CSO might decide.

4. This decision is not directed in any way against the peoples of Serbia and Montenegro.

5. The above decisions are without prejudice to the question of the future status of Yugoslavia (Serbia and Montenegro) which will be considered by the CSO as soon as possible. It is noted that the CSO will have available on that occasion information on deliberations within the United Nations and the legal opinion of the Arbitration Commission of the EC Conference on Yugoslavia.

6. The nameplate 'Yugoslavia' will be kept at CSCE meetings for the time being.

7. The exploratory mission decided by the CSO at its Twelfth Meeting will be dispatched as soon as possible to prepare recommendations, for consideration by the CSO, on the role that

further CSCE missions, of either short or long duration, might play in promoting peace, averting violence and restoring respect for human rights and fundamental freedoms in Kosovo, Vojvodina and Sandjak and in support of the efforts of the EC Peace Conference. The report of this mission will be considered by the CSO as soon as possible.

8. A Steering Group is established, consisting of Austria, Canada, the Czech and Slovak Federal Republic, Germany, Greece, the Russian Federation, Sweden, Switzerland, Turkey, the United Kingdom European Community and the United States of America, to submit recommendations to the CSO in respect of points 2, 5 and 7 above.
[*Adopted on the basis of the consensus-minus-one principle.*]

15-CSO/Journal No. 2, Annex 1

6. Decisions of the Committee of Senior Officials, Prague, 13-14 August 1992

... 2. There was consensus among participating States that the worsening crisis required greater action within the context of the CSCE. They expressed their determination to fully apply the decisions of the Helsinki Summit in order to help alleviate humanitarian problems and support the search for peace. In particular they agreed to despatch a rapporteur mission to Bosnia-Herzegovina to investigate the humanitarian situation with special reference to detention camps and to send long-duration missions to Kosovo, Sandjak and Vojvodina. They also agreed that the presence of Observers in neighbouring countries would help to avoid a spillover of tension to their territories and would help oversee the fulfilment on United Nations sanctions. ...

Decision on Missions of Long Duration
The Committee of Senior Officials, with reference to:

- the Declaration on Yugoslavia adopted by the Helsinki Summit;
- the Committee of Senior Officials' Decision of 10 June 1992 to send an exploratory mission to Kosovo, Sandjak and Vojvodina;
- the conclusions and recommendations in the report submitted to the Committee of Senior Officials by this mission;
- Chapter III, paragraphs 6-11, in the Helsinki Decisions on the political management of crises, and

In support of the efforts of the Conference on Yugoslavia, decides to establish, in co-operation with the relevant authorities, a continuous presence in Kosovo, Sandjak and Vojvodina, in the form of missions of long duration. The missions will:

- promote dialogues between the authorities concerned and representatives of the populations and communities in the three regions;
- collect information on all aspects relevant to violations of human rights and fundamental freedoms and promote solutions to such problems;
- establish contact points for solving problems that might be identified;
- assist in providing information on relevant legislation on human rights, protection of minorities, free media and democratic elections.

The missions should be sent out as soon as possible in accordance with paragraphs 9 and 10 of Chapter III of the Helsinki Decisions. Further elaboration of modalities is delegated to the Steering Group on Yugoslavia established by the Committee of Senior Officials on 8 July 1992.

The operational control of the missions will be maintained by the Chairman-in-Office assisted by the other members of the CSCE Troika and with practical support from the appropriate CSCE institution(s). Except where provided on a voluntary basis, the expenses of the missions will be borne by all participating States in accordance with the scale of distribution.

Developments regarding the missions will be reported to the Committee of Senior Officials not later than at its regular September 1992 Meeting.

16-CSO/Journal No. 3, Annex 1

7.   CSO Decision on Mission of Long Duration, 16/18 September 1992

The Committee of Senior Officials with reference to:

- its decision of 10 June 1992 to send an exploratory mission to Kosovo, Sandjak and Vojvodina and to the conclusions and recommendations in the report of 9 August 1992 submitted by this exploratory mission to the Committee of Senior Officials;
- the letter of 24 June 1992 from the Belgrade authorities accepting in principle missions of long duration to the three regions;
- its decision of 14 August 1992 that the missions of long duration establishing a continuous presence in Kosovo, Sandjak and Vojvodina will:

    promote dialogues between the authorities concerned and representatives of the populations and communities in the three regions;

    collect information on all aspects of violations of human rights and fundamental freedoms and promote solutions to such problems;

    establish contact points for solving problems that might be identified;

    assist in providing information on relevant legislation on human rights, protection of minorities, free media and democratic elections;

- the oral report presented to the CSO by the Head of the Mission, Ambassador Tore Bögh, concerning the reconnaissance trip carried out by him from 2 to 8 September 1992;
- the conclusions and recommendations dated 16 September 1992 of the Steering Group established on 8 July 1992;
- the urgency to deploy missions in the three regions;

Requests the Head of Missions to:

- begin immediately wit the establishment of a continuous presence in the three regions;
- recruit, without delay, in close consultation with the Chairman-in-Office, upon recommendation by the Steering Group, a first contingent of personnel, and to dispatch it to the three regions;
- elaborate the organisation of the missions including personnel requirements;
- elaborate on a priority basis draft modalities in co-operation with the Head of the Exploratory Mission, Ambassador Jan af Sillén, in consultation with the representatives of the relevant populations and communities and minorities in the three regions and the Belgrade authorities.

These modalities will include provisions concerning *inter alia*:

- the safety and freedom of movement for the members of the missions
- access to local populations, communities, minorities and authorities
- privileges and immunities
- location
- duration
- submit these draft modalities and financial implications within a period of three weeks to the Steering Group for consideration and recommendations to the next CSO Meeting for its approval. In view of the urgency of the matter, the open-ended *ad hoc* group established in Vienna may, if necessary, consider and approve them on a preliminary basis.

All participating States will be eligible to take part in the missions. In the elaboration of the list of composition of full-scale missions, as well as the rotation of its members by the Steering Group, appropriate consultations will be held with the participating States.

The missions will be carried out in support of the International Conference on the former Yugoslavia and in co-operation with the Ethnic and National Communities and Minorities Working Group of that Conference. The missions will co-ordinate with the EC Monitor Mission. Co-operation will be sought with relevant humanitarian endeavours of the United Nations and other agencies.

17-CSO/Journal No. 2, Annex 3

8.   CSO Decision on Missions of Long Duration and Monitor Mission to Skopje, 5/6 November 1992

The Committee of Senior Officials

1. Notes with appreciation the reports of Ambassadors Boegh and Frowick. It welcomes the establishment of the continuous CSCE presence in the three regions, decided at the Sixteenth Meting of the CSO. It approves the modalities and financial provisions agreed for these missions by the *ad hoc* group;
2. Welcomes and accepts the offer of Japan, as a participant in the London Conference, to provide a member of the Missions of long duration;
3. Also welcomes the offer of the ECMM to second five officers to the Missions of long duration;
4. Authorises Ambassador Boegh to increase the size of his missions to twenty. The financial implications accompanying this increase will be assessed by the Informal Financial Committee of Experts of the CSO and approved on a provisional basis as soon as possible by the *ad hoc* group in Vienna;
5. Requests participating States to pay their assessed contributions to the costs of the Missions as a matter of urgency.

9.   Stockholm Meeting of the CSCE Council Decisions, 15 December 1992

…

8. The Ministers stressed the importance of the work of the CSCE missions of long duration in Kosovo, Sandjak and Vojvodina. They expressed their satisfaction with the work of the CSCE. … The CSCE presence there should be maintained and expanded; the missions should increasingly focus on helping to resolve specific local differences. In particular, the Minsters agreed to increase substantially the size of the missions of long duration, with particular emphasis on Kosovo, and to take the necessary steps accordingly. They undertook to contribute urgently to these missions.

21-CSO/Journal No. 3, Annex 2

10.   CSO Decision on Missions of Long Duration and the Spillover Mission, 26/28 April 1993

…

8. The CSCE missions of long duration to Kosovo, Sandjak and Vojvodina remain essential to prevent expansion of the conflict which the international community will not tolerate. The CSO stressed that CSCE Missions are an important element in the search for peace in the former Yugoslavia. The CSO reaffirmed the importance of increasing the size of these missions to levels authorised by the Council. The CSO Vienna Group is mandated to consider was and means to improve the effectiveness of these missions in pursuit of their mandate. The CSO reaffirmed the belief that a United nations presence in Kosovo would be a positive step. The CSCE Spillover Mission to Skopje also continues to play an important role in preventing the spillover of the conflict. …

22-CSO/Journal No. 2, Annex 3

11.   CSO Decision on the Former Yugoslavia, 29/30 June 1993

…

1. Missions of Long Duration

The Missions of Long Duration to Kosovo, Sandjak and Vojvodina provide an essential means of preventing conflict by fostering dialogue between the Serbian and non-Serbian populations of these areas. Any attempt to hamper the operation of the missions or to limit their presence would constitute a serious setback to efforts to try to bring an end to the tragic conflicts in the former Yugoslavia.

Acceptance by the authorities of the Federal Republic of Yugoslavia (Serbia and Montenegro) of their presence on a long-term basis is an important test of the willingness of these authorities to contribute to the goal of long-term peace and stability in the region and must not be predicated upon any other issue.

The CSO requested the Chairman-in-Office, together with the Troika, to maintain contact with the relevant authorities in the Federal Republic of Yugoslavia (Serbia and Montenegro) to ensure continuation of the Memorandum of understanding and improved efficiency of this important long-term contribution of the CSCE to the peace process.

Pursuant to the decision of the Stockholm Council Meeting in December 1992 to increase substantially the size of these missions and in order to ensure successful continuation of the work of the missions, the CSO tasked the Vienna Group to focus in particular on expansion of activities in Kosovo, Sandjak and Vojvodina and on identifying additional categories of personnel who may be assigned there as the operation evolves.

12.   Security Council Resolution 855, 9 August 1993

[Adopted by the Security Council at its 3262nd meeting.]

The Security Council,

Taking note of the letters of 20 July 1993 (S/26121) and 23 July 1993 (S/26148) from the Chairman-in-Office of the Council of Ministers of the Conference on Security and Cooperation in Europe (CSCE),

Further *taking note* of the letters of 28 July 1993 (S/26210) and 3 August 1993 (S/26234) circulated by the authorities of the Federal Republic of Yugoslavia (Serbia and Montenegro),

Deeply concerned at the refusal of the authorities in the Federal Republic of Yugoslavia (Serbia and Montenegro) to allow the CSCE missions of long duration to continue their activities,

Bearing in mind that the CSCE missions of long duration are an example of preventive diplomacy undertaken within the framework of the CSCE, and have greatly contributed to promoting stability and counteracting the risk of violence in Kosovo, Sandjak and Vojvodina, the Federal Republic of Yugoslavia (Serbia and Montenegro),

Reaffirming its relevant resolutions aimed at putting an end to conflict in former Yugoslavia,

Determined to avoid any extension of the conflict in the former Yugoslavia and, in this context, attaching great importance to the work of the CSCE missions and to the continued ability of the international community to monitor the situation in Kosovo, Sandjak and Vojvodina, the Federal Republic of Yugoslavia (Serbia and Montenegro),

Stressing its commitment to the territorial integrity and political independence of all States in the region,

1. *Endorses* the efforts of the CSCE as described in the letters noted above from the Chairman-in-Office of the Council of Ministers of the Conference on Security and Cooperation in Europe (CSCE);

2. *Calls upon* the authorities in the Federal Republic of Yugoslavia (Serbia and Montenegro) to reconsider their refusal to allow the continuation of the activities of the CSCE missions in Kosovo, Sandjak and Vojvodina, the Federal Republic of Yugoslavia (Serbia and Montenegro), to cooperate with the CSCE by taking the practical steps needed for the resumption of the activities of these missions and to agree to an increase in the number of monitors as decided by the CSCE;

3. *Further calls* upon the authorities in the Federal Republic of Yugoslavia (Serbia and Montenegro) to assure the monitors' safety and security, and to allow them free and unimpeded access necessary to accomplish their mission in full;

4. *Decides* to remain seized of the matter.

D.   Reports of the CSCE Missions and Related Communications

CSCE Communication No. 41, Prague, 24 January 1992

1.   Report of the Human Rights Rapporteur Mission to Yugoslavia, 24 January 1992

INTRODUCTION

The CSCE Human Rights Rapporteur Mission, which was established by the fourth meeting of the Committee of Senior Officials in Prague on 22 October 1991, visited Bosnia-Hercegovina, Croatia, Macedonia, Montenegro, Serbia - including Kosovo and Vojvodina - and Slovenia between 12 December 1991 and 10 January 1992.

The Mission was led by the representative appointed by the Chairman-in-Office of the CSCE Council of Ministers and was composed of the representatives of CSCE Institutions, of the European Community and of the Conference on Yugoslavia as well as of experts from participating states (List of participants: Annex II).

The program of the visit was prepared in consultation with the Federal Government of Yugoslavia as well as the Governments of each of the above-mentioned Republics, all of which were very helpful in order to facilitate and assist the Mission. For reasons of timing and logistics the visit took place in two separate periods (12-20 December 1992 and 7-10 January 1992).

The Swiss Government provided liaison with authorities, both Federal and Republican, with private organisations and individuals as well as logistical support for the Mission. An aircraft was put at the disposal of the Mission, which could not have fulfilled its task without such effective and professional support.

As the Mission had to have a wide range of contacts and to make visits to relevant Institutions, the group in some cases split into two or three teams. Because of the very limited time available, priorities had to be set in the selection of those contacts, as meetings with all relevant groups and individuals were not possible. Therefore, not all the issues could get the attention they deserved.

During the visits to the Republics and the Autonomous Provinces, the Mission met with members of Governments and Parliaments, with representatives of parties and ethnic or religious groups, with local journalists and foreign observers, as well as with representatives of governmental and non-governmental organisations, especially in the field of human rights. (Program: Annex III) [*not reproduced*]

The Mission collected a fair amount of first-hand information and got a comprehensive picture of the human rights situation including the protection of minorities. It did however leave aside all aspects directly related to the war, as these are dealt with in other fora.

The Mission avoided to make any statement to the press at its terms of reference specifically provided for reporting to the CSCE. In some cases - in particular in Vojvodina and in Kosovo - the local authorities had made arrangements for the press to be present at the meetings. The Mission could not accept such presence as this would have prevented an open discussion.

The Rapporteur Mission of the CSCE was carried out at the eve of the formal recognition of two of the Republics on behalf of several European States, and while two other Republics formally asked for international recognition. It also took place at a time when a new cease-fire agreement was reached, that foreshadowed the possible deployment of a military peace-keeping force of the United Nations. In some cases the conclusions to which the Mission came after the contacts in the different Republics, had therefore to be adapted to the changing situation.

GENERAL REMARKS

1.   Generally speaking, there is a considerable discrepancy between legal rules and norms on the one hand and the actual implementation of such rules and norms on the other hand. Despite official declarations at various levels, human rights are frequently violated in many respects, in some places even systematically.

2. The collapse of the federal constitutional structure has destroyed the legal system of the Federal State. Therefore the Federal Authorities considering themselves to be responsible for the implementation of international and national commitments in the field of human rights, can no longer meet such responsibility. Consequently protection of human rights now exclusively lies in the hands of the Authorities of the Republics.

3. Though weakening, the influence of the communist system is still strong, since in all Republics the dominant political forces are, in many instances and under various denominations, the heirs to the Communist Party. Administrative and political structures still are widely run by the same persons who were already in power in the past. Although they have changed their political goals, many of them have not basically changed their mentality and their methods.

4. Recent developments in Yugoslavia have led to an upsurge of nationalism. As a consequence, authorities in the Republics in varying degree fail to protect minorities, often discriminate against them and sometimes violate their basic human rights. Most of the grave human rights violations in Yugoslavia are perpetrated against persons belonging to minorities.

5. While world opinion so far has concentrated on human rights violations in the war zone in Croatia, grave violations occur in other areas as well, in particular in Kosovo and Sandjak. The Mission feels that a thorough and lasting improvement of the human rights situation in Yugoslavia does require the same standards to be applied everywhere and to all ethnic groups. Concepts such as Serbs being a 'nationality' while Albanians are a 'minority', and therefore subject to a different legal regime, should be dismissed.

6. The Federal Army, which is no longer under any constitutional control, is responsible for human rights violations by drafting young conscripts in Republics, which no longer recognise the legitimacy of the drafting system. Furthermore many non-Serbian Yugoslavs, particularly in Bosnia-Hercegovina and in Vojvodina, feel intimidated by the dangerous concentration of army units and their threatening behaviour. This makes the already high volatile situation in Bosnia-Hercegovina even more explosive.

7. Moderating forces from grass-root organisations, free trade unions, NGOs, churches and religious groups are weak. This may explain the virtual absence of effective and influential movements for human rights and peace. Integration of and understanding between different ethnic groups is hampered by the fact that most political parties are actually formed along nationality lines.

8. The increase of nationalism has also led to a war in the media in particular in Serbia and Croatia. Facts are distorted, data falsified and some times atrocities invented in order to contribute to an atmosphere of mutual hatred. Neither the Government of Serbia nor that of Croatia seem to do anything to stop this incitement to ethnic hatred. This kind of nationalistic propaganda has also a negative effect on individual freedom. Anybody who does not agree with the national majority is disciplined by his colleagues and his superiors; any attempt towards moderation is looked at with suspicion.

FEDERAL AUTHORITIES OF YUGOSLAVIA

The contacts with Federal Authorities started with a comprehensive and frank discussion on human rights standards in the whole of Yugoslavia with the Deputy Minister of Justice.

The picture that emerged from the discussion indicated that generally speaking, the respect of human rights in Yugoslavia does not meet CSCE standards. The War that is taking place in Croatia is said to be the main reason, but it is certainly nor the only relevant factor. According to our interlocutors the principle of individuality has never taken roots in the region and no tradition of respect for individual rights could be established in 45 years of one party system.

In fact, while insisting, on one hand, on the necessity of a united Yugoslav State to implement all aspects of democratisation and of the rule of law, our counterpart admitted, on the other hand, the practical impossibility of achieving this aim, as the Federal Authorities have no means to enforce the law and to implement the commitments of the CSCE documents in the field of human rights and rights of minorities.

Law enforcement is therefore left to the Authorities to the republics, whose functioning now seems to be completely out of control of the Federal State.

Similar concepts were expressed at the Ministry of Foreign Affairs by the Head of the CSCE Office (Minister Loncar had resigned the day before); according to him the "secession" of some of the Republics is to be considered the main problem and the "fight of Yugoslavia against this" is inevitable; the difficulties in implementing human rights have to be seen as temporary, due to a transition period, but implementation of CSCE commitments would be ensured as soon as the unity of Yugoslavia and the authority of Federal structures are restored.

Discussions at the Federal Ministry of Defence were focused on the question of the military Draft, about which a very clear position was taken; four Republics were said to have unilaterally suspended the Federal law on drafting. However it is still considered valid and provides for sanctions against those who resist conscription. Military service is therefore to be considered as a general obligation, with no differences among nationalities.

Conscientious objection is only taken into account for religious reasons; in such cases recruitment takes place, but with no obligation to use weapons.

According to the Federal Authorities the laws establishing military service in Croatia and Slovenia are to be considered illegal; Yugoslav citizens in the national forces of Croatia and Slovenia who evade the Draft are therefore committing a crime and can be prosecuted in every part of the territory of Yugoslavia.

On the question of the legitimacy of the Federal Presidency as head of the Army, it was pointed out that the mandate to call the reservists was given when the Federal Presidency still enjoyed a full quorum of its members.

In conclusion it may be said that Federal structures have disintegrated, with the exception of the Yugoslav National Army, which is by now out of constitutional control. Even some provisions of the new Constitutions of the different Republics are considered by the Federal Authorities including the Constitutional Court at illegal, which makes the whole constitutional framework dangerously unclear and, in practical terms, ineffective.

…

6. SERBIA

A. Central Authorities and other contacts

According to Serbian authorities the origin of the present problems—both at Federal and Serbian level—depends on the fact that, in simple words, the minorities 'have gone nationalist and separatist', forcing the Republic to react and to reduce the sphere of human rights.

The question of Kosovo was raised with the Minister of Foreign Affairs, according to whom the local political movement towards secession, with disregard to Serbian as well as Federal laws and rules, was the main reason for human rights being 'not fully implemented' in that region despite the fact that as present there is no state of emergency in Kosovo.

Answering a question by the Mission on the possibility to send CSCE observers in case of elections in the autonomous provinces. Mr Jovanovic said that, when elections are held, international observers would be welcome in the autonomous province, though the results of the elections, scheduled for March 1992, would be jeopardised, since the Albanian population would anyhow refrain from voting.

Similar ideas were expressed by the Minister of Justice, the representatives of the Ministry of the Interior and the Head of Police.

Much was said about Yugoslavia having accepted most of the international agreements, including those within the CSCE: such commitments were automatically incorporated in the legal framework of the State and of the Republics and fully implemented both for individuals and for minorities. Answers to questions about the control of such implementation were less satisfactory. In particular, Albanians in Kosovo were said to be simply unwilling to enjoy the many rights (collective as well as individual) that the territorial autonomy granted to them. According to our Interlocutors, the Parliament in Kosovo, which had been dissolved by a decision of the Central Republican Authorities in Belgrade, would be re-established as soon as Albanians stopped boycotting the elections and accepted offers for co-operation with the

Serbian Authorities; Albanian schools were said to have been closed mainly for technical reasons and TV stations and newspapers in Albanian were suspended, because they "were used only for political propaganda"; people, including doctors, teachers, etc., who were left without their job, allegedly were dismissed because they simply refused to work on the conditions set by the Authorities. In contacts with both Serbian and Yugoslavian private organisations and individuals as well as with foreign observers, a somewhat different picture emerged. In general, human rights were still being violated in many ways, especially political rights, this having started well before the war. Several Serbian Authorities as well as non-official groups and organisations seemed to share the responsibility for that, while Federal bodies could practically do nothing to prevent it. The war had made things even worse, as radicalisation of feelings had made political opposition increasingly difficult. Freedom of information was seriously violated, as media were fully controlled by Republican structures. Radio and TV stations, including non-State owned ones, seem to be under heavy pressure since the demonstrations in March 1991. Private stations have in many cases, only local importance and limited influence. The main newspapers maintain a certain freedom, but are increasingly confronting difficulties since, despite the lack of censorship, which is officially abolished, the public sector still holds the monopoly of sources and technical means of information. The Mission could not find foreign newspapers in Belgrade.

There also seems to be a drastic reduction of freedom of movement, as communications are made increasingly difficult. As far as freedom of association is concerned, any activity not supporting the nationalistic attitude of the Government being in favour of actual implementation of the rule of law is considered as treacherous. Many intellectuals are now trying to emigrate to avoid the Draft and also because the radicalisation of inter-ethnic conflict does not seem likely to come to an end soon. Owing to war developments, increasing consciousness of anti-war feelings leads to an increasing number of conscientious objectors, who are not considered as such be present legislation and are therefore liable to trial: and there is no guarantee to ensure that trials in Military Courts are fair and correspond to human right standards.

The war of the media, which is developing in an extremely dangerous way, is an obvious example of the lack if implementation of CSCE commitments. ...

C. Kosovo

The Authorities of the province strongly denied any systematic mistreatment of civilians by the police and declared that the Albanians themselves have weapons and often use them to threaten civilians, committing crimes that they later ascribe to the police. The Head of the Police insisted that the Authorities have the right to enforce the law with regard to Albanians "who do not want to be loyal" by taking all disciplinary and penal measures. As far as the loss of jobs is concerned, the explanation given to the Mission was that the persons concerned did not want to accept the rules and were dismissed because they refused to work.

The situation as described by the leaders of the Albanian opposition groups of Kosovo is a most dramatic one, with thousands of Albanians left jobless, schools and University not functioning and no political representation in any decision-making body. In fact, following the dissolution of the Parliament of the autonomous province and the adoption of the law on "special circumstances" by the Serbian Parliament, about 700,000 Albanians were said to be remained without salary and social security. Moreover, the Mission was told that the local police systematically arrests, mistreats and even tortures members of the Albanian community throughout the province, treating it like an occupied territory. Private individuals of the Serbian community in Kosovo were said to have been armed in support of police forces. The Mission visited a prison in Pristina and was told by the director of the prison that there were no political prisoners on the premises. Two prisoners were interviewed.

The main problem for both sides seems to be that of the "trend to secession". Albanians, refusing to accept Serbian rules for political elections, organised a referendum about a future independent Republic of Kosovo. On the question of the relations with Albania and of a possible unification, the answers were unclear, vague and sometimes contradictory. The results of the referendum were reported to be: 87% of the electorate voted; 99% of the voters were in favour of independence. It is obvious that the Serbian Authorities would by no means be ready to accept the secession, which would mean the loss of what is considered by them to be the historical cradle of Serbia. The conclusion can be drawn that in Kosovo there is a highly unsatisfactory human rights situation. So far neither a dialogue between the Serbian and the Albanian communities nor any mediating effort take place.

CONCLUSIONS

1. The Mission deems it absolutely necessary to pursue the tenacity peace-efforts, since the rule of law cannot be restored as long as hostilities go on. To this end it is recommended to support with all energy the existing peace-initiatives, particularly those of the United nations and those of the EC in the context of the Conference of Yugoslavia.

2. After the cessation of hostilities, particular attention has to be given to the creation of a climate of reconciliation conducive to the establishment of the rule of law and the respect for human rights and the rights of all ethnic groups. Arrangements to that end could best be made on the basis of the Treaty Provisions for the Convention as proposed by the Conference on Yugoslavia. In this context it is necessary to introduce fair and non-discriminatory laws of citizenship and to establish electoral systems, which give a fair representation to all ethnic groups.

3. Participating states should respond positively to requests of competent authorities to assist them in the field of legislation, judicial administration, education-programs and other fields relevant to the protection of human rights, like the preparation and organisation of census. Since human rights seem to be particularly in jeopardy in less developed areas, assistance should also be provided in the economic and social field.

4. The Mission is of the opinion that the human rights situation should be kept under constant consideration by the CSCE. Full use should be made of the possibilities offered by the various CSCE mechanisms, in particular of the one contained in the Document of the Moscow meeting of the Conference on the Human Dimension.

5. The Mission feels that the following issues ask for immediate consideration and for consecutive action the CSCE (where appropriate, in co-ordination with the United Nations and the European Community):

6. the war in the media,

7. the explosive situation in Bosnia-Hercegovina,

8. the paralysis of public life in Kosovo, in particular

9. the human rights problems in Sanjak.

10. To that end the sending of follow-up missions should be considered, in particular with regard to the media.

11. In addition, the Mission recommends that the CSCE considers means for giving, upon request, its assistance for the preparation and organisation of census.

ANNEX I, Decision of the Committee of Senior Officials of the CSCE, Prague, October 22, 1991 [*reprinted above, Document 5.C.1*].

ANNEX II

LIST OF PARTICIPANTS

1. Prof. Dr. Thomas Fleiner-Gerster, Director of the Institute of Federalism, University of Fribourg (designated by the Chairman-in-Office of the CSCE).

2. Amb. Luchino Cortese, Director of the CSCE Office for Free Elections, Warsaw.

3. Prof. Dr. Pieter Hendrik Kooijmans, Faculty of Law, University of Leiden, (designated by the Presidency of the European Community).

4. Amb. Geert Ahrens, Ministry of Foreign Affairs, Bonn (designated by the Chairman of the Conference on Yugoslavia).

5. Prof. Dr. Roman Wieruszewski, Polish Academy of Science, Chairman of the Executive Committee of the Human Right Promotion Foundation, Peznan.

6. Dr. Paul Widmer, Head of the CSCE Office, Ministry of Foreign Affairs, Bern.

2. Republic of Serbia, Commentary Regarding the CSCE Mission on Human Rights in Yugoslavia, 6 March 1992

1. As regards the Mission's criticism of alleged discrimination against thousands *of ethnic Albanians in Serbia*, we would like to make the following observations:

Serbia has given special attention to defining and safeguarding the individual and collective rights of the Albanian national minority, so that, as the largest national minority in this Republic, the ethnic Albanians have acquired a privileged position and far greater autonomy than that envisaged for national minorities in the International Covenant on Civil and Political Rights and other relevant international instruments.

The Constitution of the Republic of Serbia guarantees the Autonomous Province of Kosovo and Metohija a form of territorial autonomy in keeping with the special ethnic, historical, cultural and other attributes of that region. By the same token, the Serbian Constitution, as the Republic's highest instrument, ensures the citizens of Kosovo and Metohija the right, through their representatives bodies (the provincial parliament and provincial government, to administer matters having to do with economic development and financing education, the use of languages, health protection, etc.

Regardless of the fact that the Constitution of the Republic of Serbia defines and guarantees the sovereignty of citizens and not a national group, the Constitution nevertheless envisages safeguards for the special rights of members of national minorities.

The ethnic Albanians have 24 newspapers and periodicals published in the Albanian language; the Albanian TV programme in Pristina broadcasts daily from 17.40 to 20.30 hours, and the Albanian language radio programme is broadcast from 8.00 to 24.00 hours.

The enrolment of ethnic Albanian children in elementary schools is 94.7, and in secondary schools it is 73.6%; in the 1989/90 academic year, 25,344 university students in Kosovo and Metohija belonging to the Albanian ethnic minority attended classes in their mother tongue. (Although there are tow and a half times more Albanians living in Albania than in Serbia, i.e. in Kosovo and Metohija, there are more than 25,000 ethnic Albanian students enrolled in the University of Pristina compared with just 19,000 at the University in Tirana.)

Furthermore, in Kosovo and Metohija the ethnic Albanians have two national theatres, the National and university libraries with over one million books, more than 140 cultural artistic societies, a film production company, 41 cinema houses, the Kosovo Archives and 12 regional archives, etc.

The ethnic Albanians exercise full freedom of confession in over 500 mosques. The ethnic Albanians engage in political activities in 15 officially registered political parties and the Union of Independent Trade Unions, which are organised along strictly ethnic lines.

In the last 15 years, ethnic Albanian representatives of the Autonomous Province of Kosovo and Metohija, have held the following state and political offices at the federal level, president of the Presidency of the SFRY, President of the Assembly of the SFRY (twice), President of the Presidency of the Central Committee of the League of Communists of Yugoslavia, Vice-President of the Presidency of the SFRY (twice), President of the Federal Chamber of the Assembly of the SFRY, President of the Chamber of Republics and Provinces of the Assembly of the SFRY, etc.

This brief review clearly shows that the Albanian national minority has rights which far exceed accepted international standards. It was a long time before the domestic and foreign public finally realised that it is the plan for the secession of Kosovo and Metohija from Serbia that lies behind the dissatisfaction with ethnic Albanian national rights. A dialogue with the Albanian alternative movement is being conducted. The deputy Prime Minister and Cabinet Ministers of the Serbian government are all taking part in it. At the moment, attention is being focused on questions of education in Kosovo and Metohija. Preparations are under way for the organisation of an international gathering, to be attended by representatives of the Serbian people, the ethnic Albanian minority, and international experts.

The Albanian minority, of their own free will, rejected the legitimate option of negotiation by boycotting the multiparty elections in Serbia. By doing so they deprived themselves of some 90 seats in parliament. It is expected that the dialogue will acquire an institutionalised form following the organisation of local and provincial elections in Serbia and in Kosovo and Metohija, which have been scheduled for the middle of this year.

The Mission's report completely overlooks the disloyalty of the ethnic Albanian minority to their home state of Serbia. It ignores the illegal nature of the activities and actions directed against the constitutional order and against the territorial integrity and sovereignty of the Republic of Serbia. The illegal proclamation of an "independent republic of Kosovo" receives no mention whatsoever in the Mission's Report, even though it is a flagrant example of the impermissible abuse of minority rights for the purpose of achieving secessionist aims. The problems in Kosovo and Metohija can be attributed not to a failure to acknowledge minority rights according to CSCE standards but rather to the abuse of these rights and systematic refusal to exercise them. The purpose of such unconstitutional behaviour is to make the ethnic Albanian minority appear the victim of alleged discrimination and persecution on the part of Serbia, in order to win over the sympathy of foreign public opinion for secessionist and separatist aims directed against the Republic of Serbia.

3. Letter to CSCE from Kosovo Political Parties & Council for the Defence of Human Rights, 6 May 1992

Respected Gentlemen,

We see it necessary to inform you about the serious violations of human, national and political rights and freedoms of the Albanian people in Kosova. Kosova has an area of around 11 thousands sq. kilometres, and circa two million inhabitants, 90 per cent of which are Albanian. (In former Yugoslavia, three mission ethnic Albanians, constituted the third largest nation). Because of its territorial, geoeconomical and ethnic compactness, Kosova has a long historic continuance of its independence, since the antique period and up to the 1974 Federation Constitution of Yugoslavia, which was in power until the moment Yugoslavia started dismembering. Pursuant this Constitution, Kosova was one of the eight constitutive elements of this federation. It was defined as such in the basic principles and the normative part of the Constitution (Articles 2 and 4). The territory and borders of Kosova could not be changed without Kosova's consent (Article 5). The constitution of Yugoslavia could not be changed without Kosova's consent, either (Art 398 and 402). Based on the Federal Constitution of 1974, Kosova had its own Constitution which defined its autonomous government, its legislative, executive and judicial powers. The autonomy of Kosova was similar to the autonomy of any of the federal units, as for the self-organization, legislation, the executive and judicial, finances, community activities, the planification of development, the social policy, the foreign policy, defence, internal affairs of Yugoslavia. Kosova was presented by its representatives in all the organs of the government and the organs of forums of the political and economic associations of the Yugoslav federation. The Yugoslav constitution of 1974 treats no longer the Albanians as a national minority, but a nationality. Article 245 of the Constitution states that all nations and nationalities in Yugoslavia are equal.

Gentlemen,

The dissipation of Yugoslavia started in Kosova and about Kosova. People that are familiar to the structure and the constitution of Yugoslavia, will understand that this fact is not casual. By exercising its domination over Yugoslavia, Serbia constantly attempted to reduce, restrict and eventually abolish the subjectivity of Kosova as a constitutive unit of the Yugoslav federation. Since 1981, Serbia openly and violently started to ruin the constitutional structure of Kosova so its hegemonist and assimilatory aspirations towards the Albanian people would become true. In order to accomplish this goal, in 1988, Serbia started the procedure for the change Constitution of Kosovo. By the amendments IX-XLIX to the Constitution of Serbia that were approved on March 28, 1989, against the plebiscitary expressed will of the Albanian people, Serbia provided arbitrarily itself the possibility to change the constitutions of Serbia without approval of Kosova, even when these changes have to do with the constitutional position of Kosovo: instead of giving its consent, now Kosova's Parliament only had the right to express its opinion, which is not of obligatory character. Facing the discontent of Albanians against he approval of these amendment, which was expressed through massive demonstrations in all of Kosova, through the well known strike of the Trepca miners, etc., on Feb. 27, 1989, one month before the amendments were to be approved, the state of emergency was installed in Kosova. The amendments to the Serbian constitution were approved in conditions of a state of emergency, in a tense political situation on March 23, 1989, in time when the Parliament of Kosova was surrounded by tanks and large police forces, when the building of the Parliament was full of members of the secret police, in conditions when even activists of the other political organizaitons and not members of the Parliament voted, and in conditions when the votes of 'in favour' and 'against' were never counted. Peopled named this act 'Constitution of Tanks'. On Sept. 28, 1990, without even asking for Kosova's opinion anymore and contrary to its own constitution, Serbia approved its new constitution, by which the autonomy of Kosova was even more radically reduced. This constitution too, was approved in conditions of a state of emergency which was virtually declared by Serbia on June 26, 1990. (The Constitution of the 'Third Yugoslavia' which is being promoted by two of eight constitutive units of former Yugoslavia, Serbia and Montenegro, has eliminated the existence of any form of subjectivity of Kosova. We aren't part of this arbitrary act, neither shall we be considered responsible).

Immediately after the violent ruin of Kosova's autonomy, Serbia started with the approval of special programs and laws on Kosova, by which the discrimination and apartheid were to be institutionalized up to the level of genocide. A direct means of functionalization of this concept is the so-called 'Program on the realization of peace, freedom, equality, democracy and prosperity in the Socialist Autonomous Province of Kosova' (Published in the 'Official Gazette of the Socialist Republic of Serbia' nr. 15/90, on March 30, 1990). This program, which has been cynically euphemized by this title, is a typical program of colonization by its content and nature. It foresees a number of concrete and systematic measures to the undertaken by Serbia in Kosova and against Albanians, in order to alter the ethnical structure of the population. For the realization of this program, Serbia approved a series of unconstitutional laws, which are being applied only in Kosova and against Albanians:

- 'The law on the activities of the republican organs in special circumstances' (published in the 'Official Gazette of the SR of Serbia' nr 3090 on June 26, 1990) which virtually established the state of emergency in Kosova for an unlimited period of time. All competences of the governmental organs in Kosova were usurped and taken over by the Serbian governmental organs;
- 'The law on the suspension of the functions of the Assembly of Kosova, its Executive Council and the discharge of functionaries of administrative organs' (published in the 'Official Gazette of SR of Serbia' nr 33/90 on June 26, 1990). By this law, a Parliament of a federal unit (Serbia), dispersed the Parliament and Government of another federal unit (Kosova), which is a unique case in any of the federal states in the world and in direct collision with the constitutions of Yugoslavia, Serbia and Kosova;
- 'The labor law on special circumstances' (published in the 'Official Gazette of the Republic of Serbia' nr 10/90 on July 26, 1990). Based on this law, Albanians are being dismissed because of their political convictions, because they dare to speak in their own mother tongue, because of the participation in a one-day general strike, because they are members of the Independent Trade-Unions of Kosova, because they voted on the Referendum, because of their activities in political parties, etc., and in all cases, without any legal proceedings;
- 'The law on the suspension of the functions of the Presidency of Kosova' (published in the 'Official Gazette of the SR of Serbia' nr. 15/91 on March 15, 1991). The law abolished the Presidency of Kosova, whose members could be elected and destituted only by Kosova's Parliament, and which represented Kosova in Yugoslavia and abroad;
- 'The law on the official use of languages and scripts' (published in the 'Official Gazette of the RS' nr 45/91, July 21, 1991). Through this law, the program on the colonization of Kosova was to be accomplished. Serbs and Montenegrins that settle in Kosova are freely given the land which is community property, and are provided with outer economic, financial and tax benefits, so the alteration of the ethnical structure of the population in Kosova would be stimulated.;
- 'The law on the restrictions of the purchase of real-estate' (published in the 'Official Gazette of the SRS', nr 30/89, on July 22, 1989, and revised on April 18, 1991, 'Official Gazette of the RS' nr 22/91). The law forbids Albanians to sell or buy any private asset without the permit of the Ministry of Finances of Serbia, which usually refuses the presented requests;
- 'The decision of the destitution of the Member of Presidency of Yugoslavia from Kosova, Riza Sanunxhiu, and the appointment of the (illegitimate) member of the Same presidency, Sejdo Bajramovic (published in the 'Official Gazette of the RS' nr 15/91, on March 18, 1991) by the Serbian Parliament. The appointment and destitution of the member of the Presidency from Kosova was in the competence of the Parliament of Kosova.

The constitutionality of these laws was contested before the Constitutional Court of Yugoslavia but, once blocked by Serbia, which Court hasn't reached any decision concerning these acts. Because of the ruin of its constitutional position of Kosova and its subjectivity in former Yugoslavia, and the application of the special discriminatory laws and the governmental repression and terror over Albanians, it could be said that, as for the violation of human, national and political rights and freedoms of Albanians, Kosova is in the worst position in Europe. Direct consequences of this situation are the following:

1. 110 people were killed and another 611 were wounded by the police and army in peaceful demonstrations and manifestations, on the streets, at the working places, in their homes, at funerals, etc. Many of the victims were children and minors. Another 54 people, while serving their military service were brought back home dead, with an explanation that all had committed suicide (they are not included in the first figure that is listed). Also, in that number are not included the other Albanian youngsters that have been killed in the wars in Slovenia, Croatia and Bosnia and Hercegovina;

2. Thousands of Albanians were beaten, tortured and mistreated physically and mentally by the Serbian police during the punishing expeditions effectuated in different villages and towns throughout Kosova (The Council for the Defence of Human Rights and Freedoms has the complete documentation about these cases).

3. Over 800,000 Albanians have been treated by the police, 2500 Albanians have been sentenced for political crimes up to 20 years of prison by the civilian and military courts, other 30 thousand Albanians have been sentenced for misdemeanors with political elements, as for example the possession of the Albanian national flag, for raising the hand in a victory sign, for having participated in the funerals of the victims, for being members of political parties and the independent Trade-Union, because of their freedom of expression, for possessing audio-cassettes, etc. 300 people were incarcerated without prior judicial decision or court order and held in different jails throughout Serbia up to four months and a half. This was the so-called 'isolation'.

4. Over 100 thousand Albanians have been dismissed from their jobs because of their political convictions, their participation in the one-day general strike, the use of their mother tongue, membership in the ITUK, activities in political parties, etc. 3650 private and state-owned commerces (ran by Albanians) were shut down up to 12 months and all the owners and heads of commerces were fined, because they too, striked;

5. 1657 Albanian medical and social workers, out of which 157 are professors, docents and instructors of the University were dismissed, automatically being denied the right to social and health insurance for the dismissed and their families. many ambulatory facilities have been shut down in villages.

6. 317 Albanian justices, district attorney and public attorneys have been discharged and were replaced by Serbs and Montenegrins. The Supreme Court of Kosova, the Provincial Prosecutors Office, the Regional Economic Court in Gjakova and another six municipal courts were abolished.

7. All the faculties and superior schools of the University of Prishtina, as well as all the high schools in Albanian were shut down. 92.000 Albanian students have been forcefully driven away from their college and school premises. 837 professors, docents and instructors of the University and 22 thousand teachers of high and elementary schools have been dismissed (The Worlds Congress of Teachers approved a special resolution condemning the actions of the Serbian government against the Albanian education in Kosova, in Oct 1991).

8. All cultural and scientific institutions of Albanians have been cut of further financiation. All directors and managing staff (Albanians) have been dismissed, and replaced by Serbs and Montenegrins;

9. The only Albanian daily newspaper 'Rijindja', as well as the radio-television broadcasting in Albanian have been banned. Over 1300 journalists and other technical staff have been dismissed, and the editors and journalists in Albanian mass-media institutions have been either sentenced to jail or investigated by the police;

10. Albanians are denied the right to the freedom of association and public gathering, or organizing any cultural, scientific manifestation. Political parties and the ITUK always faces obstacles in its activities;

11. Over 450 enterprises are under the so-called emergency management, and all Albanian managing staff has been dismissed and replaced by Serbs and Montenegrins;

12. The right to free movement is restricted for Albanians within Kosova and outside Kosova. Passports are taken away, foreign currencies as well, they are searched and maltreated while travelling, etc;

13. The violation of the right to free confession. Many mosques have been shot at, and Albanian different religious confessional leaders were either mistreated or persecuted and prosecuted;

14. Hundreds of thousands of Albanians have fled to the USA or Europe, forced to leave, running away from the recruitment in the Yugoslav army, and other political persecutions;

By these actions of violence and systematic repression over Albanians, Serbia has violated flagrantly the ten principles of the Final Document of Helsinki, reaffirmed in the Paris Charter and all other international covenants concerning human rights and freedoms. The competent international organs institutions have been informed about all these violations on the national identity of the Albanian people. By the violation of the constitutional order of Kosova and the right and freedoms of Albanians, the European Parliament, the Parliaments of Austria, Germany, Albania, Belgium as well as the US Senate and Congress have approved a series of Resolutions which condemn the Yugoslav and the Serbian government. These resolutions condemn the violation of the constitutional order in Kosova, the abolishment of the autonomy of Kosova, the violation of human rights and freedoms in Yugoslavia, the violence and systematic repression over Albanians, and demands:

• The abolishment of the state of emergency in Kosova;
• The withdrawal of the police and military forces in Kosova;
• The organization of free multi-party elections and
• The recognition of the right of self-determination to the Albanian people.

The matter of the violation of individual and collective rights of Albanians in Yugoslavia was also discussed in the UN Human Rights Committee in New York, in the UN Sub-commission on Human Rights in Geneva, in the UN Specialized Agencies (UNESCO, UNICEF, ITU), in the CSCE Session- -Human Dimension in Copenhagen and Moscow as well as other non- governmental human rights organizations such as the IHF in Vienna, Helsinki Watch in New York, Amnesty International in London and New York, etc. Based on the presented evidence and the expressed will of the Albanian people through the Constitutional Declaration of Kosova as an equal unit of the Yugoslav Federation-Confederation (July 2, 1990), the Constitution of the Republic of Kosova (Sept. 7, 1990) and the resolution on the Independent and Sovereign Republic of Kosova, as people declared themselves in favour of, in the Referendum on Sept 26-30, 1991, we have the right to expect from the state members to:

1. Condemn ruin of the constitutional order of Kosova and its colonization by Serbia;
2. Condemn the harsh violation of human, national political, economic and social rights of Albanians, by Serbia;
3. Demand the abolition of the state of emergency in Kosova and the withdrawal of the police and military forces from Kosova;
4. Support the organizaiton and effectuation of free multiparty elections in Kosova, under the supervision of the CSCE Bureau for free elections in Warsaw;
5. Recognize the right of self-determination to the Albanian people, since it was a constitutive element of the former Yugoslavia, which has stopped existing.

After all these facts and arguments that were presented, and which are very well known to the democratic international opinion, we consider that the recognition of the Serbian-Montenegrian state, the self-declared 'Third Yugoslavia', is a matter of conscience and responsibility of the countries and authorized international institutions.

Respected Gentlemen,

We feel it necessary to remind you that, any further discussion on the matter of Kosova which would ignore the plebiscitary expressed will and the rights of self-determination of the Albanian people, would be unfair on them. To reach the rightful and honest solution to the Kosova problem, no analogy to the solution of the problem of the Serbs in Croatia, of the Moslems in Sandzak or Serbs in Bosnia, is worth applying. Ksova has its on originality and continuitie independence, as well as its established borders which are guaranteed by the 1974 Yugoslav Constitution. The solution of the problem of Kosova can't serve as a compromise to solve other pending problems in former Yugoslavia, neither to give concessions to Serbia, whose direct victim is Kosova. The right solution of the matter of Kosova, is a condition to provide this region a strong and long-lasting peace, while the improper solution would be a reason for its further radicalization and a latent danger of tensions and confrontations with serious consequences for the peace and security in the Balkans and Europe.

Respectfully, Dr Ibrahim Rugova, Coordinating Body of Kosova's Political Parties; Adem Demaci, Chairman, Council for the Defence of Human Rights and Freedoms in Prishtina

4. Report of the Conflict Prevention Centre Fact-finding Mission to Kosovo, 5 June 1992

Introduction

The Committee of Senior Officials of the CSCE decided on 20 May 1992 to request the Consultative Committee of the Conflict Prevention Centre to dispatch a fact-finding mission to determine the military situation in Kosovo. On 23 May the Consultative Committee of the CPC requested the Chairman of the Consultative Committee to organise and supervise the mission. The mission was led by Ambassador David Peel of Canada and included members from the Czech and Slovak Federal Republic, Denmark, France, the Netherlands, Switzerland, the United Kingdom and a (Spanish) representative from the Secretariat of the CPC. (List of participants: Annex I.) The fact-finding mission made contact with the Vice-Chairman of the Conference on Yugoslavia and with the Chief of Staff of the United Nations Protection Force (UNPROFOR) in Yugoslavia. The mission visited Belgrade on 27 May 1992 and Kosovo from 28 May to 2 June 1992.

The mission met with representatives of the Federal Government and of the Government of the Republic of Serbia and with representatives of the Yugoslav Army (YA), Air Force and Militia (police). The mission also had considerable contact with ordinary citizens. (See Annex II.) During its time in Kosovo, the mission visited all military garrisons, most military training areas and several other installations, including border checkpoints with Albania. It visited all significant centres of population and several other settlements. Helicopter flights gave the mission the opportunity to cover the whole territory.

Section I: Background

Kosovo is situated in the southern part of Yugoslavia and covers an area of 10,887 sq. km. The population of Kosovo, approximately two million, is ethnically mixed: Albanians, Serbs, Montenegrins, Muslims, Turks and others. Albanians are approximately 90 per cent of the population; they have one of the highest birth rates in Europe. The Serbs see Kosovo as the cradle of the Serbian Orthodox church and the Serbian State. The Albanians claim to be the direct descendants of the Illyrians, and to have inhabited the Kosovo area since before the arrival of the Serbs and others. After the First World War and the break-up of the Ottoman empire, frontiers were re-established and Kosovo became part of the Kingdom of Serbs, Croats and Slovenes (Yugoslavia) in 1921. In 1944 the Federal Yugoslav Constitution of 1974 gave Kosovo the status of an autonomous province within Serbia. Kosovo was represented in the Collective Presidency, in the Federal Government and in the Federal Parliament. In 1981, demonstrations by ethnic Albanians for the status of republic in Yugoslavia led to serious riots in Kosovo. In 1969 the Republic of Serbia suspended Kosovo's status as an autonomous province; this led to further riots. In 1990 ethnic Albanian members of the parliament of Kosovo proclaimed a Republic of Kosovo. The parliament of Serbia responded by dissolving the parliament in Kosovo and by suspending local administration, including police. These functions have since been carried out by Serbian authorities. In the autumn of 1990 the dissolved ethnic Albanian parliament met and adopted a new constitution which declared Kosovo's independence. A referendum arranged by the ethnic Albanians in 1991 overwhelmingly supported Kosovo's independence. This independence has not been achieved, but in elections on 24 May 1992, arranged by the ethnic Albanians and not prevented by the Serbian authorities although they deemed them illegal, Dr. Ibrahim Rugova, who was unopposed, was elected president and a parliament was also elected. Ethnic Albanians refused to participate in the general election in Serbia on 31 May 1992.

Section II: Contacts and Perceptions

Throughout their discussions with the mission, Federal and Serbian authorities stressed the importance of Kosovo in Serbian history. Federal Government representatives said they could not accept Kosovo becoming independent or joining Albania. Military authorities described a dangerous security situation in Kosovo, including a possible threat of interference from outside. Serbian authorities emphasised that Kosovo was part of Serbia, that the ethnic Albanians are a minority in Serbia, and that boundaries could not be changed'. Serbia would defend the integrity of its territory, which is as important as that of any other country. They stressed that Albanians could have the same rights as any other Yugoslav citizen. They noted that offers had been made to the Albanians in Kosovo to negotiate great autonomy but no response had been received. The Serbians said that conflict would arise in Kosovo if a separatist movement became more active, noting that there is no internationally recognised right to secession. They stressed that any further moves by the Albanians to establish institutions would also fuel the conflict. Some said the Albanian population is well armed (a condition they admitted was common in the Balkans). The situation in Kosovo was described by one authority as a pre-conflict state of affairs. Representatives of the ethnic Albanians, on the other hand, told the mission that they would be prepared to negotiate with the Serbs, but the Serbs refused to talk on this basis. Albanians insisted that they have always been discriminated against and that they do not have equal rights, thus they refuse to participate in Serbian institutions, such as political bodies, administration, army and police. These institutions, they said, are not theirs. They insisted that the army, the police and indeed many Serbian civilians are armed while Albanians are not; as a result, their opposition could only be civil disobedience. They said that the Militia not only searches their cars and homes but uses various other forms of harassment. Kosovo remains, in their opinion, the most dangerous area in Yugoslavia. They feared the Serbs would eventually try to create an armed conflict to force the Albanians out of Kosovo. If started, it would produce a massacre and vast numbers of refugees. Some of the Albanian representatives were particularly concerned about the Serbian reaction when their newly elected parliament meets. They said that they still think a political solution is possible and hoped that Europe will do something to help them. Representatives of other ethnic groups described the situation as tense and confusing. In their view, the ethnic Albanians had decided to try to use a patient and democratic route to change, but they thought that the Serbs would never allow their demands. They feared that the situation could lead to armed conflict.

Section III: The Military Situation

The aspects of the military situation in Kosovo which the fact-finding mission investigated covered the land forces, the air forces and the Militia. The fact-finding mission had detailed discussions at command level, and visited barracks and installations, observed training at close hand and inspected military and Militia equipment. The relevant military and Militia authorities co-operated fully with the fact-finding mission. The army provided the mission with a helicopter, with no restrictions as to where it could fly or land. Territorial Defence, because it was abolished in 1992, was not a concern of the fact-finding mission.

1. The Yugoslav Army in Kosovo

a. The YA in Kosovo consists of the 52nd Corps, which as the primary task of defending the Kosovo plateau. The main military threat is seen in terms of airborne/air-landed forces on the Kosovo plateau or from a land attack into the area. The peacetime mission is to secure borders and to protect military installations. The fact-finding mission was given the detailed composition of the Corps and was allowed to verify this information.

b. A tank brigade has recently been repositioned from the former Socialist Republic of Macedonia and placed under the command of 52nd Corps. This tank brigade was withdrawn to Kosovo in accordance with agreements between Serbia and Macedonia. The tank brigade is fully equipped, but is manned with only 15 per cent of its normal peacetime strength. This repositioning has entailed some troop redeployment within the region, including the reactivation of an empty barracks.

c. The strength of the Corps was reported to the fact-finding mission as 4,000 regular personnel and conscripts and 1,200 military reservists. It is manned at 40 to 50 per cent of its normal peacetime strength; the reasons for this were explained as the lack of response to conscription by ethnic Albanians and because conscripts from the newly independent republics were no longer available. Consequently most of the conscripts are from outside Kosovo. Comparative personnel strengths for 52nd Corps for past years were given, in writing, as follows:

1988 - 11,800
1991 - 7,913
1992 - 5,200

d. Conscripts are recruited at the age of 19, and serve for a period of about 12 months. On leaving the army, conscripts become reservists with an annual call-up liability for training up to four weeks. Some are allocated to the Militia as reservists, the majority remain reservists of the armed forces. Because of manpower shortages, both conscripts and reservists are now called up more frequently, six time per year rather than twice. The mission was told that the reservists keep their uniform at home but weapons were not issued.

e. The Corps has, in total, approximately 200 tanks, mechanised and motorised infantry and normal combat support. The equipment is located in garrisons.

f. Given the general situation in the country, some efforts have been made to provide or improve the basic protection of army barracks by building earth banks and constructing trenches; barracks were guarded by sentries.

g. The Corps was reported to be at a normal state of combat readiness which means that troops had not been reinforced and peacetime duties were being carried out according to normal plans. The mission saw nothing to contradict this. The fact-finding mission had the opportunity to visit training drills (i.e. shooting, fieldcraft and weapon training). Engineer units were reported to be used in the construction of civilian roads and water supply for villages.

Conclusions:

a. The fact-finding mission saw no military movements other than normal low level routine transportation. The repositioning of the troops from Macedonia, the improvement of the basic protection of some barracks, the increased frequency in recruitment of conscripts, the additional call-up of reservists, and the transportation of conscripts into and out of Kosovo, have been interpreted by some as constituting a higher level of military activity directed against the population. However, the fact-finding mission accepts that there is a logical explanation for each of these activities, and does not consider that they were undertaken specifically against the people of Kosovo.

b. Visits to all barracks confirmed what the mission had been told about the state of their manning, equipment and training. The state of alert could be described as normal, and was demonstrably not high. Training was routine and the atmosphere in barracks and on training appeared relaxed. The impression gained was that the YA was conducting itself in a manner consistent with its role. Reinforcements would certainly be necessary before it could carry out its operational role. That said, there is sufficient manpower and equipment to deploy, without reinforcement, should the Corps be tasked with a secondary role in support of the civil power.

2. The Air Forces

The Air Force in Kosovo, based on one air base near Pristina, is not subordinated to 52nd Corps. The fact-finding mission was told that the air component consists of a squadron of fighter-bombers with the role of air intercept. The air base is defended, including air defence, and is at a normal state of alert. Aircraft carried out missions involving about 10 to 12 flying days per month. The Air Force was reported to be manned at normal peacetime strength, whereas air defence and logistic elements were reported to be at 50 per cent.

Conclusion:

The Air Force in Kosovo carried out normal military duties and tends not to feature highly in public concerns. Furthermore, because of the rapid availability of air power from outside Kosovo, the fact-finding mission considered the Air Force was not a factor which could be considered within the strict bounds of the military situation in Kosovo.

3. The Militia

a. The Militia in Kosovo comes under the authority of the Serbian Ministry of Internal Affairs. It is responsible for internal security, investigation of criminal activity, the maintenance of law and order and other police duties, such as traffic control. The fact-finding mission was told that the visibility of the Militia on the roads had been increased as a preventative measure, particularly given police concern about the high number of unregistered weapons.

b. The mission was told that the Militia consists of about 2,500 men in the active force, and about the same number of reservists on which to call; 10 to 15 per cent of reservists are called up at any one time, for short periods, to provide support for the regulars. The mission could not, of course, verify these figures but it heard no contradictory allegations. By way of contrast, officials said that in 1990 the Militia was 7,000 strong, but had no reservists. It was explained that the difference in manning resulted from the withdrawal of Federal Militia troops and because a number of other nationalities left the service, in particular over 2,000 Albanians when the local administration was suspended in 1990. The Militia in Kosovo is manned, therefore, predominantly by Serbs.

c. The Militia is equipped with light vehicles, wheeled and tracked armoured personnel carriers (some with 14.7 mm machine guns), specialised riot control vehicles, light weapons and mortars. Militia vehicles and uniforms are blue; the Militia also has special forces who wear combat uniforms similar to army uniforms. Some Militia equipment and accommodation have, in the last two years, been situated within YA barracks. The mission was told that this collocation was a matter of protection and logistic convenience, rather than an indication of close army-Militia co-operation.

Conclusions:

a. In a tense and difficult situation, the Militia provides a very visible, and essentially Serbian, presence; they are omnipresent as a result of roadblocks and patrols, both mobile and static. The Militia exercises close control over the population. The Militia claims to act within the prevailing legal framework, but the impression gained by the mission is that its activities are seen by the majority of the population as oppressive and restricting individual freedoms. It is not surprising therefore that the Militia, rather than the army, is seen as the main cause of anxiety and instrument of intimidation. The fact-finding mission heard no suggestions that Militia activities had increased recently, and it appears that the present level of activity has been the norm for the past two years.

b. Nevertheless, to the extent that the mission was able to form an impression, it seemed to be the general perception that there is often no clear distinction between the activities of the army and those of the Militia. This is possibly because of the similarity in uniforms of the Militia special forces and those of the army, reinforced by the fact that some Militia are accommodated within army barracks.

4. Unofficial Organisations and Arming of Individuals

It seems to be common knowledge that there are organisations throughout Serbia whose members are armed. Members of the Serbian community in Kosovo involved with these organisations are alleged to conduct shooting training overtly. However, the fact-finding mission has no evidence about these organisations. The mission heard several allegations that weapons are being distributed to Serbians in Kosovo; a number of people said that they had seen this taking place. According to Serbian authorities weapons had not been distributed, but they acknowledged that weapons were generally widespread among the population.

Conclusion:

While the fact-finding mission was unable to verify any assertions about the distribution of weapons to civilians, it gained the impression that certain members of the Serbian community enjoyed advantages in this respect that were not available to other communities.

Section IV: Comment

While the mandate of the mission was precisely defined, its members consider that the military situation must be seen comprehensively, within social, ethnic, economic and political circumstances. In the mission's view, it is at present not the military situation but the political situation that is the problem in Kosovo. The main problem area is the relationship between the overwhelming Albanian population and the existing Serbian administration. The aim of the ethnic Albanians, who are refusing any direct contact with the Serbian authorities, is an independent Kosovo. The Federal and Serbian authorities insist that Kosovo must remain an integral part of Serbia. Both sides understand the seriousness of the circumstances and both told the mission that they recognise the need to proceed through negotiations, but their terms for beginning negotiations are far apart. In carrying out its mandate, the

fact-finding mission did not conclude that there is mounting military tension. But the situation is a dangerous one and, if conflict is to be avoided, it must be approached with great patience and good will. The mission hopes that all parties will maintain the utmost restraint and avoid acts that could lead to misunderstanding and violence. ...

Annex No. I to the Report of the CSCE Conflict Prevention Centre
Fact-Finding Mission to Kosovo

Mission Members:

Ambassador H. David Peel (Canada), Mission Leader
Brigadier Richard F. Baly (UK)
Mr. Javier Collar (Spain - CPC Secretariat)
Sergeant-Major Poelof R. W. Fron (Netherlands)
Colonel George Ledeuil (France)
Ambassador Miroslav Polreich (CSFR)
Brigadier-General Josef Schaerli (Switzerland)
Colonel Falf Rye Vadmarn (Denmark)
Mr. Peter Taksce-Jensen (Denmark), Liaison
Mr. Alexander Pavicic, Serbo-Croat interpreter
Mr. Mohammed Zakaria Khan, Albanian interpreter

5. Report of the Exploratory Mission to Kosovo, Vojvodina and Sandzak, 2-8 August 1992

I. SUMMARY

... The deep concern with the deteriorating situation in Yugoslavia, inter alia, expressed in the reports of the two CSCE Fact-Finding Missions prompted the dispatch of a new, Exploratory, Mission to Kosovo, Vojvodina and Sandzak. The visit of the Mission took place 2- 8 August 1992.

The Mission considered its visit as part of the efforts to prevent a further deterioration of the situation. The Mission underlined in all meetings that it has been sent by the CSCE to examine the possibilities for further CSCE activities in the regions concerned. All interlocutors were asked if they agreed with the assessment of the CSCE of the situation in the three regions, and if they would accept further CSCE missions of shorter or longer duration. They were also informed that the Mission was carried out in support of the Conference on Yugoslavia.

The Mission is of the opinion that the following recommendations should be evaluated by the CSO.

1. A CSCE Mission of longer duration should be sent to Yugoslavia.
2. A mission from the Conflict Prevention Centre (CPC) should be dispatched to the Sandzak region.
3. The CSCE High Commissioner on National Minorities should visit Yugoslavia as soon as he/she has been appointed.
4. The Chairman-in-Office or the Troika should, at some stage, be engaged in talks with the Federal Government of Yugoslavia, inter alia, to facilitate further CSCE initiatives, including missions of a shorter or long duration.
5. Representatives from Yugoslavia, including representatives from Kosovo, Vojvodina and Sandzak, should be offered to participate in the seminars organised by the Warzaw Office for Democratic Institutions and Human Rights (ODIHR).

II. BACKGROUND

1. At its twelfth meeting in Helsinki 8-10 June 1992 the Committee of Senior Officials (CSO) of the CSCE decided to send an Exploratory CSCE Mission to Kosovo, Vojvodina and Sandzak in Yugoslavia (Serbia and Montenegro). The mandate of the Mission was to prepare recommendations, for consideration by the CSO, on the role that further CSCE missions, of either short or long duration, might play in promoting peace, averting violence and restoring respect for human rights and fundamental freedoms in Kosovo, Vojvodina and Sandzak and in support of the efforts of the EC Peace Conference.
2. The Yugoslav delegation at the meeting in Helsinki refused to accept the Mission, making an interpretative statement emphasising that local authorities in these regions are not authorised to concur with the Mission's visit and that, under the circumstances, Yugoslavia was not ready to receive it.

3. In a telex addressed to the Chairman-in-Office of the CSO, Mr Jan Kubis, on 22 June 1992, the Acting Federal Secretary for Foreign Affairs, Dr Vladimir Sultanovic, declared that the Yugoslav authorities were prepared to receive the Mission, provided it was 'officially requested from Yugoslavia (namely Serbia, since these regions are its integral parts)'. Such a request was sent by Mr Kubis on 23 June 1992, asking that the CSCE Exploratory Mission be accepted by the Federal Republic of Yugoslavia (Serbia and Montenegro).

4. In its reply on 24 June 1992, the Federal Secretariat for Foreign Affairs of Yugoslavia agreed to receive the Mission on the condition that the mandate of the Mission would be strictly related to human rights issues, including the rights of minorities in Kosovo, Vojvodina and Sandzak. The acceptance of any further missions of "longer or shorter duration" was said to depend "on the positions taken by the CSCE with respect to the Federal Republic of Yugoslavia". Due to these terms imposed by the Federal Secretariat in its letter of reply, the CSO subsequently decided not to send a mission.

5. At its thirteenth meeting, on 8 July 1992 in Helsinki, the CSO renewed the decision to dispatch an Exploratory Mission to Kosovo, Vojvodina and Sandzak as soon as possible. In a letter dated 17 July 1992, the Chairman-in-Office of the CSO, Mr Jan Kublis, again requested that "Yugoslavia (Serbia and Montenegro) gives full support and co-operation to this mission to its three above mentioned regions". The mandate of the Mission was the same as had been decided by the CSO at its twelfth meeting.

6. On 22 July 1992, Mr Vladislav Jovanovic, Minister of Foreign Affairs of Yugoslavia, responded by stating the readiness of the Federal Republic of Yugoslavia to accept the Exploratory Mission to Kosovo, Vojvodina and Sandzak.

II. THE WORK OF THE MISSION

1. The Mission was led by Ambassador Jan af Sillén of Sweden and included members from the Czech and Slovak Federal Republic, Germany, and Switzerland (List of Participants: Annex I).

2. The Mission met with representatives of the Yugoslav and Serbian governments in Belgrade on 3 and 7 August. On 7 August the delegation also met the President of the Federal Republic of Yugoslavia, Mr Dobrica Cosic. The Mission met twice, on 3 and 7 August, with the Prime Minister of the Federal Republic of Yugoslavia, Mr Milan Panic. The Mission, furthermore, met the Minister of Foreign Affairs of the Federal Republic of Yugoslavia, Mr Vladislav Jovanovic, and senior officials of the Federal Ministry of Foreign Affairs. The Mission also had opportunity to meet with the Federal Minster of Justice, Mr Tibor Varady.

3. On the level of the Serbian government the Mission met with the Deputy Prime Minister of the Government of the Republic of Serbia, Mr Nebojsa Mladkovic, and officials from the Ministry of Interior.

4. On 4 August the Mission met with representatives of the Serbian government in Kosovo.

5. A meeting was also held with a number of representatives of the Albanian political parties under the chairmanship of Dr Ibrahim Rugova. ....

IV. THE POLITICAL SITUATION IN KOSOVO, VOJVODINA AND SANDZAK ...KOSOVO

1. The alarming political situation in Kosovo is characterised by an extreme polarisation and absence of dialogue between the Serbian and Albanian population. The Federal and Serbian authorities have in recent times on several occasions invited the main Albanian political parties to talks, which the Albanians have refused to attend. During the same week as the Mission visited Kosovo, the Federal President, Mr Dobrica Cosic, invited national minority representatives to attend round-table discussions in Belgrade. No Albanians, however, accepted the invitation.

2. The Albanian parties have also opted out of the official political process by not participating in the latest federal and local elections held in May this year (compare the Report of the CSCE Fact-Finding Mission Regarding 31 May Elections in the Federal Republic of Yugoslavia (18-21 May 1992)). Instead, the Albanians held their own elections on 24 May, which were considered illegal by the Federal and Serbian authorities.

3. A major reason for the refusal of the Albanian side to attend any talks is that the Federal and Serbian side insists that they take place within the framework of the Serbian constitution of 1990, which suspended the autonomous status of Kosovo. According to the Albanians, the abrogation of Kosovo's status as an autonomous province by the Serbian constitution was in clear violation of the 1974 Federal Constitution. The Albanians, furthermore, emphasise that they were not consulted about the new Federal Constitution, which was passed at the end of April 1992.

4. Neither side seem to want to return to the terms of the 1974 Constitution. The Serbs because it is felt that it encouraged secessionism and led to harassment of the Serbian and Montenegrin population; the Albanians because the previous Yugoslav state has ceased to exist and that they do not want to be considered as a minority in a new Yugoslavia. The Albanians insist that in a new Yugoslavia they should be treated on an equal level and Kosovo should again become a federal unit.

5. The Albanians also say that they have had a very negative experience with previous talks and that the Federal and Serbian authorities are not interested in a real dialogue. Moreover, the Albanians point out that several of the repressive laws in force in Kosovo, inter alia, the law on special circumstances and the law on labour relations are in breach of both the past and the present Federal Constitution. The Albanians also express deep concern about the situation in the educational system and in the health services. A precondition for any serious dialogue involving the Albanian side would be the abolition of these repressive measures.

V. CONCLUSIONS

1. The Mission of the opinion that it was able to carry out the exploratory aspects of its mandate in a satisfactory manner.

2. The situation regarding human rights and the protection of minorities in the areas visited is very serious and, in certain cases even alarming. The war in Croatia and Bosnia-Hercegovina has aggravated the situation. The deepening economic crisis in Serbia and Montenegro may worsen the situation further. There is, for instance, a risk of ethnic selectivity when employment is reduced.

3. The Mission is of the opinion that the situation in Kosovo is grave, in spite of the reassurance from a local representative of the Serbian government in the province that the situation has somewhat improved.

4. For the time being the Albanians act with great caution. The lack of contacts between the authorities and the Albanians is very striking. The Mission received some indications that the Serbs would accept a silent observer in possible future direct talks between the Government and the Albanians, whereas the Albanian side wants talks under international mediation. The constitutional status of Kosovo is at the heart of the problem. Any presence of a third party in talks must not prejudice future constitutional rearrangements.

5. The authorities in Vojvodina are negative to a CSCE presence in the region, since they do not consider that the present situation warrants this. However, the Mission had other interlocutors, who expressed an interest in some kind of CSCE presence. The Mission is of the opinion that the situation in Vojvodina needs to be followed in order to secure that CSCE principles regarding human rights and protection of minorities are respected.

6. The local authorities in Sandzak do not seem to be of the opinion that a CSCE presence in the area is necessary. On the contrary, some of their representatives expressed the opinion that such a presence could aggravate the situation and stir up the local population. Leaders of the Muslim opposition, however, indicate a strong interest in the presence of the CSCE. The Mission is of the opinion that the situation in Sandzak needs further investigation.

7. The Federal and Serbian authorities in some of our discussions underlined that they felt that the CSCE principles demand that similar problems be treated on an equal footing. Thus, the application of conflict prevention instruments of the CSCE should,

in their view, be contingent on the use of these instruments also in similar situations in other CSCE countries.

8. Current developments regarding the legislation in the field of human rights and minority protection can best be described as contradictory. This reflects the confusing situation surrounding the division of power between the federal and republican level in Yugoslavia.

9. The Serbian Parliament was at the time of the visit by the Mission discussing certain laws which, if enacted, could have a negative impact on human rights. These were laws regarding increased state control of the politika publishing group, law and order, the universities and demonstrations.

10. However, at the same time the Mission noted a number of encouraging signals from the Federal Government. Several representatives of the Federal Government in talks with the Mission expressed their firm intention to implement, and in some respects expand constitutional guarantees of human rights and fundamental freedoms, inter alia, the protection of national minorities. Recently, a Federal Ministry for Human Rights and National Minorities was created to this effect. The Mission was informed that the establishment of an Ombudsman for human rights and minorities, empowered to investigate allegations of misconduct in these matters, is under consideration. There is a suggestion to upgrade the Federal Constitutional Court to an institution with wide-ranging powers. The Federal Government is also preparing a new law on federal elections, and has expressed its willingness to include representatives of the opposition parties in the work on the law. The Parliament is currently discussing a law on amnesty for conscripts who have avoided drafts and call-ups or deserted.

11. The Mission wishes to underline the extreme complexity of the situation in Yugoslavia (Serbia and Montenegro). In the view of the Mission, it is necessary to treat the issues involved with impartiality, balance, caution and good background knowledge. Many of the issues will need observation and assistance over a long period of time, if violence is to be averted and human rights respected.

RECOMMENDATIONS

The Mission is consequently of the opinion that the situation in the three regions is serious and, in some cases, even alarming. The Mission recommends to the CSO to make use of the following Helsinki process instruments to prevent a further deterioration of the situation and to avert violence and restore human rights and fundamental freedoms.

1. A CSCE Mission of longer duration, headed by a high-ranking official, should as soon as possible be sent to Yugoslavia (Serbia and Montenegro). This mission would, inter alia, be in touch with the Federal Government of Yugoslavia, the governments of Serbia and Montenegro, including regional and local authorities, representatives of political parties and ethnic groups as well as non-governmental organisations, including religious communities.

    The task of this mission should be:

    -   to collect impartial information on all aspects of violations of human rights and fundamental freedoms;
    -   to offer information on legislation in CSCE member countries in the field of human rights, protection of minorities, free media and democratic elections;
    -   to promote dialogues, and,
    -   to establish contact points for solving problems that might be brought up by the parties.

The mission could be dispatched to Belgrade and should cover activities in all three regions. At a later stage, it might be of value to consider linking this mission with the CSCE High Commissioner on National Minorities. The question regarding international presence in possible high-level political talks between the Government and the Albanians is obviously of special importance and probably of a long-term character. One possibility is that such an international presence could be the responsibility of the mission of longer duration. Another option could be that this is the responsibility of a special representative of the CSCE, the UN or the Conference on Yugoslavia.

2. The Mission suggests that the CSO should instruct the Conflict Prevention Centre (CPC) to send a mission to the Sandzak area in order to investigate the unconfirmed but worrying reports about the high military presence in the area, which in the view of the Muslims, increases tension. Such a mission was recently sent to Kosovo.

3. The Mission suggests that as soon as the CSCE High Commissioner on National Minorities is appointed, he/she should pay a visit to Yugoslavia, especially to the three regions, and communicate with all parties concerned to obtain first-hand information about the situation of national minorities and ethnic groups.

4. The High Commissioner should have at his disposal experts on various aspects relevant to the issues.

5. The Chairman-in-Office or the Troika should, at some stage, be engaged in talks with the Federal Government of Yugoslavia, inter alia, to facilitate further CSCE initiatives, including missions of a shorter or longer durations.

6. The Mission suggests that the CSCE seminars on national minorities issues, tolerance and free media organised by the Warsaw Office for Democratic Institutions and Human Rights should be offered to representatives from Yugoslavia, including representatives of the ethnic minorities in Kosovo, Vojvodina and Sandzak.

6.   Interim Report from the Head of the Missions of Long Duration, 27 September 1992

I. STATUS AS OF 27 SEPTEMBER 1992

A. Presence in the regions.

... The Mission to Kosovo is engaged in transmitting messages from the Albanian political parties to the Belgrade authorities and vice versa, in conformity with the CSO decision of August 14, 1992. For the time being such dialogue is confined to education issues. ...

E. Modalities.

The Missions have operated on the basis of the assurances given by the Belgrade government September 9. Continuous contact is being maintained about the modalities. On September 28 the Federal government will be informed that the Missions are in the process of seeking houses/flats in Prishtina, Novi Pazar and Novi Sad. There are indications that the authorities will accept a presence in the three areas, considering that the missions are already engaged in bringing about a dialogue which the parties welcome. The complex internal situation in Serbia presents problems of a legal nature. The open rift between President Milosevic and Prime Minister Panic has a paralysing effect on decision-making. This explains the reluctance on the part of the Belgrade government to authorise a continuation of the missions beyond the forthcoming elections, which may now been postponed till early December. However, there is reason to believe that a formula may be found which satisfies CSCE's need to an open-ended duration, provided the agreement contains a review clause. The Missions are in constant touch with the Federal government about the logistical arrangements and safe passage for mission members. The difficult supply situation complicates matters. Obviously, the risk element cannot be eliminated. Hitherto, Mission members have not been physically prevented from carrying out their tasks. ...

III. PROGRAMME

Beginning 28 September the Missions will have a new round of talks with the Federal government on 'Modalities' on the basis of a 'Memorandum of Understanding' originally drafted by ambassador af Sillén after his consultations during the London Conference. Also in Week 40, Mission members will go to the Vojvodina region, including the border areas with Croatia, and to Kosovo frontier areas (see Annex 1). ...

Annex 1

SPECIAL REPORT BY MISSION MEMBERS ON VISITS TO REGIONS

On September 24 - 25, members of the CSCE Mission of long duration met in Pristina, Kosovo, with leaders of the Albanian opposition and the Serbian Republic Government in Kosovo. Both sides expressed a willingness to in dialogue. It was clear, however, that for now they are entrenched in diametrically opposed positions on the fundamental political question of the statue of Kosovo in Serbia. There is some hope as to developing dialogue on the current stand-off in the education system. Teaching of an Albanian curriculum with Albanian as the language of instruction has been outlawed by Belgrade and has been replaced by a Serbian curriculum. This is unacceptable to the Albanian students who are boycotting the school system at all levels. The federal government last week proposed a 14 point plan to the Albanians to resolve the education crisis. Albanian leaders told us the political framework of the proposal was unacceptable - it includes a statement that Kosovo is an integral part of Serbia and refers to Albanians as a minority population - but indicated some of the points left room for discussion. We urged them to respond to these points. They promised to prepare either a response to the federal proposal or a counter-proposal which we offered to communicate to the federal government. The Serbian Republic official promised full co-operation with the CSCE mission, offering an open invitation to visit prisons, hospitals, police facilities, factories, etc. The visit of the Mission to Kosovo was reported in the local and national media, as well as in the Albanian opposition newspaper.

7.   CSCE Mission in Kosovo, Report on Kosovo Stalemate, 16 November 1992

Kosovo has settled into an uneasy stalemate. The Serbian Administration is safely in the saddle, maintaining control over the Province with tough emergency laws. Armed forces are stationed within and outside the Province. Members of the Serbian minority have been provided with arms to help discourage Albanian obstruction of Serbia's massive social and economic reform programme. A jet fighter makes occasional passes over the Province to remind Albanians of their opponent's military might. After three years of Serbian occupation, the Republican government must ask itself what it has achieved, whether its policies are effective, and what the prospects are for returning to normal conditions, President Milosevic intended to rebuild and stabilise Serbian influence in Kosovo, in particular by shifting the population balance in favour of the Serbs and by replacing the Albanians in all positions of political, social and economic significance. In part this was to be achieved by attracting large numbers of Serbs to settle in the Province. Conditions for settlement were made exceptionally attractive in terms of availability of employment, housing, land and virtually cost-free credit. To make room for Serbs and reduce Albanian influence, the Serbian administration initiated a policy of removal of Albanians from all sectors except the private sector. Albanians were dismissed wholesale especially from senior and middle level positions. In addition many were evicted unceremoniously from their apartments. This process is reported to be virtually completed in the public service at the central and township levels. In the educational services almost 1000 academics and administrative staff have been forced out of the University of Pristina. Public funding of educational services in Albanian has been discontinued. Most secondary schools have been shut to Albanian students and the University is boycotted on the grounds that the Albanian language has been discontinued for practical purposes. In the health sector nurses are said to have been largely replaced. With respect to medical staff the process has been slowed down because of a shortage of qualified Serbian doctors. As to the media, at least one newspaper in Albanian continues to appear daily and is subject to little if any censorship. But Albanian controlled radio and television services have ceased to exist. The judiciary has been all but cleansed of Albanian judges and magistrates. Albanians in the Kosovo police force were early victims of the cleansing operation.

In the economic sector top and middle-level management of the former socially owned and self-managed enterprises has been replaced and the process has been extended to workers as well. The parallel Federation of Free Trade Unions of Kosovo reports that at the end of September 41 per cent of its membership of 240,000 had been fired and 57 per cent were unemployed. Bearing in mind that in the past such public enterprises had neither been profit-oriented nor economically

viable, precipitant and massive replacements by generally inexperienced and frequently misqualified personnel has compounded the problems faced by these unfortunate businesses. For example Treboa which is one of Europe's largest lead/zinc mine and smelter enterprises together with over twenty associated manufacturing enterprises, is reported to be largely closed down or working on sharply reduced capacity. Several thousand miners and technical staff were fired following a major strike in early 1989. A senior official indicates that to this day sufficient replacements have not been found. Presumably they are not available in the Serbian labour market. Large brown-coal mines and nearby electric power generating plant are reported to be operating well below capacity. A ferro-nickel refinery was kept in partial operation with the help of outside technical staff on periodic visits to the plant. It has now been shut down for two months. The international sanctions have of course added to the woes of these enterprises. As yet, we have not learned of any that are in a reasonable state of health. The only sectors that have done better under Serbian occupation are agriculture, which employs 70 per cent of Kosovos population, and the private sector which benefit from entrepreneurial talent released by the massive dismissals. It is difficult to lend oredence to the Serbian claim that all dismissals were undertaken to weed out surplus and incompetent employees and to deal with massive insubordination. There is no doubt about official intentions. Firings were indiscriminate, including those of persons with a record of earlier co-operation with the Serbs.

For economic reasons alone, it is not altogether surprising that the Serbian population policy for Kosovo is failing to produce the desired effect. Officials are reluctant to discuss arrivals of Serbian settlers, but there is nowhere any sign of a rush to emigrate to Kosovo. Conditions are so uninviting that even refugees are reluctant to come. According to informal international estimation a mere 6000 have arrived so far.

The Serbian administration has welcomed Albanian emigration and has introduced efficient procedures for granting exist permits. Serbian pressure has persuaded large numbers of Albanians to seek better conditions abroad, mainly in Western Europe. But claims by Albanians that as many as 300,000 have left Kosovo during the last three years appear exaggerated.

After an initial period of consternation and confusion the Albanian population of Kosovo has responded vigorously to the Serbian challenge. In the face of overwhelmingly force the Albanian leaders have counselled against direct confrontations. Instead they have sought to develop the capacity and determination of the Albanian society to resist Serbian pressure and to unite them in the pursuit of the ultimate goal of independence. In these efforts they have sought the support of the international community. Top Serbian officials acknowledge considerable success of these initiatives. A steady stream of information of Serbian acts of repression in faxed to the world from Pristina. News is edited and redistributed in both English and French from Geneva. The Albanian leaders seek to communicate with major world leaders and travel widely to meet and influence them in favour of their objectives. Dr Ibrahim Rugova, leader of the Democratic League of Kosovo (LDK) and elected in May as President of the "sovereign and independent Republic of Kosovo", has travelled widely. In his unassuming, low-key style he has impressed the international community. Albanians appear to have been particularly effective in propagating their interpretation of the risk and dangers of Serbian occupation and the potential of drawing other Balkan powers into the conflict, if ever Serbian oppression should lead to an explosion.

While the international successes are impressive, the domestic achievements of Albanian leaders, especially Dr Rugova and his supporters, appear to us as at least equally significant. The LDK has successfully utilised Serbian oppression to unite the large majority of Albanians behind itself. Other party leaders share the aim of sovereign independence of Kosovo, but have not been able to attract similar talented and highly motivated following. Under effective LDK leadership Albanians have adopted a constitution by referendum in September last year. In May there was a general election. In the assembly LDK secured 96 out of a total of 130 seats and Dr Rugova was elected the first President of the Republic. Official interferences in these election has not been significant.

A parallel government of sorts has been formed, with several of its members in exile. What is more interesting is the degree to which this rump government has begun to provide services at the domestic level. In fact it is mostly the LDK that takes the lead. The "Ministry of Information" is excellently organised, receiving and distributing information from across the Province very quickly. The protocol services for foreign officials and non-officials visitors are enthusiastic, prompt and reliable. One of the most interesting initiatives undertaken last February was the creation of a "Financial Council" as a charitable organisation. A sophisticated province-wide taxation system has been set up to record, collect and eventually disburse resources contributed via voluntary commitments of employees and businesses. The Council ensures the maintenance of sophisticated records that are subject to periodic auditing by a commission created for the purpose. The equivalent of some 400,000 DM are reported to be collected monthly and immediately converted into foreign exchange. The funds are mainly used to pay teachers a small allowance (30 DK) and for welfare cases. An up-to-date computerised welfare role was shown to us listing province-wide some 60.000 [?] families, their status, income, and welfare receipts, if any. The Financial Council has focused in developing domestic revenue sources, but experts to generate additional income from Albanians abroad.

There is evidence of significant activity in other areas as well. The LDK has created a number of commissions covering areas of competence normally handled by ministries. The Education Commission is deeply involved in maintaining a parallel system of education from the elementary through the postgraduate level. Most elementary schools are open and instruction according to an Albanian curriculum is provided. There is little official interference from the police unless schools attempt to issue diplomats in the name of the sovereign and independent Republic of Kosovo. At the secondary and university level the situation is much more difficult in the absence of adequate facilities. The results of this educational system are of course less than satisfactory, but there is no doubt as to the determination of Albanians to cope with the situation. …

It has been somewhat of a disappointment that neither the LDK nor the Human Rights Council and the Kosovo Helsinki Committee have so far shown much interest in making use of existing procedures to seek legal redress for human rights violations. There is a distinct reluctance to use existing channels in part because of discouraging experience. It has been pointed out that unless such effort is undertaken in a credible manner, it would be difficult for this Mission to make interventions. Another reason given for this evident reluctance, shared by virtually everyone of our interlocutors, is that such action would constitute a form of tacit acknowledgement of a governmental system that is illegitimate in the Albanian view. It has been pointed out on many occasions that this interpretation is incorrect and that the defence of one's human rights within an existing system does not have anything to do with its legality or otherwise. It is hoped that in due course some Albanians will decide to seek redress through existing channels and to approach this Mission in case there is lack of an appropriate response from the official side.

Conclusion: After three years of virtual occupation Serbians have failed in their attempts to re-establish their presence in Kosovo. Attempts to take over the management of important enterprises have had particularly adverse economic consequences. In contrast, the Albanian population, under effective leadership, has strengthened its resolve and capacity to cope with the Serbian onslaught. Deep involvement in armed conflicts elsewhere in former Yugoslavia, international sanctions, a vociferous domestic opposition, control of the federal government by opponents of President Milosevic, and last but not least mounting economic problems make it seem unlikely that the Serbian government will do anything drastic to get ahead with its programme for Kosovo. Albanians speculate that the Serbian extremist elements will seek to force the hand of Belgrade by manufacturing a crisis. This hypothesis should not be discounted entirely, but against it can be pointed out that most extremists are busy elsewhere and for many of the 200,000 Serbians native to Kosovo the prospect of a confrontation with some 1.8 million Albanians is unattractive.

8.   CSCE Missions to Kosovo, Sandzak and Vojvodina, Interim Report, 17 November 1992

1. OVERVIEW
1.1. KOSOVO

The Albanian determination to stick to their passive resistance instead of engaging in one for them uncertain dialogue with the federal and Serb authorities seems to have hardened. Ibrahim Rugova has announced that the Albanians will stay away from the elections planned for December. Apart from considering it an image issue, the Albanians do not expect that the elections will bring any improvement in their situation. Although crediting some members of the federal government with good intentions, they think little of any government's power to enforce changes in Kosovo. Certain Albanian leaders, one must suspect, would view the elections as being important only to the extent that they move Serbia closer to chaos through a victory for the present Serbian regime and its supporters.

The negotiations concerning the educational system seems to be in a stalemate. The Albanians refused to attend a meeting on the subject of Novi Sad on 10 November under the auspices of the London Conference. A meeting on the subject scheduled for 17 November in Geneva, was cancelled because the Serbian minister of education would not participate. Some observers argue that the internationally sponsored negotiations process so far has done little to convince the Albanians that a dialogue is in their interest, and further, that the Albanians begin to feel that they are being used in a power struggle that is meaningless for them. On the other hand, the constant attention of visiting groups and the media is viewed as a guarantee that suppression will not be stepped up, and as something which might eventually bring about a complete internationalisation of the conflict, for example in the form of UN military presence. The army was quick to describe the incident which led to the shooting of an ethnic Albanian outside the military headquarters in Pristina on 11 November as a "terrorist attack", implying that it was premeditated. The Albanians for their part alleged that the shooting was part of an army plan. Although such reactions had to be expected, it is unfortunate that isolated events are being presented is this manner with no proof of wider involvement. The episode is unlikely to have any serious repercussions. Yet the incident illustrates the sensitivity of the situation in Kosovo and how easily a brawl can be exploited politically. There have also been speculations, in the wake of the Skopje episode, that violent conflict may spread from Macedonia to Kosovo rather than vice versa. Considering the strong conviction of the Albanian leaders in Kosovo that a longtime, non-violent, passive resistance is the best way to reach their goal, one should not draw hasty conclusions about such a scenario.

The Serbs with the possible exception of the para-military and the ultra-extremists, are hardly interested in a new front in Kosovo at this stage. The army may be needed elsewhere. The Albanians are even less interested in an armed conflict. They know that they have no chance militarily, and have instead structured themselves into a parallel state and a parallel economy. They feel they can sustain the hardship of discrimination and repression provided it does not go beyond the present level.

2. FIELD REPORTS CSCE MISSION TO KOSOVO

2.1 INTERIM FIELD REPORT, SUMMARY: Mid-November 1992

Since the Memorandum of Understanding was signed communications with the local authorities have been easier. While continuing to have regular contacts with Albanian leaders, the mission was able to meet with high-ranking representatives of the Serbian community in Kosovo, mainly in political, administrative and academic circles (among them were Mr. Momcillo TRAJKOVIC, deputy to the Parliament of Serbia and Mr. Radijvije PAPOVIC, rector of the University of Pristina). The persons met include both moderate and hard-line Serbs, whose stands on political and educational issues differ with more than nuances. All of them however strongly oppose self-determination for Albanians. For a while, the shooting incident of November 11 in Pristina (one Albanian civilian killed, two Serbian soldiers wounded) seemed to have broken the shaky quietness of the last weeks, but after some time it appeared to be an isolated event. The education issue is still in a deadlock, with about 70% of the primary schools open, practically none of the middle-level schools working, and the University closed. In the primary schools now open, the teachers are not paid because they still teach according to the Albanian programmes, refusing to apply the Serbian ones. The Albanians seem more than ever entrenched in their position to stay apart from the political system now in force in Kosovo. Illustrative hereof is their negative approach to the coming Federal and Republic elections. Observers here say that Dr Rugova and other party leaders have no choice but to boycott the election because of a widespread feeling among the Albanians that they have no longer anything to do with the power forcibly imposed on their province, all the more since they have presently their own parallel "Republic of Kosovo". The Albanians claim that tension is rising in Kosovo and that harassment of intellectuals and leading personalities is more and more frequent. The shooting incident of November 11 is claimed to be a new and serious provocation, in which Serbs have distorted the facts in order to create the impression of a terrorist attack, which would justify more repression.

The Mission has been engaged in talks with the view to obtaining appropriate documentation for approaches to the authorities about specific issues (e.g. permit for private hospital). Our experience confirms that Albanians are reluctant to employ proper grass root tactics with the authorities, often in he mistaken belief that a formal, documented approach would constitute some form of acknowledgement of the legitimacy of the regime. The mission is continuing its efforts to convince the Albanians of the benefits of proper methods, also with a view to enlisting international support. For their part, the local Serbs believe that, on the whole, the situation is "a little better now than six months ago", since many Albanians appear to have realised that they cannot but try to build a common peaceful life with Serbs "within the framework of the present system". It remains to be seen to what extent the Serbs are ready to enter into a dialogue on substantial issues in case the Albanians should accept not to include the independence option in the agenda. A suggestion by Mr TRAJKOVIC to held round table discussions on the theme "how to live together peacefully", between federal and republic representatives and political leaders from both sides, in the presence of CSCE mission members, was mentioned to Dr Rugova who appeared somewhat receptive to the idea but, expectedly, was not committal.

Interestingly enough, the Serbian parliamentarian expressed the wish to have the CSCE mission involved in an independent study of all aspects of the constitutional issue, in order to assist in the process of discussion. The importance of economic factors for the future of Kosovo was highlighted with a comparison made between the public sector, held by Serbs, and now in sharp decline due to shortage of state funding, and the private one, in the hands of Albanians and rather flourishing. The Serbs have undoubtedly suffered from the crumbling of state enterprises, even though they have filled some of the jobs left by the Albanians. Consequently, there would not be many Serbs wanting to settle in Kosovo for economic reasons, even among those who have lived here in the past. Besides, civil servants seem to be reluctant to be posted to Pristina for more than a short period.

CONCLUSION

The impression prevails that there is no strong will on either side to emerge from the present impasse. In the case of the Serbs; because they have a fairly satisfactory control of the situation, extending guarantee of safety to all their citizens in Kosovo and also because they have no clear or coherent vision of how co-existence with the Albanians should be organised. In the case of the Albanians; because they have more and more structured themselves into a parallel state and parallel economy, so that they can sustain the hardship of being discriminated and repressed provided it does not go beyond the present level of victimisation.
Pristina, 15 November 1992

2.1.1 KOSOVO - EDUCATIONAL CRISIS, Mid-November 1992

Education of Albanians in Kosovo has been in a state of acute crisis some three years. Financing by the Republic government of Albanian educational services has been virtually discontinued. Nearly all of the Albanian teaching staff in schools and at the University of Pristina have been either dismissed or declared surplus. It may be noted that these wholesale dismissals have been paralleled in other sectors such as the judiciary, the public service and the police, health and welfare, and the non-private economic sector, especially the former self-managed enterprises. Albanian students are either unwilling or unable to attend operating educational institutions with the exception of the primary level. At that level the majority of schools have remained open but without public funding. They are entirely dependent on voluntary work and insufficient private funding. In general the Serbian authorities have acquiesced to the use of Albanian curricula in these schools notwithstanding the fact that this is considered an illegal practice. The have however, attempted to suppress with ruthless measures the use of diplomas and stamps issued in the name of the Republic of Kosovo for the purpose of asserting Kosovo's independence from Serbia.

In October the Geneva Conference on former Yugoslavia initiated discussions between the Serbian authorities and representatives of the Albanian community on ways and means of returning the educational system to normal. Participation in the first two meetings held respectively in Pristina and in Belgrade was appropriate: The Serbian side was represented by ministers at the federal, republic and provincial levels. The Albanian delegation was headed by a Vice President of the Democratic League of Kosovo and included other leading political and public figures concerned with educational issues. Ambassador Ahrens led the Geneva Conference delegation to the first two meetings. The third meeting was convened by the Co-Chairman of the Geneva Conference during their visit to Kosovo on October 29. At this meeting the Republic government did not participate, but the Federal government and the Province of Kosovo were once again present at the ministerial level.

Attempts to convene a fourth meeting, first in Geneva and then in Novi Sad, capital of the Republic of Vojvodina were unsuccessful. The Geneva venue was unacceptable to the Serbs on the grounds that it would internationalise an issue that was considered domestic. The Albanian delegation had difficulties as well. One member was unable to retrieve his passport that had been confiscated in connection with an investigation of alleged involvement in illegal political activities. There were also concerns of political and logistical nature which apparently could not be resolved in the short time available. The Novi Sad venue was apparently acceptable to the Serbs but it was rejected by the Albanian side for a variety of reasons, none of which appeared entirely convincing. While Albanian leaders profess to be ready to meet in either Belgrade or Pristina, indications are that their position on educational issues may still be far from a potential compromise. Recently one of the leading Albanian negotiators has informally stated that in the absence of major concessions from the Serbians, which appeared unrealistic, a political resolution of the conflict with the Serbs should precede the tackling of the educational question.

On the substantive side, the educational discussions promptly revealed that neither Serbs nor Albanians could see their way clear to depoliticising the educational question. Education was perceived to be linked inextricably to national and ethnic identity. The Serbian side showed somewhat more flexibility in that it was ready to acknowledge more formally its unwritten acquiescence to letting Albanians employ their own curricula for primary education as they saw fit. As to secondary and post-secondary education Serbians insisted that their legislation with respect to the content and implementation of curricula be respected, and that Belgrade would remain in full control.

At the first meeting an agreed statement gave rise to the hope that about sixty primary schools would be reopened to Albanian children. However, at the second meeting difficulties with respect to complex related issues came to the fore, among them questions of the language of education and the terms and conditions for reinstating teachers. Both sides seemed increasingly concerned about potential political repercussions of reopening primary schools. Unfortunately the meeting could not be extended for a second session to enable participants to test the political waters.

The third meeting, held in Pristina, resulted in an announcement at the following press conference that primary schools would be reopened without delay and that other institutions would be the subject of further discussions with a view to early normalisation. An additional conclusion for a review of a number of discriminatory laws turned out to be extremely controversial. The next day provincial participants made explanatory statements to the media and the Republic government issued a strongly worded release denying the existence of discriminatory legislation. As to the reopening of the primary schools, the Albanians claimed that this had not been done, while the Serbian side denied that there were any closures in the first place - with a few exceptions.

To sum up, to date international effort to mediate the educational dispute in Kosovo has yielded only marginal results. While there has been no progress in resolving the dispute, it has been possible to bring together Serbs and Albanians for formal discussion of one of their major differences. The meetings can thus be considered a precedent for the use of international mediation to help resolve the problem of Kosovo. The possibility of further internationally mediated meetings on education and other, perhaps less sensitive issues such as health, should not be excluded. Finally it may be noted that the CSCE Mission was invited to participate in the series of educational meetings.

Pristina, 14 November 1992

...

3. OVERALL ASSESSMENT

3.1.1. THE INTERNAL POLITICAL SITUATION

The rift is wide open between the Serbian government and the Federal government (which survives only because of Montenegro's equal representation in the upper Federal chamber). This bizarre situation is likely to continue until the elections, scheduled for 20 December. One key issue in connection with the electoral campaign is the question of the use of the media, especially television channels. Even with a media handicap optimists among the opposition democratic parties hope for a slim majority. Another election scenario is a coalition between the Socialist (ex-communist) Party of Serbia and a nationalist party. The Kosovo Albanians, if they decide to vote, could decide the outcome. However, their participation is unlikely. It is still not clear which formal role Federal Prime Minister Panic and Federal President Cosic will have in the party line-up in the final stages of the campaign.

There is much speculation about the influence of continued and tightened sanctions on people's voting inclinations. Although inflation is staggering and unemployment has risen to unprecedented levels, the supply situation in the country has improved during the Missions' period of stay (i.e. since mid-September). At least for the time being there is little problem with petrol and heating oil, and in the cities foreign goods of high quality is available - although expensive. The most recent measures adopted by the UN Security Council may change this, so that elections will take place in a situation of extreme economic hardship. Voters are likely to react in different ways to continued international pressure. Those who have access to international information probably count on a lifting of sanctions in case of a victory for the democratic alliance. Leading opposition politicians however reckon that hardly more than ten per cent of the voters are well informed. The majority of voters tend to see sanctions only as an international reaction to the war in Bosnia, for which they are not prepared to take any blame. Therefore, these politicians conclude, the tightening of sanctions benefits the dominant socialist party.

3.2. CONSEQUENCS FOR THE INTERETHNIC RELATIONS

There is reason to believe that some of the ethnic groups, notably the Albanians, will quietly await the outcome of the elections and try not to stir up unrest in the meantime. Whatever the election result, it is evident that Serbian by the end of the year will enter a new phase in its troubled post-communist existence. The ethnic group will take their signals from that which emerges from the December contest. Clearly, the establishment of true democracy through a fair electoral process would have a positive bearing on interethnic relations. Only in a democratic environment will agreements between government and minorities on specific issues stand a chance of being observed for any length of time. However, the attempts at establishing dialogue and discouraging shrill accusations must continue also under more unfavourable circumstances. For the CSCE Missions the task will be infinitely more complex if Serbia does not adopt a moderate stand after the elections.

In a recent interview in the BORBA, one of the two leading newspapers, the Head of Missions appealed to all sides to refrain from hyperbole when reporting and commenting on ethnic-related events.

He further pointed out that Serbia was not unique in having difficult ethnic problems to cope with. The majority of countries in the world faced similar challenges. He characterised the continued existence of private armies in the federation as a special threat to ethnic groups.

4. PERSONNEL SITUATION/ADMINISTRATION

The Missions now have 11 members,

Belgrade: Tore Bögh (Head of Missions), Kaare Eltervaag

Kosovo: Philipp Hahn, Lech Skibinski, Daneil Droulers, Veniamin Karacostanoglu

Sandzak: Valentin Inzko, Jörn Ludvigsen, Douglas Dobson

Vojvodina: Ingemar Börjesson, Albert Krehbiel

A twelfth member (from the Czech and Slovak Republic) yet to be named will join the teams shortly. ...

CSCE Communication No. 409, Prague, pt. Stockholm, 11 December 1992

9.   Interim Report of Head of Missions of Long Duration to Kosovo, Sandjak and Vojvodina, 6 December 1992

1.1 INTERIM FIELD REPORT

During the reporting period the Mission has made further contacts with state officials and representatives of the ethnic groups in the area. From the wide range of our meetings we conclude that the acceptance of our Mission and, to a lesser degree, our suggestions for conflict solutions, is increasing. The political situation remains in a stalemate. Both sides try to advance their objectives, maintaining, however, a low-profile attitude. A significant increase in the number of federal army troops in Kosovo has been reported.

MISSION ACTIVITIES

As far as the Mission has been able to ascertain there have definitely been some notable troop movements or manoeuvres in the province around 20 November, especially in the area north of Pristina—by Podajevo—and south of Pristina—by Lipljan. Rockets have been observed. However, it is still impossible to say whether this involves a strengthening of the forces or whether it has been a routine army exercise.

There was a new shooting incident in Pristina 3 December when a brawl between police and some Albanian youths led to one Albanian being killed and another wounded. There was immediate contact between the Mission and the Albanian political groups, as well as between the Belgrade Mission and the central authorities. In the evening Mission members went to see the body of the person killed in the incident. It was another tragic and completely unnecessary death. This time, however, both sides refrained from making allegations about premeditated action. The Mission will closely follow the investigation in the case.

The Ahrens Group of the Geneva Conference came to Pristina on November 25 to continue discussions about the educational crisis in Kosovo. Once more the talks had to be cancelled, this time because weather conditions prevented the Belgrade delegations from attending. The Ahrens Group and the Mission made use of the occasion to review the situation with the Albanians from the health sector and to identify issues to be pursued by means of bilateral efforts. The Mission proposed a working group to consider specific local health problems caused by bureaucracy and other deficiencies. The Mission will head such a group. Talks on the education issue were resumed in Geneva 1 December. It seems, however, that little progress is likely before the elections. The Mission has been formally presented with two human rights cases, one involving the occupation by the local Serbian authorities of an apartment building under construction and paid for by Albanian, and the second involving alleged gross irregularities in court proceedings during a political trial. The first case was well substantiated, and the Mission is following up. The second needs more documentation, which should be available. The Mission urges the aggrieved parties to secure the official documents since information received on alleged human rights violations tends to be incomplete and unreliable. Also, it has been noted that Albanian human rights activists often take a political approach while being sometimes reluctant to use available facilities to pursue their objectives.

A law adopted by the Serbian Assembly is causing concern among the Albanians. The law establishes a new state enterprise for the publishing, printing and distribution of newspapers and books in Albanian, Serbian and Turkish. The enterprise will take over the assets and staff of an existing enterprise which was founded by the previous Kosovo government and controlled by Albanians. A discussion with the Kosovo Secretary of Information confirmed that the law gave the Serbian government complete control over the press media in the Province. It was pointed out to the Secretary, that the law was comparable to previous communist legislation in that control could be exercised by the party in power in Belgrade. He said that the Albanian opposition press has been subject to little if any direct censorship. The Secretary is prepared to discuss with the publishers of the Albanian papers terms and conditions to enable them to continue operation at reasonable costs. Albanians have been informed of this and have been asked to prepare their requirements. A detailed report on the publishing problem is enclosed. The Mission office in Belgrade has contacted the federal authorities in the matter. They are familiar with the complaints and consider the law unconstitutional, since publishing can hardly be considered a "public utility". We have another example here of a clash between the federal and the Serbian governments.

OBSERVATIONS/CONCLUSIONS

Some Kosovo Serbs are ready to admit the existence of serious problems in the field of human rights in the area, and to agree to the need to a normalisation of the situation. However, they are unwilling to accept a return to the previous autonomous regime (1974 constitution) which they consider to be discriminatory against them. In case of a serious escalation of tension, it is likely that these moderate Serbs would accept some form of autonomy which protects their rights. However, the Kosovo Serbs, with no exception, declare their readiness to fight for Kosovo (which they consider as the cradle of their nation) and charge the Albanians with deliberate secessionist plans from as early as the 1960's. The Albanians think that time is on their side, and seek to attract foreign monitoring and possible intervention in favour of their independence. They obviously believe that sooner or later the international community will recognise their "parallel authority" in Kosovo, if this de facto situation lasts long enough. The secessionist demand of the Albanians is not internationally accepted. However, massive and severe violation of the human rights of the Albanians of Kosovo, could lead the international community to support the Albanian objective. It should therefore be in the interest of the Serbian authorities to ensure that all internationally recognised human rights are being upheld in Kosovo. While the Serbs have the military power and the intention to use it if necessary, they hope that in the course of time the Albanians will abandon their passive resistance and make compromises. The Serbs should realise that in the long run they can win peace only through political dialogue with the Albanian population and leadership. The possibility of an autonomous regime, similar to or at variance with the one existing in the area before 1989, should be considered as one of the options.

A first positive step in the direction of better understanding could be the reopening secondary schools.

Pristina, 5 December 1992.

CSCE MISSION KOSOVO

1.1.1 Kosovo: New Press Law

At the beginning of this month the Serbian Assembly established by law a new state-owned enterprise called "Panorama" to assume effective control of newspapers, periodicals, graphical products and books in the Province of Kosovo. Publication is to take place in Serbian and in the languages of the "national minorities", i.e. in Albanian and Turkish. Panorama takes over the physical assets and human resources of the former communist enterprise "Relindja" which was formed shortly after World War II to provide similar publishing services in Albanian. It also takes over the Serbian daily "Jodinstvo" and the Turkish weekly "Tan". One of the objectives of Panorama is to resume the publication of the Albanian daily "Relindja" which was forcibly closed down in August 1990 under one of a series of "special circumstances" laws enacted in the course of that summer. Panorama was to have been set up and in operation by mid-November, but this has as yet not been achieved. Parenthetically it might be noted that as

in the case of the provincial, radio and television stations one month earlier, virtually the entire Albanian staff was forcibly removed from the premises of Relindja, with the help of heavily armed security services to forestall violence.

While Relindja was as much a monopoly as Panorama, the vital difference from the viewpoint of current Albanian leaders is that the former was under their own control, whereas the latter is in the hands of the Serbian government in Belgrade. Moreover, as with certain other enterprises in Kosovo, the new law provides that in the case of a change in ownership, e.g. some form of privatisation, 51 per cent of the stock must be held by a Serbian enterprise, in this particular case the Serbian State. This ownership legislation has come under severe criticism on the grounds that it discriminates by transferring automatically control of these enterprises into Serbian hands. Recent legislation merely formalises what since August 1990 amounted to de facto Serbian control of the publishing sector. It is interesting to note the bluntness with which the Serbian law ensures state control in this important area: the entire administrative council including its chairman, the general manager and the supervisory board of Panorama are both appointed and dismissed by the government of Serbia, which also approves the by-laws of the enterprise. Virtual monopoly is further guaranteed in that, similar to its predecessor enterprise, Panorama is fully integrated: it publishes and prints newspapers, periodicals, books and graphical and other material, operates the printing plant and distributes its publications, mainly through several hundred kiosks throughout the Province, each manned by its own salaried personnel. While independent publications are legally provided for, Panorama is the only enterprise in the entire Province that has the necessary physical plant and facilities capable of doing the job. Moreover, the Serbian authorities effectively control news print, which is currently extremely costly and in short supply.

The Mission discussed the new law with the Secretary of Information of Kosovo as well as with the editor-in-chief of the Albanian newspaper "Vujko". The latter publication was an agricultural periodical that, together with some other papers has been turned into a substitute for the banned daily Relindja. It was pointed out to the Secretary that under the new law the control exercised by the party in power in Belgrade appeared for practical purposes identical to that of the previous communist regime, with the only difference that, control had moved from the Pristina to Belgrade. For obvious reasons the Secretary rejected this view and sought to convince the Mission that Serbian media legislation did guarantee freedom of the press - by stating that the press would be free. He claimed further that newspapers in Kosovo could not exist without subsidisation. The Serbian paper "Jedinstovo" sold less than 2,000 copies a day and the former Relindja with some 25,000 copies daily had to be heavily subsidised as well. The taxpayer could not be expected to pay for Albanian secessionist newspapers. What is more significant is that the Secretary correctly noted that the Albanian daily press had an openly secessionist editorial policy, that it had not been subject to any censorship and that it would not be interfered with in future. This is of course the primary concern for the Albanian opposition which is convinced that Panorama has at its disposal the means for disrupting the publication of an opposition press. The Secretary however, was ready to consider discussing directly these concerns with Albanian representatives to alley their fears. The Mission has informed the Albanian side of this offer with the suggestion that they prepare their position on this issue and to explore mutually acceptable arrangements for a dialogue. It remains to be seen whether both Albanian and Serbs will come to an agreement on this approach and whether a meaningful dialogue on how to guarantee the freedom of the press can be initiated.

[Pristina, 30 November 1992]

CSCE MISSIONS TO KOSOVO, SANDZAK AND VOJVODINA

2. OVERALL ASSESSMENT

2.1. THE INTERNAL POLITICAL SITUATION

Federal Prime Minister Panic' decision to run against incumbent Serbian President Milosevic in the election for the highest office of the republic has initiated a new phase in the already turbulent pre-election manoeuvrings. The immediate result was a surge of support for Panic' candidacy from the opposition parties. A few days later the electoral commission declared that the Prime Minister was not eligible as a candidate since he did not meet residence requirements. This, in turn, has led some parties, including the Sandzak Muslim party, to declare that they will boycott the elections should Panic be barred from running. The supreme court is likely to overrule the electoral commission's rejection of the Prime Minister. One must expect those skirmishes to continue all the way up to 20 December, and they could jeopardise fair and orderly elections. The spontaneous support of Panic' candidacy from opposition parties seems to indicate that in spite of his failure to bring about a lifting of sanctions, he is nevertheless widely considered to be the person with the better chance of forestalling further disaster for the country. However, Milosevic' socialist party has the superior organisation as well as the media edge. Few observers dare predict the outcome of the contest, and its effect on the Bosnian war and interethnic relations in Serbia/Montenegro. ...

2.2. CONSEQUENCES FOR THE INTER-ETHNIC RELATIONS
There can be no doubt that the plight of the Serbs and their almost total international isolation have tempted other ethnic groups inside Serbia to maximise their demands. This must be expected in times of great turmoil. However, it does not necessarily mean that such groups are only waiting for the day when they will stage secessionist uprisings. In fact, many groups seem convinced that their concerns and grievances will stand a better chance of being heard if a moderate, democratic government is elected in Belgrade. This again would seem to suggest that ethnic violence on a great scale should be considered unlikely in the federation during the weeks leading up to the elections 20 December. In this connection the international community also has a responsibility. The constant reference, especially to Kosovo as "the possible next area of ethnic war" could become a self-fulfilling prophesy if repeated too often. Meanwhile, the ethnic patterns are changing, in the regions as well as in central areas of Serbia. The arrival of hundreds of thousands of refugees—mainly Serbs and Muslims—compounds the problems. ...

10.   CSCE Mission in Kosova, Elections of 20 December 1992 in Kosovo, 23 December 1992

The Mission was engaged in monitoring the elections of 20 December in the province of Kosovo. Six polling sites were visited; one in Pristina (No. 4), two in [?]; one in the village Caglavica (No. 47, 48 of the Pristina municipality). Our main observations were:
1. Voting procedure in general seems free and quiet and we did not witness any manipulation. Nevertheless, especially in urban polling sites the voting process was crowded and disorderly, conditions which leave room for irregularities. The process suffered from the supervisory committees' and the voters' lack of relevant experience, as well as the high number of registered voters at some polling stations.
2. The electoral law did not provide envelopes in which the voters should insert the ballot papers, before throwing them into the ballot boxes. This could hamper proper secrecy of the vote.
3. The lack of visually protected sites (with curtain) where the voters would secretly make their choice violated the secrecy of voting, as voters openly were making their choice and even co-operated with each other.
4. In two of the visited polling sites (both in Brosevac) an armed policeman in uniform was sitting along the supervisors committee and taking part in checking the voter's identities. In both cases Mission numbers confronted the chairman of the committee with the illegality of the policeman's presence (art. 61 of the electoral law) and the policeman left the room.
5. The vast majority of the Albanian population boycotted the elections. According to unconfirmed information less than 10 per cent the Albanians voted. In the case of Muslims, Turks and Romans the participation was much higher.
6. In most of the polling sites we visited there were no representatives of the opposition parties.
7. In some cases the ballot boxes were not properly inspected by the election committees.

11.   CSCE Mission of Long Duration Report: Concern over Police Brutality in Kosovo, 23 December 1992

The Mission is deeply concerned over the increasing number of violent incidents in the province of Kosovo. During the last few weeks, five ethnic Albanians have been killed and a number of Albanians and Serbs wounded in incidents involving Serbian police or army personnel. It seems that the excessive or abusive use of firearms and brutal physical force by the police has reached a highly dangerous point, which inflames an already very tense situation, and may even cause reprisals from the Albanian population. The Serbian and Federal authorities should be warned of the potential risks of this development. The police and the Army must be ordered to refrain from unnecessary or excessive use of force. It is essential to investigate such cases and punish those who are found responsible. However, the Serbian authorities have not shown the necessary will to start court proceedings in cases where excessive police force have been involved. Towards this background, our Missions will undertake all necessary contacts with the competent judicial and police authorities to effect a thorough investigation and to prosecute anyone held responsible for the death of Adem Zeqiraj. The Mission was first informed about his death on 20 December to the Dakovica branch of the Albanian Council for the Defence of Human Rights and Freedoms. According to the report the ethnic Albanian, Ademi Idriz Zeqiraj (37) from Brovina, near Dakovica, had been badly beaten by policemen during his detention in the police station of Ponoshec. The police had arrested him, on 17 December (17.00 hrs), during a search for firearms in his father's house, and interrogated him. His brother Sali was also arrested. The police tried to press them for information concerning their brother Rama, who is the Secretary of the local branch of the Democratic League of Kosovo (LDK), and demanded them to hand over firearms that the police claimed were in the Albanian's possession. According to the report the interrogators also daunted Sali by showing him his badly beaten brother Adem. Following the alleged hard beating and maltreatment by the police, Adem was taken on 18 December to the hospital of Dakovica. He is reported to have been in a state of shock, his kidneys (loins) had almost stopped functioning and suffered from internal bleeding. Due to his critical condition and the lack of necessary medical equipment for blood dialysis, he was transferred on 19 December (around 14.00 hrs) to the Pristina Hospital, where despite intense efforts to keep him alive, he died around 16.00 hrs. A member of the Mission was present at the hospital while the doctors made the last efforts to save the Adem. He was told by one of the doctors that he died from kidney insufficiency. On Monday, December 21, three members of the Dakovica branch of the Council for Human Rights visited the Mission and made a detailed description of the incident. Among them Dr Bosnik Bardhi, Secretary of the Council in Dakovica, who was present in Dakovica Hospital during the efforts to save Adem Zeqiraj. According to the information provided by them, no prosecutor was present during the search in Zeqiraj's house, nor was any warrant presented. They also provided us with a copy of the medical report issued by the Dakovica Hospital, according to which, the late Adem was in shock that was the consequence of serious traumatism. He had also a serious oedema and haematoma as a result of the traumatism of the limbo, in the back and in the lumber region, on both sides, but obviously on the right side. Blood and myoglobin were found in the urine. Also there was acute insufficiency of both kidneys, and the blood pressure was very low. The delegation from the Human Rights Council informed the Mission that the parents of the late Adem expressed their intention to lay charges against the police, for the death of their son.

The Mission visited the Pristina Hospital on 22 December and met with the Director of the Institute of Forensic Medicine, Professor Slevisa Dobricanin, who confirmed that an autopsy had taken place. A copy of the report should be requested from the investigation judge when the full medical report was ready. He was not willing to give details on the cause of the death, saying that he needed additional medical report to have a complete view of the matter. However, his description of the patient's condition when received at the Pristina Hospital was more or less identical with the report from the Dakovica Hospital. An additional find was that the patient had haematomas at the soles of his feet. He said that, contrary to the report of Dakovica Hospital, they did not notice any haematomas on the kidneys. He noted that violence had been used and that he had asked all relevant evidence from the police. Nevertheless, he added that the wounds were superficial and they were not connected with his internal organs. In particular he said that the kidneys had not been damaged. He also said that they considered blood dialysis but they needed more analyses for which there had been no time due to the critical condition of the injured Adem. In general he was very restrained in giving explanations or information. Some of his comments contradicted documents or testimonies which are at our disposal. The Mission underlined to the doctor the great importance of the medical report of this fatal incident, so that the case could be clarified as regards alleged excessive use of police force. If the allegations that the police had been extremely brutal were proved the perpetrators should be severely punished, the mission members stressed.

CSCE Communication No. 434/92, Prague, December 29, 1992

12. 7th Interim Report, Head of Missions to Kosovo, Sandjak & Vojvodina, 16 December 1992

The first two weeks of December have witnessed an increase tension which appears to be at least in part linked to the electoral campaign, now in its final stages. There have been at least four shooting incidents, one in Prishtina, one near the Prishtina airport, one in a small town north of Prishtina and one at the Albanian border. There were four Albanians fatalities and two Albanians and one policeman are injured. The police were involved in two incidents, both of which resulted in fatalities. The Mission has investigated them in some depth in discussions with security and police officials, investigating judges, doctors and hospitalised patients as well as several witnesses. Contrary to claims of Albanian information services no evidence has been obtained that the incidents were interconnected or that the constituted part of a province-wide premeditated attempt to exacerbate tensions. The Armed Forces were involved in the other two incidents. There were also two fatalities. The Mission has requested a meeting with the military commander of Prishtina to obtain further information. The meeting has not yet been confirmed. There has also been a significant increase in large scale police searches for hidden arms. The President of the Assembly of the Moslem Community of Serbia, Kosovo, Sandzak and Vojvodina, as well as other Moslem personalities have been arrested. The matter has been reported on separately. There are indications that the arrested may be charged with arms smuggling.

The Albanian information services dramatise incidents as evidence of an orchestrated attempt to precipitate a crisis. The Serbian newspapers and television have shown more restraint. This is in contrast to their alarmist treatment of a fatal incident on November 11 in the centre of Prishtina. The Mission has pursued several human rights/fundamental freedoms cases. It has intervened with the authorities concerning access of a lawyer and family members to one of the wounded Albanians who has been held incommunicado for over two weeks. It has visited the President of the District Court in Pec and has confirmed procedural delays in the follow-up to a political trail that resulted in the conviction of 19 Albanians. The Mission has been assured that any appeals would be in the hands of the Supreme Court of Serbia before the end of the year and was offered co-operation to help ensure the presence of one of its members as observer during the appeal hearings, if this was desired. An investigation of the occupation by Serbians of a new apartment block has confirmed the illegality of the action and produced an official undertaking for remedial action. This case required follow-up. Additional human rights cases have been brought to the attention of the Mission. There have been delays in dealing with them because promised corroborating documentation has not been forthcoming. The Mission is seeking to involve local human rights organisations in this type of work. The current focus of this organisation is on reporting of human rights violations. Experience over the past two months suggests reluctance to get involved in grass roots defence of human rights. Extensive discussions regarding the causes of the non-appearance last week of the Albanian daily (five

times) and the Serbian daily (two times) suggested a local shortage of newsprint as the immediate cause. Alleged discrimination against the Albanian daily could not be substantiated. The editor-in-chief of the Albanian daily showed himself reluctant to discuss his problems with the authorities. This was suggested to him in an effort to extract official undertakings for equitable access to newsprint, prompt receipt of revenue from the distributor, and guarantee against obstruction of his publication under a recent legislation establishing a monopolistic state owned publishing enterprise. The Mission considers pursuing the question of freedom of the press with Albanian political leaders.

The local follow-up to the health discussions recently proposed by the Kosovo Subgroup of the Geneva Conference has not yet produced any results. Instead of making proposals to improve health services, the Albanian side presented to the Mission a collection of documents intended to illustrate illegal dismissals of medical staff. The documentation was incomplete and possibly dated. The Albanians undertook to provide additional essential documents, but have not yet done so. The Mission is also following up reports of confiscations of foreign exchange from Albanian gastarbeiter by Macedonian customs officials and has contacted the CSCE Mission in Skopje in this regard. … The Ahrens group of the Geneva Conference convened two further meetings on the educational crisis in Kosovo, one in Geneva and the second in Prishtina. Neither produced any progress, but both the Serbian and Albanian delegations agreed to continue efforts to resolve the educational crisis. …

13. CSCE Mission in Kosovo, Fortnightly Report No. 1, 6 January 1993

Overview

The outcome of the December 20 elections has caused concern among Albanians in Kosovo. Dr Rugova and other Albanian leaders anticipate a radicalisation in the weeks to come. The Serbian Radical Party is confidently expected to be invited by President Milosevic to participate in the new Serbian government. The presence of Arkan, an alleged war criminal in the Serbian Assembly is viewed with great concern. Albanian pessimism about political prospects should not be taken too lightly. Election results are indeed disturbing form the Kosovo perspective but there are alternative scenarios, some of them less threatening than those envisaged by Albanian leaders. For example, it is not a foregone conclusion that the Serbian Radical Party will be asked to join in the Serbian government.

Tension immediately before and after December 29, elections continued at a high level. During the following week the authorities informed the media of the discovery of a major arms trafficking network. Throughout the Province there have been house-to-house searches for weapons and the police continue to employ brutal tactics terrorising the Albanians. At least seventy individuals, including five Serbians, were arrested. About half of them have been released according to official sources. Claims that some of the arms originate from domestic stockpiles cannot be discounted.

The Mission has received several well documented requests for assistance with alleged human rights violations. It will be recalled that in the past Albanians had appeared to hesitate involving the Mission in their human rights cases, and in particular to provide good evidence in support of their claims. It is not clear whether these approaches reflect a trend or whether they are due to increased severity of oppression. Requests originated in several parts of the Province and have been referred to the Mission by the Council for the Defence of Human Rights and Freedoms, the Democratic League of Kosovo (LDK) and by concerned individuals. The mission continues to encourage submission of solid evidence and recourse to justice in order to combat violations. There is, however, understandable reluctance to doing so. The most common reasons given are fear of police reprisals and partiality of the courts. The Council for Defence of Human Rights is however considering charges in the recent case of a death ascribed to police brutality.

Dialogue

A delegation of Albanian medical and health care representatives visited Geneva to follow up preliminary discussions held in early

December in Pristina with the Ahrens Group of the Geneva Conference. The Albanian side presented proposals for issues to be negotiated with the authorities to restore health services for Albanians in Kosovo. On its return the Albanian delegation expressed its satisfaction with the results of the meeting.

Human Rights

The President of the Moslem Community of former Yugoslavia visited the Mission and requested it to intervene with the authorities on behalf of a senior Moslem leader arrested in Prizren on suspicion of arms trafficking. A visit to Prizren confirmed the arrest and anticipated charges, but the request to see the detainee was denied.

The Mission visited the District Court of Kosovska Mitrovica to raise issues of alleged maltreatment by the police in connection with the arrest of nine subjects under investigation for illegal arms trafficking. Statements made by two detainees in court obtained from the Defence were produced in support of the allegations. In the absence of the President of the Court the Mission was received by his alternate, who proved to be discourteous and unco-operative. He claimed that the Mission was meddling and that the allegations of maltreatment were unfounded. He also denied the request of the Mission to visit the detainees. To keep the matter under active consideration the Mission has written to the President of the Court. The situation has also been brought to the attention of the appropriate authorities in Belgrade.

A visit to the President of the District Court in Pristina officially confirmed that the Police had retained control over a hospitalised detainee contrary to the law. The Kosovo Chief of Police and State Security was informed that after more than 20 days neither the family nor a lawyer had been permitted to visit the detainee. He rejected the position of the Court but agreed to look in to the matter. The Mission has since been informed that the Court has assumed responsibility for the case and that the detainee has been visited by his mother.

Alleged major human rights violations occurred in two hamlets between Pristina and Pec. A number of homes were subjected to searches for arms on Christmas Day. Several citizens visited the Mission to report details of vandalism, gross misconduct and brutality. Medical reports describing the state of several of the victims were also supplied. The Mission called on the village police Chief on the morning when several citizens had been ordered to deliver a specified number of arms, purchasing them is necessary. The local Police opined that there was nothing wrong with such a request, but declined to discuss the case further in the absence of an appropriate authorisation. The district Police Chief also declined to comment giving the same grounds. The Mission then requested the provincial Chief to look into the matter. He was advised that in addition to physical abuse of force, his men were alleged to have wantonly destroyed food supplies and abducted a three year old child, dropping it off at some distance outside the hamlet where it was found some three hours later.

In another search for arms a subject was beaten severely and subsequently died of kidney insufficiency. The Mission visited the victim in the hospital at the time he passed away. The attending doctor stated that the lack of certain dialysis equipment was the immediate cause of death. The Mission has pursued this case in various quarters. There are apparent inconsistencies in the information provided by different medical sources.

Albanian gastarbeiter on home leave have provided further documentation demonstrating the effective confiscation of large amounts of foreign exchange by Macedonian customs officials. The documentation has been delivered to the CSCE Mission in Skopje to ensure appropriate follow-up with the Macedonian authorities.

Elections

The Mission monitored the December 20 elections, visiting several polling stations within and outside the capital of Kosovo and observing the vote count at two polling stations.

Visits

The Mission received a visit from Dr Norman Balic, the President of the Party of Democratic Action which represents the interests of about 100,000 Kosovo Moslems of Slavic origin. One of the purposes of the visit was to bring to the attention of the Mission serious human rights violations by the Serbian police and security authorities. The Mission

asked for suitable evidence with a view to raising the problems with the authorities.

Media

Both prior to and after the elections the Mission was contacted by various domestic and international media representatives including correspondents and teams from Routers, BBC, ITN, Channel 4 News, Greek Channel 3, Greek Ant 1 TV, Radio Belgium BRT (Flemish) and TV Pristina.

Comment

The Mission has an increasing amount of evidence, some of it documented, that some central and Provincial authorities are not enforcing law and order on the local level. For example, administrative and court decisions, even from higher levels, have not been implemented. The wide-spread unlawful conduct of police and security officials, resulting in human rights violations to some extent also appears to be due to lack of control over local extremists. Given that at least some of the repression appears to be locally instigated and beyond the control of the government, a more decentralised operation of a strengthened Mission with some members stationed in the larger towns may have a positive effect on the human rights situation in this Province.

14.   CSCE Mission Kosovo, Substantial Deduction of the Dakovica Hospital, 15 January 1993

Our Mission was contacted by two ethnic Albanian doctors in connection with the decision of the Serbian authorities to substantially reduce the capabilities of the Dakovica Medical Centre.

According to their allegations, the Serbian government enforcing a recent law passed by the Serbian parliament is about to close nine of the 13 departments of the Dakovica Medical Centre (which includes a big hospital and other regional centres) and to subject it to the Pec Medical Centre. The reason mentioned is the economic rationalisation of the Hospital.

The reporting doctors asserted that the real reason is purely political and discriminatory against the Albanians. The objective is to essentially eliminate the Medical Centre which is the only one in the whole of Kosovo, still 90 percent staffed by Albanian doctors and other personnel. The implementation of the provision of law, said the two doctors, would harm essentially the standard of the public health services in the Dakovica municipality (with a population of about 130,000), but also in the whole of Kosovo, because a great number of patients of Albanian origin of the whole province prefer to seek medical care in Dakovica.

The Medical Centre has 546 beds, 786 employees (170 doctors) and in 1991 treated 10,063 cases (among them 6000 child-deliveries of which 50 per cent from the Dakovica area). It is considered highly qualified, well equipped and staffed. Also, contrary to other hospitals, they do not charge the patients for the services offered (mainly because the Albanians, principally occupied in the private sector of unemployed, have no social security). This is valid, as they say, both for Albanians and Serbs patients.

The staff in an effort to keep the Hospital in full operation notified the Serbian authorities that they are willing to continue working with loss or no payment and that they will manage to operate the Hospital even with reduced financial support by the State, depending on the solidarity and the support of the people.

They also claimed that the realisation of the plan would result in the dismissal of at least 50 per cent of the employees of the hospital, while it is likely that most of the rest would quit. Another consequence, they said, would be that the 17 regional medical centres of the Hospital would close too.

The highly professional standard of the Hospital as well as the inappropriate and irrational reduction of its capabilities was acknowledged (as they said) by Dr Radoljub Milosević, Counselor of the Ministry of Health of Serbia (who has been previously Minister of Health in Kosovo), as well as by Dr Bosović (Secretary for Health in Kosovo) and Mrs Vera Vesović (Director of Health Services in Pec).

The Director of the Dakovica Hospital made an appeal to the President of the Executive Council of Dakovica municipality, Mr

Obradović, urging that the Hospital does not lose its present status and capabilities. Mr Obradović seemed to be positive to the request, but is probably not to decide on the matter. The reporting doctors said that in some other cases, where the integration of hospitals had been decided, it had not been implemented in view of the position taken by their medical staff (e.g. the case of Majdanpak Hospital with Bor Hospital).

The Serbian Minister of Health has sent an inspector (Mr Milan Tubin) to examine the operation of the Dakovica Medical Centre. In his report he was in favour of the continuation of the function of the Hospital. Nevertheless, the representatives of Kosovo in the Serbian parliament proposed the reduction and integration of the Hospital. Finally, the reporting doctors proposed that the Minister of Health send a Committee to examine the matter and to evaluate the importance of the Hospital for the whole region. The Mission will make contacts with all the authorities involved, to hear their views on the issue. It seems that, if the information given by the Albanian doctors is correct, the Dakovica Medical Centre should continue its full operation. The opposite would add considerably to the interethnic tension in Kosovo, and would aggravate the already miserable living standard of the population.

15.　CSCE Mission to Kosovo, Fortnightly Report No. 2, 18 January 1993

The last fortnight has been relatively calm in comparison with the previous period. Fewer violations of human rights, and no killings have been reported. However, the Kosovo issue continues to be deadlocked by hostile feelings on both sides, total absence of contact except an educational issue, and repeated acts of violence by police or security forces. The insistence by Albanian leadership on an increased internationalisation of the conflict does not facilitate the initiation of a dialogue between the local parties. However, not all Albanian leaders support the LDK policy of rapid internationalisation of the conflict in the form of UN or other military intervention. Leaders of other Albanian political groups try to promote understanding between the two sides through democratic means. They also favour a step by step approach towards the ultimate goal of sovereignty, and recommend Albanian participation in negotiations for comprehensive autonomy.

On the Serbian side the rhetoric has grown harsher after the hard-liners won the elections and more moderate forces no longer are represented among the elected legislators from Kosovo. According to the results published here on January 4 only about 100,000 out of the 270,000 registered voters cast their ballot on December 20. Thirteen seats went to the Socialist Party, five to the Radical Party, five to the Arkan group and one to the Moslem party. The Albanian side maintains that the Serbs have clearly chosen the option of war. Conciliatory gestures do not seem likely from the next Serbian government. Should such gestures nevertheless be made they could be denounced by the extremist local forces in Kosovo who would then decide to act on their own. An undetermined number of the extreme Serb paramilitary group "White Eagles", led by Mirko Jovic is said to have arrived in the Province and to be preparing plans for a war. Provocative statements have been made by extremist leaders who call on all Serbs to reject any kind of foreign interference. In a TV interview in Pristina, the chairman of the Radical Party for Kosovo targeted the CSCE Mission, claiming it should be expelled without delay. New Serb pressure against Albanians to make them leave the country, is reported to have been applied since the beginning of the month. In mid-January the Mission received alarming reports concerning thirty-six cases of brutal mistreatment by the police from the town of Pec. Apparently more villagers have been summoned for the next few days, and the Mission is seized of the matter. The Mission has closely followed the on-going procedures in these human rights cases:

- Market incident on December 3, 1992 (one Albanian killed, another wounded). The wounded man is still under court investigation. Formal charges against him are expected shortly. His family, on their side, will charge the policeman involved in the shooting.
- Young man beaten to death in Dakovica on December 18. More forensic evidence is to be provided soon by the Albanian side.

- Religious leaders arrested in Prizren on December 14 in connection with arms trafficking. The trial will take place on 1 February. The Mission met with the two Moslem leaders, who have acknowledged the charges. The Mission has been told by the prosecutor and the President of the District Court that only criminal charges will be brought against the arrested men, thus avoiding the risk of adding to the tension by raising political charges. It will be recalled that also Serbs were involved in the arms ring and that the weapons appeared to be of Yugoslav army type.

In the economic and social fields, the Serbian government took further steps to impose its rule in Kosovo, raising bitter complaints by the Albanian leaders. Among the most important of these measures were:

- The enforcing of a new law, forcing the public enterprises in the Province to become joint ventures with Serb companies or with the Development Fund of Serbia. The latter should hold at least 51 per cent of the shares. As many as 250 enterprises appear to be affected.
- The medical centre of Dakovica is the preferred medical institution by the Albanians because of its highly qualified staff and equipment. Now the government intends to enforce a law reducing its capacity and integrating it with a similar institution in Pec.

16.　CSCE Mission Kosovo, Fortnightly Report No. 4/93, 18 February 1993

Uncertainties regarding political prospects have been removed with the recent appointment of the new Serbian cabinet. Key re-appointments including the Foreign Minister and the Interior Ministry [and the position of the ?] Radical Party of Serbia suggest continuity in the conduct of affairs in Kosovo. The political atmosphere has benefited from the departure of radical figures for theatres of renewed conflict. However, more recently there have been intensified searches for arms accompanied by intimidation, severe beatings and [occurrences?] of police brutality. ...

The economic situation remains extremely difficult. There is a very high but indeterminate level of unemployment and a virtual standstill in a large number of public (formerly "self-managed") enterprises. Albanians claim that the situation has been greatly exacerbated by the transfer of 51 per cent ownership of a large number of enterprises to interests in Serbia and describe this as pure robbery. Complaints about recent unlawful dismissals of Albanian management from several enterprises are under investigation. The impact of sanctions on the private sector of the economy is no doubt much less than claimed officially. The private sector including trade, agriculture and smaller private construction, manufacturing and other enterprises appears very active. ... currency remittances from several hundred thousand Albanians abroad are indeterminate but believed to be significant. Departures of Albanians to escape police brutality are said to continue but cannot be quantified. While these departures are regretted, it is also noted that they reduce the number of mouths to feed and possibly increase remittance.

The educational crisis continues unabated. Discussions under the auspices of the Geneva Conference to resolve it were resumed in Belgrade 17 to 19 February. The Albanian side accepted in principle five points presented by the Serbian side; but the meeting failed to produce any results.

In the health sector there has been no movement to begin negotiations for the improvement and resumption of health services which have been severely curtailed in the wake of special measures introduced by Serbia in 1990.

A meeting with the Chief Executive of the Kosovski Okrug (District) has confirmed continued official interest in closer contacts with the Mission to review issues of mutual concern, including human rights problems. Meeting with several other officials have also been encouraging in this regard, with the regrettable exception of the Police. The Mission continues to call on police stations to raise violation cases with those most directly concerned but is normally not received. Efforts to remove this obstacle to more effective work continue.

In the area of human rights and fundamental freedoms the Mission has already reported the reluctance of local human rights organisations to encourage victims of various kinds of official abuse to seek redress through available channels. In cases of police brutality reluctance is understandable. Nevertheless the Mission stresses that opportunities should be explored. In such cases as evictions from apartments or dismissals of enterprise management, there are fewer objections to litigation, but in the experience of the Mission, police brutality has not given rise to prosecution by the victims or legal aid from the human rights organisations.

The issue has once more been discussed with the President of the Council for the Defence for Human Rights and Freedoms. He indicated that the Mission's views were similar to those expressed to him by an internationally known human rights expert and undertook to raise it again with his Council.

More recently the Mission has been alerted to an increasing incidence of acts of police brutality mostly in hamlets and villages in the Pec Okrug. Among the details provided there are the names of several police officers alleged to be directly associated with the crimes. Most offences are committed in connection with searches for arms. Individuals are often told to purchase specified arms from their neighbours if they do not have any themselves and members of the victim's family are sometimes maltreated if he is absent.

The implicit application of the principle of collective responsibility has been sanctioned by the Serbian Assembly in its special programme for Kosovo adopted in March 1990.

The Albanian leadership claims that the level of frustration among the population has increased markedly and has asked the Mission to intensify its efforts to prevent abuse and help discourage explosive confrontations.

Notwithstanding threats of severe reprisals, two villages are reported to have successfully resisted attempted arrests and are now afraid of retaliation. The Mission is looking into the situation.

The human rights performance by the police has not been uniform across the Province. Since the beginning of the year Pecć has been hit worst but few if any brutalities have been reported ... Interestingly there are also signs of a more conciliatory approach in some government circles.

Thus a trial in Prizren of twenty individuals charges with arms trafficking was surprisingly non-controversial. The Mission was able to discuss the case with the Court, the Public Prosecutor and the Defence and interviewed three defendants. It attended the proceedings on the day the Defence intervened and notes that the atmosphere was courteous and that the Court was responsive to arguments of the Defence. The trial was concluded in three days and sentences were light n terms of what is provided for by law. It was also significant that the offences were treated as purely criminal cases without political content. It may be recalled that the Mission's attempt to establish contact with the Mitrovica Court about a similar arms smuggling case was rather rudely rejected.

Other cases pursued by the Mission and not previously mentioned include evictions from apartments, temporary detentions including that of a delegation of the Merhamet Humanitarian Society in the Sandzak and concerns in a large medical centre largely staffed by Albanians ...

17.   CSCE Kosovo, Fortnightly Report No. 5, 4 March 1993

Some recent incidents in the Pec area, in the villages of Nepolje, Jablanica and Dokshiq, have shown a new element or resistance by the population to arms searches by the Police. The Police are unlikely to tolerate such challenges to its authority and might change its course of action. It would however appear premature to assume a new pattern of encounters between the Albanian population and the police. These recent event may nevertheless indicate that the limit of what the Albanians are prepared to suffer ... The Police seem to be under increased pressure for many reasons: the presence of the Mission, the consequences of sanctions, international discontent with the government's conduct in Kosovo and limits of endurance of the Albanian population. ... Since the beginning of he year efforts to draft young Albanians for military service have been intensified to complete units for higher combat capability. Many young Albanians are dodging the draft. The Police have caught an unknown number of them. The Mission was informed about alleged brutality of the Police in this

context and about parents not being informed of the whereabouts of the draftees. Some enquiries have been referred to the Pristina office of the ICRC. Serbs volunteered in Pristina some weeks ago for service in the Krajina but this appears not to be the case any longer. Some military reinforcement along Macedonian and Albanian borders have been reported.

Delegations from the government and the Albanian opposition convened in Belgrade for a seventh session to negotiate a resolution of the educational crisis in Kosovo. While the results were negative, new proposals made by the government were considered by the Albanians to negotiations after the installation of new federal government. In a further meeting with the Kosovo Council for the Defence of Human Rights and Freedoms the Mission was pleased to learn that victims of human rights violations were now regularly advised to seek redress in court. It was also welcome news that charges had been laid by several victims. The Mission learned from the Democratic League of Kosovo (LDK) that it has adopted a similar policy and is issuing advice accordingly throughout the Province. Several opportunities for contributions by the Mission in this area were examined with the Council; among them significant outstanding appeals in various tribunals. The LDK has commenced a date bank of individuals subject to attention by the Police throughout the Province on the basis of reports submitted by individuals themselves and by local branches of the LDK and the Council for the Defence of Human Rights and Freedoms. The data are verifiable and a careful review suggests a high degree of reliability though it can be assumed a significant number of incidents are not captured because they are not reported. The total number of individuals with police contacts between 5 January and 28 February was 936. The District of Pec, one of the five districts in Kosovo, accounted for the overwhelming majority of the cases (864).

Members of the Pristina Office have had two meetings with Dr Milos Simovic, the Head of the Serbian administration in Kosovo. Apart from the substantial change in the official attitude towards the Mission, useful information can be drawn from his comments on the situation. It has been agreed to hold weekly working meetings with Dr Simovic and/or senior officials in various fields to address issues of concern to the Mission under the terms of its mandate. A meeting was held with Mr Bozovic, the Secretary of Health, who explained the contents of Law No. 17 on 31 March 1992 dealing with the rationalisation of the entire Serbian health system and consequential frictions with Albanian doctors, especially in the Dakovica and Glogovac Medical Centres. A visit to the Glogovac Medical Centre with the Secretary of Health was carried out on 26 February. Complaints by the Albanian Head of the Centre were reviewed in depth with him and efforts were combined to meet his concerns as best possible in the circumstances and to convince him to continue his services.

The Mission continues to receive many visits from foreign missions and from the media. Several articles and news items have also been published in the local press. Articles in the Serbian daily "Jodinstvo" sought to demonstrate that the Mission was partial to Albanian separatists.

Pec Office: The Pec Office established itself administratively and substantively during the reporting period. The Mission dealt with three serious incidents of confrontation between villagers and police forces. Subsequent to Mission repeat visits to the affected population and cordial representations to area police commanders, the situation in both places returned to normal. Violations of human rights consisted of alleged threat of use of force, police brutality and destruction of private property during searches for arms. Local Albanian representatives credit the Pec Office's rising profile and ability to approach all sides of a dispute with being a major contributing factor to what they term diminishing severity of repression. The Office has enjoyed access to and support from Serbian officials, with the exception of the Pec police commander. As the Pec District has been the focal point for Albanian complaints about human rights violations, the Mission exploited this access to establish good rapport with Serbs and Albanians, as well as to protect an image of impartiality and openness.

Prizren Office: The Prizren Office was briefed on the July 26, 1990 decision of the Serb parliament to redistrict and rename the Dragas municipality. Dragas, together with Sova Roka, Orahovac and Prizren, constitute the Prizren Okrug (District). The Parliament's decisions effectively carved out a municipality by ethnic Gorans from the majority Albanian community. The Gorans are Muslims and sympathetic to the Serb government. The newly created Municipality of Gora encompasses the town of Dragas and 17 Goran villages located to the south, with a population of approximately 17,000 of which there are 350 Albanians and 70 Serb/Montenegrins. Consequently, the region extending north of Dragas city to Prizren, known as Opoje, which comprises 24,000 Albanians in 19 villages are grafted on to the Municipality of Prizren. The new Mayor of Gora Municipality, himself a Goran, justified the redistricting on the basis of the unique linguistic, cultural and historical character of the Gorans, although he conceded Gorans in the most recent government census were recorded as Muslims. The Mayor said ethnic tensions declined with the exclusion of "aggressive, nationalistic Albanians", who did not respect the constitution and the laws of the Serb Republic. LDK activists in Opoje and Dragas claim the redistricting is a tactic to marginalise the Albanian majority, evident in the fact that Albanians are shuttled between the Gora and Prizren municipalities, but are represented by neither. Opoje residents' identification documents and passports are issued by the municipality of Gora, court cases are tried in both Gora and Prizren (with some cases bouncing back and forth), and taxes are paid to Gora. Nevertheless, the Mayor of Gora categorically stated to Mission members he does not represent Opoje residents. Mission members were advised that the number of militia in border areas adjacent to Albania has been increased significantly over the past several months. According to Albanian sources in Dragas, the normal complement of 120 border police has more than tripled to approximately 400.

18.   CSCE Mission in Kosovo, Special Report, 5 March 1993

2.1.1. THE ECONOMICS OF SEPARATIMS AND REPRESSION
The Serb Government has sought since 1989 to topple Kosovar Albanians from their position of economic dominance, brought about by their 19 years of de facto independence, by local demographic facts of life (Albanians are around 90 per cent of the population) and ... higher education and the principles of market economy. The Albanians have responded with a policy of economic and social apartheid combined with fiscal disobedience, which has denied the public sector Albanian employees and tax revenue. Using as its primary vehicle the 1990 legislative "Programme for the implementation of Peace, Equality, Democracy and Prosperity of the SAP Kosovo", and working through local Serb proxies, the Govement of Serbia fired or demoted Albanian management from public sector enterprises; merged Kosovo's state self-managed companies with industries or foundations in Serbia, ceding management control to the new Serb partners; restricted registration of private enterprises; all but halted import licenses; and denied international banking services and commercial credit instruments to the Albanian businessmen. Simultaneously, Serbs were catapulted into management positions, preferentially hired, and by the policy of the Milosevic regime, encouraged to invest and settle in. This concerted effort to diminish the Albanian community's economic power has largely failed in western Kosovo (the Pec and Pristina administrative districts). Serbian nationals own only a fraction of the region's private enterprises, retail shops and restaurants (e.g. in Prisoner, only 68 or 1600 private stores). The Albanian boycott of Serb enterprises sharply limits their potential for expansion given market demographics. Serbs find employment almost exclusively in the public sector (including state self-managed firms) and are increasingly vulnerable to the twin shocks of market-oriented reform and international sanctions. The Prisoner district administrator, noted that only 3500 - 5000 Serbs are working n Prizren, over 2000 of them in the self-managed firms. The majority of the remainder earn (shrinking) pay checks as civil servants and security force employees. Albanians control two-thirds of local real estate. Legislation requires Ministry of Finance approval for transactions between persons of different nationalities. For Serbs seeking to leave Kosovo and Albanians hoping to expand their holdings, the answer is variably "no".

The Albanian Miracle
The economic tenacity of the Albanian community is sustained by a steady flow of Deutsche Marks and Swiss Francs remitted by family members toiling abroad. ...
Industry
Following the Serbian take-over of most state self-managed enterprises, the manufacturing sector has almost ground to a halt. The giant Zastava automobile parts plant in Pec has been idle since last year. This is due to:
- Removal (or voluntary departure) of most former management (Albanians), as well as dismissal of unco-operative workers (Albanian blue collar labourers were under pressure not to sign Serbian collective wage agreements and/or were discharged for alleged political activities stemming from participation in strikes and demonstrations);
- Impact of international sanctions, which have limited supplies of inexpensive fuel and other imported inputs, as well as eliminated export markets;
- Asset stripping by new Serbian management (there is a well documented case in Dakovica which is the subject of a lawsuit), which may be intended to deny productive assets to Albanians or may just be old-fashioned corporate raiding by unscrupulous businessmen;
- The post socialism realities of the new Yugoslavia. ...
CONCLUSION
As international sanctions and fiscal irresponsibility which has led to hyper inflation, continue to erode the Federal Yugoslav Republic sector, it is highly likely that Serbs residing in Kosovo will suffer disproportionately. Economic resentment against evident Albanian prosperity and relative immunity to Serb woes, already palpable, will deepen. In this scenario, ultra-nationalist, para-military leaders such as "Arkan" will have greater opportunities to exploit aggrieved Serb chauvinism. Already the government is stepping up harassment of Albanian businessmen, through the device of legitimate auditing. A team of 100 Serb fiscal police drawn from other parts of Serbia arrived in Pec this week and are working their way through the books of Albanian businesses, looking for irregularities. If inventory of shops does not have absolutely correct documentation as to origin (most good are brought in "informally" from Greece and Turkey, as well as from middlemen in Belgrade), it is subject to confiscation on the sport. Shop employees are rarely carried formally on the books, as required by law for purposes of collecting social security levies, violations result in shops being closed.

19.   Special Report: Kosovo-Problems and Prospects, Tore Bogh, Head of Missions, 29 June 1993

...

Report: ... In the historical see-saw battle for lebensraum Serbia has suffered setbacks since the Second World War. Since World War II there has been a steady decline of the Serbian component in Kosovo's population sinking to about ten percent at present. Serbians know that in the long run their control over the provinces hinges on their ability to increase drastically their proportion of the population. Resettlement was central to the government program for Kosovo. Initially much effort was expended to make room for Serbs in higher echelons in all sectors with the notable exception of the private sector. Well in excess of 100,000 Albanians found themselves out of work for various reasons. Belgrade offered incentives to prospective colonists; heavily subsidized housing, attractive remuneration, business opportunities, and virtually cost-free land and credit for farming. Many Serbs were registered, not without some official prodding, as potential settlers in Kosovo.

Not surprisingly opinions differ whether or not Belgrade intended an ethnic cleansing to make room for several hundred thousand Serbs. Room had to be made. The province is one of the most densely settled regions in Europe. At roughly 200 persons per square kilometer the population density is well in excess of that of Denmark (120). These statistics take on added significance if it is borne in mind that most of the province is mountainous. The mineral wealth of the province is impressive, but its actual and potential economic benefit to the province remains outstanding.

There can be little doubt that the poisoned inter-ethnic relations stirred up by massive nationalistic campaigns and intensified by the Serbian program provided fertile ground for inter-ethnic incidents at the expense of the Albanians. Ethnic cleansing elsewhere in former Yugoslavia lent credence to Albanian fears that a similar fate was held in store for them. To date wholesale ethnic cleansing has fortunately not happened, notwithstanding confident predictions from several quarters including the Albanian opposition which stridently keeps insisting on an imminent Serbian holocaust.

In the tense and confrontational atmosphere the Albanian political leadership turned to a policy of concerted pacific resistance. If there have been any acts of Albanian terrorism they were isolated incidents. Interestingly, the Serbian authorities as well as radical political elements appear to have become at least equally determined to keep the crisis from getting out of hand. The level of police repression has been such as to discourage major Albanian initiatives. Police brutality and killings have however not reached such levels as to precipitate desperate acts of retaliation. Radicals make frequent and threatening appearances in Kosovo, but in the continued absence of meaningful action, their shows of force are beginning to be viewed as posturing. Today from almost any perspective, a major ethnic cleansing or massive expulsions of Albanians seem less likely. Moreover, as time passes, the likelihood of an ethnic cleansing in Kosovo may be diminishing.

At the current juncture the crucial fact is that Serbian population policy has failed. There has been no increase in the proportion of Serbs, worse still there is evidence that the outward trickle continues. Some Serbian acknowledge this setback. Albanian leaders with assistance from the average Albanian are good at reinforcing by word and deed the lack of attractiveness of Kosovo to unwanted immigrants. Though they claim otherwise, their policies contribute to isolating and ostracising Kosovars of Serbian extraction. Sharply increased radical strength at the December 20 elections both reflected and exacerbated the ethnic ill feelings. A small but significant indicator of the dimension of Serbian frustration are new obstacles in the way of departures from Kosovo. Real estate transactions of all Kosovars require government approval. Property swaps between Serbia and Kosovo are subject to review by a reputedly unsympathetic legislative committee whose decisions are beyond appeal.

Another major setback for Belgrade has been complete failure of the Serbian security apparatus to root out Albanian separatism. The Serbian program provided for draconian measures, including individual and collective responsibility for certain offenses. It is true that Belgrade retains control over internal security. It does this with an oversized repressive police apparatus supported by contingents of the state security services and backed by paramilitary forces and the Yugoslav army strategically stationed in many locations across the province. But this control is degenerating into a form of armed occupation.

At this point in time the simple fact is that notwithstanding brutal repression Albanian separatism has flourished more than at any other time in Serbia's history. Never has Serbia been confronted with such a united and highly organized opposition supported by the overwhelming majority of Albanians. Town and country have not always seen eye to eye, especially under communist rule, but the Serbian challenge has brought them together. Whereas three to four years ago there were Albanian leaders who were willing to seek a compromise, systematic Serbian rebuffs peaking in a large-scale cleansing of Albanians from positions of responsibility have created a pool of unemployed academics, managers and officials who dedicate themselves wholeheartedly to the politics of independence.

The inconsistency of the Serbian response to the Albanian challenge shows up in many quarters. For example the Albanian press has continued to propogate without censorship an openly separatist message. International travel of Albanian leaders goes on largely unmolested. International visitors, many of whom are anything but impartial, have been freely admitted to the country. Visa controls have

been imposed but the flow of inquisitive and unsympathetic visitors has not been interrupted entirely.

Perhaps the most striking Serbian failure is reflected in a successful parallel electoral process. The Serbian authorities have not scuttled a referendum held in the fall of 1991 in which an overwhelming majority of Albanians voted for a constitution establishing a sovereign and independent republic of Kosovo. In May last year, despite harrassment, there were successful elections leading to the establishment of a parallel government most of whose members are in exile. The notable exception Dr. Ibrahim Rugova, "Head of State" of the "Republic of Kosovo" with offices nearby the police/state security establishment. His frequent travels abroad with extensive exposure on the international stage have added immensely to his political stature. He has at his disposal a dedicated and enthusiastic group of talented supporters who operate an effective international information service, linking him to the world at large and especially to a militant Albanian diaspora that offers financial and moral support. His party, the Democratic League of Kosovo (LDK), is well organized and active throughout the province seeking to provide parallel administrative services. The most impressive example of parallel government is the independent system of education, virtually forced upon the Albanians when conditions in public education were made unacceptable. The parallel system indoctrinates the next generation from kindergarten through university in the spirit of independence. Much of the Albanian population participates in this national project by contributions to a voluntary taxation scheme, the proceeds of which are for the largest part invested in education. The scheme is operated by an organisation that claims to be officially registered as benevolent institution.

…

The crisis in public health has been exacerbated by several factors, but the large-scale dismissals of Albanian medical staff has contributed its share to mounting problems. There is no shortage of unemployed medics in Serbia, but it has not been possible to make them move to Kosovo. Albanian doctors have attempted to set up parallel medical services but have been less successful than in the educational field. Another problem area is the registration of real estate. Albanians and Serbs alike have refused to record their transactions in public registers in order to avoid transfer taxes. The Serbian authorities are alleged to have tried to exploit these omissions for the benefit of Serbian real estate owners who sold out to Albanians on attractive terms in the past. Apparently the number of Serbians ready to recover their land by breaking private contracts was disheartening.

In the economic sphere massive replacement of Albanians in publicly owned (formerly "self-managed") enterprises with Serbian managers, experts and workers has also backfired. Talent from Serbia could not be attracted to run these firms. The pool of provincial Serbian talent is insufficient to meet the demand. Many firms went bankrupt or are in extreme difficulties. An interesting case is the giant Trepča mining, metallurgical and manufacturing conglomerate, once among the largest in Europe. The enterprise has virtually ceased operation. Several thousand Albanian miners were dismissed in 1989 following a fierce strike against Serbian repression. There were not enough skilled miners available in all of former Yugoslavia to replace them. A number of replacements were found, but they too have been sporadically out on strike, chiefly to elicit outstanding pay from the management. Not surprisingly any concessions extracted by the miners leads to unrest among other employees in similar straights. Serbians who as a group originally benefitted from stepping into the shoes of Albanians, are now hardest hit by hyperinflation and economic decline, as it becomes ever more difficult for Belgrade to find the subsidies needed to keep afloat tottering public enterprises all over the Republic. Arrears in salaries is not unique to Kosovo, but their political cost is of a great order of magnitude in Kosovo than elsewhere.

As noted previously, the private sector has not been significantly interfered with under the Serbian program. Interestingly, there is agreement that it operates very efficiently and that business cooperation between Kosovo and Serbia has not been destroyed by the political confrontation. The level of Albanian trading talent is supposed to be reflected by the availability of some goods, such as sugar and flour, in Kosovo whereas in Vojvodina, the breadbasket of the country, these items are rarely seen on the shelves. The supply of motor fuel also seems to be better, though one cannot be sure that more favourable terms extracted by Serbian sanction busters is the sole reason for the more generous supply. Significantly the spirit of cooperation does not extend down to the retail level where prejudicial practices in the purchase of goods and services have become insuperable obstacles to some Serbian small businesses.

It is abundantly clear that Belgrade has not been able to cope with the crisis in Kosovo, a long-standing problem which it has exacerbated with its own actions. In the circumstances some government circles, after initial hesitations, have expressed increasing satisfaction with the presence and activities of the CSCE Mission of Long Duration there. Its mandate to promote dialogue with recalcitrant Albanians provides another avenue to influence more moderate Albanians and to pursue opportunities for an eventual accommodation under a regime of increased autonomy. Serbians are however divided. Some envisage total abolition of the vestiges of Kosovo's autonomy. Others have floated the idea of carving up Kosovo, giving Albanians most of the territory, but retaining areas in the north and east which are industrialized and rich in non-ferrous minerals. The northwestern corner which is of great religious significance would, according to one schemes are under serious consideration, but shortcomings have been aired and debate thereon has petered out. Belgrade realizes, of course, that it must address itself to the problem of Kosovo, and that this must be done soon and in a way that stops and reverses the setbacks suffered in recent years. Failing that Serbia can in due course expect to lost control by default. At present there are no indications what methods and means Serbia might entertain to reverse the trend.

Albanian leaders have not been greatly concerned about CSCE efforts to promote dialogue with Serbia. In the drawn-out educational talks and more recently in the negotiations to retain an independent press, they have been less flexible than their Serbian counterparts. The latter have offered significant concessions but asked in return for some form of acknowledgement of Serbian law and order. The former reject all conditions that in the narrow and at times inconsistent perception of their people could be interpreted acceptance of Serbian sovereignty over Kosovo. They perceive their benefit from the CSCE presence in terms of exposing and ameliorating human rights violations committed by the Serbian administration. Albanians see some benefit in the Missions' work but not nearly enough in terms of their needs. Sustained police criminality as well as numerous other instances of Serbian discrimination and disrespect of law and order at Albanian expense, have become nothing but proofs that Serbia has lost all claim to their province.

It is clear of course, that Serbian authorities face a dilemma. If they eliminate police repression the separatist opposition will quickly get out of hand by mounting unpalatable initiatives such as convoking the parallel assembly that is waiting in the wings. If they continue human rights violations their claim along with their capacity to govern the province will continue to erode. Albanian leaders doubt the long term prospects of Serbian rule and welcome any CSCE contribution helping them to expose internationally the incapacity of Serbia to fulfill minimum obligations towards it Albanian citizens in Kosovo. Thus some Serbians and many Albanians, each for very different reasons, perceive important benefits from CSCE missions and welcome their presence in Kosovo.

Comment: The single most important international question mark is whether and when there will be an explosion in Kosovo. The fact alone that, contrary to dire predictions, there has been no eruption since the bloody riots in 1989, should convince that neither the Serbian nor the Albanian leaders want it to happen. There is no obvious reason why they should change their minds in this matter. Evidently the political costs for one side and the potential loss in human life for the other heavily outweigh potential benefits. Since the arrival of the Missions there have been sensitive incidents and events, among them police killings successful resistance to police by villagers and one Albanian mass demonstration. None of these incidents did get out of hand. It is generally assumed that extremists exist on either side who are prepared to pay any price to achieve their political goals. Tensions are such that a major provocation or a series of incidents could escalate.

Chapter 6: Human Rights Issues

The maintenance of an increasingly desperate human rights situation in a state which considered itself to be part of Western Europe for over a decade could be seen as an indictment of the European and universal international institutions concerned with human rights questions. However, as was the case with the early involvement of the CSCE acting for the region in the Yugoslav crisis, the universal international constitutional system for the monitoring and implementation of human rights actually functioned with surprising vigour, both in relation to the Yugoslav crisis in general, and also in relation to Kosovo.

Standards and International Interest

Human rights are based in general international law, in universal conventions, and in regional and multilateral/bilateral treaties. The most basic and fundamental human rights obligations, such as the prohibition of genocide, apartheid and torture, are part and parcel of the substantive law of the international constitution. That is to say, these obligations of general international law apply to all states, whether or not they have specifically consented to them. States can never derogate from these rights or suspend their operation, even in times of armed conflict or other emergencies. Most of these fundamental obligations are also reflected in international conventions which aspire to universal membership. These human rights conventions, most notably the two United Nations Covenants on Human Rights of 1966, or the specialized Convention against Torture, also include more specific obligations, which are only in operation in relation to states that have contracted into the relevant treaties. Regional treaties will generally add even greater specificity. After all, it is assumed that states in a given region will share a certain human rights culture, and will be able to advance on the level of protection offered in relation to certain rights at the universal level. Finally, a number of individual states may wish to create a legal regime among themselves, in order to address particular human rights concerns relevant to them. For that purpose, they can establish multilateral or bilateral treaties. The latter are often concluded in relation to the protection of national minorities.

The human rights obligations binding upon the former Yugoslavia by virtue of general international law and her own specific consent were substantive, wide-ranging and clearly expressed. In addition to having to comply with human rights obligations in general international law, the former Yugoslavia was party to several universal human rights conventions (*e.g.*, the 1966 Covenant on Civil and Political Rights, the Genocide, Torture, Rights of the Child, and Elimination of Racial Discrimination Conventions). It was, however, not a member of the very sophisticated European regional system of human rights operated under the aegis of the Council of Europe. That system not only contains a very detailed catalogue of rights, but also a highly intrusive and effective machinery of human rights enforcement, including the European Court of Human Rights.

The issue of implementation, of course, is the principal weak spot of the universal human rights system. In accordance with the classical conception of international law, states must not only consent to specific obligations, in order to be legally bound by them (other than fundamental human rights contained in general international law). This consent can often be conditioned by reservations or national interpretations. In a second step, states have traditionally demanded the right to determine themselves if an international mechanism can consider the extent to which they are actually implementing the obligations they have accepted. For example, many universal conventions contain optional clauses or annexes, through which a state can agree that a special committee shall be entitled to receive petitions from individuals claiming to have been the victim of human rights violations. In the absence of such additional consent, the relevant committee lacks competence even to receive such communications.

However, the international constitutional system has developed quite significantly over the past decade. A state may no longer consider it an unlawful 'intervention' if another government, or an international organization, criticizes its human rights performance. Hence, the United Nations General Assembly, or specialized United Nations bodies such as the Commission on Human Rights and its sub-commission, will now routinely adopt resolutions condemning the human rights practices of certain states, and demand improvements. Moreover, most of the committees attached to international human rights conventions are entitled to receive and even demand reports on compliance from state parties, and to evaluate these reports critically, without the need of a further act of consent from the state in question. And the United Nations has now established a rather sophisticated system of human rights monitoring, through the United Nations High Commissioner for Human Rights and the invention of Special Rapporteurs. There are two types of Special Rapporteurs. Thematic rapporteurs consider certain types of issues or infractions, wherever they may be committed. For example, there are very active rapporteurs who consider allegations of torture, involuntary disappearances or religious intolerance throughout the world. There are also country rapporteurs, appointed by the United Nations Commission on Human Rights to consider the situation in specific states in crisis. While the states in question can opt to refuse cooperation with such rapporteurs, they will rarely do so. For, even states which systematically violate human rights are quite sensitive to international criticism, and to the condemnation by the United Nations political bodies, including the General Assembly, which a failure to cooperate might bring.

The staggering situation in the former Yugoslavia, especially in relation to Bosnia and Herzegovina, triggered significant international human rights action. In an unprecedented step, the United Nations Commission on Human Rights met in special session in August 1992. It established a Special Rapporteur for Yugoslavia, initially the high profile Tadeusz Mazowiecki, who was replaced by Elizabeth Rehn upon his resignation in the face of international inaction concerning his findings. Existing thematic rapporteurs, including those on torture and arbitrary executions, were also requested to give urgent attention to the situation in the former Yugoslavia. Subsequently, the Commission, backed by the General Assembly, requested the Secretary-General to make available resources to facilitate continuous monitoring. Indeed, in the end, after some Yugoslav resistance, efforts to establish a field office presence were successful. The resulting reports were fed into the Sub-Commission, an expert body operating under the aegis of the Commission on Human Rights, the Commission itself, the Third (Humanitarian) Committee of the United Nations General Assembly, and the plenary of the Assembly. All of these bodies adopted uncharacteristically strong resolutions, condemning FRY/Serb practices and demanding a cessation of this conduct without a hint of the usual diplomatic ambiguities.

In addition to these bodies established directly under the United Nations Charter, the Committees attached to specialized human rights conventions also became active. Yugoslavia was made to report on its conduct and its diplomats were cross-examined by the relevant committees, which then proceeded to adopt quite strongly worded findings. Yugoslavia initially cooperated with this procedure. However, by September 1992, the United Nations organs had determined that Yugoslavia could not lay claim to automatic succession of the rights of the Socialist Federal Republic of Yugoslavia. Instead, all the states which had emerged from the dissolution of Yugoslavia would be treated equally and considered new states. Hence, Yugoslavia, too, would have to apply anew for membership in the United Nations, although, in something of a diplomatic fudge, Belgrade was permitted to continue a kind of participation in certain UN bodies in the meantime.[1] Some time after this decision, Belgrade refused to participate in the work of the human rights treaty bodies, arguing that it had been wrongfully denied her claimed rights as the universal successor state to the SFRY and was in consequence placed in a position of inequality.[2] This view was rejected by the relevant committees. It was noted that, given their special humanitarian objective, human rights obligations continue to be in force for successor states to a state party. This would also include the obligation to continue cooperating with the implementation mechanisms attached to the particular convention in question.[3] Hence, the treaty committees continued to question and condemn Yugoslav practices where appropriate, also based on information outside of the state reports.

Given the proliferation of UN bodies involved in the human rights crisis in the former Yugoslavia, the General Assembly asked the Secretary-General to facilitate the coordination of the various efforts, through an annual report which summarized the findings across different agencies and described their interlocking efforts. The Secretary-General was also required to monitor the extent to which Yugoslavia complied with the Assembly's demand to cooperate with the relevant United Nations bodies, generating a more visible level of accountability for Belgrade in this respect. Overall, therefore, an integrated and in many ways unprecedented response was found to address the Yugoslav crisis.

The increasing emphasis on Kosovo is also interesting to note. It is true that the international diplomatic effort remained very much focused on the atrocities in Bosnia and Herzegovina. However, all of the human rights bodies and the General Assembly also paid attention to the developing situation in Kosovo, both when addressing the situation in the former Yugoslavia as a whole, and when adopting specific resolutions or decisions in relation to it. Moreover, the determinations by these bodies were unusually lacking in diplomatic ambiguity, identifying the individual elements of the human rights crisis clearly and demanding similarly clear remedial action.

Access

The question of access for international observers dominated international concern for Kosovo, especially after the expulsion of the CSCE long-term monitoring mission in the summer of 1993. This concern was only heightened when the full horror of Serb practices in Croatia and Bosnia and Herzegovina became apparent. Access is an issue normally handled with some care and sophistication by governments under investigation. As long as contact is maintained with human rights investigators, a state can claim to be fulfilling its human rights obligations, as is evidenced by the decision to permit transparency through the presence of monitors.[4] Often it is also possible to restrict and circumscribe the activities of monitors, to equip them with official guides, make them dependent on governmental transport and security arrangements. Rapporteurs can be fed favourable information which, in the interest of balanced reporting, will feature in their reports, whether or not creditable. More profoundly, the reporting agency will generally be minded to phrase its findings cautiously, for fear of losing the access that has been granted in response to overly vivid descriptions of the situation on the ground.

---

[1] E.g., Security Council Resolution 777 (1992), 19 September 1992, Document 5.A.16.
[2] E.g., Letter to the Chairman of the CERD Committee, 15 February 1995, Document 6.C.4.
[3] Letter from the Chairman of the CERD Committee, 6 March 1995, *id.*
[4] E.g., Letter from the FRY to the Chairman of the Commission on Human Rights, 15 February 1995, Document 6.B.6.

In this case, the UN General Assembly itself threw its weight behind the demands for access of the Special Rapporteur and others, and as indicated above, the UN Secretariat was required to report on access at the highest level, directly through the Secretary-General. Access to the Special Rapporteur was at times granted, although more frequently after the resignation of Mr Mazowiecki, who had reported in rather an outspoken way about the atrocities in Bosnia and Herzegovina. Often difficult discussions about the modalities of a visit preceded particular missions. It was also possible to conduct special investigations, for example of trials of ethnic Albanians, using observers in the field.[5] In February 1996, the FRY government agreed to the establishment of a field office in Belgrade—an action it had resisted since it had been proposed in 1992 by Mr Mazowiecki. Visits to Kosovo were undertaken by the initially two and later four members of the field office and further representations were made with a view to establishing a field office directly in that territory. That proposal was overtaken by the events of 1998. Nevertheless, during that period, the office of the High Commissioner for Human Rights did manage to maintain a continuous presence in Kosovo, although the mobility of the observers was restricted.[6]

Substantive Findings

The direct and unsubtle nature of Yugoslav/Serb action in Kosovo remains startling. When committing grave crimes against humanity in Croatia and Bosnia and Herzegovina, the leadership in Belgrade had attempted to cloak its actions in rather implausible denials. But in relation to Kosovo, repression was conducted very much officially, and under a veritable legislative programme. Serbia had formally established the purported new and subordinated status of Kosovo in its constitutional law. It had also downgraded the ethnic Albanian majority in Kosovo from a 'nationality' to a minority. More than that, many of the openly discriminatory practices applied to the territory were contained in formal acts of legislation, duly published in the official gazette of the republic. This included even specific decisions through which individuals were removed from public office or from positions of responsibility in commercial enterprises. Whether this reflected the strength of conviction in the Serb cause, was a conscious display of proclaimed ethnic superiority or merely a result of continuing legislative and administrative practices from the communist era, with its slightly odd insistence on Orwellian pseudo-legality, can probably not be answered by the outsider. But this practice certainly made it easier for international human rights bodies to form their views. It is not possible to summarize the individual findings of individual bodies, which are reproduced extensively in the documentary section. However, the general picture painted below identifies some of the principal areas of concern that were identified.

General discrimination. The existence of large tranches of openly discriminatory legislation was confirmed throughout the crisis in the Special Rapporteur reports and condemned by the General Assembly, the Commission on Human Rights and its Sub-commission and also the Committee attached to the Convention on the Elimination of Racial Discrimination. That Committee conducted a detailed dialogue with the FRY authorities about these actions. The FRY provided lengthy justifications of its policies.[7] Nevertheless, the Committee concluded that the ethnic Albanians were being discriminated against in a way in which they were "deprived of effective enjoyment of the most basic human rights provided in the Convention".[8] The General Assembly identified as early as 1993 "discriminatory policies, measures and violent actions committed against ethnic Albanians in Kosovo", demanding a cessation of "police brutality, arbitrary searches, seizures and arrests, torture and ill treatment during detention and discrimination in the administration of justice".[9] The Sub-Commission determined that such actions were taken "aiming at forcing ethnic Albanians to leave their land".[10]

Discriminatory legislation in relation to property. The Law on the Restriction of Real Property Transfers required official authorization for changes of title to real property, initially through a special commission and subsequently though the Serb Secretariat of Finance. These provisions were applied "unevenly and [were] arbitrarily implemented, depending on the applicant's ethnicity and place of residence".[11] Violations by ethnic Albanians of the relevant provisions were punished by prison sentences.[12]

Resettlement and demographic manipulation. The *Programme for the Realization of Peace, Freedom, Equality, Democracy and Prosperity* of the SAP of Kosovo of 1989 had decreed that obstacles to the "return of Serbs and Montenegrins, displaced under pressure, and all the others who wish to come and live in Kosovo" would need to be removed through direct rule.[13] In addition to limiting the transfer of property titles among Albanians, legislation had been adopted encouraging Serbs to acquire property, in particular real property. Special provisions were put into place to facilitate the taking of agricultural land by ethnic Serbs. There were financial assistance schemes in place in order to attract settlement, and an infrastructure

---

[5] Special Report, 10 September 1997, Document 6.D.14.
[6] See Report, 29 May 1998, Document 11.B.4.
[7] Documents 6.C.3, 6.C.5.
[8] CERD Concluding Observations, 15/6 March 1996, Document 6.C.4, also Concluding Observations 19 March 1998, Document 6.B.6.
[9] General Assembly Resolution48/153, 20 December 1993, Document 6.A.2.
[10] Sub-Commission Resolution 1995/10, 18 August 1995, Document 6.B.8.
[11] CERD Concluding Observations, 19 March 1998, Document 6.C.6.
[12] Special Rapporteur Report, 31 October 1997, Document 6.D.16.
[13] Document 4.B.4.

programme commenced to support this venture. On occasion, ethnic Albanians were forcibly removed from houses and apartments to make room for Serbs.[14] Finally, Serb refugees from other areas of the former Yugoslavia were directly settled in Kosovo. Ethnic Albanians who had left the territory, on the other hand, were to be de-nationalized and even some of those who remained were declared to be illegal immigrants from Albania, in an effort to change the ethnic balance.

The resettlement programme was not successful. With the exception of Serb refugees from other areas of the former Yugoslavia who had no other option, Kosovo did not prove an attractive place of 'immigration'. Ethnic Serbs remained isolated and despite Serb control over the 'official' economy, few recent arrivals prospered. While the Serb media and politicians claimed that Serbs were being subjected to significant repression from the Albanians, the human rights bodies found little evidence of a concerted campaign to that end, although there were isolated incidents. The attempt to "change the ethnic balance"[15] of the territory by removing citizenship from those who have fled the territory or moved for economic reasons was also internationally rejected. Similarly, Serb population figures based on the assertion that many ethnic Albanians were illegal immigrants from Albania were widely ignored. Hence, by 1990, there were about 90 per cent ethnic Albanians in the territory, and perhaps 8 per cent Serbs and it was generally accepted that this figure remained relatively constant throughout the period of tension of the 1990s.

Removal of ethnic Albanians from public office and from commercial enterprises. Ethnic Albanians had been dismissed wholesale from the Kosovo police force. A new police force had been created, drawing upon non-Albanians from Serbia and Montenegro and Kosovo itself. Albanian judges and prosecutors were removed from office. Teachers, too, were dismissed, many after they refused to swear allegiance to the Serb constitution and to teach a Serb syllabus decreed by Belgrade. Several Albanian staffed hospitals were 'consolidated' and effectively closed. As much of the economic system was still dominated by state enterprises, Serb control in what would elsewhere be considered the private sector could be easily established under Serb legislation. In fact, senior and middle-level managers were often removed by formal legislative decree. Some enterprises in Kosovo were merged with undertakings in Serbia. Supply of goods and services was restricted and registration of new enterprises by ethnic Albanians was also constrained.

Interference with the judiciary. The emergency legislation, later regularized under the umbrella of the new Serb constitution of 1990, permitted direct intervention by Serb courts in proceedings in the province. The judicial system in Kosovo itself was ethnically cleansed, through the removal of ethnic Albanian judges and other judicial officers. The conduct of trials by these organs was frequently criticised by human rights bodies as unbalanced and in violation of fair trial safeguards. Equally as important, although perhaps less visible, was Serb control over special economic courts and administrative review bodies. Again, these were placed at the disposal of Serb republic policies in the region. There were consistent allegations of torture as a means of extracting confessions, sometimes leading to permanent injuries. As the Special Rapporteur noted, by the beginning of 1993, "all remaining Albanian judges or magistrates have been dismissed. Under such conditions the right to a fair trial and the impartiality of the judiciary can hardly be guaranteed with regard to the Albanian population of Kosovo".[16]

Education. Educational establishments were required to teach a Serb curriculum. A widespread refusal to follow this curriculum led to the wholesale closing down of the educational system. Teachers and university professors continued to give instruction, unpaid by the state and often in private houses or other unorthodox venues, although there were Serb police raids and other measures to inhibit this activity.[17] Some 300,000 children were educated in this way, by many of the 18,000 teachers or more who had been dismissed.[18] The Serb Academy of Sciences took over the Kosovo Academy, or at least its property, and other ethnic Albanian cultural institutions were closed down.

Freedom of the press. The Albanian broadcast media were cleansed as early as 1990, with 1,300 journalists and technical staff being dismissed.[19] Newspaper offices were frequently raided and many closed. Ethnic Albanian journalists were intimidated or arrested. More profoundly, Serbia took over all sources of supplies for printing and publishing houses by consolidating the relevant undertakings into one, which was fully controlled by the republic. Nevertheless, a few publications survived.

Arbitrary Arrests. Ethnic Albanians were frequently arrested without charge, often extracted from their homes at gunpoint and at night, to participate in so-called 'informative talks'. In one six-month period alone, 1,700 persons were "subjected to police abuse in connection with the raids".[20] The Serbian authorities "have on occasion sealed off entire areas, interrogated and sometimes physically assaulted ethnic Albanians at random" and there were instances of disappearances, i.e., individuals

---

[14] E.g., Special Rapporteur Report, 1 November 1993, Document 6.D.4. Report, 21 February 1994, Document 6.D.5.
[15] E.g., General Assembly Resolution 50/190, 22 December 1995, Document 6.A.5.
[16] Report, 26 February 1993, Document 6.D.3, also Special Report, 10 September 1997, Document 6.D.14.
[17] Speical Rapporteur Report, 1 November 1993, Document 6.D.4.
[18] Special Rapporteur Report, 25 October 1996, Document 6.D.11.
[19] Special Rapporteur Report, 13 December 1994, Document 6.D.7.
[20] Special Rapporteur Report, 4 November 1994, Document 6.D.6.

never returned from police custody.[21] There were also "hostage arrests", where police detained relatives or family members of persons sought by the police.[22]

Torture and mistreatment. The systematic use of torture and other forms of mistreatment by the militia and police was frequently condemned. Such treatment was also applied to the elected ethnic Albanian political leaders,[23] against students, more or less at random, and others crossing the paths of Serb police patrols, creating a general atmosphere of intimidation.[24]

Impunity for Perpetrators. Serb officials accused of torture, harassment or killing were not held accountable in any significant way. Similarly, weapons had been made available to local groups of ethnic Serbs, who terrorized the Albanian population. Again, there was no attempt to establish responsibility for these actions, or to suppress this practice, leading to a state of insecurity and terror among the population at large.

Disproportionate use of force. Even before the outbreak of hostilities in 1988, CERD condemned the disproportionate use of force against the Albanian population, which had resulted in numerous violations of the right to life, destruction of property and in a great number of people being displaced or made refugees, of whom many were women and children, whose deaths or deprivation of their rights to security of person and protection against violence could not be condoned or justified by whatever reason. [25] This practice, of course, increased significantly in later 1997 and early 1998.[26]

Overall assessment

The crisis in the former Yugoslavia marked a new challenge for United Nations human rights bodies in the post Cold War world. Perhaps surprisingly, a coordinated effort was made across the relevant UN organs to meet this emergency. Unlike the reporting of the UN Secretary-General in the context of UN peace-keeping concerning Croatia and Bosnia (and later in relation to Rwanda), the human rights bodies were pro-active and forthright in their activities. Particular respect is due to the human rights field workers and to the Special Rapporteurs who had to brave quite uncomfortable circumstances in order to undertake fact-finding missions.

As opposed to previous practice, the determinations by human rights bodies were no longer constrained by the submissions of the target government. While information was solicited from Yugoslavia, tough and independent conclusions were reached in relation to the claims put forward by its government. This included the United Nations General Assembly. In fact, all human rights bodies, as well as the General Assembly, consistently tracked the situation in Kosovo, even while Bosnia and Herzegovina dominated the international agenda, and issued strong and appropriate demands to the FRY government.

Of course, ultimately all these activities did not lead to a marked improvement of the situation in the former Yugoslavia, including Kosovo. However, this is not due to a failing in the existing human rights machinery itself. Instead, the absence of a link between findings of fact, condemnation and demands for action on the one hand, and an enforcement mechanism when these calls remained unheeded, is to blame for this state of affairs. The failure to feed information on the human rights situation in Kosovo and other parts of the former Yugoslavia into the decision-making process, for example as it concerned the lifting of sanctions vis-à-vis the FRY before and after Dayton, might be noted in this context. The lack of collective security action in the Security Council, at a time when the human rights situation turned from deplorable into a humanitarian disaster throughout 1998, is also striking. No enforcement action was taken, other than the adoption of an arms embargo, which did not much affect Yugoslavia which had been permitted to replenish its supplies expended in Croatia and Bosnia and Herzegovina under a bilateral arrangement with Russia. Ultimately, therefore, this episode once again confirms the validity of an old truism: Where a state is determined to engage in severe human rights violations, exhortations alone will rarely bring about a change in its attitude. Human rights monitoring in those circumstances has an important role in naming and shaming the state concerned. But in the end, determination on the part of the offending government must be met with determination by the organized international community if results are to be obtained.

---

[21] Special Rapporteur Report, 25 October 1996, Document 6.D.11.
[22] Special Rapporteur Report, 31 October 1991, Document 6.D.11.
[23] Special Rapporteur Report, 4 November 1994, Document 6.D.6.
[24] Special Rapporteur Report, 31 October 1997, Document 6.D.16.
[25] CERD Decision 3 (53), 17 August 1998, Document 6.B.7.
[26] See Chapter 11 & 13.

A. Resolutions of the United Nations General Assembly

1. General Assembly Resolution 47/147, Situation of human rights, 18 December 1992

[*Adopted without a vote.*]

The General Assembly,

...

Welcoming the effort by the Conference on Security and Cooperation in Europe to prevent further human rights violations and its missions dispatched to the territory of the former Yugoslavia, including missions of long duration to Kosovo, Vojvodina and Sandjak, where the human rights situation remains a cause of great concern,

..

14. *Expresses* its grave concern at the Special Rapporteur's report on the dangerous situation in Kosovo, Sandjak and Vojvodina, urges all parties there to engage in a meaningful dialogue under the auspices of the International Conference on the former Yugoslavia, to act with utmost restraint and to settle disputes in full compliance with human rights and fundamental freedoms, and calls upon the Serbian authorities to refrain from the use of force, to stop immediately the practice of "ethnic cleansing" and to respect fully the rights of persons belonging to ethnic communities or minorities, in order to prevent the extension of the conflict to other parts of the former Yugoslavia;

...

21. *Also requests* the Secretary-General, within the overall budgetary framework of the United Nations, to make all necessary resources available for the Special Rapporteur to carry out his mandate and in particular to provide him with a number of staff based in the territories of the former Yugoslavia adequate to ensure effective continuous monitoring of the human rights situation there and coordination with other United Nations bodies involved, including the United Nations Protection Force; ...

2. United Nations General Assembly Resolution 48/153, Situation of human rights 20 December 1993

[*Adopted unanimously at the 85th meeting of the Assembly.*]
The General Assembly,

...

Welcoming the ongoing efforts of the Conference on Security and Cooperation in Europe to re-establish its presence in the Federal Republic of Yugoslavia (Serbia and Montenegro) in order to prevent further human rights violations, and deeply concerned about the decision of the authorities in the Federal Republic of Yugoslavia (Serbia and Montenegro) to expel the monitoring missions of the Conference on Security and Cooperation in Europe and the European Community of long duration to Kosovo, Sandjak and Vojvodina, where the human rights situation remains a cause of great concern,

Welcoming also the efforts of the European Union, inter alia, through its monitoring missions, to promote respect for human rights and fundamental freedoms in the territory of the former Yugoslavia,

...

Noting the discriminatory policies, measures and violent actions committed against ethnic Albanians in Kosovo, and aware of the possible escalation of the situation into a violent conflict there,

...

17. *Expresses its grave concern* at the deteriorating human rights situation in the Federal Republic of Yugoslavia (Serbia and Montenegro) particularly in Kosovo, as described in the reports of the Special Rapporteur, and strongly condemns the violations of human rights occurring there;

18. *Strongly condemns* in particular the measures and practices of discrimination and the violations of the human rights of the ethnic Albanians of Kosovo, as well as the large-scale repression committed by the Serbian authorities, including:

(a) Police brutality against ethnic Albanians, arbitrary searches, seizures and arrests, torture and ill-treatment during detention and discrimination in the administration of justice, which leads to a climate of lawlessness in which criminal acts, particularly against ethnic Albanians, take place with impunity;

(b) the discriminatory removal of ethnic Albanian officials, especially from the police and judiciary, the mass dismissal of ethnic Albanians from professional, administrative and other skilled positions in state-owned enterprises and public institutions, including teachers from the Serb-run school system, and the closure of Albanian high schools and universities;

(c) Arbitrary imprisonment of ethnic Albanian journalists, the closure of Albanian-language mass media and the discriminatory removal of ethnic Albanian staff from the local radio and television stations;

(d) Repression by the Serbian police and military;

19. *Urges* the authorities in the Federal Republic of Yugoslavia (Serbia and Montenegro):

(a) To take all necessary measures to bring to an immediate end the human rights violations inflicted on the ethnic Albanians in Kosovo, including, in particular, discriminatory measures and practices, arbitrary detention and the use of torture, other cruel, inhuman or degrading treatment and the occurrence of summary executions;

(b) To revoke all discriminatory legislation, in particular that which has entered into force since 1989;

(c) To re-establish the democratic institutions of Kosovo, including the Parliament and the judiciary;

(d) To resume dialogue with the ethnic Albanians in Kosovo, including under the auspices of the International Conference on the Former Yugoslavia;

20. *Also urges* the authorities of the Federal Republic of Yugoslavia (Serbia and Montenegro) to respect the human rights and fundamental freedoms of ethnic Albanians in Kosovo, and expresses the view that the best means to safeguard human rights in Kosovo is to restore its autonomy; ...

22. *Calls upon* the authorities of the Federal Republic of Yugoslavia (Serbia and Montenegro) to allow the immediate entry of an international human rights monitoring presence into the country, particularly to Kosovo, and strongly urges the authorities of the Federal Republic of Yugoslavia (Serbia and Montenegro) to reconsider their refusal to allow the continuation of the activities of the missions of the Conference on Security and Cooperation in Europe in Kosovo, Sandjak and Vojvodina and to cooperate with the Conference on Security and Cooperation in Europe by taking the practical steps for the resumption of the activities of those missions called for by the Security Council in its resolution 855 (1993) in order to prevent the extension of the conflict of those areas;

3. General Assembly Resolution 49/196, Situation of human rights, 23 December 1994

[*94th plenary meeting, 23 December 1994.*]

The General Assembly,

...

Welcoming the ongoing efforts of the Conference on Security and Cooperation in Europe to re-establish its presence in the Federal Republic of Yugoslavia (Serbia and Montenegro) in order to prevent further human rights violations, and deeply concerned about the decision of the authorities in the Federal Republic of Yugoslavia (Serbia and Montenegro) to expel the monitoring missions of long duration of the Conference on Security and Cooperation in Europe and the European Union to Kosovo, the Sandjak and Vojvodina, where the human rights situation remains a cause of great concern,

...

19. *Strongly condemns* the increase of police violence against the non-Serb populations in Kosovo, the Sandjak, Vojvodina and other areas of the Federal Republic of Yugoslavia (Serbia and Montenegro), and of

violations of the right to fair trial, as described in the most recent report of the Special Rapporteur;

20. *Strongly urges* the authorities of the Federal Republic of Yugoslavia (Serbia and Montenegro) to take appropriate measures to respect fully all human rights and fundamental freedoms and to take urgent action to ensure the rule of law in order to prevent arbitrary evictions and dismissals and discrimination against members of the non-Serb populations in the Federal Republic of Yugoslavia (Serbia and Montenegro);

...

26. *Urges* the Government of the Federal Republic of Yugoslavia (Serbia and Montenegro) to reconsider its refusal to allow the continuation of the activities of the missions of the Conference on Security and Cooperation in Europe to monitor the human rights conditions in its territory, particularly in Kosovo, the Sandjak and Vojvodina, and its refusal to permit the opening of a field office of the Centre for Human Rights of the Secretariat as called for by the General Assembly in its resolution 48/153; ...

4.   General Assembly Resolution 49/204, Situation of human rights in Kosovo, 23 December 1994

[*94th plenary meeting, 23 December 1994.*]

The General Assembly,

Guided by the Charter of the United Nations, the Universal Declaration of Human Rights, the International Covenants on Human Rights, the International Convention on the Elimination of All Forms of Racial Discrimination, the Convention on the Prevention and Punishment of the Crime of Genocide and the Convention against Torture and Other Cruel, Inhuman or Degrading Treatment or Punishment,

Recalling its resolution 48/153 of 20 December 1993,

Taking note of Commission on Human Rights resolution 1994/76 of 9 March 1994 and recalling Commission resolutions 1992/S-1/1 of 14 August 1992, 1992/S-2/1 of 1 December 1992 and 1993/7 of 23 February 1993

Taking note of the report of the Special Rapporteur of the Commission on Human Rights on the situation of human rights in the territory of the former Yugoslavia, in which he stated that the situation in Kosovo had deteriorated further in the course of the past six months, as well as his earlier reports, in which he described the various discriminatory measures taken in the legislative, administrative and judicial areas, acts of violence and arbitrary arrests perpetrated against ethnic Albanians in Kosovo and the continuing deterioration of the human rights situation in Kosovo, including:

(a) Police brutality against ethnic Albanians, the killing of ethnic Albanians resulting from such violence, arbitrary searches, seizures and arrests, forced evictions, torture and ill-treatment of detainees and discrimination in the administration of justice;

(b) Discriminatory and arbitrary dismissals of ethnic Albanian civil servants, notably from the ranks of the police and the judiciary, mass dismissals of ethnic Albanians, confiscation and expropriation of their properties, discrimination against Albanian pupils and teachers, the closing of Albanian-language secondary schools and university, as well as the closing of all Albanian cultural and scientific institutions;

(c) The harassment and persecution of political parties and associations of ethnic Albanians and their leaders and activities, maltreating and imprisoning them;

(d) The intimidation and imprisonment of ethnic Albanian journalists and the systematic harassment and disruption of the news media in the Albanian language;

(e) The dismissals from clinics and hospitals of doctors and members of other categories of the medical profession of Albanian origin;

(f) The elimination in practice of the Albanian language, particularly in public administration and services;

(g) The serious and massive occurrence of discriminatory and repressive practices aimed at Albanians in Kosovo, as a whole, resulting in widespread involuntary migration;

and noting also that the Subcommission on Prevention of Discrimination and Protection of Minorities, in its resolution 1993/9 of 20 August 1993, considered that these measures and practices constituted a form of ethnic cleansing,

Recognizing that the long-term mission of the Organization for Security and Cooperation in Europe to Kosovo played a positive role in monitoring the human rights situation and in preventing an escalation of conflict there and recalling in this context Security Council resolution 855 (1993) of 9 August 1993,

Considering that the re-establishment of the international presence in Kosovo to monitor and investigate the situation of human rights is of great importance in preventing the situation in Kosovo from deteriorating into a violent conflict,

1. *Strongly condemns* the measures and practices of discrimination and the violations of human rights of ethnic Albanians in Kosovo committed by the authorities of the Federal Republic of Yugoslavia (Serbia and Montenegro);

2. *Condemns* the large-scale repression by the police and military of the Federal Republic of Yugoslavia (Serbia and Montenegro) against the defenceless ethnic Albanian population and the discrimination against the ethnic Albanians in the administrative and judiciary branches of government, education, health care and employment, aimed at forcing ethnic Albanians to leave;

3. *Demands* that the authorities of the Federal Republic of Yugoslavia (Serbia and Montenegro):

(a) Take all necessary measures to bring to an immediate end all human rights violations against ethnic Albanians in Kosovo, including, in particular, the discriminatory measures and practices, arbitrary searches and detention, the violation of the right to a fair trial and the practice of torture and other cruel, inhuman or degrading treatment;

(b) Revoke all discriminatory legislation, in particular that which has entered into force since 1989;

(c) Establish genuine democratic institutions in Kosovo, including the parliament and the judiciary, and respect the will of its inhabitants as the best means of preventing the escalation of the conflict there;

(d) Reopen the cultural and scientific institutions of the ethnic Albanians;

(e) Pursue dialogue with the representatives of ethnic Albanians in Kosovo, including under the auspices of the International Conference on the Former Yugoslavia;

4. *Demands* that the authorities of the Federal Republic of Yugoslavia (Serbia and Montenegro) cooperate fully and immediately with the Special Rapporteur of the Commission on Human Rights on the situation of human rights in the territory of the former Yugoslavia in the discharge of his functions as requested by the Commission by its resolution 1994/76 and other relevant resolutions;

5. *Encourages* the Secretary-General to pursue his humanitarian efforts in the former Yugoslavia, in liaison with the Office of the United Nations High Commissioner for Refugees, the United Nations Children's Fund and other appropriate humanitarian organizations, with a view to taking urgent practical steps to tackle the critical needs of the people in Kosovo, especially of the most vulnerable groups affected by the conflict, and to assist in the voluntary return of displaced persons to their homes;

6. *Urges* the authorities of the Federal Republic of Yugoslavia (Serbia and Montenegro) to allow the immediate unconditional return of the long-term mission of the Organization for Security and Cooperation in Europe to Kosovo, called for in Security Council resolution 855 (1993);

7. *Requests* the Secretary-General to seek ways and means, including through consultations with the United Nations High Commissioner for Human Rights and relevant regional organizations, to establish an adequate international monitoring presence in Kosovo and to report thereon to the General Assembly;

8. *Calls upon* the Special Rapporteur to continue to monitor closely the human rights situation in Kosovo and to pay special attention to this matter in his reporting;

9. *Decides* to continue examination of the human rights situation in Kosovo at its fiftieth session under the item entitled "Human rights questions".

5. General Assembly Resolution 50/190, Situation of human rights in Kosovo, 22 December 1995

[*99th plenary meeting, 22 December 1995.*]

The General Assembly,

Guided by the Charter of the United Nations, the Universal Declaration of Human Rights, the International Covenants on Human Rights, the International Convention on the Elimination of All Forms of Racial Discrimination, the Convention on the Prevention and Punishment of the Crime of Genocide and the Convention against Torture and Other Cruel, Inhuman or Degrading Treatment or Punishment,

Welcoming the General Framework Agreement for Peace in Bosnia and Herzegovina reached on 21 November 1995 at Dayton, Ohio, and hoping that it will have a positive impact also on the human rights situation in Kosovo,

Recalling its resolution 49/204 of 23 December 1994 and other relevant resolutions,

Taking note of Commission on Human Rights resolution 1995/89 of 8 March 1995 and recalling previous Commission resolutions 1992/S-1/1 of 14 August 1992, 1992/S-2/1 of 1 December 1992, 1993/7 of 23 February 1993 and 1994/76 of 9 March 1994,

Taking note also of the reports of the Special Rapporteurs of the Commission on Human Rights on the situation of human rights in the territory of the former Yugoslavia, in which they describe the situation in Kosovo, the various discriminatory measures taken in the legislative, administrative and judicial areas, acts of violence and arbitrary arrests perpetrated against ethnic Albanians in Kosovo and the continuing deterioration of the human rights situation in Kosovo, including:

(a) Police brutality against ethnic Albanians, the killing of ethnic Albanians resulting from such violence, arbitrary searches, seizures and arrests, forced evictions, torture and ill-treatment of detainees and discrimination in the administration of justice, including the recent trials of ethnic Albanian former policemen;

(b) Discriminatory and arbitrary dismissals of ethnic Albanian civil servants, notably from the ranks of the police and the judiciary, mass dismissals of ethnic Albanians, confiscation and expropriation of their properties, discrimination against ethnic Albanian pupils and teachers, the closing of Albanian-language secondary schools and the university, as well as the closing of all Albanian cultural and scientific institutions;

(c) The harassment and persecution of political parties and associations of ethnic Albanians and their leaders and activities, their maltreatment and imprisonment;

(d) The intimidation and imprisonment of ethnic Albanian journalists and the systematic harassment and disruption of the news media in the Albanian language;

(e) The dismissals from clinics and hospitals of doctors and members of other categories of the medical profession of Albanian origin;

(f) The elimination in practice of the Albanian language, particularly in public administration and services;

(g) The serious and massive occurrence of discriminatory and repressive practices aimed at ethnic Albanians in Kosovo, as a whole, resulting in widespread involuntary migration;

and noting that the Subcommission on Prevention of Discrimination and Protection of Minorities, in its resolutions 1993/9 of 20 August 1993and 1995/10 of 18 August 1995, considered that those measures and practices constituted a form of ethnic cleansing,

Concerned at any attempt to use Serb refugees and other means to alter the ethnic balance in Kosovo, thus further suppressing the enjoyment of human rights there, and, in this context, noting with concern the new citizenship law awaiting approval by the Parliament of the Federal Republic of Yugoslavia (Serbia and Montenegro),

Reaffirming that the long-term mission of the Organization for Security and Cooperation in Europe to Kosovo played a positive role in monitoring the human rights situation and in preventing an escalation of conflict there, and recalling in this context Security Council resolution 855 (1993) of 9 August 1993,

Considering that the re-establishment of the international presence in Kosovo to monitor and investigate the situation of human rights is of great importance in preventing the situation in Kosovo from deteriorating into violent conflict, and, in this context, taking note of the report of the Secretary-General submitted pursuant to General Assembly resolution 49/204,

1. *Strongly condemns* the measures and practices of discrimination and the violations of the human rights of ethnic Albanians in Kosovo committed by the authorities of the Federal Republic of Yugoslavia (Serbia and Montenegro);

2. *Condemns* the large-scale repression by the police and military of the Federal Republic of Yugoslavia (Serbia and Montenegro) against the defenceless ethnic Albanian population and the discrimination against the ethnic Albanians in the administrative and judiciary branches of government, education, health care and employment, aimed at forcing ethnic Albanians to leave;

3. *Urgently demands* that the authorities of the Federal Republic of Yugoslavia (Serbia and Montenegro):

(a) Take all necessary measures to bring to an immediate end all human rights violations against ethnic Albanians in Kosovo, including, in particular, the discriminatory measures and practices, arbitrary searches and detention, the violation of the right to a fair trial and the practice of torture and other cruel, inhuman or degrading treatment, and to revoke all discriminatory legislation, in particular that which has entered into force since 1989;

(b) Release all political prisoners and cease the persecution of political leaders and members of local human rights organizations;

(c) Allow the establishment of genuine democratic institutions in Kosovo, including the parliament and the judiciary, and respect the will of its inhabitants as the best means of preventing the escalation of the conflict there;

(d) Abrogate the official settlement policy as far as it is conducive to the heightening of ethnic tensions in Kosovo;

(e) Reopen the cultural and scientific institutions of the ethnic Albanians;

(f) Pursue dialogue with the representatives of ethnic Albanians in Kosovo, including under the auspices of the International Conference on the Former Yugoslavia;

4. *Demands once again* that the authorities of the Federal Republic of Yugoslavia (Serbia and Montenegro) cooperate fully and immediately with the Special Rapporteur of the Commission on Human Rights on the situation of human rights in the territory of the former Yugoslavia in the discharge of her functions, as requested by the Commission in its resolution 1994/76 and in other relevant resolutions;

5. *Encourages* the Secretary-General to pursue his humanitarian efforts in the former Yugoslavia, in liaison with the Office of the United Nations High Commissioner for Refugees, the United Nations Children's Fund and other appropriate humanitarian organizations, with a view to taking urgent practical steps to tackle the critical needs of the people in Kosovo, especially of the most vulnerable groups affected by the conflict, and to assist in the voluntary return of displaced persons to their homes;

6. *Urges* the authorities of the Federal Republic of Yugoslavia (Serbia and Montenegro) to allow the immediate unconditional return of the long-term mission of the Organization for Security and Cooperation in Europe to Kosovo, called for in Security Council resolution 855 (1993);

7. *Welcomes* the report of the Secretary-General submitted pursuant to General Assembly resolution 49/204;

8. *Requests* the Secretary-General to continue to seek ways and means, including through consultations with the United Nations High Commissioner for Human Rights and relevant regional organizations, to establish an adequate international monitoring presence in Kosovo and to report thereon to the General Assembly at its fifty-first session;

9. *Emphasizes* the importance of laws and regulations concerning citizenship applied by the authorities of the Federal Republic of Yugoslavia (Serbia and Montenegro) being in accordance with the standards and principles of non-discrimination, equal protection before the law and the reduction and avoidance of statelessness, as set out in the relevant international human rights instruments;

10. *Calls upon* the Special Rapporteur to continue to monitor closely the situation of human rights in Kosovo and to continue to pay due attention to this matter in her reporting;

11. *Decides* to continue examination of the human rights situation in Kosovo at its fifty-first session under the item entitled "Human rights questions".

6.   General Assembly Resolution 50/193, Situation of human rights, 22 December 1995

[*99th plenary meeting, 22 December 1995.*]

The General Assembly,

16. *Condemns* police violence against the non-Serb populations in Kosovo, the Sandjak, Vojvodina and other areas of the Federal Republic of Yugoslavia (Serbia and Montenegro), particularly the systematic acts of harassment, beatings, torture, warrantless searches, arbitrary detention and unfair trials, including those directed mainly against members of the Muslim population;

17. *Strongly urges* the authorities of the Federal Republic of Yugoslavia (Serbia and Montenegro) to take appropriate measures to respect fully all human rights and fundamental freedoms and to take urgent action to ensure the rule of law in order to prevent arbitrary evictions and dismissals and discrimination against any ethnic or national, religious and linguistic group, including in the fields of education and information;

18. *Cautions* against any attempts to use Serb refugees to alter the population balance in Kosovo, the Sandjak, Vojvodina and any other part of the country, thus further suppressing the enjoyment of human rights in those areas;

...

23. *Also urges* all parties to provide full access for monitoring the human rights situation, including by allowing access to the missions of the Organization for Security and Cooperation in Europe, including in Kosovo, as called for by the General Assembly in resolution 49/196 and by the Security Council in resolution 855 (1993) of 9 August 1993, and in the Sandjak, Vojvodina and other affected areas, and requests that the Federal Republic of Yugoslavia (Serbia and Montenegro) permit the opening of a field office of the Centre for Human Rights of the Secretariat as called for by the General Assembly in resolution 49/196;

24. Urges the Secretary-General to take all necessary steps to ensure the full and effective coordination of the activities of all United Nations bodies in implementing the present resolution, and urges those bodies concerned with the situation in the territories of Bosnia and Herzegovina, Croatia and the Federal Republic of Yugoslavia (Serbia and Montenegro) to coordinate closely with the United Nations High Commissioner for Human Rights, the Special Rapporteur and the International Tribunal, and to provide to the Special Rapporteur on a continuing basis all relevant and accurate information in their possession on the situation of human rights in Bosnia and Herzegovina, Croatia and the Federal Republic of Yugoslavia (Serbia and Montenegro);

26. *Urges* the Secretary-General, within existing resources, to make all necessary resources available for the Special Rapporteur to carry out her mandate and in particular to provide her with adequate staff based in the territories of Bosnia and Herzegovina, Croatia and the Federal Republic of Yugoslavia (Serbia and Montenegro) to ensure effective continuous monitoring of the human rights situation there and coordination with other United Nations bodies involved, including the United Nations Peace Forces;

... 28. *Notes with concern* that many of the past recommendations of the Special Rapporteur have not been fully implemented, in some cases because of resistance by the parties on the ground, and urges the parties, all States and relevant organizations to give immediate consideration to them, in particular the calls of the former and the current Special Rapporteurs: ...

(d) For the Federal Republic of Yugoslavia (Serbia and Montenegro) to undertake measures to respect fully the rights of persons belonging to national or ethnic, religious and linguistic minorities; ...

7.   General Assembly Resolution 51/111, Situation of human rights in Kosovo, 12 December 1996

The General Assembly,

Guided by the Charter of the United Nations, the Universal Declaration of Human Rights, the International Covenants on Human Rights, the International Convention on the Elimination of All Forms of Racial Discrimination, the Convention on the Prevention and Punishment of the Crime of Genocide and the Convention against Torture and Other Cruel, Inhuman or Degrading Treatment or Punishment,

Taking note with concern of the reports of the Special Rapporteur of the Commission on Human Rights on the situation of human rights in the territory of the former Yugoslavia which describe the continuing grave human rights situation in Kosovo, including in particular police brutality, killings resulting from such violence, arbitrary searches and arrests, torture and ill-treatment of detainees, the deliberate maltreatment, persecution and imprisonment of political and human rights activists, the mass dismissals of civil servants, discrimination against pupils and teachers, acts which are mainly perpetrated against ethnic Albanians,

Welcoming, as a first step, the recent signature of a memorandum of understanding concerning the educational system in the Albanian language in Kosovo and calling for the proper implementation of that memorandum,

Appreciating efforts to monitor the situation in Kosovo, but at the same time expressing regret at the fact that the establishment of an adequate international monitoring presence in Kosovo has not yet been achieved,

Recalling its resolution 50/190 of 22 December 1995 and other relevant resolutions, and taking note of the resolutions on the matter adopted by the Commission on Human Rights and the resolution adopted by the Subcommission on Prevention of Discrimination and Protection of Minorities, at its forty-eighth session,

1. *Condemns* all violations of human rights in Kosovo, in particular the repression of the ethnic Albanian population and discrimination against them, as well as all acts of violence in Kosovo;

2. *Demands* that the authorities of the Federal Republic of Yugoslavia (Serbia and Montenegro):

(a) Take all necessary measures to bring to an immediate end all human rights violations against ethnic Albanians in Kosovo, including, in particular, the discriminatory measures and practices, arbitrary searches and detention, the violation of the right to a fair trial and the practice of torture and other cruel, inhuman or degrading treatment, and to revoke all discriminatory legislation, in particular that which has entered into force since 1989;

(b) Release all political prisoners and cease the persecution of political leaders and members of local human rights organizations;

(c) Allow the establishment of genuine democratic institutions in Kosovo, including the parliament and the judiciary, and respect the will of its inhabitants as the best means of preventing the escalation of the conflict there;

(d) Allow the reopening of educational, cultural and scientific institutions of the ethnic Albanians;

(e) Pursue constructive dialogue with the representatives of ethnic Albanians of Kosovo;

3. *Welcomes* the visits to Kosovo of the Special Rapporteur of the Commission on Human Rights on the situation of human rights in the territory of the former Yugoslavia and her relevant reports and calls upon her to continue to monitor closely the human rights situation in

Kosovo and to continue to pay due attention to this matter in her reporting;

4. *Urges* the authorities of the Federal Republic of Yugoslavia (Serbia and Montenegro) to allow the immediate unconditional return of the long-term mission of the Organization for Security and Cooperation in Europe to Kosovo, called for in Security Council resolution 855 (1993) of 9 August 1993;

5. *Welcomes* the report of the Secretary-General submitted pursuant to resolution 50/190, and requests him to continue his efforts to seek ways and means, including through consultations with the United Nations High Commissioner for Human Rights and relevant regional organizations, to establish an adequate international monitoring presence in Kosovo and to report thereon to the General Assembly at its fifty-second session;

6. *Encourages* the Secretary-General to pursue his humanitarian efforts in the former Yugoslavia, in liaison with the Office of the United Nations High Commissioner for Refugees, the United Nations Children's Fund and other appropriate humanitarian organizations, with a view to taking urgent practical steps to tackle the critical needs of the people in Kosovo, especially of the most vulnerable groups affected by the conflict, and to assist in the voluntary return of displaced persons to their homes in conditions of safety and dignity;

7. *Emphasizes* the importance of laws and regulations concerning citizenship applied by the authorities of the Federal Republic of Yugoslavia (Serbia and Montenegro) being in accordance with the standards and principles of non-discrimination, equal protection before the law, and the reduction and avoidance of statelessness, as set out in the relevant international human rights instruments;

8. *Decides* to continue examination of the human rights situation in Kosovo at its fifty-second session under the item entitled "Human rights questions".

8. General Assembly Resolution 51/116, Situation of human rights, 12 December 1996

The General Assembly,

... 8. *Calls upon* the Government of the Federal Republic of Yugoslavia (Serbia and Montenegro) to undertake substantially greater efforts to institute democratic norms, especially in regard to the protection of free and independent media, and full respect for human rights and fundamental freedoms;

9. *Strongly urges* the Government of the Federal Republic of Yugoslavia (Serbia and Montenegro) to revoke all discriminatory legislation and to apply all other legislation without discrimination and to take urgent action to prevent arbitrary evictions and dismissals and discrimination against any ethnic or national, religious or linguistic group;

10. *Urgently demands* that the authorities of the Federal Republic of Yugoslavia (Serbia and Montenegro) take immediate action to put an end to the repression of and prevent violence against non-Serb populations in Kosovo, including acts of harassment, beatings, torture, warrantless searches, arbitrary detention and unfair trials, and also to respect the rights of persons belonging to minority groups in the Sandjak and Vojvodina and of persons belonging to the Bulgarian minority;

11. *Calls upon* the Government of the Federal Republic of Yugoslavia (Serbia and Montenegro) to act immediately to allow free determination and full participation by all residents in Kosovo in the political, economic, social and cultural life of the region, particularly in the areas of education and health care, and to ensure that all the residents of the region are guaranteed equal treatment and protection regardless of ethnic affiliation;

9. General Assembly Resolution 52/147, Situation of human rights, 12 December 1997

The General Assembly,

... 12. *Calls upon* the Government of the Federal Republic of Yugoslavia (Serbia and Montenegro) to undertake substantially greater efforts to institute democratic norms, especially in regard to the

promotion and protection of free and independent media, and full respect for human rights and fundamental freedoms;

...

15. *Urgently demands* that the authorities of the Federal Republic of Yugoslavia (Serbia and Montenegro) take immediate action to put an end to the repression of, and prevent violence against, non-Serb populations in Kosovo, including acts of harassment, beatings, torture, warrantless searches, arbitrary detention and unfair trials, and also to respect the rights of persons belonging to minority groups in the Sandjak and Vojvodina and of persons belonging to the Bulgarian minority and to allow the immediate, unconditional return of the long-term mission of the Organization for Security and Cooperation in Europe to Kosovo, Sandjak and Vojvodina, called for in Security Council resolution 855 (1993) of 9 August 1993;

16. *Calls upon* the Government of the Federal Republic of Yugoslavia (Serbia and Montenegro) to respect the democratic process and to act immediately to allow freedom of expression and assembly and full and free participation by all residents in Kosovo in the political, economic, social and cultural life of the region, particularly in the areas of education and health care, and to ensure that all the residents of the region are guaranteed equal treatment and protection regardless of ethnic affiliation;

17. *Strongly urges* the Government of the Federal Republic of Yugoslavia (Serbia and Montenegro) to revoke all discriminatory legislation and to apply all other legislation without discrimination and to take urgent action to prevent arbitrary evictions and dismissals and discrimination against any ethnic or national, religious or linguistic group; ...

10. General Assembly Resolution 52/139, Situation of human rights in Kosovo, 1 December 1997

The General Assembly,

Guided by the Charter of the United Nations, the Universal Declaration of Human Rights, Resolution 217 A (III). the International Covenants on Human Rights Resolution 2200 A (XXI), annex. and other human rights instruments,

Taking note with concern of the reports on the situation of human rights in Bosnia and Herzegovina, E/CN.4/1998/13; see also A/52/490. the Republic of Croatia E/CN.4/1998/14; see also A/52/490. and the Federal Republic of Yugoslavia E/CN.4/1998/15; see also A/52/490. submitted by the Special Rapporteur of the Commission on Human Rights on the situation of human rights in the territory of the former Yugoslavia, which describe the continuing grave human rights situation in Kosovo,

Noting with regret that a memorandum of understanding on the educational system in Kosovo, signed in 1996, has not yet been implemented, and calling for full and immediate implementation of that memorandum,

Noting with concern the use of force by Serbian police against peaceful Albanian student protesters of Kosovo on 1 October 1997 and the failure of the Government of the Federal Republic of Yugoslavia to make reasonable accommodation to address the legitimate grievances of the students,

1. *Expresses its deep concern* about all violations of human rights and fundamental freedoms in Kosovo, in particular the repression of the ethnic Albanian population and discrimination against it, as well as acts of violence in Kosovo;

2. *Calls upon* the authorities of the Federal Republic of Yugoslavia:

(*a*) To take all necessary measures to bring to an immediate end all human rights violations against ethnic Albanians in Kosovo, including, in particular, discriminatory measures and practices, arbitrary searches and detention, the violation of the right to a fair trial and the practice of torture and other cruel, inhuman or degrading treatment, and to revoke all discriminatory legislation, in particular that which has entered into force since 1989;

(*b*) To release all political prisoners and to cease the persecution of political leaders and members of local human rights organizations;

(*c*) To allow the return in safety and dignity of Albanian refugees from Kosovo to their homes;

(*d*) To allow the establishment of genuine democratic institutions in Kosovo, including the parliament and the judiciary, and to respect the will of its inhabitants as the best means of preventing the escalation of the conflict there;

(*e*) To allow the reopening of the educational, cultural and scientific institutions of the ethnic Albanians;

3. *Urges* the authorities of the Federal Republic of Yugoslavia to pursue constructive dialogue with the representatives of the ethnic Albanians of Kosovo;

4. *Welcomes* the visits to Kosovo of the Special Rapporteur of the Commission on Human Rights on the situation of human rights in the territory of the former Yugoslavia and her relevant reports, and calls upon her to continue to monitor closely the human rights situation in Kosovo and to continue to pay due attention to that matter in her reporting;

5. *Urges* the authorities of the Federal Republic of Yugoslavia to allow the immediate unconditional return of the mission of long duration of the Organization for Security and Cooperation in Europe to Kosovo, as called for in Security Council resolution 855 (1993) of 9 August 1993;

6. *Welcomes* the report of the Secretary-General on the situation of human rights in Kosovo, A/52/502. submitted pursuant to General Assembly resolution 51/111 of 12 December 1996, and requests him to continue his efforts to seek ways and means, including through consultations with the United Nations High Commissioner for Human Rights and relevant regional organizations, to establish an adequate international monitoring presence in Kosovo and to report thereon to the Assembly at its fifty-third session;

7. *Encourages* the Secretary-General to pursue his humanitarian efforts in the former Yugoslavia, in liaison with the Office of the United Nations High Commissioner for Refugees, the United Nations Children's Fund and other appropriate humanitarian organizations, with a view to taking urgent practical steps to tackle the critical needs of the people in Kosovo, and to assist in the voluntary return of displaced persons to their homes in conditions of safety and dignity;

8. *Emphasizes* the importance of laws and regulations concerning citizenship applied by the authorities of the Federal Republic of Yugoslavia being in accordance with the standards and principles of non-discrimination, equal protection before the law and the reduction and avoidance of statelessness, as set out in the relevant international human rights instruments;

9. *Also emphasizes* that improvements in the promotion and protection of human rights and fundamental freedoms in Kosovo will assist the Federal Republic of Yugoslavia to establish the full range of relations with the international community;

10. *Decides* to continue the examination of the situation of human rights in Kosovo at its fifty-third session under the item entitled "Human rights questions".

11.   General Assembly Resolution 53/163, Situation of human rights, 9 December 1998

[*Adopted at the 85th plenary meeting, 9 December 1998.*]

The General Assembly,

...

31. Calls upon the authorities of the Federal Republic of Yugoslavia (Serbia and Montenegro) to end any torture and other cruel, inhuman or degrading treatment or punishment of persons in detention, as described in the report of the Special Rapporteur of the Commission on Human Rights on the situation of human rights in Bosnia and Herzegovina, the Republic of Croatia and the Federal Republic of Yugoslavia (Serbia and Montenegro), [*see* A/53/322 and Add.1.10/ A/53/563.] and to bring those responsible to justice;

32. Strongly urges the Government of the Federal Republic of Yugoslavia (Serbia and Montenegro) to institutionalize democratic norms, especially in regard to respect for the principle of free and fair elections, the rule of law, the administration of justice, the promotion and protection of free and independent media, and full respect for human rights and fundamental freedoms, and calls upon the authorities

in the Federal Republic of Yugoslavia (Serbia and Montenegro) specifically to repeal repressive laws on universities and the media;

33. Demands that the Government of the Federal Republic of Yugoslavia (Serbia and Montenegro) immediately cease all harassment and hindrance of journalists, whatever their ethnicity or national origin and wherever within the Federal Republic of Yugoslavia (Serbia and Montenegro) they may be practising their profession, repeal repressive laws on universities and the media, which suppress any and all internal dissent or expression of independent views, and concomitantly respect the right of free speech;

34. Urges all parties, groups and individuals in the Federal Republic of Yugoslavia (Serbia and Montenegro) to act with full respect for human rights, to refrain from all acts of violence and to act with respect for the rights and dignity of all persons belonging to minority groups;

35. Strongly urges the authorities of the Federal Republic of Yugoslavia (Serbia and Montenegro) immediately to bring to justice any persons, in particular those among its personnel, who have engaged in or authorized human rights abuses against the civilian population, including summary executions, indiscriminate attacks on civilians, indiscriminate destruction of property, mass forced displacement of civilians, the taking of civilian hostages, torture and other cruel, inhuman or degrading treatment or punishment, and in this context reminds the Government of the Federal Republic of Yugoslavia (Serbia and Montenegro) of its obligations to cooperate fully with the International Tribunal and the United Nations High Commissioner for Human Rights;

36. Calls upon the Government of the Federal Republic of Yugoslavia (Serbia and Montenegro) to revoke all discriminatory legislation and to apply all other legislation without discrimination against any ethnic, national, religious or linguistic group, to ensure the speedy and consistent investigation of acts of discrimination and violence against refugees and internally displaced persons, and to ensure the arrest and punishment of those responsible for acts of discrimination and violence;

37. Also calls upon the Government of the Federal Republic of Yugoslavia (Serbia and Montenegro) to respect the rights of all persons belonging to minority groups especially in the Sandjak and Vojvodina, and of persons belonging to the Bulgarian minority, and supports the unconditional return of the long-term missions of the Organization for Security and Cooperation in Europe, as called for by the Security Council in its resolutions 855 (1993) of 9 August 1993 and 1160 (1998) of 31 March 1998;

38. Further calls upon the Government of the Federal Republic of Yugoslavia (Serbia and Montenegro) to respect the democratic process and to act immediately to make possible the establishment of genuine democratic self-governance in Kosovo, through a negotiated political settlement with representatives of the ethnic Albanian community, to cease all restrictions on freedom of expression or assembly, to ensure that all the residents of the region are guaranteed equal treatment and protection regardless of ethnic affiliation, and calls upon all individuals or groups in Kosovo to resolve the crisis there through peaceful means;

39. Demands that the Government of the Federal Republic of Yugoslavia (Serbia and Montenegro) take immediate steps toallow for and to create conditions for the return of internally displaced persons and refugees in safety and dignity;

40. Calls upon the authorities of the Federal Republic of Yugoslavia (Serbia and Montenegro) to cooperate fully with the Office of the United Nations High Commissioner for Refugees and other humanitarian organizations to alleviate the suffering of refugees and internally displaced persons and to assist in their unimpeded return to their homes;

41. Takes note of the report of the Special Rapporteur, [*see* A/53/322 and Add.1.10/ A/53/563] in which concern is expressed about the continuing grave situation of human rights in Kosovo, as well **as** the report of the Secretary-General on the situation of human rights in Kosovo, [*see* A/53/563] while noting that the Federal Republic of Yugoslavia (Serbia and Montenegro) is allowing international verifiers into Kosovo;

42. Welcomes the establishment of a sub-office of the United Nations High Commissioner for Human Rights in Pristina in the context of the United Nations Field Operation in the Former Yugoslavia;

43. Calls upon States to consider additional voluntary contributions to meet the pressing human rights and humanitarian needs in the area, and underlines the need for continuing coordination among States, international organizations and non-governmental organizations of initiatives and programmes with the aim of avoiding duplication, overlap and working at cross-purposes;

44. Decides to continue its consideration of this question at its fifty-fourth session under the item entitled "Human rights questions".

12. General Assembly Resolution 53/164, Situation of human rights in Kosovo, 9 December 1998

[Adopted at the 85th plenary meeting, 9 December 1998.]
The General Assembly,

Guided by the Charter of the United Nations, the Universal Declaration of Human Rights,[1] the International Covenants on Human Rights[2] and other human rights instruments,

Taking note of Security Council resolutions 1160 (1998) of 31 March 1998, 1199 (1998) of 23 September 1998 and 1203 (1998) of 24 October 1998, as well as the statement made on 24 March 1998 by the Chairman of the Commission on Human Rights at its fifty-fourth session[3] and Commission resolution 1998/79 of 22 April 1998,[4]

Taking fully into account the regional dimensions of the crisis in Kosovo, particularly with regard to the human rights and the humanitarian situation, and deeply concerned at the potential adverse consequences thereof,

Taking note with concern of the report of the Secretary- General on the situation of human rights in Kosovo[5] and the report of the Special Rapporteur of the Commission on Human Rights on the situation of human rights in Bosnia and Herzegovina, the Republic of Croatia and the Federal Republic of Yugoslavia (Serbia and Montenegro),[6] which describe the persistent and grave violations and abuse of human rights and humanitarian law in Kosovo,

Gravely concerned about the systematic terrorization of ethnic Albanians, as demonstrated in the many reports, inter alia, of torture of ethnic Albanians, through indiscriminate and widespread shelling, mass forced displacement of civilians, summary executions and illegal detention of ethnic Albanian citizens of the Federal Republic of Yugoslavia (Serbia and Montenegro) by the police and military,

Concerned about reports of violence committed by armed ethnic Albanian groups against non-combatants and the illegal detention of individuals, primarily ethnic Serbs, by those groups,

Stressing, in this context, the importance of the International Tribunal for the Prosecution of Persons Responsible for Serious Violations of International Humanitarian Law Committed in the Territory of the Former Yugoslavia since 1991,

Distressed by the lack of due process in the trials of those ethnic Albanians who have been detained, charged or brought to trial in relation to the crisis in Kosovo,

Concerned by the grave infringements upon the freedom of expression in the Federal Republic of Yugoslavia (Serbia and Montenegro), in particular the adoption of the new law on public information by the Serbian Parliament and the recent closure of several independent newspapers and radio stations in the Federal Republic of Yugoslavia (Serbia and Montenegro),

1. *Welcomes* the commitment made by the authorities of the Federal Republic of Yugoslavia (Serbia and Montenegro) to address the conflict and the ongoing human rights violations in Kosovo, as manifested by agreements signed by the Organization for Security and Cooperation in Europe and the North Atlantic Treaty Organization, and the international supervision of elections and verification of the implementation of human rights commitments;

2. *Welcomes also* the withdrawal and return to garrison of a number of military and police units, as demanded by the Security Council in its resolution 1199 (1998), but cautions that such withdrawals must be genuine, complete and lasting;

3. *Welcomes further* the establishment by the Organization for Security and Cooperation in Europe of the Kosovo Verification Mission, and calls upon all parties in Kosovo to cooperate fully with the Mission and ensure the protection, freedom of movement and unrestricted access within Kosovo of its personnel;

4. *Welcomes* the conclusion of a memorandum of understanding with the United Nations High Commissioner for Human Rights, in accordance with the statement by the Chairman of the Commission on Human Rights,[3] regarding the status of the office in Belgrade, leading the way to the establishment of office premises for the Office of the High Commissioner and the deployment of additional human rights officers in Kosovo;

5. *Calls upon* the Government of the Federal Republic of Yugoslavia (Serbia and Montenegro) to respect all human rights and fundamental freedoms fully and to abide by democratic norms, especially in regard to respect for the principle of free and fair elections, the rule of law, the administration of justice, free and fair trials and the promotion and protection of free and independent media;

6. *Calls upon* the authorities of the Federal Republic of Yugoslavia (Serbia and Montenegro) and the ethnic Albanian leadership in Kosovo to condemn acts of terrorism, denounce and refrain from all acts of violence, encourage the pursuit of goals through peaceful means, and respect international humanitarian law and international human rights standards;

7. *Urges* the authorities of the Federal Republic of Yugoslavia (Serbia and Montenegro) and the Kosovo Albanian leadership to enter immediately into a meaningful dialogue, without preconditions and with international involvement, and to commit themselves both to a clear timetable, leading to an end of the crisis, and to a negotiated political settlement of the issue of Kosovo, and welcomes the current efforts aimed at facilitating such a dialogue;

8. *Strongly condemns* the overwhelming number of human rights violations committed by the authorities of the Federal Republic of Yugoslavia (Serbia and Montenegro), the police and military authorities in Kosovo, including summary executions, indiscriminate and widespread attacks on civilians, indiscriminate and widespread destruction of property, mass forced displacement of civilians, the taking of civilian hostages, torture and other cruel, inhuman or degrading treatment, in breach of international humanitarian law including article 3 common to the Geneva Conventions of 12 August 1949[7] and Additional Protocol II to the Conventions, relating to the protection of victims of non-international armed conflicts,[8] and calls upon the authorities of the Federal Republic of Yugoslavia (Serbia and Montenegro) to take all measures necessary to eliminate these unacceptable practices;

9. *Condemns* the acts of violence, including kidnappings, by armed ethnic Albanian groups, in particular against non-combatants;

10. *Strongly condemns* the denial of appropriate access to Kosovo of non-governmental organizations, the manipulation and denial of relief and basic foodstuffs, and the denial of medical care to wounded civilians, calls upon the authorities of the Federal Republic of Yugoslavia (Serbia and Montenegro) to take all measures necessary to eliminate these unacceptable practices forthwith, and recalls the commitment to allow unhindered access to humanitarian organizations and the need to facilitate the immediate return of internally displaced persons to their homes;

11. *Deeply deplores* the killing of humanitarian aid workers, as reported by the Secretary-General;[9]

12. *Calls upon* all parties, in particular those of the Federal Republic of Yugoslavia (Serbia and Montenegro), to clear the area forthwith of all landmines and booby-traps and to work with the relevant international bodies to this end;

13. *Calls upon* the authorities of the Federal Republic of Yugoslavia (Serbia and Montenegro) to comply with and build on the commitments made by the President of the Republic of Serbia in his statement of 13 October 1998, which were subsequently endorsed by the Government of the Federal Republic of Yugoslavia (Serbia and Montenegro);

14. *Also calls upon* the authorities of the Federal Republic of Yugoslavia (Serbia and Montenegro):

(a) To establish a local police force in Kosovo under local or communal direction, which will be representative of the local population;

(b) To abide by the principle that no person will be prosecuted in state courts for crimes related to the conflict in Kosovo, except for crimes against humanity, war crimes and other crimes covered by international law;

(c) To allow the International Tribunal for the Prosecution of Persons Responsible for Serious Violations of International Humanitarian Law Committed in the Territory of the Former Yugoslavia since 1991and its forensic experts complete, unimpeded access to Kosovo to examine the recently alleged atrocities against civilians;

(d) To mitigate the punishments of and where appropriate to amnesty the ethnic Albanians in Kosovo sentenced for criminal offences motivated by political aims;

(e) To respect fully all the rights of individuals in Kosovo, whatever their ethnic, cultural or religious backgrounds, so as to guarantee equitable treatment of their values and historic patrimony and so as to preserve and permit expression of their national, cultural, religious and linguistic identities in accordance with international standards and the Final Act of Helsinki of 1 August 1975;

15. *Further calls upon* the authorities of the Federal Republic of Yugoslavia (Serbia and Montenegro) to open to public observation all trials or criminal prosecutions against all those charged in relation to the conflict in Kosovo;

16. *Calls upon* the authorities of the Federal Republic of Yugoslavia (Serbia and Montenegro) to make possible the establishment of genuine democratic self-governance in Kosovo, through a negotiated political settlement with representatives of the ethnic Albanian community, as called for by the Security Council in its resolutions 1160 (1998), 1199 (1998) and 1203 (1998), to include executive, legislative and judicial bodies and police, and in so doing to respect the rights of Kosovar Albanians and all who live in Kosovo, and expresses its support for an enhanced status for Kosovo, which would include a substantially greater degree of autonomy;

17. *Also calls upon* the authorities of the Federal Republic of Yugoslavia (Serbia and Montenegro) to grant access to and free and unaccompanied movement within Kosovo for all humanitarian aid workers and international monitors;

18. *Further calls* upon the authorities of the Federal Republic of Yugoslavia (Serbia and Montenegro):

(a) To promote and respect fully freedom of expression and freedom of the press, without discrimination;

(b) To repeal those legal measures used to discriminate against ethnic Albanians, including repressive laws on universities;

19. *Calls upon* the authorities of the Federal Republic of Yugoslavia (Serbia and Montenegro) and armed Albanian groups to refrain from any harassment and intimidation of journalists;

20. *Calls upon* the authorities of the Federal Republic of Yugoslavia (Serbia and Montenegro) to work closely with and support the mission to Kosovo of the personal representative of the Chairman-in-Office of the Organization for Security and Cooperation in Europe, and with the Kosovo Verification Mission;

21. *Also calls* upon the authorities of the Federal Republic of Yugoslavia (Serbia and Montenegro) to investigate and prosecute in all cases where so warranted, notably those cases concerning its personnel, anyone suspected of torture and ill-treatment of persons held in detention;

22. *Further calls* upon the authorities of the Federal Republic of Yugoslavia (Serbia and Montenegro) to release all political prisoners, to allow unimpeded access by non-governmental organizations and international observers to those prisoners who remain in detention, and to cease the persecution of political leaders and members of local human rights organizations;

23. *Calls upon* the authorities of the Federal Republic of Yugoslavia (Serbia and Montenegro) and ethnic Albanian leaders to allow for and facilitate the free and unhindered return to their homes, in safety and with dignity, of all internally displaced persons and refugees, and expresses its concern about reports of continuing harassment or other impediments in this regard; 24. Calls upon the Government of the Federal Republic of Yugoslavia (Serbia and Montenegro) and all others concerned to guarantee the unrestricted access of humanitarian organizations and the United Nations High Commissioner for Human Rights to Kosovo, and to allow the unhindered delivery of relief items and ensure the safety and security of humanitarian, diplomatic and other affected personnel accredited to the Federal Republic of Yugoslavia (Serbia and Montenegro), including members of the Verification Mission of the Organization for Security and Cooperation in Europe;

25. *Encourages* the useful cooperation of the United Nations and the Organization for Security and Cooperation in Europe on the ground, in the light of the report of the Secretary-General on the situation of human rights in Kosovo;[5]

26. *Requests* the Secretary-General to pursue his humanitarian efforts in the Federal Republic of Yugoslavia (Serbia and Montenegro), working through the Office of the United Nations High Commissioner for Refugees, the World Food Programme, the United Nations Children's Fund, other appropriate humanitarian organizations and the Office of the United Nations High Commissioner for Human Rights, with a view to taking urgent practical steps to meet the critical needs of the people in Kosovo, and to assist in the voluntary return of the displaced persons to their homes in conditions of safety and dignity;

27. *Encourages* the Office of the Prosecutor of the International Tribunal to continue investigations at all levels on serious violations of international humanitarian law committed in Kosovo, and reaffirms that such crimes fall within its jurisdiction;

28. Demands that the authorities of the Federal Republic of Yugoslavia (Serbia and Montenegro) and the Kosovo Albanian leadership and all others concerned cooperate fully with the International Tribunal and honour all their obligations towards it by, inter alia, providing full and free access to Kosovo for the investigators of the Tribunal;

29. *Reiterates* its call upon the authorities of the Federal Republic of Yugoslavia (Serbia and Montenegro) to live up to their commitment to provide financial and material assistance to those residents of Kosovo whose homes have beendamaged;

30. *Emphasizes* that legislation on citizenship of the Federal Republic of Yugoslavia (Serbia and Montenegro) should be applied in accordance with the principles set out in relevant international instruments, in particular with regard to the standards and principles of the reduction and avoidance of statelessness;

31. *Also emphasizes* that improvement in the promotion andprotection of human rights and fundamental freedoms in the Federal Republic of Yugoslavia (Serbia and Montenegro) will assist in establishing a full range of relations with the international community;

32. *Requests* the Special Rapporteur of the Commission on Human Rights on the situation of human rights in the territories of Bosnia and Herzegovina, the Republic of Croatia and the Federal Republic of Yugoslavia (Serbia and Montenegro) to continue to monitor closely the situation of human rights in Kosovo, to pay special attention to Kosovo in his reporting and to report his findings to the Commission on Human Rights at its fifty-fifth session and to the General Assembly at its fifty-fourth session;

33. *Decides* to continue its consideration of the situation of human rights in Kosovo at its fifty-fourth session under the item entitled "Human rights questions".

---

[1] Resolution 217 A (III).

[2] Resolution 2200 A (XXI), annex.

[3] See Official Records of the Economic and Social Council,1998, Supplement No. 3 (E/1998/23), chap. III, sect. E, para. 28.

[4] Ibid., chap. II, sect. A.

[5] A/53/563.

[6] See A/53/322 and Add.1.

[7] United Nations, Treaty Series, vol. 75, Nos. 970-973.

[8] Ibid., vol. 1125, No. 17513.

[9] See A/53/563, para. 6.

B.   The UN Commision on Human Rights and its Sub-Commission

1.   Commission Resolution 1992/S-1/1, 14 August 1992

The Commission on Human Rights, meeting in special session

...

3. Expresses its alarm at all repressive policies and practices directed against members of particular ethnic groups, and also calls upon all parties to ensure the protection of the rights of persons belonging to national or ethnic, religious and linguistic minorities.

...

12.   *Requests* its Chairman to appoint a special rapporteur to investigate first-hand the human rights situation in the territory of the former Yugoslavia, in particular within Bosnia and Herzegovina, and to receive relevant, credible information on the human rights situation there from Governments, individuals, intergovernmental and non-governmental organisations, on a continuing basis, and to avail himself or herself of the assistance of existing mechanisms of the Commission on Human Rights.

13.   *Requests* the existing mechanisms of the Commission on Human Rights, in particular the Special Rapporteur on the question of torture, the Special Rapporteur on summary or arbitrary executions, the representative of the Secretary-General on internally displaced persons and the Working Group on Arbitrary Detention, to give urgent attention to the situation in the former Yugoslavia and to provide, on a continuing basis, their full co-operation, assistance and findings to the Special Rapporteur, and to accompany the Special Rapporteur in visiting the former Yugoslavia if he or she should so request.

14.   *Requests* the Special Rapporteur to visit areas of interest in the former Yugoslavia, and particularly Bosnia and Herzegovina, forthwith and to report on an urgent basis to the members of the Commission on Human Rights, providing a preliminary report no later than 28 August 1992 on the situation of human rights in the former Yugoslavia, including his or her recommendations for bringing violations to an end and preventing future violations, and requests the Secretary-General to make the report of the Special Rapporteur available also to the Security Council.

15.   *Also requests* the Special Rapporteur to report his or her findings and recommendations to the members of the Commission on Human Rights periodically thereafter until its next regular session, and to report to the General Assembly at its forty-seventh session, as well as to the Commission on Human Rights at its forty-ninth session, under agenda item 12, and requests the Secretary-General to make the reports of the Special Rapporteur available also to the Security Council.

16.   *Further requests* the special Rapporteur to gather and compile systematically information on possible violations of human rights in the territory of the former Yugoslavia, including those which may constitute war crimes, and to make this information available to the Secretary-General, and notes that such information could be of possible future use in prosecuting violators of international humanitarian law.

17.   *Requests* the Secretary-General to provide all necessary assistance to the Special Rapporteur to fulfil his or her mandate.

18.   *Requests* all United Nations bodies and the specialised agencies, and invited Governments and informed intergovernmental and non-governmental organisations, to provide the Special Rapporteur, through the Centre for Human Rights, on a continuing basis, with all relevant and accurate information in their possession on the situation of human rights in the former Yugoslavia.

19.   *Demands* that all parties in the territory of the former Yugoslavia co-operate fully with the Special Rapporteur in the implementation of the present resolution.

20.   *Requests* the Special Rapporteur to take into account and seek to complement the efforts being undertaken by the Conference on Security and Co-operation in Europe with respect to the crisis in the former Yugoslavia.

21.   *Decides* to remain seized of the issues.

2.   Commission Resolution 1992/S-2, Human rights in the former Yugoslavia, 1 December 1992

The Commission on Human Rights
Meeting in special session

...

14.   *Expresses* its grave concern at the information contained in the third report of the Special Rapporteur (A/47/66 - S/24809) on the dangerous situation in Kosovo, Sandzak and Vojvodina, and urges all parties in those areas to engage in a meaningful dialogue under the auspices of the International conference on the Former Yugoslavia, to act with utmost restraint and to settle disputes in full observance of human rights and freedoms, and calls on the Serbian authorities to refrain from the use of force and immediately to stop the practice of ethnic cleansing, and to respect fully the rights of persons belonging to ethnic communities o minorities in order to prevent the extension of the conflict to other parts of the former Yugoslavia.

3.   Commission Resolution 1993/7, Human rights in the former Yugoslavia, 23 February 1993

The Commission on Human Rights

...

Deeply concerned about the situation of human rights in Serbia, particularly in Kosovo, as well as in Sandzak and Vojvodina.

...

24.   *Expresses its grave concern* at the deteriorating human rights situation in Serbia, particularly in Kosovo, as described in the report of the Special Rapporteur, and condemns the violations of human rights occurring there, including:

(a) Police brutality against ethnic Albanians, arbitrary searches, seizures and arrests, torture and ill-treatment during detention and discrimination in the administration of justice which leads to a climate of lawlessness in which criminal acts, particularly against ethnic Albanians, take place with impunity;

(b) The discriminatory removal of ethnic Albanian officials, especially from the police and judiciary, the mass dismissal of ethnic Albanians from professional, administrative and other skilled positions in State-owned enterprises and public institutions, including teachers from the Serb-run school system, and the closure of Albanian high schools and universities;

(c) Arbitrary imprisonment of ethnic Albanian journalists, the closure of Albanian-language mass media and the discriminatory removal of ethnic Albanian staff from local radio and television stations.

25.   *Demands* that the authorities of the Federal Republic of Yugoslavia (Serbia and Montenegro) respect the human rights and fundamental freedoms of ethnic Albanians in Kosovo, and expresses its view that the best means to safeguard human rights in Kosovo is to restore its autonomy with a view to an overall political settlement of the situation in the former Yugoslavia.

26.   *Expresses its grave concern* at the report by the Special Rapporteur of violations of human rights occurring in Sandjak and Vojvodina, particularly acts of physical harassment, abductions, the burning of homes, warrantless searches, confiscation of property and other practices intended to change the ethnic structure in favour of the Serbian population.

27.   *Recognises* the courage and sacrifice of many Serbs who have refused to participate in these violations.

28.   *Urges* all parties in Serbia, particularly in Kosovo, Sandjak and Vojvodina, to engage in a substantive dialogue, act with the utmost restraint and settle disputes in full compliance with human rights and fundamental freedoms, and calls on the Serbian authorities to refrain from the use of force and the practice of ethnic cleansing and to respect fully the rights of persons belonging to minority groups in Serbia, in order to prevent the extension of the conflict to other parts of the former Yugoslavia and other States.

29. *Invites* the Security Council to consider establishing a United nations observer mission, in co-ordination with the Special Rapporteur and the Conference on security and Co-operation in Europe and its missions of long duration, to be deployed as soon as possible to investigate and report on alleged human rights violations in Kosovo, Sandjak and Vojvodina.

4.   Commission Resolution 1994/72, Human rights in the former Yugoslavia, 9 March 1994

The Commission on Human Rights

...

Deeply concerned about the situation of human rights in Serbia and Montenegro, particularly in Kosovo but also in Sandjak and Vojvodina.

25. *Expresses its grave concern* at the deteriorating human rights situation in the Federal Republic of Yugoslavia (Serbia and Montenegro), particularly in Kosovo, as described by the Special Rapporteur, and again condemns the violations of human rights occurring there.

26. *Strongly condemns* in particular the measures and practices of discrimination against and the violations of the human rights of the ethnic Albanians of Kosovo, as well as the large-scale repression committed by the Serbian authorities, including:

   (a) Police brutality against ethnic Albanians, arbitrary searches, seizures and arrests, torture and ill-treatment during detention and discrimination in the administration -language mass media and the discriminatory of justice, which leads to a climate of lawlessness in which criminal acts, particularly against ethnic Albanians, take place with impunity.

   (b) The exclusion of ethnic Albanians from positions in the police and in the judiciary, as well as from professional, administrative and other skilled positions in State-owned enterprises and public institutions, including teachers from the Serb-run school system, and the closure of the Albanian university and high schools.

   (c) Arbitrary imprisonment of ethnic Albanian journalists, the closure of Albanianremoval of ethnic Albanian staff from local radio and television stations.

   (d) Repression by the Serbian police and military.

27. *Demands* that the Federal Republic of Yugoslavia (Serbia and Montenegro) respect the human rights and fundamental freedoms of ethnic Albanians in Kosovo and declares that the best means to prevent the possible escalation of the conflict is to safeguard human rights, restore the autonomy of Kosovo and to establish democratic institutions in Kosovo.

...

29. *Urges* all parties in Serbia and Montenegro, particularly in Kosovo, the Sandjak and Vojvodina, to engage in substantive dialogue, *inter alia*, under the auspices of the International Conference on the Former Yugoslavia, and to act with the utmost restraint and settle disputes with full respect for human rights, and calls on the Serbian authorities to prevent extension of the conflict by refraining from the use of force and by respecting fully the rights of persons belonging to minority groups.

30. *Demands* that the Federal Republic of Yugoslavia (Serbia and Montenegro) permit entry into Kosovo, Sandjak and Vojvodina of United Nations observer missions and field officers of the Special Rapporteur and resumption of the missions of long duration of the Conference on Security and Co-operation in Europe.

...

5.   Commission Resolution 1994/76, Human rights in Kosovo, 9 March 1994

The Commission on Human Rights

...

Noting in the report of the Special Rapporteur on the situation of human rights in the former Yugoslavia (E/CN.4/1994/110) the continuing deterioration of the human rights situation in Kosovo including:

   (a) Police brutality against ethnic Albanians, arbitrary searches, seizures and arrests, forced evictions, torture and ill-

treatment of detainees and discrimination in the administration of justice;

   (b) Discriminatory and arbitrary dismissals of ethnic Albanian civil servants, notably from the ranks of the police and the judiciary, mass dismissals of ethnic Albanians, discrimination against Albanian pupils and teachers of primary schools, the closing of the Albanian-language secondary schools and university, as well as the closing of Albanian cultural and scientific institutions;

   (c) The intimidation and imprisonment of ethnic Albanian journalists and the systematic harassment and disruption of the news media in the Albanian language;

   (d) The dismissals of doctors and members of other categories of the medical profession of Albanian origin from clinics and hospitals;

   (e) The elimination in practice of the Albanian language, particularly in public administration and services;

   (f) The serious and massive occurrence of discriminatory and repressive practices aimed at Kosovo Albanians as a whole, resulting in widespread involuntary emigration.

1. *Strongly condemns* the discriminatory measures and practices, as well as the violations of human rights, committed by the authorities of the Federal Republic of Yugoslavia (Serbia and Montenegro) against ethnic Albanians in Kosovo.

2. *Urgently demands* that the authorities of the Federal Republic of Yugoslavia (Serbia and Montenegro):

   (a) Cease all human rights violations, discriminatory measures and practices against ethnic Albanians in Kosovo, in particular arbitrary detention and violation of the right to a fair trial and the practice of torture and other cruel, inhuman and degrading treatment;

   (b) Release all political prisoners and cease all persecution of political leaders and members of local human rights organisations;

   (c) Establish democratic institutions in Kosovo and respect the will of its inhabitants as the best means of preventing the escalation of the conflict there;

   (d) co-operate with the Conference on Security and Co-operation in Europe to enable the long-term mission to resume its activities immediately, inter alia, by permitting its return to Kosovo.

3. *Urges* the Secretary-General to explore ways and means to establish an adequate international monitoring presence in Kosovo.

4. *Calls upon* the Special Rapporteur to continue to monitor closely the human rights situation in Kosovo and pay special attention to this matter in his reporting.

5. *Decides* to remain seized of this matter.

E/CN.4/1995/153, 23 February 1995

6.   Letter from the FRY to the Chairman of the Commission on Human Rights, 15 February 1995

AIDE MEMOIRE

The Albanian Minority in the Federal Republic of Yugoslavia

The Government of the Federal Republic of Yugoslavia has underlined on several occasion that the so-called problem of the Albanian minority in Serbia is a problem of separatism par excellence. The possible forms and cases of threats or restrictions on human rights and freedoms imposed upon the members of this minority are an absolute consequence of their separatism. The refusal of the Albanian minority to be loyal to the state where they live, in compliance with the internationally accepted principles on the rights of national minorities, has resulted in the state's use of its legitimate right to control the holders of separatism and their helpers in every possible way. Hence, we resolutely dismiss any insinuations about pre-empted discrimination against the members of the Albanian or any other minority in the Federal Republic of Yugoslavia, particularly the allegation that the problem stems from the Constitution or any positive law of the country. Any such hint or allegation is a proof either of ignorance of the facts or of politically biased motives.

Hence, the states that do not want to see hat behind the so-called discontent with the enjoyment of human rights and freedoms there is a hidden scenario which has been prepared for years, aiming at the secession of Kosovo and Metohija, at the same time are closing their eyes in front of the fact that not only the existence of the national minorities in the FRY is being recognised, but also that the minority rights are guaranteed under the Constitution of the FRY and the relevant regulations, in compliance with the highest international standards in this domain. The problems of Kosovo and Metohija do not stem from non-recognition of minority rights or their non-implementation in practice, but rather from the refusal of a segment of the Albanian minority to recognise the state in which they live. This can be illustrated by the fact that the separatist leaders, in their struggle against the territorial integrity and sovereignty of Yugoslavia, have launched an illegal referendum for the secession of Kosovo and Metohija from Yugoslavia, that they have adopted a constitution of the so-called republic of Kosovo, while making use of terrorism, arms and drugs trafficking, and of other legal activities.

The members of the Albanian minority in Kosovo and Metohija, under pressure exerted by the separatists, have been persistently opposing to exercise their basic democratic rights they are entitled to in the FRY, i.e. To take part in the republican parliamentary, provincial and communal elections. By their boycotting every election held to date in Serbia and the FRY, they have been denying themselves the right to participate in the democratic decision-making process on the republican level, as well as the possibility to set up local self-government on the level of the Province.

Such an attitude testifies to their separatist aspirations, and it represents the example of extreme abuse of minority rights in Europe. It is a unique instance of a national minority refusing to enjoy the privileges of territorial and cultural autonomy guaranteed to it under the Constitution.

The separatism of the Albanian minority in Yugoslavia is not a novelty, it had been instigated in particular by the communist Albania under Enver Hoxha. It culminated in the period of dissolution of communism in East European countries and in the course of the preparations aimed at the break-up of the former Yugoslavia. At that time, the secessionist republics of the SFR of Yugoslavia were not only the inspiration for the erroneous belief of the Albanian minority that it was also entitled to secession, but they blatantly abused this false hope for their own political purposes. As for the ideologists of the Albanian separatism, they have launched a new concept whereby, since the Albanian minority in Yugoslavia has been growing to such an extent that it has, according to them, reached or even exceeded in numbers some nations of the former Yugoslavia (Macedonians, Slovenians), this very fact could serve for changing its constitutional status and proclaiming itself a nation. Accordingly, all international legal obstacles were supposed to be eliminated and the realisation of their plan for secession from Yugoslavia and unification with the Republic of Albania, accomplished.

However, the rights of the members of national minorities are not founded on their numbers, but on the Constitution as a basic law of the country, and on the international law.

Resolution of the 50th session of the Commission on Human Rights

The resolution on the situation of human rights in Kosovo and Metohija, adopted for the first time at the 50th Session of the Commission on Human Rights last year, it is true, contains no blunders in terms of promoting the Albanian minority in Kosovo and Metohija into a nation, nor does it advocate their separatism. However, in view of its very interference in the internal affairs of the FRY, it is in fact an instrument of the Albanian separatism and of the forces that hope to realise their direct or indirect objectives and interests by extending or further complicating the crisis in the territory of the former Yugoslavia, first of all in the Federal Republic of Yugoslavia.

The allegations contained in this resolution are a typical case of mistaken theses. For example, as for the allegations that discrimination has been conducted against the Albanian students and teachers, the facts prove the opposite. At the same time, it is an absurdity which probably no sponsor of this resolution could even think of is if his own country were in question: the Albanian students and teachers have arbitrarily rejected the curricula for elementary and secondary education approved by the competent Ministry of Education for the whole territory of the Republic of Serbia, which is regular practice in the countries world-wide. Instead, they have introduced certain instruction based on their own curricula, criteria and text-books, with issuing some internal diplomas which should serve their student to proceed further to higher grades.

Since the sponsors of the resolution were motivated to stress that human rights have been violated in Kosovo and Metohija, the claim contained in that resolution about massive migration of the Albanians from Kosovo and Metohija (to developed European countries), is aimed at alluding that the cause for this migration is discrimination against the Albanian minority. However, no discrimination whatsoever is in question in this case. Emigration from the FRY is a problem that affects the entire population of the FRY and it has nothing to do with the ethnic factor. It has much to do, however, with the prevailing unfavourable economic, social and other living conditions, which have been additionally and severely exacerbated by the sanctions imposed against the FRY.

The migration of the Albanian minority is neither a problem of a political nature. It is well-known that many Albanians from the FRY have not been granted political asylum in developed European countries including some of the states sponsoring this resolution. [E/1994/24; E/CN.4/1994/132 pp. 391, 393] A number of these countries recently also decided on their massive return back to the FRY. That is to say either that such countries, according to the judgement of the sponsors, are violating the Convention on the Status of Refugees by turning them back to the state where their life is in jeopardy, or that (Art. 33.1) there is no case of violation of human rights at all, which is contrary to the allegations contained in the resolution.

The claims that the conditions in Kosovo and Metohija are further exacerbating are an absurd and hollow cliché. The allegations about torturing, inhuman treatment of detainees, the judiciary discrimination etc., do not have any commendable backing in reality, nor is there any such backing in the relevant facts-founded documents of the Commission. At any rate, the proportions of such phenomena only slightly deviate from similar developments in other countries, their monitoring being a regular activity of the Commission on Human Rights, and the findings based on such monitoring do not furnish valid reasons for adopting a separate resolution. The demand that Yugoslavia co-operate with the OESC, contained in the resolution at the 50th session of the Commission on Human Rights was unfounded and dictated by various political interests. Hence, there was not, nor is there any ground at present for adopting a similar resolution on Kosovo and Metohija at the 51st Session. Even more so since, in spite of the lies launched against the Federal republic of Yugoslavia and the Serbs as a nation, the FRY has made additional efforts for the establishment of peace in the territory of the former Yugoslavia. Some prominent international factors and states have publicly given credit to Yugoslavia for such efforts. The very protagonists from among the developed countries who gave their support to violent secession of some of the former Yugoslav republics several years ago, admit at present, one by one, that approving the latters' secession from the SFRY, the way it was effected, was premature and inappropriate, and they have their share of responsibility for the consequences it entailed. Accordingly, it is evident to what extent blaming and sacrificing the Federal Republic of Yugoslavia, or rather, the peoples of the whole of Yugoslavia, has been unsubstantiated, and in particular, to what extent the adoption of a separate resolution on the situation of human rights in Kosovo and Metohija has been unfounded. Inventions, over-exaggerations and mistaken theses contained in the resolution adopted by the Commission in 1994, are manifest examples of abuse of human rights for political purposes, and of open support for the Albanian minority separatism in the FRY. Consequently, the resolution embodies a violation of international law, and of the provisions of the OESC.

At the same time, other member-states of the Commission should not identify themselves with separatism, nor do they have the right to approve separatism and various types of abuses of minority rights exercised in the Federal Republic of Yugoslavia under pretence of fighting for the protection of human rights. Being a member of the Commission on Human Rights testifies not only of a favourable position a particular state enjoys in the field of human rights but, also, enforces responsibility of objective examination of all the facts available relevant to the respect or violation of human rights and other issues raised before the Commission. This also includes the responsibility not to permit the abuse of human rights for political purposes. Yugoslavia has on many occasions so far made efforts to present those concerned ample data on the Albanian minority in Serbia, either through its national reports on the implementation of the provisions of the international instruments it has acceded to, or in its replies to special rapporteurs of the Commission on Human Rights, in its statements, etc. Ever since it has been undemocratically and unjustifiably stripped of its rights in the organs and bodies of the United Nations, the Federal Republic of Yugoslavia has been presenting these data by submitting documents and requesting that these be published as official documents for major sessions of various United Nations bodies. Such documents, including those relevant to the status of the Albanian minority in the Federal Republic of

Yugoslavia, shall be available at the 51st session of the Commission on Human Rights. The UN documents to the UN codes under which they have been published to date, primarily those within Items 12 and 20, shall be at the disposal for the 51st session of the Commission on Human Rights. In particular, note the comments by he Government of the Federal Republic of Yugoslavia on the reports by Mr T Mazowiecki.

There is nothing the Federal Republic of Yugoslavia wants to hide from the eyes of the world concerning the situation in Kosovo and Metohija. The figures issued by the Republican Ministry for Information whereby a total of 544 permanently accredited or other journalists, reporters and photographers from 26 countries visited Kosovo and Metohija in the last two years is evident proof to that effect. During the same period, 123 delegations, parliamentary and other missions of diplomatic/consular representatives stationed in the Federal Republic of Yugoslavia went on a visit to Kosovo and Metohija. Before the expiry of the Memorandum on Understanding, in 1993, the CSCE Mission held talks in Kosovo and Metohija 35 times. ...

7.   Commission Resolution 1995/89, Human rights in the former Yugoslavia, 8 March 1995

The Commission on Human Rights,

  ...

Deeply concerned at the situation of human rights in Serbia and Montenegro, particularly in Kosovo as described in the ninth and tenth reports of the Special Rapporteur (A/49/641-S/1994/1252 and E/CN.4/1995/57), but also in Sandjak and in Vojvodina, and at the situation of the Bulgarian minority,

  Recalling in particular:

(a) Police brutality against ethnic Albanians, killings, arbitrary searches, seizures and arrests, torture and ill-treatment of detainees and discrimination in the public administration;

(b) Discriminatory and arbitrary dismissals of ethnic Albanian civil servants, mass dismissals of ethnic Albanians, discrimination against ethnic Albanian pupils and teachers of primary schools, the closing of the Albanian-language secondary schools and university, as well as the closing of Albanian cultural and scientific institutions;

(c) The intimidation and imprisonment of ethnic Albanian journalists and the systematic harassment and disruption of the news media in the Albanian language;

(d) The dismissals of doctors and members of other categories of the medical profession of ethnic Albanian origin from clinics and hospitals;

(e) The massive arrests, imprisonment and Draconian punishment of ethnic Albanian political and human rights activists during the past year;

(f) The gradual elimination in practice of the Albanian language, particularly in the public administration and services;

(g) The serious and massive occurrence of discriminatory and repressive practices aimed at Kosovo Albanians as a whole, resulting in widespread involuntary emigration;

(h) The attempts at changing the ethnic structure of Kosovo, through a policy of State- sponsored resettlement of refugee Serbian populations in traditional ethnic Albanian communities, as well as through the harassment of ethnic Albanians from Kosovo wishing to return to their homeland,

Gravely concerned that any change to the Citizenship Law may lead to a further deterioration in the situation of human rights and that its purpose may be to change the demographic composition of Kosovo,

Noting with anguish the reports of the Special Rapporteur on the situation of human rights in the territory of the former Yugoslavia, in particular his seventh, eighth, ninth and tenth periodic reports (E/CN.4/1995/4, E/CN.4/1995/10, A/49/641-S/1994/1252, E/CN.4/1995/57) and his special report on the media (E/CN.4/1995/54),

  Noting with special appreciation the continuing efforts of the Special Rapporteur and those under his direction, both in field offices and at the Centre for Human Rights, and regretting that the Special Rapporteur still has not been allowed to open an office in the Federal Republic of Yugoslavia (Serbia and Montenegro),

... 29. *Strongly condemns* the discriminatory measures and practices, as well as the violations of human rights, carried out by the authorities of the Federal Republic of Yugoslavia (Serbia and Montenegro) against ethnic Albanians in Kosovo;

30. *Again demands* that the Federal Republic of Yugoslavia (Serbia and Montenegro) respect the human rights and fundamental freedoms of ethnic Albanians in Kosovo, recalling that the best means to prevent the possible escalation of the conflict is to safeguard human rights and establish democratic institutions in Kosovo;

31. *Urgently demands* that the authorities of the Federal Republic of Yugoslavia (Serbia and Montenegro):

(a) Cease all human rights violations, discriminatory measures and practices against ethnic Albanians in Kosovo, in particular arbitrary detention and violation of the right to a fair trial and the practice of torture and other cruel, inhuman and degrading treatment;

(b) Release all political prisoners and cease the persecution of political leaders and members of local human rights organizations;

(c) Respect the will of the inhabitants of Kosovo, allowing its expression by democratic means as the best way of preventing the escalation of the conflict there;

(d) Guarantee the freedom of the media throughout the country, and in particular in Kosovo, and cease the obstruction of the Albanian-language media in Kosovo;

(e) Abrogate the official settlement policy of the Government of the Federal Republic of Yugoslavia (Serbia and Montenegro), which is conducive to the heightening of ethnic tensions;

(f) Allow the Special Rapporteur to visit Kosovo in order to prepare comprehensive reports on the human rights situation there;

(g) Cooperate with the Organization on Security and Cooperation in Europe to enable the long-term mission to resume its activities immediately, inter alia by permitting its return to Kosovo;

32. *Urges* the Secretary-General to explore ways and means to establish an adequate international monitoring presence in Kosovo;

  ...

35. *Urges* all parties in Serbia and Montenegro, particularly in Kosovo, Sandjak and Vojvodina, to engage in a substantive dialogue, under the auspices of, inter alia, the International Conference on the Former Yugoslavia and the Organization on Cooperation and Security in Europe, to act with the utmost restraint and to settle disputes peacefully and with full respect for human rights;

36. *Demands* that the Federal Republic of Yugoslavia (Serbia and Montenegro) permit entry into Kosovo, Sandjak and Vojvodina of United Nations observer missions and field officers of the Special Rapporteur and resumption of the missions of long duration of the Organization on Security and Cooperation in Europe;

8.   Sub-Commission Resolution 1995/10, Human rights in Kosovo, 18 August 1995

The Sub-Commission on Prevention of Discrimination and Protection of Minorities,

Guided by the Charter of the United Nations, the Universal Declaration of Human Rights, the International Covenants on Human Rights, the International Convention on the Elimination of All Forms of Racial Discrimination, the Convention on the Prevention and Punishment of the Crime of Genocide and the Convention against Torture and Other Cruel, Inhuman or Degrading Treatment or Punishment,

Recalling its resolution 1993/9 of 20 August 1993,

Recalling also Commission on Human Rights resolutions 1992/S-1/1 of 14 August 1992, 1992/S-2/1 of 1 December 1992, 1993/7 of 23 February 1993 and 1994/76 of 9 March 1994, and General Assembly resolution 49/204 of 23 December 1994,

Taking note of the reports of the Special Rapporteur of the Commission on Human Rights on the situation of human rights in the territory of the former Yugoslavia, in which he describes the various discriminatory measures taken in the legislative, administrative and judicial areas, acts of violence and arbitrary arrests and further deterioration of the human rights situation in Kosovo including:

(a) Police brutality against ethnic Albanians, the deaths of ethnic Albanians resulting from such brutality, arbitrary searches, seizures and arrests, forced evictions, torture and ill-treatment of detainees, and discrimination in the administration of justice, including several trials, which are still going on, of former Albanian policemen,

(b) Discriminatory and arbitrary dismissals of ethnic Albanian civil servants, notably from the ranks of the police and the judiciary, mass dismissals of ethnic Albanians, confiscation and expropriation of their property, discrimination against Albanian pupils and teachers, the closing of Albanian language secondary schools and the Albanian university, as well as the closing of Albanian cultural and scientific institutions,

(c) The harassment and persecution of political parties and associations of ethnic Albanians and their leaders and activists who, on a permanent basis, are subjected to inhuman and degrading il-treatment and arrest,

(d) The intimidation, systematic harassment and imprisonment of ethnic Albanian journalists and disruption of the Albanian language news media,

(e) The dismissal of doctors and other medical staff from clinics and hospitals,

(f) The elimination in practice of the Albanian language, particularly in the public administration and services,

(g) The serious and massive occurrence of discriminatory and repressive practices aimed at Kosovo Albanians as a whole, which is resulting in widespread involuntary migration, and noting that these measures and practices constitute a form of silent "ethnic cleansing",

Gravely concerned that the new Citizenship Law awaiting approval by the Parliament of the Federal Republic of Yugoslavia (Serbia and Montenegro) may cause further deterioration of the situation of human rights and that its purpose is to change the demographic composition of Kosovo through new settlement schemes,

Recognizing that the long-term mission of the Organization for Security and Cooperation in Europe to Kosovo played a positive role in monitoring the human rights situation and preventing an escalation of the tension there, and recalling in this context Security Council resolution 855 (1993) of 9 August 1993,

Considering that the re-establishment of the international presence in Kosovo to monitor and investigate the situation of human rights is of the greatest importance in preventing the situation in Kosovo from deteriorating into a violent conflict,

1. *Strongly condemns* the measures and practices of discrimination and the violation of human rights of ethnic Albanians in Kosovo committed by the authorities of the Federal Republic of Yugoslavia (Serbia and Montenegro);

2. *Condemns* the large-scale repression by the police and military of the Federal Republic of Yugoslavia (Serbia and Montenegro) of the defenceless ethnic Albanian population and the discrimination against the ethnic Albanians in education, the administrative and judicial branches of government, health care and employment aimed at forcing ethnic Albanians to leave their land;

3. *Requests* that the authorities of the Federal Republic of Yugoslavia (Serbia and Montenegro):

(a) Take all necessary measures to bring to an immediate end all human rights violations against ethnic Albanians in Kosovo, including, in particular, discriminatory measures and practices, arbitrary searches and detention, violation of the right to a fair trial and the practice of torture and other cruel, inhuman or degrading treatment;

(b) Revoke all discriminatory legislation, in particular that which has entered into force since 1989;

(c) Release all political prisoners in Kosovo;

(d) Establish genuine democratic institutions in Kosovo, including the parliament and judiciary, and respect the will of its inhabitants as the best means of preventing the escalation of conflict there;

(e) Reopen all the cultural and scientific institutions of the ethnic Albanians;

(f) Pursue dialogue with the representatives of ethnic Albanians in Kosovo under the auspices of the International Conference on the Former Yugoslavia;

4. *Demands* that the authorities of the Federal Republic of Yugoslavia (Serbia and Montenegro) cooperate fully and immediately with the Special Rapporteur of the Commission on Human Rights on the situation of human rights in the territory of the former Yugoslavia in the discharge of his functions as requested by the Commission in its resolution 1994/76 and other relevant resolutions;

5. *Encourages* the Secretary-General to pursue his humanitarian efforts in the former Yugoslavia, in liaison with the Office of the United Nations High Commissioner for Refugees, the United Nations Children's Fund and other appropriate humanitarian organizations, with a view to taking urgent practical steps to address the critical needs of the people of Kosovo, especially of the most vulnerable groups affected by the conflict, and to assisting in the voluntary return of displaced persons to their homes;

6. *Urges* the authorities of the Federal Republic of Yugoslavia (Serbia and Montenegro) to allow the immediate and unconditional return of the long-term mission of the Organization for Security and Cooperation in Europe to Kosovo, called for in Security Council resolution 855 (1993);

7. *Requests* the Secretary-General to seek ways and means, including through consultations with the United Nations High Commissioner for Human Rights and relevant regional organizations, to establish an adequate international monitoring presence in Kosovo and to report thereon to the General Assembly;

8. *Calls upon* the Special Rapporteur to continue to monitor closely the human rights situation in Kosovo and to pay special attention to this matter in reporting;

9. *Calls upon* the relevant United Nations bodies not to recognize the legal effects which might derive from the entering into force of the Citizenship Law;

10. *Decides* to continue the examination of the human rights situation in Kosovo at its forty-eighth session, under the same agenda item.

9. Commission Resolution 1996/71, Human rights in the former Yugoslavia, 23 April 1996

The Commission on Human Rights,

...

Deeply concerned as well at the situation of human rights throughout the Federal Republic of Yugoslavia (Serbia and Montenegro), particularly in Kosovo, but also in Sandjak and in Voyvodina,

...

25. *Strongly urges* the authorities of the Federal Republic of Yugoslavia (Serbia and Montenegro) to revoke all discriminatory legislation and to apply all other legislation without discrimination, release all political detainees, allow the free return of ethnic Albanian refugees to Kosovo and take appropriate measures to respect fully all human rights and fundamental freedoms, including freedom of the press and freedom of movement and freedom from discrimination in the field of education and information, and to stop discrimination against and guarantee fully the rights of all persons belonging to any ethnic, national, religious or linguistic minority;

26. *Urgently demands* that the authorities of the Federal Republic of Yugoslavia (Serbia and Montenegro) take immediate action to put an end to the repression of and prevent violence against non-Serb populations in Kosovo, including acts of harassment, beatings, torture, warrantless searches, arbitrary detention, unfair trials, arbitrary unjustified evictions and dismissals, and also to respect the rights of persons belonging to minority groups in Sandjak and Vojvodina and of persons belonging to the Bulgarian minority;

27. *Also urgently demands* that the Federal Republic of Yugoslavia (Serbia and Montenegro) allow ethnic Albanians in Kosovo to participate fully in the life of Kosovo without discrimination and to enjoy political and educational rights, including by allowing the establishment of democratic institutions, and the right to seek, receive and impart information and ideas through any media and, in particular to improve the situation of ethnic Albanian women and children, and to

allow an international presence for monitoring of the human rights situation in Kosovo;

28. *Reiterates its call* to all parties in the Federal Republic of Yugoslavia (Serbia and Montenegro) to engage in a substantive dialogue, to act with the utmost restraint and to settle disputes peacefully and with full respect for human rights, and calls especially upon the Federal Republic of Yugoslavia (Serbia and Montenegro) to pursue dialogue with representatives of ethnic Albanians in Kosovo;

29. *Emphasizes* that improvements in the promotion and protection of human rights and political freedoms in Kosovo and the rest of its territory as well as cooperation with the Tribunal will assist the Federal Republic of Yugoslavia (Serbia and Montenegro) to establish the full range of relations with the international community;

...

45. *Decides* to extend for one year the mandate of the Special Rapporteur as revised in the present resolution, and requests that she continue her vital efforts, especially by carrying out missions to:

(a) The State of Bosnia and Herzegovina;

(b) The Republic of Croatia;

(c) The Federal Republic of Yugoslavia (Serbia and Montenegro), in particular to Kosovo, as well as to Sandjak and Vojvodina, and that she continue to submit periodic reports to the Commission on Human Rights and the General Assembly and to exchange information and advice on the human rights situation in the territories covered by her mandate with the High Representative, the Organization for Security and Cooperation in Europe and other competent organizations, and requests the Secretary-General to continue to make the Special Rapporteur's reports available to the Security Council and to the Organization for Security and Cooperation in Europe; ...

10.   Sub-Commission Resolution 1996/2, Human rights in Kosovo, 19 August 1996

The Sub-Commission on Prevention of Discrimination and Protection of Minorities,

Guided by the Charter of the United Nations, the Universal Declaration of Human Rights, the International Covenants on Human Rights, the International Convention on the Elimination of All Forms of Racial Discrimination, the Convention on the Prevention and Punishment of the Crime of Genocide and the Convention against Torture and Other Cruel, Inhuman or Degrading Treatment or Punishment,

Recalling its resolutions 1993/9 of 20 August 1993 and 1995/10 of 18 August 1995,

Recalling also Commission on Human Rights resolutions 1993/7 of 23 February 1993 and 1994/76 of 9 March 1994, and General Assembly resolutions 49/204 of 23 December 1994 and 50/190 of 22 December 1995,

Gravely concerned at the various discriminatory measures taken in the legislative, administrative and judicial areas, acts of violence and arbitrary arrests committed by the authorities of the Federal Republic of Yugoslavia (Serbia and Montenegro) and the further deterioration of the human rights situation in Kosovo, including:

(a) Police brutality against ethnic Albanians, killings, arbitrary searches, seizures and arrests, forced evictions, torture and ill-treatment of detainees, discrimination in the administration of justice, arbitrary dismissals of civil servants, notably from the ranks of the police and the judiciary, doctors and other medical staff;

(b) Discrimination against Albanian pupils and teachers, and the closing of Albanian-language secondary schools and the university, as well as other cultural and scientific institutions;

(c) The systematic harassment, persecution, intimidation and imprisonment of members of political parties, human rights organizations and journalists, the elimination in practice of the Albanian language in the public administration and services, and the disruption of the Albanian-language media;

(d) The serious and massive occurrence of discriminatory and repressive practices aimed at Kosovo Albanians as a whole, resulting in widespread involuntary migration, and the absence of

clear guarantees for their return home, and noting that these measures and practices constitute a form of silent "ethnic cleansing",

Expressing appreciation at the opening of an office of the United Nations High Commissioner for Human Rights in Belgrade and the establishment of a United States information agency in Prishtina,

Considering that the re-establishment of the international presence in Kosovo to monitor and investigate the situation there is of the greatest importance in preventing the situation in Kosovo from deteriorating into violent conflict, and recalling in this context Security Council resolution 855 (1993) of 9 August 1993,

1. *Strongly condemns* the large-scale repression, measures and practices of discrimination and the violation of human rights committed against the defenceless ethnic Albanian population by the authorities of the Federal Republic of Yugoslavia (Serbia and Montenegro), aimed at forcing ethnic Albanians to leave their land;

2. *Demands* that the authorities of the Federal Republic of Yugoslavia (Serbia and Montenegro):

(a) Take all necessary measures to bring to an immediate end all human rights violations against ethnic Albanians in Kosovo and revoke all discriminatory legislation, in particular that which has entered into force since 1989, and to apply all other legislation without discrimination;

(b) Allow the establishment of genuine democratic institutions in Kosovo, including the parliament and the judiciary, and respect the will of its inhabitants as the best means of preventing the escalation of conflict there;

(c) Reopen all the educational, cultural and scientific institutions of the ethnic Albanians;

(d) Release all political prisoners from Kosovo;

(e) Commence an internationally brokered dialogue with the representatives of the ethnic Albanians in Kosovo;

3. *Encourages* the Secretary-General to pursue his humanitarian efforts in the former Yugoslavia, in liaison with the office of the United Nations High Commissioner for Refugees and other appropriate humanitarian organizations, with a view to taking practical steps towards the safe return of the ethnic Albanian asylum-seekers from Kosovo to their homeland;

4. *Requests* the Secretary-General to seek ways and means, including through consultations with the United Nations High Commissioner for Human Rights and relevant regional organizations, to establish an adequate international monitoring presence in Kosovo and to report thereon to the General Assembly;

5. *Calls upon* the Special Rapporteur on the situation of human rights in the territory of the former Yugoslavia to continue to monitor closely the human rights situation in Kosovo and to pay special attention to this matter in her reporting;

6. *Decides* to continue the examination of the situation of human rights in Kosovo at its next session, under the agenda item entitled "Question of the violation of human rights and fundamental freedoms, including policies of racial discrimination and segregation and of apartheid, in all countries, with particular reference to colonial and other dependent countries and territories: report of the Sub-Commission under Commission on Human Rights resolution 8 (XXIII)".

11.   Commission Resolution 1997/57, Human rights in the former Yugoslavia, 15 April 1997

The Commission on Human Rights,

...

VII. Federal Republic of Yugoslavia (Serbia and Montenegro)

29. *Calls upon* the Government of the Federal Republic of Yugoslavia (Serbia and Montenegro):

(a) To undertake substantially greater efforts to institute and implement fully democratic norms, especially in regard to respect for the principle of free and fair elections and protection of free and independent media, and to ensure full respect for human rights and fundamental freedoms;

(b) To expand opportunities for the independent media, institute non-partisan management of the State-owned media and cease efforts to restrict press and broadcast journalism;

(c) To cease torture and ill-treatment of persons in detention as described in the report of the Special Rapporteur (E/CN.4/1997/9), and to bring those responsible to justice;

(d) To revoke any discriminatory legislation, to apply all other legislation without discrimination and to take urgent action to prevent arbitrary evictions and dismissals and discrimination against any ethnic or national, religious or linguistic group;

(e) To respect the rights of persons belonging to minority groups, especially in Sandjak and Vojvodina, and of persons belonging to the Bulgarian and Croatian minorities;

(f) To take immediate action, in view of the deteriorating situation in Kosovo and the danger of escalating violence there, to put an end to the continuing repression of and prevent violence against the ethnic Albanian population, including acts of harassment, beatings, torture, warrantless searches, arbitrary detention, unfair trials, and arbitrary, unjustified evictions and dismissals;

(g) To release all political detainees, allow the return in safety and dignity of ethnic Albanian refugees to Kosovo and respect fully all human rights and fundamental freedoms, including freedom of the press, freedom of movement and freedom from discrimination in the field of education and information;

(h) To allow the establishment of democratic institutions in Kosovo and the right to seek, receive and impart information and ideas through any media, and in particular to improve the situation of ethnic Albanian women and children, and to allow an international presence for monitoring of the human rights situation;

(i) Following the welcome establishment of an office of the High Commissioner/Centre for Human Rights in Belgrade and continued cooperation with the Special Rapporteur, to broaden its cooperation with institutions concerned with human rights, in particular by allowing the High Commissioner for Human Rights and the European Union to establish a presence in Pristina (Kosovo), and to allow visits by the personal representative of the Chairman in Office of the Organization for Security and Cooperation in Europe in Kosovo;

30. *Calls once again upon* all parties in the Federal Republic of Yugoslavia (Serbia and Montenegro) to engage in a substantive dialogue, to act with the utmost restraint and with full respect for human rights, and to refrain from acts of violence, and calls especially upon the Federal Republic of Yugoslavia (Serbia and Montenegro) to pursue dialogue with representatives of ethnic Albanians in Kosovo;

31. *Emphasizes* that improvements in the promotion and protection of human rights and political freedoms in Kosovo and the rest of its territory as well as cooperation with the International Tribunal will assist the Federal Republic of Yugoslavia (Serbia and Montenegro) to establish the full range of relations with the international community;

32. *Calls upon* the international community:

(a) To establish appropriate safeguards to ensure the security and fair treatment upon return of those who sought temporary protection and asylum, including appropriate measures by Governments, such as legal guarantees and follow-up mechanisms, to allow these persons to return to their homes in the Federal Republic of Yugoslavia (Serbia and Montenegro) in safety and dignity;

(b) To continue to support existing national democratic forces and non-governmental organizations in their efforts to build a civil society and achieve multi-party democracy in the Federal Republic of Yugoslavia (Serbia and Montenegro);

...

IX. Special Rapporteur

41. *Requests* the Special Rapporteur, in addition to the activities mandated in Commission resolutions 1994/72 and 1996/71:

(a) To focus her future activities on prevention and reporting of violations of, and lack of action to protect, all human rights and fundamental freedoms by governmental authorities, particularly violations that exacerbate ethnic tension, and on protecting the rights of persons belonging to minorities, women and vulnerable

groups such as children and the elderly, particularly their right to return to their homes in safety and dignity;

...

(c) To contribute to efforts for the building of democratic institutions and the improvement of the administration of justice, for the prevention and reporting of violations by civil authorities, particularly violations that exacerbate ethnic tension, and for the protection of the rights of persons belonging to minorities, women and vulnerable groups such as children and the elderly, particularly their right to return to their homes in safety and dignity;

...

(e) To provide the Commission at its fifty-fourth session with her overview of the human rights situation in the territories covered by her mandate, as requested in its resolution 1996/71;

42. *Decides* to extend for one year the mandate of the Special Rapporteur as revised in the present resolution, and requests that she continue her vital efforts, especially by continuing to carry out missions to:

(a) The Republic of Bosnia and Herzegovina;

(b) The Republic of Croatia, including Eastern Slavonia, Baranja and Western Sirmium;

(c) The Federal Republic of Yugoslavia (Serbia and Montenegro), including to Kosovo, as well as to Sandjak and Vojvodina; and that she continue to submit periodic reports to the General Assembly and the Commission on Human Rights; ...

12. Commission Resolution 1998/79, Human rights in the former Yugoslavia, 22 April 1998

The Commission on Human Rights,

...

18. *Further welcomes* the deployment of additional human rights officers in Kosovo;

19. *Endorses* the recommendations of the Special Rapporteur as contained in his report on his visit to the Federal Republic of Yugoslavia, including Kosovo (E/CN.4/1998/164), in particular:

(a) That the Federal Republic of Yugoslavia should permit forensic investigation by independent experts concerning the 28 February 1998 operations in Likosani and Cirez and the 5 March 1998 operations in Prekaz, and should also conduct its own investigation of these events;

(b) That the Kosovo Albanian leadership should commit itself to ensure that the Kosovo Albanian community shall pursue their goals only by peaceful means;

(c) That all parties should allow free access for international and humanitarian organizations and the establishment of a temporarily expanded office of the United Nations High Commissioner for Human Rights operating out of the permanent premises to be established in Kosovo;

20. *Regrets* that the Federal Republic Yugoslavia has complied only partially with the recommendations of the Chairman in Office of the Organization for Security and Cooperation in Europe regarding fostering democracy and the rule of law;

21. *Also regrets* the express refusal of the Federal Republic of Yugoslavia to allow a visit by the Special Rapporteur on extrajudicial, summary or arbitrary executions;

22. *Calls upon* authorities in the Federal Republic of Yugoslavia:

(a) To comply with the recommendations contained in the reports of the Special Rapporteur;

(b) To comply also with its obligation to cooperate with the Tribunal;

(c) To undertake substantially greater efforts to strengthen and implement fully democratic norms, especially in regard to respect for the principle of free and fair elections, the rule of law, and full respect for human rights and fundamental freedoms, and to improve its performance in the area of the administration of justice;

(d) To protect and expand opportunities for free and independent media, institute non-partisan management of the State-owned media and cease efforts to restrict press and broadcast journalism;

(e) To put an end to torture and ill-treatment of persons in detention as described in the reports of the Special Rapporteur, and to bring those responsible to justice;

(f) To repeal the 1989 Law on Special Conditions for Real Property Transactions and to apply all other legislation without discrimination;

(g) To respect the rights of persons belonging to minority groups, especially in Sandjak and Vojvodina, and of persons belonging to the Bulgarian and Croatian minorities;

23. *Condemns* violent repression of non-violent expression of political views in Kosovo, in particular the brutal police actions and the excessive use of force against the civilian population, including demonstrators and journalists among the Albanian population, condemns as well the killing of innocent civilians, equally condemns terrorism in all its forms and from any quarter, and underscores the grave concern of member States regarding the increasingly serious situation there;

24. *Urges* all parties in the Federal Republic of Yugoslavia to act with the utmost restraint and with full respect for human rights, and to refrain from acts of violence;

25. *Insists* that the Government of the Federal Republic of Yugoslavia:

(a) Take immediate action, in view of the deteriorating situation in Kosovo and the danger of escalating violence there, to put an end to the continuing repression of and prevent violence against the ethnic Albanian population, as well as other communities living in Kosovo, including acts of harassment, beatings, brutality, torture, warrantless searches, arbitrary detention, unfair trials and arbitrary, unjustified evictions and dismissals;

(b) Ensure the complete withdrawal of its special police from Kosovo;

(c) Release all political detainees, allow the return in safety and in dignity of ethnic Albanian refugees to Kosovo and respect fully all human rights and fundamental freedoms, including freedom of the press, freedom of movement and freedom from discrimination in the field of education and information, and, in particular, improve the situation of ethnic Albanian women and children;

(d) Allow the establishment of democratic institutions in Kosovo;

(e) Agree to the establishment of an office of the High Commissioner for Human Rights in Pristina;

(f) Broaden cooperation with other regional and international actors, including by allowing the return of the long-term missions of the Organization for Security and Cooperation in Europe, visits by the personal representative of the ChairmaninOffice of the Organization for Security and Cooperation in Europe and the establishment of a European Union presence in Kosovo;

(g) Implement the September 1996 "Sant'Egidio" memorandum of understanding on education in Kosovo immediately and without conditions, including at the university level, as an important first step towards reducing regional tensions, while welcoming efforts made in that regard;

26. *Emphasizes* the importance of a substantive, unconditional dialogue between authorities in Belgrade and the Kosovo Albanian leadership aimed at achieving a lasting solution to the problems of Kosovo consistent with the territorial integrity of the Federal Republic of Yugoslavia, and notes the proposals made by the Government of the Federal Republic of Yugoslavia in that direction;

27. *Also emphasizes* that improvements in the promotion and protection of human rights and political freedoms in Kosovo and the rest of its territory as well as cooperation with the Tribunal, will assist the Federal Republic of Yugoslavia to improve relations with the international community;

28. *Welcomes* positive developments in Montenegro, including in the areas of freedom of the media and the treatment of ethnic minorities, and also welcomes the formation of a multi-ethnic coalition government;

29. *Calls upon* the international community:

(a) To establish appropriate safeguards to ensure the security and fair treatment upon return of those who sought temporary protection and asylum, including appropriate measures by Governments, such as legal guarantees and follow-up mechanisms, to allow those persons to return to their homes in the Federal Republic of Yugoslavia in safety and in dignity;

(b) To continue to support existing national democratic forces and non-governmental organizations in their efforts to build a civil society and achieve multi-party democracy in the Federal Republic of Yugoslavia;

V. International Criminal Tribunal for the Former Yugoslavia

30. *Calls upon* all States and, in particular, all parties to the Peace Agreement, especially the Government of the Federal Republic of Yugoslavia, to meet their obligations to cooperate fully with the Tribunal, noting that there is no valid constitutional or statutory reason for failure to cooperate, and urges all States and the Secretary-General to support the Tribunal to the fullest extent possible, in particular by helping to ensure that persons indicted by the Tribunal stand trial before it and, as a matter of urgency, by continuing to make available to the Tribunal adequate resources to aid in the fulfilment of its mandate, including through the provision of legal and technical expertise;

...

33. *Calls upon* authorities in the Federal Republic of Yugoslavia to comply with their obligation to cooperate with the Tribunal, including with regard to events in Kosovo, on the basis of Security Council resolution 1160 (1998) of 31 March 1998, and strongly recommends that the Office of the Prosecutor of the Tribunal begin gathering information relating to the violence in Kosovo that may fall within its jurisdiction;

...

VII. Special Rapporteur

...

48. *Decides* to renew the mandate of the Special Rapporteur for one year and welcomes the appointment of a new Special Rapporteur on the situation of human rights in Bosnia and Herzegovina, the Republic of Croatia and the Federal Republic of Yugoslavia;

49. *Requests* the new Special Rapporteur, in addition to the activities mandated in Commission resolutions 1994/72 of 9 March 1994, 1996/71 of 23 April 1996 and 1997/57 of 15 April 1997:

(a) To work with the High Commissioner for Human Rights on behalf of the United Nations in dealing with the question of missing persons, including by participation in the International Commission on Missing Persons advisory group and other groups involved in missing persons issues, such as those chaired by the Office of the High Representative and the International Committee of the Red Cross, and to include in his report to the Commission on Human Rights information about activities concerning missing persons in the former Yugoslavia;

(b) To pay particular attention to the situation of persons belonging to ethnic minorities, displaced persons, refugees and returnees who fall within his mandate;

(c) To address human rights issues that transcend the borders between the States covered by his mandate and which can be addressed only through concerted action in more than one country;

50. <u>Requests</u> that the Special Rapporteur carry out missions to:

(a) Bosnia and Herzegovina;

(b) The Republic of Croatia, including Eastern Slavonia, Baranja and Western Sirmium;

(c) The Federal Republic of Yugoslavia, including to Kosovo, as well as to Sandjak and Vojvodina; ...

C. Decisions of United Nations Treaty-based Human Rights Bodies

CCPR/C/79/Add.16

1. Comments of the Human Rights Committee, FRY, 28 December 1992

1. Deeply concerned by recent and current events in the territory of the former Yugoslavia affecting human rights protected under the International Covenant on Civil and Political Rights; noting that all the peoples within the territory of the former Yugoslavia are entitled to the guarantees of the Covenant; and acting under article 40, paragraph 1 (b), of the Covenant; the Committee, on 7 October 1992, requested the Government of the Federal Republic of Yugoslavia (Serbia and Montenegro) to submit a short report on the following issues in respect of persons and events now coming under its jurisdiction:

(a) Measures taken to prevent and combat the policy of "ethnic cleansing" pursued, according to several reports, on the territory of certain parts of the former Yugoslavia, in relation to articles 6 and 12 of the International Covenant on Civil and Political Rights;

(b) Measures taken to prevent arbitrary arrests and killings of persons, as well as disappearances, in relation to articles 6 and 9 of the International Covenant on Civil and Political Rights;

(c) Measures taken to prevent arbitrary executions, torture and other inhuman treatment in detention camps, in relation to articles 6, 7 and 10 of the International Covenant on Civil and Political Rights;

(d) Measures taken to combat advocacy of national, racial or religious hatred constituting incitement to discrimination, hostility or violence, in relation to article 20 of the International Covenant on Civil and Political Rights.

… 3. The Committee welcomed the delegation, explaining that it regarded the submission of the report by the Government and the presence of the delegation as confirmation that the Federal Republic of Yugoslavia (Serbia and Montenegro) had succeeded, in respect of its territory, to the obligations undertaken under the International Covenant on Civil and Political Rights by the former Socialist Federal Republic of Yugoslavia. …

4. In its replies, the Federal Government referred exclusively to the situation in the territory of Serbia and Montenegro. It mentioned a number of instances of criminal proceedings taken against persons responsible for violations of individual freedoms (32 cases) and ethnic cleansing (5 cases). The Government affirmed that those were isolated acts and that it was not conducting any policy of ethnic cleansing. It indicated that there was no concentration camp established in its territory. It said it was dismayed by the atrocities committed in certain parts of Croatia and Bosnia and Herzegovina but declared that it could not assume responsibility for acts committed outside its territory and hence beyond its control. In regard to Kosovo, the Government did not dispute its responsibility but attributed the current state of affairs in that region to antagonism, which it was difficult to overcome, between the Serbs and the Albanian "minority". …

8. The Committee firmly urged the Federal Government to put an end to this intolerable situation for the observance of human rights, and to refrain from any support for those committing such acts, including in territory outside the Federal Republic of Yugoslavia (Serbia and Montenegro). It called upon the Government to show a clear political will and to effectively dissociate itself from the Serbian nationalist movements by totally repudiating their ideology and condemning their schemes. The Committee considers that a show of unwavering firmness on this point would deprive the extremists of support that is essential to them. The Federal Government was invited to do its utmost to foster public awareness of the need to combat national hatred and to crack down forcefully on the perpetrators of violations of individual rights by bringing them to justice. The Committee also recommended that the Federal Government put an end to the repression of the Albanian population in the province of Kosovo and adopt all necessary measures to restore the former local self-government in the province.

2. Concluding Observations, the Committee on Elimination of Racial Discrimination: Yugoslavia, 15 September 1993

509. At its 984th meeting, held on 19 March 1993, the Committee expressed its grave concern over the ongoing ethnic conflict taking place in the territory of the former Yugoslavia and requested the Government of the Federal Republic of Yugoslavia (Serbia and Montenegro), as well as other successor Governments, in accordance with article 9, paragraph 1, of the Convention, to submit further information on the implementation of the Convention, not later than 31 July 1993.

510. The report (CERD/C/248) submitted by the Federal Republic of Yugoslavia (Serbia and Montenegro) pursuant to the aforementioned decision was considered by the Committee at its 1003rd, 1004th, 1005th and 1006th meetings, held on 13 and 16 August 1993 (see CERD/C/SR.1003-1006).

511. The report was introduced by the representative of the State party, who said that disrespect for and denial of the right to self-determination to all peoples in the territory of the former Yugoslavia had led to the tragic conflict there with its resulting destruction, ethnic cleansing, mass exoduses and population displacements.

512. The representative stated that the crisis had been compounded by international interference and, in particular, the imposition of sanctions against the Federal Republic of Yugoslavia (Serbia and Montenegro) which had led to a collective condemnation of a people and which was contrary to the spirit of the International Convention on the Elimination of All Forms of Racial Discrimination. Those sanctions threatened not only the rights of the citizens of the Federal Republic of Yugoslavia (Serbia and Montenegro) but also those of the more than 600,000 refugees who had fled to the country regardless of their national or religious background. The resulting political, economic and social climate had eroded public security and the rule of law and had strengthened extremist forces pressing for intolerance and prejudice.

513. With respect to national minorities in the Federal Republic of Yugoslavia (Serbia and Montenegro), the representative stated that the legal system guaranteed minorities even greater rights than those provided for in international norms, including those agreed upon by the Conference on Security and Cooperation in Europe (CSCE). Additionally, work on the Federal Law on Minorities was in its final phase and would provide a further guarantee concerning the rights of members of minorities both as individuals and as a collectivity.

514. The representative stated that the issue of minority rights in the Federal Republic of Yugoslavia (Serbia and Montenegro) had been politicized and abused. In that connection, the Albanian national minority in Kosmet (Kosovo) and Metohija had clearly secessionist objectives and had tried to promote the "Kosovo Republic" idea in the Working Group on Ethnic and National Minorities of the International Conference on the Former Yugoslavia. That was being done despite the fact that constitutional provisions guaranteed Kosmet territorial and cultural autonomy, as well as the right to regulate questions in the fields of development, health, social protection and culture, including the use of the national minority language. Unfortunately, members of the Albanian national minority had almost completely boycotted school curricula in their own language. Similarly, there had been a decrease in the number of Albanians in the judiciary, police force and health institutions, which was due not to discrimination or expulsion from work but to their refusal to recognize the legitimate authorities of the State.

515. The situation in Vojvodina and Sandzak had also been politicized as part of the pressure being applied to the Federal Republic of Yugoslavia (Serbia and Montenegro). In Vojvodina, there were about 344,000 members of the Hungarian national minority whose ethnic, cultural, linguistic and religious identity was completely guaranteed. In places where there was a greater number of Hungarians, they held a majority in all the institutions of authority, including education, the economy and social life. With respect to the Raska (Sandzak) region, it was no more than a geographic area and the problems of the rights and status of Muslims living there had been politically imposed and artificially construed.

516. Members of the Committee expressed satisfaction that the State party had submitted further information as had been requested and that a delegation had been sent from the capital to respond to the questions posed by the Committee. Members noted that although the report contained useful information on the legal framework for the protection of national and ethnic minorities, there was little information on the actual situation of the various minorities and the extent to which their rights were protected in reality. There was also little information on the tense situation prevailing in certain regions of the State where there had been serious violations of the Convention and where ethnic tensions threatened to escalate into armed conflict.

517. Members of the Committee referred to information from other sources on the situation in the Federal Republic of Yugoslavia (Serbia and Montenegro), in particular the report of the Special Rapporteur on the situation of human rights in the territory of the former Yugoslavia (E/CN.4/1993/50). In that regard, members of the Committee wished to have further information on restrictions on the media in Kosovo and on problems that had arisen in the educational sector there following the reported changes in the school curricula which suppressed Albanian culture. Members also requested clarification on a number of laws listed in the report of the Special Rapporteur which were reported to be discriminatory in nature (see E/CN.4/1993/50, para. 156).

518. Members expressed their concern over the deterioration of the situation in Kosovo and wished to know why the autonomous status of that province had been revoked and the provincial courts there had been abolished. Regret was expressed over the fact that the Albanians there had chosen not to participate in social and public life. Emphasizing the need to foster a dialogue between the Government and the local minority leaders in Kosovo, members wished to know what active steps the Government was undertaking with a view to reducing tension and normalizing the situation there.

519. Members were particularly concerned over reports of police brutality, arbitrary arrests, disappearances and mass dismissals of the Albanian national minority in Kosovo and wished to know what had been done to investigate those reports and punish those responsible for such acts. Members also wished to know to what extent Albanian language newspapers, radio broadcasts and television programmes were still available in Kosovo. ...

522. Stressing the need for ongoing monitoring of ethnic tensions in the State party, members wished to know why the Government had so far declined to renew the mandate of the CSCE monitoring missions in Kosovo, Vojvodina and Sandzak.

523. Members also wished to have further information on the role of government officials in inciting the public to ethnic intolerance and violence; on discriminatory practices concerning employment, education and housing; on reported frequent harassment of gypsies by the police; and on the number of ethnic Bulgarians in the Federal Republic of Yugoslavia (Serbia and Montenegro), their participation in government and measures taken to facilitate the use of their language. Members also requested clarification on the extent to which the Federal army was linked to activities in neighbouring States where massive human rights violations and ethnic cleansing had been occurring.

524. Members wished to know whether the Federal Republic of Yugoslavia (Serbia and Montenegro) was considering making the declaration under article 14 of the Convention recognizing the competence of the Committee to receive individual complaints alleging violations of the Convention.

525. Replying to the questions, the representative of the State party stated that there was significant representation of minority groups at all levels of government and he provided detailed figures to that effect. With reference to problems concerning education in Kosovo, the representative stated that the ethnic Albanians were the only minority in the Federal Republic of Yugoslavia (Serbia and Montenegro) who refused to exercise their rights and had chosen to boycott the schools. As a result, there were 466 schools for ethnic Albanians in Kosovo which were not used. There were a large number of schools which had been provided for the use of other minorities in Kosovo as well as in Vojvodina and Sandzak and which were used.

526. With regard to the mass media, the representative stated that public information facilities were controlled by minority groups and

that special resources were made available to them in order to support their operation. Specific information was given indicating that there were many newspapers and weeklies as well as radio and television programmes in minority languages throughout the country. In particular, such facilities were provided in the Hungarian, Slovak, Albanian, Russian, Romanian, Ukrainian and Bulgarian languages.

527. With respect to the war crimes tribunal which was to be established pursuant to the decision of the Security Council, cooperation with that body would depend on decisions taken by Parliament, particularly concerning amnesty and extradition laws.

528. Concerning the CSCE monitoring missions in certain areas of the country, the Government had no objection to those missions and there had been cooperation in that regard. The agreement had not been extended beyond the original six-month mandate, however, because the participation of the Federal Republic of Yugoslavia (Serbia and Montenegro) in CSCE had not been clarified. The Federal Republic of Yugoslavia (Serbia and Montenegro) sought only to participate as a member of that body and, thereby, in the decisions affecting its own future.

529. The representative stressed that the Government was open to dialogue with all minorities in the country. He stated that international criticism of the Federal Republic of Yugoslavia (Serbia and Montenegro) had not been objective and that there had been mistakes and shortcomings on all sides which had contributed to the problems which the region was currently experiencing. He declared his Government's willingness to fulfil its obligations under the Convention and to cooperate with the Committee as well as other international bodies in the search for constructive solutions.

Concluding observations

530. At its 1012th meeting, held on 20 August 1993, the Committee adopted the following concluding observations.

(a) Introduction

531. The Committee noted that the report submitted by the State party contained information on the ethnic composition of the population, on the possibilities for minorities in the field of education and in public life and on the legal framework for the implementation of the Convention. However, the report did not reflect the actual situation of national and ethnic minorities in the Federal Republic of Yugoslavia (Serbia and Montenegro) or the current grave situation and tensions prevailing in certain parts of the State.

532. The Committee noted that its dialogue with the State party over the past several years had not been fruitful, with major discrepancies having become apparent between the provisions of the Convention and realities in the country. The Committee underlined the importance it attached to not only maintaining an open and constructive dialogue with States parties, but also to a practical follow-up of its suggestions and recommendations by the Federal Republic of Yugoslavia (Serbia and Montenegro).

(b) Positive aspects

533. The Committee welcomed the timely submission of the requested information and the presence of a delegation as an indication of the State party's willingness to continue the dialogue with the Committee.

534. The Committee took note of information made available to it regarding the Federal Ministry for Human and Minority Rights and of measures under consideration to provide a legal framework for the protection of the rights of members of minorities.

535. The Committee welcomed the interest shown by the delegation of the Federal Republic of Yugoslavia (Serbia and Montenegro) in an active role for the Committee with respect to re-establishing a dialogue between the interested parties in Kosovo within the framework of the early warning measures and urgent procedures devised by the Committee in its working paper of March 1993 (annex III).

(c) Principal subjects of concern

...

538. The Committee expressed alarm over the deteriorating situation in Kosovo. A number of measures had been implemented there which were in violation of the provisions of the Convention, including the enactment of discriminatory laws, the closing of minority schools, the mass dismissal of Albanians from their jobs and the imposition of restrictions on the use of the Albanian language. Such measures had

resulted in the increasing marginalization of the Albanians in Kosovo. In that regard, the Committee noted that Albanians in Kosovo did not participate in public life.

539. The Committee was deeply concerned by reports indicating that in Kosovo, as well as in Vojvodina and Sandzak, members of national minorities had been subject to a campaign of terror carried out by paramilitary organizations with the aim of intimidating or forcing them into abandoning their homes. The Committee also noted that information provided by the Government referred to such practices directed against Serbs in Kosovo. The Committee was particularly concerned that the Government of the Federal Republic of Yugoslavia (Serbia and Montenegro) had not ensured that public security and law enforcement officials took steps effectively to prohibit such criminal activities, punish the perpetrators and compensate the victims, as required under article 6 of the Convention. The Committee was also concerned that other minorities in other regions of the Federal Republic of Yugoslavia (Serbia and Montenegro) were suffering from various forms of discrimination.

540. The Committee regretted the absence of a dialogue between the Government and the leaders of the Albanians in Kosovo aimed at reducing tension and helping to prevent further massive human rights violations in the region. In that connection, the Committee regretted the recent lapse of the mission of the Conference on Security and Cooperation in Europe (CSCE), which was monitoring ethnic tension and human rights violations in Kosovo, as well as in Vojvodina and Sandzak.

541. The Committee was also concerned that Serbs in Bosnia and Herzegovina were hindering the attempts of the Government of that State to implement the Convention.

(d) *Suggestions and recommendations*

542. The Committee underlined that non-discrimination in the enjoyment of fundamental, civil, political, economic, social and cultural rights must be effectively guaranteed in law and actively protected in practice if further ethnic unrest was to be avoided. The Committee in no way encouraged unilateral trends towards separatism or secession. In that connection, the Committee noted that separatism could best be discouraged by the active promotion and protection of minority rights and inter-ethnic tolerance.

543. The Committee recommended that, in conformity with articles 2 and 4 of the Convention, the Government should prohibit racial discrimination and should urgently take vigorous steps to ban racist activities and propaganda. In that connection it was vital that paramilitary groups be disbanded, reports of ethnically motivated attacks, including allegations of arbitrary arrests, disappearance and torture, promptly investigated and those responsible punished. The Committee emphasized the importance of providing proper training in human rights norms for law enforcement officials in accordance with its General Recommendation XIII and of ensuring the equitable representation among their ranks of national minorities

544. The Committee strongly emphasized the need for urgent measures in respect of the situation in Kosovo in order to prevent persisting ethnic problems there from escalating into violence and armed conflict. The Committee recommended, in particular, that all possible measures be taken by both sides to foster dialogue between the Government and the leaders of Albanians in Kosovo. The Committee recommended that the Government of the Federal Republic of Yugoslavia (Serbia and Montenegro) strengthen the territorial integrity of the State by considering ways of assuring autonomy in Kosovo with a view to ensuring the effective representation of the Albanians in political and judicial institutions and their participation in democratic processes.

...

Further action

546. Taking into account the wish expressed by the representative of the Government and the need to promote a dialogue between the Albanians in Kosovo and the Government, the Committee offered its good offices in the form of a mission of its members. The purpose of the mission would be to help promote a dialogue for a peaceful solution of issues concerning respect for human rights in Kosovo, in particular the elimination of all forms of racial discrimination and, whenever possible, to help parties concerned arrive at such a solution. It was

understood that such a mission should have every opportunity to inform itself of the situation directly, including full discussion with central and local authorities, as well as with individuals and organizations. In that connection, no one should be victimized for, or in any way have their rights or security impaired as a result of, cooperating with the mission. The Committee requested the State party to respond by 1 October 1993 if it wished to accept that offer, in which case the Chairman, after due consultations, would designate members of the Committee for such a mission.

547. In accordance with article 9, paragraph 1, of the Convention, the Committee requested further information from the State party on measures taken to implement the provisions of the Convention, particularly in view of the concluding observations adopted by the Committee at its forty-third session. The State party was requested to provide that information by 1 January 1994 so that it might be considered by the Committee at its forty-fourth session.

CERD/C/248/Add.1, 15 September 1994

3. CERD, Supplementary Report of the FRY, 29 August 1994

... Autonomous Province of Kosovo and Metohija

13. As for the problems besetting the Autonomous Province of Kosovo and Metohija, the Federal Government wishes to take this opportunity to thank the esteemed members of the Committee for the understanding shown in assessing the situation and especially for the clearly expressed view that the Committee does not in any manner encourage unilateral trends towards separatism or secession.

14. The Constitution of the Republic of Serbia defines this Republic as a democratic State of all the citizens living in it, based on civil freedoms and human rights, with the sovereignty belonging to all its citizens. The Autonomous Province of Kosovo and Metohija, as well as the Autonomous Province of Vojvodina, have been constituted in conformity with their distinctive national, historic, cultural and other characteristics and it is in them that citizens implement their constitutional and legal rights and duties. They have a status of territorial autonomy, [?] No international act gives the right to a national minority to have its own territorial autonomy (which the Constitution of the Republic of Serbia de jure does with respect to the Albanian national minority). The highest standards in this domain (the CSCE Copenhagen Conference on the Human Dimension) provide for the *possibility of constituting local or autonomous administrative organs which correspond to the specific historic and territorial conditions for those minorities and are in tune with the policy pursued by the State concerned.* and the right to regulate matters of importance to economic development, financing, culture, education, the use of language, health care and social security, etc. The Statute is the supreme legal act of an autonomous province, and its organs include the Assembly, the Executive Council and the agencies of government administration. Persons belonging to the Albanian minority living outside the territory of the Autonomous Province of Kosovo and Metohija but within the Republic of Serbia and the Republic of Montenegro exercise their rights as guaranteed by the constitutions of these two republics and take part in their parliamentary deliberations.

15. The Constitution of the Republic of Serbia and the Constitution of the Federal Republic of Yugoslavia guarantee the highest standards in the area of protection of civil and human rights, including national minority rights. However, a large share of Albanians either do not use those rights or obstruct them on orders issued by certain representatives of the Albanian minority who regard themselves as the representatives of all Albanians living in Kosovo and Metohija, and whose aim it is to secede from the Republic of Serbia and the Federal Republic of Yugoslavia. Guided by that goal, Albanian separatist leaders have created a parallel government system, the so-called "Republic of Kosovo", and are in part responsible for the absence of the Albanian population from the 1991 population census, as well as for the non-use by them of their election rights during the vote for the government authorities of the Republic of Serbia and the Federal Republic of Yugoslavia in the period from 1990 up to the latest elections held on 19 December 1993. (They failed to turn up for the republic elections three times, for the federal election twice and were also absent from the local elections.)

16. In pursuit of their goal, the Albanian separatist forces organized in 1981 the well-known violent mass demonstrations (the use of force against the Socialist Federal Republic of Yugoslavia and the Socialist Republic of

Serbia was not condemned by the international forums at that time); the barricading of mineworkers in shafts; and the abuse of children for the purpose of simulating mass poisoning of exclusively Albanian children in schools (the biological cause which acts on a nationality basis has not been isolated to date by any domestic or international health organization). The last straw was the illegal referendum and the adoption of the so-called "Kacanik Constitution" in 1991 and the election of a segregationist parliament, inaccessible to non-Albanians in Kosovo and Metohija. Soon after this, in May the following year, the presidential election was held in the "newly-formed republic" and the leader of the Democratic Party of Kosovo (DSK) was elected as the first President. The self-same DSK called on the Albanian national minority in the same month, as well as in December of the same year, to boycott the elections in the Republic of Serbia for the deputies to the Parliaments in the Federal Republic of Yugoslavia.

17. Pursuant to its constitutional and legal commitments, but also in the spirit of international instruments, i.e. articles 37 and 40, item 3 of the document adopted at the Copenhagen session of the Conference on Security and Cooperation in Europe (CSCE), Conference on the Human Dimension, the Charter of the United Nations and the Charter of Paris, the Republic of Serbia and Yugoslavia had to protect their territorial integrity, their legal and constitutional set-up, as well as the non-Albanians and the Albanian population who offered resistance in Kosovo and Metohija to discrimination and threats to their ethnic, cultural, linguistic and religious identity, and to their property, and who opposed certain groups of Albanian secessionists and terrorists which had set as their ultimate goal the overthrow of the set-up of the Republic of Serbia (annex I.6 to the Paris Charter), by suspending for a specified time period the Assembly and the Executive Council of the Socialist Autonomous Province (SAP) of Kosovo and Metohija, but not its territorial autonomy. Meanwhile, the Republic of Serbia repealed the laws on the temporary suspension of the Assembly and the Executive Council of SAP Kosovo, as well as the Law on the Suspension of the Presidency of the SAP Kosovo, whereby conditions were re-established for the calling of provincial elections and the constitution of the provincial administration, i.e. the Assembly and its executive, which the representatives of the Albanian minority did not wish to make use of.

18. In the period between 1981 and 1988 (in the Socialist Autonomous Province of the Socialist Federal Republic of Yugoslavia) illegal Albanian terrorist groups committed over 500 assaults on military personnel and their families, along with 80 assaults on military units and 251 assaults on military installations. Nine illegal terrorist organizations and 93 groups were uncovered. A number of individual terrorist assaults were carried out by Albanians against persons belonging to the then Yugoslav People's Army (JNA)-several privates of the then JNA belonging to the Serb, Croat, Muslim and other nationalities were insidiously shot down in the barracks at Paracin. Searches led to the seizure of 5,000 guns, 427 military and 74 amateur rifles, 7 semi-automatic rifles, 117 hand grenades, 1,446 hunting rifles (without licence), 8,000 kilograms of explosives and 146 detonators. The data covering the period from 1988 to date have not been sorted out, but already point to the dramatic deterioration of the situation in this regard.

19. What is important is that the Federal Republic of Yugoslavia has strictly complied with the Convention against Torture and Other Forms of Cruel, Inhuman or Degrading Punishment or Treatment and that not a single case of death has been reported from the prisons in Kosovo and Metohija on account of alleged abuse. Currently 119 persons are on trial, suspected of having committed criminal offences against the constitutional order and security of the Federal Republic of Yugoslavia, namely: three persons for the criminal offence of sabotage; 116 persons for association and preparation to commit the criminal offence of violating territorial integrity. The perpetrators resorted to the formation of paramilitary units; illegal procurement and keeping of large quantities of armaments, ammunition, explosives and medical supplies designed to help the armed struggle against the armed forces of Serbia and Yugoslavia; organized distribution of propaganda materials calling for armed struggle; and organized fund-raising campaigns so as to purchase weaponry, ammunition and uniforms. They also formed illegal paramilitary armed formations in threesomes; organized illegal military training; introduced record-keeping on persons fit for military service; arranged for the setting up of numerous headquarters; drew up instructions on armed rebellion; developed mobilization plans; organized a military headquarters of the so-called Republic of Kosovo, etc.

20. In the period 1981-1988, over 28,000 Serbs and Montenegrins were forced to abandon their homes in the pervading atmosphere of fear, disinformation and the resulting instability, disorder, rape and plunder by Albanian terrorist-separatist forces.

21. As compared to the situation before the Second World War where the share of Serbs in the population was on a par with that of Albanians, the latter share has quadrupled. Over 400,000 Serbs and Montenegrins had to move out of the province following Albanian terror during the Second World War, the decision by the Yugoslav post-war authorities to that effect and actions by Albanian separatists in the post-war period.

22. With regard to the complaints filed by the representatives of particular parties and the associations of the Kosovo and Metohija Albanians, which refer to the situation in the judiciary, the enterprise sector, government administration, schools and universities, as well as in the health services, the Federal Government wishes to highlight the following.

23. The National Assembly of the Republic of Serbia has appointed 48 judges and 10 public prosecutors of Albanian nationality, but 28 Albanian judges and 3 Albanian Public Prosecutors refused to take an oath of allegiance before the National Assembly, whereby they have disqualified themselves for the office. Under the Constitution of the Republic of Serbia there is only one Supreme Court of Serbia and only one republican Public Prosecutor, as the highest court and the highest prosecutor in the republic respectively.

24. The Law on the Official Use of Language and Script ("Official Gazette of the Republic of Serbia", No. 45/91) stipulates that:

1. Everyone shall have the right to use his native language in proceedings before administrative agencies and to be acquainted with the facts in that language; (art. 6)

2. Proceedings before administrative agencies shall be conducted also in a national minority language which is in official use at the agency concerned (art. 12, para. 2). In Kosovo and Metohija, the Albanian language is also used alongside Serbian. This means that court proceedings in the territory of the Autonomous Province of Kosovo and Metohija are also conducted in the Albanian language. Under the Criminal Code of the Republic of Serbia, any violation of the right to the use of language and script is a criminal offence. (The Extraordinary report of the Federal Republic of Yugoslavia on the application of the Convention on the Elimination of all Forms of Racial Discrimination, which was reviewed in August 1993, contains data on the criminal proceedings regarding the mentioned criminal offence.)

25. The Republic of Serbia has not passed any decision on the closing down of schools with instruction in Albanian. The laws in effect today, as in the past, provide for the possibility that instruction be conducted in the languages of all minorities from pre-school to university levels. The main problem stems from the fact that the Kosovo and Metohija Albanians have refused to follow the school curricula approved by the competent ministries of the Republic of Serbia, and have developed their "parallel" system of education, issuing illegal school diplomas, often with the seal of the "Republic of Kosovo". It follows from all this that the Republic of Serbia and the Federal Republic of Yugoslavia have complied with the UNESCO Convention against Discrimination in Education.

26. The Federal Government adopted in the course of 1992 a comprehensive programme for the settlement of the problems in the sphere of education and culture and established a dialogue with the Albanians under the aegis of the Geneva Conference on Yugoslavia and at other meetings where the representatives of the Federal Government sought to accommodate the Albanians to the maximum extent possible by offering the following:

(a) To reach agreement which would guarantee to the maximum extent possible the preservation and development of the Albanians' cultural identity;

(b) To re-employ all Albanian teachers (with the exception of a small number of those who have committed a criminal offence);

(c) To recognize two school years to Albanian pupils which they have completed under the "parallel" and illegal system;

(d) That the Republic of Serbia shall undertake to finance all schools with instruction in the Albanian language;

(e) That instruction at all levels be conducted in the existing state-owned buildings designed for the purpose;

(f) To recognize the curriculum adopted in 1990.

27. The only demand by the representatives of the Federal and Republic Governments was for the Albanians to accept the federal and republic regulations and show respect for the reality that Kosovo and Metohija are an integral part of the Republic of Serbia and the Federal Republic of Yugoslavia (as reasserted also by the London Conference on Yugoslavia). The proposals by the Federal and Republic Governments are still valid. However, it ineluctably follows from the dialogue so far that the Albanians do not wish the problems of schooling in Kosovo and Metohija to be

effectively resolved, for the irregularity of instruction (involving some 310,000 pupils and students) is the principal argument which they invoke before the international community to prove that their human and national rights have been infringed upon. The Albanians who live outside the territory of the Autonomous Province of Kosovo and Metohija but within the Republic of Serbia regularly attend classes and follow the curricula adopted by the Republic Government. In other words, the self-induced problems of the schooling system are abused for political purposes in the struggle to achieve the secessionist goal of "an independent Republic of Kosovo". More details and information on the problems of education for the Albanian minority are given in the annex.

28. The educational authorities of the Republic of Serbia are willing to meet with the representatives of the Commission for Human Rights, CERD, CSCE, UNESCO and other international organizations, to verify and establish the extent to which the allegations made by the Albanian secessionists are false.

29. The Constitution of the Federal Republic of Yugoslavia and the Constitution of the Republic of Serbia guarantee the free choice of vocation and employment. Everyone is given equal access to a work post and an office in the society, under equal terms. Employment cannot be terminated against the will of a worker except under conditions and in the manner laid down by statute and the relevant collective contract. These rights are set forth in more detail in the Federal Law on the Basic Rights Stemming from Employment (Official Gazette of the Socialist Federal Republic of Yugoslavia, No. 60/89, 42/90 and Official Gazette of the Federal Republic of Yugoslavia, No. 42/92) and the Republic Labour Act (Official Gazette of the Republic of Serbia, No. 45/91) and the Law on Collective Contracts (Official Gazette of the Republic of Serbia, No. 6090 and 41/91).

30. The Constitution of the Federal Republic of Yugoslavia (art. 41) as well as the Constitution of the Republic of Serbia (art. 44) guarantee the freedom of trade union organization without previous approval, subject to entry in the registry of the competent agency. The federal and republic constitutions likewise guarantee (under art. 57 and art. 73 respectively) the right of the employed to strike in order to safeguard their professional and economic interests.

31. The above-mentioned freedoms and rights are elaborated in more detail and laid down by the federal and republic labour acts, the general collective contract concluded in the Republic of Serbia (Official Gazette of the Republic of Serbia, Nos. 18/90 and 10/92) and by the federal and republic laws on strikes (Official Gazette of the Socialist Federal Republic of Yugoslavia, No. 23/91, the Official Gazette of the Federal Republic of Yugoslavia, Nos. 42/92 and 37/93 and the Official Gazette of the Republic of Serbia, No. 45/91).

32. The year-long complex and very grave situation in the territory of Kosovo and Metohija, characterized by gross abuse of the rights of the Albanian national minority and direct territorial threats to the integrity of the country, as well as by extremely negative economic trends, have forced the authorities in Serbia and Yugoslavia to take appropriate stop-gap measures with a view to precluding secession and establishing the rule of law.

33. Accordingly, the Law on the Action of the Republic Agencies in Emergencies was passed (Official Gazette of the Socialist Republic of Serbia, No. 30/90) along with the Act on Employment in Emergencies (Official Gazette of the Socialist Republic of Serbia, Nos. 40/90 and 54/90) and a decision taken by the Assembly of the Socialist Republic of Serbia to the effect that special circumstances have been established in the territory of the Socialist Autonomous Province of Kosovo and a number of decisions on taking stop-gap measures in enterprises.

34. The circumstances preceding the taking of the above-mentioned measures were as follows:

(a) The paralysis of the legal set-up and the imposed state of lawlessness;

(b) Persistent assaults on the lives and property of citizens of Serb and Montenegrin nationality (wilful taking of private and socially-owned land);

(c) Blatant and even armed assaults on the law-enforcement agency personnel;

(d) Blocking or making work difficult for a large number of enterprises by boycotting working duties, by organizing strikes, and the like;

(e) Failure to honour civil duties (default on tax liabilities, rent, electricity and other utility services);

(f) Display of civil disobedience (the Albanians, among other things, refused to give data during the last Yugoslav official population census

in 1991, which is not only a civil duty but also Yugoslavia's international obligation vis-à-vis the United Nations);

(g) Constant and systematic incitement of ethnic intolerance, hatred and conflict, which posed a serious threat to the initiated democratization processes and to maintenance of peace and security in Kosovo and Metohija, in the Republic of Serbia and in Yugoslavia.

35. At the same time, the performance of the economy in Kosovo and Metohija for a number of years and in 1990 especially fell short of production potential and the level of additional investments by Yugoslavia and Serbia procured for the development of the province through the funds for the faster development of underdeveloped regions.

36. In the first semester of 1990 industrial production in Kosovo and Metohija fell by 22.5 per cent relative to the same period in 1989 (as compared to 10.9 per cent in Yugoslavia and 10.7 per cent in Serbia). A pronounced deterioration in product quality led to the building of commodity stocks which rose 4.3 times (2.5 times in Yugoslavia and 2.4 times in Serbia) and to a 22 per cent cut in the volume of exports (16.7 per cent in Yugoslavia and 16.8 per cent in Serbia), while the vigorous trend of rising imports was maintained at the level of 149.9 per cent.

37. The above-mentioned trends in material production caused a dramatic decline in the effects of all ongoing activities coupled with an increase in the economy's indebtedness ratio. Gross expenditures exceeded revenues. Generated losses increased 28.3 times (15.9 times in Yugoslavia and 27.3 times in Serbia) and material losses, which rose 22.3 times (5.9 times in Yugoslavia and 4.9 times in Serbia) reached the share of 32 per cent of total losses.

38. The principles of economic operation have been totally degraded because each Dinar invested in production required an additional Din 1.4 for procurement of raw materials and for covering other production needs (as compared to Din 0.85 in Yugoslavia and Din 0.78 in Serbia). Income, gross profits and capital formation per worker reached no more than 47 per cent (as compared to 38.6 per cent in Yugoslavia and 50 per cent in Serbia) while net personal incomes remained at the level of around 85 per cent of the Yugoslav average. The already low capital formation capacity of the economy has been almost totally depleted.

39. The situation and relations in enterprises and various institutions in Kosovo and Metohija were in those days characterized by total absence of material and financial records, destruction and appropriation of socially-owned property and an inequitable status of workers belonging to the Serb and Montenegrin nationalities. Due to the appointment exclusively of Albanians to the management boards and leading positions, good quality was sacrificed for the sake of nationality quotas.

40. To offset the adverse trends in the economy and in the social services in Kosovo and Metohija and to revive economic activity and promote human relations by eliminating distinctions among workers according to nationality affiliation, the Socialist Republic of Serbia introduced stop-gap emergency measures in the period from 5 July-11 November 1990 which were designed to protect socially-owned property in 330 enterprises and in the social services in this province.

41. The basis for the taking of stop-gap measures was the provisions of the Law on the Action of Republic Organs in Emergencies. In the course of the adoption of relevant decisions the provisions of the provincial Law on Taking Stop-gap Measures for the Social Protection of Self-management Rights and Socially-owned Property were complied with (Official Gazette of the SAPK, Nos. 40/77, 52/86 and 21/88).

42. The task of the interim organs in enterprises was to quickly and efficiently remove any hindrance to the taking of business decisions, prevent any further unlawful appropriation and destruction of corporate assets and to organize the start-up of the interrupted production process and, in the long run, to adopt programmes of economic-financial consolidation.

43. In their work, the above-mentioned organs were faced with resistance and boycotting of their decisions by managers and workers of Albanian nationality who provoked deliberate damage, engaged in sabotage activities, theft, destruction of financial records and in organized absenteeism.

44. It should be pointed out that the above-mentioned provincial Law (like the republic one) on Taking Stop-gap Measures for the Social Protection of Self-management Rights and Social Property ceased to be valid on 28 June 1991 (Official Gazette of the Republic of Serbia, No. 38/91).

45. The Law on Labour in Emergencies was passed as part of a set of measures taken by the Republic of Serbia which were given limited legal force on the territory of the Socialist Republic of Serbia where special circumstances prevailed and for as long as those circumstances were in evidence. The decision of the Assembly of the Socialist Republic of Serbia on the special circumstances in the territory of SAP Kosovo was reached on

26 June 1990. The provisions of this law were applied to labour relations in the working communities of the administrative agencies, in enterprises, the organizations of social services and in other organizations and communities where stop-gap measures were taken to protect socially-owned assets.

46. The said law has widened the powers of high-ranking government officials and managers with regard to employment, permanent or temporary reappointment to another work post which corresponds to the employee's qualification and capabilities, as well as with regard to taking decisions on disciplinary measures against particular negligent workers. The law has further introduced more stringent disciplinary measures for such workers.

47. Invoking the above-mentioned law, employers in enterprises have also terminated employment contracts with a number of staff in conformity with the regulations and in the prescribed procedure. According to data of the competent provincial organs, the main reasons for dismissal at the employer's initiative were: deliberate interruption of the work process and abandoning the work post; obstructing other workers in the execution of their working assignments and duties; refusal to accept a reappointment decision; refusal to discharge working orders; persistent and unjustified tardiness.

48. The main initiator and organizer of mass walk-out campaigns by workers belonging to the national minority was the Union of Independent Trade Unions of Kosovo (UNSK). By signing the "Declaration of Kosovo's Independence" distributed massively among the Albanian population by this trade union, any signatory terminated his employment unilaterally and deliberately.

49. This state of affairs in the area of employment in Kosovo and Metohija was followed closely and came under intensive supervision by the inspection service. Labour inspectors established a number of cases where unlawful action was taken but the monitoring of unlawful phenomena and procedures would have been simpler and more efficient had the workers, as plaintiffs, demanded the protection of their rights through regular channels on a more massive scale.

50. The Labour Inspection Service in Kosovo and Metohija, which took care of appeals at the time, was staffed by nationally mixed personnel at the communal level. The communal labour inspectorates were made up of 14 Albanians, 14 Serbs and Montenegrins, 1 Turk and 1 Muslim. The Provincial Labour Inspectorate was made up of 2 Albanians, 1 Serb and 1 Turk, while an Albanian served as the chief provincial inspector.

51. According to the files of the labour inspection service, in 1990 the service was approached by 1 Albanian and 2 Serbs, and in 1991 by 6 Albanians and 23 Serbs, with the request to postpone the taking of final decisions on the termination of their employment until the relevant court decisions took effect. These data clearly indicate that only a negligible number of dismissed workers of the Albanian national minority have complained to the inspectorates and that workers have been reluctant to do so on a larger scale.

52. Since mid-1992 a larger number of Albanian complaints have been registered with the labour inspectorates. The files of the communal labour inspectorates in the districts of Pristina, Kosovska Mitrovica, Prizren, Gnjilane and Pec for the period 1 April 1992-1 December 1993 show that a total of 183 dismissed persons lodged a complaint over dismissal in the first-instance procedure, of whom 129 were Serbs, 41 Albanians, 11 Muslims and 2 Bulgarians. In the same period, 137 persons filed complaints over reappointment in the first-instance procedure, of whom 105 were Serbs, 29 Albanians and 3 Muslims.

53. According to the files of the Ministry for Labour, Veterans' and Social Affairs of the Republic of Serbia, in the period under review complaints were lodged by 45 reappointed or dismissed persons in second-instance procedure, of whom 25 were Serbs, 15 Albanians and 3 Muslims.

54. However, on 5 March 1993 the Assembly of Serbia repealed the Law on Action by the Republic Organs in Emergencies and the Law on Labour Relations in Emergencies (Official Gazette of the Republic of Serbia, No. 18/93).

55. The freedom of trade union activities in the territory of Kosovo and Metohija is guaranteed by the federal and republic constitutions and the laws mentioned in item 1.

56. During the two months following the publication of the Decree on the Registration of Trade Union Organizations in the Republic of Serbia (Official Gazette of Republic of Serbia, No. 14/91), 792 trade unions were entered in the register, of which 5 were from Kosovo and Metohija, namely: Union of trade unions of Kosovo and Metohija, Priština; Journalists' trade union Niro Jedinstvo, Priština; Independent trade union Niro Jedinstvo, Priština; Trade union organization JP Elektroprivrede Kosova, Priština;

Trade union organization of the Elementary School ACA Markovic, Kosovo Polje.

57. Even in the former Socialist Federal Republic of Yugoslavia, the Union of Independent Trade Unions of Kosovo (UNSK) with its seat in Priština filed an application and was entered as a social organization in the register of associations, social organizations and political organizations established for the territory of Yugoslavia.

58. Although a new constitution of the Republic of Serbia has since been promulgated, the above-mentioned trade union has failed to approach the competent agency of the Republic of Serbia to be entered in the register of trade union organizations in line with the Law on Collective Contracts (Official Gazette of the Republic of Serbia, Nos. 6/90 and 45/91) and the above-mentioned Decree of the Republic of Serbia, thus boycotting the institutions of its system of authority. The reasons are exclusively of a political nature and the political platform of this trade union is secessionism. UNSK is a mononational organization which has primarily the features of a political party. The interests of its separatist policy outweigh the vital interests of Albanian workers and its methods of action affect most severely precisely those Albanian workers and citizens. By advocating work to rule, idleness, sabotage, by organizing massive walk-outs among workers and applying pressure on those who have not immediately joined hands with them, including violent extortion of membership fees, they have largely been responsible for the grave situation in which many Albanian workers and citizens have found themselves in Kosovo and Metohija.

59. The files of the judiciary in Kosovo and Metohija show that not a single person, meaning not a single union leader or UNSK activist, has ever been prosecuted for an offence or a crime committed in the course of union activities, but that a number of fines were pronounced for the offence of failing to report a gathering in keeping with the provisions of the Law on Public Order.

60. Numerous appeals and attempts, addressed by the administrative agencies and enterprises to the Albanian workers who had abandoned them to return to work, were in most cases totally ineffective, i.e. were boycotted. Ninety-five per cent of Albanians have not returned to their places of work. The homogenization of the Albanian national minority, achieved by provoking the feeling of persecution and general mobilization against all institutions of Serbia, gained the upper hand over the protection of Albanian workers' vital interests. Recognizing the pernicious nature of the method of massive walk-outs, UNSK revised their stand later on and called for a massive return to work of all workers whose employment was terminated after 15 June 1990. The demand for the massive return to work of all who have walked out or been dismissed means disregarding the relevant laws and regulations governing employment in force and the current lack of opportunities for their productive re-employment under the altered conditions of economic operation.

61. We wish to stress that in those days, as well as today, unemployment in Kosovo and Metohija was equally widespread among the Albanian and non-Albanian population alike. According to the disaggregated population figures for 1989, the non-Albanian population in the Province was characterized by higher unemployment than the Albanian population. Thus, of the total 140,824 persons seeking employment through the provincial employment service, 116,153 were Albanians and 24,671 persons of other nationalities. Likewise, of the total 12,034 persons employed through the mediation of the provincial employment service in 1989, 8,582 were Albanians and 2,014 persons of other nationalities, which bearing in mind the qualification pattern of the population gives no grounds for any claim of alleged discrimination of the Albanian population in the area of job placement.

62. It should be stressed that the total number of job-seekers, as well as the number of new applicants per month, have declined ever since 1990, which coincides with the period in which separatist forces set on dismembering Serbia have gained momentum. Thus, in 1990 the region of the employment service in Kosovo and Metohija reported 147,995 job-seekers, 133,148 in 1991, and 190,041 in 1992, and according to the latest data there were 85,887 registered job-seekers in October 1993. Objectively speaking, the decline in the number of those persons cannot be attributed to their larger-scale employment, given that, in general, and due to the deteriorating economic conditions and countless difficulties caused by the sanctions imposed against the Federal Republic of Yugoslavia, the number of new job opportunities has been minimal. The decline was, first of all, due to the failure by the jobless belonging to the Albanian national minority to register or to the lower number registered with the employment services as a way of boycotting the legal administrative agencies and the competent institutions. Persons belonging to the Albanian nationality account, by the way, for the

largest share of job-seekers registered with the employment services and make up around 83 per cent, as compared to 8 per cent for the Serbs, 3.5 per cent for the Muslims, 2.6 per cent for the Romanies and 0.8 per cent for the Turks.

63. At the same time, it is well known that persons belonging to the Albanian national minority are taken up on a considerable scale by the legal private sector and that they often moonlight with private firms as well. Apart from this, there are other forms in which they are illegally employed by employers engaged in operations which they have not registered or whose firms have not been registered at all.

64. However, persons belonging to the Albanian nationality have been claiming unemployment entitlements in every possible form, in cash and in kind, such as the facility to purchase certain products at a discount, or rebates on payments and in meeting various other liabilities.

65. The latest figures on newly-registered job-seekers in October and November 1993, which show that the number of newly registered has doubled, prove that those persons only tend to register with the employment service when they can claim an unemployment allowance or any other form of social welfare. According to the official statistics, the monthly cash allowance is claimed on average by 4,370 job-seekers registered with the employment service, of whom 98 per cent are Albanians. Apart from that, when it comes to announced vacancies to be filled, they participate on an equal footing and take up jobs by meeting identical qualifying requirements as all other unemployed persons, i.e. it all remains a matter of their own individual choice.

66. The first Constitution of the Federal Republic of Yugoslavia (art. 60) and the Constitution of the Republic of Serbia (art. 30) guarantee the right to health care to all citizens without distinction as to religion, race, gender or nationality. This right is laid down in detail in the Law on the Health Care of the Republic of Serbia (Official Gazette of the Socialist Republic of Serbia, Nos. 45/90 and 17/92) and in the Law on Health Insurance (Official Gazette of the Socialist Republic of Serbia, No. 18/92).

67. The Law on Health Care lays down the principles and general conditions for the organization and operation of the health services, the establishment of health care institutions, their scope of activity and type, fund-raising for their work, supervision of the technical work of those institutions and the like.

68. Citizens are provided with health care by health care institutions in conformity with the Law on Health Care and the health insurance enactments.

69. The provision of health care to the citizens of Kosovo and Metohija is one of the priority tasks in Serbia and is accorded special attention. The development of the health service in this province in the post-war period, in view of the grave economic conditions, has been remarkable and achieved in a relatively brief time. A medical faculty has been established with 20 specialized clinics and institutes, a public health care institute, a blood transfusion institute, and a network of other health institutions including 4 medical centres and 24 public health homes and pharmacies (a total of 50 health institutions). They employ 2,084 physicians, 321 dentists, 90 pharmacists and 6,580 health workers with post-secondary and secondary school qualifications, as well as 3,386 non-medical workers and associates. Between 64 and 66 per cent of persons employed in the health services of the province belong to the Albanian national minority.

70. The health care service of Kosovo and Metohija operates as an integral part of the single health care system of the Republic of Serbia and ensures the enjoyment of the right to health care by the citizens of the province in an identical manner to that by citizens in other parts of the Republic.

71. Regardless of the efforts geared to ensuring effective development of the health care service and the results scored in improving the health status of the population of the province of Kosovo and Metohija, certain allegations were made to the effect that the quality of work performed by the service was not in line with the level of development and with professional-medical principles recognized worldwide. The reports, made on the basis of supervision of professional work done, as well as spot-checks by competent committees made up of the most renowned experts from all over Yugoslavia in 1990, pointed to the unfavourable conditions and numerous problems in the provision of health care, mainly due to uneconomic organization of the health service and the inadequate quality of the delivered health care service. This was also reflected in the data on the inadequate rate of immunization and other measures within the health care programme, insufficient use of professional-methodological practices, poor hygienic conditions not only in towns and villages but also in numerous health institutions in the province, lack of systematic work on introducing

more up-to-date practices of eradicating, preventing, treating and rehabilitating the sick and the wounded.

72. With the worsening political circumstances in the province and deteriorating ethnic relations, the relations between the health workers of Albanian nationality and health workers of other nationalities were dramatically upset due to the outvoting of the non-Albanians by the health workers of the Albanian national minority. In numerous health institutions, there was a total split in the staff and a parallel organization emerged within the same institution, based on nationality affiliation. Numerous Albanian doctors, taking an active part in the political drives of the Albanian separatists or under pressure from the latter and exposed to direct threats, put their medical practice in the service of the tenets and policies pursued by the separatists. Their activity was based on a different treatment of patients depending on their nationality affiliation. Health workers belonging to the Albanian national minority refused to deliver health care services to citizens of Serb, Montenegrin and other non-Albanian nationality. Because of this attitude, expectant mothers of Serbian and Montenegrin nationality, as well as the sick and the wounded, started increasingly to give birth or to seek health care outside the province, in other parts of Serbia.

73. The state of the health sector in Kosovo and Metohija was also adversely affected by the very pronounced practice of unlawful disposal of financial resources and financial mismanagement. The economic standing of the health institutions in the Province worsened ever more.

74. To remove grave imbalances, abuse and unlawful transactions and to ensure normal delivery of health care services, the required level of hygiene in health institutions and the required professionalism, the Assembly of the Socialist Republic of Serbia passed a decision on stop-gap measures in 13 health institutions in the Province (4 medical centres, 7 public health homes, the Medical faculty and the Provincial Public Health Care Institute).

75. A number of health and other workers belonging to the Albanian national minority did not accept the measures of the Assembly of the Republic of Serbia. Expressing their resistance quietly or publicly, they started abandoning wilfully their work posts, discharged their duties irregularly or tardily, refused to carry out orders of their superiors, and so on. In the second half of 1990 some 1,200 workers belonging to the Albanian national minority abandoned wilfully their work posts in health institutions in this manner. They included 192 doctors. In the subsequent months, another 410 or so workers followed suit. However, only a small number of those workers were dismissed on account of lack of discipline and obstruction of the work process.

76. In the course of enforcement of the stop-gap measures, proposals were made for the vacancies on the interim management boards at various health institutions to be filled also by health workers belonging to the Albanian national minority. They most often refused to take up such duties, invoking different reasons, but the principal reason was evidently their fear of reprisals by the separatist movement and threats which they received along those lines. Cases were reported of health workers of the Albanian national minority at first accepting duties on the interim boards and two days later asking to be relieved of such duties; typically, they refrained from giving an explanation for such a course of action.

77. The cuts in the labour force of the health institutions in Kosovo and Metohija called for the supply of health personnel and teams from the Republic of Serbia to assist in the delivery of health services to the population of this province. Medical teams numbering from 60 to 118 persons spent 14-day shifts in Kosovo and were supplied from Belgrade, Niš, Vojvodina and 15 other health centres. A total of over 3,000 health workers were assigned to Kosovo and Metohija including numerous doctors, university professors and specialists in the most sought-after branches of medicine; some branches were supplied entirely with experts from Serbia.

78. Apart from that, the publicly announced vacancies were filled by new workers, including persons belonging to the Albanian national minority. The vacant work posts were filled as a rule by jobless health workers living in the province. Nevertheless, the lower number of Albanians taken on to fill the vacant posts in the health care system of the province reflects the psychological and political pressure they have been exposed to by the separatist movements.

79. The new laws of the Republic in the field of health care passed in 1992, the Law on Health Care (Official Gazette of the Socialist Republic of Serbia, No. 17/92) and the Law on Health Insurance (Official Gazette of the Socialist Republic of Serbia, No. 18/92), and the relevant by-laws and enactments have further ensured equal treatment of all health care beneficiaries, regardless of their nationality, confession and economic or other standing. Health institutions, the health inspectorate, the competent

agencies of the Republic of Serbia and the commune concerned are under the obligation to supervise the delivery of health care services and simultaneously monitor the state of human rights in the field of health care in this region.

80. The principled stand of health workers to extend adequate health care to whoever may request it regardless of his nationality, confession or any other feature lays the groundwork for regaining the lost confidence of patients of all nationalities in the health service in this region.

81. The Constitution of the Federal Republic of Yugoslavia lays down the right of national minorities to public information in their native language and the Constitution of the Republic of Serbia guarantees to every citizen the freedom of expression, of national affiliation and culture, and the freedom to use his own language and script. The legal regulation of the rights of national minorities in this field in the Republic of Serbia and the Federal Republic of Yugoslavia are in agreement with the CSCE documents. Thus, for instance, there are a large number of newspapers published and radio and television broadcasts in the national minority languages (Hungarian, Slovak, Romanian, Ruthenian, Ukrainian, Albanian, Turkish, Bulgarian and Gypsy). All media productions in national minority languages are edited by persons belonging to the minorities concerned.

82. A total of 98 papers and magazines come out in the Republic of Serbia in the languages of national minorities and the Radio Television Serbia (RTS), apart from any local and regional radio stations, has daily television and radio broadcasts in Hungarian, Albanian, Slovak, Romanian, Ruthenian, Bulgarian and Turkish.

83. In Kosovo and Metohija, 12 papers and magazines are published in the Albanian language. The daily Bujku has a circulation of 25,000 copies, the weekly Skhandia 18,000 copies, Zeri 20,000 copies, Fjalja 22,000 copies; and the monthly Ditari Islami has a circulation of 22,000 copies. Topical periodicals in the Albanian language include Kosovarja, Jeta E Re, Parparimi, Thumbi, Bat, Pioneri and Gep, highlighting a variety of issues, such as research, technology, the social status of women, etc. In addition, television and radio programming in Albanian are broadcast by RTS-RTV Priština, lasting 14 hours, and a local radio station. A 30-minute news bulletin in Albanian is also broadcast daily by RTV Belgrade.

84. Bearing in mind the talks held between the representatives of the Federal Government and the three-member CERD mission, the Federal Government is willing, as convened to the CERD mission during their visit to Belgrade in December 1993, to suggest as the first step towards opening a dialogue in the field of education the proposal by the Federal and Republic Governments on the normalization of education in Albanian as presented on the eve of the eighth session of the Working Group on Minorities of the Geneva Conference. As for the area of health and employment, the Federal Government has suggested the return of all medical personnel and employment of the unemployed who are willing to work for the government and for the social services, institutions and enterprises who have not been accused of any criminal offences, in line with the available job opportunities in view of the prevailing economic conditions. ...

[An Annex on the negotiations on education is reproduced in Chapter 5.]

A/50/18,paras.226-246, 22 September 1995

4. Concluding Observations of CERD: Yugoslavia, 15/6 March 1995

... 227. Consideration of the additional information proceeded in the absence of a representative of the State party. In that regard, the Committee had before it copies of an exchange of correspondence between the Ambassador of the Federal Republic of Yugoslavia and the Chairman of the Committee. The text of those communications reads as follows:

Letter from the Chargé d'affaires a.i. of the Permanent Mission of the Federal Republic of Yugoslavia to the United Nations Office at Geneva to the Chairman of the Committee on the Elimination of Racial Discrimination, 15 February 1995

Excellency,

With reference to the United Nations Secretary-General's note No. G/SO 237/2 (2) of 26 October 1994, and the invitation extended to the Government of the Federal Republic of Yugoslavia on 4 November 1994, for sending its representatives to a meeting of the CERD, may I transmit herewith the following position of the Government of the Federal Republic of Yugoslavia:

'The Government of the Federal Republic of Yugoslavia pointed out on several occasions its position that, being the continuation of the

international, legal and political personality of the former Socialist Federal Republic of Yugoslavia, it would strictly abide by all the commitments the SFRY had undertaken by acceding to international-legal instruments, which includes the obligations deriving from its membership in the International Convention on the Elimination of All Forms of Racial Discrimination. With regard to the fact that the delegation of the Federal Republic of Yugoslavia was unlawfully denied the right to participate in the work of the latest meeting of the States parties to the International Convention on the Elimination of All Forms of Racial Discrimination, whereby the basic rights of the FR Yugoslavia deriving from its membership in the Convention have been violated, the Government of the Federal Republic of Yugoslavia is of the view that the position of inequality, in which it is being placed by this act, makes its normal and usual cooperation with the CERD impossible. Taking into account that, regrettably, in the meantime after our latest communication (No. 56/1 of 26 January 1995), nothing has been changed in the position held towards the FR of Yugoslavia, i.e., it is not yet considered as a full member to the Convention, the Government of the Federal Republic of Yugoslavia is keeping its position and it will not participate at the above-mentioned CERD meeting. The Government of the FR of Yugoslavia is expecting that the Federal Republic of Yugoslavia will be allowed to participate on the footing of equality at the next Conference of the States parties to the International Convention on the Elimination of All Forms of Racial Discrimination and that usual cooperation with the CERD will be resumed afterwards. The Government of the Federal Republic of Yugoslavia wishes to reiterate once again its sincere interest in the equitable dialogue with the CERD, which is of mutual interest.'

Please accept, Excellency, the assurances of my highest consideration.

(Signed) Vladimir Pavicevic Ambassador"

"Letter from the Chairman of the Committee on the Elimination of Racial Discrimination to the Chargé d'affaires a.i. of the Permanent Mission of the Federal Republic of Yugoslavia to the United Nations Office at Geneva, 6 March 1995

Excellency,

I refer to your letter of 15 February 1995 which transmits the position of your Government on the invitation extended to it to participate in the consideration by the Committee on the Elimination of Racial Discrimination of the additional information supplied by your Government pursuant to a request of the Committee. May I convey to you the great regret of the Committee concerning the decision of your Government not to send a delegation to meet with it during its current session. While the absence of a delegation does not preclude consideration of the information which has been supplied, it does, however, greatly hinder the process of dialogue. The Committee considers that the continuation of the dialogue with your Government will contribute to the implementation of the Convention. Note has been taken of the reasons presented by your Government as underlying its position. In this regard the Committee would like to restate its view that it has always considered that the Federal Republic of Yugoslavia (Serbia and Montenegro) is duty bound as a State party to the International Convention on the Elimination of All Forms of Racial Discrimination and that the Committee, in its actions, will continue to proceed on the basis of this understanding. It is the hope of the Committee that your Government will reconsider its decision in sufficient time to allow for a dialogue to occur during the present session.

Please accept, Excellency, the assurances of my highest consideration.

(Signed) Ivan Garvalov"

228. Members welcomed the submission of the additional information while deploring the unwillingness of the State party to send a representative to participate in the Committee's deliberations. Members also drew attention to and stressed the importance of the findings of fact contained in the reports of the Special Rapporteur of the Commission on Human Rights on the situation of human rights in the territory of the Former Yugoslavia, Mr. T. Mazowiecki. A number of members condemned the apparent unwillingness of the State party to take seriously its international obligations concerning human rights or to cooperate with various international procedures which are intended to promote respect for the rights of all peoples and especially vulnerable minority groups.

229. With regard to articles 2 and 5 of the Convention attention was drawn to reports of patterns of discrimination perpetrated by the State party against a number of minority groups, including people of Albanian origin in the Kosovo region, people of the Muslim faith in Sandjak and those of Bulgarian origin in certain areas of Serbia. Among the discriminatory practices cited were police harassment,

deprivation of education rights, mass dismissals from employment and restrictions on freedom of expression. It was also noted that the Government persisted in refusing to assist United Nations initiatives to trace disappeared persons or to cooperate with the International Tribunal since 1991.

230. The role of the communications media in promoting ethnic and religious hatred was stressed by members and attention was drawn in that regard to the findings of the Special Rapporteur, which clearly indicate systematic and grave violations of article 4 of the Convention.

231. Members expressed concern about apparent violations of article 6 arising from reports that members of minority groups were unable to obtain adequate redress for violations of their human rights perpetrated by government authorities or by private citizens in circumstances where the government authorities failed to take preventative action.

232. Members referred to the good offices mission of the Committee which had visited Kosovo in 1993 and some expressed the view that a further mission might serve to promote respect for the Covenant in that region. In general members indicated their wish to give the fullest possible appropriate support to the Albanian minority in that region.
Concluding observations …

(a) Introduction

234. The submission of a detailed document containing the additional information requested from the State party is welcomed. However, the Committee deplores the unwillingness of the State party to send a representative to participate in the consideration by the Committee of the information before it. The Committee notes the disparity between the intentions stated by the State party in its additional information concerning cooperation with the Committee and its unwillingness to participate at the meeting.

235. The important role played by the Special Rapporteur of the Commission for Human Rights for the former Yugoslavia is acknowledged and his findings of fact are endorsed.

(b) Factors and difficulties in implementing the Convention

236. It is recognized that the State party is experiencing considerable economic difficulties which have a negative impact on the enjoyment of human rights including those protected by the Convention. It is also acknowledged that the country faces severe challenges in meeting the needs of the large number of refugees within its territory.

(c) Principal subjects of concern

237. Great concern is expressed regarding the situation of the ethnic Albanian population of Kosovo. Reports continue to be received of campaigns of discrimination, harassment and, at times, terrorization, directed against them by State authorities. Dismissals from jobs in the public sector, principally from the police and education services, continue. Numerous reports have been received of physical attacks and robbery either committed by persons in the service of the State or inadequately investigated by the police. It can be concluded that the ethnic Albanians of Kosovo continue to be deprived of effective enjoyment of the most basic human rights provided in the Convention.

…

239. Note is taken with profound concern of the large part which the media continue to play in the propagation of racial and ethnic hatred. Given the very tight State control over the media this propagation of hatred may be attributed to the State. It is further noted that the State party fails to take adequate action to either prosecute perpetrators of such acts or to attempt to redress injustices. It also fails to take action to counter the propagation of prejudice against non-Serbians through education of the population in tolerance.

240. The failure of the State party to cooperate with the Special Process on disappearances of the Commission on Human Rights is deplored. It is noted that without this cooperation no progress can be made in establishing the fate of large numbers of Croats, Bosnian Muslims and others who have disappeared.

241. The unwillingness of the State party to recognize the jurisdiction of the International Criminal Tribunal for the former Yugoslavia is also deplored and extreme concern is expressed with regard to the apparent policy of the Government to purport to bestow impunity on perpetrators of fundamental violations of international human rights and humanitarian law.

(d) Suggestions and recommendations

242. The Committee draws attention to the letter of its Chairman to the State party of 6 March 1995 and reiterates its contents. The Committee will continue to consider the Federal Republic of Yugoslavia (Serbia and Montenegro) to be bound by the terms of the Convention and looks forward to an early resumption of contact with the State party including its good-offices mission to Kosovo.

243. The Committee calls on the State party to cease immediately all policies and practices which violate rights under the Convention. It insists that victims of discrimination, including ethnic Albanians, Muslims and ethnic Bulgarians, receive redress and reparation in accordance with article 6 of the Convention.

244. The Committee recommends the immediate drafting and implementation of legislation with a view towards the outlawing of every manifestation of racial discrimination and the full implementation of the Convention. Particular attention should be paid to the legal regulation of matters such as the media and freedom of expression, employment and trade unions, the education system, and the health-care system. The Committee places itself at the disposal of the State party to make available to it any technical assistance it may require to carry out such legislative programmes.

245. The Committee insists that all perpetrators of violations of the Convention be brought to justice. It further calls on the State party to cooperate fully with the International Criminal Tribunal for the former Yugoslavia.

246. The Committee urgently suggests that the State party reconsider its failure to cooperate with the Special Rapporteur and the Special Process on disappearances of the Commission on Human Rights. It notes the important role played by both these mechanisms in promoting compliance with the terms of the Convention.

CERD/C/299/Add.17, 31 July 1997

5. CERD, Periodic Report, Yugoslavia, Addendum, 24 June 1997

… 5. In addition to a very wide range of freedoms and rights guaranteed by the Federal Republic of Yugoslavia Constitution, including personal freedoms and rights, as well as the political, cultural, social and economic rights, one should stress in particular the constitutional guarantee of the status of national minorities which will be discussed at more length later on.

6. The constitutional principle of freedom and equality of citizens regardless of any specific characteristic, which is in line with article 1 of the Convention, cannot be restricted by any means except by the equal freedoms and rights of others, and any abuse thereof is unconstitutional and punishable. Any incitement and instigation of national, racial, religious or any other inequality, as well as incitement and fanning of national, racial, religious and other hatred and intolerance, is unconstitutional and punishable.

7. The international treaties that have been confirmed and published in keeping with the the Federal Republic of Yugoslavia Constitution and the generally accepted rules of international law constitute an integral part of the domestic legal order. Since the Convention has been confirmed and published in keeping with the the Federal Republic of Yugoslavia Constitution, it can be directly applied before the courts of law and/or administrative agencies.

8. The demographic structure of the population of the Federal Republic of Yugoslavia according to the latest census available (1991) is as follows:

Total	10,304,026
Serbs	6,504,048
Montenegrins	519,765
Yugoslavs	349,784
Albanians	1,714,768

According to the census done by the Federal Statistical Office, owing to the boycott of the census by a part of the Albanian population of AP Kosovo and Metohija, as well as in the municipalities of Bujanovac and Presevo, the number of Albanians indicated in the census is an assessed number based on the summary data on the population who took part in the census and the assessed number of the Albanian population who did not take part in the census.

Hungarians:	334,147
Muslims:	336,025
Croats:	111,650

Romanies:	143,519
Slovaks:	66,863
Romanians:	42,364
Macedonians:	47,118
Bulgarians:	26,922
Others:	213,974

II. INFORMATION CONCERNING ARTICLES 2-7 …

Article 2

9. The constitutions of the member republics, the federal laws, the laws of the member republics and all other regulations and enactments shall be in harmony with the the Federal Republic of Yugoslavia Constitution, and this ensures that the Federal Republic of Yugoslavia's domestic legal acts uphold the constitutional principle on the equality of citizens and the international commitments under the Convention.

10. The State authorities and organizations exercising public powers are duty-bound to observe and to act in line with the Convention. In case a decision or any other individual act adopted by the judicial, administrative and other State agencies or organizations discharging public duties violates the principle of freedom and equality of citizens, such an act shall be invalidated in a procedure prescribed by law. In addition, any injured party has the right to compensation for any damage caused by an official, a State agency or organization which in the discharge of public office commits illegal or irregular activities, and such damage is to be compensated by the State.

11. The Federal Republic of Yugoslavia Constitution and the constitutions of the member republics prohibit any activities carried out by political, trade union or other organizations which are designed to violate the guaranteed human and civil freedoms and rights or to incite national, racial, religious and other intolerance or hatred. If a certain organization or citizens' association set out in its programme or statute objectives aimed at violating the guaranteed human and civil freedoms and rights, or at the fanning of national, religious, racial or any other intolerance or hatred, such organization or citizens' association shall not be entered in the Register of Organizations, and should such objectives be proclaimed at a later date, such organization shall be banned.

12. The decision-making procedure for banning political parties and citizens' associations is carried out before the Federal Constitutional Court, i.e. before the Constitutional Courts of the member republics, and is initiated ex officio by the government official responsible for entries in the Register of Political Parties and Citizens' Associations or by the competent Public Prosecutor.

13. The subject of protection of the freedoms and rights of members of national minorities in the legal system of the Federal Republic of Yugoslavia is primarily of a constitutional-legal nature, as regulated by the Federal Republic of Yugoslavia Constitution and the constitutions of its member republics.

14. The Federal Republic of Yugoslavia Constitution (April 1992) takes as its point of departure the concept of civil democracy and, therefore, the enjoyment of all constitutional freedoms and rights is exclusively linked to the status of citizenship identical for all citizens irrespective of their nationality. However, notwithstanding the universal human and civil freedoms and rights, the Federal Republic of Yugoslavia Constitution also provides particular rights for members of national minorities and their exercise by members of minorities gives them an additional advantage.

15. The Federal Republic of Yugoslavia Constitutional provisions directly relating to members of national minorities and governing the following rights and freedoms concern: equality on the basis of nationality; the right to preserve, develop and express ethnic, cultural, linguistic and other specificities; the right to use national symbols; the right to the official use of language and script in parallel with the Serbian language in areas inhabited by members of national minorities; the freedom to express nationality and the guarantee that the citizen shall not be obliged to state his nationality, the freedom to express one's national culture; the freedom to use one's own language and script and the right to use the services of an interpreter in criminal proceedings; the right to education in one's native language; the right to public information in one's native language; the right to set up educational and cultural organizations or associations; the right to establish and maintain unhindered mutual relations in the Federal Republic of Yugoslavia and abroad with persons belonging to one's nation, while residing in another State; the right to take part in international non-governmental organizations, but not to the detriment of the Federal Republic of Yugoslavia or either of its member republics. As a particular form of protection for persons belonging to national minorities, the Constitution prohibits, i.e. prescribes punishment for, any incitement of national hatred or intolerance. The Constitutions of the member republics contain basically the same arrangements for this area.

16. The protection of the rights and freedoms of members of national minorities is more closely regulated by laws, both at the federal and at the republican levels, in the following areas: material and criminal case law and civil legislation; citizens' political organization and associations;, public information; education; official use of languages and scripts; etc.

Federal regulations

17. The Criminal Code, article 134, defends members of national minorities by stipulating that the incitement or fanning of national, racial or religious hatred, discord or intolerance shall be punishable by a term of imprisonment ranging from 1 to 10 years.

18. Under the Law on the Association of Citizens into Associations, Social Organizations and Political Organizations being Established in the Territory of SFRY, the establishment of organizations whose programme and statutary objectives, or their carrying out, are directed toward fanning of national, racial or religious hatred and intolerance is prohibited. A similar provision, apart from the Federal Republic of Yugoslavia Constitution, also exists in the draft law on association of citizens into political parties, trade unions and citizens' associations being established in the territory of the Federal Republic of Yugoslavia, which is in the process of being adopted by the Federal Assembly.

19. The Law on the Basics of the Public Information System lays down that the programme orientation of public media shall not incite national, racial or religious hatred and intolerance.

20. The Law on Criminal Procedure stipulates that, in criminal proceedings the languages and scripts of the nations and national minorities of Yugoslavia must be used on an equal footing in conformity with the Constitution and the law; petition requests to the court may be also addressed in a minority language that is not in official use in that court if that is in line with the Constitution, the law and any other regulation in force in the territory under the court's jurisdiction, and court documents which the court communicates to members of national minorities are to be formulated in their language, provided that the language in question is in official use at the court concerned.

21. The Law on Lawsuit Procedure, like the Law on Criminal Procedure stipulates that if a court uses officially any of Yugoslavia's minority languages, it shall communicate its documents in that language to those persons taking part in the proceedings who belong to the minority in question and who use their language in the court proceedings; participants in proceedings shall address their petition requests to the court in the language of the nation or nationality to which they belong which is in official use at that court, or in a language that is not officially used by that court if this is in conformity with the Constitution, law or any other regulations in force in the territory under that court's jurisdiction; the costs of translation and interpretation into the languages of Yugoslav nations and national minorities incurred in the course of the implementation of the relevant provisions of the Constitution and the law in connection with the right of members of nations and/or national minorities to use their own language are to be borne by the court.

22. The Law on the Publication of Federal Laws, Other Laws and General Enactments stipulates that the Federal Government shall see to it that the federal laws, as well as other federal regulations which are of relevance to the achievement of national minorities' freedoms and rights, are published in the national minorities' languages and scripts in accordance with the federal law.

Regulations of the Republic of Serbia

23. The Criminal Code of Serbia, in article 100 sets out as a separate criminal offence the exposure to ridicule of a nation or a minority or ethnic group living in Yugoslavia, sanctioned by imprisonment for three months to three years.

24. The Law on Public Information stipulates that the distribution of papers and magazines and the dissemination of information by way of public media may only be prevented by a decision brought by the competent court that they instigate national, racial or religious intolerance.

25. The Law on Radio-Television Serbia stipulates that Radio-Television Serbia is to prepare and produce radio and television programming with a view, among other things, to contributing to the assertion of national values of other nations and national minorities living in the Republic of Serbia as well as to the rapprochement and intermingling of cultures of the nations and national minorities in the Republic of Serbia. RTS likewise pursues its activities through its constituent units, Enterprises RT Novi Sad and RT Priština, which prepare and produce radio and television programming in

the territory of AP Vojvodina and AP Kosovo and Metohija, both in Serbian and in the minority languages.

26. The Law on Elementary Schools stipulates that educational curricula for members of national minorities be followed in their mother tongue or bilingual instruction where at least 15 pupils so request in enrolling in the first form. If this quota is not met, the Education Minister's concurrence needs to be obtained. The Minister also has the authority to order bilingual instruction following the relevant curricula and teaching plans. Further, when a curriculum is also followed in a minority language, pupils are also required to master the contents of the subject in the Serbian language; when the curriculum is followed in Serbian, the pupils belonging to national minorities are also provided courses in their mother tongue with elements of their national culture. A school at which courses are also run in a minority language shall keep records in the minority language as well and the Principal is under the obligation to exclude from the teaching process any teacher, technical associate or educator who incites national or religious intolerance until a decision is taken on a disciplinary measure. Apart from the Republic of Serbia, i.e. the republican government, elementary ballet and music schools can be founded or run by legal and natural persons, meaning members of national minorities as well, subject to the fulfilment of all the necessary requirements stipulated by this law and by other relevant regulations.

27. The Law on Secondary Schools regulates this area on principles identical to the Law on Elementary Schools but specifies that school reports are also to be issued in the minority language in which instruction is conducted. Unlike the Law on Elementary Schools, any legal and natural person, including members of national minorities is entitled to set up any type of secondary schools without any limitation, if all the conditions are met. Identical provisions exist in other regulations as well and in that context those provisions and regulations need to be applied accordingly (the Law on Public Services, the Law on Enterprises, etc.).

28. The Law on Post-Secondary Schools stipulates that instruction at post-secondary schools can also be conducted in a minority language in which case records have to be kept on the diplomas issued in that language, whereas public documents are issued in a bilingual format. A post-secondary school may be founded by the Republic of Serbia, meaning the republican government, as well as any juridical or natural person, as is the case with secondary schools.

29. The Law on Universities includes completely identical provisions with regard to the right of persons belonging to national minorities as the Law on Post-Secondary Schools.

30. The Law on the Official Use of Language and Script regulates this matter more comprehensively than any other regulation mentioned thus far, stressing in particular that national minorities' languages and scripts are in official use in parallel with the Serbian language in the territory of the Republic of Serbia inhabited by members of national minorities, in the manner laid down by this law. For the purposes of this law, the official use of a language and script is understood to mean the use of a language and script by the government agencies or officials, by the agencies in the autonomous provinces, towns and municipalities, institutions, enterprises and other organizations when they discharge public functions, public enterprises and public services, as well as other organizations when they carry out works laid down by this law. The Law elaborates on the manner of using languages and scripts in different situations, as, for example, the use of more than one minority language, the inscription of geographical names, names of streets and squares, traffic signs and other public inscriptions, names of legal persons as well as names of persons forming part of public inscriptions, the competence to bring decisions on when and where minority languages are to be used, the use of languages and scripts in proceedings before the judiciary and administrative agencies as well as other organizations when they carry out public duties, the keeping of prescribed records, issuance of public documents and so forth.

31. The practical enforcement of the constitutional provisions and particularly the provisions of relevant laws regulating the official use of languages and scripts in the Republic of Serbia will be illustrated by the example of the Autonomous Province of Vojvodina which is unique by its national makeup: Serbs account for 57.3 per cent of its population, Hungarians 16.9 per cent, Yugoslavs 8.4 per cent, Croats 3.7 per cent, Slovaks 3.2 per cent, Montenegrins 2.2. per cent, Romanians 1.9 per cent, Romanies 1.2 per cent, Bujanovac 1.1. per cent, Ruthenians 0.9 per cent, Ukrainians 0.24 per cent and others 3.2 per cent. The Statute of the AP Vojvodina as the basic law of the province stipulates the official use in the work of the agencies of AP Vojvodina, in parallel with the Serbian language and the Cyrillic script (and the Latin script in the manner laid down by law),

of the Hungarian, Slovak, Romanian and Ruthenian languages and their respective scripts, as well as the languages and scripts of other national minorities in the manner laid down by law. Regular simultaneous interpretation into five languages is provided at the sessions of the Assembly of Vojvodina. The provincial agencies of government administration are provided with the means to ensure communication with clients (citizens) in minority languages. Courts of law in Vojvodina have the capacity to conduct proceedings in the languages which are in official use in their respective territories and in case this is not provided, the services of a professional interpreter are to be provided.

32. Of a total of 45 municipalities in the AP Vojvodina, 37 municipalities have by their statutes regulated the official use of national minorities' languages and scripts in their respective territories in such a manner that now one or more minority languages are officially used. In parallel with Serbian, the Hungarian language and script are officially used in 31 municipalities, Slovak in 12 municipalities, Romanian in 10 municipalities, Ruthenian in 6 municipalities, and there is 1 municipality where the Czech language is in official use (there are no more than 2,910 Czechs living in Yugoslavia, of whom 1,844 are residents of Vojvodina). In a large number of municipalities, several languages and scripts are used concurrently on an equal footing.

33. In the Republic of Montenegro the relevant constitutional provisions governing this area are being applied directly. Particular mention should be made here of the provision of the Constitution of the Republic of Montenegro (art. 68) by virtue of which persons belonging to national and ethnic groups are guaranteed the right to freely use their language and script, the right to schooling and the right to information in their native language.

34. The Law on Textbooks and Other Teaching Aids regulates the printing of textbooks in the languages of a national minority, thus fulfiling the preconditions for instruction in a minority language.

...

44. The Constitution of the Federal Republic of Yugoslavia goes a step further than the International Covenant on Civil and Political Rights and envisages a separate right for members of national minorities to maintain links and relations with their mother State. In this manner, the Federal Republic of Yugoslavia wishes to foster goodneighbourly relations with its neighbours on the basis of equality, observance of sovereignty, respect for territorial integrity and for mutual benefit. This is in the interest of all peoples and it serves as a basis for stability in the region. The peoples of the Federal Republic of Yugoslavia and its neighbours are destined to live side by side and members of national minorities in these States should serve as the bridge for good-neighbourly cooperation.

Article 3

45. Since the submission of the tenth periodic report, Yugoslavia has continued to meet the commitments undertaken upon the ratification of the Convention on the Suppression and Punishment of the Crime of Apartheid (ratified in 1975). Honouring its commitments under the Convention, the Federal Republic of Yugoslavia defined in its criminal law as a crime any act committed by a person who persecutes an organization or an individual on the grounds of their advocacy of the equality of men. The envisaged punishment for the mentioned crime is a term of imprisonment ranging from six months to five years.

46. Apart from that, bearing in mind the provisions of the Convention on the Prevention and Punishment of the Crime of Genocide, as well as the Convention on the Suppression and Punishment of the Crime of Apartheid, the Federal Criminal Code, article 141, prescribes the criminal act of genocide. This criminal act is committed when a person carries out certain acts deliberately and according to a plan against persons belonging to a national, ethnic, racial or religious group with a view to its total or partial destruction. The envisaged punishment for such an act is a term of imprisonment ranging from 5 to 20 years.

47. As early as in 1963, Yugoslavia adopted, in accordance with the relevant United Nations General Assembly resolutions, the law banning the holding and establishment of economic relations with the Republic of South Africa which ceased to be valid following the 1994 parliamentary elections and the establishment of democracy in that country.

Article 4

48. Yugoslavia is a signatory to all important international agreements pertaining to the condemnation and ban on any racial and other discrimination. Apart from the International Convention on the Elimination of All Forms of Racial Discrimination, Yugoslavia has also ratified the International Covenant on Civil and Political Rights, the International Covenant on Economic, Social and Cultural Rights as well as the

International Convention on the Suppression and Punishment of the Crime of Apartheid.

49. The acts prohibited by these international instruments formed the basis for the stipulation of several criminal acts by the Yugoslav criminal legislation. As a result, the criminal activities envisaged by the International Convention on the Suppression and Punishment of the Crime of Apartheid are for the most part incorporated in the institution of the criminal act of genocide as stipulated in article 141 of the Criminal Code of the Federal Republic of Yugoslavia, as mentioned above. The implementation of the constitutional principle according to which all citizens of the Federal Republic of Yugoslavia are equal and free irrespective of their distinctive features or personal characteristics is ensured under the criminal law by stipulating that any violation of the equality of citizens is a crime under the federal and republican criminal laws depending on who the crime is perpetrated by. Incitement of national or racial hatred among peoples and national minorities living in the Federal Republic of Yugoslavia likewise represents the crime of racial and other discrimination, an act prohibited by international law but not covered by any other previously mentioned incrimination. As a rule, the latter pertains to cases of discrimination against persons other than Yugoslav citizens or to acts committed abroad.

50. The provisions on citizens' equality in the Federal Republic of Yugoslavia Constitution and in the constitutions of the member republics were the basis for the definition of the criminal act of violation of citizens' equality prescribed by the federal criminal law and by the criminal laws of the member republics. The definitions of that crime given in all three laws are identical, the only difference being the characteristic of the perpetrator. The mentioned criminal acts may be committed by anyone who is in a position to deny or restrict a citizen's right or to grant citizens benefits and facilities. In most cases these are government officials, military and other responsible officials, and if the perpetrator is a government official serving in the federal agencies or a military officer, such a person shall answer under the federal criminal law, i.e. article 186 of the Criminal Code of the Federal Republic of Yugoslavia, and in case such acts are committed by anyone else, they will answer under article 60 of the Criminal Law of the Republic of Serbia or under article 52 of the Criminal Law of the Republic of Montenegro. The fact that this criminal offence is defined in almost identical terms and in all three laws is a consequence of the shared legal responsibility in the criminal-legal field of the federal State and the member republics.

51. Pursuant to article 186 of the Criminal Code of the Federal Republic of Yugoslavia, article 60 of the Criminal Law of the Republic of Serbia and article 52 of the Criminal Law of Montenegro, whoever on the ground of difference in terms of nationality, race, confession, political or other belief, ethnic origin, gender, language, education or social background, denies or restricts any citizen's right laid down by the Constitution, the law or any other regulation or enactment or ratified international treaty, or whoever grants on the grounds of this difference benefits or facilities to citizens is to be punished. The envisaged sentence for this act perpetrated against one or several citizens of the Federal Republic of Yugoslavia, is imprisonment ranging from three months to five years.

52. We wish to stress on this occasion that the above-mentioned definitions of the criminal act of violation of citizens' equality were amended in 1990 following the adoption of new amendments to the federal criminal law and the new amendments to the Criminal Law of the Republic of Serbia pursuant to article 1, paragraph 1, of the Convention, so that any discrimination made on the grounds of citizens' political or any other beliefs, as well as any denial or abridgement of the citizens' rights laid down by a ratified international treaty, is regarded as a crime. The harmonization of the Criminal Law of Montenegro with the Federal Criminal Code is under way.

53. In particular, the criminal laws of the member republics define as a crime any infringement of the citizens' right to use their mother tongue which can take the form of denial or restriction of the right to use a language or a script committed to the detriment of any citizen of the Federal Republic of Yugoslavia.

54. The Criminal Code of the Federal Republic of Yugoslavia defines as a crime the incitement of national, racial and religious hatred, discord or intolerance and any act of racial and other discrimination. Any person who incites or fans national, racial or religious hatred, sows discord or intolerance among peoples and national minorities living in the Federal Republic of Yugoslavia is to be punished by one to five years' imprisonment.

55. In case the above act has been committed under duress, through ill-treatment, by endangering someone's safety, by exposing to ridicule certain national, ethnic or religious symbols, by inflicting damage to other people's belongings, as well as desecration of monuments, memorial complexes or tombstones, the perpetrator shall be punished more severely under the law in force, namely by 1 to 10 years' imprisonment.

56. The gravest forms of the criminal offence of instigation to national, racial or religious hatred, strife or intolerance are those committed by abuse of office or powers, the sentence envisaged ranging between one and eight years of imprisonment; if resulting in riots, violence or other grave consequences for the common living of the peoples or national minorities residing in the Federal Republic of Yugoslavia, they shall be sentenced to from 1 to 10 years' imprisonment. The criminal offence referred to may be:

    (a) Violation of the fundamental human rights and freedoms recognized by the international community, on the basis of differences in race, colour, nationality or ethnic origin, with the envisaged sentence of imprisonment ranging between six months and five years;

    (b) Persecution of organizations or individuals because of their advocacy of the equality of men, the envisaged punishment also being imprisonment from six months to five years;

    (c) Spreading the idea of the superiority of one race over another, propagation of racial hatred or instigation to racial discrimination, the envisaged punishment for which is imprisonment from three months to three years.

<u>Article 5</u>

57. The Federal Republic of Yugoslavia Constitution sets forth that everyone shall be entitled to equal protection of their rights in a statutorily specified procedure, and everyone is guaranteed the right to appeal or resort to another legal remedy against a decision concerning their rights or interests stemming from the law (art. 26).

58. The Federal Republic of Yugoslavia Constitution guarantees respect for the human person and the dignity thereof in criminal and any other proceedings in case of deprivation and/or restriction of freedom, as well as during the serving of sentences. Any violence against a person deprived of freedom or whose freedom has been restricted, as well as any extortion of confessions and statements, is prohibited and punishable. The Constitution stipulates that no one may be subjected to torture or degrading punishment and treatment, prohibiting any medical or other experiments on a person without his permission (art. 25). With a view to guaranteeing respect for the human person and dignity, the Criminal Code of the Federal Republic of Yugoslavia and the criminal laws of the member republics define as a criminal offence any harassment in the discharging of office (art. 191 of the Criminal Code of the Federal Republic of Yugoslavia, art. 66 of the Criminal Law of the Republic of Serbia and art. 57 of the Criminal Law of the Republic of Montenegro - harassment in discharging office, as well as art. 65 of the Criminal Law of the Republic of Serbia and art. 56 of the Criminal Law of the Republic of Montenegro - extortion of statements).

59. The Federal Republic of Yugoslavia Constitution guarantees, for the first time in Yugoslavia, the following political freedoms and rights: freedom of the press and other mass media, guaranteed on the basis of registration of activity; censorship of the press is prohibited; political, trade union and other organizations and activities require no permission but the registration of activity; freedom of assembly and other peaceful gatherings requires no permission but notification of the assembly; the right to criticize in public the work of State organs and officials, and protection from responsibility of such criticism unless it involves the commission of a criminal offence.

60. In the sphere of personal freedoms and rights, the following are specifically spelled out, always with a view to protecting the status and rights of the citizen in the context of criminal proceedings: the obligation of the authority depriving the individual of liberty to inform the individual in his mother tongue of the reasons thereof, and the obligation of the same authority to so inform his next of kin; the stipulation to warn the individual that he is under no obligation to make any statement and to advise him of his right to counsel immediately upon his having been deprived of liberty; any torture or extortion of statements from persons deprived of freedom is prohibited. In addition, the personal freedom of movement and establishment of residence has been specifically extended to include the right to leave the country and return; personal freedom of religion has been spelled out as the freedom of the public or private practice of religion and religious rites, specifying, in particular, the right not to declare one's religious convictions. This set of freedoms and rights also includes the specific provision on the protection of personal data and of the individual's right to be informed of data collected on him.

61. The Federal Republic of Yugoslavia Constitution guarantees Yugoslav citizens of 18 years of age the right to vote and stand for elections for State

bodies, and the criminal laws of the member republics and the Federal Electoral Law envisage as criminal offences acts of violation of the right to vote, violations of freedom of choice at voting and abuse of the right to vote.

62. Members of national minorities have the right to self-organization, political organization and political representation. It is a fact that members of national minorities, apart from the Albanian national minority, are exercising this right in accordance with the Constitution and the law.

63. According to the 1990 Constitution of the Republic of Serbia, the Republic of Serbia consists of two autonomous provinces - its constituent parts (AP Vojvodina and AP Kosovo and Metohija). The autonomous provinces are constituted in compliance with the national historical, cultural and other characteristics of their respective regions. The AP authorities shall adopt their respective programmes of economic, scientific, technological, demographic, regional and social development, their respective budgets and financial statements, general decisions and general enactments, in compliance with the Constitution and law. They enforce laws, other regulations and general enactments of the Republic of Serbia, the implementation of which is within the competence of the authorities of the autonomous provinces, establish agencies and organizations and services of the autonomous province, and perform other activities stipulated by law and the Constitution. Each province has its Statute, adopted by its Assembly with the previous consent of the National Assembly of the Republic of Serbia. The authorities of the autonomous provinces are: the Assembly, the Executive Council and the administrative authorities. Such constitutional arrangements were not to the liking of ethnic Albanian secessionist leaders from Kosovo and Metohija, who discontinued every dialogue not only with institutions envisaged by the Constitution (the Government, the National Assembly and President of the Republic), but also with other national minorities, which resulted in problems and conflicts. The authorities of the Republic of Serbia are making every effort to overcome the existing problems and conflicts. However, they are not getting an adequate response. Moreover, ethnic Albanians who are willing to cooperate with the authorities are subjected not only to boycotts, threats and physical assaults by ethnic Albanian separatist forces, but also to armed and terrorist attacks, occasionally fatal.

64. The Autonomous Province of Vojvodina, in contrast to the Autonomous Province of Kosovo and Metohija, is an example of a markedly multi-ethnic community. Manifestation, preservation and promotion of ethnic affiliation and relations of tolerance against the background of cultural and ethnic pluralism are the main characteristics of the life of members of national minorities in the territory of AP Vojvodina. On many occasions have the citizens - members of national minorities in Vojvodina - declared that they consider Yugoslavia their homeland, in which they fully exercise their right to ethnic affiliation. Members of the non-dominant national minorities in Vojvodina maintain that the prerequisite for good inter-ethnic relations is the Constitution of the Federal Republic of Yugoslavia, based on democratic principles of a civil State of equal citizens irrespective of their nationality. The four largest national minority communities in Vojvodina feel that guarantees for the stability of the status of ethnic groups are to be found in the Constitution and laws, the promotion of democratic relations, tolerance and confidence, the guarantees of the State, as well as in the consistent observance in practice of the proclaimed rights and in adequate material and institutional resources. Members of these dominant, as well as other national minorities are represented in the provincial and, in particular, local authorities.

65. Based on the above, the conclusion can be reached that members of national minorities in the Federal Republic of Yugoslavia, except for almost all members of the Albanian national minority in Kosovo and Metohija, exercise their right to political organization in compliance with the Constitution and law.

66. The Federal Republic of Yugoslavia Constitution and corresponding laws guarantee and safeguard the rights specified in article 5 (d) (i) to (ix) and 5 (e) (i) to (vi) of the Convention.

67. The rights specified under article 5 (f) of the Convention have in no way been restricted in respect of anyone in the Federal Republic of Yugoslavia.

Article 6

68. Article 26, paragraph 2, of the Federal Republic of Yugoslavia Constitution guarantees everyone the right to appeal or another legal remedy against decisions concerning one's rights or interests stemming from the law. Abuse of the freedoms and rights of man and the citizen is unconstitutional and punishable, i.e. the freedoms and rights guaranteed by the Federal Republic of Yugoslavia Constitution enjoy judicial protection. In the event the violation of a guaranteed freedom or right constitutes a criminal offence, criminal proceedings shall be instituted against the perpetrator, in the majority of cases ex officio by the competent prosecutor, and in a lesser number of cases by private action of the injured party. In case of the violation of an individual's freedoms or rights of man or the citizen guaranteed under the Federal Republic of Yugoslavia Constitution by an individual act or action of judicial, administrative or other State organ or legal entity discharging public office, that individual has the right to lodge a constitutional appeal with the Federal Constitutional Court, if other legal protection has not been provided for.

69. Apart from the persons whose rights or freedoms have been violated, constitutional complaints may be lodged on their behalf by groups of citizens or another legal entity which is bound under its rules to protect the freedoms and rights of man and the citizen whose protection before the court is sought. In addition, the federal body responsible for human and minority rights is also entitled to lodge a constitutional appeal on behalf of the injured party, at the request of the latter or when the body deems it necessary.

70. If the Federal Constitutional Court establishes that a right or freedom guaranteed under the Federal Republic of Yugoslavia Constitution has been violated by an individual act of a State organ or other legal entity discharging public office, the Court shall rescind that individual act and rule that its resulting consequences be reversed. In the event of violation of the rights or freedoms in question through action of the mentioned bodies, the Court shall prohibit any further performance of such action and shall order the reversal of consequences arising from such action.

71. Everyone is entitled to compensation of material or non-material damage inflicted through the unlawful or irregular operation of an official or a State body or a legal entity discharging public office. The damages shall be compensated by the State or the legal entity discharging public office.

Article 7

72. In the sphere of education, the point of departure is the standards specified under the Convention against Discrimination in Education, adopted by the UNESCO General Conference in 1960 and ratified by Yugoslavia under a 1964 decree. This Convention prohibits any discrimination or distinction on the basis of race, sex, language, religion, political or other convictions, national or social origin, the objective or consequence of which is the annulment or impairment of equal treatment in the sphere of education. Article 5 (c) of the Convention specifically emphasizes that members of national minorities shall enjoy the right to use their own language and to carry out instruction in it, provided that such right is exercised in a way which does not prevent national minorities from understanding the culture and language of the community at large and from participating in its life, and in a way which does not endanger national sovereignty; the level of instruction in such schools should not be below the general level prescribed or approved by the competent authorities and, finally, attendance at such schools should be a matter of free choice. The aforementioned, as well as other provisions of the Convention, have been incorporated in the Yugoslav internal legal system.

73. In the Federal Republic of Yugoslavia education is accessible to all under equal conditions, with eight-year elementary education being compulsory. Regular schooling in any of the languages which are in equal official use, at the primary, secondary and higher levels, is free of charge.

74. The constitutional right to education of members of national minorities in their mother language has been spelled out in a number of republican laws and other regulations. The educational process in the languages of the nationl minorities has been organized from the preschool level to education at institutions of higher learning. ...

80. The schooling in the Autonomous Province of Kosovo and Metohija is organized in the same manner: solely out of political considerations, however, the Albanians refuse to accept the uniform educational system applied throughout the territory of the Republic of Serbia, the curricula adopted by the competent State organs, and the uniform system of diplomas and degrees. The differences in the curricula are not great, with four subjects being controversial: language, history, geography and music. All attempts at reaching an agreement, even with international mediation in Geneva, bore no fruit due to the obstructive stance of the members of the Albanian national minority; the Albanian separatists refuse to submit their curricula to the Ministry of Education of the Republic of Serbia for verification. Nevertheless, and despite everything, the Republic of Serbia is allocating considerable funds for the maintenance and provision of instruction for members of the Albanian national minority.

81. The Republic of Serbia and the Federal Republic of Yugoslavia have so far exhibited a marked willingness to make concessions so that the Albanian children do not suffer the consequences of this senseless policy. The State

organs have been willing to recognize the years of schooling spent within the unlawful school system on the condition that the diplomas should be issued by the competent authorities of the Republic of Serbia, but not even this offer has been accepted. The Albanian separatists keep insisting that the school-leaving certificates and diplomas be issued by the unlawful bodies of the non-existent and unrecognized "Republic of Kosovo".

82. In 1992, within the framework of the International Conference on the Former Yugoslavia, the Government of the Federal Republic of Yugoslavia submitted the following proposal to deal with the problem of education in Kosovo and Metohija:

(a) Agreement stipulating maximum guarantees for the preservation and promotion of the cultural identity of members of the Albanian national minority in the Federal Republic of Yugoslavia;

(b) Return to work of all Albanian teachers who left their positions of their own accord (except the few who have committed criminal offences);

(c) Recognition of two years' attendance by Albanian pupils of the parallel and unlawful educational system;

(d) Instruction at all levels to be carried out in the existing State school buildings; and

(e) Recognition of the 1990 school curriculum of the Republic of Serbia.

This proposal of the Government of the Federal Republic of Yugoslavia still stands, but the Albanian secessionist leadership in Kosovo and Metohija are adamantly refusing it.

83. On the occasion of the visit of the Committee on the Elimination of Racial Discrimination, the delegation offered their good offices in this matter taking the above proposal as the basis for negotiations.

84. As a result of the concern for education and, thus, for the future of ethnic Albanian children and youth in Kosovo and Metohija, there is an ongoing dialogue in the Republic of Serbia on the normalization of the educational system in the territory of Kosovo and Metohija.

85. According to the data for Montenegro, in the school year 1995/96, 3,118 pupils of Albanian nationality enrolled at 11 elementary schools in the territory of the Republic of Montenegro in which instruction is provided in the Albanian language.

86. According to the 1995/96 school year figures, there are three secondary schools operating in the territory of the Republic of Montenegro (in Plav, Tuzi and Ulcinj), providing instruction in the Albanian language by 83 teachers of Albanian nationality, attended by 900 pupils of Albanian nationality.

87. In view of the provisions of the Federal Republic of Yugoslavia Constitution laying down the right of national minorities to public information in their own language, as well as in view of the corresponding provisions of the republican laws on public information, international standards can be considered to have been met in this field as well.

88. According to the 1994 statistical data, the following numbers of daily papers, magazines and various bulletins were published in the Federal Republic of Yugoslavia in the following languages: 75 in Hungarian, 17 in Romanian and Ruthenian, 12 in Czech and Slovak, 25 in Albanian, 3 in Turkish, 3 in Bulgarian. Nineteen papers and 36 magazines were issued in a number of languages.

89. In accordance with the provisions of the Constitution of the Republic of Serbia and of the Law on Public Information, there are a large number of papers in Serbia published in the languages of the national minorities (Albanian, Hungarian, Slovak, Romanian, Ruthenian, Ukrainian, Turkish, Bulgarian and the Romany language). All the papers in the languages of the national minorities are edited by members of the respective national minorities.

90. In the Republic of Serbia, under the Republican Law on Public Information, the publishing of newspapers is open to all without prior permission, requiring only registration with the competent court. It is within the purview of AP Vojvodina to ensure the necessary conditions for public information to be provided also in the languages and scripts of the national minorities. For example, in 1994, funds were allocated from the budget of AP Vojvodina to subsidize the publishing of 14 dailies and 4 magazines in the languages of the national minorities.

91. Radio-Television Priština broadcasts television and radio programmes in the Albanian language, with another six local radio stations also on the air. Twenty-five dailies with an annual circulation of 21 million copies and 40 magazines with a circulation of 300,000 copies are published annually in the Albanian language.

92. Radio Priština broadcasts Albanian language programmes every day starting at 3.30 p.m. The programme basically consists of news and music.

In addition to the news, broadcast every hour, the following information programmes are also broadcast: the Midday Journal (10 minutes); Events of the Day at 3 p.m. (30 minutes); the Evening Journal at 6.30 p.m. (30 minutes) and Daily Chronicle at 10 p.m. (15 minutes). The news in Albanian broadcast by Radio Yugoslavia from 9 to 9.15 p.m. is also transmitted every day. Radio Priština broadcasts a Turkish language programme every day from 11 a.m. to 6 p.m. In addition to information broadcasts, news and journals, there are also culture, science, education, features and drama, entertainment, sports and music programmes. Also, Radio Priština broadcasts two 60-minute programmes in the Romany language (on Thursdays and Sundays, dealing with important developments in the life, culture and customs of the Romanies).

93. In addition to Radio Priština, local radio stations operate in Kosovo and Metohija such as Radio Metohija (Pes) and Radio Kosovska Mitrovica, broadcasting programmes in the languages of the national minorities (Albanian, Turkish, Romany).

94. Television Priština broadcasts every day news in Albanian (10 minutes) and a newsreel (25 minutes); on the average Television Priština broadcasts 47 minutes of Albanian - language programming daily, or 329 minutes weekly, or 17,019 minutes annually. In addition to the Albanian language, Television Priština also broadcasts programmes in the Turkish language of a total duration of 10,316 minutes annually, as well as a news magazine in the Romany language, of 1,178 minutes annually.

95. The Albanian-language programmes of Radio Priština and Television Priština, like those in the Serbian and Turkish languages, have their own desks and staff with editors-in-chief responsible for their preparation and broadcasting.

96. There is a disproportion between Serbian- and Albanian- language programmes, chiefly owing to the shortage of ethnic Albanian staff. There is a standing invitation for applications to fill the vacancies, but the response of qualified staff is inadequate, on account of the refusal of members of the Albanian national minority to work for State-financed enterprises.

97. In 1994, of the total of 285,827 hours of radio and TV broadcasts in the Federal Republic of Yugoslavia, 6,454 hours were in the Albanian language, 105 hours in the Bulgarian language, 19,543 hours in Hungarian, 3,599 in Romanian, 1,803 in Ruthenian, 5,485 in Slovak, 3,149 in Turkish, 48 in Ukrainian and 4,614 in other minority languages.

98. Radio stations in AP Vojvodina broadcast programmes in eight languages: Serbian, Hungarian, Slovak, Romanian, Ruthenian, Ukrainian, Macedonian and Romany. The radio programme in Hungarian is around the clock - broadcast 24 hours a day, in Slovak 7 hours a day on the average, in Romanian also 7, in Ruthenian 4 hours a day. These are the data for radio Novi Sad, the central station for the area of Vojvodina, with 27 regional and local radio stations in the province, 4 of which prepare and broadcast programmes in four languages, 6 of which have programmes in three languages, 8 of which have programmes in two languages, and 4 of which broadcast their programmes in one language.

99. Television Novi Sad broadcasts regular programmes in four languages in addition to the Serbian language - in Hungarian every day, and five to six times a week in the Slovak, Romanian and Ruthenian languages.

100. In 1993, the following number of books and brochures were published: 48 in Hungarian, 17 in Czech and Slovak, 16 in Romanian, 5 in Albanian, 1 in Bulgarian, and 221 books in several languages. That year, the 41 books published in the Hungarian language had an average circulation of 1,000 copies, the 7 books in Slovak had a circulation of 500 and the 6 books in Romanian and 7 in Ruthenian had a circulation of 500 copies each. The library network of Vojvodina features, in keeping with the ethnic mix of the population, the following stocks: 76.67 per cent of the books are in Serbian, 15.65 per cent in Hungarian, 1.12 per cent in Slovak, 1.04 per cent in Romanian and 0.22 per cent in Ruthenian.

101. In conformity with the provisions of the Law on Public Information of the Republic of Montenegro, a number of Albanian-language dailies are published in this republic, as well as the monthly magazine Fati, printed in Ulcinj, and the weekly Polis printed in Podgorica. Television Montenegro broadcasts 15 minutes of news in Albanian every day, on Saturdays a news and culture programme of 60 minutes, and a 30-minute news broadcast every day on the radio.

102. The interests of the minority population in the area of creative work and culture are fostered by their central cultural and publishing societies, their communities and associations which make programmes in cooperation with cultural institutions in the province and carry out activities to preserve and foster their national identity, and preserve and promote their national language, literature, art and folklore.

103. In the cultural institutions of Kosovo and Metohija no organized walkouts by members of the Albanian national minority have been staged. On the contrary, Albanians are employed in almost all cultural establishments and in fact account for the majority of the staff in many of them. Thus, for instance, in cultural centres in most of the cities there are more Albanians among the employees than Serbs. Of the eight employed in the Provincial Cultural Centre in Priština, three are Serbs, and in the Communal Cultural Centre in Glogovac all the staff are Albanian; the same is true of the State archives and museums. For instance, in the Museum of Kosovo and Metohija, of the 34 employed, 20, i.e. 60 per cent, are ethnic Albanians. In the Institute for the Protection of Cultural Monuments of Kosovo and Metohija, of the 25 employed, 10 are ethnic Albanians, and the ratio is similar in other communal institutes as well.

104. The National Theatre in Priština has two organizational units - the Serbian Drama Ensemble and the Albanian Drama Ensemble, with the latter having a larger number of actors and other artistic and technical staff. The situation is the same in the Youth Theatre and the Puppet Theatre in Priština and in the Djakovica Theatre where the majority are ethnic Albanians. These and other theatres from Kosovo and Metohija stage plays in the Albanian language not only in this province but also on tours, staging guest performances throughout the country and abroad. The National Theatre in Novi Sad has a Hungarian-language drama organizational unit.

105. The work and programmes of these institutions are financed by the State. The State also finances the protection of monuments of culture, irrespective of their national origin. ...

CERD/C/304/Add.50, 30 March 1998

6.   Concluding Observations of CERD: Yugoslavia, 19 March 1998

1. The Committee considered the eleventh, twelfth, thirteenth and fourteenth periodic reports of Yugoslavia (CERD/C/299/Add.17) at its 1260th, 1261st and 1262nd meetings, held on 11 and 12 March 1998, and adopted, at its 1272nd meeting, held on 19 March 1998, the following concluding observations.

A. Introduction

2. The Committee expresses its appreciation to the State party for the report submitted as well as for the additional information provided orally by the delegation. The Committee also expresses its satisfaction for the resumption of dialogue with the State party, interrupted since 1995, and welcomes the commitment to continue that dialogue as a means to facilitate the implementation of the Convention in Yugoslavia.

3. The Committee regrets, however, that the report contains information almost exclusively on legislation and not on the implementation of such legislation. It also regrets that the report does not respond to the concluding observations on Yugoslavia made by the Committee in 1993. The absence of any such response restricts the possibilities for a fruitful dialogue with the State party on the issues raised in those observations.

B. Factors and difficulties impeding the implementation of the Convention

4. It is acknowledged that Yugoslavia is experiencing an acute crisis with serious consequences in terms of demographic, social, economic and political developments. International sanctions, the repercussions of the war in Bosnia and Herzegovina and the presence in its territory of about 700,000 refugees adversely affect the enjoyment of human rights, including those protected by the Convention.

C. Positive aspects

5. The statement made by the State party during the oral dialogue indicating its intention to pursue cooperation with all international mechanisms for the protection of human rights is noted.

6. The Committee takes note of the statement that the Government of the Republic of Serbia is inviting the International Committee of the Red Cross to visit Kosovo and Metohija, and urges the State party to immediately grant the ICRC and other humanitarian organizations free access to Kosovo.

7. It is noted that since the Committee's good-offices mission in 1993, some progress has been made, with the participation of the Albanian population, towards the normalization of the health care system in the province of Kosovo and Metohija.

8. The Committee notes the statement made by the Government of the Republic of Serbia to the effect that all questions relating to Kosovo and Metohija should be resolved within Serbia by political means and in accordance with international standards in the field of protection of the rights of national minorities.

D. Principal subjects of concern

9. Concern is expressed at the lack of implementation of the memorandum of understanding on the normalization of education in Kosovo and Metohija, signed by President Milosevic and representatives of the Albanian population in September 1996.

10. Concern is expressed about continuing reports indicating that, despite constitutional and legal safeguards, access of certain minorities to education, public information and cultural activities in their own language is not fully guaranteed.

11. Concern is expressed at the limitations imposed by the 1989 Act on Special Conditions for Real Property Transactions, on the transactions between members of different groups and about the fact that the law is being unevenly and arbitrarily implemented, depending on the applicant's ethnicity and place of residence.

12. It is noted with regret that there has been no follow-up to the good-offices mission of the Committee in 1993. The purpose of the mission was to help promote a dialogue for the peaceful solution of issues concerning respect for human rights in the province of Kosovo and Metohija, in particular the elimination of all forms of racial discrimination, and to help the parties concerned to arrive at such a solution. As a result of the mission, the Committee proposed to the State party that a number of specific steps, particularly in the fields of education and health care, be taken with a view to normalizing the situation in Kosovo. Although the Committee expressed a willingness to continue the dialogue within the framework of the good-offices mission, no response was received from the State party.

13. Concern is also expressed at persisting violations in Kosovo and Metohija of basic human rights standards, including article 5 (a) and (b) of the Convention, requiring that arrested persons be brought promptly before a judge, and prohibiting torture and ill-treatment of persons in detention or in the course of demonstrations. Equal concern is expressed about the impunity that perpetrators of such violations seem to enjoy.

14. The Committee is concerned that disproportionate use of force by law enforcement agencies and the military against the Albanian population in the province of Kosovo and Metohija has resulted in numerous violations of the right to life, destruction of property and displacement.

15. Although the State party has argued that its recent actions in Kosovo and Metohija were carried out exclusively with a view to combating terrorism, the Committee notes with serious concern that a great number of victims of the recent events are civilians, including women and children whose deaths cannot be justified by any means. It states that any attempt to push for a military solution of the long-standing crisis in Kosovo could have distressing consequences.

16. It is regretted that the cooperation of the State party with the International Criminal Tribunal for the Former Yugoslavia remains insufficient and that individuals indicted by the Tribunal for war crimes and crimes against humanity are not put at its disposal.

E. Suggestions and recommendations

17. The Committee recommends that the information provided orally in response to a wide range of questions raised by the members be incorporated in the next periodic report due on 24 July 2000. That report should also contain information on the following issues:

(a) Cases in which the Convention has been invoked in decisions or other acts adopted by courts or administrative organs;

(b) Cases where decisions and other acts adopted by courts or administrative organs have been invalidated owing to non-compliance with the Convention;

(c) Cases where compensation has been granted for damages caused by officials or State organs involving violation of rights guaranteed by the Convention;

(d) Cases where measures have been taken against organizations carrying out activities promoting racial hatred and discrimination;

cases that might have been brought before the constitutional courts in this respect;

(e) Cases where proceedings have been instituted for the crimes of violation of citizens' right to equality, infringement of citizens' right to use their mother tongue, incitement of national, racial and religious hatred or any other act of racial discrimination.

18. Efforts should be pursued in order to guarantee full enjoyment by members of all minorities of their rights to public information and cultural activities, as well as education in their own language, whenever possible.

19. The Committee recommends that the Government of Yugoslavia take measures to incorporate human rights programmes in school curricula. Such programmes should also include the provisions of the Convention, with a view to promoting the prevention of racial discrimination.

20. Recalling its General Recommendation XXI, the Committee expresses the opinion that a solution for Kosovo and Metohija includes a status of the highest level of autonomy for this part of the State party as a means for everyone to enjoy their human rights and in particular to eliminate all forms of racial discrimination.

21. The Committee calls on all parties to ensure implementation of the memorandum of understanding on the normalization of education in Kosovo and Metohija.

22. The Committee urges the State party to carry out a full and independent investigation of the incidents that occurred in Kosovo and Metohija following the recent military operations and to bring to justice those responsible for any act involving a disproportionate use of force.

23. The Committee recommends that the State party cooperate fully with the International Criminal Tribunal for the Former Yugoslavia, in particular by handing over those indicted by the Tribunal for war crimes and crimes against humanity.

24. It is also noted that the State party has not made the declaration provided in article 14 of the Convention, and some members of the Committee request that the possibility of making the declaration be considered.

25. The Committee recommends that the State party ratify the amendments to article 8, paragraph 6, of the Convention, adopted on 15 January 1992 at the fourteenth meeting of States parties to the Convention.

1296th meeting, 17 August 1998

7. CERD, Decision 3(53) on the Federal Republic of Yugoslavia 17 August 1998

The Committee on the Elimination of Racial Discrimination,

Considering the grave developments in Kosovo and Metohija since the adoption of its concluding observations on 30 March 1998 concerning the report submitted by the Federal Republic of Yugoslavia.

Referring to its concluding observations of 30 March 1998 concerning the report submitted by the Federal Republic of Yugoslavia;

Also *referring* to General Recommendation XXI (1996);

Noting the Security Council Resolution 1160 of 31 March 1998;

1. *Calls upon* the Government of the Federal Republic of Yugoslavia and the leadership of Albanian community in Kosovo and Metohija to stop immediately all military and para-military activities or hostilities and to enter into negotiations on a just and lasting solution for Kosovo and Metohija, which shall include a status of the highest level of autonomy which will make it possible for everyone to enjoy human rights and in particular to eliminate all forms of racial discrimination.

2. *Reaffirms* that questions relating to Kosovo and Metohija can be resolved only by peaceful political means in accordance with international standards in the field of protection of human rights and in particular for the elimination of all forms of racial discrimination and should be based on respect for the territorial integrity of the Federal Republic of Yugoslavia;

3. Further *reaffirms* that all people who have been displaced or who have become refugees have the right to return safely to their homes and properties and to receive assistance to do; and to be compensated appropriately for any such property that cannot be restored to them; or

4. *Reiterates* its call that the Memorandum of Understanding on the normalization of education in Kosovo and Metohija, signed by President Milosevic and representatives of the Albanian population in September 1996, be implemented fully.

5. *Expresses* its deep concerns over:

(i) persisting grave violations in Kosovo and Metohija of basic human rights, including articles 5 (a) and (b) of the Convention;

(ii) the disproportionate use of force by the State party's law enforcement agencies and the military against the Albanian population in Kosovo and Metohija which, as reported by the United Nations High Commissioner for Refugees, has resulted in numerous violations of the right to life, destruction of property and in a great number of people being displaced or made refugees, of whom many are women and children, whose deaths or deprivation of their rights to security of person and protection against violence or bodily harm cannot be condoned nor justified by whatever reason;

(iii) acts of violence against civilians in Kosovo and Metohija based on ethnic origin committed by whatever groups or individuals.

6. *Requests* the Government of the Federal Republic of Yugoslavia, in view of article 9, para.1 of the International Convention on the Elimination of All Forms of Racial Discrimination, to provide it with information about the attempts that have been undertaken to achieve through a meaningful dialogue with the Kosovo-Albanian leadership a political solution for the status of Kosovo and Metohija including the observance of international human rights, in particular as enshrined Convention. Such information should be submitted by 15 January 1999 so that the Committee can consider it at its March session in 1999.

CRC/C/15/Add.49

8. Concluding Observations of Committee on Rights of the Child: Yugoslavia, 13 February 1996

... B. Principal subjects of concern

6. The Committee remains uncertain as to the extent to which a system for the independent monitoring of the rights of the child, such as an ombudsperson for children or a similar national institution, exists and operates in the State party.

7. The Committee raises various points of concern with reference to the implementation of article 2 of the Convention relating to non-discrimination. It expresses grave concern about the situation of Albanian-speaking children in Kosovo, especially with regard to their health and education, as well as the degree to which this population is protected from abuse by the police. From the information reported to the Committee, it appears that the rejection by the population of the Government's decision to apply a uniform education system and curriculum has been followed by the summary dismissal of 18,000 teachers and other education professionals and to more than 300,000 school-age children not attending school. The subsequent development of a parallel system of education and the tensions surrounding this development in Kosovo have resulted in further detrimental effects, including the closure of schools and the harassment of teachers.

8. The Committee also draws attention to the serious problems threatening the health-care system which have involved large-scale dismissals of health personnel, thereby adversely affecting the health and social protection of Albanian-speaking children in Kosovo.

9. Additionally, the Committee expresses its concern at the information it has received concerning the abuse of children and teachers by the police as well as at the prevailing opinion of the victims of such abuse that the police are able to act with impunity.

10. The Committee also wishes to express its concern over reports of the treatment of persons, including children belonging to a religious minority (Muslims), in Sandjak where incidents of harassment, police abuse, violent house searches and commission of human rights violations with impunity are alleged to have occurred. There have also been reports about serious incidents of discrimination against the Roma (Gypsy) population.

11. The Committee is concerned at the information brought to its attention concerning the hostile sentiments apparently broadcast by certain mass media. The Committee is worried about tendencies in the media which may lead to the incitement of hatred against certain ethnic and religious groups.

12. The Committee is deeply concerned about the absence of pluralism in the activities of the major organs of mass media, limiting the freedom of the child to receive information and the freedom of thought and conscience, as provided for in articles 13 and 14 of the Convention.
...

C. Suggestions and recommendations ...

28. The Committee strongly recommends that a solution be found to the concerns of the Committee for the situation of Albanian-speaking children in Kosovo, especially in the light of the principles and provisions of the Convention, including those of its article 3 relating to the best interests of the child. The Committee observes that the State-controlled mass media, in the interests of healing and building trust within the country, have a role and a responsibility to contribute to the efforts to foster tolerance and understanding between different groups and that the broadcasting of programmes that run counter to this objective should end. The Committee recommends that the securing and dissemination of broader and more diverse sources of information designed for children, including by broadcasting them on the mass media, would assist in ensuring further implementation of the principles and provisions of the Convention, including those of its article 17. It is also suggested that measures should be taken to improve the activities of the mass media in imparting information for children in their own language, including Albanian.

30. Note is taken of the provisions of article 2 of the Primary School Act by which certain of the aims of education laid down in article 29 of the Convention have been incorporated into school curricula. It is the view of the Committee that the principle contained in article 29 (1) (d) which stipulates that "the preparation of the child for responsible life in a free society, in the spirit of understanding, peace, tolerance, equality of sexes, and friendship among all peoples, ethnic, national and religious groups and persons of indigenous origin" is an important dimension that should be integrated into curricula at all levels of schooling. School curricula materials should be developed, if they do not already exist, which aim at educating children in the spirit of tolerance of and regard for different civilizations. ...

CAT/C/ YUGO

9. Conclusions and Recommendations of Committee against Torture: Yugoslavia, 16 November 1998.

1. The Committee considered the initial report of Yugoslavia (CAT/C/16/Add.2) at its 348th, 349th and 354th meetings, held on 11 and 16 November 1998 (CAT/C/SR. 348, 349 and 354) and has adopted the following conclusions and recommendations:

A. Introduction

2. Yugoslavia signed the Convention against Torture and Other Cruel, Inhuman or Degrading Treatment or Punishment on 18 April 1989 and ratified it on 20 June 1991. It recognized the competence of the Committee against Torture to receive and consider communications under articles 21 and 22 of the Convention.

3. The initial report of Yugoslavia was due in 1992. The Committee expresses concern over the fact that the report was submitted on 20 January 1998 only. The report contains background information, information on international instruments, on competent authorities, on court and police procedures, and information concerning the compliance with articles 2 - 16 of the Convention.

B. Positive aspects

4. As a positive aspect, it can be mentioned that the provisions of article 25 of the Constitution of the Federal Republic of Yugoslavia forbid all violence against a person deprived of liberty, any extortion of a confession or statement. This article proclaims that no one may be subjected to torture, degrading treatment or punishment. The same norm is contained in the Constitutions of the constituent republics of Serbia and Montenegro.

5. The Criminal Code of Yugoslavia defines the punishable offenses of unlawful deprivation of freedom, extortion of depositions and maltreatment in the discharge of office. Similar provisions are contained in the Criminal Codes of Serbia and of Montenegro. The Law on Criminal Procedure applicable throughout the Federal Republic of Yugoslavia contains a provision, according to which any extortion of a confession or statement from an accused person or any other person involved in the proceedings is forbidden and punishable. This Code also provides that during detention neither the personality nor the dignity of an accused may be offended.

6. The police regulations in Yugoslavia provide disciplinary and other measures, including termination of employment and criminal charges in cases of acts by police officers violating the provisions of the Convention.

7. The current legislative reform in the area of criminal law, and especially criminal procedure, envisions specific provisions which will, hopefully, contribute to the improved prevention of torture in Yugoslavia.

C. Factors and difficulties impeding the application of the provisions of the Convention

8. The Committee took into account the situation in which Yugoslavia currently finds itself, especially with respect to the unrest and ethnic friction in the province of Kosovo. However, the Committee emphasizes that no exceptional circumstances can ever provide a justification for failure to comply with the terms of the Convention.

D. Subjects of concern
...

13. With respect to the factual situation in Yugoslavia the Committee is extremely concerned over the numerous accounts of the use of torture by the State police forces that it has received from non-governmental organizations. Reliable data received by the Committee from non-governmental organizations include information describing numerous instances of brutality and torture by the police, particularly in the districts of Kosovo an Sandzack. The acts of torture perpetrated by the police, and especially by its special units, include beatings by fists, beatings by wooden or metallic clubs mainly on the head, on the kidney area and on the soles of the feet, resulting in mutilations and even death in some cases. There were instances of use of electroshock. The concern of the Committee derives also from reliable information that confessions obtained by torture were admitted as evidence by the courts even in cases where the use of torture had been confirmed by pre-trial medical examinations.

14. The Committee is also gravely concerned over the lack of sufficient investigation, prosecution and punishment by the competent authorities (article 12 of the Convention) of suspected torturers or those breaching article 16 of the Convention, as well as with the insufficient reaction to the complaints of such abused persons, resulting in the de facto impunity of the perpetrators of acts of torture. De jure impunity of the perpetrators of torture and other cruel, inhuman or degrading treatment or punishment results inter alia from amnesties, suspended sentences and reinstatement of discharged officers that have been granted by the authorities. Neither the report nor the oral statement of the Yugoslav delegation said anything about the Yugoslav government's efforts concerning the rehabilitation of the torture victims, the amount of compensation they receive, and the actual extent of redress afforded them.

15. The Committee hopes that in the future it will be possible to bridge the disconcerting discrepancy between the Yugoslav report and the apparent reality of abuse. However, the Committee is also concerned with the apparent lack of political will on the part of the State party to comply with its obligations under the Convention.

D. Selected Reports of the UN Commission on Human Rights Special Rapporteur for the Former Yugoslavia

E/CN.4/1992/S-1/9

1. Report on the Situation of Human Rights in the former Yugoslavia, 28 August 1992

… 32. In addition, there is some evidence that ethnic cleansing may be imminent in certain parts of Serbia and Montenegro where there are large communities of persons not of Serbian origin. In Kosovo, where the population of Albanian origin has complained of discrimination and oppression of many years, non-governmental organizations presented evidence of an increasing number of torture and killings. …

A/47/666, S/24809, 17 November 1992

2. Report on the Situation of Human Rights in the former Yugoslavia, 17 November 1992

… 137. Albanians, Croats, Hugarnians, Muslims and other ethnic minority groups are discriminated against in Kosovo, Vojvodina and Sandzak. In some instances, violent methods characteristic of ethnic cleansing are used, and there is a real danger that widespread violence, including armed conflict, many spread to these regions. …

A/48.92, S/25341, 26 February 1993

3. Report on the Situation of Human Rights in the former Yugoslavia, 26 February 1993

153. In his report to the General Assembly at its forthy-seventh session (A/47/6660 [reproduced immediately above], the Special rapporteur expressed his concern about the situation of human rights in Kosovo following a brief visit to Prishtina. The main issues raised concern the mass dismissal of Albanians from the public sector, police brutality, the lack of freedom of the media and problems concerning education. The situation of human rights has been constantly worsening since Kosovo lost its status as an autonomous province in July 1990. The Albanian population has been enduring various forms of discrimination as a result of new laws adopted by the Republic of Serbia and the economic situation has deteriorated to the extent that even the subsistence of many Albanian families is threatened.

154. Since his visit, the Special Rapporteur has continued to receive information from international monitors, in particular the CSCE mission, concerning the human rights in Kosovo.

Legal aspects

155. The special Rapporteur has received a list of laws reportedly discriminating against Albanians. The following paragraphs describe some of these laws.

156. Reportedly, a number of laws, programmes and decrees adopted by the authorities of Serbia contributed to the dismissal of Albanians and the appointment of Serbs and Montenegrins in their places. To this effect the Albanians cited:

(a)   The programme for the establishment of peace, liberty, equality, democracy and prosperity in the autonomous province of Kosovo (Official Gazette of Serbia 15/90 of 30 March 1990), paragraph 3 of which envisages assistance to Serbs and Montenegrins who want to move to Kosovo. Paragraph 9 of the programme implies the dismissal of Albanians form the police force, which was carried out at the time of the abolishment of the Secretariat (i.e. Ministry) of the Interior of Kosovo on 16 April 1990. The places of the dismissed Albanian policemen were taken by Serbs and Montenegrins;

(b)   The Law on police institutions (Official Gazette of Serbia 44/91 of 25 July) was used as the legal basis for taking policemen from all over former Yugoslavia to replace the dismissed Albanians;

(c)   The Law on the creation of a fund to finance the return of Serbs and Montenegrins to Kosovo (Official Gazette of Serbia 35/90 of 14 July 1990); and

(d)   The Programme for the development of the Autonomous Province of Kosovo and Metohia, aiming at the return of Serbs and Montenegrins to Kosovo and Metohia, for 1992 (Official Gazette of Serbia 54/92 of 8 August 1992) provides for assistance to Serbs for building houses, setting up private firms and enterprises, and creating cultural establishments, schools, communications and infrastructure;

(e)   The Law on labour relations in special circumstances (Official Gazette of Serbia 40/90 of 26 July 199)) provides for the right of the directors of enterprises to impose on the workers disciplinary measures envisaged by the laws. Given the fact that in a large number of cases directors are Serbs, Albanians complain that this law leads to arbitrary dismissals of Albanians. The introduction of special measures in many enterprises and social institutions led to the discontinuation of their activities and many Albanians Lost their jobs as a consequence;

(f)   The Law on the conditions, ways and means for distributing agricultural land to citizens who would like to live and work on the territory of the Autonomous Province of Kosovo and Metohia (Official Gazette of Serbia 43/91 of 20 July 1991) envisages making credit available to Serbs who want to move to Kosovo;

(g)   The Law on the Health service (Official Gazette of Serbia 17/92 of 31 March 1992) allegedly led to the dismissal of many Albanians working in the health sector;

(h)   The Law on public information (Official Gazette of Serbia 19/91 of 29 March 1991) led to the dismissal of many journalists and other staff of the Albanian nationality from newspapers, radio and television in Pristina;

(i)   The Law abolishing the Kosovo Law on the educational service (Official Gazette of Serbia 75/91 of 17 December 1991) is said to be the reason that many Albanian teachers lost their jobs.

157. Other discriminatory legal acts against the Albanians in Kosovo concerning education, cultural institutions and the use of the Albanian language were reported as follows:

(a)   The laws abolishing those adopted earlier by the legislature of the socialist Autonomous Province of Kosovo (Law on higher education, Law on university eduction, Law on the Pedagogical Academy, Law on primary education, the Law on secondary education (Official Gazette of Serbia 45/90 of 7 August 1990) and the law abolishing the law on the Education Council of the socialist Autonomous Province of Kosovo (Official Gazette of Serbia 75/91 of 17 December 1991) destroyed the established system of education for the Albanians in Kosovo on all levels;

(b)   The Law establishing the publishing house "Panorama" (Official Gazette of Serbia 80/92 of 6 November 1992) and the above-cited law on public information (Official Gazette of Serbia 19/91 from 29 March 1991) contributed to the enforcement of state control over the mass media in Kosovo. The new agency incorporates the newspaper Rilindja which has been published in Albania for more than 50 years.

(c)   The Law on the official use of the language and the alphabet (Official Gazette of Serbia 45/91 of 27 July 1991) gives priority to the official use of the Serbian language in public institutions;

(d)   The Law abolishing the Kosovo Law on the Institute of the History of Kosovo (Official Gazette of Serbia 49/92 of 21 July 1992) hampers the development of knowledge about the national history and culture of the Albanians in Kosovo. To acquire such knowledge Kosovars must address themselves to the respective Serbian institutions;

(e) The Law on the Serbian Academy of Sciences (Official Gazette of Serbia 49/92 of 21 July 1992) served as a basis for the Serbian Academy of Sciences to take over the property of the Academy of Kosovo;

(f) The Law on the universities (Official Gazette of Serbia 54/92 of 8 August 1992 envisages in its article 10 that education should be given in Serbo-Croatian. It can be given in the languages of the minorities if the board of the corresponding university or faculty agrees on this. the Albanians claim that this discriminates against them because the boards of the universities are nominated by the Serbian authorities.

158. Albanians see discrimination in the sphere of population policies:

(a) Paragraph 91 of the Programme for the establishment of peace, liberty, equality, democracy and prosperity in the Autonomous Province of Kosovo (Official Gazette of Serbia 15/90 of 30 March 1990) envisages measures for the decrease of the birth rate in Kosovo, which is among the highest in Europe;

(b) The law on public care for children (Official Gazette of Serbia 49/92 of 21 July 1992) provides for families with more than three children (and these are typically Albanian families) to receive from the State much lower allowances for the younger children. Albanians regard these provisions as discriminatory as Serbs usually have small families and thus all their children receive allowances.

159. A Declaration on human rights and the rights of persons belong to national minorities was adopted by the Serbian authorities and published in the Official Gazette of Serbia 89/92 of 7 December 1992. The Albanians, however, consider that this declaration is in total contradiction with the real facts of violations of minority and human rights in Kosovo.

Police brutality

160. Several reports indicate that, before and after the elections of 20 December 1992, the police adopted a more severe and aggressive attitude towards the Albanian population. It has been reported that searches without warrants of the houses of Albanians have been carried out on a regular basis, and that at least 70 people, including five Serbs, were arrested. According to a recent report by the CSCE mission "the President of the Assembly of the Muslim Community of Serbia, Kosovo, Sandzak and Vojvodina as well as other Muslim personalities have been arrested". According to official sources some of those arrested have been released.

161. Police action has gone beyond arrest and imprisonment and cases of death as a result of shooting or brutality by the police have been reported. During the first two weeks of December 1992, four incidents were reported from Prishtina and three other small towns during which four Albanians were said to have been killed, and two others and a policeman wounded. It has been asserted that the armed forces also participated in the recent incidents. In two clashes with the Albanian community, the armed forces have allegedly killed two people. Furthermore, the following incidents have also been reported:

(a) On 3 December 1992, in the market of Prishtina, a 19-year-old Albanian was shot dead by police and his older brother wounded in both legs, presumably while selling goods on the black market;

(b) On 18 December 1992, in Dakovica, a young man was beaten to death;

(c) On 19 December 1992, a 32-year-old Albanian from Brovina died in the hospital in Prishtina as a result of police brutality and beatings;

(d) On 24 December 1992, the police arrested a group of Albanians in Prishtina outside the Great Mosque, allegedly without giving any reason for the arrest;

(e) On 25 December 1992, in two villages between Prishtina and Pec, police abuse, maltreatment of the inhabitants and destruction of their food supply have been alleged.

According to the information received, police brutality and harassment has increased in the town of Pec and the surrounding area with the pretext of seizing and collecting arms held illegally by civilians.

162. According to the Albanians the police have adopted a variety of repressive measures in Kosovo with the aim of provoking the Albanian population.

The Situation of the mass media

163. With regard to freedom of press, the Special Rapporteur has been informed of a new Press Law adopted by the Serbian Parliament at the beginning of November 1992 to be applied in Kosovo. The federal authorities of Yugoslavia did not approve the law and declared it unconstitutional. This law has established a State-owned publishing house, Panorama, in charge of printing, publishing and distributing all newspapers, periodicals, graphics and books in the three languages, Serbian, Albanian and Turkish. Allegedly, the main objective of Panorama is to absorb all the assets and staff of the existing Albanian Publishing House run by Albanians, as well as the Serbian daily and Turkish weekly. The Government of Serbia is the only authority empowered to nominate and dismiss members of the Administrative Council, supervisory Board and the General Manager as well as to approve all the internal regulations of Panorama. Independent and private publications have not been banned by the law but, due to the high cost of printing and distribution, it is highly improbable that independent enterprises can survive. Panorama is considered by Albanian journalists, who until recently have still been able to express the Albanian point of view, as a means of censorship.

164. Since the visit by the Special Rapporteur to Prishtina all Abanian staff of the local radio and television stations have been removed from their posts. The surviving 15-minute daily television programme in Albanian is allegedly produced and presented by Serbian journalists who speak Albanian.

Dismissals

165. The Special Rapporteur was recently informed by the CSCE mission that in accordance with the law adopted by the Serbian parliament nince regional medical and the hospital of Dakovica Medial Centre were closed and integrated into the Pec Medical Centre. The authorities claimed that this decision was taken on the basis of the difficult economic situation, while Albanian physicians asserted that the reason for this law was political. The Dakovica medial Centre was among the rare organizations where the overwhelming majority of staff was still Albanian, and thus was the preferred place of treatment by the entire Albanian community of the province.

166. With regard to the judiciary, the Special Rapporteur has been informed that since his visit to Kosovo, all remaining Albanian judges or magistrates have been dismissed. Under such conditions the right to a fair trial and the impartiality of the judiciary can hardly be guaranteed with regard to the Albanian population of Kosovo.

Economic situation

167. With regard to the economic situation in Kosovo the Special Rapporteur has been informed that the regression is such that even Serbian refugees are unwilling to move there. Albanians work mostly in the private sector, mainly in small grocery stores, which allows the owners to meet their basis needs. A large number of Albanians, mainly dismissed civil servants, live in extremely poor conditions. The rate of inflation is very high and rising continuously. The few Albanians who have the opportunity to do so leave Kosovo.

168. A charitable organization, the Financial Council, financed by voluntary donations mostly from Albanians living in Western countries, has been set up by the Albanians in Kosovo. Welfare cases are taken care of by the Financial Council and about 80,000 families registered by the organization are receiving material help.

Education system

169. The Special Rapporteur was informed that the problems outlines in his previous report concerning the education system have not yet been solved. Albanian high schools and the university are closed. Some 70 per cent of the primary schools are operating following Albanian-language curricula; however, Albanian teachers do not receive any salary since they refuse to teach according to the Serbian programme and are helped by the above-mentioned Financial Council. ...

171. The conclusion to be drawn on the basis of the recent information gathered is that the human rights situation in Kosovo has not improved. On the contrary, the police have intensified their repression of the Albanian population since 1990. The Albanians continue to be deprived of their basis rights, their education system has been largely destroyed, they are victims of dismissal for political reasons and they face a very difficult economic situation. However, it must be stressed that until now they have resisted peacefully.

E/CN.4/1994/47

4.   Report on the Situation of Human Rights in the former Yugoslavia, 1 November 1993

188. The Polarization of the Albanian and Serb populations in Kosovo continues. One are affected by this polarization is the judicial system. Albanians lack confidence in the will and ability of the courts to provide an independent and effective remedy and point to the small number of Albanian judges. The CSCE monitors investigated this issue and commented: "A major reason for the lack of Albanian judges is the refusal of most Albanians to serve in the courts. Judges must take an oath to the government, which most Albanians feel would give recognition to what they see as a illegal Serb regime." However, the situation is in reality more complex and is illustrated by the experience of the Prizren District Court. Three Albanian judges have refused to serve as judges, but in June 1993, two others, both well qualified, were rejected by the Serbian Assembly in June 1993 after being described as 'separatist murderers'.

Ill-treatment and torture

189. The Special Rapporteur has continued to receive reports that the Serbian police and state security services act in excess of their powers and in breach of the law in their dealings with the Albanian population in Kosovo. These reports have increased significantly since July 1993

190. In May 1993, some 30 Albanian prisoners were serving sentences for offences involving illegal political activities; this figure does not include those given administrative sentences of up to 60 days. New trials have since taken place and are continuing; most frequently the defendants are charged under article 116 of the Serbian Criminal Code with acts against the territorial integrity of Yugoslavia. In October 1993 Albanian sources reported that 93 people had been detained since July and were in custody; they included former officers of the Yugoslav national army, as well as members of the Democratic League of Kosovo.

191. The former detainees told the Special Rapporteur's staff that in August 1993 they had been systematically beaten to induce them to confess to membership of illegal Albanian separatist movements and to provide information about armaments. In each case, the individual was asked whether he had arms himself. When this was denied, he was told to obtain gun(s) and produce them to the police.

192. Albanian human rights organizations have reported deaths following detention and ill-treatment by the police. One such case, that of Adem Zegiraj from Dakovica, was investigated by the CSCE monitors. Mr Zegiaj was arrested next day he was admitted to Dakovica hospital and then transferred to Pristina hospital, where he died on 19 December. A medical report from Dakovica hospital recorded that he had been admitted with traumatic shock, internal bleeding and a serious kidney condition.

193. The Special Reporter's staff were told by the Serbian Ministry of the Interior that 52 attacks against the police had taken place between 1 January and 30 September 1993. Two police had been killed and 15 wounded. The Deputy Minister denied that Albanians who had been in contact with CSCE monitors had been arrested. However, this denial is inconsistent with the statements made to the Special Rapporteur's staff by four people who were questioned by police after the departure of the CSCE monitors.

194. The Special Rapporteur has also received reports of police abuse in the course of searches for illegal arms. Such searches are frequent. There is frequently damage to property, including the destruction of national flags, symbols and teaching materials and removal of money and valuables.

Housing evictions

195. The Special Rapporteur's staff have received information about the eviction of Albanians from apartments in which they were lawfully resident, often without legal proceedings, in order to accommodate Serb families. In one case, a worker from the JP Elektropower enterprise of Kosovo, was evicted from the apartment of which he was a legal tenant, by two police on 7 December 1992. He remains employed, has held his job for 20 years and occupied the apartment as a member of his workers' association. The apartment was then occupied by a Serb family. Legal proceedings have commenced in the Pristina court.

Use of languages

196. Albanians are a 'national minority' under the federal Constitution and have a constitutional right to use their language in the areas in which they live and in court proceedings. The 1991 Serbian Law on the Official Use of Languages and Alphabets gives municipalities the discretion to decide which languages shall be in official use. Given the use of Albanian before 1990 and the fact that Albanians represent around 90 per cent of the Kosovo population, the Special Rapporteur believes the use of Albanian in all official matters should be normal practice, regardless of Albanian representation on municipal bodies. In practice, there has been a decline in the official use of the Albanian language.

197. The Special Rapporteur notes the issue of identity cards, births and marriage certificates and other public documents in the Serbian language. The Special Rapporteur's staff took copies of identity cards issued in Pristina: in 1984, the cards were in three languages (Albanian, Serbo-Croat and Turkish); in 1990 in two languages (Serbo-Croat and Albanian) and in 1993 in Serbian only.

198. In the Prizren District Court proceedings are now held only in Serbian, although 95 per cent of criminal defendants are Albanian. Before 1990, Albanian and Serbo Croat were of equal status, the criterion being the language of the defendant. While in principle a complaint may be made in Albanian, in practice it will not be dealt with because there is only one translator. A complaint made by an Albanian to the Prosecutor of the Pristina District Court, alleging ill treatment at the hands of the police, with a medical certificate attached, was returned the same day (27 August 1997) by the Deputy Prosecutor, with a note saying: 'We return your complaint ... so it may be translated into the Serbo-Croat language'.

199. Throughout the territories of the former Yugoslavia, street names continued to be changed in 1993 to reflect recent political changes. While in many areas this is not controversial, the Special Rapporteur's staff were told of changes in Pristina and Prizren which had the effect of giving the a Serbian character to areas in which the overwhelming majority of the population is Albanian. In Prizren, he is informed that 90 per cent of the names have been changed since 1991. For example: 'Bayran Curri' (an Albanian leader) to '27 March' (the date of the 1992 Constitution); 'League of Prizren' (Liohja e Prizreni) to 'Car Dushani' (a Serb king). Similar changes have been made in the Hungarian areas of Vojvodina.

Education   ...

201. According to the President of the Association of Albanian teachers, during the 1992-1993 school year, 274,280 pupils attended primary 'parallel' schools. This figure contrasts with official statistics showing that in 1990, more than 295,000 Albanian pupils were enrolled in state primary, secondary and tertiary education. It will be recalled that the parallel schools started after August 1990, when teachers refused to accept a new curriculum drawn up by the Ministry of Education and some 18,000 of them lost their jobs. The new curriculum is compulsory throughout Serbia and replaces, *inter alia*, curricula prepared by the educational councils of Kosovo and Vojvodina. the councils were abolished as part of a broad centralization process and with the aim of creating a common teaching system for all schools in Serbia. the 'parallel' system functions at the primary, secondary and tertiary levels. Teaching is in Albanian, according to a curriculum which is not recognized by the Serbian Ministry of Education. the schools issue their own diplomas, which are, in turn, not recognized by the Serbian educational authorities. Though teachers receive no official salary, teaching at the primary level (which is compulsory under

Serbian law) largely continues to take place in school buildings, the expenses of which are paid by the education authorities. Secondary and tertiary education takes place in private houses and premises.

202. The Serbian Minster of Education told the Special Rapporteur's staff that teaching in the Albanian language is available in the state system and both the Serbian Constitution and Serbian education laws give national minorities a right to education in their own languages. The Minister said that the teachers had refused to accept curricula decided in Belgrade. In June 1990 all national minorities had been invited to propose their own teaching programmes in certain culturally specific subjects to be included in a 'core' Serbian curriculum: literature, history, applied arts and music. The minorities in, for example, Vojvodina had done so, but the Albanians had not.

203. In March 1993, the former Rector of the University of Pristina, Professor Ejup Statovici, was arrested to serve a sentence imposed in 1992, when he was convicted on a public order charge after writing a letter to the current Rector asking for the university buildings 'which were taken by force' to be returned to Albanian teaching staff and students. The Special Rapporteur notes with concern that the conflict surrounding the University of Pristina continues and is contributing to the prevailing climate of tension.

204. Views expressed recently by the Minster of Education and by the current Rector of the University of Pristina illustrate the intellectual climate. The Ministry described education as the 'sphere in which a country manifests its identity' and criticised the University of Pristina and the former Kosovo Academy of Sciences before 1990 as 'centres of actual and theoretical separatism'. The Rector of the University, Professor Radivoje Popovic, speaking in May 1993, referred to changes in the university since 1990 in these terms:

> Our first task was to remove the hatred for all that is Serbian which had been accumulated here for decades ... This factory of evil, established with the basis intention of destroying Serbia and the Serbian name ... is now destroyed thanks to the coordinated action of the Government and university personnel. ... Our university has the ultimate object of renewing Serbian thought in Kosovo and Metohija.

205. Throughout 1993 the police have entered 'parallel' schools, questioned teachers and students and in some instances threatened or used violence. On 21 June, the CSCE monitoring team in Pec reported a 'campaign' against the parallel schools to coincide with the end of the school year. Eight schools were searched for graduation certificates issued in the name of the Republic of Kosovo. In Klina, the police searched the school and then went to the local Democratic League of Kosovo (LDK) office where a meeting was in progress which included a number of teachers. The 12 people present were arrested; 8 were beaten on the head and arms and 2 were beaten more severely, while being questioned about the school system. Similar police actions marked the start of the new school year in September 1993.

E/CN.4/1994/110

5. Report on the Situation of Human Rights in the former Yugoslavia, 21 February 1994

139. The human rights situation in Kosovo continues to deteriorate with reports of abusive and discriminatory treatment on the part of the authorities. Furthermore, the continuing absence of a dialogue between the Serbian and Yugoslav authorities on the one hand and the leadership of the Kosovo Albanians on the other has prevented any improvement on vital issues such as the 'parallel' education system of the ethnic Albanians (See E/CN.4/1994/47, paras. 200-205). In this connection, the situation of the University of Pristina remains a source of considerable tension. This is the third academic year in which enrolments, lectures, tutorials, exams and other activities of over 22,000 students and 900 teaching staff are being carried out in private homes and buildings.

140. There are continuing reports of discriminatory and abusive treatment of ethnic Albanians by the Serbian police. Allegations of beating and torture against ethnic Albanians are not uncommon. The Special Rapporteur has received, with grave concern, information from a reliable non-governmental organization about a meeting with the

President of the Pristina Regional Court in which the ill-treatment of detainees by the police was discussed. it was reported that the President of the Court supported such treatment when 'crimes against the State' where involved, 'irrespective of whether there was a conviction or not'.

141. In addition to the brutal and excessive use of force by the Serbian police, a climate of ethnic hatred and repeated harassment adds to a feeling of insecurity among the ethnic Albanian population. In one case reported to the Special Rapporteur, on 13 January 1994 the Serbian police allegedly seized gold and silver jewellery from Albanian shops in Prizren without explanation. According to information received, if there was any resistance, the police would break shop windows and shopkeepers would be arrested and ill-treated. there are also reports that police at the border crossing between Serbia and the former Yugoslav Republic of Macedonia frequently seize goods and money and confiscate passports from ethnic Albanians.

142. The Special Rapporteur has continued to receive information concerning the illegal and forced eviction of Albanians from their apartments. In most cases, the evictions take place without prior legal proceedings. Furthermore, the evicted tenants are usually replaced by Serbian families. It is reported that in January 1994 alone, the Institute for Urban Planning for Pristina issued 17 eviction notices to Albanian families, all of whom were reported to have been occupying their homes of decades and to be in possession of all the necessary supporting legal documents. Evictions are also used arbitrarily by the authorities to penalize those who do not comply with their orders. In one case in Pristina, the wife and children of an Albanian who refused recruitment into the armed forces and left the country were evicted.

143. The Special Rapporteur has continued to receive reports concerning arbitrary detention and violations of the right to a fair trial by a competent and impartial tribunal (See E/CN.4/1994/47, paras. 169-171). In particular, these violations have been associated with several criminal proceedings initiated against ethnic Albanians in Pristina, Pec, Gnjilane and Prizren, who were all accused of causing a 'threat against the territorial integrity of Yugoslavia' pursuant to article 16, paragraph 1 of the Criminal Code. Most of the accused are former officers of the Yugoslav National Army or the Territorial Defence Forces of Yugoslavia. Apparently, taking into consideration the previous military experience of the accused, the Serbian authorities have alleged that this group was setting up a military organization, forming armed units, registering conscripts for military service and collecting weapons. In December 1993, the Serbian Supreme Court extended for an additional three months the period of detention for some of the accused who were awaiting trial.

A/49/641, S/1994/1252, 4 November 1994

6. Ninth Periodic Report on the Situation of Human Rights in the former Yugoslavia, 4 November 1994

1. The situation in Kosovo

182. Regular and consistent reports indicate that the situation in Kosovo has deteriorated further in the course of the past six months. The Special Rapporteur has taken note of some particularly disturbing reports according to which, during the period January to June 1994, more than 2,000 persons were taken to police stations for so-called "informative talks", lasting from hours to several days. A majority of these persons were allegedly subjected to severe ill-treatment and torture while detained by the police.

183. During the past month, there has reportedly been a drastic increase in the number of violent house searches, raids and arbitrary arrests by the law enforcement authorities. Most of the violence has reportedly occurred when the police, under the pretext of looking for hidden arms or wanted persons, raided homes or entire neighbourhoods. During these searches, minors, women and elderly people have reportedly also been ill-treated, apparently because of their relationship to persons wanted by the police. These attacks appear to be controlled or at least condoned by the leadership of the law enforcement authorities. According to recent reports, in the period 1 January to 30 June 1994, more than 3,000 homes were searched and more than 1,700 persons subjected to police abuse in connection with the raids. A particularly

brutal incident was reported from Podujevo, where the police, while conducting an identity check on 15 September 1994, violently forced the passers-by to lie down on the ground. Fourteen of these people were subsequently beaten brutally by police using truncheons.

184. Undue delays and serious irregularities have been reported in connection with court proceedings against a large number of ethnic Albanians accused of posing a threat to the territorial integrity of the Federal Republic of Yugoslavia (Serbia and Montenegro). The majority of the accused appear to be members of the Democratic League of Kosovo (LDK). One of the latest of these trials reportedly started in Prizren on 16 September 1994 against four ethnic Albanians, members of the League. It is alleged that two of the defendants were arrested as early as 24 May 1994, and that they have been kept in detention since that date. Moreover, it appears that these persons have been subjected to severe ill-treatment during interrogations by the police.

185. Another cause for concern are the extremely difficult circumstances under which schools and other educational institutions work in Kosovo. It has been reported that, on 22 February 1994, the Government discontinued the activities of the Academy of Sciences and Arts of Kosovo and confiscated its building. Moreover, it is with great concern that the Special Rapporteur has taken note of reports according to which several Albanian primary and secondary schools have been forced to interrupt their work because of police harassment. Shortly after the beginning of the school year in early September 1994, it was reported that police entered the premises of several elementary schools. A particularly brutal incident was reported to have taken place in connection with a police raid on 1 September 1994 at the "Ibrahim Pervizi" elementary school in Mitrovica. During the raid, several teachers were reportedly severely beaten and kicked in front of their pupils by police officers. Two of the teachers allegedly had to seek medical care after the incident.

E/CN.4/1995/54, 13 December 1994

7.   Special Report on the Media of the Special Rapporteur, 13 December 1994

123. After the state of emergency was declared in Kosovo, the Serbian Government attempted to stifle the freedom of the Albanian-language media. The main targets of these efforts were TV Pristina and the Rilindja publishing house. On 5 July 1990, the Government prohibited RTV Pristina from broadcasting in Albanian. Approximately 1,300 journalists and other technical staff lost their jobs. A month later, the Serbian Parliament banned Rilindja, the only daily newspaper published in Albanian in Yugoslavia. Rilindja later resumed publishing abroad. At present, the only programme broadcast in Albanian in Kosovo merely translates information already broadcast in Serbian.

...

129. Before the breakup of the former Yugoslavia, the Albanian-language press published over 20 journals regularly. Now, there are far fewer. The largest Albanian journal, Bujku, which appears twice a week, is reported to be under the influence of the Democratic Alliance of Kosovo. There are some weekly Albanian publications including Koha, Forumi, Fjala, Shendija and Zeri.

130. There is no evidence of monopoly control over the printing or distribution networks in Serbia with the exception of Kosovo. However, in Montenegro, the Pobjeda system has a monopoly on printing and distribution, and it is reported that Monitor has often had distribution problems with Pobjeda: copies of the paper are allegedly put aside to prevent their being sold.

131. There is only one producer of newsprint in the Federal Republic of Yugoslavia, the Metroz Company; this fact could have an impact on freedom of the press.

132. The Serbian Government has created an effective monopoly on the printing and distribution network in Kosovo. Through the establishment of the enterprise Panorama in May 1993 (a forced merger of three printing and publishing companies - Rilindja, Jedinstvo and Tan), the Government gained complete control over the printing facilities of certain publications. In addition, the bank accounts of journals

previously published by these three houses were taken over by Panorama. As a result of the take-over, the Albanian-language journal Bujku at one time had to pay printing costs that were 10 times higher than those paid by the Serb-language journal Jedinstvo.

...

149. It has been reported that persecution of journalists has been the most severe in Kosovo. Almost all former editors of Albanian origin have been persecuted by the police. Some 16 cases have been reported within the period 1992-1993. ...

E/CN.4/1995/57

8.   Tenth Periodic Report on Human Rights in the former Yugoslavia, 16 January 1995

84. The Special Rapporteur continues to receive information about human rights violations in Kosovo. According to reliable international sources, the vast majority of the population live in constant fear. Allegedly, at night, paramilitary groups can be seen in the streets of Pristina. The Special Rapporteur has also received a detailed report from a Pristina-based NGO, the Council for the Defence of Human Rights and Freedoms, containing names of victims of serious human rights violations, including victims of killings and torture. This document has been sent to the Government with a request for clarification, and the matter will receive the attention of the Special Rapporteur in forthcoming reports.

85. The recent arrest of some 130 former employees of the Ministry of Interior Affairs, all of Albanian descent, has contributed to the increase of tension in Kosovo. The Special Rapporteur will seek to obtain information as to the legal grounds for that action and will attempt to monitor the matter. According to information received, some of the arrested have been tortured or ill-treated and lawyers have occasionally been denied access to their clients.

86. Allegedly the police in Kosovo continue their harassment of independent trade union activists. It has been reported that on 20 November, a number of activists of the Independent Trade Unions of Kosovo were arrested.

87. The Special Rapporteur continues to receive information about ongoing tensions between members of the local Muslim community and authorities in the region of Sandzak. It is reported that house raids in connection with so-called arms searches continue. On 26 and 27 November 1994, police reportedly raided and looted private businesses in the town of Novi Pazar. It is reported that goods were loaded on trucks and carried away. Allegedly, shop owners were harassed and ill-treated. The letters of the Special Rapporteur to the Federal Government, referred to in paragraph 194 of the 4 November 1994 report, concerning alleged human rights violations in that region have still not been answered. ...

C. Conclusions and recommendations

... 100. With regard to the additional information presented in the present report the Special Rapporteur recommends:

(a) That the Government undertake steps to remove legal and other obstacles preventing the development of a free trade union movement;

(b) That the Government undertake measures to fully respect the rights of ethnic, religious or linguistic minorities in accordance with its obligations under article 27 of the International Covenant on Civil and Political Rights and relevant provisions of the International Convention on the Elimination of All Forms of Racial Discrimination;

(c) That the freedom of the media be fully respected;

(d) That in an effort to resolve the cases of missing persons the Government cooperate with the expert designated by the Working Group on Enforced or Involuntary Disappearances in accordance with paragraph 24 of Commission on Human Rights resolution 1994/72.

9. Report by the Special Rapporteur of the Commission on Human Rights, 14 March 1996

. ... 119. During her visit the Special Rapporteur received information from non-governmental organizations and private individuals about human rights violations such as the systematic practice of torture and ill-treatment in detention centres, abuse of power by police authorities, and infringement of freedom of movement, media and association, as well as information on the situation of minorities in the areas of Vojvodina, Kosovo and Sandzak.

...

Situation of minorities

140. There are a number of concerns regarding the protection of minorities in the Federal Republic of Yugoslavia. Widespread discrimination against particular ethnic and religious groups continues to be reported in the areas of Kosovo, Vojvodina and Sandzak.

141. It is acknowledged that the Federal Republic of Yugoslavia has had severe strains placed upon its resources by the influx of refugees, particularly from the Krajina region of Croatia in 1995, and that insufficient support has been provided by the international community compared with other former Yugoslav territories. Such difficulties have also been exacerbated by the transition to a market-orientated economy. However, these obstacles should not preclude the authorities' compliance with international standards governing minority rights. The relocation of the displaced Serbian population within the territory of the Federal Republic of Yugoslavia should be exercised with caution to preserve as much as possible existing ethnic composition.

Kosovo

142. Ethnic Albanians in the Kosovo region constitute 90 per cent of the population; between 1.1 and 1.5 million people. On 27 November 1995, during her visit to the Federal Republic of Yugoslavia, the Special Rapporteur had meetings with Serb officials and representatives of the ethnic Albanian population in Kosovo. In her discussions, the Special Rapporteur requested clarification of the situation in Kosovo, as information she has received has often been contradictory.

143. It should be noted that the ethnic Albanian population has established operations of a parallel administrative system in response to the suspension of Kosovo as a federal unit in 1989-1990. The educational system for ethnic Albanian children in Kosovo, however, is far from adequate, since there is an insufficient number of trained teachers and a lack of adequate school premises and educational materials. Albanian children also suffer intimidation when not on school premises.

144. At its eleventh session, the Committee on the Rights of the Child, having considered the reports of State parties, expressed grave concern about the situation of Albanian-speaking children in Kosovo, especially with regard to their health and education. It would appear that the rejection by the Albanian population of the Government's decision to apply a uniform education system and curriculum have resulted in the summary dismissal of a large number of schoolteachers, therefore preventing some 300,000 school-age children from attending classes (CRC/C/15/Add.49, para 7).

145. Medical services are boycotted by the Albanian population due to mistrust stemming in part from an alleged poisoning incident which occurred in March 1990 during a vaccination programme carried out by Serb medical teams. Consequently, children, who are especially susceptible to illness, are not provided with adequate medical care, and inoculations against epidemic diseases have stopped. Infant mortality is high and incidents of tuberculosis have generally increased for both the young and the aged. It is of grave concern to the Special Rapporteur that it is children and the elderly who pay the price for adult mistrust.

146. The Special Rapporteur has received reports of systematic torture and ill-treatment committed by the police in Kosovo. Those who have experienced such incidents have often been refused medical assistance. Permanent disabilities have been reported by those who have been subjected to electric-shock treatment and beatings. Information provided by the Humanitarian Law Fund in Belgrade, which defended

120 cases of this nature in court, indicates that only 10 detainees were spared ill-treatment or torture whilst in detention.

147. The Special Rapporteur raised the above issue with the authorities through the Secretariat. The Minister of Justice stated that, although some incidents of abuse of power and authority had been registered in the area of Kosovo, those incidents were isolated and the perpetrators were brought to justice. The Ministry promised to forward to the Special Rapporteur the results of the proceedings and the actual number of officials charged by the court, as well as the number of those serving sentences.

148. The Special Rapporteur welcomes this initiative of the Ministry of Justice. The Special Rapporteur may consider this action as a possible mechanism for reporting human rights violations; this method could also be envisaged for establishing a dialogue with the authorities for future corrective actions.

149. A practice which appears to be widespread throughout the territory of the Federal Republic of Yugoslavia is the phenomenon of so-called "informative talks". It has been alleged that a special unit of the police entrusted with political matters invites people suspected of political involvement to report to the police stations and respond to questioning on their activities. In many instances people have been detained soon after these talks and placed in incommunicado detention. Accusations have also indicated that in some cases people have been detained for a month without their families' knowledge. ...

Conclusions

162. The human rights situation in the Federal Republic of Yugoslavia remains a serious concern.

163. Current legislation dealing with freedom of expression, freedom of movement and freedom of association should be examined with a view to the enactment of new laws.

164. The present system dealing with the question of citizenship is subjective and open to abuse.

165. The media in the Federal Republic of Yugoslavia is not assured of its independence, nor is the State-funded media impartial.

166. The education system in Kosovo is in a dire situation. Education in children's mother tongues can be beneficial, but only if different ethnic groups are provided with equivalent resources. Failing to do so can only serve to exacerbate community tensions.

167. Medical services in Kosovo are a source of mistrust for ethnic Albanians. This, coupled with the effect of sanctions on the general health of the population, has caused children and the elderly to suffer.

168. There are random home searches, arbitrary arrests and systematic beating of detainees whilst in custody in the Kosovo and Sandzak regions.

169. The Special Rapporteur acknowledges the efforts of the Government to facilitate the temporary settlement of refugees.

170. The right to express ethnic culture, language and religion could be undermined in the areas of Kosovo, Vojvodina and Sandzak if the Government does not undertake concrete measures to make effective the enjoyment of the guarantees enshrined in the Constitution.

Recommendations

171. Human rights law and standards for the population of the Federal Republic of Yugoslavia must be ensured and enforced, regardless of ethnic status.

172. Individuals should enjoy the right to fair trial and freedom from arbitrary arrest and detention.

173. The practice of so-called "informative talks" by the police should be discontinued.

174. A mechanism should be established with the relevant authorities of the Federal Republic of Yugoslavia for reporting human rights violations and for providing the Special Rapporteur with prompt responses on corrective actions undertaken by the Government.

175. Legislation regarding citizenship should take into account the provisions contained in the Universal Declaration of Human Rights and the International Covenant on Civil and Political Rights, as well as any other international legislation regarding this question.

176. Interference in broadcasting and publishing must be discontinued. Improvements must be introduced to the legislation of the Federal Republic of Yugoslavia to protect the freedom of the media, as this is a crucial indicator of democracy. Freedom of the media will be especially

important in the context of the forthcoming elections. International governmental and non-governmental organizations must assist the implementation of media freedom through financial, technical or professional support.

177. The freedom of independent trade unions must be protected and enforced by the Government. The development of independent trade unions must be furthered by the development of social and political freedoms, as the two are inextricably linked.

178. Dialogue must be established between the leaders of the ethnic Albanian population in Kosovo and the Government of the Federal Republic of Yugoslavia. The cycle of mistrust must be discontinued in order to achieve a peaceful settlement of differences. ...

E/CN.4/1997/9

10.   Periodic Report by the Special Rapporteur, 22 October 1996

Kosovo

118. On 1 September 1996, the President of Serbia, Mr. Slobodan Milosevic, and Dr. Ibrahim Rugova, President of the LDK party, signed an agreement aimed at normalizing the educational situation in Kosovo and bringing ethnic Albanian pupils back to official school facilities. It will be recalled that since 1991, Albanian students have attended classes in so-called "parallel" schools, operating without the approval of Serbian educational authorities. It is estimated that some 300,000 young Albanians currently receive primary and secondary education in these schools. Another 6,000 are enrolled in the "parallel" Albanian university in Pristina. The recent agreement is to be put into practice by a joint commission including representatives of the two parties, and preparations for the commission's establishment are now under way on both sides. It remains to be seen whether there will be progress in the actual implementation of the agreement. The majority of the ethnic Albanian population appears to have accepted the agreement's approach, but time is short and positive results will be needed very soon.

119. The Special Rapporteur continues to receive allegations of serious human rights abuses attributed to the Serbian police authorities in Kosovo. These reports include numerous cases of arbitrary arrests, ill-treatment and torture. She is particularly disturbed by recent reports according to which Albanian teachers have been ill-treated, and in some cases arrested by the police in front of their pupils.

120. Health care in the province is also a great concern of the Special Rapporteur. Much of the local population is distrustful of medical personnel of Serb nationality and has avoided treatment by them, which has placed the health of children at particular risk. A positive step towards resolving this situation was taken with the recent successful polio immunization campaign carried out by the Government in cooperation with the World Health Organization, the United Nations Childrens' Fund and the local NGO Mother Theresa.

121. As elsewhere in the former Yugoslavia, there is in Kosovo the phenomenon of "silent emergencies". For example, in Pristina the Special Rapporteur visited abandoned children who had been simply left in the children's hospital by their mothers, often due to pressures from family. Unfortunately, centres for abandoned children in the area cannot give them the protection and care they deserve. ...

134. The Government should take effective steps to halt police abuses in Kosovo, which reportedly remain widespread.

135. The Government should permit international and regional human rights monitoring organizations to establish a presence in Kosovo, a location of particular concern to the Special Rapporteur.

E/CN.4/1997/8

11.   Special Report on Minorities by the Special Rapporteur, 25 October 1996

Introduction

1. The causes of the conflict which has tormented the former Yugoslavia for the past five years are complex. Personal ambition, competition for resources, historical grievances, propaganda - all of these have been factors provoking fighting during which the most shocking human rights violations in Europe in nearly 50 years took place. But one cause of the many-sided war is absolutely clear: the failure of the former Yugoslavia's political leadership to meet the challenge of governing populations which do not share the nationality, ethnicity, religion or language of their region's dominant national group. These smaller populations, referred to in this report as "minorities", have persistently voiced resentment, fear and anger over the policies of the region's Governments which have not, in their view, respected the right of all people to express and sustain their group identities. Minorities' aspirations, and Governments' reactions to them, have led to much of the violence and many of the human rights violations which have taken place in recent years in the territory of the former Yugoslavia.

2. In response to charges that they are seeking to secure dominance by one ethnic group over others, or even to attain ethnically "pure" States, the region's Governments point to a range of legal measures they say have been taken to ensure minority rights. Such measures include constitutional and other domestic legislation, as well as accession to various international instruments. These steps have not, however, significantly almed inflamed feelings or eased the ever-present threat of conflict. Governments continue to be accused of marginalizing or repressing minority populations, and even of attempting to drive them from their States' territories altogether. At the very least, one must conclude that the participation of minority peoples in public affairs throughout the region is limited, as is their access to many of the benefits of citizenship. In some instances the law fails to provide adequate opportunities for minorities to fully exercise their rights, while in others the law is unenforced, misapplied or ignored. Both of these situations have led to a continuing high state of tension.

3. The Special Rapporteur on the situation of human rights in the territory of the former Yugoslavia has paid particular attention to the question of minorities since assuming her post in September 1995. During the past year she has made numerous visits to regions, municipalities, and even neighbourhoods where the predominant local population is of a different national or ethnic group from that which controls, either de jure or de facto, the surrounding territory. The pain and uncertainty suffered by the people she has met in these places are unmistakable. If security is one of the cornerstones upon which human rights are built, then in many parts of the former Yugoslavia minorities lack even a foundation on which to build their lives.

4. The Special Rapporteur considers that progress in the protection of minorities is now one of the most urgent human rights needs in the territory covered by her mandate, and it is for this reason that she submits the present report. The report is not an exhaustive examination of the situation of minorities throughout the territory of the Special Rapporteur's mandate. Indeed, it may be observed that in one of the countries, Bosnia and Herzegovina, the term "minority" is acutely unsatisfactory since no one national group constitutes a majority of the State's population. She has therefore decided to avoid a detailed analysis of all of the numerous and complicated situations in which one population finds itself somehow subordinate to a neighbouring larger group. Instead, the report concentrates on two countries dominated by people of one national group: the Federal Republic of Yugoslavia, which is populated mainly by Serbs, and the Republic of Croatia, which is predominantly Croat. The Special Rapporteur is of the view that the approaches taken to minority questions by the Federal Republic of Yugoslavia and Croatia are of pre-eminent importance not only for the security of these countries' own minority populations, but for the human rights of all people in the region, and for the maintenance of peace.

5. The report draws largely on the personal observations of the Special Rapporteur herself during her visits to the region. Since her appointment one year ago the Special Rapporteur has undertaken nine missions to the territory and, as noted above, has spent time in many areas with minority populations. Her impressions and conclusions derived from these visits form the major part of the report. The report also considers important legislation which has either been enacted or which could be enacted to promote protection of the human

rights of minorities, as well as political initiatives directed towards the same end. Significant recent events, including instances of serious human rights violations, are detailed in the report.

6. The report takes into consideration the international law on minority rights comprising all or parts of various instruments, including the International Covenant on Civil and Political Rights, the International Covenant on Economic, Social and Cultural Rights, the International Convention on the Elimination of All Forms of Racial Discrimination, the Convention on the Rights of the Child, the European Convention for the Protection of Human Rights and Fundamental Freedoms and the United Nations Declaration on the Rights of Persons Belonging to National or Ethnic, Religious and Linguistic Minorities, adopted by the General Assembly in 1992. The Special Rapporteur further wishes to recall pertinent resolutions of the Commission on Human Rights and the Sub-Commission on the Prevention of Discrimination and the Protection of Minorities, as well as reports of the High Commissioner for National Minorities of the Organization for Security and Cooperation in Europe. The Special Rapporteur wishes especially to highlight the constructive work of the Sub-Commission's Working Group on Minorities, established in 1995, and has taken special note of the recommendations to the Sub-Commission on the question of minority protection submitted in 1993 by Sub-Commission member Mr. Asbjørn Eide.

7. The Special Rapporteur would like to emphasize her commitment to the principles, enshrined in the Charter of the United Nations, that all States are equal in sovereignty and that their territorial integrity shall be secure from the threat or use of force. In the interest of peace, the Special Rapporteur is convinced that internationally recognized boundaries, including those of the countries of the former Yugoslavia, must be respected. She believes that while members of minority populations possess inalienable rights, they also have solemn duties with respect to the States in which they live. Nevertheless, it is clear that the Governments of the territory of the former Yugoslavia have the imperative responsibility to take new measures to promote the protection of minority rights, and indeed are well advised to do so, even if for no other reason than to ensure the lasting integrity of their States' borders.

8. The report first briefly considers the situation of national groups in the former Socialist Federal Republic of Yugoslavia, and then studies in depth the situations in the Federal Republic of Yugoslavia and the Republic of Croatia. Conclusions and recommendations are offered throughout the report, and general conclusions and recommendations are found in the report's final section.

9. The Special Rapporteur is indebted not only to the numerous interlocutors named throughout the report, but to academic authorities and studies, including materials published by the London-based Minority Rights Group

I. SITUATION OF MINORITIES IN THE FORMER SOCIALIST FEDERAL REPUBLIC OF YUGOSLAVIA

10. To better understand the present situation of minority populations in the former Yugoslavia, it is useful to recall some aspects of the unique and complex approach to nationality taken by the predecessor State in the region, the Socialist Federal Republic of Yugoslavia (SFRY). The sovereign identity of the SFRY was based both on federalism and on a liberal dispensation of autonomy among republics and provinces which conformed with the geographical concentrations of different national groups. The SFRY was a federation of republics, each of which (with the exception of Bosnia and Herzegovina) was populated predominantly by people of a single national group. The republics were Serbia (populated predominantly by Serbs), Croatia (Croats), Macedonia (Macedonians), Montenegro (Montenegrins), Slovenia (Slovenes), and Bosnia and Herzegovina (dominated by no national group, but with a plurality of Muslims and large populations of Serbs and Croats). The Socialist Republic of Serbia, furthermore, included two "autonomous provinces", created partly owing to their large non-Serb populations. To the north was Vojvodina (an ethnically diverse region with, in 1991, a slim Serb majority, but with substantial Hungarian, Croat and other populations), and to the south was Kosovo (with a large majority of ethnic Albanians, although they were a minority in the context of the Socialist Republic of Serbia as a whole).

11. Article 1 of the SFRY Constitution described the State as "having the form of a state community of voluntarily united nations and their Socialist Republics, and of the Socialist Autonomous provinces of Vojvodina and Kosovo". The reference to "nations" (in the original Serbo-Croatian version, narodi) and the connection between "nations" and "their Socialist Republics" is of particular significance. Nations in the SFRY corresponded to peoples having "their own" republics, that is, republics defined by the narodi which formed the majorities of their populations (Serbs, Croats, Slovenians, Macedonians and Montenegrins). They were differentiated under the Constitution from "nationalities" (narodnosti) who were, broadly speaking, all other minorities, whose kinfolk in most cases formed the majority of and defined neighbouring States (e.g., Hungarians, Albanians, Italians). Nations of the SFRY were considered to be "constituent nations", the foundation of the Federation, members of which held (or were believed to hold) certain advantages throughout its territory. Indeed, one of the Basic Principles of the Constitution of the SFRY emphasized the right of every nation of self-determination, including the right to secession. The nation-based republics had substantial authority over matters within their borders, although such authority could not be exercised in contravention of federal law. Each of the republics (as well as the provinces) had a presidency, a legislative assembly, a court system, and the power to confer republican citizenship.

12. The exceptional status of nations in the SFRY may help to explain the reactions of some members of nations who, after the dissolution of the SFRY found themselves in a significantly changed situation. Serbs in Croatia, for example, who, under the Constitution of the Socialist Republic of Croatia, had been a "constituent nation" of the republic on the same level as Croats, found themselves grouped by the new Constitution of the Republic of Croatia, adopted in 1991, with other national groups as "other peoples and minorities". They reacted by attempting to exercise their national right of secession as guaranteed in the Constitution of the SFRY.

13. The term "national minorities" appeared only once in the SFRY Constitution, referring in essence only to members of "constituent nations" who found themselves minorities in neighbouring States. The SFRY made significant efforts to advance the rights of these people, and of minorities generally, through several international initiatives including the submission of a draft declaration on the rights of national, ethnic, linguistic and religious minorities and taking the position that the Helsinki Final Act of the Conference on Security and Cooperation in Europe should contain references to minorities.

14. The peoples who were part of the populations of the "autonomous provinces" - Vojvodina and Kosovo - as well as other minority groups were considered "nationalities"; nations and nationalities were accorded equal rights by the Constitution of the SFRY. Nationalities had "the right to use their language and alphabet in the exercise of their rights and duties" (art. 171). Discrimination on the basis of nationality (as well as of race, sex, language, religion, education or social status) was prohibited. Advocating national inequality and incitement of national, racial or religious hatred and intolerance were unconstitutional and punishable. Freedom of religion for all citizens was guaranteed. The provinces themselves were proclaimed to be "constituent parts" of the Socialist Republic of Serbia and they exercised considerable influence at the federal level through their inclusion in high-level bodies, including the Federal Presidency.

15. Although it survived for more than 40 years, the SFRY ultimately disintegrated, starting with the proclamations of independence of the Republics of Croatia and Slovenia in 1991. These were followed by similar proclamations by the Republics of Bosnia and Herzegovina and Macedonia. The Federal Republic of Yugoslavia, comprising the remaining Republics of Serbia and Montenegro, acquired a different legal framework in 1992 with the adoption of a new Constitution. Two years before, the Socialist Republic of Serbia had altered the status of its "constituent parts", the autonomous provinces of Vojvodina and Kosovo, by significantly reducing aspects of their autonomy. A new panorama thus presented itself in the territory of the former Yugoslavia at the beginning of the 1990s.

16. The General Framework Agreement for Peace in Bosnia and Herzegovina (the Dayton Agreement) and the Basic Agreement on the

region of Eastern Slavonia, Baranja and Western Sirmium in Croatia, both concluded in late 1995, have now brought peace and an opportunity for a more considered look at the question of minority protection throughout the territory of the former Yugoslavia. The immediate outlook for the protection of minorities in the Federal Republic of Yugoslavia and the Republic of Croatia has been considerably brightened by the Agreement on the Normalization of Relations between these two countries, signed at Belgrade in August 1996. It is fervently hoped that the fate suffered by the SFRY can, and will be, avoided by the States now existing in the region.

II. SITUATION OF MINORITIES IN THE FEDERAL REPUBLIC OF YUGOSLAVIA

A. Background

17. Following a general discussion of the legal framework for minority protection of the Federal Republic of Yugoslavia (FRY), the present study will consider the situation of minorities in the country, focusing on the largest groups. The demographic situation of the FRY is described briefly below. The Special Rapporteur has taken into consideration information received from government authorities during her missions, as well as the "Report on the Status of National Minorities in the Federal Republic of Yugoslavia" submitted in May 1996 by the Federal Ministry of Justice. The Special Rapporteur is grateful to numerous local non-governmental organizations which have provided her with information and analysis including, in Belgrade, the Humanitarian Law Centre, the Belgrade Centre for Human Rights, the Helsinki Committee for Human Rights in Serbia and the Centre for Anti-War Action; in Podgorica, the Montenegrin Helsinki Committee for Human Rights; in Pristina, the Council for the Defence of Human Rights and Freedoms in Pristina; and in Novi Pazar, the Helsinki Committee for Human Rights in Sandzak.

18. The Federal Republic of Yugoslavia (FRY), composed of the Republics of Serbia and Montenegro, is a multi-ethnic society made up of a large number of different ethnic, national and linguistic groups which have lived together for centuries. Demographic data from the most recent census show that in 1991, about 67 per cent of the country's total population of 9.8 million were Serbs and Montenegrins, while the rest belonged to more than 30 different minority groups. (The second largest group was Albanians, constituting some 17 per cent of the population, followed by Hungarians comprising about 3.5 per cent). Population movements in and out of the country over the last five years have changed these proportions to some extent. Most notable among these movements have been the arrival of between 150,000 and 200,000 Croatian Serb refugees from Croatia in 1995, and the departure of thousands of non-Serbs since 1991 owing to tensions and violence connected to the conflicts in Bosnia and Herzegovina and Croatia.

19. In the Republic of Serbia the largest minority groups live mainly in three areas. The great majority of the roughly 1.5 million ethnic Albanians are concentrated in the province of Kosovo (called by the FRY Government Kosovo and Metohija), while others live nearby in other areas of southern Serbia. Most members of the Muslim minority of some 237,000 persons (according to the 1991 census) live in the area widely known as Sandzak (called by the Government the Raska district), stretching across south-eastern Serbia into northern Montenegro along the border with Bosnia and Herzegovina. The province of Vojvodina in the north of the Republic of Serbia is the most mixed region in the country, with 26 different ethnic, national or linguistic groups. In the Republic of Montenegro, meanwhile, there are small Albanian and Croat minority communities in addition to the Sandzak Muslims.

B. National and international legal standards

1. Constitutional provisions

20. The protection of minority rights in the Federal Republic of Yugoslavia has its basis in the 1992 Federal Constitution and the constitutions of the Republics of Serbia and Montenegro, promulgated in 1990 and 1992 respectively. Article 11 of the Federal Constitution is the core provision on this issue, guaranteeing to minorities their right to preserve, develop and express their ethnic, cultural and linguistic characteristics. This law is supplemented by a number of other measures in which more specific rights are defined.

21. While the official language is Serbian and the official alphabet Cyrillic, the languages of national minorities shall be in official use as regulated by statute (art. 15). The Constitution guarantees equality before the law without discrimination (art. 20), freedom of religion (art. 43), and the right of minorities to express and foster their culture and identity (art 45). Under article 46 minorities have the right to education and information in their own language, while article 47 guarantees their right to establish cultural institutions and associations. Articles 48 and 49 respectively speak of the right of minorities to maintain contacts with their co-nationals abroad, and to use their languages in dealings with administrative bodies and courts of law. Articles 38, 42 and 50 prohibit incitement to ethnic, racial or religious hatred.

22. The 1990 Constitution of the Republic of Serbia addresses the issues of minorities largely along the same lines as the Federal Constitution, emphasizing non-discrimination as the basis for equality of all citizens regardless of their ethnic, religious or other affiliation. The 1992 Montenegrin Constitution includes a few additional provisions which would appear to require affirmative action by the Government to protect and promote minority rights. For example, in chapter 5 the Constitution obliges the Republic, inter alia, to materially support cultural, educational and religious activities of national minorities, and to ensure their equal representation in public services and in State and local government.

23. Of particular significance is the provision of the Constitution of the Republic of Serbia stipulating that the areas of Kosovo and Vojvodina have the status of "autonomous provinces", with certain local political structures and areas of administrative competence prescribed by law. Some aspects of this autonomous status, as well as the consequences of the reduction in provincial authority imposed by the Republic between 1989 and 1991, are considered in detail below.

2. National legislation

24. While no single comprehensive law regulates the rights of minorities on the federal or republic level, the issue is addressed by individual laws on different subjects including education, freedom of association, the media, and the official use of languages. The laws of the FRY and its constituent republics make no provision for an ombudsman-type institution to address questions of minority rights or human rights generally.

25. Under the 1991 Law on the Official Use of Languages of Serbia, in areas inhabited by minorities their languages shall be in official use together with the Serbian language. Municipal assemblies are to specify by statute which minority languages shall be in official use in different regions. In the Republic of Montenegro, constitutional provisions on language are implemented directly, without being specified in a particular law or act. The Special Rapporteur has been informed that a comprehensive law on the use of minority languages is currently being prepared by the Federal Government.

26. Under the Republic of Serbia's Law on Primary Education, pupils belonging to minority groups are to receive instruction in their own language in schools where at least five minority students enrol for the first grade. Education in minority languages may be arranged for smaller groups of students with the approval of the Republic's Ministry of Education. The law for secondary schools is similar, providing that a minimum of 15 pupils is normally required for instruction in a minority language. In higher education, the language of instruction is Serbian but studies in minority languages may be arranged with official approval.

3. International obligations

27. The Federal Republic of Yugoslavia is a State party to the main international instruments relating to the protection of the rights and freedoms of minorities. These include the International Covenant on Civil and Political Rights, the International Covenant on Economic, Social and Cultural Rights and the International Convention on the Elimination of All Forms of Racial Discrimination. The FRY has engaged in dialogue and constructive cooperation with the treaty-monitoring bodies, although it does so only informally since the FRY's status before the United Nations needs further clarification. National legislation on minority rights largely conforms to the international standards set out in these instruments. However, as explained below, in

some areas the implementation of these guarantees needs further strengthening.

4. Citizenship

28. It is important to recall the importance of citizenship legislation to the question of minority rights. Full enjoyment of a State's protection, and for that matter the duty fully to honour one's civic responsibilities, begin with the acquisition of citizenship. The question of citizenship becomes exceptionally complicated when a State breaks apart, as happened with the Socialist Federal Republic of Yugoslavia. Minorities in successor States can face great difficulties in resolving their citizenship status.

29. The question of FRY citizenship was left essentially unregulated for several years in the absence of revised legislation corresponding to the country's new situation following the dissolution of the SFRY. However, on 16 July 1996 the Federal Assembly adopted a new law on citizenship, to come into force on 1 January 1997. Whether this law will have the positive effect of bringing more inhabitants of the FRY into the country's constitutional framework through the recognition of citizenship in appropriate cases remains to be seen. While the law's adoption is a step forward, concerns have been raised over some of its provisions, including the broad discretion in decisions to grant or deny citizenship which is vested in the federal and republican ministries of interior.

C. The situation in Kosovo

30. The presentation of the situation in Kosovo is based on information received by the Special Rapporteur and the field staff of the High Commissioner for Human Rights from both governmental and non-governmental sources. It is also based on the Special Rapporteur's impressions and conclusions formulated during the three missions she has undertaken to Kosovo since assuming her mandate in September 1995, the latest having taken place in October 1996.

31. The ethnic Albanian population of the province of Kosovo (called by the Government Kosovo and Metohija), located in the Republic of Serbia, makes up some 80-90 per cent of the province's population (most of the rest are Serbs), and some 15-20 per cent of the population of the FRY. While Kosovo's instability has a long and complicated history, the roots of the present problems may be found mainly in a series of events which occurred from 1989 to 1991.

32. As noted above, under the 1974 Constitution of the Socialist Federal Republic of Yugoslavia the autonomous province of Kosovo (like Vojvodina) enjoyed a high degree of political and territorial autonomy. The province had its own constitution, government, judiciary, parliament and presidency. The province's legislative competence extended to the areas of defence, internal security and even international relations. The province also had an independent educational system, supervised by a provincial Educational Council. In Kosovo a number of Albanian cultural institutions, such as the university and the Academy of Science and the Arts, sought to promote Albanian culture and traditions.

33. While constitutionally a part of Serbia, Kosovo as a province had the right to be directly represented in the Federal Parliament, the Presidency and other federal bodies, and was thereby in a position to veto decisions of importance for the federation. Indeed, the provinces of Kosovo and Vojvodina enjoyed in the SFRY a status close to that of the republics. However, in 1989 the Parliament of the Socialist Republic of Serbia, in a process of centralization of State administration and law-making, approved a series of constitutional changes which removed many of the attributes of autonomy from both Kosovo and Vojvodina. According to the Government, the reform was needed because Serbia was finding itself effectively paralysed by the provinces' wide-ranging independence. Most legislative and judicial functions of the provincial bodies were transferred to the Republic.

34. The changes were formalized with the adoption of Serbia's new Constitution in September 1990. Under its provisions the "autonomous provinces" retained some authority over the provincial budget, cultural matters, education, health care, use of languages and other matters, but the authority was thenceforth to be exercised only in accordance with decisions made by the Republic. In fact, the new Constitution gave the Republic the right directly to execute its decisions if the provinces failed to do so.

35. In reaction to these changes, a large number of Albanian public officials in Kosovo resigned their posts, while others were dismissed and replaced by people from other parts of Serbia. It has been alleged that in this way up to 100,000 persons were removed from posts in the State and provincial administrations, and in schools and public enterprises. Since most high-level public positions came to be filled by Serbs, the province's language for official business changed for practical purposes from Albanian to Serbian. The changes in Kosovo's status provoked widespread social unrest in the province, including large public demonstrations and other actions which were met with strong repressive measures by Yugoslav security forces. Numerous persons, mostly Albanians, were shot and killed during this time, many were hurt and numerous arrests, including arbitrary detentions, and incidents of torture were reported. A state of emergency was imposed in Kosovo by the Belgrade authorities.

36. In July 1990 the Republic of Serbia dissolved the government and parliament of the province of Kosovo, which led the provincial presidency to resign in protest. Shortly before the adoption of Serbia's new constitution in September 1990, a group of deputies from the former provincial parliament met in Kacanik and adopted a declaration on independence for Kosovo. One year later, in September 1991, Kosovo's Albanian leadership organized a referendum, illegal under the law of the Republic of Serbia, on independence, with more than 90 per cent of those voting indicating their support. Presidential and parliamentary elections for the so-called "Republic of Kosova" were held in May 1992, and the leader of the main Albanian political party, the Democratic League of Kosova (LDK), Dr. Ibrahim Rugova, was elected President. Since 1990, the majority of ethnic Albanians in Kosovo have boycotted all elections held for institutions of the Republic of Serbia and the FRY, thus virtually eliminating the Albanian minority's voice from the conduct of State affairs.

37. At present, two separate societies exist in Kosovo. Alongside the official bodies of the Republic of Serbia, a complete set of institutions maintained by the so-called "Republic of Kosova" manages most aspects of public administration and services, including a separate school system. During the last several years, the existence and activities of these "parallel" institutions have frequently been used as a pretext by the FRY authorities for the systematic abuse of the human rights of ethnic Albanians. The continuing instability has had a harmful effect both on the local Albanian population and on the province's minority Serb population. While open conflict has so far been averted, the situation remains deadlocked with both sides maintaining sharply-opposing views on the province's status and future.

38. There has recently been one promising development. On 1 September 1996 the President of the Republic of Serbia, Mr. Slobodan Milosevic, and Dr. Rugova signed a Memorandum of Understanding concerning the educational system in Kosovo, following a dialogue which had been facilitated by the Italian non-governmental organization, the Community of St. Eudigio. In the agreement the two parties declare their commitment "to proceed to the normalization of the educational system of Kosovo for the Albanian children and youth". The document expressly states that "it foresees the return of the Albanian students and teachers back to schools". The agreement further states that it was reached because of the "concern which both [parties] feel very strongly for the future of the Albanian children and youth of Kosovo". While it remains to be seen whether the accord will be implemented, it is certainly a hopeful sign.

1. Law enforcement and security of the person

39. Reports have continued to be received into the past year of systematic human rights violations perpetrated by Serbian police and security services against ethnic Albanian residents of Kosovo. These abuses have included arbitrary arrests, torture, harassment and house searches involving mainly, though not exclusively, persons active in the LDK and in the running of parallel Albanian institutions. Serbian security forces have themselves also suffered violent attacks.

40. In the spring of 1996, the level of tension in Kosovo rose sharply following a series of killings and attacks at various locations in the province. The violence started on 21 April 1996 when a 20-year-old Albanian student was shot dead on a street in Pristina. The police arrested one person, of Serbian nationality, who was subsequently

found guilty of murder. The next day four Serbs were killed when a group of armed men entered a restaurant in Decani and sprayed the room with automatic rifle fire. Almost at the same time, unidentified persons opened fire on a Serbian police patrol in Pec, wounding two policemen. A third attack took place the same day in Kosovska Mitrovica where a police vehicle was shot at. One female passenger was killed and the driver was wounded. Finally, in the village of Stimlje, a Serb police officer was killed in an ambush. These incidents reportedly resulted in widespread arrests, including arbitrary detentions, and alleged incidents of ill-treatment and torture of detainees in custody. During her visit to Pristina on 2 and 3 May 1996, the Special Rapporteur had the opportunity to speak with several Albanians who had witnessed or personally experienced ill-treatment and other arbitrary measures by local law enforcement authorities.

41. A great number of human rights abuses appear to have taken place in the summer and fall of 1996. The Special Rapporteur has been informed of, though she has been unable to confirm, hundreds of cases of persons being summoned by Serbian authorities for so-called "informative talks", during which some suspects were subjected to physical mistreatment. The Ministry of Justice has stated, however, that incidents of abuse are isolated and that perpetrators are brought to justice. The Special Rapporteur has received no documentary evidence in support of this claim.

42. Hundreds of incidents of arbitrary and violent searches of homes for weapons have been reported in Kosovo in 1996. The Serbian authorities have on occasion sealed off entire areas, interrogated and sometimes physically assaulted ethnic Albanians at random, including in an incident reported to have occurred at the Pristina market on 24 July 1996. It is further alleged that some persons are imprisoned by the Serbian authorities solely on political grounds, including Mr. Ukshin Hoti, a lecturer at Pristina University and President of the Albanian National Unity Party who was sentenced to five years' imprisonment in 1994. The "disappearance" of three ethnic Albanians who were allegedly abducted, possibly with the knowledge of the local police, while they were working in fields near Srbica in September 1996 was reported by Amnesty International on 2 October 1996.

2. Education and culture

43. In connection with the centralization process described above, in 1990 and 1991 the Government of Serbia brought the field of education under the authority of the Ministry of Education in Belgrade and established a uniform curriculum to be used throughout the country. As part of this change a number of primary and secondary schools, for example in Pec, Podujevo, Oblic, Kosovo Polje and Kijevo, were reportedly closed in the 1990/91 school year. The provincial Educational Council of Kosovo was also dissolved. It is reported that more than 18,000 teachers and other staff in local schools and faculties were dismissed or resigned owing to their refusal to implement the new educational programme, which in their view was arbitrarily imposed and did not take into account the needs of the local Albanian population. Some Albanian cultural institutions were also disbanded, including the Academy of Science and the Arts. On 8 March 1994 the last Kosovo Albanian academic institution, the Institute for Albanian Studies, was closed by a decision of the District Administrator of Kosovo.

44. Despite the measures taken for new teaching programmes, Albanian-language schools continued to follow the curricula established by the disbanded Educational Council and a large number of so-called "parallel" schools opened in private houses during the 1990/91 school year. It is estimated today that up to 300,000 pupils are attending primary and secondary classes in the "parallel" school system. An additional 6,000 students are enrolled at the "parallel" university in Pristina. Since these institutions are not operated under government authority, diplomas and degrees issued by them are not officially recognized. Harassment by Serbian police of teachers and students on the premises of "parallel" schools has been reported on numerous occasions, including an incident alleged to have occurred on 20 June 1996 at Petrovo, near Stimlje, where police raided the teachers' room of an elementary school, checked identification papers and ordered several persons to report to the local police the next morning.

45. As noted above, an event of potentially major significance occurred on 1 September 1996 when President Milosevic and Dr. Rugova signed an agreement on the normalization of education in the province. Under this framework agreement all Albanian students are to return to official schools. The accord is to be put into practice by a commission consisting of representatives of both parties. While preparations for the establishment of this commission are under way, the Special Rapporteur is concerned that there has been little progress so far in the implementation of the agreement. In the interests of Kosovo's children, it is hoped that the discussions which will take place will result in the reintegration of the two educational systems, renewed confidence in the Serbian authorities' commitment to respect the rights of the Albanian minority in the field of education, and an end to harassment of and discrimination against Albanian educators.

3. Health and child care

46. The health-care situation has also been negatively affected by the tensions in Kosovo, and as noted in earlier reports of the Special Rapporteur, it is the children who suffer the most. The Special Rapporteur has paid particular attention to this problem during her missions to Kosovo, where she has visited several local health-care centres and clinics.

47. It appears that, owing to mistrust, Albanian parents are often reluctant to have their children examined and treated by doctors and other medical staff of Serb nationality. One concrete result of this is a low immunization rate of Albanian infants against polio and other epidemic diseases. The Special Rapporteur therefore welcomes the polio vaccination campaign carried out from 27 to 29 September 1996 by the World Health Organization, UNICEF and the Albanian humanitarian organization "Mother Theresa", under the auspices of the Serbian Ministry of Health. This campaign has reportedly been successful in achieving its aim of vaccinating some 300,000 children throughout Kosovo.

48. During her most recent visit to Pristina in October 1996, the Special Rapporteur visited the local Children's Hospital, where she was informed of the tragic fate of a large number of newborn babies who had been abandoned by their mothers, many of whom were young and unmarried, immediately after their birth. This appears to be a particular problem in Kosovo. The Special Rapporteur was deeply disturbed to learn that most of these children end up in orphanages where conditions reportedly are poor.

4. The media

49. As in the rest of Serbia, the population in Kosovo relies on TV and radio for news and information. Only State-controlled stations operate in the region. Although Albanian-language broadcasts are available, few people watch them since the programmes are widely regarded as State propaganda. Some Albanians who can afford it receive TV Albania by satellite. The main Albanian daily, Bujku, which is close to the LDK party, currently is published in some 10,000 copies daily. The paper is formally under the State publishing house Panorama, which also controls its distribution and printing. Panorama reportedly keeps printing costs for Bujku at double those of other publications.

50. The independent weekly news magazine Koha (circ. 7,000) acquired its own printing facilities this year, and is now trying to establish an independent distribution network. One case of direct State interference in the work of Koha has been reported. In April 1996, the magazine published a satirical photo-montage of President Milosevic of Serbia, as a result of which State security police allegedly entered the magazine's premises, stopped operations and ordered the paper henceforth to have its contents pre-approved by the police. However, the orders have reportedly not been enforced.

5. Conclusions and recommendations

51. A complex mix of factors has resulted in a continuing pattern of human rights abuses in the province of Kosovo, and to the region's overall instability. There is no purpose served by attempting to attribute sole responsibility either to the Serbian authorities or to local Albanians and their political leadership. It will be essential in the near term for both sides to commit themselves to reopening regular channels of communication and to accepting the need to compromise in the interests of easing tension.

52. The leadership both of the Federal Republic of Yugoslavia and of the Republic of Serbia will have to acknowledge the legitimacy of the goal of the Kosovo Albanian minority to realize meaningfully their national and ethnic identity, which is consistent with the FRY's international obligations and with its domestic law. In this regard, the severe restriction by Serbia in 1990 of Kosovo's provincial authority must be seen as having been harmful to the legitimate interests of the Albanian minority. Because of the size and geographic concentration of the Albanian population, Kosovo's situation is unique, and its problems require exceptional steps in order to be resolved.

53. Kosovo's Albanian leadership should acknowledge the legitimacy of the FRY's interest in defending the integrity of the State. Both parties should now commit themselves to finding a durable solution to the Kosove question in the interest of regional peace.

54. The FRY authorities must take immediate and much stronger action to stop the trend of violent human rights abuses by Serbian security forces against the Kosovo Albanian population. Schools and homes should be secure from arbitrary and illegal searches. Political prisoners should be released forthwith.

55. The Kosovo Albanian leadership must recognize that special measures should be taken by provincial authorities to safeguard the human rights of the local Serb minority.

56. The recent agreement between President Milosevic of Serbia and Dr. Rugova on the question of education is a major step forward. Both sides should take the opportunity immediately to continue and broaden this dialogue, including through direct talks. ...

[*The same report can be found in document A/51/665, S/1996/931.*]

A/51/652, S/1996/903

12.   Report on the Situation of Human Rights in the former Yugoslavia, 4 November 1996

142. Ethnic Albanians in the Kosovo region constitute 90 per cent of the population, between 1.1 and 1.5 million people. On 27 November 1995, during her visit to the Federal Republic of Yugoslavia, the Special Rapporteur had meetings with Serb officials and representatives of the ethnic Albanian population in Kosovo. In her discussions, the Special Rapporteur requested clarification of the situation in Kosovo, as information she has received has often been contradictory.

143. It should be noted that the ethnic Albanian population has established operations of a parallel administrative system in response to the suspension of Kosovo as a federal unit in 1989-1990. the educational system for ethnic Albanian children in Kosovo, however, is far from adequate, since there is an insufficient number of trained teachers and a lack of adequate school premises and educational materials. Albanian children also suffer intimidation when not on school premises.

144. At its eleventh session, the Commission on the Rights of the Child, having considered the reports of state parties, expressed grave concern about the situation of Albanian-speaking children in Kosovo, especially with regard to their health and education. It would appear that the rejection by the Albanian population of the Government's decision to apply a uniform education system and curriculum have resulted in the summary dismissal of a large number of schoolteachers therefore preventing some 300,000 school-age children from attending classes (CRC/C/15/Add.49, para 7).

145. Medical services are boycotted by the Albanian population due to mistrust stemming in part from an alleged poisoning incident which occurred in March 1990 during a vaccination programme carried out by Serb medical teams. Consequences, children, who are especially susceptible to illness, are not provided with adequate medical care, and inoculations against epidemic diseases have stopped. Infant mortality is high and incidents of tuberculosis have generally increased for both the young and the aged. It is grave concern to the Special Rapporteur that it is children and the elderly who pay the price for adult mistrust.

146. The Special Rapporteur has received reports of systematic torture and ill-treatment committed by the police in Kosovo. Those who have experienced such incidents have often been refused medical assistance. Permanent disabilities have been reported by those who have been subjected to electric-shock treatment and beatings. Information provided by the Humanitarian Law Fund in Belgrade, which defended 120 cases of this nature in court, indicates that only 10 detainees were spared ill-treatment or torture whilst in detention.

147. The Special Rapporteur raised the above issue with the authorities through the Secretariat. The Minister of Justice stated that, although some incidents of abuse of power and authority had been registered in the area of Kosovo, those incidents were isolated and the perpetrators were brought to justice. The Ministry promised to forward to the Special Rapporteur the results of the proceedings and the actual number of officials charged by the court, as well as the number of those serving sentences.

148. The Special Rapporteur welcomes this initiative of the Ministry of Justice. The Special Rapporteur may consider this action as a possible mechanism for reporting human rights violations; this method could also be envisaged for establishing a dialogue with the authorities for future corrective action.

149.   A practice which appears to be widespread throughout the territory of the Federal Republic of Yugoslavia is the phenomenon of so-called 'informative talks'. It has been alleged that a special unit of the police entrusted with political matters invites people suspected of political involvement to report to the police station and respond to questioning on their activities. In many instances people have been detained soon after these talks and placed in incommunicado detention. Accusations have also indicated that in some cases people have been detained for a month without their families' knowledge.

E/CN.4/1997/56

13.   Periodic Report of the Special Rapporteur of the Commission on Human Rights, 29 January 1997

E. Kosovo - Police abuse, torture and arbitrary detention

147. The Special Rapporteur has continued to receive reports of widespread human rights violations attributed to Serbian police forces in Kosovo. These accounts follow a familiar pattern of arbitrary arrests, severe ill-treatment or torture and violent house searches, often targeted against political activists or persons working in so-called "parallel institutions" of Kosovo Albanians. While such cases have been reported throughout the region, in the last months of 1996 these abuses appear to have been particularly common in and around the towns of Podujevo, Stimlje and Vucitrn.

148. The Special Rapporteur was especially disturbed to learn that Mr. Feriz Blakcori, a 34-year-old teacher from Pristina, had died on 10 December 1996, allegedly as a consequence of torture in police custody. The day before, police had reportedly raided the house of the Blakcori family in Pristina in connection with an arms search. Mr. Blakcori was brought to a police station in Pristina, where he was allegedly tortured, and was later transferred to Pristina Hospital where he died. According to the hospital's letter of discharge, he had been admitted in a state of serious traumatic shock with contusions on his head and body and bruises on his buttocks and the left side of his back. The diagnosis appears to be consistent with the allegations of torture. In a letter of 16 December 1996, the Special Rapporteur urgently requested the Ministry of the Interior of Serbia to order an impartial investigation into this alarming incident, and to inform her of the results of the inquiry.

149. In November 1996, the Belgrade office of the High Commissioner/Centre for Human Rights conducted a mission to Pristina and Prizren and interviewed 12 persons, 11 of whom alleged having been subjected to ill-treatment or torture by police authorities in Kosovo. It should be noted that several of these persons wished for their identities to remain confidential, fearing repercussions from the police. Most of the persons interviewed further stated that they had not taken legal action against those responsible for their torture and ill-treatment, either because they could not afford to engage a lawyer, or because they were distrustful of the authorities and thus regarded any such attempt to achieve justice as futile. The following two testimonies, if verified, indicate clear violations of the right to freedom from torture or ill-treatment and the right not to be subjected to arbitrary arrest and

detention. They relate to police raids carried out in connection with the investigation of the murder on 25 October 1996 of Mr. Milos Nikolic, a police officer in Surkish village near Podujevo.

150. On 31 October 1996, the police reportedly raided the home of Mr. Osman Lugaliu, 73 years old, in the village of Surkish. The police entered the house without presenting a warrant or saying why they had come, and allegedly started beating and kicking Mr. Lugaliu in front of his family. The police took him to the police station in Podujevo, where he was subjected to more beatings on the soles of his feet, his legs and his hands. After several hours of beatings and interrogations he was released without any charges made against him. Mr. Lugaliu had to seek medical care for the injuries he suffered in the police station. The Special Rapporteur has received a medical statement on Mr. Lugaliu's injuries, which is consistent with the allegations of ill-treatment.

151. In the second incident, on 25 October 1996 at around midnight, police broke into the house of Mr. Ibrahim Fazliu, a 50-year-old bus driver, in Surkish village without presenting any warrant or court order. Mr. Fazliu, his 16-year-old son and three of his brothers were taken to the police station in Podujevo in a truck carrying some 30 other persons who had been rounded up in the village. Outside the police station in Podujevo, Mr. Fazliu was severely beaten and kicked by two police officers who apparently continued the ill-treatment even after he had lost consciousness. However, he told HC/CHR staff that a senior police officer intervened to halt the beating. When he regained consciousness he was taken into the police station and questioned about the murder of the police officer, Mr. Nikolic. After a short interrogation, Mr. Fazliu was allowed to leave. He was treated for his injuries at a private clinic and at the public hospital in Pristina. A statement issued by the Pristina hospital on Mr. Fazliu's injuries supports the allegations of ill-treatment.

152. On 16 December 1996, the Special Rapporteur submitted detailed information on the above incidents and two other similar cases to the Minister of the Interior of Serbia, requesting the Ministry urgently to investigate the allegations and inform her about any results. The Special Rapporteur noted that the Federal Republic of Yugoslavia is a party to the Convention against Torture and Other Cruel, Inhuman or Degrading Treatment or Punishment, and as such is obliged under article 12 to undertake prompt and impartial investigations of alleged acts of torture.

153. On 16 October 1996 two men, Mr. Avni Nura and Mr. Besim Ramaj, were reportedly arrested by the police on the road between Lubovec and Galice. However, officials refused to acknowledge their detention for 16 days. On 2 November they were brought before an investigative judge on charges of "terrorist activities", but without the presence of a lawyer. The two men were allegedly beaten during the 16 days they spent in incommunicado detention and as a result reportedly sustained injuries requiring medical attention. However, it appears that they were denied access to medical care, despite repeated requests by the men themselves and by their lawyer. The lawyer further complained that the investigative judge prevented him from discussing any case-related matters with his clients.

F. Kosovo - Return of asylum-seekers

154. Staff of the HC/CHR interviewed two Kosovo Albanian men who were returned to Kosovo in September 1996, after their applications for political asylum were rejected by Germany. Both of the men alleged that they had been physically ill-treated and harassed by the Serbian police upon their return to Kosovo. One of the asylum-seekers, Mr. Xhafer Bardiqi, stated that following his return to Kosovo on 14 September 1996, he was summoned to police headquarters in Glogovac, where he was beaten on his hands, face and chest by police officials using truncheons. After two hours of severe ill-treatment, he passed out. When he regained consciousness, he was interrogated about his stay in Germany. After several hours of questioning and beatings, he was released and told that he would be called to further interrogations. Mr. Bardiqi had to seek medical care for the injuries he sustained as a result of the ill-treatment.

155. A number of European Governments have in recent months expressed their intention to return asylum-seekers and other persons without legal residence to the Federal Republic of Yugoslavia. The vast majority of the persons who would be affected by these planned return

programmes originate from Kosovo, and many of them left the Federal Republic of Yugoslavia in the early stages of the conflict in the former Yugoslavia in order to avoid being drafted into the Yugoslav Army, or because of their political views on the Kosovo situation. On the basis of information presently available, it is difficult to determine whether the testimonies referred to above reflect isolated incidents or are representative of the general behaviour and policy of the authorities toward returnees. However, in view of the seriousness of these allegations and the overall situation in Kosovo, it is evident that any planned return programme for rejected asylum-seekers to that region should include appropriate safeguards to ensure their security and fair treatment upon return.

G. Kosovo - Education

156. In her report of 25 October 1996 on the situation of minorities in the Federal Republic of Yugoslavia, the Special Rapporteur took note of the agreement on the normalization of education in Kosovo signed by President Milosevic and Dr. Rugova on 1 September 1996, and expressed her concern about the apparent lack of progress in implementation of the accord. The agreement has been widely seen as a possible opening for a more comprehensive solution of the Kosovo situation. Both sides have now appointed their representatives to the commission whose task it is to implement the agreement, but the body has held no meetings so far. It is worth noting that the document does not define terms, conditions or dates for its implementation, which has led to disputes regarding the way to bring the process forward.

157. A major obstacle to progress appears to be a d disagreement regarding the presence of a third party in the next phase of the talks: while the Albanian side insists on the participation of a third party as a mediator in the process, the Serbian Government appears to regard implementation of the agreement as an internal matter not warranting any foreign involvement. Another contentious issue is the question of the curricula to be followed in the schools. The Serbian side insists on the reintegration of the Albanian students into the national scheme and educational programmes, as defined by the Serbian Ministry of Education. The Albanian delegation, however, maintains that the curricula developed and approved by the Kosovo Albanian "parallel" educational authorities should remain in force, and that access to the school buildings is the only issue up for discussion. Terms and conditions for the admission of Albanian students, particularly to the University in Pristina, appear to be another open issue.

E/CN.4/1998/9

14.   Special Report: Two Trials of Kosovo, 10 September 1997

Introduction

1. At the request of the Special Rapporteur on the situation of human rights in the territory of the former Yugoslavia, an observer from the Belgrade office of the High Commissioner/Centre for Human Rights attended major parts of two trials held in Pristina of 35 Kosovo Albanians. The present report is based on first-hand information gathered by the observer in Pristina, as well as on study of the charges and the trial transcripts. Furthermore, the observer spoke to the president of the court, introduced herself to the two presiding judges, and also spoke on various occasions to the Deputy Prosecutor conducting the prosecution and to lawyers for the defence.

2. This report reviews the two trials, which were held in May 1997 and in June/July 1997. They are assessed on the basis of international standards for fair trial provided in United Nations human rights instruments, in particular article 14 of the International Covenant on Civil and Political Rights. The Federal Republic of Yugoslavia is a party to that Covenant and also to the Convention against Torture and Other Cruel, Inhuman or Degrading Treatment or Punishment (The Convention against Torture), which contains several provisions in articles 12 and 15 which are particularly relevant to the trials held in Pristina. The report ends with a set of conclusions and recommendations submitted to the Government by the Special Rapporteur of the Federal Republic of Yugoslavia on the basis of the report of the trial observer

I. THE FIRST TRIAL OF 20 PERSONS, HELD IN PRISTINA IN MAY 1997

3. Between 19 and 30 May 1997, 20 Kosovo Albanian men and women were tried and sentenced by the Pristina District Court. Two were tried <u>in absentia</u>. All the accused were charged with preparing to conspire to participate in activities endangering the territorial integrity of the Federal Republic of Yugoslavia under article 136 in connection with article 116 of the Penal Code. The offences carry a maximum sentence of 10 years' imprisonment in the case of forming a group with the above aims (article 136 (1)) or of five years' imprisonment in the case of membership in such a group (article 136 (2)). Six of the defendants were in addition charged with using dangerous or violent means in attempts to threaten the constitutional order or security of the Federal Republic of Yugoslavia, acts which article 125 of the Penal Code defines as terrorism, punishable with a minimum of three years' imprisonment.

4. According to the indictment, the accused formed or belonged to a secret association called the National Movement for the Liberation of Kosovo (NMLK) aiming to attempt, by the use of force, to sever Kosovo and Metohija from the Federal Republic of Yugoslavia and unite it with Albania. The organization's main aims, according to the indictment, are increasing its membership, preparing armed rebellion by collecting various weapons and obtaining maps and blueprints of official buildings and distributing the movement's magazine <u>Qllirimi</u> (Liberation). The statute of the organization, of which only a photocopy was presented in court, advocates what it calls the liberation of all Albanians living in Serbia, Montenegro and Macedonia, an aim to be achieved, as a last resort, by armed struggle. It describes NMLK as an illegal organization, which, however, uses every opportunity to resort to legal means in pursuit of its aim.

5. The trial, which lasted six days, is the first of three involving Kosovo Albanians charged this year with having committed offences against national security. The charges in the first trial were limited to attempts and planning. Unlike the accused in the other trials, none were charged with actually having carried out acts of violence threatening the security of the State, which was the case in the second trial against 15 persons, reviewed in Section II below. Since then, 21 Kosovo Albanians, 18 of whom are in custody, have been indicted for forming what the indictment describes as a hostile terrorist organization, the Liberation Army of Kosovo, carrying out acts of violence in order to separate Kosovo from the Federal Republic of Yugoslavia. That trial has yet to take place.

6. All the accused, many of whom denied the charges against them or parts thereof, in particular the charge of terrorism, were found guilty. The main accused, who admitted to being a leader of NMLK and the editor of its magazine, was sentenced to the maximum punishment under article 136 of the Penal Code: 10 years' imprisonment. The other defendants, who included two women, one of them a 20-year-old student, were sentenced to prison terms of between two and nine years. Ten defendants claimed they had done no more than distribute the monthly magazine of the organization or write articles for it; five of them denied that they ever were members of NMLK.

A. <u>Background</u>

7. The trial took place following a series of armed attacks which had occurred in Kosovo during the previous year directed against several police officers, local government employees and persons whom the attackers have labelled "collaborators with the Serbian authorities". A previously unknown organization, the "Liberation Army of Kosovo", has claimed responsibility for most of these attacks, which started in April 1996, when six persons were killed and five others were wounded. The Special Rapporteur has repeatedly condemned these attacks. Similar incidents have been reported on a monthly basis. In reaction, the Serbian police initiated a wave of arrests on 22 January 1997, detaining around 100 people. The Belgrade office of the High Commissioner/Centre for Human Rights received testimony indicating that the police used excessive force in the course of making a number of these arrests and during subsequent interrogation of suspects.

B. <u>General Observations</u>

8. The trial was held in the District Court in Pristina. At the opening of the trial the 13 defence lawyers did not have enough space to sit and write, but the situation was promptly remedied on orders of the presiding judge the following day.

9. The presiding judge was firm but courteous to all parties, including the defendants and their lawyers. He invariably informed the defendants of their right to remain silent, a right which several defendants exercised. The judge scrupulously summarized statements from the defendants for the record, including details given by 11 defendants alleging that they were tortured, ill-treated or threatened into making "confessions" before the investigative judge and, sometimes, afterwards. This contrasts sharply with reports of lack of accurate record keeping by judicial officials during the period of pre-trial detention.

C. <u>Specific observations</u>

1. <u>Independence and impartiality of the tribunal</u>

10. Article 14, paragraph 1 of the International Covenant on Civil and Political Rights specifies that "everyone shall be entitled to a fair and public hearing by a competent, independent and impartial tribunal". The aim of this provision is to ensure that charges are brought before an independent court, established independently of a particular case and not especially for the trial of the offence in question. The United Nations observer, however, was informed by court officials in Pristina that it is customary for trials involving State security in one district in Kosovo to be brought by one public prosecutor and to be heard by one bench. The appearance of impartiality and independence of judicial and prosecution officials involved in trying political prisoners would be strengthened if these cases, like others, were heard by rotating benches and prosecutors.

11. The Pristina trial chamber consisted of a presiding judge sitting with two lay judges. Yugoslav law, in article 23.1 of the Code of Criminal Procedure - does not specify the latter's qualifications. The observer was told by lawyers that, in this case, the two lay judges were retired policemen, one of them reportedly a former head of the Criminal Investigation Department. Such a background could create an appearance of lack of impartiality. Furthermore, lawyers informed the observer that consultations between the prosecution and judges before and during trials involving political prisoners were not uncommon, and that this happened in this and the second trial.

12. Independence presupposes the judiciary to be institutionally protected from undue influence by the executive branch. The independence and impartiality of a court can be called into question when one or more of its judges are perceived to be close to one of the parties, in this case to the prosecution.

2. <u>The publicity of hearings</u>

13. The publicity of hearings is also a requirement of article 14 of the International Covenant on Civil and Political Rights. In the Pristina District Court there was little space in the public gallery. Nevertheless, many representatives of the press, embassies and non-governmental and intergovernmental organizations were present. Only one member of the family of each of the accused was permitted to attend court proceedings, but this was prompted by space limitations. The requirements of publicity were fully complied with.

3. <u>The right to adequate time and facilities to prepare a defence and to communicate with counsel of one's own choosing</u>

14. The right to adequate time and facilities is one of the most important minimum guarantees for fair trial provided in article 14.3 of the International Covenant on Civil and Political Rights. It is the most important of all the facilities which a defendant must be provided with and is of particular concern to the United Nations in this case.

(a) <u>Adequate time and facilities</u>

15. The Special Rapporteur concludes that a number of defendants were denied an adequate defence for a variety of reasons. First, several lawyers met their clients for the first time after the investigative judge had already concluded the crucial stage of investigation, the results of which the prosecution relied upon. Lawyers experienced legal and practical difficulties in obtaining access to clients at an early stage (see below under (b) and (c)).

16. Second, some defendants had lawyers assigned to them only after they entered the courtroom and thus did not have an effective opportunity to prepare a defence, although they appear to have waived their right to have a week to do so (see below under (c)).

17. Third, access to nearly all relevant trial documents was denied to defence lawyers until shortly before the start of the trial, leaving them insufficient time to prepare a defence. On 14 February 1997 the investigative judge of the District Court in Pristina, Ms. Danica Marinkovic, made the following ruling applicable to all indicted persons and their defence lawyers. She ruled that, for reasons of State security: "all documents and records, as well as objects gathered as evidence, and presence during certain stages of the investigation, namely during the examination of the indicted, and confrontation and examination of witnesses, will be denied to the defence". In practice, the order prohibited defence lawyers from having access to any trial documents other than the statement made by their own client to the investigative judge and also prevented their being present during the investigation of other accused persons. Consequently, access to any statements by the co-accused or essential documentary evidence for the preparation of a defence was only granted to the defence about one or at most two weeks before the start of the trial.

18. Article 73 (2) of the Code of Criminal Procedure, on which the judge's ruling is based, permits, by way of exception, that "during preliminary proceedings, before the indictment has been brought, examination of certain documents or certain items of physical evidence by the defence counsel may be temporarily restricted if particular reasons of national defence or national security so require". However, that provision does not appear to permit the exclusion of virtually all evidence as happened in this case. Authoritative legal commentary (by Dr. Branco Petric) explains that this provision should only be used in a very restricted manner. This did not happen. The restrictions applied to the defence regarding timely access to relevant trial documents in this case put them at such a disadvantage as to result in a violation of the important fair trial principle of "equality of arms", namely the procedural equality of the accused with the prosecutor.

(b) The right to communicate with counsel

19. Current legal standards in Yugoslavia prohibit a lawyer access to his client until he or she is brought before an investigative judge, which has to happen not later than 72 hours after arrest (article 196 of the Code of Criminal Procedure). The Constitution of the Federal Republic of Yugoslavia, in article 23, sets a higher degree of protection: it requires that arrested persons should have prompt access to counsel. However, in practice the Constitution's higher standards are not enforced, as the federal Constitution, in article 67, permits ordinary legal standards to prevail. As a result, lawyers are in practice often not granted access to their clients until three days after their arrest, that is to say when they are brought before the investigative judge. In fact most allegations of torture and ill-treatment concern that three-day period preceding the defendants' appearance before the investigative judge, when they are interrogated and denied access to a lawyer.

20. All the lawyers to whom the United Nations observer spoke stated that, when they were allowed to meet their clients, they were not permitted to communicate with them in private and to discuss their defence confidentiality. One or two prison guards were always present. One lawyer told the observer that the first time he was allowed to meet his client in private was at the opening of the trial itself. Another lawyer said that because of the constant presence of guards his client only felt able to tell him at their third meeting that he had been subjected to torture.

21. Yugoslav law in fact permits wide restrictions to be imposed on free communication between legal counsel and their clients. Article 74 (2) of the Code of Criminal Procedure permits the investigative judge to order "that the accused may converse with defence counsel only in his (the investigative judge's) presence or in the presence of some particular official". Even where free communication without surveillance between lawyers and clients is permitted and indeed when, in accordance with article 74 (3) of the Code, it is obligatory - i.e. in the period after the examination by the investigative judge has been completed or the indictment has been served ­ several lawyers maintained that such free communication continues to be denied in practice.

22. One experienced lawyer told the United Nations observer that he had referred to this legal provision when he met his client in prison after the initial investigation was concluded. The guard present at the meeting informed him that he was aware of the law. However, he also told the lawyer that he had nevertheless strict instructions from the State Security service to remain present throughout the interview between the lawyer and his client.

23. The apparent practice of not permitting defendants to communicate with their legal counsel in private is a clear violation of international human rights standards for fair trial. The Human Rights Committee, in its General Comment 13 on article 14 of the International Covenant on the Civil and Political Rights, states that article 14.3 (b) "requires counsel to communicate with the accused in conditions giving full respect for the confidentiality of their communications. Lawyers should be able to counsel and to represent their clients in accordance with their professional standards and judgement without any restrictions, influences, pressures and undue interference from any quarter". Principle 18 of the Body of Principles for the Protection of All Persons under Any Form of Detention or Imprisonment provides that, save in exceptional circumstances, the right to confidential communication between legal counsel and his or her client may not be suspended. It also provides that "Interviews between a detained or imprisoned person and his legal counsel may be within sight, but not within the hearing, of a law enforcement official."

(c) The right to defend oneself in person or through legal assistance of one's own choosing and to have legal assistance assigned in all cases where the interests of justice so require

24. The Prosecutor assured the United Nations observer that all the defendants had access to a lawyer at relevant stages of the proceedings. However, several defendants complained that when they were brought before the investigative judge they had no access to a lawyer to provide them with legal assistance. Enver Dugoli, for example, stated in court that he had been subjected to physical and mental torture that had resulted in visible injuries on his face, hands and other parts of his body, and denied the prosecution's claim that he had agreed to being questioned by the investigative judge without a lawyer. He told the judge that access to a lawyer had been forbidden to him when he had been brought before the investigative judge. One lawyer told the United Nations observer that interrogations of virtually all the defendants in this case started in the evening, when it was difficult for them to obtain the services of a lawyer. In this case, most defendants retracted in court the statements which they had previously made, often without having received legal advice, before the investigative judge, on the grounds that their statements had been extracted under torture, ill-treatment or duress. Nevertheless, the prosecution relied upon these statements as important evidence.

25. Some defendants did not have a lawyer when they entered the courtroom. Ragip Berisa, charged with an offence carrying a maximum of five years' imprisonment, had no lawyer. He explained that the lawyer who had visited him previously had not turned up in court. Although Yugoslav law does not oblige the court to appoint a lawyer in cases where offences carry a maximum punishment of five years' imprisonment, the presiding judge nevertheless proceeded to arrange for him to choose a lawyer on the spot from among the 13 legal counsel present. Mr. Berisa chose a lawyer, but he must have waived his right to postpone examination because the trial proceeded without the lawyer having time to prepare his client's defence. (Mr. Berisa was sentenced to two years' imprisonment.)

26. The main defendant, Avni Klinaku, had no lawyer when he appeared in court. Mr. Klinaku explained that he had not accepted the lawyer appointed by his family and that he would conduct his own defence. However, since he was charged with a serious offence punishable by 10 years' imprisonment, Yugoslav law requires that the accused in such a case should have defence counsel if necessary, assigned to him. The presiding judge promptly arranged for a lawyer present in court to defend the accused, who waived his right to have eight days to prepare his defence. However, article 70 (2) of the Code of Criminal Procedure requires that the accused in cases of such a serious nature "must have defence counsel at the time when the indictment is delivered". As far as can be established, this obligation was not honoured in the case of Mr. Klinaku.

4. The right to trial without undue delay

27. Sixteen of the accused were arrested between 26 and 31 January 1997, and two more on 24 April 1997. The trial started on 19 May 1997 and thus was held without delay.

5. The right to the free assistance of an interpreter if the court language cannot be understood

28. The court proceedings were held in Serbian, but most of the defendants spoke only Albanian. A court interpreter translated questions from the judge or the prosecutor to the defendants, and the latter's answers. However, discussions between the parties in court not addressed to the defendants were not translated to the defendant, who thus remained unaware of questions put and answers given concerning them in the course of the trial. It would be better if all discussions between the parties were translated to defendants in their own language throughout court proceedings, a matter which is particularly important for those defendants conducting their own defence.

6. The right not to be compelled to testify against oneself and not to be subjected to torture

29. Many defendants, when brought to court, retracted the statements which they had made previously before the investigative judge, on the grounds that had been forced to make them because they had been tortured, ill treated or had been subjected to other forms of duress.

30. The United Nations delegation received several allegations from lawyers and defendants who stated in court that the investigative judge did not wish to read their claims that defendants' statements had been extracted under torture or duress into the record, even though such statements are an essential component of testimony, which the Code of Criminal Procedure requires to be entered into the record (art. 80).

31. Eleven defendants claimed they had been subjected to torture, ill-treatment or duress. The lawyer of Duljah Salahu claims that he saw bruises on the face of his client and wanted to draw the attention of the investigative judge to other injuries on his client's body. However, the investigative judge reportedly said she did not wish him to do so. The lawyer also claimed that the investigative judge was reluctant to enter Mr. Salahu's claims of torture into the 1 February 1997 record of examination. He said that she only did so, and then only in very general terms, after Mr. Salahu had insisted that he would otherwise not sign the statement he had made before her. Evidence of beatings was still visible when Mr. Salahu was admitted to Pristina prison. The prison doctor stated on 26 February 1997: "after a detailed clinical examination we found, on admission, bruises on both hands (post contusion)". The lawyer said he requested an independent medical examination of his client, but the request was apparently not granted.

32. Ljiburn Aliju said that he was beaten with batons over the course of three days before being brought before the investigative judge. He also told his lawyer that the men whom he claimed had beaten him had visited him again in the week before the start of the trial and had threatened him that he should repeat in court what he had been made to say before the investigative judge. Hajzer Betulahu also said that his interrogators had subjected him to physical and mental torture and had threatened him by saying: "if you refuse to say in court what you told the investigative judge, we will break your bones".

33. Gani Baljija stated that he had been punched and kicked. A medical report drawn up during his detention was read out in court. Enver Dugoli alleged that his lawyer, the investigative judge and prison officials could see, when he was brought before them, the injuries on his face and hands resulting from beatings. His medical report was read out in court. A detailed statement of torture was given by Emin Salahi, who claimed that a gas mask had been put over his head, that paper had been stuffed into his mouth and that he had been given electric shocks and had been hit on the arms, legs and kidneys. He stated that he had asked for medical assistance, which had been denied.

34. Arsim Ratkoceri said that he had been beaten with batons on the hands and genitals and denied food for 24 hours. Muja Prekupi's lawyer alleged that he had been subjected to physical and mental torture for three days. Nebih Tahiri made a general statement that he had been "coerced" into making his statement and Ragip Berisa said he had done so under "duress". Sukrije Redza told the court that she had been interrogated late at night by State Security personnel and claimed she had been subjected to "mental and physical terror". In court, the

prosecutor did not deny that interrogations had taken place late at night, pointing out that there were no rules regulating the court's working hours.

35. To the Special Rapporteur's knowledge, no prompt and impartial investigations were carried out into any of the allegations that statements had been extracted by various forms of torture, ill-treatment or duress, as required under article 12 of the Convention against Torture. Nor are attempts known to have been made to comply with the requirement of article 15 of the Convention against Torture that "any statement, which is established to have been made as a result of torture, shall not be invoked as evidence in any proceedings". No such investigations were made prima facie evidence thereof in their medical records. The above allegations were carefully recorded during trial; however, it appears that the statements apparently extracted by such methods; which Yugoslav law specifically prohibits - were admitted in evidence in contravention of the requirements of the Convention against Torture and articles 83 and 219 of the Yugoslav Code of Criminal Procedure.

7. Non-compliance with several procedural requirements of Yugoslav law

36. The Code of Criminal Procedure provides a number of safeguards to protect the authenticity of legal records and the quality of evidence. Lawyers alleged in court that several of these procedural requirements had not been met. It appears that all their requests to have the evidence in question removed from the record on that ground were rejected by the court.

37. One lawyer stated that the times of beginning and ending of the interrogation of his client, Gani Baljija, had not been recorded, as the Code of Criminal Procedure requires in article 82 (2). He said that his client had been questioned for a long time in the evening and without a break. Hajzer Bejtulahu's lawyer drew the attention of the court to the fact that the interpreter had not signed the record of the interrogation, a fact not contested by the Prosecutor, who maintained, however, that such a failure was not sufficient ground to declare the statement in question inadmissible. It appears that the unsigned statement was indeed admitted in evidence, notwithstanding the clear requirement in article 82 (3) of the Code of Criminal Procedure that "the record shall be signed at the end by the interpreter if there was one".

38. Yugoslav law provides that the examining magistrate has a duty to inform all parties, including defence counsel, of the time and place of investigative procedures. Article 168 (6) of the Code of Criminal Procedure specifies that if the accused has a defence counsel, the examining magistrate shall ordinarily inform only the defence counsel. However, State Security personnel took several accused persons for further investigation, without the knowledge of the lawyers concerned, after the investigative judge had completed the initial investigation.

39. For example, after the investigative judge had completed the interrogation of Gani Baljija, he was reportedly taken back nine times to the Kosovska Mitrovica security police for further interrogation. Saban Beka stated that he had been questioned once after his investigation by the investigative judge. Majlinda Sinani stated that she had been taken out as many as 12 times after the completion of her investigation, which had usually taken place at night, between 7 and 12 p.m. Her lawyer had no knowledge of these subsequent interrogations and therefore was not present to defend her client. Since any such further interrogations cannot take place without the prior permission of the investigative judge, the judge either failed to inform the defence lawyer in accordance with the legal procedures or else these interrogations were carried out in breach of the law, without the knowledge of the investigative judge. What is clear is that Majlinda Sinani's lawyer was unable to assist her client in the course of these interrogations, when Ms. Sinani was repeatedly pressed to admit to membership of NMLK.

8. Evidence

40. The main evidence on which the prosecution relied was statements made by the defendants in the course of investigation, parts or all of which many of them subsequently retracted in court on the grounds that these statements were the result of torture or other forms of duress. Observers from organizations other than the United Nations who were in court when other evidence was presented have pointed out that no

witness testimony was presented and that the only material evidence produced was a machine-gun. Lawyers and the main accused argued that there was no proof that plans of buildings and other documents or material produced or referred to in court in support of the charges were in fact taken from the defendants, since the confiscated objects were not specified in the receipts issued after the search of the defendants' homes. Consequently, they argued, there was no evidence that the confiscated objects were in fact those produced in court and relied upon by the prosecution. Lawyers also observed that key documents presented in court, such as the Statute and the monthly magazine Qllirimi, were only presented in the form of photocopies which could not be accepted in evidence since they had not been properly authenticated. Nevertheless, this material appears to have remained on the court record and to have been used in evidence.

41. Although the United Nations observer was not able to study all the relevant documents, a review of the main evidence and a reading of the trial transcript, as well as consideration of comments made by observers present throughout the proceedings, indicate that the serious charges against the defendants were supported by little credible material evidence.

9. Trials in absentia

42. Two of the defendants were tried in absentia and sentenced to up to nine years' imprisonment. A strict interpretation of article 14.3 (d) of the International Covenant on Civil and Political Rights appears to prohibit trials in absentia, although the Human Rights Committee has held that such trials are permissible, but in strictly limited circumstances. Further observations about such trials are made in paragraph 66 below.

II. THE SECOND TRIAL OF 15 PERSONS, HELD IN PRISTINA IN JUNE/JULY 1997

43. For five days in June/July 1997 the District Court in Pristina tried 15 Kosovo Albanian men, 12 of them in absentia. According to the indictment, the accused had received military training in Albania and had subsequently formed a terrorist organization active in Kosovo with the aim of endangering the constitutional order and security of the State and of forming a separate state to be joined to Albania. Unlike the first trial held in May 1997, the accused were not only charged with preparing acts of violence, but also with responsibility for carrying out several attacks, killing 4 persons and attempting to kill 16 others. The attacks were said to have been carried out by the accused as members of the "Liberation Army of Kosovo", which had claimed responsibility for these acts.

44. All three accused who stood trial - Besim Rama, Idriz Aslani and Avni Nura - were charged under article 125 of the Penal Code with using dangerous or violent means in attempts to threaten the constitutional order or security of the Federal Republic of Yugoslavia ("terrorism"), an offence carrying a maximum penalty of three years' imprisonment. They were also charged with premeditated murder of one or more people, carrying a minimum penalty of 10 and a maximum of 20 years' imprisonment. One or more of the accused were also said to have been involved in the following incidents: the shooting of two policemen at Glogovac in an ambush in May 1993; an attack on a police car in April 1996 in which a policeman was wounded and a female convict travelling in the car was killed; the shooting of a policeman in Kosovska Mitrovica in June 1996; the throwing of two hand grenades - which did not explode - in February 1996 at a refugee camp in Vucitrn; and the throwing of bombs, which did explode but without causing casualties, in September 1996 at military barracks in Vucitrn.

45. Twelve of the 15 persons charged, including the chief defendant Besim Rama - received the maximum sentence of 20 years' imprisonment. Two defendants were sentenced to 15 years, one to 10 years and the remaining defendant, Avni Nura, had the charge of "terrorism" altered to unauthorized possession of arms and received the shortest sentence, of four years' imprisonment.

46. The observations concerning this trial should be read together with the observations made above about the first trial of political prisoners involving 20 Kosovo Albanians who were tried in May 1997 and convicted for lesser offences involving State security. Nearly all the issues and concerns raised there which stem from an assessment of international standards for fair trial provided in United Nations instruments apply equally to the trial of the 15 men in June/July 1997.

1. Specific observations

Independence and impartiality and conduct of the court

47. The bench consisted of 5 judges, including the same 3 judges who had tried the 20 accused in the first case. The same prosecutor argued for the prosecution. For reasons stated above with regard to the first trial, the appearance of independence and impartiality of the bench is not enhanced if the same judicial and prosecution officials appear to conduct all cases of a political nature; a concern compounded by the fact that several lay judges reportedly were former policemen.

48. Unlike in the first trial, the judge who presided in this trial did not promptly read into the record the claims by defendants that they had been subjected to torture. However, when this omission was pointed out to her, the presiding judge did include in the record a summary of the defendants' claims.

2. The right to be brought promptly before a judge and not to be held in unacknowledged detention

49. Article 9 of the International Covenant on Civil and Political Rights provides every person arrested on a criminal charge with the right to be brought promptly before a judge. Two defendants, Besim Rama and Avni Nura, told the court that between 16/17 September and 2 October 1996 they were held in an unknown place in unacknowledged detention, without access to anyone. Besim Rama was kept in a cell alone, but said he could hear Avni Nura being beaten. In court, Avni Nura stated that he had been arrested on 16 September 1996 and not on 29 September, the date wrongly recorded in the official records. Both men appeared before the investigative judge on 2 October 1996. Therefore, they were held for 16 days in unacknowledged detention and in breach of international human rights law and of Yugoslav law, which requires that no arrested persons can be kept longer than 72 hours without being brought before a judge.

50. For two weeks, these men had effectively "disappeared". The seriousness of any such detentions which the authorities refuse to acknowledge is underlined in article 1 of the Declaration on the Protection of All Persons from Enforced Disappearance, which states: "Any act of enforced disappearance is an offence to human dignity. It is condemned as a denial of the purposes of the Charter of the United Nations and as a grave and flagrant violation of the human rights and fundamental freedoms proclaimed in the Universal Declaration of Human Rights ... . Any act of enforced disappearance places the persons subjected thereto outside the protection of the law and inflicts severe suffering on them and their families. It constitutes a violation of the rules of international law guaranteeing, inter alia, the right to recognition as a person before the law, the right to liberty and security of the person and the right not to be subjected to torture ... ."

3. The right to access to counsel

51. International human rights standards require that such access should be prompt and that free communication between lawyer and client should be permitted. However, Idriz Aslani told the court that he had been kept for over six months without access to legal counsel to discuss his case. The first time he was allowed to meet his counsel freely to discuss his defence was on 30 May, three days before the start of the trial and then only for one minute, after which a guard came and free communication between counsel and client was made impossible.

52. The investigative judge interrogated Avni Nura and Idriz Aslani twice, on 2 and 7 October, without a lawyer even though, according to their lawyer, they had asked for legal assistance. Before that the two men had been held in unacknowledged detention, their lawyer making every effort to locate them, but obviously unable to meet them. The first day that their lawyer got permission to meet them was 8 October, but then only in the presence of a guard. However, when the lawyer showed the written authorization from the authorities, the guard reportedly informed the lawyer that he had received instructions from the investigative judge that any discussion between lawyer and client was forbidden. When the lawyer attempted nevertheless to speak with his client, asking his client about the treatment he was given in police custody, the guard said he would terminate the visit. When the United Nations observer raised these reports with the prosecutor appearing in

the case, he did not deny that guards had instructions to be present when lawyers met their clients, adding that this was done because lawyers had abused their powers in the past. However, the prosecutor did not make any specific allegation of abuse concerning the lawyers involved in this case.

53. Orders for the supervision by a guard of lawyer-client meetings, if they were indeed given, constitute not only a violation of international legal standards, but also breach article 74 (3) of the Code of Criminal Procedure, which makes free communication between a lawyer and his or her client at the conclusion of the investigation by the investigative judge mandatory. On 10 October 1997, the lawyer for the two men requested that this law be observed and that free communication be permitted, but he never received a response. The first time that their lawyer was allowed to meet his clients to discuss their defence was when the indictment was actually raised, according to the lawyer this only happened one week before the start of the trial. Given the seriousness and variety of the charges and the large number of defendants, this short period was clearly insufficient to prepare an effective defence.

4. Adequate time and facilities to prepare a defence

54. As in the previous trial, the investigative judge denied the defence lawyers access to all files, with the exception of their own client's file, and the possibility of being present during the interrogation of other accused persons. The order read: "Because of security reasons, the defence lawyers ... are denied presence during the investigation, during interrogation of the accused (except their client), the hearing and confrontation, and the examination of the file and records (except the ones relating to their client)". The defence lawyers appealed against the ruling, arguing that it was unnecessarily restrictive and went beyond the limits set in article 73 of the Code of Criminal Procedure (which permits restrictions on access to certain documents and items only), thus making it impossible for them to conduct a professional defence. However, the appeal was rejected by the President of the District Court, on 17 February 1997.

55. As observed in the first case, such broad restrictions on access to crucial documents and other evidence violates the principle of "equality of arms" between the defence and the prosecution which underlies the fair trial guarantees provided in article 14 of the International Covenant on Civil and Political Rights.

56. During the trial, defence lawyers pointed out that Besim Rama had been dismissed from military service on the grounds, as Besim Rama put it, of "pains in his head". They requested that the military service report be submitted to the court (which was done but did not prove to be conclusive) and that Besim Rama be examined by experts to establish whether he was in full possession of his mental capacities and aware of his actions at the time the crime in question was committed. The court ordered Besim Rama to be examined by three psychiatric/psychological specialists from the Belgrade prison hospital. Their report, subsequently presented in court, did not show that Besim Rama was suffering from a mental illness or backwardness and found that his capacity to understand the meaning of his acts was unimpaired. However, defence lawyers objected to the findings on the grounds that the period of examination had been too short, that the conclusions of the report did not match the examination's findings and that the findings by psychiatrists who were part of a penal establishment were biased. They requested a second examination by an independent institution or, failing that, the opportunity to question the experts in court. However, the court denied both requests. The credibility of the findings of the experts would have been enhanced if the defence lawyers had been able to question the experts in court.

5. The right not to be compelled to testify against oneself and not to be subjected to torture

57. In court the main defendant, Besim Rama, stated on 3 June 1997 that from the moment that he was arrested, until the time that he was brought before the investigative judge, the police did not stop beating him. He said that his statement before the investigative judge ­ acknowledging his participation in a number of the crimes with which he was charged - was made under duress, because he had been tortured and because the police who had beaten him stood outside the judge's office, overhearing what he said. He claimed that his face was visibly

swollen at the time. The reason for his distinct fear of the police was, he said, that he had been tortured to such an extent that he wanted to commit suicide. He said that he had informed the prison warden of the torture by his investigators, but that he had not been tortured while in prison.

58. In court Besim Rama initially acknowledged his participation in one incident, the firing on a police car in June 1996 in which one policeman was killed. Although he also admitted possessing several weapons, he denied his involvement in the other crimes with which he was charged and also that he had received military training or had gone to Albania. However, when the trial resumed on 9 July, Besim Rama retracted his statement acknowledging his involvement in the June 1996 shooting, claiming that he had made that statement out of fear of the police.

59. Basim Rama explained that he had been visited three times by police while in prison after the investigative judge had completed the investigation. He said that on 1 June, just before the start of the trial, an official, whom he identified in court as the public prosecutor in this case, had threatened him that he "would lose his head" if he failed to repeat in court what he had admitted to the police. Besim Rama maintained that two people had witnessed that threat. The public prosecutor was not in court that day and therefore could not be asked to confirm or deny this specific allegation. The court, however, is not known to have investigated this or other allegations by Besim Rama that his statement had been obtained through torture or duress, as required by the Convention against Torture. It was thus admitted in evidence, notwithstanding the provisions of international and Yugoslav law which exclude evidence being relied upon if it is established to have been extracted by such illegal methods. The same was the case for the other two defendants.

60. In court, Idriz Aslani denied all the charges against him, including possession of weapons or planning any of the attacks with which he was charged. He stated that he did not know any of the other accused. He added that all his statements to the police had been made under duress and threats and that medicines had had to be provided to him to help him recover from police torture. At one stage he had been told that he could leave the room in which he was being interrogated but not alive. The statement he had given to the investigative judge was also entirely false because he felt threatened. He saw that the same policemen, who had threatened and tortured him for three days previously, telling him what to say before the investigative judge, were standing outside the courtroom where he could see them when he made his statement to the judge.

61. Avni Nura told the court that he had been continually beaten for 10 days after arrest, after which a second group of interrogators had arrived who treated him "extremely inhumanely". He had been made to strip naked and sit on an electric heater until he fainted, then hit again. This apparently happened twice. At one stage, he had had to lean against the wall, standing one metre away from it for a prolonged period and only allowed to touch the wall with two fingers, while being beaten on the back. He had then had to do push-ups and kneel on batons, after which, he said, he had been unable to walk. He had been tied to a bed for most of the time and at night prevented from sleeping. He had been unable to eat for several days. He claimed he had been beaten mainly on the stomach, hands and legs and had had electricity applied to parts of his body so that the marks would not be clearly visible. However, his face had swollen, and he had had visible scars. On 2 October 1996, 16 days after his arrest and after these injuries had become less visible, he was taken before the investigative judge.

62. In court, he admitted possessing weapons and bombs, but claimed this was because he had been a fugitive from justice since wounding a person in a blood feud and because he had to stand guard for his brother who was an arms dealer. Of the three defendants, he alone admitted to having visited Albania, but claimed this was to escape from the blood feud.

63. On 10 October 1996 the defence lawyer requested a medical examination of Avni Nura and Idriz Aslani at the Institute of Forensic Medicine "to establish the degree and extent of physical injuries". He added that this should be done as soon as possible lest the wounds and traces of the injuries disappeared. However, he received no response

and no such examination, which could have provided important evidence of torture or ill treatment, or the lack thereof, was carried out.

6. Evidence

64. Unlike in the previous trial, a number of witnesses appeared, all of them called by the prosecution. The United Nations observer was not in court on the day of their appearance, nor has the observer been able to review the many documents referred to in court on that day. However, a reading of the trial transcript and discussions with other local and international observers about the witnesses' evidence produced in court that day indicate that none of the witnesses called produced credible material evidence to link the accused with the charges against them.

65. As in the previous case, the main evidence produced by the prosecution was the stated confessions of the accused before the investigative judge, and the admission made in court by the main accused, Besim Rama, which he subsequently retracted. There is strong evidence, however, that the statements to the investigative judge were made under torture and should therefore, according to international human rights standards which apply in the Federal Republic of Yugoslavia, not be accepted in evidence.

7. Trials *in absentia*

66. The majority of the accused (12 out of 15) were tried *in absentia*, as Yugoslav law permits. Several lawyers were present in court to represent the accused in their absence. The commentary of the Human Rights Committee on the Covenant permits trials *in absentia* in restricted circumstances: "When exceptionally for justified reasons trials *in absentia* are held, strict observance of the right of the defence is all the more necessary" (General Comment 13 (21) (d) (art. 14)). The United Nations observer was not in a position to establish whether the defendants' rights were strictly observed but the Special Rapporteur wishes to draw attention to the growing body of international opinion that such trials *in absentia* are no longer acceptable.

III. CONCLUSIONS AND RECOMMENDATIONS

A. Conclusions

67. The trials were conducted in public, without delay, as international standards require. International and local observers had full access to the trial. During the two main trials the courts generally respected, with few exceptions, Yugoslav procedural rules for trial conduct. Major breaches, however, occurred during the period of pre-trial detention. Furthermore, both trials failed to meet important minimum guarantees for fair trial provided in United Nations standards, notably the International Covenant on Civil and Political Rights and the Convention against Torture, which the Federal Republic of Yugoslavia is bound to uphold.

68. As regards the evidence presented in court, the fact that several procedural requirements of Yugoslav law regarding the authentication and production of evidence were not met ­ apparently with impunity ­ seems unfortunately not to have prevented such evidence from being admitted in court. The apparent absence of credible material evidence linking the accused to the crimes they allegedly committed is a matter of grave concern. Serious doubts remain as to whether, on the basis of the nature of the evidence presented and the illegal manner in which many statements were apparently extracted, the accused should have been found guilty as charged. By the international standards provided in human rights instruments to which the Federal Republic of Yugoslavia is a party, the accused were definitely denied a fair trial. In particular:

Defendants and their lawyers were given totally inadequate time and facilities to prepare a defence and to communicate freely;

The broad restrictions applied to defence lawyers regarding access to relevant documents and even in some cases regarding questioning their clients violated the important fair trial principle of "equality of arms";

Many statements which defendants retracted in court on the grounds that they had been extracted under torture, ill-treatment or duress were not removed from the record and were apparently admitted in evidence (despite injuries reportedly being visible to judicial officials and despite the presence of other *prima facie* evidence in medical reports);

Prompt and impartial investigations into allegations of such unlawful treatment are not known to have been ordered by any authority;

Requests for independent medical examinations which could have confirmed or denied torture allegations were refused;

Two defendants in the second trial were held for two weeks in secret detention, which the authorities refused to acknowledge, denying them their rights to personal security, to be brought promptly before a judge and to have access to a lawyer.

69. The Special Rapporteur is concerned that basic human rights standards were not met in the two trials of 35 persons convicted to very long terms of imprisonment for offences against state security. In addition questions can be raised about the independence and impartiality of the judicial process. She expresses the hope that the Government will review the issues and concerns raised in the present report and that officials and others concerned will take them into account in the course of appeals, where appropriate, as well as in future trials involving similar offences.

2. Recommedations

70. The Special Rapporteur makes the following recommendations to the Government on the basis of the United Nations trial observer's report:

(a) The Government should promptly order an impartial investigation into the claims of defendants and their lawyers that statements relied upon by the prosecution were extracted under torture or duress. If confirmed, the accused should be retried solely on the basis of evidence obtained by legal means.

(b) The appropriate authorities should ensure that any statements obtained by such methods are not admitted in evidence and are removed from the record.

(c) Trials of political prisoners for offences involving state security should be held by courts consisting of judges, including lay judges, whose background and qualifications fully meet established criteria of impartiality and independence. Such trials should be held, as is customary in other cases, before rotating benches and prosecutors.

(d) The Government should ensure that constitutional standards which provide arrested persons with prompt access to a lawyer should be immediately enforced (art. 23 of the federal Constitution). The legal provisions in the Code of Criminal Procedure which still do not permit such access effectively until 72 hours after arrest and which are currently being revised by the Ministry of Justice should be promptly brought into line with these constitutional standards.

(e) The Government should review legal provisions which permit broad restrictions to be imposed on free communication between lawyers and their clients (art. 74 (2) of the Code of Criminal Procedure), and ensure that they comply with international human rights standards which stipulate that all communication between lawyers and their clients should normally be conducted in private in full confidentiality, at most within sight but not within the hearing of any officials.

(f) The Government should introduce clear rules for the duration of interrogation of arrested persons, for the intervals between interrogations and for the recording of the identity of the persons conducting the interrogation. Late evening or night interrogations should be the exception. Sanctions should be provided for disobeying such rules.

(g) An independent investigation should be undertaken into allegations that the authorities refused to acknowledge that two defendants in the second trial were held for 16 days in September 1996 in secret detention and tortured. If the allegations are confirmed, those responsible should be brought to justice.

(h) If the impartial investigation into the allegations of torture, ill-treatment or duress described in this report confirms that these methods have been used, the Government should ensure that those responsible are brought to justice.

(i) Instructions should be given to investigative judges that torture allegations are essential elements of the testimony which should invariably be read into the record at all stages of the criminal proceedings. If there is credible evidence that statements were extracted under torture or duress, the allegations should be properly investigated and the statements concerned should not be admitted in evidence. The Government should introduce a mechanism to ensure that statements obtained from an accused person in violation of the law are forthwith invariably removed from the record and not admitted in evidence, as article 83 and 219 of the Code of Criminal Procedure and article 15 of the Convention against Torture require.

(j) Broadly phrased legal provisions permitting wide restrictions to be imposed on lawyers' access to relevant trial documents and interrogations - such as article 73 (2) of the Code of Criminal Procedure - ; should be restrictively interpreted to ensure that their application does not unduly favour the prosecution and result in violations of the important fair trial principle of "equality of arms" between defence and prosecution.

(k) Lawyers should have unhindered access to medical records of the examination of their clients in custody.

(l) The Government should introduce a mechanism to ensure that sanctions ·are invariably imposed when procedural requirements regarding the taking and recording of evidence are not met. Failure to meet such requirements should automatically result in the statements or documents concerned being excluded as evidence, unless supported by corroborative evidence.

(m) In all cases where the accused does not speak the language of the court, arrangements should be made to provide that the court interpreter translates the entire proceedings for the defendant, and not only the questions addressed to him or her by the judge and the prosecutor and his or her answers thereto. This is particularly important for those defendants conducting their own defence.

(n) The Government should ensure that, if trials have to take place in absentia, the defendants so tried are guaranteed the strictest possible observance of their rights.

A/52/490

15. Periodic Report on the Situation of Human Rights, 17 October 1997

...

In Kosovo, the first months of 1997 have been marked by increasing political and inter-ethnic tensions, which were underlined by several violent attacks, mainly against local Serb authorities and their alleged Albanian collaborators. For example, on 16 January the Rector of Prishtina University and his driver were seriously injured when their car was blown up by a bomb in central Prishtina. The so-called Liberation Army of Kosovo, believed to be behind a number of attacks mainly on police and military targets in the last year, later claimed responsibility for the act. On 5 March, after weeks of relative calm, Prishtina was again shaken by a bomb, which exploded close to the Faculty of Philosophy of Prishtina University. Four persons - two Serbs and two Albanians - were reportedly wounded in the attack.

As a reaction to those incidents, on 22 January the Serbian police began a wave of arrests throughout Kosovo. More than 100 persons were reportedly arrested and in the first week of March 57 persons were still in police custody, while some 60 had been released. Testimonies given to staff of the Belgrade office of the United Nations High Commissioner for Human Rights indicate that the police used excessive force in carrying out some arrests and in searching the homes of suspects. I have also received alarming reports and testimonies suggesting that a large number of arrested persons were subjected to torture and ill-treatment during police interrogations.

In this context, I was particularly disturbed by the tragic death of Mr. Besnik Restelica in the district prison in Prishtina on 22 February, under circumstances suggesting he died as a consequence of torture. According to the authorities, he committed suicide by hanging himself from the upper bed in his cell. However, when he was brought before an investigative judge on 4 February, injuries on his face and feet reportedly were visible, and injuries were also visible on the body one day after his death indicating possible torture. I wrote on 26 February 1997 to the Minister of the Interior of Serbia expressing my deep

concern about these allegations and requesting a prompt and impartial investigation into Mr. Restelica's death, but have not yet received a response.

Concerning education in Kosovo, I must note with regret that the Agreement signed by President Slobodan Miloevi and Dr. Ibrahim Rugova in September 1996 is yet to be implemented. While the so-called "3+3" commission given the task of putting the agreement into practice has held two meetings so far, the talks have apparently produced no concrete results.

E/CN.4/1998/15, 31 October 1997 [Also in A/52/490, 17 October 1997]

16. Report on the Situation of Human Rights in the Federal Republic of Yugoslavia, 31 October 1997

...

28. In Kosovo, there have been particularly serious violations of national and international law requiring that arrested persons be brought promptly before a judge. In June 1997 Mr. Besim Rama and Mr. Avni Nura told the Pristina District Court that they were held for more than two weeks in secret detention, from about 16 September until 2 October 1996, during which they were tortured by police in an attempt to make them confess to acts of terrorism. They appeared on 2 October before the investigating judge who wrongly recorded the date of their arrest as 29 September, so it appeared that they had been detained for only the permissible three-day period. No action is known to have been taken against those who allegedly kept the two men in illegal custody, tortured them, and provided misinformation to the judge about the real date of their arrest.

29. In previous reports, the Special Rapporteur has stated that the incidence of police abuse could be reduced if lawyers were given prompt access to their clients (see, e.g., E/CN.4/1997/56). Although proposals to that effect are now incorporated in the latest draft of the new Code of Criminal Procedure, they have not yet been enacted. The Special Rapporteur is also concerned that existing laws governing communication between lawyers and their clients are inconsistently enforced, and that some detainees are prevented from communicating with their lawyers for long periods of time.

30. The Special Rapporteur has also received a small number of reports that relatives are arrested and held as "hostages" if the person sought cannot be found. These reports are confined to Kosovo (see section IX, below).

V. ILL-TREATMENT, TORTURE AND IMPUNITY

31. The Special Rapporteur continues to receive reports of torture and ill-treatment from various parts of the country. The most serious of which come from Kosovo. She wishes in the present discussion to focus on the question of impunity which, unless addressed by the Government, will continue to facilitate further acts of torture. Torture is specifically prohibited by article 25 of the FRY Constitution and article 218 of the Code of Criminal Procedure.

32. In various communications from the Government, the Special Rapporteur has been informed that it opposes illegal methods but that from time to time aberrations could occur. The Special Rapporteur therefore welcomed invitations from the Minister of Internal Affairs and the Ministry of Justice of Serbia to submit information on possible violations to them, and she has done this in a number of cases. Among the most detailed allegations which she has submitted have been the brutal treatment of a demonstrator, Mr. Dejan Bulatovic, which she described in a letter of 13 December 1996; the torture or ill-treatment of five men in Kosovo, one of whom died allegedly as a result, described in a letter of 16 December 1996; the beatings of journalists and other peaceful participants in demonstrations (letter of 6 February 1997); and the death in police custody in Kosovo of another man (letter of 26 February 1997).

33. The Special Rapporteur is disturbed that she has received no response to any of these letters, with the exception of a detailed reply from the Minister of Justice of Serbia about medical treatment provided to Mr. Bulatovic to help him recover from beatings he had sustained. Even that letter failed to react to the principal concern that the police

had been responsible for ill-treating him. In none of the cases raised by the Special Rapporteur did the Government order an investigation or take steps to bring those responsible to justice.

34. Prosecutions against police for such practices are extremely rare. In Kosovo, where torture allegations are most numerous, only two policemen were sentenced to imprisonment for such practices between 1993 and late 1996, according to official data provided to the Special Rapporteur. The Ministry of Justice of Serbia informed OHCHR that after internal inquiries by the Ministry of the Interior, 14 policemen had been dismissed from service during 1996 or had other disciplinary measures taken against them, mostly for resorting to excessive use of force. ...

36. In most such cases, victims of torture or ill-treatment who want justice to be done have to resort themselves to initiating prosecutions. But the relevant legal provisions are difficult to enforce. Several dozen peaceful demonstrators and journalists who were seriously beaten by the police on 2-3 February 1997, some of whom required hospitalization for fractures and other injuries, put their cases to the public prosecutor in February 1997. So far he has apparently not reacted. One victim claims to have received threatening phone calls after submitting the case. The Special Rapporteur is unaware of any cases in which the perpetrators or those giving orders to use force against peaceful demonstrators in February 1997 have been brought to justice. ...

VI. RIGHT TO LIFE

38. As noted above, constitutional protection of the right to life should be clarified and the highest human rights standards should apply, meaning that the death penalty should be abolished in accordance with the FRY Constitution. Although no judicial executions have been carried out for many years, there have been a few grave incidents in which detainees have died in Kosovo prisons after torture. In her report of 29 January 1997 (E/CN.4/1997/56), the Special Rapporteur expressed grave concern about the death of Mr. Feriz Blakcori on 10 December 1996, allegedly as a result of torture in police custody. In a letter to the Chairman of the Commission on Human Rights of 3 April 1997, the Special Rapporteur also reported that Mr. Besnik Restelica had died on 22 February 1997 in the District Prison in Pristina, allegedly as a result of torture in detention. As noted above, the Government has not reacted to the Special Rapporteur's letters calling for impartial investigations into these and other allegations of torture in Kosovo. ....

VIII. THE RIGHT TO A FAIR TRIAL

42. Fair trial standards are particularly at risk in cases connected with political activities. Major breaches of international standards for due process and also of several Yugoslav procedural requirements were found by an observer from the Belgrade office of OHCHR who observed two trials of Kosovo Albanians conducted in the District Court of Pristina between May and July 1997. The cases were recently described in a special report of the Special Rapporteur (E/CN.4/1998/9). The most serious violations occurred during the period of pre-trial detention.

43. Many statements admitted in evidence by the court had apparently been extracted under torture or duress even though the Convention against Torture and articles 83 and 219 of the Yugoslav Code of Criminal Procedure specifically prohibit such evidence from being relied upon in court proceedings. A summary of the defendants' statements that they had been tortured or ill-treated was read into the record by the presiding judge. However, although lawyers said they had seen injuries resulting from torture on several defendants (one of whom had been put on a heated stove), and although several medical reports were presented which were consistent with the allegations, no investigations were ordered nor was further action taken. Lawyers' requests for independent medical examinations of clients who claimed to have been tortured and their requests to cross-examine experts appointed by the court were denied. Evidence put before the court which lacked appropriate authentication was nonetheless admitted. Considering the nature of the evidence presented, the Special Rapporteur expressed grave doubts as to whether the accused should have been found guilty.

44. Access to lawyers is another major problem. Several defendants in the Kosovo trials, including Mr. Enver Dugoli, complained that when they were brought before the investigating judge and asked for their lawyers to represent them, the judge refused the request. In fact, lawyers are specifically permitted by the Code of Criminal Procedure to be present when their client is examined by the investigating judge (art. 67). Several demonstrators arrested last winter in Belgrade and other major cities, charged with offences under the Law on Petty Offences made similar complaints. Some claimed that they were told by the judge who tried them that since they were only charged with minor offences, "they did not need a lawyer" to represent them. They were ultimately sentenced to several weeks of imprisonment. These restrictions contravene guarantees in the FRY Constitution and the International Covenant on Civil and Political Rights that defendants should have lawyers during trial. The Deputy Minister of Justice of Serbia informed the Belgrade office in March that the new draft Law on Petty Offences would guarantee the right of access to counsel at trial.

45. Under the FRY Code of Criminal Procedure, free communications between lawyer and client must be allowed after the investigation by the investigating judge is over or the indictment has been issued (art. 74). Lawyers acting for demonstrators in the Belgrade proceedings and for prisoners in the recent Kosovo trials informed the Special Rapporteur, however, that prison security guards insisted on remaining present during their consultations, preventing private communications. In Kosovo one defendant, Mr. Idriz Aslani, told the court on 3 June 1997 that he had been detained for six months without access to a lawyer and that the first time he could speak to his lawyer in confidence was three days before his trial.

46. The Special Rapporteur has also found other violations of the right to an adequate opportunity to prepare one's defence. In the trials of the Kosovo Albanians, the investigating judge denied lawyers access to essential trial documents by excluding all documents except those concerning the examination of their own clients, until about a week before the start of the trial. However, the Special Rapporteur notes that fair trial standards were met insofar as the two trials were held in public and without delay. Detailed observations about the standards for fair trial applied in the two trials of Kosovo Albanians appear in the Special Rapporteur's separate report.

X. THE SITUATION OF MINORITIES

A. Kosovo

1. Liberty and security of person

58. The Special Rapporteur has continued to receive reports of serious ill-treatment and torture committed in Kosovo against persons in police custody. This violence has been mainly, though not exclusively, reported in connection with police raids and arrests undertaken as a response to violent attacks against the Serbian police and private individuals over the last year. As noted in the Special Rapporteur's recent report, most of the defendants in trials held in Pristina in May-July 1997 allege having been subjected to torture during interrogations by the police and State security services. Throughout the reporting period, staff of the Belgrade office of OHCHR have interviewed a number of persons who witnessed or were themselves subjected to ill-treatment and other human rights abuses at the hands of the police in Kosovo.

59. In April 1997 testimony was received from four Kosovo Albanian students who alleged having been physically ill-treated by the police in Pristina. According to their account, on 19 March 1997 at around midday they were stopped by two uniformed police officers in a street in central Pristina. After checking the identity papers of the four men, the police took them into the entrance of a building nearby, where they were ordered to get undressed for a body check. One of the police officers then pulled out his truncheon and allegedly started beating the men on their legs and backs. Between the beatings the four were ordered to give information about their studies at the "parallel" university in Pristina and about a shooting incident in which a police officer was killed in Podujevo. The four men were reportedly released after 1 and a half hours of beatings and questioning.

60. The Special Rapporteur has also received a number of allegations of so-called "hostage" arrests, in which the police have detained relatives or family members of persons being sought by the police. In one such

incident on 10 June, the police entered a private house in a village near Skenderaj searching for a Kosovo Albanian man. As they failed to find the person concerned, they detained his brother instead to make the man give himself up. In an earlier incident on 29 April, special police units allegedly raided a private home in Pristina looking for "NN", the owner of the house. As he was not at home, the police allegedly harassed and ill-treated his wife and daughter. His brother, living in a house nearby, was reportedly taken to the police station.

61. The violent attacks against Serbian police and persons employed by the local authorities in Kosovo have continued in recent months. In one of the latest incidents two police officers were seriously injured on 4 August 1997 when their car came under automatic-rifle fire near Srbica. Also in August another police vehicle was damaged when it was hit by gunfire on a road near Podujevo. The previously unknown organization "Liberation Army of Kosova" has claimed responsibility for most of these attacks, in which some 30 persons have lost their lives in the last year. Following the killing of two Kosovo Albanian men and a Serbian police officer in May, the group issued a communiqué threatening to carry out more strikes against persons who "collaborated with the Serbian authorities".

2. Return of asylum seekers

62. In her last report (E/CN.4/1997/56), the Special Rapporteur took note of the alleged ill-treatment of two Kosovo Albanian men who were returned to Kosovo in September 1996 after their applications for political asylum had been rejected in Germany. In view of these allegations and the general situation in Kosovo, the Special Rapporteur recommended that any planned return programmes include adequate human rights safeguards to ensure that these people can return to their homes in safety and dignity. On 10 October 1996 the Governments of the FRY and Germany signed an agreement on the return of rejected asylum seekers and other persons without legal residence. The agreement entered into force on 1 December 1996, and the first repatriation took place in late January 1997. As of 31 July 1997, 1,600 persons had been forcibly repatriated under the agreement, and about the same number had returned voluntarily to the FRY. Around 90 per cent of them were Albanians from Kosovo. The agreement includes a human rights clause (art. 2.2), under which returns are to be carried out with full respect for returnees' human rights and dignity. While the agreement formally covers up to 130,000 Yugoslav citizens without legal residence in Germany, it is believed that 20,000-30,000 persons could be repatriated in the next three years.

63. After the agreement's entry into force, neither the Special Rapporteur nor her staff have been approached by returnees alleging that their human rights were violated upon return to the FRY. Information from local sources also indicates that, with a few exceptions, the return programme has proceeded so far without serious incidents. It is reported, however, that a number of returned asylum seekers have been verbally abused or summoned for so-called "informative talks" by the police, while others have been temporarily detained upon arrival. Isolated cases of alleged police abuse of returnees also have been reported, but the allegations have not been verified. It may be noted that a considerable proportion of the persons repatriated so far reportedly have criminal charges pending in the FRY or Germany, which may in part explain why some persons have been detained and questioned by the police. The German Embassy in Belgrade has submitted 10 cases of alleged harassment or temporary detention of Kosovo Albanian returnees to the federal Ministry of Interior, but the Ministry has reportedly not responded to these inquiries.

64. The Special Rapporteur notes that the Government of Switzerland concluded a similar agreement with the FRY on 3 July 1997. The agreement provides for the repatriation of 12,000-13,000 FRY citizens, almost all of them Kosovo Albanians, whose applications for political asylum have been rejected by the Swiss authorities. The first repatriation from Switzerland is planned to take place before the end of the year. A bilateral expert commission, composed of representatives of the Swiss and FRY Ministries of Interior, is discussing modalities for the repatriation process. The agreement, which is not limited in time, includes provisions aimed at safeguarding the human rights and dignity of the returnees.

3. Education

65. A full year has passed since the memorandum of understanding on the normalization of education in Kosovo was signed by President Milosevic and Dr. Rugova on 1 September 1996, and the Special Rapporteur notes with concern that no concrete steps have been taken to bring this agreement into practice. The joint commission tasked to implement the agreement has met several times since the beginning of the year, but the parties seem to be locked in their positions. It is estimated that some 300,000 pupils attend the "parallel" primary and secondary schools which have operated throughout Kosovo since 1990. It is reported that the Albanian "parallel" university in Pristina has enrolled 6,165 students for the next academic year. Most of these institutions operate in private houses and other temporary premises, which are clearly inadequate for teaching and training purposes. ...

Discrimination and property rights

66. The Special Rapporteur's attention also has been drawn to a number of cases relating to implementation of the 1989 Act on Special Conditions for Real Property Transactions. It is reported that from April to June 1997, more than 60 Kosovo Albanians were sentenced to 60 days in prison for purchasing property without the approval of the Serbian Ministry of Finance as required by law. The Act entered into force on 22 July 1989 and is to be applied for 10 years. This law, which applies to the whole of Serbia except for the province of Vojvodina, places severe restrictions on the purchase, sale, exchange and renting of real property between members of different ethnic groups. Under the law all property transactions have to be approved by the Serbian Ministry of Finance. Complaints against the Ministry's decisions may be filed with a Special Committee of the Serbian Parliament, whose decisions are final.

67. According to the law, approval of real-property transactions is only to be granted if the transaction is deemed to have no impact on the ethnic structure of the population and will not provoke anxiety, insecurity or inequality among persons belonging to different ethnic groups. The law further provides for sanctions only against the purchaser, in cases where transactions are carried out without the approval of the Ministry. On the face of it, the underlying logic of the law appears to be to control the migration of certain ethnic groups from areas in which they constitute a minority, thereby preventing undesired changes in the population's ethnic distribution. It may be noted that the law was passed at a time when there was a growing concern over the increasing migration of Serbs from Kosovo.

68. Cases and materials studied by the OHCHR Belgrade office suggest that the law is being unevenly and arbitrarily implemented, depending on the applicant's ethnicity and place of residence. The fact that the law is not applicable in Vojvodina would appear to place owners of property outside that province in an unequal position before the law. The exclusion of Vojvodina from the law's scope is also surprising considering the fact that some 30 different ethnic communities live in that region. The Ministry of Finance has in several cases made reference to the law, and rejected requests for authorization to purchase property filed by members of minorities in areas where there would appear to be no obvious concern about drastic changes in the population's ethnic structure. Ethnic Albanians and other members of minorities with permanent residence in Belgrade wishing to buy apartments in that city have reportedly had their applications rejected. It is also reported that members of the Turkish minority in Prizren have been prevented from purchasing property in that municipality, despite the fact that the community's population is continuously decreasing. According to local lawyers, around 98 per cent of the applications filed by Albanians or other minority members in Kosovo are rejected, and it is alleged that many transactions even between members of the same ethnic group are blocked. On the other hand, the Ministry has apparently made no objection to minority Muslims in Sandzak selling their property to local Serbs before leaving the country. The Special Rapporteur is concerned that this law places citizens in an unequal position, and that members of minorities are suffering discrimination in its implementation.

17.   Report on the Situation of Human Rights, 11 September 1998

1. Kosovo

82. In the four months since the Special Rapporteur's mission to the FRY, violence in the province of Kosovo has accelerated into a crisis with international consequences. Information about the crisis has been characterized by high-tech campaigns, political colouring of facts, and sensational headlines which, it can be argued, have affected events on the ground and attempts to defuse them. The Special Rapporteur is unable to assess the effect of the Kosovo crisis abroad, particularly on the situation of asylum-seekers, diaspora and refugees from Albania and the territory of former Yugoslavia in the countries where they now reside. He suggests that the effect of those communities on the crisis in Kosovo, and the effect of the crisis on them, deserve attention.

83. Many facts about the human rights situation in Kosovo remain elusive. New numbers of persons killed, wounded, abducted, arrested or alleged missing appear every day. The numbers in any category cannot be definitively confirmed, but there are concerns about high numbers of civilian casualties. Security considerations have often prevented access to areas of concern. After the "Moscow declaration" of 16 June 1998, diplomatic missions accredited in the FRY increased their presence in Kosovo. Diplomatic monitors have concentrated on patrolling conflict areas and gathering general information on the scope and nature of armed activity, but they have no single mandate and have not expressly stressed a human rights component to their monitoring. Yugoslav, Serbian and Kosovo Albanian leaders, as well as Montenegrin officials and representatives of different ethnic communities, have all pointed to abuses of the human rights of persons living in Kosovo and called upon the international community to take an active interest in the human rights of vulnerable groups. The Special Rapporteur observes that there is already common understanding on the need for exclusive attention to human rights in Kosovo. He trusts that his efforts and those of OHCHR can expand such common ground. These efforts would be served further by the FRY Government's consent to the opening of an OHCHR office in Kosovo.

84. In his letter of 8 April 1998, the Special Rapporteur focused on human rights concerns related to operations carried out by the Serbian Ministry of Internal Affairs in the Drenica region during late February and March 1998 and to the activity of armed Kosovo Albanians during that same period. Since that time, the geographical scope and intensity of armed hostilities between government forces and armed groups of the Kosovo Liberation Army (KLA) have increased dramatically, and gross violations attributed to both sides are reported on a daily basis. The nature of the conflict has changed from isolated attacks and retaliations to a sustained armed confrontation along fluid front lines. Concerns raised in the Special Rapporteur's letter of 8 April 1998 remain unaddressed.

85. Subsequent testimonies gathered by OHCHR staff in the field suggest that in some operations, government forces have used excessive force, including deliberate destruction of property, leading to extensive civilian casualties. International and local human rights groups have reported and investigated alleged arbitrary killings by the police in the villages of Ljubenic and Poklek on 25 and 31 May 1998, and at Orahovac on 17 to 29 July 1998. Additional research will be required to determine the actual course of events in these operations. The Serbian Ministry of Internal Affairs should promptly conduct an internal investigation of the events of 28 February, 5 March and 25 and 31 May 1998 and publicly announce its findings. If sufficient evidence is found to warrant further proceedings, it should be affirmed that officers would be subject not only to internal disciplinary measures but also to investigatory procedures applicable to all citizens. Criminal charges, as warranted, should be brought by the state prosecutor and cases brought swiftly to trial, which should be held in regular, open session.

86. Since his visit to Kosovo, during which the bodies of six Kosovo Albanian men were discovered outside Prizren, the Special Rapporteur has been alarmed by reports of Serb and Albanian civilians, as well as Serbian police officers, abducted by armed Kosovo Albanians believed to be part of the KLA. OHCHR has interviewed family members of abductees and eyewitnesses to abductions. According to Yugoslav authorities, armed Kosovo Albanians abducted 100 civilians and five policemen from January through June 1998; 14 of these were killed, six escaped, 26 were released and others are still unaccounted for. Among the unaccounted for are eight Serb civilians, aged 55 to 69, who were abducted near Decani in late April 1998. Also unaccounted for are two of four persons who were abducted from a bus on 26 June 1998; two were released through efforts of ICRC. Since June 1998, the number of abducted persons has increased. Between 17 and 21 July 1998, during clashes between government forces and the KLA in and around Orahovac, 51 Serb, Kosovo Albanian and Roma civilians, including seven Orthodox monks and a nun, were abducted by armed Kosovo Albanians in a village near Orahovac. On 22 July 1998, ICRC announced that 37 people had been released, including 27 elderly persons and eight members of religious orders. The Special Rapporteur denounces these abductions, as well as enforced disappearances attributed to state security forces, as grave violations of basic principles of international human rights and humanitarian law.

87. The Special Rapporteur has received many reports of torture during pre-trial detention in Kosovo. OHCHR has written to the Serbian Ministry of Internal Affairs concerning allegations of torture including, on 31 July 1998, a request for information concerning the death in police custody on 22 July 1998 of Rexhep Bislimi, who was arrested in Urosevac on 6 July 1998. The Special Rapporteur has expressed concern, as noted above, at the ministry's lack of response to inquiries.

2. Arrest and detention standards

88. The Special Rapporteur is alarmed at consistent disregard by Serbian state security forces throughout the Republic of international standards, as well as domestic law and procedures, governing police conduct and the treatment of pre-trial detainees. Persons are arbitrarily detained by the police for questioning for periods ranging from hours to several days, and it is common practice to hold persons in pre-trial detention longer than the period mandated by law. Lawyers report that they experience serious difficulties in gaining access to their clients. When access is granted, lawyers are as a general rule not allowed to consult their clients in private. In practice, pre-trial detainees in police (investigative) and court (post-arraignment) custody are denied access to their own physicians, and allowed access only to official physicians provided by the police or court. Beatings and ill-treatment in pre-trial detention are routine throughout Serbia. Official physicians do not report injuries sustained by detainees during police interrogations, even when those injuries are obvious, and do not provide adequate medical treatment.

89. The Special Rapporteur notes the case of attorney Destan Rukiqi, arrested in his office in Pristina on 23 July 1998, as a particular example of arbitrary process by police and judicial officials, disregard for rule of law, and violation of domestic and international standards. The same day Rukiqi was arrested, he was tried and sentenced to the maximum 60 days in prison for "disturbing public order". The Serbian Ministry of Internal Affairs brought charges against Rukiqi based on an investigative judge's claim that Rukiqi had insulted her by saying she had behaved like a policeman. Rukiqi made the remark after the judge had denied him his right as a defence attorney, guaranteed under the Law on Criminal Procedure, to unconditional review of court files relating to a client. Six days after sentencing, Rukiqi was taken to hospital suffering from kidney injuries allegedly inflicted in the Pristina prison.

90. The Special Rapporteur is concerned at abuse of the investigative procedure of "informative talks". Under the law, summons to such talks can be issued only in the event of criminal conduct or to gather direct information on criminal activity. In June 1998, Belgrade police brought summons against pensioner Vojka Kukolj to question her about the actions of a Belgrade municipal court that brought a verdict in her favour, which police repeatedly failed or refused to implement.

3. Freedom of assembly

91. Between April and August 1998, there were over 100 separate protests of Albanians and Serbs in towns within the province of Kosovo; most of these proceeded peacefully, in the presence of police. During the same period, in parts of Serbia outside Kosovo, armaments

factory workers, students, university professors, pensioners and parents of army conscripts took to the streets in several protests. Police violently dispersed several thousand students and professors who gathered in front of the Serbian Parliament on 26 May 1998 to protest the new law on universities. On 2 June 1998, in downtown Belgrade, police beat a group of students who tried to demonstrate outside the Serbian government building. The Special Rapporteur notes that in recent months, police have been more likely to react violently to small student demonstrations at Belgrade than to mass demonstrations in Pristina.

4. Refugees and displaced persons

92. Since the Special Rapporteur's mission, the latest refugees to the FRY have concentrated in Vojvodina and around Belgrade. They join the conservatively estimated 500,000 refugees from Croatia and Bosnia and Herzegovina already in the FRY. The number may well be higher, increased by the silent, steady flow of Serb refugees from Croatia during the past two years. Most refugees have found shelter in larger towns with relatives or friends; others are sheltered in collective centres throughout the country, including in Kosovo. Many have not been registered with authorities or have registered only those individual family members, usually children or the elderly, whom they deem to be in the most extreme need. Many have not applied to domestic or international humanitarian organizations, which have admitted to the Special Rapporteur and OHCHR that their stores are exhausted and their donors fatigued. An estimated additional 200,000 persons have been internally displaced by the crisis in Kosovo. The Special Rapporteur warns that the task of supporting over 700,000 persons in need, a significant portion of whom cannot return to their homes destroyed in fighting, cannot be sustained by the already overtaxed aid structure in the FRY, and is a far-reaching regional catastrophe in the making. ...

D. Concluding remarks

96. The Special Rapporteur observes that challenges facing the FRY are similar to those faced by the other countries of his mandate: to build a system based on rule of law instead of on a ruling party; foster an independent judiciary; implement in daily practice international standards and constitutional protections; create functional units of self-government and local administration; promote democracy and pluralism; support freedom of broadcast and print media; transform economic and social systems so as concurrently to create opportunity and protect the vulnerable; and heal the wounds of war. As of August 1998, the FRY faces additional challenges, and the situation of human rights in the country is grave. Without addressing here the causes of the current crisis in Kosovo - to which a political solution must be found - the Special Rapporteur emphasizes that threats to life and security of the person are the most serious violations of human rights. Every loss of life is a tragedy, regardless of the profession, ethnic identification or other categorization of the victim. Every act of violence ultimately affects a society's ability to cope with the challenges described above.

E. Reports of the United Nations Secretary-General

A/50/767

1. Report of the Secretary-General, 20 November 1995

... II. ACCESS BY UNITED NATIONS HUMAN RIGHTS MISSIONS TO THE TERRITORY OF THE FEDERAL REPUBLIC OF YUGOSLAVIA (SERBIA AND MONTENEGRO)

4. In the light of serious allegations of human rights violations and the history of tensions among the communities in the territory of the Federal Republic of Yugoslavia (Serbia and Montenegro) in general, and in the Kosovo region in particular, various efforts have been made since 1992 to establish a human rights monitoring presence. The most recent of those efforts are described below.

5. On 28 April 1995, the Special Rapporteur of the Commission on Human Rights on the situation of human rights in the territory of the former Yugoslavia, Mr. Tadeusz Mazowiecki, wrote a letter to the Minister for Foreign Affairs of the Federal Republic of Yugoslavia (Serbia and Montenegro) requesting a visit to the country and the establishment of an office in Belgrade, in accordance with paragraph 36 of Commission on Human Rights resolution 1995/89. No reply was received to that request.

6. In a letter dated 12 June 1995, the authorities of the Federal Republic of Yugoslavia (Serbia and Montenegro) extended an invitation to the United Nations High Commissioner for Human Rights to visit the country in the course of 1995, with a view to acquainting himself with the human rights situation there.

7. The High Commissioner, in his reply dated 25 July 1995, expressed regret that the Government had not granted permission for a visit by the Special Rapporteur. The High Commissioner offered to establish a dialogue between the Special Rapporteur, the Commission's expert responsible for the special process dealing with missing persons in the territory of the former Yugoslavia and the Government.

8. In subsequent conversations with the Permanent Representative of the Federal Republic of Yugoslavia (Serbia and Montenegro) to the United Nations Office at Geneva, the High Commissioner repeatedly stressed that cooperation with the human rights mechanisms was essential.

9. On 12 September 1995, a high-level delegation of the Federal Republic of Yugoslavia (Serbia and Montenegro), headed by the Federal Minister and Federal Coordinator for Activities in the Humanitarian Field, visited the United Nations High Commissioner for Human Rights. During their discussions, the Federal Minister reiterated the invitation of his Government to the High Commissioner to visit the Federal Republic of Yugoslavia (Serbia and Montenegro), emphasizing that his country was open to all those who wanted to obtain a first-hand view of his Government's respect for human rights.

10. At the same meeting, the High Commissioner reiterated his earlier request that cooperation be extended to the Special Rapporteur of the Commission on Human Rights and the Commission's expert responsible for the special process dealing with missing persons in the territory of the former Yugoslavia. He also stressed the need for full cooperation with the field officers of the Centre for Human Rights.

11. Mr. Tadeusz Mazowiecki resigned at the end of July. On 27 September, the Chairman of the Commission on Human Rights appointed Mrs. Elisabeth Rehn (Finland) as Special Rapporteur of the Commission on Human Rights on the situation of human rights in the territory of the former Yugoslavia. Mrs. Rehn conducted her first mission to the region from 9 to 15 October 1995.

12. The Special Rapporteur visited Belgrade on 13 October 1995. During meetings with the Minister for Foreign Affairs and the Federal Minister for Human Rights, she requested the opening of an office of the Centre for Human Rights to assist her in the gathering and analysis of information on the human rights situation in all parts of the Federal Republic of Yugoslavia (Serbia and Montenegro). The Minister for Human Rights replied that a written proposal should be submitted to the authorities for proper consideration.

13. On 17 October 1995, the Special Rapporteur addressed a letter to the Federal Minister for Human Rights, in which she recalled that the Centre for Human Rights had been able to establish field offices at Zagreb, Sarajevo, Mostar and Skopje. She stated that it was indeed indispensable to establish a similar presence in the Federal Republic of Yugoslavia (Serbia and Montenegro) in order to obtain direct access to information concerning the human rights situation. Without that arrangement, her ability to present reliable and objective reports would be seriously hampered. Therefore, she strongly recommended that field officers of the Centre for Human Rights be granted unimpeded access to the entire territory of the Federal Republic of Yugoslavia (Serbia and Montenegro).

14. At the time of the writing of the present report, no reply has been received from the Federal Republic of Yugoslavia (Serbia and Montenegro).

III. ACCESS BY THE CONFERENCE ON SECURITY AND COOPERATION IN EUROPE

15. On 14 August 1992, by a decision of the Fifteenth Committee of Senior Officials, the then Conference on Security and Cooperation in Europe (CSCE) established a mission of long duration in Kosovo, Sandjak and Vojvodina, Federal Republic of Yugoslavia (Serbia and Montenegro), which had as its tasks: (a) to promote dialogue between

authorities concerned and representatives of the communities in the three regions (Kosovo, Sandjak and Vojvodina); (b) to collect information on all aspects relevant to violations of human rights and fundamental freedoms and promote solutions to such problems; (c) to establish contact points for solving problems that might be identified; and (d) to assist in providing information on relevant legislation on human rights, protection of minorities, free media and democratic elections.

16. The mission maintained its presence in Kosovo for 10 months. It carried out its mandate with the formal consent and support of the authorities of the Federal Republic of Yugoslavia (Serbia and Montenegro) in accordance with a memorandum of understanding signed on 28 October 1992.

17. Following the decision by CSCE to suspend the participation of the Federal Republic of Yugoslavia (Serbia and Montenegro), the Government withdrew its formal consent for the mandate of the mission. The CSCE mission of long duration ceased its operations in July 1993.

18. Since its departure, CSCE (now OSCE), the Security Council and the General Assembly have made repeated requests to the Federal Republic of Yugoslavia (Serbia and Montenegro) for the reinstatement of the mission of long duration. The position of the Government of the Federal Republic of Yugoslavia (Serbia and Montenegro) has been that reinstatement is not possible until its full participation in OSCE is resumed. ...

A/51/556, 25 October 1996

2. Report of the Secretary-General, 25 October 1996

... II. ACCESS BY UNITED NATIONS HUMAN RIGHTS MISSIONS

4. On 23 February 1996, the Government of the Federal Republic of Yugoslavia (Serbia and Montenegro) notified the Special Rapporteur on the Commission on Human Rights, Mrs. Elisabeth Rehn, that it had approved the establishment of an office of the Centre for Human Rights at Belgrade. The Government stated that:

"in an effort to promote cooperation with you and the Centre for Human Rights, the Federal Republic of Yugoslavia is pleased to respond positively and accept your request that an office be opened in Belgrade that would be staffed with the persons of your choice and would assist you in establishing the truth about the human rights situation in the Federal Republic of Yugoslavia."

5. Requests to the Government of the Federal Republic of Yugoslavia for the opening of such an office were first made by the then-Special Rapporteur of the Commission on Human Rights on the situation of human rights in the territory of the former Yugoslavia, Mr. Tadeusz Mazowiecki, during his visits to that country in August and October 1992. The purpose of establishing such an office was to provide assistance to the Special Rapporteur in the collection and analysis of first-hand information on the situation of human rights in that country. In its resolution 1993/7 of 23 February 1993, the Commission requested the Secretary-General to "provide for the appointment of field staff in the territory of the former Yugoslavia to provide first-hand, timely reports on observance of violations of human rights in their area of assignment". Field staff of the Centre for Human Rights took up posts in 1993 elsewhere in the territory of the former Yugoslavia.

6. The Government of the Federal Republic of Yugoslavia declined repeated requests and recommendations, including recommendations from the Secretary-General, the United Nations High Commissioner for Human Rights and the Assistant Secretary-General for Human Rights for the establishment of a United Nations human rights field presence on its territory. In a letter dated 29 June 1993, the Government's Permanent Representative to the United Nations Office at Geneva wrote that the Federal Republic of Yugoslavia could not accept the appointment of a United Nations field officer in its territory since the reports of the Special Rapporteur were considered by the Government to be "one-sided, unbalanced and tendentious".

7. On 27 July 1995, Mr. Mazowiecki resigned as Special Rapporteur, and on 27 September 1995, the Chairman of the Commission on Human Rights appointed a new Special Rapporteur, Mrs. Elisabeth Rehn. Mrs. Rehn conducted her first mission to the region from 9 to 15 October 1995. On 13 October 1995, she visited Belgrade, and requested in her meetings with government officials that authorization be granted for the opening of an office of the Centre for Human Rights. She followed this with a letter to the Federal Minister for Human Rights on 17 October 1995, making the same request.

8. The Government gave its approval on 23 February 1996. On 15 March 1996, the Centre for Human Rights officially opened its office at Belgrade, and assigned an international human rights officer and a local staffperson to staff the office on a full-time basis. In September 1996 the Government authorized the assignment to Belgrade of a second international human rights officer at the request of the United Nations High Commissioner for Human Rights.

9. Since her appointment in September 1995, the Special Rapporteur has visited the Federal Republic of Yugoslavia four times, and she has travelled to the area of Kosovo twice. In addition, the staff of the Centre for Human Rights' office at Belgrade have visited Kosovo for the purpose of gathering information for the use of the Special Rapporteur. The Special Rapporteur has also visited other areas of the Federal Republic of Yugoslavia since her appointment, including the regions of Vojvodina and Sandzak. She has met with the President of the Republic of Serbia, the Minister for Foreign Affairs, the Federal Minister for Freedoms of the Citizen and National Minority Rights and other senior officials, as well as representatives of non-governmental human rights organizations and other persons concerned with human rights issues. In her report to the Commission on Human Rights dated 14 March 1996 (E/CN.4/1996/63), the Special Rapporteur stated that she was "highly encouraged by the continuing cooperation she has received from all of the parties" covered by her mandate, and she made particular note of the attention to her concerns shown by the Government of the Federal Republic of Yugoslavia. Neither the Special Rapporteur nor the staff of the Centre for Human Rights has noted any significant problems during the last year in moving throughout the country to gather human rights information.

10. The Government of the Federal Republic of Yugoslavia continues to deny permission to visit the country to the expert member of the Working Group on Enforced or Involuntary Disappearances on the special process on missing persons in the territory of the former Yugoslavia, Mr. Manfred Nowak. In a letter to the United Nations High Commissioner for Human Rights dated 12 September 1996, the Permanent Representative of the Government to the United Nations Office at Geneva reaffirmed its earlier denials of permission, stating that it had suspended cooperation with the expert since the activities he had carried out had been beyond his mandate and, thus, he had been abusing his status of expert while politicizing with extreme maliciousness the profoundly humanitarian problem of missing persons.

11. The United Nations High Commissioner for Human Rights visited the Federal Republic of Yugoslavia on 10 and 11 May 1996 ... .

III. ACCESS BY THE CONFERENCE ON SECURITY AND COOPERATION IN EUROPE ORGANIZATION FOR SECURITY AND COOPERATION IN EUROPE

... 13. The [OSCE Mission of Long Duration] maintained its presence in Kosovo for 10 months. It carried out its mandate with the formal consent and support of the authorities of the Federal Republic of Yugoslavia, in accordance with a memorandum of understanding signed on 28 October 1992.

14. Following the elections in the Federal Republic of Yugoslavia of December 1992 and its exclusion from CSCE membership, the Government withdrew its formal consent for the mandate. Therefore, the mission departed in July 1993.

15. Despite repeated requests by CSCE/Organization for Security and Cooperation in Europe (OSCE) and the General Assembly to reinstate the monitoring mission, the Federal Republic of Yugoslavia has consistently denied access.

A/52/502

3. Report of the Secretary-General, 17 October 1997

I. INTRODUCTION ...

4. At its fifty-third session, the Commission on Human Rights adopted resolution 1997/57 of 15 April 1997, by which it reiterated the requests made by the General Assembly and, in section VII, called upon the Government of Yugoslavia, inter alia, to take immediate action, in view of the deteriorating situation in Kosovo and the danger of escalating violence there, to put an end to the continuing repression of and prevent violence against the ethnic Albanian population, including acts of harassment, beatings, torture, warrantless searches, arbitrary detention, unfair trials, unjustified evictions and dismissals; to release all political detainees, allow the return in safety and dignity of ethnic Albanian refugees to Kosovo and respect fully all human rights and fundamental freedoms, including freedom of the press, freedom of movement and freedom from discrimination in the field of education and information; and to allow the establishment of democratic institutions in Kosovo and the right to seek, receive and impart information and ideas through any media, and in particular to improve the situation of Albanian women and children, and to allow an international presence for monitoring of the human rights situation.

II. ACCESS BY UNITED NATIONS HUMAN RIGHTS MISSIONS

5. Initially, the Government of Yugoslavia declined repeated requests and recommendations from the United Nations High Commissioner for Human Rights and the Assistant Secretary-General for Human Rights for the establishment of a United Nations human rights field presence on its territory. On 23 February 1996, the Government notified the Special Rapporteur of the Commission on Human Rights, Mrs. Elisabeth Rehn, that it had approved the establishment of an office of the then Office of the High Commissioner/Centre for Human Rights at Belgrade. The Government stated that: "In an effort to promote cooperation with you and the Centre for Human Rights, the Federal Republic of Yugoslavia is pleased to respond positively and accept your request that an office be opened in Belgrade that would be staffed with the persons of your choice and would assist you in establishing the truth about the human rights situation in the Federal Republic of Yugoslavia."

6. On 15 March 1996, the then Office of the High Commissioner/Centre for Human Rights officially opened its office at Belgrade. Initially, the Government agreed to permit one international human rights professional to staff the office. At the request of the United Nations High Commissioner for Human Rights, the Government in September 1996 authorized the assignment to Belgrade of a second international human rights officer. The staff of the human rights office in Belgrade frequently visits Kosovo for the purpose of gathering information for the use of the Special Rapporteur. Recently one staff member attended two trials of Kosovo Albanians charged with offences against Yugoslavia. A periodic report of the Special Rapporteur to the Commission on Human Rights documents that procedures at the trials fell short of recognized international norms for fair trials, in conformity with the International Covenant on Civil and Political Rights and the Convention against Torture, which Yugoslavia is bound to uphold.

7. From her appointment in September 1995 to September 1997, in compliance with a request from the General Assembly and the Commission on Human Rights, the Special Rapporteur visited Yugoslavia nine times and travelled to the area of Kosovo on six occasions. She has been assisted in her missions by the staff of the Office of the High Commissioner in Belgrade.

8. The Special Rapporteur has also regularly visited other areas of Yugoslavia since her appointment, including the regions of Vojvodina and the Sandak. She has met with the President of Serbia, the Minister for Foreign Affairs, the Federal Minister for Freedoms of the Citizen and National Minority Rights, the Minister of the Interior of Serbia and other senior officials, as well as representatives of non-governmental human rights organizations and other persons concerned with human rights issues. In her report to the Commission on Human Rights of 29 January 1997,3 the Special Rapporteur stated that she continued to receive generally good cooperation from all Governments covered by her mandate. Cooperation had also been good with international organizations and international and local non-governmental organizations active in the region of the former Yugoslavia as a whole. Neither the Special Rapporteur nor the staff of the Office of the High Commissioner has noted any significant problems during the last year moving throughout the country to gather human rights information. Despite repeated requests, however, the Government has refused to allow the High Commissioner to open an office in Prishtina. Thus, although the Office of the High Commissioner has unimpeded access to the region, its inability to establish a permanent presence in the area ontinues to hamper monitoring activities.

9. The Special Rapporteur remains concerned over the human rights situation in Kosovo. Since the previous report of the Secretary-General of 25 October 1996 (A/51/556), the Special Rapporteur has continued to receive reports of widespread human rights violations. These are described in the report of the Special Rapporteur that will be submitted to the General Assembly at its fifty-second session.

III. ACCESS BY THE ORGANIZATION FOR SECURITY AND COOPERATION IN EUROPE

... 12. Following the elections in Yugoslavia in December 1992 and its exclusion from CSCE membership, the Government withdrew its formal consent for the mandate. The mission therefore departed in July 1993.

13. Despite repeated requests by CSCE/Organization for Security and Cooperation in Europe (OSCE) and the General Assembly to reinstate the monitoring mission, Yugoslavia has consistently denied OSCE access to the region for general monitoring purposes. It should be noted, however, that Yugoslavia did grant OSCE permission to send an electoral observer mission to monitor presidential and parliamentary elections in Serbia, which took place on 21 September 1997.

IV. CONCLUSIONS AND RECOMMENDATIONS

14. In view of the continuing widespread violations of human rights in Kosovo as reported by the Special Rapporteur, the opening of an office of the High Commissioner in Prishtina, as well as an increased presence of other international organizations, would be indispensable for gathering reliable information on future human rights developments.

A/53/563, 30 October 1998

4. Report of the Secretary-General, 30 October 1998

...

II. Recent developments in the human rights situation

5. From April 1998, the scope and intensity of the conflict in Kosovo grew dramatically while the human rights situation deteriorated, and prospects for improvement arose only with the accord reached on 13 October 1998 between President Slobodan Milosevic and Richard Holbrooke, the envoy of the United States of America. Serious human rights abuses were being reported on a daily basis throughout the summer and early autumn. Fierce fighting took place in July and August, particularly around Orahovac, Malisevo, Djakovica and the Drenica region. At least 138 people, including 10 women, 9 minors and 19 elderly persons, were reportedly killed in clashes in the first three weeks of August. Some 700 people are believed to have lost their lives since hostilities began in the spring, while more than 240,000 people were estimated to be internally displaced in Kosovo and other parts of Yugoslavia. Another 14,000 people had fled across the border to Albania. As a result of fighting, tens of thousands of people fled their villages into the surrounding forests, and concerns deepened that the crisis would turn into a humanitarian catastrophe unless they were able to go back to their homes before the onset of winter. There were widespread reports of government forces burning and looting houses and villages in areas under their control.

6. On 24 August 1998, three aid workers of the Kosovo Albanian humanitarian organization "Mother Theresa" were killed near Vlaski Drenovac when their tractor convoy carrying relief supplies was hit by artillery shells. On 27 August eight children and three women from the same Kosovo Albanian family were killed by a mortar shell while they travelled by tractor-trailer in Grapce near Stimlje. On 27 August 1998,

government forces launched a two-day campaign involving mortars and artillery in and around the village of Senik. Government forces reportedly opened mortar fire close to a group of internally displaced persons camped on a hillside, killing 8 people and wounding 37, including women and children.

7. In mid-September, government forces mounted a large-scale campaign in the Cicevica mountains, and clashes were reported in several locations, resulting in civilian casualties and new displacement. Fighting decreased at the end of September and only sporadic exchanges were reported in the first days of October. The Milosevic-Holbrooke agreement of 13 October 1998 brought a halt to heavy fighting in Kosovo, although sporadic exchanges of fire continued to be reported in several locations. Some internally displaced persons took the opportunity of the cessation of hostilities to return to their homes. On 23 October 1998, four persons, including three children, were reportedly shot and killed by Serbian government forces while crossing the border between Albania and the Federal Republic of Yugoslavia into Kosovo. It was reported that the family had sought refuge in Albania one month earlier and, with the ceasefire, had determined to return.

8. The period since August has been marked by more discoveries of concentrations of corpses and evidence of massacres, including the massacre of Serb and Albanian civilians. Serbian authorities announced that, on 27 August 1998, in the village of Klecka, they discovered in a makeshift crematorium what they believe are the remains of civilians abducted and then killed by the Kosovo Liberation Army (KLA). Serbian Ministry of Interior officials announced that they had arrested two members of the KLA who had given statements describing the torture and execution of a number of abducted persons, including women and children. One of those arrested was brought to the scene and questioned in the presence of reporters; later, his arraignment before an investigative judge was broadcast on television. The exact number, identity, age and sex of the persons who died at Klecka has yet to be determined.

...

10. Shortly after the discovery of the Klecka site, the remains of at least 37 persons were discovered in nearby Glodjane. In contrast to the treatment of the Klecka site, Glodjane and others subsequently discovered appear to have been treated more carefully and clinically by government authorities and the media. On 29 September 1998, the bodies of 14 Kosovo Albanians, including six women, six children and two elderly men, were found in a forest close to the village of Gornje Obrinje in the Drenica region. Four of the children were under the age of 10, the two youngest being about four years of age. One of the women was pregnant. International observers who went to the scene reported that some bodies had been heavily mutilated. Most of the killed had been shot in the head at close range, and their throats had been slit. There are reports that on 26 September 1998, another 14 Kosovo Albanian men had been massacred in the village of Golubovac, a few kilometres from Gornje Obrinje. In early October 1998, the police discovered the remains of four persons believed to have been abducted by KLA in a pit close to the Volujak copper mine near Klina. Two more bodies were reportedly found on 4 October 1998 near Gremnik.

11. The fate of many Serbian, Kosovo Albanian and Roma civilians and Serbian police officers abducted by armed Kosovo Albanians, believed to belong to KLA, remains unknown. Yugoslav authorities say that 249 civilians and police have been abducted by KLA. Ninety-two of those persons were reportedly released, 9 escaped and 29 have been found dead. The International Committee of the Red Cross reports that it is currently following around 140 cases of abductions. On 21 August 1998, Djuro Slavuj, a journalist with Radio Priština, and his driver, Ranko Peranic, disappeared while on assignment in the Orahovac area. Nothing has been heard from the men since, and it is feared that they may have been abducted. In early October 1998, two more persons, State news agency journalists, were abducted while en route to Magura by armed Albanians. The political representative of KLA, Adem Demaqi, gave assurances of the journalists' well-being if they were abducted by KLA, but did not exclude the possibility that they had been abducted by non-KLA members. During his recent mission to the Federal Republic of Yugoslavia, the Special Rapporteur appealed for the release of abductees.

12. Initiatives by the European Union, the Government of the Federal Republic of Yugoslavia and international organizations, including the Office of the United Nations High Commissioner for Human Rights, calling for independent investigations into alleged massacres and arbitrary killings in Kosovo have gained momentum in the last month. The Serbian authorities have announced that their experts are investigating the killings in Gornje Obrinje and Glodjane. Upon the invitation of the Institute for Forensic Medicine of the Belgrade Medical Faculty and following correspondence between the Governments of the Federal Republic of Yugoslavia and Finland, a team of forensic experts from Finland arrived in Belgrade on 20 October 1998. The team, working under the auspices of the European Union, will assist the authorities of the Federal Republic of Yugoslavia in forensic investigations in Kosovo, but is also authorized to carry out independent investigations.

13. The Office of the United Nations High Commissioner for Human Rights continues to follow reports of persons who have been arbitrarily arrested for questioning and kept in pre-trial detention for periods well beyond the legal time limit. In addition to arrests in connection with police actions in the field, the Office has also investigated cases of arbitrary arrests and harassment of Kosovo Albanian lawyers, political activists and humanitarian workers. There are also many reports of torture and ill-treatment during pre-trial detention, including at least five alleged cases of death in custody. The Serbian Ministry of Justice has announced that more than 700 persons were currently under investigation, and that a series of trials would commence in October 1998. Some of the accused would be tried in absentia. Monitors from the Office were present when the first of the trials opened in Prizren on 22 October 1998, and would continue to follow trials scheduled for October and November 1998. Some of the defendants had reportedly been tortured under interrogation, and in such politically sensitive trials there were serious concerns regarding the independence of the courts and defendants' access to legal counsel.

III. Access by United Nations human rights missions

14. The office established by the Office of the United Nations High Commissioner for Human Rights in the Federal Republic of Yugoslavia continues its monitoring presence in Kosovo and reports regularly to the Office of the High Commissioner at Geneva and to the Special Rapporteur, Jiri Dienstbier. On 23 September 1998, the High Commissioner for Human Rights met in New York with the Foreign Minister of the Federal Republic of Yugoslavia, Zivadin Jovanovic. That meeting was followed by new rounds of working discussions in New York and Belgrade on an agreement to formalize the status of the Office of the United Nations High Commissioner for Human Rights in the Federal Republic of Yugoslavia. The parties have endorsed a final text of the agreement.

15. From 10 to 21 September 1998, the Special Rapporteur of the Commission on Human Rights, Jiri Dienstbier, conducted his second mission to the Federal Republic of Yugoslavia, travelling to the capital as well as to Montenegro, Sandzak and Kosovo. The Special Rapporteur conducted another field mission to the Federal Republic of Yugoslavia from 21 to 29 October 1998 to follow up recent developments in Kosovo, in preparation for the presentation of his report to the General Assembly. The Government of the Federal Republic of Yugoslavia has cooperated fully with the Special Rapporteur during his missions.

16. From 10 to 12 September 1998, the Special Representative of the Secretary-General for Children in Armed Conflict, Olara Otunnu, visited the Federal Republic of Yugoslavia. The Special Representative met with senior government officials and others in Belgrade and then travelled to Kosovo, where he met with local government officials, Kosovo Albanian representatives and representatives of international agencies. The mission included field trips to several locations in Kosovo.

17. In mid-October 1998, the Secretary-General sent a mission, headed by Staffan de Mistura, to the Federal Republic of Yugoslavia to establish a first-hand capacity to assess developments on the ground in Kosovo, including human rights developments. ...

Chapter 7: General Resolutions of the Security Council

The Security Council enjoys "primary" responsibility with respect to international peace and security under the United Nations Charter. It is composed of 15 members, including five permanent members (China, France, United Kingdom, United States of America, Russia). It takes substantive decisions by a majority of at least nine members, including the affirmative votes of the permanent ones (abstentions count as 'affirmative' votes). In order to employ its very strong collective security (Chapter VII) powers, ranging from calls for a cease-fire to economic sanctions and military action, it must make a finding that there exists a "threat to the peace, breach of the peace or act of aggression" under Article 39 of the Charter.

The initial inaction of the United Nations Security Council in relation to Kosovo contrasts sharply with the early but ineffective activism of the European Community/Union, the CSCE/OSCE and the human rights bodies. In fact, even the wider Yugoslav crisis triggered only a belated response from the Council, which hesitated for some three months before adopting its first resolution in relation to the fighting in Slovenia and Croatia in 1991. That resolution established an arms embargo for the former Yugoslavia, with the express consent of the government in Belgrade.

With the exception of a rather weak text, calling upon the FRY to reconsider its refusal to permit the continued operation of the CSCE Mission of Long Duration in Kosovo, Sandjak and Vojvodina, the Council failed to adopt any specific resolutions on the situation in Kosovo until 1988, when hostilities had also broken out in that territory.[1] This attitude does not appear fully in line with the famous statement of the Council of 31 January 1992, in which it described its responsibilities and functions in the post-Cold War world. The Council statement, adopted at the first meeting ever at the level of Heads of State and Governments, recognized new risks for stability and security. "Some of the most acute problems result from changes to State structures. The members of the Council will encourage all efforts to help achieve peace, stability and cooperation during these changes".[2] The Council added its determination to engage in early, prevenative action towards this end, much in accordance with the equally famous *Agenda for Peace* of the UN Secretary-General. That programmatic study on collective security also considered the new challenges and the answers which would now have to be provided by the Council, again emphasizing the need to address internal conflicts and self-determination disputes early on.

In part, the Council may have shied away from an early involvement in the crisis in order to give regional arrangements an opportunity to facilitate a peaceful resolution. Yugoslavia, after all, was initially regarded as the test case for the security architecture of the New Europe. However, Security Council backing would of course have contributed to, rather than detracted from, these efforts. Hence, the real reason for this odd reticence of the member state of the Council must be found elsewhere. It is rooted in the structure of the UN Charter and of the classical international system, which was, in a sense, at issue in this case.[3] In principle, the United Nations is not authorized by its Charter to "intervene in matters which are essentially within the domestic jurisdiction of any State or shall require the Members to submit such matters to settlement under the present Charter".[4] Of course, over time the organization has come to involve itself deeply in 'internal' matters, such as colonialist administration, apartheid, or more generally and more recently, the systematic violation of human rights. However, states have been reluctant to involve the organization, or at least the Security Council, in self-determination disputes outside of the colonial context.[5] India, for example, has struggled desperately to ensure that the Kashmir problem should not, or no longer, be directly addressed by the Security Council.[6] Other states have similar interests.[7] Until the apparent dissolution of the Socialist Federal Republic of Yugoslavia, there were objections to Council involvement in what some states still considered an 'internal matter' for Belgrade. This is precisely why the initial arms embargo against Yugoslavia of September 1991 required the positive consent from the SFRY government—otherwise China might have vetoed the resolution.

The exclusion of UN Security Council action in relation to matters falling essentially within the domestic jurisdiction of states is, however, subject to one exception. It does not apply where a situation constitutes a "threat to the peace, breach of the peace, or act of aggression". Since 1990, the concept of "threat to the peace" has undergone significant change.[8] Initially, the Council had to resort to cunning tricks in order to enable itself to take action in relation to essentially internal

---

[1] Security Council Resolution 855 (1993), 9 August 1993, Document 5.C.12.
[2] The Responsibility of the Security Council in the Maintenance of International Peace and Security, Statement of the Council adopted at the level of Heads of State and Government, 31 January 1992.
[3] See Chapter 2, Introduction.
[4] Article 2(7) UN Charter.
[5] Palestine, Katanga, Eastern Timor, Western Sahara, etc, can be classed in this category.
[6] Oddly India actually brought the issue before the Council when it first arose in a decision subsequently regretted.
[7] One might think of Sri Lanka, China, states with areas predominantly inhabited by ethnic Kurds, etc.
[8] Again, the Council had previously been active in cases of colonial self-determinaton and apartheid.

matters. It had to claim that internal situations, such as grave humanitarian emergencies, had external ramifications amounting to an international threat to the peace—say, by virtue of refugees destabilizing the region of crisis, or in view of the danger of a spread of a conflict beyond national borders—in order to be able to act under Chapter VII.[9] This charade, mainly performed for the benefit of China, was at least provisionally abandoned in December 1992, when the Council identified the "magnitude of the humanitarian tragedy caused by the conflict in Somalia" as a "threat to international peace and security".[10] That is to say, humanitarian suffering within a state could, in itself, amount to a threat to the peace, permitting the application of the collective security provisions of Chapter VII of the Charter.[11]

Despite its humanitarian dimension, identified by objective international agencies since its very beginning, Kosovo was perceived by some members of the Council as a self-determination dispute—an 'internal' matter best left to cautious diplomacy and the activities of humanitarian and human rights bodies. Significant action was delayed until humanitarian suffering was altogether too evident to ignore and until the problem had actually gained an international dimension by posing a very active threat to the stability of the region. The opportunity to adopt decisive measures which could have arrested the conflict at a far earlier stage had therefore been lost.

Resolution 1160 (1998) of 31 March 1998 was expressly adopted under Chapter VII, although it did not identify the source of a threat to the peace necessitating such action.[12] In a preambular paragraph, the resolution expressly affirmed the commitment of all member states of the UN to the "sovereignty and territorial integrity of the Federal Republic of Yugoslavia". The Council called upon the parties to negotiate a settlement based on the territorial integrity of the FRY, expressing in this context its support for an "enhanced status for Kosovo which would include a substantially greater degree of autonomy and meaningful self-administration". While this language (calls upon) may not have been directly mandatory, the binding nature of this requirement was clarified in subsequent provisions. In operative paragraph 8, the resolution imposed an arms embargo upon the FRY, including Kosovo. The decision as to whether or not the embargo would be lifted would depend on the following substantive requirements:

- substantive dialogue with a view to a settlement by the parties, with international involvement;
- withdrawal of special police units and cessation of their actions affecting civilians;
- humanitarian and human rights monitoring access and the introduction of a new OSCE presence.

When these requirements remained unfulfilled, and forcible repression instead led to an even greater displacement crisis, the Council adopted a tougher wording, although it took no further enforcement measures. It now identified the deteriorating situation in Kosovo as a threat to peace and security in the region and, acting under Chapter VII, unequivocally demanded the taking of immediate steps to improve the humanitarian situation and to avert "the impending humanitarian catastrophe".[13] It expressed grave concern at the increased fighting, including "excessive and indiscriminate use of force by Serbian security forces and the Yugoslav Army which have resulted in numerous civilian casualties and ... the displacement of over 230,000 persons for their homes". The Council also condemned "terrorism in pursuit of political goals", apparently referring to the activities of the Kosovo Liberation Army. Specifically, in relation to the FRY the Council demanded "immediate" implementation of:

- cessation of action by security forces affecting the civilian population, and now also the "withdrawal of security units used for civilian repression";
- safe return of refugees
- effective and continuous monitoring and humanitarian access;
- "rapid progress to a clear timetable" in the "dialogue with the Kosovo Albanians community with the aim of agreeing confidence building measures and finding a political solution to the problems of Kosovo".

The Council also endorsed the use of diplomatic staff accredited to Belgrade as a means of monitoring the situation, a step which had been envisaged by Yugoslavia in a joint statement with Russia of 16 June 1998, perhaps in order to avert stronger international action. This initiative had been seized upon by the United States and others, who were using the diplomatic privileges of their personnel already in Yugoslavia to create some sort of international presence in Kosovo (Kosovo Diplomatic Observer Mission, KDOM) in lieu of an OSCE presence which remained excluded.

---

[9] Early examples include resolutions on the crisis in Liberia and Resolution 688 (1991) on Iraq, although the latter resolution could in the end not be adopted under Chapter VII, due to China's attitude.
[10] Security Council Resolution 794 (1992), 3 December 1992.
[11] Similarly, the gradual promotion of 'humanitarian need' in Bosnia and Herzegovina as an issue which, in itself, permitted Chapter VII action, and Article 39 finding in relation to authorization of the French-led operation in Rwanda.
[12] Document 7.1.
[13] Resolution 1199 (1998), 23 September 1998, Document 7.4.

When the FRY failed to implement these demands, NATO threatened to use force.[14] The resulting arrangements with the FRY, including a cease-fire, the withdrawal of Yugoslav/Serb security personnel to agreed limits, a commitment to achieve an agreed settlement by a defined date, provisions for the deployment of a sizeable OSCE verification mission (KVM) and NATO aerial monitoring were endorsed by the Council in Resolution 1203 (1998) of 24 October.[15] The Council "demanded" full compliance with the key elements of this arrangement, thus turning compliance with the agreements between NATO and the OSCE and the FRY/Serbia into a legal requirement vis-à-vis the Council itself.[16]

In endorsing the result achieved by the threat of the use of force on the part of NATO, the Council appeared to add legitimacy to this measure. However, it is not possible to take the resolution as a retroactive authorization of NATO's action. The Council was careful to limit is 'welcome' to the results which had been obtained by Ambassador Holbrooke, without taking a view on the lawfulness or desirability of the process which had led to it.[17]

Again, it is of course not very useful to blame the Security Council as an institution for its lack of action before the crisis assumed proportions which, in the end, triggered the application of military force. Council practice since 1990 had clearly established that it could become active, even with respect to crises with a strong 'internal' dimension. The mechanisms for decisive action was available. At least the imposition of economic sanctions could have been expected during 1998. However, Russia had made clear in the Contact Group (where all permanent members of the Council other than China were represented) its opposition to further action. China's attitude, too, was uncertain.

In fact, even the arms embargo against Yugoslavia, much heralded at the time, did not really represent significant action on the part of the Council. By 1998, Belgrade had rearmed, under a formal cooperation agreement with Russia. Yugoslavia also boasted a significant indigenous arms industry, at least in relation to the less sophisticated weapons systems which were of relevance to the fighting in Kosovo. Instead, much like the arms embargo of 1991 in relation to the conflict between the FRY and Bosnia and Herzegovina, it froze the dominance of the FRY/Serb forces in the theatre, by denying to the armed opposition forces access to arms other than those which could be smuggled.

The initial qualification by the Security Council of the operations of the KLA as 'terrorism' may also have been somewhat unhelpful. In this way, the Yugoslav view was strengthened that it has *carte blanche* in tackling the insurrection in Kosovo, as indeed it seemed to have over the summer of 1998. The KLA, on the other hand, had little incentive to ensure that its operations would remain strictly limited to military objectives, targeted against the security apparatus in the territory. If any armed action, even if conducted in full compliance with the laws on internal armed conflicts, was qualified as terrorism, the argument for avoiding activities which can generally be termed terrorist actions, i.e., attacks on civilian Serbs, was less persuasive.

The Security Council did, however, also fulfil a positive role. In crystallizing the demands of the international community in concise and mandatory terms, it gave political legitimacy to other actors, willing to respond more strongly. Hence, the EU/EC adopted sanctions (albeit rather limited ones) going beyond the arms embargo, indicating that these were targeted precisely at terminating the practices the Security Council had so clearly condemned. When NATO threatened the use of force in September, it, too, sought to ensure that its demands corresponded precisely to those uttered by the Security Council. While this fact did not provide a legal justification for the threat in itself, the Alliance was less vulnerable to accusations of pursuing its own goals and agenda through violent means.

---

[14] See Chapter 13.

[15] Document 7.5.

[16] In relation to the Contact Group decision on enforced negotiations, it should be noted, however, that the undertaking to reach a political settlement within a short time-frame was covered by slightly less mandatory language (para 5).

[17] Similarly, the Council endorsed the result of ECOWAS action in relaton to Sierra Leone, despite the fact that the means through which this result had been obtained had been severely criticised in the Council.

1.   Resolution 1160 (1998), 31 March 1998

[*Adopted by the Security Council at its 3868th meeting, on 31 March 1998.*]

The Security Council,

Noting with appreciation the statements of the Foreign Ministers of France, Germany, Italy, the Russian Federation, the United Kingdom of Great Britain and Northern Ireland and the United States of America (the Contact Group) of 9 and 25 March 1998 (S/1998/223 and S/1998/272), including the proposal on a comprehensive arms embargo on the Federal Republic of Yugoslavia, including Kosovo,

Welcoming the decision of the Special Session of the Permanent Council of the Organization for Security and Cooperation in Europe (OSCE) of 11 March 1998 (S/1998/246),

Condemning the use of excessive force by Serbian police forces against civilians and peaceful demonstrators in Kosovo, as well as all acts of terrorism by the Kosovo Liberation Army or any other group or individual and all external support for terrorist activity in Kosovo, including finance, arms and training,

Noting the declaration of 18 March 1998 by the President of the Republic of Serbia on the political process in Kosovo and Metohija (S/1998/250),

Noting also the clear commitment of senior representatives of the Kosovar Albanian community to non-violence,

Noting that there has been some progress in implementing the actions indicated in the Contact Group statement of 9 March 1998, but stressing that further progress is required,

Affirming the commitment of all Member States to the sovereignty and territorial integrity of the Federal Republic of Yugoslavia,

Acting under Chapter VII of the Charter of the United Nations,

1. *Calls upon* the Federal Republic of Yugoslavia immediately to take the further necessary steps to achieve a political solution to the issue of Kosovo through dialogue and to implement the actions indicated in the Contact Group statements of 9 and 25 March 1998;

2. *Calls also upon* the Kosovar Albanian leadership to condemn all terrorist action, and *emphasizes* that all elements in the Kosovar Albanian community should pursue their goals by peaceful means only;

3. *Underlines* that the way to defeat violence and terrorism in Kosovo is for the authorities in Belgrade to offer the Kosovar Albanian community a genuine political process;

4. *Calls upon* the authorities in Belgrade and the leadership of the Kosovar Albanian community urgently to enter without preconditions into a meaningful dialogue on political status issues, and *notes* the readiness of the Contact Group to facilitate such a dialogue;

5. *Agrees*, without prejudging the outcome of that dialogue, with the proposal in the Contact Group statements of 9 and 25 March 1998 that the principles for a solution of the Kosovo problem should be based on the territorial integrity of the Federal Republic of Yugoslavia and should be in accordance with OSCE standards, including those set out in the Helsinki Final Act of the Conference on Security and Cooperation in Europe of 1975, and the Charter of the United Nations, and that such a solution must also take into account the rights of the Kosovar Albanians and all who live in Kosovo, and *expresses its support* for an enhanced status for Kosovo which would include a substantially greater degree of autonomy and meaningful self-administration;

6. *Welcomes* the signature on 23 March 1998 of an agreement on measures to implement the 1996 Education Agreement, *calls upon* all parties to ensure that its implementation proceeds smoothly and without delay according to the agreed timetable and *expresses its readiness* to consider measures if either party blocks implementation;

7. *Expresses its support* for the efforts of the OSCE for a peaceful resolution of the crisis in Kosovo, including through the Personal Representative of the Chairman-in-Office for the Federal Republic of Yugoslavia, who is also the Special Representative of the European Union, and the return of the OSCE long-term missions;

8. *Decides* that all States shall, for the purposes of fostering peace and stability in Kosovo, prevent the sale or supply to the Federal Republic of Yugoslavia, including Kosovo, by their nationals or from their territories or using their flag vessels and aircraft, of arms and related *matériel* of all types, such as weapons and ammunition, military vehicles and equipment and spare parts for the aforementioned, and shall prevent arming and training for terrorist activities there;

9. *Decides* to establish, in accordance with rule 28 of its provisional rules of procedure, a committee of the Security Council, consisting of all the members of the Council, to undertake the following tasks and to report on its work to the Council with its observations and recommendations:

(a) to seek from all States information regarding the action taken by them concerning the effective implementation of the prohibitions imposed by this resolution;

(b) to consider any information brought to its attention by any State concerning violations of the prohibitions imposed by this resolution and to recommend appropriate measures in response thereto;

(c) to make periodic reports to the Security Council on information submitted to it regarding alleged violations of the prohibitions imposed by this resolution;

(d) to promulgate such guidelines as may be necessary to facilitate the implementation of the prohibitions imposed by this resolution;

(e) to examine the reports submitted pursuant to paragraph 12 below;

10. *Calls upon* all States and all international and regional organizations to act strictly in conformity with this resolution, notwithstanding the existence of any rights granted or obligations conferred or imposed by any international agreement or of any contract entered into or any license or permit granted prior to the entry into force of the prohibitions imposed by this resolution, and *stresses* in this context the importance of continuing implementation of the Agreement on Subregional Arms Control signed in Florence on 14 June 1996;

11. *Requests* the Secretary-General to provide all necessary assistance to the committee established by paragraph 9 above and to make the necessary arrangements in the Secretariat for this purpose;

12. *Requests* States to report to the committee established by paragraph 9 above within 30 days of adoption of this resolution on the steps they have taken to give effect to the prohibitions imposed by this resolution;

13. *Invites* the OSCE to keep the Secretary-General informed on the situation in Kosovo and on measures taken by that organization in this regard;

14. *Requests* the Secretary-General to keep the Council regularly informed and to report on the situation in Kosovo and the implementation of this resolution no later than 30 days following the adoption of this resolution and every 30 days thereafter;

15. *Further requests* that the Secretary-General, in consultation with appropriate regional organizations, include in his first report recommendations for the establishment of a comprehensive regime to monitor the implementation of the prohibitions imposed by this resolution, and *calls upon* all States, in particular neighbouring States, to extend full cooperation in this regard;

16. *Decides* to review the situation on the basis of the reports of the Secretary-General, which will take into account the assessments of, *inter alia*, the Contact Group, the OSCE and the European Union, and *decides also* to reconsider the prohibitions imposed by this resolution, including action to terminate them, following receipt of the assessment of the Secretary-General that the Government of the Federal Republic of Yugoslavia, cooperating in a constructive manner with the Contact Group, have:

(a) begun a substantive dialogue in accordance with paragraph 4 above, including the participation of an outside representative or representatives, unless any failure to do so is not because of the position of the Federal Republic of Yugoslavia or Serbian authorities;

(b) withdrawn the special police units and ceased action by the security forces affecting the civilian population;

(c) allowed access to Kosovo by humanitarian organizations as well as representatives of Contact Group and other embassies;

(d) accepted a mission by the Personal Representative of the OSCE Chairman-in-Office for the Federal Republic of Yugoslavia that would include a new and specific mandate for addressing the problems in Kosovo, as well as the return of the OSCE long-term missions;

(e) facilitated a mission to Kosovo by the United Nations High Commissioner for Human Rights;

17. *Urges* the Office of the Prosecutor of the International Tribunal established pursuant to resolution 827 (1993) of 25 May 1993 to begin gathering information related to the violence in Kosovo that may fall within its jurisdiction, and *notes* that the authorities of the Federal Republic of Yugoslavia have an obligation to cooperate with the Tribunal and that the Contact Group countries will make available to the Tribunal substantiated relevant information in their possession;

18. *Affirms* that concrete progress to resolve the serious political and human rights issues in Kosovo will improve the international position of the Federal Republic of Yugoslavia and prospects for normalization of its international relationships and full participation in international institutions;

19. *Emphasizes* that failure to make constructive progress towards the peaceful resolution of the situation in Kosovo will lead to the consideration of additional measures;

20. *Decides* to remain seized of the matter.

2. Resolution 1186 (1998), 21 July 1998

[Adopted by the Security Council at its 3911th meeting, on 21 July 1998.]

The Security Council,

Recalling all its relevant resolutions concerning the conflicts in the former Yugoslavia, in particular its resolutions 795 (1992) of 11 December 1992, in which it addressed possible developments which could undermine confidence and stability in the former Yugoslav Republic of Macedonia or threaten its territory, and 1142 (1997) of 4 December 1997,

Recalling also its resolutions 1101 (1997) of 28 March 1997 and 1114 (1997) of 19 June 1997, in which it expressed its concern over the situation in Albania, and its resolution 1160 (1998) of 31 March 1998, in which it decided that all States shall prevent the sale or supply to the Federal Republic of Yugoslavia, including Kosovo, of arms and related *matériel* of all types and shall prevent arming and training for terrorist activities there,

Reiterating its appreciation for the important role played by the United Nations Preventive Deployment Force (UNPREDEP) in contributing to the maintenance of peace and stability and *paying tribute* to its personnel in the performance of their mandate,

Commending the role of UNPREDEP in monitoring the border areas and reporting to the Secretary-General on any developments which could pose a threat to the former Yugoslav Republic of Macedonia and by its presence deterring threats and preventing clashes, including monitoring and reporting on illicit arms flows within its area of responsibility,

Reiterating its call on the Governments of the former Yugoslav Republic of Macedonia and the Federal Republic of Yugoslavia to implement in full their agreement of 8 April 1996 (S/1996/291, annex), in particular regarding the demarcation of their mutual border,

Taking note of the letters of 15 May 1998 (S/1998/401) and 9 July 1998 (S/1998/627) from the Minister of Foreign Affairs of the former Yugoslav Republic of Macedonia to the Secretary-General, requesting the extension of the mandate of UNPREDEP and endorsing the option of an increase in its troop strength,

Having considered the reports of the Secretary-General of 1 June 1998 (S/1998/454) and 14 July 1998 (S/1998/644) and the recommendations contained therein,

Reaffirming its commitment to the independence, sovereignty and territorial integrity of the former Yugoslav Republic of Macedonia,

1. *Decides* to authorize an increase in the troop strength of UNPREDEP up to 1,050 and to extend the current mandate of UNPREDEP for a period of six months until 28 February 1999, including to continue by its presence to deter threats and prevent clashes, to monitor the border areas, and to report to the Secretary-General any developments which could pose a threat to the former

Yugoslav Republic of Macedonia, including the tasks of monitoring and reporting on illicit arms flows and other activities that are prohibited under resolution 1160 (1998);

2. *Expresses* its intention to consider further the recommendations of the Secretary-General in his report of 14 July 1998;

3. *Decides* to remain seized of the matter.

S/PRST/1998/25

3. Statement by the President of the Security Council, 24 August 1998

At the 3918th meeting of the Security Council, held on 24 August 1998 in connection with the Council's consideration of the item entitled "Letter dated 11 March 1998 from the Deputy Permanent Representative of the United Kingdom of Great Britain and Northern Ireland to the United Nations addressed to the President of the Security Council (S/1998/223) and letter dated 27 March 1998 from the Permanent Representative of the United States of America to the United Nations addressed to the President of the Security Council (S/1998/272)", the President of the Security Council made the following statement on behalf of the Council:

"The Security Council has considered the report of the Secretary-General of 5 August 1998 (S/1998/712) submitted pursuant to its resolution 1160 (1998) of 31 March 1998.

"The Security Council remains gravely concerned about the recent intense fighting in Kosovo which has had a devastating impact on the civilian population and has greatly increased the numbers of refugees and displaced persons.

"The Security Council shares the concern of the Secretary-General that the continuation or further escalation of the conflict in Kosovo has dangerous implications for the stability of the region. In particular, the Council is gravely concerned that given the increasing numbers of displaced persons, coupled with the approaching winter, the situation in Kosovo has the potential to become an even greater humanitarian disaster. The Council affirms the right of all refugees and displaced persons to return to their homes. In particular, the Council emphasizes the importance of unhindered and continuous access of humanitarian organizations to the affected population. The Council is concerned over reports of increasing violations of international humanitarian law.

"The Security Council calls for an immediate ceasefire. The Council emphasizes that the authorities of the Federal Republic of Yugoslavia and the Kosovo Albanians must achieve a political solution to the issue of Kosovo and that all violence and acts of terrorism from whatever quarter are unacceptable, and reiterates the importance of the implementation of its resolution 1160 (1998). The Council reaffirms the commitment of all Member States to the sovereignty and territorial integrity of the Federal Republic of Yugoslavia, and urges the authorities of the Federal Republic of Yugoslavia and the Kosovo Albanian leadership to enter immediately into a meaningful dialogue leading to an end to the violence and a negotiated political solution to the issue of Kosovo. It supports in this context the efforts of the Contact Group, including its initiatives to engage the authorities of the Federal Republic of Yugoslavia and the Kosovo Albanian leadership in discussions on the future status of Kosovo.

"In this regard, the Security Council welcomes the announcement by Dr. Ibrahim Rugova, the leader of the Kosovo Albanian community, of the formation of a negotiating team to represent the interests of the Kosovo Albanian community. The formation of the Kosovo Albanian negotiating team should lead to the early commencement of a substantial dialogue with the authorities of the Federal Republic of Yugoslavia, with the aim of ending the violence and achieving a peaceful settlement, including the safe and permanent return of all internally displaced persons and refugees to their homes.

"It remains essential that the authorities of the Federal Republic of Yugoslavia and the Kosovo Albanians accept responsibility for ending the violence in Kosovo, for allowing the people of Kosovo to resume their normal lives and for moving the political process forward.

"The Security Council will continue to follow the situation in Kosovo closely and will remain seized of the matter."

4.   Resolution 1199 (1998), 23 September 1998

[*Adopted by the Security Council at its 3930th meeting on 23 September 1998.*]

The Security Council,

Recalling its resolution 1160 (1998) of 31 March 1998,

Having considered the reports of the Secretary-General pursuant to that resolution, and in particular his report of 4 September 1998 (S/1998/834 and Add.1),

Noting with appreciation the statement of the Foreign Ministers of France, Germany, Italy, the Russian Federation, the United Kingdom of Great Britain and Northern Ireland and the United States of America (the Contact Group) of 12 June 1998 at the conclusion of the Contact Group's meeting with the Foreign Ministers of Canada and Japan (S/1998/567, annex), and the further statement of the Contact Group made in Bonn on 8 July 1998 (S/1998/657),

Noting also with appreciation the joint statement by the Presidents of the Russian Federation and the Federal Republic of Yugoslavia of 16 June 1998 (S/1998/526),

Noting further the communication by the Prosecutor of the International Tribunal for the Former Yugoslavia to the Contact Group on 7 July 1998, expressing the view that the situation in Kosovo represents an armed conflict within the terms of the mandate of the Tribunal,

Gravely concerned at the recent intense fighting in Kosovo and in particular the excessive and indiscriminate use of force by Serbian security forces and the Yugoslav Army which have resulted in numerous civilian casualties and, according to the estimate of the Secretary-General, the displacement of over 230,000 persons from their homes,

Deeply concerned by the flow of refugees into northern Albania, Bosnia and Herzegovina and other European countries as a result of the use of force in Kosovo, as well as by the increasing numbers of displaced persons within Kosovo, and other parts of the Federal Republic of Yugoslavia, up to 50,000 of whom the United Nations High Commissioner for Refugees has estimated are without shelter and other basic necessities,

Reaffirming the right of all refugees and displaced persons to return to their homes in safety, and *underlining* the responsibility of the Federal Republic of Yugoslavia for creating the conditions which allow them to do so,

Condemning all acts of violence by any party, as well as terrorism in pursuit of political goals by any group or individual, and all external support for such activities in Kosovo, including the supply of arms and training for terrorist activities in Kosovo and *expressing concern* at the reports of continuing violations of the prohibitions imposed by resolution 1160 (1998),

Deeply concerned by the rapid deterioration in the humanitarian situation throughout Kosovo, *alarmed* at the impending humanitarian catastrophe as described in the report of the Secretary-General, and *emphasizing* the need to prevent this from happening,

Deeply concerned also by reports of increasing violations of human rights and of international humanitarian law, and *emphasizing* the need to ensure that the rights of all inhabitants of Kosovo are respected,

Reaffirming the objectives of resolution 1160 (1998), in which the Council expressed support for a peaceful resolution of the Kosovo problem which would include an enhanced status for Kosovo, a substantially greater degree of autonomy, and meaningful self-administration,

Reaffirming also the commitment of all Member States to the sovereignty and territorial integrity of the Federal Republic of Yugoslavia,

Affirming that the deterioration of the situation in Kosovo, Federal Republic of Yugoslavia, constitutes a threat to peace and security in the region,

Acting under Chapter VII of the Charter of the United Nations,

1. *Demands* that all parties, groups and individuals immediately cease hostilities and maintain a ceasefire in Kosovo, Federal Republic of Yugoslavia, which would enhance the prospects for a meaningful dialogue between the authorities of the Federal Republic of Yugoslavia and the Kosovo Albanian leadership and reduce the risks of a humanitarian catastrophe;

2. *Demands also* that the authorities of the Federal Republic of Yugoslavia and the Kosovo Albanian leadership take immediate steps to improve the humanitarian situation and to avert the impending humanitarian catastrophe;

3. *Calls upon* the authorities in the Federal Republic of Yugoslavia and the Kosovo Albanian leadership to enter immediately into a meaningful dialogue without preconditions and with international involvement, and to a clear timetable, leading to an end of the crisis and to a negotiated political solution to the issue of Kosovo, and *welcomes* the current efforts aimed at facilitating such a dialogue;

4. *Demands further* that the Federal Republic of Yugoslavia, in addition to the measures called for under resolution 1160 (1998), implement immediately the following concrete measures towards achieving a political solution to the situation in Kosovo as contained in the Contact Group statement of 12 June 1998:

(a) cease all action by the security forces affecting the civilian population and order the withdrawal of security units used for civilian repression;

(b) enable effective and continuous international monitoring in Kosovo by the European Community Monitoring Mission and diplomatic missions accredited to the Federal Republic of Yugoslavia, including access and complete freedom of movement of such monitors to, from and within Kosovo unimpeded by government authorities, and expeditious issuance of appropriate travel documents to international personnel contributing to the monitoring;

(c) facilitate, in agreement with the UNHCR and the International Committee of the Red Cross (ICRC), the safe return of refugees and displaced persons to their homes and allow free and unimpeded access for humanitarian organizations and supplies to Kosovo;

(d) make rapid progress to a clear timetable, in the dialogue referred to in paragraph 3 with the Kosovo Albanian community called for in resolution 1160 (1998), with the aim of agreeing confidence-building measures and finding a political solution to the problems of Kosovo;

5. *Notes*, in this connection, the commitments of the President of the Federal Republic of Yugoslavia, in his joint statement with the President of the Russian Federation of 16 June 1998:

(a) to resolve existing problems by political means on the basis of equality for all citizens and ethnic communities in Kosovo;

(b) not to carry out any repressive actions against the peaceful population;

(c) to provide full freedom of movement for and ensure that there will be no restrictions on representatives of foreign States and international institutions accredited to the Federal Republic of Yugoslavia monitoring the situation in Kosovo;

(d) to ensure full and unimpeded access for humanitarian organizations, the ICRC and the UNHCR, and delivery of humanitarian supplies;

(e) to facilitate the unimpeded return of refugees and displaced persons under programmes agreed with the UNHCR and the ICRC, providing State aid for the reconstruction of destroyed homes,

and *calls for* the full implementation of these commitments;

6. *Insists* that the Kosovo Albanian leadership condemn all terrorist action, and *emphasizes* that all elements in the Kosovo Albanian community should pursue their goals by peaceful means only;

7. *Recalls* the obligations of all States to implement fully the prohibitions imposed by resolution 1160 (1998);

8. *Endorses* the steps taken to establish effective international monitoring of the situation in Kosovo, and in this connection welcomes the establishment of the Kosovo Diplomatic Observer Mission;

9. *Urges* States and international organizations represented in the Federal Republic of Yugoslavia to make available personnel to fulfil the responsibility of carrying out effective and continuous international monitoring in Kosovo until the objectives of this resolution and those of resolution 1160 (1998) are achieved;

10. *Reminds* the Federal Republic of Yugoslavia that it has the primary responsibility for the security of all diplomatic personnel accredited to the Federal Republic of Yugoslavia as well as the safety and security of all international and non-governmental humanitarian personnel in the Federal Republic of Yugoslavia and *calls upon* the authorities of the Federal Republic of Yugoslavia and all others concerned in the Federal Republic of Yugoslavia to take all appropriate steps to ensure that monitoring personnel performing functions under this resolution are not subject to the threat or use of force or interference of any kind;

11. *Requests* States to pursue all means consistent with their domestic legislation and relevant international law to prevent funds collected on their territory being used to contravene resolution 1160 (1998);

12. *Calls upon* Member States and others concerned to provide adequate resources for humanitarian assistance in the region and to respond promptly and generously to the United Nations Consolidated Inter-Agency Appeal for Humanitarian Assistance Related to the Kosovo Crisis;

13. *Calls upon* the authorities of the Federal Republic of Yugoslavia, the leaders of the Kosovo Albanian community and all others concerned to cooperate fully with the Prosecutor of the International Tribunal for the Former Yugoslavia in the investigation of possible violations within the jurisdiction of the Tribunal;

14. *Underlines* also the need for the authorities of the Federal Republic of Yugoslavia to bring to justice those members of the security forces who have been involved in the mistreatment of civilians and the deliberate destruction of property;

15. *Requests* the Secretary-General to provide regular reports to the Council as necessary on his assessment of compliance with this resolution by the authorities of the Federal Republic of Yugoslavia and all elements in the Kosovo Albanian community, including through his regular reports on compliance with resolution 1160 (1998);

16. *Decides*, should the concrete measures demanded in this resolution and resolution 1160 (1998) not be taken, to consider further action and additional measures to maintain or restore peace and stability in the region;

17. *Decides* to remain seized of the matter.

5. Resolution 1203 (1998), 24 October 1998

[*Adopted by the Security Council at its 3937th meeting, on 24 October 1998.*]

The Security Council,

Recalling its resolutions 1160 (1998) of 31 March 1998 and 1199 (1998) of 23 September 1998, and the importance of the peaceful resolution of the problem of Kosovo, Federal Republic of Yugoslavia,

Having considered the reports of the Secretary-General pursuant to those resolutions, in particular his report of 5 October 1998 (S/1998/912),

Welcoming the agreement signed in Belgrade on 16 October 1998 by the Minister of Foreign Affairs of the Federal Republic of Yugoslavia and the Chairman-in-Office of the Organization for Security and Cooperation in Europe (OSCE) providing for the OSCE to establish a verification mission in Kosovo (S/1998/978), including the undertaking of the Federal Republic of Yugoslavia to comply with resolutions 1160 (1998) and 1199 (1998),

Welcoming also the agreement signed in Belgrade on 15 October 1998 by the Chief of General Staff of the Federal Republic of Yugoslavia and the Supreme Allied Commander, Europe, of the North Atlantic Treaty Organization (NATO) providing for the establishment of an air verification mission over Kosovo (S/1998/991, annex), complementing the OSCE Verification Mission,

Welcoming also the decision of the Permanent Council of the OSCE of 15 October 1998 (S/1998/959, annex),

Welcoming the decision of the Secretary-General to send a mission to the Federal Republic of Yugoslavia to establish a first-hand capacity to assess developments on the ground in Kosovo,

Reaffirming that, under the Charter of the United Nations, primary responsibility for the maintenance of international peace and security is conferred on the Security Council,

Recalling the objectives of resolution 1160 (1998), in which the Council expressed support for a peaceful resolution of the Kosovo problem which would include an enhanced status for Kosovo, a substantially greater degree of autonomy, and meaningful self-administration,

Condemning all acts of violence by any party, as well as terrorism in pursuit of political goals by any group or individual, and all external support for such activities in Kosovo, including the supply of arms and training for terrorist activities in Kosovo, and *expressing* concern at the reports of continuing violations of the prohibitions imposed by resolution 1160 (1998),

Deeply concerned at the recent closure by the authorities of the Federal Republic of Yugoslavia of independent media outlets in the Federal Republic of Yugoslavia, and *emphasizing* the need for these to be allowed freely to resume their operations,

Deeply alarmed and concerned at the continuing grave humanitarian situation throughout Kosovo and the impending humanitarian catastrophe, and *re-emphasizing* the need to prevent this from happening,

Stressing the importance of proper coordination of humanitarian initiatives undertaken by States, the United Nations High Commissioner for Refugees and international organizations in Kosovo,

Emphasizing the need to ensure the safety and security of members of the Verification Mission in Kosovo and the Air Verification Mission over Kosovo,

Reaffirming the commitment of all Member States to the sovereignty and territorial integrity of the Federal Republic of Yugoslavia,

Affirming that the unresolved situation in Kosovo, Federal Republic of Yugoslavia, constitutes a continuing threat to peace and security in the region,

Acting under Chapter VII of the Charter of the United Nations,

1. *Endorses* and supports the agreements signed in Belgrade on 16 October 1998 between the Federal Republic of Yugoslavia and the OSCE, and on 15 October 1998 between the Federal Republic of Yugoslavia and NATO, concerning the verification of compliance by the Federal Republic of Yugoslavia and all others concerned in Kosovo with the requirements of its resolution 1199 (1998), and *demands* the full and prompt implementation of these agreements by the Federal Republic of Yugoslavia;

2. *Notes* the endorsement by the Government of Serbia of the accord reached by the President of the Federal Republic of Yugoslavia and the United States Special Envoy (S/1998/953, annex), and the public commitment of the Federal Republic of Yugoslavia to complete negotiations on a framework for a political settlement by 2 November 1998, and *calls* for the full implementation of these commitments;

3. *Demands* that the Federal Republic of Yugoslavia comply fully and swiftly with resolutions 1160 (1998) and 1199 (1998) and cooperate fully with the OSCE Verification Mission in Kosovo and the NATO Air Verification Mission over Kosovo according to the terms of the agreements referred to in paragraph 1 above;

4. *Demands also* that the Kosovo Albanian leadership and all other elements of the Kosovo Albanian community comply fully and swiftly with resolutions 1160 (1998) and 1199 (1998) and cooperate fully with the OSCE Verification Mission in Kosovo;

5. *Stresses* the urgent need for the authorities in the Federal Republic of Yugoslavia and the Kosovo Albanian leadership to enter immediately into a meaningful dialogue without preconditions and with international involvement, and to a clear timetable, leading to an end of the crisis and to a negotiated political solution to the issue of Kosovo;

6. *Demands* that the authorities of the Federal Republic of Yugoslavia, the Kosovo Albanian leadership and all others concerned respect the freedom of movement of the OSCE Verification Mission and other international personnel;

7. *Urges* States and international organizations to make available personnel to the OSCE Verification Mission in Kosovo;

8. *Reminds* the Federal Republic of Yugoslavia that it has the primary responsibility for the safety and security of all diplomatic personnel accredited to the Federal Republic of Yugoslavia, including members of the OSCE Verification Mission, as well as the safety and security of all international and non-governmental humanitarian personnel in the Federal Republic of Yugoslavia, and *calls upon* the authorities of the Federal Republic of Yugoslavia, and all others concerned throughout the Federal Republic of Yugoslavia including the Kosovo Albanian leadership, to take all appropriate steps to ensure that personnel performing functions under this resolution and the agreements referred to in paragraph 1 above are not subject to the threat or use of force or interference of any kind;

9. *Welcomes* in this context the commitment of the Federal Republic of Yugoslavia to guarantee the safety and security of the Verification Missions as contained in the agreements referred to in paragraph 1 above, *notes* that, to this end, the OSCE is considering arrangements to be implemented in cooperation with other organizations, and *affirms* that, in the event of an emergency, action may be needed to ensure their safety and freedom of movement as envisaged in the agreements referred to in paragraph 1 above;

10. *Insists* that the Kosovo Albanian leadership condemn all terrorist actions, *demands* that such actions cease immediately and *emphasizes* that all elements in the Kosovo Albanian community should pursue their goals by peaceful means only;

11. *Demands* immediate action from the authorities of the Federal Republic of Yugoslavia and the Kosovo Albanian leadership to cooperate with international efforts to improve the humanitarian situation and to avert the impending humanitarian catastrophe;

12. *Reaffirms* the right of all refugees and displaced persons to return to their homes in safety, and *underlines* the responsibility of the Federal Republic of Yugoslavia for creating the conditions which allow them to do so;

13. *Urges* Member States and others concerned to provide adequate resources for humanitarian assistance in the region and to respond promptly and generously to the United Nations Consolidated Inter-Agency Appeal for Humanitarian Assistance Related to the Kosovo crisis;

14. *Calls* for prompt and complete investigation, including international supervision and participation, of all atrocities committed against civilians and full cooperation with the International Tribunal for the former Yugoslavia, including compliance with its orders, requests for information and investigations;

15. *Decides* that the prohibitions imposed by paragraph 8 of resolution 1160 (1998) shall not apply to relevant equipment for the sole use of the Verification Missions in accordance with the agreements referred to in paragraph 1 above;

16. *Requests* the Secretary-General, acting in consultation with the parties concerned with the agreements referred to in paragraph 1 above, to report regularly to the Council regarding implementation of this resolution;

17. *Decides* to remain seized of the matter.

[For further Resolutions *see*:
    Resolution 777 (1992), Document 5.B.16.
    Resolution 808 (1993), Document 10.1.
    Resolution 827 (1993), Document 10.2.
    Resolution 855 (1993), Document 5.C.12.
    Resolution 1207 (1998), Document 10.16.]

Chapter 8: Initial Reports of the UN Secretary-General, the OSCE, NATO and Others

In response to the dramatic turn of events in Kosovo, the United Nations Secretary-General was requested to submit regular reports on the developing situation to the Council. Drawing on the OSCE, NATO and other bodies, these reports chronicle the events of April to October 1998 and the deployment of the OSCE Verification Mission (KVM).[1] While not having his own sources of information on the ground, Kofi Annan (or rather the UN Secretariat) added his own evaluations of the situation. However, there was not a great deal of diplomatic activity by the Secretary-General himself evident in the reports. According to Article 99 of the UN Charter, the Secretary-General enjoys a limited freedom of diplomatic initiative and the scope and scale of evolving drama might have merited an early response from him. The still difficult nature of the Kosovo crisis as a purportedly 'internal affair' of Yugoslavia may explain this apparent passivity. Other factors may include the dispute in the Security Council itself as to the necessary response to the crisis, and the feeling that the Contact Group was exercising the dominant role in crisis diplomacy. However, towards the end of the summer, the findings of the Secretary-General in his reports became more specific, in line with the ever-increasing drama of the displacement that was occurring.

While the OSCE reported very consistently to the United Nations on developments in the province, the silence of the EU is somewhat startling. Although the EU responded to a request from the Secretary-General and the UN Yugoslav sanctions Committee for assistance in sanctions monitoring, it did not use its EU monitoring mission to add transparency to FRY/Serb action at the UN level. This mission had already been severely criticised for failing to issue public reports on the genocide it had been observing in Bosnia and Herzegovina and also retained something of a phantom presence in the Kosovo crisis.

The change from repression to military assaults which brought about the massive displacement of Kosovo Albanians in 1998 had been triggered by increased activity of the Kosovo Liberation Army (KLA) in autumn 1997. That organization had previously consisted of tens or perhaps a few hundred individuals, mounting what were described as terrorist attacks.[2] These attacks had been generally targeted against police or other security installation, although the FRY/Serb authorities also indicated with some justification that these operations were part of a strategy of intimidation directed against Serb civilians. Attacks against Serb civilians did indeed occur, although these remained relatively isolated incidents from which the KLA dissociated itself.

While the increase in KLA operations was relatively marginal, it resulted in a change of tactic by the FRY/Serb forces in the territory. Previously, a campaign of intimidation, arbitrary arrests and forced confessions had been employed.[3] By spring 1998, FRY/Serb police and military units established more check-points on roads, also in rural areas, to limit the freedom of movement of underground fighters.[4] Then, a sequence of events familiar from the ethnic cleansing in Croatia and Bosnia and Herzegovina was employed. Ethnic Albanian villages suspected of collaborating with the KLA were surrounded by regular armed forces, including artillery and tank units and shelled. Civilians would flee or become casualties. Small units were then sent into the villages, often killing entire ethnic Albanian families, or clans, who had failed to seek shelter in the surrounding countryside. This practice was first dramatically exposed in the Drenica region, where several groups of individuals ranging in numbers from 12 to 53 had been "liquidated", several shot at close range.[5] The largest group among them included 15 women, six children and four individuals over the age of 65.

EU and KDOM diplomatic observers were denied access to areas of operation by FRY/Serb forces against villages in the region. Humanitarian supplies were also on occasion interdicted, although in general the humanitarian organizations were permitted to retain access to provide relief.[6] The conflict then spread further, involving large swathes of territory from which the KLA was progressively displaced, along with much of the ethnic Albanian population. Once more, the "wholesale destruction visited upon the Albanian villages" was reported.[7]

By early summer Serb/FRY operations were concentrated in the south-western part of Kosovo adjacent to the Albanian border, causing the first significant exodus of ethnic Albanians across that border. There were also the first reports of border incidents involving Albania directly. Although the UN Secretary-General could not find evidence of arms trafficking across the border, the FRY government justified this policy with the need to interdict support to the KLA.[8] The KLA, which had managed to establish control over certain rural regions, was increasingly pushed back in the weeks that followed. It was also internationally isolated, labelled by some governments a terrorist organization. Its position was not strengthened by reports of KLA elements involved in terrorizing isolated Serb communities in the areas still under KLA control.

---

[1] For further reports, see Chapter 13.B.

[2] Tim Judah, Kosovo's Road to War, *Survival* (Summer 1999) 13.

[3] See Chapter VI.

[4] On the 1998 conflict, *see* the excellent analysis by Stefan Troebst, in SIPRI *Yearbook 1999* (1999), Appendix 1C.

[5] High Comissioner for Human Rights Report, April 1998, Document 11.B.1.

[6] *Id.*

[7] OSCE Report, Annex V in UNSG Report, 2 July 1998, Document 8.4.

[8] UN Secretary-General's [UNSG] Report, 4 June 1998, Document 8.3.

This led to a sense on the part of the KLA and Kosovo Albanians that the international community was content to have Belgrade 'teach the KLA a lesson' as it were. Such a strategy, it was thought, would ensure that the KLA would not be in a position to obstruct the autonomy deal which was envisaged by the international community.[9] However, this plan, if it existed, had failed to consider the nature of the Yugoslav/Serb military campaign, and its consequences. In accordance with the tactics of an underground army which has neither the manpower nor the equipment to meet opposing forces directly, the KLA tended to melt away from villages that came under attack. The principal victims of FRY/Serb operations remained behind and had to flee, often under very dramatic circumstances, or risk death. With the advance of Serb/Yugoslav forces, the number of the displaced increased dramatically, reaching 100,000 by the end of July.[10]

In addition to the increasingly intolerable suffering of the civilian population, reports of the influx of small arms and ammunition from Albania surfaced, raising the prospect of an internationalisation of the conflict.[11] Moreover, corresponding to the ever larger number of displaced Albanians, and the atrocities which had led to the displacement, the KLA steadily grew in numbers. Rather than deserting the KLA on account of its lack of military success, a sense of national crisis among the Kosovo Albanians led to a feeling of solidarity, which was often transposed to the KLA, an organization that appeared to offer the only recourse in the increasingly desperate situation.

Changes were also afoot within the KLA. It had initially been dominated by a narrow cadre, reputed to maintain links with a Stalinist wing of security service officials who had survived the political changes in Albania. As the KLA grew, however, more leaders rose to prominence in their own native regions. Like most of their troops, they had resorted to arms by force of circumstances, motivated by the desire to defend their homes. Their attitude was less ideological and more pragmatic. In view of the military reverses suffered in the field, they were not always persuaded of the effectiveness of the top military and political leadership of the organization. To complicate matters still further, and contrary to media reports at the time, not all of the funds collected from the ethnic Albanian Diaspora abroad were being made available to finance the armed campaign of the KLA. The elected government, in particular, had access to considerable sums and was unwilling to transfer them to the control of an organization which it regarded with some circumspection. For, the national emergency obtaining in Kosovo had led the KLA to claim not only military, but also political leadership in Kosovo, notwithstanding the recent election result. The election of March 1998, after the fighting had erupted,had demonstrated overwhelming support for Ibrahim Rugova and his government.

At the same time, US pressure had impelled Dr Rugova to establish direct dialogue with Slobodan Milosevic, at a much publicised meeting in Belgrade. This move was not only strongly opposed by the KLA, but also by other politicians, many of whom were former supporters of Rugova's LDK party and had now formed an opposition group and were longing for power. To this climate of division and confusion, which was to haunt the Kosovo Albanians in the months to come, there was added the direct pressure from FRY/Serb forces and the need to support the large numbers of the displaced.

By September, when NATO moved towards a threat of force to terminate hostilities, Belgrade asserted that it had defeated secessionist terrorism and would soon cease operations. However, the UN Secretary-General reported on a sharp escalation of military operations as a result of an offensive launched by the Serb forces in central, southern and western Kosovo.[12] In his final report before the issuing of the threat of force, he indicated that "the level of destruction points clearly to an indiscriminate and disproportionate use of force against civilian populations", with the civilian population increasingly having "become the main target of the conflict"[13]. As of mid-September, an estimated 6,000 to 7,000 buildings in 269 villages, if not more, had been destroyed. That estimate was later raised to 20,000 when the OSCE gained access to the territory pursuant to the Holbrooke agreement. There were further reports of mass-killings of civilians in several locations, including the mutilation of ethnic Albanian bodies according to the pattern witnessed in Bosnia and Herzegovina.[14] By mid-October, there were some 280,000 to 300,000 displaced ethnic Albanians whose fate was uncertain, given the imminent onset of winter.

---

[9] Richard Caplan, International Diplomacy and the Crisis in Kosovo, 74 International Affairs (1998) 753.
[10] UNSG Report, 5 August 1998, Document 8.6.
[11] *Id.*, OSCE report, Annex 1.
[12] UNSG Report, Annex, 21 September 1998, Document 8.8.
[13] UNSG Report, 3 October 1998, Document 8.9.
[14] *Id.*

S/1998/313, 9 April 1998

1. Letter from the Secretary-General Addressed to the President of the Security Council, 8 April 1998

I have the honour to refer to Security Council resolution 1160 (1998) of 31 March 1998, in paragraph 14 of which the Council requested me to keep it regularly informed and to report on the situation in Kosovo and the implementation of the resolution no later than 30 days following the adoption of the resolution and every 30 days thereafter.

In this regard, you will recall that, on 10 March 1998, the Secretariat informed the members of the Council that the United Nations did not have a political presence in Kosovo that would enable it to provide first-hand information on the situation in the area. Such United Nations personnel as there is devoted exclusively to humanitarian assistance. As there has been no change in this regard, the Secretariat is still not in a position to independently assess the situation on the ground and to report to the Council thereon.

By means of the present letter, I should therefore like to inform the Security Council that, in discharging this part of my mandate, as well as in assessing whether the Government of the Federal Republic of Yugoslavia has complied in a constructive manner with conditions put forward by the Contact Group, I shall be relying exclusively on the information and assessments of the Contact Group, the Organization for Security and Cooperation in Europe (OSCE) and the European Union, as foreseen in paragraph 16 of the above-mentioned resolution. To this end, I have already sent requests for their cooperation to the Coordinator of the Contact Group, to the Chairman-in-Office of OSCE and to the Presidency of the European Union.

I should be grateful if you would convey this information to the members of the Security Council.

(Signed) Kofi A. ANNAN

S/1998/361, 30 April 1998

2. Report of the Secretary-General Prepared Pursuant to Security Council Resolution 1160, 30 April 1998

I. INTRODUCTION

... 3. At its first meeting, on 3 April 1998, the Committee elected Mr. Celso L. N. Amorim of Brazil as its Chairman. Kenya and Portugal were elected to serve as Vice-Chairmen. The Committee is currently considering draft guidelines for the conduct of its work. ...

II. COMPREHENSIVE REGIME TO MONITOR THE IMPLEMENTATION OF THE PROHIBITIONS IMPOSED BY SECURITY COUNCIL RESOLUTION 1160 (1998)

6. The establishment of a comprehensive regime to monitor the implementation of the prohibitions imposed by Security Council resolution 1160 (1998) would require the deployment of teams composed of qualified experts. The teams should be supported by a fully equipped communications centre. These teams would provide advice and assistance to the authorities of neighbouring and other States that bear the responsibility for enforcement of the mandatory measures in accordance with the provisions of the above resolution. In accordance with its mandate and the guidelines to be adopted by it, the Committee established by Security Council resolution 1160 (1998) would be responsible for considering reports from national authorities and regional organizations and for providing policy guidance to them. It should be noted that the United Nations is unable, within existing budgetary resources, to establish and administer the requested comprehensive monitoring regime.

7. Security Council resolution 1160 (1998) acknowledges the positive role the Organization for Security and Cooperation in Europe (OSCE) and other appropriate regional organizations could play in facilitating the implementation of the prohibitions imposed by the resolution. I believe that OSCE, with contributions and assistance from other regional organizations, as necessary, would be in a position to carry out the requested monitoring functions effectively. Those regional organizations might include the European Union, the North Atlantic Treaty Organization, and the Western European Union. They, along with the Danube Commission, contributed to the success of the former sanctions regime. The above arrangement would also facilitate the central role of the Committee established by Security Council resolution 1160 (1998).

8. If the members of the Security Council are in agreement with the concept outlined in paragraph 7 above, I would propose to explore with OSCE and other regional organizations as appropriate, their readiness to participate in a comprehensive monitoring regime with a view to submitting a more detailed proposal to the Security Council.

III. SITUATION IN KOSOVO

9. I am concerned about the deteriorating situation in Kosovo and the absence of progress in negotiations between the parties concerned. There are also alarming reports about incidents on the border with Albania. The Secretariat, however, has no political presence in Kosovo that would enable it to obtain first-hand information on the situation in the area. Such United Nations personnel as are located in the area are devoted to humanitarian assistance. In this regard, I informed the President of the Security Council in my letter dated 9 April 1998 that the Secretariat was not in a position to make an independent assessment of the situation on the ground. Therefore, in discharging this part of my mandate, as well as in assessing whether the Government of the Federal Republic of Yugoslavia has complied in a constructive manner with conditions put forward by the Contact Group, I have had to rely on information and assessments provided by the Contact Group, OSCE and the European Union, as foreseen in paragraph 16 of Security Council resolution 1160 (1998).

10. Accordingly, I sent requests for information and assessments to the Coordinator of the Contact Group, to the Chairman-in-Office of the Organization for Security and Cooperation in Europe and to the Presidency of the European Union. As of 24 April 1998, in response to my request, I had received information on the situation in Kosovo from the Presidency of the European Union (annex I) and the Chairman-in-Office of the OSCE (annex II). Whereas no information has been received to date from the coordinator of the Contact Group, one of its members, the Russian Federation, submitted its own assessment (annex III). The Chairman-in-Office further informed me that the Organization for Security and Cooperation in Europe was working on a substantive report on the crisis in Kosovo, to be submitted to the Contact Group at the end of April, and would be prepared to provide the United Nations with regular updates on the situation in Kosovo.

11. I shall endeavour to continue to present assessments to the Security Council on the basis of information obtained from various sources.

Annex I:

European Union report, 21 April 1998

1. Paragraph 16 of Security Council resolution 1160 (1998) calls for an assessment by the Secretary-General of whether the Government of the Federal Republic of Yugoslavia, cooperating in a constructive manner with the Contact Group, has:

"16. (a) begun a substantive dialogue in accordance with paragraph 4 above, including the participation of an outside representative or representatives, unless any failure to do so is not because of the position of the Federal Republic of Yugoslavia or Serbian authorities;"

2. The Government of the Republic of Serbia has issued several public invitations to representatives of "national minorities" in Kosovo, including the Kosovar Albanian community, to attend talks in Pristina. The Government has established a team, headed by Serbian Deputy Prime Minister Mr. Ratko Markovic, which has travelled to Pristina for the talks. On one occasion, the delegation of the Republic of Serbia was led by the President of the Republic, Mr. Milan Milutinovic. On 19 March, Federal President Milosevic appointed Deputy Federal Prime Minister Vladan Kutlesic as his Special Envoy for talks with the Kosovar Albanians and since then he has been a member of the team. The President of the Federal Republic of Yugoslavia has stated that he is ready to be the sponsor of the dialogue. Although representatives of some of the numerically smaller minorities have attended meetings with the Serbian Government team, the Kosovar Albanians have refused to participate.

3. The Security Council requirement on beginning a dialogue is explicitly directed at the Government of the Federal Republic of Yugoslavia. An

invitation to begin a dialogue has been issued by the Serbian Government, with the inclusion of a Federal representative. The inclusion of such a representative in a Serbian Government delegation, while a positive step in itself, does not meet the requirement. This is reinforced by the decision to issue the invitation solely in the name of the Republic of Serbia. Furthermore, the Republic of Serbia has offered to hold talks in Serbian Government offices. Moreover, although the Serbian authorities have insisted that the dialogue can take place without preconditions, the stipulation that a solution must be found within the Republic of Serbia (rather than leaving this question open) amounts to the establishment of a precondition.

4. The Serbian Government has also refused to accept the participation of an outside representative or representatives, as required by paragraph 16 (a). Acting on a proposal by the President of the Federal Republic of Yugoslavia, Mr. Slobodan Milosevic, the Serbian Government intends to hold a referendum on 23 April on the participation of foreign representatives in the solution of the Kosovo crisis. This is an attempt by the Serbian Government to seek popular confirmation of its rejection of foreign involvement.

5. Although the Kosovar Albanian parties have not attended the offered talks with the Serbian Government, their representatives have made clear their willingness to enter into dialogue without preconditions with the Government of the Federal Republic of Yugoslavia in the presence of a third party. Mr. Ibrahim Rugova, President of the Democratic League of Kosovo, has established both a 15-member team of advisers and a 4-member negotiating team in preparation for talks. The members of the advisory board have not yet agreed on a programme and some, including Mr. Rugova, continue to insist on maintaining, as an objective, independence for Kosovo. This would be in conflict with the principle of the territorial integrity of the Federal Republic of Yugoslavia affirmed in paragraph 7 of Security Council resolution 1160 (1998). On 17 April, Mr. Rugova reconfirmed the commitment of the Kosovar Albanian leadership to the dialogue. He urged that the Belgrade team meet with the Kosovar negotiating team in a neutral country/venue, with international participation, as called for by the Contact Group Ministerial meeting in Bonn, and indeed the international community.

"16. (b) withdrawn the special police units and ceased action by the security forces affecting the civilian population;"

6. The atmosphere throughout Kosovo remains extremely tense, in particular in Drenica and surrounding areas. The activities of the security forces continue, albeit at a reduced level from that of a few weeks ago, impeding the freedom of movement of the civilian population along the main routes. A major contributory factor is the presence of approximately 16 vehicle checkpoints, situated mainly on the roads going through the Drenica triangle or those bordering it and on the Pristina-Pec road. These checkpoints were set up in early March and are in addition to the long-established vehicle control points at the entry to many towns in Kosovo. Initially the new checkpoints were manned by special police forces (PJP) and Ministry of Interior Police (MUP), supported by armoured personnel carriers and heavy machine-guns. Weapon calibres included .5", 20 mm and 30 mm cannon and 2x60 mm mortars. These checkpoints have been fortified and are now of a semi-permanent nature.

7. Until 9 April, PJP forces were effectively in control of all vehicle checkpoints. Since then, there has been no evidence of uniformed PJP forces at these points. However, the armoured personnel carriers and heavy machine-guns are still present. The current strength of uniformed security forces on duty at any given time at these vehicle checkpoints is around 300. At checkpoints in the more sensitive areas, men, apparently part of the police complement, but who are not wearing normal uniform and whose role is not immediately identifiable, have been observed.

8. In some areas, the population has returned and appears to be resuming normal life. However, there are reports of harassment of civilians at checkpoints, including physical and verbal attacks and long delays apparently without good reason. Many residents of the affected areas claim that they now choose not to travel outside their home towns for fear of harassment or delay at checkpoints. On the other hand, the police have not recently sought to prevent regular demonstrations in Pristina and other towns and, although there have been isolated confrontations, have generally refrained from excessive use of force.

9. In this connection, it should be noted that the Kosovar Albanian political representatives have not yet unreservedly condemned all terrorist activity as required by paragraph 2. There have also been continuing Kosovar Albanian attacks on Serb police positions and, although responsibility has not been acknowledged, other attacks on alleged Kosovar Albanian collaborators.

"16. (c) allowed access to Kosovo by humanitarian organizations as well as representatives of Contact Group and other embassies;"

10. In contrast to the situation in the period immediately after the first incidents in the Drenica area, neither European Union (EU) embassies nor the humanitarian organizations have recently reported any specific problems in obtaining access to parts of Kosovo.

"16. (d) accepted a mission by the Personal Representative of the OSCE Chairman-in-Office for the Federal Republic of Yugoslavia that would include a new and specific mandate for addressing the problems in Kosovo, as well as the return of the OSCE long-term missions;"

11. The Federal Republic of Yugoslavia has indicated willingness to accept a mission by a Personal Representative of the EU and the OSCE Chairman-in-Office to discuss relations between the Federal Republic of Yugoslavia and the EU/OSCE, but has not agreed that the mission should include a new and specific mandate for addressing the problems in Kosovo. The Federal Republic of Yugoslavia has also sought to impose conditions on the return of the OSCE long-term missions. Informal discussions on this matter are continuing.

"16. (e) facilitated a mission to Kosovo by the United Nations High Commissioner for Human Rights;"

12. The Federal Republic of Yugoslavia has not granted the requested visa to the United Nations High Commissioner for Human Rights Special Rapporteur on extrajudicial, summary or arbitrary executions, although visas were granted for visits by the Special Rapporteur on the Former Yugoslavia and three human rights officers.

13. In addition, paragraph 17 of Security Council resolution 1160 (1998) "Urges the Office of the Prosecutor of the International Tribunal established pursuant to resolution 827 (1993) of 25 May 1993 to begin gathering information related to the violence in Kosovo that may fall within its jurisdiction, and notes that the authorities of the Federal Republic of Yugoslavia have an obligation to cooperate with the Tribunal ..."

14. The Prosecutor wrote in March to the Minister of Justice in Belgrade seeking information to help the Court assess whether the incidents in Kosovo justified an investigation. The EU understands that the Minister's preliminary response was to dispute that the International Tribunal for the Former Yugoslavia has jurisdiction in this matter. The EU further understands that the Prosecutor has sent a second letter to Belgrade upholding the Tribunal's rights of jurisdiction, reiterating her request for information and warning the authorities of the Federal Republic of Yugoslavia that their initial response did not meet the demand in Security Council resolution 1160 (1998) for full cooperation with the Tribunal.

15. With reference to paragraph 6 of Security Council resolution 1160 (1998), the parties have begun implementation of the Education Agreement. Discussions on this matter are continuing.

Annex II

Information on the situation in Kosovo and on measures taken by the Organization for Security and Cooperation in Europe

I. Situation in Kosovo

1. The situation on the ground remains relatively calm but very tense. A heavy Serbian police presence, which includes special police forces, instils in the population a sense of being under siege.

2. While there was no further large-scale violence on the scale of that reported in February and at the beginning of March, there were separate violent incidents causing a number of casualties in late March and in April.

3. There were several street demonstrations in Pristina and other towns in Kosovo in March and April, most of them organized by the Kosovar Albanians and some by the Serbian population. While all were conducted peacefully, some were dispersed by the Serbian police.

4. There has been no progress on beginning a political dialogue between the Belgrade authorities and the Kosovar Albanian community, although both sides declared their readiness to enter into such a dialogue. A delegation from Belgrade travelled to Pristina on several occasions declaring a readiness to begin a dialogue. The Kosovar Albanians declined to participate because there was no agreement on a framework and procedure for the talks. Moreover, this invitation for dialogue was issued by the Serbian Government in their Pristina offices and with the requirement that the question of the status of Kosovo be discussed only in the framework of the Republic of Serbia. This has been interpreted by the Albanian side as a precondition. At the same time, the request of the Kosovar Albanians and the international community to allow participation of an outside representative or representatives has been rejected by Belgrade. In spite of these factors, the Kosovar Albanians have formed a 15-member advisory team to prepare a platform for the talks as well as a 4-member group to

participate in the talks once they begin. The longer the talks are delayed, however, the farther apart the political sides will drift.

5. Offers by the Organization for Security and Cooperation in Europe (OSCE) to the Federal Republic of Yugoslavia to facilitate the dialogue have been rejected.

6. Adding to the deadlock between the parties, the Serbian Government, acting on the proposal of President Milosevic, decided to hold a referendum on 23 April on the question of accepting or not accepting "the participation of foreign representatives in the settlement of the problem of Kosovo and Metohija". This decision was criticized by OSCE as being a diversionary tactic and having "a disruptive effect on an already inflamed situation" (statement of the OSCE Troika, 8 April 1998). The Chairman-in-Office declined a subsequent invitation by the Minister for Foreign Affairs of the Federal Republic of Yugoslavia to observe the referendum replying that the invitation was "rather rhetorical than a meaningful effort to contribute to the improvement of the situation".

7. Access for international humanitarian organizations has improved. Also, representatives of the embassies of OSCE participating States have not reported particular obstacles to their trips to Kosovo. However, the tense atmosphere prevalent throughout Kosovo due to heavy police presence and checkpoints makes travel in the region difficult.

8. The beginning of implementation of the Education Agreement was a positive step forward, although there is a long way to go towards full reintegration of Albanians into the State system of education.

9. The situation along the borders of Albania and the former Yugoslav Republic of Macedonia is relatively normal. No evidence of a refugee flow has been reported. The danger of refugees cannot, however, be excluded in the case of renewed violence.

II. Measures taken by the Organization for Security and Cooperation in Europe

10. On 2 March 1998, the Chairman-in-Office issued a statement on Kosovo in which he expressed his deep concern over armed clashes and appealed to the sides to refrain from any further acts of violence and to start a meaningful dialogue.

11. On 10 March 1998, the Chairman-in-Office presented an action plan on Kosovo in which he requested the authorities of the Federal Republic of Yugoslavia to decrease police presence in Kosovo and for both sides to refrain from violence and prepare for dialogue. He also expressed his will to immediately dispatch Mr. Felipe Gonzalez as his Personal Representative to the Federal Republic of Yugoslavia. He called upon the Federal Republic of Yugoslavia to accept the return of the OSCE long-term missions in Kosovo, the Sandjak and Vojvodina.

12. At a special session, the OSCE Permanent Council, on 11 March, adopted Decision No. 218 which, along the lines of the Chairman-in-Office's action plan, called for the sending of Mr. Gonzalez as Personal Representative, the return of OSCE missions and the urgent beginning of a meaningful dialogue without preconditions and with the participation of an outside representative or representatives. The decision fully supported the position of the Contact Group statement adopted in London on 9 March 1998.

13. On 18 March, the Chairman-in-Office presented the mandate for his Personal Representative, Mr. Gonzalez, after consultations with the Presidency of the European Union and the members of the Contact Group. The mandate requests Mr. Gonzalez to represent OSCE in all specific areas of concern, including democratization, human rights, treatment of national minorities and the problem of the future participation of the Federal Republic of Yugoslavia in OSCE. The mandate also asks Mr. Gonzalez to address the conflict in Kosovo.

14. On 19-20 March, the Chairman-in-Office travelled to Tirana and Skopje. The main goal of his visit was to see what measures OSCE could take to prevent spillover of the Kosovo crisis. The highest authorities in both countries declared their cooperative approach to international efforts to finding a peaceful solution to the conflict.

15. Both the OSCE presence in Albania as well as the OSCE mission in Skopje have been enhanced in order to provide for monitoring of the situation on the Kosovo border.

16. At their meeting in Bonn on 25 March, the Contact Group requested the OSCE Troika (Poland, Denmark and Norway) to submit to their next meeting a "report on compliance" of the Federal Republic of Yugoslavia on Kosovo to the Contact Group demands. The work on this report is currently under way and the final document will be presented to the Contact Group at the end of April 1998.

17. On 27 March, the Chairman-in-Office visited the Federal Republic of Yugoslavia where he met authorities in Belgrade, Pristina and Podgorica.

18. During his talks with President Milosevic in Belgrade, the Chairman-in-Office reiterated the points of his plan of action and the decision of the Permanent Council. President Milosevic responded that the Federal Republic of Yugoslavia would not be ready to accept OSCE "demands" before "taking back its seat in the Organization". He indicated that Mr. Gonzalez would be welcome under the condition that his mandate would be limited to the question of readmittance of the Federal Republic of Yugoslavia to OSCE. The authorities of the Federal Republic of Yugoslavia strongly rejected any outside participation in a dialogue on Kosovo.

19. In Pristina, the Chairman-in-Office met with Mr. Ibrahim Rugova, President of the Democratic League of Kosovo, and other leaders of the Kosovar Albanians. Mr. Rugova reiterated his position that a peaceful solution to the conflict must be found through dialogue with the participation of an outside representative. He continues to maintain his objective of achieving independent status for Kosovo, a demand that may contradict the OSCE principle of territorial integrity of States.

20. In Podgorica, President Djukanovic of Montenegro presented the Chairman-in-Office with an open-minded position on the OSCE's offer to assist the Federal Republic of Yugoslavia in the democratization process and with regard to Kosovo.

21. On 26 March, a special meeting of the Permanent Council on Kosovo took place in Vienna to discuss the status of implementation of its Decision 218. In the meantime, representatives of the embassies to the Federal Republic of Yugoslavia of the OSCE participating States have continued their visits to Kosovo to monitor the situation first-hand.

22. The Ministers of the OSCE Troika met in Warsaw on 8 April and reiterated the importance of carrying out OSCE demands leading to unconditional dialogue as the only solution to bringing about a peaceful solution to the ongoing crisis in Kosovo.

III. Conclusion

23. The basic demands of OSCE have not been sufficiently considered by the authorities of the Federal Republic of Yugoslavia. The conditions required for bringing about a meaningful dialogue have not been improved and a resolution of the crisis is not in sight.

24. The existing tensions could easily escalate into new clashes with unforeseen consequences. The potential that the conflict will continue unabated threatens the stability of the Federal Republic of Yugoslavia, the region and Europe as a whole. Intensified international efforts, therefore, are indispensable, not only to prevent a further escalation of violence, but to advance a peaceful solution to the conflict. The OSCE stands ready to participate in these efforts.

Annex III

Memorandum by the Russian Federation, 14 April 1998

1. As a result of the joint efforts of the Contact Group countries, there has lately been serious progress in the implementation of the requirements of the Security Council and the Contact Group on the stabilization of the situation in Kosovo. The basis for the comprehensive dialogue, including on the issue of meaningful self-administration in Kosovo within Serbia, the Federal Republic of Yugoslavia, has been laid down.

2. The Government of Serbia has set up a delegation to participate in negotiations without preconditions. The delegation includes a special representative of the President of the Federal Republic of Yugoslavia, Deputy Premier of the Federal Government, Mr. Kutlesic. The President of the Federal Republic of Yugoslavia, Slobodan Milosevic, whose involvement in the negotiations process has been sought by all members of the Contact Group, has confirmed his intention to sponsor the dialogue.

3. The implementation of the Educational Agreement of September 1996 has begun in accordance with the document on educational issues of 23 March 1998.

4. The situation regarding the access of international representatives to Kosovo has significantly improved. The International Committee of the Red Cross, the United Nations High Commissioner for Human Rights and the field office of the United Nations High Commissioner for Refugees in Pristina have no complaints against the authorities of Serbia and the Federal Republic of Yugoslavia in this regard.

5. In accordance with the agreement of the Contact Group of 6 April 1998, in the event that foreign representatives encounter problems with trips to Kosovo or in their other activities, a respective embassy will immediately inform the embassies of the other members of the Contact Group and the OSCE "Troika" countries in order to quickly resolve those problems with the authorities in Belgrade and Pristina.

6. We have received unambiguous assurances from the high-level authorities of the Federal Republic of Yugoslavia and Serbia that the special police units have been withdrawn from Kosovo and that the overall strength of the law enforcement personnel, including anti-terrorist forces, does not exceed the level of a year ago and is defined by the crime rate and the general crime situation in the area. Our representatives in the field confirm this information.

7. In this context, new terrorist actions by the extremist forces in Kosovo and continued external support for terrorist activities there cause deep concern. We believe that, in the recommendations on the establishment of a comprehensive regime of monitoring of the implementation of measures contained in Security Council monitoring of the implementation of measures contained in Security Council resolution 1160 (1998), which the Secretary-General is to submit to the Security Council, it is necessary to clearly outline measures aimed at prevention by the States of the arming and training of terrorists, as well as providing financial support for terrorist activities. In view of this objective, such recommendations should specifically refer to ensuring effective monitoring on the borders of Albania and Macedonia with the Kosovo region.

8. The main task now is to make the parties begin negotiations. In this connection, we are disappointed by the fact that the Kosovar Albanian side has once again ignored Belgrade's proposal to begin the dialogue, all the more so now that the President of Serbia, Mr. Milutinovic, and a Deputy Premier of the Federal Republic of Yugoslavia have arrived in Pristina for that purpose. Contrary to the requirements of the Contact Group to immediately begin the dialogue without preconditions, it is the leadership of the Kosovar Albanians who set forth such preconditions, demanding the presence of international mediators and a conduct of negotiations solely with the representative of the President of the Federal Republic of Yugoslavia.

9. The issue of an international presence at the negotiations is of significant importance. In our view, there should be no direct mediation in the process of the negotiations per se. It is important to achieve the main goal which is to ensure necessary political support for the dialogue.

10. The Chairman-in-Office of the Organization for Security and Cooperation in Europe should agree with Belgrade on the mandate of his special representative as soon as possible. We believe that such a mandate should be formulated flexibly enough to provide the special representative with the opportunity to promote the solutions acceptable to both parties. The authorities of the Federal Republic of Yugoslavia should get a clear message that the successful mission of the special representative of the Chairman-in-Office will be conducive to the return of the Federal Republic of Yugoslavia to the Organization for Security and Cooperation in Europe. Such an assumption should be reflected in the special representative's mandate.

S/1998/470

3.   Report of the Secretary-General Prepared Pursuant to Security Council Resolution 1160, 4 June 1998

...

II.   SECURITY   COUNCIL   COMMITTEE   ESTABLISHED PURSUANT TO RESOLUTION 1160 (1998)

3. At its second meeting, on 6 May 1998, the Security Council Committee established pursuant to resolution 1160 (1998) adopted the guidelines for the conduct of its work to assist it in discharging its mandate pursuant to paragraph 9 of resolution 1160 (1998). The text of the guidelines was transmitted to all States and appropriate international organizations.

4. On 7 May 1998, Ambassador Celso L. N. Amorium (Brazil), Chairman of the Committee, issued an appeal on behalf of the members of the Committee to all States and international and regional organizations to provide information regarding violations or suspected violations of the prohibitions imposed by the Security Council in resolution 1160 (1998).

5. As at 29 May 1998, the following 34 States had reported pursuant to paragraph 12 of resolution 1160 (1998) to the Committee on the steps they had taken to give effect to the prohibitions imposed by the resolution: Armenia, Austria, Bahrain, Belarus, Brazil, Bulgaria, Cyprus, Czech Republic, Fiji, Finland, France, Hungary, Iran (Islamic Republic of), Italy, Japan, Malta, Monaco, Norway, Poland, Portugal, Romania, Saudi Arabia, Singapore, Slovakia, Slovenia, South Africa,

Spain, Sweden, Switzerland, the former Yugoslav Republic of Macedonia, Turkey, Ukraine, United Kingdom of Great Britain and Northern Ireland, Uruguay.

III.   COMPREHENSIVE   REGIME   TO   MONITOR   THE IMPLEMENTATION OF THE PROHIBITIONS IMPOSED BY RESOLUTION 1160 (1998)

6. In my first report (S/1998/361) dated 30 April 1998, I outlined in general terms the concept of the comprehensive regime to monitor the implementation of the prohibitions imposed by resolution 1160 (1998). Following the informal consultations of the Security Council held on 8 May 1998 to consider the report, I was informed by the President of the Security Council of the Council's wish that in exploring the establishment of a comprehensive regime to monitor the implementation of the prohibitions imposed by resolution 1160 (1998), I should take into account the existing capacities and potentials, in particular of the United Nations and the Organization for Security and Cooperation in Europe (OSCE). Accordingly, on 15 May, I addressed a letter to Mr. Bronislaw Geremek, Minister for Foreign Affairs of Poland, in his capacity as Chairman-in-Office of OSCE, in which I invited him to provide me, at his earliest convenience, with the views of OSCE on how to establish the comprehensive monitoring regime. I stated that, in doing so, OSCE could benefit from advice and support from other regional organizations which might be in a position to contribute to the success of the monitoring regime. The full text of the letter is contained in annex I to the present report.

7. In a letter dated 1 June 1998, the Chairman-in-Office of OSCE conveyed the views of his Organization on the establishment of a comprehensive monitoring regime. He confirmed the readiness of OSCE to contribute to the monitoring of the arms embargo within its capabilities. He stated that the particular comparative advantage of OSCE was its ongoing presence in the region through its missions deployed in Bosnia and Herzegovina, Croatia, Albania and the former Yugoslav Republic of Macedonia. He stated further that the monitoring activities, carried out currently by OSCE, along the border between Albania and the Federal Republic of Yugoslavia as well as the border between the former Yugoslav Republic of Macedonia and the Federal Republic of Yugoslavia, can usefully contribute to an overall arms embargo monitoring effort, under the overall responsibility of the United Nations. He added that the border monitoring capabilities of the OSCE presence in Albania were being strengthened. He concluded that, while not being able to assume a leading coordinating role with regard to an arms embargo monitoring effort undertaken by other regional organizations, OSCE might offer a flexible coordinating framework for monitoring activities in the field if so desired by participants in the effort. The full text of the letter is attached to the present report as annex II.

8. In the light of the response from OSCE and in accordance with the provisions of paragraph 15 of Security Council resolution 1160 (1998), I have written to the Secretary-General of the North Atlantic Treaty Organization (NATO) the Presidency of the European Union, the Secretary-General of the Western European Union and the Executive Director of the Danube Commission with a view to exploring their readiness to participate in the comprehensive regime, and to submit to me, on the basis of information that may be available to them, reports on suspected violations of the prohibitions imposed by the resolution, for consideration by the Security Council Committee established pursuant to resolution 1160 (1998).

9. Upon receipt of the views of the above-mentioned organizations, I shall submit my recommendation to the Security Council for a comprehensive monitoring regime, taking into account the existing potential within the United Nations and the views expressed by those organizations.

10. In accordance with the request of the President of the Security Council, I am looking into the possibility of utilizing the existing potential within the United Nations for the purposes of establishing a comprehensive monitoring regime. I have, in my latest report on the United Nations Preventive Deployment Force (UNPREDEP) in the former Yugoslav Republic of Macedonia (S/1998/454 of 1 June 1998), concluded that it would seem to be premature to proceed with a decision to withdraw UNPREDEP after 31 August 1998. I have

suggested that the Council may wish to consider extending the mandate of UNPREDEP for an additional six months, until 28 February 1999, on the understanding that the Council could review its decision, should the ongoing discussions at the international level on the possible need for an expanded military presence in the region and on the establishment of a comprehensive monitoring regime result in decisions which would affect UNPREDEP's role and responsibilities. Meanwhile, UNPREDEP will, in accordance with its mandate, continue to monitor and report on developments along the border with Albania and the Federal Republic of Yugoslavia. However, within its current strength, UNPREDEP will not be able to sustain intensive monitoring and reporting on activities at the borders. Consequently, it would be my intention, should the Council so wish, to submit before 15 July specific proposals on a possible strengthening of the Force's overall capacity, taking into consideration the situation in the region and the relevant Security Council resolutions, including 795 (1992) and 1160 (1998).

IV. SITUATION IN KOSOVO

11. The Security Council, in resolution 1160 (1998), requested me to keep it regularly informed on the situation in Kosovo and to provide an assessment on whether the Federal Republic of Yugoslavia had complied in a constructive manner with conditions put forward by the Contact Group. As the Council is aware, the situation in Kosovo is evolving daily. This report describes the situation up to the time of writing.

12. As I indicated in my first report, the United Nations Secretariat has no political presence in Kosovo. Consequently, this part of my report draws primarily on information received from a variety of non-United Nations sources, including the Chairman-in-Office of OSCE and the United States of America, as a member of the Contact Group, in response to requests from the Secretariat for information. Where indicated, it also includes specific data obtained from other sources, such as NATO. The information collected is summarized below in the remainder of section IV.

Security situation

13. Since my last report to the Security Council, the situation in Kosovo has continued to remain tense and security conditions have been steadily deteriorating. Almost daily violent clashes have occurred along the borders with Albania and in other parts of Kosovo. The authorities of the Federal Republic of Yugoslavia assert that a total of 356 terrorist assaults were perpetrated between 1 January and 27 May 1998 in Kosovo; and that the main targets were police officers, police premises and civilians, both ethnic Serbs and Albanians. The highest number of incidents was reported in the Glodovac, Decani, Srbica, Djakovica and Klina areas.

14. The Serbian special police maintain a strong presence in Kosovo. They have consolidated their positions and reinforced checkpoints, particularly in Drenica. Police heavy equipment is still in place. Special police units have been responsible for armed action against civilians, although they also have suffered casualties as a result of attacks by armed Kosovo Albanians. The Government of Serbia recently announced that it was undertaking what it termed more effective measures against terrorism in Kosovo, which entails the deployment of forces from urban barracks to field camps to restrict the manoeuvrability of the Kosovo Liberation Army (KLA) and to counter the increased sophistication of KLA weaponry. The Government reportedly does not plan to reduce its police force in Kosovo.

15. The activities of the Yugoslav Army, which maintains a large presence in Kosovo, have centred on securing the borders. Fighting continues between the Government forces and armed Kosovo Albanians in several areas, including Drenica and the Ponosevac region, near the border with Albania.

16. The upsurge in violence since mid-May has been characterized by an increase in civilian casualties and the use of heavy weapons against non-combatants. Security incidents have spread beyond Srbica and Glodovac to Klina in the Drenica region, and to the west and south into Decani and Djakovica municipalities, bordering Albania. Fighting between Serbian police and Kosovo Albanians, and KLA attacks on the Pristina-pec road, caused the Serbian authorities to close this main east-west highway for several days beginning on 11 May. This reportedly led to severe food shortages in the western part of Kosovo. During recent police operations in Klina, Ponosevac and Decani municipalities, a number of casualties on both sides were reported. According to Government sources, the clashes were provoked by the KLA attacks. Several villages were reportedly razed or burned, and there are reports that police summarily executed a number of ethnic Albanians. Total casualties in the Kosovo crisis are estimated at approximately 200 since fighting broke out there last February.

17. The Kosovo Liberation Army has increased its attacks in recent weeks, and has shown an increased propensity and ability to attack government security forces. It has issued threats against police and military, as well as against Kosovo Albanians who allegedly cooperate with the authorities of the Federal Republic of Yugoslavia. Killing and abductions of civilians and police personnel are reportedly continuing on a daily basis in different parts of Kosovo. There are also reports of attacks directed against civilian population centres.

18. Various sources report that both Serbs and Kosovo Albanians have been maltreated, harassed and beaten by police and/or unknown perpetrators at various locations. Security incidents have reportedly affected not only ethnic Albanians and Serbs, but also Montenegrins, Roma and Muslims. In a troubling new development, there have been reports of a rise in the number of incidents involving civilians attacking other civilians for ethnically motivated reasons.

19. The increased number of acts of violence on both sides and the heavy presence of the Serbian police, including special police units, as well as military forces, have been generating insecurity among the local population. According to some estimates, the number of internally displaced persons, including Kosovo Albanians and ethnic Serbs, exceeded 42,000 by the end of May.

20. The intensity of the conflict significantly increased in recent days as a result of a major Serbian police offensive operation in the south-western part of Kosovo, adjacent to the Albanian border. The most recent reports indicate extremely heavy fighting between the Serbian police and armed groups, believed to be KLA, resulting in the loss of dozens of lives. Some observers indicate that the Serbian forces used heavy weaponry, including mortars and possibly artillery. There are also reports that several villages in the area and a number of houses in the town of Decani have been burnt and destroyed. It was not possible to verify these reports as access to the area has been restricted. This new wave of violence in Kosovo caused, for the first time, a significant flow of refugees to Albania. As at 4 June, the Office of the United Nations High Commissioner for Refugees (UNHCR) registered some 6,500 refugees and the number was gradually increasing. Therefore, UNHCR has increased its planning figures to 20,000.

21. The latest fighting represents a worrying trend. There is strong apprehension that with the further escalation of hostilities the situation may get out of control and draw neighbouring States into the conflict.

22. Tension has increased along the border with Albania. Both the Federal Republic of Yugoslavia and Albania have reported a number of incidents at the border, ranging from illegal border crossings to violations of airspace.

23. No evidence was found of large-scale arms trafficking across the border between Albania and the Federal Republic of Yugoslavia, involving the transfer of heavy weapons or bulk transfers of small arms. The arms trafficking which is occurring appears to be primarily smaller-scale transfers across that border. Because of the topography of the region, the porous border and the limited monitoring, estimates of total amounts are difficult. The Government of Albania reportedly has set up checkpoints on roads leading to the border to prevent vehicles transporting weapons from reaching the border area. Albanian authorities have acknowledged difficulty in controlling the border with Kosovo, and that checkpoints could serve to prevent weapons from reaching the area of conflict.

24. In support of efforts aimed at preventing the spread of the current conflict beyond the Federal Republic of Yugoslavia, OSCE has developed its border-monitoring capacities in Albania and the former Yugoslav Republic of Macedonia. Proposals to increase the number of monitors are being considered. In Albania, temporary field offices are now established in Bajram Curri and Kukes. The OSCE mission in Albania (19 personnel) cooperates closely with local authorities, the

European Community Monitor Mission (22 personnel), UNHCR, the Spillover Monitor Mission to Skopje, and also with UNPREDEP.

25. The situation along the Federal Republic of Yugoslavia border with the former Yugoslav Republic of Macedonia is calm and relatively normal. There does not appear to be significant arms trafficking across that border. The former Yugoslav Republic of Macedonia has redeployed troops and stepped up patrols along its border with the Federal Republic of Yugoslavia. UNPREDEP conducts daily patrols along the border and reports on incidents it observes, including smuggling. UNPREDEP has not reported any incidents of arms smuggling since the adoption of resolution 1160 (1998).

26. On 2 June, NATO Secretary-General Javier Solana informed me about the discussion of the situation in Kosovo by the NATO Foreign Minister at a meeting of the North Atlantic Council held on 28 May in Luxembourg. The Foreign Ministers strongly supported the continuation of an international military presence in the former Yugoslav Republic of Macedonia after the end of the current mandate of UNPREDEP. They also supported the continuation of the mandate of UNPREDEP that contributed significantly to the stability in the region. Mr. Solana told me that NATO has two major objectives with respect to the situation in Kosovo: first, to help achieve a peaceful resolution of the crisis by contributing to the response of the international community; and secondly, to promote stability and security in neighbouring countries, with particular emphasis on Albania and the former Yugoslav Republic of Macedonia. To that end, the Foreign Ministers decided to enhance and supplement NATO's Partnership for Peace activities in both Albania and the former Yugoslav Republic of Macedonia, so as to promote security and stability in these Partner countries and to signal NATO's interest in containing the crisis and in seeking a peaceful resolution.

27. In addition, so as to have options available for possible later decisions and to confirm NATO's willingness to take further steps if necessary, the Foreign Ministers have commissioned military advice on support for United Nations and OSCE monitoring activity, as well as on NATO preventive deployments in Albania and the former Yugoslav Republic of Macedonia, on a relevant legal basis, in order to help achieve a peaceful resolution of the crisis and to strengthen security and stability in the region.

Access to Kosovo

28. Foreign diplomats and journalists have encountered some restrictions in their visits to Kosovo. In some cases the police of the Federal Republic of Yugoslavia said diplomats could not enter as roads were impassable because of fighting. Following the Serbian police offensive of 22 May, monitors of the European Community Monitor Mission were reportedly harassed and prevented from reaching the areas under siege.

29. There are concerns regarding deterioration of the humanitarian situation. The ability of humanitarian non-governmental organizations to provide relief to internally displaced persons in Kosovo has reportedly been hampered by incidents of harassment by Serbian police and by blocked access to areas with large humanitarian needs. Various sources reported that, beginning on 15 May, the authorities of the Federal Republic of Yugoslavia impeded food deliveries into Kosovo by blocking the passage of trucks carrying commercial shipments of food and supplies arriving by road. Some 200 trucks were reportedly turned back between 15 and 17 May. The Federal Republic authorities denied that a ban was in place, and stated that certain shipments had been denied entry because of incomplete or false documentation. Meanwhile, UNHCR goods from Belgrade were delivered as usual.

30. Information on the blockade caused panic among the local population, which emptied the local stores to stock up on essential foodstuffs. Almost immediately, shortages of staple foodstuffs began to appear in Kosovo. These shortages were alleviated on 21 May, when Federal Republic authorities lifted the blockade, allowing some 80 trucks into Kosovo.

31. Reacting to these worrying reports, the NATO Foreign Ministers on 28 May 1998 expressed particular concern "that the recent resurgence of violence has been accompanied by the creation of obstacles denying access by international observers and humanitarian organizations to the affected areas in Kosovo".

Dialogue between the parties concerned

32. Following intensive diplomatic efforts by European regional organizations and individual States, Ambassador Richard Holbrooke and United States Special Representative Robert S. Gelbard were able to overcome obstacles on both sides to gain agreement for the start of substantive dialogue without preconditions on Kosovo. The dialogue began in Belgrade on 15 May, with a meeting between President Slobodan Milosevic and Dr. Ibrahim Rugova, along with their respective teams. The two sides discussed the modalities of the follow-up negotiations process.

33. The Heads of State of the group of eight industrialized countries, meeting at Birmingham on 16 May, noted in their statement on the Federal Republic of Yugoslavia/Kosovo that the 15 May meeting was a "positive first step". The leaders urged both sides "to ensure that the dialogue now begun leads rapidly to the adoption of concrete measures to lower tensions and stop violence". The group of eight further noted that "it is particularly important that President Milosevic has assumed personal responsibility in the search for a resolution of the problems of Kosovo, including its future status".

34. At the meeting held on 22 May in Pristina, groups of six experts from each side discussed the framework for future talks and confidence-building measures. The initial meetings were an important first step in the dialogue process. The distance between the two parties remains great, however, and it will be important to reinforce that process. The United States has informed me that it will continue to play an active role in the negotiating process and that Special Representative Gelbard and Ambassador Holbrooke have agreed to facilitate the dialogue if called upon by the parties to do so.

35. The NATO Foreign Ministers, in their statement of 28 May 1998, expressed their conviction that the problems of Kosovo can best be resolved through a process of open and unconditional dialogue between the authorities in Belgrade and the Kosovo Albanian leadership. They acknowledged that the status quo is unsustainable and supported a political solution which provides an enhanced status for Kosovo, preserving the territorial integrity of the Federal Republic of Yugoslavia and safeguarding the human and civil rights of all inhabitants of Kosovo, whatever their ethnic origin.

36. The Federal Republic of Yugoslavia, however, has continued to reject the engagement of outside representatives in the dialogue. The referendum held in the Federal Republic of Yugoslavia on 23 April created a hurdle to direct third-party participation. I discussed this matter and the current situation in Kosovo during my meeting with Mr. Felipe González on 1 June 1998.

Measures taken by the Organization for Security and Cooperation in Europe

37. The situation in Kosovo has been the subject of discussion at the weekly meetings of the OSCE Permanent Council and the Watch Group focusing on developments in Kosovo. Furthermore, OSCE has been closely following developments in Kosovo through monitoring visits conducted by diplomatic personnel of OSCE participating States accredited to Belgrade.

38. The OSCE Troika prepared a "report on compliance" with the requirements to be met by the Federal Republic of Yugoslavia, forwarded to the Group's meeting in Rome on 29 April. The report noted, inter alia, no positive development on such central issues as the opening of unconditional dialogue, cessation of violence and the acceptance of the mission of Mr. González.

39. In a letter to President Milosevic, dated 4 May, the OSCE Chairman-in-Office noted that the situation in Kosovo was deteriorating rather than improving and urged the Federal Republic of Yugoslavia to accept the mission of Mr. González. A reply dated 7 May from Foreign Minister Jovanovic reiterated that the mission would be welcome only to discuss the relationship between the Federal Republic of Yugoslavia and OSCE, and the possible return of the OSCE missions of long duration to Kosovo, Sandjak and Vojvodina would not be considered before the participation of the Federal Republic of Yugoslavia in OSCE was restored. The Chairman-in-Office, replying to Mr. Jovanovic on 8 May, insisted on the importance of launching the mission of Mr. González to talk on all issues dealing with relations between OSCE and the Federal Republic of Yugoslavia.

40. In a statement issued on 13 May, the Chairman-in-Office welcomed the announced meeting between President Milosevic and Dr. Rugova and characterized it as an important first step and an opportunity for the two sides to agree on a format for dialogue. The Chairman-in-Office reiterated that an international representative would greatly facilitate such talks.

41. A representative of the Chairman-in-Office participated in an informal meeting of the Contact Group organized on the margins of the meeting of the group of eight at Birmingham on 16 May. On the previous day, the group of eight leaders in their final communiqué underlined the importance of cooperation with the González mission. They expressed their readiness to promote a clear and achievable path towards the full integration of the Federal Republic of Yugoslavia into the international community. At the same time the statement warned that "if Belgrade fails to build on recent progress and a genuine political process does not get under way, its isolation will deepen".

42. The NATO Foreign Ministers on 28 May also called upon President Milosevic "to agree to the readmission of the OSCE long-term mission, and to accept the mission of Mr. Felipe González, the Personal Representative of the OSCE Chairman-in-Office and the Special Representative of the European Union".

43. The Organization for Security and Cooperation in Europe remains ready to assist in the process aimed at peaceful solution of the conflict in Kosovo and maintains its expectation that the Federal Republic of Yugoslavia will accept the mission of Mr. González as OSCE and European Union representative, as well as three missions of long duration, including that in Pristina.

Implementation of the Kosovo education agreement

44. There has been progress in the implementation of the agreement signed by Serbian and Kosovo Albanian members of the "3 plus 3" commission on 23 March. In compliance with the agreement, the Institute of Albanology opened in Pristina on 31 March. The authorities of the Federal Republic of Yugoslavia turned over three faculties of the University of Pristina to the Kosovo Albanians on 15 May. Ethnic Serb protesters attempted to block the transfer, and government forces intervened to evict the protesters after they damaged the facilities.

V. OBSERVATIONS

45. I have welcomed the beginning of a political dialogue as an important step forward in the search for a just and lasting solution of the problems in Kosovo. Convinced that a non-violent approach is the way to reach a mutually accepted settlement in Kosovo, I strongly support the efforts of those committed to peaceful means. In this regard, I urge the parties concerned to continue the negotiations started in Pristina on 22 May with the aim of lowering tensions, stopping the spread of violence and opening the way for peaceful resolution of the crisis.

46. However, the situation in Kosovo continues to be extremely volatile and shows marked signs of deterioration. The armed confrontation in Kosovo has led to loss of life and there is a serious risk of a humanitarian and refugee crisis in the area. In this regard, the most recent Serbian police offensive in Kosovo is particular cause for alarm. I am gravely concerned that the mounting violence in Kosovo might overwhelm political efforts to prevent further escalation of the crisis. I deplore the excessive use of force by the Serbian police in Kosovo and call upon all parties concerned to demonstrate restraint and commit themselves to a peaceful solution. The use of violence to suppress political dissent or in pursuit of political goals is inadmissible. Terrorist activities from whatever quarter contribute to the deadly spiral of violence that jeopardizes stability in the region.

47. During a meeting with Dr. Rugova on 2 June 1998, I welcomed his non-violent approach and encouraged him to continue the search for a peaceful and mutually acceptable settlement short of independence. I reiterated that the current situation in Kosovo is unacceptable and assured Dr. Rugova that he may count on international support in his quest for such a solution.

48. I commend efforts by regional and other organizations, coalitions of States and individual Governments aimed at achieving a political solution in Kosovo. I invite all parties to cooperate fully with them. I am ready to support the efforts of the international community to resolve the Kosovo crisis with the means at my disposal.

Annex 1:

Letter dated 15 May from the Secretary-General addressed to the Chairman-in-Office of the Organization for Security and Cooperation in Europe

…

In my report to the Security Council dated 30 April 1998 (S/1998/361), I expressed the belief that the Organization for Security and Cooperation in Europe (OSCE), with contributions and assistance from other organizations, as necessary, would be in a position to carry out the requested monitoring functions effectively. In this connection, I was referring to the European Union, the North Atlantic Treaty Organization, the Western European Union and the Danube Commission, bearing in mind their contribution to the success of the sanctions regime in the case of the former Yugoslavia and the Bosnian Serb party.

Following the informal consultations of the Security Council held on 8 May 1998 to consider my first report, the President of the Council informed me of the Council's wish that, in exploring the establishment of a comprehensive regime to monitor the implementation of the prohibitions imposed by Security Council resolution 1160 (1998), I should take into account the existing capacities and potentials, in particular of the United Nations and OSCE.

I would be grateful, in particular, if in your capacity as Chairman-in-Office of OSCE, you could provide me, at your earliest convenience, with the views of your Organization for the establishment of the comprehensive monitoring regime. In doing so, you may wish to seek advice and support from other regional organizations which may be in a position to contribute to the success of the monitoring regime. In the meantime, I am looking into the possibility of utilizing existing potential within the United Nations, in accordance with the request of the President of the Security Council.
(Signed) Kofi A. ANNAN

Annex 2:

Letter dated 1 June 1998 from the Chairman-in-Office of the Organization for Security and Cooperation in Europe addressed to the Secretary-General

…

I would begin by noting that OSCE stands ready to contribute to the monitoring of an arms embargo within its capabilities. This has been confirmed in the course of consultations carried out among the representatives of the OSCE member States in Vienna. In my view, resolution 1160 (1998) places primary responsibility for enforcing the arms embargo on States. This burden falls particularly on neighbouring States and those with existing arms supplier relationships with the Federal Republic of Yugoslavia.

Within that scope, OSCE is prepared to contribute to the monitoring of an arms embargo under the overall responsibility of the United Nations. Unfortunately, OSCE has rather limited capabilities and does not have the required resources for the establishment of a comprehensive arms embargo-monitoring regime. It is my understanding of the mentioned resolution 1160 (1998) that any enforcement mechanism must relate to the entire border of the Federal Republic of Yugoslavia, and not simply to borders with the former Yugoslav Republic of Macedonia and Albania, where OSCE has a presence. This would require comprehensive monitoring of all border crossings, airports, sea- and riverports. Indeed, OSCE experience in enforcing the previous arms embargo indicates that the majority of large-scale arms shipments to the Federal Republic of Yugoslavia have entered by air or sea, rather than overland. Since OSCE does not have missions in Hungary, Bulgaria or Romania, the Federal Republic of Yugoslavia authorities are unlikely to welcome OSCE monitors to carry out this function within the Federal Republic of Yugoslavia, comprehensive enforcement of resolution 1160 (1998) appears to be out of the reach of our Organization.

Executing a less-than-comprehensive enforcement effort would be in my view problematic. Comprehensive border monitoring in Albania and the Former Yugoslav Republic of Macedonia alone would be extremely resource-intensive, and would result in the unequal application of the embargo. Clearly, the intent of the resolution was not to place a selective arms embargo on Kosovo alone.

The Organization for Security and Cooperation in Europe can, however, play a useful part in such a regime. This Organization's particular comparative advantage is its presence on the ground in the region, through the missions deployed in Bosnia and Herzegovina, Croatia, Albania and the Former Yugoslav Republic of Macedonia.

Monitoring activities along the borders between Albania and the Federal Republic of Yugoslavia, as well as the Former Yugoslav Republic of Macedonia and the Federal Republic of Yugoslavia carried out currently by OSCE, can usefully contribute to an overall arms embargo monitoring effort, under the mentioned overall United Nations responsibility, as a possible early warning indicator. I would note that the border-monitoring capabilities of the OSCE presence in Albania are undergoing a process of strengthening.

The OSCE presence in Albania provides important early warning of large-scale movements of people and weapons, and balanced reporting from the border area. It also serves as a visible symbol of the international community's abiding interest in promoting a peaceful resolution to this crisis.

The OSCE is ready to share the relevant information available as a result of its current monitoring activities with the United Nations, including its bodies responsible for arms embargo monitoring.

In conclusion, I would summarize my reaction to your request by saying that, while not able to assume a leading coordinating role with regard to an arms embargo monitoring effort undertaken by other regional organizations, OSCE may offer a flexible coordinating framework for monitoring activities in the field if so desired by the participants in the effort.

(Signed) Bronislaw GEREMEK

S/1998/608

4.   Report of the Secretary-General Prepared Pursuant to Security Council Resolution 1160, 2 July 1998

...

II.   SECURITY COUNCIL COMMITTEE ESTABLISHED PURSUANT TO RESOLUTION 1160 (1998)
2. As at 30 June 1998, the following 43 States had reported to the Committee, pursuant to paragraph 12 of resolution 1160 (1998) on the steps they had taken to give effect to the prohibitions imposed by the resolution: Armenia, Australia, Austria, Bahrain, Belarus, Belgium, Brazil, Bulgaria, Cyprus, Czech Republic, Fiji, Finland, France, Hungary, Iran (Islamic Republic of), Italy, Japan, Kenya, Latvia, Lithuania, Malaysia, Malta, Monaco, New Zealand, Norway, Poland, Portugal, Romania, Saudi Arabia, Singapore, Slovakia, Slovenia, South Africa, Spain, Sweden, Switzerland, Thailand, the former Yugoslav Republic of Macedonia, Turkey, Ukraine, United Kingdom of Great Britain and Northern Ireland, United States of America and Uruguay.
III.   COMPREHENSIVE REGIME TO MONITOR THE IMPLEMENTATION OF THE PROHIBITIONS IMPOSED BY SECURITY COUNCIL RESOLUTION 1160 (1998)
3. In my last report (S/1998/470) dated 4 June 1998, I informed the Security Council that, in the light of the response from the Chairman-in-Office of the Organization for Security and Cooperation in Europe (OSCE) dated 1 June 1998 and in accordance with the provisions of paragraph 15 of Security Council resolution 1160 (1998), I had written to the Secretary-General of the North Atlantic Treaty Organization (NATO), the Presidency of the European Union (EU), the Secretary-General of the Western European Union (WEU) and the Executive Director of the Danube Commission with a view to exploring their readiness to participate in the comprehensive regime and to submit to me, on the basis of information that may be available to them, reports on suspected violations of the prohibitions imposed by the resolution for consideration by the Security Council Committee established pursuant to resolution 1160 (1998).
4. As at 30 June, I had received an interim reply from the Secretary-General of NATO dated 11 June, as well as replies from the Secretary-General of WEU dated 18 June, the Acting President and the Secretary of the Danube Commission dated 23 June 1998 and the Presidency of the European Union dated 30 June 1998. The full text of those replies is annexed to the present report (annexes I-IV).
5. The Secretary-General of NATO informed me that a study by the NATO Military Authorities on possible support for the monitoring regime would be completed shortly, and, once it had been considered by the North Atlantic Council, the Secretary-General would contact me again. He stated that in the meantime, the NATO-led Stabilization

Force (SFOR) in Bosnia and Herzegovina was using its authority under Annex 1A of the 1995 Peace Agreement to step up its efforts, within the existing mission and capabilities, to monitor the Bosnian border with the Federal Republic of Yugoslavia to prevent the transfer of weapons. He expressed the readiness of NATO to share SFOR findings with the United Nations.
6. WEU expressed its readiness to provide any useful information that comes to its notice on the implementation of the measures imposed by resolution 1160 (1998), in particular through its Multinational Advisory Police Element (MAPE) established in Albania at the request and with the cooperation of the Albanian authorities. WEU also stated that it was in the process of considering its role with regard to the very serious developments in Kosovo and their implications for regional stability. While seeking further information on the nature of a comprehensive regime for enforcement of the prohibitions contained in resolution 1160 (1998), WEU expressed its interest in taking any relevant action in full transparency and partnership with other organizations, including EU and NATO, and in agreement with the neighbouring countries on whose territories any relevant operation would take place.
7. The Danube Commission stated that in the event that OSCE or another international organization should offer the framework for coordinating the monitoring under resolution 1160 (1998), the Commission would be prepared to contribute, within the areas of its competence and expertise, to the accomplishment of this task through its support and advice concerning navigation on the Danube and the facilitation of transit of vessels, goods and passengers in compliance with resolution 1160 (1998). At the same time, the Commission suggested that a well-defined mechanism should be devised in due course to deal with cooperation between the authorities responsible for conducting inspections under the sanctions system and organizations and representatives of the shipowners, shippers and consignees of goods on the Danube.
8. The Presidency of EU welcomed my initiative to seek its views, as well as those of other organizations, on the enforcement of Security Council resolution 1160 (1998). The member States of EU agreed to assist the Committee established pursuant to paragraph 9 of Security Council resolution 1160 (1998) by providing information on the action taken by them to implement the resolution and by making available information on alleged violations of the arms embargo. The Presidency also expressed the readiness of EU members to contribute to international efforts to monitor the embargo by asking the European Community Monitoring Mission (ECMM) to report to the Committee any relevant information on the movement of arms that should come into its possession as a result of its operations in Albania, Bosnia, Croatia, the Federal Republic of Yugoslavia and the former Yugoslav Republic of Macedonia. EU is seeking a significant increase in the number of monitors in the Federal Republic of Yugoslavia/Kosovo, in line with President Milosevic's undertaking in Moscow on increased international monitoring, and has increased the number of its monitors in northern Albania. The monitors would be tasked to be alert for any evidence relevant to the implementation of resolution 1160 (1998).
9. I will submit my recommendation, as required in paragraph 15 of the above-mentioned resolution once I have received all necessary information.
IV. SITUATION IN KOSOVO
10. As the Council is aware, the situation in Kosovo has deteriorated significantly since the submission of my last report. A new outbreak of violence in early June led to an influx of refugees to Albania and to an increase in internally displaced persons in Kosovo and Montenegro. The number of registered refugees in Albania at the end of June was 6,900. In addition, an estimated 3,150 have departed to southern Albania. It is estimated, however, that there may be as many as 13,000 refugees more in Albania. As of 19 June, the Montenegrin authorities had registered another 10,177 internally displaced persons from Kosovo. According to estimates of the Office of the United Nations High Commissioner for Refugees (UNHCR), some 45,000 people have been displaced within Kosovo itself. UNHCR is unable to assess the situation on the ground more precisely, since it cannot gain access to the affected areas.

11. Anticipating that further deterioration of the situation might lead to a major humanitarian and refugee crisis in the area, United Nations agencies expanded their activities in the region. In addition to the UNHCR office in northern Albania, the World Food Programme (WFP) also opened an emergency office there on 17 June. UNHCR continues to lead inter-agency contingency planning in the region. On 15 June, the Office of the Coordinator for Humanitarian Affairs, the United Nations Development Programme (UNDP), the United Nations Children's Fund (UNICEF), UNHCR, WFP and the World Health Organization (WHO) launched the consolidated inter-agency flash appeal for humanitarian assistance needs related to the Kosovo crisis: 1 June-31 August 1998. The appeal is aimed at obtaining US$ 18 million for multisectoral assistance for the United Nations system, of which UNHCR is seeking US$ 12.9 million. Coordinating mechanisms are operating in Pristina, Belgrade, Podgorica, Tirana and Skopje. WFP is stockpiling food in Pristina - rations are now sufficient to feed 35,000 for one month. In northern Albania, WFP is ready to start distribution of 500 tons of food assistance, which would cover existing needs until September.

12. In its resolution 1160 (1998), the Security Council requested me to keep it regularly informed on the situation in Kosovo and to provide an assessment of whether the Federal Republic of Yugoslavia had complied in a constructive manner with conditions put forward by the Contact Group. By the time of writing of the present report, I had received the relevant information from the Chairman-in-Office of OSCE, which I attach in annex V.

V. OBSERVATIONS

13. The international community is appalled by the continued violence in Kosovo. The parties concerned must demonstrate restraint and resume negotiations to find a peaceful solution to the conflict. I am increasingly concerned that, unless hostilities in Kosovo are stopped, tensions could spill across borders and destabilize the entire region. Kosovo therefore becomes a key issue for the overall stability of the Balkan region. I welcome the diplomatic efforts being made at the international level to address fundamental aspects of the situation which can only be resolved through negotiation.

14. It has been widely reported that authorities of the Federal Republic of Yugoslavia have agreed to allow foreign diplomats and accredited international organizations in Belgrade to monitor the situation in Kosovo. The process of establishing that monitoring presence is reportedly under way. Such a monitoring mission would improve the ability of the international community to assess directly the situation on the ground and could better serve the desire of the international community and the Security Council for impartial and substantive information regarding Kosovo. Should this come about, the Council may wish to review the continued need for reporting by the United Nations on the situation in Kosovo, as requested in paragraph 14 of resolution 1160 (1998), in view of the absence of a United Nations presence in Kosovo to provide an independent assessment of that situation.

Annex I:

Letter dated 11 June 1998 from the Secretary-General of the North Atlantic Treaty Organization addressed to the Secretary-General

...

As I informed you in my letter of 29 May, the North Atlantic Council has tasked the NATO Military Authorities to study possible support for the monitoring regime. This study will be completed shortly, and I will write to you again once it has been considered by the North Atlantic Council.

In the meantime, the NATO-led Stabilization Force (SFOR) in Bosnia and Herzegovina is using its authority under Annex 1A of the 1995 Peace Agreement to step up its efforts, within the existing mission and capabilities, to monitor the Bosnian border with the Federal Republic of Yugoslavia to prevent the transfer of weapons. We are making the necessary arrangements to forward any information on suspected violations in the SFOR area of operations to NATO headquarters for onward transmission to the United Nations Secretariat, via the monthly SFOR reports or on an ad hoc basis as necessary.

(Signed) Javier SOLANA

Annex II:

Letter dated 18 June 1998 from the Secretary-General of the Western European Union addressed to the Secretary-General

...

The Western European Union (WEU) welcomes your initiative to include our organization in your consultations on this important matter. WEU has repeatedly made clear its readiness to act in support of and - as appropriate - under mandates from the United Nations, as well as the Organization for Security and Cooperation in Europe.

At present, as you know, the only mission being conducted by WEU in the region concerned is the Multinational Advisory Police Element (MAPE) established in Albania at the request and with the cooperation of the Albanian authorities. MAPE is a training and advisory mission whose mandate includes assistance with the training of all Albanian police forces and advice on their future organization; its activities thus contribute to the development of the capacity of the Albanian authorities themselves, inter alia, for implementation of the embargo. WEU is ready to provide immediately, by the appropriate means, any useful information that comes to its notice on the conditions of implementation of the embargo.

WEU shares your concern for the effective implementation of resolution 1160 (1998). As indicated in the declaration recently adopted by our Ministers at their meeting in Rhodes, we are in the process of considering the role of our organization in relation to the very serious developments in Kosovo and their implications for regional stability. To make sure that the WEU Council can include in its deliberations any possible practical contributions that might be appropriate for us in that context, we would be happy to receive further information or proposals on the nature of a "comprehensive monitoring regime" for enforcement, as mentioned in your letter. I might add that we would expect to take any relevant action in full transparency and partnership with other institutions, including the European Union and the North Atlantic Treaty Organization, and in agreement with the neighbouring countries on whose territory any relevant operations would take place.

(Signed) Jose CUTILEIRO

Annex III:

Letter dated 23 June 1998 from the Acting President and the Secretary of the Danube Commission addressed to the Secretary-General

...

One of the main tasks of the Danube Commission is to ensure implementation of the provisions of the Convention concerning the regime for navigation on the Danube, which provide that "navigation on the Danube shall be free and open for the nationals, vessels of commerce and goods of all States, on a footing of equality". Hence the Danube Commission believes that any monitoring system to be established under the above-mentioned resolution and to be operated by the appropriate institutions must respect this fundamental principle of navigation on the Danube, which is based on international law and recognized by the entire international community.

Without prejudice to the provisions of resolution 1160 (1998), which must be applied in full, or to the Charter of the United Nations, it must be ensured that, when sanctions are applied by the United Nations, the interests of "innocent and neutral" transit navigation on the Danube of countries that are not the object of the sanctions are respected and protected. Not only is this navigation essential to the economies of the landlocked Danubian countries, it is also important for some 40 nations that use the Danube each year as a major European waterway.

In the event that the Organization for Security and Cooperation in Europe (OSCE) or another international organization should offer the framework for coordinating the monitoring, the Danube Commission would be prepared to contribute, within the areas of its competence, to the accomplishment of this task through its support and advice concerning navigation on the Danube and the facilitation of "innocent" transit of vessels, goods and passengers. To the extent that a control system becomes inevitable, the Danube Commission hopes that the institutions responsible for this task will take advantage of the experience of the experts of the Commission and the Danubian countries in matters related to navigation on the Danube.

At the same time, a well-defined mechanism should be devised in due course to deal with cooperation between the authorities responsible for conducting inspections under the sanctions system and organizations and representatives of the shipowners, shippers and consignees of goods on the Danube.

If the implementation of such a monitoring system causes losses to the navigation on the Danube of countries that are not the object of the sanctions but experience their consequences, a mechanism for compensating for those losses should be devised as soon as possible.

(Signed) Petru CORDOS
Acting President of the Danube Commission
Representative of Romania on the Danube Commission
(Signed) Felix P. BOGDANOV
Secretary of the Danube Commission
Representative of the Russian Federation on the Danube Commission

Annex IV:
Letter from the UK Foreign Secretary, 30 June 1998
...

The European Union welcomes your initiative in seeking its views, as well as those of other regional organizations, on the enforcement of Security Council resolution 1160 (1998), the aim of which we strongly support. The States members of the European Union have agreed to assist the committee established under paragraph 9 of resolution 1160 (1998) in its work by providing information on the action taken by member States to implement the resolution and by making available to the Committee any information available to member States on alleged violations of the embargo. I have asked member States to pool such information so that the Presidency of the day can pass this on to the committee.

The EU and its member States also stand ready to contribute to international efforts to monitor the embargo by asking the European Community Monitoring Mission (ECMM) to report to the Sanctions Committee any relevant information on the movement of arms that should come into its possession as a result of its operations in Albania, Bosnia, Croatia, the Federal Republic of Yugoslavia and the former Yugoslav Republic of Macedonia.

The European Union is seeking a significant increase in the number of monitors in the Federal Republic of Yugoslavia/Kosovo, in line with President Milosevic's undertaking in Moscow on increased international monitoring. The European Union has also increased the number of its monitors in northern Albania. The European Union will ensure that its monitors are tasked to be alert for any evidence relevant to implementation of resolution 1160 (1998). The European Union would also be willing to consider any further proposals from the Secretary-General or other regional organizations on a monitoring regime.
(signed) Robin COOK

Annex V:
Information on the situation in Kosovo and on measures taken by the Organization for Security and Cooperation in Europe
I. INTRODUCTION
The further deterioration of the situation in Kosovo and along the border between the Federal Republic of Yugoslavia and Albania since the May report to the Secretary-General has prompted the Contact Group to impose a package of economic sanctions on both the Federal Republic of Yugoslavia and Serbia to induce them to seek a political solution to the problem. For its part, the North Atlantic Treaty Organization (NATO) produced an array of crisis scenarios, and on 15 June staged a display of air power in the airspace of Albania and the former Yugoslav Republic of Macedonia, along the border with Kosovo.
II. THE DIALOGUE
On 15 May in Belgrade, President Milosevic and Dr. Rugova agreed on weekly working contacts between the two sides. However, so far only one such meeting has been held, in Pristina (on 22 May). The Albanian side contended that the military-cum-police operation unleashed on south-west Kosovo by Belgrade in late May and the whole of June precluded its participation in further meetings of this kind.

Those of the Kosovo Albanians who do not count among the supporters of Rugova's policy line have made known their displeasure with his meeting with Milosevic. Representatives of the so-called Kosovo Liberation Army (KLA) have strongly reiterated their direct objective, namely, the independence of Kosovo.

By 16 June 1998, no signs had emerged of a possibility of resumption of the Belgrade-Pristina dialogue. The issue was taken up during the Milosevic-Yeltsin meeting in Moscow on 16 June.

The two sides to the Kosovo conflict have had numerous contacts over the past month with representatives of foreign countries visiting Yugoslavia, and also with diplomats posted in Belgrade. Dr. Rugova has visited the

United States of America, Italy and France and has met with the Secretary-General of the United Nations.
III. VIOLENCE
A further deterioration of the situation was recorded in Kosovo soon after the Milosevic-Rugova meeting, notably in the Yugoslav-Albanian borderland and along the Pec-Dechani, Djakovica-Prizren and Pristina-Pec highways. Serious armed clashes were noted in those areas.

The wholesale destruction visited upon the Albanian villages in the process sent consecutive waves of refugees streaming out of the area. Casualty figures released by both sides differ considerably. The Serbs maintain that their actions had a purely anti-terrorist character and claim only a "negligible" number of victims, while the Albanians insist scores have been killed (no credible data about the number of victims are available, but some unofficial sources indicate there might be over 200 dead). Many observers agree that the range and scope of combat operations validates the contention that a guerilla war is now under way in Kosovo.

More people these days are prepared to cross illegally into the war-torn Yugoslav province from Albania, and contraband weapons are pouring into Kosovo, brought there by armed groups of ethnic Albanians.

The media quote the Belgrade office of the Office of the United Nations High Commissioner for Refugees to the effect that the combat operations in Kosovo have displaced 30,000 to 40,000 Albanians, who have now established temporary residence in other parts of the province or left for Albania (around 12,000) or Montenegro. On the other hand, there has been no confirmation of the earlier Albanian reports of their countrymen streaming into the former Yugoslav Republic of Macedonia. The Serbians argue that the Albanians overstate the facts and inflate the figures, but they do not counter them with their own information.

In the opinion of A. Demaci, Chairman of the Parliamentary Party of Kosovo, carried by the media in early June, the Kosovo Liberation Army allegedly controlled an area of 3,000 square kilometres, including some 250 villages, with a total population of 700,000 to 800,000, most of them in the Drenica region.
IV. EDUCATION
Serb students and professors in Pristina do not agree to hand over to the Albanian side a part of the premises of the local university. A student demonstration was recently dispersed by the police, while the Serb educational authorities made a hasty decision to end the academic year ahead of schedule.
V. ACCESS TO KOSOVO
The armed clashes resulted in a temporary closure in May and June of the Pristina-Pec and Pec-Decani-Djakovica-Prizren sections of the highway, with telecommunication lines severed partially within this area and a news blackout of several days imposed by the authorities. Instances of Serb troops stopping food transports and other supplies being sent from the north to Kosovo have been noted. In early June, the Serb side regained control over the aforesaid sections of the highway, which were then reopened to traffic.

Members of the KLA stop travellers in KLA-controlled areas (notably in the Drenica region), check their identification documents and often confiscate items they find of use. For instance, Japanese and American television crews were relieved of their bullet-proof vests.

The Ministry of Foreign Affairs of the Federal Republic of Yugoslavia, on 7 June, conducted a tour of Kosovo for diplomats posted in Belgrade, who reported on the widespread destruction of housing in the now-abandoned villages affected by the hostilities at the end of May/beginning of June. However, those diplomats did not confirm the allegations of some Kosovo Albanians that the Serb authorities had subjected the area to heavy artillery and aerial bombardment.
VI. RISKS OF SPILLOVER
According to the reports of the OSCE presence in Albania, the situation on the Albanian border with Kosovo remains volatile. There has been almost daily military activity in western Kosovo since the end of May, causing large-scale displacement of civilians. Over 10,000 of them have fled to Albania, most of them women, children and the elderly. The violence has caused a drastic increase in militancy on both sides of the border. Armed resistance has become very visible, including cross-border movement of arms and men. Border incidents have increased, pointing to efforts on the part of the Federal Republic of Yugoslavia to clamp down on this movement. Recent incidents also involved border violations. There is increasing evidence of mines being laid, and there have also been a number of accounts from refugees of detention of men of military age.

The refugees have been accommodated by the local population in the border region, the poorest part of Albania. For the moment, their immediate needs are being met, but the totally inadequate infrastructure makes the long-term outlook grim.

Politically, the conflict causes problems for the Government in Tirana, in that it must take into account both national sentiments of indignation and solidarity, echoed by the opposition, and international calls for restraint.
The overriding priority is to secure an early end to the fighting, followed by the deployment of a large-scale international monitoring force. This would not only enable a meaningful dialogue to take place, but also facilitate an early return of the refugees.

The OSCE mission in Skopje reports that "spillover" from the current crisis in Kosovo in the territory of the former Yugoslav Republic of Macedonia may take physical form (movement of individuals whether seeking refuge privately or coming as refugees) or political form (an adverse effect on ethnic relations in local politics). Hitherto the risks of physical "spillover" have been contained: there have been no refugees and no identifiable net inflow based on family ties; border areas are stable and calm, with life proceeding normally, albeit with increased anxiety among the local population; and there has been no serious incident, in recent months, on the country's border with Kosovo and the rest of Serbia, with reduced smuggling and illegal crossings. Any significant number of Kosovars arriving would be resented by the majority population. The key to continuing stability remains the policy approach of the Yugoslav border authorities on the northern side of the border. Should similar operations be launched to those in the Decani area, movement of refugees would be very likely, but the area has traditionally been relatively quiet.

In terms of risks of political "spillover", ethnic Albanian demonstrations in Skopje and other towns, showing solidarity with Kosovars and voicing support for the KLA, although peaceful, have caused disquiet and resentment among the ethnic Macedonian population, complicating the political scene, which is otherwise dominated by forthcoming parliamentary elections.

VII. MEASURES TAKEN BY THE ORGANIZATION FOR SECURITY AND COOPERATION IN EUROPE
Kosovo continues to be in the forefront of OSCE activities. It has become one of the priorities of its Chairmanship.

The latest developments in Kosovo have clearly demonstrated the necessity of participation by international organizations in solving the humanitarian problems in the region as well. This is why the OSCE Permanent Council stressed on 4 June the importance of free access for the International Committee of the Red Cross and other humanitarian organizations to the areas affected by fighting. The major influx of refugees arriving in Albania from Kosovo is being observed by OSCE.

At the end of May, the Chairman of the Parliamentary Assembly of OSCE, Mr. Javier Ruperez, visited the Federal Republic of Yugoslavia for talks in Belgrade and Pristina. He did not register any change in the position of the Federal Republic of Yugoslavia vis-à-vis the Gonzalez mission or a prospective OSCE mission, including one in Kosovo.

OSCE has developed relatively modest but effective monitoring capabilities in Albania. The Organization decided on 4 June to increase the number of OSCE monitors on Albania's border with Kosovo to 30.

Addressing the Central Europe Initiative meeting in Brioni on 6 June, the OSCE Chairman-in-Office came forward with the idea of a special status for Kosovo. In his opinion, it should be elaborated through the dialogue between the authorities of the Federal Republic of Yugoslavia and Kosovo Albanians. He suggested that a round table dialogue concentrating on special status for Kosovo would help resolve the dichotomy between independence and autonomy. This could be helpful in moving away from political rhetoric and turning to concrete matters, such as the functioning of legislative and executive powers there, assuring local identity, development of local government and education.

On 11 June, the Chairman-in-Office condemned violence by either side in the strongest possible terms and urged an immediate cessation of hostilities. He expressed his deep concern about the continued flow of refugees driven across the border into Albania by the violence. He called on the Belgrade authorities to facilitate the return of displaced persons and refugees.

In his address to the Permanent Council in Vienna on 17 June, the Chairman-in-Office stated that a political solution to the crisis required not only that hostilities in Kosovo be stopped and talks resumed, but also that democracy and full respect for human rights and minorities be introduced in the Federal Republic of Yugoslavia, and that the participation of that country in international organizations, including OSCE, be ensured once it applies international standards to its behaviour. The Chairman-in-Office repeated that the OSCE platform for a political solution is still available and

that the Organization would be ready to dispatch a mission to Kosovo without delay, if and when it proved to be possible.

In his letter of 19 June to President Milosevic, the Chairman-in-Office showed interest in the suggestion by the Federal Republic of Yugoslavia to hold talks with OSCE on the acceptance of the OSCE mission in Kosovo and on the participation of the Federal Republic of Yugoslavia in OSCE (this proposal was made by the Yugoslav side after the Milosevic-Yeltsin talks in Moscow on 16 June and included in the joint statement).

S/1998/644, 14 July 1998

5. Report of the Secretary-General on the United Nations Preventative Deployment Force, 14 July 1998

...

II. RECENT DEVELOPMENTS
2. It will be recalled that peace and stability in the former Yugoslav Republic of Macedonia continue to depend largely on developments in other parts of the region and that recent developments in Kosovo have highlighted the danger of renewed violence in the area and the serious repercussions such violence could have upon the external and internal security of the Republic.
3. In my report to the Security Council of 2 July 1998 (S/1998/608), prepared pursuant to resolution 1160 (1998), increased concern was expressed that, unless hostilities in Kosovo are stopped, tension could spill across the borders and destabilize the entire region. I welcomed the diplomatic efforts being made at the international level to address the fundamental aspects of the situation, which can only be resolved through negotiation. Discussions are still continuing at the international level on the possible need for an expanded international military presence in the region and on the establishment of a comprehensive monitoring regime as a consequence of the situation in Kosovo.
4. Further to his letter of 15 May 1998 (see para. 22 of S/1998/454), the Minister for Foreign Affairs of the former Yugoslav Republic of Macedonia, Mr. Blagoj Handziski, addressed a new letter to me, on 9 July 1998 (S/1998/627), reiterating his Government's recommendation for an extension of the UNPREDEP mandate for an additional period of six months, with the same mandate, structure and troop composition. The Government has endorsed the option of an eventual increase in the military as well as in the Civilian Police components, in consultation with the national authorities. Following its meeting in Bonn on 8 July 1998, the Contact Group, in its statement on Kosovo, also supported the extension of the mandate of UNPREDEP.
5. Since the start of the Kosovo crisis, UNPREDEP has intensified patrols along the borders with Albania and the Federal Republic of Yugoslavia and has also established temporary observation posts for 24-hour monitoring and reporting on activities at the borders throughout its area of operation (see para. 5 of S/1998/454). The imposition of these additional tasks has come at a time when the fulfilment of UNPREDEP's existing responsibilities have already stretched the reduced strength of the operation to the limit.
III. RECOMMENDATIONS
6. As stated in paragraph 23 of my report of 1 June 1998 (S/1998/454), I remain convinced that it would seem premature to proceed with a decision to withdraw UNPREDEP after 31 August 1998. Therefore, taking into account my recommendations set forth in paragraphs 7 to 9 below, the Security Council may wish to consider the extension of UNPREDEP's mandate for a further period of six months, until 28 February 1999.
7. In view of the constraints placed on UNPREDEP in monitoring and reporting on developments along the borders, referred to in paragraph 5 above, including the Kosovo stretch of the border, the Security Council may wish to consider increasing UNPREDEP's troop level by 350 all ranks. The majority of these troops, 230 in total, would be deployed at nine new permanently manned observation posts in the former Yugoslav Republic of Macedonia along the Kosovo (Federal Republic of Yugoslavia) and Albanian borders. The troops would, in accordance with resolution 795 (1992), monitor and report on developments in the border areas, including those developments that would have a bearing on the implementation of the relevant provisions of resolution 1160 (1998).

8. A reserve of two platoons composed of approximately 60 soldiers would perform limited ground and air patrolling duties. The reserve would be centrally located and have sufficient capacity to react in a timely manner to any developments that might require immediate attention. Because of the remote positions of observation posts and the difficult terrain in the mountainous border areas, particularly during harsh winter conditions, the reserve should be complemented by a 35-man medical unit and three helicopters to enable the Force to respond promptly to emergencies involving UNPREDEP personnel.

9. In view of the important confidence-building role played by the military observer and the civilian police elements of UNPREDEP, the Security Council may also wish to consider increasing their strength by an additional twelve and twenty-four personnel respectively. The strengthened military observers and civilian police elements would intensify community and border patrols as well as monitoring and reporting of the situation at border crossing stations.

10. Should the Security Council agree to the above-mentioned increase in force levels, I will submit an addendum on the financial implications of this report as soon as possible.

S/1998/712

6. Report of the Secretary-General Prepared Pursuant to Security Council Resolution 1160, 5 August 1998

...

II. SECURITY COUNCIL COMMITTEE ESTABLISHED PURSUANT TO RESOLUTION 1160 (1998)

2. As of 31 July, in addition to those States listed in my earlier report (S/1998/608), Greece, Germany and Liechtenstein reported to the Committee pursuant to paragraph 12 of resolution 1160 (1998) on the steps they had taken to give effect to the prohibitions imposed by that resolution.

III. COMPREHENSIVE REGIME TO MONITOR THE IMPLEMENTATION OF THE PROHIBITIONS IMPOSED BY SECURITY COUNCIL RESOLUTION 1160 (1998)

3. In paragraph 15 of resolution 1160 (1998), the Security Council requested that, in consultation with appropriate regional organizations, I include in my first report to the Council recommendations for the establishment of a comprehensive regime to monitor the implementation of the prohibitions imposed by that resolution. It also called upon all States, in particular neighbouring States, to extend full cooperation in that regard.

4. In my report to the Council dated 30 April 1998 (S/1998/361), I provided a general outline of the concept for a comprehensive monitoring regime and stated that the United Nations was unable, within existing budgetary resources, to establish and administer such a regime. I reiterate my view expressed therein that for a monitoring regime to be comprehensive, it would require the deployment at key points of teams composed of qualified experts, as well as the setting up of a fully equipped communications centre to support the work of the monitoring teams and to interact with the Sanctions Committee and its secretariat. These teams would provide advice and assistance to the authorities of neighbouring and other States that bear the responsibility for enforcement of the mandatory measures in accordance with the provisions of Security Council resolution 1160 (1998).

5. In my second report pursuant to resolution 1160 (1998), dated 4 June 1998 (S/1998/470), I stated that upon receipt of the views of the organizations I had contacted, I would submit my recommendations to the Security Council for a comprehensive monitoring regime, taking into account the existing potential within the United Nations and the views expressed by those organizations.

6. In addition to OSCE, replies were received from the European Union (EU), the North Atlantic Treaty Organization (NATO), the Western European Union (WEU) and the Danube Commission. Those communications were annexed to my earlier reports (S/1998/470, S/1998/608). On 14 July 1998, the Secretary-General of NATO informed me of his organization's decision at the current stage to proceed with the "Stabilization Force (SFOR) option" to step up its efforts to monitor the Bosnian border with the Federal Republic of Yugoslavia, and to forward to me any relevant information on suspected violations of resolution 1160 (1998) in SFOR's area of operations. The text of the letter from the Secretary-General of NATO is contained in annex II to the present report.

7. All the organizations I contacted have stated their readiness to contribute actively to the monitoring of the prohibitions imposed by resolution 1160 (1998). At this stage, however, the overall resources pledged by those organizations would not allow for the establishment of a comprehensive monitoring regime as envisaged in resolution 1160 (1998). Nonetheless, their proposed contributions, coupled with that of the United Nations Preventive Deployment Force (UNPREDEP), as outlined in my reports to the Security Council dated 1 June and 14 July 1998 (S/1998/454 and S/1998/644 respectively), provide a useful framework for reporting on violations of the prohibitions imposed by the above resolution and for assisting the Committee established pursuant to Security Council resolution 1160 (1998) in discharging its mandate.

8. Accordingly, I propose to invite the organizations mentioned in paragraph 6 above to forward to the Secretariat, for consideration by the Security Council Committee established pursuant to Security Council resolution 1160 (1998), relevant information based on reports of their own monitors or any other information that may be available to them, concerning violations or allegations of violations of the prohibitions imposed by Security Council resolution 1160 (1998).

9. On 21 July 1998, the Security Council adopted resolution 1186 (1998), by which it decided to authorize an increase in the troop strength of UNPREDEP and to extend its current mandate for a period of six months until 28 February 1999, including the tasks of monitoring the border areas and reporting to me on illicit arms flows and other activities that are prohibited under resolution 1160 (1998).

10. In the absence of an integrated coordinating mechanism, it would be essential for representatives of participating organizations, UNPREDEP and the Secretariat to hold, as necessary, periodic meetings in order to exchange information on the monitoring of the prohibitions established by resolution 1160 (1998) and to address practical issues arising in that connection.

IV. SITUATION IN KOSOVO

11. In early July, efforts by the members of the Contact Group, EU and OSCE offered hopeful signs that meaningful dialogue might be possible between the parties to the conflict. Regrettably, those hopes were not realized. I must therefore report that, as the Security Council is already aware, the situation in Kosovo continues to deteriorate. Increased heavy fighting between the security forces of the Federal Republic of Yugoslavia and the so-called Kosovo Liberation Army (KLA) has been reported from several areas in Kosovo. The numbers of civilian and military casualties are at their highest point since the outbreak of the conflict. The attitudes of the two sides appear to be hardening with every day of fighting. There is no progress on renewal of dialogue. Most disturbing are reports of increased tensions along the border between the Federal Republic of Yugoslavia and Albania. In this regard, I share the concerns expressed in the Declaration of the Presidency of the European Union of 20 July 1998 (S/1998/675).

12. The unrelenting violence has led to a dramatic increase in internally displaced persons in Kosovo and Montenegro since my last report. According to estimates by the Office of the United Nations High Commissioner for Refugees (UNHCR), more than 100,000 people have been driven from their homes by the conflict. Between 70,000 and 80,000 people were internally displaced in Kosovo by the end of July. Authorities in Montenegro had recorded 22,000 internally displaced persons from Kosovo by 22 July. As local food production has come to a standstill, food shortages could worsen sharply. With the increasing number of displaced persons and the approaching winter, Kosovo has the potential of becoming a humanitarian disaster.

13. The number of refugees in northern Albania remains approximately the same (estimated at around 13,500) with 10,300 registered refugees. The majority (some 10,000) arrived in Albania between 29 May and 9 June. While one of the main refugee locations, Tropoje, lies just 7 kilometres from the border, the proximity of the border has not created a security risk for refugees at this stage. However, with the increasing

militarization of the border region and the escalation of tensions in Kosovo, destabilization of the Albanian border region is possible.

14. United Nations agencies are intensifying their efforts to prevent a major humanitarian and refugee crisis. In response to the consolidated inter-agency flash appeal for humanitarian assistance needs related to the Kosovo crisis: 1 June-31 August 1998, however, only 9.7 per cent of assistance requirements (US$ 1.7 million) had been pledged by donors as of 14 July. Most of the funding, provided by Denmark, Germany, Luxembourg, Sweden and Switzerland, was intended for UNHCR assistance programmes for refugees and internally displaced persons in Albania and Montenegro. The World Health Organization (WHO) and the United Nations Children's Fund (UNICEF) continue to jointly assess all possible means for assisting the networks and facilities to provide vaccination for children. WHO is intensifying its coordination with health-related non-governmental organizations (NGOs) to properly address the donations of medicine. UNICEF and UNHCR are to meet with the Ministry of Education of Montenegro in order to explore ways of supporting schools hosting classes with internally displaced children. WHO is also planning an assessment of the medical and psychosocial needs of the displaced population in Montenegro.

V. OBSERVATIONS

15. The limitations on my capacity to report on the situation in Kosovo, as requested in paragraph 14 of resolution 1160 (1998), remain unchanged. At the same time, it is my understanding that there has been an increase in the presence of diplomatic observers from European and Contact Group countries in general who, as I suggested in my last report, might be better placed to provide the Security Council with a reliable flow of information concerning the situation on the ground.

16. The continuing infiltration from outside the borders of the Federal Republic of Yugoslavia of weapons and fighting men is a source of continuing widespread concern. The sharp escalation of violence and the reported use of excessive force by security forces against civilians as part of the government operations against the KLA are cause for both distress and alarm. A particularly dangerous element in the situation is the move in certain quarters away from a willingness to search for compromise on a basis of multi-ethnic communities. Centrifugal tendencies appear to be gaining ground. As indicated in paragraphs 12 and 13, the continuing conflict has led to a growing number of internally displaced persons and refugees. This in turn causes further instability. The international community risks once against being placed in a position where it is only dealing with the symptoms of a conflict through its humanitarian agencies.

17. This situation is aggravated by the failure of the authorities of the Federal Republic of Yugoslavia and the Albanian Kosovars to enter into serious negotiations on the future status of Kosovo. The continuation or further escalation of this conflict has dangerous implications for the stability of the region. Given the responsibilities of the United Nations in the wider region and the ethnic makeup in neighbouring countries, I cannot but express my alarm at this prospect. Several Security Council-mandated or Security Council-authorized operations in the region are playing a useful role in promoting dialogue and harmony among different ethnic groups. I wish to record before the Security Council my strong hope that the question of Kosovo will be examined not in isolation but in a manner that fully takes into account and embraces the broad, regional context and the principles of the Charter of the United Nations.

Annex I:

Information on the situation in Kosovo and on measures taken by the Organization for Security and Cooperation in Europe

Summary

Since mid-June, there has been further escalation of the conflict in Kosovo, with the hostilities spreading to engulf the entire south-western part of the province.

By mid-July, the crisis had reached new levels of intensity. As the fighting drew nearer Pristina, the "Kosovo Liberation Army" (KLA) removed any ambiguity as to its intention to bring the province under its control.

Numerous armed clashes were reported from the regions of Kosovo bordering Albania.

All appeals of the international community for talks and a cessation of the hostilities have remained unanswered. Prospects for a negotiated settlement appear dim and time is running out for the attainment of a peaceful solution. The Kosovo crisis entered into a phase of unpredictable consequences for regional stability and is therefore a source of deep concern for the Chairman-in-Office as it is for the entire Organization for Security and Cooperation in Europe (OSCE).

Violence and the use of force

1. The period between the 16 June meeting between President Miloevi of the Federal Republic of Yugoslavia and President Yeltsin of the Russian Federation and the end of the month was marked by a drop in the number of combat operations in Kosovo. However, units of the Yugoslav Army remained active in the border region. Isolated incidents also took place along Yugoslavia's border with the former Yugoslav Republic of Macedonia.

2. Shortly thereafter the KLA became more active, moving on from defensive actions to sporadic attacks on the Yugoslav security forces. New information continued to be received on the fighting between the KLA and the Serb security forces around Pec, Cecanice and Djakovic. Offensive operations, with heavy fighting and casualties, have been the hallmarks of the period since 20 July. The civilian population has also suffered losses and the numbers of the refugees from the area have grown.

3. Meanwhile, the OSCE presence (mission) in Albania has reported a number of serious armed clashes inside Kosovo, close to the border with Albania, with the number of such incidents increasing after 15 July. OSCE observers witnessed stepped-up military activities in the Decani area. Increased cross-border transit of KLA troops as well as shipments of arms and ammunition were recorded, as was a flare-up of the fighting on the border region on 18 July.

Situation on the Albanian/Kosovo border

4. Military activity by the Federal Republic of Yugoslavia has continued unabated since mid-May. In the border areas close to Albania, many villages and hamlets have been targeted. More recently, the larger town of Orahovac has also been the scene of fighting. This has caused an increase in the number of internally displaced persons. The refugee movement to Albania, however, has come to a virtual halt. This is probably a result of the deterrent measures by forces of the Federal Republic of Yugoslavia, including the laying of mines and increased patrols at the border.

5. The continued violence in Kosovo has reinforced overall militancy among ethnic Albanians on both sides of the border. KLA transborder activities have become increasingly overt. Regular movement of KLA arms/ammunition and manpower has been observed by OSCE across known refugee routes. There are strong indications that some of these routes have been mined on the Federal Republic of Yugoslavia side, and are targeted by direct and indirect fire. OSCE observers have recently sighted fresh shell craters 25 metres from the border on the Albanian side.

6. The increased levels of tension and armed confrontation have led to further destabilization of the north-east region of Albania. There are indications that the vital ferry link on the main supply route to the border area is under the control of the KLA.

Access to Kosovo

7. The number of visits to Kosovo by foreign diplomats posted in Belgrade has grown since the meeting between President Miloevi and President Yeltsin.

8. However, regions hit by heavy fighting and those preparing for armed operations were virtually impossible to visit. In danger zones Serbian police did grant individual passage permits while warning prospective travellers of considerable risk.

9. Units and outposts of the KLA continued to stop individuals for ID checks and sometimes refused to give access to some areas of Kosovo under its control.

10. On 6 July, the International Kosovo Diplomatic Observer Mission started work in the war-torn province, with the participation of the OSCE Troika. Observers from the United States of America, the Russian Federation and the European Union have set up offices in Pristina and operate from there.

11. On 21 July, at Belgrade, the heads of the diplomatic observer missions, representing Contact Group countries, the European Union (EU) Troika and the OSCE Chairman-in-Office, presented their first report on the situation in Kosovo.

Dialogue

12. Despite strenuous diplomatic efforts, the international community has so far failed to bring about a resumption of the dialogue between the country's authorities and representatives of the Kosovo Albanians. The Serbian side has reiterated its understanding that a dialogue should be conducted within the framework of Serbia and the Federal Republic of Yugoslavia and that the territorial integrity of Yugoslavia would first be guaranteed. Units of the Serb special forces remained in Kosovo.

13. Representatives of the Albanian negotiating team and the Chairman of the Kosovo Democratic League are of the opinion that the present-day conditions of conflict are not conducive to dialogue. In their view, a withdrawal from Kosovo of the Serb special forces, a cessation of the operations aimed against the Albanian civilian population and putting the idea of Kosovo's independence on the agenda of the negotiations would be their preconditions before a resumption of the dialogue.

14. The emergence on the Kosovar Albanian political scene of the KLA, as a force commanding considerable influence throughout the Albanian community, has introduced a new element into the idea of negotiations. Representatives of the KLA believe that the political parties should accept the existence and importance of the armed organization and that none of the parties represents the KLA. Neither do they recognize the leadership of Ibrahim Rugova. The KLA further rules out the possibility of declaring a ceasefire should the talks resume without them being accepted as one of the negotiating parties.

15. The commitment of the international community is of immense importance for the ongoing efforts to defuse the threat of a further escalation of the conflict. During their visits to both Belgrade and Pristina, international visitors have tried to pressure the two belligerent parties to stop the use of violence. The string of measures adopted with the purpose of bringing more pressure to bear on the Belgrade authorities includes the 8 June European Union decision (which went into force on 23 June) to freeze within the boundaries of the European Union all the fixed assets and financial resources of both the Federal Republic of Yugoslavia and Serbia, and the 29 June resolution of the Council of Ministers banning all flights by JAT airlines as well as other Yugoslav carriers to EU destinations.

OSCE activities

16. Following the communiqué released in Moscow on 16 June at the close of the meeting between President Yeltsin and President Miloevi, Mr. Bronislaw Geremek, Minister of Foreign Affairs of Poland and Chairman-in-Office of OSCE, wrote a letter to Mr. Miloevi requesting clarification of some points of the communiqué's paragraph dealing with OSCE. The letter elicited a response from Mr. Z. Jovanovi, Minister for Foreign Affairs of the Federal Republic of Yugoslavia, who wrote to Mr. Geremek inviting a delegation of political directors to Belgrade "to start negotiations simultaneously on the acceptance of the OSCE mission in Kosovo and Metohija and the regulation of the membership rights of the Federal Republic of Yugoslavia in the organization". In his reply Mr. Geremek proclaimed his "readiness to begin exploratory talks" between OSCE and the Federal Republic of Yugoslavia.

17. The exploratory talks, which were held at Belgrade on 3 July, revealed that the Federal Republic of Yugoslavia did not accept a return of the Gonzalez Mission and/or the OSCE Long-term Mission unless the problem of the Federal Republic's participation in OSCE had first been resolved. Moreover, the Federal Republic also rejected the idea of a step-by-step "re-establishment" of its membership. As a gesture of "good will", the Federal Republic invited an "OSCE assessment mission" to visit the Federal Republic of Yugoslavia without any preconditions.

18. As a result of the above invitation, an OSCE technical assessment mission visited the Federal Republic of Yugoslavia from 14 to 22 July 1998. Its report and conclusions are attached to the present report as a source of additional information.

   Chairman-in-Office of the Organization for Security and Cooperation in Europe. Warsaw, 24 July 1998.

Enclosure:

OSCE, Report of the technical assessment mission on its visit to the Federal Republic of Yugoslavia from 14 to 22 July 1998

I. MISSION OBJECTIVE

1. The mission had the task set by the OSCE Chairman-in-Office to go to the Federal Republic of Yugoslavia to make a preliminary assessment of the relations between OSCE and the Federal Republic of Yugoslavia, with a view to facilitating the mission of Mr. Felipe Gonzalez (as Personal Representative of the OSCE Chairman-in-Office) and a comprehensive resolution of these issues, including the re-establishment of the OSCE

Long-term Mission to the Federal Republic of Yugoslavia on the basis of OSCE Permanent Council decision 218 of 11 March 1998.

II. FRAMEWORK

2. In Belgrade, the 12-member delegation, headed by Ambassador Hansjorg Eiff of Germany, met with the Foreign Minister of the Federal Republic of Yugoslavia at the outset as well as towards the end of the visit, and had discussions with Federal and/or Serbian ministers responsible for the media, national and minority rights, and culture; the Chairman and three other members of the Foreign Relations Committee of the Parliament of the Federal Republic of Yugoslavia (representing predominantly government opinion); the Serbian Commissioner for Refugees; leaders of the political opposition; non-governmental organizations (NGOs) (including human rights groups); representatives of the independent media; and international organizations. In Belgrade it also met with representatives of regional parties from the Sandjak and Vojvodina. The Head of Mission met twice with the foreign policy adviser of President Milosevic.

3. In Kosovo, the mission met the local Serb authorities; political representatives of Kosovo Albanians (including several members of the negotiating team); the Albanian Students Union; the Helsinki Committee; and the Kosovo Diplomatic Observer Mission.

4. In Montenegro, the mission was received by President Djukanovic and met with: the Prime Minister; the Chairman of the National Assembly; the Foreign Minister and the Minister responsible for ethnic minorities; and representatives of the media and of human rights organizations.

5. The Yugoslav authorities cooperated fully with the mission and provided assistance to facilitate its work.

6. The mission focused its work on the following issues:

   • The possible return of the long-term missions to Kosovo, Sandjak and Vojvodina;

   • The mission of the Personal Representative of the Chairman-in-Office for the Federal Republic of Yugoslavia;

   • The situation on the ground in Kosovo, Sandjak and Vojvodina insofar as it would affect the work of the returned missions and the mission by the Personal Representative of the Chairman-in-Office;

   • Recent developments in the areas of concern (e.g. media, judiciary, legal and electoral systems) highlighted by Mr. Gonzalez in his 1996 report;

   • Possible participation of the Federal Republic of Yugoslavia in the work of OSCE.

III. RETURN OF THE LONG-TERM MISSIONS TO KOSOVO, SANDJAK AND VOJVODINA

7. There was a general recognition of the usefulness of the work of the three missions prior to their interruption in 1993. All regional groupings favoured a return of the missions to their areas. One Vojvodina representative suggested that that region might be covered from a base located more centrally in Belgrade, if a mission was to be established there. While some Albanians expressed reservations as to whether the mission in Kosovo could have prevented the serious deterioration of the situation, they believed that its presence could have served as a partial check on the violence. Many interlocutors noted that the missions generally could help to bridge the gap between the communities, and serve as a reassurance, and point of contact for the minorities. It was suggested that the missions could be given the mandate of an ombudsman, to receive and assess complaints about human rights violations submitted to them.

8. The Government of the Federal Republic of Yugoslavia side, both in Belgrade and in Pristina, also acknowledged the fairness and accuracy of the missions' reporting and recognized that, in the current situation, a mission could play a useful role in Kosovo. It was clear they would consider the possibility of a mission returning to Kosovo alone. They noted that OSCE missions were only dispatched to OSCE participating States. They placed the return of the mission to Kosovo firmly in the context of the agreement between President Milosevic and President Yeltsin in Moscow on 16 June and linked it to what they described as the simultaneous readmission of the Federal Republic of Yugoslavia to OSCE. The OSCE delegation stressed that the return of the missions was insufficient to secure the participation of the Federal Republic of Yugoslavia in the organization, which would require a consensus decision of all OSCE member States.

IV. ATTITUDE EXPRESSED TOWARDS THE MISSION OF THE PERSONAL REPRESENTATIVE OF THE OSCE CHAIRMAN-IN-OFFICE

9. The assessment mission emphasized to all its interlocutors its role of preparing the ground for the mission by the Personal Representative of the OSCE Chairman-in-Office, Mr. Felipe Gonzalez, and made it clear that it

was no substitute for that mission. It also stressed that Mr. Gonzalez's mandate covered the whole of the Federal Republic of Yugoslavia, including Kosovo. The Foreign Minister said the Gonzalez mission of 1996 had been completed. The Federal Republic of Yugoslavia had not been consulted on the second mission. The Federal Republic was ready to discuss this once the question of its participation in the OSCE was settled. The Chairman of the Federal Parliament Foreign Relations Committee went further, stating that the mandate could not cover internal issues and criticizing the earlier report of Mr. Gonzalez.

10. All opposition political parties to whom the mission spoke as well as all representatives of the ethnic minorities, the independent media and human rights groups favoured a continuation of the Gonzalez mission. Many said so publicly during the visit. Among the most keen were those parties which had boycotted the Serbian Republic and presidential elections in 1997 because they had believed the electoral conditions were unacceptable. Some of the Albanian representatives noted that any international mediator on Kosovo would need strong international backing, and that there were already others involved in that field.

V. KOSOVO

11. Federal Foreign Minister Jovanovic, like other government representatives, emphasized the official view that the Kosovo problem was one of separatism and terrorism, and not of national and minority rights. The Government of the Federal Republic of Yugoslavia needed to defend the interests of all the residents of Kosovo. The situation could be resolved only through direct dialogue between the parties on a series of confidence-building measures and forms of self-governance for the province, including different forms of autonomy. The outcome must respect the territorial integrity of Serbia and the Federal Republic of Yugoslavia and the rights of all nationalities and minorities, according to European standards. The Minister also highlighted the progress he said the Federal Republic had made on humanitarian issues. He called for European countries to stop what he claimed was the provision of assistance to Albanian extremists in Kosovo from groups based on their territory.

12. The mission's visit to Pristina was depressing. The total lack of trust between the two communities, which was reflected both in an absence of everyday human contact and a lack of communication between representatives of the two communities, was striking. This was one of the key reasons for the failure of the two sides to negotiate. It was very obvious that the most pressing need was for an immediate cessation of hostilities. The representatives of the local Serb authorities insisted that the Serb security forces only responded to attacks made on them by the so-called Kosovo Liberation Army (KLA). They claimed that the continuing presence of Serbian special units in the province was only necessary because of KLA attacks. They also denied that the Serbs had used disproportionate force in their engagements with the KLA. They handed the mission lists of names of 30 Albanians and 14 Serbs who they said had been killed by the KLA, together with a list of 111 Serbs, Albanians and other minority nationals who they claimed had been kidnapped since the beginning of the year. They said they were ready to continue the dialogue which had begun with the meeting between President Milosevi and Mr. Rugova on 15 May. But the Albanian side had failed to appear for the scheduled meetings since 22 May.

13. Representatives of the Kosovar Albanian political parties and community emphasized the need to find a rapid solution to the situation. They insisted that the KLA was a defensive grouping of Albanians who had taken up arms to protect themselves against the Serbian security forces. They highlighted the growing popularity of the KLA and the diminishing support for political parties as a whole. Some openly admitted that they had offered to serve as that body's political wing. But to date no party was fulfilling that role. Most significantly, no political personality distanced himself from the KLA.

14. The Albanians insisted that no dialogue could begin while, they maintained, Serb security forces continued attacking the Kosovar Albanian population. They stressed the importance of international involvement in the process, into which they said the KLA needed to be brought. All agreed that Kosovo's rights as set out in the 1974 Constitution were non-negotiable and constituted the starting point for any dialogue. Some believed that there should be an interim arrangement, including confidence-building measures, before talks on a final settlement could begin. In this context some parties looked to intervention by the North Atlantic Treaty Organization (NATO) to guarantee the security environment in the region. While some said the outcome of this dialogue should not be prejudged, it was clear that all interlocutors saw independence as the final goal. None were prepared to accept autonomy, to whatever degree, as the final outcome. There seemed to be no readiness either to accept a moratorium on the status issue.

15. The Kosovo Albanians told the mission that some 300 Albanians had been killed, and 150,000 displaced, since the beginning of the year. The Office of the United Nations High Commissioner for Refugees (UNHCR) said it had identified the whereabouts of some 57,000 internally displaced persons in the province but believed the total number was over 100,000. UNHCR said that, since mid-June, it had in principle been given free access to all areas by both the Serb authorities and the KLA. For the time being, food supplies seemed to be adequate. However, if the situation continued to deteriorate, the international community should be aware that the supply of food to the population could become very difficult once winter came. The Government of the Federal Republic of Yugoslavia said it had asked the Albanian Government to allow the Serbian Commissioner for Refugees to visit northern Albania, to meet the Kosovo refugees and to encourage them to return. So far the Federal Republic had not received any direct reply from Tirana. (This issue is being pursued by the Austrian European Union (EU) Presidency.) If a bilateral agreement could be reached, UNHCR would provide the logistics.

16. The Government of the Federal Republic of Yugoslavia said that it favoured a census held under OSCE auspices in Kosovo to establish the ethnic breakdown in the province.

...

IX. RECENT DEVELOPMENTS IN THE FIELDS OF HUMAN RIGHTS, THE MEDIA, AND JUDICIARY, LEGAL AND ELECTORAL SYSTEMS

25. The mission's findings on these issues are necessarily incomplete as it could not cover in depth the full range of questions in the time available.

A. The media

Summary. While the situation of the print media had improved and a network of independent radio and TV stations had been set up outside Belgrade, serious concern still remained in respect of the State media, the overall legislative framework governing the information sector and the Government's implementation of that legislation.

26. In the print media field, the mission noted that the number of independent publications had grown over the last two years. There is now a wide range of dailies as well as some weekly magazines, reflecting a diversity of opinion. These include a variety of publications, among them some dailies, in the Albanian language. But the mission was told that sales of newspapers were dropping and that the Yugoslav population looked mainly to the electronic media, in particular television, as its main source of information. It was also informed that the only factory producing roto-press paper in Serbia gave priority to pro-Government newspapers, which meant that many independent outlets had to import paper at higher prices.

27. In the electronic media field, the ANEM network of 33 independent local radio stations (including some stations run by municipalities in which the opposition had been victorious in the 1996 local elections) was established in 1997. The network is centred on Radio B 92 in Belgrade and covers some 60 per cent of the country. Opposition politicians said that this enabled them to gain access to the electronic media outside Belgrade. But serious problems with the legal framework governing the electronic media remain. Frequency allocation is in the hands of the Government; there is no independent regulatory council. The mission was told that the recent frequency competition (the first in five years, although it was said legislation prescribed annual competitions) was neither transparent nor strictly in accordance with the law. The Government had rejected the applications of a number of independent stations on technical grounds and had signed easily broken contracts, rather than issuing permits for the frequency licences. The media environment was governed by a series of laws and ministries at both the Federal and Republic levels, whose requirements and actions were often mutually contradictory. The Government had recently closed down independent stations (two of which were ANEM members) on the grounds that they were broadcasting without a licence, even though hundreds of others were doing likewise. These included the first attempt to establish a multi-ethnic radio station in Kosovo.

28. Concern was also expressed over the domination of the Serbian State television system, which constitutes the main source of information for the population as a whole. Its output totally supports the government line. It is the only TV network covering the whole of Serbia. Opposition leaders told the mission that they had no access to State TV and radio apart from the legally required appearances during election campaign. Independent analysis of its coverage of events during the 1997 elections showed a clear bias in favour of Government candidates. All independent media interlocutors said that Serbian State radio and TV and other pro-Government media were given preferential access to the Government's central information system, with independent outlets mainly being denied

access to official press conferences, press releases, etc. This was denied by the Government.

B. Elections

Summary. There is still a lack of confidence in the electoral system in opposition and other non-governmental circles.

29. A number of interlocutors, and in particular those members of the opposition who had boycotted the 1997 Serbian Republic and presidential elections, expressed their lack of faith in the electoral system, which the OSCE observer mission saw as flawed in many respects. The critics focused in particular on the Government's decision fundamentally to change the number of constitutional units shortly before the elections without gaining the agreement of all the main political parties; the bias of the State media; and the election process in Kosovo. The mission was unable to examine the electoral system in detail. It will be necessary to follow up these concerns in advance of the next round of elections.

C. The legal process

Summary. There is a lack of confidence in non-official circles in the legal system.

30. A large majority of non-governmental interlocutors expressed a lack of confidence in the legal institutions and processes. The mission was told that all key positions in the main institutions, including the judiciary, were filled by Government supporters. This made it difficult to seek redress against the executive branch through the judicial system. On those occasions when verdicts against the Government were handed down, they were often not implemented by the State institutions, e.g. the court decision to overrule the expulsion of a Croat family from their house in the Radical Party-controlled municipality of Zemun; and the failure by the Government to return to Radio Pirot its equipment in accordance with a court order to that effect.

31. The Serbian Parliament in May 1998 adopted a law regulating the status of universities which reduced the status of all universities to economic enterprises. The post of Rector is identical to that of a company director. He and all the deans are appointed by the Government. Each university is run by a 15-member board, including 9 nominated (6 professors, 3 students) individuals from the university, and 6 political appointees. Heads of departments are appointed by the Dean, while other teaching staff are nominated by the Dean after consulting the Education Minister. Students are not allowed to form any political, religious or ethnic organizations at the university and are separated into three groups: those paid for from the budget; those partly financed from the budget; and those self-financed.

32. The Government justified the universities' loss of autonomy on the grounds that their financier (the State) had the right to administer them. It also claimed that the law gave the universities autonomy in respect of education and scientific and research work.

X. ATTITUDE TO THE PARTICIPATION OF THE FEDERAL REPUBLIC OF YUGOSLAVIA IN OSCE

33. There was general support from both the Government of the Federal Republic of Yugoslavia and the Serbian opposition for future participation by the Federal Republic in OSCE, but a widely diverging range of views on the conditionality which it needed to satisfy to secure full participation. The Foreign Minister of the Federal Republic expressed his Government's interest in full participation in OSCE at as early a date as possible. It was wrong that the Federal Republic was the only European country excluded. He claimed that it was already applying the organization's standards despite its non-participation. He insisted on the linkage he said had been established in the Milosevi/Yeltsin agreement between the start of simultaneous talks on the return of the long-term missions and the simultaneous membership of the organization by the Federal Republic of Yugoslavia (the text actually speaks of readiness to start negotiations with OSCE simultaneously on receiving its mission to Kosovo and on the restoration of the membership of the Federal Republic in OSCE). He said that the Federal Republic did not maintain it was the sole successor State of the former Socialist Federal Republic of Yugoslavia, but it did claim to be the continuing State thereof, and indeed of Serbia and Montenegro as established by the Congress of Berlin in 1878.

34. The degree of conditionality for participation sought by interlocutors in Belgrade varied from those who thought immediate membership was necessary, to those who believed membership would play into the hands of the Government and therefore favoured greater conditionality, e.g. the return of the Gonzalez mission and a commitment to make progress on the issues it addressed.

35. For the Kosovar Albanians, this did not appear to be a major issue. But all who expressed a view on the subject linked significant progress on Kosovo, including in one case the complete solution of the Kosovo

problem, to OSCE membership. Of those advocating independence, one at least would like to see an independent Kosovo in OSCE.

36. The President of Montenegro was against participation by the Federal Republic of Yugoslavia in OSCE unless it demonstrated a cooperative attitude, not only in words but also in deeds. He reminded the mission of the Federal Republic's conduct following the suspension of Kosovo-related sanctions in May.

XI. CONCLUSIONS

37. The perceptibly deteriorating situation in Kosovo, together with the relative lack of progress on issues identified by Mr. Gonzalez in his December 1996 report, underlined the need for a rapid re-establishment of the Long-term Missions to Kosovo, Sandjak and Vojvodina and the return of the Personal Representative of the OSCE Chairman-in-Office to the Federal Republic of Yugoslavia. The Federal Republic was only prepared to consider discussing the terms of the mandate of the OSCE Chairman-in-Office's Personal Representative, Mr. Gonzalez, once the question of its participation in OSCE had been settled. There seemed to be a general willingness on all sides within the Federal Republic of Yugoslavia that the country should participate in the work of OSCE. But the degree of conditionality which it would have to satisfy to achieve this varied considerably.

38. The mission believed that its visit strongly underlined the need for the return of the Long-term Mission. Care would have to be taken that the work of the mission and other international efforts, such as the Kosovo Diplomatic Observer Mission, were not duplicated, and an assessment made, in the light of the situation at the time, of the extent to which the existing mandate was still valid. It could address issues such as the stimulation of dialogue between the two communities, serve as an ombudsman on human rights matters and provide some form of coordinating role for international activities in the area.

39. The lack of trust between the two communities in Kosovo, against the background of increasing violence, and the distance between the political positions as to how the conflict could be resolved, strongly reinforced the need for a committed high-level international involvement in the negotiation process.

40. The humanitarian situation needed to be observed carefully, as the supply of food to the population in winter could become very difficult, in particular if the situation in the province continued to deteriorate.

41. Although the scale of the problems of the Muslims in Sandjak was of a different magnitude from those of Kosovo, there was a case for a renewed presence of a long-term mission there.

42. The mission believed that the conditions in Vojvodina were such as to warrant coverage by the Long-term Mission.

43. A case can be made for the Long-term Mission to have its headquarters in Belgrade, with a sizeable presence in Kosovo and perhaps a branch office in the Sandjak.

Since the visit of Mr. Gonzalez in 1996, the situation regarding the media and the judiciary, legal and electoral systems did not appear to have improved significantly, apart from some progress in the field of print media. There was a continuing lack of confidence in non-official circles in the legal system, including the legislation relating to the election process. Developments in these fields needed to be monitored with a view to an ongoing dialogue with the authorities, including offering expertise on how progress could be made.

44. The Law on the University gave great cause for concern, as it provided for government control over the administration and teaching staff and limited the possibility of political expression by students. It fell short of relevant European standards.

45. While the Federal Republic of Yugoslavia indicated its readiness to accept the return of the Long-term Mission to Kosovo, it was only prepared to do so in return for the simultaneous participation of the Federal Republic in OSCE.

46. The mission recommends the continuation of talks between the Chairman-in-Office and the Federal Republic of Yugoslavia on issues of relevance to relations between OSCE and the Federal Republic.

Annex II:

Letter from the Secretary-General of NATO, 14 July 1998

I am writing to inform you that the military authorities of the North Atlantic Treaty Organization (NATO) have completed their assessment of possible support for a monitoring regime in connection with Security Council resolution 1160 (1998), as noted in my previous letter to you of 11 June 1998. Having considered a variety of options, the North Atlantic Council has decided at this stage to proceed with the SFOR option to step up its efforts, within its existing mission and capabilities, to monitor the Bosnian border with the Federal Republic of Yugoslavia. In this context I can confirm that the necessary arrangements have been put in place to forward any relevant information on suspected violations in the SFOR area of operations via the monthly report to the United Nations or on an ad hoc basis as necessary.

Should circumstances change I will write to you again. In the meantime allow me to take this opportunity to assure you of our continuing close cooperation.

(Signed) Javier SOLANA

S/1998/834

7.   Report of the Secretary-General Prepared Pursuant to Security Council Resolution 1160 (1998), 4 September 1998

...

II.   SECURITY   COUNCIL   COMMITTEE   ESTABLISHED PURSUANT TO RESOLUTION 1160 (1998)

2. As at 31 August 1998, in addition to those States listed in my earlier reports (S/1998/608 and S/1998/712), Albania, Chile, Croatia and the Republic of Korea reported to the Committee established pursuant to paragraph 12 of resolution 1160 (1998) on the steps they had taken to give effect to the prohibitions imposed by that resolution.

3. In a letter dated 18 August, the Permanent Representative of Austria to the United Nations, in his capacity as the representative of the Presidency of the European Union, transmitted to the Chairman of the Committee the first monthly report of the European Community Monitoring Mission containing observations on violations of Security Council resolution 1160 (1998). The report covered the Mission's activities in July and early August and was submitted in accordance with the European Union's earlier pledge to contribute to international efforts to monitor the embargo and to report to the Committee any relevant information. The Mission has instructed its regional centres in Tirana, Belgrade and Skopje, as well as its coordination centres in Pristina and Podgorica, to be particularly alert to the possibility of weapons transfers from their respective areas of responsibility into the Federal Republic of Yugoslavia.

4. At its 3rd meeting, held on 19 August 1998, the Committee decided, inter alia, to renew its appeal of 7 May 1998 to all States, international organizations and regional organizations to provide information on violations or suspected violations of the prohibitions imposed by Security Council resolution 1160 (1998). That appeal was issued on 26 August 1998 by the Chairman of the Committee, Mr. Celso L. N. Amorim (Brazil), on behalf of the Committee (SC/6564).

5. In my previous report (S/1998/712), I submitted, in accordance with paragraph 15 of Security Council resolution 1160 (1998), my observations and recommendations for the establishment of a comprehensive regime to monitor the implementation of the prohibitions imposed in paragraph 8 of the resolution. If the Council concurs with the suggested arrangements, I will proceed accordingly.

III. SITUATION IN KOSOVO

6. Continued international efforts to facilitate a political solution to the Kosovo crisis have had limited results. As the Security Council is aware, the situation in Kosovo remains volatile. In mid-July and early August, heavy fighting occurred in the towns of Orahovac and Malisevo, as well as in the Suva Reka and Stimlje areas. By mid-August, fierce fighting was raging in the western parts of Djakovica, Decani and Pec. Towards the end of August, fighting continued in several areas: west of Pec in Rugovska Klisura area, along the Stimlje-Suva Reka road, on the Komorane-Kijevo stretch of the Pristina-Pec Road and near the Pristina airport. Although the scale of fighting between the security forces of the Federal Republic of Yugoslavia and the Kosovo Liberation Army (KLA) has decreased, and the Government has announced that life is returning to normal, it is evident that the conflict continues and any prediction of its end would be premature. The negotiating process has not been renewed and tensions along the border between the Federal Republic of Yugoslavia and Albania have been evident.

Humanitarian concerns

7. An estimated 600 to 700 civilians have been killed in the fighting in Kosovo since March. The conflict has resulted in the estimated cumulative displacement of over 230,000 persons. This is a nearly tenfold increase compared to the figure of 25,000 persons estimated by the Office of the United Nations High Commissioner for Refugees (UNHCR) to have been displaced during the first four months of 1998. The vast majority of those currently displaced by the conflict are within Kosovo (170,000). Others have moved to locations in Montenegro (33,500) and Serbia (20,000). Some 14,000 refugees are currently in Albania. Deserted towns and villages, as well as destroyed houses, slaughtered livestock and burned fields, bear witness to the scale of displacement and destruction in Kosovo. However, it has not always been possible fully to gauge the level of population movement inside Kosovo, owing to the increasingly insecure environment, impediments to access and the fluidity of the population movements. Thousands of civilians are constantly in flight to escape attacks by government forces.

8. According to UNHCR estimates, there could be up to 50,000 displaced people in Kosovo who have been forced from their homes into the woods and mountains. These people are the most vulnerable and are in need of urgent help. Despite assurances from the authorities, access is hindered, and the immediate priority of the humanitarian agencies is to find these groups and to deliver essential relief. It is clear that if these people remain in their current locations over the winter, they will be at serious risk of death. It remains a priority to assist them to return to their homes, or to move them to host families, or, as a last resort, into collective centres where assistance can be more reliably provided.

9. The authorities of the Federal Republic of Yugoslavia have committed themselves to the creation of conditions for the return of refugees and displaced persons to their homes in Kosovo. The reality on the ground, however, is that inadequate security conditions and the continued destruction of homes are making return to many areas virtually impossible. There are disturbing reports that some returnees, mostly young men, were taken by police for "informative talks". In some cases, the police have prevented returnees from harvesting crops. The Assistant High Commissioner for Refugees, Mr. Soren Jessen-Petersen, who visited the area from 18 to 22 August, reported one instance when the police, occupying the house of the potential returnee, vandalized it and did not allow the owner to move back in. Such practices, as well as any potential attempts to change the ethnic balance in Kosovo, are unacceptable. I am also concerned by unconfirmed reports that some Kosovo Albanian groups, in pursuit of their political interests, may be blocking the return process in order to prolong the humanitarian crisis and maintain international attention on Kosovo.

10. In order to expedite the return process and to facilitate political progress on the Kosovo issue, there is a critical need to promote confidence-building measures between the parties in conflict. As most refugees and internally displaced persons have no trust in the willingness or ability of the Serbian or federal authorities to protect them, all necessary measures should be taken to bridge the confidence gap. In this connection, UNHCR strongly argues the urgent need to strengthen the international presence in Kosovo. The government authorities in the Federal Republic of Yugoslavia, who bear primary responsibility for the well-being and security of all its citizens, should unambiguously commit themselves to guaranteeing the safety of those returnees not proved to have participated in terrorist activities. The authorities must undertake to prosecute any member of the security forces involved in the mistreatment of innocent civilians. Another important factor is that many internally displaced persons have no place to go, since a significant number of houses have been destroyed or burned. The authorities must bring to justice all those involved in the deliberate destruction of property. They must also make every effort to provide assistance for the reconstruction of damaged and destroyed homes.

11. A prolongation of the Government's present policies is likely to result in further displacement of the wider population. This is particularly worrying because of the approaching winter, which could transform what is currently a humanitarian crisis into a humanitarian catastrophe. It is likely that most of the displacement will continue to

be concentrated within Kosovo itself, although an increasing number of those displaced appear to be electing to move to other areas within the Federal Republic of Yugoslavia (Montenegro in particular) and abroad.
12. At the beginning of 1998, there were 1,800 refugees from Croatia and Bosnia and Herzegovina housed in 28 collective centres in Kosovo. UNHCR has requested the federal authorities to transfer the refugees to safe locations outside the conflict areas, but this has not yet been done. Regular visits to the collective centres reveal that the numbers of refugees therein have dropped, as most refugees with the health and means to do so have made their own way out; their present location and condition are unknown. The options of voluntary repatriation and resettlement are being pursued. So far some 600 are being assisted to return to Croatia at their request. Interest in repatriation, especially among the elderly, is increasing and it is expected that the number of requests for return will grow in the near future. More than 1,000 refugees have now requested resettlement abroad.
13. In response to the crisis, the humanitarian agencies continue to identify the location and needs of the displaced, to provide protection when possible, and to deliver assistance from available resources. At the time of writing, the municipalities in Kosovo affected by the conflict include Decane, Djakovica, Glogovac, Istok, Klina, Lipljan, Orahovac, Pec, Srbica, Stimlje and Suva Reka. Most of the displaced within Kosovo are staying within these areas, though some have moved to other municipalities. Populations in other areas, while not directly involved in the fighting, are increasingly affected by the conflict. Many have little or no access to food supplies, as stocks in shops have, for the most part, not been replenished, and medical facilities face major supply problems. Livestock has been lost or slaughtered, crops lie unharvested in the fields, and fodder is scarce, rendered inaccessible or destroyed. It is feared that many wounded in the conflict areas have no access to medical services.
14. The most worrying problem in Montenegro is the impact of internally displaced persons on the demographic balance and the high burden they place on that Republic of the Federal Republic of Yugoslavia, since they already represent more than 10 per cent of its population. In Montenegro, UNHCR is increasing its budget to cope with the needs of new arrivals from Kosovo. The focus in the short term is on assisting the most vulnerable host families and to winterize public buildings used to shelter the internally displaced. A similar approach is required in northern Albania, although in the medium term those refugees willing to go there should be relocated to the south in order to decongest Bajram Curri and to move the refugees away from the area, which has become a KLA base. The security situation has become a major concern for the humanitarian agencies in northern Albania.

Human rights
15. The human rights situation in Kosovo has been marked by widespread violations. Acting under the mandates of the United Nations High Commissioner for Human Rights and the Special Rapporteur on the situation of human rights in Bosnia and Herzegovina, the Republic of Croatia and the Federal Republic of Yugoslavia, the Office of the United Nations High Commissioner for Human Rights is engaged in monitoring and reporting on the human rights situation in the whole of the Federal Republic of Yugoslavia. The Office of the High Commissioner opened its office in Belgrade in March 1996 and has in addition maintained a continuous monitoring presence in Pristina since March 1998.
16. The Office of the High Commissioner has received increasing reports of persons being arbitrarily arrested for questioning and kept in pre-trial detention for periods well beyond the legal time limit. It has registered more than 200 persons who are reported to be in police detention, and another 200 or more are reported by various sources as "missing". Some persons are believed to be in unacknowledged detention. While most of these people have been arrested in connection with police operations in the field, there is a growing number of cases in which Kosovo Albanian political activists, lawyers, humanitarian workers and medical personnel are being arrested and interrogated by the police. The Office of the High Commissioner has been informed that detainees have recently been transferred to Belgrade from prisons in Kosovo. Lawyers and family members say that they encounter

serious problems in obtaining permission to see those detained. Lawyers have reportedly been prevented from speaking with their clients in private for longer than five minutes and have not been allowed by the police to speak with their clients in the Albanian language. There are many reports of torture and ill-treatment during pre-trial detention, including at least four alleged cases of death in custody. The Office of the High Commissioner has on several occasions written to the Serbian Ministry of the Interior inquiring about cases brought to its attention. In Kosovo, the Office is monitoring trials of persons charged with crimes against the state, including "terrorism". Some defendants have reportedly been tortured while under interrogation. In these politically sensitive trials there are serious concerns regarding the independence of the courts and defendants' access to legal counsel.
17. Also a serious cause for concern are reports that a number of Serb, Kosovo Albanian and Roma civilians, as well as Serbian police officers, have been abducted since early April by armed Kosovo Albanians, believed to be KLA members. The Office of the High Commissioner has interviewed relatives and family members of abductees as well as eyewitnesses to abductions. The Yugoslav authorities have indicated that more than 179 civilians and police were abducted since the beginning of the conflict. On 26 and 27 August, in Klecka, 22 persons believed to be abductees reportedly were killed and their bodies burned in a makeshift crematorium. The precise number of victims and the circumstances of their death are being investigated. International monitors have also visited the site.

IV. HUMANITARIAN ACTIVITIES
18. The provision of humanitarian assistance is of great urgency, particularly with the onset of the harsh winter months in the Balkans. In cooperation with the International Committee of the Red Cross, international non-governmental organizations and local organizations, United Nations agencies are attempting to deal with the crisis in the face of difficult conditions and limited funding. Within Kosovo, UNHCR has been escorting multi-agency convoys to deliver humanitarian assistance to internally displaced persons; the first priority in this regard has been to help those living in the open, who are, unfortunately, the most difficult to reach.
19. Given the growing crisis in Kosovo and the commensurate increase in humanitarian needs, the international humanitarian assistance programme has become an indispensable factor in ensuring the provision of efficacious and cost-effective relief assistance at the local, national and regional level. UNHCR continues to act as the focal point for inter-agency coordination on issues pertaining to the crisis in Kosovo. Capacity for inter-agency and interregional information flow and coordination continues to be undertaken by UNHCR with support from the Office for the Coordination of Humanitarian Affairs. A purpose of the recent visit to Kosovo by the Assistant High Commissioner for Refugees was to assess the humanitarian situation on the ground, including issues of access, security and other operational concerns and constraints. ...
21. The military operations and civil strife of the past months, resulting in the mass displacement of civilian populations, coupled with the disruption of trade and the failure to harvest crops, have also worsened the food security situation of internally displaced persons and other affected populations. The World Food Programme's intervention in the food sector has been designed to prevent hunger and malnutrition among refugees and displaced persons, as well as among affected populations in conflict areas. UNHCR has a small provision in its budget to cover special dietary food requirements and supplementary food, to assist the most needy during the winter months of 1998 especially. A number of non-governmental organizations and the International Committee of the Red Cross/ International Federation of Red Cross Societies have funding to provide food assistance to the affected population in Kosovo as well as to internally displaced persons in Kosovo and Montenegro.
22. In the non-food sector, UNHCR provides such items as blankets, mattresses, hygienic items, heating/cooking stoves and firewood, with special emphasis on the needs of women and children. Winter clothing will be essential in the coming months. UNHCR will make clothing and footwear available from its stocks in the region; non-governmental

organizations are expected to supply substantial quantities of clothing and footwear. The United Nations Children's Fund (UNICEF) will complement the activities of UNHCR and its partners through the provision of children's garments, basic household supplies and essential hygiene items required by displaced children and women. These supplies will improve the general health status of the internally displaced persons and help to prevent the outbreak of water-borne and food-borne diseases, lice infestation and other conditions related to living in deprived circumstances.

23. The conflict and population displacement in Kosovo has led to a shortage of essential drugs and to the collapse of basic health services. Children in temporary and inadequate shelter are at risk from common diseases and there is a serious threat of a measles epidemic in the coming months. The World Health Organization (WHO) maintains a coordination role in the public health sector and provides technical guidance to agencies involved in this sector. Activities include the procurement of emergency water supply and chlorination systems, the establishment or improvement of sanitary facilities, the improvement of the emergency health surveillance system and its management, and the strengthening of the management of drugs donations and distribution. Preventive health-care activities, in particular immunization programmes and prenatal care, will be undertaken to compensate for local services which have been severely curtailed because of shortages of trained staff and essential medical supplies. In addition to the activities of WHO, UNICEF will continue to provide special paediatric essential drug kits, together with guidelines for health workers on their use. UNICEF also promotes community health and hygiene education, sound infant-feeding practices and, in collaboration with WHO, assists in the monitoring of the general health and nutritional status of the affected population. Building on the work which began in April this year, UNICEF will seek to re-establish the network of trained care providers in Kosovo, in order to provide trauma screening and psycho-social support for children and families seriously affected by the violence and conflict. WHO continues its activities of psycho-social emergency assistance to the internally displaced persons in Montenegro.

24. Accommodation is one of the major concerns in relation to the well-being of internally displaced persons and affected populations. UNHCR will provide material for emergency repairs; more substantial repairs can be carried out only once relative peace has been restored, and it is hoped that reconstruction may be possible immediately after the 1998/1999 winter. In Montenegro, where a different type of shelter assistance is required, some basic repair and maintenance of the collective centres is foreseen. Assistance will also be provided to host families in an effort to support them and encourage them to continue to extend their hospitality, as resources have already started to dwindle. However, if fighting continues in Kosovo and it is impossible for those now living outside to reach their homes, they may seek to reach Montenegro. This would necessitate the urgent provision of greater resources for collective accommodation.

25. The current conflict has taken a serious toll on education services in Kosovo. UNICEF plans to assist up to 100,000 internally displaced children in Kosovo and other parts of Serbia and up to 20,000 internally displaced children in Montenegro, so that they can start school promptly in September. In Montenegro, UNICEF will concentrate its assistance on providing necessary school materials and basic textbooks for the start of the new school year, and on providing teacher training. In areas of Kosovo with a high influx of internally displaced persons, existing schools will not have the capacity to provide classroom space for all children and alternative arrangements will have to be made. Finally, as a precautionary measure, UNICEF will prepare and print a teachers' manual and posters for use in mine awareness education in primary schools in certain parts of Kosovo. UNHCR will support UNICEF activities and will, in consultation with the Government of Montenegro, provide assistance to carry out sanitation and rehabilitation work at school buildings in Montenegro to increase their capacity. Activities in this sector in Kosovo will depend on the local situation but are expected to be limited at this stage. Working with the legal community and non-governmental organizations, the Office of the United Nations High Commissioner for Human Rights is attempting to produce educational materials that link international human rights standards with domestic law and procedures, particularly in the area of police and judicial procedures. In August, the Office began its first small grants programme for communities and organizations involved in human rights education.

26. Humanitarian agencies can continue to operate only in areas where security conditions permit and access is granted by the relevant authorities. Although access has generally improved, insecurity resulting from fighting often prevents or delays the delivery of aid. In recent weeks, the incidence of cases of restriction of movement and denial of access for humanitarian agencies to certain areas, detention of relief personnel and attacks on relief workers has increased. On 25 August, three relief workers of a local non-governmental organization, the Mother Theresa Society, were killed under fire in a Serbian offensive. In late August, a UNHCR driver of ethnic Serb background was threatened by a KLA member at a KLA checkpoint near Pagarusa while escorting a humanitarian convoy. Humanitarian aid workers must cross numerous checkpoints established by both the police and KLA, often one after another; sometimes relief workers are sandwiched between two checkpoints as neither group will allow them to pass through. Reports of landmines also give cause for concern. While guarantees of access have been given, the security and safety of aid workers remains a real issue and must be addressed by the parties.

27. The most disappointing problem is a lack of resources. Three humanitarian convoys per week do not meet the needs of the affected people. An extension of the United Nations Consolidated Inter-agency Appeal for Humanitarian Assistance Related to the Crisis in Kosovo will be launched by UNHCR and the Office for the Coordination of Humanitarian Affairs in September. It is vital that the international community responds generously to this new appeal so that United Nations agencies may meet the expanding emergency humanitarian needs. The support of donors is critical to enhance the response capacity of agencies participating in this appeal, and to allow them to do their utmost to alleviate the human suffering caused by the conflict in Kosovo.

V. OBSERVATIONS

28. I am alarmed by the lack of progress towards a political settlement in Kosovo and by the further loss of life, displacement of civilian population and destruction of property resulting from the ongoing conflict. It is essential that negotiations get under way so as to break the cycle of disproportionate use of force by the Serbian forces and acts of violence by the Kosovo Albanian paramilitary units by promoting a political resolution of the conflict. On 1 September, I wrote to President Milosevic to underline my alarm at the excessive use of force by Serbian military and police forces, noting that Kosovo Albanian extremists also bear responsibility for their acts of provocation. Persistent tensions on the border between the Federal Republic of Yugoslavia and Albania, including reports of border violations and cross-border shelling, are a further cause of serious concern. As I have indicated, this escalation of tensions risks detrimental consequences for the stability in the region. In this regard, I wish to reiterate the concern, expressed in my previous report, that United Nations operations in the region could be negatively affected by developments in Kosovo.

29. I continue to believe strongly that there can be no military solution for the crisis. I urge both parties to demonstrate restraint and to start the negotiating process as soon as possible. Efforts by the Contact Group, regional organizations and individual States to put an end to the violence and to create appropriate conditions for a political settlement of the conflict have my full support. For my part, I remain prepared to contribute to these efforts through all resources available to me.

30. As I have outlined above, recent clashes in Kosovo have led to further displacement of civilian population which have borne the brunt of the fighting since March 1998. I urge parties in the Federal Republic of Yugoslavia to assure unhindered humanitarian access to all affected areas and to ensure the security of the relief personnel. I call also on international humanitarian organizations to intensify their efforts to provide relief to Kosovo's population. To achieve this, the international community must support these efforts by providing urgently the necessary resources for assistance in Kosovo, in order to prevent a major humanitarian disaster in the region.

S/1998/834/Add1, 21 September 1998

8.   Report of the Secretary-General, Annex, 21 September 1998

1. The past four weeks have been characterized by a sharp escalation of military operations in Kosovo, as a result of an offensive launched by the Serb forces against armed groups of Kosovo Albanians in the central, southern and western regions of the province. A number of armed clashes have also been reported along the Albanina-Yugoslav border.

2. In August, the Serb forces went on the offensive after the Kosovo Liberation Army (KLA) seized control of a part of Kosovo in July. The Serb army regained control of the principal roads of Kosovo and captured a number of towns previously viewed as KLA strongholds. Many KLA fighters discarded their weapons and escaped to Albania.

3.. Continued efforts of the international community aimed at a cessation of the hostilities and for resumption of the dialogue between Belgrade and Pristina have not resulted in any breakthrough. In early August, a document of the Contact Group, featuring options for a future status of Kosovo, was transmitted to the two belligerents. No binding opinions of the said proposals have so far been forwarded by either of the opposing parties.

4. Although the invitation of the authorities of the Federal Republic of Yugoslavia to start negoations over the future status of the Kosovo province have been submitted to the Albanian leaders in Kosovo, no substantial talks have begun, mainly because of the continuing military offensive in Kosovo.

S/1998/912

9.   Report of the Secretary-General, 3 October 1998

...

II.   SECURITY COUNCIL COMMITTEE ESTABLISHED PURSUANT TO RESOLUTION 1160 (1998)

2. As at 2 October 1998, a total of 51 States, listed in my earlier reports (S/1998/608, S/1998/712 and S/1998/834), as well as Ireland and the Russian Federation, had reported to the Committee established pursuant to paragraph 9 of Security Council resolution 1160 (1998), in accordance with paragraph 12 of that resolution, on the steps they had taken to give effect to the prohibitions imposed by the same resolution. In a note verbale dated 15 September 1998, the Permanent Mission of Austria to the United Nations, on behalf of the European Union, transmitted to the Chairman of the Committee the second special report from the European Community Monitoring Mission containing its observations pertaining to the Albania/Kosovo border.

3. It will be recalled that on 21 July 1998, the Security Council adopted resolution 1186 (1998), by which it mandated the United Nations Preventive Deployment Force (UNPREDEP) to perform tasks of monitoring the border areas and to report to me on illicit arms flows and other activities that are prohibited under resolution 1160 (1998). In this connection I would like to refer to paragraph 5 of my previous report (S/1998/834) and to inform the Council that I have not yet received any suggestions on the establishment of an integrated coordinating mechanism of which UNPREDEP would form a part.

III. SITUATION IN KOSOVO

4. The present report is based on information regarding the situation on the ground from the Chairman-in-Office of the Organization for Security and Cooperation in Europe (OSCE), the European Union, the North Atlantic Treaty Organization (NATO), the Contact Group and individual Member States. My Special Representative for Children and Armed Conflict, Olara A. Otunnu, and the United Nations High Commissioner for Refugees, Sadako Ogata, visited the region from 10 to 12 September and from 24 to 29 September respectively and reported to me on their findings. As the present report was being finalized, the Secretariat received a factual report from NATO on the military situation in Kosovo following the adoption of resolution 1199 (1998). The information provided therein is reflected in the report. Reports have also been received from the Kosovo Diplomatic Observer

Mission. In addition to other information provided (see annex), the Chairman-in-Office of OSCE indicated to me that, despite a number of approaches, the authorities of the Federal Republic of Yugoslavia had not changed their position vis-à-vis the earlier requests of OSCE, including the acceptance of the mission of Felipe González or prospective OSCE missions, including one in Kosovo.

Hostilities

5. During the reporting period, fighting in Kosovo continued unabated. Government security forces conducted offensives in the various parts of Kosovo, including the areas of Licovac, Glogovac and Cicavica. In the week following the adoption, on 23 September 1998, of resolution 1199 (1998), the forces in fact intensified their operations, launching another offensive in the Drenica region and in the Suva Reka-Stimlje-Urosevac triangle. Those operations have reportedly resulted in the displacement of some 20,000 additional people. Smaller operations were conducted by the Serbian security forces in the Prizren area. Fighting continued on 28 and 29 September, contrary to the statement of the Serbian Prime Minister, Mr. Marjanovic, on 28 September, that anti-insurgency operations in Kosovo had been completed and that peace reigned in Kosovo.

6. Military activity seemed to wind down in the last days of September. There was evidence of heavily armoured formations returning to their barracks. On 29 September, Federal Minister for Foreign Affairs Zivadin Jovanovic assured me that troops were returning to the places of their permanent location. According to the most recent reports, military forces withdrew from the Drenica and Prizren areas on 1 October and observers indicated a decrease in activities of the security forces. However, the Secretariat is still receiving information that the Government's armed presence remains significant and that the operations of the special police continue.

7. The desperate situation of the civilian population remains the most disturbing aspect of the hostilities in Kosovo. I am particularly concerned that civilians increasingly have become the main target in the conflict. Fighting in Kosovo has resulted in a mass displacement of civilian populations, the extensive destruction of villages and means of livelihood and the deep trauma and despair of displaced populations. Many villages have been destroyed by shelling and burning following operations conducted by federal and Serbian government forces. There are concerns that the disproportionate use of force and actions of the security forces are designed to terrorize and subjugate the population, a collective punishment to teach them that the price of supporting the Kosovo Albanian paramilitary units is too high and will be even higher in future. The Serbian security forces have demanded the surrender of weapons and have been reported to use terror and violence against civilians to force people to flee their homes or the places where they had sought refuge, under the guise of separating them from fighters of the Kosovo Albanian paramilitary units. The tactics include shelling, detentions and threats to life, and finally short-notice demands to leave or face the consequences. There have been disruptions in electricity and other services, and empty dwellings have been burned and looted, abandoned farm vehicles have been destroyed, and farm animals have been burned in their barns or shot in the fields. For example, international observers witnessed Serb troops looting and burning houses in the Suva Reka area on 27 September.

8. The level of destruction points clearly to an indiscriminate and disproportionate use of force against civilian populations. As of mid-September, an estimated 6,000 to 7,000 buildings in 269 villages had been severely damaged or destroyed by shelling and deliberate burning in the Serb forces' main areas of operations. Information available to me from reliable sources covered only villages - not cities - in western and central Kosovo. If the rate of destruction observed in the first two weeks of September were to continue, an estimated total of 9,000 homes in nearly 300 settlements would be uninhabitable (without significant reconstruction) by early November.

Human rights

9. I am outraged by reports of mass killings of civilians in Kosovo, which recall the atrocities committed in Bosnia and Herzegovina. Following reports concerning the killing of 20 Kosovo Albanian internally displaced persons in Gornje Obrinje in the central Drenica area on 28 September, a Kosovo Diplomatic Observer Mission team

witnessed at least 14 bodies, some severely mutilated. Most were children and women at ages ranging from 18 months to 95 years. The Serb authorities denied any involvement of the police force in those atrocities. However, further killings of Kosovo civilians were reported, including the alleged summary execution of some 12 to 23 males (accounts vary) in the Golubovac area on 27 September. The Kosovo Diplomatic Observer Mission conducted a preliminary investigation in the area and observed pools of blood in the dirt, tools presumably used to stab the victims and small-calibre shell casings.

10. While the victims of the conflict are overwhelmingly ethnic Albanians, Kosovo Serbs are suffering as well. There have been a number of reports of the kidnapping and killing of Serbian and Albanian civilians by Kosovo Albanian paramilitary units. The village of Zocite, which was once half-Serb and half-Kosovo Albanian, now has only 30 Serbs, and 80 per cent of the houses were burned and destroyed during the period of several months when the village was under the control of Kosovo Albanian paramilitary units. Mass graves of Serbs were discovered in Klecka, Glodjane and Ratis. The Kosovo Diplomatic Observer Mission investigated the latest mass grave in Glodjane. The ambushing of members of the security forces by the Kosovo Albanian paramilitary units has led to reprisals, not only by the Serbian authorities, but also by armed Serb civilians, against the innocent population.

<u>Humanitarian situation</u>

11. The pattern of displacement is fast-changing and unpredictable as people flee in response to the actions and real or perceived threats of the security forces. Even though there have been some returns, the Office of the United Nations High Commissioner for Refugees (UNHCR) estimates that more than 200,000 persons remain displaced in Kosovo and some 80,000 are in neighbouring countries and other parts of Serbia. Shifting operations by Serb security forces and the Yugoslav army have continued to uproot new groups of Kosovars and to keep relief efforts off-balance. Although reporting indicated that approximately 30,000 to 50,000 internally displaced persons in Kosovo had recently returned to their homes, the total number of internally displaced persons remains unchanged, offset by the most recent government offensives. International monitors have been told that displaced persons are refusing to return home because of their fear of reprisals, and a number of displaced people have been arrested by the security forces upon returning home.

12. In Albania, while the estimated number of refugees is relatively small (some 20,000), the political and economic impact of their presence is clearly felt. The poor infrastructure and rampant lawlessness in some areas magnify the impact of the arrival of refugees. The harsh winter and insecurity in Bajram Curri led to the closure of the UNHCR office there, where only 2,500 refugees remain. The High Commissioner requested a quick decision on the allocation of land and buildings for collective accommodation in more suitable locations. The internal situation in Albania, however, is likely to delay this allocation and the adoption of legislation on refugees.

13. With 45,000 recent arrivals from Kosovo, Montenegro now has about the same number of displaced persons as at the height of the war in 1993 - some 12 per cent of the population. The High Commissioner for Refugees told President Djukanovic that while the reasons for the closure of the border with Kosovo announced on 11 September were understandable, she urged him to reverse the decision. President Djukanovic gave assurances that the decision would be implemented flexibly, with individual situations considered. He also gave assurances that there would be no more forced returns to Kosovo or expulsions to Albania. The High Commissioner pledged additional support for assistance programmes and noted a positive response to the August 1998 inter-agency appeal for the Kosovo crisis.

14. There are some 7,000 Kosovo Albanian asylum-seekers in Bosnia and Herzegovina, and the number continues to rise. The Government has finally adopted an instruction on the treatment of asylum-seekers. Finding satisfactory accommodation is now the main problem, given the already very heavy pressure on housing.

15. In the former Yugoslav Republic of Macedonia there are an estimated 3,000 to 5,000 Kosovo Albanians whose presence is directly linked to the conflict. Citizens of the Federal Republic of Yugoslavia

do not need an entry visa for a two-month stay, and the Government has just formally agreed to regularize the status of those who have exceeded this period. Some 500 persons have approached UNHCR and its partners for assistance. A large-scale influx is thought unlikely but cannot be excluded.

16. The Government claims that some 100,000 refugees have returned to their homes (independent estimates are some 30,000 to 50,000) and has pledged to facilitate the process of returns. At present, the authorities have opened 12 centres around Kosovo to provide assistance to internally displaced persons. In some of them, ethnic Albanians are employed. An immediate and fundamental change in the Serbian authorities' approach is, however, essential. Without it, indicators of different stages in the underlying cycle of violence and repression - for example, the end of one offensive, fluctuations in the number of those affected, displaced or without shelter or returnees - will have only short-term significance. The current policy and methods used by the authorities predictably cause large-scale and often repeated displacement and a well-founded fear of mistreatment by the security forces upon return. Many internally displaced persons were reportedly prevented from returning to their homes and were forced to move elsewhere. There are a number of reports of detentions and arrests of able-bodied men, some of whom are still unaccounted for. Such an attitude, combined with information about atrocities committed against civilians, has generated fear among many internally displaced persons, preventing them from returning. Thus, the absence of adequate security remains the main obstacle to return.

17. With only a few weeks before the onset of winter, the issue of the return of displaced persons and refugees remains one of the most pressing issues. Some 50,000 internally displaced persons currently lack shelter or any support network, and are ill-prepared for inclement winter weather that may arrive as early as next month. The priority of any humanitarian strategy should be to assist these people. Children and the elderly will almost certainly risk death from exposure if they remain at their current locations - especially the ones at higher elevations - into the winter.

18. While the major focus is on immediate needs, such as the return of internally displaced persons and the provision of urgent assistance to those still living in the open air, it is also necessary to address broader humanitarian issues. As most of the displaced persons in Kosovo are staying with families, assistance has to be provided to a much broader segment of the population. The host families that support most of them are beginning to deplete their personal food stocks. In this regard, an important element, in addition to providing assistance to local host families, is the removal of an unofficial blockade of Kosovo by the Serbian authorities.

19. The Government has appealed to internally displaced persons, encouraging them to return. However, after six months of hostilities, mere declarations appear to be insufficient to ensure their return. The Government of the Federal Republic of Yugoslavia must be made to assume its full responsibility of guaranteeing security for returnees as well as punishing those responsible for previous abuses and destruction.

20. I welcome the good intentions contained in the conclusions of the National Assembly of the Republic of Serbia, adopted on 28 September, regarding the speedy resolution of all humanitarian problems in Kosovo, including the reconstruction of damaged houses and the adoption of concrete measures for health care as well as the overall normalization of the economy and supply. The National Assembly also indicated that the Government of Serbia would continue to cooperate fully with the International Committee of the Red Cross (ICRC) and UNHCR with the basic goal of reducing as much as possible humanitarian problems and eliminating them soon through joint and concerted efforts, and would ensure the ability of humanitarian agencies to work unhindered. I am looking forward to seeing these assurances implemented in the most expeditious and effective way.

21. The United Nations High Commissioner for Refugees urged President Milosevic to stop the violence against civilians, the destruction and looting of deserted property and the random detention of able-bodied males. She stressed the importance of confidence-building measures such as amnesty, a reduction in the presence of a

highly visible and intimidating security force, an end to the de facto commercial blockade imposed in Kosovo and the restoration of essential services. However, even those measures would have little impact without evidence of a real change of heart and approach.

The humanitarian response

22. There has been a significant increase in operational capacity, and coordination is good on the ground. UNHCR has strengthened both this capacity and its presence in order to discharge its lead agency responsibilities effectively. Coordination with UNHCR non-governmental organization partners, with ICRC and with the Kosovo Diplomatic Observer Mission is of particular importance. UNHCR has a full-time liaison officer with the Mission.

23. Coordination with the provincial and local authorities and with representatives of the Kosovo Albanian community is no less important. The High Commissioner for Refugees underlined to President Milosevic that the beneficiaries must have confidence in the delivery of humanitarian assistance and that a key role had to be played by such agencies as the Mother Theresa Society.

24. Although aid agencies have significantly expanded their operations in Kosovo, total requirements are not being met because of the restrictive environment in which aid agencies operate. The security operations have continued to delay relief convoys travelling to populations in need until they have deemed an area "secure", have carried out protracted shelling of targets in close proximity to large groups of internally displaced persons and have displayed extremely heavy-handed behaviour when dealing with displaced persons. While overall freedom of movement for humanitarian agencies and international observers has improved, it does not apply to internally displaced persons or, in certain cases, to journalists. Moreover, continued fighting and security operations in the area have impeded the access of monitors and the delivery of humanitarian aid. There is an urgent need for non-governmental organizations to be given access and for clearance to be granted for humanitarian supplies. To date, non-governmental organizations have been denied radio clearance, thereby jeopardizing the coordination of life-saving operations and personal security.

25. It has been reported that the Federal Republic of Yugoslavia has undertaken the systematic deployment of both anti-personnel and anti-tank landmines in the border areas with Albania and the former Yugoslav Republic of Macedonia. In the areas of fighting within Kosovo itself, however, there have so far been only isolated reports of the use of anti-personnel landmines. However, a Kosovo Diplomatic Observer Mission vehicle recently hit a mine, and on 1 October an ICRC vehicle ran into an anti-tank mine in the same area. Since the laying of landmines could become a trend, the early deployment of a United Nations Mine Action Service team could become necessary. It should be given clearance to assess the situation of landmines in conflict areas. This will be fundamental to the return process and will also help to ensure the safe and free movement of humanitarian personnel and international observers.

Political settlement

26. There is a need to create a favourable climate for the process of negotiating a political settlement of the Kosovo crisis. I welcome in this regard the efforts of the international community to bring about a political solution to the problem and support the efforts of the Contact Group, and in particular Ambassador Christopher Hill, to negotiate a political settlement between the Serb authorities and Kosovo Albanian leaders, of whom Dr. Rugova remains the most prominent figure, although his leadership is contested by the Albanian opposition and Kosovar paramilitary units. Following the discussion of the Kosovo issue at the meeting of the Contact Group in London on 2 October, the Chairman communicated to me his conclusions:

"The Contact Group is united and intends to be united. We expect full and immediate compliance with Security Council resolution 1199. This has not so far been achieved.

"We heard a report on the work of the U.S. facilitator, Ambassador Hill, on the negotiating track. We endorsed a revised paper which will now be put to the parties on behalf of the Contact Group.

"We are united in condemning what is happening on the ground and in support for humanitarian efforts.

"We all concluded that time is running out."

27. I support the Chairman's conclusions and believe that there is no alternative to a direct dialogue in search of a mutually acceptable settlement in the interest of all people of Kosovo and the Federal Republic of Yugoslavia. The consequences of the current repressive approach not only affect the immediate humanitarian situation, they also have a direct and major adverse impact on the prospects for a just and lasting political solution. Even once there is a fundamentally new approach by Belgrade, the task of correcting the very deep-rooted damage of the last years, and in particular the last months, will be enormous.

IV. OBSERVATIONS

28. In the last few weeks, the international community has witnessed appalling atrocities in Kosovo, reminiscent of the recent past elsewhere in the Balkans. These have been borne out by reporting by the Kosovo Diplomatic Observer Mission and other reliable sources. I reiterate my utter condemnation of such wanton killing and destruction. It is clear beyond any reasonable doubt that the great majority of such acts have been committed by security forces in Kosovo acting under the authority of the Federal Republic of Yugoslavia. But Kosovar Albanian paramilitary units have engaged in armed action also, and there is good reason to believe that they too have committed atrocities. All those involved in the killing and mistreatment of civilians and in the destruction of property must be brought to justice. There is a need for a thorough investigation, under effective international control or with international participation, of all reported cases of atrocities and violations of human rights.

29. The Security Council has reaffirmed the commitment of all Member States to the sovereignty and territorial integrity of the Federal Republic of Yugoslavia. The authorities of the Federal Republic of Yugoslavia have the inherent right, as well as the duty, to maintain public order and security and to respond to violent acts of provocation. However, this can in no way justify the systematic terror inflicted on civilians these past few days and weeks. It is the duty of security forces to give equal protection to all citizens, not to intimidate or murder them. It is equally necessary, as called for by the Security Council, for terrorist action, including the taking of hostages by Kosovar Albanian elements, to cease.

30. If the present state of affairs persists, thousands could die in the winter. In my earlier statements on the situation in Kosovo, I have emphasized this danger repeatedly and appealed to the international community to undertake urgent steps in order to prevent a humanitarian disaster. The possibilities of asylum outside Kosovo are ever more limited, and much of the shelter available clearly is inadequate for winter. Conditions must be created that would allow for the return of a significant number of internally displaced persons. This requires a radical change of policy and behaviour and the introduction of confidence-building measures - such as a withdrawal of police units, a declaration of amnesty and a release of prisoners. The Federal Republic of Yugoslavia authorities assert that such steps have already been taken. According to reports from the field, the withdrawal so far appears limited, and it would seem that the fear that led civilians to flee remains. For all internally displaced persons, the first priority is the restoration of security. The Government must restrain police excesses and give police instructions to respect international human rights conventions. Greater efforts are also required to improve access to prisoners taken by the authorities and to secure the release of, or accounting for, hostages taken by the Kosovar Albanian side.

31. It is my earnest hope that the negotiations between the Federal Republic of Yugoslavia and the Kosovo Albanian leadership will be resumed without delay and produce early agreements, and that they will result in the restoration of confidence that is needed for a return and resettlement of all those who have fled their homes in fear. Such agreements might also envisage more far-reaching steps, possibly even institutional reforms, to address long-term needs. If there is to be a role for the international community in assisting in the implementation of such agreements, it will require a proper assessment of needs that would take humanitarian as well as rehabilitation and reconstruction requirements fully into account. The necessary operational planning must be conducted, including an appropriate division of labour, and

effective implementation and coordination mechanisms. I would like to express my hope that these considerations will be borne in mind by those involved in the negotiations. It would in my view be useful, in this regard, to initiate consultations amongst international actors to prepare to face such a challenge, without necessarily awaiting the agreements. The United Nations is prepared to play an active role in such consultations.

32. I believe that action is urgently required on several fronts. The violence on all sides has to be brought to a halt. Full humanitarian access must be granted. Conditions need to be created that will enable refugees and internally displaced persons to return to their homes with confidence that they will not face harassment or worse. It is imperative that the international presence be strengthened and made more effective. In particular, it would be helpful if, in the immediate term, the Kosovo Diplomatic Observer Mission were brought to its full strength and if the presence of human rights observers were enhanced. Also, it will be essential to ensure the closest possible coordination of international efforts in the political, humanitarian and other fields. A broad range of options could be considered in that regard.

33. In the present report, as in previous ones issued pursuant to Security Council resolution 1160 (1998), I have had to rely largely on information and analysis from sources external to the United Nations. I am grateful for these contributions, which carry conviction and are reflected in the body of the report. But, unlike reports to the Council on missions or operations where the United Nations has a direct political presence on the ground, I do not have the means necessary to provide an independent assessment of compliance, as required by the Security Council in paragraph 15 of resolution 1199 (1998), other than on the humanitarian situation. Therefore, the Council may wish to make its own judgement in this respect on the basis of the present report. As the Council has affirmed in its resolution 1199 (1998), the deterioration in the situation in Kosovo, Federal Republic of Yugoslavia, constitutes a threat to peace and security in the region. It is widely recognized in the international community that the humanitarian crisis is a consequence of what is fundamentally a political problem, which requires a comprehensive political solution through a negotiated settlement.

34. While I fully share the sense of indignation and revulsion at what has been happening in Kosovo, the international community must never lose sight of the ultimate need for a comprehensive political solution. Otherwise, we shall be treating only the symptoms of the problem, and not its causes.

Annex
Information on the situation in Kosovo and measures taken by the Organization for Security and Cooperation in Europe
General situation

The period since the previous report (S/1998/834/Add.1) has been characterized by a decrease in military operations after the offensive against armed groups of Kosovo Albanians launched by Serb forces in August.

During the second half of August only limited military actions were observed. However, house-to-house searches were carried out and the number of mine accidents increased. In the first week of September the area of Kosovo bordering north-eastern Albania was relatively calm, but continued fighting was observed towards the south, on the outskirts of Djakovica and in villages nearby. During September Yugoslav forces continued to pound villages to stamp out any traces of resistance, the burning of houses continued in the area south of Prizren and military operations commenced in the area of Orahovac with a starting line at Zrze-Orahovac and moving west.

At the end of August, Kosovo Liberation Army (KLA) fighters admitted that because of serious setbacks and lack of success with previous tactics they would resort to "hit and run" operations. Similar views were presented by Adem Demaci, leader of the Parliamentary Party of Kosovo and recently appointed political representative of the Kosovo Liberation Army. In late August, he stated to the media that the group would now adopt classic guerrilla warfare tactics against Yugoslav targets after losing territory during the recent Serbian offensive.

At the beginning of September, the United States Ambassador to the former Yugoslav Republic of Macedonia and Peace Envoy, Christopher Hill, announced that an outline agreement had been reached between the Kosovo Albanians and the Belgrade authorities on the future of Kosovo.

The agreement, based on options featured in the document of the Contact Group, envisages a three-year stabilization and normalization period to allow for the re-establishment of democratic institutions. It was also agreed that indirect talks should continue, despite the fact that indirect talks had as yet been fruitless. Still, there is confusion as to just who the Kosovo Albanians making such an agreement represent. Hitherto, there has been little success in the attempts to persuade the Albanian Democratic Movement (LDS), a party created in late June 1998 and led by Mr. Rexhep Qosja, a former ally of Rugova, to join the negotiations. Moreover, the political representative of KLA, Mr. Demaci, sees any temporary agreement as a capitulation and has pledged to continue the fighting. But the fact that some returnees have handed over their weapons to Serb forces is seen as an indication that segments of the Albanian population are prepared to accept whatever interim political agreement is reached.

In this respect there are increasing indications of splits among Albanian fighting groups. With sharp divisions within the Kosovo Albanian ranks, the problem of just who represents them will likely continue and the prospects of a ceasefire called by KLA and the Serbian authorities currently appear remote.

Monitoring activities in Kosovo

The Kosovo Diplomatic Observer Mission has continued its activity despite the growing aversion on the part of Serb security forces and KLA. The Mission is composed of several tens of people representing European Union (EU) States, the United States of America, the Russian Federation and Canada. Every week there are about 50 to 60 observation trips and a report on the situation is presented and further accepted in Belgrade by the ambassadors of the Contact Group States (the United Kingdom of Great Britain and Northern Ireland, France, Italy, Germany, Russian Federation and the United States of America) and Austria (EU Presidency) and Poland (Chairmanship of the Organization for Security and Cooperation in Europe (OSCE)).

Regardless of the missions, Kosovo has been regularly visited by employees of embassies accredited to Belgrade. Also, politicians and diplomats on a visit to the Federal Republic of Yugoslavia used to go to Kosovo.

The situation of the civilian population

Fighting has forced more than 200,000 people to flee their homes. The situation is made worse by large-scale destruction of houses, food shortages and the risk of epidemic. The threat of humanitarian catastrophe is becoming ever more real. According to the Office of the United Nations High Commissioner for Refugees (UNHCR), large numbers of displaced persons, as many as 50,000, are today living out in the open in Kosovo. Many others are living in desperate conditions as entire villages have been destroyed, livestock slaughtered and fields burned.

Although great emphasis has been given recently to the return of displaced persons, the return process is hampered by the level of destruction in some villages, and, for those who can return to relatively undamaged areas, the issue of security is paramount. The presence of Serb security forces in many areas continues to create a feeling of insecurity on the part of those wishing to return.

Several cases of large-scale detentions have been reported on different occasions where men of fighting age suspected of being separatist guerrillas were separated from the women, children and elderly by police, backed by armoured vehicles, and taken to places of detention for interrogation.

Analysis of the Kosovo conflict spillover potential

As at 1 September, UNHCR was reporting a total of 14,000 refugees in Albania of which 7,000 remained in the Tropoja district, the rest having left for other parts of the country. Still, reliable statistics are difficult to compile owing to the fluid nature of the situation. According to Albanian sources there are about 7,500 registered refugees in the Bajram Curri area and 7,500 in central Albania, particularly in the Durrës area. Out of a total of 15,000 persons (6,100 families), about 1,000 live in accommodations provided by the Government and the rest live with ordinary families.

The relative decrease in incoming refugees during the summer in the Tropoja and Has districts was caused by the tightening of the border by Yugoslav forces: the creation of a cordon sanitaire along the border west of Djakovica (Deane-Ponoevac-Djakovica road and Deane-Skrivljan-Djakovica road), heavier controls by the Yugoslav authorities on the routes over the mountains and the laying of mines. The need for refugees to find more arduous routes through this area in order to avoid detection resulted in many refugees trying to enter Albania through Montenegro. It was estimated that, by the end of August, approximately 100 to 120 refugees a day were entering the Shkodr-Koplik area through Montenegro. During the first two weeks of September, the number of refugees crossing into Albania increased steadily, indicating an opening of safe corridors through the border.

The readiness of the local population to accommodate a vast majority of the refugees, mainly elderly people, women and children, largely facilitated the immediate handling of the major influx. However, it put further strain on the local Albanian population already living under difficult or even harsh economic and social conditions. Evidence suggests that the absorption capacities are exhausted. This underlines the importance of establishing appropriate shelter facilities, preferably in other parts of Albania, in order to alleviate current and potential needs before the winter.

In this respect, in the first week of September, the Kosovo refugee issue was discussed in the Albanian Parliament, and the respective parliamentary commissions severely criticized the Government for failing to take measures to accommodate the refugees from Kosovo, particularly with winter approaching.

According to the latest figures, the number of refugees in Montenegro (640,000 inhabitants) exceeds 45,000, which have to be added to the 30,000 refugees from Bosnia and Herzegovina and Croatia. The Podgorïca authorities have begun the organized transport of about 3,000 refugees from Kosovo to Albania across the unofficial Vrmos border crossing some three kilometres from Plav (south-east of Montenegro).

Numerous incidents between KLA units and the Yugoslav army and Serb police have been reported in the border areas. Many attempts have been recorded of the illegal crossing of the border by armed Albanians. The Federal Republic of Yugoslavia and Albania have accused one another of causing incidents on the border and of shooting in the other State's territory.

Measures taken by the Organization for Security and Cooperation in Europe
On 18 August 1998, in a letter addressed to the Foreign Minister of the Federal Republic of Yugoslavia, Mr. Jovanovic, the OSCE Representative on Freedom of the Media, Mr. Duve, expressed his concerns over lack of access for foreign journalists intending to cover events in Yugoslavia in a number of instances, considered as serious incidents and not consistent with OSCE principles and commitments. On 27 August, Mr. Duve addressed the Permanent Council of OSCE, recalling the letters sent to the Yugoslav Foreign Minister and urging the Belgrade authorities to allow unimpeded access to the media to cover the events in the country, especially in Kosovo.

On 3 September 1998, Ambassador Hill addressed the OSCE Permanent Council in Vienna and assessed the current situation in the region, elaborating on the prospects for a negotiated settlement to the crisis in Kosovo. He made it very clear that violence must stop and that there can only be a peaceful solution to the problems of Kosovo, but emphasizing also that the search for political solutions should not be conditioned by the continued violence and that pursuing diplomatic action cannot wait until a ceasefire is called.

On the political negotiations, Ambassador Hill informed the Permanent Council that a new Albanian negotiating team composed of moderate and more radical Albanian participants had reached an agreement based on options featured in the document of the Contact Group. The agreement envisages a three-year stabilization and normalization period to allow for the re-establishment of democratic institutions, and after this period new approaches could be envisaged. He stressed the crucial importance of the international presence in Kosovo during the implementation period and the important role OSCE had to play in the area.

In her address to the Permanent Council on the same day, United States Secretary of State Madeleine Albright elaborated on the same issue, stating that she foresaw a special role for OSCE in a possible negotiated settlement of the Kosovo conflict, especially with regard to elections.

In its continued efforts to monitor the situation on the borders of Albania and the former Yugoslav Republic of Macedonia with the Federal Republic of Yugoslavia, on 10 September the OSCE Permanent Council approved supplementary budgets for the continued enhancement of the OSCE presence in Albania and the OSCE Spillover Monitor Mission to Skopje.

S/1998/966 19 October 1998

10.   Letter from the Secretary-General to the President of the Security Council, 14 October 1998

As you will recall, in your statement to the press on 6 October 1998 on behalf of the Security Council, you asked me to consider how to ensure that the Secretariat had a first-hand capability to assess developments on the ground, and to continue reporting to the Council on compliance with its resolutions 1160 (1998) and 1199 (1998).

Following consultations with the authorities of the Federal Republic of Yugoslavia, I wish to inform the Security Council of my intention to send an interdepartmental mission, headed by Staffan de Mistura, to the Federal Republic of Yugoslavia to look into these matters. In view of the proposed deployment of Organization for Security and Cooperation in Europe (OSCE) monitors in Kosovo to observe compliance, the mission will also assess possible modalities for coordination of activities between OSCE and United Nations agencies on the ground.

(Signed) Kofi A. ANNAN

[*For further Reports, see Chapter* 13.]

Chapter 9: Sanctions, Political Action of the European Union and Contact Group Decisions

UN and EU/EC Sanctions

Given the legal, moral and political uncertainties of military action, sanctions remain the international tool of choice when seeking to constrain a government to conform with key principles of the international constitution. In the absence of alternatives, the fact that the population of an offending state, rather than the government, mostly suffers from the consequences of sanctions is still accepted as a necessary evil, although a few sanctions, such as travel restrictions, have recently been directed specifically at public officials. While provision was made for the use of sanctions from the inception of the UN Charter, they had been rarely employed at the universal level since 1945. In view of the automatic deadlock in the Security Council, states, or rather blocks of states or alliances, used sanctions and trade restrictions outside of the UN framework quite extensively during the Cold War years. Obviously, the powerful industrialized states principally employed this technique of economic confrontation, although Western enthusiasm for this weapon waned temporarily when the Arab nations adopted an oil embargo against states cooperating with Israel in the 1970s. In principle, of course, a state is free to determine its own economic and trading relations with other states. However, the universal framework of international economic law, now principally focussed on the WTO/GATT, restricts this freedom. In addition, most states will have in place bilateral and other international arrangements with specific states, committing them to certain conduct in their mutual economic relations. The adoption of sanctions obviously interferes with these legal obligations. Such interference can be justified under four conditions:

1. A state may respond to a wrong done to it by another state. Such limited countermeasures (now generally subject to WTO/GATT rules) characterize relations even among allies, for example the US and the European Union and its members.

2. A regional organization may impose sanctions, at least against its own members. If are directed at the outside world, the states adopting sanctions will only be protected from counter-claims against the disruption of trade they may have caused if their action is also covered by one of the two remaining justifications below.

3. States may, and perhaps must, adopt sanctions in response to violations of international constitutional law of fundamental importance to the international system as a whole. Hence, a state cannot be held legally responsible for disrupting trading relations with another which is engaging in international aggression, apartheid, genocide, etc. However, some would argue that, in order to prevent abuse of this doctrine which leaves it to individual states to 'auto-interpret' when such a situation exists, sanctions should only be adopted pursuant to a Security Council decision, or perhaps confirmation by the UN General Assembly that such a severe violation has taken place, should the Council be unable to act due to the veto.

4. Finally, the Security Council can take Chapter VII measures, imposing sanctions. All member states of the United Nations are legally required to implement such sanctions, and even non-members (Switzerland) will generally cooperate. According to Article 103 of the UN Charter, states are not liable for damages resulting from the adoption of UN mandated sanctions.

Up to 1990, United Nations sanctions adopted under Chapter VII remained few and far between. Only with respect to the outcasts, Southern Rhodesia and South Africa, could the Cold War veto be overcome and limited sanctions were imposed. However, since 1990, United Nations sanctions have proliferated, starting with resolution 661 (1990), which imposed very comprehensive sanctions against Iraq and occupied Kuwait. In relation to the former Yugoslavia, the Council initially only adopted an arms embargo in Resolution 713 (1991), somewhat oddly with the express consent of the target state. However, when conflict broke out in Bosnia and Herzegovina, the rump-Yugoslavia and its client in Bosnia and Herzegovina were subjected to a Security Council sanctions regime which was in some ways even more comprehensive than the Iraq/Kuwait sanctions. Given the initial reluctance to intervene in the Bosnian crisis with military means, the prospect of lifting sanctions remained one of the few tools at the disposal of the international community to influence decision-makers in Belgrade. A somewhat symbolic suspension of sanctions occurred in October 1994, when Belgrade undertook to cease its armed support for the Bosnian Serbs.[1] Controversially, the remaining sanctions were suspended,[2] and finally terminated[3] when the rump-Yugoslavia signed and implemented the Dayton Accords on Bosnia. This total suspension and termination is controversial, inasmuch as this included the arms embargo, despite the fact that Yugoslavia/Serbia remained engaged in an increasingly violent campaign of repression in Kosovo. In fact, to Kosovo politicians, the failure to consider Kosovo when Dayton was signed and implemented appeared to confirm the abandonment by the international community of the Kosovo

---

[1] Resolution 943 (1994), adopted 23 September 1994, effective 5 October 1994.
[2] Resolution 1021 (1995), 22 November 1995.
[3] Resolution 1074, 1 October 1996.

issue. The more radical elements in the province were strengthened as a result. After all, it appeared that international attention and action would only be forthcoming in situations of extreme crisis, threatening the region as a whole or imposing great suffering on civilian populations. By March 1998, such a crisis existed. In response, the Security Council prohibited the sale or supply of arms and related equipment to the Federal Republic of Yugoslavia, including Kosovo and established a Committee to monitor compliance. In accordance with standard practice, a 'sanctions committee' composed of members of the Council and chaired by Celso L.N. Amorim of Brazil was set up. That Committee received reports from governments indicating the measures they had taken to implement the sanctions in their domestic law. In addition, the UN Secretary-General and the Committee drew upon the European institutions to help report on the importation of arms and other proscribed items into the FRY, including Kosovo. The EU, through its monitoring mission in the former Yugoslavia (ECMM), the Western European Union, which had a small presence in Albania, NATO, which also was present in Albania and in Bosnia and Herzegovina, the UN Preventative Deployment force in Macedonia (UNPREDEP), and the Danube Commission all pledged to offer assistance, although none was in a position to offer a comprehensive monitoring mission.[4] Steps were taken, however, to coordinate the monitoring efforts of these various agencies.

Despite media reports indicating otherwise, the international monitoring presence was unable to detect violations of the embargo by Yugoslavia. It did, however, receive consistent allegations of a flow of arms and other items across the Albanian border into Kosovo. It was informed by the Governments of Germany, Switzerland and Sweden that attempts were made to investigate ethnic Albanian fund-raising activities in these states, although no conclusive evidence had been found that such activities related to the acquisition of arms for the Kosovo Liberation Army (KLA).[5] As was indicated in the previous chapter, it was precisely the fact that the Rugova government refused to fund the KLA which led to considerable tension between the two bodies. However, as the conflict progressed, the KLA reportedly established its own fund-raising structure in Europe and the United States.

While the Security Council failed to respond with a tightening of sanctions when Yugoslavia increased military operations, instead of complying with the demands expressed in resolution 1160 (1998), some further action was taken at the European level. However, this occurred in a strangely haphazard and half-hearted way, given the emerging dimensions of the humanitarian crisis. The European Union/Community in fact had kept in place its own arms embargo, even after Dayton, to ensure the safety of the international peace-keeping mission in Bosnia and parts of Croatia.[6] Of course, this did not prevent the FRY from replenishing its stocks, especially from Eastern Europe and in particular from Russia. When the Security Council re-imposed the arms embargo at the universal level, the European Union/Community adopted additional sanctions. In addition to arms, non-lethal police equipment was included. There was a moratorium on government financed export credit support for trade and investment, including financing for privatisation in Serbia, and a list of senior Serb officials who would be prevented from entering the territories of member states.[7] A freezing of Yugoslav/Serb state funds and of investment in Serbia was added, when there had been no compliance with the demands of the UN Security Council and the Union,[8] and there was a ban of flights by Yugoslav carriers to and from territories of members of the Union/Community.[9] That ban was not implemented by all EU member states with similar enthusiasm. The United Kingdom, in particular, found reason not to comply immediately.

EU Political Action and the Contact Group

The initial Yugoslav crisis was supposed to have been the test case for European conflict management. The failure to influence the conflict significantly, until in the end the United States took over its management and force was used in the autumn of 1995, left a strong impression on the Europeans. However, towards the end of the decade, a new generation of leaders was taking over power in Europe, including crucially in the United Kingdom, France and Germany. Another attempt at European crisis management was to be made, this time focused on Kosovo, and in careful coordination with the United States and also Russia. Those two states were part of the 'Contact Group', also consisting of France, Germany, Italy and the United Kingdom.

The European Union had maintained in place its small civilian observer mission in the former Yugoslavia (ECMM). This group had become the symbol of European inaction or ineffectiveness, its members being clad in pure white attire, observing passively (and, to the outside world, silently) the ethnic cleansing and probable genocide in Croatia and Bosnia and Herzegovia. The EU also appointed Mr Felipe Gonzales as its Special Representative in this matter, who failed to make

---

[4] See the documents annexed to the UNSG Reports of 4 June 1998, Document 8.3; 2 July 1998, Document 8.4.

[5] Report of the Chairman of the Committee established pursuant to Resolution 1160 (1998), 26 February 1999, Document 9.A.14.

[6] Common Position, 26 February 1996, Document 9.A.3 [the relevant regulations are also reproduced in this Chapter].

[7] Common Position, 19 March 1998, Document 9.A.5.

[8] Common Positions, 7 May 1998, Document 9.A.7; 8 June 1998, Document 9.A.8.

[9] Common Position, 29 June 1998, Document 9.A.10. The implementation of the associated regulation was somewhat controversially delayed by the UK government.

much of an impact, being refused access by Belgrade.[10] The EU also repeatedly called upon both parties to the conflict to exercise restraint, and to engage in meaningful dialogue about a political settlement. In that context, it continued to emphasize the need to retain the territorial integrity of the FRY. By June 1998, the EU condemned the "wide-spread house-burning and indiscriminate artillery attacks of whole villages [indicating] a new level of aggression on the part of the Serb security forces." It expressly identified these practices as the beginning of a new phase of ethnic cleansing.[11] The EU also threatened the imposition of tough measures against the FRY/Serbia, but as was noted above, its sanctions actually remained quite limited. There was, however, a veiled threat of the use of force, although at that stage, it seemed to the Union that such measures would require a Chapter VII mandate.[12] The demands of the Cardiff European Council, which included a cessation of operations by security forces affecting civilian populations and also the withdrawals of such forces, were later found almost verbatim in Security Council Resolution 1199 (1998). This was balanced by a condemnation of "violent attacks and acts of terrorism" and a declaration that "the European Union remains firmly opposed to independence".

Just as the EU anticipated the demands made by the Security Council, the Contact Group, too, maintained a close relationship with the universal layer of collective security administered by the United Nations. The Contact Group combined three elements of persuasion. Russia was perceived as a state which could 'deliver Milosevic' due to its general support for the position of the FRY/Serbia. The EU members would be able to dangle in front of Belgrade the prospect of closer economic integration with Europe, and direct financial incentives. The United States would come to represent the driving force behind tougher action, including the possibility of the use of military force. All three combined could virtually guarantee that the Security Council would back their joint demands, inasmuch as four out of the five permanent members were represented in the Contact Group. The Group, initially established to help address the Bosnian issue, had taken an incidental interest in Kosovo in September 1997, when the first portents of wider hostilities began to emerge.[13] In January 1998, before the first news of massacres of ethnic Albanian villagers seeped out, the Group condemned both violent repression and terrorist action and urged dialogue. In March, it also condemned the excessive use of force by Serbian police against civilians.[14] Oddly, and in deference to Russia, it termed the military attacks on ethnic Albanian villages and their destruction "large scale police actions". On the other hand, the Contact Group continued to identify the armed opposition in Kosovo as terrorists. The Contact Group statement also had to note that Russia was unwilling to endorse a call for the denial of visas for senior FRY and Serbian representatives responsible for repressive action by FRY Security forces in Kosovo, and a moratorium for government finance export credit support for Yugoslavia. However, this position was to be reviewed, should Belgrade fail to cease the actions of its special police units and withdraw them, permit humanitarian access and commence dialogue with the ethnic Albanians. However, when Belgrade failed to comply within 10 days, or indeed, throughout the summer of 1998, no further action was taken within the Contact Group (and hence also not in the Security Council), and the EU/EC had to adopt limited economic sanctions outside of that framework. Instead, states were urged by the Contact Group to take action to curb the supply of what were now called "armed Albanian groups" with funds and supplies.[15] While the Contact Group was reduced to reiterating its demands, which were to be recast in the form of Security Council Resolution 1199 (1998), it also set in motion the accelerated efforts of what was to become the Hill process of negotiations. However, by October, when the NATO threat of the use of force was looming in view of the continuing humanitarian crisis, the Contact Group could only agree a three paragraph document reiterating its previous positions.[16] At the conclusion of the Contact Group meeting of 8 October, the UK Foreign Secretary could only point to "good and frank discussions" which had confirmed "a degree of unity and resolve" of all members of the Group.[17] On the other hand, he could also claim somewhat daringly that Russia would be contented to endorse the results of Richard Holbroke's diplomatic mission, despite the threat of the use of force by NATO, provided the outcome would be recast into a Security Council resolution.

---

[10] Council Conclusion on Kosovo, 31 March 1998, Document 9.B.1; Joint Action, 8 June 1998, Document 9.B.4. He had undertaken a similar mission for the OCSE as its Chairman in Office in 1996.

[11] Declaration on Kosovo, 11 June 1998, Document 9.B.5.

[12] "… to consider all options, including those which would require and authorization by the UNSC under Chapter VII". *Id.*

[13] Statement, 24 September 1997, Document 9.D.1.

[14] Statement, 9 March 1999, Document 9.D.4.

[15] Statement, 8 July 1998, Document 9.D.7.

[16] These were only 'Chairman's Conclusions', instead of the usual joint statement, 2 October 1998, Document 9.D.7.

[17] 8 October 1998, Document 9.D.9.

A.   European Union Sanctions

Official journal NO. L 227 , 22/09/1995, 495X0378, 95/378/CFSP

1.   Common Position on extension of suspension of restrictions on trade with FRY, 19 September 1995

THE COUNCIL OF THE EUROPEAN UNION,
Having regard to the Treaty on European Union, and in particular Article J.2 thereof,
    Having regard to Resolutions 943 (1994), 970 (1995), 988 (1995), 1003 (1995) and 1015 (1995) adopted on 23 September 1994, 12 January 1995, 21 April 1995, 5 July 1995 and 15 September (1995) respectively by the United Nations Security Council,
HAS DEFINED THE FOLLOWING COMMON POSITION:
Article 1. In accordance with Resolutions 943 (1994), 970 (1995), 988 (1995), 1003 (1995) and 1015 (1995) adopted on 23 September 1994, 12 January 1995, 21 April 1995, 5 July 1995 and 15 September (1995) respectively by the United Nations Security Council, the suspension of certain restrictions on trade with the Federal Republic of Yugoslavia (Serbia and Montenegro) will be extended. ...

Official journal NO. L 297 , 09/12/1995 P. 0004 - 0004, 495X0511, 95/511/CFSP

2.   Common Position on suspension of restrictions on trade with FRY and Bosnian Serbs, 4 December 1995

THE COUNCIL OF THE EUROPEAN UNION,
Having regard to the Treaty on European Union, and in particular Article J.2 thereof,
    Having regard to Resolution 1022 (1995) adopted by the United Nations Security Council on 22 November 1995,
HAS DEFINED THE FOLLOWING COMMON POSITION:
Article 1. The restrictions concerning economic and financial relations with the Federal Republic of Yugoslavia (Serbia and Montenegro) and with the Bosnian Serbs will be suspended in accordance with the provisions of Resolution 1022 (1995) adopted by the United Nations Security Council on 22 November 1995. ...

Official journal NO. L 058 , 07/03/1996 P. 0001 - 0002, 496X0184 96/184/CFSP

3.   Common Position on arms exports to the former Yugoslavia, 26 February 1996

THE COUNCIL OF THE EUROPEAN UNION,
Having regard to the Treaty on European Union, and in particular Article J.2 thereof,
    Having regard to Resolution No 1021 adopted on 22 November 1995 by the United Nations Security Council,
Whereas the European Community and its Member States decided on 5 July 1991 to impose an embargo on armaments and military equipment applicable to the whole of Yugoslavia,
HAS DEFINED THE FOLLOWING COMMON POSITION:
1. With a view to establishing peace and stability for the people of the region of the former Yugoslavia, and in particular taking into account the need to ensure the safety of the international troops and civilian personnel deployed in Bosnia and Herzegovina and Croatia during the implementation of the peace agreement, the European Union believes that restraint on the part of exporting countries will be needed even after the UN arms embargo on the States of the former Yugoslavia is lifted in accordance with UN Security Council Resolution No 1021.
2. The Council of the European Union therefore decides that:
    (i) during the period of the deployment of IFOR and UNTAES, as well as other operations including IPTF, the EU embargo on arms, munitions and military equipment[1] will be maintained towards Bosnia and Herzegovina, Croatia and the Federal Republic of Yugoslavia. Transfers of equipment needed for demining activities

are not covered by this embargo. Member States will inform the Council of these transfers;
    (ii) subject to the provisions of UN Security Council Resolution No 1021[2] export licence applications to Slovenia and the former Yugoslav Republic of Macedonia (Fyrom) shall be considered on a case-by-case basis. This provision is adopted on the understanding that the Member States will show restraint in their arms export policy toward Slovenia and the former Republic of Macedonia (Fyrom) based on the common criteria for arms exports contained in the 28 and 29 June 1991 Luxembourg European Council and the 26 and 27 June 1992 Lisbon European Council conclusions. They will also take into account the objectives of the European Union policy in the region, fundamentally aimed at pacification and stabilization in the area, including the need for arms control and reduction to the lowest level and confidence building measures;
    (iii) the European Union will deploy efforts to encourage other countries to adopt a similar policy of restraint.
3. This common position shall be reexamined before the end of the deployment of IFOR and UUNTAES.
4. This common position shall enter into force on 13 March 1996. ...

[1] The abovementioned embargo covers weapons designed to kill and their ammunition, weapons platforms, non-weapons platforms and ancillary equipment as listed in the EC embargo list of 8 and 9 July 1991. The embargo also covers spare parts, repairs, transfer of military technology and contracts entered into prior to the onset of the embargo.
[2] Paragraph 1 of UN Security Council Resolution No 1021 provides that the delivery of heavy weapons (as defined in the peace agreement), ammunition therefor, mines, military aircraft and helicopters shall continue to be prohibited to all the former Yugoslav Republics during the second 90 days following the submission of the Secretary-General's report on the formal signature of the peace agreement and until the arms control agreement referred to in Annex 1b has taken effect. After the submission of a report from the Secretary-General on the implementation of Annex 1b (agreement on regional stabilization) as agreed by the parties, all provisions of the UN arms embargo terminate unless the Security Council decides otherwise.
[*Amended by 398D0498 (OJ L 225 12.08.98 p.1), below.*]

Official journal NO. L 328 , 18/12/1996 P. 0005 - 0005, 496X0708

4.   Common Position on termination of restrictions on economic and financial relations, 9 December 1996

THE COUNCIL OF THE EUROPEAN UNION,
Having regard to the Treaty on European Union, and in particular Article J.2 thereof,
Having regard to paragraph 4 of Resolution 1022 (1995) and paragraph 2 of Resolution 1074 (1996) adopted by the United Nations Security Council,
HAS DEFINED THE FOLLOWING COMMON POSITION:
Article 1. The relevant restrictive measures concerning the former Yugoslavia, taken in accordance with Resolutions 757 (1992), 787 (1992), 820 (1993), 942 (1994), 943 (1994), 988 (1995), 992 (1995), 1003 (1995) and 1015 (1995) of the United Nations Security Council will be repealed. ...

Official journal NO. L 095 , 27/03/1998 P. 0001 - 0003, 498X0240

5.   Common Position on restrictive measures against the FRY, 19 March 1998

THE COUNCIL OF THE EUROPEAN UNION,
Having regard to the Treaty on European Union, and in particular Article J.2 thereof,
    Whereas recent events in the Federal Republic of Yugoslavia (FRY), and in particular the use of force against the Kosovar Albanian Community in Kosovo, represent an unacceptable violation of human rights and put the security of the region at risk;

Whereas the European Union strongly condemns terrorism and violent acts committed by the Kosovo Liberation Army, or any group or individual;

Whereas the Union strongly condemns the violent repression of the non-violent expression of political views;

Whereas the Union endorsed on 12 March 1998 the statement issued by the Contact Group on 9 March 1998;

Whereas the Union demands that the Government of the FRY take effective steps to stop the violence and engage in a commitment to find a political solution to the issue of Kosovo through a peaceful dialogue with the Kosovar Albanian Community, in particular by:

- withdrawing the special police units and ceasing action by the security forces affecting the civilian population,
- allowing access to Kosovo for the International Committee of the Red Cross and other humanitarian organisations as well as by representatives of the Union and other Embassies,
- committing itself publicly to begin a process of dialogue with the leadership of the Kosovar Albanian Community,
- cooperating in a constructive manner in order to implement the action set out in paragraph 6 of the Contact Group statement;

Whereas the restrictive measures in Articles 1 to 4, including the reduction of economic and/or financial relations, are deemed necessary; whereas such measures will be reconsidered immediately if the Government of the FRY takes the steps referred to in the previous recital;

Whereas the Union will move to further international measures, and specifically to pursue a freezing of the funds held abroad by the FRY and the Serbian Governments, should the above steps not be implemented and repression continue in Kosovo,

HAS DEFINED THIS COMMON POSITION:

Article 1. The European Union confirms the embargo on arms exports to the former Yugoslavia established by Common Position 96/184/CFSP.[1]

Article 2. No equipment which might be used for internal repression or for terrorism will be supplied to the Federal Republic of Yugoslavia.

Article 3. A moratorium will be implemented on government-financed export credit support for trade and investment, including government financing for privatisations, in Serbia.

Article 4. 1. No visas shall be issued for senior FRY and Serbian representatives responsible for repressive action by FRY security forces in Kosovo.

2. The persons listed in the Annex, who have been identified as having clear security responsibilities, shall be reported for the purpose of non-admission in the territories of the Member States. Other senior FRY and Serbian representatives responsible for repressive action in Kosovo would be added in the case of a failure by the FRY authorities to respond to the demands of the International Community. In exceptional cases, exemptions may be made if this would further vital Union objectives. The Council shall update the list in the light of developments in Kosovo.

Article 5. This common position shall take effect on the date of its adoption.

Article 6. This common position shall be published in the Official Journal.

___
[1] OJ L 58, 7.3.1996, p. 1.

ANNEX

Vlajko Stojlkovic (Serbian Minister for the Interior)
Vlastimir Djordjevic (Head of Public Security Department)
Dragisa Ristivojevic (Deputy Head of Public Security Department)
Obrad Stevanovic (Assistant Minister for the Interior)
Jovica Stanisic (Assistant Minister for the Interior: Head of Serbian State Security)
Radomir Markovic (Assistant Minister for the Interior: Deputy Head of State Security)
Frenki Simatovic (Chief of Special Forces of State Security)
David Gajic (Head of Security in Kosovo)
Lubinko Cvetic (Deputy Head of Security in Kosovo)
Veljko Odalovic (Deputy Head of the Kosovo Okrug)

Official Journal L 130 , 01/05/1998 p. 0001 - 0004, 398R0926

6. Council Regulation (EC) No. 926/98 on reduction of economic relations with FRY, 27 April 1998

THE COUNCIL OF THE EUROPEAN UNION,

Having regard to the Treaty establishing the European Community, and in particular Articles 73g and 228a thereof,

Having regard to Common Position 98/240/CFSP of 19 March 1998 defined by the Council on the basis of Article J.2 of the Treaty on European Union on restrictive measures against the Federal Republic of Yugoslavia[1],

Having regard to the proposal from the Commission,

Whereas the said Common Position 98/240/CFSP provides for restrictive measures against the Federal Republic of Yugoslavia, including action by the Community to reduce certain economic relations;

Whereas certain of these measures fall within the scope of the Treaty establishing the European Community;

Whereas, therefore, and notably with a view to avoiding distortion of competition, Community legislation is necessary for the implementation of these measures, as far as the territory of the Community is concerned; whereas such territory is deemed to encompass, for the purposes of this Regulation, all the territories of the Member States to which the Treaty establishing the European Community is applicable, under the conditions laid down in that Treaty;

Whereas a procedure should be provided to amend, if necessary, the list of equipment which might be used for internal repression or terrorism;

Whereas there is a need for the Commission and the Member States to inform each other of the measures taken under this Regulation and of other relevant information at their disposal in connection with this Regulation, without prejudice to existing obligations with regard to certain items concerned,

HAS ADOPTED THIS REGULATION:

Article 1. The supply or sale, directly or indirectly, to the Federal Republic of Yugoslavia of equipment which might be used for internal repression or terrorism such as that set out in the Annex hereto shall be prohibited, except under the conditions laid down therein. The Annex shall not include items specially designed or modified for military use already subject to the arms embargo established on the basis of Common Positions 96/184/CFSP[2] and 98/240/CFSP.

Article 2. As laid down in Article 3 of Common Position 98/240/CFSP, the following shall be prohibited:

(a) the provision and/or use of government and/or other official financial support, insurance and/or guarantees in respect of new export credit for trade with or investment in the Republic of Serbia or in relation to the renewal or extension of existing export credit, if the execution of the contract or transaction for which the export credit has been provided has not yet been started;

(b) the provision or use of government and/or other official financing for privatisations in the Republic of Serbia in respect of which no legally binding commitments have been entered into so far.

Article 3. The participation, knowingly and intentionally, in related activities the object or effect of which is, directly or indirectly, to promote the transactions or activities referred to in Articles 1 and 2 shall also be prohibited.

Article 4. The Council shall adopt by qualified majority amendments to the list set out in the Annex on the basis of a proposal from the Commission in conformity with Article 1.

Article 5. Each Member State shall determine the sanctions to be imposed where the provisions of this Regulation are infringed.

Article 6 . The Commission and the Member States shall, insofar as they are not otherwise obliged to do so, inform each other of the measures taken under this Regulation and supply each other with other relevant information at their disposal in connection with this Regulation, such as breaches and enforcement problems, judgments handed down by national courts or decisions of relevant international fora.

Article 7. This Regulation shall apply:
- within the territory of the Community including its airspace,
- on board any aircraft or any vessel under the jurisdiction of a Member State,
- to any person elsewhere who is a national of a Member State,
- to any body which is incorporated or constituted under the law of a Member State.

Article 8. This Regulation shall enter into force on the day of its publication in the Official Journal of the European Communities. This Regulation shall be binding in its entirety and directly applicable in all Member States.

_____
[1] OJ L 95, 27. 3. 1998, p. 1.
[2] OJ L 58, 7. 3. 1996, p. 1.

ANNEX: EQUIPMENT FOR INTERNAL REPRESSION OR TERRORISM, ENVISAGED BY ARTICLE 1
(The following list does not include items which have been specially designed or modified for military use and are covered by the arms embargo established on the basis of common positions 96/184/CFSP and 98/240/CFSP)

Helmets providing ballistic protection, anti-riots helmets, anti-riots shields and ballistic shields and specially designed components therefor.

Specially designed fingerprint equipment.

Power controlled searchlights.

Construction equipment provided with ballistic protection.

Hunting knives.

Specially designed production equipment to make shotguns.

Ammunition hand-loading equipment.

Communications intercept devices.

Solid-state optical detectors.

Image-intensifier tube.

Telescopic weapon sights.

Smooth bore weapons and related ammunition, other than those specially designed for military use, and specially designed components therefor; except:
    (1) signal pistols;
    (2) air or cartridge powered guns designed as industrial tools or humane animal stunners.

Simulators for training in the use of firearms and specially designed or modified components and accessories therefor.

Bombs and grenades, other than those specially designed for military use, and specially designed components therefor.

Body armour, other than those manufactured to military standards or specifications, and specially designed components therefor.

All-wheel-drive utility vehicles capable of off road use that have been manufactured or fitted with ballistic protection, and profiled armour for such vehicles.

Water cannon and specially designed or modified components therefor.

Vehicles equipped with water cannon.

Vehicles specially designed or modified to be electrified to repel boarders and components therefor specially designed or modified for that purpose.

Acoustic devices represented by the manufacturer or supplier as suitable for riot-control purposes, and specially designed components therefor.

Leg-irons, gangchains, shackles and electric-shock belts, specially designed for restraining human beings; except: handcuffs for which the maximum overall dimension including chain does not exceed 240 mm when locked.

Portable devices designed or modified for the purpose of riot control or self-protection by the administration of an incapacitating substance (such as tear gas or pepper sprays), and specially designed components therefor.

Portable devices designed or modified for the purpose of riot control or self-protection by the administration of an electric shock (including electric-shock batons, electric shock shields, stun guns and electric shock dart guns (tasers)) and components therefor specially designed or modified for that purpose.

Electronic equipment capable of detecting concealed explosives and specially designed components therefor; except: TV or X-rayons inspection equipment.

Electronic jamming equipment specially designed to prevent the detonation by radio remote control of improvised devices and specially designed components therefor.

Equipment and devices specially designed to initiate explosions by electrical or non-electrical means, including firing sets, detonators, igniters, boosters and detonating cord, and specially designed components therefor; except: those specially designed for a specific commercial use consisting of the actuation or operation by explosive means of other equipment or devices the function of which is not the creation of explosions (e.g., car air bag inflaters, electri-surge arresters of fire sprinkler actuators)[1].

Equipment and devices designed for explosive ordnance disposal; except:
(1) bomb blankets;
(2) containers designed for holding objects known on be, or suspected of being improvised explosive devices.

Linear cutting explosive charges (2).

Explosives and related substances as follows (3):
- amatol,
- nitrocellulose (containing more than 12,5 % nitrogen),
- nitroglycol,
- pentaerythritol tetranitrate (PETN),
- picryl chloride,
- trinitrophenylmethylnitramine (tetryl),
- 2, 4, 6-trinitrotoluene (TNT).

Night vision and thermal imaging equipment and image intensifier tubes or solid state sensors therefor.

Software specially designed and technology required for all listed items.

_____
[1] When they have obtained conclusive evidence that the end-use of the items under this indent is not for internal repression or terrorism and in accordance with Article 4 of the Regulation the competent authorities of the Member States may authorise the sale or supply of these items to the Federal Republic of Yugoslavia.

Official Journal L 143 , 14/05/1998 p. 0001 - 0002, 498X0326

7.   Common Position by the Council on freezing of funds held abroad by FRY and Serbian Governments, 7 May 1998

THE COUNCIL OF THE EUROPEAN UNION,

Having regard to the Treaty on European Union, and in particular Article J.2 thereof,

Whereas on 19 March 1998 the Council adopted Common Position 98/240/CFSP [1] on restrictive measures against the FRY;

Whereas further measures, and in particular the freezing of funds, were contemplated in Common Position 98/240/CFSP, should the conditions set out therein not be met and repression continue in Kosovo; whereas those conditions have not been met and therefore a further reduction of financial relations with the FRY should be foreseen;

Whereas, the restrictive measures set out in Article 1 will be reconsidered immediately if the FRY and Serbian Governments move to adopt a framework for dialogue and a stabilisation package;

Whereas the European Union will move to further restrictive measures, and specifically to take action to stop new investment in Serbia, if by 9 May 1998 dialogue between the parties is blocked because of the FRY and Serbian Government's non-compliance,

HAS DEFINED THIS COMMON POSITION:

Article 1. Funds held abroad by the Federal Republic of Yugoslavia and Serbian Governments will be frozen.

Article 2. This common position shall take effect from the date of its adoption.

Article 3. This common position shall be reviewed not later than six months after its adoption. ...

_____
[1] OJ L 95, 27.3.1998, p. 1. *Also: 398R1295 (OJ L 178 23.06.98 p.33).*

Official Journal L 165 , 10/06/1998 p. 0001 - 0001, 498X0374

8. Common Position on the prohibition of new investment in Serbia, 8 June 1998

THE COUNCIL OF THE EUROPEAN UNION,

Having regard to the Treaty on European Union, and in particular Article J.2 thereof,

Whereas on 7 May 1998 the Council adopted Common Position 98/326/CFSP[1] concerning the freezing of funds held abroad by the Federal Republic of Yugoslavia (FRY) and Serbian Governments; whereas a further reduction of economic and financial relations with the FRY and Serbia was foreseen in case the conditions laid down in that common position for the FRY and Serbian Government were not met;

Whereas, as such conditions have not been fulfilled so far, further action to reduce economic and financial relations with Serbia should be taken;

Whereas, the restrictive measures set out in Article 1 will be reconsidered immediately if the FRY and Serbian Governments move to adopt a framework for dialogue and a stabilisation package,

HAS DEFINED THIS COMMON POSITION:

Article 1. New investments in Serbia are prohibited.

Article 2. This common position shall take effect from the date of its adoption.

Article 3. This common position shall be reviewed not later than six months after its adoption. ...

---

[1] OJ L 143, 14. 5. 1998, p. 1

Official Journal L 178 , 23/06/1998 p. 0033 - 0035, 398R1295

9. Council Regulation (EC) No. 1295/98 on freezing of funds held abroad of FRY and Republic of Serbia, 22 June 1998

THE COUNCIL OF THE EUROPEAN UNION,

Having regard to the Treaty establishing the European Community, and in particular Articles 73g and 228a,

Having regard to Common Position 98/326/CFSP of 7 May 1998 defined by the Council on the basis of Article J.2 of the Treaty on European Union concerning the freezing of funds held abroad by the Federal Republic of Yugoslavia (FRY) and Serbian Governments[1],

Having regard to the proposal from the Commission,

Whereas the said common position provides for a freezing of funds held abroad by the Governments of the Federal Republic of Yugoslavia and the Republic of Serbia;

Whereas this measure falls within the scope of the Treaty establishing the European Community;

Whereas, therefore, and notably with a view to avoiding distortion of competition, Community legislation is necessary for the implementation of this measure, as far as the territory of the Community is concerned; whereas such territory is deemed to encompass, for the purposes of this Regulation, the territories of the Member States to which the Treaty establishing the European Community is applicable, under the conditions laid down in that Treaty;

Whereas circumvention of this Regulation, notably by entities owned by the said governments should be countered with an adequate system of information and, where appropriate, consideration of appropriate remedial measures, including additional Community legislation;

Whereas competent authorities of the Member States should, where necessary, be empowered to ensure compliance with this Regulation;

Whereas there is a need for Commission and Member States to inform each other of the measures taken under this Regulation and of other relevant information at their disposal in connection with this Regulation,

HAS ADOPTED THIS REGULATION:

Article 1. For the purpose of this Regulation:

1. 'Government of the Federal Republic of Yugoslavia' means: the Government of the Federal Republic of Yugoslavia, including the public administrations and agencies at the federal level.

2. 'Government of the Republic of Serbia' means: the Government of the Republic of Serbia, including the public administrations and agencies at the central government level in the Republic of Serbia.

3. 'Funds' means: funds of any kind, including interest, dividends or other value accruing to or from any such funds.

4. 'Freezing of funds' means: preventing any change in volume, amount, location, ownership, possession, character, destination or other change that would enable the use of the funds concerned.

Article 2. Except as permitted by Article 3:

1. all funds held outside the territory of the Federal Republic of Yugoslavia and belonging to the Government of the Federal Republic of Yugoslavia and/or to the Government of the Republic of Serbia shall be frozen.

2. No funds shall be made available, directly or indirectly, to or for the benefit of, either or both, those Governments.

Article 3. Article 2 shall not apply to funds exclusively used for the following purposes:

(a) payment for current expenses, including salaries of local staff, embassies, consular posts or diplomatic missions of the Government of the Federal Republic of Yugoslavia and/or the Government of the Republic of Serbia within the Community;

(b) transfer from the Community to natural persons resident in the Federal Republic of Yugoslavia of social security or pension payments as well as the transfer of other payments to protect entitlements in the area of social insurance;

(c) payments for democratisation projects or humanitarian activities carried out by the European Community and or the Member States, including the implementation of the Education Agreement of September 1996, signed by President Milosevic and the leader of the ethnic Albanian community Dr Ibrahim Rugova;

(d) payments of debts incurred with the Federal Republic of Yugoslavia and Serbian Governments before the entry into force of this Regulation, on the condition that these payments are made into accounts held by those Governments with banks or financial institutions within the Community;

(e) payments for essential transit services provided by the Federal Republic of Yugoslavia and Serbian Governments, on the condition that the supply of such services takes place at the usual rates.

Article 4. 1. The participation, knowingly and intentionally in related activities, the object or effect of which is, directly or indirectly, to circumvent the provisions of Articles 2 and 4 shall be prohibited.

2. Without prejudice to the Community rules concerning confidentiality, the competent authorities of the Member States shall have the power to require banks, other financial institutions and other bodies and persons to provide all relevant information necessary for ensuring compliance with this Regulation.

3. Any information that the provisions of Article 2 are being, or have been circumvented shall be notified to the competent authorities of the Member States and/or the Commission as listed in Annex.

Article 5. For the purposes of implementing this Regulation, the Commission shall be empowered, on the basis of the information supplied by the Member States, to amend the Annex.

Article 6. Each Member State shall determine the sanctions to be imposed where the provisions of this Regulation are infringed. Such sanctions must be effective, proportionate and dissuasive.

Article 7. The Commission and the Member States shall inform each other of the measures taken under this Regulation and supply each other with the relevant information at their disposal in connection with this Regulation, including information received in accordance with Article 4(3), such as breaches and enforcement problems, judgments handed down by national courts or decisions of relevant international forums.

Article 8. This Regulation shall apply:

- within the territory of the Community including its airspace,

- on board any aircraft or any vessel under the jurisdiction of a Member State,

- to any person elsewhere who is a national of a Member State,

- to any body which is incorporated or constituted under the law of a Member State.

Article 9. This Regulation shall enter into force on the day of its publication in the Official Journal of the European Communities. This Regulation shall be binding in its entirety and directly applicable in all Member States.

---

[1] OJ L 143, 14. 5. 1998, p. 1.

Official Journal L 190 , 04/07/1998 p. 0003 - 0003, 498X0426

10.   Council Common Position, Ban on flights by Yugoslav carriers between FRY and the EC, 29 June 1998

THE COUNCIL OF THE EUROPEAN UNION,
Having regard to the Treaty on European Union and, in particular, Article J.2 thereof,
    Whereas, on 19 March 1998 the Council adopted Common Position 98/240/CFSP[1] on restrictive measures against the Federal Republic of Yugoslavia;
    Whereas further measures were contemplated in Common Position 98/240/CFSP should the conditions set out therein not be met and repression continue in Kosovo;
    Whereas neither the said conditions nor those called for by the European Council at its meeting in Cardiff on 15 June 1998 have been met and therefore a further reduction of economic relations with the Federal Republic of Yugoslavia should be foreseen;
    Whereas the restrictive measures set out in Article 1 hereto will be reconsidered immediately if the Federal Republic of Yugoslavia and Serbian Governments move to adopt and implement a framework for dialogue and a stabilisation package,
HAS DEFINED THIS COMMON POSITION:
Article 1. Flights by Yugoslav carriers between the Federal Republic of Yugoslavia and the European Community will be banned.
Article 2. This Common Position shall take effect from the date of its adoption. ...

---

[1] OJ L 95, 27. 3. 1998, p. 1.
[On 30 November 1998, the Slovak Republic associated itself with this position. Amendments: *See 398R1901 (OJ L 248 08.09.98 p.1)*]

Official Journal L 209 , 25/07/1998 p. 0016 - 0017, 398R1607

11.   Council Regulation (EC) No. 1607/98 on prohibition of new investment in Republic of Serbia, 24 July 1998

THE COUNCIL OF THE EUROPEAN UNION,
Having regard to the Treaty establishing the European Community, and in particular Articles 73g and 228a,
    Having regard to Common Position 98/374/CFSP of 8 June 1998 defined by the Council on the basis of Article J.2 of the Treaty on European Union concerning the prohibition of new investment in Serbia[1],
    Having regard to the proposal from the Commission,
    Whereas this prohibition measure falls under the scope of the Treaty establishing the European Community;
    Whereas, therefore, and notably with a view to avoiding distortion of competition, Community legislation is necessary for the implementation of this measure, as far as the territory of the Community is concerned; whereas such territory is deemed to encompass, for the purposes of this Regulation, the territories of the Member States to which the Treaty establishing the European Community is applicable, under the conditions laid down in that Treaty;
    Whereas the competent authorities of the Member States should, where necessary, be empowered to ensure compliance with this Regulation;
    Whereas there is a need for the Commission and the Member States to inform each other of the measures taken under this Regulation and of other relevant information at their disposal in connection with this Regulation,
HAS ADOPTED THIS REGULATION:

Article 1. 1. It shall be prohibited, as from the date of entry into force of this Regulation, to transfer funds or other financial assets to:
        - the State or Government of the Federal Republic of Yugoslavia and of the Republic of Serbia,
        - any person in, or resident in, the Republic of Serbia,
        - any body carrying out business in, incorporated or constituted under the law of the Republic of Serbia,
        - any body owned or controlled by any of the governments, persons or bodies referred to in this paragraph,
        - any person acting on behalf of any of the above governments, persons or bodies,
in so far as such funds or other financial assets are transferred for the purposes of establishing a lasting economic link with the Republic of Serbia, including the acquisition of real estate there.
2. For the purposes of paragraph 1, 'funds and other financial assets` shall be understood to mean cash, liquid assets, dividends, interest or other income on shares, bonds, debt obligations and any other securities, or amounts derived from an interest in, or the sale or other disposal of, or any other dealing with tangible and intangible assets, including property rights.
3. The prohibition of paragraph 1 is without prejudice to the execution of contracts concluded before the entry into force of this Regulation and without prejudice to the execution of trade contracts for the supply of goods or services on usual commercial payment conditions.
Article 2. Notwithstanding Article 1, the competent authorities of the Member States may authorise the release of the funds or other financial assets on a case-by-case basis, where those funds or other financial assets are to be used solely for projects in support of democratisation, humanitarian and educational activities and independent media.
Article 3. Each Member State shall determine the sanctions to be imposed where the provisions of this Regulation are infringed. Such sanctions must be effective, proportionate and dissuasive.
Article 4. Without prejudice to the Community rules of confidentiality, the competent authorities of the Member States shall have the power to require banks, other financial institutions and other bodies and persons to provide all relevant information necessary for ensuring compliance with this Regulation.
Article 5. The Commission and the Member States shall inform each other of the measures taken under this Regulation and supply each other with other relevant information at their disposal in connection with this Regulation, such as breaches and enforcement problems, judgments handed down by national courts or decisions of relevant international fora.
Article 6. This Regulation shall apply:
        - within the territory of the Community including its airspace,
        - on board any aircraft or any vessel under the jurisdiction of a Member State,
        - to any person elsewhere who is a national of a Member State,
        - to any body which is incorporated or constituted under the law of a Member State.
Article 7. This Regulation shall enter into force on the day of its publication in the Official Journal of the European Communities. This Regulation shall be binding in its entirety and directly applicable in all Member States.

---

[1] OJ L 165, 10. 6. 1998, p. 1.

Official Journal L 248 , 08/09/1998 p. 0001, 398R1901

12.   EC Council Regulation, No. 1901/98, ban on flights of Yugoslav carriers between FRY & EC, 7 September 1998

THE COUNCIL OF THE EUROPEAN UNION,
Having regard to the Treaty establishing the European Community, and in particular Article 228A thereof,
    Having regard to Common Position 98/426/CFSP of 29 June 1998 defined by the Council on the basis of Article J.2 of the Treaty on European Union, concerning a ban on flights by Yugoslav carriers

between the Federal Republic of Yugoslavia and the European Community[1],

Having regard to the proposal from the Commission,

Whereas the developments regarding Kosovo have already led the Security Council of the United Nations to impose an arms embargo against the Federal Republic of Yugoslavia (FRY) under Chapter VII of the Charter of the United Nations, and to the consideration of additional measures in case of failure to make constructive progress towards the peaceful resolution of the situation in Kosovo;

Whereas the European Union has already decided on additional measures as envisaged by Common Positions 98/240/CFSP[2], 98/326/CFSP[3] and 98/374/CFSP[4] and the ensuing Council Regulations (EC) Nos 926/98[5], 1295/98 (6) and 1607/98[7];

Whereas the Government of the FRY has not stopped the use of indiscriminate violence and brutal repression against its own citizens, which constitute serious violations of human rights and international humanitarian law, and has not taken effective steps to find a political solution to the issue of Kosovo through a process of peaceful dialogue with the Kosovar Albanian Community in order to maintain the regional peace and security;

Whereas, therefore, Common Position 98/426/CFSP foresees a ban on flights by Yugoslav carriers between the Federal Republic of Yugoslavia (FRY) and the European Community as a further measure to obtain from the Government of the FRY the fulfilment of the requirements of UNSC Resolution 1160 (1998) and of the said Common Positions;

Whereas this further measure falls under the scope of the Treaty establishing the European Community;

Whereas, therefore, and notably with a view to avoiding distortion of competition, Community legislation is necessary for the implementation of these measures, as far as the territory of the Community is concerned; whereas such territory is deemed to encompass, for the purposes of this Regulation, the territories of the Member States to which the Treaty establishing the European Community is applicable, under the conditions laid down in that Treaty;

Whereas there is a need to provide for certain specific exemptions;

Whereas there is a need for the Commission and Member States to inform each other of the measures taken under this Regulation and of other relevant information at their disposal in connection with this Regulation,

HAS ADOPTED THIS REGULATION:

Article 1. 1. Aircraft operated directly or indirectly by a Yugoslav carrier, that is a carrier having its principal place of business or its registered office in the Federal Republic of Yugoslavia, shall be prohibited from flying between the Federal Republic of Yugoslavia and the European Community.

2. All operating authorisations granted to Yugoslav carriers are hereby revoked.

Article 2. No new operating authorisations shall be granted or existing ones renewed enabling aircraft registered in the Federal Republic of Yugoslavia to fly to or from airports in the Community.

Article 3. 1. Articles 1 and 2 shall not apply to
(a) emergency landings on the territory of the Community and ensuing take-offs;
(b) authorisations for charter series flights between Leipzig and Tivat by Montenegro Airlines.

2. Nothing in this Regulation shall be construed as limiting any existing rights of Yugoslav carriers and aircraft registered in the FRY other than rights to land in or to take off from the territory of the Community.

Article 4. The participation, knowingly and intentionally, in related activities, the object or effect of which is, directly or indirectly, to circumvent the provisions of Articles 1 and 2 shall be prohibited.

Article 5. Each Member State shall determine the sanctions to be imposed where the provisions of this Regulation are infringed. Such sanctions must be effective, proportionate and dissuasive.

Article 6. The Commission and the Member States shall inform each other of the measures taken under this Regulation and supply each other with any other relevant information at their disposal in connection with this Regulation, such as breaches and enforcement problems,

judgments handed down by national courts or decisions of relevant international fora.

Article 7. This Regulation shall apply:
- within the territory of the Community including its airspace,
- on board any aircraft or any vessel under the jurisdiction of a Member State,
- to any person elsewhere who is a national of a Member State,
- to any body which is incorporated or constituted under the law of a Member State.

Article 8. This Regulation shall enter into force on the day of its publication in the Official Journal of the European Communities. This Regulation shall be binding in its entirety and directly applicable in all Member States.

---

[1] OJ L 190, 4. 7. 1998, p. 3.
[2] OJ L 95, 27. 3. 1998, p. 1.
[3] OJ L 143, 14. 5. 1998, p. 1.
[4] OJ L 165, 10. 6. 1998, p. 1.
[5] OJ L 130, 1. 5. 1998, p. 1.
[6] OJ L 178, 23. 6. 1998, p. 33.
[7] OJ L 209, 25. 7. 1998, p. 16.

13.   FRY Statement on the Suspension of Flights of Yugoslav Airlines, 10 October 1998

At today's meeting, chaired by Prime Minister Momir Bulatovic, the Federal Government expressed its regret concerning the EU Council's decision on the suspension of flights of Yugoslav airlines; the government thinks the decision is unlawful, unilateral and an example of the policy of discrimination. The decision shall in no way contribute to the solution of Kosovo and Metohija problem; on the contrary, it could be understood as a stimulation for separatists and terrorists in Kosovo.

The enforcement of the decision overthrows the legal system of air traffic, established in 1944 by the Convention on International Aviation, as well as bilateral agreements our country has signed with the members of the European Union. The Federal Republic of Yugoslavia will therefore ask for the protection of its interests and compensation.

The Federal Government decided to continue to comply with agreements signed with EU countries; reciprocal measures will not be taken. The Federal Ministry of Transportation will continue to issue permits, in accordance with valid bilateral agreements on air traffic and Yugoslav regulations.

The Federal Government will simultaneously take steps to protect the interests of Yugoslav air traffic.

The Federal Ministry of Foreign Affairs will take measures to protect the rights of the Federal Republic of Yugoslavia.

The government decided to suspend bilateral agreements on re-admission (return of people from Kosovo that illegally abide in the EU countries), considering the fact that agreements envisage the services of Yugoslav airlines. The government will also hold up the negotiations on the agreement on re-admission, as well as the ratification procedure. ...

S/1999/216

14.   Report of the Chairman of UN Committee pursuant to SC Resolution 1160 (1998), 26 February 1999

... III.   COOPERATION WITH REGIONAL ORGANIZATIONS AND ESTABLISHMENT OF A MONITORING REGIME

... 12. The Secretary-General also felt that in the absence of an integrated coordinating mechanism, it would be essential for representatives of participating organizations to hold periodic meetings, as necessary, to exchange information on the monitoring of the prohibitions established by the Security Council and to address practical issues arising thereto. On 12 November 1998, members were briefed on the first consultation meeting held on 19 October 1998 in New York. All members supported holding such meetings periodically. The second meeting on the monitoring of the arms embargo and other prohibitions was held on 14 December 1998 at the Vienna International Centre.

IV. VIOLATIONS AND ALLEGATIONS OF VIOLATIONS

13. During the period covered by the report, the Committee received several reports on violations of the established prohibitions from organizations participating in the monitoring of the prohibitions contained in resolutions 1160 (1998) and 1199 (1998). While the Danube Commission, WEU and the NATO Stabilization Force reported

their observations on the implementation of resolution 1160 (1998), EU (the European Community Monitoring Mission), the Department of Peacekeeping Operations (UNPREDEP) and OSCE reported possible violations.

14. The Committee considers reports from participating organizations extremely useful since they enable it to approach States with a request to confirm or dispel alleged violations occurring on their territories or involving their citizens. Various reports enabled the Committee to contact the authorities of Albania with a request to provide information on reported movements of Kosovo Liberation Army (KLA) members and weapons from its territory in Kosovo. While the Committee noted with appreciation the reply received from the Albanian authorities, it reverted to them by letter for further clarification on measures taken under paragraph 8 of resolution 1160 (1998) as well as the reported presence of military camps and training facilities for KLA members inside the territory of Albania.

15. The Committee expressed concern at continued serious violations of the arms embargo and other prohibitions which, according to the information available to the Committee, had resulted in continuing military resupply and reinforcement of Kosovar Albanian armed groups. The Committee also recognized that, owing to the lack of a comprehensive monitoring mechanism, its information was limited, and that it therefore could not conclude that violations by others had been committed. It urged States, particularly those neighbouring the Federal Republic of Yugoslavia, to make every effort to comply fully with resolutions 1160 (1998) and 1199 (1998) in seeking to prevent the sale or supply to the Federal Republic of Yugoslavia, including Kosovo, of arms and related materiel of all types and to prevent the arming, training and financing of terrorist activities there. It also reiterated the responsibility of all States to support international efforts aimed at stabilizing the situation in Kosovo and enhancing the prospect of peace in the region by observing strictly the prohibitions contained in resolutions 1160 (1998) and 1199 (1998) and acting promptly when violations occur.

16. In accordance with the guidelines for the conduct of its work, the Committee regularly considers information concerning possible violations retrieved by its Secretariat from public sources. Accordingly, the Committee was apprised of the interception of arms and ammunition worth $1 million at the end of December 1998 by the Croatian authorities. In a letter addressed to the Committee, the Croatian authorities reported that an arsenal of illegal arms originating in Bosnia and Herzegovina and destined for Kosovo, Federal Republic of Yugoslavia, had been seized. The Committee commended the Croatian authorities for promptly informing it of the incident and of the legal action taken against the perpetrators of the violation. The Committee decided to seek clarification from the authorities of Bosnia and Herzegovina on the incident and the measures taken to prevent further such incidents. The Committee expressed its interest in receiving further information from the authorities of Croatia on the aforementioned incident, subject to completion of the investigation, as well as a reply from Bosnia and Herzegovina.

17. On 28 October 1998, the Government of Switzerland informed the Committee that supplementary surveillance measures had been agreed upon at a meeting between representatives of the Kosovo Foundation and representatives of the Department of Internal Affairs, which is the agency responsible for surveillance of the Foundation; as a result of this agreement, blocks on the Kosovo Foundation bank accounts were withdrawn on 23 July. In response to a press report on violations of the arms embargo and other prohibitions involving Kosovar Albanians living in Germany, the Committee was informed, on 7 December, that the German authorities, while making efforts to curb dubious fund-raising activities, had been unable to establish that the funds were intended to arm or train terrorists in Kosovo or to purchase weapons for use there. On 3 December, the representative of Sweden informed the Committee that Swedish authorities were continuing to investigate mass media reports on the financing of KLA activities from Swedish territory, however no measures had been taken. Regarding a press article on a possible violation of the prohibitions established in paragraph 8 of resolution 1160 (1998) submitted to the Committee on

29 December, a letter requesting clarification was addressed to the Bulgarian authorities.

V. OBSERVATIONS AND RECOMMENDATIONS

18. During the period under consideration, few substantive reports have been submitted by States on violations of the arms embargo and other prohibitions. With regard to States bordering the Federal Republic of Yugoslavia, only Croatia submitted an interim report, in December 1998, on an incident that occurred on its territory in contravention of resolution 1160 (1998). Given that the primary responsibility for the implementation of the prohibitions lies with States, the Committee would welcome a more proactive approach by Governments, especially with regard to their reporting on possible violations and on actions taken to prevent violations of resolution 1160 (1998). The Committee considers that it would be useful to encourage such an approach.

19. With a view to assisting and encouraging Governments in their endeavour to implement the arms embargo and other prohibitions, the Committee intends to consider sending a mission to the region, headed by the Chairman of the Committee, when appropriate.

20. All reports received so far relate to the flow of arms and funds to Kosovar Albanians in violation of paragraph 8 of resolution 1160 (1998). With the exception of one press report concerning a possible violation by the Federal Republic of Yugoslavia, all other press reports deal with the flow of arms and funds to Kosovar Albanians.

21. The Committee considers that an expert study on the military potential of the parties targeted by resolution 1160 (1998), including their external financing in violation of paragraph 11 of resolution 1199 (1998), which would be conducted within existing resources, may assist it to better understand the scope, dynamics and gravity of possible violations. The Committee intends to pursue discussion of the feasibility and possible modalities of commissioning such a report at its future meetings.

22. The Committee underlines the importance of the mandate given to UNPREDEP under Security Council resolution 1186 (1998) to monitor and report on illicit arms flows and other activities that are prohibited under resolution 1160 (1998). UNPREDEP has reported to the Committee on possible violations. Strengthened cooperation between UNPREDEP and the authorities of the former Yugoslav Republic of Macedonia, in particular its border control personnel, may allow the Committee to identify and pursue possible violations, in accordance with its mandate.

23. The Committee has noted that few States have transmitted specific information pursuant to paragraph 12 of resolution 1160 (1998) on steps taken to give effect to the prohibitions contained in paragraph 8 of the resolution. Only a few States indicated what measures in fact had been taken to give effect to the prohibitions established by the Security Council. The development of more uniform reporting requirements by the Secretariat may be of some assistance to address this issue and would also allow the Committee to provide the Council with more accurate information on States' compliance with the established prohibitions.

24. In fulfilling its mandate, the Committee continues to rely heavily on the assistance of relevant international organizations. In this context, it appreciates the commitment made by OSCE to make necessary adjustments in its reports, enabling the Committee to retrieve swiftly pertinent information on possible violations. The Committee encourages OSCE and other organizations participating in the comprehensive monitoring regime under resolution 1160 (1998) - NATO, WEU, EU and the Danube Commission, as well as the OSCE and NATO verification missions mentioned in resolution 1203 (1998) - to intensify their reporting efforts in order to further support the Committee's fulfilment of its mandate. The Committee considers that it would be useful to study ways to improve the monitoring and enforcement of the prohibitions established by resolution 1160 (1998).

25. The role of the Committee in assisting current political and diplomatic efforts aimed at fostering stability in Kosovo and peace in the region by observing States' compliance remains meaningful. Its members are determined to make every effort to maximize the Committee's contribution to achieving the objectives set out by the Council in its relevant resolutions.

B. Political Action of the Union

Bulletin EU 3-1998

1. Council Conclusions on Kosovo, 31 March 1998

Voicing concern at renewed violence in Kosovo, the Council insisted that the Serbian police be withdrawn immediately and that security forces act with restraint. It also condemned all acts of violence, including those by the Kosovo Liberation Army. The Council welcomed the 25 March declaration by the foreign ministers of the contact group and called on the authorities in the FRY and Serbia to comply fully with the demands made of them and to facilitate the mission by Mr Gonzalez, who had its total backing. It stressed that real progress in Kosovo would improve the international standing of the FRY. It went on to reiterate what it saw as an urgent need for the parties involved to begin meaningful dialogue without preconditions and welcomed in this connection the accord on implementation of the agreement on education.

PESC/98/28

2. Declaration by EU, associated countries of Central & Eastern Europe & Cyprus on Kosovo, 31 March 1998

Bulgaria, Cyprus, the Czech Republic, Estonia, Hungary, Latvia, Lithuania, Poland, Romania, Slovakia and Slovenia align themselves to the Conclusions adopted by the EU Council of Ministers on 31 March 1998 as set out in the annex to this declaration. This is the first time that associated countries have been requested to align themselves to EU Council Conclusions, in pursuit of a line of growing coherence between the associated countries and the Council.

ANNEX ...

The Council discussed the continuing tension in Kosovo, underlining its concern at the further incidents of violence in the province within the last few days. It reaffirmed its insistence that the Serbian special police force be immediately withdrawn and that FRY and Serbian security forces should act with restraint and in accordance with internationally accepted standards. It also condemned all terrorist acts, notably those by the Kosovo Liberation Army, and called on those outside the FRY who are supplying financial support, arms or training for terrorist activity in to cease doing so immediately.

The Council welcomed the statement of 25 March by the Foreign Ministers of the Contact Group. It expressed the view that the steps taken by the FRY and Serbian authorities since 9 March were insufficient to meet the full range of requirements set out on that date and reiterated on 25 March. It underlined that the measures set out in its Common Position of 19 March would not be lifted, and others would need to be considered unless these requirements had been met in full.

The Council reaffirmed its conviction that meaningful dialogue without preconditions must begin urgently between the parties. It supports neither independence nor the maintenance of the status quo as the end-result of negotiations between the Belgrade authorities and the Kosovo Albanian leadership on the status of Kosovo. It welcomed the steps already taken by Dr Rugova to prepare for negotiations and encouraged him to announce his negotiating team without delay.

The Council welcomed the agreement reached in the 3+3 Commission on the implementation of the Education Agreement and thanked Monsignor Paglia of Sant' Egidio for all his efforts in this field. Noting that the Contact Group urged all sides to cooperate with Sant'Egidio to reduce tensions in other social sectors as well, the Council called for rapid implementation by both sides of this new agreement and affirmed the European Union's readiness to give substantial assistance to this process. It asked for a rapid follow-up to the recommendations of the Presidency/Commission fact finding team currently Kosovo.

The Council expressed its full support for the mission of Mr Felipe Gonzalez as Personal Representative for the Federal Republic of Yugoslavia of the OSCE Chairman in Office and Special Representative of the European Union. It called upon President Milosevic to cooperate with this mission, which would constitute an important element in the future course of relations between the European Union and the Federal Republic of Yugoslavia.

The Council underlined its intention to continue to follow developments closely and asked the competent instances to develop further the European Union's line on this issue within the framework of the European Union's regional approach. It underlined that concrete progress to resolve the serious political and human rights issue in Kosovo will improve the international position of the FRY and prospects for normalisation of its international relationships and full rehabilitation in international institutions.

Bulletin EU 4-1998

3. European Council Conclusions on Kosovo, 27 April 1998

The Council expressed its deep concern at the mounting violence in Kosovo and called upon both parties to act with restraint. It reaffirmed its insistence that the Federal Republic of Yugoslavia and Serbian security forces conform to internationally accepted standards. It also reiterated its condemnation of all terrorist acts and called on those outside the Federal Republic of Yugoslavia who are providing support for terrorist activity in Kosovo to cease doing so immediately.

The Council underlined the fundamental importance of an urgent start to a meaningful dialogue without preconditions between the parties if further bloodshed is to be avoided. It expressed disappointment that time had passed without material progress in this respect, but welcomed indications that both sides were now trying to address the need to settle modalities for substantive discussions. The Council considered that the assistance by the international community in the process will be necessary to establish a climate of confidence between the parties. It welcomed the intention of Mr Gonzalez to arrange an early visit to Belgrade, taking up his mission on behalf of the EU and the OSCE jointly.

The Council reiterated its support for the territorial integrity of the Federal Republic of Yugoslavia. It emphasised in this context a particular responsibility that President Milosevic has to promote a peaceful settlement to the problems of Kosovo. It regretted that he had so far declined to shoulder fully this responsibility and agreed that additional measures against Belgrade would be taken in the case of continued failure to meet the international community's requirements. In this context, it noted the contingency technical work which was being taken forward by the Council instances on such measures. The Council recalled that if, on the other hand, the Federal Republic of Yugoslavia Government were to show a real willingness to cooperate with the international community and engage in meaningful dialogue, the European Community would be prepared to consider positively the Federal Republic of Yugoslavia's participation in the mechanisms of the European cooperation.

The Council underlined the importance of a cohesive international approach to this crisis. It welcomed the recent Troika visit at senior official level to Bulgaria, Romania and Hungary and will continue to cooperate closely with the countries in the region, not least, where appropriate, on the question of border security.

Official Journal L 165 , 10/06/1998 p. 0002 - 0003, 498X0375

4. Joint Action on the nomination of an EU Special Representative for the FRY, 8 June 1998

THE COUNCIL OF THE EUROPEAN UNION,

Having regard to the Treaty on European Union, and in particular Articles J.3 and J.11 thereof,

Having regard to the conclusions of the European Council, held in Amsterdam on 16 and 17 June 1997, concerning the Federal Republic of Yugoslavia (FRY),

Whereas on 29 April 1997 the Council adopted conclusions on the application of conditionality with a view to developing a coherent EU strategy applicable to relations with countries of south-east Europe which are not linked to the EU by an association agreement;

Whereas on 19 March 1998 the Council adopted conclusions nominating Mr Felipe Conzález as EU Special Representative with a view to enhancing the effectiveness of the EU's contribution to the resolution of problems in the FRY;

Whereas in its conclusions of 25 May 1998 the Council indicated that a Joint Action should be adopted on the González mission;

Whereas the EU Special Representative will work in close consultation and concurrently with the OSCE Chairman-in-Office to assist the FRY in promoting internal dialogue on democratic reforms so as to contribute to the coherence of international efforts,

HAS ADOPTED THIS JOINT ACTION:

Article 1. Mr Felipe González shall be appointed EU Special Representative for the FRY for a period ending on 31 December 1998.

The Council may review the content and duration of the mandate of the EU Special Representative, including administrative and financial aspects, as appropriate before its expiry.

Article 2. The mandate of the EU Special Representative will be to enhance the effectiveness of the EU's contribution to the resolution of problems in the FRY and to pursue the subject of FRY's future relations with the EU, its participation in OSCE and related matters.

The EU Special Representative will carry out his mandate under the authority of the Presidency and as appropriate in cooperation with the Commission.

The EU Special Representative will be guided by, and report under the authority of the Presidency to, the Council on a regular basis and as the need arises.

Article 3. 1. In order to cover the costs related to the mission of the EU Special Representative a sum of up to ECU 1 million shall be charged to the general budget of the European Communities from the date of adoption of this Joint Action.

2. The expenditure financed by the amount stipulated in paragraph 1 shall be managed in accordance with the European Community procedures and rules applicable to the general budget.

Article 4. 1. The Member States and the Community may propose the secondment of staff to work with the EU Special Representative. The remuneration of personnel, detached by a Member State, the Commission or another Community institution to the EU Special Representative shall be covered respectively by the Member State concerned, the Commission or the other Community institutions.

2. The team of the Special Representative will be composed by the Special Representative on his own responsibility in consultation with the Presidency assisted by the Commission. The Council notes that the Presidency will keep it regularly informed of developments.

3. The Council notes that the Presidency, Commission and/or Member States, as appropriate, will provide logistical support in the region.

4. The privileges, immunities and further guarantees necessary for the completion and smooth functioning of the mission of the EU Special Representative and the members of his staff shall be defined with the parties. The Member States and the Commission shall grant all necessary support to such effect.

Article 5. This Joint Action shall enter into force on the date of its adoption. It shall apply until 31 December 1998. ...

PESC/98/56

5. Declaration by the European Union on Kosovo, 11 June 1998

We are deeply concerned at the intense fighting in Kosovo. The reports of widespread house-burning and indiscriminate artillery attacks on whole villages indicate a new level of aggression on the part of the Serb security forces. We are disturbed by reports that these attacks are beginning to constitute a new wave of ethnic cleansing. We strongly condemn this action which, together with the systematic exclusion of international observers from affected areas, demonstrates that Belgrade is engaged in a campaign of violence going far beyond what could legitimately be described as a targeted anti-terrorist operation. We insist on an immediate stop to all violent action and call for the withdrawal of Special Police and Army units.

We are particularly concerned by the growing stream of refugees into northern Albania caused by the continuing conflict. This illustrates the threat posed to regional security and stability by the deteriorating situation in Kosovo. We are strongly interested in the return of refugees to their homes in Kosovo, preferably with monitoring by the UNHCR. The EU will play its part in addressing the refugee problem in a comprehensive way within the region itself.

The Council is equally concerned by the growing human cost of the violence. It is in close touch with the relevant humanitarian agencies and stands ready to offer its assistance. Full access of humanitarian organisations, in particular the ICRC, to the areas of conflict is indispensable. Furthermore, international forensic experts should have the opportunity to carry out the necessary investigation in order to clarify the circumstances in which civilians have died. The FRY authorities have an obligation to cooperate with the ICTY.

We further believe that it is time to strengthen the international monitoring capacity in Kosovo, in order to provide a more accurate picture of developments and to encourage a political solution. The EU will consider a contribution to this through the ECMM.

We continue to condemn any use of violence for political ends on either side. The European Union is determined to play its part in stopping the flow of money and weapons to the Kosovo Liberation Army (KLA). Neighbouring states have a particular responsibility to ensure that their territory is not used in support of KLA activity. We will continue to work with them to ensure that their security is not jeopardised by the continuing violence in Kosovo.

The priorities in Kosovo are to end violence and to establish a genuine political process, which is the only viable alternative to continuing conflict. We are disappointed by the very limited progress made so far in the talks between Belgrade and Pristina. We call on Belgrade to take urgent steps to reduce the tension in the province so as to create the stable environment necessary for political progress. We reaffirm our support for Ibrahim Rugova's resolve to seek a political solution through dialogue. The EU supports the granting of a special status, including a large degree of autonomy for Kosovo, within the Federal Republic of Yugoslavia.

President Milosevic bears a special responsibility as head of the FRY government for promoting a peaceful settlement to the problems of Kosovo. He should not believe that the international community will be taken in by talk of peace when the reality on the ground is ever greater repression. In the light of the grave deterioration of the situation on the ground, involving the excessive use of force by the Serb security forces, the Council has today adopted a Common Position for a ban on new investments in Serbia. The Commission will act rapidly to make the necessary proposal for implementation of the ban on new investments in Serbia. The Council will adopt the regulation on the freeze of funds of the FRY and Serbian Governments as soon as possible. The European Union remains ready to press ahead with other measures against Belgrade if the authorities there fail to halt their excessive use of force and to take the steps needed for genuine political progress. Furthermore, the EU encourages international security organisations to pursue their efforts in this respect and to consider all options, including those which would require an authorization by the UNSC under Chapter VII.

The Council regretted and condemned President Milosevic's refusal to permit the Gonzalez mission to commence work on the basis of the Council discussions and conclusions, expressed its continuing support for Felipe Gonzalez as its Special Representative and approved the Joint Action to give practical effect to this support.

DOC/98/10

6. Cardiff European Council Presidency Conclusions, Annex 2, Kosovo, 15/16 June 1998

The European Council condemns in the strongest terms the use of indiscriminate violence by the FRY and the Serbian security forces to impose the Belgrade Government's political terms. No State which uses brutal military repression against its own citizens can expect to find a place in the modern Europe. President Milosevic bears a heavy personal responsibility.

The crisis constitutes a serious threat to regional stability and requires a strong and united international response. The European Council calls for immediate action from President Milosevic in four areas in particular:

* to stop all operations by the security forces affecting the civilian population and to withdraw security units used for civilian repression;
* to enable effective and continuous international monitoring in Kosovo;
* to facilitate the full return to their homes of refugees and displaced persons and unimpeded access for humanitarian organisations; and
* to make rapid progress in the political dialogue with the Kosovo Albanian leadership.

The European Council stresses the importance of President Milosevic taking advantage of his meeting with President Yeltsin in Moscow on 16 June, which it welcomes, to announce progress on the above steps and to commit Belgrade to their implementation in full.

Unless these four steps are taken without delay, a much stronger response, of a qualitatively different order, will be required from the international community to deal with the increased threat to regional peace and security. The European Council welcomed the acceleration of work in international security organisations on a full range of options, including those which may require an authorisation by the UN Security Council under Chapter VII of the UN Charter.

Given the gravity of the situation, the European Council has agreed to supplement measures already being implemented against the FRY and Serbian Governments by taking steps to impose a ban on flights by Yugoslav carriers between the FRY and EU Member States.

A solution to the problem of Kosovo's status can only be found through a vigorous political process. The European Council calls urgently on both sides to return to the negotiating table, with international involvement, to agree confidence-building measures and to define a new status for Kosovo.

The European Union remains firmly opposed to independence. It continues to support a special status, including a large degree of autonomy for Kosovo, within the Federal Republic of Yugoslavia.

If an early reduction of tensions is to be achieved, an immediate cessation of violence will be required as well from the Kosovo Albanian side. While commending the commitment of Dr Rugova to a peaceful solution in Kosovo, the European Council calls on the Kosovo Albanian leadership to state clearly its rejection of violent attacks and acts of terrorism. The European Union will play its part in stopping the flow of money and weapons to Kosovo Albanian armed groups. The European Council calls on neighbouring States, whose security is a vital factor for the European Union, to ensure that their territory is not used in support of Kosovo Albanian armed activity.

The European Union has been concerned from the outset at the human cost of the fighting in Kosovo. The European Council agreed to take a comprehensive approach to solving the refugee problem within the region, based on the right of all the refugees from Kosovo to return to their homes in conditions of security. The European Council pledged to continue close cooperation with UNHCR and ICRC, in the first instance to provide immediate assistance from the European Community and from Member States to refugees and displaced persons.

Refugee return will require close international monitoring to generate confidence on the part of those returning that the rule of law has been re-established. The European Council decided that the Union would play its full part in an increased international monitoring effort. The European Council urges Belgrade to allow full access for investigations by international forensic experts to clarify the circumstances in which civilians have died. The FRY Government also has an obligation to allow the International Criminal Tribunal for the Former Yugoslavia (ICTY) to investigate thoroughly any possible violation of international humanitarian law in Kosovo.

The European Council expressed its full support for Felipe Gonzalez as its Special Representative to the FRY and called on President Milosevic to receive him as soon as possible in order to discuss the full range of the FRY's relations with the EU, including the democratisation of the FRY. The European Council also supported the early return of the long-term OSCE missions. The European Council warmly welcomed the outcome of the Parliamentary elections in Montenegro as an endorsement of the reform process pursued by Djukanovic and agreed to continue EU support.

PRES/98/227

7. 2111th Council Meeting, General Affairs, Luxembourg, 29 June 1998

President: Mr Robin COOK
Secretary of State for Foreign and Commonwealth Affairs of the United Kingdom
WESTERN BALKANS - Conclusions - FRY/Kosovo
The Council expressed profound concern about the heightened tension on the ground in Kosovo and underlined the urgent need for progress towards a negotiated settlement.

The Council called for full and immediate implementation of the undertakings given by President Milosevic in his meeting with President Yeltsin on 16 June. In this connection, the Council deeply regretted Belgrade's refusal to accept an increase in the size of the ECMM presence in Kosovo. The Council reaffirmed its determination to provide an increased monitoring presence in Kosovo. It reiterated the need for a comprehensive approach to the refugee issue and its intention to work with other international organisations to promote the early return of refugees and displaced people to their homes. Unhindered access for international humanitarian organisations is an essential requirement.

The Council voiced its strong disappointment that the commitments made by President Milosevic in Moscow did not cover all the requirements set out in the European Council's Cardiff Declaration, in particular the withdrawal of security units used for civilian repression; and that the conditions had not been created for rapid progress in the political dialogue with the Kosovar Albanian leadership, with international involvement. The Council stressed the importance of action by Belgrade on all these requirements if the international community were not to be compelled to respond in a qualitatively different way to the increased threat to regional peace and security.

The Council underlined its condemnation of all violence in pursuit of political goals. It reaffirmed the demand for the withdrawal by Belgrade of the security forces from Kosovo. All those in a leadership role in the Kosovar Albanian community should unite responsibly in making clear their commitment to dialogue and a peaceful resolution of the problems of Kosovo, and their rejection of violence and acts of terrorism. The Council recalled that the European Union remains firmly opposed to independence: it continues to support a special status, including a large degree of autonomy for Kosovo, within the Federal Republic of Yugoslavia.

Consistent with the decision taken in Cardiff, the Council adopted a Common Position to impose a ban on flights by Yugoslav carriers between the FRY and EU member states.

The Council reiterated its full support for Mr Gonzalez as Special Representative for the FRY, and for OSCE efforts on Kosovo and democratisation in the FRY, and called for the early return of the OSCE long-term missions to the FRY.

The Council instructed the Political Committee to keep under close review developments on the ground in Kosovo and the EU's response, against the key criterion of the continuing need to promote a meaningful political process capable of achieving rapid results.

PRES/98/240

8.   2113th Council Meeting, General Affairs, Brussels, 13 July 1998

... WESTERN BALKANS - CONCLUSIONS - FRY/KOSOVO

The Council expressed its grave concern at the continuing violence and loss of life in Kosovo particularly among the civilian population. The danger of a rapid widening of the crisis continues to exist. It reiterated its call for an immediate cessation of all hostilities and the restart of a political process with direct international involvement between the Parties. The Kosovo Albanian team for these talks must be able to speak authoritatively and therefore be fully representative of their community. The Council accordingly called on the leaders within the Kosovo Albanian community to unite and to make common cause to this end.

The Council underlined Belgrade's primary responsibility in the origin of the crisis and therefore for creating the necessary conditions for dialogue. At the same time, it insists that the Kosovo Albanian community, including the armed groups, commit themselves to dialogue and therefore refrain from violence and acts of terrorism. The Council demanded that outside assistance and support to armed Kosovo Albanian groups should cease immediately.

The Council recalled that a solution for Kosovo can be found neither through the maintenance of the status quo nor through independence, but through a special status, including a large degree of autonomy within the FRY. The Council welcomed the intention of the Contact Group to set in hand work, to which the EU is actively contributing, to define possible further elements for the future status of Kosovo with a view to making them available to the Parties. It emphasised that international involvement in the dialogue remains an essential element of credible negotiations.

The Council acknowledged the significance of the undertakings given by President Milosevic in his meeting with President Yeltsin on 16 June. It emphasised the need for them to be fully implemented, as well as the outstanding provisions of the 12 June Contact Group Statement. In this light it recalled, while acknowledging that the security forces have shown some measure of restraint recently, the necessity of further action by the Belgrade authorities on the withdrawal of security forces used for civilian repression, unimpeded access for observers, the full return of refugees and displaced persons to their homes and free and unimpeded access for humanitarian organisations and supplies to Kosovo. The Council expects that President Milosevic's commitment to allow international observers in Kosovo will permit an increase in size of the ECMM presence in Kosovo. The Council acknowledged that armed Kosovo Albanian groups also have a responsibility to avoid violence and all armed activities, and reiterated that acts of violence and terrorism are inadmissible and will not solve the problem of Kosovo.

The Council supported the adoption of a UN Security Council resolution putting the UN's authority behind the requirements expected of the Parties by the international community. Should the required steps not be taken, the Council endorsed the principle of further action under the UN Charter to bring about compliance by those who block the process. It is the understanding of the Council that such action would be under Chapter VII of the UN Charter.

The Council welcomed the UNHCR's regional approach to the refugee question and pledged its continuing support for efforts to create the conditions for an early return of refugees throughout the region. It called on the Government of Albania to cooperate actively with governments of neighbouring countries to facilitate the voluntary return of refugees to their countries of origin.

The Council notes that the Prosecutor of ICTY has expressed the view that the situation in Kosovo represents an armed conflict within the terms of the Tribunal's mandate. It calls on Belgrade and others on the ground in Kosovo to cooperate with the Prosecutor's investigation.

The Council reiterated its full support for Mr Gonzalez as Special Representative for the FRY, and for OSCE efforts on Kosovo and democratisation in the FRY, and called for the early return of the OSCE long-term missions to the FRY. ...

ALBANIA

The Council discussed the situation in Albania. It strongly encouraged the government of Prime Minister Nano to follow a policy of restraint and moderation in the Kosovo crisis, which is now more necessary than ever. It expressed its concern about the flow of arms from northern Albania to Kosovo Albanian armed groups. It called on all political organisations in Albania to support the policy of the Albanian government and to associate themselves with the line taken by the European Union on the Kosovo issue. At the same time it called upon the Albanian government to increase its efforts to stop the flow of weapons from Albania to Kosovo.

The Council called on the international community to find ways to support the Albanian government in this endeavour. It noted the decision of the WEU Permanent Council to prepare a feasibility study on possible options for an international police operation in Albania.

The Council encouraged the government of Albania to continue progress towards the democratic stabilisation of the country. It emphasised the need for further efforts by the Albanian government to fight corruption and to restore law and order and urged it to continue and strengthen this policy. The Council underlined its conviction that political questions in Albania should be discussed and solved in the structures of the Albanian state, in particular in the Albanian parliament, and urged all political organisations to play a constructive role in the democratic process. In this connection it expresses concern at the decision by the opposition Democratic Party to begin a second boycott of parliament and urges the Democratic Party to reconsider its decision and return to parliament.

The Council supported the Albanian government's proposal for an Albania conference at the appropriate time and confirmed the European Union's willingness to continue to make a particular effort to support the rebuilding of Albania. It re-emphasised the closeness of the link between strong EU support for Albania and close co-operation of Albania with the European Union and the international community in its efforts to solve the Kosovo problem.

PESC/98/77

9.   Declaration by the Presidency on behalf of the European Union on recent fighting in Kosovo, 20 July 1998

The European Union is appalled and dismayed by reports on intensified hostilities in Kosovo over the last weekend which have - according to reports - left up to 450 people unaccounted for, several dozens of whom seem to have been killed.

The EU condemns the alleged recent infiltrations of several hundred fighters from Albania into Kosovo territory as well as the violence in the Albanian-Yugoslav border area and at Orahovac/Rahovec, and calls urgently on both the armed Kosovar groups and the Serbian authorities to exercise restraint and to cease hostilities immediately. The EU is particularly concerned that VJ shelling has allegedly violated the international border and demands from the Serbian and Yugoslav authorities an immediate halt to such action. It calls on the FRY and the Albanian governments to do all in their power to reduce tensions over Kosovo.

The EU recalls that violent action will not enhance the prospects for a negotiated solution of the Kosovo problem. Indeed, each individual casualty will render an early solution more difficult.

The priorities now are a cessation of hostilities and a start of a meaningful political process.

PESC/98/128

10.   Declaration by the European Union on a comprehensive approach to Kosovo, 27 October 1998

The EU remains gravely concerned at the situation in Kosovo, in particular regarding the plight of the civilian population, refugees and displaced persons. Tens of thousands of people may still be without permanent shelter in Kosovo as winter approaches. The EU will continue to engage substantial resources towards alleviating this plight.

The EU fully supports the agreements signed in Belgrade on 16 October 1998 between the FRY and the OSCE, and on 15 October 1998 between the FRY and NATO through negotiations mandated by the Contact Group on the basis of relevant SCRs, as an important step towards a political solution to the Kosovo crisis. It welcomed UN Security Council Resolution 1203 of 24 October conferring the authority of the UN to the demand for full and immediate compliance by all parties concerned with these agreements, the unilateral commitments and UNSCRs 1160 and 1199. The focus is now on full and immediate compliance, by all Parties concerned.

Although some progress has been made, the FRY is still not respecting the provisions of UNSCR 1199, in particular with regard to the withdrawal of security forces to their positions prior to March 1998. The EU calls on all parties, and in particular on President Milosevic, to live up to their obligations and commitments, to refrain from further acts of violence in the region and to engage in immediate political negotiations. It welcomes the statement of Ibrahim Rugova on 22 October in response to the efforts of the EU Special Envoy Petritsch calling on the armed Kosovo Albanian groups to refrain from action which could be used as a provocation for new attacks by Serb/Yugoslav security forces, and expressing his support for the Milosevic-Holbrooke agreement. The need remains for pressure to be maintained to ensure compliance and to prevent a return to violence and repression. In this respect the EU will take the necessary steps to enhance the effective implementation of its own sanctions.

The EU pledges its full support for the OSCE and for the Kosovo Verification mission, to which Member States will contribute very substantially in personnel and resources. It commends the efforts of Poland, as chair-in-office of the OSCE, and Norway in this respect. Clear and effective lines of responsibility within the KVM are essential. The substantial overall European contribution to the KVM should be fully reflected in the positions of responsibility to be filled by EU nationals. The Presidency has conveyed this point to the OSCE Chairman in Office. Financial provisions should be based on the principle of equitable burden-sharing and on established OSCE procedures.

The EU welcomes the ECMM plans to considerably and quickly increase its presence in Kosovo in order to facilitate the early start of KVM. The ECMM should maintain a liaison presence in KVM HQs in Pristina for reporting purposes.

The effectiveness and security of the OSCE KVM mission are paramount concerns. The EU expects President Milosevic and those responsible in the Kosovo Albanian community to ensure the safety of the verifiers and international humanitarian personnel. The EU supports the provision of a rapid reaction capability.

The EU also supports NATO's air verification mission, and would welcome the participation of Russia and other non-NATO countries. Good coordination between air and ground verification are essential in verifying compliance.

It is urgent for the Parties to start real negotiations on the future status of Kosovo. President Milosevic must stand by his unilateral statement, which is a constitutive element in his overall agreement with Ambassador Holbrooke. The Kosovo Albanian leadership must engage in serious dialogue without preconditions, and with the widest possible representation in its negotiating team. The EU as a major factor in the stability of the Balkans will continue its efforts to restore peace in Kosovo. As part of these efforts, the EU will remain actively involved in supporting the negotiating process, notably through the activity of the EU Special Envoy, Ambassador Petritsch, on the basis of the US proposal as amended and endorsed by the Contact Group and the EU.

The EU is already contributing very substantially in Kosovo, and is prepared to continue contributing, not least in the framework of the KVM. The Commission is already urgently analysing all possibilities in the different fields of assistance to Kosovo. Member States will provide substantial assistance directly and through UN agencies, international organizations and NGOs. EU Member States are ready, in accordance with EU priorities, to make available additional financial resources to support the OSCE KVM mission and EC and Member States will

consider this for humanitarian programmes. The EU will address the issues of refugee return, winterization and reconstruction, within a plan of action, on the basis of the assessment by the Belgrade and Geneva working groups on humanitarian issues.

The EU will consider ways in which it can contribute, under the right conditions, to implementing confidence building measures among the various communities in Kosovo and to further civil society building, including community support for the implementation of the Education Agreement.

The Council has invited the Commission and competent Council bodies to prepare further proposals within this comprehensive approach for early presentation to the General Affairs Council.

11. Vienna European Council, Presidency Conclusions, 11 & 12 December 1998

The European Council emphasises the need for full and immediate compliance by both sides in the Kosovo crisis with UNSC Resolutions 1160, 1199, 1203 and 1207 in order to achieve a peaceful settlement. Deploring the lack of commitment by both parties to support the negotiating process, it urges the Government of the FRY and the leadership of the Kosovo Albanians to show the flexibility in the talks necessary for agreement to be reached on the future status of Kosovo. It reaffirms the EU's determination, as demonstrated by the active efforts of the EUSE Wolfgang Petritsch, to support the political process, to contribute to humanitarian efforts and, as soon as the parties have reached such an agreement, to assist reconstruction in Kosovo, including through a donors' conference.

C. The Response of the Western European Union

1. WEU Ministerial Council, Rhodes Declaration, 12 May 1998

...

V. KOSOVO AND REGIONAL STABILITY

Ministers held an extensive exchange of views on the situation in Kosovo. They expressed their strong concern about the increasing violence and growing polarisation in Kosovo. They condemned the excessive use of force by FRY and Serbian security forces and insisted that these forces should conform with internationally accepted standards, whilst condemning all terrorist acts, calling on those who are providing support for terrorist activity in Kosovo to cease immediately. They reiterated their support for the territorial integrity of the FRY, whilst underlining that the status quo in Kosovo was unacceptable. They agreed that the crisis in Kosovo constituted a risk to the stability of the surrounding region. They insisted that immediate steps by the parties to reduce tension and to begin an unconditional dialogue are indispensable. Ministers expressed their readiness to promote a clear and achievable path towards Belgrade's full integration in the international community, should Belgrade take the steps needed to launch substantive talks on Kosovo's political status. They also expressed their support for the efforts of the international community, including the United Nations, the OSCE, the G8, the Contact Group and countries of the region; and welcomed the recent declarations of the EU General Affairs Council, North Atlantic Council and of the Ministers of Foreign Affairs of countries of South-Eastern Europe. They deeply regretted that President Milosevic had, nonetheless, so far failed to create the conditions for a meaningful dialogue without preconditions. They noted that insufficient action by Belgrade could only lead to the deepening isolation of the FRY.

Ministers considered that WEU's Multinational Advisory Police Element (MAPE) in Albania contributes to stability in the region. They tasked the Permanent Council to consider further possible areas for cooperation with the Albanian authorities:
- extension of MAPE's advisory role to include advice on police monitoring and control in the border area, and on crowd control and other issues;
- further training and provision of equipment to improve the Albanian police capacity to monitor and control its borders.

Ministers expressed their support for the efforts under way in NATO to seek military advice on possible further contributions to security in Albania and FYROM and will propose that representatives of the WEU Military Staff be involved in the NATO assessment machinery.

Taking account of the outcome of NATO's current deliberations, WEU would be ready to examine whether any further contributions were appropriate; for example, in the field of military training and restructuring of the Albanian armed forces. ...

Turkey recognises Macedonia with its constitutional name. Turkey dissociates itself from this reference by reserving its position on this issue.

2.   WEU Ministerial Council, Rome Declaration, 17 November 1998

... To help in defining its own contribution while supporting those of others, WEU has taken part in NATO's planning for the emergency in Kosovo, and has kept in touch with the developing international responses to other aspects of the crisis including the acute human problem of displaced persons and refugees. WEU supports the missions of the OSCE and NATO and the efforts of the EU and calls on all parties to live up to their obligations and commitments, to refrain from further acts of violence in the region and to engage in immediate political negotiations.

... WEU'S PRESENCE IN ALBANIA AND CONTRIBUTION TO PEACE AND STABILITY IN THE REGION

Ministers reaffirmed WEU's resolve to continue its contribution to the efforts to promote national reconciliation and stability in Albania, notably through its Multinational Advisory Police Element (MAPE) mission directed to training, advice and evaluation for the Albanian police forces. Through a mid-term review of MAPE's current mandate the Council has identified ways to focus MAPE's work more closely on key priorities for the training and modernization of the Albanian police, and - building on initiatives by the Italian Presidency - to achieve more effective liaison and coordination with other national and international initiatives in this field. Ministers tasked the Council to ensure the rapid implementation of all measures required for these ends. In view of the grave developments in Kosovo and their consequences for the region, MAPE was tasked in June to give special priority to training, advice and assistance for Albanian border police, including the assessment of their material needs. Representatives of the WEU Military Staff have meanwhile participated in the Alliance's assessment and planning work related to the Kosovo emergency. Responding to impulsions from the European Union in the context of a comprehensive European strategy for support to Albania - including a J.4.2 decision adopted by the EU Council - WEU has studied ways to widen and better focus the geographic and functional scope of its support for the maintenance of law and order, given the necessary security conditions and material and financial support. In this context, Ministers welcomed the outcome of the Feasibility Study on international police operations in Albania and the subsequent production of a contingency plan by the Military Staff and stressed the importance of the ongoing work of the Permanent Council on that basis.

D.   The Decisions of the Contact Group

1.   Statement of the Contact Group Foreign Ministers, New York, 24 September 1997

We, the Foreign Ministers of the Contact Group countries (France, Germany, Italy, Russian Federation, United Kingdom, and the United States) meeting at the United Nations in New York on September 24 together with representatives of the Luxembourg EU Presidency, EU Commission and the Office of the High Representative, discussed the situation in Kosovo, the Federal Republic of Yugoslavia.

We voiced our deep concern over tensions in Kosovo. We call on the authorities in Belgrade and the leadership of the Kosovar Albanian community to join in a peaceful dialogue. We urge the two sides to create the conditions necessary for refugees from Kosovo to return home. As a first step, we call on all concerned to implement the Education Agreement without delay and to follow this up with additional confidence-building measures.

We warn against any resort to violence to press political demands and urge all sides to exercise maximum restraint.

Regarding the dispute over Kosovo's status, the position of the Contact Group countries is clear: we do not support independence and we do not support maintenance of the status quo. We support an enhanced status for Kosovo within the FRY. Such a status should fully protect the rights of the Albanian population in accordance with OSCE standards and the UN Charter. As a first step to reduce tensions, it is essential that dialogue begins.

2.   Contact Group Statement on Kosovo, 8 January 1998

Foreign Ministers of the Contact Group countries meeting in New York on 24 September voiced their deep concern over tensions in Kosovo and called on the authorities in Belgrade and the leadership of the Kosovar Albanian community to join in a peaceful dialogue. At the Bonn Peace Implementation Council on 9/10 December, the Council took note with increasing concern of escalating tensions in Kosovo. The decision by the delegation of the FRY to leave the PIC meeting did nothing to diminish this concern. Against this background, Contact Group Political Directors, meeting in Washington on 8 January, indicated that the Contact Group would continue to focus on Kosovo as a matter of high priority. The following principles underlie the Contact Group's continued interest in the situation in Kosovo:

- it is for the authorities in Belgrade and the leadership of the Kosovar Albanian community to assume their responsibility to promote stability and a solution to the problems between them in order to ensure a peaceful and prosperous future for their people. The Contact Group will support a mutually agreed solution that respects democratic standards;
- as a first step to reduce tensions, it is essential that dialogue begins;
- the Contact Group supports neither independence nor the maintenance of the status quo. It supports an enhanced status for Kosovo within the FRY. Such a status should fully protect the rights of the Albanian, Serb, and other residents of Kosovo in accordance with OSCE standards, Helsinki principles and the UN Charter;
- the Contact Group condemns both violent repression of non-violent expressions of political views and terrorist actions to achieve political goals, and strongly urges all sides to seek peaceful solutions to their difficulties;
- we call on the FRY to address this question urgently. Making concrete progress to resolve the serious political and human rights issues in Kosovo is critical for Belgrade to improve its international position and relations with the international community.

To facilitate dialogue, the Contact Group has decided to consider further the Kosovo issue and, in particular, how to support existing efforts to implement the Education Agreement which would be an important first step towards the promotion of stability. It will draw on the views of all those that have been working to resolve the problems of Kosovo.

3. Statement by the Contact Group on Kosovo, Moscow, Russia, 25 February 1998

At its Moscow meeting on February 25, 1998, the Contact Group confirmed its position on Kosovo, FRY, expressed in the New York Declaration of Foreign Ministers of September 24, 1997, as well as in the Washington Contact Group Declaration of January 8, 1998. It noted that since that time, despite repeated calls for dialogue to resolve the problems in Kosovo, there had been little progress on this vitally important issue. It also shared the valid expressions of concern by those in the region about the implication of the situation in Kosovo for regional security.

The Contact Group reaffirmed its commitment to uphold human rights values, and their condemnation of both violent repression of non-violent expressions of political views, including peaceful demonstrations, as well as terrorist actions, including those of the so-called Kosovo Liberation Army.

The Contact Group agreed that both sides should be reasonable and flexible and focus on immediate steps to reduce tensions -- bearing in mind the overriding need to avoid conflict and violence. It expressed continuing support for full and rapid implementation of the Education Agreement, recognizing its importance as a step for the promotion of stability in the region. It called on the authorities in Belgrade and the leadership of the Kosovar Albanian community to enter without preconditions into a full and constructive dialogue to deal with the underlying social, economic and status problems.

The Contact Group reiterated that it supported neither independence nor the maintenance of the status quo. The principles of the solution of the Kosovo problem should be based on the territorial integrity of the Federal Republic of Yugoslavia, taking into account the rights of the Kosovo Albanians and all those who live in Kosovo in accordance with OSCE standards, Helsinki principles and the UN Charter. The Contact Group supports an enhanced status for Kosovo within the FRY and recognizes that this must include meaningful self-administration.

The Contact Group reiterated their view that the FRY needs to address this question urgently, and that making progress to resolve the serious political and human rights issues in Kosovo is critical for Belgrade to improve its international position and relations with the international community. The Contact Group expressed its readiness to facilitate dialogue.

The Contact Group reaffirmed its intention to continue to pay close attention to the problem of Kosovo.

4. Statement by the Contact Group, London, 9 March 1998

1. We the Foreign Ministers of Contact Group countries, together with representatives of the European Commission and the Office of the High Representative, met in London on 9 March to discuss the increasingly tense situation in Kosovo, Federal Republic of Yugoslavia (FRY), and the unacceptable use of force over recent days. The Balkans region has seen too much bloodshed in recent years for the international community to stand aside.

2. We recalled that when we met in New York on 24 September 1997, we voiced deep concern over developments in Kosovo and called on the authorities in Belgrade and the leadership of the Kosovar Albanian community to join in a peaceful dialogue. We are dismayed that in the period since September, rather than taking steps to reduce tensions or to enter without preconditions into dialogue toward a political solution, the Belgrade authorities have applied repressive measures in Kosovo. We note with particular concern the recent violence in Kosovo resulting in at least 80 fatalities and condemn the use of excessive force by Serbian police against civilians, and against peaceful demonstrators in Pristina on 2 March.

3. Our condemnation of the actions of the Serbian police should not in any way be mistaken for an endorsement of terrorism. Our position on this is clear. We wholly condemn terrorist actions by the Kosovo Liberation Army or any other group or individual. Those in the Kosovar Albanian community who speak for the different political constituencies should make it clear that they, too, abhor terrorism. We insist likewise that those outside the FRY who are supplying finance,

arms or training for terrorist activity in Kosovo should immediately cease doing so.

4. We condemn the large-scale police actions of the last 10 days that further inflamed an already volatile situation. The violent repression at non-violent expression of political views is completely indefensible. We call upon the authorities in Belgrade to invite independent forensic experts to investigate the very serious allegations of extrajudicial killings. If these accusations are borne out, we expect the FRY authorities to prosecute and punish those responsible.

5. Our commitment to human rights values means that we cannot ignore such disproportionate methods of control. Government authorities have a special responsibility to protect the human and civil rights of all citizens and to ensure that public security forces act judiciously and with restraint.

6. In the light of the deplorable violence in Kosovo, we feel compelled to take steps to demonstrate to the authorities in Belgrade that they cannot defy international standards without facing severe consequences. The Contact Group has decided to take a broad range of action to address the current situation on an urgent basis. The Contact Group welcomes the continuation of consultations in the United Nations Security Council, in view of the implications of the situation in Kosovo for regional security. Against that background the Contact Group:

- requests a mission to Kosovo by the United Nations High Commissioner for Human Rights
- urges the office of the Prosecutor of the ICTY to begin gathering information related to the violence in Kosovo that may fall within its jurisdiction. The FRY authorities have an obligation to cooperate with the ICTY. Contact Group countries will make available to the ICTY substantiated relevant information in their possession
- supports the proposal for a new mission by Felipe Gonzalez as the Personal Representative of the OSCE Chairman-in-Office for the FRY that would include a new and specific mandate for addressing the problems in Kosovo
- supports the return of the OSCE long-term missions to Kosovo, the Sandzak and Vojvodina
- recommends that the Special Session of the OSCE Permanent Council meeting on 11 March arrange for Embassies in Belgrade of OSCE participating states to intensify their visits to Kosovo so as to provide for a continuous presence
- will continue vigorously to support Sant'Egidio's efforts to secure implementation of the Education Agreement, and identify resources to assist a fair and acceptable arrangement
- proposes the establishment of an international consortium including non-Government Organizations that would promote civil-society building in Kosovo and the distribution of humanitarian assistance.
- recognizing that neighboring countries of the FRY have legitimate security concerns stemming from violence and unrest in Kosovo, will arrange an urgent meeting of the Contact Group with representatives of governments in the region to discuss the grave consequences of an inter-ethnic conflict and its possible spillover to other parts of the region. We expect them to do all in their power to prevent support for terrorism. The meeting will in particular address:
- the possible dispatch of a short-term OSCE monitoring group to enhance the ability of the Albania mission's Shkodra field office to monitor the FRY (Kosovo) border
- the possible strengthening or the present OSCE mission in Skopje
- recommends that consideration be given to adapting the current UNPREDEP mandate, and would support the maintenance of an international military presence on the ground in the former Yugoslav Republic of Macedonia when the current mandate of UNPREDEP expires
- will monitor the situation in Kosovo by frequent joint visits to Pristina by Contact Group and other representatives

7. At the same time, it is not enough for the killing to stop; too much damage has already been done to human life and to the FRY'S credibility. Because of the gravity of the situation, we endorse the following measures to be pursued immediately:

    a) UN Security Council consideration of a comprehensive arms embargo against the FRY, including Kosovo;

b) Refusal to supply equipment to the FRY which might be used for internal repression, or for terrorism;

c) Denial of visas for senior FRY and Serbian representatives responsible for repressive action by FRY security forces in Kosovo;

d) A moratorium on government-financed export credit support for trade and investment, including government financing for privatizations, in Serbia.

The Contact Group notes that the Russian Federation cannot support measures c) and d) above for immediate imposition. But if there is no progress towards the steps called for by the Contact Group, the Russian Federation will then be willing to discuss all the above measures.

We call upon President Milosevic to take rapid and effective steps to stop the violence and engage in a commitment to find a political solution to the issue of Kosovo through dialogue. Specifically, he should within 10 days:

-    Withdraw the special police units and cease action by the security forces affecting the civilian population.

-    Allow access to Kosovo for the ICRC and other humanitarian organizations as well as by representatives of the Contact Group and other Embassies.

-    Commit himself publicly to begin a process of dialogue, along the lines in paragraph 10, with the leadership of the Kosovar Albanian community.

-    cooperate in a constructive manner with the Contact Group in the implementation of the actions specified in paragraph 6 above which require action by the FRY government.

If President Milosevic takes these steps, we will immediately reconsider the measures we have now adopted. If he fails to take these steps, and repression continues in Kosovo, the Contact Group will move to further international measures, and specifically to pursue a freeze on the funds held abroad by the FRY and Serbian governments.

The Contact Group has decided to meet again on 25 March to assess the response of the government of the FRY.

8. Belgrade's own actions have seriously set back the process of normalization of the FRY's relations with the international community. Unless the FRY takes steps to resolve the serious political and human rights issues in Kosovo, there is no prospect of any improvement in its international standing. On the other hand, concrete progress to resolve the serious political and human rights issues in Kosovo will improve the international position of the FRY and prospects for normalization of its international relationships and full rehabilitation in international institutions.

9. No one should misunderstand our position on the core issue involved. We support neither independence nor the maintenance of the status quo. As we have set out clearly, the principles for a solution of the Kosovo problem should be based on the territorial integrity of the Federal Republic of Yugoslavia, and be in accordance with OSCE standards, Helsinki principles, and the UN Charter. Such a solution also must take into account the rights of the Kosovo Albanians and all those who live in Kosovo. We support an enhanced status for Kosovo within the FRY which a substantially greater degree of autonomy would bring and recognize that this must include meaningful, self-administration.

10. The way to defeat terrorism in Kosovo is for Belgrade to offer the Kosovar Albanian community a genuine political process. The authorities in Belgrade and the leadership of the Kosovar Albanian community must assume their responsibility to enter without preconditions into a meaningful dialogue on political status issues. The Contact Group stands ready to facilitate such a dialogue

5.   Joint statement of Foreign Ministers of Countries of Southeastern Europe, Bonn, 25 March 1998

The Ministers of Foreign Affairs of Countries of South-Eastern Europe met in Bonn on 25 March 1998 to discuss the situation in Kosovo.

The Ministers expressed their high appreciation of the cooperation already established with the Contact Group states in this regard.

The Ministers agreed that the countries of the region should have a direct role in finding the solutions to the crisis in Kosovo. They expressed the readiness of their states to participate in regular consultations with the Contact Group. They also noted the importance of the dialogue on a bilateral basis between countries of the region and the Contact Group states.

The Ministers held a thorough discussion on the recent developments concerning the situation in Kosovo. They noted that there is a progress in recent days especially in view of the accord to implement the Agreement on Education.

The Ministers listened with particular interest to the intervention of Mr. Fatos Nano, Prime Minister of Albania. They expressed their appreciation of the responsible position of the Albanian government towards the crisis in Kosovo.

They agreed that the solution to the issue of the future status of Kosovo should be found on a mutually acceptable basis within the borders of the Federal Republic of Yugoslavia.

The Ministers believe that international mediation may help the conflicting parties by political means to give up their extreme demands and adopt a reconciliatory and compromising approach.

The Ministers expressed a common view that any measures against the Federal Republic of Yugoslavia should take into account the political and economic stability of South-Eastern Europe and should not harm the interests of the states of the region. Sanctions, if necessary should be political rather than economic.

The Ministers expressed the view that there should be a balanced approach of measures and incentives in order to convince both conflicting parties to actively pursue their dialogue.

The Ministers called for enhanced international monitoring in Kosovo.

They underlined the importance of the inviolability of the borders of the states in the region including those of the Federal Republic of Yugoslavia. They paid a special emphasis on the final demarcation of the border between Former Yugoslav Republic of Macedonia and the Federal Republic of Yugoslavia.

The Ministers called on the Contact Group states to incorporate these common positions of the South-East European countries in the Statement to be issued after the joint meeting.

6.   Contact Group and the Foreign Ministers of Canada and Japan, Statement, London, UK, 12 June 1998

1. Foreign Ministers of the Contact Group, meeting together with the Foreign Ministers of Canada and Japan, turned from their discussion of the recent nuclear tests carried out by India and Pakistan to address the serious deterioration of the situation in Kosovo which represents a significant threat to regional security and peace.

2. Ministers repeated that no solution to the problems of Kosovo can be found through violence. The parties must take urgent steps to end the violence and bring about a political solution to the crisis.

3. Security forces have again intervened indiscriminately causing many civilian casualties and forcing tens of thousands of inhabitants to flee their homes. Ministers condemned Belgrade's massive and disproportionate use of force which has resulted in widespread destruction and the deliberate displacement of large numbers of people. They also condemned the failure by Belgrade to take concrete steps to reduce tensions. Ministers therefore decided to put to the authorities in Belgrade a set of essential points on which they require immediate action to prevent any further deterioration in the situation. These cover concrete measures:

• to cease all action by the security forces affecting the civilian population and order the withdrawal of security units used for civilian repression;

• to enable effective and continuous international monitoring in Kosovo and allow unimpeded access for monitors;

• to facilitate, in agreement with UNHCR and ICRC, the full return to their homes of refugees and displaced persons and to allow free and unimpeded access for humanitarian organizations and supplies to Kosovo; to make rapid progress in the dialogue with the Kosovo Albanian leadership.

4. Ministers expect the Kosovo Albanian leadership to make clear its rejection of violence and acts of terrorism. It is essential that Kosovo Albanian extremists refrain from further violent attacks. A political dialogue is unlikely to take root if violence continues to be espoused by members of the Kosovo Albanian community. Our governments will

work with others, including in the region, to ensure that all those seeking to escalate the crisis through violence are denied financial and material support. Ministers also expressed support for those in the Kosovo Albanian leadership who are committed to peaceful dialogue.

5. Ministers insist that the fighting stop and effective dialogue, capable of producing meaningful early results, resume quickly. Belgrade and the Kosovo Albanian leadership must agree to a continuous dialogue to discuss confidence-building measures and to find a political solution to the problems of Kosovo, with international involvement. There must be a clear time-table for rapid progress, and President Milosevic, as President of the Federal Republic of Yugoslavia, has a special responsibility to ensure that steps are taken to achieve a political solution.

6. Ministers expect that Belgrade will take the steps in paragraph 3 above immediately. They welcomed the invitation by President Yeltsin to President Milosevic to a meeting on 16 June. They stressed the importance of President Milosevic taking advantage of this meeting to announce progress on the above steps and to commit Belgrade to their implementation in full. If the steps in paragraph 3 are not taken without delay, there will be moves to further measures to halt the violence and protect the civilian population, including those that may require the authorisation of a United Nations Security Council resolution.

7. In the meantime, faced with the growing crisis in Kosovo, Ministers also:

- urged the International Criminal Tribunal for the former Yugoslavia (ICTY) to undertake a rapid and thorough investigation of any possible violations of international humanitarian law in Kosovo;
- agreed to give active support to UNHCR and other humanitarian organisations dealing with the humanitarian cost of this crisis in the region;
- undertook to accelerate efforts to assist neighboring countries to improve their security and to cope with the humanitarian burden imposed upon them.

8. The Foreign Ministers of Canada, France, Germany, Italy, the United Kingdom and the United States confirmed their decision to implement the ban on new investment in Serbia and to freeze funds held abroad by the FRY and Serbian governments, and agreed to take steps to ban flights by Yugoslav carriers between the Federal Republic of Yugoslavia and their countries. Japan supported this approach and agreed to consider similar action. The Russian Federation does not associate itself with these measures.

9. Ministers again underlined the importance of the early launching of the mission of the Special Representative of the Chairman-in-Office of the OSCE in order to establish a dialogue across the full range of the FRY's relations with the OSCE, and of the return of the long term OSCE missions.

10. Ministers will review these decisions in the light of developments.

7.   Contact Group Statement, Bonn, 8 July 1998

1. The Contact Group met in Bonn on 8 July. It reviewed the situation in Kosovo and took stock of the parties' response to the requirements set out in the statement on Kosovo issued in London on 12 June by Foreign Ministers of the Contact Group and of Canada and Japan, and implementation of the undertakings made by President Milosevic in Moscow on 16 June.

2. The overall situation in Kosovo remains tense. The Contact Group noted with deep concern that despite vigorous efforts undertaken by the members of the Contact Croup, the prospects of a peaceful settlement have deteriorated since the Contact Group's meeting in London on June 12, 1998. Although the primary responsibility for the situation in Kosovo rests with Belgrade, the Contact Group acknowledges that armed Kosovo Albanian groups also have a responsibility to avoid violence and all armed activities. The Contact Group reiterated that violence is inadmissible and will not solve the problem of Kosovo: indeed it will only make it more difficult to achieve a political solution. The Contact Group stressed its condemnation of violence and acts of terrorism in pursuit of political goals, from whatever quarter.

3. The Contact Group assessed Belgrade's response to the requirements set out in the 12 June London statement: to cease all action by the security forces affecting the civilian population and order the withdrawal of security units used for civilian repression; to enable an effective and continuous international observer group in Kosovo and allow unimpeded access for observers; to facilitate, in agreement with UNHCR and ICRC the full return to their homes of refugees and displaced persons and to allow free and unimpeded access for humanitarian organisations and supplies to Kosovo; and to make rapid progress in the dialogue with the Kosovo Albanian leadership. The Contact Group noted that

- withdrawal of security forces used for civilian repression has not yet been carried out although the security forces have shown some measure of restraint recently
- rapid progress in the dialogue with the Kosovo Albanian leadership has not been achieved.

4. The Contact Group acknowledged the significance of the undertakings given by President Milosevic in his meeting with President Yeltsin on 16 June and emphasized the need for them to be fully implemented.

- It noted President Milosevic's commitment to allow international observers free and unrestricted access to Kosovo which is in a first stage of implementation. It expected Belgrade to cooperate fully with those states which were enhancing their capability to observe developments in Kosovo through secondment of additional personnel to their diplomatic representations in Belgrade. The Contact Group expected that President Milosevic's stated commitment to allow international observers in Kosovo will also permit an increase of size of the ECMM presence in Kosovo.
- The Contact Group noted that there has been some improvement in the access to Kosovo for international humanitarian organisations such as the UNHCR and the ICRC. But the Contact Group also urged Belgrade to do more to facilitate the return of refugees and displaced persons to their homes, in particular by agreeing to security confidence building measures. The Contact Group expressed its support for the UNHCR's regional approach to the refugee question.
- The Contact Group encouraged the European Union and other competent international organisations to continue to pursue the commitment of resources in order to create the conditions for an early return of refugees throughout the region.

5. The Contact Group called for an immediate cessation of hostilities in Kosovo to pave the way for continuous talks between Belgrade and the Kosovo Albanian leadership on additional confidence building measures and the future status of Kosovo. Contact Group members will pursue this goal through immediate talks with both Belgrade and the Kosovo Albanians. It is clear that the Kosovo Albanian team for all these talks must be fully representative of their community in order to speak authoritatively.

6. The Contact Group concluded that Belgrade needed to take further action to implement fully the undertakings made by President Milosevic in Moscow on 16 June and the requirements of the Contact Group. The Contact Group also concluded that all concerned on the Kosovo Albanian side should commit themselves to dialogue and a peaceful settlement and reject violence and acts of terrorism. The Contact Group insisted that those outside the FRY who are supplying financial support, arms or training for armed Kosovo Albanian groups should cease doing so immediately. It furthermore requested all states to pursue, as a matter of urgency, all means consistent with their domestic laws and relevant International Law, to prevent funds collected on their territory being used to contravene UNSCR 1160. Against this background the Contact Group decided to pursue United Nations Security Council consideration of the adoption of a resolution reiterating the requirements mentioned above. This resolution should underline the need for a cessation of hostilities to permit a meaningful dialogue between the parties; enshrine the undertakings made by President Milosevic in Moscow; and require the authorities in Belgrade and all those concerned on the Kosovo Albanian side to ensure the safety of international observers operating in Kosovo. Should the required steps not be taken, the Contact Group will consider further action under the United Nations Charter, including action that may require the authorisation of a UN Security Council resolution, to bring about compliance by those who block the process.

7. The Contact Group reiterated that it supports neither the maintenance of the status quo in Kosovo nor the Kosovo Albanians' claims for independence. It emphasized that international involvement in the dialogue between the Belgrade authorities and representatives of the Kosovo Albanian community was an essential element of credible negotiations.

8. With this in mind, the Contact Group agreed to recommend to the negotiating teams basic elements for a resolution of the question of Kosovo's status. Contact Group members reaffirmed their intention to work actively for the achievement of the resolution of this issue.

9. As part of this, in order to help the parties, the Contact Group set in hand work to define possible further elements for the future status of Kosovo, which would be made available to the authorities in Belgrade and the leadership of the Kosovo Albanian community for a dialogue with international involvement.

10. Should substantive talks begin, with the necessary security confidence building measures in place and the launch of the mission of the Special Representative of the Chairman-in-Office of the OSCE, then the Contact Group remains prepared to promote a clear and achievable path toward Belgrade's full integration in the international community including participation in the OSCE. The Contact Group's goal continues to be that the Federal Republic of Yugoslavia should reap the benefits of membership of international financial and political institutions.

11. The Contact Group expressed its concern about the situation in neighbouring countries. It asked competent international organisations to examine options further to stabilise the situation in Albania. The Contact Group also supported the extension of the mandate of UNPREDEP beyond 31 August.

12. The Contact Group noted that the Prosecutor of the International Criminal Tribunal for the former Yugoslavia had now expressed the view that the situation in Kosovo represented an armed conflict within the terms of the mandate of the Tribunal. It reiterated its call for Belgrade and all those in Kosovo to cooperate with the Prosecutor's investigation of possible violations of international humanitarian law; and requested international observers operating in Kosovo to supply the Prosecutor with any relevant information.

13. The Contact Group noted that a representative of the Chairman-in-Office of the OSCE met government representatives of the FRY on 3 July in Belgrade. The Contact Group supported the continuation of contacts between the OSCE and the Government of the FRY with a view to the unimpeded and early return of the long-term OSCE missions to the FRY, the early launching of the mission of the Special Representative of the Chairman-in-Office of the OSCE and a dialogue across the full range of the FRY's relations with the OSCE.

8.   Chairman's Conclusions, Contact Group meeting on Kosovo in London, 2 October 1988

The Contact Group is united and intends to remain united. We expect full and immediate compliance with UNSCR 1199. This has not so far been achieved.

We heard a report on the work of the US facilitator, Ambassador Hill, on the negotiating track. We endorsed a revised paper which will now be put to the parties on behalf of the Contact Group.

We are united in condemning what is happening on the ground and in support for humanitarian efforts.

We all concluded that time is running out.

9.   Contact Group Discussion on Kosovo, Statement by UK Foreign Secretary, 8 October 1998

FOREIGN SECRETARY: ... We had a very good and frank discussion which confirmed a degree of unity and resolve among all the nations present there. First of all we agreed that there must be full compliance with Resolution 1199. We heard from Dick Holbrooke, and also from Igor Ivanov, of their latest discussions with President Milosevic. We were disappointed to hear from Mr Holbrooke that there remain many areas where Belgrade still falls well short of full compliance with 1199, and that he has been unable to obtain satisfactory assurances so far from President Milosevic that he intends to comply fully with 1199. We agreed tonight that Dick Holbrooke should return straight to Belgrade, with the full authority of the Contact Group and the backing of all the nations represented on the Contact Group. We are also clear that compliance with Resolution 1199 must involve 6 clear measures:

- first, an end to offensive operations and hostilities by both sides;
- secondly, the withdrawal of Belgrade's security forces to their positions before March and the withdrawal of heavy weapons;
- thirdly, freedom of access for the humanitarian agencies to get on with their important relief work;
- fourthly, full cooperation with the International War Crimes Tribunal to make sure those who have committed atrocities are brought to justice;
- fifthly, the facilitation of the return of refugees to their homes without fear;
- and finally, but critically, a start to negotiations on the Hill proposals which have been endorsed by the Contact Group.

We are also agreed that any settlement that offers compliance with 1199 must be irreversible. That is why we agreed tonight that if Mr Holbrooke is successful in obtaining agreement from President Milosevic, then that agreement must be open to full and credible verification, and the provision on the ground to verify that agreement must be on a scale and with the freedom necessary for full and credible verification. Tonight the Chairman in Office of the OSCE was present and we all agreed that there may be a role for the OSCE in any such verification if an agreement is reached. But we also accepted that there is a role for all of us, and also for the UN, if there is a settlement. That is why tonight we also agreed, all of us - including all the Permanent Members of the Security Council around the table, that if there is agreement secured by Mr Holbrooke, it will be incorporated in a Security Council resolution so that any assurances or agreement offered by President Milosevic will be enshrined in a Security Council resolution which will carry the full authority of the United Nations, and that full authority will be challenged if he were to break any of those assurances. Lastly, we all recognised the urgency of the present situation. The report of the Secretary General this week has already spelt out the serious humanitarian crisis in Kosovo, particularly among the refugees. Tonight we would reinforce that message by reminding the world of the urgency of obtaining full compliance with Resolution 1199 before winter sets in and turns a humanitarian crisis into a humanitarian catastrophe.

Let me sum up the message of this meeting. That message is very simple. We all intend to see full compliance with Security Council resolutions. Dick Holbrooke returns to Belgrade with the support of a united Contact Group to get that message across.

[For further Contact Group statements, see Chapter 15.]

Chapter 10: The International Criminal Tribunal for the Former Yugoslavia

The International Criminal Tribunal for the Former Yugoslavia was established as a symbol of international impotence in relation to the events in Bosnia and Herzegovina. Throughout 1992, the international community had observed the forcible occupation of some 70 per cent of the territory of that state by Serb forces. There followed the systematic extermination of over 250,000 mainly Muslim civilians and the forcible displacement of some 2.5 million more. Calls for international intervention failed, in large part due to the reluctance of certain European governments to get involved in what was wrongly termed an 'internal' conflict. It was hoped instead that the recording of the evidence of atrocities might inhibit the practices of ethnic cleansing and probable genocide. Hence, a Commission of Experts was established in order to assemble such evidence.[1] On the basis of an interim report by the experts, the Security Council decided on 22 February 1993 to establish an international Tribunal for the former Yugoslavia.[2] Three months later, a Statute for the Tribunal was adopted by the Council.[3]

The Tribunal derives its authority directly from the Chapter VII enforcement powers of the Security Council. All UN member states are legally obliged to cooperate with it, and to recognize the pre-eminence of its jurisdiction. That jurisdiction extends to the prosecution of persons responsible for serious violations of international humanitarian law committed in the territory of the former Yugoslavia since 1991. It covers serious war crimes, genocide and crimes against humanity. The latter includes murder, extermination, deportation, imprisonment, torture, rape, persecution on political, racial and religious grounds and other inhumane acts, whether committed in international or internal armed conflict and directed against any civilian population.[4] Those actually committing the acts, as well as those organising and ordering their commissioning, can be held responsible.

While the existence of the Tribunal did not have the deterrent effect that was hoped for (the Srebrenica massacre, for example, was committed over two years after the Tribunal came into existence), it has nevertheless established its international credibility. It has vigorously researched the events during the initial Yugoslav conflict, issued indictments and begun handing down convictions—much to the surprise of its early critics. Some early procedural flaws notwithstanding, it has also achieved a reputation for even-handedness and fairness. The successes of the Tribunal are all the more impressive, given the tight budgetary restrictions imposed upon it by the United Nations General Assembly. Its resources in terms of staff and other necessary support are severely limited.

The Tribunal's public image has been mostly dominated by the persistent non-cooperation of Yugoslavia and of the Serb entity of Srpska within Bosnia and Herzegovina. This has deprived the Tribunal of the presence of several prominent Serb leaders, including the former leader of Srpska, Radovan Karadic and his military chief General Ratko Mladic. Tribunal activity in relation to other suspects, arrested on foreign soil, has also been hampered by this attitude, which has been repeatedly condemned by the UN Security Council. In addition, the Tribunal has been criticised for its failure to act in relation to the FRY/Serb leadership itself, which many believe to be ultimately responsible for the horrors that obtained in Bosnia and Herzegovina, whether or not there exists an immediate opportunity of effecting an arrest.

Although the Security Council has consistently supported the Tribunal verbally, it has failed to take effective action in the face of Yugoslav non-cooperation. In particular, no sanctions were adopted, despite the repeated pleas from the Tribunal for strong measures to obtain Yugoslav cooperation. Constraints placed upon the effectiveness of Tribunal are therefore not really to be found at The Hague, the seat of the Tribunal, but rather in New York, at UN headquarters.

Despite its limited staff, the Tribunal responded swiftly to the reports of the initial massacres of ethnic Albanians in the Drenica region. On 10 March 1998, it issued an unusual public statement, confirming its view that its jurisdiction is "ongoing and covers the recent violence in Kosovo".[5] In view of the scale of the fighting, the Prosecutor indicated, the situation in Kosovo amounted to an internal armed conflict, bringing into operation the Tribunal's jurisdiction in relation to that territory.[6] The existence of an internal armed conflict in Kosovo, at least by 1998, implies a recognition of the status of the KLA as an organized armed movement controlling a significant part of Kosovo territory. Yugoslav pleas that it was dealing with a band of gangsters or terrorists to be controlled by means of an internal 'police' action were no longer tenable at this point.

While some international organs started to refer to the KLA as an armed movement, others continued to label it a terrorist organization. The changed status of the KLA in a state of internal armed conflict, of course, did not entitle that

---

[1] Security Council Resolution 780 (1993).
[2] Resolution 808 (1993), 22 February 1993, Document 10.1.
[3] Resolution 827 (1993), 25 May 1993, Document 10.2.
[4] Statute of the ICTFY, Articles 1, 5, 25 May 1993, Document 10.3.
[5] Prosecutor's Statement, 10 March 1998, Document 10.4.
[6] Communication from the Prosecutor, 7 July 1998, Document 10.6.

organization to engage in 'terrorist' operations, such as the kidnapping and murder of Serb civilians or the killing of members of Serb security forces that had fallen into its hands. Instead, both the FRY/Serb authorities and the KLA were bound to observe the rules of internal armed conflict. Effectively, members of the KLA, too, were now subject to the prosecutorial interest of the war-crimes investigators who were starting to assemble evidence accordingly.

With respect to the FRY/Serbia, the Tribunal expressed its concern at numerous specific and credible allegations concerning wilful killings (including a number of summary executions), wanton destruction (including the use of disproportionate force in attacking an area and devastation not justified by military necessity after the attack has been successful), attacks against civilians (including reprisals), and plunder.[7]

The UN Security Council, in Resolution 1160 (1993) of 31 March confirmed the jurisdiction of the Tribunal in relation to Kosovo and urged the office of the Prosecutor of the Tribunal to begin investigations.[8] Until October 1998, the Tribunal had been able to introduce investigators into the FRY/Kosovo to collect evidence on the ground. However, the FRY government then refused the granting of visas to tribunal investigators, claiming that no jurisdiction existed.[9]

There then followed media reports which indicated that the secretive Holbrooke agreement had in some way purported to diminish the authority of the Tribunal in relation to Kosovo, leading to urgent requests for clarification from the The Hague.[10] In the event, the authority of the Tribunal is based in Security Council resolutions and could not be affected by bilateral arrangements of whatever nature. And when endorsing the principal elements of the Holbrooke agreement, the Security Council reiterated its call upon Yugoslavia to cooperate with the Tribunal.[11] However, in contrast to the presence of NATO and associated forces in Bosnia and Herzegovina, the unarmed OSCE verifiers deployed pursuant to the Holbrooke agreement in Kosovo were not in a position to effect arrests of war crimes suspects.

Yugoslavia continued to refuse cooperation and access to the Tribunal's investigators, prompting the Security Council to adopt a further resolution which again called upon the FRY authorities, as well as the leaders of the Kosovo Albanian community, to cooperate fully with the Tribunal.[12] The situation was highlighted dramatically when the Chief Prosecutor attempted to enter Kosovo from Macedonia after news was received about the Racak Massacre of January 1999. In an event captured on television and broadcast world-wide, she was refused entry and unceremoniously turned back by FRY border guards.[13] This quite dramatic footage contributed to a climate making possible the more determined attitude of the Contact Group and NATO, leading to the summons of the parties to the Rambouillet Conference.

While the Tribunal failed to gain access, it nevertheless proceeded to collect evidence as far as possible with a view to launching prosecutions. This included interviews by Tribunal staff with some of the 100,000 victims of forced displacement in the territories adjacent to the FRY. When the FRY/Serbia started the campaign of forced deportation of what seemed to be virtually the entire ethnic Albanian population of Kosovo after the collapse of the Rambouillet process, this activity was increased. However, the limited resources of the Tribunal, compared to the scale of the unfolding tragedy, hampered its efforts in this respect. Nevertheless, on the basis of the assembled evidence, the Tribunal issued indictments against the top FRY/Serb leadership during the military confrontation with NATO. This event had an important impact on the terms of the conclusion of the conflict, as will be discussed in Volume 2 of this *Series*.

---

[7] Statement by the Prosecutor, 4 November 19998, Document 10.12.
[8] Also Resolution 1199 (1998), 23 September 1998, Document 7.4.
[9] Prosecutor's Statement, 7 October 1998, Document 10.7.
[10] President of the Tribunal Statement, 14 October 1998, Document 10.8.
[11] Resolution 1203, 24 October 1998, Document 7.5.
[12] Resolution 1207 (1998), 17 November 1998, Document 10.15.
[13] Letter by ICTFY President to President of the Security Council, 16 March 1999, Document 10.20.

1. Security Council Resolution 808 (1993), 22 February 1993

[Adopted by the Security Council at its 3175th meeting.]
The Security Council,

Reaffirming its resolution 713 (1991) of 25 September 1991 and all subsequent relevant resolutions,

Recalling paragraph 10 of its resolution 764 (1992) of 13 July 1992, in which it reaffirmed that all parties are bound to comply with the obligations under international humanitarian law and in particular the Geneva Conventions of 12 August 1949, and that persons who commit or order the commission of grave breaches of the Conventions are individually responsible in respect of such breaches,

Racalling also its resolution 771 (1992) of 13 August 1992, in which, *inter alia*, it demanded that all parties and others concerned in the former Yugoslavia, and all military forces in Bosnia and Herzegovina, immediately cease and desist from all breaches of international humanitarian law,

Recalling further its resolution 780 (1992) of 6 October 1992, in which it requested the Secretary-General to establish, as a matter of urgency, an impartial Commission of Experts to examine and analyse the information submitted pursuant to resolutions 771 (1992) and 780 (1992), together with such further information as the Commission of Experts may obtain, with a view to providing the Secretary-General with its conclusions on the evidence of grave breaches of the Geneva Conventions and other violations of international humanitarian law committed in the territory of the former Yugoslavia,

Having considered the interim report of the Commission of Experts established by resolution 780 (1992) (S/25274), in which the Commission observed that a decision to establish an ad hoc international tribunal in relation to events in the territory of the former Yugoslavia would be consistent with the direction of its work,

Expressing once again its grave alarm at continuing reports of widespread violations of international humanitarian law occurring within the territory of the former Yugoslavia, including reports of mass killings and the continuance of the practice of "ethnic cleansing",

Determining that this situation constitutes a threat to international peace and security,

Determined to put an end to such crimes and to take effective measures to bring to justice the persons who are responsible for them,

Convinced that in the particular circumstances of the former Yugoslavia the establishment of an international tribunal would enable this aim to be achieved and would contribute to the restoration and maintenance of peace,

Noting in this regard the recommendation by the Co-Chairmen of the Steering Committee of the International Conference on the Former Yugoslavia for the establishment of such a tribunal (S/25221),

Noting also with grave concern the "report of the European Community investigative mission into the treatment of Muslim women in the former Yugoslavia" (S/25240, annex I),

Noting further the report of the committee of jurists submitted by France (S/25266), the report the commission of jurists submitted by Italy (S/25300), and the report transmitted by the Permanent Representative of Sweden on behalf of the Chairman-in-Office of the Conference on Security and Cooperation in Europe (CSCE) (S/25307),

1. *Decides* that an international tribunal shall be established for the prosecution of persons responsible for serious violations of international humanitarian law committed in the territory of the former Yugoslavia since 1991;

2. *Requests* the Secretary-General to submit for consideration by the Council at the earliest possible date, and if possible no later than 60 days after the adoption of the present resolution, a report on all aspects of this matter, including specific proposals and where appropriate options for the effective and expeditious implementation of the decision contained in paragraph 1 above, taking into account suggestions put forward in this regard by Member States;

3. *Decides* to remain actively seized of the matter.

2. Security Council Resolution 827 (1993), 25 May 1993

[Adopted by the Security Council at its 3217th meeting.]

The Security Council,

Reaffirming its resolution 713 (1991) of 25 September 1991 and all subsequent relevant resolutions,

Having considered the report of the Secretary-General (S/25704 and Add.1) pursuant to paragraph 2 of resolution 808 (1993),

Expressing once again its grave alarm at continuing reports of widespread and flagrant violations of international humanitarian law occurring within the territory of the former Yugoslavia, and especially in the Republic of Bosnia and Herzegovina, including reports of mass killings, massive, organized and systematic detention and rape of women, and the continuance of the practice of "ethnic cleansing", including for the acquisition and the holding of territory,

Determining that this situation continues to constitute a threat to international peace and security,

Determined to put an end to such crimes and to take effective measures to bring to justice the persons who are responsible for them,

Convinced that in the particular circumstances of the former Yugoslavia the establishment as an ad hoc measure by the Council of an international tribunal and the prosecution of persons responsible for serious violations of international humanitarian law would enable this aim to be achieved and would contribute to the restoration and maintenance of peace,

Believing that the establishment of an international tribunal and the prosecution of persons responsible for the above-mentioned violations of international humanitarian law will contribute to ensuring that such violations are halted and effectively redressed,

Noting in this regard the recommendation by the Co-Chairmen of the Steering Committee of the International Conference on the Former Yugoslavia for the establishment of such a tribunal (S/25221),

Reaffirming in this regard its decision in resolution 808 (1993) that an international tribunal shall be established for the prosecution of persons responsible for serious violations of international humanitarian law committed in the territory of the former Yugoslavia since 1991,

Considering that, pending the appointment of the Prosecutor of the International Tribunal, the Commission of Experts established pursuant to resolution 780 (1992) should continue on an urgent basis the collection of information relating to evidence of grave breaches of the Geneva Conventions and other violations of international humanitarian law as proposed in its interim report (S/25274),

Acting under Chapter VII of the Charter of the United Nations,

1. *Approves* the report of the Secretary-General;

2. *Decides* hereby to establish an international tribunal for the sole purpose of prosecuting persons responsible for serious violations of international humanitarian law committed in the territory of the former Yugoslavia between 1 January 1991 and a date to be determined by the Security Council upon the restoration of peace and to this end to adopt the Statute of the International Tribunal annexed to the above-mentioned report;

3. *Requests* the Secretary-General to submit to the judges of the International Tribunal, upon their election, any suggestions received from States for the rules of procedure and evidence called for in Article 15 of the Statute of the International Tribunal;

4. *Decides* that all States shall cooperate fully with the International Tribunal and its organs in accordance with the present resolution and the Statute of the International Tribunal and that consequently all States shall take any measures necessary under their domestic law to implement the provisions of the present resolution and the Statute, including the obligation of States to comply with requests for assistance or orders issued by a Trial Chamber under Article 29 of the Statute;

5. *Urges* States and intergovernmental and non-governmental organizations to contribute funds, equipment and services to the International Tribunal, including the offer of expert personnel;

6. *Decides* that the determination of the seat of the International Tribunal is subject to the conclusion of appropriate arrangements between the United Nations and the Netherlands acceptable to the

Council, and that the International Tribunal may sit elsewhere when it considers it necessary for the efficient exercise of its functions;

7. *Decides* also that the work of the International Tribunal shall be carried out without prejudice to the right of the victims to seek, through appropriate means, compensation for damages incurred as a result of violations of international humanitarian law;

8. *Requests* the Secretary-General to implement urgently the present resolution and in particular to make practical arrangements for the effective functioning of the International Tribunal at the earliest time and to report periodically to the Council;

9. *Decides* to remain actively seized of the matter.

3.   Statute of the International Criminal Tribunal for the Former Yugoslavia, 25 May 1993

Having been established by the Security Council acting under Chapter VII of the Charter of the United Nations, the International Tribunal for the Prosecution of Persons Responsible for Serious Violations of International Humanitarian Law Committed in the Territory of the Former Yugoslavia since 1991 (hereinafter referred to as "the International Tribunal") shall function in accordance with the provisions of the present Statute.

Article 1. Competence of the International Tribunal

The International Tribunal shall have the power to prosecute persons responsible for serious violations of international humanitarian law committed in the territory of the former Yugoslavia since 1991 in accordance with the provisions of the present Statute.

Article 2. Grave breaches of the Geneva Conventions of 1949

The International Tribunal shall have the power to prosecute persons committing or ordering to be committed grave breaches of the Geneva Conventions of 12 August 1949, namely the following acts against persons or property protected under the provisions of the relevant Geneva Convention:

    (a) wilful killing;

    (b) torture or inhuman treatment, including biological experiments;

    (c) wilfully causing great suffering or serious injury to body or health;

    (d) extensive destruction and appropriation of property, not justified by military necessity and carried out unlawfully and wantonly;

    (e) compelling a prisoner of war or a civilian to serve in the forces of a hostile power;

    (f) wilfully depriving a prisoner of war or a civilian of the rights of fair and regular trial;

    (g) unlawful deportation or transfer or unlawful confinement of a civilian;

    (h) taking civilians as hostages.

Article 3. Violations of the laws or customs of war

The International Tribunal shall have the power to prosecute persons violating the laws or customs of war. Such violations shall include, but not be limited to:

    (a) employment of poisonous weapons or other weapons calculated to cause unnecessary suffering;

    (b) wanton destruction of cities, towns or villages, or devastation not justified by military necessity;

    (c) attack, or bombardment, by whatever means, of undefended towns, villages, dwellings, or buildings;

    (d) seizure of, destruction or wilful damage done to institutions dedicated to religion, charity and education, the arts and sciences, historic monuments and works of art and science;

    (e) plunder of public or private property.

Article 4. Genocide

1. The International Tribunal shall have the power to prosecute persons committing genocide as defined in paragraph 2 of this article or of committing any of the other acts enumerated in paragraph 3 of this article.

2. Genocide means any of the following acts committed with intent to destroy, in whole or in part, a national, ethnical, racial or religious group, as such:

    (a) killing members of the group;

    (b) causing serious bodily or mental harm to members of the group;

    (c) deliberately inflicting on the group conditions of life calculated to bring about its physical destruction in whole or in part;

    (d) imposing measures intended to prevent births within the group;

    (e) forcibly transferring children of the group to another group.

3. The following acts shall be punishable:

    (a) genocide;

    (b) conspiracy to commit genocide;

    (c) direct and public incitement to commit genocide;

    (d) attempt to commit genocide;

    (e) complicity in genocide.

Article 5. Crimes against humanity

The International Tribunal shall have the power to prosecute persons responsible for the following crimes when committed in armed conflict, whether international or internal in character, and directed against any civilian population:

    (a) murder;

    (b) extermination;

    (c) enslavement;

    (d) deportation;

    (e) imprisonment;

    (f) torture;

    (g) rape;

    (h) persecutions on political, racial and religious grounds;

    (i) other inhumane acts.

Article 6. Personal jurisdiction

The International Tribunal shall have jurisdiction over natural persons pursuant to the provisions of the present Statute.

Article 7. Individual criminal responsibility

1. A person who planned, instigated, ordered, committed or otherwise aided and abetted in the planning, preparation or execution of a crime referred to in articles 2 to 5 of the present Statute, shall be individually responsible for the crime.

2. The official position of any accused person, whether as Head of State or Government or as a responsible Government official, shall not relieve such person of criminal responsibility nor mitigate punishment.

3. The fact that any of the acts referred to in articles 2 to 5 of the present Statute was committed by a subordinate does not relieve his superior of criminal responsibility if he knew or had reason to know that the subordinate was about to commit such acts or had done so and the superior failed to take the necessary and reasonable measures to prevent such acts or to punish the perpetrators thereof.

4. The fact that an accused person acted pursuant to an order of a Government or of a superior shall not relieve him of criminal responsibility, but may be considered in mitigation of punishment if the International Tribunal determines that justice so requires.

Article 8. Territorial and temporal jurisdiction

The territorial jurisdiction of the International Tribunal shall extend to the territory of the former Socialist Federal Republic of Yugoslavia, including its land surface, airspace and territorial waters. The temporal jurisdiction of the International Tribunal shall extend to a period beginning on 1 January 1991.

Article 9. Concurrent jurisdiction

1. The International Tribunal and national courts shall have concurrent jurisdiction to prosecute persons for serious violations of international humanitarian law committed in the territory of the former Yugoslavia since 1 January 1991.

2. The International Tribunal shall have primacy over national courts. At any stage of the procedure, the International Tribunal may formally request national courts to defer to the competence of the International Tribunal in accordance with the present Statute and the Rules of Procedure and Evidence of the International Tribunal.

Article 10. *Non-bis-in-idem*

1. No person shall be tried before a national court for acts constituting serious violations of international humanitarian law under the present Statute, for which he or she has already been tried by the International Tribunal.

2. A person who has been tried by a national court for acts constituting serious violations of international humanitarian law may be subsequently tried by the International Tribunal only if:

(a) the act for which he or she was tried was characterized as an ordinary crime; or

(b) the national court proceedings were not impartial or independent, were designed to shield the accused from international criminal responsibility, or the case was not diligently prosecuted.

3. In considering the penalty to be imposed on a person convicted of a crime under the present Statute, the International Tribunal shall take into account the extent to which any penalty imposed by a national court on the same person for the same act has already been served. ...

CC/PIO/302-E

4. Prosecutor's Statement Regarding the Tribunal's Jurisdiction over Kosovo, 10 March 1998

The Prosecutor of the International Criminal Tribunal for the Former Yugoslavia has in the past made it a practice not to comment on ongoing investigations. However, recent events in Kosovo are an exceptional circumstance and the Prosecutor wishes to point out that the Statute of the Tribunal, which was adopted by the United Nations Security Council in May 1993, empowers the Tribunal to prosecute persons responsible for serious violations of international humanitarian law committed in the territory of the former Yugoslavia since 1991. This jurisdiction is ongoing and covers the recent violence in Kosovo. In this regard, the Prosecutor is currently gathering information and evidence in relation to the Kosovo incidents and will continue to monitor any subsequent developments. Following her recent visit to Belgrade, the Prosecutor expects the full co-operation of the authorities of the Federal Republic of Yugoslavia in respect of investigations into the Kosovo situation.

5. Security Coucil Resolution 1166 (1998), 13 May 1998

[*Adopted by the Security Council at its 3878th meeting.*]

The Security Council,

Reaffirming its resolution 827 (1993) of 25 May 1993,

Remaining convinced that the prosecution of persons responsible for serious violations of international humanitarian law committed in the territory of the former Yugoslavia contributes to the restoration and maintenance of peace in the former Yugoslavia,

Having considered the letter from the Secretary-General to the President of the Security Council dated 5 May 1998 (S/1998/376),

Convinced of the need to increase the number of judges and Trial Chambers, in order to enable the International Tribunal for the Prosecution of Persons Responsible for Serious Violations of International Humanitarian Law Committed in the Territory of the Former Yugoslavia since 1991 ("the International Tribunal") to try without delay the large number of accused awaiting trial,

Noting the significant progress being made in improving the procedures of the International Tribunal, and *convinced* of the need for its organs to continue their efforts to further such progress,

Acting under Chapter VII of the Charter of the United Nations,

1. *Decides* to establish a third Trial Chamber of the International Tribunal, and to this end *decides* to amend articles 11, 12 and 13 of the Statute of the International Tribunal and to replace those articles with the provisions set out in the annex to this resolution;

2. *Decides* that three additional judges shall be elected as soon as possible to serve in the additional Trial Chamber, and decides also, without prejudice to article 13.4 of the Statute of the International Tribunal, that once elected they shall serve until the date of the expiry of the terms of office of the existing judges, and that for the purpose of that election the Security Council shall, notwithstanding article 13.2 (c) of the Statute, establish a list from the nominations received of not less than six and not more than nine candidates;

3. *Urges* all States to cooperate fully with the International Tribunal

and its organs in accordance with their obligations under resolution 827 (1993) and the Statute of the International Tribunal and *welcomes* the cooperation already extended to the Tribunal in the fulfilment of its mandate;

4. *Requests* the Secretary-General to make practical arrangements for the elections mentioned in paragraph 2 above and for enhancing the effective functioning of the International Tribunal, including the timely provision of personnel and facilities, in particular for the third Trial Chamber and related offices of the Prosecutor, *and further requests* him to keep the Security Council closely informed of progress in this regard;

5. *Decides* to remain actively seized of the matter.

CC/PIU/329-E

6. Communication from the Prosecutor to the Contact Group, 7 July 1998

On the eve of the meeting of the Contact Group in Bonn, the Prosecutor of the ICTY, Justice Louise Arbour, has communicated to the members of the Contact Group her position on the following issues:

KOSOVO

The Prosecutor has previously indicated that she has jurisdiction to investigate the recent events in Kosovo and to prosecute persons responsible for serious violations of international humanitarian law. The Prosecutor believes that the nature and scale of the fighting indicate that an "armed conflict", within the meaning of international law, exists in Kosovo. As a consequence, she intends to bring charges for crimes against humanity or war crimes, if evidence of such crimes is established.

The Prosecutor wishes to stress that the Tribunal's jurisdiction also includes crimes committed by persons on either side of the conflict. International law imposes obligations on combatants involved in an armed conflict to observe the laws of war, and any violations of such laws can be punished. Criminal responsibility also attaches not only to those who themselves actually commit atrocities, but equally to those in positions of superior responsibility. Under international law, a superior will be held criminally liable if he knew or had reason to know that a subordinate was about to commit criminal acts, or had done so and the superior failed to take the necessary and reasonable measures to prevent such acts or to punish the perpetrators.

Additional resources have been made available to the Office of the Prosecutor in relation to Kosovo, and investigations are likely to continue for a considerable time.

CC/PIU/349-E

7. ICTY President McDonald Statement to the Security Council, 2 October 1998

Mr. President, Members of the Security Council,

I appreciate your invitation to speak with you today and your willingness to take the time to consider this very urgent matter.

In my letter to the Security Council of September 9, 1998, I reported the continuing refusal of the Government of the Federal Republic of Yugoslavia (Serbia and Montenegro) (F.R.Y.) to cooperate with the International Tribunal. Specifically, I noted its failure to arrest and transfer to the custody of the International Tribunal three indicted persons. My letter sets out in greater detail the history of this non-compliance.

I am here today to request the Security Council to adopt effective measures to ensure there is immediate compliance by the F.R.Y. with its obligations under international law and those imposed by this body, acting pursuant to its Chapter VII authority.

In resolution 827, creating this Tribunal, the Security Council directed all States to take any measures necessary under their domestic law to implement the provisions of the resolution and the Statute of the Tribunal. Further, the Dayton Agreement requires all signatories to cooperate with the Tribunal. However, the F.R.Y. stands alone as the only signatory to the Dayton Agreement which has failed to adopt legislation to facilitate cooperation. Article 29 of the Statute of the Tribunal provides that States shall comply without undue delay with an order of a Trial Chamber for the arrest or detention of persons. The Secretary-General's Report to the Security Council transmitting the Statute of the Tribunal states that orders of the Tribunal have the status of enforcement actions under Chapter VII. Nevertheless, the F.R.Y. has refused to transfer to the custody of the Tribunal indicted persons who are nationals of that State. It contends that its Constitution prohibits the "extradition" of its citizens.

Clearly, the duty of all States to comply with orders of the Tribunal is manifest and is not subject to compromise or exception. Moreover, it is a recognized principle of international law that States may not rely on their domestic law to thwart their international obligations. Thus, there is no basis for the F.R.Y.'s failure to comply.

In Resolution 827, the Security Council noted widespread and flagrant violations of international humanitarian law occurring within the territory of the former Yugoslavia. It determined that this situation constituted a threat to international peace and security and resolved to put an end to such crimes and to have brought to justice persons who are responsible for such crimes. The Security Council concluded that the prosecution of persons responsible for these serious violations of international humanitarian law would contribute to the restoration and maintenance of peace. Thus, in your wisdom, you made the historic decision that the International Tribunal was an appropriate measure to achieve that result.

As a court of law, the Tribunal exists to dispense justice. Yet, it cannot act effectively if its orders are disregarded. As a subsidiary organ of the Security Council, and its creation, it looks to the Security Council for the support necessary to discharge its mandate. I implore you, indeed I beseech you to assist in ensuring that the Tribunal's orders are given effect.

The request I make is straightforward. The disregard of the F.R.Y. is clear and its obligation to co-operate is not subject to dispute.

The International Tribunal indicted the three individuals in question on November 7, 1995, for the alleged murder of 260 unarmed men following the fall of the city of Vukovar in November 1991. A warrant for their arrest was issued and transmitted to the Government of the F.R.Y. for execution because it was believed that they were residing on its territory. We still believe this today, a fact which has not been disputed by the F.R.Y. On April 3, 1996, a Trial Chamber concluded that "the failure to effect service of the Indictment was due to the refusal of the F.R.Y. to cooperate with the Tribunal". Thereafter, the President of the Tribunal, on April 24, 1996, reported this non-compliance to the Security Council. On May 8, 1996, the President of the Security Council reminded the F.R.Y. of those obligations, deploring "the failure to execute the arrest warrants" and calling for the immediate execution of those warrants. The Security Council remained seized of the matter.

On December 19, 1997, a Trial Chamber ordered the authorities of the F.R.Y. to serve the three accused with the Indictment and, once again, the F.R.Y. failed to respond. I should note that the President of the Tribunal has reported non-compliance by the F.R.Y. on another occasion for its failure to execute arrest warrants of the Tribunal. On July 11, 1996, the President reported to the Security Council the failure of the F.R.Y. to execute arrest warrants against Radovan Karadzic and Ratko Mladic. In response, a Presidential Statement was issued on August 8th.

Thus, almost three years after their indictment and the issuance of arrest warrants, and nearly seven years after the families of the victims lost their loved ones, the three accused I speak of today remain at liberty. And, there is no indication that the F.R.Y. is currently taking any action on this matter.

This intentional non-compliance has far-reaching consequences for international peace and security.

No State should be permitted to act as if it is "above the law". Such transgression is not only unlawful, but importantly sends a message to other States that the measures adopted by the Security Council can be ignored. Therefore, it is imperative that the F.R.Y. be brought into the fold of nations who believe in world peace and respect the authority of the Security Council.

Under Article 29 of the Tribunal's Statute, States are to comply with orders of the Tribunal "without undue delay". The F.R.Y. has been in non-compliance for almost three years. It is unconscionable for a State to be allowed to flaunt their obligations under international law. This behaviour undermines the vision of the Security Council that the Tribunal was indeed the appropriate measure to redress the commission of serious violations of international humanitarian law in the former Yugoslavia.

There comes a time when such defiance cannot be ignored. That time is now. The world community, embodied by the United Nations, must not allow this territory to revert to the catastrophy we watched begin and escalate in the early 1990s. We must learn from the lessons of the past, lest they be repeated.

The International Tribunal has made great strides in dispensing international criminal justice in the five years of its existence. We now have five ongoing trials where we apply the highest international standards of justice. The Tribunal has finally overcome many obstacles it faced in the early years. It is now effective and fully functioning. It will continue to execute the mandate given to it by the Security Council. However, the threat posed by the non-compliance of the F.R.Y. must be dealt with once and for all. The obstructionist actions of the F.R.Y. that taint the institution which you created with the expectation that peace, security and reconciliation would be achieved in the former Yugoslavia from the ashes of death and destruction must no longer be tolerated.

I know that the Security Council is fully committed to our work. I request that you not allow any State to stand in the way of the fulfilment of the mandate you charged us with when you established the International Tribunal.

Thank you for allowing me to speak with you today.

CC/PIU/351-E

8.   Statement by the Office of the Prosecutor, 7 October 1998

Up until the last few weeks, the Prosecutor has been undertaking investigations in relation to the events in Kosovo without any obstruction on the part of the Belgrade authorities. A team has just returned from Kosovo and it was the Prosecutor's intention to supplement this team with other investigators. That has not been possible because for the first time the Belgrade authorities had not issued visas in time for these other investigators to travel to Yugoslavia.

On Friday of last week the Prosecutor's staff in Belgrade sought an explanation from the Belgrade authorities as to why these visas had not been issued.

In response the representative of the Foreign Ministry indicated that the official position of the Federal Republic of Yugoslavia (FRY) regarding the Tribunal and Kosovo is that the Tribunal has no jurisdiction to conduct investigations in Kosovo and the Tribunal will not be allowed to do so.

It was further stated by the Ministry, that the Prosecutor's investigations in Kosovo represented a violation of the FRY's sovereignty. The Prosecutor's investigators would be allowed to move around in Kosovo but would not be permitted to conduct investigations. If such investigations were carried out in Kosovo, the FRY might reconsider its existing co-operation with the Tribunal and in particular might reconsider the agreement relating to the Prosecutor's Liaison Office in Belgrade.

The Prosecutor finds the position of the FRY Government to be totally unacceptable. Such a position ignores not only the express terms of the Tribunal's Statue, but also with various United Nations Security Council resolutions and Presidential Statements which unequivocally state that the Tribunal does in fact have jurisdiction over Kosovo.

For instance, UN SC Resolution 1160, which was adopted on 31 March 1998, recognised the ICTY's mandate on Kosovo. The relevant wording of that Resolution is as follows:

"Acting under Chapter VII of the UN Charter:...the Security Council ...

17. Urges the Office of the Prosecutor of the

International Tribunal established pursuant to resolution 827 (1993) of 25 May 1993 <u>to begin gathering information related to the violence in Kosovo</u> that may fall within its jurisdiction, and notes that the authorities of the Federal Republic of Yugoslavia have an <u>obligation to co-operate</u> with the Tribunal ...."

Further UN SC Resolution 1199, which was adopted on 23 September 1998, noted that:

"... he communication by the Prosecutor of the International Tribunal for the Former Yugoslavia to the Contact Group on 7 July 1998, expressing the view that the situation in Kosovo represents an armed conflict within the terms of the mandate of the Tribunal;..........."

and acting under Chapter VII of the Charter of the United Nations the Security Council:

"... 13. Calls upon the authorities of the Federal Republic of Yugoslavia, the leaders of the Kosovo Albanian community and all others concerned to co-operate fully with the Prosecutor of the International Tribunal for the Former Yugoslavia in the investigation of possible violations within the jurisdiction of the Tribunal;......"

Further, in response President McDonald's briefing to the Security Council last Friday, the President of the Security Council stated publicly that the Security Council reaffirmed the authority and jurisdiction of the International Tribunal over matters within its competence throughout the territory of the former Yugoslavia.

The Prosecutor believes that it is in the best interest of the FRY and of all people in Kosovo and Serbia, to allow the Prosecutor's investigator's to fulfill their duties and thus to contribute to the establishment of the full truth about the conflict in Kosovo and the prosecution of those responsible for the crimes falling within the Tribunal's jurisdiction, as requested by the UN Security Council.

In conclusion, the Prosecutor intends to pursue her investigations into the events in Kosovo and urges the authorities of the FRY to re-consider their position and to comply with its international obligations to co-operate fully with the Tribunal and the Prosecutor's investigations.

CC/PIU/352-E

9. Statement by the President of the International Tribunal on the Agreements on Kosovo, 14 October 1998

The President welcomes in principle the agreements on Kosovo that were provisionally concluded yesterday.

The President has not yet had the opportunity to review the agreements, and thus is not familiar with their provisions. She notes, however, conflicting media reports about whether they contain explicit provisions and mechanisms to ensure the Federal Republic of Yugoslavia's compliance with the International Tribunal.

The President further understands that the Security Council will shortly review the agreement. In this context, the President recalls that in September she wrote to the Security Council and subsequently briefed its members over the persistent failure of the Federal Republic of Yugoslavia to surrender three persons indicted by the International Tribunal in November 1995. Mile Mrksic, Miroslav Radic and Veselin Sljivancanin are charged with the murder of 260 unarmed men following the fall of the city of Vukovar in late 1991. Today they remain at liberty. The Federal Republic of Yugoslavia continues to flout the law and the will of the international community by refusing to transfer them to the International Tribunal.

Accordingly, the President would like to take this opportunity to re-iterate that the Federal Republic of Yugoslavia is legally required to co-operate with the International Tribunal. She reminds all involved parties of the need to ensure the FRY's full compliance with all of its obligations towards the International Tribunal.

CC/PIU/353-E

10. Prosecutor seeks assurance from President Milosevic regarding Kosovo investigations, 15 October 1998

The Prosecutor of the International Criminal Tribunal for the former Yugoslavia has made the following public statement:

"Following reports that the US envoy Mr Richard Holbrooke was not able to obtain any concessions from President Milosevic on Tuesday regarding the jurisdiction of this Tribunal over events in Kosovo, I wish to make a strong and unequivocal statement regarding this Tribunal's jurisdiction.

On 25 May 1993 the United Nations Security Council passed resolution 827 which created this Tribunal, giving it jurisdiction to prosecute persons responsible for Crimes Against Humanity and War Crimes, as well as other serious violations of international humanitarian law, committed in the territory of the former Yugoslavia since 1991, which includes Kosovo. Consistent with the initial resolution, the Security Council has since reaffirmed this jurisdiction in resolutions 1160 of 31 March 1998 and 1199 of 23 September 1998.

The jurisdiction of this Tribunal is not conditional upon President Milosevic's consent, nor is it dependent on the outcome of any negotiations between him and anyone else. It is for the Judges of this Tribunal to interpret such jurisdiction and for the Security Council to modify or expand.

Today I have forwarded a letter to President Milosevic informing him that it is my intention to resume investigations in Kosovo at the earliest opportunity. In respect of the next investigative mission to Kosovo, it is my intention to lead the team, which will include the Deputy Prosecutor, senior staff in my Office, together with eight other members of my team which is investigating crimes falling within this Tribunal's jurisdiction that have allegedly occurred in Kosovo during 1998.

I have also informed President Milosevic that is my intention to visit the areas where some of the alleged crimes have been committed, to meet with government and other officials, and to meet with other organisations which may assist my investigations. In accordance with normal practice investigators will also gather any relevant evidence and interview potential witnesses.

Finally, I have sought an assurance from President Milosevic that visas will be forthcoming to enable my investigations in Kosovo to continue forthwith."

JL/PIU/356-E

11. Letter from President McDonald to the President of the Security Council, 22 October 1998

... Recent efforts to find a peaceful solution to events in Kosovo have resulted in agreements between the Government of the Federal Republic of Yugoslavia (Serbia and Montenegro) (F.R.Y.) and the Organisation for Security and Cooperation in Europe and the North Atlantic Treaty Organisation. The President of Serbia has also issued a "Statement on the Principles of a Political Solution and on a Timetable Framework" [sic] (Statement of the President of Serbia). While the agreements commit the government of the F.R.Y. to accept an international verification system in Kosovo, they contain no provisions regarding the F.R.Y.'s obligation to cooperate with the International Criminal Tribunal for the former Yugoslavia (International Tribunal). Moreover, it would appear that the Statement of the President of Serbia reserves to the domestic judicial system of the F.R.Y. the right to investigate, prosecute and try offences committed in Kosovo that may fall within the jurisdiction of the International Tribunal.

This is of particular concern to the International Tribunal considering the history of its relationship with the F.R.Y., characterised by near-total non-compliance. Thus, I respectfully submit that it is imperative that the competence of the International Tribunal is unambiguously reaffirmed and that the obligation of the Government of the F.R.Y. to cooperate with it is made an explicit part of any resolution of the situation in Kosovo. As you are aware, in September of this year,

I wrote to the Security Council and subsequently briefed its members on the continuing refusal of the Government of the F.R.Y. to cooperate with the International Tribunal by failing to arrest and transfer to the custody of the International Tribunal three persons indicted by the International Tribunal. Mile Mrk{ic, Miroslav Radi} and Veselin [ljivan}anin were indicted on 7 November 1995 for the murder of 260 unarmed men following the fall of the city of Vukovar in November 1991. I recalled that in March 1996, international warrants of arrest were sent to all States, and that in April 1996, my predecessor reported the F.R.Y.'s failure to arrest the three men to the Security Council. Today, these men remain at liberty, believed to be residing in Serbia. Moreover, that Government has ignored the Security Council's decision that all States should adopt legislation necessary to implement the provisions of resolution 827 and the Statute of the International Tribunal. It stands alone among the signatories to the General Framework Agreement for Peace in Bosnia and Herzegovina in neither having adopted such legislation, nor having transferred to the International Tribunal's custody those indictees on its territory. The F.R.Y. has, thus, failed to comply with resolution 827 and the Statute of the International Tribunal, in particular Article 29.

With respect to events in Kosovo, the Security Council has confirmed on two occasions that the F.R.Y. is bound under international law to comply with the International Tribunal. Resolution 1160, passed in March of this year, inter alia, noted that the authorities of the F.R.Y. are so bound. In resolution 1199, the Security Council reiterated that obligation and called upon the F.R.Y. and other concerned parties to cooperate fully with the International Tribunal. I am, therefore, gravely concerned that the agreements concluded on the situation in Kosovo lack an explicit recognition of the F.R.Y.'s obligation towards the International Tribunal. While they do require, inter alia, the F.R.Y. to comply with the provisions of resolution 1199, there is no express commitment from the Government of the F.R.Y. to cooperate with the International Tribunal. In this regard, I note with alarm that the Statement of the President of Serbia declares that "no person will be prosecuted in state courts for crimes related to the conflict in Kosovo except for crimes against humanity and international law...". This expression of the view of the Government of Serbia does not include a reference to the International Tribunal. I fear, therefore, that it represents an implicit attempt to deny the primacy of the International Tribunal and to disregard the legal requirement that Serbia, as a part of the F.R.Y., should facilitate the work of the International Tribunal.

While I hope that the Government of the F.R.Y. will now cease its pattern of non-cooperation, I fear that in the absence of a specific commitment to obey the will of the Security Council, the International Tribunal will continue to experience further difficulties with the Government of the F.R.Y. In this regard, I note that, since my address to the Security Council last month, the F.R.Y. has taken no action to arrest the three indicted individuals referred to above. The obligation to cooperate and comply is incontrovertible. It is not subject to alteration, negotiation or abrogation by any individual or government. The Security Council, as the body with the authority to create the International Tribunal, is the only body that may revise or rescind this obligation. The Security Council has not done so and, thus, the obligation remains. Considering resolution 1199, it is clear that the F.R.Y. may not impede the work of the Prosecutor as she carries out investigations within Kosovo. It is also clear that the F.R.Y. must take all other action that is necessary to facilitate the work of the International Tribunal, including the arrest of indicted persons.

All States are subject to international law. All States must respect and ensure respect for their international obligations. In an era characterised by an increased emphasis on the human rights of individuals, the F.R.Y.'s continued flouting of the will and the law of the international community jeopardises all efforts to bring peace to the peoples of the former Yugoslavia. For these reasons, I respectfully urge the Security Council to take such action as is necessary to vindicate the status and primacy of the International Tribunal and to ensure that compliance from the F.R.Y. is now forthcoming.

CC/PIU/358-E

12. Statement by Justice Louise Arbour, Prosecutor of the ICTY, 4 November 1998

The ICTY was established by Security Council resolution 827 in 1993 and it has the power to prosecute persons responsible for serious violations of international humanitarian law committed in the territory of the former Yugoslavia, including Kosovo, since 1991. As the Prosecutor for the Tribunal, I am required to conduct the investigation and prosecution of such persons (Art. 16). As such, I have the power to question suspects, victims and witnesses, to collect evidence and to conduct on-site investigations (Art. 18(2)). Serious violations of international humanitarian law include grave breaches of the Geneva Conventions of 1949, violations of the laws or customs of war, genocide, and crimes against humanity. Of these categories of violations, all but grave breaches of the Geneva Conventions may be committed during an internal armed conflict.

There has been protracted armed violence, between Yugoslav authorities and organised armed groups in Kosovo throughout most of the year. It is my position that an internal armed conflict has existed in Kosovo during 1998 and that the ICTY has jurisdiction over persons committing serious violations of international humanitarian law during that conflict. My position is supported by several Security Council resolutions:

(a) SCR 1160 of 31 March 1998 urges the Prosecutor to begin gathering information related to the violence in Kosovo that may fall within the Tribunal's jurisdiction and notes that FRY authorities have an obligation to co-operate with the Tribunal;

(b) SCR 1199 of 23 September 1998 calls upon FRY authorities and the leaders of the Kosovo Albanian community to co-operate fully with the Prosecutor, and

(c) SCR 1203 of 24 October 1998 calls for prompt and complete investigations, including international supervision and participation, of all atrocities committed against civilians, and full co-operation with the Tribunal, including compliance with its orders, requests for information and investigations.

The Tribunal has jurisdiction over a wide range of offences which may have occurred in Kosovo. These include crimes against humanity such as murder, torture, rape and persecutions. They also include violations of the laws or customs of war such as attacks on the civilian population, murder, torture, cruel treatment, taking of hostages, outrages upon personal dignity, wanton destruction of towns and villages, and looting.

There have been numerous allegations, specific and credible enough to require further investigations, concerning wilful killings (including a number of summary executions), wanton destruction (including the use of disproprionate force in attacking an area and devastation not justified by military necessity after the attack has been successful), attacks against civilians (including reprisals), and plunder.

JL/PIU/359-E

13. Statement by Judge McDonald, President of the ICTFY, 5 November 1998

The Prosecutor and I intended to travel to the Federal Republic of Yugoslavia (Serbia and Montenegro) to attend a Conference on War Crimes Trials, organised by the Humanitarian Law Centre in Belgrade. The Prosecutor then expected to go to Kosovo to conduct investigations into possible violations of international humanitarian law committed there, as she is entitled to do pursuant to her mandate.

Yesterday evening, the Prosecutor was informed by the Government of the FRY that *"the Federal Republic of Yugoslavia does not accept any investigation of ICTY [sic] in Kosovo and Metohija generally, nor during your stay in the FR of Yugoslavia [sic]."* This statement is a blatant refusal to allow the Prosecutor to investigate events in Kosovo. This follows similar remarks made earlier this week by the Ministers of Justice of the FRY (Serbia and Montenegro) and Serbia, in which it was alleged that the International Tribunal's competence to investigate events in Kosovo had ended with the recent signing of agreements between the FRY and the NATO and the OSCE. This situation is totally unacceptable.

I would like to emphasise that the position of the Governments of FRY (Serbia and Montenegro) and Serbia have no basis in law and that the refusal to allow the Prosecutor access to Kosovo is illegal. The Security Council has on a number of occasions reaffirmed the legal right of, and indeed has directed, the Prosecutor to investigate events in Kosovo. In March of this year, the Council urged the Prosecutor to begin gathering information related to crimes that may fall within the jurisdiction of the International Tribunal. It further reiterated the obligation of the FRY (Serbia and Montenegro) to co-operate with the International Tribunal. This was subsequently restated in resolution 1199 in September of this year. Most recently, in resolution 1203, the Council called "for prompt and complete investigation, including international supervision and participation, of all atrocities committed against civilians and full co-operation with the International Tribunal for the former Yugoslavia, including compliance with its orders, requests for information and investigations."

These resolutions were adopted, and the International Tribunal was established, by the Security Council under Chapter Seven of the United Nations Charter. As a matter of international law, all States are bound by such actions. The Government of the FRY (Serbia and Montenegro) is, thus, under a clear and incontrovertible obligation to co-operate fully with the International Tribunal. It may not take any unilateral action that countermands or undermines the authority of the Security Council. The decisions and orders of the Security Council supersede any statement or assertion made by that Government. Its actions, therefore, are in direct violation of resolutions 1160, 1199 and 1203.

This conduct is a further example of the FRY's utter disregard for the norms of the international community. Essentially, it has become a rogue State, one that holds the international rule of law in contempt. The Prosecutor has written to me reporting the non-compliance of the FRY (Serbia and Montenegro), which prevents her from carrying out the functions of her office and interferes with the discharge of the International Tribunal's mandate. Later today, I shall once again report this non-compliance to the Security Council. This conduct, however, is not only an affront to the International Tribunal as an institution, it is a direct challenge to the authority of the Security Council. I will urge the Council to vindicate its authority and respond forcefully to the action of the FRY (Serbia and Montenegro).

In denying the legal entitlement of the Prosecutor to investigate the situation in Kosovo, the Government is failing to co-operate fully with the International Tribunal as an institution. In these circumstances, it is inappropriate for me to travel to the FRY (Serbia and Montenegro).

In this regard, I wish to further emphasise that by claiming that it may act outside of international law, the Government of the FRY (Serbia and Montenegro) also acts to the detriment of its own citizens. Unfortunately, the population of the FRY is being stigmatised by the policies of its Government and is suffering acute hardship as a direct result of those policies. Thus, I deeply regret that I am now unable to attend the Conference on War Crimes Trials, as it has been organised by individuals within the FRY (Serbia and Montenegro) who are dedicated to upholding the rule of law and to promoting freedom of expression. It is now time for the international community to take strong action to prevent the obstruction of the mandate that it gave the International Tribunal.

JL/PIU/360-E

14. Statement by Justice Louise Arbour, Prosecutor of the ICTFY, 5 November 1998

I was informed yesterday evening in a letter from the Ambassador of the Federal Republic of Yugoslavia in The Hague that I would not be permitted to conduct investigations in Kosovo. Specifically, the Ambassador put it to me in the following terms:

> "As you have already been informed, the Federal Republic of Yugoslavia does not accept any investigation of ICTY in Kosovo and Metohija generally, nor during your stay in the FR of Yugoslavia."

The letter also informed me that I would be granted a single entry, seven day visa, along with the Deputy Prosecutor, two members of my staff and two security officers, to attend a conference in Belgrade during the weekend, and to meet with government officials, also in Belgrade. My request had been for ten investigators to accompany me to conduct an investigative mission to Kosovo. I have decided to decline the unacceptably limited visa that was offered to me and I very much regret that I will be unable to attend the important conference to be convened in Belgrade this week end by the Humanitarian Law Center, …

I wish to stress once again that my entitlement to unrestricted and unimpeded access to Kosovo is unambiguously expressed in Article 18 (2) of the Statute of this Tribunal which provides that the Prosecutor has the power to conduct on-site investigations. I lead criminal investigations, at the request of the Security Council, in the course of which I must assemble evidence that will meet, in a court of law, a standard of proof beyond a reasonable doubt, in a public, transparent and adversarial forum. I intend to continue pursuing all legal means available to me, until I am granted access to the relevant sites, and to the witnesses that I may chose to contact in Kosovo. I will be calling on the various States and international organisations to continue to support these investigative efforts. In accordance with the applicable legal provisions, I have written to the President of the Tribunal, asking that she notify the Security Council of the failure of the Federal Republic of Yugoslavia to comply with its obligations under the Statute in this matter.

15. Letter from the President of the ICTFY to the President of the Security Council, 6 November 1998

I have the misfortune to report once again to the Security Council the continuing refusal of the Federal Republic of Yugoslavia (Serbia and Montenegro) to cooperate with the International Tribunal, as required by Resolutions of the Security Council and the Tribunal's Statute. The occasion for making this report is the failure of the Federal Republic of Yugoslavia to issue visas to investigators of the Office of the Prosecutor so that they may conduct investigations in Kosovo. In doing so, the Federal Republic of Yugoslavia has stated that it "does not accept any investigation of ICTY in Kosovo and Metohija."

Clearly this position contravenes the explicit decisions of the Security Council. In Resolution 1160 of 31 March 1998, the Security Council urged the Prosecutor of the Tribunal to begin gathering information related to the violence in Kosovo. On 23 September 1998, in Resolution 1199, the Security Council found that events in Kosovo constitute a threat to peace and security in the region. In that Resolution the authorities of the Federal Republic of Yugoslavia were obligated to "cooperate fully with the Prosecutor of the International Tribunal for the Former Yugoslavia in the investigation of possible violations within the jurisdiction of the Tribunal." Finally, less than two weeks ago, on 24 October 1998, the Security Council adopted Resolution 1203 which called for a prompt and complete investigation of all atrocities committed in Kosovo. Further, full cooperation with the Tribunal was required, "including compliance with its orders, requests for information and investigations."

By letter dated 15 October 1998, the Prosecutor advised Slobodan Milosevic, President of the Federal Republic of Yugoslavia, of her intention to lead an investigative mission to Kosovo. She sought assurance that visas would be issued to enable the investigations to continue forthwith. The failure of the Federal Republic of Yugoslavia to provide her office with the appropriate travel documents for investigators prevents her from carrying out the mandate of the Security Council. By letter of 5 November 1998, the Prosecutor requested that I notify the Security Council of the failure of the Federal Republic of Yugoslavia to fulfil its obligations under Article 29 of the Statute of the Tribunal.

Excellency, I need not remind you that this is the fourth time the President of the Tribunal has notified this body of the Federal Republic of Yugoslavia's non-compliance. …

16. Security Council Resolution 1207 (1998), 17 November 1998

[*Adopted by the Security Council at its 3944th meeting.*]

The Security Council,
Recalling all its previous relevant resolutions concerning the conflicts in the former Yugoslavia, in particular resolution 827 (1993) of 25 May 1993,
Recalling also the statement by its President of 8 May 1996 (S/PRST/1996/23),
Recalling further the General Framework Agreement for Peace in Bosnia and Herzegovina and the Annexes thereto (S/1995/999, annex), in particular its Article IX and its Annex 1-A, Article X,
Having considered the letters of the President of the International Tribunal for the Former Yugoslavia to the President of the Security Council of 8 September 1998 (S/1998/839), 22 October 1998 (S/1998/990) and 6 November 1998 (S/1998/1040),
Deploring the continued failure of the Federal Republic of Yugoslavia to cooperate fully with the Tribunal, as described in those letters,
Reaffirming the commitment of all Member States to the sovereignty and territorial integrity of the Federal Republic of Yugoslavia,
Acting under Chapter VII of the Charter of the United Nations,
1. *Reiterates* its decision that all States shall cooperate fully with the Tribunal and its organs in accordance with resolution 827 (1993) and the Statute of the Tribunal, including the obligation of States to comply with requests for assistance or orders issued by a Trial Chamber under Article 29 of the Statute, to execute arrest warrants transmitted to them by the Tribunal, and to comply with its requests for information and investigations;
2. *Calls again upon* the Federal Republic of Yugoslavia, and all other States which have not already done so, to take any measures necessary under their domestic law to implement the provisions of resolution 827 (1993) and the Statute of the Tribunal, and *affirms* that a State may not invoke provisions of its domestic law as justification for its failure to perform binding obligations under international law;
3. *Condemns* the failure to date of the Federal Republic of Yugoslavia to execute the arrest warrants issued by the Tribunal against the three individuals referred to in the letter of 8 September 1998, and *demands* the immediate and unconditional execution of those arrest warrants, including the transfer to the custody of the Tribunal of those individuals;
4. *Reiterates* its call upon the authorities of the Federal Republic of Yugoslavia, the leaders of the Kosovo Albanian community and all others concerned to cooperate fully with the Prosecutor in the investigation of all possible violations within the jurisdiction of the Tribunal;
5. *Requests* the President of the Tribunal to keep the Council informed about the implementation of this resolution for the Council's further consideration;
6. *Decides* to remain seized of the matter

17. Statement by the President of the ICTFY to the Security Council, 8 December 1998

Mr. President, Members of the Security Council
Thank you for inviting me to inform the Security Council about the implementation of Security Council resolution 1207 (17 November 1998) for the Council's further consideration. That resolution stated, *inter alia*, that the Security Council demands the "immediate and unconditional execution of those arrest warrants ... [against the three individuals referred to in my letter of 8 September 1998 to the Security Council reporting the non-compliance of the Federal Republic of Yugoslavia to the Security Council], including the transfer to the custody of the Tribunal of those individuals."

That resolution also called upon the authorities of the Federal Republic of Yugoslavia and the leaders of the Kosovo Albanian community to cooperate fully with the Prosecutor in the investigation of all possible violations within the jurisdiction of the Tribunal.

I am here to inform you that the Federal Republic of Yugoslavia has not complied with Security Council resolution 1207.

With respect to the matter relating to access by the Office of the Prosecutor to Kosovo in order to conduct investigations, as urged by the Security Council in resolution 1160 (1998), the Federal Republic of Yugoslavia has continued to deny visas to the Prosecutor's investigators in contravention to that and other Security Council resolutions (1199 and 1203). I reported that non-compliance in my letter of 6 November 1998, to the President of the Security Council. On 24 November 1998, the Registrar of the Tribunal dispatched a letter to the Ambassador of the Federal Republic of Yugoslavia in The Hague requesting his "most urgent attention" to this matter. This letter specifically referred to 14 members of the Office of the Prosecutor who requested visas four or more weeks ago and which have not been acted upon. The usual time for response is two or perhaps three weeks. She also noted that two Tribunal officials who had requested visas valid for a six-month period were given seven-day visas instead. The Ambassador has failed to respond to her requests for a meeting with him. No visas have been issued. The Prosecutor sent a letter to the President of the Security Council dated 25 November 1998 detailing the facts relating to that denial to respond to a statement by the Federal Ministry of Justice of the Federal Republic of Yugoslavia dated 10 November 1998, distributed during the current session of the General Assembly. ...

The Federal Republic of Yugoslavia is unabashedly obstructing the explicit directives of the Security Council. The UN Charter entrusts the Security Council with the primary authority for determining when a matter constitutes a threat to international peace and security and determining the appropriate measure to respond to that threat. You established the Tribunal expecting it would help to bring about and maintain international peace and security in the former Yugoslavia. We at the Tribunal strive earnestly to meet your expectations. Although the Tribunal is independent it is absolutely dependent upon you for the enforcement of the matters I bring to you today. I now turn to you, once again, for without your support it cannot discharge that mandate.

Not only does the Tribunal depend upon you, all member States look to you for the exercise of your Chapter VII authority which they ceded to you with adoption of the UN Charter. We are in your hands. Once again I implore you not to let one State stand in the way of peace. We have come a long way since 1993, but we are at a critical juncture. It is your authority and your will which is being tested by Federal Republic of Yugoslavia.

I urge you not to allow the Federal Republic of Yugoslavia's obstructionism to go unchecked for it sets a dangerous precedent, one which even transcends its non-compliance. Please show the international community that you meant what you stated when you created the Tribunal.

18. Statement by ICTFY Prosecutor Louise Arbour, 16 January 1999

I have launched an investigation into the most recent massacre in Kosovo. I will lead an investigative mission in Kosovo as soon as we can assemble our team on the ground. I have spoken to Ambassador Walker and sought his assistance.

In my recent discussions with the Minister of Justice of the Federal Republic of Yugoslavia, Mr. Knezevic, I indicated to him that any claim on his part that the ICTY has no jurisdiction in Kosovo is a legal question for the Judges of the ICTY to decide and that, if necessary, I will initiate proceedings to permit an early resolution of that issue. The Security Council has unequivocally called on my office to investigate allegations of war crimes and crimes against humanity in Kosovo.

In light of the information publicly available, the recent massacre of civilians falls squarely within the mandate of the ICTY, and the Federal Republic of Yugoslavia is required to grant access to investigators from my office. I call on the FRY authorities to facilitate our immediate access to the site.

19. Letter from the ICTFY President to Foreign Ministers Vedrine and Cook, 22 February 1999

Excellency,

In recent days I have received worrying reports concerning the progress of negotiations at the Kosovo peace talks at Rambouillet, France. I have been advised that the text currently under consideration by the parties does not contain provisions that would require them to recognise the competence of the International Tribunal (Tribunal) or to take specific measures to co-operate with the Tribunal. Rather, I understand that under the current draft of the agreement, the parties would sign only a general provision on co-operation.

Considering the attitude of the Government of the Federal Republic of Yugoslavia (F.R.Y.) to the Tribunal, as demonstrated by its record of non-co-operation with and obstructionism of Tribunal requests and orders, in my judgement, such a generic provision is not sufficient to ensure that the Tribunal will be able to discharge its mandate. As you are aware, since March 1998 both the Security Council and Contact Group have repeatedly reaffirmed that mandate with respect to Kosovo. The repeated refusal of the Government of the F.R.Y. to obey the will of the international community by recognising the competence of the Tribunal and facilitating its activities therefore renders it imperative that the agreement's provisions concerning the Tribunal make explicit reference to its legal right to access to Kosovo and to conduct investigative activities there.

I know of the commitment of France and the United Kingdom to an effective Tribunal. We cannot allow the authority of the Tribunal to be ignored or to be dismissed by omitting recognition of mandatory Chapter VII obligations in the agreement. I fear, therefore, that if there is not express reference to the matters I have mentioned, it could be well construed that, by omission, there is a tacit agreement that the Tribunal may be ignored. I urge you to use your influence as co-chair of the peace talks not to allow this to occur.

It is axiomatic that there can be no peace without justice. Thus, any agreement that fails to bind explicitly the Government of the F.R.Y. and the Kosovar Albanians to specific forms of co-operation, risks being perceived as sacrificing the principles on which the Tribunal is founded for short-term political interest.

Accept Excellency, the assurance of my highest consideration.
Gabrielle Kirk McDonald, President

20. Letter by the President of the ICTFY to the President of the Security Council, 16 March 1999

Excellency,

Once again, I have the duty to report to the Security Council the continuing refusal of the Federal Republic of Yugoslavia (Serbia and Montenegro) to co-operate with the International Tribunal, as required by numerous Resolutions of the Security Council and the Tribunal's Statute. The reason for making this report is the additional instances in which the Federal Republic has refused to permit the Prosecutor and her investigators to enter Kosovo, in order to initiate investigations into alleged crimes committed in that territory.

On 2 February 1999, I received a "Request by the Prosecutor, Pursuant to Rule 7bis(B), that the President Notify the Security Council that the Federal Republic of Yugoslavia has Failed to Comply with its Obligations Under Article 29" (hereinafter, "the Prosecutor's Request") and supporting documents. On 12 February 1999, I invited the Federal Republic of Yugoslavia to respond, no later than 26 February 1999, to the Prosecutor's assertions. I have received no such response.

The Prosecutor's Request relates, inter alia, to the failure of the Federal Republic of Yugoslavia to allow the Prosecutor and a team of her investigators to enter Kosovo on 18 January 1999, in order to initiate an investigation into alleged criminal activity occurring in Racak, Kosovo. The Prosecutor relied, in part, on Security Council resolution 1160 (1998), which urged the Prosecutor to "begin gathering information related to the violence in Kosovo that may fall within its jurisdiction." This refusal is in direct contravention of the Federal Republic of Yugoslavia's obligations under resolution 1160, which

notes "that the authorities of the Federal Republic of Yugoslavia have an obligation to cooperate with the Tribunal...," and international law generally.

The International Tribunal's Rules of Procedure and Evidence provide, under to Rule 7bis(B), that when the Prosecutor satisfies the President of the International Tribunal that a State has failed to comply with its obligations under the International Tribunal's Statute, "the President shall notify the Security Council thereof". I have made a finding, pursuant to Rule 7bis(B),that the Federal Republic of Yugoslavia has failed to meet its obligations under Article 29 of the Statute of the Tribunal.

I would also note that in Security Council resolution 1207 of 17 November1998 the Council reiterated its call for the Federal Republic of Yugoslavia to cooperate fully with the Prosecutor fully with the Prosecutor in the investigation of all possible violations within the jurisdiction of the Tribunal. In resolution 1207, the Council requested that I keep it informed "about the implementation of the resolution for the Council's further consideration."

The Security Council created the Tribunal to investigate and prosecute persons responsible for some of the most horrific violations of international humanitarian law. As a subsidiary organ of the Security Council, and because the Tribunal lacks mechanisms to enforce State compliance, we rely on the Security Council to bring non-co-operating States into compliance. Once again, I urge you to provide the support necessary to enable the Tribunal to discharge its mandate and to take measures that are sufficiently compelling to bring the Federal Republic of Yugoslavia into compliance with its obligations under international law. ...

Chapter 11: The Response of the ICRC and the UNHCR

The humanitarian emergency which resulted from the events of 1998 was in many ways overwhelming. It was addressed by a whole host of international organisations and agencies. These activities extended to the monitoring of the situation, to the provision of protection through visits to detainees and the presence of international personnel in particular areas of crisis, to intervention on behalf of individuals and groups, the distribution of relief and, ultimately, the caring for refugees who were flooding into neighbouring territories. In contrast to the situation which obtained as a result of the mass deportations undertaken by the FRY/Serbia from March 1999 onwards, many of these agencies were permitted to be present in Kosovo.

In relation to humanitarian efforts, the International Committee of the Red Cross (ICRC) exercised a particularly important function, given its special international status. Although the ICRC is a private international organisation, it enjoys significant rights of access to victims of armed conflict. In addition to its international staff, the organisation can also act in cooperation with national Red Cross societies, organised in the International Federation of Red Cross and Red Crescent Societies. In this instance the Yugoslav national society and those of neighbouring states, including Albania and Macedonia, played a particularly important role in bringing relief to those in need.

While the FRY/Serbia considered the hostilities in Kosovo an internal matter to be dealt with by way of a police action, the ICRC nevertheless managed rapidly to expand its presence in the FRY and Kosovo, to 17 expatriates and over 50 locally recruited staff (of both Serb and Albanian ethnicity). The ICRC pressed for access to areas of confrontation and to detained persons, in accordance with its mandate. It was, however, denied access to some regions while they were subjected to offensive military operations,[1] and also was not permitted to visit hundreds of detained individuals other than those who had been tried and convicted by the Belgrade authorities.[2] When it was admitted to areas of confrontation, it found many deserted and destroyed villages.[3] Often, groups of internally displaced people were found and food parcels were distributed. In addition, the ICRC sought to establish communication among members of separated families.

The ICRC also engaged in active negotiations to achieve the release of Serbs who had been 'abducted', and to provide assistance to Serb communities isolated as a result of the fighting.[4] The problem of so-called abductions was a peculiar one in Kosovo. On occasion, the KLA or other groups did take Serb civilians hostage and there were significant instances of mistreatment and even death. However, the KLA mainly captured members of the FRY/Serb security forces, at times in combat, and at times under other circumstances. For example, Serb policemen were abducted from their homes at night in some instances. The KLA considered itself in a state of armed conflict and felt entitled to detain those who were engaged in hostilities against it. In other circumstances of internal armed conflict, combatants would be detained by the 'rebel' force. As an underground force is not always in a position to house and care for those which it considers 'prisoners of war', they may sometimes be placed in the hands of a neutral power for the duration of the conflict. However, the law of internal armed conflict provides little incentive for irregular forces to care for such prisoners, inasmuch as its own members, when apprehended, will generally be tried and convicted on criminal charges by the government against which they have struggled. The reciprocity of treatment which underpins the laws of war is absent. Hence, the ICRC played a crucial role in seeking to protect Serbs who had fallen into this legal limbo and were in significant danger.

Given the scale of the atrocities, mainly and systematically committed by the FRY/Serbia, the ICRC departed from its earlier practice of not publicly commenting on developments, and issued regular reports on its findings. By September 1998, the situation had reached such proportions that the ICRC issued a formal statement on its position on the crisis in Kosovo. It confirmed that from a humanitarian perspective, "it has become apparent that civilian casualties are not simply what has become known as 'collateral damage'. In Kosovo, civilians have become the main victims—if not the actual targets—of the fighting."[5]

The ICRC reports on events are supplemented by the detailed, sometimes daily reports of the United Nations High Commissioner for Human Rights and the High Commissioner for Refugees (UNHCR). The High Commissioner for Human Rights represents an innovation at the United Nations, coordinating the human rights efforts of the organisation at UN headquarters and the UN human rights bodies based in Geneva. Given the host of relevant thematic rapporteurs, the Special Rapporteur for Yugoslavia and various other agencies, and the establishment of a human rights field mission, the need for such coordination became soon evident in the Kosovo crisis, especially in 1998, with the increase in hostilities.[6]

---

[1] E.g., ICRC Statements 11 March 1998, Document 11.A.4; 3 June 1998, Document 11.A.7.
[2] ICRC Update, 10 March 1998, Document 11.A.3.
[3] E.g., Update, 15 June 1998, Document 11.A.89.
[4] Statement, 29 July 1998, Document 11.A.14.
[5] ICRC Position, 15 September 1998, Document 11.A.20,
[6] See also Chapter 6.

Humanitarian efforts were coordinated by UNHCR, which had already exercised the function of 'lead agency' in relation to the previous episodes in the Yugoslav crisis. Coordination among humanitarian agencies has traditionally been a weak point in complex humanitarian emergencies. Even within the United System, various agencies (World Food Programme, UNESCO, UNICEF, World Health Organization, Food and Agricultural Organization, etc) have fought for autonomy and the right of independent action to the detriment of effectiveness in specific crises. Despite frequent attempts to reorganize the UN humanitarian structures, this problem has not yet been overcome. Hence the need to designate a lead agency for specific conflicts.

Matters are made more complicated by the increasing number of non-governmental organizations. While some of these have a large professional staff and possess considerable operational experience, others are only in the process of developing an adequate infrastructure. NGOs also tend to defend their independence with some vigour in relation to intergovernmental agencies. After all, this independence essentially justifies their very existence and makes operations possible which can, for bureaucratic or other reasons, not be undertaken at an 'official' level. In addition, NGOs have in the past not been given to easy cooperation with one another. Competition for donor money, the religious affiliation of some NGOs and other factors have at times led to wasteful competition.

In view of such a complex environment, the role of UNHCR in helping to organize an overall humanitarian effort was essential. The High Commissioner's staff could also draw upon established contacts with the Belgrade and regional authorities. In addition, the large-scale outpouring of refugees required its particular expertise, honed during the previous years of conflict in the Balkans. Moreover, over the past decade, UNHCR has formally embraced a mandate going beyond assistance to those driven outside of their country of origin. In-country protection has become an increasingly important focus of its activities. This area of activity was initially controversial, inasmuch as it was deemed to endanger the willingness of third states to accept refugees from an area of crisis. If there existed structures for in-country protection, it could be argued that there was no longer a 'well founded fear of persecution' on the part of the individuals benefiting from these operations. International refugee status, and the corresponding entitlements vis-à-vis third states, depends on the demonstration that there exists such a well founded fear.

The drama in the former Yugoslavia and other recent displacement crises, however, had demonstrated that this conceptual dichotomy had to be overcome. While in-country operations can contribute to an improvement of an otherwise desperate situation, they do not necessarily remove the threats and dangers entitling individuals to refugee status. Both concepts have to be applied in a complementary way. This more advanced approach characterized the humanitarian operations in relation to the Kosovo crisis.

In exercising its lead function, detailed and coordinated planning could be undertaken, based on consolidated assessments of humanitarian needs assembled by a variety of organisations. The mobilization of quite significant amounts of relief supplies was possible in this way, acquired and distributed by 'best placed' agencies, according to expertise and capacity. It was also possible to mount consolidated inter-agency appeals for emergency funds to cover the operations.

UNHCR also provided consolidated situation reports, obtained from a range of agencies active in the area. In this way, UNHCR chronicled the steady rise in the number of the displaced and refugees. By the end of September 1998, when serious consideration about the NATO threat of the use of force commenced, there were close to 200,000 internally displaced people, along with 91,000 refugees in neighbouring countries.[7]

International humanitarian agencies have received very harsh criticism when they appeared unprepared for the massive influx of refugees from Kosovo into neighbouring territories from March 1999 onwards. However, at this earlier stage, the organisations performed quite well, indeed at times heroically, in circumstances of considerable danger. Moreover, the coordination arrangements which were pioneered during 1998 greatly assisted the humanitarian aid community when it tried to address the even greater crisis which was to follow. The need to rely in this response on the military resources of some states, including NATO, however, led to considerable soul-searching on the part of a number of humanitarian organisations.[8]

---

[7] UNHCR Update, 30 September 1998.
[8] See Volume 2 in this *Series*.

A.   ICRC

1.   Kosovo: ICRC at the ready, 4 March 1998

Following the recent outbreak of violence in Kosovo, in the Federal Republic of Yugoslavia, the ICRC provided various health facilities in the region with medical assistance in the form of dressing sets. The sub-delegation in Pristina is keeping in close contact with the Yugoslav authorities and the opposition, and stands ready to assist should new needs arise. In addition, ICRC delegates are continuing to visit persons sentenced for endangering State security (some 100 since 1989).

2.   Kosovo: ICRC concerned about escalating violence, 6 March 1998

Following the recent serious incidents in Kosovo, in the Federal Republic of Yugoslavia, there are fears of further escalation in the violence in the region. The International Committee of the Red Cross (ICRC) is most concerned about these developments and reminds the relevant authorities of their duty to exercise restraint and to act with discernment, especially towards civilians who are not taking an active part in the disturbances and persons arrested in connection with the situation. The ICRC notes that the recent clashes have given rise to humanitarian needs, particularly in the medical field. It has therefore strengthened its presence in Pristina, Kosovo's main town, and has started to provide several health facilities with medical assistance. The organization hopes soon to be able to reach all communities affected by the violence. However, representations made to the authorities in this regard have been unsuccessful so far. Moreover, the ICRC intends to gain access to all persons arrested in connection with the disturbances. At present, its delegates are authorized to visit such persons only once they have been sentenced by a court of law. It is therefore essential that they also be allowed to visit people in preventive detention or under investigation without delay.

3.   Update No. 98/01 on ICRC activities in the FRY: Special focus on Kosovo, 10 March 1998

Mounting tensions during the course of last year in Kosovo culminated in unrest in the region early last week and outbreaks of violence in the area of Srbica (50km to the west of Pristina) and surrounding villages. In response, the ICRC provided medical assistance to various health centres for the treatment of the injured. After days of negotiations, the ICRC finally managed to obtain access to Srbica itself. The ICRC is in close contact with the Yugoslav authorities and representatives of the Albanian community, and is building up its supplies and staff presence in order to furnish assistance should needs arise. The ICRC has been involved in the area since 1989 and, in March 1990, started visiting security detainees held in connection with the troubles in Kosovo in the then Socialist Federal Republic of Yugoslavia. Its permanent presence was established in 1991, when the delegation in Belgrade was opened. Sub-delegations in Podgorica (Montenegro) and Pristina (Kosovo) were set up soon afterwards. There are currently four expatriates working in Belgrade and three in Pristina (including a health delegate).

ICRC ACTIVITIES

Medical

In February this year, the ICRC medical team completed its survey of the health system in Kosovo in order to assess the emergency preparedness of the local health institutions, international organizations and NGOs in terms of medical programmes. The study clearly showed that ICRC priorities would be to ensure access to medical care and assistance should the political situation in the region deteriorate. On 1 March, two medical staff based in Pristina distributed 55 dressing sets to two health structures in the region which enabled them to treat injuries following the eruption of violence on 1 and 2 March. Additional specialized supplies (sufficient for the treatment of 400 wounded) are on their way from Zagreb. Medical materials were distributed in Srbica on 8 March in order to increase the local medical structure's ability to cope with a possible influx of injured people.

Protection

In the second half of February, detention teams carried out a comprehensive round of visits to 106 prisoners (the vast majority of whom are of Albanian origin) in nine detention centres throughout the Federal Republic of Yugoslavia. The ICRC intends to gain access to all persons arrested in connection with the disturbances but, at present, its delegates are authorized to visit such persons only once they have been sentenced by a court of law. It is therefore essential that they also be allowed to visit people in preventive detention or under investigation without delay. Furthermore, the institution is worried at reports of civilians fleeing their homes and persons sheltering in the woods around Srbica and surrounding villages in the area following disturbances there. The ICRC is most concerned about the current unrest and reminds the relevant authorities of their duty to exercise restraint and to act with discernment, especially towards civilians and persons arrested in connection with the situation.

Relief

The ICRC is keenly monitoring the situation of the civilian population and is anxious to help meet humanitarian needs which might arise.

Cooperation

Following discussions with the International Federation of Red Cross and Red Crescent Societies (the Federation) and in accordance with the Seville agreement, it was agreed that the ICRC would be the lead agency for International Red Cross operations in Kosovo. Coordinating mechanisms have been established between the two institutions both in the field and at headquarters level. The Federation has decided to boost the basic food and non-food disaster preparedness stocks of the National Societies of Albania and the Former Yugoslav Republic of Macedonia.

4.   Kosovo, Federal Republic of Yugoslavia: Latest developments, 11 March 1998

In the last few days, ICRC delegates have been attempting to assess the humanitarian needs of the civilian population in the region affected by last week's violence. This task has been made all the more urgent by the bitterly cold weather which is adding to the hardships faced by the people living in the triangle formed by the towns of Srbica-Skanderai, Glogovac and Klina. Given the deserted appearance of the places visited by the delegates, it seems that some people, probably including a number of wounded, have taken refuge in the surrounding woods and hills. The ICRC would like to bring them warm clothing, food and blankets as quickly as possible. At present the ICRC's evaluation of needs in the region is only partial: its delegates have not been authorized to visit all the places affected, in particular Prekaz, Laushe and Klina. On 9 March, however, the ICRC was able to deliver dressings, medicines, food and baby items to Srbica-Skanderai. In addition, anonymous threats were made on 10 March to delegates from the ICRC and the International Federation of Red Cross and Red Crescent Societies. This situation naturally makes it more difficult for the International Red Cross and Red Crescent Movement to do its humanitarian work. The ICRC is continuing its representations with a view to visiting the persons arrested and detained in the wake of recent events. Finally, the Federation is building up stocks of food and emergency non-food items in its warehouses in Tirana (Albania), Skopje (Macedonia) and Podgorica (Montenegro), with the assistance of the National Societies concerned.

5.   Kosovo: ICRC position on invitation to head investigation, 20 March 1998

The authorities of the Republic of Serbia have approached the International Committee of the Red Cross (ICRC) to open an *ad hoc* investigation into the recent events in Kosovo. The ICRC wishes to make clear that it has informed the Serbian authorities that acting as a fact-finding commission does not lie within the scope of its mandate. The ICRC believes that taking on such a quasi-judicial task could jeopardize its primary humanitarian duty to assist and protect the victims of armed conflict or internal strife. It has recommended to the Serbian authorities that they contact an international expert in the field of international law to help them set up such a commission. The priority for the ICRC remains to fulfil its humanitarian role in Kosovo. A team led by the ICRC and including a delegate from the International Federation of Red Cross and Red Crescent Societies travelled to Pristina on Wednesday to look further into the possibilities of assisting people affected by the present crisis.

6. Update No. 98/03 on activities in response to the crisis in Kosovo, 29 May 1998

The general situation in Kosovo has continued to deteriorate in recent weeks and a political solution does not appear to be imminent, although diplomatic efforts to encourage dialogue between Belgrade and Pristina did result in the first working talks between President Milosevic of the Federal Republic of Yugoslavia (FRY) and the Kosovo Albanian leader Ibrahim Rugova on 22 May. Tension and violence has now spread from the central area around Drenica towards the south-west and the border regions with northern Albania (Decane and Djakovica), where fighting, killings, abductions and disappearances have been reported. Both the UCK (Kosovo Liberation Army) and the Serb security forces have increased their presence in the province and units of the Yugoslav army have been deployed along the Albanian border, from where outbursts of fighting have been reported.

As a result the number of dead and injured has continued to climb, supply lines between Serbia and Kosovo have been adversely affected and insecurity is widespread, prompting small but regular displacements of both Kosovo Albanian and Serb families and groups. So far, most of these movements have been limited to within the province itself.

Field trips continue
ICRC delegates carried out field trips to the troubled areas on an almost daily basis in order to gain as much information as possible about conditions in the affected towns and villages. Delegates also use these opportunities to build up contacts with local interlocutors and representatives of all sides, as well as with checkpoint personnel controlling access to various regions, providing them with information on the role and activities of the ICRC and the International Federation of Red Cross and Red Crescent Societies (Federation) in the Kosovo context. The teams regularly visit hospitals and health-care establishments to check available facilities and assess potential needs. In addition, the ICRC tries to ensure that all patients receive the treatment they need and that doctors have access to those patients. Medical structures are regularly provided with dressings and basic medicines. (Earlier this month, for example, the hospital in Pec received surgical supplies, as stocks were almost at an end. Water and sanitation conditions in the hospital were also checked.) First-aid training has been initiated for staff in health structures and first-aid posts have been set up in some of them. Ad-hoc deliveries of food, non-food and hygiene items were made to vulnerable people in villages where the lack of security prevented or hindered access to these basic supplies. Delegates are currently carrying out an assessment of water and sanitation needs with a view to developing activities in this domain, if necessary. In the meantime, support is being provided to public health institutions to improve water-quality testing and chlorination procedures.

Protection activities
The ICRC is continuing to focus on the issue of persons arrested in connection with the unrest in Kosovo and is maintaining contact with the authorities in order to be able to visit and register detainees. Delegates are also endeavouring to follow up information received from both the Serb and the Albanian communities regarding alleged abductions and disappearances, violence towards civilians and loss of contact. A Red Cross message service has been offered to help restore family links and, so far, a small number of messages have been received, mainly from family members living abroad.

Operational set-up
In response to the developing situation the ICRC has reinforced its presence in Kosovo and in neighbouring areas. Four extra delegates, including a medical delegate and a water and sanitation engineer, have been posted to Pristina bringing the total to nine expatriates, seven from the ICRC and two from the Federation. Locally-hired staff (Serb and Albanian) are assisting the delegates there, and more will be recruited in the near future. One delegate is now in place at the ICRC office in the Montenegrin capital of Podgorica and there are four delegates at the delegation in Belgrade. The ICRC mission in Skopje is being upgraded to delegation status (i.e. has a direct link to ICRC headquarters in Geneva), with the permanent placement of two delegates who will maintain contact with the authorities and the National Society. In addition to its ongoing detention and dissemination activities, the delegation in the Albanian capital, Tirana, is following events in Kosovo closely and has already visited the north-east of the country, together with the Albanian Red Cross, to assess the situation and possible needs there. Arrangements have been made to set up an ICRC office in the town of Kukes, close to the Albania/FRY border, in order to cope with a potential influx of refugees from Kosovo. Emergency stocks of food and non-food items are being built up in both Belgrade and Pristina, where there are currently enough supplies for about 15,000 beneficiaries. Surgical and medical materials sufficient for a total of 1,600 wounded are also available in both centres. The Federation is pre-positioning food and non-food items for 1,300 beneficiaries in Tirana and Skopje and will send a delegate to both places this week to assist the respective National Societies in their disaster preparedness planning.

A coordinated approach
In accordance with the Seville agreement the ICRC is the lead agency for international Red Cross operations in Kosovo. Consequently, the ICRC is now working with the Federation on the development of a plan to coordinate the activities of the Red Cross components in Kosovo. The Federation will maintain its existing programmes in favour of 15,000 Serb refugees in the region (part of a countrywide programme for over 100,000 refugees in total). In addition, the Federation is responsible for providing the local Red Cross with sufficient resources to carry out its operations effectively and for assisting in the development and training of staff and volunteers.

7. Kosovo: ICRC urgently requests access to affected area, 3 June 1998

Deeply disturbed by reports of escalating violence in the area of Decane, the International Committee of the Red Cross (ICRC) has asked the Serbian authorities for immediate and unimpeded access in order to carry out humanitarian work there. Since the crisis erupted in March, the organization's delegates have been performing protection and relief work throughout Kosovo. However, over the past two weeks they have been prevented from entering the Decane area despite a number of previous assurances from the highest authorities in Belgrade that the ICRC would be able to work unhindered in Kosovo. According to information gathered by delegates in northern Albania from the newly arrived refugees there, thousands of civilians are fleeing their homes in Decane. The sudden worsening of the situation makes it absolutely imperative for the ICRC to reach the area without delay. A team of delegates yesterday travelled to Bajram Curri, in northern Albania, where they will stay for some time to gather information from refugees there about the situation in Kosovo. Representatives of the Albanian Red Cross and the International Federation of Red Cross and Red Crescent Societies are working with ICRC delegates to respond to the refugees' immediate needs in terms of food, medicines and other supplies.

8. Kosovo: Humanitarian situation causing concern, 12 June 1998

On 10 June the International Committee of the Red Cross (ICRC) was able to reach Decane, the main town in the part of Kosovo affected by the recent fighting, for the first time since 20 May. Its access was, however, restricted to the town itself, largely deserted by its inhabitants and civilian authorities and bearing obvious traces of the clashes of the past few days. ICRC delegates could only go to the offices of the local Red Cross and were unable to establish direct contact with the civilians still remaining on the spot. The ICRC is especially worried about the initial accounts received from people having sought refuge in northern Albania and Montenegro, who report artillery attacks, threats to the lives of civilians, and the destruction of houses and property. The conditions in which the exodus is taking place also give cause for concern: the people who leave - mainly women, children and the elderly - are forced to leave all their belongings behind and to make their way on foot, avoiding inhabited areas and travelling for several days and nights before reaching a place of safety. The ICRC knows the Decane region well, having worked there on a regular basis for some months prior to the most recent events. It has brought in considerable logistic resources and has constituted stocks of food, blankets, hygiene items and other basic necessities in Belgrade and Pristina, sufficient to cover the requirements of 20,000 people, as well as medical supplies to treat 1,600 wounded. It is therefore vital that ICRC staff be allowed to return to the region in order to meet the victims' needs as a matter of urgency.

In Albania, refugees in the northern area of Bajram Curri are receiving aid from the Albanian Red Cross. So far the National Society, working with the support of the International Federation of Red Cross and Red Crescent Societies for food aid and the ICRC for medical assistance, has distributed 50 tonnes of food to about 10,000 people, utterly destitute and exhausted after days on the road.

In Montenegro, an ICRC delegate based in Podgorica is closely monitoring the situation of three to four thousand newly displaced persons from Kosovo. The Yugoslav Red Cross, with the help of the ICRC, has already come to the assistance of 500 people, and is about to distribute blankets, hygiene items, kitchen sets and other essential supplies to a further 2,000.

The ICRC, together with the Albanian and Yugoslav Red Cross Societies, is making every effort to restore contact between family members separated as a result of the conflict by enabling them to exchange Red Cross messages. From the psychological standpoint it is most important for these refugees uprooted from their homes to rapidly re-establish at least some form of contact with relatives living in other countries.

9.   Update No. 98/04 on activities in response to the crisis in Kosovo, 15 June 1998

With the renewed operations of the Yugoslav security forces against the Kosovo Liberation Army (UCK), the situation in the province of Kosovo has reached new levels of violence. After previous police operations in the Drenica region in March, the Yugoslav government is now deploying heavier military means to tighten control over the Decane/Djakovica/Pec areas close to the Albanian border. Following sustained infiltration by armed UCK elements clashes between the security forces and the insurgents have increased in violence and frequency. The confrontation is affecting more and more people and has triggered a population exodus. Thousands of people, mostly women, children and the elderly, have left their homes and sought refuge elsewhere in Kosovo, and up to 3,000 have crossed into neighbouring Montenegro. Some 10,000 have made the laborious journey across forbidding mountain passes into Albania. Their consistent reports of artillery fire, direct threats to the lives of unarmed civilians and the deliberate destruction of houses convey a disturbing picture of the situation which they have fled.

Diplomatic moves to bring about talks between ethnic Albanian representatives and the Serb government appear to have stalled because of the latest violence, signalling a deeply worrying breakdown in communication.

ICRC action

The ICRC is developing its protection and assistance activities, with the following main objectives in mind: to gather as much information as possible about the situation of the thousands of civilians reportedly still trapped in the crisis zone- following up allegations of severe harassment and arrests made - so as to substantiate its representations to the authorities and the insurgents and obtain at least a minimum of respect for the population, whether Albanian or Serb; to enable people affected by the crisis to restore contact with their relatives, both those still in the Federal Republic of Yugoslavia and those who have settled

in other countries, possibly using Albanian-language international radio programmes to broadcast family messages to people remaining in Kosovo; and to form a more accurate picture of medical and assistance needs of the population left in the crisis zone.

Kosovo

After repeated representations to the Federal Yugoslav and Serbian authorities in Pristina, Belgrade and in Geneva, on 10 June a team of delegates and interpreters were able to visit the town of Decane, the scene of fighting over the past two weeks which the ICRC had not been allowed to enter (a previous visit to Decane dates back to 19 May). In Decane, the team found barely any inhabitants and no civilian authorities in charge. Many buildings had been damaged in the recent fighting and there was a heavy police presence. The delegates distributed supplies (food and hygiene parcels, baby parcels, jerrycans, blankets etc.) to the local Red Cross and handed out food provided by the International Federation of Red Cross and Red Crescent Societies (Federation) or a group of Serb refugees. However, it proved impossible for the team to make direct contact with civilians still living in Decane and to carry out an independent and thorough assessment of the situation in the town and its surroundings. Given the disturbing character of the accounts collected from the people who have fled the area, it is imperative for the ICRC to have unimpeded access to the whole Decane area. Another ICRC team made a field trip to the Drenica area to assess the situation of internally displaced people in Glogovac and a number of nearby villages and secure the agreement of the authorities with a view to further ICRC activities in the region. The delegates talked to ethnic Albanians and Serbs, distributed some food and hygiene parcels to both and collected Red Cross messages.

Montenegro

At present, Montenegro is harbouring about 6,000 displaced people from Kosovo (3,000 since the violent events in March and up to 3,000 new arrivals over the past ten days). However, precise figures are hard to obtain as many of them have no wish to be registered by the authorities. Their most urgent needs are being met by the Montenegro Red Cross (MRC), with continued support from the ICRC, which has a delegate permanently based in Podgorica. At this point, some 2,500 displaced people are being provided with food and hygiene parcels, blankets, kitchenware etc. In addition, delegates are helping the MRC in enabling the displaced to restore familiy links via Red Cross messages.

Albania

By 11 June, some 10,000 refugees had arrived in the Bajram Curri and Tropoja areas, in northern Albania. An ICRC team, in place since 2 June, is gathering information from the refugees about the situation in Kosovo and helping the Albanian Red Cross set up a Red Cross message network for the restoration of family links. The ICRC and the Albanian Red Cross are also providing medical assistance. The National Society was the first organization on the spot to provide relief and has been distributing food, medical and other supplies (clothes, shelter materials etc.), both drawn from reserves in the country and provided by the Federation. To date, about 50 tonnes of food have been distributed, calculated to last the refugees for about 20 days.

10.   Update No. 98/05 on activities of the Red Cross and Red Crescent Movement, 26 June 1998

Access to the confrontation zone improves

In a joint statement issued after talks with the President of the Russian Federation, Boris Yeltsin, in Moscow on 16 June Yugoslav President Slobodan Milosevic expressed amongst other issues, the readiness of the Yugoslav authorities to ensure that no repressive measures would be taken against the civilian population, that the return of all refugees and internally displaced persons would be encouraged and unhindered, and that the State would provide the necessary assistance to rebuild houses damaged as a result of the fighting. The statement underlined the importance of granting unimpeded access to humanitarian organizations, namely the ICRC and the UNHCR, enabling them to respond to the needs of the people affected, and guaranteed the unobstructed distribution of humanitarian assistance across the territory of Kosovo. Following sustained representations by the ICRC to the

Yugoslav authorities, access to areas affected by the confrontation has improved significantly. Owing to the nature of the confrontation, however, working conditions for the delegates are difficult and dangerous. Usually there is no clear front line nor, in many areas, any identifiable control by either the Serb forces or the insurgents.

ICRC activities to assist the affected population

As a result of the violence, many people from both Serb and ethnic Albanian communities have been cut off or separated from their families with no means of communication. On the other hand, thousands of people have been displaced, either within the confrontation area itself (i.e. in and around Decane and Drenica), to other areas in Kosovo or to Montenegro where more than 10,000 people were registered. Some 13,000 people have fled across the border to seek refuge in northern Albania. As many of these people, particularly in Kosovo, have been given shelter by relatives not all of them have been officially registered, making it very difficult to gauge exact numbers. In response, the ICRC has kept up a constant round of field trips throughout the territory in order to gather information at all levels and develop its assistance plan accordingly.

Missions to Decane

Delegates began visiting the Decane area of Kosovo last weekend to look into the situation of a group of civilians who the ICRC had been told was being detained in Decane town, and to assess the situation in surrounding villages. The delegates had several meetings with the civilians concerned. While not detained or under house arrest, they were nevertheless in a very difficult situation as they had been unable to leave their homes owing to poor security conditions, a predicament faced by many civilians throughout central Kosovo. Information about the group's whereabouts is being relayed to their families in northern Albania who were anxious about their relatives' welfare. The mission also enabled the ICRC to assess the situation of Serbs and other civilians who remain in the area.

Missions to Junik

On 23 June, delegates reached Junik, a village a few kilometres from the Albanian border and under insurgents control. In addition to other tasks, they visited a few hundred Serb civilians stranded there. On 25 June they were back and managed to provide initial assistance to three places between Junik and the border where some 600 elderly people, women and children have taken refuge in extremely harsh conditions. Delegates distributed food parcels, hygiene parcels, baby parcels, blankets and jerrycans cans to stock water. In Junik itself, medical structures were provided with dressing material and other basic but essential supplies. Further visits will be made in the very near future.

Apart from visits to Decane (on 10, 17 and 23 June), Pec (on 17 and 23 June) and Junik (on 23 June and 25 June), delegates also travelled to Glogovac, Poklek, Vasiljevo, Stimlje, Ulcinj, Nekrovacz, Malishevo, Kidovic, Izbica, Srbica, Rudnik, Kotor and Istok. In all these localities delegates made further contact with representatives of the Yugoslav authorities and security forces, as well as with representatives of the Albanian community and the insurgents. In addition to making the ICRC's role known and promoting the rules of international humanitarian law, specific issues such as threats, arrests, allegations of abduction or summary execution, were also followed up. The ICRC also met representatives of local emergency councils, medical structures and the local Red Cross. The security conditions and food situation of the population were assessed, numbers of displaced people were taken (and verified, where possible), allegations of ill-treatment by security forces or insurgents were noted, Red Cross messages were collected and distributed and relief goods (family parcels, hygiene kits, jerrycans) were provided for vulnerable individuals and families, where necessary. Delegates also delivered medical supplies to health facilities.

In Montenegro, 2,000 food parcels are soon to be distributed in addition to the 2,500 parcels already handed out. In Kosovo, delegates have been giving out small amounts of ad hoc relief in the course of their field missions. Now that needs have been identified in many areas, larger-scale assistance can be planned and implemented shortly.

Visits to detainees

Delegates have started a new round of visits to persons detained by the government in connection with the Kosovo crisis and, on the side of the insurgents, are taking advantage of improved access to look into reports that Serb people have been abducted.

Northern Albania

The situation in the district of Tropoje is still very uncertain, concerning the exact number of refugees who have come over the border from Kosovo. The strain of supporting so many people (estimated at some 13,000) is beginning to show in the area, with an increase in the number of security incidents. Further pockets of refugees are located in Durres and Tirana. The ICRC has set up message centres in Bajram Curri -- where the ICRC maintains a permanent presence -- to enable refugees in the area to make contact with relatives in Kosovo, Albania, Montenegro, and elsewhere. The names of people and families who have arrived safely in Albania are also being broadcast regularly on radio stations. The International Federation of Red Cross and Red Crescent Societies has been supporting the Albanian Red Cross (ARC) in its work for the refugees with food and non-food assistance. The ICRC has similarly helped the ARC by providing medical support. Delegates have maintained visits to medical structures, providing them with material as necessary.

11. FRY: ICRC goes to Decane, 26 June 1998

ICRC delegates began visiting the Decane area of Kosovo last weekend to check the situation of a group of civilians which they had been told was being detained in the town of Decane and to observe conditions in surrounding villages. The delegates had several meetings with the civilians concerned. While neither detained nor under house arrest, they were nevertheless in difficulties as they had been unable to leave their homes owing to poor security conditions, a predicament faced by many civilians throughout central Kosovo. Information about the group's whereabouts is being relayed to their families in northern Albania who were anxious for news of their relatives. The mission also enabled the ICRC to assess the situation of Serbs and other civilians who remain in the area. As a result of consistent and alarming reports from refugees who left Decane in the recent exodus into northern Albania, the ICRC had tried to tour the area as a matter of urgency, but had not been allowed in the past few weeks to travel to villages around the town. It plans further visits in the coming days in order to continue its efforts to restore contact between members of separated families, to look into reports that certain individuals have been arrested and to assist those in need. ICRC staff are meanwhile making regular visits to other parts of Kosovo to conduct relief and protection work. Delegates have started a new round of visits to persons detained in connection with the Kosovo crisis and are taking advantage of improved access on the ground to look into allegations that Serbs have been abducted. The International Federation of Red Cross and Red Crescent Societies continues to provide food and other assistance to displaced people in Kosovo. ...

12. Federal Republic of Yugoslavia: ICRC reaches Kijevo, 2 July 1998

Last weekend an ICRC team managed to reach the village of Kijevo, in central Kosovo, where over 400 people - around 100 local and displaced Serb families, but also some ethnic Albanian and Romany families - have been cut off from the outside world for the past two months owing to the fighting between the Kosovo Liberation Army and government security forces. The main aim of the visit was to assess the needs of the civilian population in terms of protection and material assistance. Although food is available, medicines are scarce and, with the electricity supply having been cut three weeks ago, the water pumps are no longer functioning. The survival of the crops is also a concern in Kijevo and other areas of Kosovo where the fighting has made it unsafe for villagers to go into the fields. The delegates delivered individual food parcels, hygiene items, baby kits, blankets, candles and jerrycans to the most vulnerable people, including displaced families. The villagers welcomed not only the assistance but also the very presence of the ICRC, the only humanitarian organization to have reached Kijevo so far. ...

13.   Kosovo: ICRC calls for temporary halt to fighting in Orahovac on humanitarian grounds, 22 July 1998

Deeply concerned by the desperate plight of people affected by the recent heavy clashes in the village of Orahovac, Kosovo, the International Committee of the Red Cross (ICRC) calls on all those taking part in the hostilities to stop fighting long enough to allow the civilians and wounded to be evacuated and the bodies of the dead to be returned to their families. A team of ICRC delegates travelled yesterday from Pristina to Orahovac to assess the situation following the clashes. Another team went to Malishevo, where more than 20,000 people had arrived after fleeing Orahovac. These displaced people, several of them severely wounded, were suffering from trauma and shock. The ICRC provided them with relief supplies and distributed medical items to hospitals and first-aid posts. In Orahovac and the surrounding area, ICRC delegates saw bodies scattered along the roadside, destroyed buildings and other obvious signs of the recent fighting. They were extremely concerned about the fact that a number of severely wounded people needed to be evacuated and that many civilians remained trapped in and around the village. They also heard reports of arrests and abductions. The ICRC urgently calls on all those involved in the hostilities to treat persons who are not or are no longer taking part in the fighting with the respect they are due under the provisions of international humanitarian law.

14.   Federal Republic of Yugoslavia/Kosovo: ICRC aid for conflict victims, 29 July 1998

A dozen ICRC delegates based in Pristina travel every day to villages in the central regions of Kosovo hard hit by the recent clashes. They have observed that large numbers of civilians are having to abandon their homes to seek a safer haven. Those unable to leave take refuge in cellars or makeshift shelters. During the past week the ICRC has distributed 15 tonnes of aid (maize flour, food parcels and hygiene items) to over 20,000 displaced people who fled from Orahovac and gathered in the village of Malishevo. Medical supplies have also been distributed to various hospitals. Because of the proximity of the fighting, most of the displaced are now moving on towards Prizren, further south. Delegates also went several times to Orahovac to assess the situation and keep in touch with the traumatized civilians stranded there. The ICRC is particularly concerned about the plight of persons arrested, abducted or separated from their relatives by the events, and is doing its utmost to locate them rapidly and visit them. On 22 July delegates took charge of 35 released Serb civilians and transported them to Pristina. Thousands of other people who have been displaced to Montenegro or taken refuge in Albania are also receiving assistance from the ICRC ... .

15.   Update No. 98/06 on the crisis in Kosovo, 30 July 1998

The past weeks have seen a serious escalation in fighting in Kosovo with a series of violent clashes taking place in the centre and south west of the province between the Yugoslav forces and the Kosovo Albanian insurgents (UCK) This has undoubtedly taken a heavy toll on the civilian population with tens of thousands forced to leave their homes, many to shelter out of fear in forests and mountains, and widespread destruction of property. There are now well over a 100,000 people who have had to abandon their homes since the crisis began. The swiftly evolving situation, the large movement of displaced people and the deteriorating security situation means the ICRC faces an extremely complex and difficult environment in which to work. Nevertheless, field teams make daily visits to provide immediate help or important follow-up work (family contacts, continuing distributions, prison visits and representations with authorities).

The battle for Orahovac

In mid-July, the town of Orahovac was the scene of one of the fiercest battles so far as both sides fought for control of the town. ICRC delegates who arrived on-the-spot on Tuesday, July 21, in the immediate aftermath of the peak of the fighting were shocked to witness the visible effects of the battle with bodies scattered along

roadsides, burning buildings, and terrified civilians, mostly ethnic Albanians, trapped in their cellars. Delegates were also very much concerned by credible reports that a considerable number of Serbs had been abducted and ethnic Albanians arrested. Around 20,000 people, mainly ethnic Albanians, had fled Orahovac and its surroundings to Malishevo, north of the town. An ICRC team first visited Malishevo on Monday, 20, July where they encountered displaced people in a state of shock and trauma. Delegates were immediately able to distribute relief goods such as wheat flour, individual food and hygiene parcels and to provide medical establishments, which were quickly running out of supplies, with basic surgical equipment with which to treat the influx of wounded people. Teams returned during the following days to Malishevo to continue to distribute essential emergency supplies.

On Wednesday, July 22, the ICRC was contacted to facilitate the release of 35 Serbs from Kosovo who had been abducted during the clashes in Orahovac. The people, mainly elderly and sick and including seven priests, were collected by the ICRC and taken to Pristina. Whilst welcoming the release, the ICRC is determined to exert the same efforts in order to have access to all Serbs abducted and to all ethnic Albanians arrested because of the hostilities in Kosovo. On July 23 and 24, the delegates returned to Orahovac where they were able to meet with hundreds of civilians trapped in the town. The ICRC is now putting its efforts on normalising the life in the city and facilitating freedom of movement.

Northern Albania

As the battle for Orahovac raged, there were simultaneous clashes along the border with Albania between Yugoslav army troops and insurgents reportedly attempting to infiltrate from Albania. The clashes resulted in an influx of wounded combatants who managed to make the hazardous journey across difficult terrain to northern Albania. Albanian Red Cross representatives and ICRC delegates were immediately on-hand on the border to witness the dramatic scene and were able to provide treatment and transport for the 27 seriously wounded to the hospital in Bajram Curri.

The present situation

Since 25 July the Yugoslav forces opened by force main roads leading to UCK-controlled areas (Pec-Pristina, Suka Reva-Stimje). By Tuesday, 28 July, the UCK stronghold of Malishevo was taken by Yugoslav forces. The strategy of opening main roads has resulted in reports of destruction of villages and roadside property. The attack on Malishevo prompted the exodus of tens of thousands of people, many of whom had only recently been forced to flee Orahovac. An ICRC team is presently assessing the situation of the different groups of displaced.

Meanwhile, tension remains high around places like Junik, the scene of earlier fighting and where the ICRC has made visits to assist Serb and Albanian communities with emergency help, and around other potential flashpoints.

ICRC priorities

The main objective of the ICRC operation in Kosovo is to try to ensure that the civilian population is spared as much as possible from the damaging psychological and physical effects of the hostilities - by helping those affected and by reminding of those involved in the hostilities of their obligations to treat persons who are not or no longer taking part in the fighting the respect they are due under the provisions of international humanitarian law. The key focuses of the current ICRC action are:

- *For the displaced*, to continue to provide basic emergency relief and medical help for the increasingly large numbers of people forced to flee their homes and to re-establish family links for those who have lost contact with their relatives

- *For those trapped in their homes or cut off in their villages* to try to tackle both the psychological trauma and their material needs - such as provided recently to the people recently in Kijevo and Orahovac.

- *For the civilian victims of violence, harassment and threats*, to continue to gather relevant allegations from the affected communities by constant contact and dialogue in order to strengthen representations with the authorities where needed.

- *For the wounded, sick and for pregnant women*, to ensure material support to those providing medical care and to ensure continuing access to medical facilities for those who need it.
- *For those who lost their lives*, to ensure that their identity is established beyond doubt before their remains be given a decent burial. Ideally, families should be able to proceed to identification and burial, but where this is not possible, families must be informed of the death of a relative and the location of the grave.
- *For the abducted Serbs*, to gain immediate access to ease the anguish of their families who have no idea of their whereabouts, and facilitate their early release.
- *For the ethnic Albanians arrested*, to continue to visit them regularly.

16. Yugoslavia / Kosovo: Increasing alarm at scale of Kosovo crisis, 6 August 1998

The flight of tens of thousands of people from their homes in central Kosovo during the most recent operations by Serbian forces has resulted in a degree of desperation unprecedented since the crisis there began. ICRC teams travelling in central Kosovo have been shocked to find groups of thousands of people living in appalling conditions - surviving in the open air under makeshift shelters and in urgent need of food and medicine. In the searing heat of summer, drinking water is in especially short supply, particularly for vulnerable groups like children and old people. The risk of epidemics is on the rise. Emergency stocks of food, medicines and hygienic supplies have already started to be provided and deliveries of water are being organized as quickly as possible. On Tuesday, delegates visited Mitrovica and surrounding towns where they encountered thousands of families including elderly people and young children fleeing from the ongoing fighting in the Drenica area. Many were travelling in large tractor convoys in a state of extreme shock and trauma. ICRC staff have gone this week to Prizren, Mamusa and the Mount Berisha range to continue bringing urgent aid to those who fled Malisevo last week. Delegates saw houses either burning or already burnt to the ground. Well over 100,000 people have fled their homes since the crisis in Kosovo began. ...

17. Update No. 98/07 on Kosovo, 12 August 1998

The humanitarian crisis in Kosovo scaled new heights as the major operations launched in recent weeks by Serb forces against the strongholds of the ethnic Albanian insurgents (UCK) resulted in the biggest population movement since the crisis began and left thousands of people in a desperate plight. Operations by Serb forces have been ongoing since the battle of Orahovac in mid-July and have centered around Malishevo, the Drenica area, Junik and the triangle zone of Pec-Klina-Djakovica. Tens of thousands have scattered in many directions to take refuge in neighbouring towns and villages or to seek a precarious sanctuary in forests and mountains. ICRC teams supported by the International Federation of Red Cross and Red Crescent Societies, were quickly dispatched to all main places where the displaced have arrived, to help the traumatised people and provide emergency assistance where needed.

Population displacement and ICRC response:

The speed of events and the fluidity of population movement makes it difficult to clarify exactly the number of the recently displaced until the situation stabilises. The picture is further complicated by the fact that many of the people fleeing in recent weeks would have already moved several times in the past months. However, it is clear from information gathered from field teams who have travelled extensively in the region that the number of people who have left their homes since the crisis began is now well over 100,000.

Flashpoints:

Malishevo:

Serb forces started the attack on the UCK in the area of Malishevo at the end of July. This resulted in the exodus of almost all of the civilian population of Malishevo and surroundings, including those who had recently arrived there from Orahovac. Those who fled went either to the mountain ranges west and north east of the town (to join the large number of people who had already sought safety there) or south to Mamusa, Pagarusha, Prizren and other small places along the same route. ICRC teams were quickly on-the-spot in all these places. As delegates witnessed, the families who are sheltering in the mountains include large numbers of elderly, women and small children. They are living without adequate shelter with little food reserves, no access to medical treatment and inadequate supplies of drinking water which, in the current searing heat poses a serious health risk. Whilst ICRC was able to provide an emergency response, it is clear that much more needs to be done as quickly as possible as the situation remains precariously balanced for these desperate people. Those who left Malishevo to head south towards Prizren and the towns and villages along the way are being mainly supported by the existing community, although this inevitably puts a large strain on the already stretched resources. ICRC has delivered as a first-shot assistance, consisting in food and non-food items to displaced in a dozen places in the days since Malishevo came under Serb control. In Malishevo itself and surroundings, ICRC delegates witnessed the sight of houses burning or burnt to the ground. This disturbing phenomenon is significant in that it adds to the existing fear expressed by many of the displaced of returning to their homes.

Drenica area:

In the last few days, there has been renewed fighting in the Drenica area. Thousands have already left towards Kosovska Mitrovica, Vucitrn and surroundings. ICRC delegates managed to access the Drenica area despite ongoing fighting and gathered information that several thousands of people could be trapped. In the Drenica area the ICRC found a group of around 500 people seeking safety in a river bed. With the agreement of the Serb authorities, teams were able to return the following day to evacuate 55 of the most vulnerable in the group who wished to leave. According to further information gathered, there could be thousands more in the same predicament either too frightened or lacking the transport means to leave and it is important that those who wish are allowed to do so as soon as possible.

ICRC response and other priorities:

For the displaced:

For displaced people in a dozen villages and towns (including Prizren, Mamusa, Kosovska Mitrovica and Suha Reka) and for those who are scattered in the mountains, the ICRC, with support from the International Federation of Red Cross and Red Crescent Societies, has over the last few days provided basic emergency relief. To reach the displaced, teams have conducted over 30 field trips. So far, well over 100 metric tonnes in assistance, including individual food parcels, wheat flour, hygiene material, baby kits and other essential items from current stocks in place in Pristina were delivered. The ICRC is in the process of rebuilding its stocks in Pristina and reinforcing its team to be able to continue to respond to the growing needs.

In addition, for those who sought refuge in forests and mountains, the ICRC is endeavouring to organise for clean water supplies . Jerrycans have already been distributed to these people and water and sanitation equipment has been mobilised from existing ICRC stocks in the region. In addition, a water and sanitation engineer has just now arrived in Pristina.

Through close contact with all the groups of recently displaced, it is apparent that they are also deeply marked by the trauma of what they have experienced and the deep uncertainty which plagues their immediate future. It is clear that, particularly for those sheltering in the countryside, their present situation is not a viable option - especially with the onset of winter. Whilst some people returned to Orahovac, it is important that the conditions continue to be created by the authorities to *allow those who wish to return home to do so in safety and dignity*. The ICRC is committed to ensuring this is the case by intervening with the authorities if appropriate and by standing ready to provide the necessary practical support to the returnees.

For the sick and wounded: So far, the ICRC has delivered supplies to medical facilities in a dozen places, some of which have faced serious shortages because of the influx of wounded people. In addition, the ICRC has organised for the transport of serious and urgent medical cases for professional treatment.

For the abducted Serbs: not to spare any efforts in gaining immediate access to the more than 130 Serbs reported as abducted by their relatives to the ICRC so as to ease the anguish of their families.

For the ethnic Albanians arrested or having lost contact with their relatives: to continue to visit or gain immediate access to those ethnic Albanians who have been arrested or to gather information about their whereabouts if they are not in places of detention.

18.   Yugoslavia/Montenegro: Red Cross struggles to cope with influx of displaced from Kosovo, 19 August 1998

By mid-August the number of internally displaced persons from Kosovo registered in Montenegro was as high as 32,000, and their situation in terms of accommodation, hygiene and medical needs is starting to g ive cause for serious concern. Most of them have found refuge in the municipalities of Ulcinj, Plav and Rozaje. The displaced have now stopped entering these areas, because there is absolutely no more room left to house them. On 13 August an ICRC team reached a group of 270 displaced people from Kosovo, including 150 children, who had found shelter in stables and shepherds' huts in the village of Bandzov, in the mountains above Rozaje. They were given blankets and hygiene items to meet their most urgent needs.

In Plav, the local hotel, which has been turned into a reception centre, is currently accommodating 630 displaced persons. The premises are overcrowded and sanitation conditions inadequate. An ICRC sanitation expert will look into the possibility of providing a sufficient supply of water and proper sanitation facilities for the hotel and other collective shelters, most of which are designed for completely different purposes and are not suited to house large numbers of people.

With its distribution network and the experience in catering for the requirements of 28,000 refugees gained during the conflict in the former Yugoslavia, the Red Cross of Montenegro is doing its utmost to help the new arrivals, but is finding it increasingly difficult to meet their needs. It is working with the support of the International Federation of Red Cross and Red Crescent Societies and the ICRC, which has supplied it with emergency aid for some 15,000 displaced people and is closely monitoring developments so as to be ready to cover any further humanitarian needs that may arise.

19.   Yugoslavia/Kosovo: ICRC brings surgical team to the wounded, 28 August 1998

For the past week the ICRC has been ferrying a team of six local surgeons to various field hospitals in urgent need of assistance in Kosovo. The six, who volunteered for the task, have so far performed close to 60 operations - including 13 major ones - in three different locations. Their patients include women and children. This move follows the discovery last week by an ICRC health delegate of an exhausted surgeon who was working alone in a makeshift clinic and desperately needed help to cope with the influx of patients, many of whom were seriously wounded. The ICRC undertook negotiations with the Serb authorities in Pristina to obtain permission for the team to begin its work. Says Margaret Bryson, the ICRC health delegate who organized this assistance: "The dedication and courage shown by the team are really impressive. They realized that their skills were needed, and didn't hesitate to go". Meanwhile, ICRC teams are continuing to provide transport for particularly vulnerable people so that they can be reunited with their families or taken to centres where proper care is available. Last week the ICRC received authorization from the Ministry of Health to take four elderly people to Pristina, where they either entered a rest home or were reunited their families. They had been discovered in a very weak state and virtually abandoned in an institution near Decane, where the living conditions were appalling.

20.   ICRC position on the crisis in Kosovo, 15 September 1998

Events in Kosovo have taken a turn for the worse. The International Committee of the Red Cross (ICRC) is convinced that the situation in the region has reached a critical stage in terms of its humanitarian implications for the civilian population, forcing all those involved in

the conflict to face up to their responsibilities. At this very moment, as has been the case for several weeks now, tens of thousands of civilians are caught up in a devastating cycle of attacks and displacements. They are exposed to violence, including threats to their lives, destruction of their homes, separation from their families and abductions. Thousands of them have nowhere left to go and no one to turn to for protection. From a humanitarian perspective, it has become apparent that civilian casualties are not simply what has become known as "collateral damage". In Kosovo, civilians have become the main victims - if not the actual targets - of the fighting. The core issue to be addressed immediately is that of the safety of, and hence respect for, the civilian population. First and foremost, this means that every civilian is entitled to live in a secure environment and to return to his or her home in safe and dignified conditions.

The authorities of the Federal Republic of Yugoslavia have pledged to facilitate the return of displaced persons to their villages and have designated a dozen locations where aid will be distributed with their support. For their part, Western governments have in recent weeks put forward a number of proposals aimed at encouraging return to selected areas in Kosovo. In principle, all measures that can contribute to improving security conditions and building confidence are welcome. Indeed, a number of people are reported to have made their way back to some villages in central and western Kosovo. However, a significant discrepancy has emerged between the policy of favouring returns and the very nature of the operations carried out by the security forces in past weeks. These operations have led to further killings and wounding of civilians, to large-scale destruction of private property and to further mass displacements. They have also created a climate of deep and widespread fear. These latest events have added to the heavy price already paid by the civilian population, including the killing of dozens of Serb civilians and the abduction of over a hundred more, whose fate remains unknown. The discrepancy between the policy of inviting the displaced to return to their homes and the manner in which operations are being conducted is illustrated by certain practices witnessed by ICRC delegates in the field.

Large-scale operations have been carried out against villages and other locations where displaced people have sought refuge. These have had the following consequences:

- The killing or wounding of civilians, large-scale destruction of property, and the flight of vast numbers of residents and people who had already been displaced. This was the situation on 10 September between Istnic and Krusevac, where panic-stricken civilians were forced to take to the roads once again just when the authorities were planning to open an additional aid centre in that very place.
- Fleeing civilians becoming trapped in remote areas or very exposed terrain. Some of them have suffered further attacks, for example the shelling on 29 August of people sheltering in a gorge near Sedlare.
- The screening of entire population groups for the stated purpose of identifying individuals having taken part in operations against the security forces, ill-treatment and intimidation during interrogation, and failure to notify families of the whereabouts of those being held. For instance, this happened in Ponorac on 5 September, when several dozen men were taken away. Their families are without news of them to date.
- Difficulties in securing access to medical treatment for the wounded and the sick in hospitals in Kosovo.
- Today, thousands of civilians - Albanians, Serbs and others - are living in a climate of extreme insecurity and fear. The ICRC therefore wishes to state the following:
- Responsibility for ensuring the safety of and respect for the civilian population lies with the Serbian authorities.
- They must take every possible measure to protect civilians. Specifically, the ICRC calls on the Serbian authorities to put an end to the disproportionate use of force and to specific acts of violence directed against civilians, including the wanton destruction of property. The ICRC renews its appeal for rapid access, in accordance with its recognized working procedures, to all persons arrested in connection with the events in Kosovo.

- The ICRC calls on Albanian political representatives and on the UCK (Kosovo Liberation Army) to do everything possible to help put an end to the reported killings, and to enter into a meaningful dialogue on, and provide information about, the fate and whereabouts of abducted Serbs in Kosovo.
- Beyond the humanitarian implications lies the issue of the political settlement of the crisis. The ICRC is convinced that the international community needs to draw lessons from the experience gained in this respect elsewhere in the Balkans. The ICRC considers it crucial to keep the political and the humanitarian dimensions of the crisis clearly separate.

Displaced persons have only one wish, and that is to return home. They should be allowed to do so freely. However, until the conditions are created that enable them to do so, they should receive assistance wherever they are, and the places where humanitarian aid is provided ought not be limited to particular sites. The ICRC is well aware of its responsibility to use all available means to reach civilians both in remote areas and in their own villages, to attempt to gain access to persons arrested, to establish the whereabouts of those abducted, and to ensure that the wounded and the sick receive adequate treatment. The ICRC currently has 17 expatriates and some 50 locally recruited staff operating under difficult conditions throughout Kosovo. …The ICRC will vigorously pursue its efforts to establish a dialogue with the Yugoslav authorities and the representatives of the Albanian community with a view to finding the most appropriate humanitarian response to the present crisis. It will seek to maintain close coordination with other humanitarian agencies in the field, such as UNHCR. It will also continue to coordinate and cooperate closely with the International Federation of Red Cross and Red Crescent Societies and with the Yugoslav Red Cross. All those involved in the conflict must acknowledge and assume their respective responsibilities. This is a prerequisite if they are to succeed in alleviating the widespread insecurity and fear and in avoiding a potentially disastrous deterioration in the situation.

21. Kosovo crisis: ICRC stepping up activities, 14 October 1998

After a ten-day suspension of its field activities following a landmine incident in which a doctor was killed and three other medical staff injured, the International Committee of the Red Cross (ICRC) is resuming its activities throughout Kosovo and seeking to restore the high degree of access to persons in need that it had in recent months. Field trips will be subject to enhanced security assessments, particularly regarding the threat of landmines. A first relief convoy left Pristina this morning with 30 tonnes of food and other supplies to be distributed to displaced people in Mitrovica, north of Pristina. Further convoys are planned for the coming days. On Monday 12 October, ICRC delegates distributed food and other basic necessities to 200 wounded and sick people at Pristina hospital. Beneficiaries included patients coming from areas affected by the recent violence, refugees from Krajina, and vulnerable individuals treated at the hospital. The ICRC team in Pristina comprises five delegates working with the support of senior national staff. Last week the organization decided to stay on in Yugoslavia even in the event of airstrikes.

[For further materials see Chapter 13.]

B. The UN High Commissioners for Human Rights and for Refugees

1. UN High Commissioner for Human Rights, Field Operation in Former Yugoslavia, April 1998

A. Overview of leading human rights concerns

56. In the last weeks the OHCHR in Belgrade has followed the situation in Kosovo closely, monitored events on the ground and conducted preliminary investigations into police operations carried out in the Drenica region in late February and early March. The Drenica region has for several months been the scene of violence. Police operations have been launched in response to attacks allegedly carried out by groups belonging to the so-called "Kosovo Liberation Army" ("UCK") said to be based in the area. It is also reported that since November 1997, Serbian authorities have had serious difficulty in maintaining control over most parts of the Drenica region because of increasingly frequent armed attacks. Before the operations in late February and early March, it was reported that the police only patrolled parts of Drenica in daytime and that many post offices and other state institutions had been closed. It appears that significant police reinforcements were brought into the area during that time.

57. On 28 February it was reported that Serbian police had surrounded the villages of Likosane and Qires close to Glogovac in the Drenica region. According to a statement issued by the Serbian Ministry of Internal Affairs on 28 February, police units on regular patrol came under attack by "Albanian separatists". Four police officers were reportedly killed and two seriously wounded in the incident. In response to this attack the police reportedly pursued the attackers and launched an operation in the above-mentioned villages, killing 16 persons and arresting nine others. It appears that five of these persons are still in custody, but the police have not disclosed their identities. The Ministry also announced that it had seized large quantities of weapons and explosives

58. A second police operation was launched on 5 March when police who, according to the Ministry of Internal Affairs, had come under fire pursued their attackers and lay siege to a number of houses and family compounds in the villages of Gornji Prekaz and Donji Prekaz. The police reported that two officers were killed and four wounded in the exchange. According to the same statement, "26 terrorists" were "liquidated", among them their leader Mr. Adem Jashari. Another 30 persons were reported to have surrendered, but the police did not specify the fate and whereabouts of these people.

59. Local sources reported that, in Likosane on 28 February, a group of 12 men, including ten members of the Ahmeti family, were taken by police to an unknown location. On 2 March a private person informed relatives that the bodies of the missing persons were at the morgue in Pristina, where reportedly they later recovered 15 bodies. Witnesses who saw the corpses claim that some of the bodies bore marks suggesting that they had been mutilated, and that some of the persons appeared to have been shot at close range. On 3 March, 25 coffins were buried in Likosane. In addition to the 15 mentioned above, ten bodies were recovered in the villages, including that of a pregnant woman. According to a list compiled by a local non-governmental organization, the dead included twelve persons from Likosane, ten from Qires and three from neighbouring villages.

60. Regarding the operation on 5-7 March in and around the villages of Donji and Gornji Prekaz, it is reported that 48 bodies were brought from the Pristina morgue to the police station in Srbica on 8 March. Local sources further said that the bodies of five other people killed in the village of Lausa and in locations close to Srbica, allegedly by snipers, were brought later to Srbica. It appears that 15 women and 8 children under the age of 16 were among the dead. Four of the persons were over 65 years of age. On 10 March the Serbian Ministry of Internal Affairs acknowledged that women and children were among the dead, but stated that these persons had been killed in crossfire. The families of the deceased refused to collect the bodies for burial, demanding that an international team of forensic experts be allowed to perform an independent autopsy, as they claimed that some of the

bodies bore marks suggesting that the persons had been shot at close range. However, on 10 March the police buried the bodies in graves close to Donji Prekaz. The bodies were later exhumed and reburied by relatives. It may be noted that while many women and children fled the area in the early stages of the operation, unconfirmed reports suggest that some of the families in Prekaz had refused to evacuate the compounds that later came under fire from the police.

61. In its initial statement on casualties resulting from the above police actions, the Serbian Ministry of Internal Affairs announced that the bodies would be subject to post mortem examinations by forensic experts at the Pristina state hospital. However, it appears that no autopsies were carried out before burial of those killed in Likosane, Qires and Prekaz. Of the 53 bodies buried in Prekaz, ten were buried without having been identified. Under the Federal Law on Criminal Procedures, the authorities are obliged to carry out detailed post mortem examinations in all cases of violent death, under the authority of the investigating judge handling the case. The same law also provides for exhumation of the bodies in the event that they have already been buried, and carries an obligation for the authorities to take adequate measures to identify the dead in connection with the autopsies.

62. The OHCHR has received a number of allegations, in connection with the Prekaz operation, that unnamed members of certain families are missing. These reports have been imprecise and difficult to verify in the current charged atmosphere. The violence in Drenica also led thousands of people to flee their homes in the region. It is hard to determine whether persons initially reported as missing are indeed missing; whether they were or are detained; or whether those reported missing have simply been separated from their families. Moreover, because police sealed off most of the Drenica area for several days after the action, international humanitarian organizations -- whose regular operations might have dispelled rumor and speculation -- were unable to enter the area.

63. In recent weeks, Belgrade OHCHR has been monitoring a number of cases outside the Drenica area in which persons suspected of crimes against the state, including charges of terrorism, were arrested and detained by the police and state security services. In the only independently confirmed instance, five Kosovo Albanian men were arrested in Prizren on 27 February. It is alleged that the men were subjected to torture, including electric shock, under interrogation conducted after their formal arraignment. On 11 March, OHCHR raised questions about the Prizren allegations in correspondence with the federal and republic ministries of interior and justice. One of the men has since been released. OHCHR further discussed the allegations directly with the Serbian Ministry of Justice on 18 March.

64. On 23 March in Pristina, Serbian government officials and representatives of the Kosovo Albanians signed a document on the implementation of the September 1996 Memorandum of Understanding on education in Kosovo. Under the agreement reached on 23 March, Albanian professors and students will be allowed to return to three faculties of Pristina University by 31 May and to another seven faculties by the end of June. The Institute for Albanian Studies should also reopen by the end of March. While both signatories see the document as a success, the Pristina University Teachers' Council and some students of the university called the agreement "illegal and unconstitutional".

B. Activities

64. Developments in Kosovo have dominated the work of the OHCHR field office in the Federal Republic of Yugoslavia this month. The High Commissioner for Human Rights issued public statements concerning Kosovo on 3 March and 12 March. The "Contact Group" statement of 9 March, which requested a mission to Kosovo by the OHCHR, focused attention on the activities of the Belgrade office. From 5-19 March, two members of OHCHR Belgrade's four-person staff were on continuous field mission in Kosovo, while the other two, including the new head of office, met in Belgrade with Government officials, diplomatic representatives, staff of other international organizations, defense attorneys, and others associated with Kosovo issues. Exchanges with the Yugoslav Ministry of Foreign Affairs and the Serbian Ministry of Justice were especially informative.

65. OHCHR cooperation with other U.N. agencies operating in the FRY has heightened during the past weeks, especially with UNHCR and the U.N. Liaison Office. The Kosovo situation has enhanced the need for close contact both within the U.N. and among international organizations.

66. In addition to meeting its most urgent responsibilities, OHCHR has also been able to discuss joint efforts in commemorating the 50th anniversary of the Universal Declaration of Human Rights. An alliance of 47 NGOs has already begun a year-long series of events to promote the anniversary, and OHCHR Belgrade has begun to link efforts of independent human rights advocates, legal professionals, the international community, NGOs, and any Government commissions which may be formed to commemorate the declaration. The commemoration of the 50th anniversary will be a large-scale public event in the FRY, involving hundreds of independent initiatives and thousands of participants throughout the country.

2.   Human Rights Field Operation in the Former Yugoslavia, 30 April 1998

A. Overview of main human rights concerns

52. The situation in Kosovo has deteriorated as more violence has been directed against a broader range of targets. Following the police operations in Drenica in late February and early March, there have been several clashes between police and groups of armed civilians in the Drenica area and close to Decani and Djakovica. It is also reported that armed men presumed to be part of the so-called Kosovo Liberation Army (UCK) have maintained control over several villages in the Drenica region. The UCK has reportedly been more visible in the countryside than before. Meanwhile, Kosovo Albanians continue to hold almost daily protest marches in several locations in Kosovo. The demonstrations have mostly passed without incident or police intervention. The rising tensions and continuing violence have led more people to leave their homes in the affected areas. UNHCR estimates that 17,500 persons have now been displaced inside Kosovo and another 4,000-5,000 have been displaced to Montenegro. On 24 April, it was reported that around 1,000 Kosovo Albanians had fled their homes close to the border and entered Albania.

53. Violence has spread to villages near the Yugoslav-Albanian border and to the border itself. On 24 March a police operation was carried out in Glodjani and Dubrava close to the border. Serbian authorities reported that the action was launched in response to an attack on police in which one officer was killed and another wounded. Three persons were killed and another twenty wounded during the police operation, which continued through the day. Fourteen persons were allegedly arrested by the police. All reportedly were freed except for one man who remained in custody on charges related to "anti-state activities". It has been alleged that he has been tortured while in detention. Local sources report that others of those detained were badly beaten while in police custody.

54. Several incidents in which Yugoslav Army border guards have repelled attempted incursions by armed civilians from Albania have been reported in the last weeks. On 20 April a Yugoslav border post reportedly returned fire at five men who tried illegally to cross the border. It appears that large quantities of arms and ammunition were found at the scene of the incident. On 22-23 April it was reported that Yugoslav Army troops had intercepted a group of some 200 armed persons who tried to cross the border from Albania near Kosare. Heavy clashes reportedly went on through the night. According to initial reports 22 men were killed and 14 captured in the operation. The Yugoslav Army reported no casualties. At this writing, the Yugoslav-Albanian border is closed.

55. On 6 April the bodies of six Kosovo Albanians were found in a field outside Klina. All were reportedly kidnapped four days earlier by persons believed to be associated with the UCK. On 19 April three Serbian internally-displaced persons accommodated in Decani were reportedly detained by armed civilians identifying themselves as members of the UCK. The three IDPs were returning to their home village of Dubrava to collect their belongings when they were allegedly captured by the armed civilians. They were taken to the village of

Glodjani where they allegedly were physically assaulted before being released.

56. Despite encouraging signs in the implementation of the September 1996 Memorandum of Understanding on education, little progress has been made in resolving the Kosovo situation overall. On 20 April the office of the leader of the Democratic League of Kosova, Dr. Ibrahim Rugova, announced the main elements of the Kosovo Albanian platform for negotiations with the Yugoslav authorities. Under these terms the Kosovo Albanians would enter talks only if they were held on neutral ground and in the presence of a foreign mediator. They also insist on negotiating with the Federal Yugoslav government and not representatives of the Republic of Serbia. Over the last several weeks the Serbian republican authorities, with one federal representative in their delegation, have repeatedly invited the Kosovo Albanian side to talks in Pristina, but the Kosovo Albanian leadership has so far not accepted the invitation. On 23 April, a Serbia-wide referendum was held on the question "Do you accept the involvement of foreign representatives in resolving the problem of Kosovo and Metohija?" Kosovo Albanians boycotted the referendum; Serbian authorities reported that 75 percent of registered voters turned out and cast an overwhelming "No" vote.

57. Although developments in Kosovo have dominated the OHCHR Belgrade office's work this month, they have not been the exclusive focus. On 2 April, the commission for implementation of Article 7 of the normalization agreement between the Republic of Croatia and the Federal Republic of Yugoslavia signed a protocol on procedures for organized return. Procedures for implementation of the protocol, which has been the subject of considerable debate in Croatia, are yet to be fully elaborated.

Visit of the Special Rapporteur

58. On the request of the Commission on Human Rights as expressed in the Chairman's statement of 24 March 1998, the new Special Rapporteur, Mr. Jiri Dienstbier, made a fact-finding visit to the Federal Republic of Yugoslavia from 5-8 April 1998. The Special Rapporteur travelled to Belgrade and Pristina and met with federal and republic officials and Kosovo Albanian representatives. In his report to the Commission on Human Rights issued after the visit (E/CN.4/1998/164), the Special Rapporteur presented the following recommendations:

- The authorities should permit a forensic investigation, by independent experts including relevant U.N. authorities, of the deaths resulting from the 28 February operations in Likosani and Cirez and the 5 March operations in Prekaz. Such an investigation should have as its objective to determine whether arbitrary, summary or extra-judicial executions occurred in the course of those operations.
- The Serbian Ministry of Internal Affairs should conduct an internal investigation of the events of 28 February and 5 March, and publicly announce its findings. If sufficient evidence is found to warrant further proceedings, it should be affirmed that officers would be subject not only to internal disciplinary measures, but also to investigatory procedures applicable to all citizens. Criminal charges, as warranted, should be brought by the state prosecutor and cases brought swiftly to trial, which should be held in regular, open session.
- International standards of human rights should be scrupulously respected for persons in detention. Arrested persons should be allowed to contact their families and to receive legal assistance. They should further be provided access, whether they are in police or court custody, to their own physicians, and not only physicians provided by the police or court. Allegations of torture should be rigorously investigated and acts of torture punished.
- Police should treat the allowable periods of detention after arrest, as specified by domestic law, as maximum limits, not standard detention periods. It has been alleged in some cases that the routine confinement of detainees for the full period permitted by law has been the cause of reports that persons have gone "missing." Domestic law allows police to hold an individual up to 24 hours to determine identity, and then an additional 72 hours before arraignment before an investigative judge.
- The Kosovo Albanian leadership should make a public commitment to ensure that all members of the Kosovo Albanian

community shall pursue their goals only by peaceful means, and that they shall respect and protect the human rights of all inhabitants of the region.

- All parties should allow free access for international and humanitarian organizations to persons and areas in Kosovo affected by violence.
- The Government should authorize the opening of an OHCHR office in Kosovo. Such a presence would help substantially to promote confidence, as it did during the two-week period from 26 March-9 April when an expanded OHCHR team was active in the region.

The Government should authorize the establishment of a temporary, expanded OHCHR human rights monitoring mission in the region, operating out of premises in Kosovo, which by its presence could help to promote confidence during the difficult months which lie immediately ahead.

B. Activities

59. Developments in Kosovo, and preparation and follow-up of the visit of the Special Rapporteur dominated the work of the OHCHR Belgrade Office this month. The 24 March Chairman's Statement of the Commission on Human Rights and the 31 March Security Council resolution continued to focus international attention on the activities of OHCHR in the FRY. In response to an 11 March request from the High Commissioner, the Yugoslav government on 25 March issued visas to three OHCHR international staff. For the following fifteen days, the "expanded team" worked with Belgrade OHCHR colleagues on assignment in Kosovo and, ultimately, accompanied the Special Rapporteur on his visit to Pristina.

60. In Belgrade, OHCHR staff prepared the program of work and technical support of the "expanded team" while it also made preparations for the first visit of the new Special Rapporteur. In the weeks preceding the 25 March Contact Group meeting and the arrival of the Special Rapporteur, the Belgrade OHCHR responded to inquiries from several embassies and representatives of international organizations, many of whom visited the office. Throughout this period, OHCHR was in daily contact with the Yugoslav foreign ministry. Cooperation between the foreign ministry and OHCHR both by the Special Rapporteur and Foreign Minister Mr. Zivadin Jovanovic in their 6 April meeting. At that meeting, the foreign minister proposed preparation of a protocol to formalize cooperation and, on 7 April, the Yugoslav Government presented a draft proposal.

61. During his visit, the Special Rapporteur met in Belgrade with the Serbian Minister of the Interior, Mr. Stojiljkovic, Serbian Government Vice Premier and constitutional law professor Mr. Markovic, and the Serbian Commissioner for Refugees, Mrs. Morina. He also met with the heads of UNHCR operations in Yugoslavia and Bosnia and Herzegovina. In Pristina, Mr. Dienstbier met with Dr. Rugova, head of the Democratic League of Kosovo, as well as with representatives of international organizations and human rights and humanitarian assistance groups. Press coverage of his visit was extensive in both broadcast and print media, in official and independent organs; his report to the Commission on Human Rights was serialized and printed in its entirety by one daily.

62. Cooperation with UNHCR and other U.N. agencies grows closer. Coordination meetings organized by UNHCR with NGOs on humanitarian issues and international organizations on security matters have provided an opportunity for the new head of the OHCHR Belgrade office to meet colleagues. On 25 March, UNHCR's head of mission introduced the head of OHCHR Belgrade to UNHCR's community of donors. OHCHR is co-located with ICTY and the U.N. Liaison Office, which facilitates interaction on a daily basis.

63. During this month, OHCHR staff met at length with representatives of the Norwegian Refugee Council to explore citizenship and documentation issues affecting refugees from Croatia currently resident in Yugoslavia. OHCHR raised with the Yugoslav foreign ministry isolated reports of differential treatment accorded Serb and non-Serb visa applicants at Yugoslav consular offices in eastern Slavonia, and received assurances directly from the foreign minister that there would be equal treatment of all applicants.

64. The OHCHR Belgrade and Sarajevo offices worked together during the reporting period to inquire into the detention of a Bosnian citizen who came to Yugoslavia as part of a business delegation and was arrested at the Yugoslav border. OHCHR Belgrade made contact with defense attorneys, the Office of the High Representative, international organizations, bilateral representatives and others. After the intervention of the prime minister of Serbia, charges against the Bosnian citizen were dropped. Although Serbian authorities announced his release from detention approximately 12 hours before it actually occurred, the businessman returned to Bosnia without incident.

65. A third member of OHCHR operations in Yugoslavia arrived this month and has divided his time between Belgrade and Pristina.

3.   UNHCR Briefing Notes, 12 May 1998

UNHCR believes that the number of persons displaced as a result of the tense situation in Kosovo is on the increase. Although the situation is extremely fluid and difficult to assess, both because of limitations on UNHCR access due to the security situation and because displaced people are moving from one host family to another, UNHCR believes there are now just over 31,000 internally displaced. The Albanian NGO "Mother Theresa Society" puts the number higher, at nearly 38,000.

UNHCR continues to appeal to the Yugoslav authorites to move the Croatian Serb refugees out of accommodation places in Kosovo where they do not feel secure.

4.   Human Rights Field Operation in the Former Yugoslavia, 29 May 1998

A. Overview of main human rights concerns
Kosovo

45. Diplomatic efforts to address the growing crisis in Kosovo have continued in recent weeks. On 11-13 May, former U.S. envoy Richard Holbrooke and current envoy Robert Gelbard visited Belgrade and Pristina in an attempt to bring the two sides closer to dialogue. On 15 May, FRY President Slobodan Milosevic and the leader of the Kosovo Albanians, Dr. Ibrahim Rugova, met in Belgrade. Milosevic and Rugova agreed that "working groups" would meet on a regular weekly basis. The state-controlled media in Belgrade gave considerable publicity to the event, despite their previous campaign in support of April's referendum repudiating foreign mediation in Kosovo. Reports of serious splits within the Kosovo Albanian camps gave rise to doubts whether the talks would indeed start as agreed. However, on 25 May a state delegation headed by Serbian Deputy Prime Minister Ratko Markovic met in Pristina for a first round of talks with a Kosovo Albanian delegation led by Fehmi Agani, advisor to Dr. Rugova. After the four-hour-meeting, which took place in the premises of the Democratic League of Kosova (LDK), the spokesman for the Kosovo Albanian negotiating team said that the discussion had focused on methods, framework and modalities of the talks as well as on the steps needed to maintain momentum. The Serbian delegation issued a statement saying that the talks had been held "in a tolerant atmosphere, with the presentation of different views on the situation and ways to normalize the situation in Kosovo", adding that "the two sides reached agreement to undertake measures to promote the process of confidence building".

46. The talks come at a delicate point in time, as the strength, numbers, and visibility of the Kosovo Liberation Army (UCK) and "armed civilians" appear to be growing. The cycle of attack and retaliation continues with alarming constancy, claiming a steady toll of victims. Fighting which erupted on Friday 8 May continued for several days, forcing a closure of the main road between Pristina and Pec. The clashes raged just 12 kilometers west of Pristina, close to the airport. This was the first time a main road had been cut and the first time fighting had come that close to the provincial capital. The clashes were apparently triggered by two separate attacks on police vehicles in which six policemen were wounded. In another incident in Babaloc in Decani, one policeman was shot and killed. The Pristina-Pec road remains closed to regular traffic, as fighting continues in the area. In one of the most recent incidents, on the weekend 23-24 May, several hundred armed Kosovo Albanians were reported to have clashed with the police around the Decani-Djakovica road. The Serbian Ministry of the Interior reported that its investigators had found and identified the bodies of six Albanians killed in these clashes. Fighting is also reported to have spread towards the town of Orahovac, with an unknown number of people fleeing to Prizren. UNHCR estimates that there are now around 34,600 internally displaced persons in Kosovo.

47. In the last weeks there have been numerous reports of Serbian police officers and Serbian, Albanian and Roma civilians being abducted by groups of armed Kosovo Albanians, believed to be members of the UCK. On 23 May armed men, reportedly wearing uniforms with UCK insignia, stopped the Kosovo Polje-Pec train at Banjica, searched the passengers and forcibly removed a man in civilian clothes, a Serbian police officer travelling with his wife. On 24 May two police officers were reportedly abducted by armed Albanians while travelling by car on a road close to Decani. The whereabouts of the abducted persons remain unknown.

48. As part of the implementation of the Memorandum of Understanding on education, on 18 May the premises of the Pristina University technical college was handed over to Kosovo Albanian representatives. Before the formal hand-over, Serbian students, protesting the education accord, had occupied the college building, and Serbian police had to intervene to remove the students by force. At the same time a large number of Serbian students gathered in front of the building and started throwing stones at Albanian students who were there to officially enter the college. However, the police managed to separate the groups and a larger incident was avoided.

...

B. Activities

57. The OHCHR has maintained a continuous monitoring presence in Kosovo throughout the present reporting period, but security concerns have limited the mobility of the OHCHR team. Regular contacts have been held with both international agencies and local and international non-governmental organizations active in the region, especially as regards the deteriorating humanitarian situation in the region. Much of the work has been focused on following up a growing number of cases of missing persons and on investigating alleged human rights violations in connection with police actions. OHCHR has also monitored demonstrations and protest gatherings in Pristina. On 4-5 May, OHCHR participated in a Yugoslavia - Macedonia - Albania international interagency meeting, held in Skopje, to discuss humanitarian coordination in Kosovo.

58. Negotiations are ongoing between the OHCHR and the government of the FRY regarding formalization of the OHCHR's status. At this writing, OHCHR has just received the Yugoslav's government's response to the draft proposal submitted by OHCHR early this month.

59. Growing numbers of Serb refugees from Croatia have been coming to OHCHR's office in Belgrade, seeking advice and information about prospects for return. With the steady departure of Serbs from Croatia, representatives of human rights NGOs working in Croatia are increasingly visiting Belgrade to follow up with their clients. These, too, have made their way to OHCHR Belgrade. The Yugoslav foreign ministry, UNHCR, and the Norwegian Refugee Council have all at different times assisted OHCHR in its attempts to provide current information to refugees and their advocates. The changing, yet-unclarified state of regulations has been confusing to the refugees who have sought OHCHR's advice. Croatian state television channel HRT 1 is accessible in Belgrade even without satellite or cable, and refugees have been able to follow HRT news and commentary which, they tell OHCHR, have discouraged their return.

60. From 4-12 May, OHCHR focused on Montenegro, which the office had not been able to visit in many months. OHCHR's three international and three national staff gathered in Montenegro for a weekend to decide how to use existing resources to cope with pressing demands, in particular the growing number of missing persons, and to explore what additional material and staff resources are needed urgently short-term and long-term.

61. OHCHR met at length with the Montenegrin Prime Minister, the Minister of Justice, the Secretary of Information, and the Commissioner for Refugees. Designed to update senior Montenegrin officials on the

work of OHCHR since our last visit, the meetings produced open conversations about police practice and procedure, conformance of republican and federal law with international human rights standards, legislative interest in creation of an ombudsman, the 50th anniversary commemoration of the Universal Declaration of Human Rights, and the humanitarian situation of refugees currently accommodated in Montenegro and displaced persons arriving from Kosovo. Montenegrin officials volunteered full support to OHCHR's efforts to disseminate human rights information and urged OHCHR to develop educational television programming on human rights that could be broadcast in all languages spoken in Montenegro. As part of that effort, the Minister of Information suggested that OHCHR might wish to be a regular guest on TV Montenegro's morning magazine.

62. In Bijelo Polje, OHCHR monitored the war crimes trial of Nebojsa Ranisavljevic, accused of participating in the abduction and killing of at least 19 civilians from the Belgrade-Bar train on 27 February 1993 at Strpci. Charges under the federal law of war crimes against civilians were brought by the republican prosecutor and by attorneys for families of the identified missing. OHCHR has met with all attorneys in the case, including defense attorneys for Ranisavljevic. The trial resumes on 3 June.

63. OHCHR met with the defense attorney for over 70 members of the Roma community in Danilovgrad, restitution for whose violent ouster from their homes during riots in 1995 is still unresolved in Montenegrin courts after several actual and several postponed hearings. OHCHR raised this matter with the Montenegrin minister of justice, who pledged personal intervention to schedule a previously-postponed hearing immediately after the 31 May elections.

64. On returning from Montenegro, OHCHR attended the trial in Belgrade of artist "Nune" Popovic, who was arrested during a street performance in last year's demonstrations and accused of verbally insulting police. Independent media had aired television footage of Popovic's arrest, which showed him submitting quietly to police. The prosecution's witness did not appear at the hearing, and the trial was postponed to an indefinite date.

65. On 22 May OHCHR staff visited Kragujevac and met with representatives of the Association for Human Rights of Roma in the FRY. Discussions focused on the difficult social and educational situation of this community and on human rights cases pursued by the Association. OHCHR staff also visited a social centre and a kindergarten run by the local Roma community. In Kragujevac, OHCHR also met with representatives of the trade union of the "Zastava" weapons factory, who explained their concerns regarding the deteriorating social situation among its workers.

66. OHCHR met this month with the head of the Helsinki Committee of Sandzak to discuss issues raised in that NGO's 1997 annual report on the situation of the Muslim (Bosniak) community in the region. To coincide with the resumption of the Bijelo Polje war crimes trial, OHCHR began planning an extended field visit to Sandzak for the end of May.

5. UN Inter-Agency Update on Kosovo, Friday 24 July 1998

This report has been compiled by UNHCR with support from OCHA and with inputs from UN Agencies and other humanitarian organizations in FRY, FYROM and Albania

The conflict in Kosovo has entered a "new and potentially more deadly phase" said US Envoy to the Balkans, Robert Gelbard on Thursday, stressing that there is a "clear and urgent need for both meaningful dialogue and immediate tension-reducing measures, including a comprehensive cessation of hostilities," according to the press. The recent scene of intense fighting, Orahovac, is now reportedly under the control of the Serbian police. Belgrade media reports that life in the town was "coming back to normal" with electricity, water, and telephone links restored. Many of the inhabitants of that town who fled the fighting earlier this week, however, are yet to return, and humanitarian aid agencies are rushing to assess the priority needs of the victims, as well as to deliver critical assistance.

1. KOSOVO

1.1 Serbian Police Regain Control of Orahovac. Serbian police have reportedly assumed control of the Zrze-Bela Crkva-Orahovac road and the town of Orahovac on Tuesday evening. Belgrade media reported on 24 July that electricity, water, and phone links were reestablished. Many of the civilians displaced by the recent fighting, however, are yet to return to Orahovac, many out of fear.

1.2 Many Dead and Injured from Clashes in Orahovac. On 22 July, the Kosova Information Centre (QIK) which is close to the Democratic League of Kosovo (LDK) reported that the LDK and the Council for the Defense of Human Rights (CDHRF) chapters in Prizren obtained accounts from those who fled the fighting, and said that 16 Kosovo Albanians were known to be killed, in addition to the 34 reported earlier, bringing the total to at least 50 ethnic Albanian deaths. In addition, numerous reports indicated that many ethnic Albanians had been missing, possibly abducted or detained. As many of the dead in the town of Orahovac and in the neighbouring villages had not been identified, complete figures on casualties caused by this week's clashes remained unavailable as of today. The following figures, however, were provided by a Serbian police captain who informed reporters on Wednesday: 4 Serb civilians killed; and 51 Serbian, Albanian and Romany civilians kidnapped. The police had also arrested 223 Kosovo Albanians suspected of having aided "terrorist" activities. Most of these people were released, while 26 remained detained after questioning. Separately, Tanjug reported yesterday that a total of 79 persons had been abducted by ethnic Albanians in Kosovo between 1 January and 15 July of this year. These people included ethnic Serbs, Montenegrins, Albanians and others.

1.3 Thousands of Displaced Civilians: Mainly in Malisevo. According to Betaweek, Serbian police sources announced earlier that they had made it possible for 2,000 people from Orahovac, both Serbs and ethnic Albanians, to leave the site of conflict and evacuate safely. Figures of displacement, however, are much higher according to other sources. Kosova Information Centre (QIK) estimates that only about 5,000 people have remained in Orahovac, while some 13,000 had fled to neighbouring areas. The Mother Theresa Society (MTS), a Kosovo Albanian NGO, told UNHCR on 23 July that the arrival figures from Orahovac was at this time difficult to assess, as the influx still continued in to Malisevo. They estimated, however, that about 6,000 people remained in Orahovac. (No independent confirmation of the exact displacement figures is available to date.)

1.4 UNHCR Visits Malisevo. On 23 July, a team from UNHCR Pristina visited Malisevo, a town 15 kms north of Orahovac, to assess the overall situation with particular attention to the plight of the thousands of IDPs who were reported to have arrived from Orahovac during the last few days.

(a) Access OK, Some Roads Empty, Town Full of People - The visit proceeded smoothly without any problem faced at the check points. No traffic was seen on the road between Stimlje and Malisevo and the villages along the road appeared mostly empty. The main road in the town of Malisevo, however, was full of people with countless street shops along the road side selling produce, cigarettes and household items. (It was apparently a market day.) Regular stores were open as well.

(b) IDPs Afraid to Return - In the town of Malisevo, UNHCR met with the local chapter of the Mother Theresa Society (MTS). UNHCR also visited two households hosting IDPs in a nearby village of Oasdrozub in Malisevo commune. IDPs said there were some family members that still remained in Orahovac and that they were very eager to go back to find them, but were afraid to do so.

(c) Food Requirements - The town had plentiful seasonal produce, but both IDPs and MTS said that bread was needed the most. Wheat fields in the commune were being harvested, but the wheat could not be processed due to lack of electricity. Because the town could not be reached by private/commercial transport, other basic food items were also lacking. These items included sugar, cooking oil, rice and milk-powder.

(d) Non-food Needs - MTS said that electricity in Malisevo had been cut-off for two months. They requested a generator to at least disinfect medical equipment. As the town had been cut-off from other areas, medical supplies were lacking and local health houses were unable to treat serious cases that required hospital treatment. MTS requested vans and trucks for distribution of aid to surrounding villages. Clothing was also needed as most of the IDPs fled without much of their belongings.

(e) Serb Refugees from Croatia in Orahovac - In addition to the 21 refugees relocated from Orahovac to Pristina on 22 July (see Update #45), UNHCR Pristina relocated another 16 persons on 23 July. All 21 refugees who arrived on 22 July were moved to a collective centre in Pristina. UNHCR supplied blankets and mattresses. Six refugees chose to remain in Orahovac. ...

2.1 New Arrivals from Kosovo Decrease. For the first time in approximately one month, the daily new arrival of persons fleeing into Montenegro from the conflict in neighboring Kosovo was below 200, at 148 on 23 July. This figure was provided to UNHCR Podgorica by the Montenegrin authorities. The displaced are coming from Pec and Decane. ...

3. NORTHERN ALBANIA

3.1 KLA Fighters Train in Tropoje. According to a Reuters report of today, Kosovo Liberation Army (KLA or UCK) have "transformed the northern Albanian town of Tropoje into a virtual military base, openly engaging in weapons training." A Reuters journalist on Thursday saw "dozens of men wearing the distinctive KLA emblem practice shooting in courtyards and outside a school." Several dozen mules were "tethered alongside an open-air weapons market in the town centre." Meanwhile, insecurity in the district of Tropoje remains a serious concern for the local community, refugees, and the humanitarian aid workers in the area.

3.2 Border Situation: Concern for Both Governments. Meanwhile, on 22 July, the Albanian Ministry of Interior complained that shells from the fighting in Kosovo landed on its territory for the second time in four days, and accused Yugoslavia for threatening Albanian sovereignty. Serbian security sources reportedly have denied that shells had landed in Albania, while OSCE is reported to have said that "it did not appear that Serbian forces had been deliberately targeting Albanian territory but had been firing at the KLA," according to Reuters. On 23 July, the FRY Government decided "to extend and fortify" the border zone. FRY Prime Minister Momir Bulatovic announced that the Government would extend the border zone towards Albania to 5 kilometres. An announcement of the Federal Secretary for Information said that "the border zone will be visibly marked" and "the Army of Yugoslavia will have full authority within the zone."

6.   UN Inter-Agency Update on Kosovo, 27 July 1998

1. KOSOVO

1.1 Armed Clashes Spread to Several Fronts in Central Kosovo. Clashes between Serbian police backed by the military and armed Kosovo Albanians continued in several fronts in central Kosovo over the weekend, leaving many dead, wounded and/or displaced. According to media reports, the heaviest fighting began on 25 July and continued on the next day on (i) the Pristina-Pec road between Lapusnik and Kijevo, (ii) the Pristina-Prizren road between Stimlje and Suva Reka, and (iii) the Kosovska Mitrovica-Pec road around Srbica.

The Kosova Information Centre (QIK), which is close to the Democratic League of Kosovo (LDK), reported that the clashes were taking place not only on the main roads, but in the surrounding villages as well, resulting in immense material damage as a result of heavy shelling.

1.2 Both Sides Accuse Each Other For Starting the Offensive. The Serbian police claim that the weekend operation was a counter-offensive against an attack unleashed by the Kosovo Liberation Army (KLA) last Friday on a Yugoslav Army (VJ) convoy near Lapusnik. Kosovo Albanian sources say that the attack on the VJ was a fake and a pretext for an offensive. Meanwhile, western reporters on Monday were shown by the Serbian authorities "a network of KLA trenches, earthworks and dugouts on the high ground overlooking the valley between the villages of Komorane and Kijevo," according to Reuters. Both villages had been sealed off by armed ethnic Albanians for two months.

1.3 High Casualties Feared. On 26 July, QIK reported that at least 5 ethnic Albanians were confirmed to be killed and 24 people, including seven children, were wounded as a result of fighting on Saturday alone. It is feared that the total casualty-toll over the weekend is higher, as fighting continued beyond Saturday.

1.4 Exchange of Fire Along Kosovo-Albanian Border. Belgrade and Tirana authorities blame each other for a weekend incident along the Kosovo-Albanian border. Politika reported today that the Yugoslav Army (VJ) border guards had prevented attempts of over-night illegal border crossings between Saturday and Sunday in the vicinity of Vrbnica. The Yugoslav Army announced that their border guards who had prevented these illegal crossings were fired at from the Albanian territory. On the other hand, the Albanian Interior Ministry said on Sunday that "Serb soldiers opened fire towards the police building at the border checkpoint in Morini" in the district of Kukes. Today, the Albanian Foreign Minister Paskal Milo issued a protest against Yugoslav authorities for "provocation" against Albania's territorial integrity. ATA news agency reported that women and children were evacuated to nearby villages.

1.5 UNSECOORD Declares Kosovo as Security Phase III. The Office of the United Nations Security Coordinator (UNSECOORD) has instructed and the UN Agencies in FRY have agreed that as of today, Monday 27 July, all of Kosovo will be declared Security Phase III. This means that all UN staff must receive clearance from UNSECOORD before traveling into Kosovo.

1.6 37 Serb Refugees in Orahovac Relocated to Pristina. On 24 July, UNHCR completed its second round of assistance in relocating to Pristina a total of 37 Serb Refugees who were living in Orahovac, the site of last week's armed clashes. Most of these refugees were elderly persons, who had been displaced at least twice now, since they fled their homes during the Bosnian war. UNHCR hopes that the governments of Bosnia & Herzegovina, Croatia and FRY would swiftly enable repatriation of those wishing to return to their homes.

1.7 Resettlement Shuttle Continues. Since late June, UNHCR has been providing escorts to refugees living in various settlements in Kosovo who wished to travel to Pristina to process for resettlement to third countries, including Australia, Canada and USA. On 25 July, UNHCR escorted five refugees back from Pristina to collective centres in Djakovica and Prizren. These persons had come to Pristina for medical clearance and further interviews. UNHCR started this initiative after three refugees were kidnapped on the Djakovica-Pristina road late last month, as they were traveling towards Pristina to process for resettlement. ...

7.   UN Inter-Agency Update on Kosovo, 29 July 1998

Recent intensification of fighting in central Kosovo has affected the lives of women and children of all ethnic groups. While no organisation has been able to confirm the exact figures of displacement which continues to fluctuate on a daily, if not hourly basis, it is believed that well over 100,000 people are now displaced within Kosovo, with an additional 35,000 to 40,000 displaced elsewhere in Serbia, Montenegro, and Albania. In total, UNHCR estimates that the conflict in Kosovo has forced upto 150,000 to flee their homes. "The armed conflict must be stopped" said UNHCR's Special Envoy to the Former Yugoslavia, Nicholas Morris on Monday. Humanitarian agencies in Kosovo are struggling to find the whereabouts of the displaced civilians and ways of accessing them, as it is feared that thousands of people are hiding out of fear and panic, yet in need of urgent humanitarian aid.

1. KOSOVO

1.1 Malisevo Unblocked by the Serbian Police. Malisevo, a village in central Kosovo which has been completely under the control of the Kosovo Liberation Army (KLA/UCK) for over a month, has been unblocked yesterday evening by the Serbian police, according to both the Serbian, Kosovo Albanian, and the international media. No major fighting has been reported, as the KLA fighters and villagers, as well as the IDPs who had sheltered there, had already fled the village by the time the Serbian police had arrived.

Kosova Information Centre (QIK), close to the Democratic League of Kosovo (LDK), reported on 28 July, however, that the situation remained extremely volatile and dangerous. UNHCR tried to reach Malisevo on 29 July, but was unable to pass by either the Stimlje or Komorane routes.

1.2 More Civilians Flee. UNHCR has learned that the villagers and IDPs in Malisevo had fled to small villages around Malisevo and into the hills, as early as last Friday, out of panic and fear. These people are reportedly cut off from supplies including food and water. International aid agencies are struggling to find out where the civilians are located and how to access them, as it is feared that there are thousands of people in need of urgent humanitarian assistance. Several sources have indicated that thousands of IDPs are reported to have taken refuge in Mamusha between Orahovac and Prizren, in Nekovce, and in Mt. Berisha.

1.3 Serbian Refugee Settlement in Pristina Attacked by Grenade. After receiving a report yesterday from the local office of the Serbian Commissioner for Refugees that two grenades had been thrown to a collective centre in Pristina housing Serbian Refugees from Croatia, UNHCR Pristina visited the centre to conduct an assessment.

Serbian Refugees from Croatia in the affected building (school dormitory Grmjia) said that two hand grenades were thrown from the hill side towards the building, followed by two or three gun shots. One grenade exploded, breaking a window and making several holes in the wall. The second one did not explode, but dropped somewhere between the building and a larger main building. The unexploded grenade had already been removed by the time UNHCR had arrived. Two refugee families were in the building at the time of the incident, but remained uninjured.

The refugees expressed their fear to the UNHCR team, and pleaded for police deployment around the area. The total refugee population in the collective centre is around 130. The main building is normally shared between the refugees and local students. Currently, however, the building is occupied only by refugees, due to summer holidays. The police has investigated the incident yesterday.

1.4 Many Refugees Leave Srbica. On 28 July, UNHCR visited Srbica to assess the situation. No problem was faced in accessing the town, despite reports that another international organisation and the press were turned back at the first checkpoint earlier in the day. The town appeared largely empty of people, except for a number of villagers. Shops were empty or looted. There was a heavy presence of police in the town.

UNHCR found 16 refugees remaining in one collective centre. These refugees confirmed that the other collective centre at the Technical School was empty, saying that those who used to stay there have all left towards Kosovska Mitrovica and elsewhere due to insecurity in Srbica. Those who remained in Srbica said they heard shelling all around over the weekend, but said that Srbica itself was untouched. Bread was being provided by the police on a daily basis.

1.5 Some IDPS To Return to Obilic. Displaced persons who fled to Pristina during earlier clashes in and around the town of Belacevac in Obilic municipality have indicated their desire to return to Obilic. Local authorities were receptive to the idea of the return of IDPs, and UNHCR plans to escort these people back to their villages in the municipality. Subsequent aid delivery is planned on Thursday. According to the IDPs, approximately 1,000 of them wished to return to harvest crops, provided it was safe. Local authorities have been asked to ensure security. On 29 July, 200 returned as a first group.

2. MONTENEGRO

2.1 New Arrivals Sharply Increase Again. A sharp increase in the number of displaced persons entering Montenegro from Kosovo has been reported between 24 and 27 July, amounting to over 2,000 persons during this period alone. According to figures provided by the Montenegrin Ministry of Interior, there are now as many IDPs from Kosovo in Montenegro as the number of refugees from Bosnia & Herzegovina and Croatia who fled the previous war in the Former Yugoslavia.

Statistics as at 28 July 1998
Refugees from B&H and Croatia: 26,000
IDPs (Ministry of Interior Figures)
arrival between April and June: 23,415

estimated arrival in March: 2,500
estimated total arrival: 25,915
(Montenegrin Red Cross Figure): 25,273

2.2 Displaced Persons Continue to Come From Pec and Decane. Most of the new arrivals were from villages in and around Pec and Decane where additional clashes had been reported. No arrivals have been reported this week from Orahovac or other areas recently under intense fighting in central Kosovo. Many of them had traveled through mountain paths to avoid Serbian checkpoints, where a number of IDPs have alleged that heavy bribes were being requested.

2.3 Assistance Caseload. The Montenegrin Red Cross has registered 25,273 IDPs in need of assistance. While some cases of double registration have been noted, there is also some number of people who have not yet been registered for various reasons. Registration by the Office of the Commissioner for Displaced Persons is progressing. However, concerns are raised over the slow pace of providing new ID cards to local registration offices, as IDPs are unable to collect their rations without an ID card. UNHCR Podgorica has installed a software in the Commissioner's Office to set up a data base system for the registration process. (The Ministry of Interior simply counts the new arrivals at the check points. The Office for the Commissioner is where the registration takes place.)

2.4 Accommodation Still A Problem. The collective centres in Plav and two transit centres in Rozaje have received more persons in need of accommodation. In total, over 700 IDPs are currently accommodated in collective centres. Renovation of two hotels in Plav has been completed by Swiss Disaster Relief (SDR), improving the sanitary facilities in the hotel. UNHCR is providing financial assistance to the Office for the Commissioner of Displaced Persons to provide running costs of the hotels. ...

3. NORTHERN ALBANIA

3.1 General Security Continues to Deteriorate in Tropoje District. The working environment in the Tropoje district remains difficult and complex. The following are examples of some incidents which have affected international aid agencies last week.

(a) On 23 July, a vehicle belonging to MSF Holland was hijacked at gun point on the road 20 minutes away from Bajram Curri. Two masked men in uniform with Kalashnikov rifles and a RPG-7 anti tank rocket stopped the car and ordered the team out. MSF has consequently closed their operation in Bajram Curri and relocated to Tirana.

(b) On 25 July, Italian nuns reported to UNHCR that in Fierze commune, where they were hosting 30 refugees in their convent compound, an 18-year old Albanian man entered the small centre and threatened the refugees with a Kalashnikov. The man forced the refugees to lay face down on the floor, and kept the group in that position for one hour, claiming that the land belonged to him, and that the refugees should leave. Later in the day, he was seen shooting into the air in the vicinity of the Franciscan convent. The refugees were extremely frightened, and despite UNHCR's visit and reassurances from the chief of the criminal police, they left the centre for Tirana early morning on 26 July.

(c) At 22:00 hours on 23 July, two armed men jumped out of a bush and started following a local WFP field assistant and an international member of the OSCE who was escorting the WFP staff home. Fortunately, nothing happened as they were close to the UNHCR residency and managed to enter the compound.

3.2 Police Asked to Strengthen Security Measures. Following these incidents, UNHCR Bajram Curri held an urgent meeting with the Chief of Criminal Police and a representative of the central government of Albania. UNHCR reiterated its concerns regarding security of refugees and aid workers in the district and stressed the importance of intensified security measures.

UNHCR is now informed that police presence will be increased around residences of international staff. 40 new special forces agents have arrived in Bajram Curri last week. Movements of all international vehicles will be reported to the police, who will remain on standby for any escort requests. In addition, UNHCR Bajram Curri is now in direct radio contact with the Government's Plenipotentiary. ...

4. FYR of MACEDONIA

(While the general situation in FYROM remains calm and quiet, following are some excerpts from recent press reports.)

4.1 Another Explosion in Kumanovo. Nova Makedonija reported in its front page on 27 July that another bomb exploded in the centre of Kumanovo last Friday, 24 July. No casualties were reported, while the explosion caused panic among the citizens.

4.2 Three Albanians Detained For Illegal Border Crossing. MIC News and Vecer reported on 27 July that on 25 July, the Macedonian border patrol near the Strezimir watchtower at the Macedonian-Albanian border had attempted to prevent a large group of Albanians trying to cross the border illegally. According to the FYROM Ministry of Defense, a group of Albanian citizens with 30 pack horses had attempted to cross the border from Albania. After some shooting, three Albanians were detained, while the rest of the group returned back to Albania.

8.   UNHCR Calls for immediate action to allow the return of the uprooted in Kosovo, 21 August 1998

Soren Jessen-Petersen, the United Nations Assistant High Commissioner for Refugees, on Friday called for immediate measures to allow the safe return to their homes of more than 230,000 people uprooted by the conflict in Kosovo. Jessen-Petersen issued the statement as he left Kosovo after a two-day visit there. He was then to proceed to Montenegro to meet Milo Djukanovic, President of Montenegro, and other senior officials. He earlier visited Belgrade and Pristina and on Thursday travelled to areas engulfed in recent violence in Kosovo.

People in the conflict zone told Jessen-Petersen they felt threatened without representatives of the world community in their midst. They said they were very concerned about possible further attacks and urged UNHCR to visit them on a regular basis. "Obviously, adequate arrangements are urgently required in Kosovo that will reassure the people and encourage those uprooted from their homes that it is safe for them to return. Authorities must assume their responsibilities in establishing the necessary conditions for safe return. But clearly the displaced people lack confidence in the present circumstances. Without safe return, you leave tens of thousands of people out in the open fields and there will be a catastrophe when winter sets in," Jessen-Petersen said. On Thursday at Kotrovic village, people displaced by last week's violence south of Kosovo's second largest town of Pec said they wanted to return to their homes as soon as possible and asked how UNHCR can help them. "It is a major problem," Jessen-Petersen said. "We have seen the destruction, but if a way can be found to create conditions of safety and somehow mobilize a little bit of assistance so that they can rebuild a part of their destroyed houses, maybe they can start life again." More than 170,000 of the 230,000 people forced from their homes are displaced within Kosovo, the remainder in Montenegro and Albania. Most of them are crammed into houses of villagers, but tens of thousands remain in the open fields and in the mountains, exposed to the summer heat and occasional rains. They have little food and no clean water. Children have been suffering from malnutrition and disease. On Wednesday, Jessen-Petersen said at a news conference that only an immediate cease-fire followed by a political dialogue can avert a looming humanitarian disaster. He said authorities should send a clear and unequivocal message assuring the safety of those who wish to return and back this up with concrete action; and that those responsible for atrocities should be held accountable. He also called for stronger support to the humanitarian relief efforts.

During his visit to central Kosovo Thursday, Jessen-Petersen went to empty villages damaged by the six-month conflict in the Serb province. Junik and Malisevo were deserted except for the presence of police. In Orahovac, scene of heavy shelling in mid-July, he saw some shops had begun to reopen and a few people were out in the streets. At Ade village just outside Pristina, villagers told him they had been prevented from harvesting their fields. The houses of two families remained occupied by police. UNHCR had escorted some 200 people who had requested to return to Ade early this month. During the last month, UNHCR escorted two to three convoys per week, carrying supplies from various humanitarian agencies. Joint efforts by UNHCR and humanitarian agencies have reached many of the displaced, but the assistance requirements remain great.

9.   UN Inter-Agency Update on Kosovo, 24 August 1998

1. KOSOVO

1.1 Fresh Outbreak of Violence Results in New Displacement. A fresh outbreak of violence beginning on Saturday has prompted villagers to flee their homes over a broad area southwest of Pristina. Field reports indicated gunfire and shelling occurred in the area of Suva Reka, 40 kilometers west southwest of Pristina. A UNHCR team on its way from Prizren to Suva Reka was turned back on Monday after police at a checkpoint said the road was unsafe. A reporter on Monday told UNHCR Pristina that many displaced persons arrived in the village of Pagarusa between Malisevo and Orahovac following shelling in villages around Suva Reka. On 23 August, UNHCR received reports that fighting erupted in Komorane, site of a police checkpoint 25 kilometers outside Pristina, beginning on 22 August. Shell blasts were reported and houses were seen ablaze in a string of villages stretching 25 kilometers to the south down to Magura. Fires were seen by travelers along the Pristina-Pec road on Sunday. A UNHCR team was barred from proceeding to Magura on Monday.

According to Kosovo Albanian media sources, strongest attacks by the police took placed in the villages of Recak and Beljine. The number of people displaced by the latest fighting was not immediately known.

1.2 Some Villagers Return Home. Recently, agencies have noted return of some displaced persons in the town of Orahovac and villages in Drenica region. The returned population in these villages may be some 10 to 20 per cent of the original population.

Estimated Displacement Figures:
(as at 24 August 1998)

Displacement within Kosovo	170,000
Displacement into Montenegro	33,000
Displacement into other parts of Serbia	20,000
Refugees into Albania	14,000
Visitors into FYROM	1,000
TOTAL	235,000

1.3 UNHCR Escorts Refugees for Resettlement. UNHCR continues to provide escort services to refugees in Kosovo who have been displaced from Croatia and Bosnia & Herzegovina during the previous conflict in the former Yugoslavia. On Monday, UNHCR picked up five refugees in Prizren and surrounding areas for resettlement to third countries, and two requiring medical treatment in Pristina.

1.4 UNICEF Provides Essential Drug Kits. UNICEF has recently delivered essential drug kits to state health institutions in Decane, Prizren, and Glogovac.

1.5 Over 450 Kosovo Albanians Killed by the Conflict. According to VIP Daily New Report of 24 August, the head of the news service of the Yugoslav Army's Pristina Corps said on Sunday that Yugoslav border guards had registered 146 armed incidents in Kosovo and killed more than 450 ethnic Albanians so far. The same report says that border guards have also seized 900 rifles, 200 machine guns, 20 recoilless guns, and over 450,000 rounds of various calibre and other military equipment.

2. MONTENEGRO

2.1 Influx of Displaced Persons from Kosovo Continues. Last week saw a sudden increase in the number of people in need of aid in Ulcinj. The Montenegrin Red Cross has registered nearly 3,000 people in one week. Reasons behind this sudden increase remain unclear. Some people may have come through mountain passes without going through police checkpoints, while others may have moved internally from other areas within Montenegro. These new arrivals have made difficult an already desperate situation. UNHCR received today a report of 150 new arrivals into Tuzi, a town just miles away from Podgorica towards the Montenegro-Albanian border. As the town was already saturated by hosting 1,400 people in private homes, the 150 newly arrived people have been sheltered in a transit centre. Statistics (as at 24 August 1998): Ministry of Interior Count of New Arrivals: 32,841; Montenegrin Red Cross Registered Caseload:

Ulcinj	14,125
Rozaje	4,160
Podgorica	4,507
Plav	7,273
Others	4,119
Total	34,184

2.2 Reports of Return from Montenegro to Kosovo. According to the police, two buses with approximately 90 displaced persons from Kosovo left yesterday from Montenegro to Pec. While this report has been seconded by an Italian journalist, no further information is available to UNHCR Podgorica at this time. If this information is correct, it will be the first time a return of this scale has taken place from Montenegro to Kosovo.

2.3 Government to Maintain an Open-Door Policy. As reported earlier, the Montenegrin Government has and will maintain an open-door policy towards those displaced by the conflict in Kosovo. At the same time, however, the Republican Government increasingly stresses that Montenegro should be seen as a "transit point" for the displaced, rather than as a permanent settlement, given the current lack of means to ensure adequate coverage of the needs of the IDPs.

2.4 Assistance Coordination. The Montenegrin Deputy Prime Minister has called a meeting to take place this week with the main humanitarian agencies and line ministries, as well as with mayors from four of the most affected towns. The meeting will discuss ways to clarify what should be done to coordinate humanitarian assistance operations in order to respond to the needs on the ground in an effective manner. Separately, WHO will chair a health coordination meeting this coming Thursday.

2.5 NGOs to Open Offices in Podgorica. The Danish Refugee Council (DRC), Italian Consortium of Solidarity (ICS) and Japan Emergency NGOs (JEN) will open offices in Podgorica this week, shortly after which they will begin implementation of their programmes.

3. NORTHERN ALBANIA

3.1 Another Border Incident. Diplomatic sources reported that on 17 August, between 9:00 am and 10:10 am, several mortar bombs fell into Albanian territory, near the village of Padesh. While the situation became calm by noon and no injuries had been reported, some 40 local inhabitants temporarily moved out from the area and returned home late afternoon.

3.2 Shooting Incident Affects UNHCR. Shooting by rival gangs increased last week, one of which resulted in a random bullet hitting the UNHCR office window in Bajram Curri. On 19 August, a UNHCR car was high-jacked at gun point by two armed masked men. ...

10.   UN Inter-Agency Update on Kosovo, 26 August 1998

1.1 Fighting was reported in several areas in recent days: west of Pec in Rugarovska area, along the Stimlje and Suva Reka road, on the Komorane - Kijevo stretch of the Pristina - Pec Road and near the Pristina airport 12 km south-west of Pristina leading to new displacement. Thousands of people, mostly women and children, have fled their homes since Saturday following shelling of villages in central Kosovo. A UNHCR team visited on Tuesday the village of Pagarusa between Orahovac and Malisevo and found several hundreds encamped in the woods. Most of the new arrivals into Pagarusa are sheltered by villagers in their homes but many others were staying on a hill on the outskirts of the village. Pagarusa already was hosting some 8,000 who arrived earlier in the month. On Tuesday, the UNHCR team saw small groups of several dozen people on foot, on carts and tractors heading toward Pagarusa under overcast skies and chilly winds. The people said they came from the villages of Lower and Upper Pecan, Slapusan, Semetiste, Prestan, Studencan, Samodregja and Dobrdolan in the Suva Reka municipality and Optorusa, Reti and Zeciste which had come under heavy shelling the past three days. The people there said that on Tuesday one woman died of illness and a baby was born in the woods.

1.2 Returns. At the same time there has been considerable return of population to Orahovac. The return to Ade village remains tentative, as police continues to occupy some houses of displaced persons, while water and electricity have yet to be reconnected. Some returns have

also taken place in the Srbica area. It is estimated that 30,000 persons altogether have returned.

Estimated Displacement Figures: (as at 24 August 1998)

Displacement within Kosovo	170,000
Displacement into Montenegro	33,500
Displacement into other parts of Serbia	20,000
Refugees into Albania	14,000
Visitors into FYROM	1,000
TOTAL	235,500

1.3 Desperate Civilians Fear Further Attacks. A 34-year-old woman was bringing a 5-week-old baby in her arms to the clinic at Pagarusa for treatment of diarrhea and fever. She said the baby was born in the woods last month, when she first fled her home at Reti village in Orahovac. After four weeks in the woods, she returned to her home in Reti, seeing other villagers going back. The woman said Reti had been relatively untouched during last months bombardments and she had stayed at her home for about a week. On Saturday, however, she fled once again after hearing artillery rounds hit her village. She fled in a group of 15, but lost her 3-year-old son and 1-1/2 year-old daughter during the flight. She said she saw flames in her village and still did not know what happened to her house. The woman claimed she had nowhere to go except Pagarusa because the area was ringed on one side by Serb forces and two main roads on the two other sides with heavy police presence.

1.4 Increased Concern Over Safety and Security of Aid Workers: Three Relief Workers Killed Under Fire. According to media reports and a witness on the ground, three workers of a local relief agency run by Kosovo Albanians, the Mother Theresa Society (MTS), were killed on Monday when tank fire hit their tractor. The workers were reported to have been on their way to distribute relief supplies in the village of Vlaski Drenovac outside Malisevo. Another MTS worker who witnessed the incident from about 500 meters away told UNHCR that his tractor was raked with automatic fire but he escaped with only minor burns he suffered while trying to save some of the food packs on his trailer. The victims were on a convoy of seven tractors that had earlier picked up the supplies at the MTS warehouse at Lapcevo, 10 kilometers west of Malisevo, delivered by a UNHCR/WFP escorted multi-agency convoy just two days earlier. Safety and Security of relief workers remain to be of high concern.

1.5 More Aid Reaches Displaced Persons. UNHCR escorted a multi-agency convoy to Barane on Tuesday to deliver supplies for some 30,000 displaced people and host families in the area 12 kilometers south of Pec. The 10-truck convoy carried shipments from Doctors of the World, Mercy Corps International, Catholic Relief Services, World Food Program, Handicap International, U.S. AID, and Papa Giovanni XXIII. The convoy transported 110 tons of wheat flour, 2,000 family food parcels, oil, beans, milk power, plastic sheeting, clothes, blankets, toothbrushes, toothpaste, detergent and sanitary napkins.

1.6 Reports of Land mines. Sightings of land mines believed to have been laid by UCK have been made on dirt tracks leading north of the town of Junik as well as in areas near Malisevo and Orahovac. Diplomatic sources said they had found evidence of anti-personnel and anti-tank mines and craters made in the blasts. There were also indications rebels had set up explosives rigged from water tanks and jerry cans. There are reports of land mines laid by the Serbian authorities on the Albanian border and along the Macedonian border through the Sar Mountains to General Jankovic (Blace). ...

2. MONTENEGRO

2.1 One Thousand New Arrivals in One Day. Marking the largest single influx since mid-June, over 1,000 people arrived into Rozaje yesterday from Pec. These people apparently fled fighting taking place over the last couple of days in Rugovska Klisura, a valley west of the town of Pec. The area which is comprised of 35 villages was considered a safe area, just as recently as until last week, with no armed clashes being reported. Many people who fled recent fighting in various villages in Western Kosovo, therefore, had sought refuge in the area, before coming under fire during the last two days.

2.2 Large New Influx Confirmed by Authorities. The arrival of 1,000 newly displaced persons into Montenegro has been confirmed both by the police and by the Montenegrin Deputy Prime Minister. 500 people

out of the 1,000 have transited through Rozaje, and have proceeded to Ulcinj. This has been confirmed by the local Red Cross. As the number of IDPs have already increased to 56 per cent of the total local population of 25,000 in Ulcinj, urgent measures continue to be needed.
2.3 Thousands More May Be Fleeing. UNHCR Podgorica also received unconfirmed information that another 4,000 people are still in the mountains, and could arrive in Montenegro in the coming days. Accommodation will be a serious problem, if this influx happens.
2.4 Humanitarian Agencies Decide on Contingency Action. As a result of an urgent meeting held today between UNHCR, ICRC and the Montenegrin Red Cross, additional aid will be dispatched to the area immediately from existing stocks in the country, in preparation for a potential large influx in the days ahead. These relief items which will be donated by ICRC and UNHCR include mattresses, blankets, oil, flour, and family parcels. UNHCR offices in Podgorica and Pristina are monitoring the situation closely, as well as the ICRC team in Pec.
Statistics (as at 25 August 1998)
Ministry of Interior Count of New Arrivals: 33,336
Montenegrin Red Cross Registered Caseload:

Ulcinj	14,125
Rozaje	4,160
Podgorica	4,507
Plav	7,273
Others	4,119
Total	34,184

Average of the two figures is shown on the first page. The discrepancy may be due to the fact that the Ministry of Interior is not keeping track of IDPs traveling through mountain paths. The registration in each municipality conducted by the Commissioner for Displaced Persons' Office is proceeding slowly, with only 9,000 IDPs recorded to date. ...
3. NORTHERN ALBANIA
3.1 Food Distribution for August Completed. August distributions have been completed in Albania in Tropoje District, Tirana, Durres and Shkoder. WFP has distributed a total of 160 MT of food aid in monthly rations to more than 6,700 individuals. ...

11.   UN Inter-Agency Update on Kosovo Situation, 28 August 1998

1. KOSOVO
1.1 New clashes have been reported in the region of Dulje, on the Pristina - Prizren road, in the the town of Podujevo, the wider Drenica region and within the Klina, Glogovac and Srbica triangle and in Malisevo municipality. Fighting along the Stimlje - Suva Reka road continues. Over the last couple of days Serbian police checkpoints in Drenica, Podujevo, Lausa and Gornja Klina were reported attacked.
1.2 New displacement. New displacement has resulted from the recent clashes. UN agencies are trying to track the locations and the numbers to assess their condition.
1.3 Returns. An estimated 70%-80% of residents have returned spontaneously to Orahovac. 700 out of 2,500 villagers who fled have returned to the villages of Ade and Obilic. The returnees need help to repair houses and reconnect water and electricity. According to the field reports, most of the 180 houses remained intact in the area of Obilic. However, it is estimated that some 15,000 houses have been rendered uninhabitable, thus making it impossible for residents to return.
Estimated Displacement Figures: (as at 24 August 1998)

Displacement within Kosovo	170,000
Displacement into Montenegro	35,000
Displacement into other parts of Serbia	20,000
Refugees into Albania	14,000
Visitors into FYROM	1,000
TOTAL	237,000

1.4 Humanitarian convoys. The Serbian police stopped the UNHCR led multy-agency eight-truck convoy at Slatina near Pristina on Thursday. The convoy had been trying to deliver aid to Skivjane in the Decane municipality (4 trucks) and to Brolic in the municipality of Pec (4 trucks). The 8-truck multi-agency convoy transported 25 tons of wheat flour, 3,000 family food parcels (with 1 month food provisions for

30,000 people), 30 rolls of plastic sheeting and 120 stoves. According to the Serbian sources the convoy was denied passage due to security reasons. UNHCR spokesman in Geneva said this was the first time since the beginning of the conflict in the region that a UNHCR relief convoy had been stopped and sent back without any explanation. However, late Friday Mr Janowski told the journalists that the convoy had been granted permission to resume its journey.
1.5 Julia Taft, the US Assistant Secretary of State, Bureau for Population, Refugees and Migration accompanied by Ambassador Christopher Hill and Charge d'Affairs Richard Miles visited the villages of Kijevo and Vrnice in western Kosovo, where she was shocked by the humanitarian situation.
1.6 Pilot projects of return. Representatives of UNHCR and ICRC met on Thursday with the high level delegations from the Austrian Presidency of the European Union and Britain to discuss the proposal put forward by France and Germany to undertake pilot projects that would enable return of the displaced to selected areas in Kosovo. The EU members invited UNHCR to draft a proposal for potential returns depending on the situation on the ground. ...
2. MONTENEGRO
2.1 New Influx. Over 1,500 IDPs arrived in Montenegro following the deployment of the Serb security forces in the Rugovska Klisura. Emergency food and non-food supplies have been dispatched by UNHCR/ICRC/MRC to Rozaje and Ulcinj. According to UNHCR estimate 500 persons/day arrive in Montenegrin villages claiming insecurity due to the relative proximity of police/army forces. IDPs are unanimous in that an unknown number of people (2,000-4,000) are stranded in the forest on their way to Montengro. New arrivals were seen in Tuzi, 10 km away from Podgorica where already 1,400 IDPs are accommodated in vacant private houses. SDR/UNHCR team visited the village and requested approval from the local authorities for SDR to adapt the building turned into a temporary transit centre. UNHCR and the staff of the Commissioner for Displaced Persons visited together the municipality of Rozaje where each house hosts an average of 20 DPS. At the request of the local RC mattresses and blankets have been dispatched to the main towns to cover the urgent needs of the increased caseload. Stock is till available for 15,000 new arrivals. UNHCR and UNICEF met with the Minister of Education who stated parallel education system would not be allowed. UNHCR (SDR) will participate in rehabilitation of the school buildings while UNICEF will provide 1000 first grade textbooks. DRC opened offices in Plav and Rozaje. ...

12.   High Commissioner for Human Rights reiterates need for impartial investigation, 2 September 1998

Statement by Mary Robinson : "The last several days have brought new reports of more violence in the province of Kosovo in the Federal Republic of Yugoslavia. The death toll is rising. I am haunted and horrified by this weekend's images of charred remains in a makeshift crematorium. For many months, the violence in Kosovo has provided us with countless images of death, destruction, and human suffering. We have seen too many funerals, too many terrified faces, too many smouldering buildings, too many empty streets and villages. The humanitarian crisis is growing. The political crisis remains unresolved. I suggest that instead of concentrating on those differences that separate the parties, efforts be focused to highlight areas of common concern. Amid this continuing tragedy, I have noticed that all parties, in different ways, have publicly expressed concern over violations of human rights. At different times during this past spring, Yugoslav Government officials, representatives of Kosovo Albanians, and international and domestic human rights advocates - including the Special Rapporteur, Jiri Dienstbier, with whom I have discussed this statement - have supported independent investigation by experts, including international forensic specialists, into the violent deaths resulting from armed actions. No such investigation has occurred. The tragic developments of this past weekend further underscore the need for such investigations. Joint efforts to promote independent investigation into these tragedies are in the interest of all persons committed to human rights in Kosovo."

13. UN Inter-Agency Update on Kosovo Situation, 8 September 1998

1.1 Mass grave. At 15:30 hours today UNHCR office in Pristina was called to meet with the Prefect of Kosovo, Mr Odalovic, who stated that a mass grave had been discovered at Djakovica. Mr Odalovic was organising an immediate visit to the site for journalists and humanitarian agencies. UNHCR did not participate in the journey having no competence in the subject.

1.2 Ultimatum. The serb police and the VJ visited several villages in the area of Prizren on 5 September. The villagers were issued an ultimatum to surrender their weapons before a deadline. One of the villages was Rugovo along the Prizren-Djakovica road. KDOM saw the VJ convoy proceeding towards Ostrozub, northeast of Orahovac. According to the reports that the Serb forces launched an attack on the village of Donje Potocane, 2 km west of Orahovac on 3 September. The villagers attempted to move into the hills but were stopped. Women and children were sent to Orahovac and the men, most of whom were subsequently released, to Prizren for interrogation. UNHCR was informed of the large concentration of population in Koznik; en route to Labucevo and Ponorac, northeast of Orahovac it saw smoke rising from the villages of Kpuz and Kraljane. 50 IDPs the team saw on the road claimed that the village of Kpuz (550 inhabitants originally) was encircled and set on fire. 500 people took to the surrounding hills. No UCK presence was noted. According to the reports of IDPs the village of Zatric between Orahovac and Koznik, was burned to the ground on Thursday and Friday. According to local villagers the village of Pantina, 5 km southeast of Mitrovica was shelled on Sunday, 6 September. The KDOM team visited the place but could not confirm the reports. However, damage was evident.

1.3 Roundup. A senior foreign ministry official in Pristina told UNHCR on Monday that the government is preparing charges against 40-50 people seized during the roundup of civilians late last week in the Ponorac area of Malisevo. He said they will be given fair trial and allowed to defend themselves. Local aid workers told UNHCR that the operation forced some 20,000 people out of their homes but that some 10,000 had returned. UNHCR emphasized that returns would have negative consequences if the safety of returnees could not be guaranteed. n view of the above UNHCR visited Ponorac and was asked for urgent food and medical supplies. The team also visited Labucevo where 70% of some 100 houses are destroyed or damaged. Some 1000 local villagers and 2000 IDPs were seen returning.

1.4 Return. Villagers began returning to their homes in the area of Prizren on Saturday following a government offensive in which reportedly more than 50,000 people fled their villages. UNHCR visited Hoca Zagradska, southwest of Prizren and saw some people returning. The village underwent some destruction, but is intact for the most part. KDOM visited the Mayor of Pec and discussed the return into the villages of Grabovac, Zlopek and Lozane, north of Pec. Out of the 80 houses in Grabovac 60% are heavily damaged. In Zlopec 10% of the 50 houses are heavily damaged, while in Lozane 97% of the 70 houses remained intact. The people will need food, clothing and hygienic items. KDOM visited the area west of the Zrze - Orahovac road and found some returns have been taking place in the villages of Gede and Ratkovac. The villagers from the heavily damaged village of Radoste took shelter in the woods, but come into the village in daytime to take care of their live stock. The village of Ade is being visited regularly. Since the security situation is improving as well as the living conditions there, an increasing number of people are returning. Life in Orahovac seems to be back to normal. Over 10,000 IDPs or over 50% are estimated to have returned there.

1.5 Convoys. Two multi-agency convoys with contributions from UNHCR, WFP, Mercy Corps International, Children's Aid Direct, Doctors of the World and Handicap International delivered relief supplies on Saturday. ...

1.6 Potential danger. VJ 2nd Army based in Podgorica reported on Friday that the VJ Border Guards had prevented an attempt by a group of Albanian citizens to cross illegally the border into FRY near Grbaja post, municipality of Plav. This raises the question as to whether the UCK have started to use Montenegro to enter Kosovo from Albania.

Since the Kosovo-Albanian border is sealed and Montenegro has refused to impose the Border Belt policy decreed some 6 weeks ago by the Federal Government, this might well be the case.

Estimated Displacement Figures: (as at 4 September 1998)

Displacement within Kosovo	200,000
Displacement into Montenegro	39,628
Displacement into other parts of Serbia	20,000
Refugees in Bosnia Herzegovina	5200
Refugees into Albania	14,000
Refugees into Turkey	2,000
Visitors into FYROM	1,000
TOTAL	281,828

1.7 John Shattuck, US Deputy Secretary for Human Rughts and Bob Dole, Chairman of the International Commission for Missing Persons, having visited the conflict zone, said Sunday that they have seen "horrendous violations of humanitarian law and acts of punitive destruction on a massive scale". Shattuck said that the US believes that all situations involving violations of international humanitarian law in Kosovo should be fully investigated and prosecuted by the ICTY in The Hague. ...

2. MONTENEGRO

2.1 UNHCR field team monitored Plav and Rozaje municipalities late last week. A few families went back to the Rugovska Klisura villages to fetch their belongings and then returned to Montenegro. The road from Pec to Cakor remain closed on the Serbian side. Traffic remains possible only for non-ethnic Albanians. Daily entries by the main road to Rozaje average 100.

2.2 Assistance. The September distribution of food is planned to 42,724 IDPs. The actual quantities of what is to be distributed still depend on the complementary contributions from various donors in addition to the already available amount contributed by WFP and ICRC. IOCC opened an office in Podgorica on 7 September and plans to provide food and non food intems to IDPs, refugees and Montenegrins.

Statistics (as at 08 September 1998)
Ministry of Interior Count of New Arrivals: 36,532
Montenegrin Red Cross Registered Caseload:

Ulcinj	16,855
Rozaje	8,143
Podgorica	5,039
Plav	8,114
Berane	1,217
Bjelopolje	984
Others	2,372
TOTAL	42,724

Average of the two figures is shown on the first page. The discrepancy may be due to the fact that the Ministry of Interior is not keeping track of IDPs traveling through mountain paths. The registration in each municipality conducted by the Commissioner for Displaced Persons' Office is proceeding slowly, with only 9,000 IDPs recorded to date.

2.3 Protection. Head of Police in Podgorica informed UNHCR of a significant increase in thefts and petty crimes in the city associated with the arrival of IDPs. He expressed concern over the presence of KLA elements in the Republic, intense smuggling activites on the Albanian border and organised transport of IDPs via the lake of Skadar. He said the check-up of identity of the displaced is conducted at random, both in private accommodation and, as of recently in collective centres. Upon such an action in a collective centre in Tuzi, 50 IDPs left.

UNHCR closely monitors bus departures from Podgorica to Pec. Apparently, a few Albanian families return to Pec and the surrounding villages every day, but those without Ids do not take their chances. UNHCR saw 15 ethnic Albanian IDPs departing from Podgorica to Klina and Pec and 15 Roma returning to the latter.

3. ALBANIA

3.1 Security. The situation in the area of Padesh and Kamenica is calm. However, ECMM reports military activities in the area of Zogaj. However, 30 local Albanian families claiming insecurity left the Padesh area for Bajram Curri in the course of the last week. The security in the Tropoje District continuing tense the majority of UNHCR's international staff members are still in Tirana. Activities are reduced to the essential, mainly around Bajram Curri and the transit centre. The international organisations remaining as on 6 September are ECMM, OSCE, UNHCR and the Islamic Coordination Council.

On 1 September two serious incidents occurred at the warehouse of the Albanian Red Cross and the Islamic Coordination Council. Namely, a large group of masked, armed men threatened the guards and looted over 16 tons of food and non food items. As a result all aid for September from UNHCR, WFP, IFRC and the Islamic coordination are on stand-by in Tirana until guarranties of escort and security are given.

The situation in Kukes and Has district is calm. UNHCR is asssisting 455 refugees in the area.

3.2 New arrivals. During the week 31 August - 7 September 250 persons crossed the border in the Zogaj area. The majority are hosted at the UNHCR transit centre in Bajram Curri and all of them are registered by the Albanian Office for Refugees. Most of the assisted originate from the area of Junik and Decani who have left their homes weeks ago and waiting the propitious moment to cross the border. They report loss and burning of houses. Since the families leaving to Tirana Skodra, Durres and elsewhere in Albania do not deregister it is very hard to determine the precise number of refugees and some 6000 are estimated. ...

4. FYR of MACEDONIA

4.1 Following the IFRC Country Representative the number of families from Kosovo approaching the Macedonian Red Cross branches is slowly increasing. The MRC/Federation directly support with food, hygienic items, bedding and other some 150 people. It is noteworthy that several of the families are not ethnic Albanians, but Serbs. UNHCR is assisting some of the families wigh help in visa extensions and access to the Macedonian health care system. It is estimated that several hundred people from Kosovo are being assisted in various ways by either Red Cross or the UN system.

According to Nova Makedonija daily the control of the border between Macedonia and Kosovo will soon be strenghtened with four new observations posts, amounting to 14 observations posts on borders towards Albania and FRY.

14.   UNHCR Briefing Notes: Kosovo, 25 September 1998

The High Commissioner arrived yesterday, 24 September, in Belgrade and had a long meeting with President Slobodan Milosevic. She was disappointed that the talks revealed a wide discrepancy in their respective views of the extent of the humanitarian crisis in Kosovo. Mrs. Ogata insisted that hostilities must end immediately to avoid an even greater human tragedy. She also met with Yugoslav Deputy Prime Minister Nikola Sainovic. Today the High Commissioner will have discussions with Serbia's Refugee Commissioner Mrs. Bratislava Morina, as well as various meetings with the diplomatic community in Belgrade, before travelling to Pristina later in the day.

UNHCR's presence in Kosovo is expanding rapidly. With the arrival of additional staff and vehicles, UNHCR has been able to open two new small field offices this week, in Pec and Mitrovica, and will open a third in Prizren next week. Each of these offices has 1 international and 3 local staff. In Pristina we now have 25 staff, not including convoy leaders and telecommunications personnel seconded from Danish Refugee Council. However, it is clear that while humanitarian activities can save lives and alleviate suffering, ultimately there needs to be a poltical solution to the conflict. This is the point Mrs. Ogata is emphasising over and over during her visit.

The increase in international presence throughout Kosovo is a key element which could make return possible were there a cessation of hostilities. Displaced people have repeatedly told us that although they would like to go home, they are afraid to do so as long as fighting continues. In the field, UNHCR has received reports that at least 10,000 people have been forced from their homes in Obilic and Vucitrn municipalities, just west and northwest of Pristina, in the last few days. The continuation of fighting in that area prevents verification of these reports for the time being.

15.   UN Inter-Agency Update on Kosovo Situation, 30 September 1998

24 - 29 September 1998

This report has been compiled by UNHCR with support from OCHA and with inputs from UN Agencies and other humanitarian organisations in former Yugoslavia and Albania

KOSOVO

1. The UN Security Council has voted to demand that all parties, groups and individuals immediately cease hostilities and maintain a ceasefire in Kosovo. In its Resolution the Council said that such a ceasefire would enhance the prospects of meaningful dialogue between FRY and the Kosovo Albanian leadership. The Security Council also demanded that the FRY authorities and the Kosovo Albanian leadership take immediate steps to improve the humanitarian situation and to avert the impending humanitarian catastrophe.

2. The Resolution called on FRY to facilitate, in agreement with UNHCR and ICRC, the safe return of refugees and displaced persons to their homes and to allow free access for humanitarian organisations and supplies to Kosovo. The Resolution also called on Member States to provide adequate resources for humanitarian assistance in the region and to respond promptly and generously to the United Nations Consolidated InterAgency Appeal for Humanitarian Assistance Related to the Kosovo Crisis.

3. Several themes have emerged from public statements delivered by Mrs Ogata, the United Nations High Commissioner for Refugees, during her recent visit to FRY and Kosovo: the situation in Kosovo is not a humanitarian problem but the consequences of a political one; negotiations to achieve a fair political settlement should begin immediately; the level of internal displacement in Kosovo was a source of grave anxiety; the violence and burning of civilian houses was deplored; commerce should be re-established so that supplies can reach the communities in need, thus avoiding continued dependence on humanitarian assistance; the police presence should be reduced to give the displaced the confidence to return home, particularly in light of the onset of winter; returnees should not be subjected to harassment; the Government's declared policy to assist the return of the displaced was welcomed.

4. Mrs Ogata stated that UNHCR's policy is to identify IDPs living in the open air and with host families; and to provide assistance in the form of food, shelter, clothing and medical help to the displaced and the returnees; she also called on the authorities to continue to facilitate humanitarian agencies' access to populations in need to enable them to carry out their work.

5. The United Nations system and international NGOs are rapidly expanding in Kosovo in order to meet increased humanitarian needs in the province. UNHCR has opened satellite offices in Pec, Mitrovica and Prizren and now has 28 staff, twice its strength one month ago. WFP has also increased its staff to more than 20 primarily with a view to improving its monitoring capacity. There are now more than 30 International NGOs in Kosovo, at least five of whom have arrived during the past month.

6. The International Committee of the Red Cross (ICRC) has issued a statement dated September 1998 summarising its activities in Kosovo. In the field of protection ICRC is currently visiting 155 people in prisons in Kosovo and in other parts of FRY, 66 of whom are sentenced for offences against state security. ICRC has also received confirmation from the authorities that a further 54 people are detained. ICRC is aware of many other cases of alleged detention, reported by various sources. ICRC is also following up on 140 people who have been reported as abducted by the Kosovo Liberation Army (KLA) or who have lost contact with their families. Efforts are being made to restore family links through the exchange of Red Cross messages.

Internal Displacement

7. During the period under review clashes between the KLA and the Serbian police occurred in the triangle defined by Suva Reka, Stimlje and Urosevac, South of Pristina, resulting in casualties on both sides. On 28th September a UNHCR assessment team in the area was told that 15,000 people from 13 villages in the Suva Reka area had been on the move since the previous day. To the North-West of Pristina,

fighting between the KLA and the Serbian police in the Cicavica mountains continued to cause widespread civilian displacement, although hostilities between the two sides eased during the weekend.

8. The recent trip by the UN High Commissioner for Refugees to Kosovo illustrates the extent to which displaced populations move around within the province due to a combination of insecurity and poor weather. On 25th September UNHCR staff saw an estimated 15,000 displaced in Resnik, a village situated two kilometres west of the road linking Pristina and Vucitrn. These people were fleeing serious fighting in the Cicavica Mountains. On 26th September the delegation of the High Commissioner for Refugees visited Resnik and discovered approximately 2,000 displaced. On 27th September staff from UNHCR's Pristina office visited the same village and discovered only a handful of displaced. The remaining displaced said that police had arrived with buses the previous night and transported women, children and many others to Vucitrn.

9. The most immediate response to those suffering in Resnik was provided by ICRC. On 25th September ICRC provided medical treatment for 30 wounded in Resnik and evacuated the most seriously injured. Three trucks, with 47 tonnes of food, 11,500 blankets as well as plastic sheeting were also brought to the village.

10. During the weekend of 26-27 September a Kosovo Diplomatic Observer Mission (KDOM) team discovered several thousand displaced 5 km South-West of Komorane in Glogovac municipality, an area believed to be under the control of the KLA. The team estimated that 1,800 people were living in the open air in urgent need of security, food and medical care.

UNHCR Estimated Displacement / Refugee Figures: (as at 29 September 1998)

Displacement within Kosovo	200,000
Displacement into Montenegro	41,800
Displacement into other parts of Serbia	20,000
Refugees in Bosnia Herzegovina	6,800
Refugees into Albania	18,000
Refugees into Turkey	2,000
Refugees into Slovenia	2,000
Non-visa guests into FYROM	1,000
TOTAL	291,600

...

Access

11. The ability of humanitarian organisations to gain access to populations in need remains sporadic. WFP attempted to visit Vucak (in Glogovac municipality) following reports of 6,000 - 8,000 people living in the open air but were blocked by the Police due to fighting in the vicinity. At the outskirts of Vucak the team observed that many houses were on fire and that the village appeared deserted. On 25th September humanitarian organisations, including UNICEF and UNHCR, were turned back at Slatina 10 kilometres west of Pristina on the Pristina-Pec road. In the afternoon aid agencies saw smoke emanating from several villages in the Drenica area, through which this road passes.

Relief Distribution

12. On 24th September joint convoys delivered emergency aid for some 28,000 people in Pec and Istinic in Western Kosovo. The 12 trucks carried family food parcels, wheat flour, pasta, medicine, soap, detergent, plastic sheeting, hygienic parcels and stoves. Participating agencies include Children's Aid Direct, Doctors of the World, Mercy Corps International and the Centre for the Protection of Women and Children(a local NGO). The convoy was led by UNHCR. ...

[*For further reports, see Chapter 13.*]

Chapter 12: The NATO Threat of Force and the Holbrooke Agreement

The United States had uttered threats of the use of force in relation to Kosovo since 1992. "In the event of conflict in Kosovo caused by Serbian action, the United States will be prepared to employ military force against the Serbs in Kosovo and Serbia proper", then President George Bush reportedly wrote to Slobodan Milosevic in December of that year—a threat echoed the following February by the Clinton Administration.[1] However, the neglect of the Kosovo issue let that threat recede into the background for several years. It was only when hostilities commenced early in 1998 that NATO professed a "legitimate interest in developments in Kosovo, *inter alia* because of their impact on the stability of the whole region which is of concern to the Alliance."[2] In April, the alliance confirmed its willingness to support UN or OSCE monitoring activities and indicated that it was considering NATO preventative deployments in Albania and in the former Yugoslav Republic of Macedonia, and further "deterrent measures".[3] To this end, Partnership for Peace collaborations with Albania and Macedonia were increased. NATO also activated Permanent Joint Council consultations with Russia. In June, there followed joint air exercises in Albania and Macedonia, with the agreement of those two states, involving no less than 68 fighter aircraft and 17 support aircraft from 13 NATO states. The mission flew up to 15 kilometres to the borders with Yugoslavia/Kosovo.[4] In August and September, joint exercises of land forces were held in Albania and Macedonia, involving NATO troops, but also contingents from a number of other partnership for peace states.[5]

By the end of September, the humanitarian situation was dramatic. There were 300,000 displaced persons. Only one third of them had made it into neighbouring territories, where adequate relief and shelter could be provided. The others were dispersed in the rugged countryside of Kosovo. With the onset of winter, a humanitarian catastrophe was feared. The day after the Security Council adopted Resolution 1199 (1998), on 24 September, the North Atlantic Council approved the issuing of an 'ACTWARN' decision for both a limited air operation and a phased air campaign in Kosovo, taking NATO to an increased level of military preparedness.[6] Against this background, in early October, the United States dispatched its Special Envoy Richard Hoolbroke to Belgrade, to obtain, finally, compliance with the mandatory demands made by the Security Council in Resolutions 1160 (1998) and 1199 (1998). He had a reputation of being able to persuade Milosevic, having been the key negotiator at the Dayton Conference, but failed on this occasion. US President Bill Clinton then announced that he had instructed his delegation to NATO to vote for authorization "for military strikes against Serbia if President Milosevic continues to defy the international community".[7] Secretary of State Albright echoed that the Alliance "has the legitimacy to act to stop a catastrophe,"[8] adding: "Milosevic knows what he needs to do to avoid NATO action. He must immediately end all military and police operations in Kosovo; withdraw all units to their bases and cantonments in a way that can be verified; provide international organizations and diplomatic observers unfettered access to Kosovo; agree to a timetable for a political settlement based on the draft that the Contact Group has endorsed; and co-operate with the War Crimes Tribunal."

In the meantime, Richard Holbrooke had returned to Belgrade and news of a breakthough in his talks appeared to emerge. Nevertheless, on 13 October, NATO issued an activation order for both limited air-strikes and a phased air campaign, to commence after the expiry of a period of approximately 96 hours. That breathing space was intended to permit the Holbrooke deal to be consolidated. [9] The issuing of this ultimatum was unprecedented, not only in NATO's history.[10] While the demands of the Security Council had been made in two mandatory Chapter VII resolutions, there existed no mandate for the military enforcement of its decisions. Instead, this action could only be justified with reference to the humanitarian emergency in the region. The United Kingdom argued that such authority existed in international law in view of the "exceptional circumstances of Kosovo". It added that in such circumstances, "a limited use of force was justifiable in support of purposes laid down by the Security Council but without the Council's express authorization when that was the

---

[1] Quoted from a newsreport in Richard Caplan, International Diplomacy and the crisis in Kosovo, 74 *International Affairs* (1998) 753.
[2] NAC statement, 5 March 1998, Document 12.1.
[3] NAC Statement, 30 April 1998, Document 12.2.
[4] Operation 'Determined Falcon', 13 June 1998, Document 12.6, 15 June 1998, Document 12.7.
[5] Exercises Cooperative Assembly 17-22 August 1998, Document 12.8; and Cooperative Best Effort, 10-18 September 1998, Document 12.9.
[6] Statement by NATO Secretary-General, 24 September 1998, Document 12.10.
[7] Remarks by US President, 8 October 1998, Document 12.12.
[8] Statement, 8 October 1998, Document 12.7.
[9] Statement of NATO Secretary-General, 13 October 1998, Document 12.9.
[10] A number of ultimata had been issued by NATO in relation to Bosnia and Herzegovina. However, in that case there had existed an enforcement mandate from the Council.

only means to avert an immediate and overwhelming catastrophe."[11] The conditions for humanitarian 'intervention' in general international law expressed here could be married to the facts of this case in the following way:[12]

- *Overwhelming humanitarian necessity.* In this instance, it was claimed that the lives of tens of thousands of internally displaced were at stake. The existence of life-threatening distress of a significant magnitude could not really be denied. In addition, the ongoing military operations were likely to add further to the numbers of displaced.
- *Instancy.* Many of the displaced were already living in highly unstable conditions, without supplies of food and shelter. The onset of a Balkan winter made a humanitarian emergency of large proportions inevitable should the situation not be remedied within a short time-frame. Indeed, rapid action was required to ensure that large numbers of people in need would be moved to areas in Kosovo where their needs could be provided for, especially in the light of the large-scale destruction of houses and the civilian infrastructure.
- *Objective determination of facts.* The existence of an imminent humanitarian catastrophe had been confirmed by disinterested objective agencies, best placed to assess the situation, including the Security Council and UNHCR.
- *Exhaustion of other options.* Throughout the year, attempts had been made to persuade Yugoslavia to accept the demands of the Security Council, by Russia, the Contact Group, the EU Special Representative and finally the US Special Envoy. Given the instancy of the situation, it could be argued that there was no time for other options, such as the adoption of more comprehensive economic sanctions, to achieve compliance.
- *Objective determination of legitimate aims.* The demands made by NATO were precisely the ones which the Security Council had enunciated repeatedly (cessation of hostilities, withdrawal of forces, humanitarian and monitoring access, substantive dialogue leading to a settlement within a short time-frame). Hence, it could not really be argued that NATO was pursuing aims of its own, rather than acting on the basis of genuine humanitarian motives.
- *Minimum force.* The application of military force would be kept at the minimum necessary to achieve the stated aims. To that end, a strategy of either symbolic strikes, or of phased strikes had been put in place.

In contrast to the actual application of military force some months later, the NATO ultimatum and threat of force did not trigger wide-spread objection among other governments. This was seen, at the time, as further confirmation that forcible humanitarian action without a Security Council mandate is politically and legally acceptable.[13] Perhaps wider discussion was precluded by the apparent rapid success of the threat, and by the fact that its result was formally endorsed by the Security Council, in Resolution 1203 (1998).

The actual Holbrooke agreement is rather a complex arrangement, much of which was cast into more formal terms a few days after the Holbrooke mission. The package had been negotiated with President Milosevic, who announced on 13 October that a settlement had been achieved which would eliminate the danger of military intervention and was fully in keeping with Yugoslav national interests.[14] It was left to the Serb government, however, to announce its acceptance of an 11-point political framework for the settlement of the Kosovo issue.[15] This permitted Serbia to continue to argue that the fate of Kosovo lay exclusively within its own hands, and was not a matter for disposition by the FRY, although the Federation subsequently endorsed this plan. The Serb statement contained an undertaking to achieve the completion of an agreement containing core elements for a political settlement in Kosovo by November, using as a basis the paper proposed by the Contact Group (the first Hill proposal).[16]

With respect to military matters, it was agreed that the Federal Republic of Yugoslavia/Serbia would withdraw security forces introduced into Kosovo after February 1998 These comprised 10,021 special police (MUP). In addition, heavy weapons brought into the territory or transferred from the Yugoslav Army to the MUP after that date were to be withdrawn. Other heavy weapons would be returned to cantonment areas or police stations. Similarly, Yugslav Army forces (VJ) and their additional equipment brought into the territory after February would be removed. VJ force levels would thus be limited to approximately 11,300. The remaining VJ units would return to their regular garrisons and remain there, with the exception of three company-sized teams to protect lines of communication. Police forces would also be withdrawn from certain areas and their movements and the use of armoured patrols would be significantly restricted. The Kosovo

---

[11] UK Parliamentary Testimony, November 1998/January 1999, Document 12.27.

[12] E.g., the UK view on humanitarian intervention in Iraq: "the practice of states does show over a long period that it is generally accepted that in extreme circumstances a state can intervene in another state for humanitarian reasons. I think before doing so though a state would have to ask itself several questions. First of all, whether there was a compelling and an urgent situation of extreme humanitarian distress which demanded immediate relief. It would have to ask itself whether the other state was itself able or willing to meet that distress and deal with it. Also whether there was any other practical alternative to intervening in order to relieve the stress, and also whether the action could be limited in scope." Testimony by FCO Legal Counsellor Tony Aust, Parl. Papers 1992-1993, H.C., Paper 235-iii, pp. 85ff, also reproduced in Harris Cases and Materials on International Law (5th ed., 1998) 921.

[13] Issue of humanitarian 'intervention' will be briefly addressed again in Chapter 15, and at considerable length in Volume 2 of this *Series*.

[14] Statement by President Milosevic, 13 October 1998, Document 12.15.

[15] Serbian Government statement, 13 October 1998, Document 12.16.

[16] Document 14.B.2.

diplomatic observer mission would receive continuous reports on the activities of VJ and MUP units. These military undertakings were formalized in a 'record of a meeting' between the FRY Prime Minister, a senior offical from the Serb Interior Ministry and NATO Generals Klaus Nauman and Wesley Clark in Belgrade. Strictly speaking, this document, previously not in the public domain, is not directly a formal agreement. Instead, the NATO representatives "took note" of certain undertakings given by the Yugoslav/Serb representatives.[17] Hence, Belgrade could argue that it had not consented to a definite international obligation with respect to its troop deployments in Kosovo, but merely informed NATO of its intentions concerning such deployments. Further modalities were agreed in an 'understanding' between the Kosovo Diplomatic Observer Mission (in fact the US KDOM Chief) and the Ministry of the Interior of Serbia, concluded on the same day.[18] That understanding provided for the dismantling of specific check points by security forces, with the exception of 27 "observation points" which would be created along important lines of communication. In addition, police forces would be withdrawn from certain locations, along certain roads.

While the commitments relating to force deployments were concluded in this circuitous way and remained confidential, two formal agreements had been concluded already on 15/16 October respectively. In the Kosovo Verification Mission agreement, the Federal Republic of Yugoslavia agreed to an "air surveillance system for Kosovo". The aim was ostensibly to verify compliance of all parties with the provisions of Security Council Resolution 1199 (1998), although, in fact, it would enable NATO to monitor compliance with the military arrangements subsequently formalized. The agreement provided for the right of overflight, according to certain modalities, of unarmed NATO reconnaissance platforms (unmanned vehicles, low and medium level reconnaissance aircraft and U-2 missions). In contrast to the no-fly zones which had been imposed upon northern and southern Iraq for humanitarian purposes, FRY fighter aircraft continued to be entitled to fly within Kosovo at all times, except when NATO manned low and medium altitude flights were being undertaken. However, air defence weapons or critical components of such systems would be removed from Kosovo and from a 25 km safety zone along its border.

Finally, an agreement was concluded with the OSCE for the deployment of 2,000 unarmed 'verifiers' plus expert personnel on the ground, again to monitor compliance with the terms of Security Council Resolution 1199 (1998).[19] After completion of these two agreements, NATO issued a statement indicating that it would maintain its readiness to launch air operations.[20] On 27 October, the NATO Secretary-General could report that substantial force withdrawals were taking place and that the situation was stabilizing. However, "if we see evidence of substantial non-compliance in the future with UNSC Resolution 1199 we will be ready to use force", he indicated, confirming that the ACTORD remained in place, both for limited air strikes and a phased air campaign.[21] In addition, an "extraction force" of 1,500 NATO troops would be sent to Macedonia, to ensure the protection and eventual evacuation of the OSCE verifiers, should that become necessary.[22] NATO also emphasized that the Kosovar Albanian side would need to comply with the terms of Resolution 1199 (1998) and cooperate with the verification mission. The Kosovo Albanians had not been party to any of the agreements that had been reached and were, in fact, not informed of the contents of the military undertakings and the precise nature of the overall package. Nevertheless, there was a commitment to a cease-fire and the KLA participated in arrangements for a cooperative disengagement of forces.

Just like the eventual use of force by NATO in relation to Bosnia and Herzegovina at the end of the summer of 1995, it appeared to some that the Holbrooke agreement had delivered peace to the region. However, the more astute observers noted that the agreement could also be interpreted by Belgrade as a sign that the threat of force was not, in fact, a real one. The US negotiator, it seemed, had seized upon quite informal commitments by the Yugoslav government, which had not been noted over the past 10 years for compliance with its undertakings. It was also questioned whether the OSCE mission could make a significant impact on the territory, being unarmed and effectively having to rely on FRY/Serb support. The exclusion of the Kosovo Albanians from the arrangements was also a source of concern, especially as the attitude of the KLA was not unambiguously clear. Given these doubts, the widely shared assessment was that the Holbrooke deal might provide for a useful pause which could be used for proper negotiations. It would not in itself resolve the crisis and, unless supplemented by further steps, would merely permit the parties to sit out the winter before resuming armed action.

---

[17] Record of NATO-Serbia/FRY Meeting in Belgrade, 25 October 1998, Document 12.23.

[18] Understanding, 25 October 1998, Document 12.24.

[19] *See* Chapter 13.

[20] NAC/NATO Secretary-General Statement, 16 October 1998, Document 12.21

[21] NATO Secretary-General Statement, 27 October 1998, Document 12.25

[22] The activation order for that force was adopted on 4 December, see Document 12.29 , 5 December 1998.

1.   North Atlantic Council Statement on the Situation in Kosovo, 5 March 1998

The North Atlantic Council is profoundly concerned by the violent incidents which took place in Kosovo the last few days, and in particular the Serbian police's brutal suppression of a peaceful demonstration in Pristina on 2nd March 1998. It condemns unreservedly the violent repression of non-violent expression of political views as well as terrorist acts to achieve political goals. The North Atlantic Council calls on all sides to take immediate steps to reduce the tensions. The Federal Republic of Yugoslavia (FRY) in particular has the obligation to undertake early initiatives to avoid a deterioration of the situation. A rapid and full implementation of the Education Agreement would represent an important step forward. The North Atlantic Council calls on the authorities in Belgrade and leaders of the Kosovar Albanian community to enter without preconditions into a serious dialogue in order to develop a mutually acceptable political solution for Kosovo within the Federal Republic of Yugoslavia (FRY) on the basis of the principles outlined by the international community, and most recently the Contact Group on 8th January and 25th February 1998. The North Atlantic Council welcomes international efforts to facilitate this process, including by the OSCE. NATO and the international community have a legitimate interest in developments in Kosovo, inter alia because of their impact on the stability of the whole region which is of concern to the Alliance.

2.   North Atlantic Council Statement on the Situation in Kosovo, 30 April 1998

The North Atlantic Council is profoundly concerned by the further deterioration of the situation in Kosovo with the risk of escalating conflict in the region. The Council condemns the increase in violence in recent days in Kosovo, in particular the excessive use of force by the Yugoslav Army, and the proliferation of arms in the territory. The Council is firmly opposed to independence for Kosovo and to a continuation of the unacceptable status quo. It rejects all use of violence, either by state security forces to suppress political dissent or by terrorist groups to seek political change. The Council calls on political leaders in the Federal Republic of Yugoslavia (FRY) and the neighbouring countries to exercise maximum restraint, fully respect human rights, prevent the introduction of arms and of armed groups from outside, and condemn terrorism. It calls on the countries of the region to confirm their respect for territorial integrity and for the inviolability of internationally recognized borders. The Council expects the FRY to respect the inviolability of borders of neighbouring countries, and calls on neighbouring states not to allow their territory to be used for organizing violence and notes the responsibility of neighbouring states to exercise control over their own borders with the Federal Republic of Yugoslavia. The Council calls upon the authorities in Belgrade and the leadership of the Kosovar-Albanian community to take all possible steps to prevent further outbreaks of violence and to begin urgently and without preconditions the process of dialogue necessary to resolve the differences between them on the basis of United Nations Security Council Resolution (UNSCR) 1160. The Council supports all efforts of the international community to facilitate this process, including those of the Contact Group and the OSCE, and calls for the immediate dispatch of the Gonzalez mission. The Council considers it of utmost importance that security and stability of the neighbouring countries not be jeopardized. The Secretary General's visit to Albania on 12 March and to the former Yugoslav Republic of Macedonia on 30 April signal the importance NATO attaches to stability in the region and to the security of its Partners. Within the framework of the Euro-Atlantic Partnership Council and Partnership for Peace, NATO is working with its Partners to make the best use of available tools to promote such stability and security and is considering possible further measures. The Council will continue to closely monitor the situation with regard to Kosovo.

3.   Statement of Ministerial Meeting, North Atlantic Council, Luxembourg, 28 May 1998

We are deeply concerned by the situation in Kosovo. We deplore the continuing use of violence in suppressing political dissent or in pursuit of political change. The violence and the associated instability risk jeopardising the Peace Agreement in Bosnia and Herzegovina and endangering security and stability in Albania and the former Yugoslav Republic of Macedonia. It is particularly worrying that the recent resurgence of violence has been accompanied by the creation of obstacles denying access by international observers and humanitarian organisations to the affected areas in Kosovo.

We are firmly convinced that the problems of Kosovo can best be resolved through a process of open and unconditional dialogue between authorities in Belgrade and the Kosovar Albanian leadership. The status quo is unsustainable. We support a political solution which provides an enhanced status for Kosovo, preserves the territorial integrity of the Federal Republic of Yugoslavia (FRY), and safeguards the human and civil rights of all inhabitants of Kosovo, whatever their ethnic origin.

President Milosevic has a special responsibility to ensure that steps are taken to achieve a political solution in Kosovo. The Kosovar Albanian leadership, represented by Dr. Rugova, also has a crucial part to play in bringing about a political solution. We therefore urge both sides to ensure that the dialogue that has now begun leads rapidly to the adoption of concrete measures to lower tensions, stop the spread of violence and open the way to a peaceful resolution of the crisis. The dialogue process should take into account the views of all communities in Kosovo. We welcome all efforts of the international community to these ends. We support strongly the continuation of an international military presence in the former Yugoslav Republic of Macedonia after the end of the current mandate of UNPREDEP. We support the continuation of the mandate of UNPREDEP, which has contributed significantly to stability in the region. We have two major objectives with respect to the situation in Kosovo:

-    to help achieve a peaceful resolution of the crisis by contributing to the response of the international community; and
-    to promote stability and security in neighbouring countries, with particular emphasis on Albania and the former Yugoslav Republic of Macedonia.
-    We have decided to enhance and supplement PfP activities in both Albania and the former Yugoslav Republic of Macedonia to promote security and stability in these Partner countries and to signal NATO's interest in containing the crisis and in seeking a peaceful resolution:
-    We are launching NATO-led assistance programmes to help Albania and the former Yugoslav Republic of Macedonia to secure their borders, based on enhanced PfP activities and on bilateral assistance.
-    We are upgrading a PfP exercise in the former Yugoslav Republic of Macedonia, scheduled to take place in September.
-    We are scheduling by the end of August a PfP exercise in Albania involving ground and air forces.
-    We are establishing a NATO/PfP Cell in Tirana, which will play a direct role in the implementation of Albania's Individual Partnership Programme and which, with the other measures we are taking, will help to enhance the capabilities of Albania's armed forces to ensure the security of its borders.
-    We are elaborating a concept for the establishment of PfP training centres, including the possible future use of the Krivolak training area in the former Yugoslav Republic of Macedonia.
-    We are authorising the visit of NATO's Standing Force Mediterranean (STANAVFORMED) to the port of Durres in early July.
-    We will prepare to support the UNHCR in the event of a humanitarian crisis in the area.

In addition, in order to have options available for possible later decisions and to confirm our willingness to take further steps if necessary, we have commissioned military advice on support for UN and OSCE monitoring activity as well as on NATO preventive deployments in Albania and the former Yugoslav Republic of Macedonia, on a relevant legal basis, in order to help achieve a peaceful resolution of the crisis and to strengthen security and stability in the region.

We will continue to monitor closely the situation in and around Kosovo and we task the Council in Permanent Session to consider the political, legal and, as necessary, military implications of possible further deterrent measures, if the situation so requires.

We are in close consultation with the governments of Albania and the former Yugoslav Republic of Macedonia about the measures involving their countries. We have informed Partners of the development of NATO's thinking prior to this meeting. With Russia, we have consulted in a special meeting of the PJC. We will use the meetings of the NATO-Russia Permanent Joint Council, the NATO-Ukraine Commission and the Euro-Atlantic Partnership Council, both here in Luxembourg and in the future, with a view to seeking the cooperation of Russia, Ukraine and our other Partners with our efforts to help achieve a peaceful resolution of the crisis in Kosovo. We have invited the Secretary General to inform the UN Secretary General, the OSCE Chairman-in-Office, the WEU Secretary General and other appropriate international organisations with a view to suggesting the coordination of the activities of the various international organisations involved in Albania and the former Yugoslav Republic of Macedonia.

We call upon President Milosevic to agree to the re-admission of the OSCE Long-Term Mission, and to accept the mission of Mr. Felipe González, the Personal Representative of the OSCE Chairman-in-Office and the EU Special Representative.

We are determined, through the ongoing activities of the Alliance through Partnership for Peace and the additional measures we have decided today, to contribute to the international efforts to solve the crisis in Kosovo and to promote regional security and stability.

(Turkey recognises the Republic of Macedonia with its constitutional name.)

4. Statement issued on behalf of the UN Secretary-General, 5 June 1998

The Secretary-General is deeply disturbed by the latest reports of an intensifying campaign against the unarmed, civilian population in Kosovo. He reiterates in the strongest possible terms his condemnation of the atrocities committed by Serbian military and para-military forces. They must not be allowed to repeat the campaign of 'ethnic cleansing' and indiscriminate attacks on civilians that characterized the war in Bosnia. If the world had learned anything from that dark chapter in history, it is that this kind of aggression must be confronted immediately and with determination. The Secretary-General is encouraged by the North Atalantic Treaty Organization's resolve to prevent a further escalation of the fighting and reiterates his call for a negotiated settlement that will facilitate a peaceful and democratic future for the people of Kosovo.

5. Statement issued at the Meeting of the North Atlantic Council in Defence Ministers Session, 11 June 1998

We are deeply concerned by the situation in Kosovo which has deteriorated seriously in recent days. Reports have indicated a new level of violence on the part of the Serb security forces. We condemn any use of violence for political ends by either the authorities in Belgrade or Kosovar Albanian extremists. We are particularly concerned by the number of refugees and displaced persons.

We call upon all parties to avoid actions which prolong the violence. NATO continues to support a political solution which brings an end to the violence, provides an enhanced status for Kosovo, preserves the territorial integrity of the Federal Republic of Yugoslavia, and safeguards the human and civil rights of all inhabitants of Kosovo, whatever their ethnic origin. On this basis, we intend to contribute to the response of the international community.

NATO also remains determined to contribute to efforts promoting stability and security in neighbouring countries, with particular emphasis on Albania and the former Yugoslav Republic of Macedonia. In this regard, we support the continuation of UNPREDEP following the end of its current mandate and reviewed the progress made in implementing the measures agreed by Foreign Ministers in Luxembourg to enhance and supplement PfP activities in the two Partner countries.

We reviewed the serious security situation, drawing also on a report from the assessment team which is currently in Albania and the former Yugoslav Republic of Macedonia. Against this background, we, as Defence Ministers, took the following additional decisions:

• We directed the NATO Military Authorities, subject to the agreement of the governments of Albania and the former Yugoslav Republic of Macedonia, to conduct an appropriate air exercise in these two countries as quickly as possible, with the aim of demonstrating NATO's capability to project power rapidly into the region.

• We directed the NATO Military Authorities as soon as possible to assess and develop for further Council consideration and decisions as appropriate a full range of options with the mission, based on the relevant legal basis, of halting or disrupting a systematic campaign of violent repression and expulsion in Kosovo; supporting international efforts to secure the agreement of the parties to a cessation of violence and disengagement; and helping to create the conditions for serious negotiations toward a political settlement. The study will give priority to options which are effective and readily available. Together with the measures already commissioned in Luxembourg, these new options should also contribute to preventing spillover of violence into neighbouring states.

We also decided to accelerate the provision of advice mandated by NATO Foreign Ministers on possible support for UN and OSCE monitoring activity and on possible NATO preventive deployments in Albania and the former Yugoslav Republic of Macedonia, on a relevant legal basis; agreed the details of the PfP exercise to take place in Albania in August; and we recommend that the Euro-Atlantic Disaster Response Coordination Centre support the UNHCR and other international organizations by the coordination of national humanitarian assistance.

We will use the occasion of tomorrow's meetings of the NATO-Russia Permanent Joint Council, the NATO-Ukraine Commission and the Euro-Atlantic Partnership Council to consult with our Partners on measures being undertaken. NATO is also consulting directly with the governments of Albania and the former Yugoslav Republic of Macedonia.

NATO will continue to monitor closely the situation in and around Kosovo. We are determined to play our part as Defence Ministers in helping to achieve a resolution of the conflict by the international community and in providing stability and security in the region.

6. Statement by NATO Secretary General on Exercise "Determined Falcon", 13 June 1998

Following the decision by NATO Ministers of Defence on 11 June 1998, NATO will hold Exercise "DETERMINED FALCON" on 15 June 1998. This is an air exercise in Albania and the Former Yugoslav Republic of Macedonia which is taking place with the agreement of these two governments. The objective of this exercise is to demonstrate NATO's capability to project power rapidly into the region. A variety of NATO aircraft will be participating in this exercise including fighters, reconnaissance, airborne early warning, tankers and helicopters. The aircraft are provided by a number of NATO nations. The aircraft will originate at bases in NATO countries, fly to the exercise area for specific events and then return to their originating bases. The Fifth Allied Tactical Air Force (FIVEATAF) Combined Air Operations Centre at Vicenza, Italy, will be responsible for the conduct of the exercise. NATO continues to support a political solution which brings an end to the violence in Kosovo, provides an enhanced status for Kosovo, preserves the territorial integrity of the Federal Republic of Yugoslavia, and safeguards the human and civil rights of all inhabitants of Kosovo, whatever their ethnic origin. On this basis, we intend to contribute to the response of the international community.NATO also remains determined to contribute to efforts promoting stability and security in neighbouring countries, with particular emphasis on Albania and the Former Yugoslav Republic of Macedonia.

7. Press Release: Determined Falcon demonstrates NATO's resolve for peace, stability, 15 June 1998

NATO successfully concluded Determined Falcon, a very complex air exercise in the skies of Albania and the Former Yugoslav Republic of Macedonia which underscored NATO's ability to project power in the region. The exercise is part of several initiatives taken by NATO to promote stability, cooperation and security in the region surrounding Kosovo and support the international community in the achievement of a peaceful resolution. All 14 NATO nations with air forces contributed to Determined Falcon. Lt General Michael (Mike) C. Short, commander, Allied Air Forces Southern Europe and Lt General Arnaldo Vannucchi, commander, 5th Allied Tactical Air Force held a press conference at the end of Exercise Determined Falcon at Aviano, Italy at 1 p.m. The mission was executed through the coordination of General Vannucchi operating out of the Combined Air Operations Center in Vicenza, Italy, the same center that is supporting the SFOR mission over the skies of Bosnia-Herzegovina. Sixty-eight fighters and 17 support aircraft from 13 nations launched from six European countries and flawlessly executed the NATO plan. NATO's aircraft flew mainly from Italy, but also from France, Germany, the United Kingdom, the Netherlands, and Greece. The aircraft flew over the Adriatic Sea, where they refueled, before flying into Albanian and then the Former Yugoslav Republic of Macedonia (FYROM) airspace, approximately 15 miles from the nations' borders. No ordnance was dropped during the exercise. The exercise went exactly as planned, said Gen. Short. Two aircraft that had systems problems, flown by the mission commander and a key mission planner, were instantly replaced by their spares and backup personnel with no effect on the mission, demonstrating flawless execution. Throughout the press conference, Short stressed the unanimous support of all NATO nations for peace and stability in the region. He added that this exercise sent a signal of our concern and NATO's strong resolve for peace and stability in the region ...

8. Exercise Cooperative Assembly 98, NATO Press Release, 6 August 1998

1. Fources from 14 Allied and Parnership for Peace (PfP) countries and observers from another six will conduct a PfP (live/field) training exercise near tirana, Albania, from 17-22 August 1998.

2. this exercise, Cooperative Assembly 98 (CA98), is designed to develop a common understanding of peace support operations, doctrine and training and to practise interoperability between participating nations' military forces.

3. Air, maritime and land forces from 14 countries will practise together various skills, to include search and rescuer, close air support, medical evacuation, and air drop procedures as well as infantry peace support operations skills. This training will help refine and validate the procedures and requirements necessary for military forces from NATO and Partner nations to operate effectively together. Forces participating come from: Albania, Belgium, Canada, France, Germany, Greece, Italy, Lithuania, Netherlands, Russia, Spain, turkey, United Kingdom and the United States. ...

9. NATO Exercise Cooperative Best Effort, NATO Press Release 3 September 1998

1. Troops from various NATO and Parter nationas will participate in the Partnership for Peace Exercise Cooperative Best Effort 98 which will take place in the Krovolak Training Area in the former Yugslav Republic of Macedonia, between 10 and 18 September 1998. This exercise is evidence of the great importance with the Alliance attaches to the further development of PfP cooperation with the former Yugoslav Republic of Macedonia and of the significant contribution of the former Yugoslav Republic of Macedonia to the overall PfP programme. It is the first exercise of its kind to be held in the former Yugoslav Republic of Macedonia.

2. Cooperate Best Effort 98 is designed to exercise infantry from different NATO and Partner Nations in a typical peacekeeping scenario. It aims to foster mutual understanding and improve interoperability between NATO and Partner Nation soldiers. The exercise will also demonstrate the important contribution, which PfP can make to the fostering of stability and security in the region, a goal which the Alliance considers to be of significant importance.

3. To date, 26 Nations have committed themselves to gar to take part in the exercise. The exercise is planned and conducted by Headquarters Allied Forces Northwestern Europe, based near High Wycombe in the UK. It will be conducted at Krovolak, which is about 100 kms from Skopje in the central part of the Republic. Personnel from the following nations will participate: NATO-Canada,, Denmark, France, Germany, Greece, Italy, Netherlands, Norway, Portugal, Spain, turkey, United Kingdom and United States; and PfP-Albania, Austria, Azerbaijan, Bulgaria, Estaonia, the former Yugoslav Republic of Macedonia, Georgia, Hungary, Latvia, Moldova, Poland, Romania and Ukraine. Finland is not participating but will provide technical support.

4. Participating units will begin arriving in the former Yugoslav Republic of Macedonia in the week of 7-10 September. ...

10. Statement by NATO Secretary-General following ACTWARN Decision, Vilamoura, 24 September 1998

Just a few moments ago, the North Atlantic Council approved the issuing of an ACRWARN for both a limited air option and a phased air campaign in Kosovo. The ACTWARD will take NATO to an increased level of military preparedness. In particular, the ACTWARD will allow NATO Commanders to identify the assets required for these NATO air operations. Let me stress that the use of force will require further decisions by the North Atlantic Council. But today's decision is an important political signal of NATO's readiness to use force, if it becomes necessary to do so. Finally, let me express the strong support of all Allies for [the] firm Resolution that was adopted in New York last night by the UN Security Council. That Resolution makes it clear what President Milosevic must do:

- he must stop his repressive actions against the population;
- he must seek a political solution to the Kosovo crisis based on negotiations, as must the Kosovar Albanians;
- and he must take immediate steps to alleviate the humanitarian situation.

The Resolution and today's decision by NATO underline the unity of the international community and our resolve to find a solution to the Kosovo crisis.

S/1998/921, Annex, 6 October 1998

11. Statement by the Government of the Russian Federation, 4 October 1998

The air strikes which the North Atlantic Treaty Organization (NATO) is planning to carry out against objectives located in the territory of the Federal Republic of Yugoslavia on the pretext of "giving fresh impetus" to the settlement of the Kosovo problem arouse deep disquiet in Moscow. The Russian Government feels compelled in this connection to emphasize yet again that use of force against a sovereign State without the due and proper approval of the Security Council would constitute a serious violation of the Charter of the United Nations, and would compromise the entire system of international relations as it now stands. The Russian Government is deeply convinced that extremely complex ethnic conflicts—as is evidently the nature of the conflict in Kosovo—cannot be resolved through military means. Painstaking work is necessary to establish a legal mechanism to ensure that people of different nationalities and religious persuasions can live together in freedom and full security. There is undeniably a problem in Kosovo. Responsibility lies with the authorities in Belgrade, who have not taken in good time the necessary measures for a political settlement of the situation in the region, but also with the leaders of the Kosovo Albanians, who have not renounced their separatist aims and have refused to enter into constructive dialogue.

Military intervention in the internal Yugoslav conflict would not only fail to tackle the causes of the problem, it would, in fact, merely serve to considerably strengthen resistance in Kosovo and counter the diplomatic efforts currently being made by the international community to initiate dialogue between Serbs and Albanians. The security of the peacekeeping forces in Bosnia and Herzegovina would be compromised, as would the outcome of the peace process in the territory of the former Yugoslavia and the prospects for stability in the Balkans in general. The Government of the Russian Federation invites Belgrade to strictly apply the Moscow accords of 16 June 1998, which opened the way to a peaceful settlement of the Kosovo problem. The authorities of the Federal Republic of Yugoslavia and the leaders of the Albanian community in Kosovo must fully respect the provisions of Security Council resolution 1199 (1998) of 23 September 1998, immediately end acts of hostility, urgently take steps to prevent the impending humanitarian catastrophe and begin negotiations with a view to a peaceful settlement of the Kosovo crisis. This is the only way to restore peace in Kosovo.

12.   Remarks by US President on Kosovo, 8 October 1998

As a result of the unconscionable actions of President Milosevic, we face the danger of violence spreading to neighboring countries, threatening a wider war in Europe. We face a humanitarian crisis that could be a catastrophe in the making, as tens of thousands of homeless refugees risk freezing or starving to death as winter comes on. Our goal is simple: It is full compliance with United Nations Security Council resolutions by President Milosevic. My Special Envoy, Richard Holbrooke, has just completed three days of talks with Mr. Milosevic, making absolutely clear that he must meet the demands of this Security Council resolution -- end the violence, withdraw his forces, let the refugees return to their homes, give the humanitarian relief workers full and free access to the people who need them, and begin negotiations with the Kosovar Albanians on autonomy for their region, which is provided for under the law of their nation. Yesterday I decided that the United States would vote to give NATO the authority to carry out military strikes against Serbia if President Milosevic continues to defy the international community. In the days ahead, my counterparts in Europe will be making similar decisions. We would prefer -- we would far prefer -- to secure President Milosevic's compliance with the will of the international community in a peaceful manner. But NATO must be prepared to act militarily to protect our interests, to prevent another humanitarian catastrophe in the Balkans.

13.   Statement by Secretary of State Madeleine K. Albright, Situation in Kosovo, 8 October 1998

... I have just met with Secretary-General Solana. I have also been briefed by Ambassador Holbrooke who has just returned from his mission to Belgrade where he held three lengthy sessions with President Milosevic in Belgrade. Despite his best efforts, I am not satisfied that President Milosevic understands the seriousness of the current (Situation). It is also clear that he has not complied fully with the demands of the international community. I have asked Ambassador Holbrooke to return to Belgrade to convey a very clear and simple message to President Milosevic: he must comply in a manner that is both durable and verifiable with the long-standing political, humanitarian and military demands of the international community or face the gravest of consequences. Later today I will meet my Contact Group colleagues in London. I look forward to a good exchange with them on how to ensure Serbian compliance with the demands of the international community and the way ahead. The Secretary-General and I have discussed NATO's role in this crisis. I fully concur with his assessment that the Alliance has the legitimacy to act to stop a catastrophe. Speaking for the United States, I believe it is time for the Alliance to move to the next phase of its decision-making, that is to take the difficult but necessary decision to authorise military force if Milosevic fails to comply. I've come to that conclusion for several reasons. First, it is true, but also not surprising, that Serbian forces have avoided provoking us in the last few days. That is only because they face military action and they hope they can use this to drive a wedge in the unity of the international community. That will not happen. We

must be prepared to take action because we know that, if we are not, there is nothing to stop them from going back to business as usual.

Second, the situation on the ground has not changed fundamentally. Yugoslav infantry, artillery and armoured units are still deployed at key points in Kosovo. Special police are still deployed in heavy numbers along roads. Many are digging in for the winter; others are still occupying the houses of civilians they have driven into the hills. The central region of Drenica remains effectively sealed off by security forces. Tens of thousands of refugees are still afraid to go home. What we have seen is a televised show of soldiers leaving Kosovo. What we need is a complete and verifiable withdrawal of the forces responsible for the violence.

Third, we have to take into account not only this week's snapshot of events on the ground but Milosevic's long-standing unwillingness to negotiate seriously, and the accumulated barbarity of the last three months. Time and again, Milosevic has promised us to do things he had no intention of doing. Time and again, he has taken half measures to avoid the consequences of his actions. Yet even in the last two weeks, even as he made cosmetic gestures in the direction of compliance, his forces committed some of the worst atrocities of the war. We must assume that Milosevic will continue to do the minimum necessary to avoid NATO action. But he has to understand that the minimum is not good enough. The only thing that is good enough is full compliance. Milosevic knows what he needs to do to avoid NATO action. He must immediately end all military and police operations in Kosovo; withdraw all units to their bases and cantonments in a way that can be verified; provide international organisations and diplomatic observers unfettered access to Kosovo; agree to a timetable for a political settlement based on the draft that the Contact Group has endorsed; and, co-operate with the War Crimes Tribunal. He had months to do all these things. Now he has but a few days, which is frankly all he ever needed. Let me stress that we have worked hard in the last few weeks to build a consensus for what we must now be prepared to do. Diplomats from every Contact Group country have gone the extra mile for peace. Our concerns have been reflected in a strong UN Security Council resolution. We have made it clear to Milosevic and Kosovars that we do not support independence for Kosovo – that we want Serbia out of Kosovo, not Kosovo out of Serbia. But one of the keys to good diplomacy is knowing when diplomacy has reached its limits. And we are rapidly reaching that point now. We are not going to stop this conflict by constantly evaluating the situation, and simply waiting to see what happens. We need to act now to compel a realistic and durable settlement, and then see that it is implemented.

Finally, let me say that I believe that we are at a crossroads in the history of the Balkans as well as NATO. The decisions we take in the days ahead will be crucial for us all. NATO is our institution of choice when it comes to preserving peace and defending Western values on the continent. It must be prepared to act when a threat of this nature exists on Europe's doorstep. ....

14.   Statement by the Secretary-General Following Decision on the ACTORD, 13 October 1998

A few hours ago we were briefed by Ambassador Holbrooke reporting that there has been progress. He stressed that the process [sic.] was largely due to the pressure of the Alliance in the last few days and that we have to maintain this pressure in order to ensure that the process continues. In response, just a few momements ago, the North Atlantic Council decided to issue activation orders—ACTORDs—for both limited air strikes and a phased air campaign in Yugoslavia, execution of which will begin in approximately 96 hours. We took this decision after a thorough review of the situation in Kosovo. The Federal Republic of Yugoslavia has still not complied fully with UNSCR 1199 and time is running out. Even at this final hour, I still believe diplomacy can succeed and the use of military force can be avoided. The responsibility is on President Milosevic's shoulders. He knows what he has to do.

15. President Milosovic Announces Accord on Peaceful Solution, Belgrade, 13 October 1998

Yugoslav President Slobodan Milosevic on Tuesday addressed the Yugoslav public to inform it about his talks with U.S. Envoy Richard Holbrooke over the past several days. President Milosevic said:

"Honorable citizens, I wish to inform you about the talks we have had in the past several days. Accord has been reached that problems in Kosovo and Metohija and in connection with Kosovo and Metohija be resolved by peaceful means, by political means. The accords we have reached eliminate the danger of military intervention against our country. As for the political solution, it will be directed towards the affirmation of the national equality of all citizens and all national communities in Kosovo and Metohija. In the immense pressures we have been exposed to, I would say, for years and, especially, in the past weeks and days, the commitment that good solutions can be reached only by peaceful means has nevertheless prevailed. The accords we have reached are fully in keeping with the interests of our country, the interests of the Republic of Serbia and all its citizens, and with the interests of all citizens and national communities in Kosovo and Metohija. The next task is to step up the political process and to step up the economic recovery of our country as a whole. In conclusion, I wish to thank all the citizens at home and abroad who were sending me all this time messages of strong support. These messages also contained the duty to preserve our country's sovereignty and territorial integrity, in other words to preserve its dignity. And, on the other hand, to secure that problems which burden life in Serbia's southern Province be peacefully resolved. I believe that we have accomplished this. I thank you all."

16. Serbian Government Endorses Accord Reached by President Milosevic, Belgrade, 13 October 1998

The Serbian Government held a session on Tuesday chaired by Prime Minister Mirko Marjanovic to discuss a report presented by Serbian President Milan Milutinovic on the political talks held by the President of the Federal Republic of Yugoslavia Slobodan Milosevic with the special US envoy Ambassador Richard Holbrooke, the Serbian Information Ministry said in a statement. President Milutinovic informed the Government of the talks held during several days by President Milosevic and Ambassadors Holbrooke and Christopher Hill and on the definite accord reached Monday on resolving the problems in Serbia's southern Province of Kosovo-Metohija in a peaceful way and by political means. President Milutinovic presented to the Government a full report on the talks and especially on the interest of the international community in full-scale monitoring of the situation in Kosovo-Metohija. It has been agreed that this task should be carried out by an OSCE mission as the best way of enabling the international community to verify the positive trends underway. The fact that a positive approach has been adopted is very important, as it will form the basis for a lasting political solution for the autonomy of Kosovo-Metohija within Serbia, in line with the principles of equality of all citizens and ethnic communities living in this area.

In addition, a political framework has been worked out and agreement has been reached on the principles of a political solution and on a timetable framework for its realization, which is an important achievement. The principles are the following:

1. Political approach and a peaceful solution of problems in Kosovo, achieved through dialogue are the only acceptable means for reaching any lasting, just and humane solution of all open issues;
2. Violence and terrorism, as inadmissible means, contrary to all international norms, must stop immediately;
3. Any solution for Kosovo must respect the territorial integrity and sovereignty and internationally recognized boundaries of the Federal Republic of Yugoslavia, in full compliance with the basic principles of the UN Charter, the Helsinki Final Act and the Paris Charter of the OSCE;
4. The solution has to be based on the full respect of equality of all citizens and national communities in Kosovo. Full affirmation and equal treatment of their national, confessional, cultural values and historic patrimony should be guaranteed;

5. The future of Kosovo lies in peace, equality, integration, economic prosperity and free and common life, not in ethnic, confessional, cultural or any division and isolation;
6. The legal arrangements establishing Kosovo's self-governance and legal frameworks of the Republic of Serbia and the FRY are to be harmonized, and be in accordance with international standards and the Helsinki Final Act;
7. Citizens in Kosovo shall govern themselves democratically through assemblies, executive and judicial organs of Kosovo. Within nine months, there will be free and fair elections for Kosovo authorities, including those on the communal level. The Government of the FRY hereby invites the Organization for Security and Cooperation in Europe (OSCE) to supervise those elections to ensure their openness and fairness;
8. Members of the national communities shall have additional rights, in order to preserve and express their national, cultural, religious and linguistic identities in accordance with international standards and the Helsinki Final Act. The national communities shall be legally equal and shall not use their additional rights so as to endanger the rights of other national communities or other rights of citizens;
9. In the context of the political settlement for Kosovo, which will devolve many responsibilities to the communal level, police under local - communal direction will be established. These local police, which will be representative of the local population, will be coordinated by administrative organs of Kosovo. The settlement must address the security of all citizens and national communities;
10. No person will be prosecuted in state courts for crimes related to the conflict in Kosovo except for crimes against humanity and international law, as set forth in Chapter XVI of the Federal Penal Code. In order to facilitate full transparency, the state will allow complete, unimpeded access for foreign (including forensics) experts, along with state investigators;
11. The competent organs shall reexamine, with the aim of extraordinary mitigation of the punishments, the sentences of the sentenced members of the national communities in Kosovo and Metohija for criminal offenses motivated by political aims.

TIMETABLE

- By Wednesday, October 14, it will be agreed on a comprehensive timetable, building on the following elements:
- By October 19 - an agreement on the status of the international presence, including verification, OSCE and other elements;
- By November 2 - the completion of an agreement containing core elements for a political settlement in Kosovo using as a basis the paper proposed by the Contact Group (October 2, 1998);
- By November 9 - the completion of a rules and procedures for elections.

The Serbian Government has fully endorsed the accords that have been reached as they fully preserve the territorial integrity and sovereignty of the country, avert a conflict and lay the conditions for a political dialogue on the basis of the principle that all solutions must be within the framework of the legal systems of the Republic of Serbia and the Federal Republic of Yugoslavia. The Serbian Government decided to propose to the Yugoslav Government to accept the accords that have been reached, the statement says.

17. Statement of the Federal Government of the Federal Republic of Yugoslavia, 14 October 1998

At its meeting this evening, chaired by Momir Bulatovi}, the President of the Federal Government, the Federal Government fully supported the agreement between the President of the Federal Republic of Yugoslavia Slobodan Milosevic and American envoy Richard Holbrooke. This agreement ensures that all issues in Kosovo and Metohija be resolved in a peaceful manner, solely by political means, respecting the territorial integrity and sovereignty of the Republic of Serbia and the FR of Yugoslavia and eliminates the threat of military intervention against our country.

The Federal Government fully supported the decisions and positions which, with a view to implementing the agreement, were agreed upon by the President of the Republic of Serbia Milan Milutinovic and the Government of the Republic of Serbia.

The Federal Government approved the text of the Agreement between the Federal Government of the FR of Yugoslavia and the Organization for Security and Cooperation in Europe on the OSCE Kosovo verification mission. The Federal Government has authorized the Federal Minister for Foreign Affairs, Zivadin Jovanovic, to sign, on behalf of the Federal Government of the Federal Republic of Yugoslavia, this agreement with the Chairman-in-Office of the OSCE, Bronislaw Geremek, Minister for Foreign Affairs of Poland.

As part of the verification process and compliance with the United Nations Security Council resolution 1199, the Federal Republic of Yugoslavia will permit non-combat aircraft to observe, for purposes of peaceful verification, the situation in Kosovo.

The Federal Government assessed that the achieved agreement provided for the preservation of peace, not only in the FR of Yugoslavia but in the region and Europe as well, and enabled that creative energy be directed at accelerated economic prosperity and development, good-neighbourliness and comprehensive cooperation in the region.

18. Press Conference, UK Foreign Secretary and Defence Secretary, 14 October 1998

FOREIGN SECRETARY: … First of all, can I begin by saying that Britain has played a leading part in securing the agreement that has now created a new opportunity for the Kosovo people. It was Mr Robertson who, in Portugal, brokered the agreement to the twin-track approach of intensive diplomacy led by the Contact Group, backed up by a credible throat of force by NATO. The events of the last few days have shown that that was the right strategy and without both tracks we would not have secured this agreement. But it is not over yet. We have opened up a way forward for the Kosovo people, but we have a long way to go before we can say with confidence we have achieved peace and stability and a satisfactory political settlement in Kosovo. We are prepared to go the distance with the people of Kosovo. Britain, having played that leading part in this agreement, now is willing to make a leading contribution to making the agreement work. I can announce today that Britain will be making a major contribution to the OSCE mission to make sure that the agreement is verified and that Milosevic is obliged to stick to it. We will be offering immediately an advance party of experienced personnel who are ready to leave from tomorrow when we get clearance from the OSCE. We are also offering a further immediate contribution of 150 personnel who will be ready to leave within the next week or two. We will be discussing with the OSCE how quickly they can receive this contribution and how well they can be deployed in the best places. They will be people of calibre, able to give this mission the eyes and the ears which the international community needs to make sure we keep tabs on President Milosevic. We would hope eventually to provide one-tenth of the verification mission of 2,000 people. As well as the presence on the ground, Britain will not be abandoning the intensive effort we have put into the diplomacy around the Kosovo crisis. Next week I will be touring the neighbouring countries of Yugoslavia in order to discuss the crisis with them and to reassure them of Britain's continuing commitment to stability and security in the region. In particular I will be visiting Macedonia and hope to visit the site where the NATO cell will be provided for the communications, the control of the verification mission in the air and the coordination with the people on the ground.

Secondly, Britain is the current President of the Security Council. We are determined that this agreement should be endorsed by the Security Council in a resolution which makes it clear that this agreement has the authority and the backing of the United Nations. Tomorrow I go to the meeting of the Contact Group in Paris where I will be discussing with our colleagues in the Contact Group how we can take forward that resolution and how strong we can make it. The Contact Group played an important part in getting this agreement by sending Dick Holbrooke back with a mandate from all the nations of the Contact Group. Tomorrow we will be looking to all the nations of the Contact Group to play their part in making this agreement work. But the most urgent task first is to get humanitarian relief through to the refugees on the hillside. Without this agreement they would have faced very shortly snow and frost in the open, on the hillsides, without proper shelter or food. Britain will now be working closely with the UN High Commissioner for Refugees, with the Red Cross, to make sure that as quickly as possible we get relief to the people and that they are able to return without fear to the valleys and to settlements where they can get through the winter.

My last message is that we must all understand that the outcome of the negotiations with Belgrade is not the end of the story, it is a new beginning. That agreement will only work if we make it work, and Britain is determined to play its part in doing that.

DEFENCE SECRETARY: I would just like to highlight the fact that here is another example of diplomacy backed up by the credible threat of military force. I visited last Tuesday our Harrier pilots at Gioia dell Colle air base in southern Italy, those who would have been in the forefront of the air campaign had it been required, if it is required. They were there to serve their country, to serve the Alliance. Some of them faced the near certainty of action that could have caused death or injury, and they did so with bravery and with commitment and professionalism, and they are there today partly responsible for the climb-down by President Milosevic, the retreat from the precipice that we have seen in the last two days, the success of diplomacy, so far the beginning of a process that we hope will bring lasting peace to the area. And I would also underline the point that Robin has made, Britain in the forefront first of all with the dual track of the UN Security Council and the Contract Group and the diplomatic channel, and the or else being contributed by the Alliance, that that track has taken us forward, and indeed we are now willing to be in the forefront of the next stage for the future of Kosovo. The personnel for the verification force from this country are ready to go now and can be in Kosovo by the weekend. We are now going to offer a senior and experienced individual to take part in the running of the verification mission that will be based in Pristina, and we will be contributing British Canberra planes to the aerial surveillance of Kosovo which is going to play such a big part in the verification of the agreements that we hope will be signed by President Milosevic by the end of this week. Two Canberras at least will be going there, an elderly plane but with, as those of you who are experts in this room will know, state of the art surveillance equipment able to detect very small details on the ground in Kosovo. …

FOREIGN SECRETARY: Thank you, George. And I would stress that the Foreign Office and Ministry of Defence have worked very closely on this throughout the crisis and Goorge and I have been in daily contact.

QUESTION (Mike Evans, Times): How happy are you that the protection of the OSCE force is going to be in the hands of the Yugoslav security forces?

FOREIGN SECRETARY: The protection is not going to be in the hands of the Yugoslav security forces and we ourselves will make sure that it is understood in Belgrade that we stand behind these people, they are our people, we will not tolerate any threat to their security, But the agreement that President Milosevic has signed up to makes it quite clear that he has to respect both their security and also their right of movement to go wherever they think right. They can flood the whole of Kosovo.

QUESTION: But there won't be anyone actually there to protect them?

FOREIGN SECRETARY: They are going in as unarmed verifiers because it is not their job to enforce the agreement. The enforcement of that agreement, if needed, is a job for the whole of NATO.

QUESTION: Do you regard, and can the people of Kosovo regard, Kosovo as a safe haven?

FOREIGN SECRETARY: The purpose of this agreement was not to construct a safe haven in terms of Iraq, in the way for instance that it has been used in northern Iraq, the purpose of this agreement was to stop the hostilities, to get the Yugoslav security forces to pull back, to enable the refugees to return, free from fear and with the security of knowing that the international community is watching closely what is happening. That is what we have delivered.

QUESTION (Mark Laity, BBC): The Americans are saying that they expect to see an over the horizon force outside Kosovo ready to move in to protect. Do you also expect an over the horizon force and if so what kind of force are you talking about and would Britain be prepared to play a part in that?

FOREIGN SECRETARY: Britain is prepared to play a part in everything that is necessary to make this agreement stick and there will indeed be a NATO cell in Skopje [in Macedonia], at the site I will be visiting next week, and there will be British personnel who will be there. My understanding is that the Americans themselves, when they consider this option, are mainly considering their own Marines on the aircraft carriers.

DEFENCE SECRETARY: We are already in the area. I think it is a point worth making that 58% of all of the troops that are presently in Bosnia just now are European troops, and of course the biggest contributor to that are British troops. So we are in the area, we are very conscious of our responsibilities here, but this agreement is designed to make sure that people in the short term get the safety and security to go back to where they were living before.

FOREIGN SECRETARY: It is a fair point that there are now tens of thousands of NATO and other armed personnel within the western Balkans theatre.

DEFENCE SECRETARY: The threat of force has not been removed here. The Alliance has mobilised, the planning has been done, that planning will stand us in good stead to make sure that these agreements are adhered to.

QUESTION: Foreign Secretary, ... you said that President Milosevic has promised full cooperation with the International War Crimes Tribunal, but in fact isn't it the case that the Yugoslavs won't accept the jurisdiction of The Hague Tribunal in Kosovo at all?

FOREIGN SECRETARY: First of all, President Milosevic has agreed explicitly, clearly and in terms in this agreement to full compliance with the UN Security Council resolution and one of those paragraphs in that resolution requires him to cooperate with the War Crimes Tribunal. Also I do have to say that it is not up to Belgrade to decide where the jurisdiction of the War Crimes Tribunal extends, that is a matter for the tribunal and the Prosecutor has made it quite clear that she regards that she does have jurisdiction in Kosovo.

...

19.   NATO/FRY Kosovo Verification Mission Agreement, FRY, 15 October 1998

The North Atlantic Treaty Organisation, hereafter called NATO represented by General Wesley K. Clark Supreme Allied Commander, Europe and The Federal Republic of Yugoslavia, hereafter called FR|Y represented by Colonel General Memeilo Feridle, Chief of General Staff of the Army of Yugoslavia

Have agreed on the NATO Kosovo Verification Mission as follows:

NATO KOSOVO VERIFICATION MISSION

Introduction: In order to provide air surveillance to verify compliance by all parties with the provisions of UNSCR 1199, complementing the ground verification to be established by the OSCE. NATO and FRY agree to the establishment of an air surveillance system for Kosovo, to be known as the NATO Kosovo Verification Mission, and agree that NATO will implement it. This document establishes the terms of reference and governing procedures for this NATO Kosovo air verification system. The NATO Kosovo air verification system will be comprised of NATO aerial vehicles (UAVs), and low and medium altitude manned reconnaissance platforms such as the F-3, Canberra, DeHaviland-7 ARL and comparably configured non-combatant platforms.

Flight Control Requirements

In order to create a co-operative and safe operating environment for the NATO Kosovo air surveillance mission and for the FRY Air Force and Air Defence Forces (FAADF), the following procedures shall apply:-

• A mutual Safety Zone encompassing FRY airspace within a radius of 25km from the contiguous boundary of Kosovo will be established, within which FRY Air Force Fighter aircraft and Air Defence Forces will not conduct operations during the period of flight operations by NATO manned non-combatant reconnaissance platforms. This Mutual Safety Zone will be identified for all aircraft as follows: from latitude-longitude to latitude-longitude (to be specifically defined). Additionally, NATO Aircraft operating in support of the Kosovo Air Verification Mission will avoid all published instrument approach fixes within Kosovo and the Mutual Safety Zone.

Per manned low and medium altitude reconnaissance platforms, NATO flight operations will consist of a defined period to include a thirty-minute safety margin before and after announced NATO flights, and may be conducted at all times within the confined of Kosovo. For U2 and unmanned reconnaissance platforms, flight operations may be conducted at all times and do not require this thirty-minute safety margin.

• In order to permit the FRY air force to comply with this requirement, the NATO flight operations co-ordinator will provide a weekly schedule of NATO non-combatant reconnaissance platform flight operations. NATO weekly schedules will make all attempts to provide FAADF appropriate training requirements. In case of an emergent situation or weather and visibility problems, NATO may fly any of its non-combatant reconnaissance platforms with a one-hour notice. NATO authorities will contact FAADF fighter aircraft can clear the Kosovo and Mutual Safety Zone airspace immediately.

• Commercial, civilian private aircraft, military air transport and rotary wing flight operations by FRY entities may be operated at any time without restriction, including during the period of NATO non-combatant reconnaissance platform operations. These FRY flight operations may operate anywhere in the sovereign airspace of the FRY. Prior co-ordination with the NATO Flight Operations co-ordinator is not required for these flights; however, FRY flights will be operated to avoid interference with declared NATO flight operations.

• FRY fighter aircraft may fly within Kosovo and the Mutual Safety Zone at all times except when NATO manned low and medium altitude, non-combat reconnaissance platforms are operating as described above.

• NATO aircraft will conduct aerial reconnaissance missions on a mutual non-interference basis.

• Airspace entry and exit points for manned non-combatant platforms will be through Albania and FYROM except if co-ordinated in advance.

FRY Integrated Air Defence System Requirements

During the duration of the NATO Kosovo Verification Mission, the following conditions apply within Kosovo and the Mutual Safety Zone:

• Early warning radars may operate unrestricted at all times.

• All SAMS and air defence weapons (includes acquisition target tracking or other fire control radars, radar controlled gun and man-portable air defence systems; will either be removed from Kosovo and the established Mutual Safety Zone, or placed in cantonment sites and not operated. Cantonment sites will be declared, geographic positions identified and open for inspection. SA-6 missiles and launchers may remain in deployed sites if separated from their cantoned acquisition, target tracking and fire control radars.

• All SAMS and air defence weapons outside the Mutual Safety Zone must refrain from acquisition, target tracking or otherwise illuminating (except with early warning and air non-combatant reconnaissance platforms.

• Training and maintenance may be conducted on systems precluded from operation with 24 hour notification and approval. Additionally, systems in cantonment areas and deployed may be removed to areas outside Kosovo and the Mutual Safety Zone following the same provisions of this agreement.

• No SAMs or air defence weapons not initially identified in the Kosovo and Mutual Safety Zone may be brought into Kosovo.

Force Protection

Violations of any provisions of this agreement, to include unauthorised flight or activated of FRY Integrated Air Defence Systems (IADS) within Kosovo and the Mutual Safety Zone, will be immediately arbitrated through appropriate bilateral channels to determine liability and appropriate action to be taken.

Command and Control

In order to help assure the safe conduct of the NATO Kosovo air verification system, 'Air Defence Liaisons' comprised of FRY and NATO representatives will be established at appropriate offices in Belgrade, and at the Combined Air Operations Centre (CAOC) in Vicenza, Italy.

The NATO Kosovo Air Verification Mission air surveillance activities and OSCE Kosovo Verification Mission ground surveillance activities will be co-ordinated between the OSCE Verification Mission Headquarters and NATO.

Status and Conditions

• The FRY government hereby guarantee the safety and security of the NATO Kosovo Verification Mission and all its members;

• The FRY government and its entities will designate formal liaison officers to work with the NATO Kosovo Verification Mission in Belgrade.

Implementation and Transition Period

Implementation of this agreement is subject to the following provisions:

• Communications and liaison channels will be established between FAADF in Belgrade and CAOC, Vicenza as soon as possible following conclusion of this agreement;

• D2 and UAV operations may commence within 72 hours of establishing communications and liaison channels;

• Within 15 days, 25km boundary defining the Mutual Safety Zone will be agreed and identified by both parties on a common reference map;

• FAADF will be provided 15 days after concluding this agreement to allow movement and cantonment of air defence systems and establish internal operations procedures of compliance;

• NATO will conduct a flight profile with a manned non-combatant reconnaissance platform prior to full initiation of the Kosovo Air Verification Mission to determine the operations concepts of this agreement. If during this validation profile, flight conduct and safety concerns are identified, NATO and FRY will agree to immediately establish changes to the provisions of this agreement to address the concerns of both parties.

Done at Belgrade on the 15th day of October 1998, in two original, in the English, French and Serbian languages.

In the event of any dispute on the interpretation of the present Agreement, the English text will be authoritative.

20.   Press Points by the NATO Secretary-General, 15 October 1998

I have come to Belgrade today, accompanied by the Chairman of the Military Committee, General Nauman, and SACEUR, General Clark, to deliver a simple but strong message to President Milosevic. He must comply fully and immediately with the requirements of of the UN Security Council Resolution 1199.

Three weeks have elapsed since that Resolution was adopted but still we are far from seeing the full compliance that the international community demands. I have told President Milosevic about the many army and special police units that, according to our information, remain in Kosovo even though their barracks are outside Kosova territory. These units must be withdrawn immediately. Let there be no doubt: we will keep the situation in Kosovo under the closest scrutiny. NATO will maintain its pressure until we have evidence that compliance has been fully achieved. We will remain ready and willing to act if these obligations are not met. NATO prefers compliance to conflict.

We have just signed with the government of this country an agreement to establish a NATO/Kosovo air verification regime, to be operated by NATO. We intend to beging implementation in the very near future. Along with the OSCE mission on the ground in Kosovo, NATO's role will be crucial in verifying that President Milosevic intends to keep his word and to help stabilize the situation in Kosovo. I also made clear to President Milosevic that we expect the full cooperation of the Yugoslav government in carrying out the agreement on the air verification regime over Kosovo strictly. Any attack or hostile intent against our NATO verification aircraft will have the gravest consequences.

We also expect the full cooperation of the Yugoslav authorities, including its security forces, with both the NATO and the OSCE verification missions.

I want to emphasize that the agreement that we have signed today and the agreement that the OSCE will sign shortly are not the end of the story. They are but the first step in ending the conflict in Kosovo and in relieving the urgent humanitarian situation. These agreements represent an opportunity for the leaders of Yugoslavia to solve problems in a peaceful and more constructive way. I urge President Milosevic and the Kosovar Albanians not to squander this opportunity.

Finally, I would like to address a few words to the peoples of Yugoslavia. There has been too much suffering, too much intolerance and too much violence in this country and this region over the past few years. Much of this has been caused by political leaders who have misused their political power. And the closure of independent newspapers is the latest one. Apart from the terrible human tragedy, the result is that Yugoslavia has been increasingly isolated from the European democratic family of nations. I urge you to open a new chapter in your history and to work for solutions through dialogue and reconciliation. The Alliance is there to help you in this endeavour; but you too must accept your responsibility and look to the future.

21.   NATO Statement on Kosovo following North Atlantic Council meeting, Brussels, 16 October, 1998

The North Atlantic Council at its meeting today took stock of the State of Compliance in Kosovo. We are still some distance from full compliance. There is clear evidence that many army and special units, that are normally based outside Kosovo, are still deployed in Kosovo. As the Secretary General made clear in Belgrade, the North Atlantic Council expects these units to be withdrawn immediately. While in Belgrade, the Secretary General impressed upon President Milosevic the urgent need to comply fully with UNSCR 1199. The NAC therefore decided to maintain its readiness to launch air operations against

Yugoslavia, including the deployment of substantial air forces in the region. The NAC has decided that the period before execution of air strikes will be extended until 27th October. The Council will continue to monitor developments very closely. The NAC calls on President Milosevic to take urgent steps to ensure that full compliance is achieved in this time period.

22.   Letter from the FRY to the Secretary-General of the United Nations, 23 October 1998

All activities of the security forces in Kosovo and Metohija ceased on 28 September 1998. Since terrorists have been neutralized, the need for engaging special anti-terrorist security forces has ceased and they have been withdrawn with their weapons and equipment to places of their permanent encampment. Accordingly, only regular police effectives, maintaining public peace and order and guaranteeing the safety of citizens and of their property, as well as freedom of traffic and movement, are now deployed in Kosovo and Metohija. Also deployed in the Province are the regular effectives of the Army of Yugoslavia, carrying out regular activities, including the protection and security of the international border.

Full freedom of movement and the activities of all diplomatic representatives, unhindered access of humanitarian organizations, particularly of UNHCR and ICRC personnel and convoys, have been ensured on the entire territory of the Province, as well as their cooperation with State authorities at all levels - from the Federal to local ones. This is borne out also by statements made by representatives of those organizations, as well as by the reports of diplomatic representatives (KDOM).

The State authorities have taken comprehensive measures to solve humanitarian problems efficiently. This is evinced, among other things, by the functioning of an extensive network of humanitarian distribution centres (about 100) with large quantities of aid in food, medicine, building material, distributed every day to all citizens in need, without any discrimination.

Special attention has been devoted to measures aimed at the return of displaced persons and their accommodation, which include the Government's public calls and guarantees of full security to all, enabling unhindered return to more than 100000 displaced persons to their homes.

The State makes a clear distinction between the vast majority of its citizens of Albanian nationality and a small number of terrorists, whose aim is secession of the Province of Kosovo and Metohija from Serbia and the FR of Yugoslavia and creation of the so-called "Greater Albania".

The provisional Executive Council of the Autonomous Province of Kosovo and Metohija of multi-ethnic composition is in charge of all major questions of development of the Province. Elected local security organs, reflecting the national composition of a given place, successfully in 92 localities. All forms of public rail, bus, air - are maintained in the Province. The system in Albanian, Serbian and Turkish languages is in place. The same applies to the media, health, administrative and other public services. A vast number of citizens has returned arms that terrorists gave or sold them through blackmail and force. Citizens are returning to work, production and everyday duties.

The State is committed to a peaceful, democratic and stable solution of all questions on the basis of equality of all citizens, national and ethnic communities and the highest international sandards of human and national minority rights in accordance with the Framework Convention of the Council of Europe on the Protection of National Minorities. All the solutions to be arrived at through unconditional dialogue have to proceed from the respect of the territorial integrity and sovereignty of Serbia and the FR of Yugoslavia.

This commitment to a peaceful political solution has been affirmed in the recent agreements of the President of the FR of Yugoslavia, Slobodan Milosevic, and the US Special Envoy, Richard Holbrooke. Within the implementation of the agreements:

1. The President of the Republic of Serbia, M. Milutinovic, and the Government of the Republic of Serbia promulgated on 13 October 1998 a framework political solution (11 points) and a timetable (Annex 1);

2. An Agreement on the OSCE Kosmet verification mission was signed between the Government of the FR of Yugoslavia and the OSCE on 16 October 1998, the implementation of which is under way. Constructive and fruitful talks were conducted on this subject with the Director of the Mission, Ambassador William Walker, in Belgrade yesterday and today.

3. As part of the verification process and compliance with the United Nations Security Council resolution 1199, the FR of Yugoslavia will permit non-combat aircraft to observe, for purposes of peaceful verification, the situation in Kosovo and Metohija.

The Government of the FR of Yugoslavia is fully committed to a consistent implementation of all agreements it made and signed and, to this effect, expects support and cooperation by all international factors.

However, it is concerned that no adequate measures have been taken to root out all channels of financing terrorism, recruitment, training and infiltration of terrorists into Kosovo and Metohija, which is explicitly requested from member-States by Security Council resolutions. This is the case, in particular, with Albania where terrorist centres (Bajram Curri, Tropoje, Kuks) continue to operate.

In light of the presented facts, the Government of the FR of Yugoslavia is deeply concerned over the unfounded pressures and threats, including even the threat of military intervention which is contrary to international law and constitutes a violation of the Charter of the United Nations. The Government of the FR of Yugoslavia is also concerned over the double standards in the treatment of separatism and terrorism, as global threats of the present-day world. It is not possible to accept that some States are recognized the right to self-defence and struggle against terrorism, while, at the same time, other States are denied that legitimate right.

It is time to direct all energy towards supporting the implementation of the agreements reached, in particular towards establishing the OSCE Kosovo and Metohija Verification Mission, continuing unconditional dialogue in accordance with the agreed political framework. In doing so, it is necessary to eliminate all pressures and threats which only encouraged the opponents of dialogue and the proponents of terrorism also in the past and had general negative repercussions on all hitherto efforts to reach a peaceful political solution.

We believe that the facts presented above will contribute to an objective assessment of the situation in Kosovo and Metohija and of the measures being taken to normalize it by the Governments of the Republic of Serbia and the FR of Yugoslavia. We hope that the ongoing visit of the Mission of the Secretariat, headed by your envoy Mr. de Mistura, will constitute a contribution to the same goal. ...

23. Record of NATO-Serbia/FRY Meeting in Belgrade, 25 October 1998

1. The meeting was attended by Milan Milutinović, President of the Republic of Serbia; Nikola Šainović, Vice Prime Minister of the Federal Government of the FRY; Colonel General Momcilo Perišić, Chief of the General Staff of the Yugoslav Army; Colonel General Vlastimar Đorđević, Chief of Public Security of the Ministry of Interior of the Republic of Serbia; and their delegation. The NATO Military authorities were represented by General Naumann, Chairman of the Military Committee; General Clark, Supreme Allied Commander Europe; and their delegation.

2. The purpose of the meeting was to discuss specific steps to be taken to achieve full compliance by the FRY with the requirements of the United Nations Security Council Resolution 1199.

3. The position of the FRY and Serbian authorities is reflected in the attached statement. The NATO Military Representatives took note of the statement.

For The Federal Republic of Yugoslavia: Nikola Šainović, Vice Prime Minister

For The Republic of Serbia: Colonel General Vlastimir Đorđević, Chief of Public Security of the Ministry of Interior of the Republic of Serbia

For The NATO Military Authorities: General Klaus Naumann, Chairman of the Military CommitteeGeneral Wesley K. Clark, Supreme Allied Commander, Europe

Attachment: Yugoslav Statement

Recognising UNSCR 1199 and proceeding from the fact that organised terrorism has been defeated in Kosmet and that all actions against terrorists have ceased as of September 29, 1998 the authorities of the Federal Republic of Yugoslavia have decided, among other measures, to undertake a series of actions that would help further confidence-building among citizens, members of all national communities living in Kosmet, as well as the resolution of all pending humanitarian problems, especially the speedy return to their homes of all displaced persons. These measures are undertaken with a clear view of ensuring the return to full normality of life as soon as possible throughout Kosmet, while continuing to secure the safety and well-being of all citizens, members of all national communities living in Kosovo and Metohija to carry on their everyday life free from any threat and constraint, which includes full freedom of movement for all citizens and state authorities representatives, as well as normal activity of all State organs.

In order to further encourage the return to peace and normality, the state authorities of the FRY will bring down the level of presence and the equipment of security forces (MUP and VJ) throughout Kosmet to normal levels, i.e. to the levels preceding the outbreak of terrorist activities, with the clear intention of creating conditions that would help the speedy resumption of the political process and resolution of all outstanding political and humanitarian issues.In this process the State authorities of the FRY are counting on the assistance and support of the OSCE Verification Mission, KDOM and international humanitarian and other organisations.With these goals in mind, the State authorities of the FRY have announced the following measures:

1. Special police units deployed to Kosovo after February 1998 will be withdrawn from Kosovo. Combined police/special police strength in Kosovo will be reduced to their February 1998 duty level.

2. Any additional (that is, brought in or transferred after February 1998) heavy weapons (12.7mm or above) or equipment brought into Kosovo or transferred from the VJ to the police/special police will be withdrawn from Kosovo or returned to the VJ.

3. Police/special police will resume their normal peacetime activities. Heavy weapons and equipment remaining under MUP control in Kosovo will be returned to cantonments and police stations.

4. All VJ units and additional equipment brought into Kosovo after February 1998 will be withdrawn from Kosovo.

5. Except for those VJ currently augmenting border guards, all VJ elements remaining in Kosovo will return to garrison except for three company-sized teams which will remain deployed, each to protect lines of communications between a) PEC-LAPUSNIK-PRISTINA, b) DAKOVICA-KLINA, and c) PRIZREN-SUVA REKA-PRISTINA. These three company-sized teams will return to garrison not later than one week after signature of the Political Agreement.

6. VJ border guards will remain in position along the international border of FRY and conduct ongoing border security operations.

7. The withdrawals and deployments described above will be completed by 1200 hours, 27 October 1998, except for the three company-sized teams in paragraph 5 above. On commencement, movements will be notified to KDOM and the new structures and numbers will be given to KDOM not later than 1200 hours 29 October 1998.

8. In order to ensure verification of these provisions, VJ and MUP commanders will provide to KDOM/OSCE detailed weekly reports of manning, weapons, and activities of their forces and will provide immediate notification to KDOM/OSCE of any deployments contrary to these provisions and will explain the circumstances regarding such deployments.

The FRY intends to comply unconditionally with UNSCR 1199 and the actions described in Para. Ll above. It calls on all other parties to also comply unconditionally with this Resolution. The FRY remains committed to seek solutions to all outstanding issues and problems peacefully and in consultation with the OSCE. However, as a last resort, and consistent with the right of self defense, the State authorities retain the right to respond adequately and proportionately to any form of terrorist activity or violation of law which could jeopardize the lives and safety of citizens and representatives of the State authorities.

24.   Understanding between KDOM and the Ministry of the Interior of the Republic of Serbia, 25 October 1999

1. All check-points will be dismantled. The FRY authorities will establish 27 observation points will be manned initially. The number of observation points will be kept under constant review in consultation with KDOM/OSCE, with the final intent of dismantling them completely:

Observation points on lines of communication:
1. Lapusnik-Dolac total 7
2. Oriate-Malisevo total 4
3. Kosovska Mitrovica-Gornja Klina-Rakos total 7
4. Pec-Djakovica total 3
5. Stimlje-Dulje total 6

The overview of observation points will be completed by October 29, 1998.

2. In case of incidents or increased tension, the police will have the right, upon notifying KDOM/OSCE, to perform patrol duties in armored vehicles equipped with machine guns up to 7.9 mm which will be used exclusively in self-defense and with restraint.

3. The police will withdraw its stationary forces from: Dragobilje, Ostrozub, Opterusa, Dobrodeljane, Studencani, Samodraza, Pecane and Klecka and will keep them in Malisevo, Orahovac, Zociste, Restane, Suva Reka and Dulje. The police will use the road Orahovac -Suva Reka- Dulje-Malisevo and in the coming 15 days it will not move along the Malisevo-Orahovac road. The Malisevo-Orahovac road must remain fully open at all times for unimpeded and free traffic and flow of people and goods.

The Republic of Serbia: Colonel General Vlastimir Dordevic
Chief of Public Security of the Ministry of Interior of the Republic of Serbia
Shaun M. Byrnes, U.S. KDOM Chief

25.   Statement by NATO Secretary General following Meeting of the North Atlantic Council, 27 October 1998

Two weeks ago, NATO issued an ACTORD for limited air operations and a phased air campaign against Yugoslavia. We took this decision in order to back up diplomatic efforts to achieve peace in Kosovo and open the way for a political solution to the crisis. From the outset we have insisted on full and unconditional compliance by President Milosevic with United Nations Security Council Resolution 1199 and 1203. Since the ACTORD was issued, we have continued to put President Milosevic under pressure. General Nauman, SACEUR and I have been to Belgrade to make it clear to him that he has no option but to comply. I have also written to President Milosevic to stress the gravity of the situation. In this pressure and out credible threat to use which have changed the situation in Kosovo for the better. NATO's unity and resolve have forced the Yugoslav Special Police and military units to exercise restraint and reduce their intimidating presence in Kosovo. We have been able to reduce the level of violence significantly and to achieve a cease-fire which has held, despite some sporadic incidents. This improvement in the security situation in Kosovo has first and foremost allowed an immediate improvement in the humanitarian situation. International relief organizations have re-started their operations in Kosovo. They now have unrestricted access for their convoys. Thousands of displaced persons have returned to their villages. At the same time, the improvement in the security situation is creating the conditions for a meaningful political dialogue to begin between Belgrade and the Kosovar Albanians.

Over the past few days, NATO's aerial surveillance assets and the Kosovo Diplomatic Observer Mission have been verifying whether Mr Milosevic actions match the commitments he has made to us. I am pleased to report that over the past 24 hours over 4,000 members of the Special Police have been withdrawn from Kosovo. Police and military units that are normally based in Kosovo are now moving back to their barracks together with their heavy weapons. Check points have been dismantled. In addition, most police and military units that are normally based elsewhere in Yugoslavia have left Kosovo. The Security forces are returning to the level they were at before the present crisis began.

Despite these substantial steps, NATO's objective remains to achieve full compliance with UNSC Resolutions1199 and 1203. As a result, we have decided this evening to maintain the ACTORD for limited air operations. Its execution will be subject to a decision and assessments by the North Atlantic Council. We will also maintain our ACTORD for the phased air campaign and will continue our activities under Phase Zero. We have requested our Military Authorities to remain prepared to carry out these air operations should they be necessary and to maintain forces at appropriate readiness levels for the operations under both ACTORDs. The North Atlantic Council will keep the situation in Kosovo under constant review. If we see evidence of substantial non-compliance in the future with UNSC Resolution 1199 then we will be ready to use force. We know that President Milosevic only moves when he is presented with the credible threat of force. The burden of proof of compliance clearly rests with him.

The Kosovar Albanians must equally comply with the UNSC Resolutions and cooperate with the international community. I call on the Kosovar Albanian armed groups to maintain the cease-fire that they have declared. Our immediate focus will now be on ensuring the effectiveness of the verification regime. Our NATO verification flights over Kosovo are beginning. We welcome the possible association of Russia and other partner countries in NATO's air verification regime. NATO and OSCE have been working closely together to co-ordinate their activities in carrying out the verification mission. The Alliance is also expediting planning for a NATO force for the extraction of OSCE verifiers on the ground in Kosovo. We welcome UNSC Resolution 1203 which endorses the establishment of two verification missions.

Despite the progress we have made, this crisis is far from over. A lot of work remains to be done. It is high time that the two parties in the conflict understand that the international community will not tolerate a continuation of the status quo. There has been too much human suffering. Clearly, a political solution must be found. I urge both sides to take advantage of the opportunity that now exists to move the political process forward and to secure this unique opportunity to work for a better future for Kosovo, and also for Yugoslavia as a whole.

26.   Secretary of State Albright, Remarks on Kosovo, Washington, DC, 27 October 1996

SECRETARY ALBRIGHT: … Two weeks ago, NATO took the historic step of authorizing the NATO commander to launch air strikes for only the second time in its fifty year history. The Alliance insisted that President Milosevic comply with the repeated political, humanitarian and military demands of the UN Security Council with respect to the treatment of the people of Kosovo. The Alliance made clear that continued failure to comply would result in the use of force. Today the Alliance was able to report that President Milosevic is in very substantial compliance with Security Council Resolution 1199, and that this compliance is sufficient to justify not launching air strikes at this time. This is an important and welcome development. It would not have happened if we had not combined diplomacy with the threat by NATO to use force. The key now is to ensure that Belgrade sustains compliance and for the parties to make progress towards a political settlement. To these ends, we will continue to pursue diplomacy combined with a credible threat of force. Let me repeat -- NATO's threat to use force if necessary remains. Over the past two weeks, as a result of NATO's resolve, there have been tangible changes in Serb behavior and in the situation on the ground in Kosovo. Army units brought into Kosovo from outside have been withdrawn. Kosovo-based units are moving back to their garrisons and progress is being made toward placing heavy weapons in storage. Equally important, we are seeing the withdrawal of thousands of police reinforcements from outside Kosovo and the return of other units to garrisons. Yesterday, the Kosovo Diplomatic Observer Mission witnessed the withdrawal of more than 4,000 Serbian special police, the units responsible for the lion's share of violence. In addition to the numbers, we have a commitment from Milosevic -- that will have to be tested -- that remaining units will not engage in the aggressive behavior that has caused so much repression and terror. Relief agencies are now able to operate without major impediments. Food, blankets and medical kits are being delivered. Although more remains to be done, progress has been made in providing shelter. Thousands of Kosovar Albanians who had been displaced by the violence have already left the mountains to return to their villages and begin rebuilding their lives.

These developments should result in a safer and more secure climate in which those still displaced may also return home. The result, if all goes well, will be the prevention of further humanitarian catastrophe. It is vital to understand that even if the humanitarian crisis is averted, the political crisis remains. This crisis can only be resolved at the bargaining table. This is a vital point, for not even NATO military force can resolve the tensions, rivalries and disagreements that are at the heart of the problems of Kosovo. Politically, the Serbs and Kosovar Albanians have resumed a dialogue with the goal of an interim agreement that would give Kosovars democratic self-government, including their own police, and elections supervised by the international community. To support those negotiations, we have also delivered a clear message to the leadership of the Kosovo Liberation Army: there should be no attempt to take military advantage of the Serb pull-back. Neither side can achieve a military victory in Kosovo.

This message is starting to have an effect. In recent days, we've seen a new degree of restraint on the part of the Kosovo Liberation Army, which has been willing to negotiate the disengagement of forces in several key areas. Future progress will be enhanced if Kosovars have confidence that the international community is engaged and determined to prevent a return to repression and terror. The Kosovo Diplomatic Observer Mission is in the field reporting to ensure that Milosevic is complying with our demands not only on paper, but also on the ground. NATO already has begun air verification missions. Their efforts will soon be augmented by the OSCE's new Kosovo Verification Mission, led by US Ambassador Bill Walker. I'm not here to tell you today that in Kosovo all is well; it is not. We have made considerable progress over the past ten days, but have to do far more than look at this week's snapshot of events. We must consider Milosevic's track record, his long-standing unwillingness to negotiate seriously and the accumulated barbarity of the past months. Time and again, Milosevic has taken half-steps to avoid the consequences of his actions. We are not interested in further promises, only continued compliance. We assume that Milosevic will act responsibly only when all the other alternatives have been exhausted. That's why we are maintaining the threat of force and not letting down our guard. That's why today at NATO, we have decided on an integrated package of steps to ensure Milosevic's complete and verifiable compliance with our demands. This regime will include the following elements:

-   First, NATO will soon activate the full air verification regime to ensure Serb compliance with the military provisions of the agreement.
-   Second, I've been working with my NATO counterparts to accelerate planning for a reaction force with forward elements in the Former Yugoslav Republic of Macedonia if the government of Skopje agrees. Its purpose will be to ensure that Alliance forces are on call to respond if needed.
-   Third, the authority for NATO to launch air strikes remains in place.
-   And fourth, NATO forces remain prepared to act promptly if and when that is necessary.

Milosevic should be under no illusions. NATO will be overhead and next door. The OSCE will have an intrusive presence on the ground. NATO will remain willing and able to act. NATO military authorities will provide regular assessments for the NATO Council on Milosevic's track record on compliance. These assessments will be developed with inputs from the Kosovo Verification Mission. ...

QUESTION: Madame Secretary, even with those new mechanisms, mindful of how many meetings had to be held, how many allies had to be consulted, the trips you had to make, the laborious preparations, should -- and it's not hypothetical, given his track record -- he should renege on this agreement, would it take a long time for NATO to get to the point again of hitting him, of attacking him, should he violate the agreement; or would there have to be meetings of the Contact Group, all sorts of mechanisms to satisfy? Could he be playing for time?

SECRETARY ALBRIGHT: Well, frankly, Barry, what I think is that there has been the best of all possible contact and coordination with the NATO allies. I've spent a lot of time with them on the phone -- not so much in an effort to persuade, but in an effort to stay in touch. I think that because it's not easy to assure and assess all these facts, and there's been a lot of stuff going on with General Clark and General Naumann going to Belgrade -- so there's been a lot. What I've found whether they're Contact Group meetings or individual conversations, that we do not have a disagreement about the fact that Milosevic needs to comply nor the fact that the threat of the use of force has been useful in terms of getting the kinds of progress that we have had. So I do not see any delay. What I'd like to do, because I think it's the clearest, is to read to you from the Solana statement on this that explains how that Act Ord remains in effect. Let me just read this. "Despite these

substantial steps, NATO's objective remains to achieve full compliance with Security Council Resolutions 1199 and 1203. As a result, we have decided this evening to maintain the Act Ord for limited air operations. Its execution will be subject to a decision and assessment by the North Atlantic Council. We will also maintain our Act Ord for the phased air campaign, and will continue our activities under Phase 0. We have requested our military authorities to remain prepared to carry out these air operations, should they be necessary, and to maintain forces at appropriate readiness levels for the operations under both Act Ords." So it would be my sense, Barry, first of all, that they actually had a choice: they could have suspended the Act Ords; they didn't do that. What they did was keep them in effect and simply use the fact that we would have to stay in contact and that the execution would be subject to a decision and assessments by the NAC. I think given the kinds of exchanges and interchanges we're having on an hourly basis, that we're all pretty much on the same track. ...

27. United Kingdom Parliamentary Testimony on the Threat or Use of Force, November 1998 & January 1999

[House of Lords, Written Answers, WA11, 2 November 1998; The Parliamentary Under Secretary of State, Foreign and Commonwealth Office (Baroness Symons of Vernham Dean)]: The legal basis for the use of force can only be considered in the light of all the circumstances at the time. In the exceptional circumstances of Kosovo, it would be justified on the grounds of overwhelming humanitarian necessity, without Security Council authoritization. The rules of international humanitarian law of course apply. ...

[16 November 1998, WA 139f, Baroness Symons of Vernham Dean]: The prohibitions on the use of force contained in the UN Charter do not preclude the use of force by a state or group of states in self-defence in accordance with Article 51 or under the authorization of the Security Council acting under Chapter VII of the Charter. There is no general doctrine of humanitarian necessity in international law. Cases have nevertheless arisen (as in northern Iraq in 1991) when, in the light of all the circumstances, a limited use of force was justifiable in support of purposes laid down by the Security Council but without the council's express authorization when that was the only means to avert an immediate and overwhelming catastrophe. Such cases would in the nature of things be exceptional and would depend on an objective assessment of the factual circumstances at the time and on the terms of relevant decisions of the Security Council bearing on the situation in question.

[House of Commons, Session 1998-99, Foreign Affairs Committee, Minutes of Evidence, HC188i, 26 January 1999]: Memorandum submitted by the Foreign and Commonwealth Office, Kosovo: Legal Authority for Military Action, 22 January 1999]:

"1.   This memorandum responds to the Committee's request for information on the specific legal authority upon which military action in Kosovo would be based, following the Foreign Secretary's answer in the House of Commons on 19 January that:

'Preparations continue and have not ceased, on what might be the appropriate military response if one is required.'

2.   The legal basis for any military action would need to be considered in the light of the circumstances at the time. A range of possibilities is conceivable in relation to the situation in Kosovo. Any military action by British forces would have to be lawful under international law.

3.   Military forces could be sent to the Federal Republic of Yugoslavia, including Kosovo, in support of a political settlement. This would normally be based upon the agreement of the parties and be backed by a resolution of the United Nations Security Council.

4.   Circumstances may arise in which military action would be based on the right to individual or collective self-defence recognised in Article 51 of the Charter, including the right to rescue nationals when the local authorities are unable or unwilling to do so. Action might also be based on an authorization given by the Security Council of the United Nations under Chapter VII of the United Nations Charter.

5.   There may also be cases of overwhelming humanitiarn necessity where, in the light of all of the circumstances, a limited use of force is justifiable as the only way to avert a humanitarian catastrophe." ...

[Testimony by Mr Tonly Lloyd, Minister of State]: We had no doubt whatsoever about the legal base for action last year. There were some 50,000 people living rough in the mountains facing death through starvation, facing death through cold, facing deprivation of an almost unimaginable kind, so yes, the humanitarian situation at the time did demand rapid action.

[Mr Rowlands]: I am asking: can one nation define the situation in Kosovo?

[Reply]: ... I remember, and Mr Rowlands will certainly remember, that not so long ago there was a time when Tanzania intervened in Uganda. ... At that time, if the Committee recalls, there was the most massive violence committeed by the government of Uganda against its own people. On that basis the Tanzanians invoked international law as a justification for their intervention. Precedent would therefore say, and if Mr Rowlands accepts—I certainly do—that at the time the intervention of the Tanzanians was legitimate, we could say that yes, one country could put that interpretation on it.

28. Press Statement by the North Atlantic Council on Kosovo, 19 November 1998

NATO is deeply concerned about the deteriorating security situation in Kosovo. Since the beginning of November there has been a sharp increase in tension resulting from incidents created in some cases by Serbian Security forces and in other cases by armed Kosovar elements such as the UCK. The incidents risk creating a dangerous cycle of provocation and response which, if continued, could destabilize the ceasefire, reverse the recent improvement in the humanitarian situation and jeopardize the arrangements being put into place by NATO and OSCE for verification of compliance with the relevant UN Security Council resolutions. NATO is monitoring the situation closely has made its concerns clear to the Government of the Federal Republic of Yugoslavia and the Kosovar Albanians. NATO insists that all parties must comply fully with the relevant UNSCRs and their other commitments; in particular by observing the ceasefire, avoiding provocation, and moving promptly to negotiations on a political settlement which alone can be the basis of a lasting peace in Kosovo.

29. NATO Press Statement on the Extraction Force, 5 December 1998

NATO has developed plans in the context of UN Security Council Resolution 1203 in consultation with the OSCE for an Extraction Force that will extract OSCE verifiers or other designated persons from Kosovo in an emergency. Under these plans, and with the agreement of the government of the Former Yugoslav Republic of Macedonia (FYROM), the standing element of this Extraction Force will be stationed in FYROM and will compromise about 1500 personnel from several NATO countries. The North Atlantic Council authorised last night the sending of the Activation Order for the deployment to FYROM of the Extraction Force. This deployment will start shortly. The deployment of the Extraction Force in no way relieves the government of the Federal Republic of Yugoslavia (FRY) government of its primary responsibility for the safety and security of the OSCE verifiers deployed in Kosovo, stipulated in Security Council Resolution 1203 and in the agreement signed between the FRY government and the OSCE. (Turkey recognizes the Republic of Macedonia with its constitutional name.)

30. NATO Statement on Kosovo, 8 December 1998

1. NATO's aim has been to contribute to international efforts to stop the humanitarian crisis in Kosovo, end the violence there and bring about a lasting political settlement. NATO's decisions in October made a crucial contribution to the withdrawal of forces of the Federal Republic of Yugoslavia (FRY) from Kosovo and helped to avert a humanitarian disaster. The Alliance's enhanced state of military readiness continues.

2. The security situation in Kosovo remains of great concern to us. Since the beginning of November, violent incidents provoked in some cases by Serbian security forces and in others by armed Kosovar elements have increased tension. These incidents show that both the Belgrade authorities and the armed Kosovar elements have failed to comply fully with the requirements set out in UN Security Council Resolutions 1160, 1199 and 1203. We call upon the armed Kosovar

elements to cease and desist from provocative actions and we call upon the FRY and Serbian authorities to reduce the number and visibility of MUP special police in Kosovo and abstain from intimidating behaviour.

3. We insist that both sides maintain scrupulously the ceasefire and comply fully with the UN Security Council resolutions. We also expect them to facilitate the war crimes investigations by the International Criminal Tribunal for the former Yugoslavia (ICTY). In this connection, we deplore the denial of visas to ICTY investigators. Continued violence between FRY and Serbian forces and armed Kosovar elements jeopardises prospects for a political settlement for which an opportunity now exists.

4. We remain firmly convinced that the problems of Kosovo can only be resolved through a process of open and unconditional dialogue between the authorities in Belgrade and representatives of the Kosovar leadership. We therefore strongly urge all parties to move rapidly in a spirit of compromise and accommodation to conclude the negotiating process led by Ambassador Hill in which they are engaged. We reaffirm our support for a political solution which provides an enhanced status for Kosovo, a substantially greater degree of autonomy and meaningful self-administration, and which preserves the territorial integrity of the FRY, and safeguards the human and civil rights of all inhabitants of Kosovo, whatever their ethnic origin. We believe that stability in Kosovo is linked to the democratisation of the FRY and we support those who are genuinely engaged in that process. In this regard, we condemn recent actions taken by President Milosevic to suppress the independent media and political pluralism in Serbia. We welcome the steps the Government of Montenegro has taken to protect the independent media, promote democratic reforms and ensure respect for the rights of all its citizens.

5. We will continue the Alliance's air verification mission, Operation "Eagle Eye", in accordance with the agreement between the FRY and NATO, and communicate periodically to the UN Secretary-General NATO's views on compliance.

6. We intend to cooperate fully with the OSCE Kosovo Verification Mission (KVM). The security and safety of the OSCE verifiers is of the utmost importance to us. We call on the FRY government to meet its responsibilities in this regard, as set out in UNSCRs 1199 and 1203 and the OSCE-FRY agreement of 16th October. We expect the FRY and Serbian authorities, as well as the Kosovar communities, to cooperate fully with the OSCE KVM, in particular by respecting its freedom of movement and right of access and by ensuring that its personnel are not subject to the threat or use of force or interference of any kind. We also expect the FRY and Serbian authorities to continue to allow unhindered access to international relief organisations including by issuing the necessary visas.

7. The North Atlantic Council has authorised an Activation Order (ACTORD) for a NATO-led Extraction Force, Operation "Joint Guarantor". We will quickly deploy the standing elements of this force in the Former Yugoslav Republic of Macedonia to provide the ability to withdraw personnel of the OSCE KVM in an emergency. We greatly appreciate the cooperation and support of the authorities of the former Yugoslav Republic of Macedonia for providing facilities for the basing of NATO forces.

8. We welcome the willingness of Partner countries to join with NATO in contributing to the solution of the Kosovo crisis either by participating in the NATO-led air verification mission or by offering the use of their airspace or other facilities in support of NATO's efforts. We will continue to consult closely with all Partner countries on the Alliance's actions in respect of the Kosovo crisis.

Chapter 13: The OSCE Verification Mission

The OSCE had been excluded from Yugoslavia since 1993. Persistent demands for a reintroduction of its Mission of Long Duration, made not only by the OSCE organs, but also by the United Nations General Assembly and the Security Council, had been ignored. Instead, an international presence had been building up in neighbouring Macedonia and Albania. Both countries required international assistance in order to retain or restore domestic stability. In Macedonia, inter-ethnic relations were often described as a powder keg. If conflict were to erupt in that former Yugoslav state, boasting an ethnic Albanian minority of between 20 to 30 per cent, the entire region would be affected, and some analysts were predicting a spreading of the conflict reaching as far as Greece and Turkey. It was feared that continued strife in Kosovo, which shares a border with Macedonia, might spark such an explosion. Although ethnic Albanian leaders in Macedonia were pursuing a very cautious and moderate policy, there had been some indications that the KLA was obtaining support from ethnic Albanians in that state, most of whom lived in territories contiguous with the Kosovo border. Police raids had uncovered a number of arms dumps and other facilities.

To address concerns about the instability of Macedonia, a small but quietly effective UN peace-keeping force had been deployed to the territory (UNPROFOR, later UNPREDEP) early in the conflict sparked by the dissolution of Yugoslavia. The OSCE had also established a 'Spill-over Mission', hoping to reduce the risk of a spreading of the conflict.. Relations with those missions were somewhat delicate. On the one hand, their presence was vital to prevent the outbreak of civil strife. On the other hand, the missions also added an international dimension to what the Macedonian majority regarded as an internal minority problem, and was seen to embolden the demands for equal participation in the political system by ethnic Albanian citizens.[1]

In Albania, the post-communist transition had already led to the eruption of violence in 1997—answered with the deployment of an Italian-led peace-keeping mission (with some enforcement powers) to help restore civil society and governance. That mission had been accompanied by OSCE, WEU and even NATO activities, designed to rebuild Albania's civil and military institutions. However, just at the point when the mission was about to declare itself a success and start winding down, renewed unrest appeared to grip hold of the country in the autumn of 1998 and the outbreak of further civil strife could not be excluded. At the same time, Albania came under considerable pressure to curb arms smuggling to Kosovo and the granting of training and supply bases on its territory. While Albania was in no position to give significant military or financial assistance to the KLA, rumours persisted that it was engaged, somewhat unintentionally, in a two track approach to the mounting violence in Kosovo. At the level of the official government, it stoutly defended the rights of the Kosovo Albanians. At the same time, it supported the Hill and later Rambouillet peace-process, although its enthusiasm for it had to be awakened and maintained by the United States and others. However, it was also rumoured that there existed another tier of governance, left over from the previous neo-Stalinist regime in Albania and still in control of part of the security apparatus, including the intelligence service. These elements, it was alleged, were encouraging and supporting a hard-line attitude of quite small KLA cells, who had risen to prominence and positions of control within that organization, and who saw no room for compromise and a peaceful resolution of the Kosovo issue. Instead, a pan-Albanian agenda was pursued within a framework of a rather rigid ideological framework.

Given this somewhat ambivalent nature of its position, the Albanian government permitted actions which were designed to ensure domestic stability and to avert Yugoslav raids against KLA facilities on its territory. Hence, there was an increase of OSCE personnel and cooperation with NATO was significantly strengthened, culminating in joint military exercises held in August 1998. Albania, however, remained hostile to the idea of introducing an international force which would monitor its border region with Kosovo. This might have disrupted the 'unity of fate' between Albania and Kosovo which had been proclaimed, and which was designed to forestall the application of the strategy of containment which had been applied to the Bosnian conflict by the outside world. That strategy had held that strife and ethnic cleansing in Bosnia and Herzegovina could not be influenced from the outside, at least not without significant human cost. Instead, there was maintained an ineffective UN presence which was reliant on the cooperation of the parties. Effective international measures concentrated on isolating the rest of the region from the events in Bosnia, however shocking they may have been. It was only when this strategy of containment finally collapsed, in the wake of the Srebrenica massacre of 1995 and with the determination by Islamic states that they would no longer comply with the arms embargo against Bosnia, that decisive international intervention was mounted which immediately terminated the fighting.

This experience had taught the Albanian government (and others) that human suffering alone was not sufficient to generate the international involvement necessary to advance the cause of the Kosovo Albanians or even to save them from a Bosnia-style campaign of ethnic cleansing and possible genocide. Instead, the prospect of a widening of the conflict had to be

---

[1] Macedonia officially disputed that there were up to 30 per cent ethnic Albanians on its territory.

maintained—a somewhat difficult balancing act, given Albania's own political instability and military and economic impotence. An altogether too intrusive international presence along the border with Kosovo would have limited the necessary freedom of action in this respect and would have fostered an international view that it might be possible, after all, to manage the developing Kosovo crisis through containment.

In addition to strengthening its limited monitoring presence in Albania and Macedonia, the OSCE revived its calls for permission to deploy in Kosovo when hostilities erupted in earnest in February and March 1998.[2] Through its Troika of Foreign Ministers (previous, present and next Chairman in Office), it requested cooperation with its own organs and the EU/OSCE Special Representative Filipe Gonzalez. The FRY reiterated its position that the mission of long duration could not return until the modalities for the resumption of full participation in the OSCE organs had been agreed.[3] The United Nations Security Council, following upon a suggestion from the UN Secretary-General[4] and an invitation from Macedonia, increased the strength of UNPREDEP to 1,050 and extended its mandate to 28 February 1999, "to continue by its presence to deter threats and prevent clashes, to monitor the border area."[5]

The FRY sought to deflect international pressure for more decisive action. On 16 June 1998, in a joint statement with his ally, President Boris Yeltsin, Mr Milosevic solemnly committed himself to the implementation of the demands made by the Security Council in Resolution 1160 (1988). However, since 1991 the Milosevic government had given assurances in relation to its armed activities which were generally not kept. Hence, particular attention was paid to the issue of monitoring the implementation of the Yugoslav undertakings and the Security Council had demanded the reinstatement of the OSCE Mission of Long Duration to that end. On that crucial point, the statement merely reiterated the well-known position which effectively precluded a permanent OSCE presence by linking even the 'beginning' of talks to the reinstatement of the FRY to full membership privileges:[6]

> To announce the willingness of the Federal Republic of Yugoslavia to begin negotiations with the Organization for Security and Cooperation in Europe (OSCE) on receiving the mission sent by that organization to Kosovo and on the reinstatement of the Federal Republic of Yugoslavia as a member of OSCE.

Given this dilemma, a number of states seized upon a further paragraph in the joint statement which referred to the presence of foreign diplomatic representatives in Yugoslavia whose freedom of movement was not to be restricted. While their number was limited to those 'accredited' to Yugoslavia, this nevertheless gave impetus to the use of diplomatic staff, provisionally in lieu of the OSCE. In contrast to EU monitors whose findings have always been kept confidential, and whose role has been marginal, some of these observers issued regular and public reports on events in Kosovo—especially in the case of the US, which made the reports available on the internet. In fact, the US element in what was to become the Kosovo Diplomatic Observer Mission was quite substantial, and was later accorded a special, and less public role in relation to the verification of the Holbrooke agreement.

Despite the involvement of KDOM, the conflict escalated, and the number of the displaced and refugees reached beyond 100,000 by early summer. The attention of international agencies remained focussed on containing the conflict, increasing the monitoring and, with ever greater urgency, the provision of humanitarian relief. This prompted the UN Secretary General, who had held a key position in the UN Secretariat managing peace keeping operations during the Bosnia debacle, to observe in July that "the international community risks once again being placed in a position where it is only dealing with the symptoms of a conflict through its humanitarian agencies".[7] But, by September, increased monitoring and diplomatic initiatives had not achieved much. The number of the displaced and refugees was climbing to 300,000. Kofi Annan noted:[8]

> In the last few weeks, the international community has witnessed appalling atrocities in Kosovo, reminiscent of the recent past elsewhere in the Balkans. These have been borne out by reporting by the Kosovo Diplomatic Observer Mission and other reliable sources. I reiterate my utter condemnation of such wanton killing and destruction. It is clear beyond any reasonable doubt that the great majority of such acts have been committed by security forces in Kosovo acting under the authority of the Federal Republic of Yugoslavia. But Kosovar Albanian paramilitary units have engaged in armed action also, and there is good reason to believe that they too have committed atrocities.

The situation changed after the ACTWARN decision of NATO, adopted on 24 September.[9] Although the initial Holbrooke Mission of early October remained without success, on 6 October the FRY government addressed the OSCE Chairman in Office, inviting the OSCE to "witness [at] first hand the positive evolution of the most crucial processes in

---

[2] OSCE Permanent Council Decision NO. 218, 11 March 1998, Document 13.A.1.
[3] UN Secretary General's Report, 4 June 1998, Document 8.3.
[4] UN Secretary-General's Report, 14 July 1998, Document 8.5.
[5] UNSC Resolution 1186 (1998), 21 July 1998, Document 7.2.
[6] Joint Statement by Boris Yeltzin and Slobodan Milosevic, Moscow, 16 June 1998, Document 13.A.2.
[7] UN Secretary-General's Report, 5 August 1998, Document 8.3.
[8] UN Secretary-General's Report, 3 October 1998, Document 8.9.
[9] *See* Chapter 12.

Kosovo and Metohija".[10] However, the Chairman in Office replied that now it was imperative to achieve compliance with all demands of the United Nations Security Council. The OSCE would be ready to undertake a role within that framework. The opportunity to exercise such a role then presented itself a few days later, when the Holbrooke agreement was reached. On 14 October, the FRY government authorized its Foreign Minister to conclude an agreement with the OSCE for the deployment and operation of a Verification Mission. That agreement was signed two days later, on 16 October, supplemented by the NATO aerial verification agreement and certain other undertakings.

According to the OSCE Agreement, the mission (KVM) would be established under an OSCE Permanent Council decision, but pursuant to a Security Council resolution. In this way, Yugoslavia could assure itself of a modicum of indirect control over the operation, through Russia's presence in the Security Council. In addition, this permitted the FRY to avoid an altogether too obvious u-turn in relation to its refusal to accept an OSCE mission until her participation in that organization had been fully restored.[11]

The agreement was concluded for one year, with the unusual possibility of unilateral extensions at the request of either the FRY or the OSCE. However, as the mission was established under both OSCE and Security Council mandates, its operation was not quite as open-ended as might be presumed.

The Agreement provided for the presence of 2,000 unarmed OSCE 'Verifyers', principally based in Prishtina (headquarters) and in every municipal district in Kosovo, plus a liaison office in Belgrade. The additional use of experts for election monitoring or other tasks was also permitted, providing the option of deploying significantly more than 2,000 personnel. The functions of the mission were broad, being directed towards verification by all parties of compliance with their commitments under Security Council Resolution 1199 (1998). In addition, the OSCE would 'supervise' rather than monitor elections in Kosovo. As the Mission would verify compliance of all parties, and as it would effectively run elections in Kosovo, it is interesting to note that none of the elected representatives of Kosovo, or indeed, no representative of Kosovo at all, was consulted about its terms. Nor was Kosovo invited to accede to the agreements.[12] This fact is all the more surprising, inasmuch as the mission was also supposed to support the establishment of a political settlement, and would assist in the building of political institutions in Kosovo, including a new indigenous police force.

The military aspect of the mission's mandate was also somewhat confusing. It was expressly charged with reporting on the maintenance of a cease-fire by all parties and also to verify the numbers and locations of FRY/Serb military forces and police forces. However, a significant number of senior members of the mission were not given access to the actual undertakings that had been made by Belgrade in relation to these issues. Instead, it appears that KDOM, which should in principle have become superfluous with the establishment of the OSCE mission, and its US element, would also exercise a verification role in this respect. In fact, rather than winding down this presence, towards the end of the mission, the US contributed no less than 143 members to KDOM, compared to 33 furnished by all EU states combined.

The OSCE appointed US Ambassador William Walker to head KVM, and formally established the mission on 25 October.[13] By that time, the other elements of the Holbrooke deal had been translated into a series of military undertakings, and the Security Council had endorsed the mission the day before. UNHCR reported that winter was setting in, the first snowfalls having been observed, and that rapid arrangements were being put into place to provide for the return of the displaced and refugees and to assure their supply with foodstuffs, medicine, stoves and building materials.[14] A detailed survey of the state of villages and buildings was undertaken, to ensure that returnees would receive the support they required. Once again, the integration of effort between the UN agencies, KVM, KDOM and non-governmental agencies was impressive, in contrast to many previous experiences of humanitarian agencies in complex emergencies.

Almost in parallel with the partial pullout of FRY/Serb forces from Kosovo or their return to barracks in Kosovo, the first returns of refugees and the displaced were being noted. While the humanitarian situation improved somewhat, it was reported that FRY/Serb repression continued. The increased international presence also resulted in the discovery of corpses, apparently of victims of summary execution. Some 1,500 ethnic Albanians were still being detained by FRY/Serb authorities, their future uncertain. There were also retaliatory actions by Kosovo forces, who now enjoyed a greater freedom of movement, and by returning villagers, against Serbs.[15]

---

[10] OSCE Press Release, 7 October 1998, Document 13.A.3.

[11] Of course, FRY participation in the UN itself remained somewhat in limbo, but in a less visible way, as FRY delegates continued to represent the FRY in relation to the Security Council.

[12] Hence, there ensued intense US efforts to persuade KLA leaders to abide by the agreement. However, a month after the conclusion of the Holbrooke agreement, the UN Secretary-General reported that the position of Kosovo Albanian paramilitaries remained unclear, although respect for a cease-fire was, by and large, expected. There was evidence that paramilitaries were exploiting the FRY/Serb withdrawals to enhance their positions and to replenish their supplies. Report, 12 November 1998, Document 13.B.4.

[13] OSCE Permanent Council Decision 263, 25 October 1998, Document 13.A.9.

[14] UN Inter-Agency Update, 21 October 1998, Document 13.B.2.

[15] UN Secretary-General Report, 12 November 1998, Document 13.B.4.

Serb security measures were increased in November and early December, including the re-establishment of security check-points and heavy security presences especially in villages along the Albanian border. Arbitrary arrests and the practice of 'informative talks' at Serb detention centres continued "on a massive scale," along with 'abductions' of Serb individuals (four reported since mid-October, although the actual figure is likely to be higher).[16] Then, a Serb policeman was shot after having been kidnapped. On 14 December, six Serb teenagers were killed while playing pool when two masked gunmen sprayed a café in Pec with bullets.[17]

Early December also saw occasional violations of the cease-fire and localized fighting. The still tense situation was not improved upon by the fact that by that time, the OSCE had only managed to establish an advance headquarters in Kosovo and to introduce 50 staff. As the OSCE does not have significant staff of its own, and as prospective KVM members had to be seconded from or nominated by member states, and then trained and familiarized with local circumstances, this is, of course, not altogether surprising.[18]

On Christmas Eve, the UN Secretary-General reported that 100,000 Kosovo Albanians had returned to their homes, while 200,000 remained displaced.[19] While no new 'abductions' had been reported to the Secretary-General, no progress to clear up the fate of 282 Serb civilians and police who had disappeared during the conflict was made. In turn, the amnesty of detained ethnic Albanians, envisaged in the Serb government statement upon the conclusion of the Holbrooke agreement, was not progressing. On the positive side, the presence of the OSCE mission had increased very significantly, with a total personnel of 908, although this included 392 local staff. Regional OSCE Centres also started to become operational. However, rather than stabilizing the situation, it soon deteriorated dramatically.

Over the Christmas period, the FRY/Serb forces commenced a major offensive operation, leading to a renewed exodus of refugees, now in the harsh conditions of mid-winter. This operation was seen by international observers to be aimed at probing the determination of the international community, especially NATO, and its timing was seen as significant in that context. It was also a sign that Serbia would not be willing to permit the emergence of a situation in which it would lose effective control over Kosovo to the benefit of the Kosovo military and political leadership.

The OSCE managed to negotiate a truce after four days of renewed hostilities. These hostilities were again marked by direct attacks against civilian concentrations, rather than limited counter-insurgency operations. However, in early January, further attacks were mounted, culminating in the Racak massacre. This atrocity was in fact only one of several. However, it had been discovered by the international media and was therefore widely reported upon. In Racak, 45 ethnic Albanians had been killed; 22 of whom were found together in a gully, killed execution-style. This included several elderly men and one child. The scene of the atrocity was quickly visited and the action was immediately condemned by the UN Secretary-General, the OSCE, including its Head of Mission, and various other international bodies. The Security Council adopted a Presidential statement reflecting the view that the FRY was responsible for the atrocity. The Council also noted with concern that 5,500 civilians had fled Racak during the operation of FRY forces in the area. Finally, it deplored the decision of Belgrade to declare the OSCE Head of Mission *persona non grata*, in consequence of his clear condemnation of the act.[20]

A report of a Finnish/EC forensic team later confirmed that none of the victims appeared to have been "anything other than unarmed civilians".[21] An investigation of the incident by the International Criminal Tribunal was precluded by the FRY, which denied access to the Tribunal's staff. The Finish team, too, endured rather difficult circumstances, including the removal of the corpses and various bureaucratic obstacles.

Throughout January, further fighting was reported, triggering another Presidential Statement from the Security Council.[22]NATO military commanders journeyed to Belgrade, to impress upon Milosevic NATO's continued determination to use force, if necessary. Nevertheless, NATO reported that armed formations had been re-introduced by the FRY/Serbia into Kosovo in violation of the Holbrooke agreements. Incidents of abduction continued, now also affecting the ethnic Albanian population. There were further shootings of civilians by unidentified gunmen, again directed at both segments of the population.

---

[16] Secretary-General Report, 4 December 1998, Document 13.B.7.
[17] UN Inter-Agency Update, 24 December 1998, Document 13.B.10.
[18] See Ettore Greco, The OSCE Verification Mission, 4 *International Peacekeeping* (1998) 117.
[19] Report of the Secretary-General, 24 December 1998, Document 13.B.11.
[20] *See* Documents 13.B13-20. That decision was subsequently not withdrawn, but 'frozen', after the OSCE Chairman in Office negotiated directly with President Milosevic.
[21] Report of the EU Forensic Team, 17 March 1999, Document 13.B.29.
[22] Statement by the President of the Security Council, 29 January 1999, Document 13.B.23.

While the Rambouillet talks were under-way, another FRY/Serb offensive was launched, leading to the displacement of the KLA from key positions and to further forced movements of civilians. The total of those who had been unable to return to their homes or had been driven out rose again to around 211,000.[23]

Between the conclusion of the Rambouillet conference on 23 February and the commencement of NATO action on 24 March, an additional 30,000 ethnic Albanians had been displaced, bringing the total close to the number which had triggered the threat of force by NATO in September 1988 and the negotiation of the Holbrooke agreement in the first place.[24]

The three week hiatus in negotiations between the Rambouillet talks and the Paris follow-on conference was characterized by a steady build-up of FRY/Serb armed forces, including heavy weaponry.[25] It later emerged that Belgrade had just about deployed double the forces permitted under the Holbrooke terms. There occurred armed border incidents with Albania, raising the spectre of the spreading of the conflict. And the newly strengthened FRY/Serb troops continued to encircle villages, shell, empty and occupy them.

On 19 March, the Paris follow-on talks ended, having failed to achieve FRY/Serb agreement to the Rambouillet package. That day, in view of the increasingly impossible security situation, the OSCE Chairman in office, Norwegian Foreign Minister Knut Vollebaek, decided on the immediate withdrawal of the OSCE verifiers. By that time, their number had reached 1,400, just over two thirds of the number that had been agreed six months earlier. The failure of the Holbrooke agreement and of the OSCE mission can, however, not really be ascribed to the hesitant deployment of the verifiers. Their mission was made difficult if not impossible by the requirement imposed upon them of having to rely on the cooperation of the parties. That meant that their presence would be obstructed where it was not desired, although the verifiers did on occasion quite courageously manage to escape from this stricture. At a deeper level, the Mission had been charged with verifying an arrangement which probably had no chance of success from the beginning.

The Holbrooke deal placed Belgrade in an odd position. It retained a very significant military presence in Kosovo. Nevertheless, it was supposed to restrict the freedom of movement of these forces. Practically, this meant that local control would gradually be taken over by ethnic Albanian forces. They had been constrained over the summer to retreat from the countryside they had previously partially controlled. Now, they were filtering back into their old positions and beyond. Even with moderation on the part of the KLA this could not really be avoided. Most of the KLA fighters were ordinary villagers seeking to return to their home regions and they were organized in regionally-based groups.

The failure to tie the Holbrooke agreement to a political settlement was also crucial in this respect. When NATO had permitted the 2 November deadline for FRY/Serb acceptance of the Hill plan for a settlement to pass without consequence, the chance for a political arrangement had been lost. In the absence of settlement providing for an orderly devolution of power with international involvement, Serbia had to continue to rely on repression and the use of force to keep its administration of the province afloat, whether or not that involved the violation of the Holbrooke terms. The FRY/Serbia soon adopted the tactics that had been employed in Bosnia and Herzegovina vis-à-vis UNPROFOR. It sought to restrict the movement of the very verifiers who were supposed to ensure restrictions on the movement of FRY/Serb forces. It also gradually increased offensive operations, testing as it went along NATO's determination to respond to infractions of the agreement by using force. As there was no forcible response, which would have jeopardised the Holbrooke agreement to which the OSCE and NATO were now committed, further action was taken, culminating in the Christmas offensive. In addition, operations were now being carried out by FRY/Serb 'unattributable forces', who sought to prevent the return of ethnic Albanians to the areas from which they had been cleansed. This salami tactic was only disrupted by the accidental discovery of the Racak massacre, which made it difficult for NATO to legitimise its inaction.

In fairness, it would have been very difficult for NATO to justify the application of military force, at least before the Christmas offensive. The Holbrooke agreement was based on the hope of KLA cooperation. However, should this hope not be fulfilled, it did in fact permit the FRY/Serbia to respond to provocations by the KLA. Belgrade was also entitled to retain control over main roads and highways through permanent observation posts and special patrols. As the use of force was, therefore, permissible to a certain extent, NATO would have had to judge on particular instances of uses of force, to determine whether or not these were necessary in order to maintain the degree of control over the territory which had been granted to the FRY/Serb forces in the agreement. The agreement was therefore indeed a perfect example of the kind of ill-considered policy making on the hoof, obtained in a marathon negotiating session with Mr Milosevic without having thought through its consequences.

---

[23] Report of the Secretary-General, 17 March 1999, Document 13.B.30.
[24] Report of the Secretary-General, 23 March 1999, Document 13.B.32.
[25] Letter of the Secretary-General, Annex, 25 March 1999, Document 13.B.33.

A. Establishment of the OSCE Verification Mission

OSCE, 156th Plenary Meeting, PC Journal No. 156, a.i. 3, PC/DEC/218, 11 March 1998

1. OSCE Permanent Council Decision No. 218, 11 March 1998

The Permanent Council meeting in special session,

Deeply concerned about the crisis in Kosovo, Federal Republic of Yugoslavia (FRY), and urging those involved to cease unconditionally any form of violence,

Condemning the excessive and indiscriminate use of force during Serb police actions in Kosovo, which have led to the death of some 80 people over
the past week,

Stressing the unacceptability of any terrorist action and calling on all concerned actively to oppose the use of violence to achieve political aims,

Recalling the statements of the Chairman-in-Office of 2 March and 10 March 1998 on the situation in Kosovo,

Recognizing that the crisis is not solely an internal affair of the FRY because of the violtions of OSCE principles and commitments on human rights and because it has a significant impact on the security of a region, as well as taking into account the need for immediate efforts by the international community to prevent further escalation,

Calling on the authorities in Belgrade and the leadership of the Kosovar Albanians to assume their responsibility to enter without preconditions into meaningful dialogue, based on full observance of the OSCE principles and commitments, including those of the Helsinki Final Act, and expressing the readiness of the OSCE to assist in this process,

1. *Takes positive note* of the activities of the Chairman-in-Office undertaken with regard to the crisis in Kosovo and encourages him to continue efforts aimed at an effective OSCE contribution to its peaceful resolutions.

2. *Supports* a new mission by Mr Felipe Gonzales as the Personal Representative of the Chairman-in-Office for the FRY which would include a mandate for addressing the problems in Kosovo;

3. *Expresses* gratitude for the work of Mr Max van der Stoel, whose experience and expertise remain invaluable in helping the OSCE in its efforts to resolve the problems in the region;

4. *Authorizes* the following operational measures to be taken to allow adequate observation of the borders with Kosovo, FRY, and possible spillover effects, as already requested by the Chairman-in-Office:
- The monitoring capabilities of the OSCE Presence in Albania and, as appropriate, the OSCE Spillover Monitor Mission to Skopje will be temporarily enhanced for the fulfillment of those tasks;
- The respective Heads of Mission will report regularly on their observations;

5. *Requesting* the representative of OSCE Troika members accredited in Belgrade to co-ordinate arrangements for continuous monitoring of the situation in Kosovo by diplomatic representatives in Belgrade of the OSCE participating states. The Permanent Council will be kept informed about relevant findings;

6. *Calls* on FRY authorities:
- To halt excessive use of force in Kosovo, to vigorously investigate and accept international investigation and reported summary executions and to bring to justice those found responsible;
- To co-operate fully with the OSCE Chairman-in-Office's Personal Representative to the FRY, MR Felipe Gonzales;
- To initiate a meaningful dialogue with Kosovar Albanian representatives which will lead to concrete steps towards the resolution of ongoing political problems in the region;
- To allow access to Kosovo for the International Committee of the Red Cross and other humanitarian organizations;
- To implement without delay the Education Agreement and seek agreements on further confidence-building measures;

- To accept without preconditions, an immediate return of these missions as essential for future participation in the OSCE by the FRY.

S/1998/526, Annex, 17 June 1998

2. Joint statement by President of Russian Federation and President of FRY, Moscow, 16 June 1998

The Presidents reaffirm their position of principle on the necessity of preserving the territorial integrity and respecting the sovereignty of the Federal Republic of Yugoslavia, and condemn all forms of terrorism, separatism and armed activity which affect the civilian population. n an effort to stabilize the situation in Kosovo and Metohija, the Yugoslav side announces its willingness:
- To resolve the existing problems by political means, based on the equality of all citizens and national communities in Kosovo;
- In line with this goal, to continue without delay the negotiations between representatives of the State and representatives of Kosovar Albanian political parties, which were begun by President Milosevic and Mr. Rugova, leader of the Kosovar Albanians. Negotiations on all of the problems in Kosovo, including forms of autonomy in accordance with internationally recognized standards, shall be pursued continuously according to the timetable established by the parties with a view to achieving significant and speedy progress;
- To refrain from taking any repressive measures against peaceful populations;
- As a means of strengthening confidence-building measures, to guarantee complete freedom of movement throughout the territory of Kosovo. No restrictions shall be imposed on diplomatic representatives of foreign countries and international organizations accredited to the Federal Republic of Yugoslavia who wish to learn about the situation;
- To guarantee free access to the above-mentioned territories by humanitarian organizations, the International Committee of the Red Cross (ICRC) and the Office of the United Nations High Commissioner for Refugees (UNHCR), and to allow the unimpeded entry of humanitarian supplies into those territories;
- To allow the free return of all refugees and displaced persons on the basis of the programmes agreed upon with UNHCR and ICRC. State assistance shall be provided for the reconstruction of homes which have been destroyed;
- To the extent that terrorist activities are halted, to reduce the presence of security forces outside the areas in which they are permanently deployed;
- To announce the willingness of the Federal Republic of Yugoslavia to begin negotiations with the Organization for Security and Cooperation in Europe (OSCE) on receiving the mission sent by that organization to Kosovo and on the reinstatement of the Federal Republic of Yugoslavia as a member of OSCE.

Both Presidents stated their firm intention to develop multilateral cooperation in the interest of the peoples of the two countries and of peace and stability in Europe.

No. 58/98

3. Press Release by Professor Bronislaw Geremek, Chairman-in-Office the OSCE, Warsaw, 7 October 1998

Professor Bronislaw Geremek, the OSCE Chairman-in-Office, has received yesterday evening a letter from the Foreign Minister of the Federal Republic of Yugoslavia, Zivadin Jovanovic, in which he invited the OSCE "to witness first hand the positive evolution of the most crucial processes in Kosovo and Metohija."

The OSCE Chairman-in-Office emphasized that the best conditions for accepting this invitation will appear when the FRY satisfies the requirements contained in the OSCE Permanent Council Decision 218, as well as United Nations Security Council Resolutions 1160 and 1199.

Minister Geremek recalls the OSCE's long-standing readiness to give its contribution to the democratic processes in the FRY and to the solution of the crisis in Kosovo, where appalling human suffering is occurring, and where there is the risk of its aggravation in the near future. At the same time, Mr. Geremek recalls and confirms the OSCE's long-standing readiness to contribute to a durable solution and stability in the area.

The Chairman-in-Office confirms this readiness and hopes that conditions will soon allow the OSCE to undertake appropriate initiatives.

The Chairman-in-Office also draws attention to the fact that Foreign Minister Jovanovic's proposal does not refer to the contents of the OSCE Permanent Council Decision No. 218, regarding the invitation of the long-term Missions to Kosovo, Sandjak and Vojvodina, or to the mission of Felipe Gonzalez as Personal Representative of the Chairman-in-Office for the FRY. The Chairman-in-Office also notes that the relation between the mission proposed by Minister Jovanovic and the diplomatic monitoring activities currently underway in Kosovo and organized by the Contact Group with OSCE participation, was not mentioned by Minister Jovanovic. OSCE monitoring could be an important element of the settlement process of the solution of the crisis in Kosovo. This would also mean acceptance of the requirements of the international community addressed to President Milosevic, as stated in the UN Security Council Resolution 1199.

Minister Geremek underlines that it is now up to the FRY, through full compliance with the terms of the above-mentioned documents, to enable the OSCE to make its contribution to the resolution of the crisis over Kosovo.

4.   FRY Federal Government Statement, Extract, 14 October 1998

... The Federal Government defined the text of the agreement between the Federal Government of the Federal Republic of Yugoslavia and the OSCE on the OSCE's mission for verification in Kosovo. The Federal Government authorized Foreign Minister Zivadin Jovanovic to sign the agreement with the OSCE Chairman Bronislaw Geremek, Polish Foreign Minister. As a part of the verification process and the implementation of the Security Council's Resolution 1199, the Federal Republic of Yugoslavia shall permit the observing flights in Kosovo. The Federal Government thinks the agreement will preserve the peace, not only in Yugoslavia but in the whole region and Europe; it also provides the development of economy, neighbourly relations and comprehensive cooperation in the region.

[For the full statement, see Document 12.16.]

5.   Press Release: US Special Envoy for Kosovo Addresses Permanent Council, Vienna, 15 October 1998

Ambassador Christopher R. Hill, US Special Envoy for Kosovo, briefed the special session of the OSCE Permanent Council today on the negotiations which led to the agreement to establish an OSCE verification mission for Kosovo. He also reported on this morning's Paris Contact Group Meeting which discussed how to implement the agreement. Ambassador Hill made clear that the agreement placed an enormous burden on the OSCE - both to verify the agreement and to help the Kosovars build effective democratic institutions. He also stated that it was his view that the OSCE was fully capable of taking on this burden and executing its responsibilities effectively.EU special envoy and Austrian Ambassador to the FRY, Wolfgang Petritsch, was also in Vienna to attend the Permanent Council meeting.

OSCE Permanent Council, PC.DEC/259/98, 15 October 1998, 189th Plenary Meeting, PC Journal No. 189, a.i. 2.

6.   OSCE Permanent Council, Decision No. 259, 15 October 1998

The Permanent Council,

Acting within the framework of the United Nations Security Council Resolution No. 1199,

Recalling the Permanent council Decision No. 218 paragraph 1, and the statement of the Chairman-in-Office of 7 October 1998 confirming the OSCE's long-standing readiness to give its contribution to the peaceful solution of the crisis in Kosovo,

1.   *Declares* the preparedness of the OSCE to embark upon verification activities related to compliance of all parties in Kosovo with the requirements set forth by the international community with regard to the solution of the crisis in Kosovo;

2.   *Supports* the Chairman-in-Office's efforts to arrange with the FRY authorities for the OSCE to make such contribution;

3.   *Expresses* its readiness to consider in an urgent manner any further specific steps necessary to meet the requirements for efficient verification in Kosovo

OSCE Document CIO.GAL/65/98

7.   OSCE-FRY Kosovo Verification Mission Agreement, 16 October 1998

Preambular Language

Devoted to the respect of the principles of the UN Charter and to the Principles of the Helsinki Final Act on peace, stability and cooperation in Europe, as well as to the Paris Charter,

Considering in particular the importance of reaching a peaceful, democratic and lasting solution of all existing problems in the Province of Kosovo and Metohija, based on the equality of all citizens and national and ethnic communities,

Devoted to the respect of the sovereignty and territorial integrity of all states in the region,

Agreeing to comply with and willing to contribute to the FRY implementation of Resolutions 1160 and 1199 of the UN Security Council,

The Federal Government of the FR of Yugoslavia, on one side, and, The OSCE, on the other, have reached the following AGREEMENT:

Establishment and Termination

The OSCE Kosovo Verification Mission will be established by the OSCE Permanent Council pursuant to a resolution of the United Nations Security Council calling upon OSCE to establish the Mission.

The FRY government has informed the OSCE Chairman-in-Office of its endorsement of the establishment of the Mission.

OSCE will request member states to contribute personnel and funding for the Verification Mission in accordance with established procedures.

OSCE will establish coordination with other organizations it may deem appropriate to allow the Verification Mission to accomplish all its objectives most effectively.

KDOM will act in place of the OSCE Verification Mission pending its establishment. Once OSCE is operational, KDOM will be absorbed by the Verification Mission.

The FRY government hereby guarantees the safety and security of the Verification Mission and all its members.

In the event of an emergency situation in Kosovo which in the judgement of the Mission Director threatens the safety of members of the Verification Mission, the FRY shall permit and cooperate in the evacuation of Verification Mission members.

The FRY government will accept the OSCE Verification Mission as a diplomatic entity in terms of the Vienna Convention on Diplomatic Relations. The Mission will enjoy the privileges and immunities conferred by such status, as will its members, in accordance with the Vienna Convention.

The FRY government and its entities will designate formal liaison officers to work with the Verification Mission in Belgrade, Pristina and field locations. The FRY, Serbian and Kosovo authorities will undertake to provide full cooperation and support to the Verification

Mission. This will include, but not be limited to, billets, frequency or frequencies, visas and documentation, customs facilities, vehicle registration, fuel, medical support, airspace access for support aircraft and access to Belgrade, Pristina and other airports in accordance with normal procedures.

The OSCE and the FRY agree on a Verification Mission for one year, with extensions upon the request of either the OSCE Chairman-in-Office or the FRY government.

General Responsibilities, Roles and Missions

To verify compliance by all parties in Kosovo with UN Security Council Resolution 1199, and report instances of progress and/or non-compliance to the OSCE Permanent Council, the United Nations Security Council and other organizations. These reports will also be provided to the authorities of the FRY.

To establish permanent presences at as many locations throughout Kosovo as it deems necessary to fulfil its responsibilities;

To maintain close liaison with FRY, Serbian, and, as appropriate, other Kosovo authorities, political parties and other organizations in Kosovo and accredited international and non-governmental organizations to assist in fulfilling its responsibilities;

To supervise elections in Kosovo to ensure their openness and fairness in accordance with regulations and procedures to be agreed. For the elections, the Mission may be augmented with elections support personnel;

To report and make recommendations to the OSCE Permanent Council, the UN Security Council and other organizations on areas covered by UN Security Council Resolution 1199.

Specific Terms of Reference

The Verification Mission will travel throughout Kosovo to verify the maintenance of the cease-fire by all elements. It will investigate reports of cease-fire violations. Mission personnel will have full freedom of movement and access throughout Kosovo at all times.

The Verification Mission will receive weekly information from relevant FRY/Serbian military/police headquarters in Kosovo regarding movements of forces during the preceding week into, out of or within Kosovo. Upon request of the Verification Mission Director, Mission personnel may be invited to accompany police within Kosovo.

The Verification Mission will look for and report on roadblocks and other emplacements which influence lines of communication erected for purposes other than traffic or crime control. The Mission Director will contact the relevant authorities upon receipt of such reports. These authorities will explain the reasons for the emplacements or else direct that the emplacements be removed immediately. The Verification Mission will also receive notification should emergent circumstances lead to the establishment of a roadblock for other than traffic or crime control-related reasons. The Mission Director may request the removal of any roadblock.

The Verification Mission will maintain liaison with FRY authorities about border control activity and movements by units with border control responsibilities through areas of Kosovo away from the border. The Verification Mission, when invited by the FRY authorities or upon its request, will visit border control units and accompany them as they perform their normal border control roles.

When invited or upon request, the Verification Mission will accompany police units in Kosovo as they perform their normal policing roles.

The Verification Mission will, to the extent possible, assist UNHCR, ICRC and other international organizations in facilitating the return of displaced persons to their homes, the provision of facilitative and humanitarian assistance to them by the FRY, Serbian and Kosovo authorities as well as the humanitarian organizations and NGOs. The Mission will verify the level of cooperation and support provided by the FRY and its entities to the humanitarian organizations and accredited NGOs in facilitating procedural requirements such as issuance of travel documentation, expedited customs clearance for humanitarian shipments and radio frequencies. The Mission will make such representations as it deems necessary to resolve problems it observes.

As the political settlement defining Kosovoâ's self-government is achieved and implementation begins, the Mission Director will assist, both with his own resources and with augmented OSCE implementation support, in areas such as elections supervision, assistance in the establishment of Kosovo institutions and police force development in Kosovo.

The Mission Director will receive periodic updates from the relevant authorities concerning eventual allegations of abusive actions by military or police personnel and status of disciplinary or legal actions against individuals implicated in such abuses.

The Verification Mission will maintain liaison with FRY, Serbian and, as appropriate, Kosovo authorities and with ICRC regarding ICRC access to detained persons.

The Mission Director will, as required, convene representatives of national communities and authorities to exchange information and provide guidance on implementation of the agreement establishing the Verification Mission.

The Mission Director will report instances of progress and/or non-compliance or lack of full cooperation from any side to the OSCE and other organizations.

Composition and Facilities

A Director, together with headquarters staff to be determined by Verification Mission requirements.

2000 unarmed verifiers from OSCE member states will be permitted. Headquarters and support staff included in this total. The Mission may be augmented with technical experts provided by OSCE.

A headquarters in Pristina.

Field presence in locations around Kosovo to be determined by the Mission Director.

A small liaison office in Belgrade.

Vehicles, communications and other equipment along with locally-hired interpreters and support staff which the Director deems to be required for the performance of the responsibilities of the Mission.

Field Presence

Coordination centers will be established in the capitol of each opstina in Kosovo with specific areas of responsibility, under the Mission Director located in Pristina. Many opstina coordination centers will have one or more sub-stations in smaller towns/villages in the opstina. The number and location of sub-stations will vary from opstina to opstina, depending on the verification environment and past conflict situation.

The chief of each coordination center will maintain a liaison relationship with the opstina authorities and the local leadership of the ethnic Albanian and other communities. Each sub-station will be responsible for coordination with the local authorities including the local leadership of main ethnic groups.

The number of verification personnel assigned to each coordination center and sub-station would depend on the complexity of verification issues in the particular area. Each coordination center and sub-station would have appropriately configured vehicles with which to patrol its assigned area of responsibility.

For the Organization for Security and Cooperation in Europe H.E. Bronislaw Geremek, Chairman-in-Office; For the Federal Republic in Yugoslavia, H.E. Zivadin Jovanovic, Minister of Foreign

8. OSCE Appoints Head of Kosovo Verification Mission, Warsaw, 17 October 1998

The OSCE Chairman-in-Office, Minister Bronislaw Geremek, appointed today Ambassador William Graham Walker of the United States as Head of the OSCE Kosovo Verification Mission. Ambassador Walker has had a distinguished 37-year career in the Foreign Service, serving as Ambassador to El Salvador from 1988-92 and as Deputy Assistant Secretary of State from 1985-88. He also held diplomatic assignments in Bolivia, Honduras, Brazil, Japan and Peru. Most recently, he served as Special Representative of the UN Secretary General as head of the United Nations Transitional Administration for Eastern Slovonia (UNTAES), in Croatia. ...

9. Press Release, Foreign Ministers of the OSCE Troika Meet in Oslo, 21 October 1998

The OSCE Troika, the Foreign Minister of Poland, Bronislaw Geremek, the Foreign Minister of Norway, Knut Vollebaek and the Foreign Minister of Denmark, Niels Helveg Petersen, met here today to review pressing issues facing the OSCE. The Secretary General of the OSCE, Giancarlo Aragona, also took part. Their primary focus was on the progress toward establishing the OSCE Kosovo Verification Mission (KVM). The Ministers also reviewed a number of regional issues of particular concern to the OSCE and evaluated the work of several OSCE missions in the field. The Ministers expressed their satisfaction with the signing of the agreement between the OSCE Chairman-in-Office and the Federal Republic of Yugoslavia and their expectation that it will be rapidly implemented. They expressed the hope that the agreement will become a turning point in international efforts to bring about a peaceful settlement in Kosovo and expressed their determination to contribute their utmost to that effect. However, the Ministers were disturbed by reports of renewed fighting in Kosovo and urged both sides to abstain immediately from further use of force and work toward a peaceful settlement. The Ministers stressed the importance of ensuring the security of the KVM personnel. They called on both sides to live up to their responsibilities to this end. Also, Ministers agreed that close liaison with NATO shall be maintained. They welcomed the appointment of Ambassador William Walker as Head of the Mission. Ambassador Walker was also present at the meeting. The Ministers welcomed the offer from the Norwegian Government to assume responsibility for the set-up and operation of the Kosovo Mission headquarter in Pristina, in co-operation with the OSCE Secretariat. The Ministers were encouraged by the broad support of OSCE States for an OSCE role in Kosovo and appealed to them to contribute quickly to setting up the Mission and to strengthening the Secretariat. They were pleased that a technical assessment team had visited Belgrade and Kosovo, and that a KVM Support Unit in Vienna has been formed. They agreed that financing the KVM should be based on the scale of contributions for large Missions and projects adopted at the 1997 Copenhagen Ministerial. The Ministers also expressed the need for voluntary contributions to ensure that the Mission becomes operational as soon as possible. The Ministers also welcomed the initiative by the OSCE Office for Democratic Institutions and Human Rights (ODIHR) to convene a meeting in Warsaw with all organizations involved with human rights. The meeting should co-ordinate a strategy for human rights action in Kosovo. ...

OSCE Permanent Council, PC.SEC/263/98, 25 October 1998, 193rd Plenary Meeting, PC Journal No. 193, a.i. 1

10. OSCE Permanent Council Decision 263, 25 October 1998

The Permanent Council,

Acting in accordance with its Decision No. 259 (PC.DEC.259) and the agreement signed by the Chairman-in-Office of the OSCE and the Foreign Minister of the FRY (CIO.GAL/65/98),

Noting the United Nations Security Council Resolution 1203,

Decides:

1. To establish the Kosovo Verification Mission (KVM) in accordance with the mandate contained in the agreement signed by the CiO (CIO.GAL/65/98);

2. To authorize immediate start-up deployment of the KVM;

3. To establish the KVM for one year, with extensions upon the request of either the OSCE Chairman-in-Office or the FRY government;

4. To request hereby OSCE States to contribute Personnel and funding for the KVM in accordance with established procedures;

5. To task the Secretary-General, taking account of offers of voluntary contributions, to establish urgently the budget for the KVM for the approval of the Council.

11. Richard Holbrooke & William Walker, Press Conference, 28 October 1998

MR. RUBIN: Before turning the podium over to Ambassador Holbrooke, let me just introduce two people -- at least two people -- with him. First, we have Ambassador William Walker, who has the job of holding President Milosevic's feet to the fire in terms of compliance. It is his people who will be doing the verification. As we know, that is no easy task. He will run the Kosovo Verification Mission as soon as the OSCE gets it up and running. He is sitting to Ambassador Holbrooke's left. His success running the peace-keeping operation in eastern Slavonia and dealing, at that time, in *mano a mano* discussions with Milosevic and Tudjman make him the right choice to supervise the roughly 2,000 international personnel that will be allowed to verify compliance on security and humanitarian aspects. In addition, we have Ambassador Pardew, sitting to his left, who has been appointed by the Secretary as U.S. Special Representative for Kosovo Implementation. Actually, Assistant Secretary Marc Grossman made that appointment specifically. He will lead a team in the Bureau of European Affairs and will serve as the single point of contact in the Department for implementation issues related to Kosovo. He is currently U.S. Special Representative for Military Stabilization in the Balkans, and will continue to carry out those functions while assuming his new responsibilities for Kosovo. In addition, to his left, is Larry Rossin, the Office Director for Southern and Central Europe; and then my next-door neighbor, Jim O'Brien, is sitting over there, who is senior advisor to Secretary Albright, who has been assigned by the Secretary, with the strong encouragement of Ambassador Holbrooke, to go over and spend time with President Milosevic, along with Ambassador Hill, in trying to pull the necessary teeth to get progress on Kosovo in both the political and other sides. With that introduction, let me turn the podium over to Ambassador Holbrooke, who will bring others to the fore as appropriate.

AMBASSADOR HOLBROOKE: Thanks, Jamie. It's good to be back and to see you again. Let me try to give you a couple of brief headlines and then take your questions. In the last month, we have been conducting this intense negotiation with Belgrade, the outcome of which is now beginning to become apparent. I will review the details in a minute, but I want to make two overarching points.

First, what has been agreed to represents -- and here I'm not speaking only from my own point of view, but quoting such observers as *The Financial Times*, *The Economist* and Roger Cohen in *The New York Times*. What has been agreed to by Belgrade represents enormous concessions -- provided, of course, they're carried out; but I'll get to that in a minute. I stress this because there seems to be some doubt about that among some observers who talk about NATO blinking or comparing it to other parts of the world. So let me be clear -- starting in 1989, the authorities in Belgrade began taking the rights of the Albanian people in Kosovo away from them. The world protested; President Bush issued his famous Christmas warning, repeated by this Administration. But until the last month, nothing was done about it that was effective. In fact, Milosevic and his colleagues threw all international presence out of Kosovo in the early 1990s; took away property rights; broke down the Albanian police; and did immense -- I hope not irreparable -- damage to the Albanian political and social structure; and then this summer launched what can only be described as a rampage through the countryside of Kosovo.

The President of the United States, Secretary Albright, and other American officials made clear, starting early this year, how strongly they opposed what had happened. It was not until the last few days and weeks that we were able to achieve the present situation, which is a hell of a lot better than it was. What has happened, in a nutshell, is that the Kosovo problem has become internationalized; notwithstanding the fact that on April 23 of this year, a referendum was held in Serbia, where well over 90% of the people voted that there should be no foreign interference -- a referendum which Belgrade used as justification for keeping the OSCE and the international community out. All of this has now, I believe, begun to turn the other way.

Now, again, I stress, the proof is in the implementation. That is why Ambassador Walker, Ambassador Pardew and others have joined me here today, because Jamie Rubin and I wanted you to meet the team that's going to do the hard part, which is implementation. I would remind those of you who were at Dayton on November 21, 1995, that when we initialed that agreement I said that day that implementation is going to be the hard part. And as those of you who have read my book -- copies on sale in the lobby -- know, I consider the early implementation phase on the civilian side in Bosnia to have been a failure -- with consequences which were not reversed until Madeleine Albright and Jamie made their historic trip -- historic for different reasons -- in the spring of 1997.

The implementation is the key. But let's focus for a minute on what happened. We are going to have an air verification mission, which you have been fully briefed on. The radars will be turned off, the anti-aircraft will go into cold storage; we will fly when and where we wish. We are going to have 2,000 or more OSCE verifiers on the ground, and I want to stress a couple of points about them. First, they are verification people; they are compliance verifiers. I know you are not going to find that phrase in your dictionary; but they are not monitors, they are not observers. They are verifiers. Milosevic wanted the words observer and monitor. Those are bureaucratic babble words. Verification, compliance are active words. This is going to be a hands-on activist mission. And if you read the agreement -- and I hope that you all have read the agreement, I want to highlight a few points on it, and in a minute or two you will see that there is a significant mission here.

Second: I keep reading up to 2,000 or maybe we won't reach 2,000. Read the agreement -- it is 2,000 or more. Ambassador Walker has the right, under this agreement, to bring in any additional people at any time. I quote, "Two thousand unarmed verifiers from OSCE member states will be permitted, headquarters and support staff included. The mission may be augmented with technical experts provided by OSCE." President Milosevic and I agreed clearly that if Ambassador Walker wants more people to conduct elections -- and I stress the election will be conducted by OSCE -- or if he wants additional people to train local police, and that is one of his most important missions, he will get them. He doesn't need to apply for permission to go over 2,000; 2,000 is a floor, not a ceiling. So my second point is we have the ground verification system.

Point number three -- that ground verification system will include some extraordinarily important activities which I believe will reverse the trend of the last/next decade if implemented -- again, if implemented. Number one, we are going to supervise the elections within 9 months. Now, all of you who have been to Kosovo know that the Albanians are not going to trust an election conducted by the Serbs. But an internationally supervised election -- and the word is the word in the Dayton agreement, and any of you who covered the elections in Bosnia know that it would be run by OSCE -- know that that means internationally run. That's very important.

Secondly, the police will be -- local Albanian police -- will be trained and advised by OSCE. These are major events -- again, if implemented. But implementation has to be preceded by agreements, and the agreements, if they work, can retroactively and retrospectively later be regarded as turning points, perhaps, arguably, historic turning points. We can revisit that in a year or two. I stood at this podium after Bosnia and heard a lot of doubts about it and predictions that the fighting would resume. Three years later, the fighting hasn't resumed. Let's see how things go in Kosovo.

The fourth thing that has come out of the last few weeks is the explicit public description of Chris Hill and his team as the negotiators or mediators between the Albanian and Serb sides -- a tremendous step forward. As Jamie said a moment ago, Jim O'Brien is here today. He and Chris Hill are the senior members of the negotiating team. As we speak, Chris is in Pristina, in Kosovo, meeting with leading members of the Albanian factions. Jim is backstopping the effort here, along with Larry Rossin, who is the head of the office in the European Bureau. That is without question the most complicated part of this negotiation. And I wish to stress, we did not ask any Albanians to sign anything or agree to anything last week or the week before -- nothing -- nor did we sign or agree to anything with the Serbs. The announcement on the 11 points concerning politics was a unilateral announcement of the Belgrade authorities -- far short of what we think is desirable and necessary. But since it was a unilateral step in the right direction, if an inadequate step, it should be recognized as such. Those are the main ingredients of the process. I left one out I should add, and that is Macedonia -- F.Y.R.O.M. It is extremely important that there will be a NATO force in the country next door, The Former Yugoslav Republic of Macedonia. Secretary Albright discussed this for the first time in public yesterday. It's something that she and I have long believed, going back at least 2 or 3 years, was an essential concomitant of stability in the southern Balkans. The UNPREDEP forces there, including 300 Americans, are very important. An additional NATO force, which will not -- repeat, not -- include American combat troops, but may have a small American liaison cell of some sort, for obvious reasons, because we need uplinks to the NATO planes overhead and we need links to the American-led force in Bosnia and we need links to NATO headquarters elsewhere. But this force in The Former Yugoslav Republic of Macedonia is immensely important. Details cannot come from this podium -- they must come from NATO headquarters. The British and the French are in extended talks on this now. Secretary Albright has, if I'm not mistaken, Jamie, been in constant communication with Robin Cook and Hubert Vedrine and Solana on this point for the last week. I stress the importance of the announcement she made yesterday.

So those are the headlines. One last generic point: Foreign policy is not architecture, no matter what Dr. Brzezinski and others like to compare it to. In architecture, you make a plan down to the last nut, the last bolt, the last stress beam, and then you build the thing. Foreign policy, in my view, is more like jazz; it's an improvisation on a theme, and you change as you go along. Dean Acheson did not have a clear vision of what is now his legacy when he started out. He created the best he could taking account the domestic factors, Euro factors, the Russians, and so on. I want to stress that this is a work in progress, but it is of enormous historic consequence. It begins with this Administration's decisions to make the United States a resurgent presence in Europe, working in partnership in the post-Cold War world so that resurgence should not be misunderstood to mean unilateralism, working in close partnership with our NATO allies in enlarging NATO, in the Bosnia events, the bombing, IFOR, SFOR, and so on, and now Kosovo. History will decide how this movie comes out -- whether it succeeds or fails -- but Kosovo and Bosnia, while totally different in almost every technical detail, are bound together by the commonality of the area of the world they are in, by the core problem which emanates from the leadership in Belgrade and always has, and by the fact that the crises in Bosnia and Kosovo have required the United States to try to forge new rules and new alliances and new relationships for the post-Cold War world. These are of immense importance. We think that, if implemented successfully, what has happened this week will be of tremendous long-term importance. If it is not implemented successfully, the ACTORD is going to be reactivated. The threats which were essential to reach this point are still available and we have learned a lot in the last few weeks about how to pull together a situation without any precedent in NATO's history; and, although there were many bumps along the way, in the end the Alliance held together and performed very well. Let nobody in Belgrade or anywhere else misunderstand us: The coalition whose threat was credible and which will remain viable is ready to be reactivated at any time that the situation on the ground necessitates.

QUESTION: I want to invite you to "Take the A Train" with us -- the Albania train, speaking of jazz, and tell us if you would where that side of the equation is headed. Now, the U.S. Government says they're not in favor of independence, they're in favor of self-rule, but, for heaven's sake, only the U.S. was able to stop Milosevic. This has got to have improved the optimism of Albanians that they will be able to go beyond self-rule to a state. Isn't that likely to lead to a new flair-up, to new conflict? Nobody likes parallels because, as Albright says, we don't have a cookie-cutter foreign policy. You've restrained yourselves in the Middle East, although we know you are down the road to statehood for the Palestinians. Aren't you down the road to statehood for the Albanians? Do you think Milosevic is going to stand for that, especially *Anschluss* with Albania, or federation of Albania?

AMBASSADOR HOLBROOKE: Is this question about *Anschluss* or the Palestinians? (Laughter.)

QUESTION: The question is about the other side of this diagram, which you haven't addressed. What have you done for the Albanians? How can you stop them from pushing for statehood? Do you intend to and if you do, what's about to happen?

AMBASSADOR HOLBROOKE: First of all what has been done -- I don't want to use "we" because this was a collective effort that involved not only the United States but our allies and even the Russians. What has been achieved for the Albanians is, first of all, they are coming home out of the forests and the hills. Jim Pardew talked to Shaun Byrnes this morning again. The returns are continuing. There are some minor incidents along the way -- booby-trapped refrigerators, some booby-trapped foxholes. Jim tells me that some of the Serbs are cooperating and identifying them. But people are coming home and that's real -- that's not an abstraction of foreign policy. Serb police checkpoints are disappearing, and we are making real progress there. In regard to the political goals that you are talking about, Barry, I said a minute ago that these are the most difficult. It is demonstrably true that the core stated objective of most Albanian political leaders in Kosovo is independence, and that is not supported by the European Union, the United States, or any other international entity that I am aware of for many different reasons. That's a long-standing policy, and therefore we are going to have to sort this out as we go along. There's no way to answer your question except that everyone is aware of the dilemma and the problem.

QUESTION: The flash point?

AMBASSADOR HOLBROOKE: I don't think the flash point is the

difference in goals; that's well understood. I think the flash point, if there were one, would be if either side provoked the other deliberately in a way designed to re-escalate the fighting. Many of you have already written about the danger that fighting could break out again at any time and particularly in the spring. We're well aware of that problem. And when I said if implemented, repeatedly in my opening comments, that's what I was referring to. That could happen any time.

QUESTION: This force --

AMBASSADOR HOLBROOKE: But that -- excuse me for interrupting, that could happen any time. No, I'm not even going to say it's less likely. It's one of our major concerns; it is why the Administration and Madeleine Albright and myself, Marc Grossman, Chris Hill, Jim O'Brien, Larry Rossin have all been engaged, along with our colleagues at the NSC, in an intense evaluation of how to deal most effectively with people who are members of the UCK or the KLA. Shaun Byrnes has been in constant contact at the checkpoints and in the field with KLA commanders, talking to them, making clear to them that it takes two to have a cease-fire, insisting from them on guarantees for the safety of the OSCE verifiers. Larry Rossin has been having meetings all over Europe and the United States with people who have ties with the KLA to insist to them on the importance of this. This is a very important part of our policy. We do not ask people to renounce their dream of independence. But we do insist that they work within the framework of the UN resolution 1199 for peaceful resolution of it. If either side provokes the other into breaking down the cease-fire, we're going to have real problems.

QUESTION: Yesterday in talking about the force in Macedonia, the Secretary talked about the size and the limitations. She didn't talk about the role. It's since been described elsewhere as an extraction force. Is that what it's mean to be?

AMBASSADOR HOLBROOKE: I'm going to let NATO describe the force -- its mission, its size, its configuration, its leadership. All I want to say is its presence on the Yugoslav border is an enormously important part of stabilizing the region. What she said yesterday struck me as exactly correct.

QUESTION: On the subject of humanitarian situation, I understand from the experts at DOD that there are enough shelters for those who are now outdoors, coming back to their villages, to get by the winter -- stay warm enough to survive. There's going to be enough food, I believe, if there isn't already, on the ground. My basic question is, was this agreement -- did it come in time, really, to save the humanitarian disaster that was impending with the onset of winter?

AMBASSADOR HOLBROOKE: I think the answer to that is a qualified yes. Anyone who's still alive is not, in my view, in any danger anymore. That couldn't have been said a few weeks ago. Are you comfortable with that Larry? But a lot of people died already, including as recently as 2 or 3 days ago. For them, the disaster has already occurred. We just feel heartsick that we weren't standing up having this kind of briefing 3 or 4 months ago.

QUESTION: Have they got housing if they go back home?

AMBASSADOR HOLBROOKE: Yes, this is not Rwanda. There's been a tremendous amount of houses damaged, but there's a tremendous resilient spirit in the countryside. People are rebuilding as fast as they can. There is material down there. The UNHCR is out in force without any opposition. The OSCE document that we negotiated in Belgrade specifically empowers Ambassador Walker's Kosovo Verification Mission to assist the UNHCR and other humanitarian organizations -- a very minor point to all of you, but a very big point for anyone who ever was in Bosnia and watched the OSCE people refusing to help the UNHCR people 15 feet away because "it isn't in our mission." It is in the mission. So any one of the verification mission members can, at Bill Walker's direction, help on this issue.

QUESTION: I just want to understand better the policy now on political recognition of Kosovo independence. The starting point, from the Clinton Administration's point of view, is that one side wants independence and the other side doesn't want to give it, and they should negotiate from that point; is that correct?

AMBASSADOR HOLBROOKE: Well, no, it's a little more complicated than that. The international community's position, including our own, is that the boundaries of the Federal Republic of Yugoslavia, as currently shown on a map, are the correct boundaries. We are not supporting the separatist movement for independence; although I think everyone who knows the Kosovar Albanians understands their desire for it and has great sympathy for the motivations that led them there. The ultimate political settlement of the future is for the people themselves to work out. Chris Hill and Jim O'Brien are going to be the leaders of the team, now formally acknowledged -- even though they've been working for months, they'd always worked in a kind of a limbo status. Now they have been explicitly, formally announced

towards that resolution. It may take a while. It is far and away the toughest part of this. I described in my last press meeting, which was in Belgrade, I described the differences between the crisis and the emergency. The crisis is a decade old and hasn't been solved. That's the issue you're talking about -- the question of Kosovo. The emergency, which was caused by the summer rampage and which led us to the brink of war, now appears -- the resolution of the emergency appears to be within sight. By the way, I just want to take a diversion here. I saw a distinguished former ambassador of the United States say on television yesterday that NATO was bluffing. So let me just be very clear on something. When our team, Larry Rossin, Jim O'Brien, Chris Hill, General Short, General Thrasher, myself, Dick Miles, got to Belgrade, all of us thought that bombing was almost certainly going to happen. In the middle of our negotiations, we moved the B-52s forward to the U.K. -- not for theater but to get them ready for 6-hour deployment. I judged the chances of military action -- that is, an aerial war -- as well over 60% when we started. That was not a bluff. I want to be clear with everybody because it should be understood, especially in Belgrade. It was the credible threat of the use of force. The President, the Secretary of State, the Secretary of Defense, and NATO were all ready to move. The targets had been picked and we knew exactly where we were and we knew exactly how to get everyone out if we needed to. In fact, as you know, we did get everyone out.

QUESTION: The North Atlantic Council approved the Activation Order only after you visited the Council and briefed them on your deliberations. Some have said, including another former ambassador, that they may not have approved that Activation Order if you had not been able to give them as optimistic a report -- this is now that Monday -- as you were able to give them. Are you confident that they would have approved that Activation Order even if you had come back with, say, a less hopeful assessment?

AMBASSADOR HOLBROOKE: I'm a little confused by your comment. Jim, you came up with me to Belgrade, to Brussels. The way I envisage it -- Jim may have a different view -- I thought that there were only two possible choices that night: an Activation Order with a suspension, or an Activation Order without a suspension. It was what you call the optimistic report, and I would call a status report, that led the NAC to decide to do the Activation Order but tell General Clark to hold off on launching the planes. If we had given a totally bleak picture, absent the OSCE document, absent the air verification, then the bombing would have been authorized without a pause, and we would now be in the middle of an aerial war. So that's how I remember it. So whoever has talked to you, I think, is perhaps a little out of sync. Is that your memory, Jim?

QUESTION: The idea being that perhaps some allies approved that in the belief that they were already convinced it wouldn't be necessary.

AMBASSADOR HOLBROOKE: That's in their minds. These are ambassadors in a room with a round table doing what they are instructed. The real heavy lifting was being done by the Secretary of State and Jim Steinberg, Sandy Berger and others -- even from the Wye Plantation, by the way -- to make sure the key allies were on board. We had to make sure the Russians understood what was happening. And there was a New York component. The only choices that night were to bomb or to authorize bombing and give an additional pause for compliance; there was no third choice. What you call the optimistic report, which was two pieces of paper -- this is one of them -- and Geremek was there too that night, remember, so we briefed Geremek for the first time. He was stunned by it, but very enthusiastic. That led immediately to Ambassador Walker's designation by Madeleine as the head of this mission. All of this created the sense that maybe the credible threat of NATO use of force was going to produce a result, but we weren't quite there yet -- so let's keep the planes aimed at our targets, but not quite have them start down the runways yet. That's what happened. After the 96 hours ran out, a lot of the people in this room or elsewhere reported that NATO had blinked and made invidious comparisons to other parts of the world and said that we had given them a reprieve. But that was not at all what the Administration and NATO thought they were doing. What the Administration and NATO were intending was to keep the pressure on Belgrade. Somehow it came out quite the opposite -- I remember reading the paper Saturday a week ago, reading the newspapers and kind of saying, this is amazing; the newspaper account is 180 degrees off the intention. So we had a bad week with you guys because you thought NATO had blinked.

QUESTION: You didn't talk to us.

AMBASSADOR HOLBROOKE: That's true, I didn't talk to you, Sid. But that's personal, so -- (laughter). No, I didn't talk to you because I really didn't think it was necessary. I thought what was happening was so clear. I had done the media the first day and then I had gone off and done other things. But when that happened, we all realized that there had been a miscommunication with the public and with the press. I hope at least now, retrospectively, you all understand what happened. The extension after the 96 hours was because there was no way he could get his forces back that quickly. The KLA was still in the field doing a lot of stuff which made it complicated. Who started this incident in Malisevo? Are you going to start bombing because of an argument at a checkpoint that turned into a shooting match, when that shooting match may well have been started by an Albanian, you don't know? We had to sort out. But we wanted to keep the pressure on, and that's what happened.

QUESTION: You said a few moments ago that you feel heartsick that you weren't here 3 or 4 months ago. Why didn't that happen 3 or 4 months ago? And I have a follow-up.

AMBASSADOR HOLBROOKE: Oh, God, that is -- I'm sorry I said that. Heartsick because if we had been here 3 or 4 months ago, we wouldn't have had all that destruction, that photograph of all those burned-out buildings, people who died, a polarization of a society that was already ripped to hell by this thing. Your question is why weren't we here?

QUESTION: Why weren't you there 3 or 4 months ago?

AMBASSADOR HOLBROOKE: Well, now that we're in a position we feel pretty good about, I don't want to go back and do a blame-game business. But it was a combination of several factors. I would lump all of them except the Russian factor, which is separate -- and you're all aware of that -- under one general headline, which is called "democracies take a while to get their act together." At the risk of repeating something I've said from this podium before, it takes a while for democracies to get their act together; but when they get it together, they have more strength and unity and effectiveness than anyone else. The British and the French and the Germans had a very well-publicized view -- and you're all aware of this -- that NATO's action required a prior UN Security Council resolution. That was not our view, but we had to work that through and it took time. That was, I think, something that Madeleine Albright spent most of the summer on. And there were other factors. So it took a little while longer than it should have, just as it did in Bosnia. But in Bosnia, it took 4 years longer than it should have. Kosovo, I would put the time delay at something like 12 to 15 weeks. If you compare the two crises and the American-led NATO alliance response, I think it's demonstrably true that we're doing better. The Russians are working more closely with us; the British and the French are sorting it out. A very key factor was the German election. But then President Clinton saw Gerhard Schroeder at that decisive meeting on Friday 2 weeks ago, and the next morning Jim O'Brien and Chris Hill and I went in to see Milosevic and we said, "The Germans are on board and any residual thought you had that the election in Germany would change the outcome, forget it." At that point, Prodi's Government fell and other people were saying, aha, okay, now we have a crisis in Rome. The Italians said it doesn't matter. All of this takes time; that's what I mean by democracies.

QUESTION: When you said that you're not asking people to give up the dream of independence, are you -- it sounds to me like you might be holding the door a open a little bit more than you had in the past to perhaps the United States --

AMBASSADOR HOLBROOKE: No, you misread me. We are not supporting independence. But I am not going to stand up here and tell people who dream about it that they shouldn't dream that dream. I just want to be honest. Larry Rossin and I and Jim have spent a lot of time with the Albanian-American leadership in the United States -- in New York and elsewhere. They all understand this. They all want independence; they understand our position and within that agreement to disagree we're trying to work out ways we can all go forward together.

QUESTION: Can I just follow up on that? If you're going to mediate between the two parties -- if you're not, then say so -- then by definition you have to go into that without a position. In other words, leaving open the possibility that the two parties could agree on independence. How do you square that?

AMBASSADOR HOLBROOKE: I would say that chances of that happening range from zero to zero.

QUESTION: Which -- mediation or --

AMBASSADOR HOLBROOKE: No, that the two parties would agree to independence. There is no possible chance that Belgrade will agree to independence. I'm not speaking on behalf of the Belgrade authorities; I'm just giving you a self-evident fact.

QUESTION: Just to follow up on the point of why something couldn't have been done earlier, you said you put the time frame at 12 to 15 weeks. But why couldn't the war have been prevented before it even started, back in February, when the Secretary said that the United States was not going to

allow what happened in Bosnia to happen in Kosovo? Why couldn't preventative action have been taken?

AMBASSADOR HOLBROOKE: Well, first of all, let's be clear -- what the Secretary said did turn out. What happened in Kosovo is not what happened in Bosnia. Bosnia had 300,000 killed and 2.5 million homeless. As a percentage of population, what happened in Kosovo is far, far smaller. Nonetheless, I take your point. If you want to change my number from 15 weeks and backdate it to February -- I don't know how many additional weeks that is -- I accept it; because my own personal concern has run much longer than that. But in February, the fighting had not yet reached a very significant level. I was thinking of the -- my first trip out there was in May with Bob Gelbard, then I went out again in June; I went out in July. We could just see it coming, and we couldn't stop it.

QUESTION: I guess my sort of question is, why, instead of waiting for the fire to break out, why can't action be taken to prevent it from breaking out in the first place?

AMBASSADOR HOLBROOKE: I answered that question -- I think it was your question. You're the one who asked why it took us so long. I've answered already, Michael. It takes a while for the democracies to get their act together, particularly when you also have to work with the Russians and you have all these different issues -- the UN, NATO, and so on. I'm not defending that delay. It drove Madeleine Albright and I and the people sitting along that wall who were then involved in policy such as Jim O'Brien and Larry Rossin, when he joined the team, and Jim Pardew, who is watching from his equip-and-train perch from Bosnia, we were doing everything we could to move forward the process for it. But let me say this -- without yielding to what is sometimes criticized in Europe as American triumphalism, I don't think it is unfair to say that without the leadership of the Administration of the United States, we would not be where we are today. There were a lot of factors involved. By the way there is another factor we haven't mentioned which is important, which is the congressional factor. ...

QUESTION: On the same subject, how do you assess the role of Greece to diffuse the crisis -- (inaudible) --

AMBASSADOR HOLBROOKE: Ah, yes, well, thank you; finally a question on your subject that I will answer. (Laughter.) We were very gratified by the position of the Greek Government, very gratified. Foreign Minister Pangalos made calls to Belgrade during the crisis making absolutely clear to the Yugoslav authorities that Greece was part of NATO and would support the process, although with certain specific reservations that they had with their own right. Because of the special ties between Greeks and Serbs, the fact that the Greeks were so supportive was something that we deeply appreciated. Ambassador Burns -- in fact Ambassador Hill went down to Athens to see the Greek Government in that regard. ...

QUESTION: Ambassador Walker, your verifiers are unarmed and presumably out among the population. What happens if things go sour? How are you going to protect them?

AMBASSADOR WALKER: I think Ambassador Holbrooke has mentioned the force that will be in Macedonia next door. I think we are taking a good look at that as to how it might react in terms of an extraction in case things really go wrong or something less than that if it is not quite as serious as I think you are implying.

QUESTION: Will they at any point be accompanied by any armed people?

AMBASSADOR WALKER: Verifiers? No, the agreement is my verifiers will be unarmed.

QUESTION: They can't be accompanied by paramilitary police or whatever?

QUESTION: (Inaudible) -- Serb police to protect your people?

AMBASSADOR WALKER: Let me preface my remarks by saying that I've been in the job for exactly 9 days -- of which 5 were spent going to some of these places that Ambassador Holbrooke and the other fellows sitting on the wall there have spent the better part of their last year or two in. I spent a couple of hours with President Milosevic and we went over this point. He accepts, as he did in the agreement, responsibility for the safety, security, well-being and very lives of the verifiers. So up until we have evidence to the contrary, we will take that assurance. But other people are looking at other options, should his compliance not be total.

QUESTION: (Inaudible) -- emergency evacuation?

AMBASSADOR WALKER: Yes, exactly.

12. **Council of Europe, Final Communique, 103rd Session of the Committee of Ministers, Strasbourg, 3-4 November 1998**

... The Ministers expressed concern about the situation in the Federal Republic of Yugoslavia and, in particular, Kosovo. They encouraged their Chairman and the Secretary General to pursue contacts with the OSCE to discuss ways in which the Council of Europe might participate in the international monitoring of human rights and in contributing to democratisation in general, as well as with other relevant international organisations and countries of the region.

PC.DEC/266, PC Journal No. 196, Agenda item 1

13. **Organization for Security and Co-operation in Europe, Permanent Council Decision No. 266, 11 November 1998**

The Permanent Council,
Recalling Decision No. 8 of the Copenhagen Ministerial Council (MC(6).DEC/8),
Recalling its Decisions Nos. 260 (PC.DEC/260), 263 (PC.DEC/263) and 265 (PC.DEC/265) on the establishment and funding of the Kosovo Verification Mission (KVM),
  - Approves the 1998 budget for the KVM in the amount of ATS 756,530,264 as set out at Annex 1. The budget will be implemented on the basis of the proposal circulated by the Secretary General on 9 November 1998 (PC.IFC/75/98). The post table for the KVM Secretariat augmentation and the international contracted staff in Kosovo is attached at Annex 2;
  - Calls upon participating States, partners for co-operation, Mediterranean partners for co-operation and other States, as well as international organizations and institutions, to consider making voluntary contributions, including in-kind contributions, towards this budget;
  - Decides that in-kind contributions from participating States of items specifically requested by the KVM and contained in this budget may, exceptionally and without precedent, be credited against assessed contributions, in accordance with procedures to be established by the Secretary General.
This budget shall be billed in accordance with the provisions of the Decision on a scale for large OSCE missions and projects (MC(6).DEC/8). The residual financing, if any, once voluntary contributions have been taken into account, shall be billed following the presentation of a report from the Secretary General on the state of expenditures under this budget. [*An annex listing expected expenditure has been omitted.*]

MC(7).JOUR/2 , 2 December 1998, Annex 1

14. **Organization for Security and Co-operation in Europe Ministerial Council Declaration, Oslo, 2 December 1998**

I. We have discussed the challenges to security in our region, the OSCE's contribution to meeting them and how this can be developed in future. We stress the need for the international community to develop co-ordinated responses to such challenges. 1998 has been an important year in this regard, including for the OSCE. The crisis in Kosovo has come to the forefront of the OSCE's concerns and action. We urge the parties to stop all violence and to co-operate in the negotiation of a political settlement. The Kosovo Verification Mission (KVM) is the largest and most difficult operation ever put into the field by the OSCE. It marks the international community's recognition of the Organization's developing potential and expertise to contribute to security. Success for the KVM requires not only the use of internal mechanisms for transparent consultations, but also effective co-operation with other inter-governmental bodies, as well as with non-governmental organizations; and it requires adequate allocation of resources by participating States. ....

MC(7).JOUR/2, 2 December 1998, Annex 2

15. **OSCE Ministerial Council Statement on Kosovo, Oslo, 2 December 1998**

The plight of so many people in Kosovo caught up in violent confrontation and fleeing their homes in fear has moved us all.

Involvement in Kosovo represents a challenge and an opportunity for the OSCE. It shows that security, democracy, human rights and fundamental freedoms are inseparable.

Thanks to the vigorous efforts of the international community, including the OSCE, there is now a ceasefire. It is still fragile, but it marks a great step forward. Displaced persons and refugees are starting to return to their homes. Now further diplomatic efforts are underway to find a political solution. Those efforts have our strong support.

There is still violence in Kosovo, and this is of deep concern to us. We urge all parties involved to stop the violence and to resolve their differences by peaceful means. We urge the FRY authorities, Serbian authorities and all Kosovo Albanians to co-operate in the search for a political settlement, so that substantial political dialogue could start as soon as possible. The international community is determined to help. But only the parties can overcome their differences. The sooner they do so, the sooner the reconstruction and development of Kosovo can make headway.

United Nations Security Council Resolutions 1160 and 1199 set out what is required of the parties to bring the confrontation to an end. Those resolutions have confirmed also the need to respect the sovereignty and the territorial integrity of the FRY, while securing a political settlement for Kosovo, involving substantive, broad and meaningful self-administration. The OSCE has taken on the task of verifying that all parties are complying with these Resolutions.

The OSCE is setting up its largest ever operation, the Kosovo Verification Mission. Besides verifying compliance, the KVM will help to implement the political settlement to be reached by the parties by supervising elections, providing support in building up democratic institutions and assisting with police force development in Kosovo. We intend to do this effectively, and in a manner in which the views of governments contributing to KVM are taken fully into account.

The head of the KVM, Ambassador Walker, his team and the OSCE Secretariat have worked very hard in the past few weeks to establish the Mission. Numbers are building up quickly. We encourage all those involved to continue their excellent work. The OSCE will continue to work in close co-ordination with other international organizations and NGOs involved in the international effort in Kosovo.

We urge all parties to the conflict to respect the ceasefire, to comply fully with relevant Security Council Resolutions, and to co-operate closely with the KVM so that it can carry out its duties unimpeded throughout Kosovo. The OSCE, for its part, will respect fully the terms of the agreement on the establishment of the KVM signed by Foreign Minister Geremek as the CiO, and Foreign Minister Jovanovic. We stress that its implementation will be important for any future consideration of FRY participation in the OSCE.

The staff of the KVM must be able to carry out their duties safely. The OSCE verifiers are not a fighting force. Although their true protection is compliance by all parties with the terms of agreement, security must be in place to protect them. The OSCE welcomes the commitment of other organizations to provide assistance and protect the OSCE and its verifiers in its mission in Kosovo, in case it would be required.

It is our hope and belief that the KVM will make the path to a settlement to the conflict in Kosovo easier. We will continue to give it our full support. But it is for the parties themselves to go down that path and to ensure that Kosovo can look forward to a peaceful future.

B.   Events following upon the Establishment of the Verification Mission

S/1998/966 19 October 1998

1.   Letter from the UN Secretary-General to the President of the Security Council, 19 October 1998

As you will recall, in your statement to the press on 6 October 1998 on behalf of the Security Council, you asked me to consider how to ensure that the Secretariat had a first-hand capability to assess developments on the ground, and to continue reporting to the Council on compliance with its resolutions 1160 (1998) and 1199 (1998).

Following consultations with the authorities of the Federal Republic of Yugoslavia, I wish to inform the Security Council of my intention to send an interdepartmental mission, headed by Staffan de Mistura, to the Federal Republic of Yugoslavia to look into these matters. In view of the proposed deployment of Organization for Security and Cooperation in Europe (OSCE) monitors in Kosovo to observe compliance, the mission will also assess possible modalities for coordination of activities between OSCE and United Nations agencies on the ground.

(Signed) Kofi A. ANNAN

2.   UN Inter-Agency Update on Kosovo Situation, 21 October 1998

... 3. The text of the Agreement on the OSCE Kosovo Verification Mission addresses humanitarian issues as follows: " The Verification Mission will, to the extent possible, assist UNHCR, ICRC and other international organisations in facilitating the return of displaced persons to their homes, the provision of facilitative and humanitarian assistance to them by the FRY, Serbian and Kosovo authorities as well as the humanitarian organisations and NGOs. The Mission will verify the level of co-operation and support provided by the FRY and its entities to the humanitarian organisations and accredited NGOs in facilitating procedural requirements such as issuance of travel documentation, expedited customs clearance for humanitarian shipments and radio frequencies. The Mission will make such representations as it deems necessary to resolve problems it observes."

4. The Agreement on the OSCE Kosovo Verification Mission also makes provision for ICRC's detention work: "The Verification Mission will maintain liaison with FRY, Serbian and, as appropriate, Kosovo authorities and with ICRC regarding ICRC access to detained persons." It is also intended that the Verification Mission, which will have an initial lifespan for one year, will provide support in areas such as elections supervision, assistance in the establishment of Kosovo institutions and police force development in Kosovo.

5. At the meeting of the OSCE Permanent Council on 15 October representatives from both UNHCR and OSCE emphasised the importance of maintaining a coordinated approach to the Kosovo crisis in order to pave the way for a political settlement and lasting peace. Discussions are ongoing to determine in more detail the respective roles and responsibilities of UNHCR and OSCE in Kosovo.

United Nations Assessment Mission in FRY

6. In response to the request of the Security Council in the President's statement to the press, and in lieu of a personal visit, the UN Secretary-General has despatched a mission to FRY to consider how to ensure that the UN Secretariat has a first-hand capability to assess developments in FRY and to continue reporting to the Security Council on compliance with resolutions 1160 and 1199. The mission will assess present and proposed arrangements for cooperation and information-sharing among UN entities, the OSCE and other international actors present in the region. The mission will also assess the current situation in Kosovo and investigate the possibilities for expanding the UN presence in Kosovo, if so requested by Member States. The mission will take place from 17-24 October and will travel to Belgrade, Kosovo and Montenegro. The mission includes representatives from the political, peace-keeping, humanitarian and human rights components of the United Nations system.

UN Humanitarian Strategy for Kosovo

7. On 14 -15th October the UNHCR Special Envoy for former Yugoslavia chaired an Interagency Regional Strategic Planning meeting in Sarajevo. The meeting included UN agency representatives from Sarajevo, Belgrade, Zagreb, Tirana, Skopje and Geneva. The International Council of Voluntary Agencies (ICVA) was also present to represent the views of the NGOs. The participants of the meeting welcomed the recent political progress made with regard to Kosovo and, after extensive discussion, decided to revise humanitarian strategy in Kosovo as follows:

Strategy within Kosovo

to promote and assist the safe return of the displaced to their homes, or to host families where their homes are too severely damaged; to provide the necessary humanitarian assistance to all the affected population (food, blankets, mattresses, stoves etc); to provide immediate winterisation of damaged dwellings -- to a minimum of one room weatherproof; to support self-help house repairs; to ensure Serbian authorities deliver promised material assistance; to restore essential services (electricity, water and restocking/repair of health clinics); to support reactivation of education and extend winterisation assistance to damaged schools; and to support seeds programmes for spring planting.

Strategy outside Kosovo

Assistance should continue to be given to the estimated existing Kosovo Albanian caseload in Albania, Bosnia and Herzegovina, FYROM, Montenegro and other parts of Serbia until Spring, with return taking place thereafter. If earlier return is possible resources would be shifted to Kosovo as necessary.

Population Movements

8. Humanitarian agencies have reported that the onset of winter, epitomised by the first light snow fall in Kosovo on 14th October, has obliged increasing numbers of displaced living under plastic in the hills and mountains to seek shelter, despite their continuing security-related concerns. Many of those dislocated from their homes have now sought refuge in major towns such as Podujevo, Mitrovica, Vucitrn, Urosevac and Pristina. In these towns many of the houses contain three to four times the number of their original occupants. Barns are used for shelter and tents and covered wagons can be seen in the courtyards of many homes. The Kosovo Diplomatic Observer Mission (KDOM) also reported increased IDP returns, particularly in the areas of Malisevo, Orahovac, Suva Reka, Djakovica and Decani, as well as in the Drenica region. However, there has also been some renewed displacement in the Malisevo area and in the area South of Komorane and Lapusnik in the wake of skirmishes between Government forces and the KLA over the weekend of 17-18 October during which 3 Serbian policemen were reportedly killed and 4 wounded. ...

UNHCR Estimated Kosovo Displacement / Refugee Figures:
(as at 13 October 1998)

Kosovo[1]	200,000
Montenegro[2]	42,000
Other parts of Serbia	20,000
Bosnia Herzegovina[3]	8,600
Albania[4]	20,500
Turkey[5]	2,000
Slovenia[6]	2,000
FYROM[7]	3,000
TOTAL	298,100

[1] Estimated figure based on information from various organisations in Kosovo.

[2] Average based on figures provided by the Montenegrin Ministry of Interior and the Montenegrin Red Cross.

[3] UNHCR estimate.

[4] Figures provided by Albanian Government's Office for Refugees and endorsed by UNHCR..

[5] UNHCR estimate.

[6] UNHCR estimate.

[7] Estimate of those whose presence is directly linked to the conflict in Kosovo.

... MONTENEGRO

22. Although cross-border movement of Kosovo displaced remains fluid with Kosovo Albanians both entering and leaving Montenegro,

there has been a higher level of return during the period under review than vice versa. On 17th October the Montenegrin Commissioner for Displaced Persons reported that 5,000 Kosovo displaced had returned to their areas of origin since the start of the talks between Ambassador Holbrooke and President Milosevic. The police in Rozaje told UNHCR that 60-70 displaced per day were currently returning to Kosovo via mountain paths. The police attributed this movement to the poor living conditions of the displaced in mountain villages. On the other hand some sources in Plav and Rozaje reported a continuing influx of displaced. On one occasion a woman and 10 children were sent back to Kosovo by the Montenegrin border police suggesting that Government pledges to treat the most vulnerable displaced in a "flexible" manner had not been communicated to the appropriate border officials. UNHCR and the Government of Montenegro are currently planning a joint re-registration programme to determine the numbers of Kosovo displaced more accurately. ...

ALBANIA

26. UNHCR's office in Kukes in North-east Albania reports that approximately 100 Kosovars crossed into Albania through Zogaj (opposite Dakovica) during the past week. There was little evidence of any refugees returning into Kosovo and many of those interviewed expressed a reluctance to return to their destroyed houses during the Winter. The slowdown in the refugee influx into Albania during the past week is attributable to fears of an increased prevalence of landmines at the border as well as an improvement in security conditions in Kosovo. During the past week five refugees were reportedly killed and three wounded in separate mine-related incidents at the border near Kukes.

3. UN Inter-Agency Update on Kosovo Situation, 28 October 1998

UN Security Council Resolution 1203 (1998)

1. Acting under Chapter VII of the UN Charter, which allows for enforcement, the United Nations Security Council on 24th October endorsed and supported the agreements signed in Belgrade on 16 October by the Federal Republic of Yugoslavia and the Organization for Security and Cooperation in Europe (OSCE), and on the following day by FRY and the North Atlantic Treaty Organization (NATO). The Russian Federation and China abstained on the text, which was adopted with 13 votes in favour as Resolution 1203 (1998).

2. The Security Council demanded that the Federal Republic of Yugoslavia comply fully and swiftly with its resolutions on Kosovo, and cooperate fully with the OSCE Verification Mission and with the NATO Air Verification Mission in accordance with agreements reached. The Council also demanded that the Kosovo Albanian leadership and all other elements of the Kosovo Albanian community comply fully and swiftly with its resolutions and cooperate with the OSCE Verification Mission.

3. With respect to humanitarian issues, the Security Council demanded immediate action from the Belgrade authorities and the Kosovo Albanian leadership to cooperate with international efforts to improve the humanitarian situation and to avert the impending humanitarian catastrophe. The Council also called on the FRY Government and the Kosovo Albanian leadership to take all steps to ensure that international and humanitarian personnel are not subjected to the threat or use of force. Reaffirming the right of all refugees and displaced persons to return to their homes in safety, the Council underlined the Federal Republic of Yugoslavia's responsibility in creating the necessary conditions towards that end. The Council also urged Member States and others concerned to provide adequate resources for humanitarian assistance in the region and to respond promptly and generously to the UN Inter-Agency Consolidated Appeal for Humanitarian Assistance Related to the Kosovo Crisis.

Compliance with UN Security Council Resolution 1199

4. On 27 October the Kosovo Diplomatic Observer Mission (KDOM) reported that approximately 4,500 Serbian police had left Kosovo during the course of the previous day. KDOM Team Orahovac reported that Serbian security forces had withdrawn from the area between Orahovac and Malisevo and reduced their presence almost to February

1999 levels. KDOM Team Prizren noticed a "massive pulll-out" of police and military forces from the area between Prizren and Pristina. KDOM in Mitrovica reported a similar large-scale reduction in police and military presence in their area of operations.

Returns

5. There are clear indications that the retreat of the Serbian security forces has encouraged many displaced to return to their areas of origin. However, at the time of writing the international humanitarian community has not yet had the opportunity to verify with any accuracy the true extent of return since the reduction of the police presence in Kosovo. The plight of the estimated 3,500 displaced living rough in the hills at Kisna Reka has attracted a high level of publicity. In a recent meeting with Mr Andjelkovic, Prime Minister of Kosovo's Temporary Executive Committee, UNHCR was informed that the displaced would be able to return to their villages in the Komorane area after the withdrawal of the police from the area. There have also been reports that the Kosovo Liberation Army (KLA) has been moving into areas vacated by the security forces in the Drenica area.

6. UN agencies and NGOs in Kosovo are planning an interagency survey on a municipality by municipality basis over the next few weeks in an attempt to gather more reliable information on the number of displaced, conflict-affected families and returns in each region.

Security of Humanitarian Personnel

7. Threats to the security of humanitarian personnel working in Kosovo remain. On 23 October KLA soldiers in uniform started shooting at a relief convoy on the outskirts of Jablanica. They immediately stopped when they realised that they were firing at a UNHCR vehicle. On 27 October a UNHCR team travelling near Malisevo noted that a vacated police station appeared to be booby-trapped. ...

UNHCR Estimated Kosovo Displacement / Refugee Figures:
(as at 13 October 1998)

Kosovo	200,000
Montenegro	42,000
Other parts of Serbia	20,000
Bosnia Herzegovina	8,600
Albania	20,500
Turkey	2,000
Slovenia	2,000
FYROM	3,000
TOTAL	298,100

...

Human Rights

14. The United Nations Office of the High Commissioner for Human Rights (OHCHR) has finalised a Status Agreement with the FRY Government. The Agreement provides for standard privileges and immunities as well as full freedom of movement and access throughout the country for human rights related activities and confirms OHCHR's status as the sole international organisation with a broad mandate for human rights protection and promotion throughout FRY. OHCHR plans to strengthen its activities in Kosovo through the deployment of additional human rights officers.

Health

15. The UNICEF office in the Federal Republic of Yugoslavia has received a US$ 500,000 loan from its internal Emergency Programme Fund. The loan will e used to enhance UNICEF's capacity to respond to the crisis in Kosovo and will hopefully be reimbursed through contributions made against the forthcoming UN Consolidated Appeal. The loan will be used to meet the needs of women and children in four different areas; the provision of winter clothing and shoes for children; the provision of immunisation supplies (including cold chain inputs, syringes and needles and measles vaccines) for approximately 150,000 children; the promotion of breast feeding and printing of guidelines on infant feeding in emergencies; and the provision of water containers and baby hygiene items. UNICEF will also strengthen its field presence through the deployment of additional international staff to its offices in Pristina and Podgorica.

MONTENEGRO

16. UN interagency assessments in Plav and Rozaje have revealed that relatively few displaced children from Kosovo are benefiting from

education. According to the director of the Gusinje primary school (near Plav) there are currently only 60 displaced children from Kosovo in primary schools in the Gusinje area. In Rozaje municipality, which includes 28 villages, only 35 displaced are attending school in the area. During the mission UNICEF distributed winter jackets to the school children in Gusinje and Rozaje. The Danish Refugee Council is helping UNICEF to distribute school equipment to displaced children in the mountainous area near Plav and Rozaje.

ALBANIA

17. After deliberations with UNHCR, IFRC, the Albanian Red Cross (ARC) and the Ministry of Local Governments, WFP and ARC have decided to resume the October food aid distribution in Tropoje district in Northern Albania. Distributions were halted on 12 October due to poor security and distribution and the Ministry of Local Government has pledged to work with the police to ensure security in the area where the distributions will take place. UNHCR, WFP and ARC believe that the estimated 2,500 Kosovo Albanians remaining in Tropoje district are among the most vulnerable of the refugee population in Albania.

18. WFP and other food supply agencies have drafted a food distribution plan for the month of November in Albania. WFP estimates that it will provide rations to 7,000 of the 21,000 refugees registered in Albania. WFP will continue to support a bakery project which provides bread on a daily basis to 5,700 refugees in the Durres area. ...

S/1998/1068, 12 November 1998

4.   Report of the Secretary-General, 12 November 1998

... IV. SITUATION IN KOSOVO

5. This section of the report is based on information provided by the Chairman-in-Office of OSCE (annex I), the European Union, NATO (annex II), the Kosovo Diplomatic Observer Mission and individual Member States. It also draws upon the report of a United Nations mission to the Federal Republic of Yugoslavia that visited the region from 17 to 27 October 1998 (hereinafter referred to as the United Nations mission; see sect. V), as well as contributions provided by the Office of the United Nations High Commissioner for Refugees and the United Nations High Commissioner for Human Rights.

Political framework

6. The accord reached by the President of the Federal Republic of Yugoslavia, Slobodan Milosevic, and the United States Special Envoy, Richard Holbrooke, on 13 October 1998 (see S/1998/953, annex), as well as the agreements signed in Belgrade on 15 October 1998 between the Federal Republic of Yugoslavia and NATO, and on 16 October 1998 between the Federal Republic of Yugoslavia and OSCE, have contributed towards defusing the immediate crisis situation in Kosovo and have created more favourable conditions for a political settlement.

7. The authorities of the Federal Republic of Yugoslavia welcomed the Agreement of 16 October establishing the Kosovo Verification Mission and indicated their readiness to cooperate fully with the Mission. They pledged to ensure full freedom of movement for the Kosovo Verification Mission monitors and undertook to inform them of possible dangers. The Minister of the Interior of Serbia, in particular, indicated the Government's intention to inform the Mission promptly of all incidents that might occur in the region excluding, however, incidents that the authorities might classify as "criminal activity".

8. Government officials informed the United Nations mission that they were considering holding elections in Kosovo in about nine months. The Kosovo Executive Council, that is, the local administration established by the Government, had recently became functional, albeit with no Kosovo Albanian participation. The Deputy Prime Minister of the Federal Republic of Yugoslavia indicated to the United Nations mission the need for joint national and international efforts to address the humanitarian situation in Kosovo and pledged to promote active cooperation with humanitarian organizations on the ground to that end.

9. The Kosovo Albanian leaders, in their contacts with the United Nations mission, expressed reservations about the 13 October accord and the 16 October agreement, although they appreciated the fact that Kosovo was no longer considered to be exclusively an internal problem of the Federal Republic of Yugoslavia. They still insisted on their right to self-determination and signalled their continuing wish for an international armed presence on the ground.

10. The position of Kosovo Albanian paramilitary units remained unclear. The authorities of the Federal Republic of Yugoslavia expressed concern that members of those units might try to provoke the police and military in Kosovo and trigger a reaction from the Government. The Kosovo Albanian leaders indicated, with various degrees of certainty, that Kosovo Albanian paramilitary units would respect the 13 October accord by and large. Nonetheless, they could not rule out the possibility that some small splinter armed groups might continue attacks, thus giving the authorities of the Federal Republic of Yugoslavia a pretext for violent retaliation.

Recent military situation

11. Both the parties to the conflict and the international observers on the ground acknowledge that the military situation has stabilized recently and that, despite some serious but isolated incidents, there has been no major fighting since 1 October. Many local people indicated to the United Nations mission that the situation had improved in the two weeks following the ceasefire, although several villages had reportedly been destroyed recently by the Serbian police. Tensions persist, however, in many areas dominated by Kosovo Albanian paramilitary units, with guerrilla-style attacks on police and military positions and frequent reports of sporadic gunfire exchanges and shelling by Government forces.

12. Between 28 September and 19 October 1998, the Ministry of the Interior reported a total of 117 attacks of varying intensity, in which a total of 10 policemen were killed and 22 were injured. Seven members of the Yugoslav army were also reported killed and two injured during the incidents. The demarcation between police and Kosovo Albanian paramilitary units was not always clear at the time of the visit of the United Nations mission; in some cases their respective positions were only several hundred metres apart. Accordingly, in almost all cases, it was difficult to determine which side had initiated hostilities.

13. Recent attacks by Kosovo Albanian paramilitary units have indicated their readiness, capability and intention to actively pursue the advantage gained by the partial withdrawal of the police and military formations. Reports of new weapons, ammunition and equipment indicate that the capacity of those units to resupply themselves is still fairly good.

14. The army and police presence in Kosovo has been significantly reduced since early October. The presence and disposition of the remaining Government forces indicate a strategy based on containing pockets of resistance and on control of high ground and the main arterial routes in areas dominated by Kosovo Albanian paramilitary units. Tripwires and anti-personnel mines have reportedly been laid at the approaches to some police positions as an early warning measure. Since 27 October, there has been a continued withdrawal of the Serbian security forces from Kosovo and numerous checkpoints and fortified positions have been dismantled. The Serbian police retain control over key roads. Mobile police checkpoints have been established on major roads in some areas.

15. Kosovo Albanian paramilitary units are asserting their own authority to supplant that of the Serbian police in areas from which the police have withdrawn, and have established their own checkpoints on a number of secondary roads.

16. While the ceasefire is generally holding, there are continued reports of sporadic violations, including armed provocations against police and police harassment of ethnic Albanians. The presence of Kosovo Albanian paramilitary units is reportedly on the increase in several areas, and they appear to be responsible for some of the reported violations, including attacks on civilians. Serbian police raised security measures around a coal mine and power plant outside Pristina following an attack by Kosovo Albanian paramilitary units on 3 November in which three Serbian workers were injured.

17. Kosovo Albanian paramilitary units denied access to Kosovo Diplomatic Observer Mission teams to some areas, requesting a letter

from their political representative. On 5 November, a clearly marked OSCE vehicle was fired on as it drove close behind a Federal Republic of Yugoslavia military convoy between Suva Reka and Stimlje.

Security

18. The overriding concern of both ethnic Serbs and Albanians is the security of their families. While the Serbian authorities told the United Nations mission that they needed a large police presence in designated parts of Kosovo to protect ethnic Serbs living in the province and to ensure that at least main highways remained safe and free for travel, the Kosovo Albanian representatives stated that police units were used as another arm of the military, intent on intimidating local Albanians. Police and military personnel have occupied some village homes, making their owners' return impossible. Furthermore, many deserted villages have a presence of some five to eight police, who remain purportedly to prevent or give early warning of attempts by Kosovo Albanian paramilitary units to reoccupy territory previously taken by Government forces. This presence was cited almost universally by the internally displaced persons as the primary reason for people not returning to their homes.

19. Government authorities informed the mission that they had established local police units with Kosovo Albanian participation in some 100 "secured" villages. The only ethnic Albanian police officers met by the mission were three elderly officers involved in food distribution near Dakovica.

Humanitarian situation

20. As of mid-October, the United Nations High Commissioner for Refugees (UNHCR) estimated that some 200,000 persons were still displaced inside Kosovo. The number of people who had fled to other areas was estimated at 42,000 in Montenegro, 20,500 in Albania, 3,000 in the former Yugoslav Republic of Macedonia, 10,000 in Bosnia and Herzegovina and some 20,000 in Serbia. In 11 European countries recently surveyed by UNHCR, the total number of applications by asylum-seekers from the Federal Republic of Yugoslavia increased from 11,000 in the first quarter of 1998 to 28,000 in the third. Some 80 to 90 per cent of the applicants are asylum-seekers from Kosovo.

21. Significant progress was made in the return of displaced persons in Kosovo following the ceasefire and the 13 October accord. UNHCR estimates that up to 50,000 people have returned to their original villages, including 2,000 internally displaced persons from Montenegro. Since the military withdrawal on 27 October, thousands of displaced persons have returned to their villages. Many of the returnees whose houses were intact indicated that they would stay and would shelter neighbours who had lost their homes. Others are repairing homes to bring back their families. In some areas, villagers were preparing to plant the winter crop of wheat. Although there were some reports of harassment and obstruction by security forces, most returnees encountered few problems.

22. As of mid-October, people living in the open presented one of the major concerns to the international community. Of the 10,000 internally displaced persons estimated to be living under plastic sheeting before the 27 October military withdrawal, almost all had either returned to their villages or were staying with host families. There were still, however, a number of villages that remained deserted.

23. There are still many displaced families remaining with host families and in towns that have been untouched by the hostilities. This, in turn, has created problems. In many towns private dwellings are packed to three or four times their normal capacity, creating serious sanitary hazards.

24. UNHCR estimates that there are some 20,000 damaged houses, of which approximately 60 per cent are currently inhabitable. From 2 to 4 November, United Nations agencies, non-governmental organizations and the Kosovo Diplomatic Observer Mission conducted a village-by-village survey in order to get an accurate picture of the number of returnees and the condition of houses. The results of the survey are expected to help aid agencies in planning emergency shelter assistance and relief supplies. Preliminary indications are that some 370 villages have suffered varying degrees of damage. UNHCR, together with non-governmental organizations, is currently distributing 3,000 emergency shelter kits, pending a more systematic distribution of shelter materials upon completion of the inter-agency survey.

25. Access by humanitarian agencies to internally displaced persons has generally improved since the time of my previous report, although delays in obtaining entry visas from the authorities of the Federal Republic of Yugoslavia for their staff and difficulties in obtaining radio licences persist.

26. The encouraging response from donors to the current United Nations Consolidated Inter-agency Appeal for Humanitarian Assistance to Kosovo has enabled United Nations humanitarian agencies to step up emergency assistance to the victims of the conflict. From 28 October to 4 November, UNHCR escorted multi-agency convoys that delivered relief aid for 208,700 people in various parts of Kosovo. Supplies came from UNHCR, the World Food Programme (WFP), Mercy Corps International, Children's Aid Direct, Catholic Relief Services and Oxfam. Convoys are currently running three times a day, six days a week.

27. The initiative of the authorities of the Federal Republic of Yugoslavia to establish distribution centres throughout Kosovo has been welcomed by United Nations agencies as a constructive step. However, many potential beneficiaries interviewed by the mission stressed that the decision to delegate management of the centres to the local police is likely to dissuade Albanian internally displaced persons from taking advantage of such facilities. In line with the United Nations principle that assistance should be delivered where it is most needed, most agencies have so far opted to continue to distribute aid mainly through the Mother Teresa Society, which has a wide network and enjoys the trust of the Albanian population. Since it is questionable whether any Serb in need in Kosovo would be in a position to use the Albanian-managed Mother Teresa centres, assistance to needy Serbs is channelled through the Yugoslav Red Cross Society.

28. The situation of refugees and internally displaced persons in Montenegro, which hosts the biggest number of internally displaced persons outside Kosovo, remains of concern. The decision by the Government of Montenegro to close its border to internally displaced persons from Kosovo on 11 September is still in force. The authorities have justified this decision on economic and security grounds, voicing particular concern about potential destabilization in Montenegro as a result of the situation in Kosovo.

29. With almost half of the Montenegrin population living under the poverty line and with refugees and internally displaced persons comprising up to 12 per cent of the total population, Montenegro may indeed face a lack of capacity to cope with the problem. Economic sanctions against the Federal Republic of Yugoslavia and the general downturn in Montenegro's economy have made it virtually impossible for the Government, through the local Red Cross, to continue on its own to provide comprehensive assistance to the 42,000 new arrivals from Kosovo, in addition to a refugee caseload of 25,000 from the former Yugoslavia. However, considerable assistance is being provided by the international community to these persons.

30. A recent assessment mission by the Food and Agriculture Organization of the United Nations (FAO) to the Federal Republic of Yugoslavia concluded that the conflict in Kosovo was affecting the agricultural sector through uncertain access by returnees to their land, the collapse of local cereal production, a shortage of farming equipment and a decline in livestock. FAO will appeal for essential agricultural inputs to enable basic food production activities.

Mines

31. There have been many reports of mines being laid in Kosovo by both the Government forces and the Kosovo Albanian paramilitary units. The Deputy Chief of the General Staff of the Federal Republic of Yugoslavia asserted that the Yugoslav army had laid mines only on the borders with Albania and the former Yugoslav Republic of Macedonia, but not in the interior; that they were properly and accurately recorded in accordance with international conventions; and that the army was in a position to lift all mines without the assistance of the United Nations or other agencies. There are, however, some reports of small protective minefields being laid by police around their positions in central Kosovo. Reports of mined areas in the territories dominated by Kosovo Albanian paramilitary units are mostly undetailed.

32. Landmines and booby traps are becoming a growing problem in Kosovo, both for displaced persons returning to their homes and for humanitarian personnel. As internally displaced persons returned to their villages, several people were reportedly killed by anti-personnel mines or booby traps laid around houses, buildings and wells. Vehicle mines are also present on a number of dirt roads in the province. The reported presence of mines has restricted humanitarian access in several areas. This situation will be exacerbated by the onset of winter, when snow will cover traces of landmine locations. Humanitarian agencies have asked local communities to seek the assistance of Kosovo Albanian paramilitary units in removing landmines in the areas that they control. Efforts are under way to train relief staff in mine awareness and first aid. In the absence of a technical mine survey mission, the general uncertainty regarding mined areas poses a particular threat.

Human rights

33. The Office of the United Nations High Commissioner for Human Rights continues its monitoring presence in Kosovo and reports regularly to the United Nations High Commissioner for Human Rights and the Special Rapporteur of the Commission on Human Rights, Jiri Dienstbier. From 21 to 29 October, the Special Rapporteur conducted his third visit to the Federal Republic of Yugoslavia. His report on human rights in Bosnia and Herzegovina, Croatia and the Federal Republic of Yugoslavia, including Kosovo, is contained in documents A/53/322 and Add.1.

34. Reports on the situation of human rights are consistent with the categories of serious violations of human rights that have characterized the crisis in Kosovo for many months. The human rights situation appears not to have changed significantly since the signing of the 16 October agreement. Violations have been attributed to Serbian security forces, Kosovo Albanian paramilitary units and village defence groups. Retaliatory and armed action, torture and ill-treatment, arbitrary detention, forced disappearances, harassment and discriminatory treatment are widely reported.

35. Religious and cultural monuments have been damaged and vandalized, both in conflict-affected areas and in urban areas where no fighting has taken place. In discussions with the Special Rapporteur and the staff of the Office of the United Nations High Commissioner for Human Rights, Government representatives in Pristina confirmed that in some locations Government forces had been responsible for deliberate and retaliatory destruction of property owned by Kosovo Albanians. Returning internally displaced persons and Government officials have also confirmed the practice of the "screening" of internally displaced persons, in which men are separated from women and children and then held for questioning for periods ranging from hours to several days. It is reported that many of those detained are beaten and ill-treated during interrogation.

36. The Serbian Ministry of Justice has also confirmed that more than 1,500 persons, including 500 in absentia, are currently being investigated under suspicion of involvement in anti-state activities and in activities of the Kosovo Albanian paramilitary units. Some persons have already been convicted and sentenced. Five cases of death in custody have been reported so far. The Office of the United Nations High Commissioner for Human Rights monitors these trials, the first of which began on 22 October in Prizren. The Serbian Minister of the Interior has observed that an amnesty law can be discussed only after a political agreement has been finalized, a census and elections held, and new organs of local government subsequently formed.

37. The need for independent investigations into alleged arbitrary executions gained renewed urgency with the discovery of additional concentrations of corpses in several locations in Kosovo. The United Nations mission also received reports of alleged extra-judicial killings and massacres at Gornje Obrinje, Klecka, Golubovac, Volujak, Malisevo, Rausic, Glogovac and Gremnik. As a result of efforts by the European Union and other international organizations, including OHCHR, and initiatives by the Government of the Federal Republic of Yugoslavia, a group of Finnish forensic experts arrived in the Federal Republic of Yugoslavia on 20 October to assist the authorities in investigations into alleged arbitrary killings and mass graves. According to the Finnish Ministry for Foreign Affairs, the group also

intended to carry out independent investigations as necessary. Unfortunately, the Government of the Federal Republic of Yugoslavia failed to cooperate fully with the International Tribunal for the Former Yugoslavia. A team of Tribunal officials, led by Chief Prosecutor Louise Arbour, was unable to visit Kosovo since the requested visas were not issued by the Federal Republic of Yugoslavia.

38. There are growing concerns as to the fate and whereabouts of the 140 to 150 civilians and police officers who are still missing after having been abducted by the Kosovo Albanian paramilitary units. The authorities of the Federal Republic of Yugoslavia report that 249 civilians and police have been abducted by Kosovo Albanian paramilitary units. The most recent of these cases involves two journalists of the state news agency, who went missing on 18 October; despite assurances about their well-being and imminent release, reports now indicate that they have been "sentenced" to 60 days' imprisonment. During his visit to Kosovo, the Special Rapporteur has appealed for the release of all abductees.

V.   UNITED NATIONS MISSION TO THE FEDERAL REPUBLIC OF YUGOSLAVIA

39. In a statement to the press on 6 October 1998 on behalf of the Security Council, the President of the Council requested me to consider how the Secretariat might be ensured a first-hand capability to assess developments on the ground, and to continue reporting to the Council on compliance with its resolutions 1160 (1998) and 1199 (1998). In response to that request, and following consultations with the authorities of the Federal Republic of Yugoslavia, I dispatched a United Nations interdepartmental mission, headed by Staffan de Mistura, Director of the United Nations Information Centre in Rome, to the Federal Republic of Yugoslavia to look into those matters. In view of the expected deployment by OSCE of the Kosovo Verification Mission, the United Nations mission also assessed possible modalities for the coordination of activities between OSCE and United Nations agencies on the ground.

40. Between 17 and 27 October, the mission visited the Federal Republic of Yugoslavia, including Kosovo and Montenegro, as well as the OSCE secretariat in Vienna. Members of the mission met with a number of government and local officials, as well as with representatives of the Kosovo Albanian community. They also held consultations with international organizations, international and local non-governmental organizations and members of the diplomatic community in the Federal Republic of Yugoslavia. The mission visited various parts of Kosovo (see map), and interviewed a number of local citizens of different ethnic backgrounds. The head of the mission held consultations with senior OSCE and Kosovo Verification Mission officials.

41. So far, the Secretariat's capability to assess developments on the ground has been limited mainly to the humanitarian and human rights situation. Information in these areas has effectively been provided on a regular basis by UNHCR in its capacity as lead agency, and OHCHR, which has contributed to the Secretary-General's monthly reports prepared pursuant to resolution 1160 (1998). The Office of the High Commissioner for Human Rights, through the Special Rapporteur, has a separate mandate to report to the General Assembly and the Commission on Human Rights on human rights violations in the former Yugoslavia. Although the United Nations liaison office in Belgrade informs the Secretariat on political and military developments in the Federal Republic of Yugoslavia, including in Kosovo, it does not have a mandate to report to the Security Council on these issues, nor does it have a presence in Kosovo. It thus does not have the capacity to provide to the Council consistent, comprehensive first-hand information on the situation on the ground. Meanwhile, OSCE and NATO confirmed to the United Nations mission their preparedness to report to the Security Council on the situation in Kosovo in accordance with their newly approved mandates. Having explored various modalities for providing the Council with first-hand information on the situation in Kosovo, Mr. de Mistura prepared several alternatives for my consideration.

42. In doing so, he has taken into account that UNHCR, as the lead humanitarian agency in the region, has enhanced its coordinating role with arrangements to encompass other humanitarian partners

operating in Kosovo and the increasing number of international and national non-governmental organizations represented on the ground. Weekly meetings chaired by UNHCR are held to coordinate the provision of assistance and to avoid the duplication of activities between partners. UNHCR also has good working relations with federal and local authorities. Effective coordination arrangements are thus in place to ensure comprehensive reporting on the humanitarian situation. The activities of the Office of the High Commissioner for Human Rights in the Federal Republic of Yugoslavia, in particular in Kosovo, are to be strengthened in the fields of monitoring, training and capacity-building, by increasing the number of Office personnel in the field. The memorandum of understanding between OHCHR and the Government of the Federal Republic of Yugoslavia was concluded on 9 November 1998.

43. It is self-evident that OSCE, with 2,000 Kosovo Verification Mission monitors due to be deployed on the ground, is becoming the lead political organization dealing with the Kosovo crisis. The principal task of the Mission will be to monitor compliance with Security Council resolution 1199 (1998). The Mission will not enforce compliance, nor will it respond to local disturbances, react to hostilities or enforce access by relief organizations.

44. Pending the establishment of the OSCE Kosovo Verification Mission, United Nations agencies, through the UNHCR liaison office with the Kosovo Diplomatic Observer Mission in Pristina, will continue to cooperate with the Kosovo Diplomatic Observer Mission, which is expected in the transitional period to start acting as the Kosovo Verification Mission and eventually to be absorbed by it. Initial consultations by Mr. de Mistura with the head of the Kosovo Verification Mission, William Walker, and with the pre-deployment logistical team for the Mission, as well as with OSCE Secretary-General Giancarlo Aragona and the central planning team of the Mission, reflected a strong desire on the part of both organizations to ensure that there is early agreement on coordination issues, in order to avoid the danger of overlapping or any misconception of the roles of each organization, and to ensure the optimal use of the international community's resources.

45. To this end, it is envisaged that the United Nations role in Kosovo will focus on humanitarian and human rights issues and UNHCR is thus expected to remain the lead agency in the humanitarian field and OHCHR in the field of human rights. In order to facilitate coordination between the Kosovo Verification Mission and UNHCR on the ground, UNHCR has established close liaison with OSCE in Vienna, and with the Kosovo Verification Mission advance party in the field. The Office for the Coordination of Humanitarian Affairs is also expected to establish a presence in Pristina, under the UNHCR umbrella, to assist in coordination efforts and longer-term reconstruction/post-conflict development plans in Kosovo. For its part, OHCHR is planning to open a sub-office in Pristina and, with the Kosovo Verification Mission and UNHCR, will establish an effective system of information sharing on cases of human rights violations in Kosovo. While liaison with NATO is expected to be maintained primarily through the NATO liaison office at United Nations Headquarters, it is anticipated that coordination on the ground will be established in Pristina.

VI. OBSERVATIONS AND RECOMMENDATIONS

46. I welcome the accord reached by the President of the Federal Republic of Yugoslavia and the United States Special Envoy on 13 October 1998 and the agreements of 15 October between the Federal Republic of Yugoslavia and NATO and of 16 October between the Federal Republic of Yugoslavia and the OSCE. I believe the establishment of the Kosovo Verification Mission can contribute to the peaceful settlement of the Kosovo crisis, and I call upon all parties concerned to cooperate with the mission. For its part, the United Nations will continue its humanitarian and human rights activities and will support the efforts of the Kosovo Verification Mission, regional organizations and individual Member States aimed at restoring peace and stability to the region. The complexity and the scope of tasks in Kosovo require coordinated and concerted efforts by all organisations on the ground. All United Nations agencies operating there will establish their lines of communication with the Kosovo Verification

Mission to this end. Moreover, the United Nations is prepared to provide assistance to the Mission operation through the United Nations Logistics Base at Brindisi and the United Nations Staff College in Turin.

47. I also welcome the efforts of Christopher Hill of the United States of America, supported by European Union Envoy Wolfgang Petrisch of Austria, in promoting a political dialogue between the Serbian authorities and the representatives of the Albanian community in Kosovo and I call on all parties to cooperate with them in their endeavours.

48. While welcoming reports of the withdrawal of Government forces in Kosovo to agreed levels, I urge all the parties concerned to honour their commitments and to comply fully with the Security Council resolutions. In this regard, reports of the return of Kosovo Albanian paramilitary units to positions vacated by Government forces and particularly by their continued attacks against security forces and civilians are disturbing. This situation makes it all the more urgent that early deployment of Kosovo Verification Mission monitors take place, with a 24-hour presence in order to restore stability and confidence and to enable continuous verification of events on the ground.

49. I am also disturbed by the denial of cooperation on the part of the Government of the Federal Republic of Yugoslavia with the International Tribunal for the Former Yugoslavia. I urge the authorities of the Federal Republic of Yugoslavia to comply with the demands of the international community including, inter alia, paragraph 14 of Security Council resolution 1203 (1998).

50. Despite the beginning of the mass return of internally displaced persons to their homes, the situation on the ground indicates that their needs must be further addressed at the international, regional and local levels. In this connection, the effective and well-established coordinating role played by UNHCR as the lead agency for humanitarian activities in Kosovo should be maintained and reflected in a formal agreement with OSCE. The coordinating role of UNHCR will be further reinforced by the larger involvement of the Office for the Coordination of Humanitarian Affairs in facilitation of coordination efforts and longer-term reconstruction and post-conflict development plans in Kosovo. More attention will also need to be paid to the humanitarian needs of refugees in Montenegro, as well as to those of the half a million refugees in Serbia.

51. Given the fact that legitimate personal security fears were the overriding obstacle to the return of internally displaced persons, political action to ensure real security to the people is a requisite for any solution to the humanitarian crisis. Such a process would be facilitated if the authorities of the Federal Republic of Yugoslavia were to extend guarantees to all returning civilians so as to avoid the blanket interrogation of male internally displaced persons. The issuance of appropriate amnesty legislation to permit this to happen would be crucial in this regard. Likewise, Kosovo Albanian paramilitary units must stop any armed actions to provoke the Federal Republic of Yugoslavia security forces and must put an immediate end to abductions and other violent activities.

52. The persistent fear expressed about returnees' security highlights the need to actively monitor the activities of and to train local police forces, particularly in the area of human rights. Unless this issue is addressed on an urgent basis, the return process will be seriously undermined by a lack of confidence in the ability or the desire of the local police to protect returnees. If requested and deemed appropriate, the United Nations Civilian Police Unit would be prepared to provide advice in this area. The Office of the High Commissioner for Human Rights will provide existing manuals and other training resources on the subject.

53. The establishment of a United Nations human rights sub-office in Kosovo will allow OHCHR to perform its expanded monitoring and promotional tasks in close cooperation with the Kosovo Verification Mission and UNHCR and other international and national institutions and organizations. Early, effective and coordinated action in cases of human rights abuses will be critical in building confidence for the return of refugees and displaced persons.

54. It is necessary to establish a capability to initiate a comprehensive and integrated mine action plan, including mine

awareness, education, information, mine-marking and mine clearance. The United Nations Mine Action Centre will study the possibility of providing assistance in this area.

55. The immediate crisis in Kosovo should not overshadow the necessity to assess the medium-term rehabilitation and reconstruction needs of the Federal Republic of Yugoslavia. As conditions allow, the World Bank, the United Nations Development Programme and bilateral donors should play a major role in this process, particularly in post-conflict projects in Kosovo.

56. With regard to the issue of a first-hand capability to assess the situation on the ground (see sect. V above), it is recalled that subsequent to its request to me, the Security Council endorsed the establishment of the Kosovo Verification Mission by OSCE. Under the 16 October agreement between the Federal Republic of Yugoslavia and OSCE, the Kosovo Verification Mission has been assigned, inter alia, the responsibility of reporting to the Council. In my view, this should subsume the reporting on the situation in Kosovo from a political perspective, a function that the Secretariat has been carrying out with considerable difficulty, for lack of an independent presence on the ground in the past few months. It is quite obvious that any need that might have existed for such a presence has been superseded by the decision to establish the Kosovo Verification Mission. Taking this into account and having considered the options presented by Mr. de Mistura, I have decided against recommending a United Nations political presence in Kosovo, thus avoiding parallel reporting channels that might lead to confusion and overlapping in the field, as well as unnecessary financial expenditure. I consider it important at this stage, therefore, to develop clear channels of communication between the United Nations and OSCE on this issue. If necessary, short-term missions could be sent to the region to look into specific aspects at the Council's request. Should the future situation require an expanded United Nations presence on the ground, the Council could revert to this issue at a later stage.

57. In its resolution 1203 (1998), the Security Council requested me, in consultation with the parties concerned with the agreements signed in Belgrade on 16 October 1998 between the Federal Republic of Yugoslavia and OSCE, and on 15 October 1998 between the Federal Republic of Yugoslavia and NATO, to report regularly to the Council regarding implementation of that resolution. The agreement between the Federal Republic of Yugoslavia and OSCE, however, indicates that the latter will report directly to the Council. I suggest that OSCE and NATO report to the Council through me (as do the Stabilization Force and the Office of the High Representative), while I would continue to report to the Council on the humanitarian and human rights situation in Kosovo. As to the frequency of these reports, this should be determined in consultation with the Kosovo Verification Mission and NATO. It is my opinion, however, that under the present circumstances and in view of the stability achieved on the ground, quarterly reports would suffice, unless otherwise requested by the Council or necessitated by events in the area.

Annex I

Information on the situation in Kosovo and measures taken by the Organization for Security and Cooperation in Europe

(September/October 1998)
General situation

1. The period since the previous report of 21 September 1998 has been characterized by relative calm, with sporadic fighting throughout Kosovo and specific operations launched by Yugoslav security forces in several locations. Burning and looting of houses, destruction of property and shelling of villages continued, especially in the Djakovica and Prizren areas.

2. By the end of September, for the first time since the conflict erupted, Serb security forces launched operations not only in central Kosovo and along the border to Albania, but also in an area north of Pristina, between Mitrovica and Podujevo, the so-called Shala region …

3. During the second week of October, armed forces of the Federal Republic of Yugoslavia were observed redeploying personnel and equipment away from some of the larger Kosovo towns to locations near the border.

4. Despite announcements by both the Serbian Government and the Kosovo Liberation Army (KLA), declaring their readiness to show "self-

restraint" in response to a call from the Security Council last month, cases of fighting, as well as destruction of property, continue to be reported.
Monitoring activities in Kosovo

5. The Kosovo Diplomatic Observer Mission continued its activity in the province, monitoring the situation and compliance with Security Council resolutions 1160 (1998) and 1199 (1998).

6. At the beginning of October, the most noticeable response to international demands was the partial withdrawal of units, in particular those of the Yugoslav army. The security forces behaved in a more discrete fashion, but with still noticeable presence. Observers deemed this presence necessary given the likelihood that KLA, emboldened by the circumstances, could take advantage of the depleted security arrangements.
The situation of the civilian population

7. According to the Office of the United Nations High Commissioner for Refugees (UNHCR), the continued crackdown by the Serbian police and military against KLA strongholds has forced an estimated 300,000 people to flee their homes. Out of these, 200,000 are displaced within Kosovo and an estimated 50,000 internally displaced persons still remain in the open. Fear is still a major factor inhibiting their return and an additional concern is the destruction of housing, which raises the question of what they can return to.

8. Generally, the conflict has continued to cause more displaced persons and refugees than returnees. In addition, internally displaced Kosovars have experienced increasing difficulties in entering Montenegro from Serbia.
Influx of refugees

9. As at 13 October, UNHCR was reporting a total of 20,500 refugees in Albania, out of which 7,000 remain in the Tropoje district. During the reporting period, the major flow of refugees entering Albania came from Montenegro, as crossing the border with the Federal Republic of Yugoslavia Province of Kosovo became more hazardous for refugees.

10. A critical juncture was reached during the second half of September, when a sudden large influx of more than 4,500 Kosovar refugees expelled from Montenegro were driven by Montenegrin authorities to the border crossing point of Bashkim, in the remote northern valley of Vermosh, from which the refugees tried to make their way to Shkodra. Most of them came from the Decane area, reflecting the ongoing fighting there. The refugees found a much deteriorated security situation, suffering several ambushes, which only added to the very difficult conditions of the roads.

11. At other parts of the border between Albania and the Federal Republic of Yugoslavia, refugees continued to enter Albania, although in smaller numbers than before, since the first snows in mountainous areas created additional difficulties for those trying to cross the border. During the first week of October, limited numbers of refugees continued to enter Albania through the Has district and via Shkodra lake. UNHCR has estimated that some 3,000 remain in the Tropoje district and around 900 in the Kukes/Has district.
Spillover potential of the Kosovo conflict

12. The missions of the Organization for Security and Cooperation in Europe (OSCE) in Tirana, Skopje and Sarajevo were instructed to follow closely the spillover potential of the Kosovo conflict.

13. The refugee situation in Albania during the reporting period became even gloomier following the influx in the north, making it very difficult for the Albanian authorities to handle. UNHCR expressed its readiness to declare a humanitarian state of emergency if the authorities were unable to provide sufficient accommodation.

14. The problem of refugees in Albania acquired much wider political dimensions because it appeared impossible to hold all the refugees in the north-east. Of the perhaps 25,000 refugees that have crossed into Albania, many have moved abroad, and significant numbers have taken refuge in Tirana and Durres. A few of this latter group will be persuaded to move to collective accommodation.

15. Enforcement of law and order in the north-east of Albania remained extremely weak and very much depended on family ties, giving the international community continued cause for concern. The unpredictable security situation, along with deteriorating weather conditions, caused most international agencies to abandon the area.

16. In Shkodra, despite high tension connected to events in Tirana, the situation remained relatively calm during the reporting period, although the local police apparently teamed up with ex-police related to the Democratic Party. In Bajram Curri, ongoing lawlessness resulted in the heavy looting of the UNHCR warehouse, and most humanitarian agencies working in the area decided either to cease activities in the region or severely cut back on their operations.

17. As regards border incidents, by the end of September, a serious clash took place near the Morina border post, as about 30 soldiers of the Federal Republic of Yugoslavia opened fire on Albanian territory after a truck of the Federal Republic of Yugoslavia struck a mine believed to have been laid by KLA. This incident was followed by the shelling of the Albanian village of Padesh from the Federal Republic of Yugoslavia. By mid-October it was reported that units of the Federal Republic of Yugoslavia in the areas bordering Albania were reinforced far beyond normal staffing just before threats of air strikes by the North Atlantic Treaty Organization (NATO).

18. During the first week of October, an increase in KLA activities in the Has and Tropoje districts was observed, with KLA moving openly in some border areas. Internationals observed what appeared to be a training facility in Babine and a KLA logistics base at Papaj. The Padesh plateau and the town of Tropoje, both former strongholds of KLA, are virtually empty of irregular fighters.

19. The political crisis in Albania in mid-September, which deteriorated into a situation of violence, with shooting and looting of official buildings and private property in Tirana, did not help to enhance the already weak State presence in northern Albania and thus the control by Albanian authorities of the border with the Federal Republic of Yugoslavia.

20. Prime Minister Nano received considerable criticism from all political parties concerning a declaration he made in Lisbon in early September, a few days before his resignation, calling for a Kosovo within a democratic Yugoslav Federation.

21. It remains clear that an unresolved Kosovo problem will continue to link Albania to the crisis in the Yugoslav province and that an unstable Albania, used as a base or housing numbers of disenchanted former fighters, will only add to the difficulties of finding a long-term solution. Therefore, initiatives like the Friends of Albania Group serve as stabilization, not only in Albania, but in the region as a whole.

22. In the former Yugoslav Republic of Macedonia, the situation at the northern border remained calm during the first half of October, without substantive incidents and with all border crossings open and functioning normally. There have been no significant incidents; illegal crossings and smuggling have been less than at any time since independence, attributable in large part to the presence of Yugoslav security forces on the northern side of the border and the increased risks of illegal crossing during the Kosovo crisis. On the western border with Albania there has been no substantive change in the pattern of activity. Periodic incidents continue to occur of attempted illegal entry, sometimes armed, of small groups from Albania. These groups sometimes engage security forces of the former Yugoslav Republic of Macedonia, and are sometimes fired upon.

23. According to UNHCR there are 3,000 people in the former Yugoslav Republic of Macedonia whose presence is directly linked to the conflict in Kosovo.

24. The potential risks of spillover from Kosovo to the former Yugoslav Republic of Macedonia seem to be dividing public opinion along ethnic lines as the ethnic population of the former Yugoslav Republic of Macedonia fears the consequences of military action and an implicit endorsement of such action by many in the ethnic Albanian community. The leader of the principal political party representing the Serb minority, the Democratic Party of Serbs in the former Yugoslav Republic of Macedonia, warned that an attack on Serbia would be interpreted as an attack on Serbs generally. Still, during the parliamentary election campaign, Kosovo was not a major issue, attracting minimal public comment.

25. By the second week of October, an estimated 7,800 refugees from Kosovo had settled in Bosnia and Herzegovina, the great majority of whom have come to the Sarajevo area. The peak rate of this inflow came in mid-September (approximately 800 weekly arrivals) and it has declined rapidly since. Almost all the refugees are Muslim, ethnic Albanians; only a handful of Serb refugees from Kosovo have been reported. Limited preparations have been made to provide refugee camps. Only three are currently operational, and another three are planned. Some 1,000 are sheltered at a Coca Cola plant in the Sarajevo suburb of Hadzici, while the other two camps house around 100 each. The remaining refugees have dispersed throughout Bosnia and Herzegovina finding shelter most often through the hospitality of relatives.

26. Though no specific incidents have been reported, OSCE field staff have noticed a "domino effect" on the general level of reconciliation in those areas experiencing inflows of refugees from Kosovo. In areas already struggling with return issues, the additional presence of refugees from Kosovo has added tension. In those areas, other returnees regard the new arrivals from Kosovo as competitors for precious available accommodations.

Measures taken by the Organization for Security and Cooperation in Europe

27. On 6 October, the Minister for Foreign Affairs of the Republic of Yugoslavia, Zivadin Jovanovic, sent a letter to the OSCE Chairman-in-Office, Polish Foreign Minister Bronislav Geremek, inviting OSCE "to witness first-hand the positive evolution of the most crucial processes in Kosovo and Metohija". In a press release issued the following day, the Chairman-in-Office emphasized that the best conditions for accepting this invitation would appear when the Federal Republic of Yugoslavia satisfied the requirements contained in decision No. 218 of the OSCE Permanent Council, as well as Security Council resolutions 1160 (1998) and 1199 (1998). He underlined that it was up to the Federal Republic of Yugoslavia, through full compliance with the terms of the above-mentioned documents, to enable OSCE to make its contribution to the resolution of the crisis over Kosovo.

28. On 15 October 1998, the OSCE Permanent Council, recalling paragraph 1 of its decision No. 218 and the statement of the Chairman-in-Office of 7 October 1998 confirming the long-standing readiness of OSCE to give its contribution to the peaceful solution of the crisis in Kosovo, adopted decision No. 259 supporting the efforts of the Chairman-in-Office to arrange with the authorities of the Federal Republic of Yugoslavia for OSCE to make such contribution.

29. Based on arrangements reached by Richard Holbrooke, United States Special Envoy and representing also the Contact Group, and Yugoslav President Milošević, the OSCE Chairman-in-Office, and the Minister for Foreign Affairs of the Federal Republic of Yugoslavia signed an agreement on the establishment of an OSCE Kosovo Verification Mission in Belgrade on 16 October 1998.

30. The overall task of the Verification Mission will be to verify compliance by all parties in Kosovo with Security Council resolution 1199 (1998) and to report instances of progress and/or non-compliance to the OSCE Permanent Council, the Security Council and other organizations. Further, the Verification Mission will be tasked to supervise elections in Kosovo in order to ensure their openness and fairness.

31. The Verification Mission, unprecedented in size, will be composed of up to 2000 unarmed verifiers and will establish a permanent presence at as many locations throughout Kosovo as it deems necessary to fulfil its responsibilities. The current Kosovo Diplomatic Observer Mission will act in place of the OSCE Verification Mission pending its establishment, and will subsequently be absorbed by the new Mission.

32. During the talks on 16 October in Belgrade, the Minister for Foreign Affairs of the Federal Republic of Yugoslavia made a number of promises to the effect that the Federal Government would do its best to implement the agreement and expressed hope that the Verification Mission would contribute to assessing the situation "in an objective, truthful and unbiased manner". He also made a solemn promise to care for the security of the personnel of the Verification Mission in accordance with the Vienna Conventions. He confirmed that the Verification Mission would have all possibilities of movement and access to desired information on the ground.

33. On the same day, the OSCE Chairman-in-Office met in Pristina with Ibrahim Rugova. The leader of the Albanian community in Kosovo expressed the view that the agreement signed in Belgrade contained many weak points that could cause disappointment in the Albanian community. He also voiced disappointment that no representatives of the Albanian community from Kosovo had been a party to the negotiations.

34. In spite of these critical moments, Mr. Rugova welcomed the agreement and unequivocally expressed the view that the Albanian community in Kosovo would cooperate with the Verification Mission. He sees this act as an important step towards enlarging the international presence in Kosovo, which should facilitate negotiations for a political solution to the crisis, recognition of the Albanian community institutions, including local police, and deciding over the future of Kosovo.

35. The agreement on the OSCE Kosovo Verification Mission and the agreement on the NATO-Kosovo air verification regime, signed on 15 October in Belgrade, are aimed at supporting international efforts to solve the crisis in Kosovo and constitute an important step towards development of a political framework to ensure compliance with the demands set out in Security Council resolution 1199 (1998). The agreements highlight the verification of compliance with the said resolution, as stipulated in paragraph 16 thereof.

36. Once this important political support is secured, the OSCE Chairman-in-Office would be ready to begin immediately deployment of the Verification Mission on the ground. It has already been decided to dispatch

to the Federal Republic of Yugoslavia a small OSCE technical advance mission to start preparation of the operation, the scope of which goes beyond previous OSCE experience. Consequently, the 13-member OSCE technical advance mission arrived on 17 October in Belgrade and started talks with the authorities of the Federal Republic of Yugoslavia regarding the preparations for establishing the OSCE Kosovo Verification Mission. On 18 October, the OSCE technical advance mission arrived in Pristina to assess conditions for deployment of the Verification Mission.

37. Acting as OSCE Chairman-in-Office, Mr. Geremek decided to appoint William Graham Walker as Head of the OSCE Kosovo Verification Mission, effective 17 October 1998. Mr. Walker has recently served as Special Representative of the Secretary-General as Transitional Administrator for the United Nations Transitional Administration for Eastern Slavonia, Baranja and Western Sirmium (UNTAES), in Croatia.

38. On 17 October, the OSCE Chairman-in-Office sent a letter to the Secretary-General informing him of the signing of the agreement with the authorities of the Federal Republic of Yugoslavia and expressing his hope that the agreements would be acknowledged and supported by the Security Council in an appropriate resolution in order to make these acts effective and to ensure the safety and security of international verifiers.

39. The OSCE Chairman-in-Office and the OSCE Representative of the Freedom of the Media, Helmut Duve, have on several occasions expressed their concern over the treatment of foreign journalists, as well as domestic, independent media, by the authorities of the Federal Republic of Yugoslavia. In a press release issued on 16 October, Mr. Duve called upon the Belgrade Government to stop repression of the media. Reacting to a government decree leading to the closure of Nasa Borba, a leading independent newspaper, the previous day, he noted that "a free media is one of the elements that will ensure the success of the difficult task of bringing peace to Kosovo".

Annex II

Letter dated 27 October 1998 from the Secretary-General of the North Atlantic Treaty Organization addressed to the Secretary-General

...Further to my letter of 22 October, I am writing to inform you that the North Atlantic Council today decided to maintain the activation order for the limited air response on the understanding that execution would be subject to a further Council decision and assessments that the Federal Republic of Yugoslavia was not in substantial compliance with Security Council resolution 1199 (1998). The Council also decided to continue the present air activities as part of the phased air campaign. This decision was reached by the North Atlantic Treaty Organization (NATO) after a thorough assessment by NATO of the level of compliance by the Federal Republic of Yugoslavia with the provisions of Security Council resolution 1199 (1998). NATO aerial surveillance assets and the Kosovo Diplomatic Observer Mission have confirmed that Federal Republic of Yugoslavia and Serb security forces have withdrawn in substantial numbers towards pre-March levels. Also, the necessary conditions are being established for the return of refugees and displaced persons. However, NATO will continue to monitor the situation very closely. In this context, NATO welcomes the recent adoption of Security Council resolution 1203 (1998), which, inter alia, endorses and supports the verification agreements signed between the Federal Republic of Yugoslavia and NATO and OSCE, respectively. We are continuing our work to ensure close coordination between NATO and OSCE and hope that both missions can be fully operational in the very near future. Our military authorities are developing planning for the possible extraction of OSCE verifiers in an emergency. Meanwhile, NATO military authorities have begun technical discussions with some nations within the Partnership for Peace about associating the latter with the NATO air surveillance mission. I will continue to keep you informed of further important developments.

(Signed) Javier SOLANA

5. UN Inter-Agency Update on Kosovo Situation Report 72, 26 November 1998

14 November - 25 November 1998
UN Security Council on Kosovo
1. On 19 November the UN Security Council met to discuss the UN Secretary-General's most recent report on Kosovo. After the meeting the President of the Security Council said that Council members welcomed the recent agreements on Kosovo, which were helping to defuse the immediate crisis and create more favourable conditions for a political settlement which respects the full rights of all the people of Kosovo. He said that members of the Security Council reaffirmed their commitment to the sovereignty and territorial integrity of FRY. However, Council members were concerned about the persisting tensions in many areas described in the report. He said the Council members called on all parties concerned to comply fully with the Security Council Resolutions, to cooperate with the Kosovo Verification Mission (KVM), to honour their commitments and to provide for the security of all KVM personnel.

2. On 16 November the UN Security Council adopted Resolution 1207 acting under Chapter 7 of the UN charter. The Resolution deplored the continued failure of the Federal Republic of Yugoslavia to cooperate fully with the International Criminal Tribunal for former Yugoslavia (ICTY). With regard to Kosovo the Resolution reiterated its "call upon the authorities of the Federal Republic of Yugoslavia, the leaders of the Kosovo Albanian community and all others concerned to cooperate fully with the Prosecutor in the investigation of all possible violations within the jurisdiction of the Tribunal." As at 25 November the Tribunal's investigators had still not been granted entry visas by the Yugoslav authorities. ...

Security

12. Local sources reported that the ceasefire held from 17-22 November although tensions remained high in the Malisevo and Decane areas, and in Podujevo where two police were killed in an apparent KLA ambush. Some elements of the KDOM engaged in intensive discussions with both senior Serbian officials and the area KLA commander in Podujevo concerning the recent kidnapping of one Serb and two ethnic Albanians, which has greatly increased tensions in the area. The Serbian detainee was subsequently released on 24 November. Such incidents are clearly not conducive to return movements.

Shelter

13. From 2-4 November United Nations agencies and NGOs conducted a joint shelter survey in Kosovo. Of the 285 villages assessed 210 had been damaged by the conflict. Nearly 40 percent of the homes were found to be habitable, requiring basic shelter materials, plastic and plywood to close windows or seal off doors. About 30 percent of the homes were damaged or destroyed and will need to be renovated next spring, if the fragile return process holds. UNHCR's is liaising with the Yugoslav authorities on the distribution of basic shelter materials such as tiles, bricks and windows which the FRY Government must provide in accordance with the provisions of United Nations Security Council Resolution 1199. ...

ALBANIA

25. Security remains tight along villages on the border with Albania, where illegal traffic in arms continues. Early this month, troops detained an entire village population for 24 hours while they conducted a house-to-house search for weapons. As a result, the number of refugees returning to Kosovo is slight although a few refugee families from northern Albania have returned along Kosovo's western frontier villages.

26. Albania hosts some 20,000 refugees from Kosovo. Lawlessness and bandit attacks on aid agencies in the northern Albanian town of Bajram Curri have created a precarious security situation which has influenced the decision of refugees to return home for lack of options. UNHCR is working to relocate these refugees to safer areas within Albania, thus avoiding involuntary returns. Plans are underway to assist the relocation of the first group of 53 refugees to Velipolje, which is near Shkodra.

6. Yugoslavia/Kosovo: ICRC steps up food distribution, 3 December 1998

Working in close cooperation with the World Food Programme, the ICRC has pinpointed the areas where people need more assistance and has begun to provide additional food for various distribution centres throughout Kosovo. On 30 November six trucks coming from Belgrade loaded with 60 tonnes of wheat flour, vegetable oil, sugar, salt, yeast and pasta reached Glogovac, in central Kosovo. Further convoys will bring 90 tonnes of food to Srbica and Kosovska Mitrovica (centre and north) this week. The assistance is meant to supplement regular ICRC relief operations in the field. From 1 to 26 November over 260 tonnes of food and thousands of blankets, shoes, clothing articles, hygiene items and baby kits were delivered to various towns and villages in the Pec, Prizren, Pristina and Drenica regions.

A total of 21 ICRC expatriates and 99 local staff members are currently engaged in medical, detention, tracing, relief and water and sanitation operations in Kosovo. Yugoslavia/Kosovo: ICRC steps up food distribution, 3 December 1998

S/1998/1147, 4 December 1998

7. Report of the Secretary-General, 4 December 1998

...

6. This section of the report deals with humanitarian and human rights aspects of the situation in Kosovo, as I recommended to the Council in my previous report. It is based on information provided by the Chairman-in-Office of the Organization for Security and Cooperation in Europe (OSCE) (see annex), the Kosovo Diplomatic Observer Mission and individual Member States, as well as contributions provided by the Office of the United Nations High Commissioner for Refugees (UNHCR) and the Office of the United Nations High Commissioner for Human Rights.

Humanitarian situation

7. No major combat between military forces has occurred in Kosovo since the time of my last report, but the situation on the ground is still far from peaceful. Sporadic ceasefire violations were reported by both the Serbian authorities and Kosovo Albanian sources. In most cases it was impossible to identify who initiated the clashes.

8. Since the withdrawal of the Serbian police and Yugoslav military forces on 27 October the return of internally displaced persons to their homes has significantly increased. With the onset of winter, villages across Kosovo are being repopulated, as people uprooted by eight months of fighting are looking for better shelter than plastic tents in the woods, the crammed houses of friends or relatives in urban centres and rented space they could no longer afford in neighbouring countries and territories. As at 24 November, UNHCR estimates that some 75,000 displaced persons have gone back to their villages in hard-hit central and western Kosovo. About 175,000 people remained displaced within Kosovo. Many of them have returned to their villages to find their homes reduced to rubble. These returnees are forced to stay in the houses of their more fortunate neighbours and thus are still displaced, albeit within their own villages.

9. A trickle of several refugee families from northern Albania have returned to Kosovo's western frontier villages. Albania hosts some 24,000 refugees from Kosovo. Lawlessness and bandit attacks on aid agencies in the northern Albanian district of Tropoja have created a precarious security situation, in view of which some of the approximately 2,500 refugees located there decided to return home for lack of other options. UNHCR is working to relocate such refugees to safer areas within Albania, thus avoiding involuntary returns.

10. The Montenegrin Red Cross reported that, as at 24 November, it had provided assistance to some 34,000 internally displaced persons; however, UNHCR believes that the number is now closer to 30,000. Some 10,000 to 12,000 internally displaced persons have returned from Montenegro to Kosovo, but it is impossible to estimate at this time how many have remained there. Many internally displaced persons have returned again to Montenegro, others have gone to Albania or have moved to Western Europe. Only upon receiving the November distribution figures will it be possible to have a more accurate count of the displaced persons still in Montenegro. It will also take a few weeks to establish with more certainty the whereabouts of those displaced persons that have departed from Montenegro.

11. The return process is fragile, and those returning home often sleep with their belongings still packed beside them. Many families come only during the daylight hours, returning to their host families each evening. The fluidity of the movement back makes it almost impossible for the humanitarian organizations to accurately assess the number of people returning at present, but it appears that the number of returnees is growing and that the number living with host families will continue to decrease.

12. At the end of each month, UNHCR and the humanitarian organizations in Kosovo will hold meetings to assess the number of internally displaced persons and returnees inside Kosovo. These meetings will be attended by UNHCR staff from Montenegro and Albania, where information can be shared and the actual numbers more accurately counted.

Obstacles to returns

13. Uncertainty and continuing danger appear to be the main deterrent to returns. People who have returned spontaneously have done so mainly in search of survival during the expected harsh winter months. In the villages where internally displaced persons have gone back, many have prepared just one room to endure winter conditions.

14. Returns continue to be tentative and little permanent reconstruction is being undertaken. Returnees hesitate to put money into something that they fear they may well lose later. In the towns, businessmen appear to be holding back on investments, awaiting signs that a political settlement may be forthcoming.

15. In many cases, the internally displaced persons have returned to find their houses totally destroyed, prompting them to remain in the towns, where they feel they can at least be assured of continuing relief aid. Another major factor preventing returns is damaged infrastructure - lack of schools, no electricity and polluted wells.

16. International monitors observe increased returns of displaced persons to areas located in Malisevo, Orahovac, Suva Reka, Djakovica, Decani and Drenica municipalities. However, during the reporting period, in the wake of skirmishes between the government forces and Kosovo Albanian paramilitary units, renewed displacement was reported in areas such as Malisevo, south of Komorane and Lapusnik.

Confidence-building for returnees

17. Most returnees say they will feel more secure when teams of the Kosovo Diplomatic Observer Mission are around them. They anxiously await the arrival of the monitors of the OSCE Kosovo Verification Mission.

18. Where the presence of the Observer Mission is most visible, substantial returns have taken place. For example, between 70 and 100 per cent returns have been reported in the villages of Dragobilje, Ostrozub, Banja, Dobrodeljane and Pagarusa. The Mission has either maintained an outpost or conducted regular patrols in those villages, which have a combined population of more than 10,000. The same is true of seven villages in the Suva Reka region. Since the Mission began to deploy there, 13,000 of the 30,000 residents have returned.

Aid and shelter programmes

19. UNHCR, together with the World Food Programme and the non-governmental organization community, is continuing to provide aid to the displaced and returnee populations. The frequency of UNHCR-escorted convoys has increased to six days per week. During the third week of November, 120 trucks provided food and non-food assistance for 100,000 beneficiaries in 21 different locations.

20. UNHCR has satellite offices in Pec, Prizren and Mitrovica. Coordination of food and non-food assistance will be decentralized and the number of convoys per week is expected to increase to over 150 trucks by the beginning of December.

21. The UNHCR-non-governmental organization shelter assessment of 2-4 November covered 285 villages, of which 210 had been damaged by the conflict. Nearly 40 per cent of the homes were found to be habitable, requiring basic shelter materials - tiles, bricks, windows - which the Government of the Federal Republic of Yugoslavia should provide, pursuant to Security Council resolution 1199 (1998).

Security

22. A ceasefire called last month has generally held, although there have been arbitrary detentions, killings and kidnappings blamed on both Serbian security forces and the Kosovo Albanian paramilitary units. For the first time in the conflict, self-appointed groups on both sides of the ethnic divide have taken part in these actions, threatening to unravel the fragile peace.

23. Although security checkpoints were dismantled following the 27 October pullback, police continued to control checkpoints on highways, moving to less visible positions on strategic hills. Mobile checkpoints

have been established by Serbian security forces and Kosovo Albanian paramilitary units. These have not impeded the access of staff or vehicles of the office of the United Nations High Commissioner for Human Rights during this reporting period. However, at traffic checkpoints established by Serbian police, the Office has both directly observed and received reports of the questioning and search of passengers on regular intercity bus lines. While the pullback has resulted in freer movement, fear of being accosted on the street by police remains.

24. Security remains tight in villages along the border with Albania, where illegal traffic in arms and movement of members of Kosovo Albanian paramilitary units continue. Recently, troops detained an entire village population for 24 hours while they conducted a house-to-house search for weapons.

25. In the meantime, Kosovo Albanian paramilitary units have taken over checkpoints left by Serbian police in the interior villages, provoking incursions by Serbian armoured vehicles and triggering occasional gun battles. In many villages, members of Kosovo Albanian paramilitary units returned with the villagers - often their own family members - and acted as protectors. However, they seem to be in no mood to resume full-scale fighting and are battening down for the winter, as are the Serbian police.

Human rights

26. The situation of human rights in Kosovo continues to be characterized by the abduction and arbitrary detention of persons, as well as reports of summary execution of persons detained. Reports of systematic severe ill-treatment of persons in police detention and pre-trial detention continue.

27. In November the Office of the High Commissioner for Human Rights devoted all its country-wide staff resources to monitoring court proceedings in Kosovo against persons charged with terrorism, violating or endangering constitutional order or contributing to anti-state activity. Over a month after the accord of 13 October between the President of the Federal Republic of Yugoslavia, Slobodan Milosevic, and the United States Special Envoy, Richard Holbrooke, implementation of the last two points of the accord, which concern prosecution in state courts, remains unclear. The Serbian Minister of Justice has sent teams of prosecutors to district courts in Kosovo to examine individual cases, and court officials have confirmed to the Office of the High Commissioner that they have participated in working sessions with representatives of the Serbian Ministry of Justice and the office of the President of Serbia. The Ministry of Justice, together with the Federal Ministry for Foreign Affairs and the office of the President of Serbia, have solicited the cooperation of the Office of the High Commissioner in the ongoing resolution of individual cases and categories of cases pending in Kosovo to which the Office or the Special Rapporteur have drawn particular attention. These efforts have resulted in the release of several individuals from pre-trial detention and/or detention pending appeal, but new arrests, trials and sentencing continue. Kosovo Albanian media have taken an intense interest in reports of the ill-treatment of detainees and in the court proceedings themselves, particularly the potential application of "paraffin glove evidence". To the knowledge of the Office of the High Commissioner, however, no clear position has been enunciated by the Kosovo Albanian political leadership on amnesty or pardon for detainees. The Kosovo Albanian defence attorneys continue to pursue strongly the interest of their individual clients, as cases come up for trial.

28. The Office of the High Commissioner concentrated its efforts in the district courts of Prizren and Pec, where the bulk of armed activity has occurred and approximately 1,350 cases are pending, far exceeding the number of cases in the courts of Kosovska Mitrovica, Pristina and Gnjilane combined. The district court in Prizren, which had been holding trials related to allegations of terrorism and anti-state activity on a regular daily basis, suspended trials from 31 October to 9 November so that, according to the court president, case review could be conducted. The district court in Pec, however, has continued to hold up to four trials a day, except when weather or security conditions have prevented the transport of defendants to court. The Office of the High Commissioner has to date recorded 92 completed decisions of courts of first instance throughout Kosovo, but that figure is by no means comprehensive and only includes court documents at hand. Of that number, nearly all decisions have been convictions, with eight acquittals. Sentences range from 60 days to 13 years, with the majority of sentences from two to five years. For sentences of less than five years, until they have been confirmed by a court of a final instance, detention is not mandatory during the appeal process, but most so sentenced have been detained.

29. The number of persons in actual custody is difficult to obtain, as "custody" includes persons in pre-arraignment detention by Serbian police, under the auspices of the Ministry of Interior, and investigative or post-sentencing detention, under the auspices of the Ministry of Justice. On a massive scale, Serbian security officials in Kosovo have arrested and held in police detention large numbers of individuals for periods ranging from several hours to several days. The routine police "screening" of male returnees, however, has abated in recent weeks. Persons in police detention are routinely held incommunicado, without access to attorneys, longer than the three-plus-one days of pre-arraignment detention allowed by law. Their families are not informed of their arrest or of their release from police detention. The number of persons subsequently arraigned and held in investigative detention is unclear, as the International Committee of the Red Cross (ICRC) is not routinely and regularly informed of arraignments by the Ministry of Justice. As a result, the Office of the High Commissioner can only estimate, as have the Serbian Minister of Justice and defence attorneys, that from 1,500 to 1,900 cases are pending on charges related to terrorism, anti-state activity and/or aiding and abetting such activity. This does not include persons in police detention or persons called for "informative talks" by the police, whose number is absolutely unknown and whose names are known only anecdotally or when reported by non-governmental organizations.

30. Since the accord of 13 October and the Agreement of 16 October, information on the activity of Kosovo Albanian paramilitary "tribunals" has become public. The activity of the "tribunals" suggests a pattern of arbitrary arrest and summary execution. On 30 October, two League of Democratic Kosova activists were "arrested" by the Kosovo Albanian paramilitaries in Malisevo and have been "charged" with advocating the surrender of weapons to Serbian authorities. On 3 November, the "KLA Military Police Directorate" issued a communiqué stating that the two men had been arrested and were "under interrogation". The communiqué also acknowledged that two additional individuals had been executed and that Kosovo Albanian paramilitary units were seeking to arrest a member of the presidency of the League of Democratic Kosova. On 31 October, in "policing" activities, members of Kosovo Albanian paramilitary units arrested three men and killed a fourth near Podujevo for "alleged criminal activity".

31. On 1 November, a "Military Court" of Kosovo Albanian paramilitary units sentenced two abducted Tanjug journalists to 60 days of detention for "having committed violations and ignorance of the internal regular civilian-military book of regulations of the KLA, chapter VIII, respectively the military police book of regulations, item 5, page 27". Representatives of international agencies, including ICRC and the Office of the High Commissioner in the Federal Republic of Yugoslavia, have not been allowed to visit the abductees.

32. On 9 November, in Srbica, Kosovo Albanian paramilitary units abducted the third and fourth Serb civilians taken since mid-October, Zlatan Ivanovic and Bojan Pavlovic. In retaliation, on the evening of 11 November, family members of the victims and villagers from Leposavic organized the arbitrary detention of roughly 25 Kosovo Albanian passengers from an intercity bus. It is reported that the detention occurred with the knowledge of Serbian police who, at a minimum, did not intervene to stop it. During the night of 11 November, all but seven of the passengers were released; the seven were held in exchange for the two abducted Serbs. On 12 November, through the intervention of the Kosovo Diplomatic Observer Mission, an exchange took place.

33. On 17 November, near Podujevo, members of Kosovo Albanian paramilitary units abducted a Serbian police officer, Goran Zbiljic. In the same area on the same day, a Kosovo Albanian, Hakif Hoti, was also abducted. On 23 November, Kosovo Albanian paramilitary units issued a communiqué stating that it had "arrested" Mr. Zbiljic and other

Albanian "collaborators". On 24 November, through the actions of the Observer Mission, Mr. Zbiljic was released. Nothing is known about the fate of Mr. Hoti or other Serb, Albanian and Roma civilians and police officers abducted by armed Kosovo Albanians.

34. The Yugoslav authorities have reportedly authorized the team of Finnish experts acting under the European Union auspices to start investigations at six locations in Kosovo and in any other locations where forensic investigation proves to be justified. The choice of places, however, remains the prerogative of the Serb authorities since the forensic investigation, as part of the criminal investigation in general, can be initiated only on the basis of a Court order issued by an investigating judge.

V. OBSERVATIONS

35. After eight months of fighting, there are indications that displaced persons and refugees from Kosovo have begun returning to their homes, many destroyed. This is a difficult process and the United Nations agencies on the ground are making every effort to assist in the restoration of normal life in Kosovo. These activities, however, require close cooperation with the Kosovo Verification Mission and the support of the international community.

36. The extent to which the internally displaced persons and refugees are willing to return to their homes still varies by area. The reluctance to return permanently is mainly due to Kosovo Albanian paramilitary units and security forces remaining concentrated in certain areas, thus posing the potential of continuing clashes. Among other constraints hampering the return process are mines and booby traps and the destruction of utilities and dwellings. However, it is to be hoped that, as a result of the ceasefire, the increased international presence in the region and unhindered humanitarian assistance, the rate of returns will accelerate.

37. Nevertheless, humanitarian efforts cannot be an alternative to the political process. I am therefore concerned that, after the end of major hostilities in Kosovo, the advance towards a political solution remains slow. I commend the efforts of Ambassador Christopher Hill of the United States and of the Contact Group, and call upon the parties to engage in a meaningful dialogue aimed at finding a peaceful settlement in Kosovo to benefit all its people.

38. It is evident that the relative tranquillity in Kosovo is very deceptive. It is neither stable, nor irreversible. According to various reports, members of the Kosovo Albanian paramilitary units, which have been reappearing in greater numbers throughout Kosovo, seem to be motivated, well armed and ready for renewed action. The Government has enough security forces in the area to launch a new crack-down should these units engage in provocative actions. I urge all parties concerned to show restraint so as not to undermine the efforts for a political settlement.

39. Abductions and arbitrary arrests, coupled with fear of such actions, pose the most dangerous potential threats to the security and human rights of all persons in Kosovo. I strongly urge the Serbian authorities to stop the practice of arbitrary arrests and to cooperate fully with the international community in the field of human rights. I also urge Kosovo Albanian paramilitary units to immediately release all abductees without any preconditions.

40. As earlier stated, it is expected that the early deployment of the OSCE Kosovo Verification Mission will be a critical factor in building the confidence necessary for the return of those who fled their homes in the past months. It will also greatly assist in providing the Security Council with cogent information on the situation in the region. ...

Annex

Information on the situation in Kosovo and measures taken by the Organization for Security and Cooperation in Europe

General situation

1. The period since the last report, of 20 October, has been calm, without major operations being undertaken by Federal Republic of Yugoslavia or Kosovo Liberation Army (KLA) forces. Sporadic skirmishes and incidents of hostage-taking have occurred and tension has increased accordingly in many areas.

2. During the early part of the period, military activity was observed in western Kosovo between the towns of Pec, Gjakova and Dakovica. This area, adjacent to the Albanian border, has been an area of heavy fighting since the beginning of June. On 16 October, amid clear indications of withdrawal of Federal Republic of Yugoslavia security forces, the KLA "General Staff" announced a unilateral ceasefire but stated that it would also respond to any provocation.

3. Special Yugoslav police units were still present all over the province mostly on main roads, in the Drenica and Maljiševo areas, but in significantly decreased numbers. Federal Republic of Yugoslavia forces adopted a more discreet stance with troops hiding in the woods and mobile patrols. Many checkpoints were still in place and manned, particularly south-east of Kosovo and in the Drenica region. Freedom of movement was affected in some areas: Kosovo Diplomatic Observer Mission staff were prevented from entering a military base near Kosovska Mitrovica, and denied access to western regions by KLA forces near Glogovac. In the Shala region (the triangle between Kosovska, Mitrovica, Podujevo and Vucitrn) an Observer Mission team was stopped and denied onward access by the KLA.

4. KLA presence has become more significant in many areas over the last fortnight. KLA fighters were allegedly reported in the Orahovac area and in the Rugova Canyon, west of Pec. KLA seem to be filling the vacuum left by departing Federal Republic of Yugoslavia forces: many of them were spotted in abandoned MUP positions.

5. The ceasefire was violated several times in November through incidents such as an attack on mineworkers in Grabovac, a shoot-out between a heavily-armed KLA patrol and police resulting in five dead KLA members, attacks on the Maljiševo and Orahovac police stations and the burning of a school in Sipitula (west of Priština) with mutual accusations flying between Serb security forces and local Albanian population.

6. During the reporting period, the presence of large numbers of security forces, increasing tension and clashes were reported in the Dragobilje area, although it appeared difficult to establish who was responsible. The situation in Maljiševo remained tense with Serb security forces and Kosovo Albanians blaming each other for sporadic shootings. The situation was complicated by the arrest of two leading members of the League of Democratic Kosova chapter in Maljiševo by KLA on 30 October. In small villages in the area of Pec an increasing number of cases of harassment, arbitrary arrest and intimidation were reported.

7. The situation on the northern border of the former Yugoslav Republic of Macedonia with the Federal Republic of Yugoslavia (Kosovo) has remained stable and calm throughout the reporting period. All border crossings have continued to function normally. There have been no significant incidents; illegal crossing and smuggling have remained at a lower level than at any time since independence, attributable in large part to the presence of Yugoslav security forces on the northern part of the border of the former Yugoslav Republic of Macedonia. On the western border with Albania there has been no substantive change in the pattern of activity. Periodic incidents continue to occur of attempted illegal entry by small groups from Albania, sometimes armed, which sometimes engage Macedonian security forces, and are sometimes fired upon. The arrival of the first winter snow can be expected to dampen activity.

The situation of the civilian population

8. By the end of October, the Head of the Office of the United Nations High Commissioner for Refugees (UNHCR) in the Federal Republic of Yugoslavia indicated that the fear of winter had forced some 30,000 internally displaced persons to return to their homes and repair them before the winter, in spite of security fears. It is estimated that some 10,000 internally displaced persons still remain exposed in the open on high ground. Internally displaced persons accommodated in other people's homes are estimated at 60,000 in Priština, 42,000 in Kosovska Mitrovica and 20,636 in the Pec area. In some cases, such as a camp in the area of Kormorane with an estimated 1,500 internally displaced persons, people spend the day in their villages rebuilding, returning to the camp at night.

9. Refugee returns are occurring but trends vary according to region. In some villages south-east of Maljiševo approximately 90 per cent of the population has returned; but the area closest to the Albanian border and to Junik remains deserted, as do all the small villages to the east. There are no signs of spontaneous return of refugees.

10. Urgently required aid has been delivered by UNHCR and all other agencies at a rate of 14 convoys a week, supplying some 100,000 internally displaced persons. Humanitarian agencies have encountered considerable problems, many of which centre on security fears and trust among the internally displaced persons. An incident that typifies the precarious

situation occurred on 23 October, when, for the first time in the experience of UNHCR in Kosovo, an aid convoy came under KLA fire in a case of mistaken identity.

11. A medical team assessed the general health situation of people living in Kosovo as very poor. Owing to the conflict situation and subsequent collapse of medical supplies and availability of treatment, especially in the rural areas, a significant increase of various infectious diseases is to be expected.

12. Another issue of concern is that of missing persons, whether ethnic Albanians or Serbs. In this respect the International Committee of the Red Cross in Kosovo has drawn attention to 119 missing Serbs.

Refugee influx

13. A significant number of refugees have continued to enter Albania via Montenegro, while in the north-east of Albania very few refugees were reported to have crossed into the country. This is thought to be a result of the first heavy snowfalls, which are making for very harsh winter conditions, the increased number of Federal Republic of Yugoslavia patrols in the area and reports of newly laid mines.

14. By the end of October, UNHCR claimed that an average 12 refugees were still crossing the border each day and the number of refugees in Kukes, Has and Zogaj was 1,106. The deployment of the Kosovo Verification Mission has brought demands for early repatriation from refugees who remain in the north of the country who are extremely wary of returning without solid guarantees for their security. Still, some of the registered refugees voiced their intention to stay in Albania during the winter months.

15. The inadequate security situation in the Tropoje district continues to seriously hamper the registration process of refugees, a prerequisite for their continued aid. The situation of refugees in the area is deteriorating, little aid has arrived in the district since September, and locals have stolen previous supplies. Action to improve the security situation in the district by the appropriate Albanian authorities is considered grossly inadequate.

16. The current number of refugees from Kosovo in the former Yugoslav Republic of Macedonia is 2,800, although the figure is difficult to verify. The number of Kosovars visiting and staying on a temporary or extended footing with friends or relatives has remained broadly stable. The great majority of those staying wish to remain out of public view, shun officialdom and appear to wish to return to Kosovo as soon as they judge it is safe to do so. There has been little sign to date of any significant number returning.

Kosovo conflict spillover potential

17. The OSCE presence in Albania, the OSCE spillover mission to Skopje and the OSCE missions to Bosnia and Herzegovina and to Croatia have been instructed to continue to follow closely the spillover potential of the Kosovo conflict.

18. OSCE monitors in Albania observed convoys of Federal Republic of Yugoslavia security vehicles regrouping and moving in the border area, suggesting that some elements have withdrawn from there. Despite these withdrawals heavy border patrolling continued, especially in traditional refugee crossing points, in the north-east and north of the country.

19. Additional mines have been laid by Federal Republic of Yugoslavia forces and an increased number of people have been killed or injured by newly laid mines. Laying of mines is seen as an attempt to limit the activity of the KLA, and is regarded as provocative at a time when the peace process is at an embryonic stage and does nothing to instill hope in the refugees who wish to return to their homes.

20. Movement and training of fighters continue to be observed in the north-eastern border areas of Albania, and it is apparent that cross-border activity is continuing, albeit more limited than in the past, owing to the heavy presence of Federal Republic of Yugoslavia forces. There have been a number of actions inside the Federal Republic of Yugoslavia, and some wounded fighters were being treated later in local Albanian hospitals.

21. A number of border incidents have occurred during the reporting period, sometimes triggered by KLA activity. One incursion by a Federal Republic of Yugoslavia patrol was reported as being a kilometre inside Albanian territory. Another border incident occurred on 1 November when the Serb forces fired several mortar rounds at Koshara BP and one round landed on the Albanian side of the border.

22. Albanian Prime Minister Majko, while following the policy established by his predecessor, Mr. Nano, has been introducing some changes in the Government's public approach to the Kosovo issue. Pointing out that the Albanian State will not play an active role in giving advice to the Kosovo Albanian people to find their political identity, Mr. Majko stressed indirectly the idea of an ethnic Albanian solution as an offer for the Albanians in Kosovo. Nevertheless, the Kosovo crisis is far from being the dominant topic in Albanian politics, which focused on the International Conference on Albania, called by the Government of Albania under the auspices of "Friends of Albania" (a group co-chaired by OSCE and European Union), held on 30 October, the first large gathering of this nature since the traumatic events of early 1997.

23. Law and order enforcement in the north-east of Albania remained extremely weak and the continuing lack of government control in the region is still a source of serious concern also in the context of the Kosovo crisis.

24. In the former Yugoslav Republic of Macedonia, the situation in the northern border with the Federal Republic of Yugoslavia remained mostly calm during the reporting period. In a shooting on 11 November, a Macedonian border patrol killed an Albanian male on the border between the former Yugoslav Republic of Macedonia and Albania. The potential risks of spillover from Kosovo to the former Yugoslav Republic of Macedonia are, however, at the moment regarded as slight, in particular in view of the increase in troops of the United Nations Preventive Deployment Force from 850 to 1,050 and the stationing of the NATO "Extraction Force" on Macedonian territory in support of the Kosovo Verification Mission.

25. During the campaign for the second round of the parliamentary elections, the crisis in Kosovo was a dominant issue and the leading coalition, VMRO-DPMNE/DA, continue to stress its commitment to dealing with the problems of the economy as a first priority. Macedonian officials said that the government had a basic policy of an "equal relationship" with all neighbours and that regional cooperation was to be promoted to achieve its objectives. Speaking of rumours of Macedonian Albanians joining the KLA, an official stated that Albanians were well integrated in the former Yugoslav Republic of Macedonia. The attitude of people in the former Yugoslav Republic of Macedonia can best be described as "apprehensive", owing to the problems in neighbouring countries, but neither of the ethnic groups is militant.

26. Referring to the explosions in Gostivar, Skopje, Kumanovo and Prilep, the Minister of the Interior reported that 12 persons of Albanian origin were arrested and that direct material evidence had been found, as well as supplies of weapons. Press speculation was that the KLA were responsible but the Interior Ministry confirmed that the 12 were members of an interior group associated with radical political parties inside the former Yugoslav Republic of Macedonia and connected with foreign countries.

Measures taken by the Organization for Security and Cooperation in Europe

27. Following negotiations between Ambassador Holbrooke and President Milosevic, the Government of the Federal Republic of Yugoslavia signed two agreements designed to verify compliance with Security Council resolution 1199 (1998) of 23 September which called, inter alia, for a cessation of hostilities in Kosovo. On 15 October an agreement was concluded between the authorities of the Federal Republic of Yugoslavia and NATO that permitted unarmed NATO aircraft to fly over Kosovo. An agreement between OSCE and the Federal Republic of Yugoslavia was then signed on 16 October between the Chairman-in-Office, Bronislaw Geremek, and Federal Republic of Yugoslavia Minister of Foreign Affairs Jovanovic, agreeing to the establishment of an OSCE Verification Mission. The Permanent Council of OSCE declared "the preparedness of OSCE to embark on verification duties related to compliance of all parties in Kosovo" in its decision 259.

28. OSCE study teams have since undertaken detailed examinations to establish the operational requirements of the OSCE Kosovo Verification Mission. The Verification Mission Support Unit, consisting of planning, personnel, logistics and communications cells, was formed in Vienna. The working groups produced the concept of operations document, which was approved by the Head of Mission, Ambassador William Walker, who first visited Pristina on 22 October and permanently took up his duties there on 11 November 1998.

29. The Verification Mission's immediate financial requirements were covered by the OSCE Contingency Fund and a spending authority allocated by the Secretary-General. The OSCE Permanent Council, in its decision 266 of 11 November, authorized the 1998 budget for the Mission in the amount of ATS 756,530,264. This enabled the Mission to make the major investments required this year; it additionally enabled augmentation of the secretariat's departments in Vienna.

30. The Verification Mission's advance headquarters has been established in Pristina, and Norway has assumed the responsibility for providing initial staffing and communications links. The Activation Unit has been replaced by Mission staff. A training location (the Kosovo Verification Mission Induction Centre) has been identified in Brezovica, outside Pristina, where three-day training courses will begin on 23 November for OSCE verifiers.

31. Cooperation between the OSCE Kosovo Verification Mission, humanitarian and other international organizations is a key ingredient of the Mission's concept of operations. The successful outcome of the Mission depends largely on coordination at headquarters level and close collaboration in the field.

32. NATO has a pivotal role in supporting the implementation of the mandate and underpinning the Mission's security plan; a number of meetings have taken place between the two organizations in Brussels and in Vienna.

33. An early example of this kind of cooperation is the target-oriented meeting organized by the OSCE Office of Democratic Institutions and Human Rights in Warsaw on 5 November 1998 to bring together international and humanitarian organizations, non-governmental organizations and OSCE institutions for an exchange of views on this subject.

34. On 5 November the Chairman-in-Office of OSCE, Bronislaw Geremek, received in Warsaw Ambassador William Graham Walker, head of the OSCE Kosovo Verification Mission. During the meeting it was agreed that, at this stage of Verification Mission planning, the main concern is to assure the security of Mission personnel on the ground. Minister Geremek emphasized his strong support to Ambassador Walker and provided him with his view on the major problems regarding deployment of the OSCE verifiers in Kosovo. He underlined the need for cooperation with the authorities of the Federal Republic of Yugoslavia and NATO, as well as immediate deployment of the personnel in Kosovo.

35. The same day the Chairman-in-Office of OSCE, accompanied by Ambassador Walker, met with the deputies of the Kosovo Verification Mission and delivered them their nominations.

36. Preparations for the deployment of the Mission were going relatively well. By the date of the OSCE Ministerial Meeting in Oslo, that is by 2 December, the aim is to have around 800 verifiers on the ground in Kosovo, with further deployment capacity of 200 to 250 a week. Allowing for Christmas and the New Year, by mid-January the Mission should reach 1,500 to 1,600 personnel. By mid-November, the leadership group of the Mission was already in the field.

37. The following international Kosovo Verification Mission and Kosovo Diplomatic Observer Mission personnel are already present on the ground in Kosovo:

Kosovo Verification Mission headquarters:
    50 personnel and 11 soft-skinned vehicles
Kosovo Diplomatic Observer Mission:
    United States: 183 personnel and 13 armoured vehicles
    European Union:30 personnel and 13 armoured vehicles
    Russian Federation: 17 personnel and 3 soft-skinned vehicles
    United Kingdom: 50 personnel and 20 armoured vehicles
    France: 15 personnel and 8 armoured vehicles
    Kosovo Verification Mission: 12 personnel and 2 soft-skinned vehicles
    Induction Centre:

38. The Organization for Security and Cooperation in Europe is making all efforts to verify Yugoslav compliance with Security Council resolutions 1160 (1998), 1199 (1998) and 1203 (1998), as well as in supporting the establishment of proper political conditions to start unconditional peace negotiations between the parties to the conflict.

8. Press Release, OSCE Chairman-in-Office Condemns Kosovo Violence, Warsaw, 15 December 1998

The Chairman-in-Office of the OSCE, Polish Foreign Minister Bronislaw Geremek, strongly condemns the recent violence in Kosovo which comes at a critical juncture in the efforts of the international community to relax tensions and support the peace process. Yesterday's violence cost the lives of over 30 people. Mr. Geremek offers his condolences to the family members of those who were killed. Mr. Geremek warns that continued violence could reverse the progress made over the past couple of months towards a peaceful settlement of the conflict. While the OSCE remains steadfast in its commitment to carry out its mandate, it can't do it alone. The Federal Yugoslav authorities and the people of Kosovo must commit themselves to negotiations, and not resort to further violence. Fighting will not lead to peace and prosperity, but to a future of instability. The OSCE renews its full support to the negotiations led by US envoy Christopher Hill and supported by the EU representative Wolfgang Petritch as the only way to come to a peaceful settlement. The OSCE continues to build -

with the Kosovo Verification Mission - a strong international presence on the ground. As our numbers grow, so too will our efforts to deter violence and promote stability.

9. ICRC Update on the Response to the Crisis in Kosovo, 22 December 1998

<u>General situation:</u> Ten weeks after the agreement between the Organization for Security and Cooperation in Europe (OSCE) and the Federal Republic of Yugoslavia (FRY) was signed, the situation in Kosovo remains volatile. The month of December saw some of the most serious incidents since the cease-fire was established, including clashes along the border between the Federal Republic of Yugoslavia and Albania, as well as what appear to be the first deliberate attacks on public places in urban areas. While there is still an expectation that the growing presence of the Kosovo Verification Mission (KVM) of the OSCE will contribute to a stabilization of the security situation, the lack of discernible progress in the political negotiations raises lasting concerns for the future. Against this unstable background, and in view of the harsh winter conditions, humanitarian actors, including the International Committee of the Red Cross (ICRC), have continued to address specific needs throughout Kosovo, as well as in other areas of Serbia and in Montenegro. ...

Protection

Further progress was made in the ICRC's efforts to visit detainees. Since the end of October, some 400 persons held by the Serbian authorities in connection with the Kosovo conflict were visited, including persons still under investigation. In addition, the Serbian authorities have officially notified the ICRC of approximately another 420 detainees.

Although the ICRC has still not been able to reach a generalized access agreement with the Serbian authorities and must therefore continue to present requests for visits to detainees to investigating magistrates, the growing number of notifications and the more widespread access to persons under investigation represent a considerable improvement.

As for access to persons allegedly held by the Kosovo Liberation Army (KLA), there has to date not been any significant development, in spite of the recent release of six persons by the KLA.

<u>Cooperation with OSCE Verification Mission</u>

As a result of consultations between the OSCE and the ICRC, which began within days of the signing of the OSCE-FRY agreement, delegates of the International Red Cross have, since the end of November, been taking part in the briefing sessions for KVM staff arriving in Kosovo.

The objective is to present the mandate and specific tasks of the ICRC and the broader International Red Cross and Red Crescent Movement. By the end of the year, the ICRC will have taken part and made presentations in ten such sessions.

This activity is undertaken in parallel to the institutional and operational dialogue established with the KVM and the OSCE in Pristina, Belgrade, Vienna and elsewhere.

10. UN Inter-Agency Update on Kosovo Humanitarian Situation, 24 December 1998

United Nations Consolidated Interagency Appeal

1. On 17 December the United Nations launched the Consolidated Interagency Appeal for Bosnia and Herzegovina, Croatia, Federal Republic of Yugoslavia, The former Yugoslav Republic of Macedonia and Albania. The Appeal covers the period January - December 1999. Programmes included in the Appeal are divided into two distinct but related categories: transitional programmes which address needs following the 1995 General Framework Agreement for Peace (Dayton Agreement) and more emergency-orientated programmes which focus on humanitarian needs in Kosovo. Projects included in the Appeal are divided into five different sectors: Human Rights, Protection and Promotion of Solutions; Food; Health, Education and Community Services; Relief and Rehabilitation; and Multi-sectoral Assistance and Programme support.

2. The Appeal seeks a total of US $ 359.4 million, US $ 104 million of which is earmarked for programmes in the Federal Republic of Yugoslavia (FRY). UNHCR is the largest appealing agency for FRY seeking US $ 60.5 million. Almost two thirds of the amount requested by UNHCR for FRY will be used to assist over 500,000 refugees from Bosnia and Herzegovina and Croatia.

3. Within the FRY, it is estimated that 460,000 persons affected by the crisis in Kosovo will require assistance in the first six months of 1999. Of these, 400,000, including displaced, returnees and host families, are in Kosovo, 20,000 in other parts of Serbia and 40,000 in Montenegro. For planning purposes it is assumed that 100,000 persons will require direct support in the second half of 1999. For the longer term, developmental support and activities aimed at improving the economic conditions of the country are required.

4. For countries within the region affected by an influx of Kosovo refugees, namely Albania, Bosnia and Herzegovina and The former Yugoslav Republic of Macedonia, the 1999 planning scenario involves the provision of continued protection and assistance to meet the needs of existing caseloads until spring when programmes will be reviewed. Should conditions allow earlier voluntary repatriation, the resources foreseen for countries of asylum would be redeployed to assist the returnees.

UN High Commissioner for Refugees visit to the FRY

5. From 20-22 December the UN High Commissioner for Refugees visited the Federal Republic of Yugoslavia. The High Commissioner travelled to Kosovo with the principal purpose of establishing a link with the Organisation for Security and Cooperation in Europe Kosovo Verification Mission (OSCE/KVM), which is charged with the responsibility of verifying the cease-fire on the ground, seeking to ensure security for all citizens and promoting conditions for a political settlement. UNHCR is charged with the responsibility of lead role for the protection and assistance of refugees and displaced within and from Kosovo.

6. The High Commissioner met a number of key Government and diplomatic officials, including President Milosevic and the Head of the OSCE/KVM mission, Ambassador Walker. During the course of her visit the High Commissioner stressed the strong and continuous support of UNHCR to more than 500,000 refugees from Bosnia and Herzegovina and Croatia and underlined her commitment to maintaining UNHCR's active search for solutions and financial support to the refugees. She welcomed the ceasefire and the successful implementation of a major humanitarian assistance programme in Kosovo, which ensured that a humanitarian catastrophe had been averted, and permitted all displaced to reach proper shelter. The fact that some 100,000 of the former displaced were back in their home villages/towns was a source of great satisfaction. However, she noted that many houses had been destroyed and remained empty and that 175,000 - 200,000 people remained displaced within Kosovo even though they had adequate shelter.

Human Rights

7. The Office of the UN High Commissioner for Human Rights estimates that between 1,500 and 2,000 Kosovo Albanians have been detained since the Holbrooke/Milosevic Agreement of 13 October 1998. During her recent visit to FRY the UN High Commissioner for Refugees deplored these arrests and the fact that the ICRC has no access during the period up to trial of detainees. She also deplored the abduction of the estimated 150 civilians by the Kosovo Liberation Army (KLA) and strongly denounced the terrible murders which had taken place during the past week in Pec, Kosovo Polje and Podujevo.
...

Security

10. On 14 December two major incidents set back the search for peace in Kosovo. On the western border, security forces killed at least 36 armed Albanians, part of a group of some 140, while they were attempting to cross into the Serbian province from Albania before dawn. Later in the evening in Kosovo's second major town of Pec, masked men sprayed gunfire on the Panda Cafe, killing six Serbian teenagers as they played pool. These two events were the most severe since the cease-fire came into effect two months ago. In another incident, police found the body of the deputy mayor of Kosovo Polje on 18 December near Pristina airport. The official was kidnapped from his home the previous night. On 21 December a policeman was shot dead in Podujevo. During the past week protests have been held in Kosovo's major towns against abductions attributed to the KLA. On 18 December the head of the OSCE/KVM met families of Serbian kidnapping victims in an attempt to defuse tension in Kosovo. Meanwhile, every effort to secure the release of the abducted, or news of their fate, continues.

11. Threats to the security of humanitarian personnel are also increasing. On 11 December Serbian civilians, protesting the kidnapping of two Serbians in July, briefly detained three aid workers, including an international staff member of Cap Anamur, the German NGO. It was the first time an expatriate worker had been held by Serbians while on an aid mission in Kosovo. The aid workers were on their way to distribute relief aid at Jezerce village when they were stopped and held by Serbians at Nerodimlje village just outside Urosevac. UNHCR alerted representatives of the Kosovo Diplomatic Observer Mission, who intervened to secure the release of the three within a few hours.

Coordination

12. On 16 December UNHCR chaired a coordination meeting in Pristina on behalf of the relief and donor community to facilitate planning and to identify areas to be targeted for assistance during 1999. In presentations delivered by representatives from UN agencies, the UN Secretariat, donors and the OSCE several target areas emerged, including human rights, protection, women and children and local capacity building. ...

MONTENEGRO

22. On 11 December a landslide near Kolasin in the North of Montenegro caused severe damage to the main road rendering it unusable. The Automobile Club of Yugoslavia told UNHCR that it could take several months to make the necessary repairs. If initial reports are correct, the implications are serious as this route is used to transport food and other relief items from Bar, the main port of entry in Montenegro, to Kosovo, Northern Montenegro and, to a lesser extent, other parts of the Federal Republic of Yugoslavia. The one alternative route is not a serious option as it is a narrow mountain road which is frequently blocked by snow. Humanitarian agencies are currently investigating other options such as the use of the railway or local purchase to ensure that there is no interruption in the supply of humanitarian items to Kosovo and Northern Montenegro.

23. The UNHCR-funded registration of displaced in Montenegro is due to start shortly. In the meantime the December food distribution is underway for 34,385 displaced beneficiaries. The displaced receive a ration of 12 kg flour, 1 kg pasta, 1 litre of oil, salt and yeast. The International Orthodox Christian Church and Samariter Arbeitshilfer are also distributing food parcels. UNHCR reports that the refugees from Bosnia and Herzegovina and Croatia have received no food since October 1998. According to WFP 7,000 MT wheat flour is awaiting customs and sanitary clearance in Bar and distributions to refugees are scheduled to begin in January 1999.

24. The final draft of the Memorandum of Understanding on the provision of education to displaced children from Kosovo has been submitted by UNHCR and UNICEF to the Government of Montenegro for signature. UNICEF reports that there are currently 1,600 children of school age in Montenegro. In meetings with school principals UNICEF and UNHCR have found practical solutions to ensure that children are able to attend school. ...

S/1998/1221, 12 December 1998

11.   Report of the Secretary-General, 24 December 1998

... 3. This section of the report is based on information provided by the Office of the United Nations High Commissioner for Refugees (UNHCR) and the Office of the United Nations High Commissioner for Human Rights, the Kosovo Diplomatic Observer Mission and individual Member States.   The report also includes information submitted by the Chairman-in-Office of OSCE (see annex I).

4. Since my last report was issued, the situation in Kosovo has not significantly improved and there are alarming signs of potential deterioration. While various sources report that the ceasefire is still holding, there are indications of growing tensions on the ground. During the first half of December, violence reached its highest level since the 16 October Agreement; more than 50 persons have died in violent attacks.

5. Meanwhile, despite the efforts of Ambassador Christopher Hill of the United States of America and the European Union Envoy, Ambassador Wolfgang Petritsch of Austria, to bring the parties concerned to the negotiation table, there has been no progress in the political dialogue in Kosovo. Recent statements by both sides regarding the draft agreement proposed by Ambassador Hill indicate that there is considerable distance between the positions of the parties and that they are far from engaging in meaningful negotiations.

6. Though no additional abduction cases have been reported since mid-November, the fate and whereabouts of abducted persons remain unknown and family members and others have begun to organize public protests and appeals to representatives of OSCE. These protests, which have also addressed arbitrary detentions, have failed to obtain satisfactory results or information. Reports continue to be received concerning arbitrary detention and systematic ill-treatment of persons in police detention and pre-trial detention.

Returns

7. Despite tensions, displaced persons continue to return to their homes. UNHCR estimates that some 100,000 people have now returned, while some 200,000 remained displaced within Kosovo. The estimated number of internally displaced persons has increased based on the evidence obtained from the first phase of the shelter survey, and on figures cited by the Yugoslav state media on 14 December.

8. As winter's cold weather has arrived, more people are seeking to return home, encouraged in part by the growing presence of humanitarian agencies and the Kosovo Verification Mission. Returns began even to such "sensitive" locations as Junik, near the Albanian border; the Djakovica area; and Lodja, a village near Pec. Potential returnees have made tentative visits even to the Malisevo area. According to UNHCR, some 1,300 of the 6,000 residents of Junik who had fled during the Government offensive in August have returned, although the army and police have maintained a heavy presence in the area as they consider it one of the key routes in trafficking of illegal weapons and personnel of Kosovo Albanian paramilitary units. On 11 December, UNHCR and the Observer Mission escorted the first group of 16 displaced persons back to Lodja. They had expressed a wish to rebuild their houses which had been severely damaged last August. The return was preceded by assurances from police officials in Pec that returnees would not be harmed. Since the area has been almost totally destroyed, the repair of the local school will take priority so that it can be used as a temporary shelter while returnees rebuild their homes.

9. These returns indicate the genuine desire of many displaced persons to return home. However, the process is impeded by the lack of housing and adequate security mechanisms to monitor returnees' reintegration into their respective communities. Other returns, however, have taken place in situations of continued tension and sporadic clashes and under far from ideal conditions, apparently as a result of desperation and the lack of other options. Difficulties in paying for accommodation in the places of refuge and the worsening winter weather prompted many of the displaced to opt for return.

10. Among those who have returned are some 10,000 who previously sought safety in Montenegro. The number of displaced in Montenegro is at present estimated at 27,000. Bosnia and Herzegovina now hosts an estimated 10,000 refugees from Kosovo, of whom 6,700 have registered with UNHCR. Some of them have already requested assistance to repatriate. According to the latest registration of refugees from Kosovo in Albania, there are some 24,000 persons there. In addition, it is estimated that there are still some 20,000 displaced persons from Kosovo in other areas of Serbia. The latter figure might be growing, as there are some indications of fear among the Serbian inhabitants of remote villages as Kosovo Albanians return.

Obstacles to returns/security

11. On 20 November, two policemen were killed and three injured in a suspected ambush by Kosovo Albanian paramilitaries in Prilep. On 3 December, 12 Albanians were killed in separate incidents, 8 by Yugoslav Army border guards in the area of the Gorozup watchtower, 1 by Kosovo Albanian paramilitaries along the Pristina-Pec road and 3 others on a main street in downtown Pristina under circumstances which are unclear.

12. Not only has the number of persons killed increased dramatically, but during the reporting period there were violent incidents in heavily populated urban centres. On 4 December, an armed confrontation between Serbian security personnel and Kosovo Albanian paramilitaries occurred in the hospital compound in Pec, resulting in the death of one of the Kosovo Albanians. On 11 December, three Kosovo Albanian men - a policeman, and two state company employees - were killed in Glogovac. On 14 December, 34 violent deaths occurred in two separate incidents. Thirty Albanians were killed and 12 wounded near the Gorozup and Liken border posts in fighting between Yugoslav border guards and a group of armed Albanians. That same day, two masked men entered and attacked patrons in a cafe in Pec, killing six Serbs. On 18 December, the Deputy Mayor of Kosovo Polje was kidnapped and murdered.

13. Following the 13 October accord between President Slobodan Milosevic and United States Special Envoy Richard Holbrooke, Kosovo Albanian paramilitary units have taken advantage of the lull in the fighting to re-establish their control over many villages in Kosovo, as well as over some areas near urban centres and highways. These actions by Kosovo Albanian paramilitary units have only served to provoke the Serbian authorities, leading to statements that if the Kosovo Verification Mission cannot control these units the Government would. The local authorities have indicated to UNHCR that they would not allow "terrorists to take over Kosovo". Government officials have warned that recent incidents, particularly attempts by the armed groups to cross into Kosovo from Albania and killings of civilians, would justify a renewal of operations against Kosovo Albanian paramilitary units.

14. In this regard, serious apprehension of a new cycle of major hostilities has been expressed by different sources. While Kosovo Albanian paramilitary units are taking an increasingly bold stance, the Serbian police force is responding by increasing patrols and the use of mobile checkpoints. Some reports suggest that the number of Yugoslav Army and Serbian special police units deployed in Kosovo may exceed agreed figures.

15. The persistent insecurity reinforces UNHCR's position of not promoting return from areas outside Kosovo. However, where individuals clearly express their wish to repatriate, UNHCR will facilitate their return, seeking clearance, ensuring that they possess the necessary documentation and providing transport assistance, if appropriate. UNHCR will monitor the security situation of returnees and of those who remain displaced within Kosovo and will assess their material needs.

Abductions

16. The lack of information about the fate of persons abducted by Kosovo Albanian paramilitaries has given rise to growing impatience among the families and their affected communities. According to information received from the authorities of the Federal Republic of Yugoslavia, as of 7 December, 282 civilians and police have been abducted by Kosovo Albanian paramilitary units, 136 of whom are sill unaccounted for. On 9 December, the political spokesperson of the Kosovo Albanian paramilitary units, Adem Demaqi, noted publicly that he had made efforts to release abducted Serb civilians and that he expected "the Serbian side" to do the same. However, Mr. Demaqi admitted that he feared that many persons listed as missing had been killed in clashes between the police and Kosovo Albanian paramilitary units during the summer offensive. On 10 December, Kosovo Serbs from Orahovac organized a march to the Kosovo Albanian paramilitary-controlled area of Dragobilje, demanding information about the fate of the missing. The march proceeded without incident, owing mainly to the mediation of the Kosovo Diplomatic Observer Mission, and concluded with a meeting between Serb and Kosovo Albanian representatives. On 11 December, Serb civilians from the

Urosevac area held a group of five national and international humanitarian workers for approximately eight hours, demanding that they be exchanged for two Serbs abducted in July. The group was released through the intervention of the Observer Mission. On 14 December, relatives and supporters of abducted Serbs demonstrated outside the OSCE headquarters in Pristina; a letter was submitted to Ambassador Walker requesting OSCE to take concrete steps to resolve the issue.

Visit of the United Nations High Commissioner for Refugees to the Federal Republic of Yugoslavia

17. The purpose of the visit of the High Commissioner for Refugees to the Federal Republic of Yugoslavia from 20 to 22 December was to review the effectiveness of the United Nations humanitarian action in the new situation and to ensure that there was a solid foundation for close cooperation between the Kosovo Verification Mission and the humanitarian action led by UNHCR. In Kosovo she met senior government officials and Ambassador William Walker, the Head of the Verification Mission, with whom she visited returnees who in some cases were repairing their homes, and met Croatian refugees at a collection centre. In Belgrade, the High Commissioner met with President Milosevic and other senior officials.

18. In her meeting with the President at the end of her mission, the High Commissioner reviewed the assistance programme and discussed possible solutions for the problem of over 500,000 refugees from earlier conflicts in the region as well as the humanitarian situation in Kosovo. With regard to the latter issue, the High Commissioner noted significant positive changes that had occurred since her last meeting with the President three months ago. The conflict which had caused large-scale displacement had effectively ceased in October and many persons had returned to their villages, if not to their homes. The humanitarian operation was now able to meet the challenge and an immediate humanitarian catastrophe had been averted.

19. The High Commissioner strongly condemned acts of violence and intimidation against all civilians. She noted that many Kosovo Albanians feared detention on suspicion of having been involved in the conflict and that this was adversely affecting the prospects for the return of those still displaced, as well as the sustainability of the returns that had occurred. A number of those she had met had asked her about an amnesty and she recalled earlier exchanges on the subject with President Milosevic and the authorities. The High Commissioner expressed her concern that the necessary safeguards on return would not be in place at the time they were most needed, and requested the President to adopt an amnesty law as soon as possible. Such an amnesty was a key component of confidence-building in any post-conflict return and would contribute to the declared aim of the authorities of finding a political solution without delay.

20. The High Commissioner also underlined the importance of the restoration of essential services, such as electricity, and the need to help health and education services recover from the effects of the conflict. President Milosevic said that the restoration of such services was a high priority, but adversely affected by acts of violence committed by "terrorists".

Aid/shelter programmes

21. UNHCR and non-governmental organizations (NGOs) are conducting the second phase of the shelter survey, which will cover some 500 more villages in western and central Kosovo.

22. At the same time, UNHCR is providing assistance to those returnees undertaking major repairs of their houses. Some 450 houses in 31 villages are currently undergoing repairs using startup kits from UNHCR and other aid agencies, including heavy-duty tarpaulin and wooden beams and fillets, battens for window and door frames, boards, nails and tools. UNHCR has also distributed 4,500 shelter kits for minor repairs, which include plastic sheets, wood, nails and hammers, thus facilitating the preparation of at least one room in the house for the winter.

23. One of the most significant problems in Kosovo facing people affected by the fighting has been the lack of food. Wheat flour stored for the winter has often been either looted or burned. Thousands of livestock have been killed. Farmers missed the October planting

season. Thus many displaced persons will depend on donated food supplies well into 1999.

24. In addition to the six-days-per-week deliveries of food and other humanitarian assistance coordinated by UNHCR from Pristina, aid distribution has begun in Pec. Convoys from Pec will deliver assistance to nearby villages and remote areas in Decane and Klina. Another distribution centre is scheduled to begin operations from Prizren and will distribute food supplies to 10 municipalities in southern Kosovo. These decentralized distribution centres will expand the capacity of UNHCR and other humanitarian organizations to deliver needed relief supplies to a larger group of people, targeting more areas.

Security of the humanitarian personnel

25. Humanitarian agencies in general have unhindered access to all areas of Kosovo. Although Kosovo Albanian paramilitary units have not directly posed a threat or any obstacles to the delivery of humanitarian aid, their practice of laying mines and engaging in sporadic clashes with the Serbian police clearly create a risk for humanitarian workers. No harassment of aid workers by the Government forces has been reported.

Coordination with the Kosovo Verification Mission

26. Although the Kosovo Diplomatic Observer Mission has significantly increased in size and presence, the operational date and deployment of the Verification Mission remain delayed and expectations of large-scale presence of international verifiers on the ground have not been met. OHCHR field staff report that civilians in urban areas and villages are pointing increasingly to unfulfilled expectations and to even further delays in deployment likely to be caused by the traditional winter holidays. The combination of unfulfilled expectations of international confidence-building, dramatic incidents of urban-area violence and border clashes is exacerbating an already grave human rights situation.

27. UNHCR has systematically continued briefings for the incoming observers of the Verification Mission at their induction sessions. With four liaison officers now in place, UNHCR maintains daily contact between the Mission and the humanitarian agencies on staff security and humanitarian issues. The basis is being laid for a functional and effective working relationship, similar to the one developed with the Diplomatic Observer Mission. As with the Observer Mission, UNHCR, on behalf of all humanitarian agencies, is establishing a mechanism for exchange of information with the Verification Mission to promote conditions that would spur returns to those areas where return is feasible.

28. The Head of the Verification Mission assured the High Commissioner for Refugees during their meeting that the Mission would support the humanitarian action in every way possible consistent with its mandate and primary task. The High Commissioner assured him of close coordination on the part of UNHCR in order to make the best possible use of the potential of the Mission to contribute, with its rapidly expanding field presence, to creating conditions that allowed sustainable return and in helping identify humanitarian needs. They recognized that a good foundation for this cooperation had already been laid, including, for example, with information provided for the humanitarian actors by the Verification Mission Mine Action and Information Centre, with which UNHCR works very closely.

Trials and detainees

29. The trials reported upon at length in my previous report continue on a daily basis, according to a regular court schedule. Trials have now been scheduled additionally in the court districts of Gnjilane and Prokuplje. Several proceedings were delayed or rescheduled for the period of the traditional December holidays, which are not observed as holidays in the Federal Republic of Yugoslavia. The Office of the United Nations High Commissioner for Human Rights observes that the proceedings so rescheduled involve especially large groups of defendants or incidents and operations of an especially sensitive nature. The Office's complement of trial monitors will not decrease during the December holiday period and the Office continues to meet with court officials, prosecutors and defence attorneys, and to monitor proceedings.

30. The absence of an amnesty law continues to be a major hindrance to confidence among the population. While paragraph 10 of the Serbian Government's statement of 13 October on the accord between President Milosevic and United States Special Envoy Richard Holbrooke envisaged an amnesty, the present practice of the Serbian authorities contradicts it. UNHCR expressed its concern over this situation in a letter dated 9 December addressed to the Deputy Federal Prime Minister, highlighting the importance of an amnesty in the context of confidence-building and requesting an opportunity to discuss with the competent officials the specific provisions of such a law while it was still in draft form.

31. In view of regular reports of ill-treatment of detainees and of the continuing absence of an elaborated policy to implement paragraphs 10 and 11 of the 13 October accord, the Office of the High Commissioner for Human Rights pursued its efforts to review implementation options. To that end, the Office met with representatives of the Kosovo Albanian political leadership and continues to correspond with the Serbian Ministry of Justice. On 18 November, the Ministry responded in writing to inquiries by the Office regarding the whereabouts and status of named detainees, largely humanitarian and medical workers and juveniles. On 27 November, the Office asked the ministry about 46 additional cases of reported human rights violations, largely of the elderly, young persons and invalids.

Forensic investigation

32. On 10 December, Serbian security forces refused to allow a team of Finnish forensic investigators, accompanied by the Ambassador of Finland to the Federal Republic of Yugoslavia, to proceed without a police escort to the site of Gornje Obrinje. Serbian authorities pointed to a provision of the forensic investigators' terms of reference which permits Serbian Government presence during the investigations. The Finnish team noted, however, that the excessive police and military presence (two buses of security forces, two armed personnel carriers and six armoured vehicles) was likely to provoke action by Kosovo Albanian paramilitary units and would thus endanger the team. After a formal protest, the chief of the forensic team met with the Minister of Justice of Serbia. The Minister reportedly assured him that such an incident would not be repeated and proposed that only one investigative judge and two Serbian forensic experts accompany the team.

IV. OBSERVATIONS

33. It bears repeating that the problems in Kosovo can be resolved only by political means through negotiations between the parties directly concerned. I urge all parties concerned to engage without delay in such negotiations; the lack of agreement so far has a direct bearing on the current volatility. The tireless efforts of Ambassador Christopher Hill of the United States and of the European Union Envoy, Ambassador Wolfgang Petritsch, aimed at finding a peaceful political settlement in Kosovo merit the support of all those wishing to set Kosovo on a positive course. Progress in this direction is all the more pressing in view of the increased levels of violence in Kosovo in December and its spread to urban areas, which earlier remained relatively untouched by the hostilities. These actions put at risk the entire peace process and could trigger a renewal of fighting in the coming months.

34. Should the worst happen, it would be very difficult for the humanitarian action to meet the resulting needs, still less encourage those affected to return and rebuild their homes and lives once more, which reinforces my conviction that those in a position to influence developments must spare no effort to find a negotiated settlement in early 1999, before it is too late.

35. I urge all the parties concerned to honour their obligations under the 16 October Agreement and to refrain from actions that could provoke resumed hostilities that would only lead to the further suffering of civilians. Continued instability in Kosovo impedes the return process and has the potential to jeopardize humanitarian efforts.

36. In this regard, the completion of the full deployment of the Kosovo Verification Mission should become a decisive factor for stability and confidence-building in Kosovo. The United Nations agencies that have a presence on the ground will continue developing their cooperation with the Verification Mission in order to coordinate efforts aimed at the restoration of normal life in Kosovo. It is my hope that the Verification Mission will soon be fully deployed and that it will be in a position to provide the Security Council with information on the compliance by the parties by the time of my next report as well as on the situation in Kosovo in accordance with the Security Council request in resolutions 1160 (1998) and 1199 (1998). With regard to the absence of a field capacity on the ground, except in the humanitarian and human rights field, I would hope that the Kosovo Verification Mission would assume such reporting by early February and would accordingly discontinue it, except as concerns the humanitarian and human rights situation, in order to eliminate duplication.

Annex I

Information on the situation in Kosovo and measures taken by the Organization for Security and Cooperation in Europe

General situation

1. Low-intensity conflict with incidents and moments of increased tension has continued in Kosovo since 20 November. A single armed clash in mid-December between armed Kosovo Albanians, later described as "our soldiers" by the Kosovo Liberation Army (KLA), and forces of the Federal Republic of Yugoslavia near Prizren was a significant exception to this trend.

2. The principal area of concern continues to be the western region of Kosovo, centred on the triangle formed by Malisevo and the border zone adjacent to the towns of Pec, Dakovica and Prizren. KLA activity in the area of Podujevo to the north of Pristina is an emergent source of tension. The number of demonstrations by members of the Serb community is increasing. There are indications that they may be politically motivated and that the Kosovo Albanian community is poised to follow suit.

3. There have been a number of violations of the ceasefire during the reporting period. These include KLA attacks on Serb police (MUP) vehicles, typically carried out with rocket-propelled grenades and small arms fire. Incidents like these were reported in Prilep, Dolovo, Klina and Zociste. Police also invited the Kosovo Diplomatic Observer Mission (KDOM) to investigate two other incidents on the Decani-Djakovica road in which police vehicles had been destroyed. A joint patrol of MUP and KDOM was fired upon in the general area of Belanci.

4. Armed clashes between uniformed groups of Kosovo Albanians and the Serbian security force continue to occur. The most significant of these occurred on 14 December where 31 Kosovo Albanians were killed in the border region near Prizren and 9 were taken prisoner. An attack by two gunmen in a Pec bar later that day killed six Serb youths and worsened a tense situation. The Serb authorities blamed the KLA; the KLA blamed criminals. Further reports of clashes were investigated by KDOM during the reporting period, notably in Planeja, west of Prizren, where eight corpses and ammunition were found at the scene. The funeral that followed in Velika Krusa was attended by 2,000 to 3,000 people and 25 uniformed members of the KLA.

5. Incidents of kidnap and abduction continue to create tension and division in Kosovo. KDOM successfully negotiated the release of a Serbian policeman held by the KLA since 19 November and two Tanjug journalists who had been held by the KLA for two months. Demonstrations and protests by members of the Serbian community about the missing have increased, with activity centred on the Serb town of Orahovac, east of Dakovica. The area encompassed by such protests has begun to spread. A group of 700 protestors, led by the mayor of Orahovac, marched from Orahovac to the KLA-dominated town of Dragobilja in a potentially tense confrontation largely defused by members of the Organization for Security and Cooperation in Europe (OSCE) Kosovo Verification Mission (KVM). Demonstrations have taken place twice outside the KVM headquarters at Pristina in which the crowd requested action to release Serb abductees.

6. Local agreements brokered by KDOM have proved useful in decreasing tension in some areas but levels of KLA cooperation differ; some local commanders agree to maintain a discreet posture in their areas of operation, while others are more assertive. Central control and unified political and military strategy are increasingly visible aspects of KLA activity and it remains true that KLA forces seek to fill the vacuum left by the withdrawal of Serb forces. This trend has created perceptible frustrations among the Serb authorities and an unwillingness to further cede "control" of territory. This is now marked in Podujevo, a town north of Pristina astride the principal road into Kosovo from northern Serbia, where the KLA have been seen constructing bunkers overlooking the route.

7. Isolated incidents of vandalism directed at the international community were reported, resulting in minor damage to parked vehicles. Occasional verbal abuse and stone throwing was also reported by KVM and NGO staff.

Situation of the civilian population

8. Sources of the Office of the United Nations High Commissioner for Refugees (UNHCR) estimate that 75,000 internally displaced persons (IDPs) have returned to their homes in central and western Kosovo. There are now no refugees known to be living in the open in the region but serious sheltering problems remain. Uncertainty or fear in the minds of IDPs remains the principal factor affecting returns. Where KVM and KDOM presence has been frequent, permanent returns have been substantial; in areas where such presence has been less visible, or where MUP presence has continued, the pace of return has been affected. Return trends continue to vary by region. In Decari and Junik, south of Pec, significant returns have occurred; returns to areas close to the Albanian border have been more tentative; and there have been few returns to the area of Malisevo, north of Prizren, though many of the houses in the area remain habitable.

9. MUP presence, particularly in Malisevo, continues to hamper the refugee return process. Examples include complaints by the villagers of Semetesite (north-west of Suva Reka) of harassment at a MUP checkpoint, and returnee concern about the proximity of a MUP observation point in Vitak (south-east of Klina). In the Serb village of Svinjare (south of Mitrovica), KDOM officials were informed that some members of the Serb community were refugees from neighbouring areas and were afraid to return home because of KLA threats. KDOM received complaints about a MUP checkpoint in the area of Movjalne (north-west of Prizren). MUP maintained it was vital for the protection of 15 Serb families living there; Kosovar Albanians complained that it was preventing the return of Kosovo Albanians to an essentially Albanian area. KDOM members patrolling Podujevo (north of Pristina) were informed that the KLA had been denying Serb IDPs access to villages in the area to the north of the town.

10. UNHCR published a survey of the shelter situation in 20 of the 29 municipalities of Kosovo, which, in conjunction with other NGOs, assessed the needs of 285 villages in those areas. Two hundred ten of them were found to have been affected by the conflict, with 30 per cent of the houses destroyed, a further 30 per cent of houses suffering minor to major damage and 40 per cent left undamaged. Whereas the pre-conflict population of the villages was 349,657, the current population was 88,950 and the IDP population was 24,177, some 24 per cent of the total.

11. UNHCR has reorganized its regional structure to reflect that of the OSCE Kosovo Verification Mission, with distribution points now decentralized to the main towns of Pec, Prizren and Mitrovica. Food delivery responsibilities have been divided by area with Catholic Relief Services, Mercy Corps International and the World Food Programme (WFP). Aid delivery operations by humanitarian organizations have been hampered by winter weather and food supply shortages. The International Committee of the Red Cross (ICRC) has assisted with the shortfall. Kosovo's current food requirement stands at 3,600 tons per month, to feed 300,000 IDP returnees and host families.

Refugee influx

12. The situation of refugees in Albania is closely followed by the OSCE presence in Tirana. There was a slight improvement during the reporting period. The number of refugees currently in Albania remains unclear but is estimated to be 23,000. The registration process, crucial for accurate and targeted supplies, is not properly under way. This has caused instances of food shortages and of oversupply and has made the calculation of future needs difficult.

13. The situation of refugees is especially difficult in the north-east of Albania where the number of refugees is estimated at 3,000. Refugees in the Tropoje District, numbering up to 1,500, have not received aid for almost two months owing to the lack of security for aid agencies in the area. These refugees have been offered transport to other locations where the security situation permits aid agencies to supply them on a regular basis. OSCE gave initial assistance in providing administrative arrangements for their transport. A large number of the refugees who decided to leave Bajram Curri chose to go to Tirana and Durres and not to collection centres.

14. Refugees in the districts of Kukes and Has suffered food shortages owing to miscalculation of the number of refugees in the area (1,100), coupled with the fact that supplies were delayed in reaching the districts. Relief agencies are unwilling to stockpile food because of the security situation. The appalling road conditions, together with the weather and the scarcity of transport, are additional difficulties faced in determining whether refugees received aid.

15. The number of crossings from Kosovo into Albania during the reporting period was estimated to be very low, with most taking place in the area of Dobruna.

16. The Holbrooke Agreement raised expectations that a safe return to Kosovo would be feasible in the near future and resulted in a number of representatives of refugees in Albania approaching OSCE field offices requesting that their return be facilitated as soon as possible. It was initially feared that many refugees would try to return on their own initiative, running the risk of entering minefields or being mistaken by Federal Republic of Yugoslavia forces as KLA infiltrators. By mid-November, only a limited number of refugees had crossed using this dangerous route and the message that they should wait a few more months before returning in an orderly manner seems to have been accepted, not least because many are still unhappy with the current security situation in Kosovo. The issue of refugee return is one that will need to be addressed between the relevant authorities in Albania and the Federal Republic of Yugoslavia.

Kosovo conflict spillover potential

17. The OSCE presence in Albania, the OSCE spillover mission to Skopje and the OSCE missions to Bosnia and Herzegovina and to Croatia continue to follow closely the spillover potential of the Kosovo conflict.

18. During the reporting period, the situation on the Albanian border with Kosovo (Federal Republic of Yugoslavia) was relatively calm. Some isolated incidents occurred. Bad weather and poor road conditions continued to hamper movement and monitoring along the border areas. By mid-December, tension had increased at the border between Albania and Kosovo (Federal Republic of Yugoslavia) after several border incidents. This was seen as an indication that the KLA had become more active after a quieter preparatory period.

19. Very limited KLA movement was observed in the Has District, although the existence of a KLA training camp with about 10 fighters near the border was reported at the beginning of December. Overall activity remains limited and is probably constrained by poor weather.

20. During December, poor weather conditions limited OSCE Mission members' movement, precluding accurate observation, but no movement of any kind could be seen within the immediate areas of Kosovo adjacent to the border.

21. Few border incidents occurred during the period but previous incidents had led the Albanian Foreign Minister in mid-December to state that the Federal Republic of Yugoslavia authorities were ignoring an agreement on border incidents signed by both countries obliging the parties to verify and confirm any border incidents through a bilateral commission.

22. In his address to the OSCE Ministerial Council Meeting in Oslo on 2 December, Foreign Minister Milo of Albania said that his Government is ready "to cooperate with OSCE and other international organizations committed to Kosovo". He added that pressure should continue to be applied on Belgrade to find a satisfactory political solution and welcomed the new flexibility that, in his view, the KLA was showing with regard to demands for independence, stating that Albania was working with the KLA to convince them to be more realistic.

23. Speaking in Brussels on 7 December, Foreign Minister Milo voiced pessimism over a solution to the crisis, reaffirmed that Tirana did not subscribe to the idea of a greater Albania and rejected allegations that armed groups were being trained in its territory and sent to Kosovo.

24. The security situation remained tense during the campaign for the referendum on the Constitution held on 22 November. Media distortion and veiled threats of violence, some directed at the international community, and at OSCE in particular, were the main cause.

25. In northern Albania, in a letter sent to central government officials, the Tropoja District Council, the Mayor of Bajram Curri and political parties described the security situation as one of total lawlessness and chaos brought about by the absence of working judicial institutions and effective policing and called upon the Government to take urgent measures.

26. The situation on the northern border between the former Yugoslav Republic of Macedonia and the Federal Republic of Yugoslavia remained stable and calm during the reporting period, without substantive incident. All border crossings remained open and functioned normally. Similarly, the western border has been quiet.

27. The Federal Republic of Yugoslavia objected strongly to the intention of the North Atlantic Treaty Organization (NATO) to deploy an extraction force in the former Yugoslav Republic of Macedonia in relation to the Kosovo Verification Mission and sought to put pressure on the new Government over the issue. However, shortly after its endorsement by Parliament, the Government approved the stationing of NATO forces on Macedonian territory. Prime Minister Georgievski announced that the basis of the decision was the country's wish to achieve NATO membership as soon as possible, in addition to its commitments under the Partnership for Peace and certain status-of-forces agreements.

Measures taken by the Organization for Security and Cooperation in Europe

28. The process of fully establishing the Kosovo Verification Mission has continued since the Agreement between OSCE and the Federal Republic of Yugoslavia of 16 October 1998 and OSCE Permanent Council Decision 263 of 25 October 1998 that formally established the Mission. Its strength on 19 December stood at 888, including 392 local staff, with 180 international staff in headquarters in Pristina and 111 in Regional Centre One (RC1), Prizren. Two coordination centres are established as RC1 sub-stations, in the towns of Orahovac and in Suva Reka. KDOM strength is now at 217. Prizren Regional Centre became fully operational on 11 December; Regional Centre 2 (Mitrovica) became operational on 19 December. All five regional centres will be fully established by the end of January 1999. Staff have now been selected for all regional centres. Liaison offices have been established in Belgrade and Tirana.

29. Patrols by KVM personnel have begun and are coordinated closely with KDOM. KVM submits a regular interim report, instituted as a temporary measure in order to inform OSCE participating States and other international organizations of developments in the Mission area pending full establishment of the Mission. Reporting will subsequently reflect the full range of KVM's verification tasks.

30. Training of KVM verifiers began on 23 November at the Kosovo Verification Mission's induction centre in Hotel Narcis in Brezovica, outside Pristina. Five training courses have been completed; they were conducted by a KVM training team with support from other OSCE missions, OSCE institutions, UNHCR and ICRC. The syllabus consists of a four-day course with a capacity of up to 125 per course. Subjects taught include communications, policing issues, security, the human dimension and reporting procedures.

31. KVM and OSCE institutions continue to work in close cooperation with other international and humanitarian organizations in Kosovo. A fact-finding visit to Belgrade and Kosovo, led by Ambassador Stoudmann of the Office for Democratic Institutions and Human Rights, was conducted from 22 to 26 November in order to carry out a preliminary assessment of conditions for elections in the region. The group included representatives from the European Commission, the Council of Europe and the International Foundation for Election Systems. KVM and UNHCR hosted a meeting of key humanitarian agencies on 14 December in Pristina to discuss the outlook for the civil population of Kosovo over the winter period.

32. The OSCE Ministerial Meeting was held at Oslo on 2 December and issued a consensus-based statement declaring that "security, human rights, democracy and fundamental freedoms are inseparable". It went on to say that "the ten basic principles of the Helsinki Final Act, together with the current operational capabilities the OSCE has gained throughout the years, have contributed to making this Organization one of the best-suited instruments to address the crisis in Kosovo" (see annex II). Ambassador William Walker, the head of KVM, briefed the OSCE Ministerial Meeting about the situation regarding the KVM. He also briefed the North Atlantic Council in Brussels.

33. Discussions between members of KVM and the Government of the former Yugoslav Republic of Macedonia took place on 8 December to determine arrangements concerning the Mission. The Government agreed to allow KVM members to make emergency use of medical facilities in Skopje and allowed emergency access by air and road under these conditions.

34. KVM carried out its first verification at the barracks of the Yugoslav Army's 549th Motorized Brigade in Prizren on 11 December. This consisted of a meeting at the base followed by an inspection of a company team position in Dobruste, west of Prizren. KVM officials were prevented from conducting an inspection inside the barracks as planned and lodged an official complaint.

35. NATO has begun deployment of an advance force in the former Yugoslav Republic of Macedonia. Secure communications links have been established between KVM headquarters and the Kosovo Verification Coordination Centre in Skopje.

Structure

36. The Prizren Regional Centre has temporarily extended its area of operations to include the Djakovica municipality. Although this falls outside the boundaries of the Prizren political district, there is an operational need for KVM to patrol the area. When the Pec Regional Centre is established, it will undertake KVM patrolling of Djakovica.

37. KVM headquarters received 11 orange-coloured cargo vehicles during the period. There has been a delay in the arrival of armoured vehicles. The first were scheduled to be in Pristina on 18 December.

38. Current strength of KVM and KDOM on the ground in Kosovo is as follows:

KVM

Headquarters mission members: 179 personnel and 2 armoured vehicles[a]
Headquarters temporary mission members: 20 personnel
Induction centre: 33 instructing personnel
Prizren: 108 personnel and 21 armoured vehicles
Mitrovica: 56 personnel
Belgrade : 8 personnel Pec (embryonic regional centre): 38 personnel
Gujilane (embryonic regional centre): 8 personnel
Pristina (embryonic regional centre): 13 personnel
KVM Local Staff (all locations): 445 personnel
Total: 908

KDOM

United States: 143 personnel (33 of these are in Belgrade or Skopje) and 37 armoured vehicles
European Union: 33 personnel and 14 armoured vehicles
Russian Federation: 11 personnel
Canada: 3 personnel and one armoured vehicle

Plus 30 armoured vehicles on loan from the United Kingdom of Great Britain and Northern Ireland, and 1 from Sweden; 70 soft skinned vehicles.

12. UN Inter-Agency Update on Kosovo Humanitarian Situation, 11 January 1999

24 December 1998 - 10 January 1999

Population Movements

1. UNHCR estimates that there are currently some 180,000 civilians displaced within Kosovo, including the 5,000 who fled their homes in Podujevo municipality (See point two below). Approximately 110,000 people have returned to their villages, including 12,000 from Montenegro.

2. Fighting between Serbian security forces and the Kosovo Liberation Army (KLA) erupted in Podujevo municipality on 24 December and continued for four days, ending in a truce negotiated by the OSCE Kosovo Verification Mission (KVM) on 27 December. Some 18 people are believed to have been killed during the four-day period. The conflict centred primarily on the villages of Obrandze, Velika Reka and Lapastica, causing more than 5,000 people to leave although little damage was reported in these villages. Hundreds of residents have since returned to their homes but the majority remain in overcrowded temporary shelters in nearby villages with little sanitation facilities. Podujevo town, which has a population of more than 20,000, remains tense and some residents (mostly women and children) have begun to leave, fearing the spread of fighting.

3. In other parts of Kosovo, the coordinated approach adopted by UNHCR and OSCE KVM has helped to encourage returns. One important example is the town of Malisevo, the former KLA headquarters abandoned by its 3,000 residents last July during an assault by government security forces. Some 1,000 people have returned to Malisevo where the police maintain a reduced presence. The returnees say they were encouraged by assurances given by Mrs Ogata, the UN High Commissioner for Refugees and Ambassador Walker, the head of the OSCE Kosovo Verification Mission, during a visit on 21 December. OSCE KVM now has a permanent presence in Malisevo which acts as a source of reassurance for returnees.

Security Situation

4. In addition to the fighting in Podujevo, the most serious incident since the declaration of the ceasefire in October 1998, the period under review has witnessed an increase in the number of murders (allegedly perpetrated by the KLA), which have prompted vigorous retaliatory action by government security forces. During the past 11 days 21 people are known to have been killed through random violence in urban centres throughout Kosovo. On 5 January an explosive device detonated outside a cafe in Pristina, injuring 3 Serbian youths and triggering retaliatory attacks by Serbian civilians on Albanians. This is the first time that such an incident has occurred in the capital. On 8 January the KLA captured 8 Yugoslav soldiers near Kosovska Mitrovica and OSCE KVM verifiers are currently trying to secure their release. In the meantime tanks and armoured cars have been deployed

in the areas around Kosovska Mitrovica and Podujevo. In a separate incident 3 Serbian police were reportedly killed near Suva Reka.

Impact of deteriorating security on Humanitarian Operations

5. The deteriorating security environment is posing increased threats to the operational capability of humanitarian organisations. In one development a vehicle operated by Norwegian Church Aid was targeted by an under-car explosive-device. The device exploded in early morning causing superficial damage to the vehicle. No casualties were sustained. International organisations have been alerted to the need to take precautionary measures to minimise the effectiveness of such attacks.

6. The delivery of relief supplies to vulnerable civilians is becoming more challenging in the current environment. On 7 January hundreds of armed Serbian civilians sealed off the roads into Pristina in protest over the killing of a Serbian man, urging President Milosevic to take urgent action to protect them against spiralling violence in Kosovo. Four inter-agency convoys led by UNHCR had left Pristina before the civilians took to the streets. One convoy of four trucks went to Orahovac in central Kosovo without any problems and returned in mid-afternoon to Pristina after offloading supplies. The three other convoys managed to deliver aid to their destinations, one after skirting the demonstrators on the Pristina-Skopje road. However, the 10 trucks in the three convoys were unable to return to Pristina and spent the night in Mitrovica and Malisevo. Other aid workers were also stranded. At nightfall, UNHCR negotiated with police to allow 14 NGO vehicles blocked at Kosovo Polje just outside Pristina to proceed to the capital.

7. On 9 January armed Serbian civilians seized medicines from Medecins du Monde (MDM) outside Suva Reka in central Kosovo. The medicines were taken to a local hospital. The four MDM staff sought refuge in the nearby woods and were extricated by OSCE KVM later in the evening after UNHCR requested intervention at its headquarters in Pristina and spoke to police authorities.

...

13.   UN Secretary-General, Statement on the Racak massacre, New York City, 16 January 1999

I am shocked to learn today of the alleged massacre of some 40 individuals, apparently civilians, in Kosovo. I have received a full briefing from his excellency, Mr. Knut Vollebaek, Foreign Minister of Norway and Chairman-in-Office of the Organization for Security and Cooperation in Europe (OSCE). I am gravely concerned at this latest development and call for a full investigation by the competent authorities. I appeal once again to all sides in Kosovo to refrain from any action that would further escalate the tragic situation.

14.   Chairman's Concluding Statement, Special Meeting of Permanent Council, Vienna, 18 January 1999

The Chairman of the Permanent Council of the OSCE following today's discussion in the Permanent Council, expresses shock over the killings of ethnic Albanian civilians in southern Kosovo on Friday, 15 January. He condemns these atrocities, which the OSCE mission has determined were committed by F.R.Y. military and police against unarmed civilians. All available information indicates that many of the victims of the latest atrocities were brutally executed. A full investigation must be carried out by the F.R.Y. authorities and by the International Criminal Tribunal for the former Yugoslavia, to bring those responsible for this tragedy to full account. In this context, the F.R.Y. authorities must without delay give prosecutor Louise Arbour and ITCY experts full access to the scene of the violence as well as to the suspects. The latest violence is by far the worst setback to the ongoing efforts to solve the Kosovo crisis since the 16 October agreement between Foreign Ministers Geremek and Jovanovic and constitutes a clear violation of this agreement. As a result of this violence, several thousand inhabitants fled the area. There is now a climate of fear in Kosovo, in particular among the displaced persons and those who have returned to their villages. The prospects of sustainable return, which the KVM -- together with the UNHCR -- has done much to promote have been

damaged. It is now essential that a climate of security be re-established to promote the return process and prevent further displacement. The F.R.Y. must put an immediate end to its use of force in Kosovo. The parties must comply immediately with the cease-fire. They must now demonstrate restraint and abstain from violence and retaliation, which can only lead to more suffering and destruction. The security of verifiers is of paramount importance to the OSCE and to the functioning of the KVM. The 15 January attack on OSCE verifiers is to be condemned. The OSCE Mission will, with the full support of the Permanent Council, fulfill its role in promoting stability and dialogue. All parties must firmly respect the commitments they have undertaken. The F.R.Y. has not complied with the Geremek/Jovanovic agreement; it must be fully implemented. The legitimate requests of the KVM must be met. The cease-fire must be restored and maintained by the F.R.Y. as well as by the KLA. The recent tragic events underline the urgent need to find a political settlement to the conflict. The efforts made by representatives of the international community to this effect, in line with all relevant UN Security Council resolutions have the full support of the OSCE. The parties must now negotiate seriously and reach a solution promptly.

15.   U.S. Representative to OSCE, Statement at Extraordinary OSCE PC Meeting, Vienna, 18 January 1999

The United States is appalled and outraged by the massacre at Racak, and by the F.R.Y. authorities' scandalous attempt to present the cold-blooded slaughter and mutilation of civilians as a military operation against terrorists. Our sense of outrage and shock engendered by the massacre itself is compounded by Serbian President Milosevic's January 17 statement that the OSCE Kosovo Mission -- one which we strongly support -- impeded investigation of this crime, falsified evidence, and displayed partiality toward the KLA. These groundless accusations are especially despicable coming only one week after OSCE verifiers risked their lives to secure the liberation of eight Serbian soldiers. In the absolute brazenness of this fabrication, Milosevic aspires to take his place beside this century's chief perpetrator of the Big Lie, and Milosevic yields no ground to Goebbels as the Big Lie's propagandist. If Belgrade hopes to salvage even a shred of credibility with the international community after its horrific actions of the past few days, at a minimum it must do three things:

First, Belgrade must publicly and unequivocally accept the jurisdiction of The Hague Tribunal for all of Kosovo. It must grant chief prosecutor Arbour and ICTY team immediate, unrestricted access to investigate this and other incidents, and Belgrade must cooperate fully with the ICTY team. F.R.Y. authorities must help identify those responsible for the Racak massacre and hand over any and all suspects to the ICTY for prosecution, if the ICTY requests.

Second, Belgrade should cease immediately its dissemination of deliberate misinformation about the OSCE Mission's activities. This misinformation constitutes a hostile act against the OSCE and the international community as a whole. Moreover, President Milosevic must retract the baseless charges he has already made against the mission and personally against Mission Director Walker.

Third, Belgrade must cooperate fully with the OSCE Kosovo Mission in a whole host of areas where cooperation has been heretofore lacking. The F.R.Y. authorities must provide accurate and complete information with regard to the deployment of F.R.Y. and MUP units in the region as well as prior notification of significant movements. Belgrade must return military and police units to garrisons in accordance with its commitments in order to stabilize the current tense situation and ensure the safety of both the local population and international personnel, including OSCE verifiers. The F.R.Y. authorities must take immediate action to bring VJ and MUP deployments and force levels into compliance with the commitment Milosevic has already made. Belgrade must also allow OSCE verifiers full and unimpeded access to all areas and access to prisoners, when requested, in a timely fashion.

The United States expects Belgrade to facilitate all of the OSCE Missions' support requests, including access for the OSCE's

MEDIVAC helicopter, and full provision of a range of key security-related requests. We call on President Milosevic to fulfill the commitments made in his 11-point unilateral statement, including amnesty for Kosovar Albanian prisoners. ...

16. Kosovo: Ogata condemns atrocities, appeals for access, 18 January 1999

The UN High Commissioner for Refugees Sadako Ogata on Monday called for the immediate cessation of hostilities in Kosovo, warning that fighting in the Stimlje area has once again forced people to flee into the hills and that children are reported to be dying in the cold. "There are hundreds of people who have spent the past three nights in the woods in freezing weather. Most of them are women and children. My staff are trying to help them, but the only way to do this is for the two sides to stop fighting and allow these people to seek shelter," Ogata said. Renewed fighting since Christmas Eve has forced more than 20,000 people to flee at least 23 villages in the municipalities of Decane, Podujevo, Stimlje, and Suva Reka. UNHCR staff report that the conflict area in Kosovo seems to be widening. Field workers in the Stimlje area on Monday could hear gunfire and artillery rounds coming from the surrounding villages. They met a group of displaced people who told them that two babies had died in the woods during the night.

"It is devastating that the current round of fighting is happening just when the presence of the Kosovo Verification Mission was clearly starting to make a difference. I was shocked to learn of the massacre at Racak and I condemn it in the strongest possible terms," Ogata said. The cease fire called in October averted a humanitarian catastrophe in Kosovo. The tens of thousands of people who were living out in the open in the wooded hills at that time came down to seek warm shelter before winter. "I was encouraged by that development, but now we are again seeing people in the hundreds encamped in the woods. A new upsurge of violence will undermine what we have accomplished to date," said the High Commissioner. She said there would be "dramatic consequences" for both Serbian and Albanian civilians in Kosovo, unless the fighting stops.

UNHCR has been leading aid convoys throughout Kosovo since the beginning of the crisis last year. A UNHCR team which tried to deliver food and blankets to Racak on Sunday, 17 January, was blocked by Serbian security forces from entering the village. The convoy unloaded its supplies at Stimlje, one kilometer from Racak, in the hope that the aid would reach the neediest people. By Sunday evening, however, most of the 2,000 residents of Racak had fled, heading for the woods and for the town of Stimlje. Aid workers in Stimlje on Sunday evening said there was a steady stream of displaced people arriving on foot, in horse-drawn carts and tractors. UNHCR workers reported that around 3,500 villagers had also left the nearby areas of Petrovo, Malopolje and Rance.

17. Council of Europe condemns massacre in Kosovo, 18 January 1999

"The Serbian authorities are responsible for the mass murder of Kosovo Albanian civilians in Racak, which constitutes a crime against humanity", the Bureau of the COUNCIL OF EUROPE Parliamentary Assembly stated today at its meeting. "According to the reports by the Kosovo Verification Mission there was no doubt that the victims, including women and children, were executed, at close range, by the Serb security forces". The Bureau recalled the Assembly's position that the International Criminal Tribunal for the former Yugoslavia has a jurisdiction in Kosovo. It called for an immediate dispatching of Tribunal investigators to the site of the massacre, in order to make sure that perpetrators and instigators of this horrendous crime are brought to justice. The Bureau said that the Serbian government's reaction to the killings, blaming the victims and representatives of the international community, was outrageous and utterly unacceptable. The Bureau also decided to propose to the Assembly that the deteriorating situation in Kosovo be debated under urgent procedure at the next part-session, to be held from 25 to 29 January 1999 in Strasbourg. Mr Alain CHÉNARD, President of the COUNCIL OF EUROPE's Congress of

Local and Regional Authorities of Europe, made the following declaration today:

"I strongly condemn the latest developments in Kosovo, which mark a return to the worst tradition of war crimes, genocide and ethnic cleansing. While the Congress has made proposals on the future status of Kosovo in its Recommendation 44 (1998) and has co-operated in this area with the Commission for Democracy through Law in liaison with the international negotiators, the obvious failure of the current strategy undermines all negotiations aimed at a future status for Kosovo. We had hoped that the spirit of cooperation could replace the "logic of war". The recent massacre of civilians by Serbian forces leaves no more hope for that solution in the immediate future. I therefore appeal to the international community and all those who have the power to act on the ground, in particular NATO, to take all the necessary measures to guarantee the most fundamental human rights and the protection of the civilian population in the region by all appropriate means, especially those that enable real pressure to be exerted on President Milosevic. Moreover, those responsible for war crimes must be arrested and brought before the International Tribunal in The Hague. Unless strong action is taken, there is a danger of a worsening spiral of violence of the kind already seen in Bosnia-Herzegovina, with a real risk of the whole region exploding. Only when the peoples' most fundamental rights to life and security have been restored will it be possible to resume dispassionate dialogue on the future autonomous status of the Kosovo."

18. Statement by James P. Rubin, US Spokesman, 18 January 1999

Kosovo Verification Mission and Ambassador Walker

The U.S. notes with outrage the FRY Foreign Minister's decision that OSCE Kosovo Verification Mission Director Ambassador William Walker must depart the country within 48 hours. The reasons given by the FRY for this unacceptable step are spurious and unworthy. The United Nations Security Council, the OSCE, and other concerned governments have also spoken out, demanding the FRY decision be reversed. The FRY authorities have for some time failed to fulfill their commitment to the OSCE with regard to the security of KVM personnel. Despite the binding obligation on the FRY of their October 16, 1998 agreement with the OSCE, they have done nothing to ensure the security of the KVM. To the contrary, they have denied all security-related requests by Amb. Walker and have engaged in a media war against the KVM that has in fact diminished the KVM's security. We are alarmed by the continuing attacks on the KVM in the government controlled press in Serbia. In a January 17 press statement, Serbian Republic President Milutinovic unleashed a vitriolic personal attack against KVM Director Amb. William Walker. The FRY has now declared Walker "persona non grata", as Serbian and FRY authorities pursue their transparent attempt to divert attention from the tragic massacre in Racak. The security of the OSCE KVM personnel is of paramount importance to the United States and all OSCE members. We will not tolerate actions that could imperil their safety, and we will not tolerate anything less than full FRY cooperation with the OSCE, the KVM and Ambassador Walker.

19. ICRC Takes action in Aftermath of Racak violence, 18 January 1999

Staff from the International Committee of the Red Cross (ICRC) today returned to the Racak area to try to aid hundreds of people who fled the violence that erupted as Serbian forces entered the village last Friday. A team of relief and medical delegates set out for the village of Dremnjak, south-east of Racak, to bring food and other items to several hundred people who had sought sanctuary there and to check reports that some were wounded and in need of treatment. Delegates who initially went to Racak on Saturday in response to reports that civilians had been displaced, and some wounded, were profoundly shocked to find scores of bodies - apparently civilians - and a community badly traumatized by the violence. The ICRC deplores what appears to be a deliberate attack against civilians in Racak. In light of the escalating violence involving both sides in recent weeks, the ICRC reiterates its condemnation of all attacks on civilians and calls on both sides to comply with international humanitarian law and spare those not, or no longer, involved in the fighting.

S/PRST/1999/2, 19 January 1999

20.   Statement by the President of the Security Council, 19 January 1999

At the 3967th meeting of the Security Council, held on 19 January 1999 in connection with the Council's consideration of the item entitled "Letter dated 11 March 1998 from the Deputy Permanent Representative of the United Kingdom of Great Britain and Northern Ireland to the United Nations addressed to the President of the Security Council (S/1998/223); Letter dated 27 March 1998 from the Permanent Representative of the United States of America to the United Nations addressed to the President of the Security Council (S/1998/272)", the President of the Security Council made the following statement on behalf of the Council:

"The Security Council strongly condemns the massacre of Kosovo Albanians in the village of Racak in Southern Kosovo, Federal Republic of Yugoslavia, on 15 January 1999, as reported by the Organization for Security and Cooperation in Europe (OSCE) Kosovo Verification Mission (KVM). It notes with deep concern that the report of the KVM states that the victims were civilians, including women and at least one child. The Council also takes note of the statement by the Head of the KVM that the responsibility for the massacre lay with Federal Republic of Yugoslavia security forces, and that uniformed members of both the Federal Republic of Yugoslavia armed forces and Serbian special police had been involved. The Council emphasizes the need for an urgent and full investigation of the facts and urgently calls upon the Federal Republic of Yugoslavia to work with the International Tribunal for the former Yugoslavia and KVM to ensure that those responsible are brought to justice.

"The Security Council deplores the decision by Belgrade to declare KVM Head of Mission Walker persona non grata and reaffirms its full support for Mr. Walker and the efforts of the OSCE to facilitate a peaceful settlement. It calls upon Belgrade to rescind this decision and to cooperate fully with Mr. Walker and the KVM.

"The Security Council deplores the decision by the Federal Republic of Yugoslavia to refuse access to the Prosecutor of the International Tribunal and calls upon the Federal Republic of Yugoslavia to cooperate fully with the International Tribunal in carrying out an investigation in Kosovo, in line with the call for cooperation with the International Tribunal in its resolutions 1160 (1998) of 31 March 1998, 1199 (1998) of 23 September 1998 and 1203 (1998) of 24 October 1998.

"The Security Council notes that, against clear KVM advice, Serb forces returned to Racak on 17 January 1999 and that fighting broke out.

"The Security Council considers that the events in Racak constitute the latest in a series of threats to the efforts to settle this conflict through negotiation and peaceful means.

"The Security Council condemns the shooting of personnel of the KVM on 15 January 1999 and all actions endangering KVM and international personnel. It reaffirms its full commitment to the safety and security of the KVM personnel. It reiterates its demands that the Federal Republic of Yugoslavia and the Kosovo Albanians cooperate fully with the KVM.

"The Security Council calls upon the parties to cease immediately all acts of violence and to engage in talks on a lasting settlement.

"The Security Council also strongly warns the 'Kosovo Liberation Army' against actions which are contributing to tensions.

"The Security Council considers all of these events to be violations of its resolutions and of relevant agreements and commitments calling for restraint. It calls upon all parties to respect fully their commitments under the relevant resolutions and affirms once again its full support for international efforts to facilitate a peaceful settlement on the basis of equality for all citizens and ethnic communities in Kosovo. The

Council reaffirms its commitment to the sovereignty and territorial integrity of the Federal Republic of Yugoslavia.

"The Security Council takes note with concern of the report of the United Nations High Commissioner for Refugees that five and a half thousand civilians fled the Racak area following the massacre, showing how rapidly a humanitarian crisis could again develop if steps are not taken by the parties to reduce tensions.

"The Security Council will remain actively seized of the matter."

21.   Press Statement by James P. Rubin, US Spokesman, 23 January 1999

The United States welcomes the release today by Serbian authorities of nine Kosovar Albanian detainees. We also welcome the release of the Serbian civilians who were kidnapped from their village early Friday morning. These actions represent constructive steps toward reducing tension in Kosovo.

These releases highlight the importance of the role of the Kosovo Verification Mission (KVM) in managing the cease-fire and defusing tensions as they seek to build compliance with UN Security Council resolutions and the October agreement.

We call on both sides to release all detainees and to cease further detentions. Such action would serve to build confidence on both sides, help maintain the cease-fire, and facilitate progress in the negotiations on a political settlement. We strongly urge both sides to treat detainees humanely, and to afford them due process of law, and to allow access by the International Committee of the Red Cross, KVM, and other international observers

22.   UN Inter-Agency Update on Kosovo Humanitarian Situation, 25 January 1999

Population Movements

1. Approximately 30,000 people have fled fighting since late December in some 25 villages in the municipalities of Podujevo, Decane, Stimlje, Suva Reka and Kosovska Mitrovica. The four days of fighting in late December at Podujevo led to the departure from the suburbs and surrounding villages of an estimated 5,500 people. As little damage was done to buildings, return to the villages started as soon as a ceasefire was brokered. However when eight soldiers were kidnapped, tension rose again leading to new displacement. Since the OSCE Kosovo Verification Mission (KVM) negotiated the release of the eight soldiers, over 5,000 have returned to the Podujevo / Mitrovica area. In the second week of January, there were clashes in the Decane municipality, prompting some 4,000 people to flee from five villages; UNHCR estimates that over 500 of these have now returned to two of the villages.

2. Serious fighting broke out in Stimlje / Suva Reka on 15 January. KVM's attempts to intervene were not accepted, and following the reported massacre of some 45 people in the village of Racak, 6,400 villagers fled from six villages. Most of these people found shelter in Stimlje, Suva Reka, Lipljan, Urosevac and Pristina. However, an estimated 300-400 people were obliged to remain in the open under makeshift shelters, afraid to approach roads where security forces were present. Displaced leaving these encampments told UNHCR and KVM that at least three babies had died in the cold.

3. On 20 January 5 policemen were injured by alleged KLA mortar fire on the outskirts of Mitrovica. Police action in nearby villages such as Sipolje and Vaganica continued until the next day resulting in the evacuation of the population as well as the people from their homes on the outskirts of Mitrovica. The displaced started to return on 22 January when the police withdrew from the area.

4. Where peace has held, there have been continuing returns, usually slow and gradual. In Malisevo more than half of the 3,000 who left in July have come back and a degree of normalcy is being established. At Lodja near Pec, work on the school which is to serve as a home for some families while they repaired their houses stopped following the murders in the Pec cafe, but is expected to start again now. Representatives of twenty families from Opertusa, a village in Suva Reka, have asked UNHCR for assistance to return home. At Junik, a

village from which 10,000 fled in August 1998, there have been 1,500 returns, primarily from Albania and Djakovica, despite ongoing tensions between the local population and the police.

5. Government sources have informed UNHCR that some 90 villages previously of mixed population have seen the flight of all their Serbian citizens. Some are displaced inside Kosovo, while the Government estimates that there are 50,000 displaced from Kosovo living elsewhere in Serbia.

6. At the beginning of 1999 UNHCR estimated that some 180,000 remained displaced within Kosovo. Although some 30,000 people have since fled their homes for reasons of insecurity, an estimated 7,000 people have been able to return to their home areas and a further 3,000 to areas not affected by recent conflict. Thus, UNHCR estimates that there are 200,000 persons displaced within Kosovo as at 22 January. It is difficult to give a definitive assessment of the numbers of displaced / returnees as many people flee their homes for one day before returning. Some have fled and returned to their home areas several times.

Security of humanitarian personnel

7. UNHCR has continued to conduct mine-awareness seminars and security briefings for all agencies working in Kosovo in order to alert relief agencies to areas where fighting is in progress. Regular warnings have been issued over the presence of land mines. More than 140 areas have been identified where the presence of land mines and explosive devices has been confirmed. ...

S/PRST/1999/5, 29 January 1999

23.   Statement by the President of the Security Council, 29 January 1999

At the 3974th meeting of the Security Council, held on 29 January 1999 in connection with the Council's consideration of the item entitled "Letter dated 11 March 1998 from the Deputy Permanent Representative of the United Kingdom of Great Britain and Northern Ireland to the United Nations addressed to the President of the Security Council (S/1998/223); Letter dated 27 March 1998 from the Permanent Representative of the United States of America to the United Nations addressed to the President of the Security Council (S/1998/272)", the President of the Security Council made the following statement on behalf of the Council:

"The Security Council expresses its deep concern at the escalating violence in Kosovo, Federal Republic of Yugoslavia. It underlines the risk of a further deterioration in the humanitarian situation if steps are not taken by the parties to reduce tensions. The Council reiterates its concern about attacks on civilians and underlines the need for a full and unhindered investigation of such actions. It calls once again upon the parties to respect fully their obligations under the relevant resolutions and to cease immediately all acts of violence and provocations.

"The Security Council welcomes and supports the decisions of the Foreign Ministers of France, Germany, Italy, the Russian Federation, the United Kingdom of Great Britain and Northern Ireland and the United States of America (the Contact Group), following their meeting in London on 29 January 1999 (S/1999/96), which aim at reaching a political settlement between the parties and establish a framework and timetable for that purpose. The Council demands that the parties should accept their responsibilities and comply fully with these decisions and requirements, as with its relevant resolutions.

"The Security Council reiterates its full support for international efforts, including those of the Contact Group and the Organization for Security and Cooperation in Europe Kosovo Verification Mission, to reduce tensions in Kosovo and facilitate a political settlement on the basis of substantial autonomy and equality for all citizens and ethnic communities in Kosovo and the recognition of the legitimate rights of the Kosovo Albanians and other communities in Kosovo. It reaffirms its commitment to the sovereignty and territorial integrity of the Federal Republic of Yugoslavia. The Security Council will follow the negotiations closely and would welcome members of the Contact Group keeping it informed about the progress reached therein.

"The Security Council will remain actively seized of the matter."
S/1999/99, 30 January 1999

24.   Report of the Secretary-General, 31 January 1999

... Violence

3. The human rights situation in Kosovo has remained consistently grave for nearly 11 months. The October 1998 ceasefire did reduce the number of internally displaced persons and civilian casualties, the use of heavy weaponry, and the destruction of property and means of livelihood. However, during the reporting period, violence in Kosovo, including violations of the ceasefire, has continued, and the situation of human rights has further deteriorated, culminating with the massacre of Kosovo Albanian civilians in Racak.

4. The most disturbing new element is the spread of violence in Kosovo and the transformation of the nature of that violence. Prior to the ceasefire hostilities were limited to certain geographic locations, with fluid lines of engagement, although sniper fire did occur sporadically outside the discrete areas of encounter. In many cases, the civilian population fled from threatened locations to areas of perceived relative safety, some to urban areas within Kosovo but many others to exposed conditions with poor access to shelter and food. Following the ceasefire, many internally displaced persons began returning to their homes, but many continue to express fear of government forces and paramilitary units in and around villages. Calculated acts of violence followed by retaliatory measures now occur frequently in cities that, until winter, had been notably exempt from violence, even during the influx of internally displaced persons into urban areas whose social resources were already overtaxed. With the exception of some isolated incidents, the resident communities of Kosovo's large multi-ethnic cities, where most of its population resides, have not turned violently upon each other. However, targeted acts of violence and growing expressions of public rage during the past month might seriously threaten peace in urban areas.

5. In December, field staff of the Office of the United Nations High Commissioner for Human Rights in the Federal Republic of Yugoslavia attempted to follow up acts of discriminate violence, interviewing victims, families and community leaders, not only in the immediate aftermath of incidents but long after them. While some violent acts were widely publicized, it would appear that most were less well known, particularly in cases in which the perpetrators, be they Serb police or Kosovo Albanian paramilitary units, still maintained positions or control in or near the area. The Office of the United Nations High Commissioner for Human Rights observed that the transformation of the nature of violence in Kosovo had reduced the geographic area of perceived safety and had resulted in a real increase in the number of persons who live in apprehension of direct experience of violence or arbitrary treatment. During this period, assailants have selectively fired directly upon urban sidewalks and cafés, as well as civilian passenger vehicles - in at least one instance, on a car clearly transporting a family group.

6. The violence and arbitrary treatment characterizing this period have surgically targeted influential individuals and localities known for open-mindedness and flexibility in community relations. The Office of the United Nations High Commissioner for Human Rights concluded with concern that a message was being transmitted throughout Kosovo, where codes based on individual reputation have for generations governed social relations within and among all regional communities, that a reputation for open-minded and flexible behaviour was no guarantee of personal safety. The responsibility for targeted killings is increasingly a matter of attribution by one side or another. Frequently, assailants have been identified simply as "masked men", and witness interviews by the Office of the United Nations High Commissioner for Human Rights have indicated that the "masked men" have exhibited signs of unfamiliarity with their immediate surroundings. Moreover, public responsibility is rarely claimed for acts of violence, further fuelling polarization and fear. Perpetrators of acts of violence, gross official misconduct and crimes against humanity committed throughout the crisis still have not been brought to justice, suggesting that such acts are committed with impunity.

7. A brief summary of casualty figures is insufficient to illustrate how the nature of violence against civilians has been transformed or to suggest how it has fuelled an atmosphere of fear. A narrative of the

time and place of major incidents better suggests how tensions have spread.

8.   The abduction and murder on 16-17 December of the deputy mayor of Kosovo Polje, noted in my last report, sparked several days of public protests from the Serb community. On 22 December, armed assailants attacked a café in Kosovska Mitrovica, killing one Kosovo Albanian immediately, while another, who was reportedly a member of the newly created municipal government's local security force, died later of his wounds.   On 27 December, Kosovo Albanian paramilitary units claimed responsibility for the 26 December killing of an elderly Serb from the village of Obranza, shot on the doorstep of his home. On 27 December, three Roma were found dead in Kosovska Mitrovica. On 29 December, the bodies of five Kosovo Albanians were found, left alongside roads or bridges, in three municipalities, two in Prizren, two in Kosovska Mitrovica and one on the Pec-Decani road.   On 30 December, a Kosovo Albanian was killed near the village of Dremnjak. On 31 December, a Serb janitor in the Urosevac agricultural school was found dead on the outskirts of the town.

9.   On 2 January, the bodies of several Serbs were demonstrably left in the Roma neighbourhood of Kosovska Mitrovica.   The same day, unknown assailants killed a Kosovo Albanian in front of his house in Stimlje.   During the night of 4-5 January, two Kosovo Albanians were killed at a gasoline station in Vitina, south-west of Gnjilane, a region of comparatively little violence.   On 5 January, a grenade exploded outside a Serbian café in Pristina, followed by shooting in Pristina, as well as vandalism directed at cafés frequented by Pristina's Albanian community.   The 6 January killing outside Pristina of a Serb electric company employee from Kosovo Polje sparked angry armed demonstrations by Serb civilians, who effectively sealed all roads in and out of Pristina on 7 January.   On 9 January, one Kosovo Albanian was killed and another wounded by unknown attackers who opened fire on them from a car.

10. On 11 January, the director of the Kosovo Information Centre, Enver Maloku, was killed by unknown assailants while getting out of his car in a Pristina suburb.   On the same day, a Kosovo Albanian man was shot and killed in a car near Pec.   On 13 January, one Kosovo Albanian man was shot and killed in front of his house in Kosovska Mitrovica by unknown assailants and another was reported to have been killed in Urosevac.   Also on 13 January, the mutilated body of a local forest caretaker, a Serb, was discovered at the same spot on a highway outside Pristina where the dead body of Kosovo Polje's deputy mayor had been left less than one month before.

The Racak massacre

11. During the period from 15 to 18 January, fighting occurred in and around the village of Racak, near Stimlje.   On 15 January, the Serb police and, as indicated in some reports, paramilitary units entered Racak.   On 16 January, the Kosovo Verification Mission reported that the bodies of 45 Kosovo civilians, including 3 women, at least 1 child and several elderly men, were found, 11 in houses, 23 on a rise behind the village and others in various locations in the immediate vicinity of the village.   Many of the dead appeared to have been summarily executed, shot at close range in the head and neck.   The Council is aware of the developments in the aftermath of the Racak massacre that prompted the presidential statement of 19 January 1999 (S/PRST/1999/2).   Detailed information on this incident was contained in the special report by the Kosovo Verification Mission attached to my letter of 17 January 1999 addressed to the President of the Security Council and in the report of the Kosovo Verification Mission attached to my letter of 20 January 1999 addressed to the President of the Security Council.

12. The Special Rapporteur on human rights in the territory of the former Yugoslavia, in a statement issued on 16 January from Prague, and the United Nations High Commissioner for Human Rights, in a letter of 19 January to President Milosevic, condemned the massacre and called for an immediate investigation of the Racak deaths. However, investigative and forensic efforts in the wake of this massacre have been wilfully obstructed by the lack of cooperation by the authorities of the Federal Republic of Yugoslavia with the international community.   In an attempt to enter the Federal Republic of Yugoslavia to investigate the Racak deaths, the Chief Prosecutor of the

International Tribunal for the Former Yugoslavia, Louise Arbour, was turned back, without a visa, at the border of the Federal Republic of Yugoslavia on 18 January 1999; the Government of the Federal Republic of Yugoslavia continues to assert that the International Tribunal for the Former Yugoslavia does not have jurisdiction to investigate alleged war crimes in Kosovo.   In order to resolve this problem, the Chief Prosecutor proposed to the authorities of the Federal Republic of Yugoslavia that she would publicly state that her access to Kosovo would not prejudice the position of the Federal Republic of Yugoslavia on jurisdiction, nor would she use the access as evidence that the Federal Republic of Yugoslavia has voluntarily submitted to the jurisdiction of the Tribunal.   The authorities, however, continued to deny the Chief Prosecutor's entry to Kosovo.

13. Meanwhile, on 18 January, the bodies of the victims were moved from the site to Pristina, where autopsies were performed in the presence of monitors of the Kosovo Verification Mission.   The authorities of the Federal Republic of Yugoslavia, however, failed to respond to the appeal of the head of a Finnish forensic team to postpone examinations until the arrival of Finnish experts.   The forensic team arrived in Pristina on 21 January.   By that time, 16 autopsies had been carried out without the Finnish experts being present.   The Finnish team, together with Serb and other foreign experts, performed autopsies on the remaining bodies and examined the autopsies performed earlier.

Abductions and taking of hostages

14. During this period, no new information emerged or was volunteered on the whereabouts or fate of persons abducted or reported missing.   On 26 December, after the Head of the Kosovo Verification Mission, William Walker, met with the families of persons abducted from Orahovac, the Mission announced that it had opened a special office to investigate reports of abductions.   The office, staffed in shifts by two international verifiers, takes testimony on reported abductions.

15. From 24 December to 2 January, during fighting around Podujevo, it was reported that 11 Serbs and Kosovo Albanians were captured by Kosovo Albanian paramilitaries and released with the intervention of the Kosovo Verification Mission and the Kosovo Diplomatic Observer Mission.

16. On 8 January, as the OSCE Chairman-in-Office, Knut Vollebaek, began his visit to Albania and the Federal Republic of Yugoslavia, Kosovo Albanian paramilitary units attacked a Yugoslav Army convoy north-east of Kosovska Mitrovica, capturing eight army personnel, including several conscripts.   This action led to the largest build-up of infantry, armour and artillery since the deployment of the Kosovo Verification Mission.   Representatives of the Verification Mission initiated negotiations for the captives' release, which continued intensively throughout the Chairman's visit, and, on 13 January, the eight were released.   The release did not, however, lead to a reduction of forces of the Federal Republic of Yugoslavia deployed throughout the area.   Yugoslav Deputy Prime Minister Sainovic and all Serbian government officials emphasized that the release of the army personnel had been absolutely unconditional.   On 14 January, a communiqué issued by Kosovo Albanian paramilitary units asserted that the eight had been released as part of an exchange for nine "prisoners".

Detention and trials

17. Reports of arbitrary detention and systematic ill-treatment of persons in police detention and under the jurisdiction of the Ministry of Justice continue.   Measures that would build confidence among communities are not forthcoming.   Of particular importance would be implementation of points 10 and 11 of the 13 October accord between President Slobodan Milosevic and United States Special Envoy Richard Holbrooke, release of information as to the whereabouts of those reported abducted and missing, and full cooperation by all parties with the International Committee of the Red Cross regarding persons held in detention.

18. Court proceedings on criminal charges of alleged terrorist and anti-State activity, as well as conspiracy to aid and abet such activity, continue to be held regularly in all district courts in Kosovo. Related proceedings have also begun in the military courts of Belgrade and Nis. The Office of the United Nations High Commissioner for Human Rights continues to monitor proceedings directly and to obtain court records of proceedings it cannot physically attend.   The efforts of the

Office to illuminate the legal and procedural issues raised by the proceedings have expanded informal working exchanges between and among court officials, prosecutors, defence attorneys, defendants and national and international organizations interested in the administration of justice. As part of this process, the Office makes repeated inquiries into judicial practice in the area of detention. Its consultations have contributed to a re-evaluation of detention decisions in cases throughout Serbia and, in some proceedings in Kosovo, to critical evaluation of evidence previously used to bring criminal charges or to justify continued detention. A small but growing body of precedent is being established as courts have released from detention, or dropped charges against, roughly 40 persons who were the specific subject of inquiry by the Office of the United Nations High Commissioner for Human Rights. However, hundreds of Kosovo Albanians remain in detention and the wave of violence described in this and my previous report has led to sweep arrests, police detentions, or "informative talks" in the search for perpetrators. As of 18 January, the Serbian Ministry of Justice had not responded to the Office on approximately 50 inquiries pending since late November. At the political level, no policy on implementation of points 10 and 11 has been enunciated, although existing federal and Serbian laws and procedures already include means for implementing, inter alia, federal and republic-level executive amnesty, termination of proceedings, suspension of charges, mitigation of sentences and release from detention.

19. Several proceedings involving especially large groups of defendants or incidents and operations of an especially sensitive nature were scheduled during the traditional December and January holidays. In monitoring many trials, the Office of the United Nations High Commissioner for Human Rights has observed violations of domestic judicial procedure in the treatment of selected groups of Kosovo Albanians. Courtroom observation also indicates obvious differences in the physical condition and demeanour of prisoners held in Lipljan and Gnjilane prisons, both under the jurisdiction of the Pristina district prison administration, from those held in the jurisdiction of the Prizren district prison administration. Reports of ill-treatment at Lipljan are received regularly, and two prisoners have already died in custody in Gnjilane. During this period, the Office repeatedly observed the transport of Lipljan prisoners in the 40-member Kosovo Albanian "Orahovac group" by heavily armed special police, who, holding automatic weapons, were permitted by the presiding judge to remain in the courtroom, at a ratio of one policeman to one defendant, instead of regular court guards. Such prisoners were chained on arrival in the courtroom, remained in a submissive head-down position throughout the proceeding, looked to individual police guards before answering even cursory questions put to them by the court and were rechained on removal from the courtroom. In contrast, imprisoned Kosovo Albanians kept in the Prizren prison jurisdiction were transported in handcuffs by prison guards who carried light arms and handguns; prisoners did not appear ill or malnourished, and they looked attorneys, judges and even family members in the eye during court proceedings.

20. The Office of the United Nations High Commissioner for Human Rights monitored several trials during this period that included the conviction and sentencing of persons in absentia. As a general rule, persons convicted in absentia received higher sentences than those present for trial.

21. The Office of the United Nations High Commissioner for Human Rights monitored trials in which several Kosovo Albanian defendants, in open court testimony, indicated that their statements during police detention and after arraignment before an investigative judge were made under ill-treatment or torture. Of the 26-member "Urosevac group" arrested in June 1998 and brought before the Pristina district court in late December and mid-January, two defendants had died while in police custody, and all nine standing trial (the others were in absentia) claimed that they had been tortured and still had visible traces of injuries inflicted by police and State security officials, including after arraignment. Of the 15-member "Kacanik group" arrested in August 1998 and tried in Pristina in mid-December, all present (eight were in absentia) testified to having been subjected to ill-treatment ranging from beatings to electric shock. Neither the presiding judge nor the prosecutor made further inquiry into these allegations. All

members of the group were convicted of sentences ranging from three to nine years, and those sentenced to less than three years were not released pending appeal, even though such provision exists in domestic law for sentences of under five years.

<u>Forensic investigation of mass graves</u>

22. Following the incident at Gornje Obrinje referred to in my previous report, the Finnish forensic team discussed the matter with the Serb authorities and representatives of Kosovo Albanian paramilitary units. Both parties suggested independently that since for the moment it was dangerous to carry out investigations at Gornje Obrinje (and also Golubovac), the Finnish team should instead start work at other locations currently not under the control of Kosovo Albanian paramilitary units, investigating in the first instance sites at Glodjane and Orahovac. The team, however, did not consider it possible to continue its field work at any other locations and therefore decided to leave Pristina on 20 December for a Christmas break. Under the prevailing circumstances, it remains uncertain whether in the foreseeable future there will be any prospect of making another attempt at Gornje Obrinje.

23. The difficulties experienced by the Finnish forensic team in performing their task were discussed at a meeting with the European Union Heads of Mission, and the Federal Republic of Yugoslavia Vice-Prime Minister and Head of the Government Commission for Cooperation with the Kosovo Verification Mission, Mr. Sainovic, on 29 December 1998 in Belgrade. Mr. Sainovic indicated his Government's readiness to discuss the problems, but only once the Finnish team was back in the Federal Republic of Yugoslavia.

<u>Coordination with the Kosovo Verification Mission</u>

24. Since the arrival of the Technical Assessment Team and throughout the build-up of the Kosovo Verification Mission, the Office of the United Nations High Commissioner for Human Rights has briefed representatives of OSCE and the Kosovo Verification Mission on the situation of human rights and has provided regular introductions to human rights issues to Verification Mission inductees. In December, the Office of the United Nations High Commissioner for Human Rights provided the services of a consultant on mission to the Kosovo Verification Mission, who advised the Mission on plans for sustained human rights training of its verifiers. UNHCR and the Office of the United Nations High Commissioner for Human Rights also met with the OSCE Chairman-in-Office and the OSCE secretariat delegation during its mission to the Federal Republic of Yugoslavia.

<u>Humanitarian situation</u>

25. Since late December, more than 20,000 people have fled from some 23 villages in the four municipalities of Decane, Podujevo, Stimlje and Suva Reka. The four days of fighting in late December at Podujevo led to the flight from the suburbs and surrounding villages of an estimated 5,000 people. As little damage was done to buildings, return to the villages started as soon as a ceasefire was brokered. However, following the capture of eight Yugoslav soldiers, tension rose again, leading to new displacement. From a total of 11 villages in the Podujevo-Mitrovica area some 15,000 inhabitants fled, of whom over 5,000 people later returned.

26. In the second week of January, clashes in the Decane municipality prompted some 4,000 people to flee from five illages. UNHCR estimates that over 500 of these have now returned to two of the villages. As a result of serious fighting in Stimlje/Suva Reka and following the massacre in Racak on 15 January, 6,400 Kosovo Albanian civilians fled from six villages.

27. Meanwhile, from some 90 villages, principally in central and western Kosovo, all Serbian inhabitants have left, estimated to total some 1,500 people.

28. Where peace has held, there have been continuing returns, usually slow and gradual. For example, in Malisevo more than half of the 3,000 who left in July have come back, returns are continuing and some normalcy is being established. At Lodja near Pec, work stopped on the school that is to serve as a home for some families while they repair their houses following the murders in the Pec café, but is now expected to start again. Representatives of 20 families from Opertusa, a village in Suva Reka, have asked UNHCR for assistance to return home. At Junik, a village from which 10,000 fled in August, there have been

1,500 returns; however, some trouble between the villagers and the police last week prompted about 200 to flee the village again. Returns to Junik appear to be from Albania and Djakovica and, despite the recent incident, appear to be continuing.

29. At the start of 1999, UNHCR estimated that some 180,000 civilians remained displaced within Kosovo, the vast majority of whom are Kosovo Albanians, including some 5,000 displaced in the last days of 1998. Some 110,000 were thought to have returned to their villages, if not their homes, in the last quarter of 1998. The great majority of these returns were from displacement within Kosovo, but included were some 12,000 returnees from Montenegro. No other significant returns were reported from outside Kosovo.

30. With regard to those still displaced or refugees outside Kosovo as a result of the conflict, at least 20,000 from Kosovo are thought to have moved to other parts of Serbia, and there are indications that the figure may be higher. Some 25,000 displaced persons are in Montenegro. Numbers in neighbouring countries are estimated as follows: Albania, 22,000 (of whom only some 500 remain in the Tropoje district); Bosnia and Herzegovina, 10,000; and the former Yugoslav Republic of Macedonia, 3,000. It is estimated that some 93,890 persons from the Federal Republic of Yugoslavia sought asylum in other countries in Europe in 1998, of whom 85 to 90 per cent are Kosovo Albanians.

31. In the first three weeks of 1999, some 20,000 persons are thought to have fled their homes for reasons of insecurity. Of these and those displaced at the end of 1998, some 7,000 have already been able to return, and a further 3,000 have returned to areas not affected by recent conflict. As at 20 January, UNHCR therefore estimated that some 190,000 remained displaced within Kosovo.

III. OBSERVATIONS

32. I am shocked and dismayed by reports of the atrocities committed in Racak on 15 January and urge the Yugoslav authorities to launch an urgent investigation of this crime with the participation of international experts. Sadly, the massacre and events surrounding it appear indicative of the pattern of disproportionate use of force by the authorities of the Federal Republic of Yugoslavia in retaliation for provocations by Kosovo Albanian paramilitaries. It is imperative that the perpetrators be brought to justice in order to deter further violence and to give peace in Kosovo a chance. Any appearance of impunity for the perpetrators could become a real obstacle to the process of finding a peaceful solution to the conflict through negotiation. In this regard, I urge that unconditional respect be given to the authority of the International Tribunal for the Former Yugoslavia throughout all of the territory of the former Yugoslavia.

33. The violence since 24 December, and in particular the massacre at Racak on 15 January and subsequent events, has been a major setback for the humanitarian operation, just when the deployment of the Kosovo Verification Mission was beginning to help create and consolidate conditions for return of the internally displaced, even to the most difficult areas such as Malisevo. Civilians have once again had to flee for their lives; many have had to spend bitter nights in the open. Continued violence would undermine what has been achieved by the humanitarian operation to date.

34. Fear of fighting between the security forces and Kosovo Albanian paramilitary units and continued violence against civilians are the overriding obstacle to return and to the sustainability of those returns that have taken place. The humanitarian operation has demonstrated its capacity to deliver large-scale assistance, but without an end to violence and the establishment of a climate of security this will not suffice. I am deeply concerned about the risk of a return to the situation that existed in Kosovo before October 1998, and I urge those in positions of public authority to put an end to the spiral of violence and to seek the path of constructive dialogue.

35. I am increasingly concerned that the spread of violence and the nature of the attacks could lead to a situation of all-out civil war in Kosovo, which might have unpredictable repercussions for the entire region. Violence, from whatever quarter, can only lead to further suffering for the civilian population in Kosovo, which has been the main target and victim of the conflict. Full and unconditional acceptance of peaceful negotiations is the only way to resolve the crisis in Kosovo. I therefore once again urge the parties to engage in negotiations on a peaceful settlement in Kosovo without further delay and without preconditions, as demanded by the international community and, in particular, by the Security Council in its resolutions 1160 (1998), 1199 (1998) and 1203 (1998).

36. I support the efforts of OSCE and of the Head of the Kosovo Verification Mission, Mr. Walker, to facilitate such a settlement and call upon the Yugoslav authorities to honour their obligations under the 16 October agreement and to cooperate fully with Mr. Walker and the Kosovo Verification Mission. I also call upon the authorities of the Federal Republic of Yugoslavia to honour their obligation to cooperate fully with the Prosecutor of the International Tribunal for the Former Yugoslavia as requested in Security Council resolutions 1160 (1998), 1199 (1998) and 1203 (1998).

37. I expect that the OSCE Chairman-in-Office, in consultation with the Head of the Kosovo Verification Mission, will henceforth be in a position to provide the Council with regular information on the political aspects of the situation in Kosovo. ...

Annex II
Letter from the Secretary-General of NATO, 22 January 1999

I am writing to bring you up to date with regard to the actions and decisions of the North Atlantic Treaty Organization (NATO) in the Kosovo crisis. As you know, the situation has deteriorated significantly in recent weeks culminating in the massacre of Kosovar Albanians in the village of Racak last Friday.

Following its meeting on 17 January to assess the situation, the North Atlantic Council called on the Yugoslav authorities to cooperate fully with the International Tribunal for the Former Yugoslavia, in accordance with United Nations resolutions, and to take immediate steps to bring those responsible for the massacre to justice. It also expressed its full support for the mission of the Organization for Security and Cooperation in Europe (OSCE) in Kosovo, as established by Security Council resolution 1203 (1998), and called on President Milosevic to comply fully with his commitments to NATO and OSCE, based on Security Council resolution 1199 (1998) and the undertakings provided to the Alliance last October on force levels and posture.

At the request of the Council, NATO's senior military authorities, the Chairman of the Military Committee, General Klaus Naumann, and the Supreme Allied Commander Europe (SACEUR), General Wesley K. Clark, visited President Milosevic personally on 19 January to underline its concern and reinforce the need for him to honour his obligations. Regrettably, until now, he has failed to do so. The North Atlantic Council is accordingly now assessing the situation and considering how best to help the international community achieve a political solution to the crisis.

The North Atlantic Council also agreed on 20 January 1999 that I would provide a report to the United Nations on compliance by the parties to the conflict. Accordingly I enclose, for your information and for distribution as you deem appropriate, an assessment of compliance trends derived from various public and official Alliance sources. The report covers significant trends and incidents over the past month, but is not intended as a complete compilation. As you will see from the report, neither side in the conflict has respected the ceasefire; and there have been a number of cases of kidnappings and attacks by Kosovar armed elements. The activities of the Yugoslav Army (VJ) and the Special Police (MUP), however, have been wholly disproportionate and excessive, particularly bearing in mind the operations conducted during the period from 10 to 16 January 1999.

I will keep you informed of any further important developments and am looking forward to an exchange of views on these and other issues with you on 28 January. I am sending a copy of this letter to the Chairman-in-Office of the Organization for Security and Cooperation in Europe.

Enclosure: North Atlantic Treaty Organization compliance report for Kosovo 13 December 1998-19 January 1999

Table 1, United Nations Security Council resolution 1199 (1998)

Resolution tenet	Related activity
1. Federal Republic of Yugoslavia and Kosovo Albanians: Cease hostilities and maintain ceasefire	13-19 Dec.: VJ units begin deployment to Podujevo area. VJ kills 31 Kosovo Albanians crossing border. UCK, in separate incidents, kill 8 Serb civilians, 1 MUP officer. UCK kidnap and kill Deputy Mayor of Kosovo Polje. 20-26 Dec.: UCK attack MUP patrol; 2 UCK killed. UCK kill MUP officer in Podujevo, local security official in a café in Kosovska Mitrovica. VJ forces, reinforced with armour and artillery, attack villages in and around Podujevo. 27 Dec.-VJ continue shelling civilian 2 Jan. facilities and UCK positions in and around Podujevo resulting in the deaths of at least 15 Kosovo Albanians. UCK kill Serb judge in Podujevo. 3-9 Jan.: UCK kill 3 MUP officers in ambush. UCK blamed for grenade attack against Serb bar, death of Serb official in Polje, Serb guard at a power plant and 6 MUP. UCK capture 8 VJ soldiers (later released, unharmed). VJ/MUP shell villages in Podujevo area; attack UCK positions. 10-16 Jan.: VJ tanks fire on Lapastika. VJ/MUP operations with artillery support in Decane area. VJ/MUP operations in Suva Reka and Stimlje. VJ heavy shelling in Racak. VJ/MUP believed (including by Head of the Organization for Security and Cooperation in Europe (OSCE) Kosovo Verification Mission) to be responsible for 45 civilian deaths in Racak.
2. Federal Republic of Yugoslavia: Take steps to improve humanitarian situation.	On 17 December, the Government of the Federal Republic of Yugoslavia has announced but has not yet implemented plans to build humanitarian centres and new houses and to reconstruct damaged houses. Federal Republic of Yugoslavia operations around Podujevo, Suva Reka have displaced over 7,000 persons.
3. Federal Republic of Yugoslavia and Albanian-Kosovars: Enter into dialogue, with international involvement, to end crisis.	Nothing significant to report.
4. Federal Republic of Yugoslavia: Cease all action by security forces affecting the civilian population and order the withdrawal of security units used for civilian repression.	3-9 Jan.: MUP accused by civilians of firing on villages of Djakavica, Sipitula and Belince. 10-16 Jan.: MUP/VJ forces conduct counter-insurgency operations in Stimlje, Decane, Suva Reka and Racak; see entry 1 above.
5. Federal Republic of Yugoslavia: Enable effective and continuous international monitoring, including access and complete freedom of movement.	Throughout the reporting period, VJ and MUP forces have denied access, in selected areas, to Kosovo Diplomatic Observer Mission and OSCE personnel.
6. Federal Republic of Yugoslavia: Facilitate with the Office of the United Nations High Commissioner for Refugees (UNHCR) and the International Committee of the Red Cross safe return of refugees and internally displaced persons to their homes.	There is no overt example of cooperation by the Federal Republic of Yugoslavia with UNHCR to assist in the safe return of refugees and internally displaced persons. The most recent fighting in the Stimlje area has created a new situation with estimates of up to 6,000 internally displaced persons fleeing their homes in the Stimlje/Racak regions. Many of these people are without shelter.
7. Federal Republic of Yugoslavia and Kosovo Albanians: Set a timetable aimed at confidence-building measures and political solutions.	Nothing significant to report.
8. Federal Republic of Yugoslavia: Cooperate with the International Tribunal for the Former Yugoslavia in the investigation of possible violations.	10 Dec.: Serb police blocked the Finnish forensics team from carrying out the first exhumations of Kosovo massacre victims in a dispute over Serb access to a UCK-controlled area. A Serb contingent, consisting of an associate police commander and nearly two dozen policemen wearing flak jackets and carrying automatic weapons, stopped the Finnish convoy on the road to Trstenik. The UCK in the area said that the police were unwelcome but that the Finnish team could proceed. The Serb police were not satisfied with this arrangement and therefore prohibited the investigators from proceeding to the grave site. The Finnish team leader has accused the Serb side of obstruction, adding that the Serb action violated the diplomatic immunity of the Finnish Ambassador for Human Rights who accompanied the team. 19 Jan.: The Government of the Federal Republic of Yugoslavia denied the chief of the International Tribunal for the Former Yugoslavia, Louise Arbour, entry to Kosovo to evaluate the alleged massacre of 45 civilians in Racak. The authorities of the Federal Republic of Yugoslavia have moved the bodies from a mosque in Racak to Pristina and have begun their own autopsies.
9. Federal Republic of Yugoslavia: Bring to justice security force members involved in mistreatment of civilians and the deliberate destruction of property.	There is no indication that the Government of the Federal Republic of Yugoslavia has assisted in this effort. See entry 8 above.
10. Kosovo Albanian leadership: Condemn all terrorist activity.	There has been no public declaration by either the political or the military leadership to denounce alleged UCK acts of terrorism during the reporting period.

Table 2 Modalities for Kosovo Federal Republic of Yugoslavia security force reductions and operations agreed to by the North Atlantic Treaty Organization and the Federal Republic of Yugoslavia on 25 October 1998

Modality	Actions by the Federal Republic of Yugoslavia
1. Special Police units deployed to Kosovo after February 1998 will be withdrawn from Kosovo. Combined police/Special Police strength in Kosovo will be reduced to their February 1998 duty level.	There is strong evidence that Special Police detachments from Serbia proper continue to operate within Kosovo. There are no indications that externally based detachments are being withdrawn.
2. Any heavy weapons (12.7 mm and above) or equipment brought into Kosovo or transferred from the VJ to the police/Special Police after February 1998 will be withdrawn from Kosovo or returned to the VJ.	In violation of this provision, MUP has and is employing heavy weaponry in Kosovo.
3. Police/Special Police will resume their normal peacetime activities. Heavy weapons and equipment remaining under MUP control in Kosovo will be returned to cantonments and police stations.	See table 1, entry 4. Excessive traffic patrolling, fortification of observation posts and unauthorized checkpoints continue.
4. All VJ units and additional equipment brought into Kosovo after February 1998 will be withdrawn from Kosovo.	VJ forces may have been reinforced with personnel from outside Kosovo.
5. Except for those VJ currently augmenting border guards, all VJ elements remaining in Kosovo will return to garrison, with agreed exceptions.	VJ units clearly began to violate this requirement in mid-December and continue to deploy units above the agreed-to limits in size and location.
6. VJ and MUP commanders will provide to the Kosovo Diplomatic Observer Mission/OSCE detailed weekly reports on manning, weapons and activities of their forces and will provide immediate	VJ and MUP reporting has been inaccurate and misleading. VJ and MUP units have failed to account for equipment and personnel numbers and activities.

notification and explanation to the Kosovo Diplomatic Observer Mission/OSCE of any deployment contrary to these provisions.

Federal Republic of Yugoslavia-Kosovo Diplomatic Observer Mission verification modalities

7. All checkpoints will be dismantled.	MUP continue to maintain and build unauthorized checkpoints throughout Kosovo. Some include kitchens and sleeping facilities.
8. In case of incidents of increased tension, the police will have the right, upon notifying the Kosovo Diplomatic Observer Mission/OSCE, to perform patrol duties in armoured vehicles.	See entry 6 above. Notification is usually relayed after the fact as a statement of action already carried out.

Table 3 United Nations Security Council resolution 1203 (1998)

Resolution tenet	Related activity
1. Federal Republic of Yugoslavia: Cooperate fully with the Organization for Security and Cooperation in Europe (OSCE) Kosovo Verification Mission and Air Verification Mission.	Kosovo Air Verification Mission continues uninhibited with full support of the Federal Republic of Yugoslavia. On 18 January, the Government of the Federal Republic of Yugoslavia declared the Head of the OSCE Kosovo Verification Mission, Ambassador William Walker, "persona non grata" and ordered him to leave the Federal Republic of Yugoslavia within 48 hours.
2. Federal Republic of Yugoslavia: Comply immediately with Security Council resolutions 1160 (1998) and 1199 (1998).	Offensive operations conducted by VJ and MUP forces, inter alia, from 23 to 27 December in the Podujevo area and, from 15 to 21 January in the Stimlje region. See table 1, entries 1 and 4.
3. Federal Republic of Yugoslavia and Kosovo Albanians: Respect freedom of movement of OSCE Kosovo Verification Mission and other international personnel.	Both parties prohibit access in some areas and at some facilities. To date, the Federal Republic of Yugoslavia has not allowed Kosovo Verification Mission personnel access to border operations nor to some MUP facilities.
4. Federal Republic of Yugoslavia: Ensure the safety and security of all diplomatic personnel, including OSCE Kosovo Verification Mission personnel and all international and non-governmental organization humanitarian personnel.	On 17 January, without warning, MUP began mortar and automatic weapons fire in Racak, seriously endangering Kosovo Verification Mission personnel in the vicinity.
5. Federal Republic of Yugoslavia and Kosovo Albanians: Ensure personnel are not subject to the threat or use of force or interference of any kind.	On 15 January, UCK small arms fire wounded two Kosovo Verification Mission personnel. UCK claims firing was not intentional.
6. Federal Republic of Yugoslavia and Kosovo Albanians: Cooperate with international efforts to improve the humanitarian situation and avert pending humanitarian crisis.	Nothing significant to report.
7. Federal Republic of Yugoslavia: Create the conditions that allow internally displaced persons to return home.	See table 1, entry 6.
8. Federal Republic of Yugoslavia: Conduct prompt and complete investigation of all atrocities committed against civilians through the Hague-based International Tribunal for the Former Yugoslavia.	See table 1, entry 8.

S/1999/161, 12 February 1999

25.   Report of the Secretary-General, 12 February 1999

I. INTRODUCTION

1. The present report is submitted pursuant to Security Council resolution 1186 (1998) of 21 July 1998, by which the Council decided to authorize an increase in the troop strength of the United Nations Preventive Deployment Force (UNPREDEP) up to 1,050 and to extend its mandate for a period of six months until 28 February 1999, including to continue by its presence to deter threats and prevent clashes, to monitor the border areas, and to report to the Secretary-General any developments which could pose a threat to the former Yugoslav Republic of Macedonia, including the tasks of monitoring and reporting on illicit arms flows and other activities that are prohibited under resolution 1160 (1998). The present report covers developments in the mission area since my last two reports of 1 June and 14 July 1998 (S/1998/454 and S/1998/644).

II. COMPOSITION, STRENGTH AND MANDATE OF THE UNITED NATIONS PREVENTIVE DEPLOYMENT FORCE

2. During the period under review, the mandate of UNPREDEP has remained unchanged. The mission is headed by my Special Representative, Fernando Valenzuela Marzo, who succeeded Henryk J. Sokalski on 9 January 1999 (see S/1998/1191 and S/1998/1192). The military component is headed by the Force Commander, Brigadier-General Ove Strømberg (Norway).

3. The increase in UNPREDEP's military component by 300 all ranks, authorized by the Security Council in resolution 1186 (1998), was completed by the beginning of January 1999, thus bringing its strength to 1,050 troops (see annex). At the same time, the total number of observation posts and patrol bases has been increased from 8 to 16, all of which are situated at strategic locations and sensitive points along the borders with Albania and the Federal Republic of Yugoslavia. Reconfiguration of the augmented military component and the increase in the number of observation posts and patrol bases have enabled UNPREDEP to fulfil its mission in the entire area of responsibility.

4. The military component consists of two mechanized infantry battalions: a Nordic composite battalion and a United States Army task force, with 650 and 350 personnel respectively, supported by a 50-strong heavy engineering platoon from Indonesia. In addition, there are 35 military observers and 26 civilian police monitors. The authorized strength of the civilian component, including the local staff, is 203. The international civilian and military personnel are drawn from 50 countries.

5. During the past six months, the military units of UNPREDEP have actively patrolled their respective areas of operation, while the military observers and civilian police monitors have continued their community and border patrols. On average, UNPREDEP military personnel have conducted some 400 patrols per week, including 300 border and community patrols, established 80 temporary observation posts (from 3 to 24 hours), and conducted 15 helicopter patrols. In addition, the civilian police monitors conduct approximately 100 patrols per week.

6. Pursuant to Security Council resolution 1186 (1998), UNPREDEP has undertaken the new task of monitoring and reporting on illicit arms flows and other activities that are prohibited under resolution 1160 (1998). UNPREDEP has developed new techniques to enhance its capacity to ascertain whether arms smuggling is actually taking place in its area of operation. Mobile reaction teams have been established, which, while paying due attention to safety, respond to sighted smuggling activities by moving quickly to continue observation at a closer distance, thus providing more accurate information on whether arms, ammunition or explosives are involved. However, it should be underlined that while UNPREDEP, within it current mandate, can monitor and report, it does not have the authority to interdict and inspect cross-border traffic. Although smuggling incidents have been observed, UNPREDEP has so far not detected any direct evidence of arms smuggling across the borders of the former Yugoslav Republic of Macedonia with Albania or the Federal Republic of Yugoslavia.

7. The civilian component of UNPREDEP has been effectively monitoring and reporting on developments in the country that could

affect its peace and stability. It has continued to implement the good offices mandate vested in my Special Representative by conducting an active dialogue with the authorities and all other major political forces in the country; encouraging cross-party dialogue and a better understanding among the various segments of the population with a view to easing inter-ethnic tensions; and promoting the application of international standards of human rights.

8. In pursuing a comprehensive model of preventive action, UNPREDEP has also been involved in a wide range of programmes related to good governance and the rule of law, strengthening of national capacity and infrastructure, institution- building and human resources development in the governmental and civil sectors. The mission has worked with many groups in the society to encourage them to contribute to the country's development and to serve as agents of conflict prevention and promoters of democracy and human rights. International expertise has been made available to the host country through long-term programmes and activities aimed at enhancing social peace and stability. These programmes have been funded from extrabudgetary resources mobilized by the office of the Special Representative, which have now reached nearly US$ 8 million in cash and kind.

9. UNPREDEP has continued its close cooperation with the Spillover Monitor Mission to Skopje of the Organization for Security and Cooperation in Europe (OSCE) and the European Commission Monitoring Mission in the country. It has also established a working relationship with the North Atlantic Treaty Organization (NATO) Kosovo Verification Coordination Centre and the NATO Extraction Force recently deployed in the host country. ...

IV. RECENT DEVELOPMENTS

20. Since my last report dated 14 July 1998 (S/1998/644), the situation in Kosovo (Federal Republic of Yugoslavia) has been a matter of continued grave concern to the international community. Issues relating to the situation in the region were addressed in my report to the Council of 30 January 1999 (S/1999/99), prepared pursuant to resolutions 1160 (1998), 1199 (1998) and 1203 (1998).

21. The bilateral relations of the former Yugoslav Republic of Macedonia with some of its neighbours have strengthened during the reporting period. Relations with Albania have improved significantly following the recent parliamentary elections in the host country and the inclusion, at the invitation of the winning coalition, of a coalition of the ethnic Albanian Party for Democratic Prosperity of Albanians and the National Democratic Party (PDPA/NDP) in the new Government. High-level bilateral visits and agreements on mutual cooperation between the two countries, as well as efforts by the new Government to improve inter-ethnic relations, have had a further positive impact on bilateral relations.

22. The steady increase in trade and collaborative ventures with Greece, as well as official visits by that country's leadership, reflect improved bilateral relations between the two neighbours despite the still unresolved name-related dispute. Relations with Bulgaria are also strengthening, with both countries expressing a renewed determination to overcome the language dispute while simultaneously increasing economic and other forms of cooperation.

23. Relations between the former Yugoslav Republic of Macedonia and the Federal Republic of Yugoslavia have been strained owing to the host country's decision to authorize the deployment of the NATO Extraction Force on its territory. This decision prompted a strong protest by the Federal Republic of Yugoslavia. There has also been no progress on the issue of demarcation of the border between the two countries and the Joint Border Commission, after a hiatus of six months, has yet to resume its deliberations.

24. The most significant positive development on the domestic political scene during the reporting period was the holding of the third parliamentary elections in October and November 1998. The elections, which were held in a peaceful atmosphere, resulted in a change of Government. The new Government represents a coalition of three parties, including the ethnic Albanian coalition (PDPA/NDP). The elections were held in accordance with the new electoral laws, which enjoyed wide political consensus when adopted by the Parliament. They were monitored by international observers from the Office for Democratic Institutions and Human Rights (ODIHR) of OSCE, the Parliamentary Assembly of the Council of Europe and international NGOs, all of whom assessed the overall electoral process to be well conducted and in accordance with OSCE and Council of Europe standards.

25. The new Prime Minister, Ljubco Georgievski, in his policy statement before assuming office, underlined that the fostering and development of inter-ethnic relations will be one of the fundamental tenets of his Government. The formation of a new inclusive Government has been a demonstration of that commitment and has eased inter-ethnic relations in the country.

26. In keeping with this declared policy of seeking inter-ethnic harmony, the first legislative act of the newly constituted Parliament was to adopt the law on amnesty to pave the way for the release of the ethnic Albanian mayors and chairmen of the municipal councils of Gostivar and Tetovo. The trial and heavy sentencing, in particular of the then mayor of Gostivar, Rufi Osmani, in September 1997, had heightened inter-ethnic tensions in the country (see S/1997/911, para. 20). Despite President Gligorov's initial veto of the promulgation of the law, owing to his objections to some aspects of it, the Parliament adopted it at its second reading on 4 February 1999. The subsequent immediate release of the imprisoned ethnic Albanian local government officials is expected to contribute further to the easing of inter-ethnic tension in the country. ...

VI. OBSERVATIONS

30. Peace and stability in the former Yugoslav Republic of Macedonia continue to depend largely on developments in other parts of the region, in particular in Kosovo. In my report to the Council of 30 January 1999 (S/1999/99), I expressed my increasing concern that the spread of violence and the nature of the attacks in Kosovo could lead to a situation of all-out civil war in the province, which might have unpredictable repercussions for the entire region. It is a matter of satisfaction that, until now, the former Yugoslav Republic of Macedonia has not been adversely affected by the conflict in Kosovo. However, the potential serious repercussions that continued violence in Kosovo could have upon the external and internal security of the country cannot be ignored given the large proportion of ethnic Albanians in the population of the former Yugoslav Republic of Macedonia.

31. As stated in my report to the Council of 1 June 1998 (S/1998/454, para. 21), the presence of UNPREDEP has so far contributed successfully to preventing the spillover of conflicts elsewhere in the region to the former Yugoslav Republic of Macedonia. By contributing significantly to promoting dialogue among the various political forces and ethnic communities in the country, UNPREDEP continues to have a stabilizing effect. The confidence inspired by its presence has been useful in defusing tensions that could have arisen as a result of the continued crisis in Kosovo.

32. The Minister for Foreign Affairs of the former Yugoslav Republic of Macedonia, in a letter addressed to me on 29 January 1999 (S/1999/108), presented his Government's arguments for an extension of the mandate of UNPREDEP for an additional six months, with its existing composition and structure. In his letter, the Minister for Foreign Affairs pointed, in particular, to his Government's concern over the danger of a spillover of the conflict in Kosovo into neighbouring countries, the increase in tensions on the Albanian-Yugoslav border, the still unstable situation in Albania, which has burdened his Government's efforts to prevent arms trafficking to Kosovo, and the lack of progress in the demarcation of the country's border with the Federal Republic of Yugoslavia.

33. As the present report is being written, the Contact Group on the former Yugoslavia is actively engaged in seeking a political solution to the Kosovo crisis. At the same time, discussions are continuing within the framework of NATO concerning the possible deployment of an international military presence in the region. The outcome of such deliberations and the medium- to long-term impact they will have on the former Yugoslav Republic of Macedonia, and on UNPREDEP itself, cannot be foreseen at this time.

34. Against the backdrop of developments in and relating to the region, and taking into account, in particular, the arguments adduced by the

Government of the former Yugoslav Republic of Macedonia, the Security Council may wish to consider extending the presence of UNPREDEP, with its existing mandate and composition, for a further period of six months until 31 August 1999, on the understanding that it would review its decision should the discussions referred to in paragraph 33 above result in developments which would affect UNPREDEP's role and responsibilities.

35. Finally, I should like to thank my Special Representative, Fernando Valenzuela Marzo, and his predecessor, Henryk J. Sokalski, as well as the Force Commander, Brigadier-General Ove Strømberg, and all the military and civilian personnel under their command for their dedication and perseverance in carrying out the tasks entrusted to them by the Security Council.

Annex

Composition and strength of the military and civilian police elements of the United Nations Preventive Deployment Force, February 1999[*]

Country	Contingent strength	Military observers	Civilian police
Argentina	-	1	-
Bangladesh	-	2	-
Belgium	-	1	-
Brazil	-	2	-
Canada	-	1	-
Czech Republic	-	1	-
Denmark	87	1	-
Egypt	-	1	-
Finland	199	1	6
Ghana	-	1	-
Indonesia	51	2	-
Ireland	-	2	-
Jordan	-	1	2
Kenya	-	2	-
Nepal	-	1	-
New Zealand	-	1	-
Nigeria	-	1	4
Norway	152	2	-
Pakistan	-	2	-
Poland	-	2	-
Portugal	-	1	-
Russian Federation	-	3	2
Sweden	198	1	-
Switzerland	-	1	4
Turkey	-	-	4
Ukraine	-	1	4
United States of America	362	-	-
Total	1 049	35	26

[*] The number of military personnel and civilian police monitors may vary owing to rotations.

26. UN Inter-Agency Update on Kosovo Humanitarian Situation, 22 February 1999

Population Movements

1. Clashes between the Kosovo Liberation Army (KLA) and Serbian security forces during the period under review led to new displacement in Studencane and Ristane (Southwest of Pristina in Suva Reka municipality) and in several villages in Vucitrn municipality (approximately 25 km Northwest of Pristina). UNHCR estimates that some 9,000 civilians have been forced to flee their homes in these two areas although some have since returned. The area between Pristina and Podujevo remains deserted by all its inhabitants.

Security

2. The murder of Albanian and Serbian civilians has continued, with bodies killed by gunshot wound found daily. More than 40 murders have occurred in the first three weeks of February 1999. The President of the Kosovo Temporary Council told UNHCR that he could no longer guarantee the safety of Serbs living in Kosovo. Consequently, UNHCR will continue to be active in the protection of minorities living in Kosovo in the post-Rambouillet environment. The Organisation for Security and Cooperation in Europe Kosovo Verification Mission (KVM) has maintained its presence throughout Kosovo with the exception of Leposavic north of Pristina where verifiers were driven out by Serb civilians and the Mayor.

Relief Distribution

3. During the period under review UNHCR led convoys carrying food and non-food items to thousands of displaced, host families and returnees in the municipalities of Klina, Orahovac, Kosovska Mitrovica, Srbica, Glogovac, Suva Reka and Obilic. Humanitarian agencies supplying relief items include UNHCR, WFP, Children's Aid Direct, Doctors of the World, Mercy Corps International and Mother Teresa Society.

Coordination

4. The first "Principals' Meeting" was held in Pristina on Friday 19 February. The meeting arose following ongoing discussions between UNHCR and OSCE KVM since November 1998 and is intended to facilitate coordination and cooperation on humanitarian issues at the highest level. Chaired by UNHCR the meeting also included representatives from OSCE/KVM (Ambassador Walker), the NGO Executive Committee (International Rescue Committee and Mercy Corps International) and ICRC. OCHA acted as secretary to the meeting.

5. The agenda covered the security situation, the likely scenarios post Rambouillet and the need for strong coordination of humanitarian and reconstruction assistance. After the conclusion of the Rambouillet talks UNHCR stated that it would continue its humanitarian programme, concentrating on returns and provision of necessary protection as well as delivery of relief until alternative arrangements were in place. UNHCR would not directly engage in reconstruction, but would take an active role in coordination of reconstruction activities and the recently-completed UNHCR-sponsored shelter survey could be used as a reference document for donors and implementing bodies involved in reconstruction.

6. ICRC said that it would continue its traditional activities, seeking free access for humanitarian assistance, access to the detained, and the development of the local Red Cross. IRC and MCI said that NGOs would continue with their long-term programmes and welcomed the opportunity to be closely involved in coordination post-Rambouillet. NGOs were also given the chance to raise any other outstanding issues of concern. It was decided that the Principals' meetings should continue under the chairmanship of UNHCR with relevant agencies joining as they came on board.

Health

7. The second workshop on basic epidemiology in emergencies organised by WHO was completed on 23 February 1999. Participants were eight medical doctors from Mother Teresa medical branch and eight medical doctors from the Institute of Public Health (IPH) Pristina and its branches in other parts of Kosovo. The aim of the second workshop was to empower local doctors to use EpiInfo6 software package especially designed for surveillance of infectious diseases. ...

S/1999/214, 26 February 1999

27. Letter from the Secretary-General to the President of the Security Council, 26 February 1999

I have the honour to convey the attached communication, dated 20 February 1999, which I have received from the Chairman-in-Office of the Organization for Security and Cooperation in Europe (OSCE). The enclosed report on the situation in Kosovo is submitted pursuant to requirements set by the Security Council in resolution 1160 (1998) of 31 March 1998 and resolution 1203 (1998) of 24 October 1998, and in compliance with the Council's wish to be kept informed on the situation in Kosovo.

As I indicated to the Council in my reports dated 12 November 1998 (S/1998/1068) and 24 December 1998 (S/1998/1221), it was my intention, as soon as OSCE was in a position to provide the Security Council with information on the compliance by the parties, to discontinue reporting on the situation in Kosovo accordingly, except as concerned the humanitarian and human rights situation. I therefore intend to complement the OSCE communication with a report on the humanitarian and human rights aspects of the situation in Kosovo, which will be submitted to the Council separately.

Annex
Letter dated from the Chairman-in-Office of the OSCE to the Secretary-General, 20 February 1999
... Enclosure
Monthly report on the situation in Kosovo
Mid-January 1999 - Mid-February 1999
I. General situation
Security situation
During most of the reporting period the situation in Kosovo remained tense and volatile. In February however, the level of direct military engagement between the security forces of the Federal Republic of Yugoslavia (FRY) and the Kosovo Liberation Army (KLA) dropped significantly compared with late December and the month of January. The main areas of military tension remained the same as during the previous period - the Podujevo region in the northern Kosovo, the Decani region in the west of the Province and the area around Stimlje, south of Pristina.

While the level of military conflict was reduced in February, KLA attacks on the Serb police, isolated clashes and sporadic exchange of gunfire, including at times the use of heavy weapons by the VJ, continued to take place. The main feature of the last part of the reporting period has been an alarming increase in urban terrorism with a series of indiscriminate bombing or raking gunfire attacks against civilians in public places in towns throughout Kosovo. Although all of these attacks remained non-attributable, and it was not clear whether they were criminally or politically motivated, these incidents led to disruption and the spread of an atmosphere of fear.

The reporting period started with FRY security forces operations in the Stimlje and Mitrovica areas. The Urosevac Deputy Head of Police was killed in the Racak area on 19 January. KVM HQ was informed that he had been escorting an investigation team to Racak. Two other policemen were injured and evacuated by helicopter to Pristina.

On the 20 January police search operations in the Mitrovica area ended in exchanges of fire and the deaths of two KLA members. The incident was observed by the KVM throughout its development. The police surrounded two houses and called for the occupants to surrender. The residents replied with small arms fire. Further negotiations brokered by the KVM failed when the occupants of the house opened fire with an anti-tank rocket launcher. The police responded with anti-aircraft artillery fire. The bodies of two armed KLA members were found. It was estimated that 10 other occupants had escaped.

The KLA abducted five elderly Serb civilians from Nevoljane (West of Vucitrn) on 22 January. The KVM was told by the KLA that the hostages would be released to the OSCE as long as the police did not carry out operations in the Vucitrn area. KVM liaison officers carried out the negotiations and facilitated the releases of the hostages on 24 January. The KVM strongly condemned the abduction of these civilians by the KLA as an act of terrorism.

Five Kosovo Albanians (two adult males, one adult female and two children aged approximately 10 and 12 years old) were killed on the evening of 25 January in Rakovina (northeast of Djakovica). They were travelling along the road on a tractor and trailer when they were killed by small arms fire. Verifiers assess approximately 300 rounds were fired from a prepared position. The day after the killings the FRY Health Minister, Miodrug Kovac, stated that the five died in a traffic accident. KVM's inquiry into the Rakovina incident continues.

Towards the end of January serious breaches of the ceasefire were reported in the Podujevo area. On 28 and 29 January mortar, tank and machine-gun fire was reported south of Podujevo in the direction of the village of Kisela Banja. No casualties were reported, but a large number of displaced persons were observed in that area. The continued KLA and security force stand-off in this area with both sides digging trenches and preparing positions has been a particular concern throughout the period. Though the fighting has since subsided, neither the KLA nor the VJ has withdrawn as required under United Nations Security Council resolutions. VJ forces in the field exceed the limits set by the NATO-FRY Agreement signed on 25 October 1998. The KVM has been protesting this non-compliance by both parties.

A number of incidents occurred in the border region between Djakovica and Prizren. On 27 January a six-man patrol vehicle encountered and exchanged fire with an armed group of men in the Djakovica area. Two policemen were injured and two members of the other group, allegedly KLA, were killed. A VJ liaison officer informed the KVM that on the same day the KLA also attempted to infiltrate into Kosovo from Albania near the village of Damnjane south of Djakovica. There were reports of fighting in that area and a large number of IDPs were seen leaving the nearby village of Romaja.

On 29 January, 25 Kosovo Albanians and one Serb policeman were killed in the village of Rogovo, midway between Djakovica and Prizren. The Yugoslav authorities informed the KVM that the incident at Rogovo began when shots were fired at a police patrol and a policeman was killed. KVM verifiers confirmed that four of the Albanians were in KLA uniform. A local KLA commander later acknowledged that 18 of 25 Albanians killed in Rogovo were KLA members. The FRY authorities agreed to a joint investigation of the incident by their specialists and by a Finnish forensic team.

Urban violence increased significantly in February. Pristina, Mitrovica, Pec, Urosevac have all been subjected to such incidents in which five people have been killed and more than a dozen injured. In the most serious of these an explosive device detonated outside a small Albanian grocery store in Pristina on 6 February, killing the owner and two passers-by, including a teenage girl.

More reports were received of the KLA "policing" the Albanian community and administering punishments to those charged as collaborators with the Serbs. In the area of Pec several Albanians said to be loyal to the Serbs were murdered in separate incidents. Most of the victims were highly educated males, described by Serbs as "loyal citizens of Serbia" and killed by shots to the head. Incidents of abduction of Albanians were also reported. During the funeral in Racak on 11 February eight Kosovo Albanians were abducted (the KLA term was "arrested") by KLA members. Only after KVM's intervention were they released.

Two Serb policemen were allegedly abducted on 10 February in Kosovo Poljc. A third was abducted in Novo Selo (south of Vucitrn) but later escaped. The KLA at first denied the abduction and detention of police officers, but later engaged in contacts with KVM on the matter. This issue has yet to be resolved. ...

II. OSCE activities
Activities of the Chairman-in-Office and the Permanent Council
On 20 January the OSCE Troika, the foreign ministers of Norway, Austria and Poland, discussed the situation caused by the FRY decision to declare Ambassador Walker persona non grata. They demanded that the decision be rescinded. On 21 January 1999 OSCE Chairman in Office (CiO) Knut Vollebaek had meetings in Belgrade with President Milosevic of the FRY and Foreign Minister Jovanovic to insist that the FRY Government rescinded its decision to declare the Head of Mission (HOM) of KVM, Ambassador William Walker, persona non grata. As a result of these meetings, and the unanimous support given by the international community, this decision was frozen. The CiO then visited the KVM Headquarters in Pristina, where he briefed the KVM staff on these developments. The OSCE Chairmanship convened themed Kosovo meetings in Vienna during the reporting period, dealing with, among other issues, the humanitarian situation and reconstruction in Kosovo, UNHCR's Special Envoy to the former Yugoslavia, Mr. Nick Morris and Mr. Fabrizio Barbaso from the European Commission addressed meetings of the Informal Watch Group. The CiO participated at the 29 January meeting of the Contact Group initiating the Rambouillet negotiations. On 1 February the OSCE Permanent Council expressed full support for the efforts of the international community to achieve a political settlement to the conflict in Kosovo. The CiO attended the opening of the Kosovo peace talks at Rambouillet in France, which began on February 6. He was accompanied by Ambassador Walker. The CiO, his team and representatives from the KVM are closely following the progress of the talks. The CiO also participated at the Contact Group meetings on 14 and 20 February.

KVM operations
The build up of the Kosovo Verification Mission continued during the period covered by the report. The Regional Centres (Prizren, Pec, Mitrovica, Gnjilane and Pristina) opened new municipality-based

Coordination Centres (CCs) and village-based Field Offices (FOs). Prizren Regional Centre has CCs in Suva Reka, Orahovac and Prizren, with FOs in Rastane, Velika Krusa, Malisevo, Zur and Slapuzane, Mitrovica Regional Centre has CCs in Vucitrn, Srbica and Sipolje with FOs in Trepca, Vaganica, Donje Stanovce, Leposovic, Svecan, Zubin Potok and Rudnik. Pec Regional Centre has CCs in Klina, Istok, Decani and Djakovica with FOs in Junik and Rogovo. Gnjilane Regional Centre has CCs in Vitina and Kamenica with FOs in Ogoste, Ranilug, Ugljare, Zitinje, Prozaranje and Smira. Pristina Regional Centre has CCs in Urosevac, Pristina and Glogovac with FOs in Lipljan, Kacanik, Strpce and Stimlje. The total number of CCs is 16 and the FOs is 24. The strength of the Mission at 20 February was 1,306 international staff and 1,263 local staff (total 2,569). The KVM continued to monitor the situation throughout Kosovo, verifying the maintenance of the ceasefire regime and investigating reports of ceasefire violations, emplacements of roadblocks and checkpoints for purposes other than traffic and crime control. Besides mandated verification tasks the KVM, as during the previous reporting period, was involved in overall activity to reduce tension, negotiating the release of hostages and engaging in confidence building measures such as the establishment of Field Offices. KVM police verifiers began monitoring the conduct of the local police in the course of their investigative duties. The KVM Headquarters Reconstruction Unit, in cooperation with the KVM Coordination Centre in Orahovac (Prizren Regional Centre), initiated a series of contacts between the Serb and Albanian local representatives in order to assist in restoration of vital communal services in villages in the area of Malisevo. Regional Centre Pec organized a series of local initiatives to reconnect the electricity supplies to local villages. By accompanying Serb technicians to Albanian villages enough confidence was achieved to enable vital repairs to be carried out.

KVM operational status: Personnel

KVM HQ: 250
KVM Induction Centre instructors: 39
KVM Induction Centre under training: 55
KVM Prizren: 204
KVM Mitrovica: 177
KVM Pec: 186
KVM Gnjilane: 144
KVM Pristina: 217
KVM Belgrade: 7
KVM Skopje: 6
KVM Tirana: 3
KVM Associated (temporary) members: 18
KVM International staff (all locations): 1 306
KVM Local staff (all locations): 1 263
Total: 2 569
US KDOM: 7; EUAG: 21

Vehicles: Armoured: 124; Soft skin: 247

II. Cooperation and compliance by the parties

This Section is designed to focus solely on the requirements set down by UNSCR 1199 and to assess, on the basis of information available to the KVM, whether the FRY authorities and the Kosovo Albanian leadership, including the KLA, have complied with its tenets during the reporting period. Both the present and previous reports from the OSCE CiO indicate that neither the FRY authorities nor the KLA have complied fully with the provisions of UNSCRs 1160 (adopted 31 March 1998) and 1199 (adopted 23 September 1998); nor have these parties fully complied with the additional tasks outlined in the OSCE/FRY (16 October 1998) and NATO/FRY (25 October 1998) Agreements.

Hostilities. UNSCR 1199 makes several demands (para. 1, 4 a and 6) with reference to cessation of military and security force activity:

"... demands that all parties, groups and individuals immediately cease hostilities and maintain a cease-fire in Kosovo ...;"

"... demands further that the FRY ... cease all action by the security forces affecting the civilian population and order the withdrawal of security units used for civilian repression ...;"

"... insists that the Kosovo Albanian leadership condemn all terrorist action, and emphasizes that all elements in the Kosovo Albanian community should pursue their goals by peaceful means only."

There has been a general failure by both the FRY authorities and the Kosovo Liberation Army (KLA) to abide by these strictures. The cycle of confrontation can be generally described, in no set order, as relatively small-scale KLA attacks on the MUP (Serbian police), generally on police vehicles, buildings and individuals; a disproportionate response by the FRY authorities, often in the form of large cordon and search operations by the MUP, supported by the VJ (Yugoslav Army) and occasionally including the use of heavy weapons including mortars, anti-aircraft cannon and tanks; resultant population movement; and renewed KLA activity elsewhere. The battle to dominate roads of strategic importance often provided the catalyst for conflict. It should be noted that during the period under review it is likely that a number of breaches in the ceasefire were the result of attacks by the KLA against Serb police vehicles and patrols.

Main incidents are as follows:

(a) Stimlje. 20-21 January. A major cordon and search operation by the MUP in Stimlje, following KLA ambushes that killed 4 policemen, declined in intensity January 20-21. KVM staff reported hearing "heavy mortars" firing. (On the 18th January, contrary to arrangements agreed between the OSCE Chairman-in-Office and the FRY Foreign Minister Jovanovic, armed police had again entered the village and fighting with the KLA resumed.)

(b) Mitrovica. 20 January. MUP opened fire on a house in which suspected KLA personnel were harboured. Despite KVM attempts to arrange a ceasefire the KLA opened fire with small arms, Rocket Propelled Grenades (RPG) and anti-aircraft cannon killing two men inside. Military uniform and KLA insignia were found on the bodies.

(c) Sipolje. MUP conducted a cordon and search operation on 20 January which resulted in the temporary displacement of some 5,000 residents (UNHCR estimate).

(d) Rakovina. 25 January. KVM attended the scene of a shooting incident in which 5 Albanian civilians were killed by gunfire, including a woman and 2 children whilst travelling on a tractor and trailer. KVM assessed that 300 rounds were fired at them from a prepared position.

(e) Luzane. 27 January. Tanks were observed firing in the area. A MUP liaison officer alleged that Luzane police station had been attacked by the KLA during the night of 26 January. No return fire was observed from KLA positions. Neither side attempted to withdraw.

(f) Rogovo. 29 January. Twenty-five Kosovo Albanians killed and 1 Serb policeman. A KLA sector commander in Pec later said that 18 of the 25 were members of the KLA.

(g) Djakovica. On 4 February the KLA ambushed 4 MUP personnel in their vehicle on the northern outskirts of the town.

The Kosovo Albanian leadership has failed to "condemn all terrorist action" and to provide that all elements in the Kosovo Albanian community "pursue their goals by peaceful means only" as required in the UNSCR 1199. The KLA has continued its attempts to consolidate its military strength in areas left by the FRY army and the Serb police forces. A number of reports of border incidents indicate that the infiltration of personnel and weapons across the Albanian border has continued. Urban violence has increased, characterized by grenade and bomb attacks on both Serb and Albanian property; some of these attacks may be ascribed to organized crime. Incidents of kidnap and abduction continue to increase tension in Kosovo and are a potent source of destabilization amongst the civil community; public protests about this issue have become increasingly common. The Pec District, where the number of recorded incidents of kidnap is high, is particularly affected. Adem Demaci, a political representative of the KLA, claimed on 25 January that the KLA held no Serbs, only Albanians who had been tried and convicted of misdemeanours.

(a) The KLA kidnapped 5 civilians at Nevoljane on 22 January and refused to release them until the FRY authorities released the

prisoners taken in the border ambush incident on 14 December 1998.
(b) Racak. 11 February. During the Racak funeral 8 Kosovo Albanians were abducted by the KLA.

Humanitarian issues. UNSCR 1199 makes two demands (para. 2 and 4 (c)) with reference to humanitarian assistance:

"... demands that the authorities of the FRY and the Kosovo Albanian leadership take immediate steps to improve the humanitarian situation ..."

"... demands further ... that the FRY ... facilitate, in agreement with the UNHCR and the ICRC, the safe return of refugees and displaced persons to their homes and allow free and unimpeded access for humanitarian organisations and supplies ..."

Military operations cannot easily be separated from their humanitarian effect: wherever there is fighting in inhabited areas groups of IDPs tend to be created. The kind of cordon and search operations carried out by the MUP (paras. 5.a and 5.c above are examples of this) inevitably cause suffering amongst the target populations as a secondary effect. Nevertheless, the overall level of cooperation by the parties with humanitarian organizations and NGOs has been generally good. Improvements have been noted by the ICRC on the part of the FRY authorities in providing information on detainees and access to them. KVM human rights verifiers have also noted improvements in some District Court procedures, notably in the towns of Prizren, Pec and Pristina. Prevention of humanitarian access has not been a significant problem but has occurred.

(a) On 4 February Serb civilians from Nevodimlje denied access to UNHCR aid vehicles taking aid to Jezerce, an Albanian village in the Urosevac area; the Serbs said that Albanian villagers had abducted two Serbs during the summer conflict and insisted on inspecting the contents of the vehicle before refusing access.

Access and freedom of movement. UNSCR 1199 makes one demand (para. 4 b) with reference to access and freedom of movement for those engaged in international monitoring:

"... demands further that the FRY ... enable effective and continuous international monitoring in Kosovo by the European Community Monitor Mission and diplomatic missions accredited to the FRY, including access and complete freedom of movement of such monitors to, from and within Kosovo unimpeded by government authorities, and expeditious issuance of appropriate travel documents to international personnel contributing to the monitoring ..."

There have been several occasions on which KVM verifiers have been denied access to areas; others in which threats have been used; and others where weapons were used in a threatening manner. Examples are:

(a) KVM were denied access to the village of Tanes Do on 25 January 1999 by the VJ.
(b) MUP officers threatened a KVM patrol in Nevoljane with sniper rifles and an anti-tank weapon on 27 January. The patrol had escorted Albanians to their homes to remove personal effects.
(c) A KVM patrol was denied access to 5 km border zone by VJ near Planeja. A number of incidents of this type have now occurred since the VJ's attempt to introduce a restricted border zone.
(d) The KLA denied a KVM patrol access to Ziljivoda on 2 February, asking for prior notice.
(e) Pristina airfield. 10 February. A KVM patrol was denied passage and then blocked by a VJ check-point. The VJ demanded that the interpreter leave the vehicle, then attempted to physically remove him.

Political solution. UNSCR 1199 makes two demands (para. 3 and 4 d) with reference to the imperative to search for a political solution to the conflict:

"... calls upon the authorities in the FRY and the Kosovo Albanian leadership to enter immediately into a meaningful dialogue without preconditions and with international involvement, and to a clear timetable, leading to ... a negotiated political solution to the issue of Kosovo ..."

"... demands further that the FRY ... make rapid progress to a clear timetable, in the dialogue referred to in paragraph 3 with the Kosovo Albanian community called for in UNSCR 1160, with the aim of agreeing confidence-building measures and finding a political solution to the problems of Kosovo ..."

The FRY authorities have repeatedly refused to negotiate with what they described as "terrorists"; the Albanian side has remained divided and adamant that the FRY authorities could not be trusted. There was no effort by either party to negotiate and this remained true until the parties accepted the summon of the Contact Group to assemble for negotiations at Rambouillet.

Cooperation with ICTY. UNSCR 1199 refers to the need for cooperation with ICTY (para. 13):

"... Calls upon the authorities of the FRY, the leaders of the Kosovo Albanian community and all others concerned to cooperate fully with the Prosecutor of The International Tribunal for the Former Yugoslavia in the investigation of possible violations within the jurisdiction of the Tribunal ...;"

There was no progress on the part of the FRY authorities in compliance with the requirements to cooperate fully with the Prosecutor of the International Tribunal for Former Yugoslavia. Despite repeated calls by the international community, the CiO and the head of the KVM, Ambassador Walker, the FRY authorities have refused to cooperate with ICTY and refused Prosecutor Louise Arbour permission to enter Kosovo to conduct investigations. There is no evidence that the authorities of the FRY have brought to justice those members of the security forces who have been involved in the mistreatment of civilians and the deliberate destruction of property.

28. ICRC assists Civilians caught up in Clashes, 11 March 1999

ICRC teams have been travelling daily to villages in the area of Kosovo bordering on the Former Yugoslav Republic of Macedonia to assist civilians caught up in the fighting which erupted there last week between Serbian security forces and the Kosovo Liberation Army.

Earlier this week, the ICRC was the only organization to reach civilians trapped in the village of Globocica, where it delivered food and other relief items to around 400 people. It also visited Kotlina, Lac and other villages in the same area following successful negotiations with both sides for access to the frightened civilians. Along with the relief supplies, the ICRC brought a medical team to perform on-the-spot surgery on the wounded and arranged for over 50 women, children and elderly persons to be evacuated. Robin Bovey, ICRC relief delegate based in Pristina, said: "The situation of these people is pitiful. They are completely surrounded by the fighting and extremely frightened. We have been coordinating our work with other agencies such as UNHCR, and the ICRC has been concentrating on the most exposed communities. It is impossible to know exactly how many people are caught up in the fighting and we will continue to visit the areas involved to find out exactly what the needs are and attempt to meet them."

29. Report of the EU Forensic Team on the Racak Incident, 17 March 1999

These comments are based on the medicolegal investigations by the EU Forensic Expert Team in Pristina as locally authorized by the District Court of Pristina in accordance with the Yugoslav Law on Criminal Procedure. It should be emphasized, that medicolegal investigations constitute only a part -- but do not cover the whole spectrum -- of criminal investigations. The comments represent the personal view of the author, Dr. Helena Ranta, and should not in any manner be construed as an authorized communication on behalf of the Department of Forensic Medicine, University of Helsinki or the EU Forensic Expert Team.

1. TERMS OF REFERENCE OF THE EU FORENSIC EXPERT TEAM
The EU Forensic Expert Team consisting of Finnish experts has been involved in the investigation of alleged atrocities in Kosovo since

October 1998. When the Racak tragedy was discovered on 16 January 1999, the OSCE turned to the European Union for assistance. Since an EU Forensic Team was already available, it was decided that the Team should also embark on the investigation of the Racak victims.It should be emphasized that the terms of reference of the EU Forensic Team cover solely the medicolegal autopsies of the 40 victims brought to the hospital. They do not concern the full scale of criminal investigations. Accordingly, to mention one important example -- there was no possibility to conduct scene investigations at the actual site of the presumed crime -- which could have rendered important additional information concerning the manner of death of the victims. The findings by the experts are therefore based almost entirely on information derived by investigating the bodies at the morgue. Furthermore, the investigation of the bodies at the hospital was greatly complicated by the fact that the start of autopsies by the EU experts became possible only approximately a week from the estimated time of death of the victims. More importantly, there was no chain of custody by the EU forensic experts of the bodies from the moment of death until the time the investigations started on 22 January 1999 in Pristina. What may or may not have happened to the bodies during that time is difficult to establish in connection with the autopsies with absolute certainty.It should be noted that the EU experts now have completed only a part of the overall investigations concerning the events in Racak -- namely the medicolegal investigation of the victims. For a more complete picture of what took place in Racak a full criminal investigation into the events would be required, combining scene investigations, interrogation of witnesses and analysis of the evidence with the autopsy findings of the EU experts.The original mission of the EU forensic experts was authorized to investigate in an impartial and independent manner, sites of alleged killings of civilians in Kosovo, i.a. in Glodjane, Golubovac, Gornje Obrinje, Klecka, Orahovac and Volujak. The investigations concerning Klecka and Volujak, initiated last year, are to be completed by the end of March 1999 when the DNA analysis will be available. Thereafter, the Team will as soon as possible resume preparations for the investigations with respect to Glodjane, Golubovac, Gornje Obrinje and Orahovac.The first crucial step that one would normally expect to be implemented at any alleged crime scene would be the isolation of the area and the exclusion of unauthorized access. The scene should then be photographed and videotaped, any evidence be collected and victims localized and marked at site. This step should also include sampling for a gunshot residue (GSR) analysis. Victims should then be placed in individual body bags for transport to the morgue. With respect to Racak none of this was done at all -- or was done only partially or improperly. Therefore, important information at the site may have been lost.

2. DETAILS OF THE RACAK INCIDENT

According to various sources of information, the incident in Racak most probably took place on or around 15 January 1999. The EU forensic experts only started working in Pristina on 22 January when the bodies had already been brought to the morgue. The Team therefore has no first hand information on the events at Racak. Concerning the site of the events and the circumstances surrounding the deaths of the victims the Team has to rely entirely on the information from the OSCE/KVM and EU/KDOM observers who visited the site on 16 January 1999, and from reports in the media. According to these sources altogether some 45 bodies were found in Racak. Yet, only 40 were taken to the Department of Forensic Medicine, University of Pristina to be investigated.Based on the information obtained from the KVM and KDOM observers the total of 22 men were found in a gully close to the village of Racak. They were most likely shot where found. Most of them have been turned over at some stage. The rest of the victims were found at or close to the village and had either been turned over or moved after death into houses in the village.The more time elapses, the more difficult it usually becomes to establish the assumed time of death. When the Finnish experts had the possibility to start investigations, more than a week had already passed since the discovery of the bodies at Racak. However, the temperature both at the mosque in Racak, where the bodies were first brought, and at the Pristina hospital morgue was close to OC, which has contributed to

their preservation. Most that can be said is that the victims appear to have died approximately at the same time.

Most of the victims wore several warm jackets and pullovers. No ammunition was found in the pockets. It is likely that no looting of the bodies has occurred, because money (bank notes) was found on them. The clothing bore no identifying badges or insignia of any military unit. No indication of removal of badges or insignia was evident. Based on autopsy findings (e.g. bullet holes, coagulated blood) and photographs of the scenes, it is highly unlikely that clothes could have been changed or removed. Shoes of some of the victims, however, had been taken off, possibly before the bodies were carried inside the mosque. Among those autopsied, there were several elderly men and only one woman. There were no indications of the people being other than unarmed civilians.

The Racak events have been described as a "massacre". However, such a conclusion does not fall within the competence of the EU Forensic Team or any other person having participated solely in the investigation of the bodies. The term "massacre" cannot be based on medicolegal facts only but is a legal description of the circumstances surrounding the death of persons as judged from a comprehensive analysis of all available information. Thus, the use of this term is better suited to be used by organs conducting criminal investigations for the purpose of initiating legal proceedings. Moreover, medicolegal investigations cannot give a conclusive answer to the question whether there was a battle or whether the victims died under some other circumstances. A full criminal investigation combined with the interrogation of witnesses by appropriate investigative entities could shed more light on the circumstances prior to and at the time of the death. It should be noted that especially persons not familiar with criminal investigations may have a natural tendency to interpret some observations made at the site of the tragedy as signs of post-mortem mutilation. These, however, are most likely related to animal activity -- such as stray dogs, which are in abundance in the area, and other wild animals -- or traces on the dead bodies caused by the high pressure of projectiles. No indication of tampering or fabrication of evidence was detected.Traditionally, a paraffin test has been used in gunshot residue analysis (GSR). To remove residues from the hand, casting with paraffin has been suggested. This test lacks specificity, however, and at the Interpol meeting in 1968 it was officially stated that it no longer should be used. The most successful technique to date for the analysis of GSR analysis is without doubt the Scanning Electron Microscope with an Energy Dispersive X-Ray Analyzer (SEM-EDX). Only this method has the ability of determining the metallic content without concern about environmental contamination. With the SEM-EDX, the sample is virtually unaffected by the analysis and can be re-examined, if necessary, many times. The sample for the GSR analysis is collected by means of a tape-lift taking into consideration routine precautions (contamination). Paraffin test was for the above reasons not used by the Finnish Team. Test samples for SEM-EDX were taken and they proved to be negative.

3. CO-OPERATION BETWEEN ORGANS AND TECHNICAL ARRANGEMENTS

At the professional level, the Team experienced no problems in collaboration with Yugoslavian or Belorussian pathologists. After a demonstration autopsy, all agreed upon common methods and procedures. Furthermore, local criminal and autopsy technicians contributed to the cooperative working atmosphere. The Team was able to complete its investigations without any outside pressure put upon it in Yugoslavia or elsewhere.In Finland, the presence of media in autopsy theatres is unacceptable. Prior to initiating the autopsies it was agreed that media coverage should be minimized. Nevertheless, the Head of the Pristina Institute of Forensic Medicine, Professor Dobricanin, allowed television teams and photographers to enter the premises. When asked, he confirmed that this was in accordance with his instructions.

Confusion has been caused by statements and premature conclusions drawn by local experts while the investigations were not completed. In Finland, on-going investigations are not commented upon. After the completion of the autopsies in January, the Serbian and Belorussian pathologists decided to draw up common reports summarizing their findings. The Finnish Team declined to sign these which was erroneously interpreted as disagreement on the findings between the local experts and the Finnish Team. The view of the Finnish Team is that no professional conclusions on the basis of the autopsies should be made without a comprehensive analysis of the data gathered from the corpses. The analysis and tests were conducted at the Helsinki University Department of Forensic Medicine only after the Team returned from Kosovo. Therefore, arriving at conclusions or signing of reports in January would have been premature and thus out of place.

Bearing in mind the complex nature of the investigations, it is the view of the Finnish experts that nothing could have been achieved by unnecessarily speeding up procedure. The involvement of the Team began after 16 autopsies had already been performed by local pathologists. With respect to these corpses, the EU experts were in the position only to verify that the work had been done properly.

There was no information available from the scene of the alleged crime at the time when autopsies were being performed, which further complicated a systematic approach. All histological, toxicological, and DNA analysis had to be performed afterwards in Helsinki. For safety reasons films had to be developed in Helsinki. All radiographs were digitized and incorporated into a data base. In all, more than 3000 photos were taken and 10 hrs of video film taped. There is a court order by the Investigative Judge authorizing the Team to conduct the medicolegal autopsies. According to Yugoslav law, the autopsy reports will therefore have to be handed over to the District Court of Pristina. A copy of the autopsy reports will also be conveyed to the Department of Forensic Medicine, University of Pristina. The European Union Presidency will be notified of the results of the investigations accordingly.It should be emphasized that the medicolegal investigations undertaken by the EU forensic experts constitute only part of the normal investigation of alleged crimes. Comprehensive picture over the sequence of events in Racak can only be achieved by combining the medicolegal findings of the EU Forensic Team with other possible information from different sources eventually available at a later stage.

S/1999/293, 17 March 1999

30. Report of the Secretary-General, 17 March 1999

… Violence

4. The humanitarian and human rights situation in Kosovo remains grave. The general insecurity, combined with continuing and unpredictable outbreaks of violence, has resulted in a cycle of displacement and return throughout Kosovo. During the reporting period, targeted killings of civilians, summary executions, mistreatment of detainees and new abduction cases were reported almost daily. Since 20 January, the Office of the United Nations High Commissioner for Human Rights (UNHCHR) has registered more than 65 cases of violent death, including one in custody. The Office's background investigations of targeted violence further confirmed the observations expressed in my previous report that the nature of violent activity in Kosovo, which has now spread to urban areas, has increased the number of persons who live in fear of being directly affected by violence or arbitrary treatment.

5. While clashes between the Serbian security forces and Kosovo Albanian paramilitary units continued at a relatively lower level, civilians in Kosovo are increasingly becoming the main target of violent acts. An increasingly common pattern of individual killings throughout the region accounts for the majority of deaths. Most violent incidents have remained unclaimed. This has contributed to the climate of fear and insecurity, causing deep distrust among communities and adding to the humanitarian and social problems in Kosovo.

6. The following narrative of when and where major incidents occurred suggests how violence against civilians in Kosovo continues to spread. On 18 January 1999, a Serb man was killed after reportedly failing to stop at a Kosovo Liberation Army's (KLA) roadblock in Nedakovac, near Kosovska Mitrovica. On 19 January, the body of a Kosovo Albanian teacher was discovered near Istok. On 20 January, two Serbian women (mother and daughter) were wounded after unidentified persons opened fire on their house, apparently targeting the father. On 21 January, a Kosovo Albanian man and woman were killed when their car was fired upon at an intersection outside Orahovac. The same day, the body of a Kosovo Albanian doctor was found near the Pec-Mitrovica highway.

7. On 24 January, five Kosovo Albanians, two men, one woman and two boys, aged 11 and 12, were killed on the Rakovina-Jablanica road, while repairing their tractor. According to international observers, some 60 spent cartridges were found on the scene of the incident and the bodies revealed multiple bullet wounds.

8. On 25 January, a Kosovo Albanian was killed and his son severely wounded near Decani when masked assailants fired a reported 55 rounds into their car. On 26 January, a Serb man was severely wounded in an attack directed at his house in the Istok municipality. The body of a 23-year-old Serb was found under a driveway in the outskirts of Kosovska Mitrovica on 27 January; the body may have been moved to that location after the victim was killed elsewhere.

9. On 29 January, Kosovo Albanian sources reported that the body of a Kosovo Albanian was found in Bistrazin village and that another Albanian, close to the Democratic League of Kosovo (LDK), was seriously wounded in front of his apartment by two shots fired by unknown persons. On 30 January, a 36-year-old Kosovo Albanian from Pec was found shot in the head on the Pec-Pristina road. That same day, the body of another reputed "Kosovo Albanian loyalist", a physics teacher from Djakovica, was found in the village of Gradis. In Istok municipality, an elderly Serb was killed and his 72-year-old wife was injured when unidentified persons threw a grenade into their house in the village of Rakos.

10. On 31 January, the body of a Kosovo Albanian from the village of Begov Vukovac was found, shot in the head, south of Istok. That same day, in Stimlje municipality, masked gunmen reportedly broke into a house in the village of Donje Godance and wounded one man and two boys.

11. Attacks and killings in urban areas continued during the first half of February. On 4 February, bodies of three Kosovo Albanians were found in a car between the villages of Istinic and Gornja Lika, in Decani municipality, and the body of a Serb was found near the village of Rastavica. All had been shot. On 4 February, a Serb male was killed by automatic weapon fire while travelling on the Pec-Djakovica highway.

12. On 7 February, bodies of two Kosovo Albanians reported missing since 3 January were found in Kacanik, south of Urosevac. During the night of 7-8 February, the body of an unidentified man aged about 30 was found in the village of Livadja in Lipljan municipality. At this writing, UNHCHR is attempting to clarify several reports of bodies found in or around Djakovica on 8 February. The bodies of two young persons, one a 17-year-old boy and one a 20-year-old woman, were reported found in two different locations in a Djakovica suburb. The body of a Kosovo Albanian male, dead from gunshot wounds, was found in his car in the Djakovica area, near the village of Trakanic. The same day, again in Djakovica, bodies of a male and an elderly woman were also found. Both victims, who are believed to be from the Roma community, died of gunshot wounds to the neck. Bodies of two Kosovo Albanians from the village of Goden near Djakovica were found on 10 February.

13. On 11 February, four more bodies were discovered in different areas of Kosovo. According to media reports, the body of the Kosovo Albanian owner of an Istok tea room was found on the Zac-Zablace road; he had been shot in the head. Two men, one a Kosovo Albanian shot in the head, the other, as-yet-unidentified, were found in separate locations in Novo Selo, near Pec. The body of an unidentified male was found in a pond in Klina.

14. Targeted violence against civilians in Kosovo is taking new, even more dangerous, forms. In particular, recently increased terrorist acts against Serb and Albanian establishments in urban areas, including grenade attacks on cafes and shops, are a cause of serious concern. Since the end of January, at least 10 such incidents in Pristina, Pec, Kosovska Mitrovica and Urosevac have been reported. The investigation by UNHCHR indicated that in many cases these establishments had been frequented by Serbs and Albanians and no incidents between them had previously been reported. The latest

attack, on 13 February in the main town square in Urosevac, was particularly horrible: 12 people were wounded and about 20 neighbouring shops and several cars parked nearby heavily damaged. On 17 February, another explosive device planted at the Urosevac market was discovered and deactivated by the Kosovo Verification Mission. The result of these attacks is the growing alienation of the Serb and Albanian communities, a pervasive feeling of insecurity and the shrinking of the remaining ground for coexistence.

15. Following these grenade attacks and a number of killings in Pristina and in the areas of Pec and Djakovica, UNHCHR field staff have expressed concern that, particularly in these three urban areas, civilians known for open-mindedness and flexibility in community relations, as well as professionals, intellectuals and moderate community activists, have been targeted. Increasing pressure on the urban elite in Pristina, Pec and Djakovica has also frequently been cited to UNHCHR staff as a source of tension and apprehension in Prizren.

Racak investigation

16. On 10 February 1999, the 40 remaining bodies of the Kosovo Albanian victims of the Racak massacre were handed over to their families. A funeral was held in Racak on 11 February. The release of the bodies had become a point of contention between the Government of the Federal Republic of Yugoslavia and the Kosovo Verification Mission. As of 1 February, the team of Finnish forensic experts had completed or monitored autopsies on 24 of the 40 bodies brought from the Racak mosque to Pristina. Sixteen bodies had been autopsied by Serbian forensic specialists before the arrival of the Finnish team. Five bodies of the total of 45 dead at Racak were reportedly removed from the village by families and were not autopsied. The Finnish team stressed, during its two-week stay in the Federal Republic of Yugoslavia, that it was not carrying out an investigation into the events at Racak, but an examination of the bodies moved from the place of death to the mosque in Racak and then to the Pristina morgue. After the events at Racak, the scene was not isolated; the circumstances of evidence-gathering and the chain of custody of evidence remain unclear. The Finnish team indicated that it would release the results of its examination in Racak to the European Union and to the Pristina district court in early March. There is no indication at this time of action by the authorities of the Federal Republic of Yugoslavia to bring the perpetrators of the Racak massacre to justice.

Abductions and taking of hostages

17. During this period, no new information emerged or was volunteered on the whereabouts and fate of persons abducted or reported missing. Eleven persons were abducted, 10 Serbs, among whom five were released and one escaped, and one Kosovo Albanian, who was found dead. On 21 January, five Serb civilians (three men and two women) were abducted in the village of Nevoljane, Vucitrn municipality, and released on 23 January through mediation by the Kosovo Verification Mission. The KLA spokesman in Pristina stated that the five were not kidnapped. Instead, he claimed that "stopping, disarming and the arrest of the five members of the Serb nationality ... were performed in accordance with the international conventions and norms, and for the reason of public security and order in that village".

18. During the night of 8-9 February, one Serb civilian went missing near Kosovska Mitrovica. The following night, two Serb civilians were abducted near Novo Selo on the Pristina-Vucitrn road. One managed to escape and reported that he was kidnapped by persons wearing KLA uniforms and insignia. On 10 February, the body of a Kosovo Albanian from Urosevac, who had been kidnapped the day before, was discovered. On 11 February, Serbian sources reported that two plainclothes police officers were abducted the night before, after having last been seen off-duty in Kosovo Polje, outside Pristina.

Detention and trials

19. Reports of arbitrary detention and systematic ill-treatment of Kosovo Albanians in police detention and under the jurisdiction of the Ministry of Justice continue to emerge from UNHCHR field interviews and during court testimony. According to information released by Serbian Public Prosecutor, Dragica Krsmanovic, 2,007 persons in Kosovo have been charged with criminal offences of terrorism, endangering the territorial integrity of the country and seditious activity. Of those, 1,060 are currently in detention and 824 are under

indictment. As earlier reported, the number of Kosovo Albanians detained, questioned, subjected to "informative talks" or arrested and subsequently released by police is not known.

20. On 16 January it was reported that Halit Aliaj, aged 48, who was arrested the day before, died while in police custody in the Djakovica police station. UNHCHR is making further inquiry into this case. Three other persons are known by UNHCHR to have died in 1998 while in police custody in Djakovica.

21. UNHCHR staff continue to monitor proceedings in which Kosovo Albanian defendants are accused of alleged terrorist or anti-state activity. The number of persons already sentenced in courts of first instance is relatively small. Most proceedings are still pending. Regardless of the size of the group of defendants or the number of witnesses to be called, most proceedings monitored by the Office have been discontinued after a hearing lasting only one working day or less, and subsequent hearings in the same case are frequently postponed for only a few days short of the maximum postponement allowed by law. As a result, defendants remain in detention indefinitely. On 8 February, proceedings against 24 "Orahovac group" defendants were once again postponed until 10 March. The group was arrested on or about 21 July 1998 and has been in detention, under systematic abuse, at Lipljan prison ever since. The hearing on 8 February was the first time any of the accused gave court testimony after more than six months' detention and after repeated postponements.

22. During this reporting period, sentences were handed over on 5 February in the "Urosevac group" case. Of the 28-member Urosevac group, 11 were arrested in June 1998; two of those defendants died while in police custody, allegedly as a result of torture. The nine remaining defendants were first brought before the Pristina district court in late December and mid-January. Seventeen defendants were tried in absentia. All nine standing trial claimed they had been tortured and still had visible traces of injuries allegedly inflicted by police and state security officials, including after their arraignment before an investigative judge. The defendants, including those tried in absentia, were sentenced to periods ranging from two and a half to 15 years.

23. On 10 February, the district court of Prizren sentenced eight men from Orahovac municipality to five years' imprisonment on charges of terrorism. The accused had all been charged with membership in the "so-called 'KLA'". Individual charges included providing medicine, food and fuel to KLA, possession of weapons, carrying out patrols and opening fire on patrols of the Ministry of the Interior. The decision of the court relied on confessions of the accused made before the investigating judge and photocopies of alleged lists of KLA membership. No originals of these documents were submitted by the prosecution as evidence. In earlier proceedings, defendants had maintained that their statements were made under coercion and torture, allegations not examined by the court. In explaining why the court did not consider these allegations, the presiding judge, on pronouncing his sentence, stated that the court would have considered these allegations seriously were it not for the fact that some of the accused had admitted they were KLA members. The court's final judgement did not indicate which acts had been proved to have been committed by each individual accused. The presiding judge did indicate in his explanation of his judgement that the strategy of defence attorneys had compelled him to issue heavy sentences.

Displacements

24. To keep count of the numbers of displaced is difficult, but the Office of the United Nations High Commissioner for Refugees (UNHCR), in consultation with non-governmental organization (NGO) partners, believes the number inside Kosovo stands at some 211,000, while there are an estimated 25,000 displaced in Montenegro. To assess the numbers of returns is even more difficult, given the long-term displacement of some, the short-term and sometimes repeated displacement, combined with return, of others. Therefore, UNHCR believes that it is more appropriate at this stage to address the humanitarian needs of the war-affected, including displaced, returnees, host families and those who never moved but lost their property and means of livelihood. The United Nations humanitarian agencies and NGOs are together providing relief assistance to some 420,000 persons in Kosovo and Montenegro.

25. A resumption of hostilities in Kosovo in January and February resulted in new displacement of population. Clashes between Kosovo Albanian paramilitary units and Serbian forces in the Podujevo area have prevented the return of some 15,000 displaced from about 17 villages. Serb and Albanian homes along the main Pristina-Podujevo road remain deserted, as intermittent fighting occurs some 3 kilometres to the west. This area has witnessed a pattern of displacement, return and fresh displacement. In Drenica, Suva Reka, Stimlje, Prizren and Vucitrn similar clashes also led to a new displacement of population. In some cases return took place, at least of some of the displaced, as soon as the violence passed; in other places, where the presence of Serbian security forces or Kosovo Albanian paramilitary units continued, fear prevented early return.

26. February was also marked by the continuing departure of the Serbian population from towns and villages where they had been in the minority, or where clashes between Kosovo Albanian paramilitary units and security forces occurred. According to information provided by the Serbian Commissioner for Refugees, some 90 villages in central and western Kosovo have lost their entire Serbian population in recent months, while towns like Podujevo and Kosovska Mitrovica have seen a reduction of the Serbian population. The estimated number of displaced Serbs within Kosovo is 10,000 while 30,000 more have moved to other parts of Serbia. In contrast, Kosovo Albanians who have lost or never had identity documents are afraid to move from their villages for fear of harassment by the security forces. UNHCR is seeking to prevent further displacement and to facilitate visits of persons without documentation to the appropriate police stations in order to secure identity documents.

Return movements

27. Throughout the reporting period, some returns have continued to take place, especially where the OSCE/Kosovo Verification Mission has established a continuing presence. In Slapuzane, south of Pristina, for example, 1,200 formerly displaced persons have returned. In Malisevo more than half of the former 3,000 residents are back in their village, while in Junik, more than 1,500 of the inhabitants are back in their homes. Following the burial, on 13 February, of 40 of those killed at Racak, the OSCE/Kosovo Verification Mission established a continuing presence there and some villagers have since returned. In Lodja, a village on the outskirts of Pec that was almost totally destroyed last summer, UNHCR and NGOs are assisting a group of about 16 families in repairing the largely undamaged school building. These families are now living in the school while undertaking the major task of rebuilding their homes.

Humanitarian assistance

28. Delivery of humanitarian assistance has continued almost uninterrupted throughout the month of February, despite the violence and severe weather. UNHCR has coordinated and led three multi-agency convoys six days per week, bringing systematic assistance to the displaced, the returned and to the war-affected population. Some relief assistance by NGOs working outside the escorted convoy system has been disrupted. There were reports of confiscation by the Serbian security forces of local trucks contracted by an NGO and of relief items belonging to another. Moreover, cases of harassment of relief NGOs were also reported. Some NGOs have been repeatedly visited by the regular and the financial police and questioned about their activities, others reported aggressive behaviour by KLA members.

Shelter survey

29. UNHCR and UNICEF worked with 14 NGOs from November 1998 to February 1999 to undertake a shelter survey covering 654 villages in 19 municipalities affected by the conflict in Kosovo, 440 villages were directly affected by the conflict, with damage ranging from slight to complete destruction. These villages had a total of 66,686 family houses before the conflict. Half of these houses have differing degrees of damage and 22,239 houses require major reconstruction. The resulting Shelter Report catalogues the extent of damage, village by village, for each of the 19 municipalities surveyed, and will prove an important document in the planning of priorities for repair and reconstruction.

30. UNICEF, in cooperation with five international NGOs, has conducted a school damage assessment survey in 13 municipalities.

The survey indicated that out of 900 schools, 163 have been destroyed or seriously damaged, while the remaining have minor damages or have been looted.

IV. OBSERVATIONS

31. UNHCR and its United Nations and NGOs partners will continue their efforts, in these risky conditions, to protect and assist the large number of refugees and displaced persons, and to support the population affected by the 12 months of conflict in Kosovo. There is strong apprehension, however, that violence against civilians and clashes between Serbian security forces and Kosovo Albanian paramilitary units will continue, with the resultant displacement of the civilian population. Cooperation between UNHCR and the Kosovo Verification Mission will remain crucial in monitoring developments and reacting rapidly in order to meet the needs of the displaced and their host communities. UNHCR and its partners have updated contingency and preparedness plans, but it is clear that any break in the continuity of humanitarian action would create further suffering.

32. I share the strong concerns of the UNHCHR about the spread of violence against civilians in Kosovo. Beyond the unacceptable actions of the Serbian security forces, the recent dangerous terrorist bombings are causing a growing number of victims. Terror tactics by Government forces, ethnically motivated violence, arbitrary treatment, targeted killings, abductions and bomb attacks must be halted by those responsible.

33. It is obvious that the humanitarian problems in Kosovo are a consequence of the armed conflict and the political crisis and they are difficult to separate from security issues. I am increasingly alarmed that continued confrontation in Kosovo, including persistent breaches of the ceasefire, has led to a substantial aggravation of the situation. According to OSCE, the current security environment in Kosovo is characterized by disproportionate use of force, including mortar and tank fire, by the Yugoslav authorities in response to persistent attacks and provocations by the Kosovo Albanian paramilitaries. As tensions mount in Kosovo, the number of Yugoslav troops deployed in the field exceeds the agreed level by a factor of five. Kosovo Albanian paramilitary units are consolidating their presence throughout Kosovo, including areas they did not control before. As a result, fighting now affects areas previously untouched by hostilities, leading to further deterioration of the situation and new displacements of civilian population.

34. Further fighting has rendered the October 1998 ceasefire agreement almost meaningless. I urge both parties to halt military activities in Kosovo, to comply fully with relevant Security Council resolutions and honour their commitments under the October 1998 agreements. In particular, the Yugoslav authorities should immediately reduce the number of troops deployed in the field to the level established in October 1998 and Kosovo Albanian paramilitary units should refrain from any provocative actions.

35. I strongly support efforts by the Contact Group to provide a political framework for a settlement of the crisis. I encourage the parties to seize this opportunity to achieve peace and autonomy for the people of Kosovo by negotiation, while respecting the national sovereignty and territorial integrity of the Federal Republic of Yugoslavia.

31. OSCE Chairman-in-Office Pulls out OSCE Personnel out of Kosovo, Oslo, 19 March 1999

The OSCE Chairman-in-Office, Norwegian Foreign Minister Knut Vollebaek, today made the decision to withdraw the OSCE mission (the Kosovo Verification Mission) from Kosovo immediately. The decision has been made in the light of the unsuccessful negotiations in Paris and following extensive consultations with the foreign ministers of the Contact Group and the other members of the OSCE troika: Austria and Poland. The OSCE Chairman-in-Office says that the situation for the unarmed OSCE verifiers has gradually deteriorated. Conditions have made it increasingly difficult for the Mission to carry out its tasks, and it is at present not justifiable to keep the personnel in Kosovo. Vollebaek emphasizes the responsibility of the Yugoslav authorities for the safety of the OSCE personnel and calls on the parties to show restraint and refrain from any action that can put the personnel at risk. "The OSCE Mission has made an important contribution to stability in Kosovo under very difficult conditions. But as OSCE Chairman-in-Office, responsible for the safety of approximately 1400 verifiers from many different countries in Kosovo, I have no other choice in the present situation than to withdraw the OSCE personnel", says Foreign Minister Vollebaek. The Norwegian Foreign Minister deplored the negative outcome of the Paris negotiations. "The Yugoslav authorities have taken on a heavy responsibility in refusing to sign the peace agreement, says Vollebaek. "This may lead to a further escalation of the conflict, with much human suffering as a result."

S/1999/315, 23 March 1999

32.   Letter from the UN Secretary-General addressed to the President of the Security Council, 23 March 1999

Annex
Letter from the OSCE Chairman-in-Office to the Secretary-General, 20 March 1999

...

I. General situation
Security situation
The situation on the ground in Kosovo remained grave. Localised clashes between KLA and Serb security forces continued. Unprovoked attacks by the KLA against the police continued and the number of casualties sustained by the security forces has increased. A new area of military tension emerged in the south of the Province at the border with the former Yugoslav Republic of Macedonia. Military operations affecting the civilian population intensified in mid-March. The overall number of Yugoslav army (VJ) units deployed outside their Kosovo barracks was greater than previously agreed in the Naumann/Clark Agreement of 25 October 1998. Indiscriminate urban terrorist attacks targeting civilians continued. The number of security incidents involving OSCE personnel increased significantly. There has been a steady erosion of KVM's ability to fulfil its tasks. Intensive movement of VJ convoys, including tanks and armoured personnel carriers, has been observed within the Province since mid-February. The VJ strengthened their positions in border areas and upgraded their defensive capabilities both in terms of weapon types and number of troops and equipment deployed. Increased KLA activity was noted in certain areas of Kosovo.

Due to the deteriorating security situation the OSCE Chairman-in-Office, Foreign Minister Knut Vollebæk of Norway, on 19 March decided to temporarily withdraw the Mission from Kosovo to the former Yugoslav Republic of Macedonia. On 20 February exchanges of fire between the security forces and the KLA were observed in the area of Rastane and Studencane villages, west of Suva Reka. Large numbers of KLA were seen in Studencane. A VJ liaison officer informed the KVM that the engagements in Studencane were the result of a KLA attack on a routine police patrol. The OSCE patrols confirmed that the KLA were at a high state of alert on that day and that the local KLA commander referred to orders to engage the police if they passed in that area.

Fighting was reported west of Vucitrn on 22 February in the vicinity of Doljak, Jezero and Taradza. Approximately 200 VJ soldiers, supported by two tanks, and reinforced by the police, attacked KLA positions near these villages but later withdrew to barracks in Mitrovica which continued until the beginning of March and caused a displacement of the civilian population from the nearby villages. The situation in the area remains highly charged and volatile. Reports of fighting in the Kacanik area were received on 28 February when the security forces were attacked by the KLA near Gajre. One police officer, the commander of the Kacanik police station, was killed and four policemen wounded. An estimated 2,000 people fled half a dozen villages in the Kacanik area. Many of them tried to cross the Yugoslav-Macedonian border. On 10 March the Commander of the Police in Kosovo informed the OSCE that the security force operation in the area had been completed. OSCE verifiers were shown a stockpile of weapons, ammunition and military uniforms, apparently seized in

Kotlina and Ivaja. On 11 March OSCE teams gained access to those areas and found Straza village deserted, with 12 of the 50 houses burned and others damaged. More than 50% of the houses in Ivaja were also burned. On 11 March VJ and MUP conducted a joint operation against the KLA, using tanks and support weapons, in the area south-west of Prizren. Heavy bombardment of Jeskovo and burning houses were observed. The following day the OSCE teams were shown the bodies of seven armed men in KLA uniforms, apparently killed at Jeskovo during the security force operation. The OSCE were not able to confirm that these men had died where they were found. In a separate incident. One policeman was seriously wounded when a MUP observation point at Ljumbarda, south of Pec, was engaged by KLA small arms fire.

On the afternoon of 13 March three separate explosions occurred, two in Podujevo and one in Mitrovica. The timing and the location of the incidents (a market and a nearby post office in Podujevo, and a market in Mitrovica) indicated the deliberate targeting of the civilian population. Six people were killed immediately, one died later and more than fifty were wounded, many of them severely. Towards the end of the period under review intensive exchanges of fire and significant security force activity continued in the areas south west of Vucitrn and south of Mitrovica. OSCE verifiers observed heavy shelling and houses burning in Drvare, Salce and Mijalic. Security forces operations that included the use of mortars were carried out in the area of Dubrave west of Kacanik, as well as in Svrhe and Dus, south of Klina.

Non-attributable murders continued and most victims of these were Albanian. The recent abduction of al Albanian civilian employed by the Prizren police revealed that a centrally controlled KLS "security force" carried out the act. Eyewitness accounts described a 10-man uniformed unit wearing KLA insignia seizing the victim. The KLA have admitted to holding the man. This year, in the west of the Province in the area from Pec to Prizren, several eyewitnesses have given similar descriptions of a KLA unit seizing Albanians loyal to the Serbs. Previous claims the at the perpetrators of these murders were rogue KLA elements are now less plausible than the conclusion that some "punishment shootings" are being initiated at the highest levels of KLA Command.

The number of security incidents involving OSCE personnel increased during the reporting period. The most serious case took place on 21 February when uniformed and armed policemen physically assaulted two OSCE verifiers. In the period 25 to 26 February a number of KVM vehicles were detained by FRY Customs officials on the border crossing between the FRY and the former Yugoslav Republic of Macedonia. At one point there were 21 mission members and 8 OSCE vehicles detained at the border. The situation escalated to a point at which the KVM HQ had to temporarily stop all OSCE movement across the border. The OSCE Chairman-in-Office and the KVM strongly protested those actions as a contravention of the Vienna Convention, and a violation of the Mission's freedom of movement. The VJ has since late February carried out preparations that would enable it to destroy infrastructure and block roads in and out of Kosovo. During the last week of the reporting period, leading NATO Military Officials expressed serious concern over the security of the unarmed OSCE Verifiers.
Political situation
Uncertainty regarding the FRY/Serbian authorities' and the Kosovo Albanians' positions on the plan for an Interim Agreement presented to the delegates in Rambouillet remained a significant characteristic of the overall political situation in Kosovo. At the same time developments on the ground and continued fighting demonstrated a lack of political will for reconciliation. Adem Demaci resigned as a political spokesman for the KLA on 2 March, in what appeared to be an indication of a shift within the KLA towards acceptance of the Interim Agreement advocated at Rambouillet. On 3 March the eight Kosovo Albanian political parties, including the Democratic League of Kosovo (LDK) of Ibrahim Rugova, represented in a shadow "Parliament of the Republic of Kosova", called on Kosovo Albanians to support the Rambouillet Interim Agreement.

On 5 March Ibrahim Rugova told a press conference in Pristina that, despite difficulties on the ground, wide-ranging efforts to build support for the Rambouillet accord across the whole spectrum of the Kosovo Albanian community were continuing. He expressed his belief that the terms of the Interim Agreement had been receiving overwhelming support by the people in Kosovo. On 6 March Serbian President Milan Milutinovic and Deputy Prime Minister Ratko Markovic sent letters to the Foreign ministers of the Contact Group countries saying that the proposed text of the Interim Agreement had been neither discussed nor accepted at the Rambouillet talks. On 8 March Yugoslav President Slobodan Milosevic received German Foreign Minister Joschka Fischer and the EU Commissioner for Foreign Affairs Hans Van den Broek. Following the meeting the President's office issued a statement ruling out the deployment of any foreign troops as an implementation force. President Milosevic stated the same position during a meeting with Russian Foreign Minister Igor Ivanov on 12 March. On 13 March the Kosovo Albanian delegation left Pristina for the Paris talks. The OSCE facilitated the movement of the delegates from the KLA and the FRY authorities co-operated with the arrangements.

Humanitarian Situation

According to the UNHCR and other humanitarian organisations, some 30,000 persons have fled their homes since the end of the Rambouillet negotiations on 23 February. Military operations in the Prizren, Vucitrn and southern border areas had caused the displacement of as many as 18,000 people. About 12,000 of these were able to return after a short absence. UNHCR reported that returns continued in places where there was no violence, and especially where OSCE had established a continuous presence. At least 230,000 persons are now displaced within Kosovo as a result of the conflict. A further 170,000 have fled the province in the past year, and several hundred thousand who have not been displaced nevertheless remain affected by the conflict. The departure of Serbs and other minorities from Kosovo continued. Serbs have abandoned some 90 villages in west and central Kosovo since October 1998. The fighting in Podujevo and Mitrovica areas have left many Serbian homes empty, barred and shuttered.

Human rights issued

The increased fighting and police and VJ activity during the reporting period was accompanied by tightened restrictions on freedom of movement and the right to liberty. Ethnic Albanian men continue to be detained by the police, who inform KVM that they are checking for identification documents. With regard to IDPs, a pattern has emerged in which police have tended to separate the men from women and children. The men are then taken to the police station for questioning. Many of those men that were subsequently released had reported that the police beat them. Complaints have also been received that the VJ is pillaging and stealing goods from homes in villages after they have seized control. The non-attributable murder of civilians continues. Because the police were not robustly investigating such killings it remained difficult to determine whether the deaths were the result of criminal activity or whether they constituted human rights violations. The number of incidents of abduction remained alarmingly high.

During the reporting period, the OSCE Human Rights Division continued to monitor trials of ethnic Albanians charged with "terrorism" related offences. Concern has been voiced by the KVM that many convictions are based either on confessions which the defendants later retract and content were obtained through the use of force and ill treatment, or on the basis of a paraffin glove test. Rarely are the defendant's attorneys permitted to call witnesses or to cross-examine the prosecution's experts. It has also been confirmed that the KLA has detention facilities and is detaining Albanians who are alleged to be 'collaborators as well as criminals'. The KLA vehemently denies that it is detaining any Serbs.

Kosovo conflict spillover potential

The OSCE Presence in Albania, the OSCE Spillover Mission to Skopje and the OSCE Missions to Bosnia and Herzegovina and to Croatia continue to follow closely the Kosovo conflict spillover potential. During the reporting period, the situation on the border between Albania and Kosovo (FRY) remained relatively calm in spite of increased Yugoslav military activities inside Kosovo and intermittent border incidents. Yugoslav forces remained on high alert and patrolled the border regularly. Albanian military personnel reinforced the border with Kosovo and conducted training exercises in the region. Observation of movement along the border continued to be hampered by inclement weather and heavy snowfalls. Illegal movement across the border between Albania and Kosovo (FRY) was negligible during the reporting period, as it appeared that the border area adjacent to the former Yugoslav Republic of Macedonia was used more often. The Kosovo Liberation Army (KLA) maintained a low profile during this period with only one attempted crossing reported. It has been noticed that the passage of information between police on either side of the Albanian-Macedonian border relating to illegal crossings has been poor. Meanwhile, smuggling has continue across the border in both directions between Albania and Montenegro via the Shkodra Lake.

OSCE Field Offices in Kukes/Krume and Peshkopi reported on a number of disturbing cross-border incidents, some involving the use of weapons. On 4 March, an exchange of gunfire between Yugoslav soldiers and Albanian civilians in the border village of Letaj occurred. After the incident, a meeting of the Joint Border Commission was convened between the Yugoslav Border Commander and the regional Albanian Commander, the first for many months.

Kosovo has been the dominant preoccupation of politicians and the media since the Rambouillet talks were suspended on 23 February. The Albanian Government welcomed the achievements of the international negotiators in what it described as "the first phase of a process", and committed itself to co-operating closely in the full implementation of the plan "through the implementing instruments of NATO and OSCE". The Government clearly played a helpful role behind the scenes in trying to persuade the Kosovo negotiators, and the KLA in particular, of the advantages of agreement at the resumed talks. Foreign Minister Milo went to Paris for talks with the Kosovo team in the final days of the talks in Rambouillet, and Hashim Thaci, together with Rexhep Qosja, came to Tirana for talks with President Meidani on 1 and 2 March. The Democratic Party, for its part, criticised the Government for its alleged failure to come out sufficiently firmly in favour of a referendum on independence for Kosovo. On 4 March the Albanian Parliament unanimously adopted a new declaration on Kosovo, encouraging the Kosovo Albanians to sign the Agreement "as soon as possible" and calling on NATO to ensure implementation. In the former Yugoslav Republic of Macedonia, the situation on the northern border with Yugoslavia has been unstable and characterised since the beginning of March by continued fighting in the Kosovo salient south of Kacanik.

The reporting period was dominated by the marked increase in the numbers of those from Kosovo seeking refuge. The Office of the United Nations High Commissioner for Refugees (UNHCR) and the Red Cross have registered 4,000 people seeking the status of humanitarian assisted persons since the beginning of March. Unofficial government estimates put the total number of Kosovars staying on an extended basis at over 6,000, a figure which broadly coincides with estimates by the OSCE Spillover Monitor Mission to Skopje. On 10 March the Red Cross total of arrivals over the last 12 months was 7,081. The UNCHR figure on 11 March was 7,271.

Reception arrangements worked efficiently and new arrivals were absorbed by host families in the ethnic Albanian community. The OSCE Missions observation of registration by the police in the remotest northern border areas indicated that there is a positive and constructive relationship between the police and the ethnic Albanian population in some of the most vulnerable and exposed communities regarding the new arrivals. The Government published its outline plan for the reception of up to 20,000 refugees and identified four principal points of expected entry: Vesala north west of Tetovo in the Sar mountains; near Jazinic; Gorno Blace; and on the northern border near Kodra Fura.

Relations between the former Yugoslav Republic of Macedonia and FRY have deteriorated in the last weeks following military threats made by Serbian Vice President Vojislav Seselj. The Macedonian Government sent a note of protest to the Yugoslav Embassy which was answered by another note of protest from the Yugoslav Embassy regarding a recent statement made by Dosta Dimovska, vice premier of the Macedonian Government during a visit to Bulgaria.

II. OSCE activities

Activities of the Chairman in Office and the Permanent Council

The OSCE Chairman-in-Office (CiO), Foreign Minister Knut Vollebæk of Norway met the Yugoslav President Slobodan Milosevic on 1 March in Belgrade, as well as with Foreign Minister Jovanovic, Deputy Prime Minister Sainovic and Serbian and Serbian President Milutinovic. The OSCE CiO urged President Milosevic and the Yugoslav leadership to sign the draft Interim Agreement, and emphasised that the OSCE would not be able to implement a political settlement for Kosovo without a robust international military presence on the ground in Kosovo.

On 2 March the OSCE CiO met in Pristina with members of the Kosovo Albanian delegation who had participated in the Rambouillet talks, and expressed his optimism that the Kosovo Albanians would sign the draft Interim Agreement. He also met with representatives of the Serbian population in Kosovo, Momcilo Traikovic and Father Sava, who expressed concern that they had not been properly informed of the content of the draft Interim Agreement, and were worried of the implications it would have for them. In order to improve this situation, the CiO sent a member of the CiO team at Rambouillet to Pristina to brief the Serbian representatives.

The EU Special Envoy to Kosovo, Wolfgang Petritsch, addressed the OSCE Permanent Council in Vienna on 4 March in order to update the Council on developments in Rambouillet and to report on progress in achieving a settlement. He stated that he felt that the KVM's objective and unbiased role in Kosovo had been an important asset during the negotiations. He emphasised that a strong implementation force was considered a *sine qua non* of a durable settlement.

The Head of the KVM, Ambassador William Walker, addressed an informal meeting of the Permanent Council on 10 March and updated a full meeting of the Permanent Council on 11 March. He then briefed the Euro-Atlantic Partnership Council at NATO Headquarters in Brussels on 12 March. The Chairmanship initiated a planning process to elaborate a comprehensive plan for meeting possible new tasks for the OSCE in Kosovo, in the event that the Interim Agreement should be signed by the Parties. The OSCE in Secretariat gathered a team of experts in Vienna, including members of the OSCE KVM and other OSCE Missions, to further this process. Key job descriptions have been circulated to OSCE Delegations in order to reduce the lead-time for recruitment of experts. A comprehensive planning document will be circulated as soon as preliminary planning is complete.

Due to the deteriorating security situation, the CiO on 19 March decided to temporarily withdraw the Mission to the former Yugoslav Republic of Macedonia, after having consulted with the OSCE troika as well as with other OSCE Countries.

Liaison KVM operational status

A new KVM office was opened in Podgorica, Montenegro, to assist with logistic support to the Mission. The number of municipality-based Co-ordination Centres was increased to 26. The number of village-based Field Offices was 14. By noon on 20 March all international members of the OSCE Kosovo Verification Mission had departed from the Federal Republic of Yugoslavia. At the time of the temporary withdrawal the KVM consisted of 1381 international members and 1693 local employees, a total of 3074. The Mission will remain in the former Yugoslav Republic of Macedonia for the time being, in order to enable a quick return to Kosovo. Personnel in Belgrade and Podgorica were withdrawn to Zagreb. Visas were cancelled and ID cards withdrawn at the border. Consequently, the Mission members will have to obtain new visas when the Mission returns to Kosovo.

III. Cooperation and compliance by the parties

18 February - 18 March 1999

Hostilities UNSCR 1199 makes several demands (operative paragraphs 1, 4a and 6) with reference to cessation of military and security force activity:

"...demands that all parties, groups and individuals immediately cease hostilities and maintain a cease-fire in Kosovo...;"

"...demands further the FRY ...cease all action by the security forces affecting the civilian population and order the withdrawal of security units used for civilian repression...;

"...insists that the Kosovo Albanian leadership condemn all terrorist action, and emphasises that all elements in the Kosovo Albanian community should pursue their goals by peaceful means only."

Main incidents are as follows:

On 25 February the VJ started a military firing exercise in the area of Bukos south of Mitrovica which continued until the beginning of March and caused an active displacement of civilian population from the nearby villages. The situation in the area remained highly charged and volatile with sporadic fire exchanges between the KLA and the VJ continuing throughout the reporting period.

On 26 February an OSCE patrol was fired upon by the KLA in the village of Stitarica north of Podujevo. No casualties resulted. The patrol was in the vicinity of VJ forces. The KLA apologised for the "mistake", indicating they were firing at the VJ and were unaware of the KVM presence.

On 27 February a police patrol was ambushed west of Pristina airfield with one police offer killed and one wounded, apparently by KLA sniper fire.

A new area of military engagement emerged at the end of February as KLA from other regions moved to villages south-west of Kacanik near the southern border with the former Yugoslav Republic of Macedonia. That was followed by an increased concentration of VJ and police forces. Reports of fighting in that area were received on 28 February when the security forces were attacked by the KLA near Gajre south west of Kacanik. One police office, the Commander of the Kacanik police station, was killed and four policemen wounded. An estimated 2,000 people fled villages in the Kacanik area some trying to cross a border to the former Yugoslav Republic of Macedonia.

Three police officers were wounded and one of them later died in Pristina hospital after a static police patrol was attacked at a bridge in the centre of Podujevo on 3 March.

On 4 March the KLA informed OSCE verifiers they would attack any police convoy attempting to pass through the area of Srbica and Glogovac. KLA reinforcements were observed in that area.

On 5 March approximately 15 to 20 KLA members ambushed a police patrol in an area south-west of Pristina airport. According to police sources 11 policemen were wounded, six of them seriously, and two police vehicles were destroyed by rocket-propelled grenades.

On 5 March there was an explosion at a Serbian restaurant in Pec. Six people were injured, one seriously. Later on the same day seven people - all Albanians - were wounded after an Albanian café in Pristina was sprayed with automatic weapon gunfire by unknown attackers. One of the wounded subsequently died at the scene.

On 7 March two policemen were killed and a third was wounded in an Albanian suburb of Pristina while attempting to serve an arrest warrant for three suspected criminals. The incident prompted a heavy-handed response by the police during a house to hours search operation that reportedly resulted in about fifteen Albanians requiring medical assistance.

On 8 March a police vehicle hit an anti-tank mine near the village of Smonica west of Djakovica, two policemen were killed and six wounded.

On 15 March OSCE patrols reported an active VJ movement north-east of Podujevo with large convoys heading south from the vicinity of the border with Serbia proper.

On 10 March an exchange of fire and shelling by VJ of villages in the area west of Vucitrn were reported and OSCE confirmed that a dozen of approximately forty houses in Salce were burned.

On 11 March VJ and police conducted a joint operation against the KLA using tanks and support weapons, in the area south-west of Prozren. In a separate incident one policeman was seriously wounded when a police observation point at Ljumbarda south of Pec was engaged by KLA small arms fire.

On 13 March the VJ informed KVM that they had intercepted a group of 10 to 20 KLA members crossing from Albania near Gorozup south west of Prizren, which withdrew after an exchange of fire. The OSCE team observed a scene of what appeared to be an intercepted attempt of an infiltration into Kosovo across the border from Albania. A large quantity of equipment including ammunition, grenades, sniper rifles, rocket-propelled grenades, military clothing and a dozen of rucksacks.

Fighting continued on 14 and 15 March at Luzane between Pristina and Podujevo. The OSCE Field Office was evacuated.

Humanitarian issues UNSCR 1199 makes two demands (operative paragraphs 2 and 4c) with reference to humanitarian assistance:

"...demands that the authorities of the FRY and the Kosovo Albanian leadership take immediate steps to improve the humanitarian situation..."

"...demands further ... that the FRY ... facilitate, in agreement with the UNHCR and the ICRC, the safe return of refugees and displaced persons to their homes and allow free and unimpeded access for humanitarian organisations and supplies ..."

Although the overall level of cooperation by the parties with humanitarian organisations and NGOs has been generally good, military operations and clashes cannot easily be separated from their humanitarian effect: wherever there has been fighting in inhabited areas groups of IDPs have been created.

Prevention of humanitarian access has not been a significant problem but has occurred. On 25 of February three French NGO members were arrested by police in Sofalija, but later released.

On 5 and 6 March the KLA blocked evacuation by the UNHCR of some 200 displaced persons that remained in the open in the Kacanik area. The KLA denied access to the IDPs. In a public statement by the UNHCR such actions were condemned as unacceptable.

Human rights issues UNSCR 1199 refers to the need to ensure that the rights of all inhabitants of Kosovo are respected (preamble paragraph 11):

"Deeply concerned also by reports of increasing violations of human rights and of international humanitarian law, and emphasising the need to ensure that the rights of all inhabitants of Kosovo are respected..."

In the absence of a functioning human rights protection mechanism in Kosovo, the KVM continues to receive individual complaints of alleged human rights abuses by the Serb authorities and by the KLA.

Serbian authorities informed the International Committee of the Red Cross (IRRC) that approximately 1,000 people are in detention following being either sentenced or accused of offences against the security and integrity of the State in connection with the conflict in Kosovo. ICRC reported that they have visited 682 persons who are in detention. ICRC is also following up the cases of 146 persons reportedly abducted by the KLA or otherwise unaccounted for in areas under KLA control. According to the ICRC "for some 50 percent of these people, witnesses claim that they were abducted by KLA members, while the other half are assumed to be in the hands of KLA, given that they went missing in territories under KLA control." ICRC is working on the cases of some 200 Albanians, who have been "allegedly arrested, but whose names are not on the notification list submitted by the Justice Ministry of Serbia".

Incidents of kidnap and abduction continued. On 20 February leader of Kosovo Democratic Initiative Selim Topoljani was abducted from his house in the village of Doganovic south of Urosevac by a group of armed KLA members.

Two Serbian residents of Bukos (west of Vucitrn) were abducted by the KLA on 22 February and one of them was beaten to death. The attempt by the police to investigate resulted in a clash the following day in which one local TV reporter and five police officers were wounded. The KVM secured the release of another Serb from the KLA on 27 February. KLA "zone commander" told KVM that the abductions were carried out by "uncontrolled elements".

Three Albanian men were reported missing on 23 February in Orahovac area. This was followed by reports on 27 February, that three Serbian men were abducted in the Prizren area.

On 27 February two Serb brothers were abducted near the village of Velika Hoca south of Orahovac. The KLA first admitted holding the men, but then distanced itself from the incident. One of the hostages was shot dead by kidnappers. On 1 March his body was handed over by the KLA to the KVM and the other one was released alive, but apparently having been severely beaten. The KVM condemned the abductions as an action detrimental to a political settlement.

On 3 March two Serb civilians were shot and killed by the KLA at a "checkpoint" in the village of Mijalic located between Pristina and

Vucitrn. The two Serbs were presumed to be relatives searching for a third family member, a VJ soldier, who had been earlier detained by the KLA.

On 9 March Prizren Regional Centre reported that an Albanian from Pirane was abducted by a group of masked men wearing black uniforms with KLA insignia. The police said the Albanian was a civilian working as a document clerk in the Prizren police station. The KLA confirmed their involvement and the OSCE started negotiating to secure his release.

Access and Freedom of Movement UNSCR 1199 makes one demand (operative paragraph 4b) with reference to access and freedom of movement for those engaged in international monitoring:

"...demands further that the FRY ... enable effective and continuous international monitoring in Kosovo by the European Community Monitor Mission and diplomatic missions accredited to the FRY, including access and complete freedom of movement of such monitors to, from and within Kosovo unimpeded by government authorities, and expeditious issuance of appropriate travel documents to international personnel contributing to the monitoring..."

OSCE/FRY Agreement (paragraph 6) provides: "The FRY government ... guarantees the safety and security of the Verification Mission ..."

On 20 February OSCE patrols were denied access by the VJ in Gniljane area, although the road remained open for local traffic.

On 20 February the VJ told OSCE to evacuate Field Offices in Zur and Dragas.

On 24 February the VJ soldiers and Serb villagers in Devet Jugovica north-east of Obilic threatened OSCE patrols.

On 25 February VJ denied access to OSCE in the area of Firza.

On 25 and 26 February a number of OSCE vehicles were detained by FRY Customs officials at the Djenera Jankovic border crossing between the FRY and the former Yugoslav Republic of Macedonia. At one point there were 21 mission members and eight OSCE vehicles stopped at the border. The situation escalated to a point at which KVM Headquarters had to temporarily stop all OSCE movement across the border.

On 28 February two OSCE verifiers were assaulted while off duty in Prizren by a group of civilians (mostly youngsters joined later by adults), who beat them to the ground before the verifiers managed to get away.

On 6 March an OSCE patrol while observing a VJ checkpoint near Prizren was ordered out of the area by the VJ.

On 6 March the VJ liaison officer refused entry to the OSCE verifiers to Bukos west of Vucitrn, despite previously reached agreement on such a visit.

On 8 and 9 March OSCE patrols were denied access by the security forces to the villages in the Kacanik area affected by the fighting.

On 11 March in the area of Pec the VJ were hostile towards OSCE verifiers by pointing their weapons at the OSCE patrol. In a separate incident the VJ east of Pristina stopped an OSCE patrol and verifiers were ordered to get out of the vehicle or to leave the local interpreter with the VJ. These orders were refused and the OSCE patrol turned back.

On 12 March Prizren Regional Centre teams were denied access to the VJ position at Dulje west of Stimlje which is one of the three authorised VJ Combat Team locations as agreed in the 25 October 1998 NATO/FRY Agreement. That was the second time that access had been recently denied, although previously the VJ co-operated with verification visits.

On 15 March an OSCE team was stopped by the VJ at the village of Donja Budriga in the Gniljane district was not permitted into a five-kilometre zone to the border.

On 16 March verifiers from RC Mitrovica were ordered out of the area of Mitrovica railway station by the VJ when attempting to observe the arrival of a convoy that included 7 T-72 (M 84) Main Battle Tanks.

Political Solution UNSCR 1199 makes two demands (operative paragraphs 3 and 4d) with reference to the imperative to search for a political solution to the conflict:

"...calls upon the authorities in the FRY and the Kosovo Albanian leadership to enter immediately into a meaningful dialogue without preconditions and with international involvement, and to a clear time-table, leading to ... a negotiated political situation to the issue of Kosovo ..."

"...demands further that the FRY ... make rapid progress to a clear time-table, in the dialogue referred to in paragraph 3 with the Kosovo Albanian community called for in UNSCR 1160, with the aim of agreeing confidence building measures and finding a political solution to the problems of Kosovo ..."

The latest round of the Rambouillet process in Paris was adjourned on 19 March due to the lack of progress. Talks will not resume unless the Serbian party expresses willingness to sing the draft Interim Agreement.

Cooperation with ICTY UNSCR 1199 refers to the need for full cooperation with ICTY (operative paragraph 13):

"Calls upon the authorities of the FRY, the leaders of the Kosovo Albanian community and all others concerned to co-operate fully with the Prosecutor of The International Tribunal for the Former Yugoslavia in the investigation of possible violations within the jurisdiction of the Tribunal..."

There was no progress on the part of the FRY authorities in compliance with the requirements to co-operate fully with the Prosecutor of the International Tribunal for Former Yugoslavia.

S/1999/338, 25 March 1999

33.   Letter from the Secretary-General addressed to the President of the Security Council, 25 March 1999.

... Annex
Letter from the Secretary-General of NATO the Secretary-General, 23 March 1999

... The situation has recently deteriorated significantly. The requirements of the United Nations for a ceasefire are being disregarded by both sides and President Milosevic is flouting last October's undertakings to NATO to reduce and redeploy his forces in Kosovo. Following the withdrawal of the Kosovo Verification Mission of the Organization for Security and Cooperation in Europe (OSCE) on 20 March, the Federal Republic of Yugoslavia has increased its military activities and is using excessive and wholly disproportionate force, thereby creating a further humanitarian catastrophe. I am writing to you separately about the next steps in dealing with this deepening crisis but in the meantime I attach for your information and distribution as you deem appropriate a detailed update of significant trends and incidents since my last report to you, of 22 January 1999. ...

Enclosure
NATO compliance report for Kosovo, 16 January-22 March 1999
Table 1, United Nations Security Council resolution 1199 (1998)

Resolution tenet	Related activity
1. Federal Republic of Yugoslavia and Albanian-Kosovar insurgents: cease hostilities and maintain ceasefire	16-23 Jan.: MUP/VJ continue security operations in Decane and Stimlje areas.

UCK fire on MUP investigative team in Racak.
24-30 Jan.: UCK attacks MUP element in vicinity of Bistrazin. One MUP policeman is wounded, two UCK are killed.
UCK attacks a MUP police station near Rogovo; one MUP officer is killed. MUP respond in a security operation that leaves 24 Kosovo-Albanians dead.
VJ respond with tank fire to UCK attempt to seize VJ bulldozer.
UCK kills two MUP policemen in Gornji Streoc.
31 Jan.-6 Feb.: VJ/MUP shelling in Podujevo against civilian targets.
7-14 Feb.:VJ/MUP forces fire on the village of Lapastica, near Podujevo.
UCK conducts harassing attacks against VJ positions near Dulje and Gornja Lapastica. No injuries reported.
15-22 Feb.:UCK opens fire on a MUP patrol in the vicinity of Lapusnik and attack a police station in Orahovac.
VJ forces in the vicinity of Luzane open fire on targets in the direction of the village of Godisnjak. Targets include a mosque.
VJ shell Studecane, causing thousands of civilians to leave the area for safety.
1 Mar.: Bukos for live-fire "exercises" engaged UCK forces with automatic weapons and tank fire. MUP and Serbian civilians are trapped in a house in Bukos as UCK forces fired on them. Five MUP are injured in the siege. VJ forces reinforced with MUP and supported by two tanks and an unspecified quantity of mortars launch an attack against UCK positions near Vucitrn.   Sporadic fighting continues in this area through 27 February.
UCK and MUP clash in Randubava leaves two Kosovar Albanian civilians dead.
UCK ambushes a MUP patrol in Krivovo leaving one MUP policeman dead and another seriously wounded.
UCK ambush near village of Gajare, outside Kacanik, leaves one Serbian policeman killed and four wounded.
2-8 Mar.: Combined VJ/MUP security operations continue in the Federal Republic of Yugoslavia-former Yugoslav Republic of Macedonia border area for the entire week. Force activity is most notable in the Kacanik area, where villages inhabited by civilians are shelled. Serb force activity causes a large number of civilians to leave their homes.
VJ live-fire "exercises" continue in the Bukos area.   UCK retaliate with mortar attacks against some VJ positions.
UCK attack a MUP convoy near Vrsevec (Vucitrn area). Eleven MUP are injured.
UCK attack a MUP convoy along the Pristina-Pec highway. |

Resolution tenet	Related activity	Resolution tenet	Related activity
	VJ forces fire on the village of Gjurica with at least 10 tanks. Combined VJ/MUP security operations targeted against known and suspected UCK strongholds begin in the Kovoska Mitrovica area. Combined VJ/MUP security operations begin in the Vucitrn and Malisevo-Orahovac areas. By the end of the week, these operations extend to the area south-west of Prizren. UCK attack a MUP patrol near Zur. 9-16 Mar.: Combined VJ/MUP sweep operations continue through the week near Vucitrn, Malisevo-Orahovac, Dus, the Cicavica Mountains and the Federal Republic of Yugoslavia-former Yugoslav Republic of Macedonia border. UCK attack MUP patrol in Zur; clashes follow. VJ employ artillery and tank fire against UCK positions near Streoce, Mijalic, Drvare and Osilane. UCK conduct attacks against Serb police stations and VJ convoys. 17-22 Mar.: VJ forces attacked UCK-held areas in the Shale and Llap UCK sub-zones, as well as UCK positions in the Podujevo areas. VJ units near the village of Glogovac fire on UCK fighters and their positions with artillery. Concurrent with the cessation of negotiations in Paris and the subsequent departure of OSCE/KVM from Kosovo, VJ and MUP intensify military operations in central and north-central Kosovo, supported by tanks and heavy artillery. In the course of this broadened operation, several Albanian villages are reported under heavy destructive fire and the inhabitants are fleeing.		villagers fleeing their homes. 15-22 Feb.: Thousands of civilians depart the Studecane area as a result of VJ/MUP shelling. Army reserve personnel are observed emplacing mines on a major bridge leading from the former Yugoslav Republic of Macedonia into Kosovo. KVM confirms the bridge is prepared for demolition. VJ emplaces obstacles along the south-west border between Kosovo and Albania. 23 Feb.- 1 Mar.: VJ inflicts heavy shelling and tank fire on Pustenik. KVM reports approximately 2,000 civilians from the Pustenik area attempt to cross border into the former Yugoslav Republic of Macedonia but are prevented by border guards. 2-14 Mar.: Aggressive Serb attacks on villages suspected of harbouring UCK forces or command centres. 17-22 Mar.: The ongoing Serb security force sweep operations continue to drive civilians from their homes. Serb Security Forces revert to the previous practice of destroying homes and villages in UCK areas by direct weapons fire, deliberate burning or demolition.
2. Federal Republic of Yugoslavia: Take steps to improve humanitarian situation.	There are few examples of overt evidence that the federal government of the Federal Republic of Yugoslavia is actively participating in actions to improve the humanitarian situation.	5. Federal Republic of Yugoslavia: Enable effective and continuous inte-national monitoring, by the European Community Moni-toring Mission and diplomatic missions including access and complete free-dom of movement.	1-20 Feb.: VJ deny KVM access to villages of Zjum, Planeza, Kiselja Banja, Ponosevac, Donje Ljupce and Sukovac. MUP and VJ forces deny KVM patrol access to the Pristina airfield.
3. Federal Republic of Yugoslavia and Albanian-Kosovars: Enter into dialogue, with international involvement, to end crisis.	On 19 March the Kosovar Albanians sign the Interim Peace Agreement. Federal Republic of Yugoslavia authorities refuse to do so.		
4. Federal Republic of Yugoslavia: Cease all action by security forces affecting the civilian population and order the withdrawal of security units used for civilian repression.	31 Jan.-6 Feb.: VJ forces harass inhabitants of the village of Djeneral Jankovic.		MUP stop a KVM convoy as it tries to enter Prizren. Four OSCE vehicles are stopped by border police and denied entry into Kosovo from the former Yugoslav Republic of Macedonia. KVM patrol is denied access by the VJ to the five kilometre border security zone north-west of Kusnin. KVM patrol is stopped and held at gunpoint by VJ at Donja Kusce. Four VJ soldiers enter a KVM field office in Zur and instruct the verifiers to leave the office by the end of the day. KVM verifiers remain in place. A Serb demonstration comprised of at least 150 Serb civilians occurs at the KVM field office in Laposavic. VJ forces prohibit two KVM vehicles from following a convoy. KVM verifiers prohibited from departing Prizren at gun point. When verifiers attempt to follow a VJ convoy through Prizren, they are forced from their vehicle at gun point and personally searched. Two KVM members are stopped by VJ forces south of Gniljane. The verifiers are forced out of their vehicles and ordered to surrender their maps. A VJ liaison officer arrives on the scene and the verifiers are released.
	7-14 Feb.: MUP harass civilians attending funeral services for 9 of the 24 killed in Rogovo. MUP forces harass the inhabitants of Gusica. MUP forces forcibly occupy civilian homes in the village of Foniq. VJ operation in the Lapusnik area results in 50		

Resolution tenet	Related activity
	23 Feb.-1Mar,: KVM patrol is prevented from patrolling around Firza by VJ. On 25 Feb. eight OSCE vehicles and 21 KVM employees are forcibly detained by customs officials of the Federal Republic of Yugoslavia at Djeneral Jankovic border crossing. Contingent allowed to proceed to Pristina late on 26 February after vehicles are forcibly searched. 2-8 Mar.: Federal Republic of Yugoslavia authorities continue to interfere with KVM attempts to cross the border at the Djeneral Jankovic crossing site on the former Yugoslav Republic of Macedonia border. Federal Republic of Yugoslavia interference also occurs at the border crossing south of Gnjilane. Federal Republic of Yugoslavia turns back KVM verifiers because they refused to submit to vehicle searches. Other KVM verifiers agree to searches in order to be allowed into or out of Kosovo. 9-16 Mar.: In addition to increased incidents of restricted freedom of movement, OSCE and NGO personnel are threatened and in some cases assaulted by official personnel of the Federal Republic of Yugoslavia and by civilian antagonists. The trend of harassment coincides with increased VJ and MUP security operations. 17-22 Mar.: [KVM withdraws on 20 March.]
6. Federal Republic of Yugoslavia: Facilitate with UNHCR and ICRC safe return of refugees and internally displaced persons to their homes. …	There is no overt example of Federal Republic of Yugoslavia cooperation with UNHCR to assist in the safe return of refugees and internally displaced persons. …

Table 2, Modalities for Kosovo Federal Republic of Yugoslavia security force reductions and operations agreed by the North Atlantic Treaty Organization and the Federal Republic of Yugoslavia on 25 October 1998

Modality	Actions by the Federal Republic of Yugoslavia
1. Special Police units deployed to Kosovo after February 1998 will be withdrawn from Kosovo. Combined police/special police strength in Kosovo will be reduced to their February 1998 duty level.	MUP force numbers in Kosovo are now assessed to be approximately 2,500 to 3,500 personnel above the agreed limit of 10,021.
2. Any additional (that is, brought in or transferred after February 1998) heavy weapons (12.7 mm and above) or equipment brought into Kosovo or transferred from the VJ to the police/special police will be withdrawn from Kosovo or returned to the VJ.	MUP possesses and continues to employ heavy weaponry in Kosovo.
3. Police/special police will resume their normal peacetime activities. Heavy weapons and equipment remaining under MUP control in Kosovo will be returned to cantonments and police stations.	Excessive traffic patrolling, fortification of observation posts and unauthorized checkpoints continue. MUP continue to conduct road security patrols in their areas of control and to operate unauthorized checkpoints with no regard to the prohibition to do so.
4. All VJ units and additional equipment brought into Kosovo after February 1998 will be withdrawn from Kosovo.	VJ forces in Kosovo have been reinforced and now number about 3,500-5,000 personnel above the authorized strength of approximately 11,300.
5. Except for those VJ currently augmenting border guards, all VJ elements remaining in Kosovo will return to garrison except for three company-sized teams which will remain deployed, each to protect the lines of communications.	Estimates now indicate that 5,000-5,500 Pristina 52nd Corps personnel are deployed out of garrison in Kosovo. These forces remain concentrated in the north near Podujevo, near Vucitrn and Orahovac in central Kosovo and near Kacanik in the southern border region. As of 16 March, VJ tanks from units in Serbia and Montenegro have been transported into Kosovo, via rail, possibly to reinforce battle groups in Kosovska Mitrovica and Podujevo.
6. VJ border guards will remain in position along the international border of the Federal Republic of Yugoslavia and conduct ongoing border security operations.	9-16 Mar. VJ forces augment border guard battalions. The amount of equipment and personnel deployed into the border area near Kacanik probably amounts to two company-sized elements. See entry 5 above.
7. The withdrawals and deployments … will be completed by 1200 hours, 27 October 1998, except for the three company-sized teams.	See entry 5 above.
8. In order to ensure verification	Reporting has been

Modality	Actions by the Federal Republic of Yugoslavia
of these provisions, VJ and MUP commanders will provide to the Kosovo Diplomatic Observer Mission/OSCE detailed weekly reports of manning, weapons, and activities of their forces, and will provide immediate notification to the Kosovo Diplomatic Observer Mission/OSCE of any deployment contrary to these provisions and will explain the circumstances regarding such deployments.	inaccurate and misleading. VJ and MUP units have failed to account for equipment and personnel numbers and activities. VJ officials fail to notify OSCE of intention to conduct military training in Kosovo. This information was only offered in explanation after VJ forces were observed conducting activities claimed to be live-fire exercises in the vicinity of occupied villages.
9. All checkpoints will be dismantled.	MUP continue to maintain and build unauthorized checkpoints throughout Kosovo.
10. In case of incidents of increased tension, the police will have the right, upon notifying the Kosovo Diplomatic Observer Mission/OSCE, to perform patrol duties in armoured vehicles.	See entry 8 above. Notification is usually not timely and does not seek permission or approval, but is relayed as a declaration of actions already committed.
11. The police will withdraw its stationary forces from: Dragobilje, Oztrozub, Opterusa, Dobrodeljane, Studencani, Samordraza, Decane and Klecka. Police forces may remain in Malisevo, Orahovac, Zociste, Restane, Suva Reka and Dulje. The police will use the road Orahovac-Suva Reka-Dulje-Malisevo. The police will not move along the Malisevo-Orahovac road beginning on 25 Oct. - this road must fully open for free traffic flow.	Continued reports of heavy MUP presence in and around Podujevo, Stimlje, Racak, Decane and Malisevo persist. Malisevo is an approved police location, but Albanians complain MUP presence there is menacing and that it has inhibited the return of some internally displaced persons.

Table 3, United Nations Security Council resolution 1203 (1998)

Resolution tenet	Related activity
1. Federal Republic of Yugoslavia: Cooperate fully with the OSCE Verification Mission and Air Verification Mission.	On 18 March, KVM observers sight an air defence radar at Prizren airfield normally associated with surface to air missiles. This represents a violation of the air verification agreement.
2. Federal Republic of Yugoslavia: Comply immediately with Security Council resolutions 1160 (1998) and 1199 (1998).	Currently, Federal Republic of Yugoslavia security forces are not fully in compliance with resolutions 1160 (1998) and 1199 (1998).
3. Federal Republic of Yugoslavia and Kosovar-Albanians: Enter immediately into meaningful dialogue without preconditions and with international involvement ... leading to an end to the crisis.	On 19 March, the Kosovar Albanian Delegation signs the Interim Peace Agreement. Federal Republic of Yugoslavia authorities refuse to do so.
4. Federal Republic of Yugoslavia and Kosovar-Albanians: Respect freedom of movement of OSCE Verification Mission and other international personnel.	Both KVM and UNHCR report increased movement control by both Federal Republic of Yugoslavia and UCK forces. The overwhelming majority are committed by VJ forces - in some instances at gunpoint.
5. Federal Republic of Yugoslavia: Ensure the safety and security of all diplomatic personnel to include OSCE Verification Mission, all international and NGO humanitarian personnel.	Against the background of Federal Republic of Yugoslavia refusal to negotiate an interim peace agreement, and an increasingly hostile environment on the ground in Kosovo, the OSCE withdraws its verification mission on 20 March.
6. Federal Republic of Yugoslavia and Kosovar-Albanians: Ensure personnel (see entry 5 above) are not subject to the threat or use of force or interference of any kind.	See entry 5 above.
7. Federal Republic of Yugoslavia and Kosovar-Albanians: Cooperate with international efforts to improve the humanitarian situation and avert pending humanitarian crisis.	Nothing to report.
8. Federal Republic of Yugoslavia: Create the conditions that allow internally displaced persons to return home.	The overall security environment for civilians remained unchanged. The ongoing Federal Republic of Yugoslavia security force sweep operations continue to drive civilians from their homes. Federal Republic of Yugoslavia security forces revert to their previous practice of destroying homes and villages in UCK areas by direct weapons fire, deliberate burning or demolition. Approximately 100,000 internally displaced persons have been generated since fighting between Serb security forces and

Resolution tenet	Related activity
	UCK began in late December 1998. Many of these individuals, however, have returned to find their homes destroyed and are most likely residing with neighbours, friends or relatives. Given the level of Serb security force operations over the last week, the rate of displacement has increased sharply. As many as 20,000 internally displaced persons may have been generated by VJ/MUP operations against the UCK between 15 and 19 March. Fighting on 20 March reportedly generated 4,000 internally displaced persons in the Podujevo region and another 5,000-10,000 in the Srbica-Glogovac region.
9. Federal Republic of Yugoslavia: Conduct prompt and complete investigations of all atrocities committed against civilians through the Hague-based United Nations International Tribunal on the Former Yugoslavia.	Nothing to report.

Chapter 14: The Hill Process

Throughout the crisis, attempts were made to persuade the FRY/Serbia and the Kosovo Albanians to reach a peaceful settlement. Early on, this might have been comparatively easy. Until the declarations of independence of Croatia and Slovenia in June 1991, a re-negotiated Yugoslav Federation would have been possible. Within such a looser Federation, the position of Kosovo could have been restored at the federal level. After all, even when responding to the unilateral change of her status by Serbia in 1990, Kosovo had not immediately declared independence. Instead, she had merely adopted a constitutional declaration, which sought to establish the territory as an equal constituent unit *within* the Federation of Yugoslavia.[1] But, of course, Serbia was in no mood to give up the gains she had made on two fronts. On the one hand, she now dominated the Federation as a whole, and had proven unwilling to give in to Slovenia's and Croatia's demands for more independence within a re-negotiated federal structure. As there was no scope for compromise, a war of secession followed, rapidly leading to the dissolution of the Socialist Federal Republic as a whole. On the other hand, Serbia was similarly determined to extend and consolidate, rather than reverse, the control now exercised by Belgrade over Kosovo. The 'return' of Kosovo to Serbia had become the centrepiece of political rhetoric which had brought Slobodan Milosevic to power as Serbia's President, and later as the President of the rump-Yugoslavia.

When the forcible dissolution of the Federation began in 1991, Kosovo really had no option other than a declaration of independence. Her separate legal status had been entrenched in the federal structure. With the Federation gone, she would have remained trapped exclusively within the Serb republic, having lost her status as an entity entitled to separate rights and partial international legal personality. Precisely this happened, of course, when the rump-Yugoslavia consisting only of Serbia and Montenegro gave itself a new federal constitution. That constitution merely mentioned Kosovo and Vojvodina as forms of 'territorial autonomy' within Serbia and accorded no legal status or rights to either entity.[2] Even the status of the ethnic Albanians as a 'nationality' had been removed. Now, they were a 'minority' in their own territory, despite the fact that 90 per cent of the population was ethnic Albanian. And they were subject to a system of governance which was openly aiming for the 'Serbianization' of their land. This was supposed to be achieved through an official settlement programme for Serbs, the preclusion of property transfers among ethnic Albanians and the suppression of Kosovo Albanian culture and language.[3] At the same time ethnic Albanians were being politically disenfranchised in Kosovo, their organs of governance having been taken over by Belgrade. They were systematically removed from all forms of public authority, including the police, judiciary, education and even the medical and social services, and instead subjected to a regime of arbitrary arrests, torture and disappearances.[4]

In the face of these pressures, Kosovo's declaration of independence of 1991, after the secession of Croatia and Slovenia, may have been a desperate act. It was, however, not a naïve decision by reckless politicians, leading an entire population into a romantic but dangerous adventure. The risks of such a step were well known and appreciated by the ethnic Albanians who overwhelmingly expressed themselves in favour of independence in a referendum. There was simply a lack of alternatives.

Once independence had been declared, Kosovo struggled to be noticed by the international community. A request for recognition addressed to the European Conference on Yugoslavia remained unanswered.[5] Similarly, the OSCE did not permit the expression of the views by the Kosovo leadership.[6] The initial Carrington Conference on Yugoslavia considered the question of Kosovo only as an afterthought, in a hastily added provision which did not even dare refer to the territory by name.[7] At the second major attempt to address the Yugoslav crisis as a whole, the London Conference of August 1992, Kosovo was not permitted to enter the conference chamber, and instead had to make do with separate sessions with important personalities like Lord Carrington in a *chambre séparé*.

Even when the international human rights machinery started to report on the nature and extent of abuses perpetrated by the Belgrade government in relation to the territory, interest remained muted. The Kosovo issue was permitted to languish into a silent death at the Geneva follow-on talks to the London Conference. The Special Group on Kosovo only concerned itself with the practical issue of education, and even that problem was not addressed with any vigour over a period of some four years. It was left to a small religious NGO to broker a fragmentary education agreement, which was however never

---

[1] Constitutional Declaration, 2 July 1990, Document 4. C.2.
[2] Constitution of the Federal Republic of Yugoslavia, April 1992, Document 4.B.17.
[3] See the materials reproduced in section 4.B.
[4] The developments are extensively chronicled in Chapter 6.
[5] Letter from Dr Rugova to Lord Carrington, 22 December 1991, Document 5.A.5.
[6] Kosovo sent repeated communications to the various CSCE organs requesting to be heard, but was refused.
[7] Carrington Drafts, 18 October 1991, Document 5.A.1.; 1 November 1991, Document 5.A.2.

implemented.[8] When Belgrade finally came under pressure from the Security Council in 1998, suddenly an agreement to implement the initial education agreement emerged, a further 18 months having expired.[9] However, the agreement on the agreement too remained unimplemented, armed conflict having taken hold by then.

Throughout this period, the Kosovo Albanian population had suffered more or less in silence. The moderate Rugova government had formed the view that confrontation with Serbia would be suicidal. Instead, much effort was expended on making the situation somehow tolerable, through the system of parallel schools and parallel health care and social security, funded from voluntary contributions (a 3 per cent tax) and contributions from the Kosovo Albanian diasphora. However, after eight years, this approach appeared to have been counter-productive. It seemed to have allowed the international community to register duly and then forget the United Nations official reports on widespread human rights abuses and intolerable conditions. Such resolutions were adopted every year, condemning Belgrade's actions and praising the moderate stance of the Kosovo leadership.

It is sad to note that change only occurred when more radical elements in Kosovo took the matter in hand. The KLA's armed campaign, which really started only in autumn of 1997, triggered even greater FRY/Serb repression. The more visible level of suffering of the Kosovo Albanians, especially their displacement in large numbers, raised international interest. More than that, the KLA now played the card which Rugova had been unwilling to use. It started to put in motion a chain of events which might lead ultimately to Western Europe's the nightmare scenario—a spreading of the conflict to Albania and Macedonia and possibly beyond. This finally led to United Nations Security Council involvement, including the invocation of Chapter VII collective security powers. One of the key demands of the Council was the achievement of a political settlement. However, no more decisive action was taken to follow up on this demand and the fighting dragged on throughout the summer, creating a massive displacement crisis.

The initial involvement by the Security Council was answered with a two-pronged strategy by the FRY/Serbia, supported by Russia.[10] On the one hand, a referendum was held, proclaiming the view of over 90 per cent of the participating Serb population that the matter was an internal one which could not be subject to international involvement.[11] On the other hand, an attempt was made to engage the Kosovo leadership under Dr Rugova, recently re-elected by an overwhelming majority, in direct talks. Under very heavy US pressure, Rugova agreed to meet with President Milosevic in Belgrade—an act seen as treachery by the KLA and others.[12] There was established a team of 15 advisers for these negotiations, and a smaller groups of negotiators. However, the talks came to nothing, and the Kosovo leadership withdrew from them when FRY/Serb offensive operations continued.

Almost a decade after the unilateral changes to Kosovo's status, the first real international attempt to achieve a settlement was then commenced. That attempt was directed by the Contact Group (France, Germany, Italy, United Kingdom, Russia, United States, USA) and spearheaded by US Ambassador to Macedonia Chris Hill, who had played a role in the Dayton accords.[13] While Kosovo had always hoped for such international involvement, its leadership responded with caution. Over the summer of 1998, the number of victims of armed FRY/Serb operations climbed from 100,000 to 300,000 displaced—a significant part of the entire population of Kosovo. Even those who had not been displaced were subjected to repression and hardly a family remained unaffected. This situation was not conducive to a position of compromise and instead led to a swelling of the ranks of the KLA and of the more radical political parties affiliated with it. The KLA and the parties supporting it now openly challenged the legitimacy of the Rugova government, arguing that it had never really existed.

At its Bonn meeting of 8 July 1998, the Contact Group agreed to recommend to its negotiating team basic elements for a resolution of the question of Kosovo's status, emphasizing that it supported neither the maintenance of the status quo, nor independence for Kosovo.[14] Under strong US pressure, the Rugova government nominated a small, but informal negotiating team mainly composed of members of the majority LDK party, which could receive and consider proposals for a settlement, without thereby prejudicing Kosovo's position.

While it seemed that the Contact Group mandate had finally envisaged talks on the issue which lay at the heart of the problem, the status of Kosovo, the initial efforts of the Hill mission, conducted through shuttle diplomacy, were soon directed in another way. After the Contact Group had presented to the parties various options for a settlment, it was clear that agreement on Kosovo's status would impossible. The FRY/Serbia was unwilling to move, and the Kosovo leadership, too, would not be able to abandon its position, in view of the dramatic developments of the summer. Instead, Ambassador Hill reported to the OSCE that an informal understanding had been reached about a three-year stabilization and

---

[8] St Egidio Education Agreement, 1 September 1996, Document 5.B.8.
[9] Agreed Measures, 23 March 1998, Document 5.B.8.
[10] Memorandum by the Russian Federation, 14 April 1998, Document 8.1. Annex.
[11] *See* Documents 14.A.3-5, April 1999.
[12] FRY Statement on Talks, 15 April 1999, Document 14.A.9.
[13] See EU Council General Affairs Meeting, 13 July 1998, Document 9.B.8.
[14] Statement issued by the Contact Group, 8 July 1998, Document 9.B.7.

normalization period to allow for the re-establishment of democratic institutions, and after this period new approaches could be envisaged. He stressed the crucial importance of an international presence in Kosovo during the implementation period and the important role which the OSCE would have to play in that area.[15]

Although it appeared that the succession of drafts for a settlement which were produced emanated from Ambassador Hill and another veteran of Dayton, the quite brilliant legal advisor Jim O'Brian, the Contact Group as a whole retained considerable influence over the contents of these documents. In addition, a draft produced by the Council of Europe Venice Commission for Democracy through Law proved influential—in fact so influential that the equally gifted and resourceful legal officer of the Venice Commission was later seconded to support the European Union envoy Wolfgang Petrisch at the Rambouillet talks.[16]

After some further explorations during late summer, the first formal and complete draft was presented to the parties on 1 October 1998.[17] It represented a genuine attempt at a balancing of interests. In particular, it avoided altogether the issue of the status of Kosovo and instead focussed on a pragmatic assignment of powers to different levels of administration. For the FRY/Serbia, this approach was painful, inasmuch as it avoided an explicit confirmation of the continuation of the territorial integrity and sovereignty of the FRY or even Serbia. Kosovo, too, was hesistant. While the draft did not directly prejudice its status, being silent on the issue, it nevertheless had one very significant shortcoming. The source of public power, it seemed, would be located not in the Kosovo institutions. Instead, it was based in the individual communes, or local districts. This meant that Kosovo as an entity would not enjoy any significant element of legal personality—a fact which might seriously damage its quest for an enhanced legal status at some future date. In deference to Serbia, the draft also contained very detailed provisions which, it was feared, would subject Kosovo to devisive ethnic politics.

The actual assignment of public authority provided for in the draft was quite complex. Residual authority over all matters not regulated elsewhere would lie with the communes, which were also granted significant direct powers of self-administration. This included the power to arrange for local police, representative of the ethnic composition of the commune. Moreover, communes could unite to form 'self administering regions comprising multiple communes'. While most communes in Kosovo had an ethnic Albanian majority, a few had a Serb majority. Hence, this provision appeared to be one which would permit the formation of an ethnic Serb entity within Kosovo based on a collection of communes. Such division had not proved fruitful before, bearing in mind the establishment of Srpska in Bosnia and Herzegovina.

In addition, a further layer of authority was introduced on behalf of 'national communities', i.e., all ethnic groups whether or not they constituted a majority in a particular commune. These communities would enjoy 'additional rights' going somewhat beyond traditional minority rights and have additional organs of self-administration, including even courts. Kosovo was much opposed to this concept, which once again appeared to be based on ethnic division, rather than a multicultural society with equal rights for all. However, the determination of the FRY/Serbia to ensure a separate status for Serbs, and incidentally also others, was very strong throughout the negotiations, including the Rambouillet process, and the concept of national communities would be strengthened over time.

Kosovo itself was equipped with a number of organs (Assembly, Chairman, Government, Administrative Organs, Ombudsman) which would exercise powers established in the draft. The Assembly would enjoy quite wide legislative competence in relation to political, economic, social and cultural areas, including the power to adopt 'organic documents' of Kosovo, i.e., its own constitution and associated texts. Voting of the Assembly, however, could be obstructed by any national community, again introducing the prospect of ethnic politics into Kosovo.

The Chairman would be directly elected and head a government. There was no President—a proposition not engendering immediate support from Dr Rugova. The government would include at least one member from each national community and supervise the functioning of the administrative agencies. A separate annex dealt with law enforcement. It provided for an ethnic Albanian Minister of the Interior, and a Serb Deputy, and a similar arrangement for the Chief of Staff for Communal Police Issues. The Kosovo police, confusingly named Kosovo Communal police, would be limited to a ceiling of 2,500 active duty personnel. The extent of municipal (i.e., commune) police would depend on the size of the local population.

The Federation would exercise powers in relation to territorial integrity, a common market, monetary policy, defence and foreign policy. There would also be a Federal police presence with jurisdiction over crimes with implications for the Federation. Crucially, the was no mention of Serbia in the draft.

A very significant element of the draft related to the concluding provisions. It provided for "a comprehensive assessment of the agreement, with the aim of improving its implementation and considering proposals by either side for additional steps,

---

[15] OSCE Report, Annexed to UN Secretary-General's Report, 3 October 1998, Document 8.3.
[16] *See* the Venice Commission Outline, Document 14.B.1.
[17] Document 14.B.2.

which will require mutual agreement for adoption". This provision meant that the agreement was not, in fact, a genuine interim agreement. It could not be terminated or changed, unless both sides so agreed.

While Kosovo was formulating its response to the initial draft, the Holbrooke agreements were concluded. One of the elements of the Holbrooke agreement was a unilateral statement by Serbia, outlining a political framework which it claimed had been agreed.[18] This 11-point framework would furnish the basis of a political settlement, to be completed by 2 November on the basis of the initial Hill draft. However, in contrast to the Hill document, the Serb text included an express provision respecting the territorial integrity and sovereignty of the FRY. It also provided for harmonization of legal arrangements establishing Kosovo's self-governance within the legal systems of both the FRY and Serbia, implying a continued subordination of Kosovo also to the latter entity.

The unilateral presentation of a purported framework for a settlement, and the commitment to reach an agreement by 2 November, without consulting the other party was extraordinary. Kosovo was at no stage during the Holbrooke mission involved in these developments. In fact, up to that time, Kosovo had only unofficially commented on the Hill drafts. While formally indicating that these could not furnish 'as basis for a settlement', it had nevertheless, though its delegation, furnished constructive comments in relation to them. Faced with the Holbrooke deal, Kosovo issued its own statement on fundamental principles for a settlement.[19] By that time, on 2 November, a new, far more detailed Hill draft had emerged.[20] That draft had, in fact, enhanced the status of Kosovo as a legal entity in its own right somewhat. In addition, Kosovo would now also have a President and the role of the Kosovo courts was developed in greater detail. On the other hand, the provisions on communes and national communities, of essential concern to the FRY/Serbia, had also been further entrenched.

Despite the pledge made in the Holbrooke agreement, Serbia did not commit itself on 2 November to the Hill document that had been presented.[21] This failure to take Serbia by its word, as it were, may have lost a crucial opportunity to achieve a settlement, for this draft might also have been acceptable to Kosovo. Instead, on 18 November, Serbia organized its own conference, attended, inter alia, by representatives, or purported representatives, of the 'national communities' in Kosovo. This meeting resulted in a counter-proposal, supported by the FRY, Serbia and Kosovo Serb, Gorani, Egyptian, Romani, Turk and Muslim 'national communities'.[22] While this proposal mirrored some of the language of the Hill texts, it was seen by Kosovo as a cynical attempt to undermine the internationalised Hill process. In addition to substantive changes, in particular in relation to national communities and the position of Serbia, the draft did not provide for signature by Kosovo, but by all individual national communities. To the Kosovo Albanians, it reflected the attempt, once again, to turn them into a political minority in a land where they constituted the overwhelming demographic majority. Moreover, Kosovo noted that the representatives of the national communities supporting the Serb text were either members of Mr Milosevic's party, or they had been hand-picked by Belgrade and had, in fact, in part been disowned by these groups in Kosovo.

While rejecting the Serb draft, Kosovo's chief 'informal' negotiator, Dr Fehmi Agani, went further than before in embracing the Hill process and the progress made thus far.[23] This optimism was to prove premature, inasmuch as the following day a new Hill draft was submitted, which provided for express powers of Serbia in relation to Kosovo. In fact, the draft was immediately reject by both sides and, despite new attempts at shuttle diplomacy by the Hill team to keep the dialogue open, the peace process seemed to have reached a dead end. This feeling of gloom was only strengthened by the FRY/Serb Christmas offensive and the ensuing hostilities of January. Depite this setback, the Hill team continued its work and produced one more draft, two days before the Contact Group decision to summon the parties to talks at Rambouillet.[24] This draft was very detailed. Several alternative proposals for certain provisions previously placed in brackets had been removed. Of particular interest were new provisions relating to the withdrawal of Yugoslav Army and Serb special police forces, and the provisions on international implementation.

---

[18] Serbian Government Endorses Accord, 13 October 1999, Document 12.16
[19] Kosovo Statement, 3 November 1998, Document 14.B.5.
[20] Document 14.B.4.
[21] FRY Statement, 10 November 1998, Document 14.B.6.
[22] Proposal, 20 November, and Declaration in Support of Joint Proposal, 25 November 1998, Documents 14.B.9-10.
[23] Kosovo Press Release, 1 December 1998, Document 14.B.11.
[24] Final Hill Proposal, 27 January 1999, Document 14.B.16.

A. Bilateral Attempts to Achieve a Settlement

1. FRY statement: Serbia-Kosovo Methohija-Dialogue, 13 March 1998

Head of the Serbian govermental and parliamentary delegation, professor Ratko Markovic, after the political representatives of the Albanian national minority failed to show up again on Friday for talks in Pristina, said that the Government invitation for talks remained open.

"The Government of the Republic of Serbia remains ready for unconditional talks about all issues relating to Kosmet, whenever and wherever in the territory of Serbia," Markovic said at a press conference, held after waiting 45 minutes for ethnic Albanian representatives, who were sent personal invitations yesterday to attend the meeting. Markovic said that the fact that they did not come for talks on Friday showed that the representatives of ethnic Albanians had ulterior motives for refusing dialogue with the state of Serbia, as the excuse made the previous day by some Albanian leaders that the invitation was not adressed to anyone could no longer stand. It appears that they want to talk under certain conditions, Markovic said, and repeated the position of the Government of Serbia that the dialogue can raise all issues and that a solution for all those issues can be sought by political means.

"The position of Serbia is that Kosmet is in Serbia, that it is an internal affair of Serbia and that a consensus existed among all political factors in that respect," Markovic recalled. The delegation of the Republic of Serbia was again in full formation on Friday: Ministers Ratomir Vico, Andreja Milosacljevic and Ivan Sedlak, representatives of Serbian parliamentary groupings - Tomislav Nikolic (Serbian Radical Party), Milovan Bojic (Yugoslav Left), Vojislav Zivkovic (Socialist Party of Serbia) and Antal Bijaci (Alliance of Vojvodina Hungarians). Nikolic assessed that talks with ethnic Albanian political representatives were "decided by the fact that Serbia had openly made it known to the entire world what it wanted to do in Kosovo and Metohija."

"Albanian national minority members should think twice who are their political leaders - if those people wanted to talk or wage war and would they let their children take part in terrorist actions or leave that up to poor Albanians," Nikolic said. Bojic said that the not showing up on Friday has unmasked a dangerous scenario of "inciting terrorism by the political mentors of ethnic Albanian representatives." Bijaci, after expressing regret that ethnic Albanian representatives have not come for talks, said that his party was ready to take part in dialogue at any time, as it wishes to help solve Kosmet problems. The latest developments in Kosovo and Metohija, according to Zivkovic, have shown that political parties in Serbia and the Serbian people were firm in their determination that problems in the region of Kosmet can be resolved only in the Republic of Serbia. Zivkovic said he hoped direct contact with Albanian representatives would be established in the near future, regardless of the problems that are arising. "We have information that, besides foreign pressures on Albania itself, even the Albanians themselves (from Kosmet) have not agreed who should represent them at the talks with Serbian Government representatives. We believe that they will reach an agreement in the near future and propose their people," Zivkovic said.

2. FRY, Serbian Government again invites ethnic Albanians to Dialogue, 14 March 1998

Despite the fact that ethnic Albanian representatives in Serbia's southern province of Kosovo-Metohija have failed to come to talks with Serbian Government officials, the Serbian Government on Friday issued another written invitation for dialogue to ethnic Albanian parties, associations and public and cultural figures, the Serbian Information Ministry said in a statement.

Among those invited again are Democratic League of Kosovo party leader Ibrahim Rugova, Parliamentary Party of Kosovo leader Adem Demaqi, Social Democratic Party leader Loleta Pula-Beqiri, Christian Democratic Party leader Mark Krasniqi, President of the Union of Independent Trade Unions Hajrua Gorani, Peasants' Party leader Hivzi Islami as well as Mahmut Bakalli, Azem Vllasi, Remzi Kolgeci, Kaqusha Jashari, Gani Jashari and other public figures, the statement said. The invitation, signed by Serbian Deputy Prime Minister Ratko Markovic, said:

"Dear Sir,

"The Serbian Government invites you to take part in talks with its representatives at the Serbian Government's office in Pristina, 2 Vidovdanska Street, at 11 a.m. on Monday, March 16, 1998.

"In line with conclusions adopted at its session of March 10, 1998, the Serbian Government appointed its negotiators in the talks with leaders of ethnic Albanian parties and associations in Kosovo-Metohija with a view to upgrading political processes and resolving specific issues of vital importance to citizens in Kosovo-Metohija.

"The Government expresses its openness to unconditional dialogue and its determination to deal by political means with all questions which determine the exercising of human and civil rights of all citizens in Kosovo-Metohija, as well as matters of a speedier economic and cultural development in line with the Constitution of the Republic of Serbia, European and international standards, principles of the OSCE (the Organization for Security and Cooperation in Europe), the Paris Charter and the U.N. Charter, and also in keeping with the principles contained in the Council of Europe's framework convention on the protection of national minorities.

"Taking part in these talks on behalf of the Serbian Government will be Deputy Premier Ratko Markovic and Ministers Ratomir Vico, Andrea Milosavljevic and Ivan Sedlak.

"Also taking part in the talks will be representatives of parliamentary parties in the Serbian Parliament."

3. FRY: Yugoslav President Milosevic calls for Referendum, 2 April 1998

The President of the Federal Republic of Yugoslavia, Slobodan Milosevic, sent on Thursday morning a letter to Serbian President Milan Milutinovic, Serbian Prime Minister Mirko Marjanovic and Serbian National Assembly President Dragan Tomic. The following is the integral version of the text of the letter:

To the: President of the Republic of Serbia
Prime Minister of Serbia
President of National Assembly of the Republic of Serbia

It is well known that we have rejected the participation of foreign representatives in the resolution of the internal affairs of our country, and especially in the resolution of the problems in Kosovo and Metohija, which are the internal affair of Serbia. I believe that this position has a fundamental significance for the preservation of our country's sovereignty and territorial integrity. Because of that, our country once again faces the threat of all possible forms of pressure. Those who want to dictate to the entire world how it should live and even think, have an extremely negative and aggressive stand towards our determined position to resolve our problems as a sovereign state, without foreign interference.

Over the past few days, we have heard how they have nothing against our people, that they even love us and are sorry that the people will be subject to pressures because the leadership is taking such a stand. I believe that we cannot accept such cynicism which serves to justify pressure exserted in the name of democracy. I believe that, during the entire period of the crisis in the territory of the former Yugoslavia, we conducted a national policy, rather than a personal or even party one. In this instance too, our refusal to allow foreign factors to participate in the resolution of the internal issue of the Republic of Serbia - Kosovo and Metohija, also represents a national policy, not a personal or party one. Whether this is true, can only be decided by the citizens. This is why I am proposing that, in keeping with the Constitution and laws of Serbia, you initiate proceedings for holding a referendum which would provide an answer to the question:

Do you accept the participation of foreign representatives in the resolution of the problems in Kosovo and Metohija?

I am using this opportunity to say that, at the same time, it is necessary to intensify efforts in the constructive resolution of the problems which burden Kosovo and Metohija. This implies the speedy start of a dialogue and steps which will represent a solution for the equal affirmation of the interests of all who live in Kosovo and Metohija.

Sincerely,
Slobodan Milosevic

4. Serbian President Milutinovic issues statement on President Milosevic's Letter, 2 April 1998

Serbian President Milan Milutinovic on Thursday supported Yugoslav President Slobodan Milosevic's initiative that Serbian citizens decide in a referendum whether foreign representatives should be included in efforts to resolve the problem in Kosovo and Metohija. Following is Milutinovic's statement communicated by his Office:

"Citizens of Serbia know under what kind of pressures our country is because of the determination to preserve Serbia within its constitutional and historical boundaries and develop it as a state of equal citizens, in which all rights of national minorities will be guaranteed under the highest international standards. "Under the Constitution of the Republic of Serbia, the sovereignty belongs to all citizens of Serbia and they exercise that sovereignty in a referendum. There are not many situations that so clearly call for a direct stating of opinion by all citizens of the Republic of Serbia, as is the issue of sovereignty and preservation of its territorial integrity.

"Aware that, in relation to this crucial matter, we need to ask for a verification of our policy from the citizens, themselves, I fully support the initiative of President of the Federal Republic of Yugoslavia Slobodan Milosevic that the citizens of Serbia decide in a referendum whether they accept that foreign representatives be included in our efforts toward resolving the problem in Kosovo and Metohija.

"Starting from stands contained in the March 18 Declaration on the political process in Kosovo and Metohija, I believe that only through a constructive and intensive political dialogue can we arrive at solutions, which will be in the long-term interest of all those living and working in Kosovo and Metohija."

5. Serbian Government proposes calling of a Referendum, 2 April 1998

The Serbian Government on Thursday unanimously accepted Yugoslav President Slobodan Milosevic's initiative that Serbian citizens decide in a referendum whether foreign representative should be included in the resolution of problems in Kosovo and Metohija. According to a statement issued by the Serbian Information Ministry, at the beginning of the Thursday's session Serbian Premier Mirko Marjanovic informed members of the Cabinet about the contents of the letter sent to him by President Milosevic. The Government unanimously adopted the Yugoslav President's initiative and decided, in line with the law, to submit to the Serbian Parliament a proposal for calling a referendum in which Serbian citizens would decide whether they accept that foreign representatives be included in the resolution of problems in Kosovo and Metohija, the statement said. The Government believes that the referendum on this issue is the right way for a direct expression of the citizens' will and thereby for an affirmation of the constitutional principle of the sovereignty of the people. The Government unanimously decided to propose to the Parliament that the question posed in the referendum be worded as follows:

"Do you accept the participation of foreign representatives in the resolution of problems in Kosovo and Metohija?"

[*Note: On 23 April 1998, it was announced that the referendum had resulted in a vote of 94.73 per cent against participation of foreign representatives in the resolution of the problemsin Kosovo. The poll had been boycotted by ethnic Albanians.*]

6. FRY, Letter of the Vice-President of Serbia to the President of the Democratic Alliance of Kosovo, 26 April 1998

Dear Dr Rugova,

Ahead of our fortcoming talks, I should like to present to you the essential elements of the approach of interest to all participants and to propose a constructive and open attitude towards dialogue. I consider that the responsability to reach a viable political settlement lies both with yourself as well as with us who represent the Government.

The differences existing in the present posititon can only be resolved in an atmosphere of mutual respect. I consider that everyone should enter into dialogue without preconditions and that none of the participants should attempt to predeterminate the outcome. Any solution reached through dialogue should be in accordance with the principles of the UN Charter, the OSCE Final Document and the standards of the Council of Europe. In that sense, any solution must guarantee equal civil and human rights of all. All citizens of Kosovo and Metohija - Serbs, Montenegrins, Albanians, Muslims, Romany, Turks and members of other ethnic groups have equal rights and have the right to live without fear or persecution.

Violence is not an acceptable tool to attain any political goals. We deem it extremely important that the agreements reached through dialogue are fully implemented. In this context, full support for cooperation in the further implementation of the 1996 Education agreement should be mutually expressed. The modality regarding the conduct of dialogue should be mutually agreed, including:

- mutual agreement on the timing and other details of the future meetings;
- the delegations attending the talks shall be freely and independetly composed by the participants of the dialogue;
- meetings and consultations could be held in plenary, or reduced number of participants;
- the talks will be private but not secret, and the facts on dialogue should be a metter of public reccord;
- the aggenda will be mutually agreed upon;
- the participants of the dialogue should give mutual
- assurance that all agreements will be respected in good faith, and that they will not be abandoned or undermined.

I am confident that the above represents a clear and, at the same time, wide framework for the start of substantive dialogue. Therefore I propose that we reach our first agreement thereon at our forthcoming meeting schelduled for 28 April 1998, in Pristina.

Sincerely,
Prof Dr Ratko Markovic, Vice-President of the Government of Serbia

7. FRY: Ethnic Albanian Representatives fail to appear at Talks once more, 28 April 1998

The Serbian Government delegation met in Pristina on Tuesday with the representatives of national minorities in Kosovo and Metohija, minus the political representatives of the Albanian national minority who failed to appear for the 12th time. The Government delegation, headed by Serbian Vice Premier Ratko Markovic, also included the Yugoslav President's special envoy Vladan Kutlesic, as well as Tomislav Nikolic, Ratomir Vico, Ivan Sedlak, Andreja Milosevljevic and Vojislav Zivkovic. Present were the representatives of the Romany, Turkish and Muslim national minorities, ethnic Egyptians and some individual Albanians. Markovic said during the talks and at a press conference afterwards that the government believes that a solution to the Kosovo and Metohija problem can only be reached through talks between partners who respect each other. An alternative to agreement can only be a dictate, a one-sided decision, which is a form of violence. The most brutal from of violence is terrorism and we can testify that in Kosmet terrorism is gaining in strength in contrary proportion to the dialogue on the Kosmet problems. Thus, direct responsibility for terrorism lies with those who refuse to participate in the dialogue, Markovic said.

"This is why when a part of the international community supports the Albanian side which rejects a dialogue, it stimulates terrorism and pushes a dialogue into a blind alley," Markovic said. He set out that at the previous talks a list was made of all rights of national minorities included in international acts and that determined was that domestic constitutions and laws guarrantee almost all these rights. Markovic said that the ethnic Albanians' human rights are threatened in the bigest degree by the ethnic Albanians themselves. Some other Albanians are stopping them from voting at elections, using their political rights, with the exception of those with which they express their rejection of the state of Serbia, they prevent them from obtaining a university education, using health institutions, etc., Markovic said.

Today's talks focused on local self-rule as a form of participation of national and ethnic communities in public services, especially in a multinational environment, such as that in Kosmet. Concrete agreement on that issue was reached - said Markovic. According to that, he emphasised that mutual aim is to adhere to the democratic institutions of the Serbian State. According to him, a democratic Serbia should be the creation of the free citizens, in it all freedoms should be realized - ranging from personal to ethinc and other collective freedoms and it can be realized only through democratic methods. The method towards reaching such a Serbia in Kosmet, is the method being offferred by the Serbian Government at these talks, Markovic said. He did not say when the talks would resume, but set out that the Republican Government delegation remains open and willing to take part in talks and that the pulbic and the representatives of national minorities in Kosmet would be informed about this.

8. FRY: Serbian Vice Premier Markovic invites minorities to Talks on May 12, 5 May 1998

Serbia's Vice Premier and Chief Negotiator Ratko Markovic invited on Tuesday ethnic minorities in the province of Kosovo and Metohija to open talks with the Serbian Government on Tuesday, May 12, a Government statement said. The proposed agenda for the talks, to be held in the Serbian Government building in Kosovo and Metohija's chief city of Pristina, 2 Vidovdanska street, is as follows:

1. Draft provisional statutory decision on the Autonomous Province of Kosovo and Metohija;
2. Bill on local self-rule;
3. The Council of Europe framework convention for the protection of ethnic minorities.

The Government reaffirms its determination to seek, in an open and direct dialogue with representatives of the Albanian and other minorities in Kosovo and Metohija, generally acceptable solutions to all concrete questions concerning the exercise of their human and civic rights and self-rule in line with existing European and world standards, the statement said.

9. Statement on the talks of the FRY President S. Milosevic with Dr Ibrahim Rugova and his Delegation, 15 April 1998

The President of the Federal Republic of Yugoslavia Slobodan Milosevic received today Dr. Ibrahim Rugova and members of his delegation Pajazit Nusi, Mahmut Bakali, Fehmi Agani and Veton Suroi. These talks should mark the beginning of a peaceful resolution of problems in Kosovo and Metohija, President Milosevic said at the outset of the meeting, which took place in the spirit of openness to presenting the positions on the most important issues concerning the resolution of these problems. President Milosevic pointed out that it is only by political means - through a direct dialogue on the basis of principle - that peaceful, human, just and lasting solutions to the problems in Kosovo and Metohija can be found. These solutions should be based on the equality of all citizens and ethnic communities in Kosovo and Metohija. President Milosevic stressed that the common future and life in equality of Serbs, Montenegrins, Albanians, Muslims, Romanies, Turks and other citizens in Kosovo and Metohija are mutual respect and tolerance, which is equally in the interest of all of them, just as the violence and terrorism in particular are their common enemy.

President Milosevic stated that he believed that a dialogue was the best way for overcoming, in a peaceful manner, the outstanding issues which will be discussed at the forthcoming meetings of the delegations. It was agreed that meetings should be held every week. The first meeting will take place as early as the end of next week. The State delegation, to be headed by Dr. Ratko Markovic, Deputy Prime Minister of the Republic of Serbia, will also include Mr Tomislav Nikolic and Dr Milovan Bojic, Deputy Prime Ministers of the Republic of Serbia, as well as Mr Ivan Sedlak, a Member of the Government of the Republic of Serbia, and Dr Vladan Kutlesic, Deputy Prime Minister of the Federal Republic of Yugoslavia and Mr Radoslav Rajakovic, Assistant Minister. The Kosovar Albanian delegation will be composed of Messrs Pajazit Nusi, Mahmut Bakali, Fehmi Agani, Veton Suroi and another two members which will be designated subsequently. Also present at the talks was the Secretary General of the President of the Federal Republic of Yugoslavia, Mr Goran Milinovic.

10. FRY on talks in Pristina, including statement by Albanian side read by B. Salja, 22 May 1998

The State delegation, headed by Prof. Dr. Ratko Markovic and the delegation of the representatives of political parties of the Albanians from Kosovo and Metohija, headed by Dr. Fehmi Agani, started today in Pristina a dialogue on the political resolution of issues in Kosovo and Metohija. The first meeting took place in an atmosphere of tolerance, while different views on the situation and the ways of normalizing the situation and relations in Kosovo and Metohija, were presented in an open fashion. The questions of organization and methods for successful conducting of talks were discussed in particular. The importance of the reception and talks that the delegation, headed by Dr. Ibrahim Rugova, had with the President of the Federal Republic of Yugoslavia, Mr. Slobodan Milosevic, was underscored. The need for the peaceful solution of existing problems in Kosovo and Metohija was commonly agreed. The goal is to reach just, humane and permanent solutions, based on the equality of all citizens and ethnic communities in Kosovo and Metohija, on their mutual respect, tolerance and security. In order to achieve this, violence, and in particular terrorism, as well as all other phenomena causing fear and uncertainty of the citizens, must be eliminated. It was agreed that measures, which will encourage the process of the building of confidence as a prerequisite for the accomplishment of these goals, will be undertaken by both sides. In the interest of an early normalization of the situation and relations, readiness was expressed to invest mutual efforts, which will help affirm the atmosphere of dialogue, in order for the concrete results to be achieved as soon as possible. It was agreed that, as a rule, the meetings of delegations will take place once a week. The next meeting will be held during the course of next week. Participants in the dialogue agreed that the meetings and consultations may be held in plenary or as expert level exchanges, whereas the information about the outcome of the meetings will be communicated to the public in a way reinforcing the atmosphere of confidence in the dialogue. Delegations have agreed to be flexible to possible changes in their composition, depending on how the forthcoming meetings proceed. Participants in the dialogue have undertaken to respect reached agreements in good faith, without abandoning or undermining them.

PRESS RELEASE READ BY B. SALJA: The Albanian team from Kosovo, appointed by Dr. Ibrahim Rugova met today with the delegation appointed by President Slobodan Milosevic, within the framework of the process initiated by Ambassadors Holbrooke and Gelbard, on the basis of last week's talks between Dr. Rugova and President Milosevic. On that occasion, discussions were held on the framework and modalities of negotiations, on security and confidence-building measures to be undertaken with a view to preserving the negotiation process, as well as on the political status of Kosovo.

Contrary to obvious differences regarding the assessment of the current situation in Kosovo, as well as the ways to resolve the issue of Kosovo, readiness of both sides to provide prerequisites which would assist the negotiation process, was expressed in this meeting.

11.   Press Release of the Ministry of the Interior of the Republic of Serbia, 5 June 1998

Talks between the State delegation of the Republic of Serbia and a delegation of representatives of political parties of Albanians from Kosovo and Metohija were not held today. The State delegation, headed by Serbian Vice President Ratko Markovic, arrived in Pristina but the ethnic Albanian delegation did not turn up. The statement, read out by the head of the State delegation of the Republic of Serbia Ratko Markovic, is as follows:

"A state delegation, headed by Ratko Markovic, today arrived to a meeting, which the two delegations had agreed to hold at 11 a.m. (0900 GMT) on Friday, June 5, 1998. The meeting should have focused on the measures of security confidence and other issues important to the normalisation of life of all citizens in Kosovo and Metohija. In the spirit of agreements reached at the first meeting, the state delegation has prepared for detailed and open talks on all listed questions. The head of the State delegation informed the ethnic Albanian delegation that the State delegation was rady to start with the agreed dialogue. However, without offering an explanation, the ethnic Albanian delegation did not show up for hours after the scheduled time. This ethnic Albanian delegation's move clashes with the atmosphere of dialogue, achieved in a meeting between President of the Federal Republic of Yugoslavia Slobodan Milosevic and Dr. Ibrahim Rugova. On that occasion, it was agreed that the two delegations would hold meetings in Pristina at least once a week.

Every interruption and delay in a dialogue means a loss towards positive changes, creation of space for terrorist actions and infliction of losses of human lives and property. The State delegation points at a serious delay in the dialogue since one date for the meeting of two delegations' had already been missed due to a visit abroad by some members of the ethnic Albanian delegation. The behaviour of the ethnic Albanian side is all the more surprising since in all its meetings abroad it had been said that the finding of solutions for the crisis in Kosovo and Metohija was possible only through political means, primarily dialogue, and since the idea on an independent Kosovo and terrorism as a means for achieving political goals had been unequivocally rejected. Precisely at the time when there was no dialogue, there has been the largest escalation of terrorist activities with a large number of human victims, blockade of roads and prevention of free movement with serious consequences to the citizens' normal and safe life.

The State delegation remains on the position that political means, which should be established in an unconditional dialogue, are the only way to resolve the crisis in Kosovo and Metohija without human losses and violation of preconditions for the co-existence of all citizens and national communities in Kosovo and Metohija. In keeping with this, the State delegation expresses its readiness to resume the dialogue," the statement said. The state delegation also included Yugoslav Deputy Prime Minister Nikola Sainovic and Serbian Ministers Ivan Sedlak, Leposava Milicevic and Jorgovanka Tabakovic as well as Yugoslav Assistant Justice Minister Radivoj Rajakovic.

B.   The Hill Process

1.   Venice Commission Outline for Main Elements for Agreement on Kosovo, undated

[*Note: The European Commission for Democracy through Law, or Venice Commission, operates within the Council of Europe*].
Introduction
1.   This outline was prepared by a working group of the Venice Commission with the participation of Messrs Scholsem (Belgium), Bartole (Italy) and Malinverni (Switzerland), as well as Mr Marko (Austria). Mr Cuatrecasas and, at the second meeting, Mr Locatelli represented the Congress of Local and Regional Authorities of Europe. This outline does not claim to be a complete blueprint for a solution of the Kosovo conflict and was prepared without the participation of representatives of the parties to the conflict. The ideas set down in the outline will have to be submitted to representatives of the parties and may then serve as the basis for negotiations between them.
Analysis of the present situation
2.   At present, the status of Kosovo is laid down only in the Constitution of Serbia of 1990. Its preamble describes Serbia as the "democratic State of the Serbian people in which members of other nations and national minorities will be able to exercise their national rights". According to Article 6 "the Republic of Serbia includes the autonomous province of Vojvodina and the autonomous province of Kosovo and Metohia, these being the forms of territorial autonomy".
3.   Articles 108-112 of the 1990 Constitution set down the main elements of this "autonomy". The degree of autonomy is very low. The powers of the autonomous provinces are powers to execute, within the framework of the Constitution and the law (Article 109 of the Serbian Constitution). The territory of the provinces is determined by law (Article 108 of the Serbian Constitution). The law also determines to what extent the autonomous provinces may collect revenues (Article 109 in fine). The statute of the autonomous province, although enacted by its Assembly, must be submitted for prior approval to the Serbian National Assembly (Article 110 § 2). Finally, the basis for this autonomy, i.e. the Serbian Constitution, may be revised according to the modalities foreseen in its Articles 132-134 without the possibility for the population of the autonomous provinces to object to the revision.
4.   This present status is in contrast to the extremely wide degree of autonomy enjoyed by the autonomous provinces of Kosovo and Vojvodina under the Yugoslav Constitution of 1974. Even though these provinces were part of the Socialist Republic of Serbia, they had the status of constituent parts of the Federation and participated in federal affairs. In particular, the constitutional basis for the status of the autonomous provinces was set down by the Constitution of the Federation. Their territory could not be modified without their consent. The Federal Constitution could not be revised without the agreement of all republics and autonomous provinces.
5.   Obviously, this very large degree of autonomy under the 1974 Constitution has to be interpreted in the light of the political regime during this period and the communist party's control of all levers of power.
6.   The present situation is clearly unsatisfactory for the Albanian-speaking population of Kosovo. This outline aims to give Kosovo a large degree of self-government in order to enable the Albanian-speaking majority to preserve and develop its culture while fully respecting the rights of other people living within Kosovo. On the other hand, a high degree of self-government also implies less interest in the running of federal affairs and the present paper therefore does not grant Kosovo as strong a participation in federal affairs as was the case under the 1974 Constitution.
The respective powers of the Federation and of Kosovo
NB.The following lists are in no way definitive and will have to be subject to negotiations between the parties.

A. Responsibilities of the Federation

The federal organs and institutions shall have on the territory of Kosovo, subject to respect for the other parts of the Agreement to be negotiated, exclusive responsibility for the following matters:

foreign affairs and international relations; (but cf. para. 10 below)

national defence; (but cf. para. 26 below)

foreign trade;

customs, free movement of persons and goods;

guarding the borders of the State, immigration and emigration, extradition; (but cf. para. 27 below)

status of foreigners and right to asylum;

taxes allocated by the Agreement to the Federation;

roads and airports of international importance, international transport by air and train;

post and telecommunications,;

the issuing of currency, the central bank;

weights and measures;

civil and commercial law with the exception of family law and the law of succession, labour law;

criminal code;

civil and criminal procedure, procedure before the administrative courts; (but cf. Paragraph. 32 below)

intellectual property;

citizenship.

B. Responsibilities of Kosovo

8. Kosovo shall be responsible for all subject matters which are, according to the Constitution of the Federal Republic of Yugoslavia, within the responsibility of the Republics.

9. Kosovo shall be exclusively responsible for all subject matters not specifically mentioned as within the powers of the organs and institutions of the Federation or of Kosovo in the Agreement.

10. The organs and institutions of Kosovo shall have on the territory of Kosovo, subject to respect for the other provisions of the Agreement, exclusive responsibility in particular for the following matters:

organisation of the political institutions and form of government (Constitution, Parliament, government and judicial system);

organisation and number of local and regional authorities, their powers and borders and their civil service; (but cf. para. 17 below)

local and regional elections; (but cf. para. 18 below)

housing;

public works with the exception of projects of national importance;

communications, roads and transport within the territory of Kosovo;

water, forests, nature reserves;

protection of the environment and nature;

regional and spatial planning;

hunting and fishing;

agricultural policy and law, including agricultural property law;

culture, museums, historical monuments; (but cf. para. 20 below)

teaching and education at all levels; (but cf. paras. 15 and 16 below)

relations with religious communities; (but cf. para. 20 below)

sport;

tourism;

public health, hospitals;

police, maintenance of public order; (but cf. para. 29 below)

civil protection, fight against fires and natural catastrophes;

administration of justice in criminal, civil and administrative matters, subject to review of the application of federal law by the federal courts of last instance;

family law and law of succession;

mining and exploitation of natural resources;

energy policy;

privatisation of public enterprises;

taxes with the exception of taxes reserved to the Federation by the Agreement, budget of Kosovo;

social security;

symbols, flag and emblems of Kosovo;

official languages in Kosovo;

civil service of Kosovo;

media, including radio and television

11. With respect to the subject matters for which it is responsible, Kosovo may enter into international and transfrontier agreements or agreements with the member Republics of the Federal Republic of Yugoslavia which may not contradict the provisions of the Agreement, the Constitution of the Federal Republic of Yugoslavia to the extent it is compatible with the Agreement or international commitments entered into by the Federal Republic of Yugoslavia.

C. Co-operation between Kosovo and the Federation

12. The competent authorities of the Federation and of Kosovo may agree to co-operate with respect to subject matters within the responsibility of either the Federation or Kosovo.

Protection of human and minority rights within Kosovo

13. The material provisions of the European Convention for the Protection of Human Rights and Fundamental Freedoms (ECHR) and of the Framework Convention for the Protection of National Minorities of 1995 as well as Article 7 of the European Charter for Regional or Minority Languages shall be directly applicable within Kosovo as part of the Agreement. The Parties might wish to examine which further provisions of the Charter might be made part of the Agreement.

14. The Serbian language (and other minority languages) may be freely used in private, social and business life and each individual shall have the right to use the Serbian language in contacts with the public authorities or before courts established in the minority population areas defined in the Appendix to the Agreement.

15. Within these minority population areas Kosovo shall offer education in the Serbian language.

16. Throughout Kosovo private schools using the curriculum of the Republic of Serbia may be freely set up and shall be financially supported by Kosovo on an equal footing with other schools.

17. Within minority population areas, the borders of municipalities shall not be changed without the consent of the population concerned.

Electoral law shall ensure a – at least proportional - representation of minorities in all elected bodies of Kosovo and the local and regional authorities within Kosovo, without any threshold applying to minorities.

The principle of proportional representation shall also be applied, as far as possible, in the public administration.

20. Kosovo shall respect the independence and the property of the Serbian Orthodox Church and protect the national monuments belonging to the Church. These monuments shall be under the joint protection of the Federation and of Kosovo.

Participation of Kosovo in the organs and institutions of the Federal Republic of Yugoslavia

21. Since Kosovo shall enjoy a large degree of self-government under the Agreement, it seems justified to reduce the participation of Kosovo in decision-making at the level of the Federation. Kosovo shall therefore not be represented in the Chamber of the Republics. By contrast, citizens of the Federal Republic of Yugoslavia residing in Kosovo shall participate in the same way as all other citizens in the elections to the Chamber of Citizens of the Federal Republic of Yugoslavia.

22. The Republic of Serbia exercising no powers with respect to the territory of Kosovo, citizens of the Federal Republic of Yugoslavia residing in Kosovo shall have no right to participate in elections to organs of the Republic of Serbia unless the Republic of Serbia expressly grants such a right to all or some of them.

23. The President of Kosovo shall be a full member of the Supreme Defence Council of the Federal Republic of Yugoslavia.

24. In appointments to any offices and posts of the Federation citizens residing in Kosovo shall be considered on the same basis as all other citizens of the Federal Republic of Yugoslavia.

Other issues

A number of issues will have to be addressed separately and in detail in the agreement. Without prior contacts with the parties, only a preliminary outline can be given here.

Borders

25. The borders of Kosovo shall be the borders of the present autonomous province. These borders may be changed only by

agreement between the Federation and Kosovo. There shall be no border controls between the territory of Kosovo and other parts of the Federal Republic of Yugoslavia.

b) Military issues

26. The military forces of the Federal Republic of Yugoslavia shall be withdrawn from Kosovo and may not enter any part of Kosovo, except at the specific invitation of the President of Kosovo, with the exception of a zone along the international borders between the Federal Republic of Yugoslavia and Albania and "the Former Yugoslav Republic of Macedonia" defined in a map appended to the Agreement. The government of the Federal Republic of Yugoslavia shall endeavour to enter into agreements with the governments of Albania and "the Former Yugoslav Republic of Macedonia" on the demilitarisation of their mutual borders and the Yugoslav military forces shall be withdrawn from the respective frontier zones of Kosovo upon the entry into force of such agreements.

Border police

27. Posts at official crossings along the international borders of the Federal Republic of Yugoslavia on the territory of Kosovo shall be manned jointly by border police of the Federal Republic of Yugoslavia and the Kosovo police. Patrols along those borders shall be carried out by joint units of the Federation border police and the Kosovo police.

Police

28. Police of the Federation and of the Republic of Serbia shall be withdrawn from Kosovo and may enter the territory of Kosovo only with the express consent of the government of Kosovo.

29. The ethnic composition of the police force of Kosovo shall reflect that of the population of Kosovo. Any police unit stationed in minority population areas shall reflect the ethnic composition of the area.

Property

30. Property issues will have to be addressed in the Agreement, including who is the owner of public enterprises or of assets of public enterprises on the territory of Kosovo.

Taxes

31. The distribution of taxes between the organs of the Federal Republic of Yugoslavia and Kosovo will have to be defined in the Agreement. The Federation may only collect those taxes on the territory of Kosovo which are specifically mentioned in the Agreement.

Public Prosecutor's office

32. The Public Prosecutor's office of Kosovo shall be independent from the Federal Public Prosecutor and the Federal Public Prosecutor may not appear before the Kosovo courts.

Status of the agreement

33. The Agreement shall prevail with respect to any inconsistent provisions of the Constitutions and the laws of the Federal Republic of Yugoslavia, Kosovo and the Republic of Serbia. It may be amended only by mutual agreement between the Federal Republic of Yugoslavia and Kosovo.

34. This principle shall be set out in the Constitutions of the Federal Republic of Yugoslavia, the Republic of Serbia and of Kosovo.

35. Within one year after the entry into force of the Agreement, the Federal Republic of Yugoslavia, the Republic of Serbia and Kosovo shall amend their respective Constitutions to ensure their conformity with the Agreement.

36. Federal law shall apply on the territory of Kosovo to the extent that the organs of the Federation enjoy powers under the Agreement. The Kosovo authorities shall respect and apply all such law of the Federation. The law of the Republic of Serbia shall not be applicable on the territory of Kosovo.

Guarantees for the implementation of this agreement

37. A Special Court shall be established to ensure compliance with the Agreement. Three judges of the Special Court shall be elected by the Chamber of Citizens of the Federal Republic of Yugoslavia and three by the Assembly of Kosovo. During a period of 20 years from the entry into force of the Agreement three judges appointed by the European Court of Human Rights following consultations with the governments of the Federal Republic of Yugoslavia and Kosovo shall sit on the Court. These judges shall not be citizens of the Federal Republic of Yugoslavia or a neighbouring country.

38. The Special Court shall enjoy jurisdiction with respect to all subject matters arising under the Agreement.

39. In particular, the Special Court shall rule:

at the request of the President, the government, the Chamber of the Republics or the Chamber of Citizens of the Federal Republic of Yugoslavia or of the President, the government or the Assembly of Kosovo:

in case of disagreement or doubt as to the compatibility of federal or Kosovo legislation or of the federal or the Kosovo Constitution with the Agreement;

in case of disagreement on the rights and obligations of the Federation or Kosovo under the Agreement;

following the exhaustion of ordinary remedies, at the request of any natural or legal person, association or municipality, on complaints that rights granted to the plaintiff by the Agreement, including by the provisions of international treaties incorporated into the Agreement, have been violated by a public authority.

40. If a court on the territory of the Federal Republic of Yugoslavia considers that a law, on whose validity its ruling in a case before it depends, may be inconsistent with the Agreement, it shall stay the proceedings and seek a ruling from the Special Court as to the compatibility of the law with the Agreement.

41. If the Constitutional Court of the Federal Republic of Yugoslavia considers that a provision of the Constitution of the Federal Republic of Yugoslavia, on whose validity its ruling in a case before it depends, may be inconsistent with the Agreement, or if the Constitutional Court of Kosovo considers that a provision of the Constitution of Kosovo, on whose validity its ruling in a case before it depends, may be inconsistent with the Agreement, it shall stay the proceedings and ask for a ruling by the Special Court.

42. The decisions of the Special Court shall be final and binding and shall be executed by all public authorities on the territory of the Federal Republic of Yugoslavia. The Special Court shall establish its own rules of procedure.

International guarantees

43. In addition to the setting up of the Court, further international guarantees for the implementation of the Agreement seem advisable. It is not up to the Venice Commission to decide to what extent other States may be willing to witness or guarantee the implementation of the Agreement. It would seem obvious that compliance with the Agreement will be a commitment to be entered into by the Federal Republic of Yugoslavia upon admission to the Council of Europe. Compliance with the Agreement should also be a condition set out in future economic treaties between the European Union and the Federal Republic of Yugoslavia.

44. Further possibilities include:

- the witnessing of the Agreement by neighbouring States or the States of the Contact Group, who would pledge to respect and guarantee its terms;
- reference to the Agreement in resolutions of the UN Security Council;
- reference to the Agreement by the OSCE.

2. First [Hill] Draft Agreement for a Settlement of the Crisis in Kosovo, 1 October 1998

1. All citizens in Kosovo have equal rights and duties as set forth in this Agreement in Kosovo, members of each national community have additional rights as set forth below.

2. Nothing in this Agreement shall be interpreted as authority or Federal and Republic organs to intervene in the work of the organs of Kosovo. The areas of competence of the respective organs shall be defined in this Agreement.

3. The organs of Kosovo shall follow principles of full respect for human rights, democracy, and national communities.

4. Citizens in Kosovo shall enjoy, without limitation, human and democratic rights and shall be given the opportunity to be represented in all organs of authority.

5. Every person in Kosovo shall have the right to apply to international institutions, including the European Court of Human Rights, for the

protection of their rights in accordance with the procedures of such institutions.

6. Each side will implement the Agreement in accordance with its procedures including for the Republic of Serbia and the Federal Republic of Yugoslavia their respective legal systems, and international standards, including the Helsinki Final Act.

II. RIGHTS AND DUTIES OF CITIZENS IN KOSOVO

1. Kosovo shall retain its current boundaries.

2. Persons in Kosovo shall concern themselves democratically through legislative, executive, and judicial organs established in this Agreement. The rights and duties of citizens in Kosovo will include the right to democratic-government and to participate in free and fair elections.

3. The basic unit of government will be the communes. All responsibilities not expressly assigned elsewhere by this Agreement will be the responsibility of the communes.

4. The Federal authorities will have responsibility in Kosovo for territorial integrity, maintaining a common market within the Federal Republic of Yugoslavia, monetary policy, defense, foreign policy consistent with the Constitution of the Federal Republic of Yugoslavia, customs services, and other functions specified in the Agreement.

5. The organs of Kosovo shall not interfere in the additional rights described in Part 3 of this Agreement.

III. RIGHTS OF NATIONAL COMMUNITIES

1. Members of the national communities shall have additional rights determined by this Agreement in order to preserve and express their national, cultural, religious, and linguistic identities in accordance with international standards and the Helsinki Final Act.

2. The national communities shall be legally equal and shall not use their additional rights as to endanger the rights of other national communities or the rights of citizens.

3. Each national community shall select through democratic means, in accordance with procedures it shall decide, a National Council to administer the affairs of the community in Kosovo. Each Council will establish its own executive organs and procedures.

4. The national communities shall be subject to decisions of the Assembly of Kosovo, provided that any decisions concerning national communities must be nondiscriminatory. The Assembly shall decide upon a procedure for resolving disputes between national communities.

5. The additional rights of the national communities are to:

(i) preserve and protect their national cultures, including by: using their languages and alphabets. inscribing local names of towns and villages, of squares and streets, and of other topographic names in the language and alphabet of the national community, consistent with decisions about style made by the communal organs. providing information in the language and alphabet of the national community. establishing educational, cultural and religious associations, for which relevant authorities will provide financial assistance. enjoying unhindered contacts with their respective national communities outside of the Federal Republic of Yugoslavia. using and displaying national symbols. providing for education, in particular for schooling in their own language and alphabet and in national culture and history. protecting national practices on family law by, if the community decides, arranging rules in the field of heritage, family, and matrimonial relations; tutorship and adoption. the preservation of sites or religious, historical, or cultural importance. implementing public health and social services. operating religious institutions in cooperation with religious authorities.

(ii) adopt procedures for dispute resolution, as provided in Article V(1)(b) of this Agreement;

(iii) be guaranteed at least one radio and TV frequency, which it shall administer subject to non-discriminatory, technical standards;

(iv) finance activities of the national communities by collecting charges a National Council decides to levy on members of its own community.

6. Members of national communities will also be guaranteed: the right to participate in regional and international non-governmental organizations in accordance with procedures of these organizations; and equal access to employment in public services.

IV. THE ORGANS OF KOSOVO
PART I: GENERAL

1. The organs of Kosovo are the Assembly, the Chairman, the Government, the Administrative Organs, and the Ombudsman.

The Assembly

2. The Assembly.

(a) (i) The Assembly shall comprise ( )Members, of which ( ) Members shall be directly elected in accordance with Article VII(4). (ii) The remaining) Members shall be allocated among the national communities with at least)% of the population, each of which shall elect Members democratically according to its own procedure.

(b) The Assembly shall he responsible for enacting all decisions of Kosovo, including those regulating relations in political, economic, social, and cultural areas consistent with this Agreement. Its areas of responsibility include:

The adoption of the organic documents of Kosovo;

The adoption of regulations on the organization and procedures of the organs of Kosovo;

The adoption of budgets and annual accounts of the Organs of the Government;

Cooperation with Federal and Republic authorities;

Ensuring freedom of movement;

Financing activities of the Organs of the Provisional Government;

Coordination among communes or national communities when necessary, including the enactment of laws or decisions necessary and property for inter-communal issues; and

Confirmation of the members of the Governing Board and judges of the courts.

(c) Decisions of the Assembly shall be taken by majority of those present and voting, except as provided in paragraph(d).

(d) When a majority of the Members of a national community covered by paragraph (a)(ii) assert that a proposed decision affects the vital interests of their national community, that decision shall require for approval a majority that includes the majority of the Members present and voting from the affected national community. If a majority of Members from the asserting community is not present and voting, the regular voting rule shall apply.

(e) A procedure for resolving disputes over the sue of the procedure established in paragraph (d) will be agreed.

(f) A majority of Members present shall constitute a quorum.

(g) The Assembly will decide its own rules of procedure and select its officers. Each national community covered by paragraph (a)(ii) shall be represented in the leadership. The Presidency of the Assembly shall rotate each term of office among those national communities in alphabetical order but may not be from the same national community as the Chairman.

The Chairman

3. There shall be a Chairman, who shall be directly elected.

The Chairman shall be responsible for:

Chairing meetings of the Government-

Representing all persons in Kosovo before any international Federal, or

Republic body, with the President of the Assembly when required by this Agreement.

Meeting regularly with the National Councils and with other representatives of the national communities and other persons.

Conducting foreign relations consistent with the Constitution of the Federal Republic of Yugoslavia.

Signing agreements on behalf of Kosovo after they are approved by the Assembly.

Serving on the Joint Implementation Commission established by this Agreement. Meeting regularly with the president of the Federal Republic of Yugoslavia, the President of Montenegro, and the President of Serbia to discuss issues of mutual concern.

Government

4. Executive power shall be exercised by the Government.

(a) The Government shall comprise ( ) Members, including at less one person from each national community.

(b) The Government shall be responsible for implementing and enforcing decisions of the Assembly and, when devolved to their competences, of other governmental organs.

(c) Decisions of the Government shall require a majority of members present and voting. The Government shall otherwise decide its own rules of procedure.

Ombudsman

6. (a) There shall be an Ombudsman of Kosovo, who shall monitor the implementation of this Agreement, particularly with regard to the rights of the national communities.

(b) The selection, term, and termination of the Ombudsman shall be set forth in the Agreement.

(a) The Ombudsman shall have complete, unimpeded and immediate access to any person, place, or information upon his or her request. He or she shall have the right to intervene before any Federal or other domestic authority upon his or her request.

PART II: THE COMMUNES

1. Kosovo shall have ( ) communes, with boundaries determined by

2. Communes may by mutual agreement form self-administering regions comprising multiple communes.

3. Each commune shall have a Council and such executive bodies as each Council may establish. Each national community with at least ( )% of the population of the commune shall be represented on the Council in proportion to its share of the regional population or by one member, whichever is greater.

4. The communes shall have exclusive responsibility for carrying out typical function of local and regional government, including:

Providing law enforcement, including criminal investigations, prosecution, and punishment.

Regulating and, when appropriate, providing childcare. Establishing and regulating the work of medical institutions and hospitals.

Special arrangements will be made for institutions owned by government entities.

Protecting the environment.

Regulating commerce and privately owned stores.

Regulating hunting and fishing.

Planning and carrying out public works of communal or Kosovo-wide territorial importance, including roads and water supplies.

Regulating land use, town planning, building regulations and housing construction.

Designing and implementing programs of economic, scientific, technological, demographic, regional and social development, and programs for the development of agriculture and of rural areas.

Developing programs for tourism, the hotel industry, catering, and sport.

Organizing fairs and local markets.

Organizing public services of communal importance, including fire, emergency response, and police.

Financing the work of communal organs, including raising revenues, taxes, and preparing budgets.

4. Each commune shall conduct its business in public and shall maintain publicly available records of its deliberations and decisions.

Part 3. Representation of Kosovo in Federal and Republic Bodies.

(a) The participation of Kosovo in Federal institutions shall be discussed, in particular to obtain appropriate representation in Federal organs responsible for developing and implementing defense and economic policies and to take into account developments in Yugoslavia since 1991.

(b) The following is without prejudice to the rights of persons in Kosovo to decide whether to accept the offer and to the review described in section VIII(3):

Kosovo shall be offered at least (ten) deputies in the House of Citizens of the Federal Assembly and (twenty) deputies in the National Assembly of the Republic of Serbia.

Each national community in Kosovo shall be offered at least one place in the Federal Government and in the Government of the Republic of Serbia.

Each national community in Kosovo shall be offered at least one judge on the Federal Court of the Federal Republic and three judges on the Supreme Court of Serbia.

(c) In order to monitor the protection of additional rights of the national communities, a Council for the protection of members of the national communities shall be established.

V. RESOLVING CONFLICTS AND MAINTAINING PUBLIC ORDER

(1) Dispute Resolution.

(a) Courts in Kosovo.

The Assembly shall establish common and supreme courts for Kosovo with jurisdiction over constitutional, civil, and criminal matters. Appeals from these courts?

(b) National Communities

Each community may establish procedures for resolving conflicts concerning inheritance, family law, matrimonial relations, tutorship, adoption, civil lawsuits as decided by the Assembly of Kosovo, and criminal cases for which imprisonment of up to one year is prescribed in the currently applicable penal code. These procedures must ensure that practices are consistent with internationally recognized human rights. They shall have jurisdiction only when all parties to a dispute agree.

Decisions of the national community dispute resolution mechanism shall be honored by other courts in Kosovo and the Federal Republic of Yugoslavia in accordance with applicable rules.

(2) Police.

(a) Police shall be sworn to uphold the law impartially, fairly, and with equal treatment for all persons.

(b) All police operating in Kosovo must be trained to internationally accepted standards for police operations, in particular with regard to human rights.

PARAGRAPHS(c)AND(d) TO BE DEVELOPED FURTHER

(c) Each commune shall establish local police, which shall have membership representative of the commune. Police (such as customs police) from other governmental levels shall recruit members of national communities so that the composition of such police forces in Kosovo will be representative of the population there.

(d) The local police shall he exclusively responsible for maintaining public order and peace. Federal and Republic police shall not carry out this responsibility. Federal and Republic authorities, in accordance with their respective responsibilities, shall retain responsibility for external security, border police, and the investigation of international and extra-Kosovo crime.

(e) Each commune shall establish commission to review and make recommendations on all matters concerning the police, including in particular complaints about violations of human rights. Every national community in the commune will have the right to participate on the commission. These commissions shall have the complete cooperation of both sides and unimpeded access to any person, place, document, and information it requests.

VI. FINANCING

1. The bodies established in Sections II-IV shall have the right to keep all revenues from their own taxes or other charges. They shall also have a part of revenue otherwise derived in Kosovo (including duties or fees). The organs of Kosovo shall participate in the collection of customs and other duties within Kosovo according to procedures to be agreed.

2. In recognition of the fact that this Agreement confers new responsibilities upon bodies in Kosovo, Republic and the Federal authorities shall examine how to provide resources necessary for the conduct of its responsibilities. These resources shall include funds (including tax remission), equipment, and training.

3. Federal and Republic authorities shall also facilitate, to the extent of their respective authorities, the delivery of resources from international sources to Kosovo.

VII IMPLEMENTATION PERIOD

1. This Agreement shall be implemented as quickly as possible. The signatories of this Agreement take the obligation to allow, insofar as

possible, it's adequate implementation even before the adoption and undertaking of all acts and measures fixed in the Agreement.

2. The sides will start without delay an any and all legal changes, necessary for the full implementation of this Agreement. They acknowledge that complete implementation will require the adoption of necessary state regulations and other general acts of the organic document of Kosovo, political acts and measures, and the elections of establishment of institutions and bodies established by this Agreement.

3. Each national community in Kosovo is authorized to start exercising the additional rights determined by this Agreement, to the extent possible, immediately upon signature.

4. Within ( ) months, there will be elections for all bodies established by this Agreement. The Government of the FRY hereby invites the Organization for Security and Cooperation in Rome (OSCE) to conduct those elections.

5. Under international supervision, an objective and free census of the population in Kosovo shall be carried out when the international supervisor determines that conditions allow an accurate census.

6. All relevant governmental institutions shall provide the organs of Kosovo with all necessary records about the places of residence, citizenship, voters' lists, and other data.

7. The signatories of this Agreement shall provide active support, cooperation, and participation for the successful implementation of the Agreement.

8. Laws and institutions currently in place in Kosovo shall remain until replaced by a decision of a competent body established by this Agreement.

VIII AMENDMENTS

1. Amendments to the Agreement shall be adopted by signature of the parties.

2. Each signatory may propose amendments at any time and will consider and consult with the other with regard to proposed amendments.

3. In three years, the sides will undertake a comprehensive assessment of the Agreement, with the aim of improving its implementation and considering proposals by either side for additional steps, which will require mutual agreement for adoption.

IX FINAL PROVISIONS

1. This Agreement is concluded in the ( ) languages.

2. This Agreement shall enter into force upon the completion of the internal process of each side.

FOR

Federal Republic of Yugoslavia
Republic of Serbia

Kosovo

3. Draft Law Enforcement and Security Annex, 1 October 1998

I. GENERAL PRINCIPLES

1. The Parties agree to cooperate on law enforcement matters of mutual interest consistent with the procedures outlined below.

2. All Kosovo, Republic and Federal law enforcement and military authorities shall be obligated, in their respective areas of authority, to ensure freedom of Movement and safe passage for all persons, vehicles and goods.

3. In exercising authorities under this annex, all law enforcement and military components shall observe internationally recognized standards of human rights, due-process and fundamental fairness.

4. Police forces at the communal and municipal levels under the supervision of civilian authorities will have primary responsibility for maintaining public order and security in Kosovo.

5. All law enforcement bodies operating in Kosovo will be representative of the population.

6. An international civilian police mission will be undertaken in the territory of Kosovo to monitor the enforcement of this agreement and guide the implementation of the agreement. The Parties agree to cooperate fully with the international civilian police mission.

II. THE MINISTRY OF INTERIOR

A. Leadership
The Ministry of Interior will be headed by a Minister of Interior and a Deputy Minister of Interior. In every possible circumstance, decisions will be taken jointly by the Minister of Interior and the Deputy Minister of Interior. At a minimum, the Minister will inform, and consult with, the Deputy Minister on all significant matters.

Minister of Interior.
The Minister will be of Kosovar Albanian ethnicity.

2. Deputy Minister of Interior.
The Deputy Minister will be of Serb ethnicity and will be a permanent resident of Kosovo. He or she will be appointed and removed by the Kosovo authorities in consultation with the Kosovo Security Commission. The Deputy Minister will serve as the deputy principal officer for law enforcement and the administration of justice in Kosovo and will support the Minister in the management of all law enforcement personnel reporting to the Ministry.

1. Chief of Staff for Communal Police Issues:
The Chief of Staff, and his or her deputy, will coordinate police issues and provide guidance to communal commanders.

The Chief of Staff will be of Kosovar Albanian ethnicity, appointed by the Minister of Interior, with concurrence of the Deputy Minister of Interior, following consultations with the Kosovo Security Commission. He or she will report to the Minister and Deputy Minister of Interior.

3. Deputy Chief of Staff for Communal Police Issues:
The Deputy will assist the Chief of Staff in all functions.

The Deputy Chief of Staff will be of Serb ethnicity, appointed by the Minister of Interior, with concurrence of the Deputy Minister of the Interior, following consultations with the Kosovo Security Commission. He or she will report to the Minister and Deputy Minister of Interior.

B. Structure.
A Ministry of Interior building will be established in Pristina. All headquarters offices of the Ministry of Interior will be located within this building.

C. Authorities
The Ministry of Interior will have responsibility for all law enforcement matters in Kosovo.

Consistent with international standards of democratic policing and human rights and the rule of law and subject to the exceptions noted in this Annex, the Ministry will have the authority to: initiate and implement, through its law enforcement bodies, the full range of law enforcement operations; order the arrest and/or detention of individuals for suspected criminal activity; establish administrative and personnel procedures necessary to carry out its tasks; and employ and remove personnel.

D. Financing
The Ministry of Interior, including salaries for all personnel serving directly in the Ministry or in its component law enforcement bodies, will be financed by Kosovo.

III. LAW ENFORCEMENT STRUCTURES

The following law enforcement structures, all reporting to the Ministry of Interior, shall be established to provide for civilian security within Kosovo:

A. Kosovo Communal Police Units
1. Duties and Functions- There shall be established communal police units in Kosovo, organized and stationed at the communal and municipal levels, which will have primary responsibility for the protection of life and property in Kosovo.

The specific responsibilities of the communal police will include:

  a. Police patrols and crime prevention
  b. Criminal investigations
  c. Arrest and detention of criminal suspects
  d. Crowd control
  e. Traffic control

2. Structure and Composition
    a. Size. The total number of communal police operating within Kosovo shall not exceed 2,500 active duty law enforcement officers (exclusive of administrative officers).
    b. Civilian Staff. Communal police units will be coordinated by a civilian staff located at the Ministry of Interior.
3. Communal/Municipal Level: Communal police operations will be undertaken by personnel assigned at the communal level and, within communes, at the municipal station level. Force size for each commune will be determined on the basis of the size and population of the commune. The ethnic balance of a communal police unit will be representative of the ethnic balance of the commune in which it operates.
    a. Personnel:
        i) Communal Commander; Each commune will have a police commander to manage day-to-day operations and personnel issues within the commune. The commander will be appointed on the recommendation of the commune government (following consultation with the Communal Security Commission) by the MOI Chief of Staff, with the concurrence of the Deputy Chief of Staff. The Chief of Staff must appoint the communal government's nominee absent a showing of good cause for not doing so. The Chief of Staff will have authority to remove communal commanders.
        ii) Deputy Communal Commander: Each commune will have a deputy police commander to assist the communal commander in all his/her duties. The deputy commander will be appointed by the Chief of Staff, with the concurrence of the Deputy Chief of Staff, on the recommendation of the commune government (following consultation with the Communal Security Commission). The Chief of Staff must appoint the communal government's nominee absent a showing of good cause for not doing so. The Chief of Staff will have authority to remove the deputy communal commander. The deputy communal commander must be a member of the largest minority ethnic group where that ethnic group comprises at least 10% of the commune's population.
        iii) Municipal Station Chiefs: The communal commander, with the concurrence of the deputy commander and in consultation with the Communal Security Commission, will appoint, and have removal authority over, municipal station chiefs who will oversee operations at each municipal police station. The municipal station chiefs will report directly to the communal commander and his/her deputy.
    b. Municipal Stations: The communal government, with the concurrence of the communal police commander, shall establish such municipal police stations in the commune as it deems necessary to prevent, detect and investigate criminal activity and maintain public order. These stations will be manned by communal police assigned to the commune.
4. Salaries: Salaries for all police personnel, regardless of where they are assigned, will be paid by the Kosovo Ministry of Interior.
5. Recruitment Communal police recruitment will be conducted primarily at the communal level. Each commune government, in consultation with the communal security commission and the communal police commander and deputy commander will nominate officer candidates. Appointments to the academy basic recruit course will be made by the academy director and deputy director, with the concurrence of the MOI Chief of Staff and Deputy Chief of Staff. While participating in the basic recruit course, police candidates will receive meals, lodging and a modest stipend from the Ministry of Interior. Offers of employment will be made by the Chief of Staff, with the concurrence of the academy director and deputy director, only after the candidate has successfully completed the academy basic recruit course. New police officers will be assigned by the Ministry of Interior to the commune from which they were nominated. For as long as the international civilian police mission is present, recruitment, selection and training will be provided by and/or in cooperation with the international civilian police mission with the assistance of international bilateral donors.

6. Equipment
All police officers, with the exception of crowd control units, will wear a standard solid dark blue uniform, the precise design of which will be developed by the Ministry of Interior and agreed to by the Minister and Deputy Minister of interior. Such uniform will include a badge, picture identification, and nametag. Aside from insignias noting officer rank, the only patches or insignias which may be worn on the uniform are a "Communal Police" patch, and a patch which notes the name of the officer's assigned commune. If an officer is assigned to a specialized unit such as a crowd control or traffic control unit, the name of the unit also may be noted on the uniform. Police officers will be equipped with a sidearm, handcuffs and a baton. Each commune may keep, either at the communal headquarters or at municipal stations, no more than 20 long-barreled weapons without special permission from the Chief or Deputy Chief of Staff (and international civilian police mission as long as it is present). Long-barreled weapons may be carried or used only with the permission of the communal police commander (and the international civilian police mission for as long as it is present). When not in use, all weapons will be securely stored and each commune will keep a registry of all weapons assigned to it. Crowd control units will receive equipment appropriate to their task, including batons, helmets and shields.
7. Use of Force
Police personnel are authorized to use force in performance of lawful duties. The force used must be the minimum force that is reasonable and necessary under the circumstances. Allegations of inappropriate use of force will be investigated by the Ministry of Interior's Internal Affairs Unit. The penalty for inappropriate use of force will be proportional to the seriousness of the offense and may include dismissal, criminal charges or civil penalties.
B. The VIP Protection Unit
1. Duties and Functions. This unit will provide personal protection for senior government officials and visiting dignitaries.
2. Structure and composition
    a. Chief of the VIP Protection Unit. The chief of the unit will be a Kosovar Albanian appointed and removed by the Minister of Interior with the concurrence of the Deputy Minister of Interior. He or she will manage all aspects of the unit, from operations to administrative matters, reporting to the Minister and Deputy Minister of Interior.
    b. Deputy Chief of the VIP Protection Unit. The deputy chief of the unit will be of Serb ethnicity appointed and removed by the Minister of Interior with the concurrence of the Deputy Minister of Interior.
    c. Within the Unit, there will be separate divisions for government protective security and foreign dignitary security. Within the government protective security division, the governmental officials involved may chose the ethnicity of the officers charged with their protection.
3. Recruitment
Individuals may apply to the Chief of the VIP Protection Unit for employment in the protective service. The Unit will develop a common form that all candidates must complete. Selection of candidates for training will be made jointly by the Chief and Deputy Chief of the Unit, with the concurrence of the Minister of Interior. Formal job offers will be made by the Chief of the Unit, with the concurrence of the Deputy Chief and the Academy Director only after candidates have successfully completed a course of intensive training at the Kosovo law enforcement academy (or, until that academy is operational, they have successfully completed a course of training provided by bilateral donors in cooperation with the international civilian police mission). Officers will be dismissed by the Chief of the Unit, with the concurrence of the Deputy Chief. The names of all personnel serving within the VIP Protection Unit will be provided to the Kosovo Security Commission.
4. Use of Force
Officers of the unit are authorized to use force in performance of lawful duties. The force used must be the minimum force that is reasonable and necessary under the circumstances. Allegations of inappropriate use of force will be investigated by the Ministry of interior's Internal

Affairs Unit. The penalty for inappropriate use of force will be proportional to the seriousness of the offense and may include dismissal, criminal charges or civil penalties.

C. The Internal Affairs Unit

1. Duties and Functions

The Internal Affairs Unit will undertake, sua sponte or at the request of the Minister or Deputy Minister of Interior, a communal police force chief, or the Security Commissions., investigations into allegedly inappropriate, wrongful, and/or possibly unlawful conduct by law enforcement personnel employed by the Ministry of Interior. Such conduct could include, but is not limited to, inappropriate use of a firearm, violation of a suspect's human rights, or involvement in organized crime or police corruption. The Unit will operate independently and on a confidential basis, including undercover, while its investigations are ongoing. However, it will prepare a report of findings and the conclusion or dismissal of each investigation for the Minister and Deputy Minister of Interior. These reports will be made available on a timely basis to the relevant communal police force chief and to the Kosovo Security Commission unless the Internal Affairs Unit can show good cause for not doing so. The reports also will become part of an officer's permanent personnel file and will be considered in promotion decisions and future assignments. The Unit may be armed with sidearms and will have arrest authority.

2. Structure and Composition

a. Chief of the Internal Affairs Unit. The Chief of the unit will be a Kosovar Albanian appointed and removed by the Minister of Interior with the concurrence of the Deputy Minister of Interior. He or she will manage all aspects of the unit, from investigations to administrative matters, reporting to the Minister and Deputy Minister of Interior.

b. Deputy Chief of the Internal Affairs Unit. The deputy chief of the unit will be of Serb ethnicity appointed and removed by the Minister of Interior with the concurrence of the Deputy Minister of Interior.

c. The Unit will be based in Pristina in a building near the Ministry of Interior. The unit will establish such communal offices as it deems necessary on a permanent or temporary basis to successfully carry out its tasks. All levels and branches of the Ministry of Interior law enforcement bodies will cooperate fully with Internal Affairs Unit investigations. d. The ethnic makeup of the Unit will be representative of Kosovo as a whole.

3. Recruitment

The members of the Internal Affairs unit will be selected through the basic police application process by the Chief of the Internal Affairs unit, on the recommendation of the police academy director and deputy director.

4. Use of Force

Officers of the unit are authorized to use force in performance of lawful duties. The force used must be the minimum force that is reasonable and necessary under the circumstances. Allegations of inappropriate use of force will be investigated by the Ministry of Interior's Internal Affairs Unit. The penalty for inappropriate use of force will be proportional to the seriousness of the offense and may include dismissal, criminal charges or civil penalties.

D. Interim Police Academy

1. Functions

Under the supervision of the international community, an interim Police Academy will offer mandatory and professional development training for all personnel serving in law enforcement functions under the Ministry of Interior. Such training will include:

-- a basic recruit program
-- advanced investigative and forensic skills
-- crowd control
-- traffic control
-- VIP protection

Priority will be given to establishing the basic recruit program. The Academy will play a role in the selection and advancement of law enforcement personnel, providing recommendations and evaluations based on individuals' performance in academy programs . The Academy will provide certificates upon completion of training programs and will maintain adequate training records.

2. Structure and Administration

a. Academy Director. The director will be a Kosovar Albanian appointed and removed by the Minister of Interior with the concurrence of the Deputy Minister of Interior and in consultation with the Kosovo Security Commission. He or she will manage all aspects of the academy, from student selection to program development, approval and evaluation. The director will report to the Minister and Deputy Minister of Interior.

b. Academy Deputy Director. The deputy director will be of Serb ethnicity appointed and removed by the Minister of Interior with the concurrence of the Deputy Minister of Interior, and in consultation with the Kosovo Security Commission.

c. All costs relating to the functioning of the academy, including facility maintenance, travel, costs and salaries for instructors and academy administrative personnel, will be paid by the Ministry of Interior.

3. Facilities

The Academy will provide lodging, meals, classrooms and appropriate training facilities, including a firing range.

4. Faculty

The staff of the Academy will he selected and removed with the concurrence of the Academy Director and Deputy Director and will be representative of the ethnic balance of Kosovo.

5. Basic Program of Study

Once the police academy becomes operational, all police candidates will be required to successfully complete a course of police studies which include principles and methods of democratic policing. Candidates who do not satisfactorily complete the course will not be permitted to join the police force.

IV. SECURITY COMMISSIONS

V. The parties shall a establish a Kosovo Security Commission with competence throughout Kosovo, and Communal Security Commissions within each commune. The Commissions shall address and attempt to resolve problems concerning law enforcement and security in Kosovo.

1. Functions of the Commissions.

a. Review, and make recommendations regarding the recruitment, selection and training of police officers.

b. Review, and make recommendations regarding communal police and other law enforcement issues.

c. Consider complaints regarding police practices filed by individuals or national communities.

d. In the Kosovo Security Commission only: In consultation with designated local and Federal police liaisons, supervise jurisdiction sharing in cases of concurrent jurisdiction between Kosovo and Federal authorities.

2. The membership of the Kosovo Security Commission and each Communal Security Commission shall be representative of the population and shall include:

a. In the Kosovo Security Commission
    i.   a representative of each commune
    ii. a representative of the Federal Special Investigations unit
    iii. a representative of the border police
    iv. a representative of each national community
    v.   a representative of the Ministry of Interior
    vi. a representative of the ICPM, during its period of operation in Kosovo.

b. In the Communal Security Commissions:
    i.   a representative of the communal police
    ii. a representative of the Federal Special Investigations Unit, if the unit maintains an office in the commune.
    iii. a representative of the border police, if border police are present in the commune.
    iv. a representative of each national community
    v.   civilian representative of the communal government
    vi. a representative of the ICPM, during its period of operation in Kosovo.

3. Each Security Commission shall meet at least monthly.

V. COORDINATION AND COOPERATION ON MUTUAL SECURITY MATTERS

A. Joint Coordination Committee

A Joint Coordination Committee (JCC) will be established to provide a forum for coordinating and cooperating on mutual security matters. The JCC will be an advisory body with 3-5 representatives each from the FRY, Serbia, Montenegro, Kosovo, and the ICPM during its period of operation in Kosovo. The Kosovo and Montenegro Interior Ministries will select their own representatives. The JCC will meet not less than monthly and ad hoc sessions will be called within 48 hours at the request of any member. Hosting responsibilities for JCC meetings will alternate among the members.

B. TECHNICAL ASSISTANCE

Communal police forces and the Kosovo Border Police may request technical assistance from Federal and Republic authorities in cases requiring forensic assistance and other forms of specialized expertise.

VI. FEDERAL AND REPUBLIC POLICE OPERATIONS IN KOSOVO

A. Except as specifically permitted in this Agreement, it shall be the exclusive responsibility of communal police forces to patrol the territory of Kosovo and investigate crimes. Republic and FRY law enforcement personnel will not patrol, investigate, or otherwise operate individually or collectively within the territory of Kosovo without the express consent, or at the express request, of the Kosovo Minister of Interior. The consent to or request for such operations will specify any restrictions on the movements and the authorities of the Federal or Republic law enforcement personnel permitted in Kosovo.

B. Federal Special Investigative Unit

1. Federal law enforcement authorities may establish a Federal Special Investigative Unit (FSIU) in Kosovo staffed with Federal police officers to investigate the following crimes with potential Federal and cross-border consequences.

The sale and distribution of significant quantities of narcotics.
Kidnappings that may involve the transport of victims across the Kosovo border
Smuggling
Counterfeiting Money
Forgery of Federal Government Documents
Espionage
Murder or Aggravated Assault of Republic or Federal authorities
Destruction of Republic or Federal property
Fraud or Embezzlement or Acceptance of Bribes, committed by Federal or Kosovo authorities in the course of performing

4. Revised Hill Proposal, 1 November 1998

I. INTRODUCTION

1. All citizens in Kosovo have equal rights and duties as set forth in this Agreement and the international agreements specified in Annex 1. In Kosovo, members of each national community have additional rights as set forth below.
2. The authorities of Kosovo, acting in accordance with this Agreement, are autonomous. The Parties accept and will abide by the principle that their powers and authorities in Kosovo are as specified by this Agreement, which shall prevail over contradictory legal authority of any Party. The Parties shall take all necessary legal steps within their respective systems to carry out this Agreement.
3. The authorities of Kosovo shall follow principles of full respect for human rights, democracy, and national communities.
4. Citizens in Kosovo shall enjoy, without limitation, human and democratic rights and shall be given the opportunity to be represented in all institutions of authority.
5. Every person in Kosovo shall have the right to apply to international institutions [, including the European Court of Human Rights,] for the protection of their rights in accordance with the procedure of such institutions.
6. Each side will implement the Agreement in accordance with its procedures and international standards, including the Helsinki Final Act.

II. GOVERNANCE IN KOSOVO; PART I: GENERAL

1. Citizens in Kosovo shall govern themselves democratically through legislative, executive, judicial, and other institutions established in this Agreement. The rights and duties of citizens in Kosovo will include the right to democratic self-government and to participate in free and fair elections.
2. The basic [territorial] unit of [local] government will be the communes. All responsibilities not expressly assigned elsewhere by this Agreement will be the responsibility of the communes.

[Option 1: 3. The authorities of Kosovo shall have responsibility for all areas except the following, which shall be within the competence of the Federal Republic save as specified in paragraph four: (a) territorial integrity, (b) maintaining a common market within the Federal Republic of Yugoslavia, which power shall be exercised in a manner that does not discriminate against any particular region or area of the Federal Republic, (c) monetary policy, (d) defense, (e) foreign policy consistent with the Constitution of the Federal Republic of Yugoslavia, (f) customs services [, and (g) other functions specified in the Constitution of the Federal Republic of Yugoslavia].* Citizens in Kosovo shall continue to participate in areas reserved for the Federal Republic through their representation in Federal institutions.
4. Kosovo shall retain the following powers in the areas otherwise reserved for the Federal Republic:
(a) No change to the borders of Kosovo shall
be made without the consent of the Kosovo   Assembly and [President] [Presidency];
(b) No armed attacks shall be launched from the territory of Kosovo without the prior consent of the [President] [Presidency] of Kosovo. Deployment and use of force in Kosovo shall be governed by Annex 2 of this Agreement;
(c)Kosovo officers and institutions shall have the authority to conduct foreign relations [in cultural, economic, and other fields] consistent with the present Constitution of the Federal Republic of Yugoslavia ;
(d) Citizens in Kosovo serving as Federal customs officers shall play a role in carrying out customs activities in Kosovo. Customs officers shall be representative of the national communities of Kosovo.]

[Option 2 :
3. The authorities of Kosovo will not have responsibility in Kosovo for the following areas: (a) territorial integrity, (b) maintaining a common market within the Federal Republic of Yugoslavia, (c) monetary policy, (d) defense, (e) foreign policy except as consistent with the Constitution of the Federal Republic of Yugoslavia, (f) customs services [, and (g) other functions specified in the Constitution of the Federal Republic of Yugoslavia].** It is understood that Federal authorities will carry out these responsibilities. Citizens in Kosovo shall continue to participate in areas reserved for the Federal Republic through their representation in Federal institutions.]

The authorities of Kosovo shall not interfere in the additional rights described in Part V of this Agreement.

* Note: A proposal may be made to expand the list of Federal responsibilities
** Note : See supra Note

PART   II :   ASSEMBLY,   [PRESIDENT] [PRESIDENCY], COUNCIL OF MINISTERS, AND ADMINISTRATIVE BODIES
The Assembly
1. There shall be an Assembly, which shall
comprise [ ] Members.
(a) [   ] Members shall be directly elected in accordance with Article X (4) and Annex 4.
(b) The remaining [   ] Members shall be
allocated [equally] [by the formula set forth in Annex 5] among the national communities with at least [   ] % of the population of Kosovo, each of which shall elect Members democratically according to its own procedure. Each national community

recognized under the principle set forth in Annex 5 shall have at least one Member in the Assembly.

2. The Assembly shall be responsible for enacting [Decisions] [laws] of Kosovo, including those regulating relations in political, economic, social, and cultural areas consistent with this Agreement. Ist areas of responsibility shall include:

- The adoption of the [Basic Law] [Constitution] of Kosovo consistent with this Agreement, which shall not be subject to change or modification by authorities of the Republics or the Federal Republic of Yugoslavia ;
- The adoption of regulations concerning the organization, procedures, and functioning of the administrative bodies of Kosovo;
- The adoption of budgets and annual accounts of the Administrative bodies and other institutions of Kosovo, with the exception of communal and national community institutions unless otherwise specified by this Agreement;
- Cooperation with Federal Assemblies, and with the Assemblies of the Republics;
- Ensuring freedom of movement of goods, services, and persons inside Kosovo and between Kosovo and other parts of the Federal Republic of Yugoslavia, consistent with Federal responsibilities;
- Financing activities of Kosovo institutions, including by levying taxes or other charges;
- Conduct of relations with foreign entities consistent with this Agreement and the [Basic Law] [Constitution] of Kosovo;
- Coordination among communes or national communities when necessary, including the enactment of [Decisions] [laws] concerning inter-communal issues;
- Designing programs for regional development;
- Protection of the environment where inter-communal issues are involved; and
- Confirmation of the Ministers and Justices of the Supreme Court and the Constitutional Court.

3. [Decisions] [Laws] of the Assembly shall be taken by majority of those present and voting, except as provided in paragraph 4.

4. When a majority of the Members of a national community selected pursuant to paragraph 1(b) assert that a proposed decision affects the vital interests of their national community, that decision shall require for approval, in addition to the majority specified in paragraph 3, a majority of the Members present and voting from that national community. If a majority of Members from the asserting community is not present and voting, the regular voting rule shall apply. Any other national community wishing to assert that the same proposed decision also affects its vital interests must make ist claim within two days after the privilege is first asserted. After that two day period has elapsed, no national community may assert the privilege set forth in this paragraph with respect to the same proposed decision.

5. The following procedure shall be used to resolve disputes regarding the exercise of the national community privilege set forth in paragraph 4:

(a) The national community or communities asserting the privilege will give reasons to the Assembly explaining its concerns. Members of the Assembly supporting the proposed decision will given an opportunity to respond. The [President] [Presidency] of Kosovo shall mediate the dispute and attempt to reach a settlement agreeable to all affected national communities.

[Option 1:

(b) If mediation does not produce a mutually agreeable result within seven days, there shall be a vote of the Assembly. The proposed decision shall take effect if it receives the support of [4/5] of the Members of the whole Assembly.

[Option 2:

(b) If mediation does not produce a mutually agreeable result within seven days, the matter will be given to the Constitutional Court for decision. The Court shall determine whether as a matter of law the vital national interests of national community or communities asserting the privilege set forth in paragraph 4 are

[affected] [substantially harmed] by the proposed decision. The Court shall hear argument and rule within ten days.

(c) The decision of the Court may be appealed to the [President of the European Court of Human Rights] [Special Court provided for in this Agreement].]

6. A majority of Members shall constitute a quorum. The Assembly will decide its own rules of procedure. Members of Assembly shall be immune from civil or criminal proceedings on the basis of opinions expressed or votes cast in the Assembly.

7. The Assembly shall elect from among its Members a President, two Vice-Presidents, and other leaders as it deems proper. Each national community covered by paragraph 1(b) shall be represented in the leadership.

(a) The President of the Assembly shall represent the Assembly, call its sessions to order, chair ist meetings, coordinate the work of any Committees it may establish, and perform other tasks prescribed by the rules of procedure of the Assembly.

[Option 1:

8. The President of the Assembly may not be from the same national community as the [President] [Chair of the Presidency] of Kosovo.]

[Option 2 :

No text.]

[President] [Presidency] of Kosovo

[Option 1:

9. There shall be a President of Kosovo.

(a) The President shall be selected for a [three] year term. No person may serve more than two terms as President. The President shall be elected directly by the people of Kosovo.]

[Option 2:

9. There shall be a President of Kosovo.

(a) The President shall be elected for a [three] year term. No person may serve more than two terms as President. The President shall be elected [by vote of the Assembly.] [by majority vote of the communal governments. Each commune shall receive one vote, and shall cast that vote as it decides by a majority vote of the communal assembly.]

[Option 3:

9. Kosovo shall have a collective Presidency, which shall consist of one Serbian of Kosovo, one Albanian of Kosovo [, and others].

(a) Each member of the Presidency shall be elected for a [three] year term. No person may serve more than two terms as a member of the presidency. Candidates for the Presidency shall run for office together on interethnic slates. A slate shall be selected for the Presidency directly by the people of Kosovo.

(i) There shall be a Chair of the Presidency, who shall be selected from among the members of the Presidency by majority vote of the Assembly.

(ii) The Presidency shall decide its own rules of procedure. It shall endeavour to act by consensus. Subject to the privilege set forth in section (a) (iii) of this paragraph, decisions may be taken [by the Chair] [by majority vote] where all efforts to achieve consensus have failed.

(iii) Within four days of the adoption of a Decision of the Presidency, a Member of the Presidency may assert that the Decision affects a vital interest of his or her national community. The issue shall be promptly referred to [the National Council of] his or her national community. If the national community affirms within ten days by a decision taken under its own democratic procedures that its vital interests are affected, the Decision shall be rescinded.* [Dissenting Members of the Presidency may petition the Constitutional Court to have a

(iv) Decision reinstated. The Court shall decide within ten days whether the vital interests of the national community are [substantially] affected as a matter of law.] [The decision of the Constitutional Court may be further appealed by either party to the Special Court, which shall rule within ten days.]]

(b) The [President] [Presidency] shall be responsible for:

- Representing all citizens in Kosovo before any international or Federal body, or any body of the Republics.

• Proposing to the Assembly candidates for Prime Minister and Justices of the Supreme Court and the Constitutional Court.

• Meeting regularly with [the National Councils and with other] democratically selected representatives of the national communities and other persons.

• Conducting foreign relations consistent with the Constitution of the Federal Republic of Yugoslavia.

• Concluding agreements on behalf of Kosovo, consistent with the Constitution of the Federal Republic of Yugoslavia, after they are approved by the Assembly.

• Serving or designating a representative to serve on the Joint Commission and Joint Council established by Article VIII of this Agreement.

[* Note: The privilege to block a Decision of the Presidency as affecting a vital interest could be limited to certain categories of important Decisions. This will be a subject for further discussion.]

• Meeting regularly with the President of the Federal Republic of Yugoslavia, the President of Montenegro, and the President of Serbia.

Council of Ministers

10. Executive power shall be exercised by the Council of Ministers.

(a) The Council of Ministers shall consist of a Prime Minister and [   ] Ministers, including at least one person from each national community.

(b) The candidate for Prime Minister shall put forward a list of Ministers to the Assembly. The Prime Minister and his or her proposed Ministers shall be approved by a majority of those Members present and voting in the Assembly. In the event that the Prime Minister is not able to obtain a majority for the Council of Ministers, the [President] [Presidency] shall propose a new candidate for Prime Minister within ten days.

(c) The Council of Ministers shall be responsible for implementing and enforcing [Decisions] [laws] of the Assembly and actions of other government authorities when such responsibilities are devolved by those authorities. Ministers of the Council shall head the Administrative Bodies of Kosovo, and shall also have independent authority to propose [laws] [Decisions] to the Assembly.

(d) The Prime Minister shall call meetings of the Council of Ministers, represent the Council of Ministers in appropriate settings, and organize its work. Decisions of the Council shall require a majority of Members present and voting. The Prime Minister shall cast the deciding vote if the Ministers are equally divided. The Council shall otherwise decide its own rules of procedure.

Administrative Bodies

11. Administrative Bodies shall be responsible for implementing [Decisions] [laws] of Kosovo and, where devolved to them, of other authorities.

(a) Employees of administrative bodies shall be fairly representative of the population of Kosovo.

(b) Any citizen of Kosovo claiming to have been aggrieved by the decision of an administrative body shall have the right to judicial review of that decision. The Assembly shall enact administrative law to regulate this review.

(c) An administrative body of Kosovo shall have responsibility for all enforcement matters in Kosovo, in accordance with Annex 2 to this Agreement.

PART III : COURTS IN KOSOVO

General

1. Kosovo and ist Communes shall establish courts for Kosovo. There shall be a Constitutional Court, a Supreme Court, and Communal Courts. [There shall also be a special Court for purposes of monitoring the implementation of this Agreement.] Justices and judges of the Kosovo courts shall not be held criminally or civilly liable for any acts carried out within the scope of their duties.

2. The courts of Kosovo shall have jurisdiction over all legal matters arising under the [Basic Law] [Constitution] of Kosovo and [Decisions] [laws] of the Assembly, and international law to be applied in Kosovo including, but not limited to, matters relating to the application and interpretation of the international human rights agreements listed in Annex 1.

3. The courts of Kosovo shall also have jurisdiction as specified in this paragraph over matters arising under federal law or raising questions of federal law.

(a) Kosovo courts shall adjudicate all civil cases in Kosovo arising under Federal law or raising federal law questions in the first instance. Unless otherwise specified in this Agreement, Kosovo courts shall also adjudicate criminal cases in Kosovo arising under federal law. Disputes presenting federal questions may be appealed to the Federal courts after all appeals available under the Kosovo system have been exhausted. Kosovo courts shall be the final authority as to the meaning of Kosovo legal authorities.

[Option 1:

(b) Those federal criminal matters specified in [   ]* shall be adjudicated entirely by the courts of the Federal Republic of Yugoslavia. Appropriate Federal courts of first instance shall be established in Kosovo for this purpose. The courts of the Federal Republic shall conduct these proceedings in a manner fully in keeping with all international human rights standards.]

[Option 2:

(b) Those federal criminal matters specified in [   ] ** shall be adjudicated in the first instance by the courts of the Republic of Serbia, with appeal to the Federal courts. The Courts of the Republic of Serbia and the Federal Republic shall conduct these proceedings in a manner fully in keeping with all international human rights standards.]

[* This section of the Agreement will set forth a list of serious crimes with cross border implications, such as counterfeiting of money and narcotics trafficking. The list will be a subject for negotiation between the parties.

** Id.]

Constitutional Court and Supreme Court

4. **Composition.** The Constitutional Court shall consist of [five] Justices. The supreme Court shall consist of [nine] Judges.

(a) The Justices and Judges shall be distinguished jurists of the highest moral character. The two tribunals shall be broadly representative of the national communities of Kosovo. [Each national community representing at least [   ] % of the population of Kosovo shall have at least one Justice and one Judge on each of the two tribunals.] [Another procedure to allocate seats.]

(b) The Justices and Judges shall each be selected for a term of five years, and may not be reappointed. They shall be required to retire at age 70, and may resign at any time. Justices and Judges may otherwise be removed only for cause. Removal for cause shall require the consensus of the other Justices or Judges of the tribunal.

5. Jurisdiction of the Constitutional Court

The Constitutional Court shall have sole authority to resolve disputes relating to the [Basic Law] [Constitution] of Kosovo. That authority shall include, but is not limited to, determining whether decisions or actions of the [President] [Presidency], the Assembly, the Council of Ministers, the Communes, and the National Communities are compatible with the [Basic Law] [Constitution] of Kosovo.

The Court shall also have jurisdiction to decide whether the actions of any official or institution are compatible with the European Convention for Human Rights and ist Protocols, and with the other human rights agreements listed in Annex 1, and with the Human Rights and Fundamental Freedoms and rights of National Communities set forth in this Agreement.

(a) Matters may be referred to the court by the [President] [Presidency] of Kosovo, the President or Vice-Presidents of the Assembly, the Prime Minister, the Ombudsman, the communal assemblies and councils, and any national community acting according to its democratic procedures.

(b) Any Kosovo court, which finds in the course of adjudicating a matter that the dispute depends on the answer to a question within the Court's jurisdiction, may refer the issue to the Court for a preliminary decision.

(c) The Court shall have appellate jurisdiction over cases raising matters within its authority after all other avenues for appeal have been exhausted, including the Supreme Court.

(d) [Questions relating to the compatibility of official actions with the European Convention for Human Rights and its Protocols may be further appealed to the European Court of Human Rights. In such matters, the decisions of the European Court shall be final.] [Where a matter falls within the jurisdiction of the Special Court, appeals may also be taken to that tribunal consistent with this Agreement.] Questions of Federal law may be appealed to the courts of the Federal Republic of Yugoslavia.

6. Jurisdiction of the Supreme Court. The Supreme Court shall hear appeals from the Communal Courts. It shall be the final appellate tribunal of Kosovo for all matters of Kosovo law falling outside the jurisdiction of the Constitutional Court [and the Special Court]. Questions of Federal law may be appealed to the courts of the Federal Republic of Yugoslavia.

7. Functioning. The two tribunals shall adopt decisions by majority vote of all the Justices or Judges. They shall hold public proceedings, and issue published opinions setting forth the reasons for their decisions along with any dissenting views.

Communal Courts

8. The Communes shall establish such tribunals of first instance as they deem proper to address matters falling within the jurisdiction of the Kosovo courts. Judges shall be unbiased, and a representative percentage shall be selected from each national community in the Commune after consultations with the national communities.

National Community Dispute Settlement Mechanism

9. Each national community may establish procedures for resolving conflicts concerning inheritance, family law, matrimonial relations, tutorship, adoption, civil lawsuits as decided by the Assembly of Kosovo, and criminal cases for which imprisonment of up to one year is prescribed in the currently applicable penal code.

(a) These procedures must ensure that practices are consistent with internationally recognized human rights. They shall have jurisdiction only when all parties to a dispute agree.

(b) Decisions of the national community dispute resolution mechanism shall be honored by other courts in Kosovo and the Federal Republic of Yugoslavia in accordance with applicable rules.

[Special Court

10. General. A Special Court shall be established to ensure compliance with this Agreement. Three judges of the Special Court shall be elected by the Chamber of Citizens of the Federal Republic of Yugoslavia and three by the Assembly of Kosovo. During a period of [twenty] years from the entry into force of the Agreement, three judges appointed by the European Court of Human Rights following consultations with the Government of the Federal Republic of Yugoslavia and Kosovo Council of Ministers shall sit on the Court. These judges shall not be citizens of the Federal Republic of Yugoslavia or any neighboring state. The Special Court shall establish its own rules of procedure.

11. Jurisdiction and Powers. The Special Court shall have jurisdiction to decide matters arising under this Agreement and its Annexes. In particular, it shall hear cases under the following circumstances:

(a) At the request of the President, the Government, the Chamber of the Republics, or the Chamber of the Citizens of the Federal Republic of Yugoslavia; of the President, the Government, or the National Assembly of the Republic of Serbia, of the [President] [Chairman of the Presidency], the Council of Ministers, the Assembly, or the Ombudsman of Kosovo; or the Chair of the Joint Commission:

(i) In case of disagreement as to the compatibility of Federal Republic of Serbia, or Kosovo legislation or of the Federal Republic of Serbia Constitution or the [Basic Law] [Constitution] of Kosovo with this Agreement; or

(ii) In case of disagreement as to the rights and obligations of the Federation, the Republic of Serbia, or Kosovo under this Agreement.

(b) At the request of the [President] [Chair of the Presidency]. the Council of Ministers, the Assembly, the Ombudsman, a National Community, a Commune, or the Chair of the Joint Commission in the case of a disagreement as to the rights or obligations of the requesting body under the Agreement.

(c) Upon appeal from a ruling of the Constitutional Court as to whether a proposed Decision [or law] of the Assembly [substantially] affects the vital interest of a national community.

(d) Following the exhaustion of other legal remedies, at the request of any natural or legal person or association on a compliant that any rights granted by this Agreement, including by the provisions of international treaties incorporated herein, have been violated by a public authority.

12. If a court on the territory of the Federal Republic of Yugoslavia considers that a law, on whose validity its ruling in a case before it disputes, may be inconsistent with this Agreement, it shall stay the proceedings and seek a ruling from the Special Court as to the compatibility of the law with this Agreement.

13. If the Constitutional Court of the Federal Republic of Yugoslavia considers that a provision of the Federal Republic of Yugoslavia Constitution, on whose validity its ruling in a case before it depends, may be inconsistent with this Agreement, or if the Constitutional Court of the Republic of Serbia considers that a provision of the Constitution of the Republic of Serbia, on whose validity ist ruling in the case before it depends, may be inconsistent with this Agreement, it shall stay the proceedings and ask for a ruling by the Special Court.

14. Decisions of the Special Court shall be final and binding, and shall be executed by all public authorities on the territory of the Federal Republic of Yugoslavia.]

PART IV. THE OMBUDSMAN

General

1. There shall be an Ombudsman of Kosovo, who shall monitor the protection of human rights and fundamental freedoms and the protection of the rights of national communities under this Agreement.

(a) The Ombudsman shall be an eminent person of high moral standing who possesses a demonstrated commitment to human rights. He or she shall be appointed for a non renewable [four] year term. The Ombudsman shall be independently responsible for choosing his or her own staff. He shall have two Deputies, one drawn each of the two national communities representing the largest percentage of the population of Kosovo.

(b) The first Ombudsman shall be appointed by the Federal Republic of Yugoslavia from a list of candidates prepared by [the Chairman-in-Office of the Organization for Security and Cooperation in Europe (OSCE).] [the President of the European Court of Human Rights.] Federal authorities shall consult with the other parties to this Agreement and the National Communities of Kosovo to guide their selection. The initial appointee may not be a citizen of the Federal Republic of Yugoslavia or of any neighboring state.

(c) Subsequent appointees shall be selected on the basis of consensus between the [President] [Presidency] of Kosovo and the President of the Federal Republic of Yugoslavia, after consultation with the national communities of Kosovo.

2. The Office of the Ombudsman shall be an independent agency of Kosovo. In carrying out its mandate, no person, institution, or entity of the Parties may interfere with its functions.

3. The salaries and expenses of the Ombudsman and his or her staff shall be determined jointly by the Federal republic of Yugoslavia and Kosovo. The salaries and expenses shall be fully adequate to implement the Ombudsman's mandate.

4. The Ombudsman and members of his or her staff shall not be held criminally or civilly liable for any acts carried out within the scope of their duties. When the Ombudsman and members of the staff are not citizens of the Federal Republic of Yugoslavia, they and their families shall be accorded the same privileges and immunities as are enjoyed by diplomatic agents and their families under the Vienna Convention on Diplomatic relations.

Jurisdiction

5. The Ombudsman shall consider:

(a) alleged or apparent violations of human rights and fundamental freedoms in Kosovo, as provided in the European Convention for the Protection of Human Rights and Fundamental Freedoms and the Protocols thereto, the international agreements listed in Annex 1 of this Agreement, and Article IV of this Agreement, and

(b) alleged or apparent discrimination on any ground such as sex, race, color, language, religion, political or other opinion, national or social origin, association with a national minority, property, birth or other status arising in the enjoyment of any of the rights and freedoms provided for in the international agreements listed in Annex 1 of this Agreement, where such violation is alleged or appears to have been committed by the Parties, including by any official, institution, or entity of the Parties, or any individual acting under the authority of such an official, institution, or entity, and

(c) violations of the rights of National Communities specified in this Agreement.

6. All citizens in Kosovo shall have the right to submit complaints to the Ombudsman. The Parties agree not to take any measures to punish persons who intend to submit or who have submitted such allegations, or in any other way to deter the exercise of this right.

Powers and Authority

7. The Ombudsman shall investigate alleged violation falling within the jurisdiction set forth in paragraph five. He may act either on his own initiative or in response to an allegation presented by any Party or person, non-governmental organization, or group of individuals claiming to be the victim of a violation or acting on behalf of alleged victims who are deceased or missing. The work of the Ombudsman shall be free of charge to the person concerned.

8. The Ombudsman shall determine which allegations warrant investigation and in what priority, giving particular priority to allegations of especially severe or systematic violations.

9. The Ombudsman shall have complete, unimpeded, and immediate access to any person, place, or information upon his or her request.

(a) He shall have access to and may examine all official documents, including classified documents, and he can require any person, including officials of Kosovo, the Republics and the Federal Republic of Yugoslavia to cooperate by providing relevant information, documents and files.

(b) The Ombudsman may attend administrative hearings, meetings of other Kosovo institutions, and meetings and proceedings of the Republics and the Federal Republic of Yugoslavia in order to gather information.

(c) He may examine facilities and places where persons deprived of their liberty are detained, work, or are otherwise located.

(d) The Ombudsman and staff shall maintain the confidentiality of all confidential information obtained by them, unless the Ombudsman determines that such information is evidence of a violation of rights falling within his or her jurisdiction, in which case that information may be revealed in public reports or appropriate legal proceedings.

(e) Where an official impedes an investigation by refusing to provide necessary information, the Ombudsman shall contact the official's superior or the public prosecutor for appropriate penal action to be taken in accordance with the law. Where the competent authority fails to take action, the Ombudsman may, in substitution for that authority, institute disciplinary proceedings against the official responsible or where appropriate before a criminal court.

10. The Ombudsman shall issue finding and conclusions in the form of a published report promptly after concluding an investigation.

(a) A Party, institution, or official in Kosovo identified by the Ombudsman as a violator shall, within a period specified by the Ombudsman, explain in writing how it will comply with any prescriptions the Ombudsman may put forth for remedial measures.

(b) In the event that a person or entity does not comply with the conclusions and recommendations of the Ombudsman, the report shall be forwarded for further action to the Joint commission set forth in Article VIII of this Agreement, to the Presidency of the appropriate Party, and to any other officials or institution that the Ombudsman deems appropriate.

11. The Ombudsman shall have the right to appear and intervene before any Federal, domestic, or (consistent with the rules of such bodies) international authority upon his or he request [including the Special Court].

(a) The right of intervention shall include the power to appear in support of the application of any person claiming violation of the rights set forth in paragraph five before any tribunal or proceeding of Kosovo, the Republic, or the Federal Republic of Yugoslavia.

(b) The Ombudsman may support appropriate applications to [the European court of Human rights and other] international bodies.

(c) The Ombudsman shall promptly report to the International Criminal Tribunal for the Former Yugoslavia evidence of war crimes, crimes against humanity, and other fundamental violations of international humanitarian law that may fall within the jurisdiction of that tribunal.

PART V: COMMUNES

[Option 1 :1. Kosovo shall have the existing communes.]

[Option 2 :1. Kosovo shall have [   ] communes within the boundaries specified in annex 6 of this Agreement.]

[Option 1 :

2. Communes may by mutual agreement form self-administering regions comprising multiple communes. These regions shall have the authorities of communes, unless the agreement establishing them expressly determines otherwise.]

[Option 2 :

2. Communes may develop relationships among themselves for their mutual benefit.]

3. Each Commune shall have an Assembly, a Council, and such executive bodies as the commune may establish. Each national community with at least [   ]% of the population of the commune shall be represented on the Council in proportion to its share of the regional population or by one member, whichever is greater.

4. The communes shall have exclusive responsibility for:

- Law enforcement, as specified in annex 2 of this Agreement.
- Regulating and, when appropriate, providing childcare.
- Establishing and regulation the work of medical institutions and hospitals. Special arrangements will be made for institutions owned by government entities.
- Providing and regulating education, consistent with the rights and duties of national communities.
- Protecting the communal environment.
- Regulating commerce and privately owned stores.
- Regulating hunting and fishing.
- Planning and carrying out public works of communal importance, including roads and water supplies, and participating in the planning and carrying out Kosovo-wide public works projects in coordination with other communes and Kosovo authorities.
- Regulating land use, town planning, building regulations, and housing construction.
- Designing and implementing programs of economic, scientific, technological, demographic, and social development, and programs for the development of agriculture and of rural areas.
- Developing programs for tourism, the hotel industry, catering, and sport.
- Organizing fairs and local markets.
- Organizing public services of communal importance, including fire, emergency response, and police consistent with Annex 2 of this Agreement.
- Financing the work of communal institutions, including raising revenue, taxes, and preparing budgets.

5. Each commune shall conduct its business in public and shall maintain publicly available records of its deliberations and decisions.

6. Members of national communities may avail themselves of Federal institutions and institutions of the Republics, in accordance with the procedures of those institutions and without prejudice to the ability of communes to carry out their responsibilities.

IV. HUMAN RIGHTS FUNDAMENTAL FREEDOMS

1. The Parties shall ensure that the highest level of internationally recognized human rights and fundamental freedoms is secured for the

people of Kosova. The Parties shall take every measure to ensure the protection and preservation of these rights.

(a) Applicable rights and freedoms shall include those specified in the European Convention for the Protection of Human Rights and Fundamental Freedoms and its protocols, and the other international agreements listed in Annex 1 of this Agreement including, but not limited to, those to which the Federal republic of Yugoslavia is already a party.

(b) All competent authorities shall cooperate with and provide unrestricted access to the supervisory bodies established by any of the international agreements listed in Annex 1 of this Agreement and the international Criminal Tribunal for the Former Yugoslavia.

2. The rights referred to in paragraph 1 shall be directly applicable in Kosovo and in any matter involving a person of Kosovo, and shall take precedence over all other law of the Parties. All courts, agencies government institutions, and instrumentalities of the Parties and all of their officials and employees shall conform to these human rights and fundamental freedoms. Applicable rights include:

(a) The right to life.

(b) The right not to be subjected to torture or to inhuman or degrading treatment or punishment.

(c) The right not to be held in slavery or servitude or to perform forced or compulsory labor.

(d) The right to peacefully assemble and freely associate with others.

(e) The right to liberty and security of person.

(f) Freedom of thought, conscience and religion.

(g) Freedom of expression, and the right to freely receive information and ideas without interference or threats.

(h) The right to a fair hearing in civil and criminal matters, and other rights relating to criminal proceedings.

(i) The right to liberty and security of person.

(j) The right to marry and found a family.

(k) The right to property.

(l) The right to education.

(m) The right to liberty of movement and residence.

3. The rights and freedoms provided for in this Article and detailed in the international agreements listed in Annex 1 shall be enjoyed without discrimination on any ground such as race, color, language, religion, political or other opinion, national or social origin or membership in a particular national community, property, birth, or other status.

V. RIGHTS AND DUTIES OF MEMEBERS OF NATIONAL COMMUNITIES

1. Members of the national communities shall have additional rights determined by this Agreement in order to preserve and express their national, cultural, religious, and linguistic identities in accordance with international standards and the Helsinki final Act.

2. The national communities shall be legally equal and shall not use their additional rights so as to endanger the rights of other national communities or the rights of citizens.

[Option 1 :

3. Each national community shall select through democratic means, in accordance with procedures it shall decide, institutions to administer its affairs in Kosovo.]

[Option 2 :

3. Each national community shall select through democratic means, in accordance with procedures it shall decide, a National Council to administer the affairs of the community in Kosovo. Each Council will establish its own executive institutions and procedures.]

4. The national communities shall be subject to [Decisions] [laws] of the Assembly of Kosovo, provided that any action concerning national communities must be nondiscriminatory. The Assembly shall decide upon procedure for resolving disputes between national communities.

5. The additional rights of the national communities are to:

(a) preserve and protect their national culture, including by:

- using their language and alphabets,
- inscribing local names of towns and villages, of squares and streets, and of other topographic names in the language and alphabet of the national community [in addition to signs in Serbian,] consistent with decisions about style made by the communal institutions,
- providing information in the language and alphabet of the national community,
- establishing educational, cultural and religious associations, for which relevant authorities will provide financial assistance,
- enjoying unhindered contacts with their respective national communities outside the Federal Republic of Yugoslavia.
- using and displaying national symbols [as well as the symbols of the Federal Republic of Yugoslavia and Serbia],
- providing for education, in particular for schooling in their own language and alphabet and in national culture and history,
- protecting national practices on family law by, if the community decides, arranging rules in the field of inheritance, family and matrimonial relations; tutorship; and adoption,
- the preservation of sites of religious, historical, or cultural importance
- implementing public health and social services,
- operating religious institutions in cooperation with religious authorities.

(b) adopt procedures for dispute resolution, as provided in Article II. Part 3(g) of this Agreement.

(c) be guaranteed at least one radio and TV frequency, which it shall administer subject to non-discriminatory, technical standards;

(d) finance activities of the national communities by collecting charges [a National Council] [the national community] decides to levy on members of its own community.

6. Each national community may exercise these additional rights through Federal institutions, or institutions of the Republics.

7. Members of national communities will also be guaranteed:

- the right to participate in regional and international non-governmental organizations in accordance with procedures of these organizations; and
- equal access to employment in public services

VI. REPRESENTATION OF KOSOVO IN FEDERAL INSTITUTIONS

1. The participation of Kosovo in Federal institutions shall be discussed in accordance with Article XI(3) ;

2. The following is without prejudice to the rights of persons in Kosovo to decide whether to accept the offer and to the review described in section XI (3);

- Kosovo shall be offered at least [thirty] deputies in the House of Citizens of the Federal Assembly.
- Each national community in Kosovo shall be offered at least one place in the Federal Government.
- Each national community in Kosovo shall be offered at least one judge on the Federal court of the Federal Republic.
- The [President] [Presidency] of Kosovo shall be a full member of the Supreme Defence Council of the Federal Republic of Yugoslavia.

VII. FINANCING AND OTHER ECONOMIC ISSUES

Financing

1. The authorities established to levy and collect taxes and other charges are set forth in this Agreement. Except if otherwise expressly provided in this Agreement, those bodies have the right to keep all revenues from their own taxes or other charges.

2. In recognition of the fact that this Agreement confers new responsibilities upon authorities in Kosovo, [Republic and] Federal authorities shall examine how to provide resources necessary for the conduct of the new responsibilities. These resources shall include funds (including tax remission), equipment, and training.

3. The authorities of Kosovo shall have part of revenue otherwise derived in Kosovo (including duties or fees0. Authorities collecting such revenue shall be representative of the population in Kosovo. Federal taxation and revenue collection in Kosovo, and the rules governing any additional contribution to Federal Republic of Yugoslavia institutions from which Kosovo benefits, shall be governed by the terms and conditions specified in Annex 3 of this Agreement.

4. Federal and other authorities shall also facilitate, to the extent of their respective powers, the delivery of resources from international sources to Kosovo.

Other Economic Issues

5. Annex 3 of this Agreement shall specify, in terms consistent with this Agreement, arrangements for the disposition of government owned assets in Kosovo; the resolution of disputes over pension and social insurance contributions; and the resolution of other matters relating to economic relations between the parties.*

[* Note: The Parties are encouraged to convene expert working groups forthwith to examine these technical issues in detail]

VIII. JOINT COMMISSION AND JOINT COUNCIL

Joint Commission

1. A Joint Commission will serve as the central mechanism for monitoring and coordination the implementation of this Agreement. It will be comprised of Federal [and Republic] representatives, representatives of the national communities in Kosova, representatives of Kosovo political institutions including the [President] [Presidency] of Kosovo and the Ombudsman, and international representatives (including the Kosovo Verification Mission), the Contact Group, and others as agreed).

[Option 1 :

2. The members of the Joint Commission shall select a Chair to organize its work.]

[Option 2 :

2. A person of high moral character will be selected to serve as Chair of the Joint Commission. The Chair will coordinate the work of the Joint Commission, and shall have other powers and authorities as set forth in this Agreement.

(a) For [ten] years following the entry into force of this Agreement, the Chair shall be a person chosen by the Chair in Office of the OSCE after consultation with the Parties. During this initial period, the Chair of the Joint Commission shall not be citizen of the Federal republic of Yugoslavia or a surrounding state. The Chair shall organize the work of the Joint Commission, and supervise the overall implementation of this Agreement.

(b) After the initial period, the Chair shall be elected by consensus between the President of the Federal Republic of Yugoslavia, and the [President] [Presidency] of Kosovo.]

3. The sides shall cooperate completely with the Commission and its Chair.

The Joint Commission as a whole and the Chair individually on his or her own initiative shall have safe, complete, and unimpeded access to all places, persons, and information (including documents and other records) both within Kosovo and, where the Joint Commission or the Chair deem it relevant, within the Federal Republic.

Joint Council

4. The national communities shall establish a Joint Council to coordinate their activities under this Agreement, and to provide an informal mechanism for the resolution of disputes. The Joint council shall consist of one member from each of the national communities. It shall meet no less than once each month. The Joint Council shall encourage the creation of similar mechanisms at the communal level, building on the example of local commissions established pursuant to Article IX(5) of this Agreement.

IX. CONFIDENCE BUILDING MEASURES

1. Violence in Kosova shall cease. Alleged violations of the cease-fire shall be reported to international observers and will not be used to justify violence in response. All persons held by the Parties without charge shall be released.

2. [An agreement on the status of security forces in Kosovo, to be added after expert consultations.]

3. [An agreement on the status of police forces in Kosovo, to be added after expert consultations.]

4. Each side shall encourage all persons displaced during the conflict to return to their homes as the security situation permits. There will be no impediments to the normal flow of goods in Kosovo. International humanitarian organizations will be freely permitted to provide building materials and other assistance to persons returning to their homes in Kosovo.

5. In each community a local commission, representative of all national communities there, will assist international humanitarian agencies in the delivery and distribution of food, medicine, clothes, construction materials, the restoration of electricity and water supply, and in encouraging return.

6. International personnel, including the Kosovo Verification Mission and members of non-governmental organizations, shall be allowed unfettered access, at any time, throughout Kosovo. It is expected that international personnel will be present at all times in selected communities.

7. Each side shall respect tits obligation to cooperate in the investigation and prosecution of war crimes, crimes against humanity, and other violations of international humanitarian law. In acknowledgement that allegations of atrocities cannot be resolved to the satisfaction of the other, each side will allow complete, unimpeded, and unfettered access to international experts including forensics experts-authorized to investigate such allegations. Each side will provide fully support and cooperation to the activities of the International Criminal Tribunal for the Former Yugoslavia.

[Option 1 :

8. Rebupolic and Federal authorities shall re-examine, for extraordinary mitigation of punishments, all sentences pronounced on members of national communities from Kosovo for acts motivated by political goals.]

[Option 2 :

8. There shall be a general amnesty for all persons in Kosovo accused or convicted of committing politically motivated crimes. The amnesty shall not apply to those accused for or convicted of committing war crimes, crimes against humanity, or other fundamental violations of international humanitarian law.]

X. IMPLEMENTATION PERIOD

1. This Agreement shall be implemented as quickly as possible. The signatories of this Agreement take the obligation to allow, insofar as possible, its adequate implementation even before the adoption and undertaking of all acts and measures fixed in the Agreement.

2. The sides will start without delay on any and all legal changes necessary for the full implementation of this Agreement. They acknowledge that complete implementation will require the adoption of necessary state regulations and other general acts, of the [Basic Law] [Constitution] of Kosovo, political acts and measures, and the election and establishment of institutions and bodies set forth in the Agreement. This Agreement shall take precedence over all existing legal authorities of the parties.

3. Each national community in Kosovo is authorized to start exercising the additional rights determined by this Agreement, to the extent possible, immediately upon signature.

4. Within [nine] months, there shall be elections in accordance with Annex 4 of this Agreement for all authorities established by this Agreement, according to an electoral list prepared to international standards. The Government of the Federal Republic of Yugoslavia hereby invites the organisation for Security and Cooperation in Europe (OSCE) to supervise those elections to ensure openness and fairness.

5. Under the supervision of the OSCE and with the participation of Kosovo authorities, Federal authorities shall conduct an objective and free census of the population in Kosovo, which shall be carried out when the OSCE determines that conditions allow an accurate census.

(a) The first census shall be limited to name, place of birth, address, gender, age, citizenship, nationality, and religion.

(b) The institutions and authorities of the parties shall provide the institutions of Kosovo with all records necessary to conduct the census, including data about places of residence, citizenship, voters' lists, and other information.

6. The signatories of this Agreement shall provide active support, cooperation, and participation for the successful implementation of the Agreement.

7. Laws and institutions currently in place in Kosovo shall remain until replaced by a decision of a competent body established by this Agreement.

The initial elections called for in paragraph four of this Article will be conducted pursuant to the procedures in Annex 4.

XI. AMENDMENTS

1. Amendments to this Agreement shall be adopted by signature of all the parties.

2. Each signatory may propose amendments at any time and will consider and consult with the other with regard to proposed amendments.

3. In three years, the sides will undertake a comprehensive assessment of the Agreement, with the aim of improving the implementation and considering proposals by either side for additional steps, which will require mutual agreement for adoption.

XII. FINAL PROVISIONS

1. This Agreement is concluded in [   ] languages.

2. This Agreement shall enter into force upon the completion of the internal process of each side.

FOR

Federal Republic of Yugoslavia
Republic of Kosovo
Republic of Serbia

ANNEX 1: HUMAN RIGHTS AND FUNDAMENTAL FREEDOMS
Human Rights Agreements

- 1948 Convention on the Prevention and Punishment of the Crime of Genocide
- 1949 Geneva Conventions I-IV on the Protection of the Victims of War, and the 1977 Geneva Protocols I-II thereto
- 1950 European Convention for the Protection of Human Rights and Fundamental Freedoms, and the Protocols thereto
- 1951 Convention relating to the Status of Refugees and the 1966 Protocol thereto
- 1957 Convention on the Nationality of Married Women
- 1961 Convention on the Reduction of Statelessness
- 1965 International Convention on the Elimination of All Forms of Racial Discrimination
- 1966 International Covenant on Civil and Political Rights and the 1966 and 1989 Optional Protocols thereto
- 1966 Covenant on Economic, Social, and Cultural Rights
- 1979 Convention on the Elimination of All Forms of Discrimination Against Women
- 1984 Convention Against Torture and Other Cruel, Inhuman, or Degrading Treatment or Punishment
- 1987 European Convention on the Prevention of Torture and Inhuman or Degrading Treatment or Punishment
- 1989 Convention on the Rights of the Child
- 1990 Convention on the Protection of the Rights of All Migrant Workers and Members of Their Families
- 1992 European Charter for Regional or Minority Languages
- 1994 Framework Convention for the Protection of National Minorities

Other Annexes
The following additional annexes will be a part of the completed Agreement:
Annex 2 : Police and Security Matters
Annex 3 : Financing and Other Economic Issues
Annex 4 : Conduct and Supervision of Elections
Annex 5 : National Communities
[Annex 6: Communal Boundaries]

5. Kosovo Statement on Fundamental Principles for a Settlement, 3 November 1998

The Government of the Republic of Kosova has studied with interest the proposals for a settlement put forward by Ambassador Hill. On the basis of expert advice received, this proposal has been found to be fundamentally incompatible with the democratic mandate bestowed upon the Government of the Republic of Kosova by the people of Kosova. The Government of the Republic of Kosova declares that it cannot furnish a basis for discussion.

Despite the outrages suffered by the population of Kosova at the hands of FRY/Serb armed forces, special police forces and other instrumentalities of the Belgrade regime, the Government of the Republic of Kosova remains committed to the search for a peaceful solution of the crisis in the region. However, the terms of a possible settlement, and the path towards it, must obviously be influenced by these latest atrocities which have resulted the death of thousands, in immense suffering by tens of thousands, and in over 400,000 displaced members of the civilian population a large number of whom are dwelling at the edge of death through exposure and starvation.

The Government of the Republic of Kosova will engage in further talks once all the demands made by the United Nations Security Council in legally binding resolutions, adopted under Chapter VII, have been implemented by the FRY. It must be noted that it is not for any delegation, or group of states, unilaterally to relieve the FRY from the mandatory demands of the Security Council. Instead, in its latest resolution 1203 (1998), adopted in response to the so-called Holbrooke agreement of 12/13 October, the Security Council expressly reiterated its demand that the FRY must comply 'fully and swiftly' with its previous resolutions 1160 (1998) and 1199 (1998). This further resolution was also expressly adopted under Chapter VII of the UN Charter.

The Government of the Republic of Kosova was not consulted about the terms of the so-called Holbrooke agreement. Despite serious reservations relating to the arrangement, it has consented (for an initial period of three month, to be automatically extended for further periods of three months unless revoked by the Government of the Republic of Kosova) to the presence of the proposed verification force on its territory, and to the overflight of monitoring aircraft. It is also actively participating in the administration of the humanitarian operations which are now being conducted.

The Government of the State of Kosova has, for its part, fully implemented all aspects of Resolutions 1160 (1998), 1199 (1998) and 1203 (1998). Matters of compliance which are outstanding on the FRY/Serb side, and which must be resolved before talks can progress, include:

- The cessation of the campaign of violence and intimidation by the FRY/Serb forces, principally directed against the civilian population;
- The full withdrawal of FRY/Serb armed forces and special police forces, as required by mandatory Security Council resolution;
- The establishment of freedom of movement, including free and unhindered access for humanitarian aid;
- The creation of conditions necessary for the protection and safe return in dignity of the displaced;
- Full access to all areas of Kosova to international monitors, including human rights monitors, and war crimes investigators;
- Full acceptance by the FRY of its duty to cooperate with the ICTFY war-crimes investigation, including the furnishing of full access to all persons and materials that may be requested.

The Government of the Republic of Kosova proposes the creation of a neutral Implementation Commission, composed of two representatives nominated by the Government of the Republic of Kosova, two nominated by the FRY, and three individuals from outside of the region, to be nominated by the UN Secretary-General acting jointly with the Presidency of the European Union. The members of the Commission will evaluate the extent to which the parties have complied with the mandatory demands of the Security Council and will, by a majority decision, advise the parties, the United Nations Security Council and other relevant bodies of its findings.

The Implementation Commission will adopt its initial report on compliance within two weeks of its coming into being. It is entitled to receive information from all sources, and will be given access to the reports of the verification mission and others, and will enjoy full freedom of movement and access to all individuals and places it might deem relevant. The decisions of the Commission shall be reasoned and public.

Once compliance has been certified by the Commission, negotiations on an interim settlement will commence. The Commission will remain active to monitor continued compliance during the negotiating period. In cases of substantial violations of the demands imposed upon the parties under mandatory Security Council Resolutions, it will adopt a decision to this effect by a simple majority, and will so report publicly to the Security Council, the EU Presidency and other relevant bodies within a week of having obtained knowledge of significant alleged violations.

Either of the parties shall be entitled to submit to the Commission allegations of violations, together with the relevant evidence. The Commission shall immediately seek the views of the party which is alleged to have committed the allegation and mount an investigation. It shall publish its findings within one week of having received the allegation and bring them to the attention of the relevant international bodies to which reference is made above.

Once it has been established that the parties have achieved substantive compliance, negotiations about an interim agreement shall commence. These talks shall be conduced in Geneva, starting seven days after certification of compliance has occurred.. In addition to the delegations of the Republic of Kosova and of the FRY, there will be international involvement in the talks, in the form of three guarantor states and representatives of implementing organizations to be designated.

1. There will be no pre-conditions for the substantive outcome of such talks. Instead, each party will be free to formulate its views as to a desirable interim arrangement adopted at the level of international law. Without prejudice to its legal position, and reserving the right to amend and modify its views in the light of subsequent developments, the Government of the Republic of Kosova will seek an agreement on the basis of the following principles:

2. The Republic of Kosova is a self-determination entity through which the people of Kosova have actualized their international and constitutional right to obtain independence upon the dissolution of the Socialist Federal Republic of Yugoslavia, and in the light of the repression suffered at the hands of an unrepresentative regime. An interim agreement need not expressly confirm the status of Kosova as an independent state, but it must not prejudice it. The interim agreement must recognize the inalienable right to self-determination.

3. The Republic of Kosova's territorial definition shall be the same as under the 1974 SFRY constitution. The Republic of Kosova has no territorial claims in relation to the other states of the region, and, unless this is provided in an overall regional settlement, it will not seek to merge with other states. It exercises foreign affairs powers.

4. The Republic of Kosova is a multi-ethnic state. Public authority is exercised on the basis of parliamentary democracy based on the equality of all citizens.

5. Kosova has already adopted its own constitution and has re-established indigenous structures of public authority. An interim agreement must be based on the legal personality of Kosova as a whole, and on the exercise of principal public authority through the organs of Kosova on the basis of its own legal order. Kosova is willing to subject its constitutional structure to a further internal referendum, internationally monitored, and will hold parliamentary and local elections with international involvement.

6. The exercise by FRY or other non-indigenous public organs of any remaining authority in the territory of the Republic of Kosova or in relation to it will be progressively reduced and removed. As this phasing out process takes place, the Republic of Kosova will engage in certain co-operative arrangements in relation to issues of common concern.

7. The transfer of all aspects of state activity to the organs of Kosova will be conducted in a way to ensure that public authority is exercised at a national and local level in a way which is representative of the population. To reassure minority populations, there will occur joint police patrols with international involvement in certain locations to be agreed during the interim period.

8. Kosova has already embraced international standards on the treatment of minorities, religious and cultural freedoms and other international human rights standards. It is willing to reiterate its commitment to these standards in a legally binding way, along with the FRY. It will also accept significant international involvement in the interpretation and application of these standards.

9. The organs of the Republic of Kosova will give full effect to and vigorously enforce human rights and minority rights provisions on the basis of full equally. All parties will collaborate with the relevant international organs in the pursuit of war criminals who have committed offences against the civilian population and others, whatever their religious or ethnic appurtenance.

10. At the conclusion of the interim period, the future status of Kosova will be determined or confirmed in accordance with the principle of self-determination of the people of the Republic of Kosova. A referendum will be conducted with international involvement.

11. The interim agreement will be subject to international guarantees and will be implemented with strong international involvement, also on the ground.

6.　Press Release by the Yugoslav Federal Ministry of Foreign Affairs, 10 November 1998

In the wake of various speculations in the general public that the Republic of Serbia and the FR of Yugoslavia are informed of the alleged "new plan of Ambassador Christopher Hill for a peaceful resolution of the problem in Kosovo and Metohija", the Federal Ministry of Foreign Affairs wishes to inform that the authorities of the Republic of Serbia and the FR of Yugoslavia have not in any way been informed of the "new plan of Ambassador C. Hill", and in that sense, have not discussed or adopted any position on the said plan. The only matter that was discussed and agreed upon, in the framework of the talks of the President of the FR of Yugoslavia, Mr. Slobodan Milosevic, and Ambassador Richard Holbrooke, of which the general public has been informed of in detail, was the question of principles, expressed in 11 points, which are the basic framework for a political solution. On 13 October 1998, the Government of the Republic of Serbia fully supported the said 11 points because by them the territorial integrity and sovereignty of our country was fully maintained, the conflict was avoided and conditions were created for a political dialogue based on the stated principles, which proceed from the point that all solutions must be within the frameworks of the legal systems of the Republic of Serbia and the Federal Republic of Yugoslavia. he same position was adopted also by the Federal Government.

7.　Statement by Milan Milutinovic, President of Serb Republic, Pristina, 18 November 1998

Distinguished Gentlemen,

I would like to express my great pleasure at having the representatives of all national communities living in Kosovo and Metohija present at this meeting.

I view this as a big interest in the promotion of political process and continuation of the dialogue through which we will jointly arrive at the solutions to the problems in Kosovo and Metohija.

Assessing that the conditions have been created to have a direct meeting and talks to seek political solutions to the problems in Kosovo and Metohija, I considered it necessary to personally chair this meeting.

Distinguished Gentlemen,

The major breakthrough and the greatest contribution to the continuation of political process in Kosovo and Metohija was made by the agreement between the President of the Federal Republic of Yugoslavia Slobodan Milošević and Ambassador Richard Holbrooke. It represents the definite agreement with the international community to have the problems in Kosovo and Metohija resolved peacefully by political means. The Agreement was supported by the Governments of the Republic of Serbia and of the Federal Republic of Yugoslavia, and it has also been overwhelmingly supported by the citizens of our country. The agreement brought enormous relief in Kosmet. The international community endorsed it through the decisions of the UN Security Council and the Organization for Security and Cooperation in Europe (OSCE).

The Agreement represents a basis comprising clear principles committing all national communities to seek solutions to the problems in Kosovo and Metohija through dialogue, in a peaceful manner. It provides the conditions to make it operational through a meaningful dialogue, and arrive at just and democratic solutions; to encourage the forces of peace and tolerance; to open a chapter of development and ensure the future for all national communities and all citizens in Kosovo and Metohija.

Serbia is firmly committed to having the problems in Kosovo and Metohija resolved politically. Serbia is a civil State and it does not divide its citizens according to their national, religious or any other background. But at the same time, Serbia is a multi-ethnic, multi-confessional and multi-cultural State guaranteeing to all national communities additional rights for the preservation and expression of their national identity, script, language, religion, customs, culture and tradition.

I would like to underline that peace and common life are possible in Kosmet only with genuine, not just formal equality of all national communities. This has been confirmed by the fact that we have honored all obligations and deadlines set forth in the agreements with the international community; that civilian structures are functioning and getting stronger by the day in Kosmet; that the situation in all fields, particularly economic, social and humanitarian is being increasingly normalized in Kosmet.

It is necessary to ensure peace and security in the interest of all, to reach democratic, just and acceptable solutions, proceeding from clearly defined principles, established political framework and the best forms.

As far as the principles are concerned, the basic ones are: equality of all national communities; additional rights with a view to preserving the identity of a national community.

As far as political framework is concerned - legal, i.e. constitutional framework of our country is broad enough to ensure consistent implementation of international standards in the field of protection of rights of national communities, with full respect of the existing practice.

Once the above is honored, the form is clear - democratic self-governance within the Republic of Serbia, and consequently, in the Federal Republic of Yugoslavia. In that respect, it should be clear to all that any solution for Kosmet has to respect the territorial integrity and sovereignty and internationally recognized borders of the Federal Republic of Yugoslavia, in accordance with the fundamental principles of the Charter of the United Nations, Helsinki Final Act and the OSCE Paris Charter.

I would particularly like to emphasize that the solutions should be based on the respect and equality of all citizens and national communities in Kosmet. It practically implies that each national community shall enjoy additional rights enabling them to preserve and express their national, cultural, religious and linguistic identity, in line with accepted international standards. All of this will be realized through democratic self-governance through parliamentary, executive and judiciary authorities and local police which will be constituted through direct, democratic and multi-party elections, once the necessary conditions are ensured.

It is highly important that the political solution embrace the position that no national community shall realize its additional rights to the detriment of other national communities and that they will pursue a constructive approach in searching concrete institutional models to use the rights they are granted.

There is no true agreement without compromise, without building confidence and mutual respect and tolerance. In that context, the State shall, in appropriate legal procedures, i.e. in line with the legislation, offer amnesty to all persons proven not to have committed the crimes against humanity and international law; it will mitigate the sentences to those who cooperated with investigative authorities, were forcibly drafted or voluntarily handed over arms.

With all those measures, we wish to encourage trust and accelerate the political process. Only in this we see the preconditions to solve the problems in Kosovo and Metohija which will enable the national communities to realize democratic self-governance, guarantee territorial integrity and sovereignty of our State, ensure peace and development in Kosovo and Metohija but also stability in the region of the Balkans and South-Eastern Europe and the inclusion of the peoples and States from these parts in broader political, economic, cultural and other integration processes, organizations and institutions.

Distinguished Gentlemen,

We need relatively fast solutions but we also need patience to reach them. We need the solutions which will not take us back in any respect - be it legal arrangement or institutions, there is no going back to the times that generated the problems. We need modern democratic solutions which will guarantee to all national communities full equality, prevent the abuse of majority vote, while creating the conditions for development, better life and high living standards of all citizens.

Though it is easy to say, it is difficult to define it in one act, in one agreement. It is even more difficult to have everybody respect it. But it is our shared obligation to jointly reach such solutions. Of course, all well-intentioned outside ideas are welcome, those that can help us reach a political solution, but no one except those at this table and the citizens of Kosmet themselves, can do a better job defining that.

I therefore expect your constructive contribution in our today's talks.

I expect your proposals, ideas, suggestions, comments; when you make them, I expect you take into account the ideas of other national communities; when you criticize, I expect you to take into account the interests of others living with you in Kosmet; I expect you to recognize the responsibility we have towards the members of all national communities, towards all citizens and the international community.

I repeat my deep conviction - the future of Kosovo is in peace, equality, common life, development and not in conflicts and divisions, on any grounds.

In order to achieve that, we need courage, commitment, we need to be well organized and patient. Accelerated political process has permanently discarded force as a way of thinking and resolving this problem and it will reinforce tolerance, understanding and trust. This approach is the best way to eliminate all exclusiveness, extremism and hatred.

Serbia has reaffirmed, both by its state policy and at the diplomatic level, that it is firmly committed to a political way of resolving the problems in Kosovo and Metohija. Exactly for being consistent in this approach, I emphasize that Serbia is ready to fully defend and ultimately defend the achieved peace and safety of all its citizens.

Nothing can be gained by terrorism, and the latest attacks of the defeated terrorist gangs will not derail the political process. Nevertheless, those attacks of terrorist gangs against security forces should be energetically prevented. They should also be condemned by the international community and by all Albanian political parties. That would be a proof that they, too, are committed to a peaceful resolution of the problems. That would eliminate any doubt among the terrorists that they enjoy any backing or support.

I would particularly like to emphasize that the future of Kosmet is not in conflicts and attempts at apartheid or self-imposed isolation of national communities. Kosmet has vast economic and natural resources and they can and should be rapidly used to ensure better life of all those living in this province of Serbia. Our goal is to open up the perspective of development of Kosovo, and end the spiral of conflicts, xenophobia, chauvinist, religious and historical prejudice, in short - all that divides our peoples and nations. That is the future of Kosmet.

It is up to us to open up the perspectives for such future. I wish this meeting to be a major contribution to that goal.

8. Concluding Remarks by the President of the Republic of Serbia, Pristina, 18 November 1998

Distinguished Gentlemen,

I assess our today's talks as positive, both in terms of the presence of all national communities and the way we held our discussions, including the ideas that were presented, and readiness to continue in the same vein and jointly come to the outcome acceptable to all.

Unfortunately, our meeting today was not attended by the representatives of leading political parties of Albanians from Kosmet. This is not the first time that they did not respond to our calls to a political dialogue. Such an attitude of these political parties in itself, speaks a lot to our public and all those well-intentioned in the world because any further delay and refusal, under lame and transparent excuses and conditionalities, can only result in derailing the process of searching political solutions.

Moreover, this is contrary to the interests of Albanian national community itself as well as against the interests of all those living in Kosovo and Metohija. On the other hand, it serves the interests of those forces who seek to turn this region into a testing ground to pursue their own goals. By acting in this manner, these parties are used as a pretext for further pressures against our country. That is why, regardless of their failure to attend the meeting today, we remain patient and open for a constructive dialogue as the only way to reach the solution which will be in the long-term interest of all those living and working in Kosovo and Metohija. In that sense, I personally stand ready, once the representatives of these political parties so decide, to meet with them at any time and discuss the vital issues we discussed here today.

I wish to thank all individual representatives of each national community present here for their constructive contribution, ideas, proposals and suggestions. It is good indeed that we discussed all questions in a democratic and open manner; in a manner not ruling out anything, leaving enough room for further discussions, for new proposals and ideas in the pursuance of better and more acceptable solutions to all. The participants in the debate advanced critical remarks regarding the paper presented by Ambassador Christopher Hill. The remarks are legitimate and I assign to them. The above paper does not rely on the Milosevic-Holbrooke Agreement as a whole, it does not respect full equality of all national communities in Kosmet and is in many respects contrary to the legal system of the Republic of Serbia and of the Federal Republic of Yugoslavia. I therefore feel personally obliged - in view of the positions and opinions presented here - sometimes conflicting, pertaining to the important issues under dissuasion - and I shall personally engage, with the help of all of you, to have your proposals and ideas once again considered, further elaborated and, in line with basic initial principles, respected to the fullest. Practically, it implies that I would again talk to a representative of each national community assigned by you, and if possible, with the representatives of political parties of Kosmet Albanians not present here - in order to be able advance my position accommodating the comments and suggestions with a view to working out a platform for a political solution to the problems in Kosovo and Metohija. I hope that at our next meeting we shall be able to embark upon a meaningful dialogue on the platform to reach concrete solutions.

Distinguished Gentlemen,

I am convinced that we have opened a new page in the dialogue leading to the political solution in the interest of all citizens and national communities living in Kosovo and Metohija. It is what they expect and demand from us. I express my conviction that by resuming these talks soon, we shall live up to their expectations.

9. Joint Proposal on Political Framework of Self-Governance in Kosovo and Metohija, Belgrade, 20 November 1998

The political solution to the problems in Kosovo and Metohija was considered in Pristina on 18 November and in Belgrade on 19 November, with the delegations of the National Party of Kosovo, Kosovo Democratic Initiative, representatives of the National Community of the Turks, National Community of the Gorancies, National Community of Muslims, National Community of Romanies, National Community of Egyptians, representatives of Parliamentary parties from Kosovo and Metohija, as well as with the representatives of the Socialist Party of Serbia and Presidents of the Serbian Radical Party and the Yugoslav United Left Party. President Milutinoviæ also held consultations on the same issues on 20 November with the Presidents of the Serbian Renewal Movement, New Democracy and Alliance of the Vojvodina Hungarians.

At all these talks and consultations, full support was given to the Agreement between President Milosevic and Ambassador Richard Holbrooke, particularly to the political framework for the resolution of problems in Kosmet, expressed in 11 points of the Government of Serbia. Also, many concrete comments and suggestions were made on the ways to achieve an institutionalized and political solution to the problems in Kosovo and Metohija.

The result of all these talks and consultations is the following: ...

Signatories to this Agreement,

Considering that, in view of the complex national structure in Kosovo and Metohija, it is necessary to protect the development and existence of each individual national community;

Firm in their commitment to the position that all national communities, regardless of their numbers, are mutually equal and that, therefore, in relations among them there can be no discrimination;

Considering that persons belonging to all national communities in Kosovo and Metohija should be enabled to exercise fully their ethnic, cultural, linguistic and religious identity, in accordance with the highest international standards and basic documents of the United Nations, Organization on Security and Cooperation in Europe, Council of Europe (the Charter of the United Nations, Universal Declaration on Human Rights, Helsinki Final Act, Paris Charter, European Convention on Human Rights, Council of Europe Framework Convention on the Rights of the Persons belonging to National Minorities), etc;

Considering that it is necessary to set up appropriate democratic institutions in order to create the atmosphere of tolerance and dialogue;

Determined in their position that broad self-governance within national communities and in the territory of Kosovo and Metohija is a precondition for overcoming inter-ethnic tensions and conflicts;

Bearing in mind the most positive experience and legal solutions developed through long-standing common life;

Have agreed as follows:

I. PRINCIPLES

1. Political approach and peaceful solution of problems in Kosovo and Metohija achieved through dialogue are the only acceptable way to reach a lasting, just and humane solution to all outstanding questions;

2. All solutions for Kosovo and Metohija must respect the territorial integrity and sovereignty and internationally recognized borders of the Federal Republic of Yugoslavia, in compliance with the basic principles of the UN Charter, the Helsinki Final Act and the Paris Charter of the OSCE.

3. The solution has to be based on full respect of equality of all citizens and national communities in Kosovo and Metohija. Full affirmation and equal treatment of their national, religious, cultural values as well as historic heritage shall be guaranteed;

4. The future of Kosovo and Metohija lies in peace, equality, integration, economic prosperity and free and common existence, not in ethnic, religious, cultural or any divisions and isolation;

5. The legal arrangements establishing self-governance in Kosovo and Metohija should be in line with legal systems of the Republic of Serbia and of the FR of Yugoslavia, and with international standards and basic documents;

6. Citizens of Kosovo and Metohija shall exercise their rights democratically through assembly, executive, and judicial organs.

7. Citizens and members of each national community in Kosovo and Metohija shall enjoy, without limitations, human and democratic rights and shall have the opportunity to be represented in all organs of authority.

8. Members of national communities shall have additional rights, in order to be able to express and preserve their national, cultural, religious, and linguistic identity, in accordance with international standards and fundamental international documents.

The national communities and their members shall be equal before the law, they shall abide by all State laws and shall not use their additional rights to endanger the rights of other national communities or other rights of citizens, especially territorial integrity and state sovereignty of the Federal Republic of Yugoslavia.

9. The responsibilities of organs in Kosovo and Metohija shall be set forth in this Agreement. The organs in Kosovo and Metohija acting within their competencies, shall be independent.

10. All citizens of Kosovo and Metohija shall have the right to apply to international institutions, including the European Court of Human Rights, for the protection of their rights, after all legal means envisaged by domestic legislation are exhausted.

II. RIGHTS OF CITIZENS

1. The rights of citizens of Kosovo and Metohija shall be realized through assembly, executive and judicial organs established by this Agreement. These rights make up democratic self-governance, including:

- the adoption of the Statute of Kosovo and Metohija;
- the adoption of regulations on the organization and procedures of organs of Kosovo and Metohija;
- adoption of the budget and annual accounts;
- regulation and provision of child care;
- establishment and regulation of the functioning of health institutions and hospitals, except those owned by the State;
- protection of environment;
- regulation of trade and private stores in accordance with republican and federal laws;
- regulation of hunting and fishing;
- planning and execution of public works of communal importance or of importance to Kosovo and Metohija;
- regulation of the land use, town planning and civil engineering, in accordance with republican and federal regulations;
- adoption and implementation of programs of economic, scientific, technological, demographic, regional and social development, as well as programs for development of agriculture and rural areas;
- adoption of tourism development programs, catering and sports;
- organization of fairs and local markets;
- setting up of public services of communal importance and of importance to Kosovo and Metohja;
- financing of the activities of communal organs and organs of Kosovo and Metohija.

2. The organs of Kosovo and Metohija shall not interfere with the additional rights of the members of national communities.

3. A commune shall be the basic unit of local self-governance.

III. ADDITIONAL RIGHTS OF MEMBERS OF NATIONAL COMMUNITIES

1. The members of national communities shall have additional rights set forth this Agreement. The additional rights shall preserve and express national, cultural, religious, and linguistic and other characteristics of members of national communities, in accordance with international standards and the Helsinki Final Act.

2. National communities shall be equal in terms of law and may not use their additional rights to threaten additional rights of other national communities or rights of citizens of the Republic of Serbia or of the Federal Republic of Yugoslavia.

3. Each national community shall select, in accordance with procedures it shall establish, a National Council which will make decisions on additional rights of national communities in Kosovo and Metohija. Each Council shall establish its own executive organs.

4. Additional rights of the national communities include:

- Using their language and alphabet;
- Inscribing local names of towns and villages, squares and streets, and of other topographic names, in the language and alphabet of the national community, along with inscriptions in Serbian;
- Providing information in the language and alphabet of the national community.
- Establishment of educational, cultural and religious associations, to which the State authorities will provide financial assistance.
- Maintenance of unimpeded contacts with their respective national communities outside the Federal Republic of Yugoslavia.
- Using and displaying national symbols, along with the State symbols of Serbia and the FR of Yugoslavia;
- Providing education, in particular for schooling in their own language and alphabet, in subjects related to national culture and history. National communities are encouraged to coordinate curricula with the republican authorities concerning some subjects (for example to ensure that pupils satisfy certain standards in subjects like math or science);
- Protection of national customs in the field of family law, if a community so decides, by establishing regulations in the field of heritage, family and matrimonial relations, adoption and tutorship;
- Each commune shall be able to establish a procedure for resolving disputes in these areas, with the consent of the parties to a dispute. These regulations have to be in accordance with internationally recognized human rights;
- Protecting the sites of religious, historical, or cultural importance to national communities.
- Setting up public health and social services;
- Operation of religious institutions in cooperation with religious authorities.
- Determining procedures of the courts of national communities as provided for in this Agreement and ensure the funds for the implementation of the decisions of those courts;
- Guaranteeing the right to at least one radio and TV frequency, which it shall administer subject to non-discriminatory technical standards;
- Financing activities of national communities by collecting duties which the National Council decides to levy on members of its own community.
- Participating in regional and international non-governmental organizations in accordance with the procedures of these organizations;
- Having equal access to employment in public services.

IV. THE ORGANS OF KOSOVO AND METOHIJA

1. The Assembly

1. The Assembly shall be elected directly. The Assembly shall have two Chambers: Chamber of Citizens and Chamber of National Communities.

2. Members of the Chamber of Citizens shall be elected directly in line with the principle one citizen - one vote.

3. Members of the Chamber of National Communities shall be elected democratically, within each national community. Each national community shall have a delegation with equal number of members in the Chamber.

4. The Assembly shall be responsible for:

- the adoption of the Statute of Kosovo and Metohija;
- making decisions and adoption of other acts regulating some questions related to rights of citizens of Kosovo and Metohija;
- the adoption of budgets and annual accounts;
- cooperation with Federal and Republic Assemblies;
- financing activities of the organs established by this Agreement;
- coordination among communes or national communities when necessary, including decisions concerning inter-communal issues, and
- election of members of the organs set forth in this Agreement.

5. Decisions of the Assembly shall be taken by majority in both Chambers, except as provided for in paragraph (6).

6. If members of one national community assert that a proposed decision affects the vital interests of this national community, such decision shall require majority vote, which includes the majority among the members of that national community delegation in the Council of National Communities.

7. If a decision cannot be taken on account of reasons referred to in paragraph 6, but needs to be taken, the National Assembly of Serbia

shall make an interim decision pending the one taken pursuant to paragraph 5.

8. The Assembly shall elect the Presidency of the Assembly which shall consist of one representative from each national community. The Presidency shall have a President, which function shall rotate among members of Presidency each year, in alphabetical order.

The Presidency shall be responsible for:

- calling the meetings of the Assembly and proposing the agenda;
- representing the Assembly;
- regular contacts with National Councils and other representatives of the national communities in order to facilitate the work of the Assembly.

Each national community shall be represented in the leadership of the Assembly. The President of the Presidency of the Assembly cannot be a member of the same national community as the President of the Executive Council and Ombudsman.

2. Executive Council

Executive Council shall exercise executive power.

The Council shall comprise at least one person from each national community. Members shall be proposed by the Presidency of the Assembly and shall be elected by both Assembly Chambers on the basis of equality.

The Executive Council shall be responsible for implementing the decisions of the Assembly and regulations of the State authorities, when authorized for their implementation.

Decisions of the Council shall be adopted by majority vote of Members present and voting, except on questions affecting vital interests of a certain national community. In that case, the principle valid for voting in the Assembly shall apply.

3. Administrative organs

The administrative organs of Kosovo and Metohija shall have responsibility for the implementation of decisions and general acts, in accordance with this Agreement.

Executives in administrative organs in Kosovo and Metohija shall be representative of the local population.

4. Ombudsman

The Ombudsman shall monitor the realization of the rights of members of national communities.

The Ombudsman shall be nominated by the Presidency of Assembly and shall be elected by the Assembly, each term from another national community.

The Ombudsman shall have a right to review the acts and unimpeded access to any person or place and shall have the right to appear before any domestic organ.

V. THE COMMUNES

1. Communes shall be basic units of self-governance.

2. Each commune shall have an Assembly and Executive Council and such administrative organs established by Executive Council. The organs of a commune shall be organized along the same principles as the organs of Kosovo and Metohija.

3. The duties of local self-governance in a commune include:

- Providing child-care;
- Health institutions and hospitals, except those owned by the State;
- Educational institutions except those State-owned;
- Protection of environment;
- Public works of communal or regional importance, including roads and water supplies.
- Land use;
- Tourism, hotel industry, catering, and sport.
- Fairs and local markets.
- Public services of communal importance, including fire department, emergency response, and local police.
- Financing the work of communal organs, levying duties in accordance with the law.

VI. REPRESENTATION OF THE CITIZENS OF KOSOVO AND METOHIJA IN FEDERAL AND REPUBLIC BODIES

1. Citizens of Kosovo and Metohija shall be represented by at least ten deputies in the Chamber of Citizens of the Federal Assembly and at least twenty deputies in the National Assembly of the Republic of Serbia.

2. From among the citizens of Kosovo and Metohija at least one member shall be elected to the Federal Government and the Government of the Republic of Serbia.

3. From among the citizens of Kosovo and Metohija at least one judge in the Federal Court and three judges in the Supreme Court of Serbia shall be elected.

4. There shall be a Council of the Republic of Serbia for the protection of the rights of the members of national communities. The President of the Republic of Serbia shall preside over the Council of the Republic of Serbia for the protection of the rights of members of national communities.

VII. COURTS AND LOCAL POLICE

1. Courts of National Communities

Each national community may establish, in accordance with the law, courts and determine procedures for resolving disputes concerning inheritance, family law, matrimonial relations, tutorship, adoption and trials for which imprisonment of up to one year is prescribed by the Penal Code. The competence of these courts may be established only if parties to a dispute agree.

The judges shall be appointed by the National Councils and approved by the Assembly. The judges of these courts have to meet criteria necessary for the selection of judges in the corresponding State courts.

2. Local police

Each commune may, if it so decides, establish its local police representative of the population in the commune.

The local police shall be trained in specialized state police schools to respect human rights, particularly the rights of national communities.

The members of local police shall be sworn in to uphold the law impartially, fairly, equally treating all persons.

The local police shall be responsible for the maintenance of public order.

The members of the local police may use, as means of coercion, only guns, rubber truncheons and handcuffs and passenger transportation vehicles and adequate means for communication. The members of the local police cannot use means of coercion against the members of another national community.

If necessary, local police shall be obliged to place itself under control of the State police in fulfilling its tasks in accordance with the law.

A commune may establish a commission to monitor the work of local police. Each national community in a commune shall have the right to participate in the work of the commission.

VIII. FINANCING

1. The organs established in Sections II-IV shall be entitled to income from their own duties and to a share of State taxes.

2. In view of the fact that this Agreement establishes new responsibilities for the organs of Kosovo and Metohija, the Republic and Federal authorities shall consider possibilities to ensure additional resources to exercise the competencies of the organs in Kosovo and Metohija established by this Agreement. These resources shall include funds (plus tax deductions), equipment and training.

IX. CONFIDENCE-BUILDING MEASURES

1. No person shall be prosecuted for acts related to the conflicts in Kosovo and Metohija except for crimes against humanity and international law as set forth in Chapter XVI of the Federal Penal Code. In order to facilitate transparency, the State shall grant access to foreign experts (including forensics), along with state investigators.

2. The competent organs shall, through the relevant judicial procedure based on the law, grant amnesty to persons for whom it is proved that they had not committed crimes against humanity and international law, mitigate the sentences to those who cooperated with investigative authorities, those who had been forcibly drafted or voluntarily handed over weapons.

X. IMPLEMENTATION OF THE AGREEMENT

1. The signatories to this Agreement undertake the obligation to implement it as soon as possible.

2. The State authorities shall undertake the amending of regulations necessary for the implementation of the Agreement, without delay.

3. The competent State organs shall organize, as soon as possible, an objective and free census of the population in Kosovo and Metohija, under the OSCE supervision. The census shall provide necessary information on the places of residence, citizenship, voter lists, and other data relevant for conducting elections.

4. Within nine months, there shall be free and fair elections for all organs in Kosovo and Metohija. The Government of the FR of Yugoslavia invites the OSCE to monitor the elections.

5. The signatories to this Agreement shall extend active support and cooperation to, and shall participate in the implementation of the Agreement.

6. The State authorities shall ensure initial and necessary conditions for the functioning of organs established by this Agreement.

XI. AMENDMENTS

1. Amendments to this Agreement shall be made by agreement of the signatories.

2. Each signatory may propose amendments to this Agreement. The signatories undertake to duly consider proposed amendments.

3. After three years, the signatories shall comprehensively review this Agreement with a view to improving its implementation and shall consider the proposals of any signatory for additional measures, whose adoption shall require the consent of all signatories.

XII. FINAL PROVISIONS

1. This Agreement is concluded in the Serbian language and the languages of national communities (Albanian, Romany, and Turkish) in Kosovo and Metohija.

2. This Agreement shall enter into force on the day of its signature.

FOR THE REPUBLIC OF SERBIA
FOR THE NATIONAL COMMUNITIES IN KOSOVO AND METOHIJA (in alphabetical order)
FOR THE FR OF YUGOSLAVIA

10. Declaration in Support of Joint Proposal for Agreement, Belgrade, 25 November 1998

Representatives of national communities and political parties
- National Party of Kosovo, Kosovo Democratic Initiative, National Community of Turks, National community of Goranies, National Community of Muslims, National Community of Romanies and National Community of Egyptians, together with the representatives of parliamentary parties from Kosovo and Metohija, with the representatives of parties in the National Assembly of Serbia and the State delegation, at the meeting in Pristina of 25. November 1998, with respect to the joint proposal of the Agreement on the political frameworks of self-governance in Kosovo and Metohija, adopted the following:

DECLARATION

1. The signatories to the Declaration assess that the joint proposal of the Agreement on the political frameworks for self-governance in Kosovo and Metohija represents a just and democratic political solution to the problems in Kosmet and emphasize that its adoption and implementation will be of key importance to peace, stability and development of this Province.

2. The signatories to the Declaration assess that the Joint Agreement on political frameworks for self-governance in Kosovo and Metohija entirely affirms full equality of all national communities, as well as that all legal solutions for the establishment of self-governance in Kosovo and Metohija should be in accordance with the legal systems of the Republic of Serbia and the FR of Yugoslavia, as well as with the international standards and basic documents.

It was jointly assessed that broad self-governance, based on the equality of national communities, is a cornerstone for the political solution and a condition for overcoming tensions and conflicts.

3. The signatories to the Declaration particularly point out that the proposed Agreement defines principles, creates institutional prerequisites of the broad democratic self-governance of national communities in Kosmet, sets forth the rights and obligations and ensures that they be efficiently realized and protected within the rule of law - in the interest of every national community and all citizens in Kosovo and Metohija.

They point out that the proposed Agreement provides a new atmosphere of tolerance, dialogue, trust and life and work in peace, freedom and equality.

4. The signatories to the Declaration decide to establish a single Commission to organize the elaboration of legal documents and undertake necessary acts and procedures in the process of realization of the jointly proposed Agreement.

The Joint Commission will be composed of members of the State delegation, representatives of national communities and representatives of political parties in Kosovo and Metohija.

5. The signatories to this Declaration invite all other political parties from Kosovo and Metohija to join the Agreement, i.e. to consider the Agreement open for accession by all other parties, and as an invitation to make their full contribution (through observations, suggestions and in other ways) to its elaboration and realization in the interest of all people living in Kosmet, in the interest of peace, development and prosperity.

6. This Declaration has been signed in Serbian and in the languages of the members of national communities (Albanian, Turkish) in Kosovo and Metohija.

For the Republic of Serbia, Dr Ratko Markovic

For the national and political parties in Kosovo and Metohija:
Kosovo Democratic Initiative, Faik Jasari
National Party of Kosovo, Aron Abazi
National Community of Goranies, Ibro Vait
National Community of Egyptians, Cerim Abazi
National Community of Muslims, Refik Senadovic
National Community of Romanies, Ljuan Koka
National Community of Turks, Zejnelabedin Kurejs
Democratic Party of the Turks, Sadik Tanjol
Parliamentary parties from Kosovo and Metohija, Radenko Krulj

For the FR of Yugoslavia, Dr Vladan Kutlesic

11. Kosova Press Release: Hill draft plan should be further improved, 1 December 1998

Dr. Fehmi Agani, head of the Kosova negotiating team, told a press conference held in the KIC Press Center in Prishtina today the team, although not complete, had done a significant job in advancing the interests of Kosova in the negotiating process mediated by U.S. envoy Chris Hill. Hill's plan has undergone changes for the better, according to Agani, who said "30 hours of our discussions" have been incorporated in it. The Kosova negotiating team has commented on all articles and formulations of the Hill draft plan, he said, adding that the team has produced three written statements of objections/remarks, "an entire body of written complaints/objections". Dr. Agani said representatives of the UÇK (Kosova Liberation Army) and the LBD, the coalition group of opposition parties chaired by Rexhep Qosja, should join the negotiating team. "In a way they have been participating in the negotiations, because Ambassador Hill has contacted both the parties and presented them with the text of the draft plan".

The Kosova Albanian side "has serious objections to the Hill draft plan", Dr. Agani said, adding that the draft plan should be improved "to reflect a reality and other equitable political relations".

All the political parties represented in the Parliament of the Republic of Kosova have subscribed to the idea of an interim settlement for Kosova, Dr. Fehmi Agani said. This is not, however, to drop the independence goal, he added, "but rather an attempt to facilitate and secure in the interim period a lasting resolution".

It would be good that even an interim solution be put to the people of Kosova in a referendum, Agani said, noting that the three-year interim solution proposed by the Kosova side does not "get off track" of the independence referendum of 1991.

The talks have been going on through Ambassador Chris Hill "under a tacit agreement by Prishtina and Belgrade", the Kosova negotiator said.

Dr. Agani called a proposed plan on Kosova presented by the Serbian 'disastrous', adding that it constituted a stumbling block to the negotiating process. Serb President Milutinovic's paper is an attempt to legalize the fait accompli situation created by the Serbian Constitution of 1990. "That constitution had been adopted without and against the will of the [Kosova] Albanians", Dr. Agani said, adding that the aim was to degenerate the position of Kosova and the Albanians in former Yugoslavia.

The chief Kosova negotiator mocked Serbia's efforts to de-structure (fragmentize) Kosova, to treat it as an association of national communities, and exposed Belgrade's idea of representation of these communities. The representation is an institutions, and only one who is elected and authorized to represent is a representative, Agani said. "Luan Koka is a Gypsy. This in itself does not mean that he is a Gypsy representative", the Kosova negotiator concluded.

The Serbian regime has picked up the representatives of the national communities in Kosova, all of whom members of the two parties chaired by the Milosevic-Markovic couple in Belgrade.

12. 3rd Hill Draft Proposal for a Settlement of the Crisis in Kosovo, 2 December 1998

I. INTRODUCTION

1. All citizens and peoples in Kosovo have equal rights and duties as set forth in this Agreement. Members of each national community shall have additional rights as set forth below. The national communities shall be legally equal and shall not use their additional rights so as to endanger the rights of other national communities or the rights of citizens.

2. The authorities of Kosovo shall follow principles of full respect of human rights and democracy, and for the equality of all citizens and national communities. Citizens in Kosovo shall enjoy human and democratic rights and shall be given the opportunity to be represented in all institutions in Kosovo. All citizens and national communities in Kosovo shall be guaranteed full affirmation and equal treatment of their national, confessional, and cultural values and historic patrimony.

3. The authorities in Kosovo, acting in accordance with this Agreement, shall be independent. Citizens in Kosovo shall have the right to democratic self-government through assemblies, executive, judicial, and other institutions established in accordance with this Agreement. The right of democratic self-government shall include the right to participate in free and fair elections.

4. Every person in Kosovo shall have the right to apply to international institutions for the protection of their rights in accordance with the procedures of such institutions.

The Parties accept and will abide by the principle that their powers and authorities in Kosovo are as specified by this Agreement, which shall prevail over any other legal provisions of the Parties. In implementing this Agreement in accordance with their procedures and international standards, the parties shall harmonize their governing practices and documents. All parties shall make the necessary political and legal commitments to implement this Agreement fully.

II. GOVERNANCE IN KOSOVO

PART I: GENERAL

1. The basic territorial unit of local government will be the communes. All responsibilities of government and public authority affecting Kosovo not expressly assigned elsewhere by this Agreement will be the responsibility of the communes.

2. The Federal Republic's authority in Kosovo over the following areas shall not be affected by this Agreement, except as specified in paragrapf 3:

(a) territorial integrity;

(b) maintaining a common market within the Federal Republic of Yugoslavia;

(c) monetary policy;

(d) defense;

(e) foreign policy;

(f) federal taxation;

(g) customs services; and

(h) [   ].*

3. The Federal Republic of Yugoslavia shall act in Kosovo in a manner consistent with Kosovo's democratic self-governance. This includes, but is not limited to, the following undertakings:

a)   No change to the external or internal borders of Kosovo shall be made without the consent of the Kosovo Assembly and Presidency.

b) Deployment and use of Federal military forces in Kosovo shall be governed by Annex 2 of this Agreement.

c) Kosovo officers and institutions shall have the authority to conduct foreign relations within the areas for which they are responsible, subject to respect for the sovereignty and territorial integrity of the Federal Republic of Yugoslavia and Article 109 (6) of the Constitution of the Republic of Serbia.

(d) Citizens in Kosovo will have the opportunity to paricipate in carrying out customs activities in Kosovo. They shall serve this function as Federal customs officers. Custom officers in Kosovo shall be representative of the national communities of Kosovo.

e)   All Federal taxes and duties applicable within Kosovo shall be set in a non-discriminatory way at uniform rates applicable for the whole territory of the Federation.

f) Martial law shall not be declared in Kosovo without the consent of the Kosovo Presidency.

g) Federal measures having a differential, disproportionate, or discriminatory impact on Kosovo shall not take effect in Kosovo without the

consent of the Kosovo Presidency.

h) The institutions and officers of the Federal Republic shall abide by this Agreement in its entirety.

4. Within Kosovo the institutions established by this Agreement shall exercise all competences currently exercised by the Republic, except for the following competences and any other competences expressly reserved for the Republic by this Agreement:

a) The Republic may continue to maintain a system of health care, of education, and of care for war veterans and disabled persons, which shall be available equally to the members of all national communities. This authority shall not be interpreted to limit the authority of Kosovo institutions to establish similar systems in their areas. Arrangements will be made in Annex 3 for the treatment of existing health care and educational facilities.

[* Note: A proposal may be made to expand the list of Federal responsibilities to include other matters.]

b) The Republic shall have the authority to enact measures relating to the protection of workers' safety and health, provided that all such measures shall be administered in a nondiscriminatory manner throughout the Republic.

c) The Republic may maintain systems of social protection and social security and provide other public services to citizens in Kosovo. These programs shall not discriminate on the basis of membership in a particular National Community, and participation and use (including payment of any taxes necessary to fund participation in or use of such services) shall be on a voluntary basis. This authority shall not be interpreted to limit the authority of Kosovo institutions to establish systems and provide services in these areas.

5. Kosovo, Federal and Republic authorities shall not interfere with the exercise of the additional rights described in Article IV of this Agreement.

PART II: ASSEMBLY, PRESIDENCY, AND ADMINISTRATIVE BODIES

The Assembly

1. There shall be an Assembly, which shall comprise [   ] Members.

(a) [   ] Members shall be directly elected in accordance with Article IX (4) and Annex 4.

(b) The remaining [   ] Members shall be allocated equally among the national communities with at least [   ] % of   the population of Kosovo, each of which shall elect Members democratically according to its own procedure. Each applicable national community shall have at least one Member in the Assembly.

2. The Assembly shall be responsible for adopting the Constitution of Kosovo and enacting Decisions of Kosovo, including those regulating relations in political, economic, social, and cultural areas. The Constitution and Decisions of the Kosovoa Assembly shall not be subject to change or modification by authorities of the Republics or the Federation so long as they are consistent with this Agreement and within the scope of the jurisdiction herein provided for Kosovo.

a) The Assembly's areas of responsibility shall include:

- Financing activities of Kosovo institutions, including by levying taxes and duties on sources within Kosovo;
- The adoption of budgets and annual accounts of the Administrative bodies and other institutions of Kosovo, with the exception of communal and national community institutions unless otherwise specified by this Agreement;
- The adoption of regulations concerning the organization, procedures, and functioning of the Administrative Bodies of Kosovo;
- Approving candidates put forward by the Kosovo Presidency for Kosovo judicial offices;
- Ensuring freedom of movement of goods, services, and persons consistent with the responsibilities of other authorities;
- Conducting relations with foreign entities and approving agreements within its areas of responsibility, consistent with the authorities of Kosovo institutions under this Agreement;
- Cooperating with the Federal Assembly, and with the Assemblies of the Republics;
- Establishing, in accordance with this Agreement, the main rules of local self-government, including in particular rules on elections, finance, the status of elected local officials, and on local government employees;
- Coordination among communes or national communities when necessary, including the enactment of Decisions concerning inter-communal issues;
- Protection of the environment where inter-communal issues are involved; and
- Designing and implementing programs of economic, scientific, technological, demographic, regional, and social development of agriculture and of rural areas.

b) The Assembly shall also have authority to enact Decisions on areas whithin the responsibility of the Communes if the matter cannot be effectively regulated by the Communes or if regulation by individual Communes might prejudice the rights of other Communes or if uniform legislation is necessary to ensure throughout Kosovo the equality of rights granted by this Agreement to individuals. In the absence of a specific Decision by the Assembly validly taken within this authority that preempts communal action, the Communes shall retain their authority.

3. Decisions of the Assembly shall be taken by majority of those present and voting, except as provided in paragraph 4.

[Option 1:

4. When a majority of the Members of a national community selected pursuant to paragraph 1(b) assert that a proposed decision affects the vital interests of their national community, that decision shall require for approval, in addition to the majority specified in paragraph 3, a majority of the Members present and voting from that national community. If a majority of Members from the asserting community is not present and voting, the regular voting rule shall apply. Any other national community wishing to assert that the same proposed decision also affects its vital interests must make its claim within two days after the privilege is first asserted. After that two day period has elapsed, no national community may assert the privilege set forth in this paragraph with respect to the same proposed decision.

5. The following procedure shall be used to resolve disputes regarding the exercise of the national community privilege set forth in paragraph 4:

(a) The national community or communities asserting the privilege will give reasons to the Assembly explaining its concerns. Members of the Assembly supporting the proposed decision will given an opportunity to respond. The Presidency of Kosovo shall mediate the dispute and attempt to reach a settlement agreable to all affected national communities.

[Option 1a:

(b) If mediation does not produce a mutually agreable result within seven days, there shall be a vote of the Assembly. The proposed decision shall take effect if it receives the support of [4/5] of the Members of the whole Assembly, including a simple majority of the members representing each of at least two national communities selected pursuant to paragraph 1(b).]

[Option 1b:

(b) If mediation does not produce a mutually agreable result within seven days, the matter will be given to the Constitutional Court. The Court shall determine wether as a matter of law the vital national interests of the community or communities asserting the privilege set forth in paragraph 4 are affected by the proposed decision. The Court shall hear argument and rule within ten days.

(c) The decision of the Court may be appealed by either party to the [Director of the Kosovo Verification Mission so long as the mission remains in place, or alternatively the designee of the OSCE Chair in Office] [Chair of the Joint Commission], who shall resolve the matter acting in a quasi-judicial capacity. He or she shall rule within ten days. The judgement shall be final.]]

[Option 2:

Decisions of the Assembly are presumed valid. If a majority of the members from any national community delegation selected pursuant to paragraph 1(b) believes that its vital interests are adversely affected by a Decision, the delegation may seek review of the Decision before the Constitutional Court and, on appeal, the [Director of the Kosovo Verification Mission so long as the mission remains in place, or alternatively the designee of the OSCE Chair in Office] [Chair of the Joint Commission]. Decisions determined to affect adversely a national community's vital interests will be set aside.]

6. A majority of Members shall constitute a quorum. The Assembly will decide its own rules of procedure. Members of Assembly shall be imune from civil or criminal proceedings on the basis of opinions expressed or votes cast in the Assembly.

7. The Assembly shall elect from among its Members a President, two Vice-Presidents, and other leaders in accordance with the procedures of the Assembly. Each national community covered by paragraph 1(b) shall be represented in the leadership.

(a) The President of the Assembly shall represent the Assembly, call its sessions to order, chair its meetings, coordinate the work of any Committees it may establish, and perform other tasks prescribed by the rules of procedure of the Assembly.

[Option 1:

b) The President of the Assembly may not be from the same national community as the Chair of the Kosovo Presidency.]

[Option 2: No text.]

Presidency

8. Executive power shall be exercised by the Presidency, which shall consist of one representative from each National Community qualifying under the terms set forth in Annex 5.

(a) Each member of the Presidency shall be selected by the Assembly for a [three] year term. No person may serve more than two terms as a member of the presidency.

(i) There shall be a Chair of the Presidency, who shall be selected from among the members of the Presidency by majority vote of the Assembly. The Chair shall call meetings of the Presidency, represent it in areas within its competence, and organize its work.

(ii) The Presidency shall decide its own rules of procedure. It shall endeavor to act by consensus. Subject to the privilege set forth in section (a) (iii) of this paragraph, decisions may be taken by the Chair where all efforts to achieve consensus have failed.

(iii) Within four days of the adoption of a Decision of the Presidency, a Member of the Presidency may assert that the Decision affects a vital interest of his or her national ommunity.

a) The issue shall be promptly referred to his or her national community. If the national community affirms within ten days by a decision taken under its own democratic procedures that its vital interests are affected, the Decision shall be rescinded.*

b) Dissenting Members of the Presidency may petition the Constitutional Court to have a Decision reinstated on the grounds that the vital interests of the national community asserting the privilege are not adversely affected. The Court shall decide within ten days.

[* Note: The privilege to block a Decision of the Presidency as affecting a vital interest could be limited to certain categories of important matters. This will be a subject for further discussion.]

c) The ruling of the Constitutional Court may be further appealed by either party to the [Director of the Kosovo Verification Mission so long as the mission remains in place, or alternatively the designee of the OSCE Chair in Office] [Chair of the Joint Commission] who shall resolve tha matter acting in a quasi-judicial capacity. The decision shall be final.

b) The Presidency shall be responsable for:

Representing all citizens in Kosovo before any international or Federal body, or any body of the Republics.

- Implementing the Decisions of the Assembly and of other authorities when authorized by those authorities.
- Selecting officers of the Administrative Bodies to assist in carrying out these executive responsibilities.
- Proposing to the Assembly candidates for the Constitutional Court, the Supreme Court, and other Kosovo judicial offices.
- Proposing Decisions to the Assembly.
- Meeting regularly with the democratically selected representatives of the national communities and other persons.
- Conducting foreign relations and concluding agreements on behalf of Kosovo
- after they are approved by the Assembly, consistent with the authorities of Kosovo institutions under this Agreement.
- Serving or designating a representative to serve on the Joint Commission and Joint Council established by Article VII of this Agreement.
- Meeting regularly with the President of the Federal Republic of Yugoslavia, the President of Montenegro, and the President of Serbia.
- Other duties specified in this Agreement.

Administrative Bodies

9. Administrative Bodies shall be responsible for assisting the Presidency in implementing Decisions of Kosovo and, where authorized, of other authorities.

(a) Employees of administrative bodies shall be fairly representative of the population and national communities of Kosovo.

(b) Any citizen of Kosovo claiming to have been directly and adversely affected by the decision of an executive or administrative body shall have the right to judicial review of that decision after exhausting any avenues for administrative review. The Assembly shall enact administrative law to regulate this review.

(c) An administrative body of Kosovo shall have primary responsibility for all criminal law enforcement matters in Kosovo, in accordance with Annex 2 to this Agreement.

PART III : COURTS IN KOSOVO

General

1. Kosovo shall have a Constitutional Court, a Supreme Court, District Courts, and Communal Courts. The Kosovo Supreme Court shall, upon approval by the Kosovo Assembly, promulgate rules of procedure consistent with this Agreement to guide the courts' activities.

[Option:

a) Until such time as the parties mutually agree to discontinue this arrangement or the Federal Republic becomes member of the Council of Europe and appeals are possible under its rules to the European Court of Human Rights, a majority of judges on the Constitutional Court shall be selected from a list presented by the Committee of Ministers of the Council of Europe pursuant to Council Resolution (93) 6.]

2. The Kosovo courts shall shall have jurisdiction over all legal matters arising under the Constitution of Kosovo, Decisions of the Assembly, and laws of the Republic of Serbia. Disputes presenting solely questions of Republic law may be appealed to the Supreme Court of Serbia after all appeals available in the Kosovo courts have been exhausted.

3. The Kosovo courts shall also have jurisdiction as specified in this paragraph over matters arising under federal law or raising questions of federal law. Disputes presenting federal questions may be appealed to the Federal courts after all appeals available under the Kosovo system have been exhausted.

(a) Kosovo courts shall adjudicate all civil and administrative cases in Kosovo arising under Federal law or raising federal law questions in the first instance. Except as specified in Section 3 (b) of this Part, Kosovo courts shall also adjudicate criminal cases in Kosovo arising under federal law.

(b) Those federal criminal matters specified in [   ]* shall be adjudicated enterely by the courts of the Federal Republic of Yugoslavia. An appropriate branch of the Federal Court shall be established in Kosovo for this purpose.

4. The Republic of Serbia shall continue to maintain separate courts in Kosovo. Citizens in Kosovo may opt to have civil and administrative disputes to which they are a party adjudicated by the Republic courts, which shall apply applicable Kosovo legal authorities and shall refer matters falling within paragraph 6 (b) to the Constitutional Court. Criminal defendants may opt to have their cases decided by a Republic court pursuant to the same provisos applicable to civil and administrative cases, except with respect to these cases involving federal matters specified in Section 3 (b) of this Part.

[* This section of the Agreement will set forth a list of serious crimes with gross-border implications, such as counterfeiting of money and narcotics trafficking. The list will be a subject for negotiation between the parties.]

Members of the Judiciary

5. Composition. The Constitutional Court shall consist of [nine] judges. The Supreme Court shall consist of [nine] judges. The Assembly shall determine the number of other judges necessary to meet current needs.

(a) The judges shall be distinguished jurists of the highest moral character.

(b) The judges shall be broadly representative of the national communities of Kosovo. There shall be a least one Constitutional Court judge and one Supreme Court judge from each national community representing at least []% of the population of Kosovo.

(c) Removal of a Kosovo judge shall require the consensus of the judges of the Constitutional Court. A Constitutional Court judge whose dismissal is in question shall not participate in the deliberations on his case.

6. Jurisdiction of the Constitutional Court

The Constitutional Court shall have sole authority to resolve disputes relating to the meaning of the Kosovo Constitution. That authority shall include, but is not limited to, determining wether decisions or actions of the Presidency, the Assembly, the Council of Ministers, the Communes, and the national communities are compatible with the Kosovo Constitution.

(a) Matters may be referred to the court by the Presidency of Kosovo, the President or Vice-Presidents of the Assembly, the Ombudsman, the communal assemblies and councils, and any national community acting according to its democratic procedures.

(b) Any court, which finds in the course of adjudicating a matter that the dispute depends on the answer to a question within the Court's jurisdiction, shall refer the issue to the Court for a preliminary decision.

(c) Following the exhaustion of other legal remedies, the Court shall at the request of any natural or legal person or association have jurisdiction over complaints that human rights and fundamental freedoms and the rights of members of national communities set forth in this Agreement have been violated by a public authority.

(d) The Constitution of Kosovo may provide that the Court shall have jurisdiction over other questions arising under it. The Constitutional Court

shall have such other authorities and jurisdiction as may be specified elsewhere in this Agreement.

7. Jurisdiction of the Supreme Court. The Supreme Court shall hear appeals from the District Courts and the Communal Courts. Subject to the specific powers of the Constitutional Court, and to paragraphs 2, 3, and 4 of this Part, the Supreme Court shall take the final decision in all cases arising within Kosovo. Its decisions shall be recognized and executed by all public authorities on the territory of the Federal republic of Yugoslavia.

8. Functioning of the Courts. The Constitutional and Supreme Courts shall each adopt decisions by majority vote of their members. All Kosovo courts shall hold public proceedings, and issue published opinions setting forth the reasons for their decisions along with any dissenting views.

National Community Dispute Settlement Mechanism

9. Each national community may establish procedures for resolving conflicts concerning inheritance, family law, matrimonial relations, tutorship, adoption, civil lawsuits as decided by the Assembly of Kosovo, and criminal cases for which a monetary fine is prescribed as punishment in the currently applicable penal code.

a) Dispute settlement mechanisms established under this provision shall have jurisdiction only when all parties consent.

b) Within the framework of these procedures, no decisions on arrest or detention of a person may be taken. If a competent authority established under this provision considers during its review of a criminal case that a sentence of imprisonment might be appropriate, it shall refer the case to the competent court.

c) Procedures established under this provision must maintain practices consistent with internationally recognized human rights. At the request of one of the parties, the Constitutional Court of Kosovo shall review whether any decision taken within this framework respects the provisions of this Agreement, including in particular the human rights guarantees set forth in Article III.

d) Decisions of the national community dispute resolution mechanism shall be honored in accordance with applicable rules by Kosovo courts, Republic courts, and the courts of the Federal Republic of Yugoslavia.

PART IV. THE OMBUDSMAN

1. There shall be an Ombudsman, who shall monitor the realization of the rights of members of national communities and the protection of human rights and fundamental freedoms in Kosovo.

(a) The Ombudsman shall be an eminent person of high moral standing who possesses a demonstrated commitment to human rights and the rights of the national communities.

(b) He or she shall be nominated by the Presidency and shall be elected by the Assembly from a list of candidates prepared by the President of the European Court for Human Rights for a non-renewable [four] year term.

2. The Ombudsman shall be independently responsible for choosing his or her staff. He or she shall have two Deputies. The Deputies shall each be drawn from different national communities, and neither shall be from the same national community as the Ombudsman if he or she is a member of a national community in Kosovo.

3. The Ombudsman shall have a right to review the acts and shall have unimpeded access to any person or place and shall have the right to appear and intervene before any domestic, Federal, or (consistent with the rules of such bodies) international authority upon his or her request. The Ombudsman shall have other powers and jurisdiction as set forth in Annex 1.

PART V: COMMUNES

[Option 1 : 1. Kosovo shall have the existing communes.]

[Option 2 : 1. Kosovo shall have [   ] communes within the boundaries specified in annex 6 of this Agreement.]

2. Communes may develop relationships among themselves for their mutual benefit.]

3. Each Commune shall have an Assembly, a Council, and such executive bodies as the commune may establish. Each national community with at least [   ]% of the population of the commune shall be represented on the Council in proportion to its share of the regional population or by one member, whichever is greater.

4. The communes shall have exclusive responsibility for:

- Law enforcement, as specified in annex 2 of this Agreement.
- Regulating and, when appropriate, providing childcare.
- Establishing and regulating the work of medical institutions and hospitals.
- Providing and regulating education, consistent with the rights and duties of national communities.
- Protecting the communal environment.
- Regulating commerce and privately owned stores.
- Regulating hunting and fishing.
- Planning and carrying out public works of communal importance, including roads and water supplies, and participating in the planning and carrying out Kosovo-wide public works projects in coordination with other communes and Kosovo authorities.
- Regulating land use, town planning, building regulations, and housing construction.
- Developing programs for tourism, the hotel industry, catering, and sport.
- Organizing fairs and local markets.
- Organizing public services of communal importance, including fire, emergency response, and police consistent with Annex 2 of this Agreement.
- Financing the work of communal institutions, including raising revenues, taxes, and preparing budgets.

5. The commune shall also have responsibility for all other areas not expressly assigned elsewhere by this Agreement, subject to the provisions of Article II, Part II.2 (b).

6. Each commune shall conduct its buseness in public and shall maintain publicly available records of its deliberations and decisions.

III. HUMAN RIGHTS AND FUNDAMENTAL FREEDOMS

1. The Parties shall ensure that the highest level of internationally recognized human rights and fundamental freedoms is secured for all persons in Kosovo.

2. Applicable rights and freedoms shall include those specified in the European Convention for the Protection of Human Rights and Fundamental Freedoms and its protocols.

a) The European Convention shall be directly applicable in Kosovo and in any matter involving a person of Kosovo, and shall take precedence over all other law.

b) All courts, agencies, government institutions, and instrumentalities of the Parties and all of their officials and employees shall conform to these human rights and fundamental freedoms.

IV. RIGHTS AND DUTIES OF MEMEBERS OF NATIONAL COMMUNITIES

1. Members of the national communities shall have additional rights determined by this Agreement in order to preserve and express their national, cultural, religious, and linguistic identities in accordance with international standards and the Helsinki final Act.

2. Each national community shall select through democratic means, in accordance with procedures it shall decide, institutions to administer its affairs in Kosovo.

3. The national communities shall be subject to Decisions of the Assembly of Kosovo, provided that any action concerning national communities must be nondiscriminatory. The Assembly shall decide upon procedure for resolving disputes between national communities.

4. The additional rights of the national communities, acting through their democratically selected institutions, are to:

(a) preserve and protect their national culture, including by:

- inscribing local names of towns and villages, of squares and streets, and of other topographic names in the language and alphabet of the national community in addition to signs in Serbian, consistent with decisions about style made by the communal institutions.
- providing information in the language and alphabet of the national community.
- establishing cultural and religious associations, for which relevant authorities will provide financial assistance.
- providing for education and establishing educational institutions, in particular for schooling in their own language and alphabet and in national
- culture and history, for which relevant authorities will provide financial assistance. National communities are encouraged to coordinate curricula with Republic authorities concerning some subjects (for example, to ensure that pupils satisfy common standards in subjects such as math and science).
- enjoying unhindered contacts with representatives of their respective national communities, within the Federal Republic of Yugoslavia and abroad.
- using and displaying national symbols, along with symbols of the Federal Republic of Yugoslavia and the Republic of Serbia.
- protecting national practices on family law by, if the community decides, arranging rules in the field of inheritance, family and matrimonial relations; tutorship; and adoption.
- the preservation of sites of religious, historical, or cultural importance to the national community, in cooperation with other authorities.
- implementing public health and social services.
- operating religious institutions in cooperation with religious authorities.
- participating in regional and international non-governmental organizations in accordance with procedures of these organizations.

(b) adopt procedures for dispute resolution, as provided in Article II, Part III(g) of this Agreement.
(c) be guaranteed at least one radio and television frequency, which they shall each administer subject to non-discriminatory, technical standards;
(d) finance their activities by collecting charges the national communities may decide to levy on members of their own communities.
5. Members of national communities shall also be individually guaranteed:
the right to enjoy unhindered contacts with members of their respective national communities elsewhere in the Federal Republic of Yugoslavia and abroad.
- equal access to employment in public services at all levels.
- the right to use their languages and alphabets.
- the right to use and display national community symbols on private occasions.
- the right to participate in democratic institutions that will determine the national community's exercise of the collective rights set forth in this Article.

6. Each national community and, where appropriate, their members acting individually may exercise these additional rights through Federal institutions and institutions of the Republics, in accordance with the procedures of those institutions and without prejudice to the ability of Kosovo institutions to carry out their responsibilities.

V.   REPRESENTATION OF KOSOVO IN FEDERAL INSTITUTIONS
1. Kosovo shall be offered the following representation, without prejudice to the rights of persons in Kosovo to decide whether to accept this offer;
a) At least [   ] deputies in the House of Citizens of the Federal Assembly.

b) At least [   ] deputies in the National Assembly of the Republic of Serbia.
c) The opportunity for the Kosovo Assembly to present to the appropriate authorities a list of candidates from which shall be drawn:
(i) at least one citizen in Kosovo to serve in the Federal Government, and at least one citizen to serve in the Government of the Republic of Serbia.
(ii) at least one judge on the Federal Constitutional Court, one judge in the Federal Court, and three judges on the Supreme Court of Serbia.
2. There shall be a Council of the Republic of Serbia for the protection of the rights of the members of national communities. The President of the Republic of Serbia shall preside over this Council.

VI.   FINANCING AND OTHER ECONOMIC ISSUES
Financing
1. The authorities established to levy and collect taxes and other charges are set forth in this Agreement. Except if otherwise expressly provided in this Agreement, those bodies have the right to keep all revenues from their own taxes or other charges.
2. In accordance with the provisions of Annex 3, the authorities of Kosovo shall forward to Federal authorities a fair share of revenue collected within Kosovo, if necessary for funding of Federal responsibilities within Kosovo and not covered by revenue from Federal taxes from Kosovo.
3. In accordance with the provisions of Annex 3, revenue from certain Kosovo taxes and duties shall accrue to the Communes, taking into account the need for an equalization of revenues between the Communes based on objective criteria. The Communes shall also be able to levy local taxes, in accordance with the provisions of Annex 3.
4. Federal and other authorities shall also ensure, to the extent of their respective powers, the delivery of resources from international sources to Kosovo.
Other Economic Issues
5. Annex 3 of this Agreement shall specify, in terms consistent with this Agreement, arrangements for the disposition of government owned assets in Kosovo; the resolution of disputes over pension and social insurance contributions; and the resolution of other matters relating to economic relations between the parties.

VII.   JOINT COMMISSION AND JOINT COUNCIL
Joint Commission
1. A Joint Commission will serve as the central mechanism for monitoring and coordinating the implementation of this Agreement. It will be comprised of Federal and Republic representatives, representatives of the national communities in Kosovo, representatives of Kosovo political institutions including the Presidency and the Ombudsman, and international representatives (including the Kosovo Verification Mission and Contact Group).
2. A person of high moral character will be selected to serve as Chair of the Joint Commission. The Chair will coordinate and organize the work of the Joint Commission, supervise the overall implementation of this Agreement, and shall have other powers, authorities, and duties as set forth herein or as may be later agreed by the Parties.
(a) For [ten] years following the entry into force of this Agreement, the Chair shall be a person chosen by the Chair in Office of the OSCE after consultation with the Parties. During this initial period, the Chair of the Joint Commission shall not be citizen of the Federal Republic of Yugoslavia or a surrounding state.
(b) After the initial period, the Chair shall be selected by consensus between the President of the Federal Republic of Yugoslavia, and the Presidency of Kosovo. In the event the parties cannot reach an agreement, the Chair shall be a person selected by the Chair in Office of the OSCE after consultations with the Parties.
3. The Parties shall cooperate with the Commission and its Chair. The Joint Commission as a whole and the Chair individually on his or her own initiative shall have safe, complete, and unimpeded access to all places, persons, and information (including documents and other records) both within Kosovo and, where the Joint Commission or the Chair deem it relevant, within the Federal Republic.

4. In the event of disagreement as to the meaning of any provision of this Agreement a Party may petition the Chair of the Join Comission, who shall have final authority to resolve such disputes. The Parties agree to abide by the Chair's decision.

Joint Council

5. The national communities shall establish a Joint Council to coordinate their activities under this Agreement, and to provide an informal mechanism for the resolution of disputes. The Joint Council shall consist of one member from each of the national communities. Its activities shall be founded equally by the once each month. The Joint Council shall encourage the creation of similar mechanisms at the communal level, building on the example of local commissions established pursuant to Article VIII(5) of this Agreement.

VIII. CONFIDENCE - BUILDING MEASURES

1. Violence in Kosova shall cease. Alleged violations of the cease-fire shall be reported to international observers and will not be used to justify violence in response. All persons held by the Parties without charge shall be released.

2. [An agreement on the status of security forces in Kosovo, to be added after expert consultations.]

3. [An agreement on the status of police forces in Kosovo, to be added after expert consultations.]

4. Each side will encourage all persons displaced during the conflict to return to their homes as the security situation permits. There will be no impediments to the normal flow of goods in Kosovo. International humanitarian organizations will be freely permitted to provide building materials and other assistance to persons returning to their homes in Kosovo.

5. In each community a local commission, representative of all national communities there, will assist international humanitarian agencies in the delivery and distribution of food, medicine, clothes, construction materials, the restoration of electricity and water supply, and in encouraging returns.

6. International personnel, including the Kosovo Verification Mission and members of non-governmental organizations, shall be allowed unfettered access, at any time, throughout Kosovo. It is expected that international personnel will be present at all times in selected communities.

7. Each side shall respect its obligation to cooperate in the investigation and prosecution of war crimes, crimes against humanity, and other violations of international humanitarian law. In acknowledgement that allegations of atrocities cannot be resolved to the satisfaction of the other, each side will allow complete, unimpeded, and unfettered access to international experts - including forensics experts - authorized to investigate such allegations. Each side will provide full support and cooperation to the activities of the International Criminal Tribunal for the Former Yugoslavia.

8. No person shall be prosecuted for crimes related to the conflict in Kosovo, except for those who have committed war crimes, crimes against humanity, and other fundamental violations of international humanitarian law.

[Option 1 :

Republic and Federal authorities shall reexamine, for extraordinary mitigation of punishments, all sentences pronounced on members of national communities from Kosovo for acts motivated by political goals.]

[Option 2 :

There shall be a general amnesty for all persons in Kosovo convicted of committing politically motivated crimes related to the conflict in Kosovo.

This amnesty shall not apply to those properly convicted of committing war crimes, crimes against humanity, or other fundamental violations of international humanitarian law.]

IX. IMPLEMENTATION PERIOD

1. This Agreement shall be impemented as quickly as possible. The Parties undertake to allow, insofar as possible, its adequate implementation even before the adoption and undertaking of all acts and measures required to implement this Agreement.

2. The Parties will start without delay on any and all legal changes necessary for the full implementation of this Agreement. They acknowledge that complete implementation will require the adoption of necessary state regulations and other general acts, of the Constitution of Kosovo, political acts and measures, and the election and establishment of institutions and bodies set forth in the Agreement. This Agreement shall take precedence over all existing legal authorities of the parties.

3. Each national community in Kosovo is authorized to start exercising the additional rights determined by this Agreement, to the extent possible, immediately upon signature.

4. Within [nine] months, there shall be elections in accordance with and pursuant to procedures specified in Annex 4 of this Agreement for all authorities established herein, according to an electoral list prepared to international standards. The Government of the Federal Republic of Yugoslavia hereby invites the Organisation for Security and Cooperation in Europe (OSCE) to supervise those elections to ensure openness and fairness.

5. Under the supervision of the OSCE and with the participation of Kosovo authorities, Federal authorities shall conduct an objective and free census of the population in Kosovo, which shall be carried out when the OSCE determines that conditions allow an accurate census.

(a) The first census shall be limited to name, place of birth, address, gender, age, citizenship, nationality, and religion.

(b) The institutions and authorities of the Parties shall provide the institutions of Kosovo with all records necessary to conduct the census, including data about places of residence, citizenship, voters' lists, and other information.

6. The Parties shall provide active support, cooperation, and participation for the successful implementation of the Agreement.

7. Institutions currently in place in Kosovo shall remain until the establishment of the bodies created by this Agreement.

8. Martial law shall be repealed. Laws compatible with this Agreement shall remain in force until replaced by the decision of a competent body established herein.

X. AMENDMENTS

1. Amendments to the Agreement shall be adopted by agreement of all the parties.

2. Each Party may propose amendments at any time and will consider and consult with the other with regard to proposed amendments.

3. In three years, the Parties will undertake a comprehensive assessment of the Agreement, with the aim of improving ist implementation and considering proposals by either side for additional steps, which will require mutual agreement for adoption.

XI. FINAL PROVISIONS

1. This Agreement is concluded in [ ] languages.

[?]

6. This Agreement shall enter into force when each Party has notified the others of the completion of ist internal process.

FOR

Federal Republic of Yugoslavia, Republic of Serbia, Kosovo

ANNEX 1: THE OMBUDSMAN

General

1. The Office of the Ombudsman shall be an independent agency of Kosovo. In carrying out its mandate, no person, instituttion, or entity of the Parties may interfere with ist functions.

2. The salaries and expenses of the Ombudsman and his or her staff shall be determined and paid by the Kosovo Assembly. The salaries and expenses shall be fully adequate to implement the Ombudsman's mandate.

3. The Ombudsman and members of his or her staff shall not be held criminally or civilly liable for any acts carried out within the scope of their duties.

Jurisdiction

4. The Ombudsman shall consider:

a) alleged or apparent violations of human rights and fundamental freedoms in Kosovo, as provided in the Constitutions of the Federal Republic and theRepublic of Serbia, and the European Convention for the Protection of Human Rights and Fundamental Freedoms and the Protocols thereto; and

b) alleged or apparent violations of the rights of national communities specified in this Agreement.

5. All citizens in Kosovo shall have the right to submit complaints to the Ombudsman. The Parties agree not to take any measures to punish persons who intend to submit or who have submitted such allegations, or in any other way to deter the exercise of this right.

Powers and Authority

6. The Ombudsman shall investigate alleged violations falling within the jurisdiction set forth in paragraph five. He may act either on his own initiative or in response to an allegation presented by any Party or person, non-governmental organization, or group of individuals claiming to be the victim of a violation or acting on behalf of alleged victims who are deceased or missing. The work of the Ombudsman shall be free of charge to the person concerned.

7. The Ombudsman shall have complete, unimpeded, and immediate access to any person, place, or information upon his or her request.

   a) He shall have access to and may examine all official documents, and he can require any person, including officials in Kosovo, the Republic of Serbia, and the Federal Republic of Yugoslavia to cooperate by providing relevant information, documents, and files.

   b) The Ombudsman may attend administrative hearings, meetings of other Kosovo institutions, and meetings and proceedings of the Republics and the Federal Republic of Yugoslavia in order to gather information.

   c) He may examine facilities and places where persons deprived of their liberty are detained, work, or are otherwise located.

   d) The Ombudsman and staff shall maintain the confidentiality of all confidential information obtained by them, unless the Ombudsman determines that such information is evidence of a violation of rights falling within his or her jurisdiction, in which case that information may be revealed in public reports or appropriate legal proceedings.

   e) The Parties undertake to ensure cooperation with the Ombudsman's investigation. Willful and knowing failure to comply shall be a criminal offense prosecutable in any jurisdiction of the Parties. Where an official impedes an investigation by refusing to provide necessary information, the Ombudsman shall contact that official's superior or the public prosecutor for appropriate penal action to be taken in accordance with the law.

8. The Ombudsman shall issue findings and conclusions in the form of a published report promptly after concluding an investigation.

   a) A Party, institution, or official identified by the Ombudsman as a violator shall, within a period specified by the Ombudsman, explain in writing how it will comply with any prescriptions the Ombudsman may put forth for remedial measures.

   b) In the event that a person or entity does not comply with the conclusions and recommendations of the Ombudsman, the report shall be forwarded for further action to the Joint Commission set forth in Article VII of this Agreement, to the Presidency of the appropriate Party, and to any other officials or institutions that the Ombudsman deems proper.

9. The Ombudsman shall promptly report to the International Criminal Tribunal for the Former Yugoslavia evidence of war crimes, crimes against humanity, and other fundamental violations of international humanitarian law that may fall within the jurisdiction of that tribunal.

Other Annexes: The following additional annexes will be a part of the completed Agreement: Annex 2 : Police and Security Matters; Annex 3 : Financing and Other Economic Issues; Annex 4 : Conduct and Supervision of Election; Annex 5 : National Communities; [Annex 6: Communal Boundaries]

13.   Kosova Press Release: UCK won't settle for anything less than full independence, 5 December 1998

The Kosova Liberation Army (UÇK) stands firm in its commitment to the "just fight towards the creation of our independent and democratic state", the General Staff of the UÇK said in a statement, referred to as Political Declaration # 19, carried by today's Albanian-language press in Prishtina. The UÇK will not accept any political solution which "harms the ideals of our people for independence, or else would

sanction, be it even temporarily, an imposed co-existence in an anti-Albanian and anti-democratic edifice, such as Yugoslavia - Greater Serbia would be".The statement contravened remarks Mr. Adem Demaçi, the UÇK Political Representative, made last Tuesday in a press conference in Prishtina. He stated the UÇK would be willing to accept republic status for Kosova - on a par with Serbia and Montenegro within 'Yugoslavia' - on a temporary basis, with guarantees that in three years' time the people of Kosova would determine their future in a referendum. The General Staff of the UÇK called on the international community, first and foremost the United States of America, to support Kosovar independence, "which would mean also the triumph of democratic principles in this part of the volatile Balkans, and would result in a lasting peace in the future". The Serbian aggressor's forces have been attacking the civilian Albanian population in certain parts of Kosova, and the UÇK has been responding to such attacks in defense of the population, the General Staff of the UÇK said. "We are making efforts to preserve the cease-fire that we have ourselves declared", the UÇK said. "Although unjustly excluded from the agreement on the deployment of international observers in Kosova, and therefore not obligatory to us", the UÇK welcomes their arrival and will undertake all measures within its power to cooperate with them as well as to ensure their security, the statement said.

14.   Kosova Press Release: Demaci rejects Hill's Plan, 8 December 1998

Mr. Adem Demaçi, the main political representative of the Kosova Liberation Army (UÇK), called the new Hill draft on an interim solution for Kosova "utterly unacceptable". The current draft is an essential degraded version of the previous draft, "which was also unacceptable", Adem Demaçi said in a press conference in Prishtina on Tuesday. "Mr. (Chris) Hill is either unfamiliar with the Albanian question or else is taking sides" with the Serbs, "accommodating their demands", Demaçi said. The UÇK representatives urged the State Department, "if it is possible, to review the work of Mr. Holbrooke and Mr. Hill, especially the latter, and find people who do not have the prejudices of Dayton, who do not have some deficiencies which we see as the causes of such oscillations which have astonished the Albanian and international public". Demaçi said he would like the State Department to review Hill's record and, possibly, "find a man who would be free of the past and committed to serious efforts...in pursuit of a real solution, a solution that would be lasting against the backdrop of the Albanian-Serbian context". Demaçi said the UÇK is very much in agreement with the position the chief Kosova negotiator Fehmi Agani took with regard to the latest Hill draft plan. "I think the time has come for us, Albanians, to offer our own proposal, that we ourselves offer our assistance to the solution of this problem", he added. "We have the right and obligation to offer our own plan and to stand behind it", Demaçi underlined. Asked to say whether he had made hasty statements on the UÇK supporting third republic status for Kosova within the Yugoslav Federation, Demaçi said that was not a proposal but rather agreement with the step-by-step approach to the resolution of the Kosova issue. "We have not come up with any proposal that would preclude the ultimate goal of an independent and sovereign Kosova". Adem Demaçi said it was his "historic mission" to unite the Albanians, so that "we be united in force and politics and create our state."

15.   Kosova Press Release: Kosovo Parliament's commissions discuss draft Plan, 11 December 1998

The Commission for Constitutional Issues and the Foreign Relations Commission of the Parliament of the Republic of Kosova met Thursday afternoon in a joint session in Prishtina to discuss the Kosova negotiating process, namely Ambassador Hill's draft on an interim solution to the Kosova issue. Mr. Fatmir Sejdiu and Ms Edita Tahiri, chairpersons of the respective commissions, chaired the meeting.

Dr. Fehmi Agani, head of the Kosova negotiating team, said the most recent U.S. draft plan was "a return to the old and unacceptable proposals".The December draft includes Serbia's demands that Kosova remain not only within Yugoslavia, "but also within Serbia", Agani said. The draft does not envision that the Parliament of Kosova have legislative powers, he went on to say, noting that the Parliament would not be able to adopt laws but only acts, which are inferior by nature. The formation of the Kosova government is not provided by the draft; in addition Kosova would not have a President, but only a Presidency, and this latter consisted of representatives of national communities, Dr. Agani told the members of the two Kosova Parliament's commissions.

The chief Kosova negotiator pointed out that the previous draft, the November one, likewise presented by Ambassador Hill, had been more "promising", and was much more defined than the last one, as an temporary arrangement for Kosova, which had been opposed by Serbia. The members of the Parliament of Kosova's constitutional and foreign relations commissions discussed the matter at length. All the speakers lent their support to the Kosova negotiating team, and appreciated its presentation and comments on the current draft plan for Kosova.

The Kosova MPs were united in their position that no kind of political solution within Serbia could be accepted, adding that all efforts should lead towards the implementation of the will of the people of Kosova for independence, in line with the 1991 national referendum for Kosovar independence and sovereignty. The Parliament of the Republic of Kosova can in no way be sidelined, the two commissions' members said, emphasizing that the consent of the Parliament should be sought and obtained for any solution to the Kosova issue. The Commission for Constitutional Issues and the Foreign Relations Commission of the Parliament of the Republic of Kosova adopted a number of conclusions at the end of their joint meeting on Thursday. They supported the Negotiating team's work so far, urging it to work in line with its mandate, upholding the independence bid for Kosova. Both the interim settlement and permanent solution should based on the "principle of the right to self-determination of the people of Kosova", as well as the possibility of establishing an international protectorate in Kosova", the commissions said. The commissions said they pressed for the Parliament of the Republic of Kosova "and all its mechanisms" to be in permanent cooperation with the Negotiating team and assisting the negotiating process in all its stages. The commissions called on the President of the Republic of Kosova Ibrahim Rugova to enlarge the Negotiating team, to add new members to it, so that it be more representative in its political and professional specters, a statement issued from Thursday's meeting said.

16. Final Hill Proposal, 27 January 1999

I. INTRODUCTION

1. All citizens in Kosovo have equal rights and duties as set forth in this Agreement. National communities and their members shall have additional rights as set forth below. The national communities shall be legally equal and shall not use their additional rights so as to endanger the rights of other national communities or the rights of citizens.

2. All authorities in Kosovo shall fully respect principles of human rights, democracy, and the equality of citizens and national communities.

3. Citizens in Kosovo shall have the right to democratic self-government through legislative, executive, judicial, and other institutions established in accordance with this Agreement. They shall have the opportunity to be represented in all institutions in Kosovo. The right of democratic self-government shall include the right to participate in free and fair elections.

4. Every person in Kosovo shall have the right to apply to international institutions for the protection of their rights in accordance with the procedures of such institutions.

5. The Parties accept that their powers and authorities in Kosovo are as specified by this Agreement, which shall prevail over any other legal provisions and shall be directly applicable. In implementing this Agreement in accordance with their procedures and international standards, the parties shall harmonize their governing practices and documents. All parties commit to implement this Agreement fully.

6. The Parties invite the OSCE to carry out the functions set forth in this Agreement. They agree to cooperate fully with all international organizations working in Kosovo on the implementation of this Agreement. The Kosovo Verification mission shall have the authority to call upon international organizations for additional assistance as necessary.

II. GOVERNANCE IN KOSOVO

PART I: GENERAL

1. The basic territorial unit of local government in Kosovo will be the communes. All responsibilities not expressly assigned elsewhere by this Agreement will be the responsibility of the communes.

2. The authorities of Kosovo shall have responsibility for all areas except the following, which shall be within the competence of the Federal Republic of Yugoslavia save as specified in paragraph three:

   (a) territorial integrity

   (b) maintaining a common market within the Federal Republic of Yugoslavia, which power shall be exercised in a manner that does not discriminate against any particular region or area of the Federal Republic of Yugoslavia

   (c) monetary policy

   (d) defense

   (e) foreign policy

   (f) customs services, and

   (g) federal taxation.

   Citizens in Kosovo shall continue to participate in areas reserved for the Federal Republic of Yugoslavia through their representation in Federal institutions.

3. Kosovo shall retain the following powers in the areas otherwise reserved for the Federal Republic of Yugoslavia:

   (a) No changes to the borders of Kosovo shall be made without the consent of the Kosovo Assembly and President;

   (b) Deployment and use of police and public security forces in Kosovo shall be governed by Annex 2 of this Agreement;

   (c) Citizens in Kosovo shall not be conscripted for Federal military service without the consent of the President of Kosovo;

   (d) Kosovo officers and institutions shall have authority to conduct foreign relations within their areas of responsibility equivalent to the power provided to Republics under Article 7 of the Constitution of the Federal Republic of Yugoslavia;

   (e) Martial law shall not be declared in Kosovo without the consent of the President of Kosovo;

   (f) Federal measures having a differential, disproportionate, or discriminatory impact on Kosovo

shall not take effect in Kosovo without the consent of the Kosovo President.

4. There shall be no interference with the right of citizens and national communities in Kosovo to call upon institutions of the Republic of Serbia for the following purposes on a purely voluntary basis:

   (a) assistance in designing school curricula and standards;

   (b) participation in social benefits programs, such as care for war veterans, pensioners, and disabled persons; and

   (c) other voluntarily received services, provided that these services are not related to police and security matters which shall be governed by Annex 2, and that any Republic personnel serving in Kosovo pursuant to this paragraph shall be unarmed social service providers acting at the invitation of a national community in Kosovo; the Chair of the Joint Commission shall have the authority to limit the exercise of this right to ensure the protection of all national communities.

5. Kosovo, Federal, and Republic authorities shall not interfere with the exercise of the additional rights described in Article IV of this Agreement.

6. All candidates for appointed, elective, or other public office in Kosovo, and all office holders in Kosovo, shall meet the following criteria:

   a) No person who is serving a sentence imposed by the International Criminal Tribunal for the Former Yugoslavia, and no person who is under indictment by the Tribunal and who has failed to comply with an order to appear before the Tribunal, may stand as a candidate or hold any office; and

   b) All candidates and office holders shall renounce violence as a mechanism for achieving political goals; past political or resistance activities shall not be a bar to holding office in Kosovo.

PART II: ASSEMBLY, PRESIDENT, GOVERNMENT, AND ADMINISTRATIVE BODIES

The Assembly

1. There shall be an Assembly, which shall be comprised of one hundred Members.

    (a) Sixty Members shall be directly elected.

    (b) The remaining forty Members shall be elected by the members of qualifying national communities. The

seats shall be divided equally among the national communities meeting a threshold determined as follows:

        (i) After the completion of the census specified in Article IX.5, those national communities representing at least five percent of the population of Kosovo as determined by the census shall be eligible for seats allocated under this paragraph.

        (ii) Prior to the completion of the census, the national communities eligible for seats in the Assembly under this paragraph shall be decided by the Head of the Kosovo Verification Mission based on his estimation of which national communities meet the five percent population threshold. His decision shall take into account previous census data and other information.

        (iii) The Serbian and Albanian national communities shall be presumed to meet the necessary population threshold.

    (c) Elections for all Members, whether under paragraph l(a) or l(b), shall be conducted democratically, consistent with the provisions of Article IX.4 and Annex 3.

2. The Assembly shall be responsible for adopting the Constitution of Kosovo and enacting laws of Kosovo, including those regulating relations in political, economic, social, and cultural areas. The Constitution and laws of the Kosovo Assembly shall not be subject to change or modification by authorities of the Republics or the Federation.

    (a) The Assembly's areas of responsibility shall include:

- Financing activities of Kosovo institutions, including by levying taxes and duties on sources within Kosovo;
- The adoption of budgets and annual accounts of the Administrative Bodies and other institutions of Kosovo, with the exception o fcommunal and national community institutions unless otherwise specified by this Agreement;
- The adoption of regulations concerning the organization, procedures, and functioning of the Administrative Bodies of Kosovo;
- Approving the Government proposed by the President of Kosovo; Approving candidates put forward by the Kosovo President for Kosovo judicial offices;
- Adoption of laws ensuring free movement of goods, services, and persons in Kosovo consistent with the responsibilities of other authorities;
- Conducting relations with foreign entities and approving agreements within its areas of responsibility, consistent with the authorities of Kosovo institutions under this Agreement;
- Cooperating with the Federal Assembly, and with the Assemblies of the Republics;
- Establishing, in accordance with this Agreement, the main rules of local self-government, including in particular rules on elections consistent with the rules and regulations of the Central Election Commission, finance, the status of elected local officials, and on local government employees;
- Coordination among communes or national communities when necessary, including the enactment of laws concerning inter-communal issues;
- Protection of the environment where inter-communal issues are involved; and
- Designing and implementing programs of economic, scientific, technological, demographic, regional, and social development, as well as programs for the development of agriculture and of rural areas.

    (b) The Assembly shall also have authority to enact laws in areas within the responsibility of the Communes if the matter cannot be effectively regulated by the Communes or if regulation by individual Communes might prejudice the rights of other Communes or if uniform legislation is necessary to ensure throughout Kosovo the equality of rights granted by this Agreement to citizens in Kosovo. In the absence of a law enacted by the Assembly validly taken within this authority that preempts communal action, the Communes shall retain their authority.

3. Laws shall be enacted by majority of those present and voting, except as provided in paragraph 4.

4. If a majority of the Members of a national community present and voting elected pursuant to paragraph l(b) make a motion that a law adversely affects the vital interests of their national community, that law shall remain in force subject to completion of the dispute settlement procedure in paragraph 5. Vital interest motions shall be made within five days of a law's enactment.

5. The following procedure shall be used in the event of a motion asserting that the vital interest of a national community has been adversely affected:

    (a) The national community or communities asserting that its vital interest has been adversely affected will give reasons explaining its concerns to the President of Kosovo. Members of the Assembly supporting the law will be given an opportunity to respond. The President of Kosovo shall mediate the dispute and attempt to reach a settlement agreeable to all affected national communities.

    (b) If mediation does not produce a mutually agreeable result within seven days, the matter shall be given to the Constitutional Court. The Court shall determine whether as a matter of law the vital interests of the national community or communities asserting the privilege set forth in paragraph 4 are adversely affected by the law. The Court shall hear argument and rule within fifteen days. Its judgment shall be final.

    (c) A law determined by the President of Kosovo or, if applicable, the Constitutional Court to adversely affect the vital interests of a national community shall be void. The law shall stay in effect pending the completion of any appeal to the Constitutional Court.

6. A majority of Members shall constitute a quorum. The Assembly will decide its own rules of procedure. Members of the Assembly shall be immune from all civil or criminal proceedings on the basis of opinions expressed or other acts performed in their capacity as Members of the Assembly.

7. The Assembly shall elect from among its Members a President, two Vice-Presidents, and other leaders in accordance with the procedures of the Assembly.

8. Each national community meeting the threshold specified in paragraph l(b) shall be represented in the leadership. The President of the Assembly shall not be from the same National Community as the President of Kosovo.

9. The President of the Assembly shall represent the Assembly, call its sessions to order, chair its meetings, coordinate the work of any Committees it may establish, and perform other tasks prescribed by the rules of procedure of the Assembly.

President of Kosovo

10. There shall be a President of Kosovo, who shall be selected by the Assembly for a three year term. No person may serve more than two terms as President of Kosovo.

11. The President of Kosovo shall be responsible for:

- Representing Kosovo before any international or Federal body, or any body of the Republics.
- Proposing to the Assembly candidates for Prime Minister, the Constitutional Court, the Supreme Court, and other Kosovo judicial offices. Meeting regularly with the democratically elected representatives of the national communities and other persons.
- Conducting foreign relations and concluding agreements on behalf of Kosovo after they are approved by the Assembly, consistent with the authorities of Kosovo institutions under this Agreement.
- Serving or designating a representative to serve on the Joint Commission and Joint Council established by Article VII of this Agreement.
- Meeting regularly with the President of the Federal Republic of Yugoslavia, the President of Montenegro, and the President of Serbia.
- Other duties specified in this Agreement.

Government

12. Executive power shall be exercised by the Government. The Government shall be responsible for implementing and enforcing the laws of Kosovo, and of other government authorities when such

responsibilities are devolved by those authorities. The Government shall also have the authority to propose laws to the Assembly.

(a) The Government shall consist of a Prime Minister and Ministers, including at least one person from each national community meeting the threshold specified in paragraph l(b). Ministers shall head the Administrative Bodies of Kosovo.

(b) The candidate for Prime Minister proposed by the President shall put forward a list of Ministers to the Assembly. The Prime Minister and the proposed Ministers shall be approved by a majority of those present and voting in the Assembly. In the event that the Prime Minister is not able to obtain a majority for the Government, the President shall propose a new candidate for Prime Minister within ten days.

(c) The Government shall serve at the confidence of the Assembly, and may be dissolved by majority vote of the Assembly. In the event of dissolution of the Government by the Assembly or because of resignation by the Prime Minister, the President shall select a new candidate for Prime Minister who shall seek to form a Government under the rules set forth in paragraph 12(b) of this Part.

(d) The Prime Minister shall call meetings of the Government, represent it in appropriate settings, and coordinate its work. Decisions of the Government shall require a majority of Ministers present and voting. The Prime Minister shall cast the deciding vote in the event Ministers are equally divided. The Government shall otherwise decide its own rules of procedure.

Administrative Bodies

13. Administrative Bodies shall be responsible for assisting the Government in carrying out its duties.

(a) Employees of administrative bodies shall be fairly representative of the population and national communities of Kosovo.

(b) Any citizen of Kosovo claiming to have been directly and adversely affected by the decision of an executive or administrative body shall have the right to judicial review of that decision after exhausting all avenues for Administrative review. The Assembly shall enact administrative law to regulate this review.

(c) An administrative body of Kosovo shall have primary responsibility for all criminal law enforcement matters in Kosovo, in accordance with Annex 2 to this Agreement.

PART III: COURTS IN KOSOVO, General

1. Kosovo shall have a Constitutional Court, a Supreme Court, District Courts, and Communal Courts. The Kosovo Supreme Court shall, upon approval by the Kosovo Assembly, promulgate rules of procedure consistent with this Agreement to guide the courts' activities.

2. The Kosovo courts shall have jurisdiction over all matters arising in Kosovo under the Constitution and laws of Kosovo and laws of the Assembly except as specified in paragraph 4.

3. The Kosovo courts shall also have jurisdiction over matters arising in Kosovo under federal law or raising questions of federal law. Disputes resenting questions of federal law may be appealed to the Federal courts on those federal legal questions after all appeals available under the Kosovo system have been exhausted.

4. Citizens in Kosovo may opt to have civil disputes to which they are a party adjudicated by the Republic courts, which shall apply applicable Kosovo law and shall refer matters falling within paragraph 6(b) to the Constitutional Court of Kosovo. Criminal defendants may seek access to and participation of Republic officials in Kosovo proceedings.

Members of the Judiciary

5. Composition. The Constitutional Court shall consist of nine judges. The Supreme Court shall consist of nine judges. The Assembly shall determine the number of other judges necessary to meet current needs.

(a) The judges shall be distinguished jurists of the highest moral character.

(b) The judges shall be broadly representative of the national communities of Kosovo. There shall be a least one Constitutional Court judge and one Supreme Court judge from each national community qualifying for seats in the Kosovo Assembly under paragraph l(b) of this Part.

(c) Until such time as he parties mutually agree to discontinue this arrangement or the Federal Republic of Yugoslavia becomes a party to the European Convention for the Protection of Human Rights and Fundamental Freedoms, a majority of judges on the Constitutional Court shall be selected from a list presented by the Committee of Ministers of the Council of Europe pursuant to Council Resolution (93)6.

(d) Removal of a Kosovo judge shall require the consensus of the judges of the Constitutional Court. A Constitutional Court judge whose dismissal is in question shall not participate in the deliberations on his case.

6. Jurisdiction of the Constitutional Court.

The Constitutional Court shall have sole authority to resolve disputes relating to the meaning of the Kosovo Constitution. That authority shall include, but is not limited to, determining whether decisions or actions of the President, the Assembly, the Government, the Communes, and the national communities are compatible with the Kosovo Constitution.

(a) Matters may be referred to the Court by the President of Kosovo, the President or Vice-Presidents of the Assembly, the Ombudsman, the communal assemblies and councils, and any national community acting according to its democratic procedures.

(b) Any court which finds in the course of adjudicating a matter that the dispute depends on the answer to a question within the Court's jurisdiction shall refer the issue to the Court for a preliminary decision.

(c) Following the exhaustion of other legal remedies, the Court shall at the request of any natural or legal person or association have jurisdiction over complaints that human rights and fundamental freedoms and the rights of members of national communities set forth in this Agreement have been violated by a public authority.

(d) The Constitution of Kosovo may provide that the Court shall have jurisdiction over other questions arising under it. The Constitutional Court shall have such other authorities and jurisdiction as may be specified elsewhere in this Agreement.

7. Jurisdiction of the Supreme Court. The Supreme Court shall hear appeals from the District Courts and the Communal Courts. Subject to the specific powers of the Constitutional Court, and to paragraph 4 of this Part, the Supreme Court shall take the final decision in all cases arising within Kosovo. Its decisions shall be recognized and executed by all public authorities on the territory of the Federal Republic of Yugoslavia.

8. Functioning of the Courts. The Constitutional and Supreme Courts shall each adopt decisions by majority vote of their members. All Kosovo courts shall hold public proceedings, and issue published opinions setting forth the reasons for their decisions along with any dissenting views.

PART IV. THE OMBUDSMAN

1. There shall be an Ombudsman, who shall monitor the realization of the rights of members of national communities and the Protection of human rights and fundamental freedoms in Kosovo.

(a) The Ombudsman shall be an eminent person of high moral standing who possesses a demonstrated commitment to human rights and the rights of the national communities.

(b) He or she shall be nominated by the President and shall be elected by the Assembly from a list of candidates prepared by the President of the European Court for Human Rights for a non-renewable three year term.

2. The Ombudsman shall be independently responsible for choosing his or her own staff. He or she shall have two Deputies. The Deputies shall each be drawn from different national communities, and neither shall be from the same national community as the Ombudsman if he or she is a member of a national community in Kosovo.

3. The Ombudsman shall have unimpeded access to any person or place and shall have the right to appear and intervene before any domestic, Federal, or (consistent with the rules of such bodies) international authority upon his or her request. The Ombudsman shall have other powers and jurisdiction as set forth in Annex I.

PART V. COMMUNES

1. Kosovo shall have the existing communes. Changes may be made to communal boundaries by act of the Kosovo Assembly.

2. Communes may develop relationships among themselves for their mutual benefit.

3. Each commune shall have an Assembly, a Council, and such executive bodies as the commune may establish.

(a) Each national community whose membership constitutes at least five percent of the population of the commune shall be represented on the Council in proportion to its share of the communal population or by one member, whichever is greater.

(b) Prior to the completion of a census, disputes over communal population percentages for purposes of this paragraph shall be resolved-by the Head of the Kosovo Verification Mission or his designee taking into account past census data and other information.

4. The communes shall have responsibility for:

- Law enforcement, as specified in Annex 2 of this Agreement.
- Regulating and, when appropriate, providing child care.
- Establishing and regulating the work of medical institutions and hospitals.
- Providing education, consistent with the rights and duties of national communities, and in a spirit of tolerance between national communities and respect for the rights of the members of all national communities in accordance with international standards.
- Protecting the communal environment.
- Regulating commerce and privately owned stores.
- Regulating hunting and fishing.
- Planning and carrying out public works of communal importance, including roads and water supplies, and participating in the planning and carrying out of Kosovo-wide public works projects in coordination with other communes and Kosovo authorities.
- Regulating land use, town planning, building regulations, and housing construction.
- Developing programs for tourism, the hotel industry, catering, and sport.
- Organizing fairs and local markets.
- Organizing public services of communal importance,
- including fire, emergency response, and police consistent with Annex 2 of this Agreement.
- Financing the work of communal institutions, including raising revenues, taxes, and preparing budgets.

5. The communes shall exercise the authorities specified in paragraph 4 and shall also have responsibility for all other areas not expressly assigned elsewhere by this Agreement, subject to the provisions of Article II, Part II.2(b).

6. Each commune shall conduct its business in public and shall I maintain publicly available records of its deliberations and decisions.

III. HUMAN RIGHTS AND FUNDAMENTAL FREEDOMS

1. The Parties shall ensure respect for internationally recognized human rights and fundamental freedoms in Kosovo.

2. Applicable rights and freedoms shall include those specified in the European Convention for the Protection of Human Rights and Fundamental Freedoms and its Protocols.

(a) The rights and freedoms set forth in the European Convention for the Protection of Human Rights and Fundamental Freedoms and its Protocols shall apply directly in Kosovo. These shall have priority over all other law.

(b) All courts, agencies government institutions, and instrumentalities of the Parties and all of their officials and employees shall conform to these human rights and fundamental freedoms.

IV. RIGHTS AND DUTIES OF NATIONAL COMMUNITIES AND THEIR MEMBERS

1. National communities and their members shall have additional rights determined by this Agreement in order to preserve and express their national, cultural, religious, and linguistic identities in accordance with international standards and the Helsinki Final Act.

They shall have these rights without regard to their representation as a percentage of the Kosovo population.

2. Each national community shall elect through democratic means in a manner consistent with the provisions of Annex 3 institutions to administer its affairs in Kosovo.

3. The national communities shall be subject to the laws enacted by the Kosovo Assembly, provided that any action concerning national communities must be nondiscriminatory. The Assembly shall decide upon a procedure for resolving disputes between national communities.

4. The additional rights of the national communities, acting through their democratically elected institutions are to:

(a) preserve and protect their national cultures, including by: inscribing local names of towns and villages, of squares and streets, and of other topographic names in the language and alphabet of the national community, consistent with decisions about style made by the communal institutions.

providing information in the language and alphabet of the national community.

providing for education and establishing educational institutions, in particular for schooling in their own language and alphabet and in national culture and history, for which relevant authorities will provide financial assistance; curricula shall reflect a spirit of tolerance between national communities and respect for the rights of members of all national communities in accordance with international standards.

enjoying unhindered contacts with representatives of their respective national communities, within the Federal Republic of Yugoslavia and abroad.

using and displaying national symbols, including symbols of the Federal Republic of Yugoslavia and the Republic of Serbia;

protecting national practices on family law by, if the community decides, arranging rules in the field of inheritance, family, and matrimonial relations; tutorship; and adoption.

the preservation of sites of religious, historical, or cultural importance to the national community, in cooperation with other authorities.

implementing public health and social services.

operating religious institutions in cooperation with religious authorities.

participating in regional and international non-governmental organizations in accordance with procedures of these organizations.

(b) be guaranteed at least one radio and one television frequency, which they shall each administer subject to non-discriminatory, technical standards;

(c) finance their activities by collecting charges the national communities may decide to levy on members of their own communities.

5. Members of national communities shall also be individually guaranteed:

- the right to enjoy unhindered contacts with members of their respective national communities elsewhere in the Federal Republic of Yugoslavia and abroad.
- equal access to employment in public services at all levels.
- the right to use their languages and alphabets.
- the right to use and display national community symbols.
- the right to participate in democratic institutions that will determine the national community's exercise of the collective rights set forth in this Article.
- the right to establish cultural and religious associations, for which relevant authorities will provide financial assistance.

6. Each national community and, where appropriate, their members acting individually may exercise these additional rights through Federal institutions and institutions of the Republics, in accordance with the procedures of those institutions and without prejudice to the ability of Kosovo institutions to carry out their responsibilities.

V. REPRESENTATION OF KOSOVO IN FEDERAL AND REPUBLIC INSTITUTIONS

1. Kosovo shall be offered the following representation, without prejudice to the rights of persons in Kosovo to decide whether to accept this offer:

(a) At least 10 deputies in the House of Citizens of the Federal Assembly.

(b) At least 20 deputies in the National Assembly of the Republic of Serbia.

(c) The opportunity for the Kosovo Assembly to present to the appropriate authorities a list of candidates from which shall be drawn:

(i) at least one citizen in Kosovo to serve in the Federal Government, and at least one citizen to serve in the Government of the Republic of Serbia.

(ii) at least one judge on the Federal Constitutional Court, one judge on the Federal Court, and three judges on the Supreme Court of Serbia.

VI. FINANCING AND OTHER ECONOMIC ISSUES

Financing

1. The authorities established to levy and collect taxes and other charges are set forth in this Agreement. Except if otherwise expressly provided in this Agreement, those bodies have the right to keep all

revenues from their own taxes or other charges. In particular, Republic authorities shall have no right to levy or collect taxes on Kosovo sources.

2. Revenue from certain Kosovo taxes and duties shall accrue to the Communes, taking into account the need for an equalization of revenues between the Communes based on objective criteria. The Assembly shall enact appropriate nondiscriminatory legislation for this purpose. The Communes shall also have authority to levy local taxes in accordance with this Agreement.

3. Federal and other authorities shall facilitate the delivery of resources from international sources to Kosovo to the extent of their respective powers, and in particular shall allow unfettered access of persons delivering such resources.

Other Economic Issues

4. The Parties agree to the following arrangements for: the disposition of government owned assets in Kosovo (including educational institutions and hospitals); the resolution of disputes over pension and social insurance contributions; and the resolution of any other matters relating to economic relations between the parties not covered by this Agreement.

(a) The Parties shall make a good faith effort to mediate these disputes under the auspices of the Head of the Kosovo Verification Mission or his designee.

(b) In the event the Parties cannot reach agreement, the Head of the Kosovo Verification Mission shall arbitrate the disputed issues. His decision shall be final and binding on the Parties.

VII. JOINT COUNCIL AND JOINT COMMISSION

Joint Council

1. The national communities shall establish a Joint Council to coordinate their activities under this Agreement, and to provide an informal mechanism for the resolution of disputes. The Joint Council shall consist of one member from each of the national communities. Its activities shall be funded equally by the participating national communities. It shall meet no less than once each month. The Joint Council shall encourage the creation of similar mechanisms at the communal level, building on the example of local commissions established pursuant to Article VIII-5 of this Agreement.

Joint Commission

2. A Joint Commission will serve as the central mechanism for monitoring and coordinating the implementation of this Agreement. It will be comprised of Federal and Republic representatives, representatives of the national communities in Kosovo, representatives of Kosovo political institutions including the President and the Ombudsman, and international representatives of the Kosovo Verification Mission.

3. The head of the Kosovo Verification Mission shall serve as the Chair of the Joint Commission. The Chair will coordinate and organize the work of the Joint Commission, supervise the overall implementation of this Agreement, and shall have other powers, authorities, and duties as set forth herein or as may be later agreed by the Parties.

4. The Parties shall cooperate with the Commission and its Chair. The Joint Commission as a whole and the Chair individually on his own initiative shall. have safe, complete, and unimpeded access -6c all places, persons, and information (including documents and other records) both within Kosovo and, where the Joint Commission or the Chair deem it relevant, within the Federal Republic of Yugoslavia.

5. In the event of disagreement as to the meaning of any provision of this Agreement a Party may petition the Chair of the Joint Commission, who shall have final authority to resolve such disputes.. The Parties agree to abide by his decisions.

VIII. CONFIDENCE-BUILDING MEASURES

1. Violence in Kosovo shall cease. Alleged violations of the cease-fire shall be reported to international observers and will not be used to justify violence in response. All persons held by the Parties without charge shall be released. The Parties shall grant full and immediate access by the ICRC to all detainees, wherever they might be held.

2. The status of police and security forces in Kosovo shall be governed by the terms set forth in Annex 2. The parties shall abide by its provisions completely. The existence of any paramilitary or irregular

force in Kosovo is incompatible with the spirit and terms of this Agreement.

3. The Parties shall facilitate the safe return of refugees and displaced persons to their homes. The Parties shall allow free and unimpeded access for humanitarian organizations and supplies to Kosovo, including materials for the reconstruction of homes and structures damaged during the conflict.

4. In each community a local commission, representative of all national communities there, will assist international humanitarian agencies in the delivery and distribution of food, medicine, clothes, construction materials, the restoration of electricity and water supply, and in encouraging returns.

5. There will be no impediments to the normal flow of goods into Kosovo. All goods and materials entering Kosovo at an international border or transiting the Federal Republic of Yugoslavia for entry into Kosovo to be used by international organizations (whether governmental or nongovernmental) assisting in the reconstruction and development of Kosovo or the implementation of this Agreement shall enter without duties or taxes of any kind.

6. International personnel, including the Kosovo Verification Mission, shall be allowed unfettered entry, movement, and access to anyplace at any time throughout Kosovo. The Federal Republic of Yugoslavia shall waive all visa, customs, or licensing requirements of persons or things for the Kosovo Verification Mission, UNHCR, and other international organizations and NGOs working in Kosovo. The FRY shall provide all necessary facilities, including frequencies for radio communications, to all humanitarian organizations responsible for delivering aid in the region. It is expected that international personnel will be present at all times in selected communities.

7. The Parties shall immediately comply with all Kosovo Verification Mission support requests. KVM shall have its own broadcast frequencies for radio and television programming in Kosovo.

8. All Parties shall comply with their obligation to cooperate in the investigation and prosecution of war crimes, crimes against humanity, and other serious violations of international humanitarian law. The parties will allow complete, unimpeded, and unfettered access to international experts-including forensics experts and investigators from the International Criminal. Tribunal for the Former Yugoslavia (ICTY)-to investigate such allegations. Pursuant to the terms of UN Security Council resolution 827 and subsequent resolutions, the Parties shall provide full support and cooperation for the activities of the ICTY, including complying with its orders and requests for information, and facilitating its investigations.

9. The Parties shall not Prosecute anyone for crimes related to the conflict in Kosovo, except for those who have committed war crimes, crimes against humanity, and other serious violations of international humanitarian law.

10. With respect to persons already convicted, there shall be a general amnesty for all persons in Kosovo convicted of committing politically motivated crimes related to the conflict in Kosovo. This amnesty shall not apply to those properly convicted of committing war crimes, crimes against humanity, or other serious violations of international humanitarian law at a fair and open trial conducted pursuant to international standards.

11. Recognizing the importance of free and independent media to the development of a political climate necessary for the reconstruction and development of Kosovo, the Parties shall ensure the widest possible press freedoms in all mediums, including print, television, and radio. Prior to the election of Kosovo officials pursuant to this Agreement, the head of the KVM shall promulgate such rules as may be necessary to ensure the flourishing of independent media in keeping with international standards, including allocation of radio and television frequencies.

IX. IMPLEMENTATION PERIOD

1. This Agreement shall be implemented as quickly as possible, under the supervision of the head of the KVM pursuant to a schedule that he shall specify. The Parties undertake to allow insofar as possible implementation of individual elements, not conditioned on the adoption and undertaking of other acts and measures required to implement this Agreement.

2. The Parties acknowledge that complete implementation will require political acts and measures, and the election and establishment of institutions and bodies set forth in this Agreement. The Parties agree to proceed expeditiously with this task under the supervision and direction of the head of the KVM.

3. Each national community in Kosovo is authorized to start exercising the additional rights determined by this Agreement, to the extent possible, immediately upon signature.

4. Within nine months, there shall be elections in accordance with and pursuant to procedures specified in Annex 3 of this Agreement for authorities established herein, according to a voter registry prepared to international standards by the Central Election Commission. The Government of the Federal Republic of Yugoslavia hereby invites the Organization for Security and Cooperation in Europe (OSCE) to supervise those elections to ensure openness and fairness.

5. Under the supervision of the OSCE and with the participation of Kosovo authorities and experts nominated by and belonging to the major national communities of Kosovo, Federal authorities shall conduct an objective and free census of the population in Kosovo under rules and regulations agreed with the OSCE in accordance with international standards. The census shall be carried out when the OSCE determines that conditions allow an objective and accurate enumeration.

    (a) The first census shall be limited to name, place of birth, place of usual residence and address, gender, age, citizenship, national community , and religion.

    (b) The institutions and authorities of the Parties shall provide each other and the OSCE with all records necessary to conduct the census, including data about places of residence, citizenship, voters' lists, and other information.

6. The Parties shall provide active support, cooperation, and participation for the successful implementation of the Agreement.

7. Unless otherwise specified herein or in any Annex hereto, institutions currently in place in Kosovo shall remain until the establishment of the bodies created by this Agreement. The head of the KVM may order existing institutions to cease operations on the grounds that they are functioning in a manner contrary to the spirit or terms of this Agreement. During this transitional period, the KVM head may also designate persons to serve on an interim basis in administrative and judicial capacities and shall also have the authority to remove officials from office.

8. Martial law shall be repealed. Laws compatible with this Agreement shall remain in force until replaced by the decision of a competent body established herein, and shall become part of the law of the entity responsible according to this Agreement.

X. AMENDMENTS

1. Amendments to the Agreement shall be adopted by agreement of all the parties.

2. Each Party may propose amendments at any time and will consider and consult with the other with regard to proposed amendments.

3. [In three years, there shall be a comprehensive assessment of this Agreement under international auspices with the aim of improving its implementation and determining whether to implement proposals by either side for additional steps, by a procedure to be Determined taking into account the Parties' roles in and compliance with this Agreement.]

XI. FINAL PROVISIONS

1. This Agreement is concluded in the Albanian, English, and Serbian languages. Each version shall be equally authentic, but in the event of a conflict the English text shall be definitive.

2. This Agreement shall enter into force upon conclusion of the document.

    Federal Republic of Yugoslavia; Serbia; Kosovo

ANNEX 1: THE OMBUDSMAN, General

1. The Office of the Ombudsman shall be an independent agency of Kosovo. In carrying out its mandate, no person, institution, or entity of the Parties may interfere with its functions.

2. The salaries and expenses of the Ombudsman and his or her staff shall be determined and paid by the Kosovo Assembly. The salaries and expenses shall be fully adequate to implement the Ombudsman's mandate.

3. The Ombudsman and members of his or her staff shall not be held criminally or civilly liable for any acts carried out within the scope of their duties.

Jurisdiction

4. The Ombudsman shall consider:

    (a) alleged or apparent violations of human rights and fundamental freedoms in Kosovo, as provided in the Constitutions of the Federal Republic of Yugoslavia and the Republic of Serbia, and the European Convention for the Protection of Human Rights and Fundamental Freedoms and the Protocols thereto; and

    (b) alleged or apparent violations of the rights of national communities specified in this Agreement.

5. All persons in Kosovo shall have the right to submit complaints to the Ombudsman. The Parties agree not to take any measures to punish persons who intend to submit or who have submitted such allegations, or in any other way to deter the exercise of this right.

Powers and Authority

6. The Ombudsman shall investigate alleged violations falling within the jurisdiction set forth in paragraph five. He may act either on his own initiative or in response to an allegation presented by any Party or person, non-governmental organization, or group of individuals claiming to be the victim of a violation or acting on behalf of alleged victims who are deceased or missing. The work of the Ombudsman shall, be free of charge to the person concerned.

7. The Ombudsman shall have complete, unimpeded, and immediate access to any person, space, or information upon his or her request.

    (a) He shall have access to and may examine all official documents, and he can require any person, including officials of Kosovo, the Republic of Serbia, and the Federal Republic of Yugoslavia to cooperate by providing relevant information, documents, and files.

    (b) The Ombudsman may attend administrative hearings, meetings of other Kosovo institutions, and meetings and proceedings of the Republics and the Federal Republic of Yugoslavia in order to gather information.

    (c) He may examine facilities and places where persons deprived of their liberty are detained, work, or are otherwise located.

    (d) The Ombudsman and staff shall maintain the confidentiality of all confidential information obtained by them, unless the Ombudsman determines that such information is evidence of a violation of rights falling within his or her jurisdiction, in which case that information may be revealed in public reports or appropriate legal proceedings.

    (e) The Parties undertake to ensure cooperation with the Ombudsman's investigations. Willful and knowing failure to comply shall be a criminal offense prosecutable in any jurisdiction of the Parties. Where an official impedes an investigation by refusing to provide necessary information, the Ombudsman shall contact that official's superior or the public prosecutor for appropriate penal action to be taken in accordance with the law.

8. The Ombudsman shall issue findings and conclusions in the form of a published report promptly after concluding an investigation.

    (a) A Party, institution, or official identified by the Ombudsman as a violator shall, within a period specified by the Ombudsman, explain in writing how it will comply with any prescriptions the Ombudsman may put forth for remedial measures.

    (b) In the event that a person or entity does not comply with the conclusions and recommendations of the Ombudsman, the report shall be forwarded for further action to the Joint Commission set forth in Article VII of this Agreement, to the President of the appropriate Party, and to any other officials or institutions that the Ombudsman deems proper.

9. The Ombudsman shall promptly report to the International Criminal Tribunal for the Former Yugoslavia evidence of war crimes, crimes against humanity, and other serious violations of international humanitarian law that may fall within the jurisdiction of that tribunal.

ANNEX 2: POLICE AND SECURITY; I. GENERAL PRINCIPLES

A. In exercising authorities under this Annex, all law enforcement and military components shall act in compliance with this Agreement and shall observe internationally recognized standards of human rights, due process, and fundamental fairness.

B. The KVM shall monitor the enforcement of this Annex and related provisions of the Agreement, and supervise their implementation. The Parties agree to cooperate fully with the KVM and to comply with its directives.

C. In addition to other responsibilities specified in this Annex and the Agreement, the KVM shall have the authority to:

1. Monitor, observe, and inspect law enforcement activities, personnel, and facilities, including associated judicial organizations, structures, and proceedings;

2. Advise law enforcement personnel and forces and, when necessary to bring them into compliance with this Agreement and Annex, issue appropriate binding directives;

3. Participate in and guide the training of law enforcement personnel;

4. Assess threats to public order and advise on the capability of law enforcement agencies to deal with such threats;

5. Advise and provide guidance to governmental authorities on the organization of effective civilian law enforcement agencies; and

6. Accompany the Parties' law enforcement personnel as they carry out their responsibilities, as the KVM deems appropriate.

D. All Kosovo, Republic and Federal law enforcement and military authorities shall be obligated, in their respective areas of authority to ensure freedom of movement and safe passage for all persons, vehicles and goods. This obligation includes a duty to permit the unobstructed passage into Kosovo of police equipment which has been approved by the KVM for use by Kosovo police.

E. The Parties undertake to provide one another mutual assistance in the extradition of those accused of committing criminal acts within a Party's jurisdiction, and in the investigation and prosecution of cross-border offenses. The Parties shall develop agreed procedures and mechanisms for responding to these requests. The head of the KVM or his designee shall resolve disputes on these matters.

II. LAW ENFORCEMENT COMPONENTS.

A. Communal Police Units

1. Communal police units, organized and stationed at the communal and municipal levels, shall have primary responsibility for law enforcement in Kosovo. The specific responsibilities of the communal police will include:

    a. Police patrols and crime prevention

    b. Criminal investigations

    c. Arrest and detention of criminal suspects

    d. Crowd control

    e. Traffic control

2. Number. The total number of communal police operating within Kosovo shall not exceed 2,700 active duty law enforcement officers.

3. Criminal Justice Administration. Communal police units shall be coordinated by the Criminal Justice Administration (CJA), which shall be an Administrative Body of Kosovo. The CJA shall report to the Government of Kosovo.

4. Communal Commanders. Each commune will appoint, and may remove for cause, a communal police commander with responsibility for police operations within the commune.

5. Service in Police.

    a. Communal police recruitment will be conducted primarily at the local level. Local and communal governments, upon consultation with communal security commissions, will nominate officer candidates to attend the Kosovo Police Academy. Offers of employment will be made by communal police commanders, with the concurrence of the academy director, only after the candidate has successfully completed the academy basic recruit course.

    b. Recruitment, selection and training of communal police officers shall be conducted under the direction of the KVM during the period of its operation.

    c. There shall be no bar to service in the communal police based on prior political activities. Members of the police shall not, however, be permitted while they hold this public office to participate in partisan Political activities other than belonging to a political party and voting for candidates at elections.

    d. Continued service in the police is dependent upon behavior consistent with the terms of this Annex and the Agreement. The

KVM shall supervise regular reviews of officer performance, which shall be conducted in accordance with international due process norms. The KVM shall have the authority to dismiss or discipline officers for cause.

6. Uniforms and Equipment

    a. All communal police officers, with the exception of officers participating in crowd control functions, will wear a standard dark blue uniform. Uniforms will include a badge, picture identification, and name tag.

    b. Communal police Officers will be equipped with a sidearm, handcuffs, a baton, and a radio.

    c. Each commune may maintain, either at the communal headquarters or at municipal stations, no more than 20 long-barreled weapons.

        i. Long-barreled weapons may be carried or used only with the permission of the communal police commander in response to serious law enforcement problems clearly justifying their release from storage. When no--- in use, all weapons will be securely stored and each commune will keep a registry of all 'weapons assigned to it.

        ii. If the head of the KVM determines that a long barreled weapon has been used by a communal police force in a manner contrary to this Annex, he may take appropriate corrective measures; such measures may include reducing the number of such weapons that the communal police force is allowed to possess. d. Communal police officers engaged in crowd controls functions will receive equipment appropriate to their task, including batons, helmets and shields.

B. Interim Police Academy

1. Under the supervision of the KVM, the Kosovo CJA shall establish an interim Police Academy that will offer mandatory and professional development training for all communal police officers. All police candidates will be required to successfully complete a course of police studies before serving as communal police officers.

2. The Academy shall be headed by a Director appointed and removed by the CJA in consultation with the Kosovo Security Commission and the KVM. The Director shall consult closely with the KVM and comply fully with its recommendations and guidance.

III. SECURITY COMMISSIONS

A. The parties shall establish a Kosovo Security Commission and Communal Security Commissions. The Commissions shall be forums for cooperation, coordination and the resolution of disputes concerning law enforcement and security in Kosovo.

B. The functions of the Commissions shall include the following:

    a. Monitor, review, and make recommendations regarding the operation of law enforcement personnel and policies in Kosovo, including communal police units.

    b. Review, and make recommendations regarding the recruitment, selection and training of communal police officers and commanders.

    c. Consider complaints regarding police practices filed by individuals or national communities, and provide information and recommendations to the head of the KVM for consideration in its reviews of officer performance.

    d. In the Kosovo Security Commission only: In consultation with designated local, Republic and Federal police liaisons, monitor jurisdiction sharing in cases of overlapping criminal jurisdiction between Kosovo, Republic and Federal authorities.

C. The membership of the Kosovo Security Commission and each Communal Security Commission shall be representative of the population and shall include:

1. In the Kosovo Security Commission:

    a. a representative of each commune.

    b. the head of the Kosovo CJA.

    c. a representative of each Republic and Federal law enforcement component operating in Kosovo (for example, Customs police and Border police).

    d. a representative of each national community.

    e. a representative of the KVM, during its period of operation in Kosovo.

    f. a representative of the VJ.

2. In the Communal Security Commissions:
  a. the communal police commander.
  b. a representative of any Republic and Federal law enforcement component operating in the commune.
  c. a representative of each national community.
  d. a civilian representative of the communal government.
  e. a representative of the KVM, during its period of operation in Kosovo.
  f. a representative of the VJ, who shall have observer status.

D. Each Security Commission shall meet at least monthly, or at the request of any Commission member.

IV. POLICE OPERATIONS IN KOSOVO

A. The communal police established by this Agreement shall have exclusive law enforcement authority and jurisdiction and shall be the only police or security presence in Kosovo, with the exceptions set forth in this Article and Article V of this Annex.

1. The Republic of Serbia shall immediately withdraw its security forces in Kosovo (hereinafter referred to as "MUP") to 2,500 officers, and shall in no event exceed that level of deployment with the exception of separate provisions for border police in Article V.A of this Annex. All anti-terror forces, special forces, special police, armored vehicles - including APC's, self-propelled Air Defense Artillery (ADA), and armored reconnaissance vehicles weighing more than six tons - and all weapon systems of 12.7 millimeters and above shall be withdrawn from Kosovo immediately.

2. The remaining MUP shall carry out only normal policing duties at the direction of the head of the KVM, and shall withdraw according to a progressive schedule to be determined by the KVM head. As communal police are trained and become available for deployment, law enforcement responsibility shall be transferred to the local police. It is expected that this transfer will occur in phases. The head of the KVM may specify particular regions or localities for withdrawal of all MUP and early transfer to local policing during this transitional period.

3. During the period of phased withdrawal, MUP in Kosovo shall serve under the supervision and direction of the head of the KVM. The head of KVM shall have the authority to order Individual MUP officers or units to leave Kosovo at any time, and to take, or refrain from taking, any action he deems necessary to effect the implementation of this Agreement.

4. Notwithstanding paragraph 2, all MUP shall be withdrawn no later than 12 months after the entry into force of this Agreement with the exception of Border Police as specified in Article V.A. The head of KVM shall have the discretion to extend this deadline for up to an additional 12 months if necessary to meet operational needs.

B. Concurrent Law Enforcement in Kosovo

1. With the exception of IV.A above, Federal and Republic law enforcement officials may only act within Kosovo in cases of :
  a) Hot pursuit of a person suspected of committing a felony criminal offense who has entered Kosovo in order to flee arrest.
    (i) Federal and Republic authorities shall as soon as practicable, but in no event later than one hour after their entry into Kosovo, notify the nearest Kosovo law enforcement officials that the pursuit has crossed into Kosovo. Once notification has been made, further pursuit and apprehension shall be coordinated with Kosovo law enforcement. Following apprehension, suspects shall be placed into the custody of the authorities originating the pursuit. If the suspect has not been apprehended within four hours, the original pursuing authorities shall cease their pursuit and immediately depart Kosovo unless invited to continue their pursuit by the CJA or the head of the KVM.
    (ii) In the event the pursuit is of such short duration as to preclude notification, Kosovo law enforcement officials shall be notified that an apprehension has been made and shall be informed prior to the detained person being moved.
    (iii) The same rules will apply to hot pursuit of suspects by Kosovo law enforcement authorities to Federal territory outside of Kosovo.
  b) The President of Kosovo may on a purely voluntary basis request that Federal and Republic law enforcement officials assist in law enforcement matters in Kosovo. Federal and Republic officials shall comply with reasonable requests for assistance.

V. SECURITY ON THE INTERNATIONAL BORDERS

The Government of the FRY will maintain official border crossings on its international borders (Albania and FYROM). Personnel-from the organizations listed below may be present along Kosovo's international borders and at international border crossings, and may not act outside the scope of the authorities specified in this Annex.

A. Republic Border Police

1. The Border Police shall continue to exercise authority at Kosovo's international border crossings and in connection with the enforcement of Federal Republic of Yugoslavia immigration laws. The total number of border police shall be limited to 75. All border police in excess of this figure shall immediately leave Kosovo.

2. Membership. While maintaining the personnel threshold specified in paragraph one, the ranks of the existing Border Police units operating in Kosovo shall be supplemented by new recruits so that they are representative of the Kosovo population.

3. Training. All Border Police stationed in Kosovo must attend police training at the Kosovo police academy.

B. The Federal Army (VJ)

1. VJ garrisons shall be limited to pre-February 1998 Border Guard Battalions located in Djakovica, Prizren, and Urosevac and subordinate facilities within 5 km of the FRY-Albania and FRY-FYROM border (specified on the attached map). There shall be no more than 1,506 members of the VJ present at any time in Kosovo. Border Guard units at the above locations shall be limited to weapons of 82 millimeters and below. Border Guard units shall not maintain armored vehicles above six tons - including APC'S, BOV's, and BRDM's - or Air Defense Artillery weapons in Kosovo. The VJ shall immediately withdraw from Kosovo all forces and equipment above this level. VJ units shall not deploy mines.

2. VJ units shall be permitted to patrol in Kosovo only within 5 km of the international border, and solely for the purposes of defending the borders against external attack and maintaining their integrity.

3. The VJ may travel through the territory of Kosovo to reach its duty stations and garrisons only along routes that have been agreed upon between the VJ and communal police commanders. In the event that they are unable to agree, the head of the KVM shall have binding authority to resolve disputes. VJ forces transiting and deployed in Kosovo shall be permitted to act only in response to direct threat to life or property, pursuant to rules of engagement agreed with the head of the KVM.

C. Customs Officers

1. The FRY Customs Service will continue to exercise customs jurisdiction at Kosovo's official international border crossings and in such customs warehouses as may be necessary within Kosovo. The total number of customs personnel shall be limited to 50. All customs personnel in excess of this figure shall immediately leave Kosovo.

2. While maintaining the personnel threshold specified in paragraph 1, the FRY Customs Service shall recruit persons of Kosovar Albanian ethnicity to work as officers within the Customs Service. Within eight months of the effective date of this agreement, each unit of Customs officers working at an international border or elsewhere within Kosovo shall include at least one officer of Kosovar Albanian ethnicity.

3. Kosovar Albanian officers of the Customs Service shall be trained and compensated by the FRY. The FRY shall receive all customs duties collected at Kosovo's international borders.

VI. OTHER SECURITY ISSUES

1. No Party shall deploy mines anywhere in Kosovo. The Parties shall provide the KVM with all information in their possession as to the location of existing minefields to, facilitate humanitarian demining efforts.

2. Within three months of the conclusion of this Agreement, all existing paramilitary and irregular forces in Kosovo shall disband in accordance with the timetable and rules to be promulgated by the KVM director. The KVM will supervise the disbandment of paramilitary and irregular forces, which shall turn in to the KVM all weapons having a caliber of greater than 7.62 millimeters. The KVM will arrange for the destruction of these weapons. No new paramilitary and irregular forces will be permitted while this Agreement is in force.

VI. ARREST AND DETENTION

A. Except as noted in Article IV of this Annex and in the following paragraphs, only officers of the communal police shall have authority to arrest and detain individuals in the territory of Kosovo. Officers may use reasonable and necessary force proportionate to the circumstances for these purposes. Immediately upon making such arrests, communal police authorities shall notify the detention, and the location of the detainee, to the appropriate communal security commission.

B. Border Police officers shall have authority within Kosovo to arrest and detain individuals who have violated criminal provisions of the immigration laws. Immediately upon arrest, Border Police officers shall notify the detention, and the location of the detainee to the appropriate communal security commission.

C. Officers of the Customs Service shall have authority within Kosovo to arrest and detain individuals for criminal violations of the customs laws. Immediately upon arrest, Customs Service officers shall notify the detention, and the location of the detainee, to the appropriate communal security commission.

VII. ADMINISTRATION OF JUSTICE

A. Authorities

1. Except in accordance with paragraph 2, any person arrested within Kosovo shall be subject to the jurisdiction of the Kosovo courts.

2. Any person arrested within Kosovo, in accordance with the law and with this Agreement, by the Border Police or Customs Police shall be subject to the jurisdiction of Federal Republic of Yugoslavia courts. If there is no applicable court of the Federal Republic of Yugoslavia to hear the case, then the Kosovo courts shall have jurisdiction.

B. Prosecution of Crimes

1. Kosovo shall create an Office of the Prosecutor responsible for prosecuting individuals who violate the criminal laws of Kosovo before the criminal courts of Kosovo.

2. The CJA shall appoint, and have the authority to remove, a Chief Prosecutor with responsibility for the Office of the Prosecutor.

C. PRISONS

1. Kosovo and its constituent communes shall establish jails and risons to accommodate the detention of criminal suspects and the imprisonment of individuals convicted of violating the laws of Kosovo.

2. Prisons shall be operated consistent with international standards. Access shall be provided to international personnel, including the ICRC.

ANNEX 3: CONDUCT AND SUPERVISION OF ELECTIONS

Conditions for Elections

1. The Parties shall ensure that conditions exist for the organization of free and fair elections, which include but are not limited to:

a) freedom of movement for all citizens;

b) an open and free political environment;

c) an environment conducive to the return of displaced persons;

d) a safe and secure environment that ensures freedom of assembly, association, and expression;

e) an electoral legal framework of rules and regulations complying with OSCE commitments, which will be implemented by a Central Election Commission representative of the population of Kosovo in terms of national communities and political parties;

f) free media, effectively accessible to all registered political parties and candidates, and available to voters throughout Kosovo;

2. The Parties request the OSCE to certify when elections will be effective under current conditions in Kosovo, and to provide assistance to the Parties to create conditions for free and fair elections.

3. The Parties shall comply fully with Paragraphs 7 and 8 of the OSCE Copenhagen Document, which are attached to this Agreement.

The OSCE Role

4. The Parties request the OSCE to adopt and put in place an elections program for Kosovo and supervise elections is set forth in this Agreement.

5. The Parties request the OSCE to supervise, in a manner to be determined by the OSCE and in cooperation with other international organizations the OSCE deems necessary, the preparation and conduct of elections for:

a. Members of the Kosovo Assembly;

b. Members of Communal Assemblies;

c. other officials popularly elected in Kosovo under this Agreement and the laws and Constitution of Kosovo at the discretion of the OSCE.

6. The Parties request the OSCE to establish a Central Election Commission in Kosovo ("the Commission").

7. Consistent with Article IX.4, the first elections shall be held within nine months of the entry into force of this Agreement. The President of the Commission shall decide, in consultation with the Parties, the exact timing and order of elections for Kosovo political offices.

The Central Election Commission

8. The Commission shall adopt electoral Rules and Regulations on all matters necessary for the conduct of free and fair elections in Kosovo, including rules relating to: the eligibility of candidates, parties, and voters; ensuring a free and fair elections campaign; administrative and technical preparation for elections including the establishment, publication, and certification of election results; and the role of international and domestic election observers.

9. The responsibilities of the Commission, as provided in the electoral Rules and Regulations, shall include:

a) the preparation, conduct, and supervision of all aspects of the electoral process, including development and supervision of political party and voter registration, and creation of secure and transparent procedures for production and dissemination of ballots and sensitive election materials, vote counts, tabulations, and publication of elections results;

b) ensuring compliance with the electoral Rules and Regulations, established pursuant to this Agreement;

c) ensuring that action is taken to remedy any violation of any provision of this Agreement, including imposing penalties such as removal from candidate or party lists, against any person, candidate, political party, or body that violates such provisions; and

d) accrediting observers, including personnel from international organizations and foreign and domestic non-governmental organizations, and ensuring that the Parties grant the accredited observers unimpeded access and movement.

10. The Commission shall consist of the Head of the OSCE Kosovo Verification Mission or his representative, representatives of national communities and political parties in Kosovo, and any such other persons as the Head of the Kosovo Verification Mission may decide. The Head of the Kosovo Verification Mission shall act as the President of the Commission. In the event of disputes within the Commission, the decision of the President shall be final.

11. The Commission shall enjoy the right to establish communication facilities, and to engage local and administrative staff.

Chapter 15: The Rambouillet Conference

The Rambouillet Conference represents a unique attempt of enforced negotiations. The venture was supported by the demands of the United Nations Security Council and the actions of the Contact Group, which included Russia, an ally of Yugoslavia. However, the unity of the Contact Group and other actors involved proved to be fragile. The attempt by leading powers to assume the task of 'reordering the Balkans' and impose a settlement in the face of a significant threat to the survival of a civilian population and to regional stability was therefore undermined from the beginning. In some aspects, the conferences was more a shambles than a grand design aimed at imposing reason upon the parties. But it was a heroic failure nevertheless, which at one stage appeared to come close to success.

I. The Summons to the Conference and the Renewed Threat of Force

By early December 1998, the efforts of US Ambassador Hill and his team to mediate a settlement for Kosovo had reached a dead end. Both parties had rejected the latest incarnation of the Hill draft. Yugoslavia had instead put forward its own draft agreement. While that document was designed to mirror some of the language and content of the mediator's proposals, it preserved Serbia's dominant position in relation to Kosovo and was immediately rejected by its elected leadership. Kosovo, in turn, had observed that the original Hill project was gradually being modified in accordance with key Yugoslav demands, reflected in the original 11-point outline presented by Belgrade in the context of the Holbrooke agreement of late October. This development placed in jeopardy the fragile consensus among the parties in Kosovo to participate at least indirectly in the Hill initiative, by way of the informal group lead by Dr Fehmi Agani and loosely connected with the Rugova government. Through that means, the Rugova government had been able to declare that it did not regard the Hill plan as a basis for a settlement, while at the same time seeking to improve it through comments provided by Dr Agani's team. Moreover, it had been miraculously possible to persuade the leadership of the KLA that an interim agreement might, in principle, be acceptable and preferable to outright confrontation. But the increased emphasis on a formal determination of the legal status of Kosovo as a part of Yugoslavia and the Serb Republic in both the Yugoslav and the Hill proposals was seen as evidence of the fact that the Hill process was designed to lure Kosovo into a negotiating process which would in the end be incompatible with its basic requirements. Those requirements were that any agreement would need to leave open the question of status and that it would be of a genuinely transitory nature.

The impetus for the Rambouillet process

The Contact Group negotiators had been aware that an agreement would need to be reached before spring, when a renewed outbreak of hostilities would be made possible by favourable weather. Now, however, it emerged that their worst fears were being realized ahead of schedule. The Yugoslav military offensive, launched on Christmas Eve, threatened a further outpouring of refugees. Not only did it directly affect the civilian populations of the villages that came under attack, but more profoundly, it appeared to indicate that the Verification Mission was not an effective means of constraining Yugoslav military operations which went significantly beyond the limited measures claimed by Belgrade to be necessary in order to hunt down 'terrorists' in the territory. In that sense, the Christmas offensive appeared to be designed to test the resolve and capacity of the OSCE verifiers and, more importantly, of NATO. The Alliance, after all, still maintained the threat of the use of force in order to obtain Yugoslav compliance with the terms of the Holbrooke agreement. Again, the NATO governments did not appear to have an appetite to make good their threats which were in consequence rapidly losing their credibility.

While it is generally assumed that it was the discovery of the massacre of some 45 Kosovo Albanians in the village of Racak which prompted the Contact Group to adopt a more vigorous attempt to achieve a settlement, this is only partially true. In reality, it became clear already in late December that the Holbrooke agreement would not even succeed in guaranteeing a space for further mediation until the beginning of spring. Hence, in early January, before the Racak massacre took place, the members of the Contact Group started a process of informal soundings about the prospect of success of an accelerated move towards a negotiated interim settlement. The idea of a concerted push for such a settlement within a short period of time along the lines of the Dayton conference on Bosnia and Herzegovina was mooted within the Contact Group and, cautiously, in relation to representatives of both sides or other persons in contact with either party. As one diplomat put it at the time "We cannot afford failure—that would be too embarrassing; we need a guarantee of success".

Kosovo indicated that it would be prepared to participate in such a conference, provided the question of the status of the territory would not be addressed and provided the result would be a genuine interim agreement. Yugoslavia, while reiterating her willingness to engage in direct talks with a Kosovo delegation on the basis of the 11-point plan, expressed reservations about a conference at which the KLA 'terrorists' would be represented. There were also doubts about the obvious internationalisation of what Yugoslavia considered an internal matter of the Serb Republic which an international conference would bring. Hence, there was no advance guarantee of success for the conference. In fact, when Contact

Group political directors met in London on 22 January to lay the groundwork for the conference, there was not even an assurance that both parties would definitely turn up at such an event.

To increase pressure upon the parties to attend and to come to an agreement, it would have been deemed preferable to obtain a Chapter VII resolution, requiring constructive participation of both delegations and uttered in conjunction with a further threat of force from NATO. However, even after the Racak massacre, it was judged unlikely that such a direct and significant involvement of the Council in the matter would be acceptable to some of its members. Nevertheless, it did prove possible to involve the United Nations and also Russia to some extent in the unorthodox project of the Rambouillet conference.

On 26 January, Secretary of State Albright met Russian Foreign Minister Ivanov. They issued a Joint Statement, declaring that "the sides in Kosovo must work harder to achieve an interim political settlement providing substantial autonomy for Kosovo and should engage in meaningful intensive negotiations for that purpose."[1] The wording was carefully chosen. The term 'meaningful' reflected a demand for talks bringing about real results. 'Intensive' referred to the idea of seeking to obtain such a result within a defined and short space of time. Finally, the use of the word 'negotiations' indicated that the time of shuttle diplomacy was now over and that a more direct format of discussions was required. In terms of substance, Russia was reassured by a further reiteration of the determination that "a settlement should respect the territorial integrity and sovereignty of the FRY," which was once again added to the formula of 'substantial autonomy for Kosovo'. There was no indication of a NATO threat of force however.

Further consultations were then held within NATO, which, two days later, expressed its support for an "early conclusion of a political settlement under the mediation of the Contact Group, which will provide an enhanced status for Kosovo, preserve the territorial integrity of the Federal Republic of Yugoslavia and protect the rights of all ethnic groups".[2] That day, the United Nations Secretary-General took the unusual step of giving a Statement to the North Atlantic Council at NATO Headquarters, linking together the efforts of the Alliance, the Contact Group and the UN. That statement was quite strongly worded, drawing upon "our experience in the Bosnian war" and indicating that the situation in Kosovo was now no longer one where "horror threatens", but instead where "it is present, in the lives of hundreds of thousands of the people of Kosovo whose lives have been disrupted violently".[3] The Secretary-General even appeared to give an endorsement of a threat of force by NATO, when targeting his words at "particularly those with the capacity to act" (i.e., NATO) and referring to the "need to use force, when all other means have failed".

The Contact Group and NATO decisions

On 29 January, the Contact Group issued its summons to negotiate to the parties.[4] This statement was remarkable in several respects. In terms of substance, it 'insists' that a settlement must be based upon principles established by the Contact Group. These principles were contained in the Hill drafts which, according to the Contact Group, merely required refining in a limited number of points. Of course, at that stage both sides had rejected the Hill draft and elements of the basic approach which underpinned it. In terms of process, the six governments summoned the parties to Rambouillet within a week, to negotiate a settlement with direct involvement of the Contact Group, principally within a further week. If progress was sufficient, the talks could be extended for a further period of less than a week. The Contact Group concluded by reiterating that negotiations would have to be completed within a total of 21 days from the date of its summons. "The Contact Group will hold both sides accountable if the fail to take the opportunity now offered to them". The Security Council in a Presidential statement immediately declared that it "welcomes and supports" the decisions of the Contact Group.[5] In language reminiscent of a Chapter VII resolution (but not contained in such a resolution), it "demands that all parties should accept their responsibilities and comply fully with these decisions and requirements".

The somewhat ambiguous determination of the Contact Group to hold both sides accountable was rephrased more aggressively by the North Atlantic Council the following day. On the one hand, the NAC reiterated that force might be used in order to obtain compliance with the Holbrooke agreement, in particular a cessation of hostilities, the reduction and redeployment of Yugoslav military and paramilitary forces and the termination of the excessive and disproportionate use of force by them. On the other hand, NATO added a further requirement, namely a positive response to the demand that a political settlement be achieved within the framework established by the Contact Group. In support of these aims, the "Council has therefore agreed today that the NATO Secretary-General may authorize air strikes against targets on FRY territory".[6]

---

[1] Joint Statement by Secretary of State Albright and Russian Foreign Minister Ivanov, 26 January 1999, Document 15.A.1.
[2] Statement to the Press by Dr Javier Solana, 28 January 1999, Document 15.A.3.
[3] Statement by Kofi Annan, 28 January 1999, Document 15.A.4.
[4] Contact Group Statement, 29 January 1999, Document 15.A.6.
[5] S/PRST/1999/5, 29 January 1999, Document 15.A.7.
[6] Statement by the North Atlantic Council on Kosovo, 30 January 1999, Document 15.A.8.

Justification for the threat of the use of force

As was the case when NATO issued its original threat of the use of force which resulted in the Holbrooke agreement of October 1998, the threat raised difficult questions in international law. On the face of it, the action appeared inconsistent with a key pillar of the international constitutional order contained in Article 2(4) of the United Nations Charter. That provision, which enjoys the highest legal authority and applies to all states under all circumstances, prohibits not only the use, but also the threat of the use of force. In its Advisory Opinion on the *Legality of the Threat or Use of Nuclear Weapons*, the International Court of Justice had held only a few years earlier:[7]

> Whether a signalled intention to use force if certain events occur is or is not a "threat" within Article 2, paragraph 4, of the Charter depends upon various factors. If the envisaged use of force is itself unlawful, the stated readiness to use it would be a threat prohibited under Article 2, paragraph 4. Thus, it would be illegal for a State to threaten force to secure territory from another State, or to cause it to follow or not follow certain political or economic paths. The notions of "threat" and "use" of force under Article 2, paragraph 4, of the Charter stand together in the sense that if the use of force itself in a given case is illegal—for whatever reason—the threat to use such force will likewise be illegal.

While NATO was not aiming to secure territory, it was clearly determined to cause Yugoslavia to follow a certain political path. Of course, NATO had been careful to tailor its threat to match demands which had been established by the United Nations Security Council. Initially, in October, NATO's aims reflected the Chapter VII demands contained in Resolutions 1160 (1998) and 1199 (1998). These resolutions had been adopted pursuant to a formal finding that the situation in Kosovo constituted a threat to international peace and security and required, *inter alia*, the cessation of armed action and repression by Yugoslav military and paramilitary forces, their withdrawal and the commencement of a substantive dialogue about a political settlement. With the conclusion of the Holbrooke agreement, the Alliance could also rely upon Chapter VII resolution 1203 (1998), which endorsed the deal brokered by the US emissary. That deal itself had included a Serb undertaking to accept a settlement by November 1998.

Absence of an express Security Council mandate to threaten or use force

A finding by the Security Council that a situation constitutes a threat to international peace and security confirms that the matter can no longer be considered an internal one. Demands issued by the Council under Chapter VII are legally binding and require immediate and unconditional compliance. But neither of these two elements taken individually, nor both of them taken together, amount to a legal authorization for third states to intervene forcibly, or to implement the demands of the Council through the threat or use of force. In fact, when adopting Resolution 1203 (1998), the Council had cautiously emphasized this fact by including an unusual preambular paragraph emphasizing that under the Charter of the United Nations, "primary responsibility for the maintenance of international peace and security is conferred on the Security Council".

One might perhaps argue that the Council had in fact exercised its prerogative when it had welcomed the decision of the Contact Group to summon the parties to the Conference at Rambouillet in its Presidential Statement. The statement clearly endorsed the project as one which was fully in accordance with its previous, repeated calls for negotiations about a political settlement within a short time-frame. In fact, the Statement may have somewhat elevated this request and turned it into a requirement. Previous resolutions had used the slightly less mandatory form of words. It "calls upon" the parties to enter into meaningful dialogue, possibly indicating that this step was merely recommended. And in past practice, the Council has been very reluctant to involve itself through the application of Chapter VII powers in the actual settlement of disputes, especially self-determination disputes.

However, Resolution 1160 (1998) had already listed the commencement of substantive dialogue as one of the conditions (in fact the first) which would have to be fulfilled before a lifting of the newly imposed United Nations sanctions could be considered. Hence, it appears that the Council did indeed intend from the beginning to impose a binding obligation to negotiate upon the parties. To that was added in Resolution 1199 (1998) the requirement of a "clear time-table, leading to an end of the crisis and to a negotiated political solution to the issue of Kosovo". In Resolution 1203 (1998), finally, the Council called for an implementation of Yugoslavia's commitment, given in the context of the Holbrooke agreement, to complete negotiations by 2 November 1998. This deadline not having been met, the Presidential statement of 29 January 1999 not only welcomed and supported the decision of the Contact Group of the same day, but also "demands that the parties should accept their responsibilities and comply fully with these decisions and requirements".

As this 'demand' was not enshrined in a Chapter VII resolution, it is not possible to argue that it constituted in itself an enforcement decision through which the Council directly adopted the Contact Group decision as its own and turned it into a legal obligation binding upon the parties according to Articles 24, 25 and 103 of the Charter, requiring the parties to attend the talks and reach a settlement. Still, the same result was achieved in a slightly less direct way. Through its

---

[7] 1996 (I) ICJ 246.

Presidential Statement, the Council confirmed its understanding that compliance with the decision of the Contact Group would be required in fulfilment of its previous resolutions. That is to say, having been unable to engage in meaningful and successful dialogue over the past year, and given the progressive deterioration of the situation, the Council now recognized that constructive participation in the Rambouillet talks would be the only means of fulfilling its previous, more general requirements in this respect. In this circuitous way, the Council had therefore endorsed the Contact Group's decision to the full. This is not altogether surprising, inasmuch as Russia was part of the Contact Group which had taken the initial decision now supported by the Council.

No express retroactive approval from the Security Council for regional action

NATO's claim to act in support of the aims not only of the Contact Group, but also of the 'international community' as a whole in backing the summons to negotiate is therefore not entirely unfounded. Nevertheless, it is one thing to offer political support to a decision which has the backing of the Security Council and another to threaten or use force in order to obtain compliance with that decision. Of course, it might be argued that the Presidential Statement also implied retroactive authorization granted to a regional agency, substituting for a formal Chapter VII or Chapter VIII mandate granted in advance.[8] While such informal action has no formal basis in the United Nations Charter, it is in fact established in practice, as the recent episodes of regional action in relation to Liberia and Sierra Leone demonstrate. However, in view of the rather ambiguous formulation adopted by the Contact Group ('will hold both sides accountable') and given the known hesitations relating to intervention in the domestic affairs of states and the potential use of force of individual members of the Council, legislative intent directed towards the granting of such an informal mandate appears unlikely. The response of some members of the Council after the outbreak of hostilities in March 1999 bears this out. Moreover, the Council Statement followed upon the Contact Group decision, but preceded the NATO decision. It is not clear how the Council could retroactively approve that which had not yet happened.

No implied enforcement authority for NATO

Still, NATO's decision was targeted towards the implementation of aims established by the Security Council, and the Alliance claimed it was not threatening the use of force for its own purposes but on behalf of the international community as a whole. It was acting, as it were, as the enforcement agent of Security Council, albeit a self-appointed one. However, this argument, too, is unpersuasive. After all, only a few months earlier, the members of the Security Council had strongly opposed United States and United Kingdom armed action against Iraq. That action had purportedly been undertaken in order to enforce demands made by the Security Council relating to Baghdad's obligation to cooperate with United Nations arms inspectors. Indeed, in that instance, the binding Chapter VII character of the requirements of the Council which were to be enforced was even more clearly established. Nevertheless, the thesis that states or groups of states can bestow upon themselves the authority to use force in pursuit of aims enunciated by the United Nations was rightly rejected.[9]

Forcible humanitarian action

While the decisions taken by the Security Council were not in this instance sufficient to justify the threat of force issued by NATO, they were still useful in this context. For they added credibility to the final line of argument which could be deployed, again in accordance with the practice followed in the October episode: forcible humanitarian action. Humanitarian 'intervention' is seen by some as a further exception to the prohibition of the use of force in international law. It permits the application of force in response to significant and widespread violations of human rights in foreign territory, at least when such violations have generated an overwhelming humanitarian emergency. A more advanced view argues that forcible humanitarian action can only occur in very limited circumstances, where a government or effective authority can no longer conceivably claim the exclusive power to represent a population or a constitutionally significant segment thereof. For example, where a government exterminates a large segment of its population, denies a population that which is necessary for its survival, or forcibly displaces it, that government is no longer legally competent to oppose international action on behalf of that population. Instead, where such a circumstance of fundamental dissociation between government or population has taken place, the United Nations Security Council, regional organizations or states and alliances can act directly on behalf of the threatened population.[10]

The North Atlantic Council decision of 30 January took great pains to link the purported aims of the international community as they had been specifically formulated to humanitarian need:

---

[8] In fact, NATO does not formally consider itself a regional organization, although it has exercised mandates typically bestowed upon regional organizations when acting under Council authority in relation to Bosnia and Herzegovina.

[9] In fact, at least the United Kingdom appeared to be somewhat discomforted by this argument, preferring instead to rely on the equally unpersuasive assertion that the violation of cease-fire Resolution 687 (1991) had revived the forcible mandate granted to states cooperating with the government of Kuwait in the liberation of that state in 1990.

[10] It is, of course, not possible to rehearse here in full the debate about the legality or otherwise of humanitarian 'intervention'. This question will be addressed at greater length in Volume 2 of this *Series*. On the theory of fundamental dissociation see Weller, Access to Victims: Reconceiving the Right to Intervene, in Heere, ed., *International law and The Hague's 750th Anniversary* (1999) 353.

The crisis in Kosovo remains a threat to peace and security in the region. NATO's strategy is to halt the violence and support the completion of negotiations on an interim political settlement for Kosovo, *thus averting a humanitarian catastrophe* [emphasis added].

Even for those who support the doctrine of humanitarian 'intervention' in international law, this assertion in itself does not provide a full justification of the threat of force in this instance. The doctrine of forcible humanitarian action establishes strong criteria which must be fulfilled before it can be applied. While these criteria—and indeed the existence of a doctrine of humanitarian 'intervention' in international law—are still disputed, one might argue that the threat or use of force for humanitarian purposes must meet the following requirements:

- there must have arisen a fundamental dissociation between population and purported government, in this type of circumstance manifested by an actual or imminent humanitarian catastrophe of significant proportions;[11]
- this fact must have been identified by a best placed, competent and objective international agency;
- the action taken must be appropriate, necessary and proportionate;
- and the action must be carried out subject to the requirements of transparency, Security Council review and accountability.

In October, the forced displacement of 300,000 civilians from Kosovo as a result of the military and paramilitary operations of Belgrade evidenced a circumstance of fundamental dissociation. Or, in other words, the Belgrade government could, at that moment, no longer claim to be competent fully and exclusively to represent internationally the very people it was disenfranchising and persecuting on such a massive scale in Kosovo. Instead, international action could be taken directly on behalf of that population to the extent necessary to preserve it from destruction.

The United Nations Security Council itself had authoritatively identified the situation as a threat to international peace and security, and it has established the minimum requirements necessary in order to remedy that threat (cessation of repression, withdrawal of Yugoslav/Serb military and paramilitary forces and an expeditious settlement). NATO's threat of force was precisely tailored to achieve these minimum aims. By January, however, it was argued by some that the emergency had subsided. Most of the displaced had returned to their villages and those unable to return had managed to find shelter over the winter elsewhere, it was asserted. In fact, there remained no less than 200,000 displaced people in Kosovo and abroad, and the latest round of fighting had already led to a renewed displacement of approximately 30,000.[12]

Preventative humanitarian action

It could therefore be argued that NATO action was in fact an answer to an actual humanitarian emergency. Alternatively, it could be argued that the action anticipated one. The violations by Belgrade of the Holbrooke agreement, consisting of a renewed use of disproportionate and excessive force against civilians and the interference with the Verification Mission were seen to presage a development which would inevitably lead to a renewed exodus of refugees. Seen in this light, NATO action had a preventative, rather than a palliative character.

Preventative humanitarian operations can be lawful, provided it is clear that an overwhelming emergency will necessarily arise unless international action is taken. For example, in 1992 an international coalition of states imposed, through the threat of the use of force, an aerial exclusion zone over southern Iraq. This action was taken after reliable information had been obtained from an objective and best placed international agency which confirmed that the Shiite population of southern Iraq was under an imminent threat of a military assault from the Baghdad regime. This limited, preventative action did not trigger significant international criticism.[13]

In the instance of Kosovo, the international community appeared to be witnessing a repetition of the pattern of practice which had brought about the initial emergency in 1998. Given that experience, it was clear that another displacement crisis of similar proportion—this time under the harsh conditions of mid-winter—would have catastrophic humanitarian consequences. The first requirement for preventative humanitarian action was therefore met, and a good case can be made that a humanitarian crisis of some proportion was in fact already under way.

Authoritative determination of an actual or imminent humanitarian emergency

The second requirement for lawful humanitarian action was also fulfilled. In order to minimize the risk of abuse of the doctrine of humanitarian action by states for their own purposes, the existence of an actual or imminent emergency of sufficient intensity to generate a dissociation between population and government must be confirmed by competent, best placed and objective international agencies. 'Competent' means that the agencies in question must have a constitutional mandate and recognized expertise in evaluating situations of this kind. 'Best placed' requires that the agency is in a position

---

[11] See also the introduction to Chapter 12.
[12] See Chapter 13.
[13] This development is chronicled in Weller, *Iraq and Kuwait: The Hostilities and Their Aftermath* (1993) 723ff.

to judge the concrete circumstances of the particular emergency. And, to avoid the allegation of bias, the agency must not be a representative of a particular state, group of states or interest group. Instead, it must have a track record of reliably assessing similar cases on their merits.

Here, the OSCE Verifiers, a host of humanitarian organizations, and the Security Council itself, through its Presidential Statement of 29 January, had confirmed the existence of an imminent humanitarian disaster evidencing a fundamental dissociation between population and government.[14]

Appropriate, necessary and proportionate action

Humanitarian action must be appropriate, in that the action taken must be capable of achieving the desired humanitarian objective. It must be necessary inasmuch as no means other than the threat of use of force must be available to this end, all other options having been exhausted. And it must meet the criterion of proportionality, that is to say, the injury done to the target state must not outweigh the humanitarian good that is being pursued.

The assertion that the achievement of a political settlement was appropriate, necessary and proportionate in order to avert a humanitarian disaster may have been somewhat daring—it certainly was an innovative extension of the doctrine of humanitarian 'intervention'. There had been previous instances when the Security Council had mandated complex United Nations peace support operations, which would also include an attempt to bring the parties to an international conflict to a settlement and to reconstruct the constitutional structure of civil society of a state which had suffered from prolonged internal strife. However, in this instance, there was no direct Council mandate, the settlement was to be obtained by a self-selected group of states (the Contact Group, backed by the Alliance), and the terms of the settlement, it appeared, were to be imposed upon the parties, at least in broad terms. The direct and unambiguous threat of the use of force to obtain acceptance of such a settlement was entirely unprecedented in post UN Charter history and somewhat reminiscent of an exercise of Great Power diplomacy in the classical balance of power system of the post Napoleonic Concert of Europe.

Of course, in this instance, the states involved did not really pursue classical hegemonic policies. Instead, they acted—quite reluctantly—to counter the threat of a humanitarian catastrophe. They may also have been propelled into action by the hope of saving that area of Europe from a military confrontation which might have spread beyond Kosovo, involving Albania and Macedonia and, ultimately, perhaps others. But this additional motivation does not undermine or necessarily taint the humanitarian objective which had been enunciated.[15] Still, the question remains whether a right of humanitarian action can extend beyond military measures which are directly related to the protection of a civilian population from significant and widespread actual or imminent harm and which were strictly necessary, all peaceful alternatives having been exhausted.

The initial threat of force in October had been aimed at terminating the excessive use of force by Yugoslav military and paramilitary forces by imposing a cessation of hostilities. It is difficult to dispute that a cessation of the very acts which were directly causing the refugee flow was strictly necessary in order to terminate the humanitarian emergency and that the threat of the use of force was an appropriate means of seeking to achieve this aim. Hence, given the failure of other options, and in view of the urgency of the situation, it was legally defensible as a forcible humanitarian action. This cease-fire was to be stabilized by a withdrawal of forces to a level they had held before the Yugoslav spring offensive of 1998 and by essentially cantoning some of the remaining troops. Again, in view of the treatment which the civilian Albanian population of Kosovo had received, and also in view of the record of Yugoslav actions in Bosnia and Herzegovina, this demand, too, appears to be necessary in order to reverse the humanitarian consequences of Belgrade's actions. But was it also reasonable to claim, as NATO did in January, that the acceptance of the Contact Group plan for Kosovo, then encapsulated in the Hill proposals, was strictly necessary to avert a humanitarian catastrophe? And did such a demand not impose upon Belgrade requirements which may have been disproportionate to the purported aim of a strictly humanitarian act?

A political settlement as a humanitarian necessity?

A justification for such an expansive approach can only be found in the overall context of this episode. NATO would draw attention to the prolonged and repeated history of ethnic cleansing and perhaps even genocide perpetrated by the government in Belgrade, first in Croatia, then in Bosnia and Herzegovina and finally in Kosovo. A peaceful attempt to reign in Yugoslav practices had been made in relation to Kosovo since 1992, when it was hoped to stabilize the situation through the presence of the OSCE long-term monitoring mission and the parallel track of negotiations flowing from the London Conference of summer 1992. However, Yugoslavia had unilaterally terminated the OSCE presence in Kosovo and the Geneva negotiating track had never been pursued in earnest by Belgrade. Other attempts to arrest the situation of perennial

---

[14] S/PRST/1999/5, Document 15.A.7.
[15] In fact, the threat to peace and stability in the wider region might be considered an independent source of authority to act. However, only the Security Council, acting directly or through a regional organization or arrangement, can authorize forcible responses to such abstract threats.

crisis and replace it with political accommodation had also failed, whether driven by non-governmental intercession, such as the St Eugidio initiative, or the formal process of Ambassador Hill's shuttle diplomacy.

The more intrusive and coercive attempt to avert a humanitarian emergency through the initial NATO threat followed by the Holbrooke agreement, with its restrictions on permitted numbers, locations and activities of Yugoslav military and paramilitary forces, had also failed, it appeared. And Yugoslavia's pledge of October to facilitate a political settlement within weeks had not been fulfilled, notwithstanding the demand of the Security Council. In fact, the Council had found a settlement to be a necessary condition for the restoration of peace and stability in the region. Hence, NATO could argue that the only remaining avenue to address this persistent crisis and its likely further humanitarian consequences was finally to insist on the achievement of a settlement under international auspices within a very short period of time, before more widespread fighting would erupt again. Such a settlement would need to be guaranteed through an effective international implementation presence. Whether the requirement to reach such a settlement was reasonable, or necessary and proportionate, must depend on the actual content of the proposals put forward at Rambouillet, and the process through which agreement in relation to them was to be achieved.

II.   The Conference Process

Enforced negotiations

The Rambouillet Conference represented an odd example of enforced negotiations. As already noted, the presence of Yugoslavia at the talks was to be obtained through the threat of the use of force. Yugoslavia responded to this threat with a formal protest, seeking the protection of the United Nations Security Council.[16] It subsequently compared the Rambouillet process to the Munich conference on Czechoslovakia.[17] Nevertheless, Yugoslavia received United Kingdom Secretary of State for Foreign Affairs Robin Cook and the 'Contact Group Non-negotiable Principles/Basic Elements' for the talks he brought with him. In spite of hesitations relating to the presence of KLA representatives at Rambouillet, Yugoslavia decided to participate in the conference and, indeed, attempted vigorously to engage the Kosovo delegation, including the KLA, in direct negotiations. Moreover, Yugoslavia formally accepted the 'Non-negotiable Principles' during the conference process.

In fact, the Non-negotiable principles bear in many respects a striking similarity to the 11-point declaration on a settlement made unilaterally by Belgrade on 13 October in the context of the Holbrooke agreement.[18] That declaration was, of course, itself obtained within the context of the initial threat of force by NATO. However, it effectively summarized points of agreement between the Hill proposals, which had been formulated on behalf of the Contact Group, and Belgrade's position. Hence, the threat of force may have been effective in terms of requiring Yugoslavia to attend a conference with a view to achieving a settlement quickly. But the terms that were to be 'imposed' upon the parties were in many respects co-extensive with Belgrade's own proposals and with the minimum demands of the Security Council, at least at a level of general principle contained in the Non-negotiable Basic Elements.

The extent of the efficacy of the threat of force in relation to Yugoslavia can perhaps also be judged in the light of the final outcome of the conference. After all, in the end Belgrade refused to sign the overall agreement which emerged from the talks, in the full knowledge of the possible consequences. Hence, its leadership did not appear to make its decisions dependent on the threat. Perhaps in the knowledge of this fact, the negotiations were actually conducted in a way which made very significant concessions to Yugoslavia, in order to obtain consent relatively freely given.

Yugoslavia was aware of the doubtful credibility of the threat of force. NATO had struggled very hard not to have to implement it in October. After the Racak massacre and other significant violations of the terms of the Holbrooke agreement, NATO dispatched its military leaders to Belgrade to demonstrate decisiveness. But there was no action and this mission may well have proved counter-productive. Whether the political resolve and unity of the NATO states would be sufficient even to launch airstrikes, merely in response to Belgrade's failure to sign an agreement, was by no means clear. Even if strikes were to be launched, they were likely to be limited and symbolic, targeting relatively isolated military infrastructure assets—more appeared unlikely at that stage, given the hesitations of Italy, Germany, Greece and others. After all, NATO had committed itself to a graduated plan of military action, which required at each stage of escalation the consensus of the North Atlantic Council. Thus, it appeared that Yugoslavia would be able to absorb whatever strikes might be launched without great sacrifice. Once air strikes had occurred without achieving great effect in relation to the Belgrade leadership, NATO would have played and lost its trump card. Yugoslavia could then have mounted a gradual campaign against the KLA, while offering a settlement on its own terms. Given NATO's offensive military action, its role, or rather the role of NATO members in the Contact Group, could have been minimized in the context of such a settlement. After

---

[16] Letter of 1 February 1999, S/1999/107, 2 February, Document 15.A.13.

[17] Speech by Professor Sur, Counsel and Advocate for Yugoslavia, in the International Court of Justice, CR99/14, 10 May 1999. The proceedings in the Court will be reproduced and analyised in *Volume 2* of this Series.

[18] See Document 12.B.16.

all, it would have appeared unreasonable to accept as neutral mediators or as participants in a weakened verification mission the very forces which only a short time before had been involved in an armed attack against Yugoslavia.

The situation of Kosovo was somewhat different. In principle, the threat of the use of force also applied to it, or perhaps more specifically, the KLA. In reality, however, it was clear that NATO would not really be able to use military force against a grassroots armed movement like the KLA, which possessed little in the way of heavy armament or installations which could be subjected to air-strikes. The military threat against the KLA was therefore an indirect one. NATO states would take effective steps to inhibit further funding of its operations from the Albanian Diaspora around the world, especially from the US and Germany (and, if possible, neutral Switzerland). In a bid to shut down its support network abroad, the KLA would be declared a 'terrorist' organization and legally pursued accordingly. Secondly, pressure would be applied to Albania to close logistical and training facilities it was allegedly granting to the KLA. NATO might even patrol the Albania-Kosovo and Macedonia-Kosovo borders, in an attempt to inhibit the continued supply of the organization with men and equipment. It is not clear that such action would not have been fully effective, given the nature of the terrain, even if it had been possible to force Tirana to accept such a step. However, if implemented, this would have significantly reduced the effectiveness of the KLA as a fighting force. In fact, the organization would probably have had to abandon its ambition to function as an organized underground army capable of engaging Yugoslav military and paramilitary forces. Instead, it would have had to resort to 'terrorist' tactics against the Serb infrastructure in the territory—a fact which had not escaped its leadership which was keenly interested in developing the profile of a legitimate political movement.

More damaging still was NATO's political threat. If Kosovo refused to go along with the Rambouillet project, NATO states, including the United States, would simply declare the situation hopeless and withdraw their involvement in the crisis. Given the realities of the military situation vis-à-vis Yugoslavia, Kosovo's only hope was to even the odds on the political field through strong international involvement. To lose the element of 'internationalisation' of the crisis would have meant a far greater disaster for its leadership than any military reverses. In that sense, the NATO threat and the Contact Group summons represented a grave risk for Kosovo. There really was no option but to participate in the conference. However, being by far the weaker party in the negotiations, participation might well have resulted in an agreement fundamentally inconsistent with the requirements of Kosovo—an agreement Kosovo would not be in a position to reject, but which it would also probably not be able to deliver, given the position of the KLA.

Structural inequality

The concerns of Kosovo were reinforced by the structural inequality of the parties. Yugoslavia's insistence on the maintenance of its continued sovereignty and territorial integrity had, from the beginning, been shared by the Security Council, the Contact Group and practically all other agencies involved in the crisis. After all, these two principles were cornerstones of the international order in which all governments have a stake and which none wished to undermine. The language emphasizing a level of self-governance for Kosovo and the restoration of human rights as the principal aim of a negotiating effort appeared to Kosovo to betray a certain lack of appreciation of the situation. Yugoslavia had demonstrated over a decade that its human rights practices were unlikely to be constrained by yet further international obligations. And promises of self-governance seemed to ring hollow as well. Even when Serbia was one of eight republics and autonomous provinces in the Socialist Federal Republic, it had been able unilaterally to modify and then abolish Kosovo's autonomy. Now, with Yugoslavia consisting merely of two republics and that rump Federation being dominated by Serbia, a regime for self-governance, it was feared, would be easily undermined by Belgrade.

It was also noted that the international community consistently referred to a restoration of self-governance, or 'meaningful self-administration'. This wording appeared to be chosen to fall below the level of authority which Kosovo had enjoyed as an autonomous province. Hence, it appeared that Serbia's usurpation of authority and the removal of Kosovo's direct federal status would now be essentially internationally legitimised and instead a lesser status of self-administration within Serbia would be imposed. To Kosovo's leadership, even a full restoration of autonomy appeared insufficient, in view of the sacrifices made by its population over the past decade and given the absence of a strong federal system which might have protected Kosovo's exercise of autonomous powers from Serbia's desire to restore its supremacy. The attachment of the international community to the principles of territorial integrity and sovereignty therefore made it unlikely that the conference would produce anything which might be acceptable to Kosovo's increasingly radicalised constituents at home.

Procedure

Belgrade's 11 points of 13 October were obtained directly by the Contact Group, through Ambassador Holbrooke. Kosovo had no involvement in their formulation. In fact, Kosovo never actually received a full text of the Holbrooke agreements from the Contact Group. To see the unilateral Serb points on a political settlement directly reflected in the Non-negotiable principles, which had been presented to the parties after the Contact Group decision, appeared to be designed to reassure Yugoslavia, paying little regard to Kosovo's position.

The rules of the conference provided for the tabling of detailed elements of a settlement based on the Non-negotiable principles. The Contact Group drafts would stand, unless either party could persuade its negotiators that a change would be required in order to better implement a specific provision, or if both sides agreed on a change. The inequality in formulating the Non-negotiable principle would therefore be directly injected into the conference proceedings through drafts based upon them, which could not be easily deviated from.

Of course, the devil is in the details, and much would depend on the actual formulation of the Contact Group drafts. The actual drafting lay in the hands of a small group of highly skilled legal advisors to the three Contact Group negotiators, Ambassadors Hill (USA), Petritsch (European Union) and Mayorski (Russia). The drafts were provided on the basis of instructions from the Contact Group and were reviewed by it.

Negotiating theory has identified a number of different models of international mediation. There can be entirely neutral mediators, or there may be one or more 'committed' mediators who have a special and long-standing relationship with one of the parties. The strong links between the United States and Israel may serve as an example in the context of Middle Eastern peace negotiations. In this instance, Russia clearly acted as a 'committed' mediator on the side of Yugoslavia, threatening to disrupt the Contact Group consensus should proposals be adopted which appeared inconsistent with Belgrade's basic position. The role of Russia as the advocate of Yugoslavia also extended beyond internal Contact Group discussions and was very much felt in the actual negotiations. The nuanced differences between the statements by the negotiators at their joint press conferences given during the Rambouillet talks provide a somewhat faint but still visible image of this fact.[19]

While Russia acted as Yugoslavia's advocate, its attitude was nevertheless consistently praised by the other members of the Contact Group. The expectation was that Russia would fight Belgrade's corner and would thus place itself in a position to persuade the Milosevic government to sign. As will be seen from the presentation which follows, in accordance with this plan, the original Contact Group draft was changed significantly in order to persuade Yugoslavia to accept the Rambouillet package. However, in the end, neither these concessions nor Russia's attitude managed to deliver acceptance.

On the other hand, no state within the Contact Group could be considered a 'committed' mediator on behalf of Kosovo, at least at the outset. Instead of seeking to advance Kosovo's position, the other members of the Contact Group acted according to what they regarded as a reasonable compromise when approving or modifying drafts for discussions among the parties. Only towards the conclusion of the Rambouillet conference, when Kosovo appeared unwilling to accept the package on offer, did the United States change tack and started to defend the position of Kosovo to some extent.

The initial phase of negotiations

The Conference was opened at the ancient Chateau Rambouillet on 6 February 1999. The inequality of the parties was somewhat symbolized by the fact that for long and anxious hours the Belgrade government refused to allow the Kosovo delegation to leave for Paris. However, rather than intimidating the Kosovars, the worrisome time spent awaiting transport forced the somewhat disparate Kosovo delegation closer together and gave its members a first opportunity to attempt to find some cohesion. This tentative cohesion was demonstrated when the entire delegation refused to leave without the KLA delegates, as had been demanded by Yugoslavia.

Once both delegations had safely arrived at the Chateau, rather special conference badges were issued to them. While security badges ordinarily provide access to a conference site, in this instance the badges indicated to the French security forces guarding the Chateau that those unfortunate enough to wear them would not be permitted to leave the grounds, which were surrounded by heavy iron fences. Apparently the plan had been to isolate both delegations from the oxygen of publicity. At the Dayton conference, where a similar policy was attempted with greater success, it had been possible to isolate the delegations to some extent from their constituencies and political headquarters at home.

Rambouillet, of course, was different in several respects. It was not located in the isolated vastness of Ohio. Instead, the centre of Paris was just a 30 minute ride away on the local transport system. The mobile telephone infrastructure of Western Europe provided for direct communication links to the Balkans and to the editorial office of the New York Times and other media present in Paris. However, the crucial difference lay elsewhere. In the case of Dayton, the international community had managed to persuade Slobodan Milosevic, after a sustained use of force in Bosnia and Herzegovina, that his position in that territory was crumbling. By August/September 1995, the military forces of the Bosnian Serbs were being demoralized by NATO attacks against their infrastructure. Precisely at that moment, an alliance of Bosnian government and Croatian forces was starting to roll back Serb troops on the ground, taking territory which they had held since the outbreak of hostilities in spring of 1992. To freeze this situation and prevent further losses, President Milosevic simply abandoned the fiction of a separate Serb 'state' in Bosnia and Herzegovina, headed by Dr Radovan Karadic and General Mladic. He

---

[19] *See* the materials reproduced in section 15.B.

simply arrogated to himself the power to represent the 'Srpska' republic at Dayton and personally determined its future destiny at that conference.

At Rambouillet, on the other hand, the situation was different. Yugoslavia had not been beaten on the ground and the issue of Kosovo was seen to be a far more essential interest of Belgrade than the fate of the Bosnian Serbs might have been. Belgrade had little interest in achieving a settlement, which would, due to international involvement, inevitably lead to a result less favourable than the status quo. Hence, in the best possible case, the conference would fail, and this failure would be attributable to the Kosovo delegation. In that case, the threat of the use of force would collapse, and Yugoslavia would be left to consolidate its control over the territory.

Given this background, Mr Milosevic did not appear in person at Rambouillet. In fact, the Yugoslav delegation styled itself the Delegation of the Republic of Serbia, led by Professor Dr Ratko Markovic. Although the delegation had the full support of the Yugoslav Federal Foreign Ministry and was run by it, this was meant to indicate that the entire matter was really an internal affair of the Serb Republic. Hence, the delegation at Rambouillet could negotiate for the best deal possible. The Yugoslav government could then hope to extract further concessions back in Belgrade, when it came to persuading Mr Milosevic to sign a deal. Alternatively, Belgrade could disown any accord which its negotiators might arrive at, hoping that NATO would be lacking in its resolve to use force, or to sustain the use of force.

The Yugoslav/Serb delegation itself was composed somewhat oddly. A significant number of representatives were in fact supposed to be delegates from Kosovo, or rather from the non-Albanian minorities in Kosovo. Picked by Belgrade, several of these delegates were, however, disowned by the ethnic groups they were supposed to represent back in Kosovo.

The composition of the delegation of Kosovo, too, was not without controversy. The LDK party and Ibrahim Rugova had been elected twice by an overwhelming majority. However, during 1997/8, several former supporters of Rugova had left the party, being disillusioned by the lack of success of his non-violent campaign. The United Democratic Movement (LBD) in particular had attracted some important supporters. That party, led by the noted Academician Rexhep Qosja, was reputed to be ideologically closer to the KLA. And like the KLA, many of its members attempted to undermine the claims to democratic legitimacy of the elected 'government' and President. In fact, bitter attacks had been mounted against the LDK leadership and its claim to have formed a government which had been active over some seven years was discounted by these groups. By the second half of 1998, when the informal group under Dr Fehmi Agani formulated responses to the successive Hill drafts, a great deal of pressure existed to establish a broader-based negotiating team.

At the same time, the United States was pressing for the establishment of a delegation which would also include the KLA directly. It was considered too dangerous to arrive at an agreement, either through the Hill shuttle, or later through the Rambouillet conference, which might be opposed by the KLA. This might put any implementation force for the agreement in a position of being targeted by more radical elements of the KLA—a potential nightmare for the United States, in view of their peace-keeping experiences in Lebanon and Somalia. The 'delivery' of the KLA therefore became a key priority, whatever its credentials may have been at the time in terms of democratic representation of the population of Kosovo. This proposed feat was not made easier by the divergence of views within the KLA on key aspects. The views of its political leadership cadre may not have been at all times fully reflective of the commanders in the field, who had risen to arms at a time of national emergency and were less ideologically minded.

The Kosovo delegation in the end consisted roughly of one-third LDK representatives (including elected President Rugova and Prime Minister Bukoshi), one-third LBD and one-third KLA. In addition, there were two independents, Veton Surroi and Blerim Shala, both distinguished journalists and intellectuals. Overall, this meant that the more radical LBD and the KLA representatives dominated the delegation by two to one. Thus, instead of the elected President Ibrahim Rugova, the delegation was led by Hashim Thaci, a then 29-year-old, highly intelligent and determined KLA leader whose *nom de guerre* 'the snake' had been earned during the previous months of confrontation. He had a reputation of great effectiveness in consolidating previously divergent views within the KLA and was viewed by the Belgrade government with particular hatred.[20]

The Conference was opened with some ceremony by the President of France, Jaques Chirac, and the two co-Chairmen of the Conference, the UK and French Foreign Ministers Cook and Vedrine on 6 February. Both parties were then handed an initial draft, consisting of a Framework Agreement, a constitutional annex, and annexes on elections and the proposed Ombudsman.[21]

On the day of the opening of the conference, a bomb exploded in Prishtina, triggering a joint condemnation by both parties.[22] The negotiators considered this to be a promising sign of a spirit of cooperation and compromise. Both parties

---

[20] Belgrade issued wanted posters for Mr Thaci during the Rambouillet Conference and sought his arrest by Interpol.
[21] Document 15.B.5.
[22] Document 15.B.6.

also issued general statements of their positions in the first days of the conference. The negotiators then reported to the outside world that the delegations had requested computers and had set to work in a business-like way. While computers and other conference equipment had certainly been requested, it was in fact only Kosovo which gave evidence of constructive activity by devising detailed and substantive comments on the drafts which had been put forward by the Contact Group. The Yugoslav/Serb delegation simply fell silent. Its members became known as the 'Tea Club', as they were seen lounging about the public areas of the chateau, enjoying refreshments throughout the day. At one stage, an informal protest was made against the singing of Serb patriotic songs deep into the night in the Yugoslav/Serb delegation room, which disrupted the sleep of the sizeable delegations from the Contact Group, the OSCE, the EU and others who were accommodated in the chateau.

The Kosovo delegation, on the other hand, had formed a small drafting committee, chaired by Dr Agani and consisting of at least one representative of the LDK, the LBD and the KLA and one of the two independent members, plus one of the two external legal advisers who had placed themselves at the disposal of the delegation.[23] That committee went through the drafts which had been submitted and formulated detailed comments in a very draining process, the difficulty of which may not have been fully appreciated by the conference chairs and the negotiators. The draft comments were then subjected to very serious debate in the plenary of the entire delegation and frequently modified. The working language of the delegation was Albanian. But it was felt preferable to present the negotiators with an English version, rather than having to rely on the work of their translators who might well have misunderstood the very nuanced formulations which had been arrived at. This process of translation too was not without complexity. [24]

Despite these difficulties, Kosovo managed to submit substantive comments on all documents it had received in the first week (an Annex on Economic issues was added on 12 February). It took great care to declare that all these documents were in principle 'acceptable', subject to a limited number of technical amendments which could be negotiated. Throughout, Kosovo reserved its position, however, emphasizing that consent could only be achieved in relation to the overall package, which in its view would have had to include robust NATO-led enforcement.

On 14 March, the Contact Group Foreign Ministers assembled again in Paris, pronouncing themselves somewhat disappointed with the slow state of progress, but agreeing to extend the Conference for a second week, to terminate on Saturday, 20 February at 12 noon. The Ministers also gave the negotiators "discretion to table the remaining annexes on the implementation of a settlement".[25] This was somewhat odd, as it was rumoured at the time that the details of the military implementation annex had still not been fully agreed among the Contact Group and instead remained a source of some controversy. In fact, the implementation annexes were only tabled two days before the supposed final deadline of the conference amid reports that Russia was not supporting their contents.

The Yugoslav/Serb delegation maintained its silence until Ambassador Hill travelled, together with one senior member of that delegation, to Belgrade for direct discussions with Mr Milosevic.[26] It appears that during those talks, which apparently were undertaken by way of a unilateral US initiative, Yugoslavia identified the key requirements which would have to be met if its delegation was to engage in serious negotiations at Rambouillet. At that time, there emerged, ten days after the opening of the conference, and three days before its scheduled conclusion, a very lengthy FRY/Serb document fundamentally challenging the drafts which had been submitted thus far. While the negotiators had not responded in any way to the comments Kosovo had continually furnished over that period, they now engaged in a feverish effort to refine the detailed Yugoslav/Serb comments into a list of some eight crucial points which would require discussion.

The second phase of negotiations: the draft of 18 February and proximity talks

While the negotiators, or rather their legal experts, had spent difficult hours with the Yugoslav/Serb delegation, attempting to hone down their voluminous comments to points that might actually be discussed, the Kosovo delegation was still not receiving any feedback whatever in response to its comments. An initial meeting between the Kosovo drafting committee and the Contact Group committee of legal experts on 17 February proved rather disappointing to it. According to the Contact Group legal experts, very few of the proposals the delegation had put forward appeared to offer realistic possibilities of modification of the initial draft. According to the procedures of the Conference, no changes to the original

---

[23] Both delegations had been issued with five revolving badges, which could be used to bring different experts into the Chateau every day. This posed considerable problems for Kosovo, as the three parties were keen to introduce as frequently as possible those who they considered to be 'their' advisers. However, after some initial dispute it was agreed that at least the two external lawyers would need to be present throughout the conference and they were exempted from the daily struggle for badges.

[24] Unfortunately, the comments on the framework agreement had been put forward orally and in Albanian at a time when the legal advisors had not yet been let into the Chateau by the vigorous French security forces. As the framework agreement covered crucial issues, including the interim nature of the agreement and provisions for a final settlement, this may have meant that a few but important points of divergence were not noted sufficiently early by the negotiators and no discussion took place in relation to them until the very end of the Conference.

[25] Chairman's Conclusion, Contact Group Meeting, Paris, 14 February 1999, Document 15.B.9.

[26] Kosovo protested against this violation of the isolation purportedly imposed upon the delegations. By way of compensation, Mr Thaci too was subsequently permitted to travel back home for brief consultations.

Contact Group draft would be admissible, unless they were accepted by the other side, or unless the negotiators were persuaded that they would better serve to implement the provisions of the original draft. There had at that stage been no 'trading' of concessions by both sides through the negotiators, as is customary in genuine proximity talks. Yugoslavia/Serbia appeared to have made proposals which fell significantly outside of the initial draft and which could not be considered proposals for its more efficient implementation. Hence, it appeared that the original Contact Group proposal would remain principally unaltered.

The following day, however, the negotiators submitted a revised draft for a political settlement.[27] The new draft had, in view of the Kosovo delegation, been fundamentally changed in accordance with demands which had apparently been put forward by President Milosevic as a precondition for substantive participation in the talks. In essence, the new draft reintroduced the issue of the legal status of Kosovo/a into the constitutional settlement, and sought to resolve it firmly in favour of Belgrade. The actual exercise of authority by the Kosovo organs was also severely limited. And there was re-introduced a veto mechanism for members of all national communities which would effectively have paralysed legislative action in Kosovo. By contrast, very few of the suggestions proposed by the Kosovo delegation had been adopted.[28]

The new draft was presented by the negotiators along with the invitation to the parties to consider it to be the final version of a political settlement. This invitation was declined by both sides. In fact, the delegation of Kosovo issued a strongly worded protest, indicating that it considered the submission of a substantially new document two days before the scheduled conclusion of the conference, apparently as the result of talks conduced directly with Belgrade, a breach of faith and that it refused even to receive this document.[29] This gesture was meant to communicate to the negotiators a serious warning that the fundamental change of the draft in favour of the side which had obstructed progress in the talks until the last minute jeopardized further constructive participation from the Kosovo delegation. The Kosovo delegation would not be in a position to accept any settlement irrespective of its contents, and could not continue to be taken for granted. In fact, the introduction of the new draft had infused into the delegation a feeling of betrayal which would be very difficult to overcome in the days that followed. Once again, it seemed to the Kosovars as if the outside world was conspiring to deprive the ethnic Albanians of their entitlements.

The protest from the Kosovo delegation was not understood as a constructive warning by the Contact Group and instead severely criticised as being impetuous and ill-founded. As there appeared to be no prospect of reverting to the original draft, the Kosovo delegation reluctantly prepared a very short non-paper of less than a page, indicating crucial changes which would have to be made if discussions were to be continued with any prospect of success. For its part, the FRY continued to demand changes on a number of key points. Hence, the day before the deadline for acceptance of the agreement, a significant number of substantive issues had not even been negotiated. Moreover, the crucial annexes on civilian and military implementation had only just been presented by the parties (or at least to the Kosovo delegation).

The reasons for the delay in presenting the military annex appeared to have been two-fold. It appeared that the Contact Group itself remained divided in relation to the functions, modalities and powers of NATO implementation of the agreement. In fact, Russia remained opposed to military implementation in principle, although certain understandings were reached as to the presentation to the parties of the military annex in the end. In addition, as it had been announced that no proposals for changes to the implementation annexes would be entertained, it may have been considered unnecessary to acquaint the parties with the content of a document which they were expected to accept without changes.

Whatever the merits of this strategy, it had the disadvantage that the Kosovo delegation, and especially its military elements, had not had the opportunity to discuss in depth with NATO representatives and others the way in which the NATO annex would be interpreted in practice.[30] As the annex provided for the demilitarisation of the KLA, it could not have come as a surprise to the negotiators that some reassurances as to the implications of this concept would have to be given to a delegation which was effectively dominated by the KLA and a political party close to it. Similarly, the negotiators lost the opportunity to explain certain provisions to the FRY/Serb side, which were later presented as evidence of entirely unacceptable demands on the part of the Contact Group, or rather NATO. This concerns especially the famous Annex B to the military enforcement section, of which more will be said later.

Despite these uncertainties, on 20 February, shortly before the expiry of the noon deadline, the parties were presented with a short document of less than a page, in which they would indicate acceptance of the agreement, subject only to technical changes which would be made later by experts. Unfortunately, at that time the negotiators had not been able to provide the delegations with the actual text of the agreement as it stood at that time. In fact, it was known that negotiations continued

---

[27] Document 15.B.15.

[28] One exception to which the negotiators pointed frequently was the introduction of a technical commission to deal with economic claims.

[29] Statement by Kosovo, 18 February 1999, Document 15.B.17.

[30] There had been one briefing on military implementation before the text of the security annex had been made available. That briefing left the KLA and its supporters in something of a state of shock and was evidently not designed to reassure the military elements of the Kosova delegation on whose consent the entire process would, in the end, depend.

with the FRY/Serb delegation in relation to the further substantive concessions it had demanded, which were manifestly not mere technical changes.

When it became obvious a few hours after the expiry of the deadline that neither the FRY delegation nor the Kosovo delegation were in a position to sign this text, the Contact Group decided to prolong negotiations until 3 p.m. on 23 February. It was at this stage that a sense of panic set in among some members of the Contact Group (other than Russia). Hitherto, some of its members had watched in awe in the Contact Group office the CNN reports of the deployment of US heavy bombers to pre-strike positions. Now, suddenly, it appeared as if the strategy of obtaining a settlement through the threat of force if necessary was failing spectacularly. The Western members of the Contact Group had assumed that the Kosovo delegation was fully 'on board'. The fact that they had not really been negotiated with had been deemed irrelevant. If the Kosovars were smart, the reasoning went, they would accept any political settlement, whatever its content, provided it brought a withdrawal of FRY/Serb forces and the deployment of a NATO implementation force with it. Under this umbrella, democratic Kosovo institutions would be established which would necessarily be dominated by ethnic Albanians, given the demographics of the region.

To the individual members of the Kosovo delegation, this logic was less persuasive. They would, after all, have to live under the terms of whatever settlement might emerge. They would be held responsible by their constituents for the result of the conference. And what appeared to the Contact Group negotiators to be matters of detail, for example provisions on economic management or voting in the Kosovo Assembly, would actually be of tremendous importance in practice. At a broader level, the Contact Group had failed to engage the Kosovo delegation in dialogue on the two issues which were known from the beginning to constitute the principal points of difficulty: the demilitarisation of the KLA and provisions on the period after the expiry of the interim period, in particular the uniform demand among all Kosovo parties for a referendum.

When it became known that Kosovo might not sign the draft agreement, attention of the Contact Group, especially the US, switched. Over the next few days, Secretary of State Albright spent a significant amount of time in the chateau, summoning key members of the Kosovo delegation for meetings. Encounters with Hashim Thaci, the KLA Chairman of the delegation, appeared to be particularly draining. In addition, negotiations on finalizing the political settlement were now suddenly being conducted in the way of genuine proximity talks. Substantive proposals by one side were transmitted through the group of legal experts. A number of these proposals were accepted by the other side. Where no agreement was forthcoming, the Contact Group representatives would seek to reduce the scope of the respective proposals through very tough and skilful negotiation and refine it until they could become acceptable. In this way, it was possible to produce a consolidated text of the entire agreement in advance of the expected signature on 23 February.

At the insistence of the FRY/Serb delegation, that text now no longer consisted of a brief Framework Agreement, tying together a number of substantive annexes. Instead, all the annexes had been incorporated into an overall document, entitled Interim Agreement for Peace and Self Government in Kosovo. Some of the provisions from the Kosovo constitutional annex (now Chapter) had been moved into the general introductory part of the agreement. This was meant to preclude demands from Montenegro to be given similar constitutional safeguards.

A belated but intensive effort was finally begun to persuade the KLA and its supporters of the merits of signing the agreement. This included briefings by military experts, including, at the very final stage of the negotiations, by NATO itself. Through these contacts, the KLA was to be assured as to the actual meaning of demilitarisation in practice. One government also offered to record its willingness to contribute to the transformation of the KLA in full compliance with the terms of the accords. Nevertheless, two days before the deadline, a straw poll in the Kosovo delegation had resulted in a vote of 7 to 9 against the agreement, only the LDK and independent members supporting signature.

An intensive diplomatic effort was then made to persuade the KLA and its supporters to change their attitude. Albania sent its Foreign Minister Milo to Paris and a particularly respected Albanian novelist resident in Paris sent an important and emotional letter to the leader of the KLA friendly LBD delegates. On the other hand, Albanian exile groups were bombarding the delegation with demands to refuse a settlement. The FRY/Serbia also increased pressure upon the Kosovo delegation. On the ground, it launched further offensive operations leading to significant KLA losses. A request for an arrest warrant against Hashim Thaci was forwarded to Interpol and there were death threats. The FRY/Serb delegation also reiterated its willingness formally to sign the non-negotiable principles, hoping that the Kosovo delegation would not find this a convenient step to take. An attempt would then have been made to claim that Kosovo was in fact obstructing progress. Demands for direct negotiations were also reiterated, with strong support from the Russian mediator.

In terms of substance, a determined effort was made to address the issue of the final settlement which would take place after the interim period of three years. This attempt was spearheaded by the United States and led to some tension in the Contact Group. Apparently it had been agreed in the Group that on no account there would be a provision on a referendum after the expiry of the interim period. To the Kosovo delegation, however, this issue was non-negotiable. There was no point in having an interim agreement, if there was no prospect of significant change after the interim. To satisfy the requirements of the Kosovo delegation, an important addition was made to the final section of the agreement, referring to "the will of the people", rather than a referendum. In addition, as a result of quite dramatic all night negotiations, the US delegation offered to give bilateral assurances to the effect that this formulation did indeed refer to a right of the people of Kosovo to make manifest their will in relation to the future status of the territory through a referendum.[31] The KLA was also promised assistance in the process of 'transformation' from a military to a civil force, to induce it to change its stance.

In the meantime, tense but quite productive proximity negotiations had continued with the FRY/Serb side. Kosovo, now fully focused on the issue of the referendum, agreed to a number of substantive changes required by that delegation. These related to the political decision-making structure within Kosovo and the special rights of national communities. Despite the grave reservation of the Kosovo delegation, the reference to the 'sovereignty and territorial integrity' of the FRY had been retained, although in a slightly modified form. This, probably, was the key non-negotiable demand for the FRY/Serb delegation. Hence, it appeared as if an agreement could, after all, be possible. On the other hand, the possibility of agreement appeared to extend only to the political settlement. The FRY/Serbia still objected to any military presence in Kosovo, not to speak of a NATO presence, although it did contemplate an 'international presence' of a civilian character.

Despite the further direct intervention of US Secretary of State Albright, neither Kosovo nor the FRY/Serb side was in a position formally to sign the agreement by the deadline of 23 February. In fact, her personal intervention had helped sway the majority of the Kosovo/a delegation. This result coincided with a change in the leadership of the KLA in Kosovo itself. But, according to news reports, the Chairman of the Presidency of the Kosovo delegation was unable to support signature.[32] As the delegation had agreed at the outset of the talks to act according to the consensus principle, his vote made formal signature impossible at that stage.

On the other hand, Dr Rugova, until then not overly active in the negotiating process, quite courageously offered to sign the agreement himself, not as a member of the delegation's Presidency, but in his function as the elected President of Kosovo. All this left the international mediators in a state of considerable bafflement. They had heard of a vote of 16 to one in favour of signature, and were sitting in the delegation room expecting a decision according to this clear vote. In the confusion which followed, a carefully drafted legal statement announcing the intention of Kosovo to sign was rewritten on the spot in Albanian by an independent member of the delegation and under the eagle eyes of the delegation's chairman. That text was then, perhaps not entirely reliably, translated by US staff into English. A somewhat oddly formulated document emerged, in which Kosovo 'understands that it can sign the agreement in two weeks after consultations with the people of Kosovo, political and military institutions'.[33] The declaration also noted that in order to facilitate such consultations, the delegation had voted in favour of the Agreement as presented in the negotiations on 23 February.

The position of the FRY/Serb delegation too was not free of ambiguity. It was clear that there would be no signature forthcoming, but the means and modalities of presenting this result depended very much on Kosovo's attitude. If Kosovo failed to sign and its delegation fell apart, as then seemed possible, the threat of the use of force would have dissipated. In that case, the FRY/Serbia could give some evidence of its own constructive attitude and add further significant demands of its own before signature could be contemplated. If, on the other hand, Kosovo signed there and then, the FRY/Serbia would need to indicate that it, too, had in principle accepted a political settlement, although the modalities of implementation would need to be discussed. This division between the political and military aspects of the agreement would undermine the resolve of the less hawkish NATO states to permit the use of force. Finally, if Kosovo requested further negotiations, then the FRY/Serbia, too, could display a reasonably constructive attitude, while adding demands for a re-negotiation of key aspects of the political settlement.

The evolving actions of the FRY/Serb delegation were in a sense somewhat comical. Through a Russian member of the Contract Group, the delegation was periodically updated on the latest twists and turns in the Kosovo delegation chamber, where the mood shifted minute by minute from a break-up of the delegation to the possibility of formal signature. In accordance with this conflicting information, the FRY/Serbia issued no less than three versions of its final statement to the Contract Group. The first version appeared when the Kosovo delegation appeared to be nearing collapse. It noted that important progress had been made, but also that "we did not reach an agreement on important elements", adding a lengthy list of points that would need be satisfied.[34] A second statement omitted the detailed listing of essential issues of disagreement. Instead, it merely "pointed to eight vital issues" for the FRY/Serbia and again emphasized the need to "extend the positive spirit of the meeting" through further talks. The FRY/Serbia also expressly agreed to discuss the scope and character of an 'international presence' in Kosovo to implement an agreement.[35] The final statement no longer

[31] Draft provision for Chapter 8, 22 February 1999, Document 15.B.29.
[32] Jeffrey Smith, Kosovar Rebel Upset Western Strategy, *International Herald Tribune*, 25 February 1999, p. 6.
[33] Kosovo Statement, 23 February 1999, Document 15.B.34.
[34] Letter, 23 February, Document 15.B.31.
[35] Document 15.B.32.

mentioned the eight essential points, but instead referred to the need to clarify the definitions contained in the agreement, to facilitate its actual implementation. Again, there was an offer also to discuss an international implementation presence.

Hence, in its final statement, delivered the moment US Ambassador Hill entered the Kosovo delegation room to obtain an undertaking to sign the agreement, the FRY/Serbia appeared to indicate that there had been agreement in principle on the political settlement, although some refining work needed to be done. The issue of implementation, too, could be addressed, although there was only a reference to an 'international presence' as opposed to an international military presence. However, this formulation was not necessarily inconsistent with the non-negotiable principles of the Contact Group, which had provided for an implementation presence by the OSCE "and other international bodies as necessary". The acceptance of the political aspects of the Rambouillet in principle contrasts with the subsequent attitude of the FRY government, which claimed that Rambouillet was an entirely unacceptable diktat which would inevitably lead to the detachment of Kosovo from the Serb motherland.

The end result of the Rambouillet conference remained somewhat confusing. Kosovo argued that its delegation had in fact accepted the text as the definite outcome of the negotiations and that it would probably sign subject to consultation at home. This position was taken to avoid a further dilution of the text. Throughout the conference process, the text had been fundamentally revised in order to tempt the FRY/Serbia into signing. It was feared that this would now continue, outside of the conference process, perhaps through another Holbrooke mission.

This attitude was consistent with the indication given by the negotiators, who had in fact invented the idea of a further meeting to follow upon the Rambouillet talks as a means of preventing the collapse of the talks. In their view, a further conference would be in the nature of a signature conference, in accordance with the precedent of the 1995 agreement on Bosnia and Herzegovina. While the negotiators in Dayton initialled the texts, the document was formally signed in Paris some weeks after negotiations had been concluded. The FRY/Serbia, on the other hand, regarded the process of negotiations as by no means terminated.

The Contact Group then issued Chairmen's Conclusions, which were perhaps not fully reflective of the intention of either of the parties. It was noted that a political framework was now in place and the groundwork had thereby been laid for finalizing the implementation chapters of the agreement, including the modalities of the invited international civilian and military presence in Kosovo. As it was essential that the agreement be completed and signed as a whole, the Contact Group indicated the parties had committed themselves to attend a further conference, covering all aspects of implementation on 15 March.[36] Hence, it appeared that the conference would neither be a simple signature conference, nor a conference at which the discussions about a political settlement would be re-opened. Instead, talks were apparently intended to focus only on implementation—the very issues which had been declared to be non-negotiable through the entire Rambouillet process thus far.

III. The Political Interim Settlement

The issue of status and the basic distribution of powers

The non-negotiable principles had reflected the FRY/Serb demand that the territorial integrity of the FRY and its neighbouring countries be respected. The government of Kosovo had responded that it would be willing to attend the Rambouillet talks, provided a proposed settlement would not prejudice the status of Kosovo, in accordance with the approach that had been adopted in the initial Hill proposals. The first draft of the agreement presented to the Conference was in accordance with this idea of leaving out express statements on issues on which no agreement could be achieved. It contained, in what started out as the Draft Framework Agreement, merely a preambular which recalled the commitment *of the international community* to the sovereignty and territorial integrity of the FRY. Hence, in signing this text, Kosovo itself would not have had to take an express view in this matter. There was also a reference to United Nations and OSCE principles. As these contain both the rule of territorial unity and the principle of self-determination this reference was also acceptable to Kosovo, while it provided reassurance to the FRY/Serbia. The Constitution (initially Annex 1) did not contain a preamble and, instead of addressing the status of Kosovo/a and the legal quality of its relations with the FRY or even Serbia, it focused on a reasonable division of competences.

When the second draft of the agreement was presented on 18 February, a preamble had been added which referred to "democratic self-government in Kosovo grounded in respect for the territorial integrity and sovereignty of the Federal Republic of Yugoslavia, from which the authorities of governance set forth herein originate." While the Contact Group attempted to assert that this was an insubstantive addition, it did in fact fundamentally change the nature of the entire interim settlement. To avoid a failure of the Rambouillet process on account of this unilateral change made without explanation two days before the deadline for signature, the following compromise was in the end adopted:

---

[36] Co-Chairmen's Conclusions, 23 February 1999, Document 15.B.36.

> Desiring through this interim Constitution to establish institutions of democratic self-government in Kosovo grounded in respect for the territorial integrity and sovereignty of the Federal Republic of Yugoslavia and from this Agreement, from which authorities of governance set forth herein originate,

Even as amended, this provision almost led the Kosovo delegation to reject the agreement. Still, the formulation permitted Kosovo to argue that acceptance of the territorial integrity and sovereignty was limited to the interim period.[37] In any event, this commitment and the legal personality and powers of Kosovo were rooted in the Agreement, rather than in a grant of autonomy by the FRY.

Another important change that had been made in the draft of 18 February related to the assignment of powers. According to Article I (2) of the initial draft of what then was Annex 1, Kosovo as an entity would enjoy responsibility for "all areas" other than those where authority was expressly assigned to the FRY. Those areas of authority were enumerated exclusively and their exercise was subjected to important restrictions and safeguards for Kosovo. In the draft of 18 February, the express presumption in favour of Kosovo authority had been abandoned. Instead, a new paragraph had been added, indicating that Serbia, too, would exercise competence in relation to Kosovo as specified in the agreement.

The FRY/Serbia strongly insisted on the inclusion of a further provision in the introductory section of the agreement (formerly the Framework Agreement), stating that the parties would only act within their powers and responsibilities in Kosovo as specified by this agreement. Acts outside those powers and responsibilities would be null and void. Kosovo would have all rights and powers set forth in the agreement, in particular as specified in the Constitution. While the FRY/Serb delegation might have intended this provision as a safeguard against creeping jurisdiction by the Kosovo organs, the delegation of Kosovo interpreted it as a helpful confirmation that the powers of Kosovo were indeed based in the agreement, and not in a sovereign grant of rights by the FRY. In addition, this formulation supported the view that FRY/Serb exercises of powers in relation to Kosovo would be strictly limited to competences that have been expressly granted to them.[38]

The issue of legal personality for Kosovo as a whole was also clarified in some measure through a provision concerning the communes. One of the difficulties with the initial Hill proposal was its insistence that Kosovo communes would be the basic unit of self-governance in Kosovo and that they would exercise all authority not assigned to other Kosovo organs. While the latter element was retained,[39] it was clarified in what was to become Article I (8) of Chapter 1 of the final text that the communes were merely the basic unit of *local* self-government. The insertion of the word local ensured that this provision no longer diluted the overall legal personality of Kosovo as a whole.

The Kosovo institutions and their powers

The principal organs of Kosovo according to the agreement were the Assembly, the President of Kosovo, the Government and Administrative Organs, judicial organs and the communes.[40] The Assembly was to be composed of 120 members, of which 80 would be directly elected. The other 40 members would be elected by members of qualifying national communities. Communities whose members constitute more than 0.5 per cent of the Kosovo population but less than 5 per cent were to divide ten of these seats among themselves. Communities whose members constituted more than 5 per cent of the Kosovo/a population (in fact only the ethnic Albanians and Serbs) would divide the remaining 30 seats equally.

The draft of 18 February had unilaterally introduced as an additional feature a second chamber of the Assembly as a result of FRY/Serb pressure. In that Chamber of 100 seats, the Turks, Goranies, Romanies, Egyptians, Muslims and any other group constituting more than 0.5 per cent of the population (hence also including the ethnic Albanians and Serbs) would be equally represented. The Chamber would have had the right of consultation in relation to legislative acts of the Assembly, and any of the groups represented within it could have initiated so-called vital interest motions which would amount to an attempted veto of legislation.

The FRY/Serb delegation itself abandoned the concept of the second chamber and instead focused on attempting to strengthen the power of veto of national communities in the Assembly. According to the initial draft and the draft of 18 February, the decision as to which legislative acts would violate the vital interests of a national community and would thus be null and void would have been taken by the Constitutional Court of Kosovo. The Kosovo delegation had grave reservations about the very concept of special powers for ethnic groups, including separate elections according to ethnic

---

[37] A proposal to entitle Chapter 1 'Interim Constitution' was not adopted. However, given the overall title of the Agreement, the specific reference to the interim period in this preambular provision, and the concluding provisions, this was not seen by the Kosova delegation as a significant setback.

[38] Federal functions were still expressly, and in the view of Kosovo/a, exhaustively listed: territorial integrity, maintaining a common market within the Federal Republic of Yugoslavia, monetary policy, defence, foreign policy, customs services, federal taxation, federal elections and other areas specified in this agreement.

[39] See also Article VIII (5) of Chapter 1, and the important reference contained therein to Article II (5) (b) of Chapter 1.

[40] On the national communities and their institutions, see the section which follows.

criteria. While strongly endorsing the notion of equal rights for members of all ethnic groups, the idea of separate representation appeared to grant to very small groups broad rights of co-decision which were unrepresentative and hence undemocratic. Moreover, the example of ethnic politics in Bosnia and Herzegovina had demonstrated the divisive nature of an ethnic organization of a political system. Finally, a legislative system which was subjected to the constant threat of a veto by any ethnic group would result in perennial paralysis.

Despite these concerns, and in view of the strong position of the FRY/Serbia in this matter, the Kosovo delegation endorsed, however reluctantly, the concept of special representation for ethnic groups for the interim period. However, this concession was dependent on a judicial process to check vital national interest motions in the Assembly, in order to avoid an arbitrary use of this procedure leading to constant deadlock in the legislature. The Contact Group disregarded this view and gave way to a Serb/FRY proposal of settling disputes about vital national interest motions outside of the judicial system. According to Article II (8) (c) of Chapter 1, the final agreement provided that the decision about such motions would be rendered by a panel comprising three members of the Assembly: one Albanian, one Serb, each appointed by his or her national community, and a third Member of a third "nationality" to be selected within two days by consensus of the Presidency of the Assembly. As the Serb national community was guaranteed a member of the Presidency of the Assembly (in fact, actually the President of the Assembly), it appeared that this nominating process itself could be blocked by a factual veto.

Decisions of the Assembly which had been challenged according to the vital national interest procedure were to be suspended in regard to the national community having brought the challenge, pending completion of the dispute settlement procedure. Hence, it might appear as if a Serb veto in relation to Assembly decisions was introduced through the back door. However, as this veto would depend on an abuse of process in frustrating the nomination of the third member of the arbitration panel, the general dispute settlement mechanism attaching to the agreement as a whole, or the general powers of the Constitutional Court, would probably be brought to bear on a matter of this kind. It should also be noted that the decision on the merits of a vital interest motion, while conducted by a political body, was to be made according to legal criteria.[41]

The substantive powers of the Assembly were reasonably wide, covering most aspects of governance. Importantly, this included the power to set the framework of, and to coordinate, the exercise of competences assigned to the communes. The first elections in Kosovo were to be held within nine months of the entry into force of the agreement under international supervision.

The President of Kosovo was to be elected by the Assembly by a majority vote. His or her functions included representation before international, FRY or republic bodies, the conduct of foreign relations consistent with the authorities of Kosovo institutions, proposing to the Assembly candidates for Prime Minister and for the principal courts of Kosovo, etc. The Government, also to be approved by the Assembly, would have general authority for implementing the laws of Kosovo, etc. At least one minister would have been a member of the Serb national community.

The powers reserved for the communes were being narrowed down somewhat in comparison with earlier drafts. However, while there was provision for coordination on a Kosovo-wide basis, the police was to be organized on a communal basis and limited to a ceiling of 3,000 active law-enforcement officers throughout Kosovo. In addition, there was authority in relation to education, child care, the communal environment, local economic issues, etc.

The judiciary consisted of a Constitutional Court composed of nine judges. At least one judge would have been a member of the Serb national community and five other judges would have been selected from a list drawn up by the President of the European Court of Human Rights. The powers of review of the Constitutional Court were quite wide. They included, but are not limited to, determining whether laws applicable in Kosovo, decisions or acts of the President, the Assembly, the Government, the Communes, and the national communities are compatible with the Constitution.

The Supreme Court composed of nine judges, including one member of the Serb national community, would hear final appeals from subordinated courts in Kosovo, including communal courts.

A special feature related to the right of citizens in Kosovo to opt to have civil disputes to which they are party adjudicated by other courts in the FRY, which would apply the law applicable in Kosovo. In criminal cases, a defendant would be entitled to have a trial transferred to another Kosovo court designated by him or her. In effect, this meant that a defendant could opt to be tried in the local court of a specific commune, which would be principally composed of members of his or her ethnic appurtenance. In criminal cases in which all defendants and victims were members of the same national community, all members of the judicial council would be from the national community of their choice if any party so requested. A defendant in a criminal case could also insist that one member of the judicial council hearing the case would be

---

[41] A vital interest motion shall be upheld if the legislation challenged adversely affects the community's fundamental rights as set forth in Article VII, or the principle of fair treatment.

from his or national community. This might include judges of courts in the FRY serving as Kosovo/a judges for these purposes.

Human rights and additional rights of national communities

The provisions on human rights were strangely short and undeveloped in the Constitution and throughout the agreement. There was no listing of fundamental human rights to be applied in Kosovo/a. Instead, Article VI (1) of the Constitution stated rather generally that all authorities in Kosovo must ensure internationally recognized human rights and fundamental freedoms. As opposed to the Dayton agreement, which included a long list of human rights instruments identifying what internationally recognized human rights and fundamental freedoms are, the agreement in Article VI (2) rather ingeniously incorporated by reference the terms of the European Convention for the Protection of Human Rights and Fundamental Freedoms and its Protocols which "shall apply directly in Kosovo". In this way, a very sophisticated body of human rights law, refined in decades of jurisprudence by the European Court and Commission of Human Rights would have been instantly available in Kosovo. The Kosovo Assembly also had the power to enact into law other internationally recognized human rights instruments.

The rights and freedoms established in this way would have priority over all other law. Interestingly, all "courts, agencies, governmental institutions, and other public institutions of Kosovo or operating in relation to Kosovo shall conform to these human rights and fundamental freedoms" (Article VI (3)). This means that FRY and republic authorities would also have had to exercise their competences in relation to Kosovo in accordance with these standards. As the FRY was not a party to the European Convention and its Protocols, this would have placed it in an unusual position.

While the human rights provisions were compact, the additional rights granted to national communities were extensive, but not unlimited. Firstly, these rights were tied to the specific purpose of preserving and expressing their national, cultural, religious and linguistic identities. This was to be done in accordance with international standards and in accordance with human rights and fundamental freedoms.

More controversially, each national community could elect and establish its own institutions—a feature which it was feared would give rise to a parallel state structure within Kosovo. However, national community institutions would have to act in accordance with Kosovo law and not take discriminatory action. National communities could arrange for the inscription of local names of towns and villages, etc, in the language and alphabet of the respective community, issue information in that language, provide for education and schooling in that language and in national culture and history, reflecting a spirit of tolerance between communities and respect for the rights of members of all national communities, display national symbols, including those of the FRY and Serbia, protect national traditions on family law, arrange for the preservation of sites of religious, historical or cultural importance in cooperation with other authorities, implement public health and social services on a non-discriminatory basis, operate religious institutions in cooperation with religious authorities and participate in non-governmental organizations.

National communities could also enjoy unhindered contacts with representatives of their respective national communities within the FRY and abroad. They must be guaranteed access to and representation in the media and my finance their activities by collecting contributions from their members. Importantly, every person has the right freely to choose to be treated or not to be treated as belonging to a national community.

Final status

The draft presented to the parties at the outset of the Conference restated the concluding provision from previous Hill proposals providing for amendments to the Agreement to be adopted by agreement of all the parties. Each party was to be entitled to propose such amendment at any time. However, after three years, there would occur a comprehensive assessment of the Agreement under international auspices with the aim of improving its implementation and determining whether to implement proposals by either side for additional steps.[42] The means of undertaking this assessment, and the procedure to be adopted, were left unclear.

The Kosovo delegation argued strongly that, in accordance with the interim character of the agreement, provision would need to be made for a further international conference on a final settlement for Kosovo. The decisions of that conference should be based on the will of the people of Kosovo, made manifest in a referendum. The negotiators pointed out that they were not authorized by the Contact Group to adopt language on a referendum. However, even the non-negotiable principles had at least provided for "a mechanism for a final settlement after an interim period of three years". In the dramatic final phase of the conference, it became possible to obtain significant changes to the final provision, in reflection of this wording. The final text of what became Article I (3) or Chapter 8 reads:

---

[42] This formulation actually represented a slight retreat from the final Hill draft, put forward on 27 January, which had referred to a 'procedure' for considering such additional steps to be determined taking into account the Parties' roles in and compliance with this agreement.

Three years after the entry into force of this agreement, an international meeting shall be convened to determine a mechanism for a final settlement for Kosovo, on the basis of the will of the people, opinions of relevant authorities, each Party's efforts regarding the implementation of this Agreement, and the Helsinki Final Act, and to undertake a comprehensive assessment of the implementation of this Agreement and to consider proposals by any Party for additional measures.

This wording stops short of actually establishing a mechanism for a final settlement, contrary to what might have been expected in view of the language contained in the non-negotiable principles. However, startlingly, it was accepted that this mechanism shall be established and/or operate, inter alia, on the basis of the will of the people.[43] On the other hand, this mechanism would be created by "an international meeting" the composition, remit and authority of which was not defined. All organs of the international community had consistently ruled out the possibility of independence and it would not be surprising if the "international meeting" might hold a similar view. These uncertainties were not entirely removed by the unilateral interpretation offered by the US in a draft side letter, which confirmed that Kosovo could hold a referendum on independence after three years. In any event, that side-letter was in the end not formalized, given the failure of the Kosovo delegation to sign the agreement by the stipulated deadline at Rambouillet.

IV. Implementation

The provisions for implementation contained in the Rambouillet text were complex and distributed throughout the interim agreement. They consisted principally of the introductory section of the agreement entitled Framework, Chapter 2 on Police and Public Security, Chapter 3 on the Conduct and Supervision of Elections, Chapter 4 (a) on Humanitarian Assistance, Reconstruction and Development, Chapter 5 on the Civilian Implementation Mission in Kosovo, Chapter 6 concerning the Ombudsman and Chapter 7 on 'Implementation II', that is to say, military implementation. For reasons of space it will only be possible to review some of the principle features of this implementation structure here.

Confidence building

Upon signature of the agreement, a cease fire was to come into force immediately. Alleged violations of the cease-fire were to be reported to international observers and could not be used to justify use of force in response. The status of police and security forces in Kosovo, including withdrawal of forces was to be achieved according to Chapter 7. Paramilitary and irregular forces in Kosovo were deemed incompatible with the terms of the agreement. The latter provision gave rise to some difficulty, inasmuch as the KLA did not consider itself a paramilitary or irregular force. However, it was clear that it, too, was addressed through Chapter 7 of the agreement.

All abducted persons or other persons detained without charge were to be released, including persons held in connection with the conflict in Kosovo. No one was to be prosecuted for crimes related to the conflict, except for persons accused of having committed serious violations of international humanitarian law. Persons already convicted for committing politically motivated crimes related to the conflict were to be released, provided these convictions did not relate to serious violations of humanitarian law obtained in a fair and open trial conducted pursuant to international standards.

The agreement confirmed the obligation, already contained in mandatory Security Council resolutions, to cooperate with the Hague International Criminal Tribunal for the Former Yugoslavia. This included the obligation to permit complete access to tribunal investigators and compliance with the orders of the Tribunal. This provision was somewhat contested at Rambouillet. Kosovo attempted to strengthen its scope, as did, indirectly, the Tribunal itself. However, in the face of determined opposition from the FRY, a rather short paragraph was adopted which did not greatly improve upon the obligations already contained in the demands of the Security Council.

The parties also recognized the right to return of all persons to their homes, including those who have had to leave the region. There was to be no impediment to the normal flow of goods into Kosovo, including materials for the reconstruction of homes and structures. The FRY would not require visas, customs or licensing for persons or things connected with international implementation.

NATO-led implementation and the withdrawal of forces

The military implementation chapter was the most detailed element of the entire accords. The parties would have agreed that NATO would establish and deploy a force (KFOR) operating under the authority and subject to the direction and the political control of the North Atlantic Council (NAC) through the NATO chain of command. However, contrary to much speculation afterwards, a Chapter VII mandate was to be obtained from the Security Council from the beginning. Other states would be invited to assist in military implementation. While this is not spelt out, it was envisaged that KFOR would be of a strength of approximately 28,000 troops. This would include a sizeable Russian contingent according to the precedent SFOR/IFOR in

---

[43] In a dramatic night negotiating session delegation towards the very end of the conference, the Kosovo delegation was able to extract from the negotiators an even better formulation, referring to the 'expressed will of the people'. However, this concession was lost when the delegation was not immediately able to sign the final text and when the Contact Group overruled it afterwards.

Bosnia and Herzegovina. In accordance with that precedent, KFOR would be authorized to take such actions as required, including the use of necessary force, to ensure compliance with Chapter 7. As opposed to the arrangements of Dayton, it was made clear at the beginning that KFOR would not only be available to ensure compliance with the military aspects of the agreement, but that it would also actively support civilian implementation by the OSCE and others as part of its original mandate. As in the Dayton agreement, the mandate of KFOR could have been broadened through further action by NATO, in this instance acting through the North Atlantic Council.

A Joint Implementation Commission would have been established to consider complaints by the parties and other matters. It would have been composed of FRY military commanders and FRY/Serb officials, Kosovo representatives and representatives of the military and civilian implementation missions. The agreement envisaged that final authority to interpret the provisions of Chapter 7 would rest with the KFOR military commander.

The regular armed forces of the FRY (VJ) would have been subjected to a rigorous regime of redeployment and withdrawal according to fixed deadlines. This included the removal of assets such as battle tanks, all armoured vehicles mounting weapons greater than 12.7mm and all heavy weapons of over 82mm. Within 180 days of the agreement coming into force, all VJ units, other than 1,500 members of a lightly armed border guard battalion deployed close to the border would have had to be withdrawn from Kosovo. An additional 1,000 support personnel would be permitted in specified cantonment sites. The border guards would have been limited to patrolling the border zone and their travel through Kosovo would have been subjected to significant restrictions. Moreover, the air defence system in Kosovo would be dismantled and associated forces withdrawn, as would other FRY or Serb forces, including the Ministry of Interior Police (MUP). The MUP would initially be reduced to a size of 2,500, and be entirely withdrawn upon the establishment of a Kosovo police within one year. Upon entry into force of the agreement, all other forces would have had to commit themselves to demilitarisation, renunciation of violence, to guarantee security of international personnel, etc. The definition of the term 'demilitarisation' had been subject to some discussion, especially as it applied to the KLA. It would have included the surrender of heavy armaments and some small arms.

The military chapter was accompanied by two Appendices, which were both published along with the agreement. The rather extravagant claims, that they reveal a secret agenda by NATO for the virtual occupation of all of Yugoslavia, made some time after the conclusion of the conference are entirely without substance. Appendix A established cantonment sites for FRY/Serb forces. The famous Appendix B established what in other contexts would be the standard terms of a status of forces agreement for KFOR, very much in line with the precedent of IFOR/SFOR in Bosnia and Herzegovia and United Nations peace-keeping operations. A provision which permits transit through Yugoslavia for NATO and affiliated forces falls within these standard terms, although it may have been phrased slightly more broadly than would have been usual. If, as was subsequently claimed, the terms of the Appendix, or this particular provision, was what rendered Rambouillet unacceptable, it remains to be explained why the FRY did not seek clarification or even modification of this provision at the Paris follow-on conference. That conference was exclusively dedicated to negotiations on the implementation aspects of the agreement, which had not been available at Rambouillet itself.

Civilian implementation

The OSCE would have been charged with principal responsibility over the civilian elements of implementation, operating under a Chief of the Implementation Mission (CIM). The implementation mission would monitor, observe and inspect law enforcement activities in Kosovo, which would be established principally at communal level. The Kosovo police force of around 3,000 was to be only lightly armed. The authority of Federal and Serb police would have been very significantly restricted. Importantly, the CIM would have had final authority to interpret the provisions of the agreement in relation to civilian implementation.

All aspects of civilian implementation would have been coordinated and monitored by a Joint Commission, including Federal, Republic and Kosovo representatives and others, and chaired by the CIM exercising a final right of decision in this rather powerful body. In addition, an ombudsman would monitor the realization of the rights of members of national communities and the protection of human rights and fundamental freedoms. Elections were to be held at communal and Kosovo level within nine month from entry into force of the agreement once the OSCE would have certified that conditions had been established for a free and fair ballot. Finally, the agreement provided for the administration of humanitarian aid and reconstruction principally through the organs of Kosovo, with strong involvement by the European Union. In fact, throughout the conference, the European Union, through its negotiator and through representatives of the Commission, exercised a considerable influence, also and especially in relation to this issue. Great emphasis was placed on careful planning, rapid and unbureaucratic deployment of resources once needs have been identified, and close cooperation with the beneficiaries of such aid.

V. Conclusion

The Rambouillet Conference on Kosovo represented a significant departure in international mediation. The presence of the parties at the talks had been ensured through the threat of the use of force by NATO. Acceptance of the political interim settlement for Kosovo was to be obtained, if necessary, through the threat or use of force. The implementation of the agreement was to be assured through the presence of a 28,000 strong NATO-led force, in addition to a sizeable OSCE element. Acceptance of this presence, too, was to be obtained through the threat of the use of force, if necessary. At the time of the conference, there existed no express United Nations Security Council mandate for the threat or use of force in relation to the parties. Instead, NATO had to rely on the justification of forcible humanitarian action in general international law to justify its posture. However, the Security Council had expressly supported the Contact Group decision which required the parties to attend the conference, and which was supported by NATO in this way.

In terms of its substance, the Rambouillet settlement might have represented a further step in the development of innovative mechanisms to resolve self-determination conflicts. In fact, it combines within it, and advances upon, some of the elements pioneered in the innovative responses to others crises that may have appeared irresolvable. The Dayton settlement provided for the retention of the territorial unity of a state (Bosnia and Herzegovina) which had come under unbearable pressure as a result of armed strife, while at the same time granting very substantive powers of self-governance to the entity that needed to be contained within it (Srpska). The Good Friday agreement on Northern Ireland and the Palestine accords introduced the concept of the allocation of authority at differing levels of governance, without necessary prejudicing questions of legal status. Eritrea and Chechnya introduced the notion of an interim agreement pending an exercise of the will of the people.

Conceptionally, one might argue that the conference represented an attempt by the international community to advance on these precedents by actually imposing reason upon parties which appeared to be unreasonable. The FRY/Serbia had persisted over a decade in a policy of repression which had been clearly rejected. However, all attempts to reverse Belgrade's actions had failed. The Kosovars, on the other hand, had committed themselves to independence—an attitude which was identified as unreasonable by the international community. Hence, the international community, at the level of the Security Council, had identified, at a general level the outcome that was to be obtained: significant self-governance with human rights within the FRY/Serbia. Rather than seeking to impose a permanent settlement, the Hill process had revealed that the cooperation of both parties would be more likely if an interim agreement could be achieved. Insistence on an interim agreement was also more in line with the justification for an 'imposed' settlement, i.e., the ongoing humanitarian emergency and the destabilization of the region.

The actual terms of the settelement, anticipated in the basic non-negotiable principles, had of course been refined over time in cooperation with the parties, through the Hill process. The definition of a reasonable political settlement which the parties could be expected to accept, at least for the interim, was therefore not quite as arbitrary as it seemed. The initial draft presented to the parties provided for a sensible sharing of authority without touching upon issues of status. However, when a second text was presented shortly before the conclusion of the talks, it had been fundamentally altered in accordance with Belgrade's demands. If the first version had been deemed to reflect that which was inherently reasonable, it was difficult to explain to Kosovo why now a substantially different document was equally as reasonable. Kosovo gave in on most matters of the assignment of public authority changed in the draft, or rather, it was offered no choice in the matter. Hence, in terms of the assignment of public authority, the Rambouillet text fell short of a restoration of the autonomous powers Kosovo had enjoyed before its status was unilaterally modified. In addition, there was introduced the notion of national communities, which provided ethnic Serbs and others with very extensive and disproportionate powers of representation and co-decision making, to the point of undermining the functioning of the Kosovo institutions under the terms of the agreement.

On the issue of status, the FRY/Serbia obtained an express recognition of the continued territorial integrity and even sovereignty of the FRY. This language had to be bought with a counterveiling reference to an expression of the will of the people at the termination of the three year period when it emerged that Kosovo would not sign. While it is clear that the wording 'will of the people' would have permitted the holding of a referendum, this would not, in fact, have necessarily determined the issue of status. Even according to the wording proposed in the US side letter, it was confirmed that the will of the people would only be one of the elements to be taken into consideration when determining the mechanism for a final settlement after three years. Given the fact that the establishment of the mechanism for a final settlement would lie in the hands of the international community which had declared itself consistently against the granting of independence for Kosovo, there was no automaticity of self-determination for Kosovo, although the case for it had been strengthened.

On the side of military implementation, the Contact Group itself, due to Russia's position, was unable to present a united view as to what was reasonable and could be imposed upon the parties. However, the FRY/Serbia gave up the opportunity to test to what extent it could advance its position on implementation at the follow-on Paris conference, which was expressly devoted to the issue of implementation. Most observers had expected an attempt to undermine NATO's determination to use force at Paris. Had the FRY/Serbia signed up to the political part of the agreement and offered, for example, to accept an OSCE or UN-led implementation mission of more limited dimensions, it is not at all certain that NATO could have maintained a consensus on the threat or use of force.

Instead, the FRY started to question the political settlement which it previously appeared to have regarded as a reasonable compromise and which, ironically, could have brought with it for a period of at least three years the international protection of the territorial integrity of that state. Evidently, Belgrade was unable to embrace the concept of self-rule for ethnic Albanians and a reversal of its policies in relation to that territory, co-administered by the organized international community. Perhaps there was also a recognition that in the longer term it would be impossible to constrain an ethnic Albanian population in the FRY, if the tools of repressing that population had been removed from Belgrade.

Throughout the talks, significant rifts in the Contact Group were visible, relating to the political settlement, to the implementation force and to the threat or use of force as a tool of achieving a settlement. These divisions became more pronounced towards the conclusion of the conference, when a collapse of the talks appeared likely. In fact, one might say that towards the end, the talks were less about Kosovo and more about relations within the Contact Group. The rifts in the Contact Group, and the uncertain position of the Kosovo delegation itself, significantly undermined the effect of the threat of force. In view of this disunity, and of the actual conduct of the negotiations, at least in relation to the FRY/Serbia, the characterization of Rambouillet as a settlement imposed by a number of powerful states according to the model of the Concert of Europe appears somewhat shaky.

With the commencement of NATO action some weeks after Rambouillet, much thought has been expended on the question of whether Rambouillet represented a serious attempt to achieve a settlement, or whether it was instead a US 'setup', designed to manoeuvre Yugoslavia into a position in which the initiation of military action appeared justified. The oscillating nature of the negotiations, and the very substantive concessions made to the FRY/Serbia would appear to rule out such conspiracy theories. Similarly, the influence of other members of the Contact Group on the conduct of the talks is often underestimated. The Contact Group had developed the Hill package on which Rambouillet was principally based. It had to approve with consensus all major developments in the drafts as the talks progressed. When the US unilaterally offered last-minute concessions to Kosovo to ensure that it would, after all, sign, these were in fact in part overruled by the Contact Group. Towards the end of the talks, there was a true sense that an agreement might be possible after all, although this was being achieved through concessions which in fact jeopardized Kosovo's ability to sign the agreement.

The conspiracy theory also fails to take into account the inability of US policy to conceive and carry through long-term foreign policy. Had there existed a plan to 'frame' Yugoslavia, it would have been essential to ensure that the Kosovo Albanians were on board and conduct themselves according to the script. As the developments at Rambouillet amply demonstrated, no such effort had been made. In fact, US policy-makers had failed to develop an understanding of the dynamics within the Kosovo delegation, and of the positions that would likely be taken by its members.

Whether or not the FRY/Serbia could have been reasonably expected to accept the Rambouillet package depends in the end on what standard is applied to identify what is reasonable. The defenders of the draft agreement and of the Rambouillet process would argue that this standard had been raised by Yugoslavia's own conduct over the previous decade. In fact, even up to the events of 1998, Serbia would probably have been able to satisfy international demands for the restoration of meaningful self-governance in Kosovo by accepting a more modest autonomy regime for the province. In the autumn of 1998, the FRY could have accepted a political settlement similar to the one on offer at Rambouillet in the shape of the Hill draft put forward on 2 November. Such a settlement would not have had attached to it strong implementation provisions, including a NATO-led presence. Instead, significant FRY/Serb armed forces would have remained in the territory. After the Christmas offensive and the Racak massacre, conducted under the noses of the OSCE's unarmed verification mission, the attitude to implementation changed, at least among NATO states. It was no longer deemed reasonable to expect the Kosovo Albanians to rely on further agreements or promises by the Belgrade government in the absence of the strong enforcement presence envisaged in the Rambouillet agreement.

The result which obtained after a failure to embrace Rambouillet, and after the extraordinary campaign to expel virtually the entire ethnic Albanian population from its homeland, must strike the observer as somewhat ironic. A NATO presence was introduced, without any significant opportunity for Belgrade to determine the modalities and powers of this force. No political settlement exists, which would guarantee the rights of the Serb 'national community'—a concept not now likely to attract vigorous support from the ethnic Albanian politicians who are assuming control over the territory. In fact, Belgrade's only hope to retain its 'territorial integrity' lies in the hand of NATO and the international community.

A.   The Summons to the Conference

1.   Joint Statement by Secretary of State Albright and Russian Foreign Minister Ivanov, Moscow, 26 January 1999

Secretary Albright and Foreign Minister Ivanov expressed their preoccupation with the recent deterioration in the situation in Kosovo. They noted positively the outcome of the Contact Group Political Directors meeting in London January 22. The sides in Kosovo must work harder to achieve an interim political settlement providing substantial autonomy for Kosovo and should engage in meaningful intensive negotiations for that purpose. Such a settlement should respect the territorial integrity and sovereignty of the FRY. Russia and the United States, backing the efforts of Ambassadors Hill and Petritsch, will continue to press the sides to agree on such a political settlement, and will collaborate in the Contact Group toward that end.

Secretary Albright and Foreign Minister Ivanov expressed their complete commitment to the unimpeded functioning of the OSCE Kosovo Verification Mission under the leadership of Ambassador William Walker. All attacks on and threats to the OSCE KVM must cease immediately. It is incumbent upon everyone in Kosovo to ensure the safety of KVM and other international personnel. They call on FRY authorities and media to create a supportive atmosphere for the activities of the KVM and its Head of Mission. The FRY authorities should facilitate the work of the KVM by fulfilling the Head of Mission's requests for adequate security arrangements and other measures to make fully effective the agreement between the OSCE and the FRY.

The United States and Russia firmly demand that the FRY comply fully with the resolutions of the UN Security Council, particularly with regard to police and military units, and its agreements with the OSCE and other international entities. They call on the FRY to do so without delay. The United States and Russia reiterate their indignation at the massacre of Kosovar Albanians in Racak, which cannot be justified. Those responsible must be brought to justice. The FRY authorities must give their full cooperation to the International Criminal Tribunal for the Former Yugoslavia, as required by resolutions of the UN Security Council. The FRY authorities must conduct a fully investigaiton of what happened at Racak with the participation of the Tribunal. Judge Louise Arbour and ICTY investigatory should be allowed to enter and work in Kosovo, to participate in the investigation of the massacre at Racak. The FRY authorities should identify the officers operating in Racak at the time of the massacre and suspend them until the results of the investigation become available.

The United States and Russia urge the Kosovo Albanians to fulfill all their obligations and commitments. "Kosovo Liberation Army" provocations have contributed significantly to the renewed deep tensions in Kosovo. The United States and Russia condemn such provocations and demand they end immediately. Measures should be developed to discourage such activity whenever feasible, in the interest of ensuring full compliance with the commitments and obligations undertaken by the sides, including implementing the arms embargo under the relevant UN Security Council resolutions.

Hostage taking must cease. All hostages should be released. Secretary Albright and Foreign Minister Ivanov appreciated the work of the KVM in such situations. They called upon the Serbian authorities to carry out the commitments in their 11 point Statement of Principles of a Political Settlement of October 13, 1998, in particular to mitigate the sentences of persons detained in connection with the Kosovo conflict and to provide due process to all detainees. Such steps would contribute to easing tensions. Recent escalated hostilities in Kosovo have displaced thousands more civilians. This has put at risk progress made since last year in averting a humanitarian catastrophe. The sides must avoid actions that affect the civilian population and must facilitate the work of international and non-governmental organizations providing humanitarian assistance. The FRY authorities should provide all necessary facilities including radio communication to humanitarian organizations and remove impediments they have encountered.

Secretary Albright and Foreign Minister Ivanov decided to maintain close contacts on the matter of Kosovo in order to coordinate U.S. and Russian support for a resolution of the crisis.

2.   Statement by US Department of State Spokesman James P. Rubin, 27 January 1999

Having achieved agreement with our allies on a strategy aimed at resolving the crisis in Kosovo by combining diplomacy with a credible threat of force, Secretary Albright looks forward to joining her Contact Group colleagues in London on Friday to help implement this strategy.

3.   Statement to the Press by Dr Javier Solana, NATO Secretary General, Brussels, 28 January 1999

Good evening, ladies and gentlemen. I would like to make the following statement on behalf of the North Atlantic Council:

NATO fully supports the early conclusion of a political settlement under the mediation of the Contact Group, which will provide an enhanced status for Kosovo, preserve the territorial integrity of the Federal Republic of Yugoslavia and protect the rights of all ethnic groups. The Federal Republic of Yugoslavia authorities must immediately bring the Yugoslav Army and the Special Police force levels, posture and actions into strict compliance with their commitments to NATO on 25 October 1998 and end the excessive and disproportionate use of force in accordance with these commitments. All Kosovar armed elements must immediately cease hostilities and any provocative actions, including hostage taking. All parties must end violence and pursue their goals by peaceful means only.

The appropriate authorities in Belgrade and representatives of the Kosovo Albanian leadership must agree to the proposals to be issued by the Contact Group for completing an interim political settlement within the timeframe to be established. NATO demands that the parties to the conflict in Kosovo cooperate fully with the Organisation for Security and Cooperation in Europe Verification Mission, ensure the security of its personnel and provide full freedom of movement and lift all restrictions on institutions monitoring the situation in Kosovo. We demand that the Federal Republic of Yugoslavia authorities fully respect all commitments undertaken in relation to the Organisation for Security and Cooperation in Europe, and ensure that Ambassador Walker is able to continue to carry out his responsibilities fully as Head of the Kosovo Verification Mission.

4.   Statement by UN Secretary General to North Atlantic Council, NATO HQ Brussels, 28 January 1999

Secretary-General Solana, Ambassadors, Friends, …

The bloody wars of the last decade have left us with no illusions about the difficulty of halting internal conflicts - by reason or by force - particularly against the wishes of the government of a sovereign state. But nor have they left us with any illusions about the need to use force, when all other means have failed. We may be reaching that limit, once again, in the former Yugoslavia.

Friends,

I have looked forward to this meeting as an exchange of views, and so I will only briefly outline three areas of common interest that I believe will affect our relations in the years to come.

Let me begin with Kosovo. When I addressed the NATO Conference in Rome last June, I expressed the hope that we were beginning to draw the right lessons from our experience in the Bosnian war - about such critical factors as credibility, legitimacy and the morality of intervention and non-intervention. But I added that there is only one way in which we can prove that we have done this; by applying those lessons practically and emphatically where horror threatens. Alas, the horror no longer threatens. It is present, in the lives of hundreds of thousands of the people of Kosovo whose lives have been disrupted violently. And now, Racak has been added to the list of crimes against humanity committed in the former Yugoslavia.

I know that you and your member states are engaged in intense consultations - in the Contact Group and elsewhere - in order to restore the fragile agreement that halted the killings last time round and bring the parties to the negotiating table. Therefore, let me ask only that we all - particularly those with the capacity to act - recall the lessons of Bosnia.

That means full and unconditional respect for the human rights of all citizens in Kosovo; full and unconditional acceptance of peaceful negotiation as the only way to resolve the conflict in Kosovo; and full and unconditional respect for the authority of the United Nations War Crimes Tribunal throughout all of the territory of the Former Yugoslavia.

Ultimately, however, it means providing the people of Kosovo with the degree of autonomy that is consistent with their need to live lives free from terror and violence. What form such autonomy will take will depend not only on the wishes of the Kosovars, but also on the actions of the Yugoslav authorities. We can only hope that they, too, have learned the lessons of Bosnia.

5. Statement to the Press by NATO Secretary General, Dr Javier Solana, 29 January 1999

Good Evening Ladies and Gentlemen, I would like to make the following statement on behalf of the North Atlantic Council:
NATO fully supports the early conclusion of a political settlement under the mediation of the Contact Group, which will provide an enhanced status for Kosovo, preserve the territorial integrity of the Federal Republic of Yugoslavia and protect the rights of all ethnic groups. The Federal Republic of Yugoslavia authorities must immediately bring the Yugoslav Army and the Special Police force levels, posture and actions into strict compliance with their commitments to NATO on 25 October 1998 and end the excessive and disproportionate use of force in accordance with these commitments. All Kosovar armed elements must immediately cease hostilities and any provocative actions, including hostage taking. All parties must end violence and pursue their goals by peaceful means only.

The appropriate authorities in Belgrade and representatives of the Kosovo Albanian leadership must agree to the proposals to be issued by the Contact Group for completing an interim political settlement within the timeframe to be established. NATO demands that the parties to the conflict in Kosovo cooperate fully with the Organisation for Security and Cooperation in Europe Verification Mission, ensure the security of its personnel and provide full freedom of movement and lift all restrictions on institutions monitoring the situation in Kosovo. We demand that the Federal Republic of Yugoslavia authorities fully respect all commitments undertaken in relation to the Organisation of Security and Cooperation in Europe, and ensure that Ambassador Walker is able to continue to carry out his responsibilities fully as Head of the Kosovo Verification Mission. NATO fully supports and shares the demands of the international community that the parties must cooperate fully with the International Criminal Tribunal for the former Yugoslavia including by granting immediate and unrestricted access to its representatives to carry out their investigation of the Racak massacre and by ensuring the safety of its personnel. We also demand that the Federal Republic of Yugoslavia authorities take immediate steps to ensure that those responsible for the massacre are brought to justice.

We reaffirm our support to international efforts to bring peace to Kosovo and to avoid a humanitarian catastrophe, including by the Security Council of the United Nations, Organisation for Security and Cooperation in Europe, the European Union, the countries of the region, and the current efforts of the Contact Group. NATO stands ready to act and rules out no option to ensure full respect by both sides of the demands of the international community, and in particular observance of all relevant Security Council Resolutions. NATO is also intensively studying how to support measures to curb arms smuggling into Kosovo. It calls upon the international community, particularly neighbouring countries, to take all necessary steps to prevent the smuggling of arms and will work with other international bodies to this end.

In addition to the measures implemented last week, the North Atlantic Council has decided to increase its military preparedness to ensure that the demands of the international community are met. The North Atlantic Council will follow developments closely and will decide on further measures in the light of both parties' compliance with international commitments and requirements and their response to the Contact Group's demands.

That concludes the statement of the North Atlantic Council.

I would like to add for my own part that we are at a critical turning point in the Kosovo crisis. The next few days will be decisive. What we have seen in Yugoslavia during the past decade is that it is very difficult to stop internal conflicts if the international community is not willing to use force -- and when all other ans have failed. We may be reaching that limit, once again, in the Former Yugoslavia

The Contact Group meeting in London tomorrow will launch an important initiative. It will be fully backed by NATO's military capabilities. We are ready to act, if necessary. The parties must seize this opportunity. It is the only way to overcome the Kosovo conflict and prevent a humanitarian catastrophe. The entire international community has come together to push for a diplomatic solution. You have seen from the visit of the United Nations Secretary General to NATO earlier today that the United Nations shares our determination and objectives. In this endeavour, NATO has a key role to play and will make a full contribution - but the parties must finally face up to their responsibilities. We will keep them under strong pressure until they do so. The North Atlantic Council will be meeting round the clock and we will be ready to take further measures as the situation develops.

6. Contact Group Statement, London, 29 January 1999

1. Contact Group Ministers met in London on 29 January to consider the critical situation in Kosovo, which remains a threat to peace and security in the region, raising the prospect of a humanitarian catastrophe.
2. Despite the intensive efforts of the international community, violence remains a daily occurrence in Kosovo. Ministers unreservedly condemned the massacre of Kosovo Albanians at Racak which resulted in several thousand people fleeing their homes. The escalation in violence - for which both Belgrade's security forces and the KLA are responsible - must be stopped. Repression of civilians by the security forces must end and those forces must be withdrawn. Ministers of the Contact Group deplore the failure of the parties to make progress towards a political settlement, and cannot accept that this should permit the crisis to continue. Time is of the essence in reaching a solution, and the Contact Group is therefore assuming its responsibility.
3. Ministers called on both sides to end the cycle of violence and to commit themselves to a process of negotiation leading to a political settlement. To that end, the Contact Group:

- insisted that the parties accept that the basis for a fair settlement must include the principles set out by the Contact Group;
- considered that the proposals drafted by the negotiators contained the elements for a substantial autonomy for Kosovo and asked the negotiators to refine them further to serve as the framework for agreement between the parties;
- recognised that the work done by the negotiators had identified the limited number of points which required final negotiation between the parties;
- agreed to summon representatives from the Federal Yugoslav and Serbian governments and representatives of the Kosovo Albanians to Rambouillet by 6 February, under the co-chairmanship of Hubert Vedrine and Robin Cook, to begin negotiations with the direct involvement of the Contact Group. The Contact Group recognised the legitimate rights of other communities within Kosovo. In the context of these negotiations, it will work to ensure their interests are fully reflected in a settlement;
- agreed that the participants should work to conclude negotiations within 7 days. The negotiators should then report to Contact Group Ministers who will assess whether the progress made justifies a further period of less than one week to bring the negotiations to a successful conclusion.

4. The Contact Group demanded that the parties seize this opportunity to reach a settlement offering peace to the people of Kosovo. The

Contact Group praised the present role of the OSCE Kosovo Verification Mission in working to reduce tensions in Kosovo and create the conditions for political dialogue, and recognised the continuing role of KVM. The Contact Group recognised that continuing international engagement would be necessary to help the parties implement a settlement and rebuild the shattered province. It required that the parties accept the level and nature of international presence deemed appropriate by the international community.

5. In the meantime, the Contact Group demands that the FRY:

- stop all offensive actions/repression in Kosovo;
- comply fully with the OSCE/FRY and NATO/FRY agreements and relevant SCRs;
- promote the safe return of all those who have been forced to flee their homes as a result of the conflict. This includes bringing much needed relief to Kosovo;
- cooperate fully with the OSCE and permit the KVM and its Chief of Mission to continue to carry out their responsibilities unhindered;
- cooperate fully with ICTY as required by relevant SCRs;
- conduct a full investigation of Racak with the participation of ICTY, allowing the Chief Prosecutor and ICTY investigators to enter and work in Kosovo to participate in the investigation of the massacre;
- identify and suspend the VJ/MUP officers operating in Racak at the time of the massacre until the results of the investigation become available;
- mitigate the sentences of those imprisoned in connection with the conflict and provide due process to all detainees.

6. The Contact Group emphasised that compliance with SCRs 1160, 1199 and 1203 applied equally to the Kosovo Albanians. It condemned all provocations by the UCK which could only fuel the cycle of violence, and insisted that all hostages should be released. The Contact Group believes that the framework it has set out meets the legitimate aspirations of the Kosovo Albanians and demanded that their leaders rally behind negotiations to reach a settlement and end provocative actions which would impede the political process.

7. The Contact Group asked Robin Cook to travel to Belgrade and Pristina to transmit these messages to the parties.

8. The future of the people of Kosovo is in the hands of leaders in Belgrade and Kosovo. They must commit themselves now to complete the negotiations on a political settlement within 21 days to bring peace to Kosovo. The Contact Group will hold both sides accountable if they fail to take the opportunity now offered to them, just as the Group stands ready to work with both sides to realise the benefits for them of a peaceful solution me.

S/PRST/1999/5

7. Security Council Presidential Statement, 29 January 1999

The Security Council expresses its deep concern at the escalating violence in Kosovo, Federal Republic of Yugoslavia. It underlines the risk of a further deterioration in the humanitarian situation if steps are not taken by the parties to reduce tensions. The Council reiterates its concern about attacks on civilians and underlines the need for a full and unhindered investigation of such actions. It calls once again upon the parties to respect fully their obligations under the relevant resolutions and to cease immediately all acts of violence and provocations.

The Security Council welcomes and supports the decisions of the Foreign Ministers of France, Germany, Italy, the Russian Federation, the United Kingdom of Great Britain and Northern Ireland and the United States of America (the Contact Group), following their meeting in London on 29 January 1999 (S/1999/96), which aim at reaching a political settlement between the parties and establish a framework and timetable for that purpose. The Council demands that the parties should accept their responsibilities and comply fully with these decisions and requirements, as with its relevant resolutions.

The Security Council reiterates its full support for international efforts, including those of the Contact Group and the Organization for Security and Cooperation in Europe Kosovo Verification Mission, to reduce tensions in Kosovo and facilitate a political settlement on the basis of substantial autonomy and equality for all citizens and ethnic communities in Kosovo and the recognition of the legitimate rights of the Kosovo Albanians and other communities in Kosovo. It reaffirms its commitment to the sovereignty and territorial integrity of the Federal Republic of Yugoslavia.

The Security Council will follow the negotiations closely and would welcome members of the Contact Group keeping it informed about the progress reached therein.

The Security Council will remain actively seized of the matter.

8. Statement by the North Atlantic Council on Kosovo, 30 January 1999

NATO reaffirms the demands set out in its statement of 28th January 1999. It stands ready to act and rules out no option to ensure full respect by both sides in Kosovo for the requirements of the international community, and observance of all relevant Security Council Resolutions, in particular the provisions of Resolutions 1160, 1199 and 1203. NATO gives full support to the Contact Group strategy of negotiations on an interim political settlement which are to be completed within the specified timeframe. It welcomes the Presidential Statement of the United Nations Security Council of 29th January 1999. NATO recalls that those responsible for the massacre at Racak must be brought to justice and that the FRY authorities must cooperate fully with ICTY. They must also cooperate fully with the OSCE Kosovo Verification Mission and ensure the security of its personnel.

The crisis in Kosovo remains a threat to peace and security in the region. NATO's strategy is to halt the violence and support the completion of negotiations on an interim political settlement for Kosovo, thus averting a humanitarian catastrophe. Steps to this end must include acceptance by both parties of the summons to begin negotiations at Rambouillet by 6 February 1999 and the completion of the negotiations on an interim political settlement within the specified timeframe; full and immediate observance by both parties of the cease-fire and by the FRY authorities of their commitments to NATO, including by bringing VJ and Police/Special Police force levels, force posture and activities into strict compliance with the NATO/FRY agreement of 25 October 1998; and the ending of excessive and disproportionate use of force in accordance with these commitments.

If these steps are not taken, NATO is ready to take whatever measures are necessary in the light of both parties' compliance with international commitments and requirements, including in particular assessment by the Contact Group of the response to its demands, to avert a humanitarian catastrophe, by compelling compliance with the demands of the international community and the achievement of a political settlement. The Council has therefore agreed today that the NATO Secretary General may authorise air strikes against targets on FRY territory. The NATO Secretary General will take full account of the position and actions of the Kosovar leadership and all Kosovar armed elements in and around Kosovo in reaching his decision on military action. NATO will take all appropriate measures in case of a failure by the Kosovar Albanian side to comply with the demands of the international community. NATO is also studying how to support measures to curb arms smuggling into Kosovo. NATO's decisions today contribute to creating the conditions for a rapid and successful negotiation on an interim political settlement which provides for an enhanced status for Kosovo, preserves the territorial integrity of the FRY and protects the rights of all ethnic groups. NATO is resolved to persevere until the violence in Kosovo has ended, and a political solution has been reached.

9. Statement to the Press by NATO Secretary General, Javier Solana, 30 January 1999

Good evening Ladies and Gentlemen, NATO stands ready to act. We rule out no option to ensure full respect by both sides in Kosovo for the requirements of the international community. We welcome the results of the Contact Group meeting. NATO gives full support to the Contact Group strategy of negotiations. We will put all of our capabilities behind this push for an interim political settlement. Today, we have made clear that we are maintaining all of our demands on both sides and which I gave in my warning last Thursday evening. If these demands are not met, NATO is ready to take whatever measures are necessary. Therefore, the Council has agreed today that I may authorise air strikes against targets on Yugoslav territory. I will take my decision in the light of both parties' compliance with international commitments and requirements, including in particular assessment by the Contact Group of the response to its demands, to avert a humanitarian catastrophe, by compelling compliance with the demands of the international community and the achievement of a political settlement.

I will also take full account of the position and actions of the Kosovar leadership and all Kosovar armed elements in and around Kosovo in reaching my decision on military action. NATO will take all appropriate measures in case of a failure by the Kosovar Albanian side to comply with the demands of the international community. NATO is studying how to support measures to curb arms smuggling into Kosovo. NATO's decisions today contribute to creating the conditions for a rapid and successful negotiation on an interim political settlement which provides for an enhanced status for Kosovo, preserves the territorial integrity of the Federal Republic of Yugoslavia and protects the rights of all ethnic groups. NATO is resolved to persevere until the violence in Kosovo has ended, and a political solution has been reached.

10.   US Secretary of State Albright, Statement on NATO Final Warning on Kosovo, Washington, DC, January 30

I strongly support NATO's decision today to authorize air strikes if Belgrade does not comply with the demands of the international community. Our strategy of diplomacy backed by the threat of force is the only way to ensure that both sides halt the violence and come immediately to the negotiating table. The people of Kosovo and indeed of the FRY as a whole now have a window of opportunity -- if only their leaders will seize this opportunity. The choice is truly up to the leadership on both sides, especially the authorities in Belgrade. Either they cease fighting and agree upon a peaceful interim settlement, or they will face the consequences NATO has spelled out today.

11.   Contact Group Non-negotiable Principles/Basic Elements, 30 January 1999

General Elements
Necessity of immediate end of violence and respect of cease-fire
Peaceful solution through dialogue
Interim agreement: a mechanism for a final settlement after an interim period of three years
No unilateral change of interim status
Territorial integrity of the FRY and neighbouring countries
Protection of rights of the members of all national communities (preservation of identity, language and education; special protection for their religious institutions)
Free and fair elections in Kosovo (municipal and Kosovo wide) under supervision of the OSCE
Neither party shall prosecute anyone for crimes related to the Kosovo conflict (exceptions: crimes against humanity, war crimes, and other serious violations of international law
Amnesty and release of political prisoners
International involvement and full co-operation by the parties on implementation
Governance in Kosovo
People of Kosovo to be self-governed by democratically accountable Kosovo institutions
High degree of self-governance realized through own legislative, executive and judiciary bodies (with authority over, intern alia, taxes, financing, police, economic development, judicial system, health care,

education and culture (subject to the rights of the members of national communities), communications, roads and transport, protection of the environment
Legislative: Assembly
Ececutive: President of Kosovo, Government, Administrative bodies
Judiciary: Kosovo court system
Clear definition of competencies at communal level
Members of all national communities to be fairly represented at all levels of administration and elected government
Local police representative of ethnic make-up with coordination on Kosovo level
Harmonisation of Serbian and Federal legal frameworks with Kosovo interim agreement
Kosovo consent required inter alia for changes to borders and declaration of marial law
Human Rights
Judicial protection of human rights enshrined in international conventions and rights of members of national communities
Ombudsman selected under international auspices
Role of OSCE and other relevant IOs
Implementation
Dispute resolution mechanism
Establishment of a joint commission to supervise implementation
Participation of OSCE and other international bodies as necessary

12.   Response of Kosova to Views Adopted by the Contact Group, 30 January 1999

The Government of the Republic of Kosova has considered in a constructive spirit the statement issued by the Contact Group at its Meeting in London of 29 January 1999. While reserving its position in view of possible further developments, including the tone and content of the response and further actions of the Federal Republic of Yugoslavia (FRY), the Government of the Republic declares the following:

The Government of the Republic of Kosova joins the Contact Group in the condemnation of the escalation in violence. The people of Kosova cannot continue to bear the brunt of the brutal acts to which they have been subjected and which, in the words of the Contact Group, constitute a threat to international peace and security and have raised the prospect of a humanitarian catastrophe. The Government of the Republic of Kosova has repeatedly declared its readiness to lend its full support to all measures of international verification and action which can bring to an end this intolerable suffering. It has repeatedly insisted that all sides must comply fully and unconditionally with the mandatory demands of the United Nations Security Council, made in Resolutions 1160 (1998), 1199 (1998) and 1203 (1998), which continue to be flouted by the FRY authorities. The Government of the Republic of Kosova remains willing to cooperate fully in the adoption of further effective measures which may be taken to ensure such compliance.

The Government of the Republic of Kosova remains committed to the search for a peaceful settlement of the crisis, as was indicated in its statement of 3 November 1998. As was reconfirmed then, the Government of the Republic of Kosova is willing to engage in genuine negotiations about such a settlement, with strong international involvement, including that of the United States and others. The Government of the Republic of Kosova remains ready and willing to participate in such international talks at an international venue, also according to an accelerated time-table. These talks should be inclusive, due regard being paid to the democratic legitimacy bestowed upon the elected Government of the Republic of Kosovo by the overwhelming vote of the people of Kosova, whose very survival and future will be at stake in these talks. The Government of the Republic of Kosova is ready to nominate an inclusive negotiating team for this purpose. The Government of the Republic of Kosova has considered the work thus far conducted by Ambassador Hill and his team. It has indicated that the present draft proposal cannot furnish, in its present form, a basis for a settlement. However, the Government of the Republic of Kosova also recognizes positive elements upon which further progress can be based.

The Government of the Republic of Kosova remains willing to entertain the concept of an interim agreement in order to help stabilize the situation. Such an agreement would be concluded at the international level, with international guarantors, and in accord with the will of the population of Kosova. The agreement would not prejudice the status of the Republic of Kosova in one way or another. It would be subject to a genuine review after a significant period of confidence building. That review must not be restricted to questions of the further implementation of the interim agreement and it must take due account of the legitimate right of the people of Kosova to determine their political structures and status. The interim agreement would establish institutions and principles of governance for the entity of Kosova. This would include a Parliamentary Assembly, based on internationally accepted principles of representative democracy, in which principal constitutional and legislative authority in all its aspects would be vested, and subordinate structures of local governance.

There is no place in Kosova, neither now nor in the future, for any form of discrimination, on religious, ethnic, linguistic or any other grounds.

There would be adequate, proportionate and fair provision for representation of all segments of the population of Kosova at all levels of public authority. However, there must not be created parallel structures which would render the entity of Kosova effectively ungovernable. The Republic of Kosova reiterates its clear and unambiguous willingness and positive desire to accept substantive and significant provisions for the safeguard of human and minority rights in the entity of Kosova. This can be achieved through provisions in the interim agreement, provisions in the new Kosova constitution and international legal standards. In addition, the Government of the Republic of Kosova is ready to accept significant international involvement in the monitoring and, during the period of confidence building, in the administration of human and minority rights.

The Government of the Republic of Kosova is also willing to cooperate in good faith and in a constructive spirit in arrangements for an orderly and peaceful transfer of power of the ground. It recognizes that the establishment, under Kosova authority, of a representative police force, an appropriate educational system, the local administration of justice, etc., will need to be conducted in a way which does not generate anxieties among segments of the population. Hence, the Government of the Republic of Kosova is willing to go beyond the present proposals for international involvement in the transfer of authority in sensitive aspects of public administration, including especially policing during a period of confidence building. The Government of the Republic of Kosova has noted that present proposals would strictly limit the exercise of FRY authority, including military activities, while such strictly limited activities remain permitted during an interim period. Given the past history of FRY commitments in this respect, including the failure of the FRY to fulfil the requirements of mandatory Security Council Resolutions and its own undertaking given to Ambassador Holbrooke, there would need to be deployed during this interim period a significant international military presence to prevent the abuses which have, the past, had such tragic results.

The above views, which represent an important, and its is believed, helpful evolution of the position of the Government of the Republic of Kosova, have been formulated in order to facilitate genuine progress in negotiation. They should inform the "refining" of present proposals put to the parties as a framework for a settlement. On that basis, the Government of the Republic of Kosova will cooperate in addressing the other remaining points which will need to be identified jointly.

The Government of the Republic of Kosova will judge the extent to which its constructive attitude is matched by the FRY in its own response concerning the forthcoming negotiations, and especially also in relation to its willingness finally to comply fully with all elements of the mandatory demands of the United Nations Security Council and the demands made by the Contact Group in paragraph 5 of its Statement of 29 January 1999.

S/1999/107, 2 February 1999

13.   Letter from Yugoslavia to the President of the Security Council, 1 February 1999

I have the honour to transmit, enclosed herewith, the letter of H.E. Mr. Zivadin Jovanovic, Federal Minister for Foreign Affairs of the Federal Republic of Yugoslavia, requesting that an emergency meeting of the Security Council be convened in order to prevent aggression against the Federal Republic of Yugoslavia following the decision of the North Atlantic Council to empower its Secretary-General to authorize air strikes by the North Atlantic Treaty Organization against my country (see annex). Enclosed also are the letter from Mr. Javier Solana, Secretary-General of the North Atlantic Treaty Organization to H.E. Mr. Slobodan Milosevic, President of the Federal Republic of Yugoslavia (see enclosure) and the statement of the North Atlantic Council on Kosovo (see appendix). ...

(Signed) Vladislav JOVANOVIC
Chargé d'affaires a.i.

Annex, Letter dated 1 February 1999 from the Minister for Foreign Affairs of the Federal Republic of Yugoslavia addressed to the President of the Security Council

I am writing to you regarding the letter that the Secretary-General of the North Atlantic Treaty Organization (NATO) addressed to the highest authorities in the Federal Republic of Yugoslavia on 30 January 1999, and regarding the statement by the North Atlantic Council on the province of Kosovo and Metohija, attached thereto. The decision by NATO, as a regional agency, to have its Secretary-General authorize air strikes against targets on territory of the Federal Republic of Yugoslavia, as well as the positions contained in the letter that this was a "final warning", represents an open and clear threat of aggression against the Federal Republic of Yugoslavia as a sovereign an independent State Member of the United Nations. Article 53, paragraph 1, of the Charter of the United Nations stipulates that "... no enforcement action shall be taken under regional arrangements or by regional agencies without the authorization of the Security Council ...". In this specific case, the Security Council has not authorized NATO to take enforcement action against the Federal Republic of Yugoslavia. Therefore, NATO's threat directly undermines the sovereignty and territorial integrity of the Federal Republic of Yugoslavia and flagrantly violates the principles enshrined in the Charter of the United Nations, particularly Article 2, paragraph 4, thereof, and it undercuts the very foundations of the international legal order. In view of the above, I call on you to inform all Council members of this letter and to convene an emergency session of the Council in order to take appropriate measures available under the Charter to prevent aggression against my country. I take this opportunity to emphasize once again that the Federal Republic of Yugoslavia pursues an open policy of peace, good-neighbourly and equal cooperation with all countries and organizations accepting such cooperation; it does not threaten anyone, nor is there any threat from its territory against any side. Consistently following the policy of peaceful settlement of all outstanding issues, the Federal Republic of Yugoslavia is a factor of peace and stability in the region. It is determined to protect its legitimate State and national interests, primarily its sovereignty and territorial integrity in accordance with the principles embodied in the Charter of the United Nations, the Helsinki Final Act and the Paris Charter.

(Signed) Zivadin JOVANOVIC

Enclosure, Letter dated 30 January 1999 from the Secretary-General of he North Atlantic Treaty Organization addressed to the President of the Federal Republic of Yugoslavia

Further to my letter of 28 January 1999, I am writing to underscore NATO's profound concern with the situation in Kosovo and our determination to ensure that the demands of the international community concerning this crisis are met. To this end, the North Atlantic Council has this evening authorized me to send you a final warning, a text of which is attached.

I urge you to heed this warning and to take immediate steps to fulfil your obligations to the international community, including those established by the United Nations Security Council, the Organization for Security and Cooperation in Europe, the European Union, the North Atlantic Treaty Organization and the Contact Group.

I have sent a similar message to Dr. Rugova.

(Signed) Javier SOLANA

...

B. The Proceedings of the Rambouillet Conference

1. Address by Jacques Chirac, President of the Republic of France, 6 February 1999

Ladies and Gentlemen,

There are some rare moments in time when the future course of history lies in the hands of a few people. It is the case today as you come to the negotiating table. You will determine the future of Kosovo, but most of all you will determine the future of the men, women and children of Kosovo. The Contact Group has outlined precise guidelines for your negotiations. Principles for substantial autonomy will be put to you. You now have to specify and define them so that within the present borders all the inhabitants of the province, whatever their origins, can live in peace, with both their physical integrity and their rights being protected.

I hope that your talks will bring you not to a useless battle of words and concepts but rather to consider pratical measures to ensure that the desirable autonomy can be truly implemented, day after day so that peace may return to the minds and hearts of the people. You can either prolong the tragedies of the past or endorse the hopes being expressed today. It is not a question of forgetting. No one can forget a lost son or a destroyed village. Justice will have to be done and the culprits tried.

As you know, France has suffered the horrors of war. It has looked barbarity in the eye. But it has healed what were thought to be ever-lasting wounds. It has overcome supposedly ancestral hatreds. What France is saying today is that the will for peace can outweigh the temptation of war. This is particularly meaningful here where General De Gaulle and Chancellor Adenauer built new future together. In building peace you must also turn your gaze to a new horizon: Europe.

You represent peoples who fully belong in Europe. This is also why the idea of war in Kosovo is unbearable to us. Europe has reconciled enemies. Europe has overcome the divisions of 50 years of Cold War. And today, with its partners, Europe is by your side in the quest for a peaceful settlement.

In urging you to make peace I ask you to take as your own the basic values of the European Union - freedom, democracy and tolerance. Thus, you will resume your rightful place in the European family. This too is one of the major challenges of the conference starting today. The entire international community has decided to act. Its actions are not aimed against anyone. We are acting for the benefit of all. Yet you must realize that neither France, nor its European, American and Russian partners will allow such a conflict to go on, a conflict which violates the basic principles of human dignity. Nor will we allow this spiral of violence to threaten the stability of the whole of south-eastern Europe. We want peace to prevail on our continent.

Let me express once more my trust in the representatives of the Contact Group, and especially in the British and French ministers who have been chosen to chair the meetings. The Contact Group, thanks to the support of the Security Council, and therefore of the entire international community, and thanks to the means at its disposal, has the necessary authority to ensure that law, justice and peace triumph.

We will also have to devise the appropriate mechanism to help implement the agreement. The OSCE will have a vital role to play, similar to the brave and effective work of the KVM, to which I pay tribute. We feel an international deployment, accepted by all, must take place to ensure arms are kept quiet. You can rest assured that France, as it has always done since the start of the conflicts in the former Yugoslavia, will assume its responsibilities. We owe it to our European ambition. We owe it to our sons who died on Yugoslav soil for this ideal of peace, dignity and freedom which we will continue to serve with determination.

Let me say this to both parties, Serbs and Kosovo Albanians: peace is in your hands. I call upon your sense of duty. I call upon your courage. Not the courage that leads to battle, to revenge and never-ending violence. But true courage, a greater and nobler form of courage. The courage to negotiate and make peace.

Ladies and Gentlemen,

In the coming days you will have a unique opportunity to take a significant step on the road to reconciliation; to start a process leading to substantial autonomy for Kosovo and respect for each other's rights. You will need strong-will and perseverance. One thing is certain: when you leave Rambouillet a page in Europe's history will have been turned.

I urge you to let the forces of life triumphs over the forces of death. The world is watching you. It is waiting for you.

2. Address by Mr Hubert Vedrine, French Foreign Minister, Rambouillet, 6 February 1999

Today is a solemn day. Robin Cook and myself have been asked by our American, Russian, German and Italian partners to inaugurate and co-chair the Rambouillet negotiations as well as to make ourselves available at all times. Yet, from now on the entire world looks to you. What is at stake is peace in Kosovo. For nearly a year now the international community, through the Contact Group, the United Nations Security council, the European Union, NATO and the OSCE, has striven to achieve a political settlement enabling Serbs and Kosovo Albanians to coexist. I pay tribute to the sense of duty of both parties - the authorities in Belgrade and the representatives of the Kosovo Albanians. Ladies and gentlemen, you have answered the Contact Group's call and come to Rambouillet because you have understood that direct negotiations could not be delayed any longer. France is happy to put this chateau at your disposal. I honestly hope that this historical setting will help you to achieve the success which now depends on you. Only you can decide to put an end to the violence between the two camps. The Contact Group's only ambition is to help you do so by facilitating a political settlement. Over the last few months it has tried to define basic principles and elements for substantial autonomy for Kosovo. It has chosen three representatives to help you in your negotiations: Ambassadors Hill, Petritsch and Mayorski. The presence here today of representatives of all the member states of the Contact Group bears witness to their unity and shared determination which will be important every day of this conference.

At this crucial moment in time, it is only normal that you should first think of those you represent and of their demands, their fears and their rights. But now the time has come to think of the future, the future of your peoples, the future of the Balkans in tomorrow's Europe. To reject the inevitability of violence and war, to ward off historical curses, to exorcise the past, to dare to think out coexistence and invent peace you will need courage, a lot of courage. Be brave and rise above the tragedy!

3. Opening Remarks by Robin Cook, UK Secretary of State, Rambouillet, 6 February 1999

We meet today with the world watching. We meet with the authority of the Security Council, the support of the European Union and the OSCE, and the backing of NATO. We are here as representatives of the Contact Group and of the two sides in the conflict in Kosovo. We meet because of that conflict. There are some things we agree on. We are united by the commitment, which both sides have expressed, to search for a peaceful solution. We are united by the belief that people from different ethnic groups ought to be able to live together in peace: that diversity should be strength, not weakness. That is a key principle on which the modern Europe is founded. We want the countries of the Former Yugoslavia to join us in that modern Europe and in the structures that bind us together. But that will only be possible through acceptance of that same principle of mutual respect for all people whatever their ethnic group or religion. It also requires respect for international law, including recognition that it is not acceptable in today's world to seek to change borders by violence.

I would congratulate France on having found such an excellent site for our talks. There could not be a more discrete location nor a more attractive environment in which to pursue our challenging task. The countries of the European Union know from our own history how difficult it can be to build peace in place of war. This chateau has not always been so peaceful. The castle which stood on this site has been attacked three times by the English. However, today Britain and France preside jointly over these talks - a symbol of the strong partnership which we have forged. Like all countries of the European Union we have learned that our peoples and their economies have gained far more from peace and stability than they ever gained from war or conflict. The greater the strength of our partnership, and the peace between us, the stronger are each of our countries. We want to share the lessons of our experience with the communities of your region. But it is not just Britain and France that we represent on this platform. We represent all the countries of the Contact Group who are equally determined that these talks should end with agreement. On the way here, I spoke by phone to Igor Ivanov, the Russian Foreign Minister who repeated the strong commitment that Russia had made to the holding of these talks and to the practical arrangements for their success.

Throughout the talks Hubert Védrine and I will be reporting to all our colleagues in Italy, the United States and Russia, as well as Germany, which has a particularly important role as presidency of the European Union. We want to be able to report to them that the talks are proceeding in a business-like manner between two sides seriously committed to finding solutions. All our countries have shown our commitment to restoring peace to Kosovo. For four months, Ambassadors Hill and Petritsch have worked hard on a detailed framework document which provides a good basis for these negotiations. It is the result of intensive consultations with both sides. It offers the basis for a democratic self-governing Kosovo with control over its own internal affairs. It provides entrenched rights for the national communities of Kosovo and full protection for the different cultures, languages and religions within Kosovo. It enables both sides to make progress in building a stable peaceful Kosovo without surrendering any of their own views as to what should be the long term future for Kosovo after three years. There are representatives of communities in Kosovo on both sides of these negotiations. All representatives from Kosovo, on whichever side they sit in these negotiations, should welcome the opportunity presented by the framework document for a peaceful, democratic Kosovo in which all opinions can be freely and fairly expressed and represented.

In summoning these talks, and in preparing the framework document, the Contact Group has shown its commitment to ending the conflict. We now require the same commitment from all of you. I know it is not going to be easy for us to reach agreement. A distinguished former resident of this chateau, President Clemenceau, once said: "It is much easier to make war than make peace." I understand the bitterness and distress created by the violence of the past year. But we do not honour those who have given their lives by prolonging the conflict in which more people will be killed. We serve their memory best by giving our fullest commitment to finding a settlement that will end the killing. We meet today in a place of tranquillity and beauty but we are here to change a scene of violence and fear. We meet a long way from the people for whom we are negotiating. But throughout the next two weeks, we must keep them firmly in our minds. It is the people in Kosovo and elsewhere in the Federal Republic who will pay the price of failure in these talks. We owe it to them to end these talks with an agreement that gives both Albaians and Serbs the hope of peace in place of fear of bloodshed. Let us now get down to work to find that agreement.

4.   Joint Press Conference by Mr Vedrine and Mr Cook, Rambouillet, 6 February 1999

Mr. Védrine: Ladies and gentlemen, good evening. As you know, Robin Cook and I were chosen by our American, Russian, German and Italian Contact Group partners to chair the negotiations which are starting now. The President of the French Republic, Mr. Jacques Chirac, made a statement and spoke to the two delegations, after which we opened the negotiations as co-chairmen. Naturally, we will remain available and attentive to every aspect as the talks move forward, and ready to intervene at any time; Right up to the last moment, before the talks, as co-chairmen, we'd already had to overcome a number of difficulties. But as a result of international pressure, unprecedented on this matter of Kosovo, the negotiations are now beginning at Rambouillet; We believe you know the texts of the three short statements which have just been made so we're here now to supplement them by answering your questions Mr. Cook: I'd like to add to what Hubert has just said that so far everything is going well. We've

managed three stages. We managed to achieve unanimity in the Contact Group and international community on looking for an agreement and bringing pressure to bear to that end. Second, we obtained a commitment from the two sides to participate and reached a situation in which the two parties are actually present. And we overcame the first obstacle to the talks which was to make sure that the two parties could participate. And this afternoon, the talks duly got off to a start. The negotiations will not be easy but we are approaching them with real determination to ensure that they succeed. This is the best chance the people of Kosovo and the Federal Republic of Yugoslavia will have to reach an agreement and implement it successfully. Hubert Védrine and myself are working in close collaboration with the mediators so that it actually produces results.

Q. - Mr. Minister, is the international deployment being discussed during the conference and if yes, how? How would you assess the role that Russia has played and is playing in the conference?

Mr. Cook: If you mean by that deployment of forces on the ground, that presupposes first achieving a political settlement. So that's the first point to reach. Russia is fully engaged in the talks. I talked with the Russian foreign minister this morning, as did Hubert, and he is wholeheartedly supporting the negotiations. Russia is part of the troika of three ambassadors with representatives of Russia, the United States and the European Union who are therefore going to be working as a team.

Mr. Védrine: On the question of deployment, I can confirm that this matter will be examined when the time comes along with the possibility of achieving a political agreement. As for Russia, it is a very important partner in the Contact Group; it has been fully involved in the entire process which led up to the meeting at Rambouillet and we were able to verify only a short while ago that it intends to participate fully in the search for a solution;Q. - Mr. Minister, Albanian public opinion and world opinion in general expects a great deal from the conference. Why wasn't it held a year ago and then the tragedy in Kosovo could have been avoided? The Contact Group and NATO have the means. Can we say this evening that after the Rambouillet conference there will be no more terrible images of the tragedy in Kosovo?

Mr. Védrine: The aim of the Rambouillet conference, as the Contact Group wanted, is precisely to stop the never-ending cycle of tragedy We invited the two parties to come to the meeting and they came. So I'd like to think that they came because they share that goal.

Q. - It's been reported that certain delegations were not able to come with all their advisers and also that a number of issues for discussion have been imposed by the international community. Is that true?

Mr. Védrine: With regard to the second point, a format had to be defined for each delegation if only for reasons of place and for the negotiations to be efficient and direct. The two parties had originally decided on delegations that were too large and the two parties adjusted to the conditions that we had set for the negotiations. As for the issues under discussion, over the course of the past several weeks the Contact Group worked out a number of basic principles which form the core of the possible solution. The discussions around these central principles should make it possible to complete and make clear what still hasn't been settled.   Q. - Mr. Minister, why did Mr. Milosevic not come to the international conference on Kosovo today? As you know, Karadjic said that Mr. Milosevic had not been out of Yugoslavia for two or three years? Mr. Védrine: The Rambouillet meeting was not convened or organized at head-of-state level.

Q. - Mr. Minister, you mentioned international pressure. What kind of international pressure are you going to put on the two parties to reach a solution? Are we talking about military pressure when the time comes?

Mr. Cook: Let's be clear. We've brought the parties together so that they can be here for seven days. The seven day deadline has been agreed to, and so you've got international pressure for reaching a settlement. It is planned for the two sides to get down to business immediately. They have seven days to reach an agreement. After the seven days, we will review the situation with our Contact Group colleagues, and if necessary, with the authority of the Security Council, the OSCE and NATO we will support the negotiations with international pressure so that they produce results.

Q. - Can you give us some details about the famous basic principles you mentioned, the main lines set out by the Contact Group? And do the two delegations agree on how the discussions are going to take place? Will there be direct discussions between the two delegations?

Mr. Védrine: I can't exactly go into the detail about the principles because I'm keeping all possibilities open for the talks to move forward and conclude successfully. But I would remind you that we've proposed substantial autonomy which already says a great deal. It means autonomy that goes very far in the framework of respect for existing and recognized

international borders. As for the method, all methods are good when they allow things to move forward.

Mr. Cook: I'd simply like to add that the framework document which has been prepared wasn't drafted in an empty room miles from Belgrade. It was discussed intensively with the two sides. Three quarters of the solution is already there in this framework document. But we've done enough shuttling back and forth. In order to complete the work and fill in the remaining 25% we have to have the parties together, which is the purpose of this meeting.

Q. - The first part of the question concerns the NATO summit in Washington in two months: is there an objective with a view to this summit or is it really, as President Chirac said in his speech, to achieve genuine stability in the region? Supposing an agreement is obtained this time, what's going to happen at the end of three years?
Is there going to be a second Rambouillet to gain independence for Kosovo?

Mr. Védrine: Regarding your first point. You'll have seen that it is by getting all the institutions and all the international organizations to pull together that the international community took back the initiative in the tragedy of Kosovo. And among the various organizations, there is NATO. Even though the general political line was decided in the Contact Group, all that has no particular link to the table at a summit. All organizations have regular summit meetings. The two things are not linked. As for the second point: what is to happen at the end of a certain period of time? Well, that is precisely the purpose of the negotiations. So as co-chairmen, we can't give you an answer this evening. But the purpose of all these tremendous efforts everyone is making is to reach a political solution.

Mr. Cook: Indeed, I can't tell you if there will be a Rambouillet 2, but our putting this effort into it implies obtaining a success in achieving an interim agreement, and that has to be the thrust of our efforts.

Q. - You mentioned the framework document which refers to autonomy, to self-government for Kosovo. These are strong words, does that mean in the long run independence for Kosovo?

Mr. Cook: The point of our efforts is to show the importance of reaching an interim agreement with powers devolving on the assemblies and local administrations so they can handle their own defense, their own single market and do so in the context of their own authority from parliament. So these are strong words which have been used deliberately. The document provides for the devolution of basic democratic rights so as to protect communities having their own language and culture in order to make Kosovo still more democratic at local government level, and only those who are against the democratic process should oppose this agreement.

Q. - In the case of an international deployment, would the eventual deployment of troops take place in a matter of days or weeks, and are the Europeans satisfied with U.S. guarantees in such an event?

Mr. Védrine: I think it is positive to observe that several very important countries, in Europe and also the United States, have already expressed their readiness to this end, and a converging readiness. But nothing has been negotiated yet, nothing is decided yet.

Mr. Cook: We have begun contingency planning and we are trying to make sure that if plans go as scheduled, the interval is as brief as possible. Of course, if the two parties reach an agreement tomorrow, then we'd be taken up short. But it is a problem we'll consider with pleasure once the talks have ended.

Q. - Do you think that Montenegro will be the sole loser in the conference? Can the European Union guarantee that this will not be the result for Montenegro?

Mr. Cook: The principles which Montenegro refers to have been fully explained and applied. Montenegro has absolutely no reason to be worried about results coming out of this conference that would go against it.

Mr. Védrine: I would like to add that to my mind, the continuation of the tragedy in Kosovo is much more threatening than the prospect of a solution. And I would like to say after Robin that no country in the Contact Group, and especially not us, will be looking for a solution that would in any way be injurious to Montenegro.

Q. - In the days prior to the opening of the conference, the Slav party kept on insisting that it would refuse to talk to the Kosovo Liberation Army, calling it a terrorist organization. How do the mediators intend to overcome the problem and how meaningful would an agreement be if the Kosovo Liberation Army were not a party to it?

Mr. Védrine: You will certainly have noticed that in every conflict of this kind the moment negotiations start to draw close, every party states its positions of principle rather firmly--and they appear to be absolutely incompatible. It is the negotiators' task to manage to get the work started in spite of that and to see that it is successfully concluded. And one result has been achieved already in that they are here, not far from us.

Mr. Cook: I agree with Hubert. Look at the ground that we've covered. The two parties agreed to come, they met in the same room. We've just had the opening meeting, and that is real progress. But in the end, negotiating peace means you have to negotiate with those making war. You don't talk peace with your friends.

Q. - When you talk about substantial autonomy, one gets the impression that the decisions, if decision there is in these negotiations, have been made in advance. What are the margins for the negotiations, what can the negotiators say yes and no to?

Mr. Védrine: Autonomy is a general principle but if you look around the world, especially at a number of places where tragedies have been resolved by this approach, there is very great diversity in the forms of autonomy. It's an area for negotiation just like the one mentioned earlier by Robin Cook in response to a question on the interim period. But admittedly the Contact Group has shouldered its responsibilities by proposing a body of principles because it was impossible to leave matters as they were.

Mr. Cook: To be more specific about what I said a moment ago, the FRY retains responsibility for foreign policy, defense, customs and the single market. The other responsibilities will therefore be under the authority of the assemblies, local administrations and elected offices in Kosovo. Of course, these responsibilities may be discussed further by the various parties as to the breakdown, but don't forget that it is a document which is the result of three months of talks, it didn't simply fall out of the sky. So there remains the responsibilities to be settled by the parties, not simply by this constant shuttling back and forth between the cities.

Q. - There are reportedly differences of views among the Albanian leaders. Do you think that this my have some bearing on the success of the conference?

Mr. Védrine: It is one of the many problems that have to be addressed, that have to be resolved, that the negotiators have to surmount. There are an infinite number of them. There are matters on either side, problems that must be worked out to be successful in spite of everything.

Mr. Cook: No one is saying that things will be easy. We all recognize that there are problems. The important thing is not to see these problems as obstacles but as challenges that we can overcome. But that presupposes that each party comes with the goodwill to overcome these challenges and to reach a solution..

5. Interim Agreement for Peace and Self-Government in Kosovo, Initial Draft, 6 February 1999

Contents: Framework Agreement
Annex 1:   Constitution of Kosovo
Annex 3:   Elections
Annex 6:   Ombudsman

Framework Agreement

Convinced of the need for a peaceful solution of the Kosovo conflict as a prerequisite for stability in the whole region.

Determined to refrain from the further use of violence.

Reaffirming their commitment to United Nations and OSCE principles, in particular to the Charter of Paris on a new Europe.

Recalling the commitment of the international community to the sovereignty and territorial integrity of the Federal Republic of Yugoslavia.

Recognising the need for self-government of Kosovo on the basis of the full participation of the members of all national communities in political decision-making.

Desiring to ensure the protection of the human rights of all individuals living within Kosovo, including in particular the rights of the members of all national communities.

Recognising the ongoing contributions of the OSCE's Kosovo Verification Mission to peace and stability in Kosovo.

Having regard to Security Council Resolutions 1160, 1199, and 1203.

Noting that the present Agreement has been concluded under the auspices of the States members of the Contact Group and of the European Union and undertaking with respect to these States and with respect to the European Union to abide by the Agreement.

Aware that full respect for the Agreement will be central for the development of relations with European institutions.

Have agreed as follows:-

Article I: Principles

1. All citizens in Kosovo have equal rights and duties under this Framework Agreement and its annexes (hereinafter referred to collectively as 'the Agreement'). National communities and their members shall have additional rights specified in Annex 1. Kosovo, Federal, and Republic authorities shall not interfere with the exercise of these additional rights. The national communities shall be legally equal as specified herein, and shall not use their additional rights to endanger the rights of other national communities or the rights of citizens.

2. All authorities in Kosovo shall fully respect principles of human rights, democracy, and the equality of citizens and national communities.

3. Citizens in Kosovo shall have the right to democratic self-government through legislative, executive, judicial, and other institutions established in accordance with the Agreement. They shall have the opportunity to be represented in all institutions in Kosovo. The right of democratic self-government shall include the right to participate in free and fair elections.

4. Every person in Kosovo shall have the right to apply to international institutions for the protection of their rights in accordance with the procedures of such institutions.

5. The Parties accept that their powers and responsibilities in Kosovo are as specified by the Agreement and that Kosovo shall have all rights and powers set forth herein, including in particular as specified in the Kosovo Constitution attached to this Framework Agreement as Annex 1. The Agreement shall prevail over any other legal provisions of the Parties and shall be directly applicable. In implementing the Agreement in accordance with their procedures and international standards, the Parties shall harmonise their governing practices and documents. All Parties commit to implement the Agreement fully.

6. The Parties invite the Organisation for Security and Co-operation in Europe (OSCE) through its Kosovo Verification Mission (KVM) to carry out the civilian implementation functions set forth in the Agreement. The head of the KVM shall have primary responsibility, in consultation with the members of the Joint Commission, for all matters relating to the civilian implementation of the Agreement. The Parties agree to co-operate fully with all international organisations working in Kosovo on the implementation of the Agreement.

Article II: Confidence Building Measures

End of Violence

1. Violence in Kosovo shall cease immediately. Alleged violations of the cease-fire shall be reported to international observers and will not be used to justify violence in response.

2. The status of police and security forces in Kosovo including MUP withdrawal, shall be governed by the terms set forth in Annex 2. The Parties shall abide by its provisions completely. The existence of any paramilitary or irregular force in Kosovo is incompatible with the spirit and terms of the Agreement.

Return of Refugees and Displaced Persons

3. The Parties shall facilitate the safe return of refugees and displaced persons to their homes, including taking all measures necessary to readmit to Kosovo returning refugees and displaced persons.

4. The Parties shall co-operate fully with all efforts by UNHCR and other international and non-governmental organisations in relation to arrangements for the repatriation and return of refugees and displaced persons, including those organisations' monitoring of the treatment of displaced persons and returnees following return.

Reconstruction

5. The Parties shall allow free and unimpeded access for humanitarian organisations and supplies to Kosovo and to the people of Kosovo, including materials for the reconstruction of homes and structures damaged during the conflict.

6. The Parties shall assist returning refugees and displaced persons to re-occupy their real property or to re-assert their occupancy right to State-owned property and to recover their property and possessions.

Access for International Assistance

7. There will be no impediments to the normal flow of goods into Kosovo. The Federal Republic of Yugoslavia shall waive all visa, customs, or licensing requirements for persons of things for the Kosovo Verification mission, UNHCR, and other international and regional organisations and NGO's working in Kosovo.

8. All staff, whether national or international, working with international or non-governmental organisations shall be allowed unrestricted access to the Kosovo population for purposes of delivering humanitarian assistance. All persons in Kosovo shall similarly have safe, unhindered, and direct access to the staff of humanitarian organisations.

9. The Parties shall immediately comply with all KVM support requests. The KVM shall have its own broadcast frequencies for radio and television programming in Kosovo. The Federal Republic of Yugoslavia shall provide all necessary facilities, including frequencies for radio communications, to all humanitarian organisations responsible for delivering aid in the region.

Detention of Combatants and Justice Issues

10. All persons held by the Parties without charge shall be released. The Parties shall grant full and immediate access by the International Committee of the Red Cross (ICRC) to all detainees, wherever they might be held.

11. The Parties shall provide information on all persons unaccounted for the ICRC, and shall co-operate fully with its efforts to determine the whereabouts and fate of such persons.

12. The Parties shall not prosecute anyone for crimes related to the conflict in Kosovo, and shall release any persons being held on such charges, except for those who have committed war crimes, crimes against humanity, and other serious violations of international humanitarian law.

13. With respect to persons already convicted, there shall be a general amnesty for all persons convicted of committing politically motivated crimes related to the conflict in Kosovo. This amnesty shall not apply to those properly convicted of committing war crimes, crimes against humanity, or other serious violations of international humanitarian law at a fair and open trial conducted pursuant to international standards.

14. All Parties shall comply with their obligation to co-operate in the investigation and prosecution of war crimes, crimes against humanity, and other serious violations of international humanitarian law.

    (a) The Parties will allow complete, unimpeded, and unfettered access to international experts - including forensics experts and investigators from the International Criminal Tribunal for the Former Yugoslavia (ICTY) - to investigate such allegations.

    (b) Pursuant to the terms of UN Security Council Resolution 827 and subsequent resolutions, the Parties shall provide full support and co-operation for the activities of the ICTY, including complying with its orders and requests for information, and facilitating its investigations.

Independent Media

15. Recognising the importance of free and independent media to the development of a democratic political climate necessary for the reconstruction and development of Kosovo, the Parties shall ensure the widest possible press freedoms in Kosovo in all mediums, including print, television, and radio.

Article III: Amendment and Comprehensive Assessment

1. Amendments to the Agreement shall be adopted by agreement of all the Parties.

2. Each Party may propose amendments at any time and will consider and consult with the other with regard to proposed amendments.

3. In three years, there shall be a comprehensive assessment of the Agreement under international auspices with the aim of improving

its implementation and determining whether to implement proposals by either side for additional steps.

Article IV: Final Clauses

1. The Agreement consists of this Framework Agreement and its [ ] annexes, which shall be considered as incorporated herein. Acceptance of this Framework Agreement constitutes acceptance of the Agreement in its entirety.

2. The Agreement is concluded in the English language. After conclusion of the Agreement, authoritative translations will be made into the Albanian and Serbian languages. Each version shall be equally authentic, but in the event of a conflict the English text shall be definitive.

3. The Agreement shall enter into force upon conclusion of the document.

Federal Republic of Yugoslavia;

Republic of Serbia;

Kosovo

Annex 1, Constitution

Article I: Principles of Democratic Self-Government in Kosovo

1. Kosovo shall govern itself democratically through the legislative, executive, judicial, and other institutions specified herein. Officers and institutions of Kosovo shall exercise their authorities consistent with the terms of the Framework Agreement and its annexes (hereinafter 'the Agreement').

2. All authorities in Kosovo shall fully respect the principles of human rights, democracy, and the equality of citizens and national communities.

3. The authorities in Kosovo shall have responsibility for all areas except the following, which it is understood shall be within the competence of the Federal Republic of Yugoslavia save as specified in paragraph four: (a) territorial integrity, (b) maintaining a common market within the Federal Republic of Yugoslavia, which power shall be exercised in a manner that does not discriminate against any particular region or area of the Federal Republic of Yugoslavia, © monetary policy, (d) defense, (e) foreign policy, (f) customs services, and (g) federal taxation. Citizens in Kosovo shall continue to participate in areas reserved for the Federal Republic of Yugoslavia through their representation in Federal institutions.

4. Kosovo shall have the following powers in the areas otherwise reserved for the Federal Republic of Yugoslavia:
   (a) No changes to the borders of Kosovo shall be made without the consent of the Kosovo Assembly and President;
   (b) Deployment and use of police and security forces in Kosovo shall be governed by Annex 2 of the Agreement;
   (c) Kosovo officers and institutions shall have authority to conduct foreign relations within their areas of responsibility equivalent to the power provided to Republics under Article 7 of the Constitution of the Federal Republic of Yugoslavia;
   (d) Martial law shall not be declared in Kosovo without the consent of the President of Kosovo;
   (e) Federal measures having a differential, disproportionate, or discriminatory impact on Kosovo shall not take effect in Kosovo without the consent of the President of Kosovo.

5. There shall be no interference with the right of citizens and national communities in Kosovo to call upon institutions of the Republic of Serbia for the following purposes on a purely voluntary basis:
   (a) assistance in designing school curricula and standards;
   (b) participation in social benefits programs, such as care for war veterans, pensioners, and disabled persons; and
   (c) other voluntarily received services, provided that these services are not related to police and security matters which shall be governed by Annex 2, and that ant Republic personnel serving in Kosovo pursuant to this paragraph shall be unarmed social service providers acting at the invitation of a national community in Kosovo.

6. The basic territorial unit of local government in Kosovo shall be the communes. All responsibilities and authorities of Kosovo not expressly assigned elsewhere shall be the responsibility of the communes.

7. To preserve and promote democratic self-government in Kosovo, all candidates for appointed, elective, or other public office, and all office holders, shall meet the following criteria:
   (a) No person who is serving a sentence imposed by the International Criminal Tribunal for the Former Yugoslavia, and no person who is under indictment by the Tribunal and who has failed to comply with an order to appear before the Tribunal, may stand as a candidate or hold any office; and
   (b) All candidates and office holders shall renounce violence as a mechanism for achieving political goals; past political or resistance activities shall not be a bar to holding office in Kosovo.

Article II: The Assembly

1. Kosovo shall have an Assembly, which shall be comprised of one hundred Members.
   (a) Sixty Members shall be directly elected.
   (b) The remaining forty Members shall be elected by the members of qualifying national communities. The seats shall be divided equally among the national communities meeting a threshold determined as follows:
      (i) After the completion of the census specified in Article [ ] Annex 5, those national communities representing at least [ ] percent of the population of Kosovo as determined by the census shall be eligible for seats allocated under this paragraph.
      (ii) [A procedure to determine national communities eligible for these seats in the Assembly prior to the completion of a census.]
      (iii) The Serbian and Albanian national communities shall be presumed to meet the necessary population threshold
   (c) Elections for all Members, whether under paragraph 1(a) or 1(b), shall be conducted democratically, consistent with the provisions of Annex 3.

2. The Assembly shall be responsible for enacting laws of Kosovo, including those regulating relations in political, economic, social, and cultural areas. This Constitution and the laws of the Kosovo Assembly shall not be subject to change or modification by authorities of the Republics or the Federation.
   (a) The Assembly's areas of responsibility shall include:
   - Financing activities of Kosovo institutions, including by levying taxes and duties on sources within Kosovo;
   - The adoption of budgets and annual accounts of the Administrative Bodies and other institutions of Kosovo, with the exception of communal and national community institutions unless otherwise specified herein;
   - The adoption of regulations concerning the organisation, procedures, and functioning of the Administrative Bodies of Kosovo;
   - Approving the Government put forward by the Prime Minister;
   - Approving candidates put forward by the President of Kosovo for judicial office;
   - Adoption of laws ensuring free movement of goods, services, and persons in Kosovo consistent with the responsibilities of other authorities;
   - Conducting relations with foreign entities and approving agreements within its areas of responsibility, consistent with the authorities of Kosovo institutions;
   - Co-operating with the Federal Assembly, and with the Assemblies of the Republics;
   - Establishing the main rules of local self-government, including in particular rules on elections consistent with Annex 3 and the rules and regulations of the Central

Election Commission, finance, the status of elected local officials, and on local government employees;

- Co-ordination among communes or national communities when necessary, including the enactment of laws concerning inter-communal issues;
- Protection of the environment where inter-communal issues are involved; and
- Designing and implementing programs of economic, scientific, technological, demographic, regional, and social development, as well as programs for the development of agriculture and of rural areas.

(b) The Assembly shall also have authority to enact laws in areas within the responsibility of the Communes if the matter cannot be effectively regulated by the Communes or if regulation by individual Communes might prejudice the rights of other Communes or if uniform legislation is necessary to ensure throughout Kosovo the equality of rights granted to citizens in Kosovo. In the absence of a law enacted by the Assembly validly taken within this authority that preempts communal action, the Communes shall retain their authority.

3. Laws shall be enacted by majority of those present and voting, except as provided in paragraph 4.

4. If a majority of the Members of a national community present and voting elected pursuant to paragraph 1 (b) make a motion that a law adversely affected the vital interests of their national community, that law shall remain in force subject to completion of the dispute settlement procedure in paragraph 5. Vital interest motions shall be made within five days of a law's enactment.

5. The following procedure shall be used in the event of a motion asserting that the vital interest of a national community is adversely affected:

   (a) The national community or communities asserting that its vital interest is adversely affected will give reasons explaining its concerns to the President of Kosovo. Members of the Assembly supporting the law will be given an opportunity to respond. The President of Kosovo shall mediate the dispute and attempt to reach a settlement agreeable to all affected national communities.

   (b) If mediation does not produce a mutually agreeable result within seven days, the matter shall be given to the Constitutional Court. The Court shall determine whether as a matter of law the vital interests of the national community or communities at issue are adversely affected by the law. The Court shall hear argument and rule within fifteen days. Its judgment shall be final.

   (c) A law agreed in mediation to adversely affect the vital interests of a national community, or a law so adjudicated by the Constitutional Court, shall be void.

6. A majority of the Assembly's Members shall constitute a quorum. The Assembly will decide its own rules of procedure. Members shall be immune from all civil or criminal proceedings on the basis of opinions expressed or other acts performed in their capacity as Members of the Assembly.

7. The Assembly shall elect from among its Members a President, two Vice-Presidents, and other leaders in accordance with its procedures. Each national community meeting the threshold specified in paragraph 1 (b) shall be represented in the leadership. The President of the Assembly shall not be from the same National Community as the President of Kosovo.

8. The President of the Assembly shall represent the Assembly, call its sessions to order, chair its meetings, co-ordinate the work of any Committees it may establish, and perform other tasks prescribed by the rules of procedure of the Assembly.

Article III: President of Kosovo

1. There shall be a President of Kosovo, who shall be elected by the Assembly by vote of a majority of its members for a three year term. No person may serve more than to terms as President of Kosovo.

2. The President of Kosovo shall be responsible for:

- Representing Kosovo before any international or Federal body, or any body of the Republics.
- Proposing to the Assembly candidates for Prime Minister, the Constitutional Court, the Supreme Court, and other Kosovo judicial offices.
- Meeting regularly with the democratically elected representatives of the national communities and other persons.
- Conducting foreign relations and concluding agreements on behalf of Kosovo after they are approved by the Assembly, consistent with the authorities of Kosovo institutions under the Agreement.
- Serving or designating a representative to serve on the Joint Commission and Joint Council established by Article [ ] of Annex 5.
- Meeting regularly with the President of the Federal Republic of Yugoslavia, the President of Montenegro, and the President of Serbia.
- Other duties specified herein.

Article IV: Government and Administrative Bodies

1. Executive power shall be exercised by the Government. The Government shall be responsible for implementing and enforcing the laws of Kosovo, and of other government authorities when such responsibilities are devolved by those authorities. The Government shall also have the authority to propose laws to the Assembly.

   (a) The Government shall consist of a Prime Minister and Ministers, including at least one person from each national community meeting the threshold specified in paragraph 1 (b) of Article II. Ministers shall head the Administrative Bodies of Kosovo.

   (b) The candidate for Prime Minister proposed by the President shall put forward a list of Ministers to the Assembly. The Prime Minister and the proposed Ministers shall be approved by a majority of those present and voting in the Assembly. In the event that the Prime Minister is not able to obtain a majority for the Government, the President shall propose a new candidate for Prime Minister within ten days.

   (c) (c) The Government shall serve at the confidence of the Assembly, and may be dissolved by majority vote of the Assembly. In the event of dissolution of the Government by the Assembly or of resignation by the Prime Minister, the President shall select a new candidate for Prime Minister who shall seek to form a Government.

   (d) The Prime Minister shall call meetings of the Government, represent it in appropriate settings, and co-ordinate its work. Decisions of the Government shall require a majority of Ministers present and voting. The Prime Minister shall cast the deciding vote in the event Ministers are equally divided. The Government shall otherwise decide its own rules of procedure.

2. Administrative Bodies shall be responsible for assisting the Government in carrying out its duties.

   (a) Employees of administrative bodies shall be fairly representative of the population and national communities of Kosovo.

   (b) Any citizen of Kosovo claiming to have been directly and adversely affected by the decision of an executive or administrative body shall have the right to judicial review of that decision after exhausting all avenues for administrative review. The Assembly shall enact administrative law to regulate this review.

Article V: Judiciary

1. <u>Structure of the Judiciary</u>. Kosovo shall have a Constitutional Court, a Supreme Court, District Courts, and Communal Courts.

2. <u>Jurisdiction</u>. The Kosovo courts shall have jurisdiction over all matters arising in Kosovo under the Constitution and laws of Kosovo and laws of the Assembly except as specified in paragraphs 3 and 5. The Kosovo courts shall also have jurisdiction over matters arising in Kosovo under federal law or raising questions of

federal law. Disputes presenting questions of federal law may be appealed to the Federal courts on those federal legal questions after all appeals available under the Kosovo system have been exhausted.

3. Optional Jurisdiction. Citizens in Kosovo may opt to have civil disputes to which they are a party adjudicated by the Republic courts, which shall apply applicable Kosovo law and shall refer matters falling within paragraph 5 (b) to the Constitutional Court of Kosovo. Criminal defendants may seek access to an participation of Republic officials in Kosovo proceedings.

4. Composition. The Constitutional Court shall consist of nine judges. The Supreme Court shall consist of nine judges. The Assembly shall determine the number of other judges necessary to meet current needs.

   (a) The judges shall be distinguished jurists of the highest moral character.

   (b) The judges shall be broadly representative of the national communities of Kosovo. There shall be at least one Constitutional Court judge and one Supreme Court judge from each national community qualifying for seats in the Kosovo Assembly under paragraph 1 (b) of Article III.

   (c) Until such time as the Parties mutually agree to discontinue this arrangement or the Federal Republic of Yugoslavia becomes a party to the European Convention for the Protection of Human Rights and Fundamental Freedoms, a majority of judges on the Constitutional Court shall be selected from a list presented by the Committee of Ministers of the Council of Europe pursuant to Council Resolution (93) 6.

   (d) Removal of a Kosovo judge shall require the consensus of the judges of the Constitutional Court. A Constitutional Court judge whose dismissal is in question shall not participate in the deliberation on his case.

5. Jurisdiction of the Constitutional Court. With the exception of Article I. 3-5, the interpretation of which shall be charged to the Chair of the Joint Commission, the Constitutional Court shall have sole authority to resolve disputes relating to the meaning of this Constitution. That authority shall include, but is not limited to, determining whether decisions or actions of the President, the Assembly, the Government, the Communes, and the national communities are compatible with the Kosovo Constitution except as specifically charged above to the Chair of the Joint Commission.

   (a) Matters may be referred to the Court by the President of Kosovo, the President or Vice-Presidents of the Assembly, the Ombudsman, the communal assemblies and councils, and any national community acting according to its democratic procedures.

   (b) Any court which finds in the course of adjudicating a matter that the dispute depends on the answer to a question within the Court's jurisdiction shall refer the issue to the Court for a preliminary decision.

   (c) Following the exhaustion of other legal remedies, the Court shall at the request of any natural or legal person or association have jurisdiction over complaints that human rights and fundamental freedoms and the rights of members of national communities set forth in the Agreement have been violated by a public authority.

   (d) The Constitutional Court shall have such other authorities and jurisdiction as may be specified elsewhere in the Agreement.

6. Jurisdiction of the Supreme Court. The Supreme Court shall hear appeals from the District Courts and the Communal Courts. Subject to the specific powers of the Constitutional Court and the Chair of the Joint Commission, and to paragraph 3, the Supreme Court shall take the final decision in all cases arising within Kosovo. Its decisions shall be recognised and executed by all public authorities on the territory of the Federal Republic of Yugoslavia.

7. Functioning of the Courts. The Kosovo Supreme Court shall, upon approval by the Kosovo Assembly, promulgate rules of procedure consistent with the Agreement to guide the courts' activities. The Constitutional and Supreme Courts shall each adopt decisions by majority vote of their members. All Kosovo courts shall hold public proceedings, and issue published opinions setting forth the reasons for their decisions along with any dissenting views.

Article VI: Human Rights and Fundamental Freedoms

1. The Parties shall ensure respect for internationally recognised human rights and fundamental freedoms in Kosovo.

2. Applicable rights and freedoms shall include those specified in the European Convention for the Protection of Human Rights and Fundamental Freedoms and its Protocols.

   (a) The rights and freedoms set forth in the European convention for the Protection of Human Rights and Fundamental Freedoms and its Protocols shall apply directly in Kosovo. These shall have priority over all other law.

   (b) All courts, agencies, government institutions, and instrumentalities of the Parties and all of their officials and employees shall conform to these human rights and fundamental freedoms.

Article VII: National Communities

1. National communities and their members shall have additional rights determined by the Agreement in order to preserve and express their national, cultural, religious, and linguistic identities in accordance with international standards and the Helsinki Final Act.

2. Each national community shall elect through democratic means in a manner consistent with the provisions of Annex 3 institutions to administer its affairs in Kosovo.

3. The national communities shall be subject to the laws enacted by the Kosovo Assembly, provided that any action concerning national communities must be non-discriminatory. The Assembly shall decide upon a procedure for resolving disputes between national communities.

4. The additional rights of the national communities, acting through their democratically elected institutions, are to:

   (a) preserve and protect their national cultures, including by:

   - inscribing local names of towns and villages, of squares and streets, and of other topographic names in the language and alphabet of the national community, consistent with decisions about style made by the communal institutions.

   - providing information in the language and alphabet of the national community.

   - providing for education and establishing educational institutions, in particular for schooling in their own language and alphabet and in national culture and history, for which relevant authorities will provide financial assistance; curricula shall reflect a spirit of tolerance between national communities and respect for the rights of members of all national communities in accordance with international standards.

   - enjoying unhindered contacts with representatives of their respective national communities, within the Federal Republic of Yugoslavia and abroad.

   - using and displaying national symbols, including symbols of the Federal Republic of Yugoslavia and the Republic of Serbia;

   - protecting national practices on family law by, if the community decides, arranging rules in the field of inheritance, family, and matrimonial relations; tutorship; and adoption.

   - the preservation of sites of religious, historical, or cultural importance to the national community, in co-operation with other authorities.

   - implementing public health and social services.

   - operating religious institutions in co-operation with religious authorities.

- participating in regional and international non-governmental organisations in accordance with procedures of these organisations.

(b) be guaranteed at least one radio and one television frequency, which they shall each administer subject to non-discriminatory, technical standards;

(c) finance their activities by collecting charges the national communities may decide to levy on members of their own communities.

5. Members of national communities shall also be individually guaranteed:

   - The right to enjoy unhindered contacts with members of their respective national communities elsewhere in the Federal Republic of Yugoslavia and abroad.
   - Equal access to employment in public services at all levels.
   - The right to use their languages and alphabets.
   - The right to use and display national community symbols
   - the right to participate in democratic institutions that will determine the national community's exercise of the collective rights set forth in this Article.
   - The right to establish cultural and religious associations, for which relevant authorities will provide financial assistance.

6. Each national community and, where appropriate, their members acting individually may exercise these additional rights through Federal institutions and institutions of the Republics, in accordance with the procedures of those institutions and without prejudice to the ability of Kosovo institutions to carry out their responsibilities.

Article VIII: Communes

1. Kosovo shall have the existing communes. Changes may be made to communal boundaries by act of the Kosovo Assembly after consultation with the authorities of the communes concerned.

2. Communes may develop relationships among themselves for their mutual benefit.

3. Each commune shall have an Assembly, a Council, and such executive bodies as the commune may establish.

   (a) Each national community whose membership constitutes at least [   ] percent of the population of the commune shall be represented on the Council in proportion to its share of the communal population or by one member, whichever is greater.

   (b) [A procedure to resolve disputes over communal population percentages for purposes of this paragraph prior to the completion of a census.]

4. The communes shall have responsibility for:

   - Law enforcement, as specified in Annex 2 of the Agreement.
   - Regulating and, when appropriate, providing child care.
   - Establishing and regulating the work of medical institutions and hospitals.
   - Providing education, consistent with the rights and duties of national communities, and in a spirit of tolerance between national communities, and respect for the rights of the embers of all national communities in accordance with international standards.
   - Protecting the communal environment.
   - Regulating commerce and privately owned stores.
   - Regulating hunting and fishing.
   - Planning and carrying out public works of communal importance, including roads and water supplies, and participating in the planning and carrying out of Kosovo-wide public works projects in co-ordination with other communes and Kosovo authorities.
   - Regulating land use, town planning, building regulations, and housing construction.
   - Developing programs for tourism, the hotel industry, catering, and sport.
   - Organising fairs and local markets.

- Organising public services of communal importance, including fire, emergency response, and police consistent with Annex 2 of the Agreement.
- Financing the work of communal institutions, including raising revenues, taxes, and preparing budgets.

5. The communes shall have the responsibilities specified in paragraph 4 and shall also have responsibility for all other areas within Kosovo's authority not expressly assigned elsewhere herein, subject to the provisions of Article II.2 (b) of this Constitution.

6. Each commune shall conduct its business in public and shall maintain publicly available records of its deliberations and decisions.

Article IX: Representation

1. Kosovo shall have available to it the opportunity for the following representation, without prejudice to the right of citizens in Kosovo to decide whether to exercise it:

2. At least 10 deputies in the House of Citizens of the Federal Assembly.

3. At least 20 deputies in the National Assembly of the Republic of Serbia.

4. The opportunity for the Kosovo Assembly to present to the appropriate authorities a list of candidates from which shall be drawn:

   (i) at least one citizen in Kosovo to serve in the Federal Government, and at least one citizen to serve in the Government of the Republic of Serbia.

   (ii) at least one judge on the Federal Constitutional Court, one judge on the Federal Court, and three judges on the Supreme Court of Serbia.

Article X

1. The Assembly of Kosovo may by a majority of two-thirds of its members, which majority must include a majority of those members elected pursuant to Article II 1 (b) from each national community so qualifying, adopt further Articles of this Constitution. These Articles may supplement, but may in now way contradict, the Articles of the Constitution appearing in this Annex.

2. This Constitution shall enter into force upon the conclusion of the Agreement.

Annex 3

Conduct and Supervision of Elections

Article I: Conditions for Elections

1. The Parties shall ensure that conditions exist for the organisation of free and fair elections, which include but are not limited to:

   (a) freedom of movement for all citizens;

   (b) an open and free political environment;

   (c) an environment conducive to the return of displaced persons;

   (d) a safe and secure environment that ensures freedom of assembly, association, and expression;

   (e) an electoral legal framework of rules and regulations complying with OSCE commitments, which will be implemented by a Central Election Commission, as set forth in Article III of this annex, which is representative of the population of Kosovo in terms of national communities and political parties; and

   (f) free media, effectively accessible to all registered political parties and candidates, and available to voters throughout Kosovo.

2. The Parties request the OSCE to certify when elections will be effective under current conditions in Kosovo, and to provide assistance to the Parties to create conditions for free and fair elections.

3. The Parties shall comply fully with Paragraphs 7 and 8 of the OSCE Copenhagen Document, which are attached to this annex.

Article II: Role of the OSCE

1. The Parties request the OSCE to adopt and put in place an elections program for Kosovo and supervise elections as set forth in the Agreement.

2. The Parties request the OSCE to supervise, in a manner to be determined by the OSCE and in co-operation with other international organisations the OSCE deems necessary, the preparation and conduct of elections for:
   (a) Members of the Kosovo Assembly;
   (b) Members of Communal Assemblies;
   (c) other officials popularly elected in Kosovo under the Agreement and the laws and Constitution of Kosovo at the discretion of the OSCE.

3. The Parties request the OSCE to establish a Central Election Commission in Kosovo ('the Commission').

4. Consistent with Article [   ] of Annex 5, the first elections shall be held within nine months of the entry into force of the Agreement. The President of the Commission shall decide, in consultation with the Parties, the exact timing and order of elections for Kosovo political offices.

Article III: Central Election Commission

1. The Commission shall adopt electoral Rules and Regulations on all matters necessary for the conduct of free and fair elections in Kosovo, including rules relating to: the eligibility of candidates, parties, and voters; ensuring a free and fair elections campaign; administrative and technical preparation for elections including the establishment, publication, and certification of election results; and the role of international and domestic election observers.

2. The responsibilities of the Commission, as provided in the electoral Rules and Regulations, shall include:
   (a) the preparation, conduct, and supervision of all aspects of the electoral process, including development and supervision of political party and voter registration, and creation of secure and transparent procedures for production and dissemination of ballots and sensitive election materials, vote counts, tabulations, and publication of elections results.
   (b) ensuring compliance with the electoral Rules and Regulations, established pursuant to the Agreement;
   (c) ensuring that action is taken to remedy any violation of any provision of the Agreement,
   (d) including imposing penalties such as removal from candidate or party lists, against any person, candidate, political party, or body that violates such provisions; and
   (e) accrediting observers, including personnel from international organisations and foreign and domestic non-governmental organisations, and ensuring that the Parties grant the accredited observers unimpeded access and movement.

3. The Commission shall consist of the head of the OSCE Kosovo Verification Mission or his representative, representatives of national communities and political parties in Kosovo, and any such other persons as the head of the Kosovo Verification Mission may decide. The head of the Kosovo Verification Mission shall act as the President of the Commission. In the event of disputes within the Commission, the decision of the President shall be final and binding.

4. The Commission shall enjoy the right to establish communication facilities, and to engage local and administrative staff.

Annex 6
The Ombudsman
Article I: General

1. There shall be an Ombudsman, who shall monitor the realisation of the rights of members of national communities and the protection of human rights and fundamental freedoms in Kosovo. The Ombudsman shall have unimpeded access to any person or place and shall have the right to appear and intervene before any domestic, Federal, or (consistent with the rules of such bodies) international authority upon his or her request. In carrying out its mandate, no person, institution, or entity of the Parties may interfere with the functions of the Ombudsman.

2. The Ombudsman shall be an eminent person of high moral standing who possesses a demonstrated commitment to human rights and the rights of the national communities. He or she shall be nominated by the President and shall be elected by the Assembly from a list of candidates prepared by the President of the European Court for Human Rights for a non-renewable three year term.

3. The Ombudsman shall be independently responsible for choosing his or her own staff. He or she shall have two Deputies. The Deputies shall each be drawn from different national communities, and neither shall be from the same national community as the Ombudsman if he or she is a member of a national community in Kosovo.
   (a) The salaries and expenses of the Ombudsman and his or her staff shall be determined and paid by the Kosovo Assembly. The salaries and expenses shall be fully adequate to implement the Ombudsman's mandate.
   (b) The Ombudsman and members of his or her staff shall not be held criminally or civilly liable for any acts carried out within the scope of their duties.

Article II: Jurisdiction

1. The Ombudsman shall consider:
   (a) alleged or apparent violations of human rights and fundamental freedoms in Kosovo, as provided in the Constitutions of the Federal Republic of Yugoslavia and the Republic of Serbia, and the European Convention for the Protection of Human Rights and Fundamental Freedoms and the Protocols thereto; and
   (b) alleged or apparent violations of the rights of national communities specified in the Agreement.

2. All persons in Kosovo shall have the right to submit complaints to the Ombudsman. The Parties agree not to take any measures to punish persons who intend to submit or who have submitted such allegations, or in any other way to deter the exercise of this right.

Article III: Powers and Duties

1. The Ombudsman shall investigate alleged violations falling within the jurisdiction set forth in Article II.1. He may act either on his own initiative or in response to an allegation presented by any Party or person, non-governmental organisation, or group of individuals claiming to be the victim of a violation or acting on behalf of alleged victims who are deceased or missing. The work of the Ombudsman shall be free of charge to the person concerned.

2. The Ombudsman shall have complete, unimpeded, and immediate access to any person, place, or information upon his or her request.
   (a) He shall have access to and may examine all official documents, and he can require any person, including officials of Kosovo, to co-operate by providing relevant information, documents, and files.
   (b) The Ombudsman may attend administrative hearings and meetings of other Kosovo institutions in order to gather information.
   (c) He may examine facilities and places where persons deprived of their liberty are detained, work, or are otherwise located.
   (d) The Ombudsman and staff shall maintain the confidentiality of all confidential information obtained by them, unless the Ombudsman determines that such information is evidence of a violation of rights falling within his or her jurisdiction, in which case that information may be revealed in public reports or appropriate legal proceedings.
   (e) The Parties undertake to ensure co-operation with the Ombudsman's investigations. Willful and knowing failure to comply shall be a criminal offense prosecutable in any jurisdiction of the Parties. Where an official impedes and investigation by refusing to provide necessary information, the Ombudsman shall contact that officials' superior or the public prosecutor for appropriate penal action to be taken in accordance with the law.

3. The Ombudsman shall issue findings and conclusions in the form of a published report promptly after concluding an investigation.
   (a) A Party, institution, or official identified by the Ombudsman as a violator shall, within a period specified by the Ombudsman, explain in writing how it will comply with any prescriptions the Ombudsman may put forth for remedial measures.

(b) In the event that a person or entity does not comply with the conclusions and recommendations of the Ombudsman, the report shall be forwarded for further action to the Joint Commission set forth in Annex 5 of the Agreement, to the President of the appropriate Party, and to any other officials or institutions that the Ombudsman deems proper.

4. The Ombudsman shall promptly report to the International Criminal Tribunal for the Former Yugoslavia evidence of war crimes, crimes against humanity, and other serious violations of international humanitarian law that may fall within the jurisdiction of that tribunal.

6. Statement of both Delegations on a Bomb Explosion in Pristina, 7 February 1999

The three negotiators of The Rambouillet talks announce that the two participating delegations received with regret and indignation the news of the February 6 bomb explosion in Pristina, which caused the deaths of innocent civilians. The two participating delegations condemn in the strongest terms this act and demand the perpetrators be found and brought to justice as soon as possible.This and similar cowardly acts are directed against efforts now underway in Rambouillet, where the two participating delegations are working intensively towards a peaceful political solution to the problem in Kosovo.Kosovo Albanian Delegation Resident in the Chateau

Fehmi Agani
Idriz Ajeti
Ramë Buja
Bujar Bukoshi
Mehmet Hajriri
Xhavit Haliti
Hydajet Hyseni
Bajram Kosumi
Jakup Krasniqi
Rexhep Qosja
Ibrahim Rugova
Blerim Shala
Veton Surroi
Azem Syla
Edita Tahiri
Hashim Thaqi

FRY/Sertian Delegation Resident in the Chateau

Cerim Abazi
Sokolj Cuse
Faik Jasari
Ljuan Koka
Zejnclabidin Kurejs
Vladan Kutlesic
Ratko Markovic
Guljbchar Sabovic
Nikola Sainovic
Kefik Senadovic
Vladimir Stambuk
Ihro Vait; Vojislav Zivkovic

7. Press Briefing by the three Negotiators, Rambouillet, 9 February, 1999

Ambassador Christopher Hill: Well, thank you very much. It is a pleasure to meet you and to get out of the Chateau for a few minutes. We are all experiencing a certain amount of "chateau fever" being cooped up in there but we are persevering okay.

Ambassador Boris Mayorskiy: It is fever, not fatigue.Ambassador Hill: Yes, right. I know that you have had some briefings in the last couple of days by the Contact Group spokesman, Phil Reeker. But we thought we would take this opportunity and tell you how we see this situation from the inside and how we see this proceeding. Let me first assure you that this is not easy and frankly it is not a lot of fun. But I think my colleagues join me in saying that we are making progress. We are moving ahead through some very difficult

territory. As we speak now, we have a working group of our experts going through the text and responding to comments from the working group from the Albanian delegation. We have continued this procedure of meeting with the delegations and going through their comments. We have received preliminary comments from both delegations. I want to stress that what we are doing in these first few days is going through what we call the framework elements of the political settlement. There will be security elements in the future, but we have been rather insistent that we want to nail down the political elements. That is, what Kosovo is going to look like in this three year interim accord. And, most importantly, to make sure that the elements of these papers can actually be implemented on the ground, and that people will understand what their lives. will look like after this agreement goes into effect. So, it is not easy, but I am very pleased with the progress. I don't want to imply for a minute that either of the delegations is particular happy. There are a lot of problems they see. They come forward with a lot of extra ideas. It is always good to encourage ideas, but sometimes the supply of them exceeds the demand, and we have been rather clear at times that we have got to remain on task, as we see the task. And there are times when people sort of jump ahead and discuss other ideas when what we want them to do is work on the political settlement. And we are holding very hard to that. So, I would like to have my colleagues speak. We work very much together, we meet together, we see the delegations together - sometimes we will see them individually - but then we come back together to discuss what we have clone individually. We are working very much as a team and we are looking forward to continuing this job until we get it done.

Ambassador Wolfgang Petritsch: Thank you. Let me add a few words on the basis of our proposals. The negotiations have started in various working groupe. This is a very positive sign, so that it is well and firmly established that the proposals of the Contact Group are the basis for these negotiations. This has been accepted. The structure of the negotiations has emerged. I believe we have pretty well arrived to where we can say, "Ok, this is now a very flexible and unanimously accepted structure for our talks, and for our negotiations." So this helps to push forward and come to an early agreement. When Chris said that it is not easy, I absolutely agree, but I must tell you one thing. The shuttling between rooms in Rambouillet is much easier than the shuttling between Pristina and Belgrade. So there is quite substantial progress, at least for Chris and myself who have been traveling and shuttling between Pristina and Belgrade for the past couple of months. Also, I would like to stress that the team is working very well. I have known Chris and Boris for a long time. They are excellent experts on the Balkans, and I believe that the mechanisms of the team are well in place. Let me just add that I am representing the European Union here, and I am very proud of the participation of the individual European Union member countries, in particular of the presidency, and above all the co-hosts, the United Kingdom and France. So we have a structure, we have a lot of European input into the negotiations (I should not forges to also mention the Commission), so I believe that we are on the right track Ambassador Boris Mayorsky: May I add that one of the reasons for meeting you here today was just to show you that our faces are not scratched, that fingers are there, limbs are there - so everything is in good shape. Yes we work quite a lot together. I am asking myself how we should live after the conference is over I think we should reconsider some of the family arrangements, maybe. There is perfect understanding, which doesn't mean that we don't argue sometimes, but we argue for a good and benign reason. And the conference, if you ask me how I assess the conference, I would use the French phrase "ça bouge" (English : it's happening). Yes, we set it in motion, there are no miracles, there are no surprises. Because I would say that what are faced with today, we could sort of imagine long before the beginning of the conference.And it is understood, and I think it is a firm agreement between all of us, that for the sake of the negotiations, the success of the negotiations, the details of what we are faced with will not be discussed in public. And I request the understanding of that. Believe me, we have all the tropes for successful ending of this exercise which is fascinating, challenging and very, very difficult at the same time. As far as my country is concerned, and I represent Russia in the troika, we are firm believers in political settlement, and only political settlement, of the crisis.

Question - BBC - You mentioned that you perhaps had more ideas than was helpful. How much are the ideas, or the leaked ideas, of the Albanians and the Serbs distracting the agenda, and how unhelpful are the number of leaks? And would you like to do something about the amount of information that seems to be being published? And is it holding up the negotiations and diverting them?

Ambassador Hill: I am sure our opinions will differ on that I don't think it has been a big problem. I mean, this is an era of cellphones and that has changed the world of sequestered conferences, but we are managing to live with that. And frankly, with the excessive number of complaints and comments and ideas, etc that are leaking out' I would hope that people would understand this. Because most of them are so contradictory and don't make a lot of sense, that really, one shouldn't pay too much attention to them. So I am not too worried about that. You know, this is, I forget... what day is today ?... this is Tuesday... OK... this is only the beginning of the third day of the actual negotiations, and the first couple of days were taken up with a lot of organizational issues within the delegations. They needed to form working groups, etc and that was probably the primary reason for, you know, why news has been slow to come out about developments to the agenda, but I think we are making progress now. I am very pleased with it.

Ambassador Petritsch: Let me just add regarding the leaks. Although some of the issues that are being brought forward by the two warring parties, the two negotiating parties, might have a strong connection with the 19th century, in regard to spinmeisters, they are quite up to where we are.

Ambassador Mayorskiy: My opinion, if you want a direct answer to your question, is that leaks are very unhelpful, of course. Because they create extra excitement outside the negotiation quarters. And it doesn't help, but as Chris said, these are facts of life. We get excited ourselves for five minutes after we read the newspaper, and then we go on working. So if you want to help us, don't use those leaks, and be friendly in your publications to what we do. After it is finished, I will give you my autograph. Ok ? If you want me to write something.

Press: No, we should write something.

Ambassador Mayorskiy: Write something good.

Question - Jim Bitterman, CNN - I take it, from your comments, that you have not gotten the two sides together around the same table yet. At what stage will you do that, if ever ?

Ambassador Hill: I am not sure at what stage we will do that' but we haven't tried to get them together. What we have tried to do is get them to react to our texts, also if they don't like something to give us some language that they can live with. And we are very successful with that. I imagine as we get further on, that is as the issues become fewer but more critical, perhaps there will be a need to bring people together, but we are certainly not working on that right now.

Ambassador Petritsch: If I may add, there are some indications that eventually they will get together. So I believe we are making progress there as well.

Ambassador Mayorskiy: But then, in the Rambouillet environment, it doesn't really matter at which table you sit. We are all together, all the same.

Question - Financial Times - Mr. Hill, your comments about wanting to focus now on the political side, and leave the security issues to later, seems to raise the possibility, I suppose, of a partial or a preliminary agreement. So that something might be signed and that you might move on to other issues. Is that a possibility ? Might it focus on the elements or the so-called "non-negotiable elements" ? Might you try to package those into some kind of preliminary agreement ? Or is it all one ball of wax and nothing is agreed until everything is agreed ?

Ambassador Hill: I think one ball of wax is probably the right way to go. We are not interested in a partial agreement' We are interested in a settlement that works. And we are not interested in a piece of paper that describes a settlement, unless we can make the settlement work. And we have a strategy for how to negotiate that, and it starts with working on the institutions that would be formed in Kosovo. Now, as I have said, some people want to jump ahead and look at some of the other elements of how that would work. And what we have stressed to them is, you know, we expect them to eat their vegetables first, and then we will talk later about other issues that we need to do. But I want to stress, by the end, we will have a settlement that works, that can be implemented and will function. And so people will understand what their lives are like in Kosovo, and everyone is going to feel comfortable in Kosovo, and that is the important goal.

Ambassador Mayorskiy: When the cart is in front of the horse, of course it can move, but it is very uncomfortable.

Question - Jane Perlez, New York Times - I understand that negotiations have a momentum of their own. Mrs. Albright, I think is expected here at the weekend. So, is it correct that to assume, or to think, that you will be bringing in the security issues, which are so troublesome to both sides and to various parties, after her departure and after the Contact Group meeting at the weekend ?

Ambassador Hill: I think that at this point it is difficult to speculate where we are, where we will be on the weekend. I am really in constant communication with Secretary Albright, who is very much - for the U.S. - the person behind participation in these negotiations. And as I understand it, we don't have complete decisions on precisely when she will be in Rambouillet. When she does come, I can assure you there will be important issues to be discussed and resolved, but I am not prepared at this time to say precisely what those are. What I am telling you is, we are working very hard on the political settlement'. We are working very hard on the shape of the institutions that will be charged with making Kosovo function, and we have got to get progress on that before we can discuss other issues. That is the bedrock and we have got to get that framework built first.

Question - The two co-presidents of the conference are expected today to meet the delegation. They were supposed to come only if it was necessary to put their weight in the talks. Does it mean that you are getting through at the moment to a specific crisis or any problem in particular ?

Ambassador Petritsch: We are going to have a meeting which was already prearranged quite some time ago, with the two co-hosts today.

Ambassador Mayorskiy: We don't have any prearranged crisis, no.

Ambassador Hill: But let me say that as co-hosts, you know, the idea was always that they would check in and see how things are going, and make contributions where needed. We intend to have a very good discussion with them today, and make sure they are very much directly briefed by us on where the problems are, where we feel we are making progress and where we feel we would like to make more progress. So we are very pleased they are coming today and look forward to talking to them.

Ambassador Mayorskiy: And we appreciate very much their interest in our work.

Question - What is your opinion of the quality of the delegations?

Ambassador Petritsch: I believe that both sides are represented in such a way that we can conduct successful negotiations. And this is really the gist of the matter. Both sides have sent both politically competent people in regard to the negotiating process - experts. So I believe both sides have sent their best people, and we are optimistic about their input and the eventual outcome of the negotiations.

Question - Jonathan Landay, Christian Science Monitor: The KLA yesterday issued a statement saying that they had presented you with a demand for an immediate cease fire, for the release of all political prisoners, for amnesty for their political exiles. And I am wondering if that was transmitted to the Serbian delegation and what their response was.

Ambassador Hill: Well, first of all, I am not going to talk about what goes on inside, and certainly not on the basis of statements made to the outside. Suffice it to say that we have continued to be in close contact with them. In fact, I just got out of a meeting forty-five minutes ago, which included the KLA. We discussed some of these issues and we are moving ahead. I mean, we have no blockages here.

Ambassador Mayorskiy: And I would like to add to this. This information stems really from the Albanian delegation directly. They are breaking the rules of the game. Because it was clearly agreed among everyone there that such outside communications, about what is going on between the delegations and between us, should not take place. So when you ask us to comment on something which is a result of leakage, you embarrass us a little bit. Please keep it in mind.

Ambassador Petritsch: It is something quite apart from what you just asked, of course, but we are very much concerned about the security situation on the ground The Contact Group is extremely concerned that nothing happens on the ground that would in one way or another influence the negotiations. So, of course, we appeal to both sides to stick to the ceasefire, which is one of the non-negotiable basic elements, on the basis of which the two, parties are here in Rambouillet.

Question - Phil Smucker, U.S. News - For the Russian if you don't mind: the key to international involvement appears to still be the ground force, and I just want to ask you if Russia feels comfortable with a NATO-led ground force. And have the Serbs been queried as to their preferences? This ground force issue seems to be the dominant force of the international involvement.

Ambassador Mayorskiy: You remember the answer that Jesus Christ save to Pilate when he was interrogated there ? He said "you said it". I return it to you.

Question - Just to pick up on that, and hope we can get a longer answer than that. The Albanians are very concerned that if they sign the agreement, who will guarantee it ? Because NATO has been sort of invisible, versus what the situation was in Dayton, and there are fears that no matter how many agreements we sign here, things will still not work out on the ground and this agreement will not be implemented.

Ambassador Hill: 1 could just answer by reiterating that what we want is a settlement in Kosovo. It makes no sense to have a settlement which cannot be implemented. That is, any settlement we have, where the prestige of the international community is behind it, must be fully implemented.

Ambassador Mayorskiy: And it should have a proper mechanism.

Ambassador Hill: And I can assure you that, at the end of the day, whenever that comes, however many days we are here, we will have a settlement that is fully implemented.

Question - Jeff Albridge, Associated Press - On this, if you leave the military question until the end, which is what it looks like you are doing, is that not an awful lot to accomplish in a very short period of time, given the importance of it? And is there another forum somewhere where these issues are in fact being worked on right now?

Ambassador Mayorskiy: Forgive me, did we say anything about military questions during this press conference?

Question - Jeff Albridge - I am asking the question.

Ambassador Mayorskiy: No, no, you said the military questions are likely, from what we said, to be postponed to the end. We didn't say anything of the kind. So this is your supposition. No, the security issue and military issue are two different issues, please. Let us not have a semantic discussion here, but security questions and military questions are two different aspects.

Ambassador Hill: There is a certain logical sequence, that when you talk about implementation of institutions of a political framework, that the implementation discussion should take place after you have had at least a substantial discussion and a substantial agreement on what it is you are implementing. So that is the logical sequence. It doesn't mean that you get to the implementation issues after everything is buttoned clown on the actual institutional framework. But certainly you have to make a lot of progress to know what that institutional framework is going to look like, before you figure out how you are going to insure that it is implemented. So that is the only point I was making. I was not suggesting that we were only doing the political institution building.

Question - I have a question for Mr. Hill and Mr Mayorskiy. Do you think that at Rambouillet there is any obstacle to allowing Kosovo to have special rights with Albania - like Dayton allowed the two parts of Bosnia special relations with Serbia and Croatia?

Ambassador Hill: I am sorry. You are asking whether there would be special rights created between Kosovo and Albania?

Question - Yes.

Ambassador Mayorskiy: Let me remind you that the basic principles that were adopted by the Contact Group, and under which we are acting now, provide for the territorial integrity of Yugoslavia and its neighbours.

Ambassador Hill: But let me just add to that, I don't know if it will help much, but what we would like to see in the Balkans is what we have seen in the rest of Europe. That is, borders that join rather than divide. We would like people to feel free to move, we would like commerce, industry, ideas, to be shared. We would like to see the Balkans join Europe, and we would like to see the Balkans have modem borders, to create economic space for themselves, and to begin to operate as the rest of Europe does. And that is our challenge We are not talking about special rights. We are talking about rights that every European enjoys.

Ambassador Petritsch: Let me just add that we Europeans are interested in getting the borders down, not to erect new ones. That also implies that relations between neighbours should be improved, and I am sure that this agreement will contribute to an improvement of overall relations in the whole region.

8.   Annex 4, Economic Issues, dated 12 February 1999

Article I

1. The authorities established to levy and collect taxes and other charges are set forth in the Agreement.   Except as otherwise expressly provided, all authorities have the right to keep all revenues from their own taxes or other charges consistent with the Agreement.

2. Certain revenue from Kosovo taxes and duties shall accrue to the Communes, taking into account the need for an equalisation of revenues between the Communes based on objective criteria. The Assembly of Kosovo shall enact appropriate non-discriminatory legislation for this purpose. The Communes may also levy local taxes in accordance with the Agreement.

3. The Federal Republic of Yugoslavia shall be responsible for the collection of all customs duties at international borders in Kosovo. There shall be no impediments to the free movement of persons, goods, services, and capital between Kosovo and other parts of the Federal Republic of Yugoslavia.

4. Federal authorities shall as necessary allocate resources to Kosovo to ensure it receives a proportionate and equitable share of Federal resources.

5. Federal and other authorities shall to the extent of their respective powers and responsibilities ensure the free movement of persons, goods, services, and capital to Kosovo, including from international sources. They shall in particular allow access to Kosovo without discrimination for persons delivering such goods and services.

Article II

1. The Parties agree to reallocate ownership and resources in accordance with the distribution of powers and responsibilities set forth in the Agreement, in the following areas:

    (a) government-owned assets (including educational institutions, hospitals, natural resources, and production facilities);

    (b) pension and social insurance contributions;

    (c) revenues to be distributed under Article I.4 of this Annex; and

    (d) any other matters relating to economic relations between the Parties not covered by the Agreement.

2. The Parties agree to resolve any dispute between them on matters referred to in paragraph 1 in accordance with the following procedures:

    (a) The parties to the dispute shall make good faith efforts to resolve it through mediation by the Head of the KVM or a person designated by him.

    (b) In the event that the parties to the dispute cannot reach agreement under the procedure set forth in subparagraph (a) within 30 days, the dispute shall be submitted at the request of any of them to arbitration in accordance with the following provisions:

        (i) Each party to the dispute shall appoint one arbitrator within 14 days of the submission of the dispute to arbitration.

        (ii) The Head of the KVM shall appoint one arbitrator within the same period who shall serve as Chairman. In the event that there are three parties to the dispute, the Head of the KVM shall appoint an additional arbitrator within the same period.

        (iii) The decision of the arbitrators shall be taken by majority vote. The proceedings shall otherwise be conducted in accordance with rules determined by the Head of the KVM.

        (iv) The arbitrators shall issue their decision as soon as possible, and in any event within 60 days of the appointment of the last arbitrator.

        (v) The decision of the arbitrators shall be final and binding. The parties to the dispute shall implement it without delay.

9.   Chairman's Conclusion, Contact Group Meeting, Paris, 14 February 1999

Contact Group Foreign Ministers met at Paris on 14 February following a week of negotiations for an interim political settlement in Kosovo on the basis of the principles and basic elements agreed in London on 29 February. On the basis of a report from our three negotiators, Ambassadors Hill, Petritsch and Mayorsky, we assessed the state of the negotiations. Progress has been slower than we had hoped when we met in London on 29 January, but essential ground clearing work has been carried out. It is now crucial that the parties immediately reach agreement on the hard issues outstanding. On this basis we have decided, as provided for in the conclusions of our last meeting, to continue the negotiations. They must be concluded by 1200 noon on Saturday 20 February. We agreed that this is a decisive moment for peace efforts over Kosovo. Time is now very short to reach a negotiated settlement, which is the only way to avoid further large scale violence leading to humanitarian catastrophe. We consider that the Contact Group approach and the documents being tabled to the parties, provide the basis for the interim political settlement. We therefore expect both parties to use the few remaining days to: - agree very rapidly on the Contact Group's detailed proposals for self-government in Kosovo which have now been under negotiation for a week. - accept the implementation arrangements needed to establish this self government, including the development of a local police force, and measures to end the military confrontation in Kosovo. We underlined our total support for our three negotiators. We endorsed their determination to intensify the peace of negotiations so as to conclude them within a week at the latest. The two Co-Chairmen, Hubert Vedrine and Robin Cook, made clear their readiness to return to Rambouillet whenever necessary to work with the negotiators in pushing the talks forward. We agreed that the negotiators have discretion to table the remaining annexes on the implementation of a settlement. Provided that the parties are ready to live up to their responsibilities to reach an interim political settlement, the international community is willing to devote significant civilian and military resources to helping all the people of Kosovo to rebuild their lives in conditions of security. But we reiterate what we said at London: we will hold both sides accountable if they fail to take this opportunity.

10. Secretary of State Albright, Briefing following Contact Group meeting, 14 February 1999

SECRETARY ALBRIGHT: Good afternoon. I want to begin by thanking Foreign Minister Vedrine for hosting the Contact Group today, with his co-chairman Robin Cook, for doing so much to get the Rambouillet talks off to a strong start.

I made this quick trip to Paris at President's Clinton request to assess the progress the parties have made toward an agreement. I am particularly pleased that I was able to bring the leaders of the two delegations together for the first time earlier today. Both sides assured me that they recognize that the time is short and that the killing must stop. I hope that this joint meeting will be a model for further discussion in the days ahead.

I have had extensive discussions with my Contact Group colleagues, and I have spoken with the negotiators Chris Hill, Wolfgang Petritsch and Boris Mayorskiy, and heard their frank assessment of where we stand after one week of talks.

The Contact Group agreed that the sides have begun to grapple with the central issues in good faith. On that basis we have extended the Rambouillet talks for a second and final week.

But it is clear to us all that the most difficult work is only beginning.

Not surprisingly many of the thorniest issues remained unsettled. As they enter the final stage of talks, the parties need to remember that this is not a conventional negotiation.

I reminded both sides today that the Contact Group proposals were not put forward to provide opportunities for bickering and delay. Rather they are a road-map for peace. The parties may choose to take the path toward a rational solution that will achieve peace and justice for all the people of Kosovo, or they may turn back to disaster, chaos and more killing.

Let me also say that based on my talks with the Kosovo Albanian leadership today, I believe that they recognize that the plan is a fair deal for the people of Kosovo. And they gave me every indication that they will be ready to sign on to it by the time the conference closes.

My Contact Group colleagues and I continue to make it clear that the prospect of peace with international involvement will not remain on offer beyond February 20. The parties are well aware of the consequences of failure to work productively at Rambouillet or to continue to wage war in Kosovo. The threat of NATO air strikes remains real. And I am confident that our negotiators will have the full support of the Contact Group as they work to conclude an agreement in the week ahead. Contact Group unity backed by the threat of NATO force has brought serious negotiators for both sides to the table to look hard at Kosovo's future, and nothing less than decisive actions from NATO and the Contact Group will keep both sides focused on the task at hand.

In my talk with America's NATO allies and European partners including Russia, I also stressed that an agreement without a strong international presence is no agreement at all. That means a robust civilian mission, building on the work of the OSCE to support human rights, democratic reforms, and reconstruction in Kosovo.

And it means a NATO led peacekeeping force that gives both sides the confidence to lay down their arms.

It is clear, as President Clinton said yesterday, that American participation in such a force is critical to achieving that confidence, and that America has important national interests at stake. Quote, "If there is an effective agreement and a clear plan," he said, "America should contribute to securing peace in Kosovo."

I will fly tonight to meet President Clinton in Mexico, and I will brief him on the state of the talks and on the road ahead. I will not be able to say that the path to an agreement is clear, or that success is in sight.

But I will say that there is a great deal at stake here -- for the people of Kosovo, for their neighbors, for Europeans and for Americans who believe in security, cooperation, respect for human rights and an adherence to the rule of law.

And I will say that I see every sign that if the international community stands together, we can lead the way towards peace. I would be happy to take your questions.

QUESTION: When you say that (inaudible) Albanians gave you every indication they consider this a fair deal, does that mean they consider it fair to have self rule but not independence at least for three years? Is that issue pretty much dealt with now?

SECRETARY ALBRIGHT: Let me say that they know what the plan is on the table, and how it is to be carried out for an interim period, and in my discussions, I have to say that it is a sense that I got from the way that they were talking about what could be done. It's an indication not a promise.

QUESTION: Madame Secretary, you characterized out at Rambouillet a little bit of the Serb reaction, saying they were very interested and listening to what you had to say, but can you elaborate on that a little bit, as to what their response was and what the Serb President's response was to your message, because we've a different characterization from someone who talked to the Serbs that they were rather angry with the presentation.

SECRETARY ALBRIGHT: Well, that's very interesting. I think that my presentation to them was clear-cut and realistic. I definitely did point out that there were two roads forward, that we were in a fork in those roads right now, and that one road led to chaos and killing and definitely, the further disintegration of the former Republic of Yugoslavia, and that the other road had possibilities. One, developing a functional and decent and appropriate relationship with the people of Kosovo in which the Kosovar Albanians would have a high degree of self-autonomy and other minority groups, their rights would be respected. That what we were dealing with was a question of democracy and human rights and not independence. And I think that I pointed out that if they chose the first road, they were leading their country into a deep dark hole, and if they chose the second, there was not only generally light at the end of the tunnel, but that was the road -- that way down it would ultimately lead to some kind of reintegration, and I did not note any anger. I think they actually were quite surprised about my personal relationships and past as a child that I spent in Belgrade, and my ability to understand everything they were saying when they were speaking Serbian. So, I did not feel any sense of anger. With President Multinovic, I had a sense that they know what they have to do, but that it is very difficult.

QUESTION: Madam Secretary, I was surprised to learn that there are three American advisors with the Albanian delegation. Can you tell us a little bit about their background and what role they are playing out in Rambouillet?

SECRETARY ALBRIGHT: I think that every delegation is entitled to whatever advisors they want. It is not up to me to tell you their background. Ask them.

QUESTION: Without getting into too many details, how would you qualify the negotiators? Who would be the most stubborn, the Serbs or the KLA?

SECRETARY ALBRIGHT: Well, I guess, I don't think it's fair to characterize anybody at the moment. I think there is no question that the slow-down this week was due to the Serbs. But I think that both sets of negotiators believe that they are looking out for their sides' best interests. I think the problem is for them to determine what is really in their best interest, and I think that if they were to really carefully study the documents, and all the documents now the negotiators have the discretion to put them down whenever they want, I think they would see that this is a comprehensive and fair agreement that deals with a long-standing and difficult problem, and that stubbornness is not the way to achieve peace for one's people, that the only way that one can actually achieve peace is to compromise, that is what negotiations are about.

QUESTION: Madam Secretary, are you excluding totally any going beyond the February 20 deadline at mid-day if it's close to an agreement? Can you not envisage extending it by two or three days, or by another week if that's necessary?

SECRETARY ALBRIGHT: Let me say that I found very interesting that the Contact Group members all agreed on putting a final deadline on this. I see no value in talking about an extension. I think many of you know that I'm a former professor, and people who come in and ask for extensions before they've done the work are not very well received.

QUESTION: Secretary Albright, the issues of sovereignty on the one hand, and independence on the other have been largely spoken about as being a conflict, but it seems from some things that at least President Milutinovic has said that the notion of sovereignty on this part of the Serbs is rather extensive and conflicts with many other aspects of the draft accord that we've seen, for example, withdrawing troops, for example international control of the police within Kosovo. I wonder if you could sort of comment on that.

SECRETARY ALBRIGHT: I actually both with President Milutinovic and then with both groups -- we had a fairly interesting discussion about sovereignty and independence and political structures as we enter the 21st century. As I told you, I'm sorry to act like the professor, but were I still in my former business of a political scientist teaching about international relations, I think that we are in the process of developing different kinds of entities, and that great nations who understand the importance of sovereignty at various times cede certain portions of it in order to achieve some better good for their country. Arms control agreements for instance, are ways of making agreements that in some way, say to a highly sovereign country, I'm not going to have all the weapons that I really could produce because I think that there is value to my people if I limit my weapons so that the other side limits theirs. The way we are all operating as a global community means that we are looking at how the nation-state functions in a totally different way than people did at the beginning of this century and will be doing at the beginning of the next. I also think that the model that is now being described for Kosovo is really very, very imaginative. It gives the Kosovar Albanians, or everybody who lives in Kosovo, an ability to run their daily lives in a way that they had not been able to before when they were under a communist system. They will be able to have elections, local police, schools, various sets of institutions both at the local and their higher level, and they will have tremendous power and control over their own lives. So that the terms are not as absolute -- sovereignty, independence. What they are, are terms now that I think need to be looked at in a way that allows countries to operate in the freest possible way and get along with their neighbors.

QUESTION: Is it your sense that the Serbs were beginning to accept some of this imaginativeness?

SECRETARY ALBRIGHT: The questions is foreign troops on your territory. There is a big difference. If the troops invade or if they are invited and are a result of an agreement. And there are many cases throughout the world now where there are troops in a country that are there to implement a peace, that are not there as an invasion force. There can be no forces on anybody's territory without agreement and the Serbs, I hope, will understand that those forces there will also serve a purpose of enforcing the peace out of which they are also beneficiaries, and that the killing will stop.

QUESTION: I want to ask you something that concerns the Republic of Montenegro. It is a question as to whether there is anything in the political document of the Contact Group that says that Kosovo will one day become a third republic, or that Kosovo has a possibility of becoming a third republic of Yugoslavia?

SECRETARY ALBRIGHT: No, that is not an issue here. We are talking here about a high degree of self-autonomy for Kosovo for a three-year interim period.

11.   Press Briefing by Spokesman for Contact Group Negotiators, Rambouillet, 16 February 1999

PHIL REEKER: The negotiations continue inside the Chateau at a very solid pace following the visits of the six Contact Group Foreign Ministers over Sunday and Monday. As you know, the Contact Group Foreign Ministers decided on Sunday to continue the Rambouillet talks until 12:00 noon on Saturday. As of this morning, the negotiators had been presented with comprehensive comments and responses to the Contact Group draft Interim Agreement from both the Kosovar Albanian and the FRY Serbian delegations. The negotiators and their experts and advisors are reviewing those comments to see where adjustments may be made to the Agreement, and as usual we are not prepared to discuss any specific details of the negotiations or of the text. So I think we will stop there and let you go ahead and ask any questions.

QUESTION : (AFP) Can you please tell us the progress of this past weekend in the negotiations ?

PHIL REEKER : Well I think, speaking on behalf of the three negotiators, my statement does indicate something you might consider progress, that is that both delegations have handed over to the negotiators comprehensive comments and responses to the Contact Group draft Interim Agreement.

QUESTION : When you say handed over, does this mean that the Serbian delegation is now giving written comments ?

PHIL REEKER : Yes, that was, if I can make that clear, they have both now presented written comments.

QUESTION : The Albanians have been handing over written comments for about a week now. Have the mediators got back to them on any of those points or have they waited until they get the Serbian comments before talking about them ?

PHIL REEKER : I don't have an answer for you on that. I know that they have both the sets of comments in full on the draft text and they will obviously be going over those, as I have said, with the experts and advisors in order to see where these things may be incorporated and then taken back to the two parties.

QUESTION : Does that mean that right now there is a bit of a lull in the work, that it is now, the emphasis is on Mr. Hill and his colleagues to get back to them, that they have now completed their work on the text and are just waiting ?

PHIL REEKER : I think the two delegations are continuing to have discussions among themselves and meeting with the negotiators even this morning and with some of the experts just to go over various points' but they do have those responses now in full in written form.

QUESTION : Can you please confirm if the military aspects of the documents are non-negotiable ?

PHIL REEKER : We aren't discussing any specifics of any aspects of the negotiations, of anything. Let me just remind you that at the Contact Group Ministerial on Sunday, the Ministers agreed that the negotiators have the discretion to table remaining annexes on the implementation of the settlement, and I think that is as far as we can go.

QUESTION : Is Russia coming along as far as support from the (Implementation Force?) or (inaudible) ?

SERGEY BAZDNIKIN : I would appreciate it if you would direct the question to the Russian officials. I am not here representing the country, I am representing our Ambassador Mayorskiy. He is the negotiator at the talks.

QUESTION : Can the Serb delegation sign an agreement without Mr. Milosevic's presence because, as we hear so open in the press, that the Yugoslavian parliament of Serbia who decides whether or not to sign ?

PHIL REEKER : I don't think that is a question that we are at a position to think about at this point.

FRANCOIS RIVASSEAU : If I could add something. You know that we have always considered that the delegation who came to Rambouillet has the authority to commit. The word "commit" is pretty clear.

QUESTION : Are we expecting NATO observers to arrive and if so when ?

PHIL REEKER : I don't have any information on NATO observers.

QUESTION : We are given to understand that at some stage, there will be a NATO presence here.

PHIL REEKER : I don't have any particular information on anything about NATO.

QUESTION : Can we expect the arrival of Minister Cook and Vedrine tomorrow...eventually, or any other Minister from the Contact Group ?

CHARLES HAY : My understanding is that Mr. Cook still intends to come to Rambouillet tomorrow as he indicated over the weekend, but I don't have any clear details of when that would be exactly.

FRANCOIS RIVASSEAU : I don't have any confirmed details on Mr. Vedrine's intentions at this point, but it's a possibility of course.

QUESTION : (Financial Times) Just further to Mr. Reeker's answer about both delegations should have or had authority to commit their sides to the Agreement. What happens if the Serbian Yugoslav side say "Well, this is OK by us but it has to go back to Belgrade to be approved by the Yugoslav federal or Serbian parliament. Would that be an acceptable procedure ?

PHIL REEKER : I think it was very clear from the Contact Group statement on Sunday that the deadline for an agreed upon political settlement for Kosovo is 12:00 noon on Saturday.

FRANCOIS RIVASSEAU : And to complete the answer, I think there is a hypothetical part, and we don't like to answer the question beginning by "if".

QUESTION : I have several questions but I will only ask one. We know that the Albanians demand independence; is there a hope for the Albanians to have a referendum on Kosovo after three years? If not, how can we assuage a whole population who have already experienced so much tragedy?

PHIL REEKER : Let me just reiterate again that the focus of the Rambouillet talks is to negotiate an interim three year settlement that immediately grants self-government to the people of Kosovo, ending the violence and replacing Serb security forces with Kosovo local police.

QUESTION : In principle, if both parties agree to an Agreement by Saturday mid-day, could it be possible that they sign at a later date, after their parliaments have approved the agreement?

PHIL REEKER : I think that would be a decision for the Contact Group Ministers and I don't have an answer for you on that.

OK, if you don't mind, thank you very much. We'll let you know tomorrow morning if there will be any press (events?) expected for tomorrow. Don't hesitate to check at the Sous-Prefecture for tomorrow's activities.

QUESTION (BBC) : In simple terms that people can understand, the significance of the fact that the Serbs are now giving written answers - What does it mean? Can we say it is a breakthrough?

PHIL REEKER : I think we see that these talks are moving ahead after Sunday's discussions with the various Ministers and the Contact Group Ministerial decision to extend the talks by one week until noon on Saturday, but now both parties have turned over comprehensive responses and answers to the draft of the Contact Group which they were presented a week ago. So it is important now to take those comments and move on ahead and continue the discussions and the talks, and we have four more days to go.

QUESTION : How significant is it. I mean would you characterize it. Is it a breakthrough. Is it. I mean how important to the ordinary person is this ?

PHIL REEKER : I would say obviously, it is the kind of-stuff that the Contact Group Ministers were expecting to see to move these talks forward, and that is why they were extended on Sunday.

QUESTION : Would you characterize this week more effective than the previous one ? PHIL REEKER : No, not necessarily. I wouldn't make any characterization because the week has just started.

QUESTION (APTN) : Can you just confirm (inaudible) ?

PHIL REEKER : No, I can't confirm after three years because we are not deciding that.

QUESTION (APTN) : (inaudible) any indications at all (inaudible) ?

PHIL REEKER : Yes, I just don't think that is one of the issues we are dealing with. We are looking at three years in creating democratic institutions in Kosovo so that people can get on with their lives, live in security, and feel at home where they live.

12.   Letter from Delegation of Kosova to Contact Group Negotiators, Rambouillet, 17 February 1999

HE Ambassador C. Hill
HE Ambassador W. Petritsch
HE Ambassador B. Maiorsky

Rambouillet, 17 February 1999

Your Excellencies,

The delegation of Kosova feels constrained to put forward the following observations in strong terms:

1. The delegation of Kosova expresses its concern at the increasing signs that the rules of the conference are violated and unilaterally changed without any consultation. The delegation of Kosova expresses, in this context, its grave concern that a member of the delegation of the FRY was permitted to travel to Belgrade contrary to rules which are being enforced strictly in relation to the Kosova delegation. This violation is but one instance of the kind of treatment of this delegation which has led it to doubt the value of these talks and the fairness of this process.

2. The delegation of Kosova has worked very hard, contributing constructively and expeditiously within the format of the conference established by the Contact Group. There can be no unilateral change of the format, rewarding the thus far obstructive attitude of the FRY.

3. Kosova's comments have been carefully crafted fully to remain within the terms proposed by the Contact Group and do not amount to a reopening of issues. They are necessary to add substance to the proposals and make then workable in actual practice. Kosova's constructive proposals must be given special weight, inasmuch as they concern its own self-governance.

4. The FRY has only now, after 11 days, seen fit to make available written comments. From what is known thus far, these fall outside of the framework for a settlement and cannot even constitute a basis for dicussion. Again, this evident lack of cooperation cannot result in procedural or any other concessions to the FRY delegation and must be clearly condemned.

5. There does not appear to be any reason for the Kosova delegation to engage in proximity or any other talks with a delegation put forward by the FRY which, according to the FRY Prime Minister, is entirely lacking in competence in terms of negotiating and expressing consent. This point has now been borne out by the trip of Ambassador Hill to Belgrade. There cannot be one set of agreements established here, and then an additional set of concessions extracted by Belgrade thereafter.

We use this opportunity to assure you once again of the highest consideration of this delegation.

Yours sincerely,

The Presidency of the Kosova Delegation, Hashim Thaci, Chairman

13.   NATO-Russia Permanent Joint Council Meeting at Ambassadorial Level, NATO HQ, 17 February 1999

Ambassadors discussed the situation in Bosnia and Herzegovina and in Kosovo. They stressed the importance of and expressed their full support for the ongoing peace talks at Rambouillet, and urged the parties to work responsibly and intensively in order to achieve an interim political agreement by Saturday 20 February.

NATO and Russia agreed to continue their close consultations in light of the ongoing negotiation process.

Ambassadors received a briefing on the meeting of military representatives under the auspices of the PJC held on 4 February 1999.

Following presentations by NATO and Russia, Ambassadors discussed strategy as part of their ongoing exchanges on strategy and defence policy, the military doctrines of NATO and Russia, and budgets and infrastructure development programmes.

The next meeting of the PJC is scheduled for 17 March 1999.

14.   Joint Press Briefing given by Messrs Vedrine & Cook, Paris, 17 February 1999

M. VEDRINE - Robin Cook and I have come back to Rambouillet today, as the whole of the Contact Group asked. We were asked to follow things very closely, day by day. We feel things are moving slightly, that a lot of work is being done here, both between the negotiators and each of the parties and also we hope now between the negotiators and both parties. But there is very little time left. We have reminded both sides of the deadline of Saturday 12.00 noon. Time is running out and there are still some considerable obstacles to overcome. There are still some serious decisions to be made, which require true political courage on both sides. That's the position. I think it is time to repeat that the agreement proposed by the Contact Group, both as regards its political and military dimensions, is quite obviously the only way to satisfy the legitimate aspirations, requires, concerns of the two parties. We are repeating once again that it's a compromise and, as such, it requires sacrifices, the parties to give up things, thus political courage. It's the only way to build the future on new foundations. Both parties are now faced with these choices.

MR COOK - I agree absolutely with what my friend, Hubert Védrine, has said. We came here today for a full report from the negotiators and we have met with both delegations. There is some movement, but that movement needs to pick up a lot of speed if it is going to complete its work with successful agreement on Saturday. Hubert Védrine and I said to both of the delegations that we are looking to them to redouble their efforts. The Contact Group has set a very clear deadline on Saturday and we have reminded them of that deadline and urged them to work to meet that deadline. I welcome the fact that the Serb delegation has now moved off its position of insisting on a statement of principles first. That is welcome, but it is very important that they now apply themselves and that the Albanian side also apply themselves to reaching an agreement within the timetable set by the Contact Group.

Q. - Tell us about Mr Hill's visit to Belgrade and the declarations that came out of Belgrade ?

MR COOK - Mr Milosevic really confined himself to something as brief as saying "No", and we are quite clear that there have been instructions given to the Serb delegation and one would expect that, and they are engaged in the work, we met with them today, they have put in a number of comments on the political text. We would hope that we can achieve an agreement on the broad principles of that political text within the very near future. The work does continue here.

Q. - Was Mr Hill's visit to Belgrade a success?

MR COOK - The test of whether it was a success will be on Saturday at noon.

Q. - How about disarming the KLA? Is there any chance that you could persuade the Albanians to do that and therefore help the process?

MR COOK - Hubert and I represent two countries that are willing to commit troops as part of an international military force. Between us France and Britain will commit a clear majority of the troops that are currently committed to that force. We are both clear that we are only going to supply our troops as part of that international force if there is a ceasefire and demilitarisation on both sides. We have made that clear to the Kosovo Albanians, it is in their interests that that military force is supplied, they therefore do have to reach agreement on a political settlement first. (...)

Q. - How do the Kosovars react when you say the only way they can get a NATO force is if they are actually willing to hand in their arms ?

MR COOK - They heard what we said, they understand what we say. It is certainly in the interests of the people of the Kosovo Province that they do achieve that international force that can make sure that they have stability, that they have peace, that they have the ability to develop a democratic self-governing Kosovo. It is now in their hands whether they seize that opportunity..

15.   Interim Agreement for Peace and Self-Government in Kosovo, 2nd Draft, 18 February 1999

The Parties to the present Agreement,

Convinced of the need for a peaceful and political solution in Kosovo as a prerequisite for stability and democracy.

Determined to establish a peaceful environment in Kosovo.

Reaffirming their commitment to the Purposes and Principles of the United Nations, as well as to OSCE principles, including the Helsinki Final Act and the Charter of Paris on a new Europe.

Recalling the commitment of the international community to the sovereignty and territorial integrity of the Federal Republic of Yugoslavia.

Recalling the basic elements/principles adopted by the Contact Group at its ministerial meeting in London on January 29, 1999.

Recognising the need for democratic self-government in Kosovo, including full participation of the members of all national communities in political decision-making.

Desiring to enhance the protection of the human rights of all persons in Kosovo, as well as the rights of the members of all national communities.

Recognising the ongoing contribution of the OSCE to peace and stability in Kosovo.

Noting that the present Agreement has been concluded under the auspices of the members of the Contact Group and the European Union and undertaking with respect to these members and the European Union to abide by the Agreement.

Aware that full respect for the present Agreement will be central for the development of relations with European institutions.

Have agreed as follows:

Framework

Article I: Principles

1. All citizens in Kosovo shall enjoy, without discrimination, the equal rights and freedoms set forth in this Agreement.

2. National communities and their members shall have additional rights specified in Chapter 1. Kosovo, Federal and Republic authorities shall not interfere with the exercise of these additional rights. The national communities shall be legally equal as specified herein, and shall not use their additional rights to endanger the rights of other national communities or the rights of citizens, the sovereignty and territorial integrity of the Federal Republic of Yugoslavia, or the functioning of representative democratic government in Kosovo.

3. All authorities in Kosovo shall fully respect human rights, democracy, and the equality of citizens and national communities.

4. Citizens in Kosovo shall have the right to democratic self-government through legislative, executive, judicial, and other institutions established in accordance with the Agreement. They shall have the opportunity to be represented in all institutions in Kosovo. The right to democratic self-government shall include the right to participate in free and fair elections.

5. Every person in Kosovo may have access to international institutions for the protection of their rights in accordance with the procedures of such institutions.

6. The Parties accept that their powers and responsibilities in Kosovo are as specified by the Agreement and that Kosovo shall have all rights and powers set forth herein, including in particular as specified in the Constitution at Chapter 1. The Agreement shall prevail over any other legal provisions of the Parties and shall be directly applicable. The Parties shall harmonise their governing practices and documents with the Agreement.

7. The Parties agree to cooperate fully with all international organisations working in Kosovo on the implementation of the Agreement.

Article II: Confidence-Building Measures

End of Use of Force

1. Use of force in Kosovo shall cease immediately. In accordance with the Agreement, alleged violations of the cease-fire shall be reported to international observers and shall not be used to justify use of force in response.

2. The status of police and security forces in Kosovo, including withdrawal of forces, shall be governed by the terms set forth in the Agreement. Paramilitary and irregular forces in Kosovo are incompatible with the terms of the Agreement.

Return of Refugees and Displaced Persons

3. The Parties recognise that all refugees and displaced persons have the right to return to their homes. The Parties shall take all measures necessary to facilitate the safe return of refugees and displaced persons. All persons shall have the right to reoccupy real property, assert their occupancy rights in state-owned property, and recover their other property and personal possessions. The Parties shall take all measures necessary to readmit to Kosovo returning refugees and displaced persons.

4. The Parties shall cooperate fully with all efforts by the United Nations High Commissioner for Refugees (UNHCR) and other international and non-governmental organisations concerning the repatriation and return of refugees and displaced persons, including those organisations' monitoring of the treatment of displaced persons and returnees following return.

Access for International Assistance

5. There shall be no impediments to the normal flow of goods into Kosovo, including materials for the reconstruction of homes and structures. The Federal Republic of Yugoslavia shall not require visa, customs, or licensing for persons or things for the Kosovo Verification Mission (KVM), [1] the UNHCR, and other international organisations, as well as for non-governmental organisations working in Kosovo as determined by the Head of the KVM.

6. All staff, whether national or international, working with international or non-governmental organisations including with the Yugoslav Red Cross, shall be allowed unrestricted access to the Kosovo population for purposes of international assistance. All persons in Kosovo shall similarly have safe, unhindered, and direct access to the staff of such organisations.

7. The Parties shall immediately comply with all KVM support requests. The KVM shall have its own broadcast frequencies for radio and television programming in Kosovo. The Federal Republic of Yugoslavia shall provide all necessary facilities, including frequencies for radio communications, to all humanitarian organisations responsible for delivering aid in Kosovo.

---

[1] Or however this enhanced mission is renamed.

Detention of Combatants and Justice Issues

8. All abducted persons or other persons held without charge shall be released. The Parties shall also release and transfer in accordance with other provisions in the Agreement all persons held in connection with the conflict. The Parties shall cooperate fully with the International Committee of the Red Cross (ICRC) to facilitate its work in accordance with its mandate, including ensuring full access to all such persons, irrespective of their status, wherever they might be held, for visits in accordance with the ICRC's standard operating procedures.

9. The Parties shall provide information, through tracing mechanisms of the ICRC, to families of all persons who are unaccounted for. The Parties shall cooperate fully with the ICRC and the International Commission on Missing Persons in their efforts to determine the identity, whereabouts, the fate of those unaccounted for.

10. Each Party:
    (a) Shall not prosecute anyone for crimes related to the conflict in Kosovo, except for persons accused of having committed serious violations of international humanitarian law. In order to facilitate transparency, the Parties shall grant access to foreign experts (including forensics) along with state investigators.
    (b) Shall grant a general amnesty for all persons already convicted of committing politically motivated crimes related to the conflict in Kosovo. This amnesty shall not apply to those properly convicted of committing serious violations of international humanitarian law at a fair and open trial conducted pursuant to international standards.

11. All Parties shall comply with their obligation to cooperate in the investigation and prosecution of serious violations of international humanitarian law.
    (a) As required by UN Security Council resolution 827 (1993) and subsequent resolutions, the Parties shall fully cooperate with the International Criminal Tribunal for the Former Yugoslavia in its investigations and prosecutions, including complying with its requests for assistance and its orders.
    (b) The Parties shall also allow complete, unimpeded, and unfettered access to international experts - including forensics experts and investigators to investigate allegations of serious violations of international humanitarian law.

Independent Media

12. Recognising the importance of free and independent media for the development of a democratic political climate necessary for the reconstruction and development of Kosovo, the Parties shall ensure the widest possible press freedoms in Kosovo in all media, public and private, including print, television, radio and internet.

Chapter 1
Constitution

Affirming their belief in a peaceful society, justice, tolerance, and reconciliation.

Resolved to ensure respect for human rights and the equality of all citizens and national communities.

Recognising that the preservation and promotion of the national, cultural, and linguistic identity of each national community in Kosovo are necessary for the harmonious development of a peaceful society.

Desiring to establish institutions of democratic self-government in Kosovo grounded in respect for the territorial integrity and sovereignty of the Federal Republic of Yugoslavia, from which the authorities of governance set forth herein originate.

Recognising that the institutions of Kosovo should reflect the existence of the national communities in Kosovo and foster the exercise of their rights and those of their members.

Recalling and endorsing the principles/basic elements agreed at the Contact Group ministerial meeting in London on January 29, 1999.

Article I: Principles of Democratic Self-Government in Kosovo

1. Kosovo shall govern itself democratically through the legislative, executive, judicial, and other organs and institutions specified herein. Organs and institutions of Kosovo shall exercise their authorities consistent with the terms of Agreement.

2. All authorities in Kosovo shall fully respect human rights, democracy, and the equality of citizens and national communities.

3. The Federal Republic of Yugoslavia has competence in Kosovo over the following areas, except as specified elsewhere in the Agreement: (a) territorial integrity, (b) maintaining a common market within the Federal Republic of Yugoslavia, which power shall be exercised in a manner that does not discriminate against Kosovo, (c) monetary policy, (d) defense, (e) foreign policy, (f) customs services, (g) federal taxation, (h) federal elections, and (I) other areas specified herein.

4. The Republic of Serbia shall have competence in Kosovo as specified in the Agreement, including in relation to Republic elections.

5. Citizens in Kosovo shall continue to participate in areas in which the Federal Republic of Yugoslavia and the Republic of Serbia have competence through their representation in the relevant institutions.

6. With respect to Kosovo:
    (a) There shall be no changes to the borders of Kosovo;
    (b) Deployment and use of police and security forces shall be governed by Chapter 2 to the Agreement;
    (c) Kosovo shall have authority to conduct foreign relations within its areas of responsibility equivalent to the power provided to Republics under Article 7 of the Constitution of the Federal Republic of Yugoslavia;
    (d) Martial law shall not be declared without the consent of the Assembly of Kosovo; and
    (e) Federal measures having a differential, disproportionate, injurious, or discriminatory impact on Kosovo shall not take effect in Kosovo without the consent of the President of Kosovo.

7. There shall be no interference with the right of citizens and national communities in Kosovo to call upon appropriate institutions of the Republic of Serbia for the following purposes:
    (a) assistance in designing school curricula and standards;
    (b) participation in social benefits programs, such as care for war veterans, pensioners, and disabled persons; and
    (c) other voluntarily received services, provided that these services are not related to police and security matters governed by Chapter 2, and that any Republic personnel serving in Kosovo pursuant to this paragraph shall be unarmed service providers acting at the invitation of a national community in Kosovo.

[*sic*] The Republic shall have the authority to levy taxes or charges on those citizens requesting services pursuant to this paragraph, as necessary to support the provision of such services.

8. The basic territorial unit of local self-government in Kosovo shall be the commune. All responsibilities in Kosovo not expressly assigned elsewhere shall be the responsibility of the communes.

To preserve and promote democratic self-government in Kosovo, all candidates for appointed, elective, or other public office, and all office holders, shall meet the following criteria:
    (a) No person who is serving a sentence imposed by the International Criminal Tribunal for the Former Yugoslavia, and no person who is under indictment by the Tribunal and who has failed to comply with an order to appear before the Tribunal, may stand as a candidate or hold any office; and
    (b) All candidates and office holders shall renounce violence as a mechanism for achieving political goals; past political or resistance activities shall not be a bar to holding office in Kosovo.

Article II: The Assembly

1. Kosovo shall have an Assembly, which shall consist of the Chamber of Citizens and the Chamber of National Communities.

Chamber of Citizens

2. The Chamber of Citizens shall be comprised of 120 Members.

    (a) Eighty Members shall be directly elected.

    (b) A further 40 seats shall be elected by the members of qualifying national communities.

        (i) Communities whose members constitute more than 0.5 per cent of the population but less than 5 per cent shall have ten of these seats, to be divided among them in accordance with their proportion of the overall population.

        (ii) Communities whose members constitute more than 5 per cent of the Kosovo population shall divide the remaining thirty seats equally. The Serb and Albanian national communities shall be presumed to meet the 5 per cent population threshold.

Chamber of National Communities

3. The Chamber of National Communities shall consist of 100 Members, who shall be elected democratically by the members of qualifying national communities. Each of the following national communities shall qualify for seats in the Chamber of National Communities: National Community of Turks, National Community of Gorancies, National Community of Romanies, National Community of Egyptians, and National Community of Muslims. In addition, any other national community whose members constitute more than 0.5 per cent of the population in Kosovo shall be eligible for seats in the Chamber of National Communities. Seats shall be divided equally among qualifying national communities.

Other Provisions

4. Elections for all Members shall be conducted democratically, consistent with the provisions of Chapter 3. Members shall be elected for a term of three years.

5. Allocation of seats in the Assembly shall be based on data gathered in the census referred to in Chapter 5. Prior to the completion of the census, for purposes of this Article declarations of national community membership made during voter registration shall be used to determine the percentage of the Kosovo population that each national community represents.

6. Members of the Assembly shall be immune from all civil or criminal proceedings on the basis of words expressed or other acts performed in their capacity as Members of the Assembly.

Powers of the Assembly

7. The Assembly shall be responsible for enacting laws of Kosovo, including in political, security, economic, social, educational, scientific, and cultural areas as set out below and elsewhere in the Agreement. This Constitution and the laws of the Kosovo Assembly shall not be subject to change or modification by authorities of the Republics or the Federation.

    (a) The Assembly shall be responsible for:

        (i) Financing activities of Kosovo institutions, including by levying taxes and duties on sources within Kosovo;

        (ii) The adoption of budgets of the Administrative organs and other institutions of Kosovo, with the exception of communal and national community institutions unless otherwise specified herein;

        (iii) The adoption of regulations concerning the organisation and procedures of the Administrative organs of Kosovo;

        (iv) Approving the list of Ministers of the Government including the Prime Minister;

        (v) Coordinating educational arrangements in Kosovo, with respect for the authorities of national communities and Communes;

        (vi) Electing candidates put forward by the President of Kosovo for judicial office;

        (vii) Enacting laws ensuring free movement of goods, services, and persons in Kosovo consistent with the Agreement;

        (viii) Approving agreements concluded by the President within the areas of responsibility of Kosovo;

        (ix) Cooperating with the Federal Assembly, and with the Assemblies of the Republics, and conducting relations with foreign legislative bodies;

        (x) Establishing a framework for local self-government;

        (xi) The enactment of laws concerning inter-communal issues and relations between national communities when necessary;

        (xii) Enacting laws regulating the work of medical institutions and hospitals;

        (xiii) Protection of the environment where inter-communal issues are involved;

        (xiv) Adopting programs of economic, scientific, technological, demographic, regional, and social development, as well as urban planning;

        (xv) Adopting programs for the development of agriculture and or rural areas;

        (xvi) Regulating elections consistent with Chapter 3;

        (xvii) Regulation of Kosovo-owned property; and

        (xviii) Regulation of land registries.

    (b) The assembly shall also have authority to enact laws in areas within the responsibility of the Communes if the matter cannot be effectively regulated by the Communes or if regulation by individual Communes might prejudice the rights of other Communes. In the absence of a law enacted by the Assembly under this subparagraph that preempts communal action, the Communes shall retain their authority.

Procedures

8. Laws and other decisions of the Assembly shall be adopted by majority of those present and voting in the Chamber of Citizens, after consultation with the Chamber of National Communities.

9. If a majority of the Members of a national community present and voting elected to the Chamber of Citizens pursuant to paragraph 2 (b0 make a motion that a law or other decision adversely affects the vital interests of their national community, that law or decision shall remain in force subject to completion of the dispute settlement procedure in paragraph 11. Vital interest motions shall be made within five working days of a law or decision's enactment.

10. Any national community represented in the Chamber of National Communities may request immediate consultation with the members of the Chamber of Citizens if they believe that a proposed or enacted law adversely affects the vital interests of their national community. They may further petition relevant national community delegations in the Chamber of Citizens to make a motion pursuant to paragraph 9 in order to protect vital interests of their national community.

11. The following procedure shall be used in the event of a motion under paragraph 9 asserting that the vital interests of a national community are adversely affected:

    (a) The national community or communities asserting that its vital interest is adversely affected will give reasons explaining its concerns to the President of Kosovo. Members of the Assembly supporting the law will be given an opportunity to respond. The President of Kosovo shall mediate the dispute and attempt to reach a settlement agreeable to all affected national communities.

    (b) If mediation does not produce a mutually agreeable result within seven days, the matter shall be given to the Constitutional Court. The Court shall determine whether the vital interests of the national community or communities at issue are adversely affected by the law. A law shall be deemed to adversely affect the vital interests of a national community in particular if it would involve serious violations of the additional rights of national communities under Article VII. The Court shall rule within fifteen days. Its judgment shall be final.

    (c) A law agreed in mediation to adversely affect the vital interests of a national community, or a law so adjudicated by the Constitutional Court, shall be void.

12. In each chamber, a majority of the Members shall constitute a quorum for that chamber. The chambers will otherwise decide their own rules of procedure.

Leadership

13. Each chamber shall elect from among its Members a Presidency, which will consist of a President, two Vice-presidents, and other leaders in accordance with the chamber's procedures. Each national community meeting the threshold specified in paragraph 2(b) (ii) shall be represented in the leadership. The President of the Chamber of Citizens shall not be from the same National Community as the President of Kosovo.

14. The President of each chamber shall represent the respective chamber, call its sessions to order, chair its meetings, coordinate the work of any Committees it may establish, and perform other tasks prescribed by the rules of procedure of the chamber.

Article III: President of Kosovo

1. There shall be a President of Kosovo, who shall be elected by the Chamber of Citizens by vote of a majority of its members, in consultation with the Chamber of National Communities. The President of Kosovo shall serve for a three-year term. No person may serve more than two terms as President of Kosovo.

2. The President of Kosovo shall be responsible for:
   (i) Representing Kosovo, including before any international or Federal body or any body of the Republics.
   (ii) Proposing to the Assembly candidates for Prime Minister, the Constitutional Court, the Supreme Court, and other Kosovo Judicial offices.
   (iii) meeting regularly with the democratically elected representatives of the national communities.
   (iv) Conducting foreign relations and concluding agreements within this power consistent with the authorities of Kosovo institutions under the Agreement; such agreements shall only enter into force upon approval by the Assembly.
   (v) Designating a representative to serve on the Joint Commission established by Article I.2 of Chapter 5.
   (vi) Meeting regularly with the Federal or Republic Presidents.
   (vii) Other functions specified herein or by law.

Article IV: Government and Administrative Organs

1. Executive power shall be exercised by the Government. The Government shall be responsible for implementing the laws of Kosovo, and of other government authorities when such responsibilities are devolved by those authorities. The Government shall also have competence to propose laws to the Assembly.
   (a) The Government shall consist of a Prime Minister and Ministers, including at least one person from each national community meeting the threshold specified in paragraph 2 (b) (ii) of Article II. Ministers shall head the Administrative organs of Kosovo.
   (b) The candidate for Prime Minister proposed by the President shall put forward a list of Ministers to the Chamber of Citizens. The Prime Minister, together with the list of Ministers, shall be approved by a majority of those present and voting in the Chamber of Citizens. In the event that the Prime Minister is not able to obtain a majority for the Government, the President shall propose a new candidate for Prime Minister within ten days.
   (c) The Government shall resign if a no confidence motion is adopted by a vote of a majority of the members of the Chamber of Citizens. If the Prime Minister or the Government resigns, the President shall select a new candidate for Prime Minister who shall seek to form a Government.
   (d) The Prime Minister shall call meetings of the Government, represent it as appropriate, and coordinate its work. Decisions of the Government shall require a majority of Ministers present and voting. The Prime Minister shall cast the deciding vote in the event Ministers are equally divided. The Government shall otherwise decide its own rules of procedure.

2. Administrative Organs shall be responsible for assisting the Government in carrying out its duties.

(a) National communities shall be fairly represented at all levels in the administrative organs.

(b) Any citizen in Kosovo claiming to have been directly and adversely affected by the decision of an executive or administrative body shall have the right to judicial review of the legality of that decision after exhausting all avenues for administrative review. The Assembly shall enact a law to regulate this review.

Article V: Judiciary

General

1. Kosovo shall have a Constitutional Court, a Supreme Court, District Courts, and Communal Courts.

2. The Kosovo courts shall have jurisdiction over all matters arising under this Constitution or the laws of Kosovo except as specified in this paragraph and paragraph 3. The Kosovo courts shall also have jurisdiction over questions of federal law, subject to appeal to the Federal courts on these questions after all appeals available under the Kosovo system have been exhausted.

3. Citizens in Kosovo may opt to have civil disputes to which they are party adjudicated by the courts of the Republic of Serbia, which shall apply the law applicable in Kosovo and shall refer matters falling within paragraph 5(b) to the Constitutional Court of Kosovo. Defendants in criminal cases may have access to and participation of Republic officials in Kosovo proceedings.

Constitutional Court

4. The Constitutional Court shall consist of nine judges. There shall be at least one constitutional court judge from each national community qualifying for seats in the Kosovo Assembly under paragraph 2 (b0 (ii) or Article II. Until such time as the Parties agree to discontinue this arrangement, 5 judges on the Constitutional Court shall be selected from a list presented by the President of the European Court of Human Rights.

5. The Constitutional Court shall have authority to resolve disputes relating to the meaning of this Constitution. That authority shall include, but is not limited to, determining whether laws applicable in Kosovo, decisions or acts of the President, the Assembly, the Government, the Communes, and the national communities are compatible with this Constitution.
   (a) Matters may be referred to the Constitutional Court by the President of Kosovo, the President or Vice-Presidents of each chamber of the Assembly, the Ombudsman, the communal assemblies and councils, and any national community acting according to its democratic procedures.
   (b) Any court which finds in the course of adjudicating a matter that the dispute depends on the answer to a question within the Court's jurisdiction shall refer the issue to the Constitutional Court for a preliminary decision.

6. Following the exhaustion of other legal remedies, the Constitutional Court shall at the request of any person claiming to be a victims have jurisdiction over complaints that human rights and fundamental freedoms and the rights of members of national communities set forth in this Constitution have been violated by a public authority.

7. The Constitutional Court shall have such other jurisdiction as may be specified elsewhere in the Agreement or by law.

Supreme Court

8. The Supreme Court shall consist of nine judges. There shall be at least one Supreme Court judge from each national community qualifying for seats in the Kosovo Assembly under paragraph 2(b) (ii) of Article II.

9. The Supreme Court shall hear appeals from the District Courts and the Communal Courts. Except as otherwise provided in this Constitution, the Supreme Court shall be the court of final appeal for all cases arising under law applicable in Kosovo. Its decisions shall be recognised and executed by all authorities in the Federal Republic of Yugoslavia.

Functioning of the Courts

10. The Assembly shall determine the number of District and Communal court judges necessary to meet current needs.

11. Judges of all courts in Kosovo shall be distinguished jurists of the highest moral character. They shall be broadly representative of the national communities of Kosovo.

12. Removal of a Kosovo judge shall require the consensus of the judges of the Constitutional Court. A Constitutional Court judge whose dismissal is in question shall not participate in the deliberations on his case.

13. The Constitutional Court shall adopt rules for itself and for other courts in Kosovo. The Constitutional and Supreme Courts shall each adopt decisions by majority vote of their members.

14. Except as otherwise specified in their rules, all Kosovo courts shall hold public proceedings. They shall issue published opinions setting forth the reasons for their decisions.

Article VI: Human Rights and Fundamental Freedoms

1. All authorities in Kosovo shall ensure internationally recognised human rights and fundamental freedoms.

2. The rights and freedoms set forth in the European Convention for the Protection of Human Rights and Fundamental Freedoms and its Protocols shall apply directly in Kosovo. Other internationally recognised human rights instruments enacted into law by the Kosovo Assembly shall also apply. These shall have priority over all other law.

3. All courts, agencies, governmental institutions, and other public institutions of Kosovo or operating in relation to Kosovo shall conform to these human rights and fundamental freedoms.

Article VII: National Communities

1. National communities and their members shall have additional rights determined by the Agreement in order to preserve and express their national, cultural, religious, and linguistic identities in accordance with international standards and the Helsinki Final Act. Such rights shall be exercised in conformity with human rights and fundamental freedoms.

2. Each national community may elect through democratic means, in a manner consistent with the principles of Chapter 3, institutions to administer its affairs in Kosovo.

3. The national communities shall be subject to the laws applicable in Kosovo, provided that any act or decision concerning national communities must be non-discriminatory. The Assembly shall decide upon a procedure for resolving disputes between national communities.

4. The additional rights of the national communities, acting through their democratically elected institutions, are to:

(a) preserve and protect their national, cultural, religious, and linguistic identities, including by:

  • inscribing local names of towns and villages, of squares and streets, and of other topographic names in the language and alphabet of the national community in addition to signs in Albanian and Serbian, consistent with decisions about style made by the communal institutions.

  • providing information in the language and alphabet of the national community.

  • providing for education and establishing educational institutions, in particular for schooling in their own language and alphabet and in national culture and history, for which relevant authorities will provide financial assistance; curricula shall reflect a spirit of tolerance between national communities and respect for the rights of members of all national communities in accordance with international standards.

  • enjoying unhindered contacts with representatives of their respective national communities, within the Federal Republic of Yugoslavia and abroad.

  • using and displaying national symbols, including symbols of the Federal Republic of Yugoslavia and the Republic of Serbia;

  • protecting national traditions on family law by, if the community decides, arranging rules in the field of inheritance, family, and matrimonial relations; tutorship and adoption.

  • the preservation of sites of religious, historical, or cultural importance to the national community, in cooperation with other authorities.

  • implementing public health and social services on a non-discriminatory basis as to citizens and national communities.

  • operating religious institutions in cooperation with religious authorities.

  • participating in regional and international non-governmental organisations in accordance with procedures of these organisations.

(b) be guaranteed access to, and representation in, public broadcast media, including provisions for separate programming in relevant languages under the direction of those nominated by the respective national community on a fair and equitable basis.

(c) finance their activities by collecting contributions the national communities may decide to levy on members of their own communities.

5. Members of national communities shall also be individually guaranteed:

  • the right to enjoy unhindered contacts with members of their respective national communities elsewhere in the Federal Republic of Yugoslavia and abroad.

  • equal access to employment in public services at all levels.

  • the right to use their languages and alphabets.

  • the right to use and display national community symbols.

  • the right to participate in democratic institutions that will determine the national community's exercise of the collective rights set forth in this Article.

  • the right to establish cultural and religious associations, for which relevant authorities will provide financial assistance.

6. Each national community and, where appropriate, their members acting individually may exercise these additional rights through Federal institutions and institutions of the Republics, in accordance with the procedures of those institutions and without prejudice to the ability of Kosovo institutions to carry out their responsibilities.

7. Every person shall have the right freely to choose to be treated or not to be treated as belonging to a national community, and no disadvantage shall result from this choice or from the exercise of the rights connected to that choice.

Article VIII: Communes

1. Kosovo shall have the existing communes. Changes may be made to communal boundaries by act of the Kosovo Assembly after consultation with the authorities of the communes concerned.

2. Communes may develop relationships among themselves for their mutual benefit.

3. Each commune shall have an Assembly, an Executive Council, and such administrative bodies as the commune may establish.

(a) Each national community whose membership constitutes at least three per cent of the population of the commune shall be represented on the Council in proportion to its share of the communal population or by one member, whichever is greater.

(b) Prior to the completion of a census, disputes over communal population percentages for purposes of this paragraph shall be resolved by reference to declarations of national community membership in the voter registry.

4. The communes shall have responsibility for:

  • Law enforcement, as specified in Chapter 2 of the Agreement.

  • Regulating and, when appropriate, providing child care.

  • Providing education, consistent with the rights and duties of national communities, and in a spirit of tolerance between national communities and respect for the rights of the members of all national communities in accordance with international standards.

  • Protecting the communal environment.

  • Regulating commerce and privately owned stores.

  • Regulating hunting and fishing.

  • Planning and carrying out public works of communal importance, including roads and water supplies, and participating in the planning and carrying out of Kosovo-wide public works projects in coordination with other communes and Kosovo authorities.

- Regulating land use, town planning, building regulations, and housing construction.
- Developing programs for tourism, the hotel industry, catering, and sport.
- Organising fairs and local markets.
- Organising public services of communal importance, including fire, emergency response, and police consistent with Chapter 2 of the Agreement.
- Financing the work of communal institutions, including raising revenues, taxes, and preparing budgets.

5. The communes shall have the responsibilities specified in paragraph 4 and shall also have responsibility for all other areas within Kosovo's authority not expressly assigned elsewhere herein, subject to the provisions of Article II.2 (b) of this Constitution.

6. Each commune shall conduct its business in public and shall maintain publicly available records of its deliberations and decisions.

Article IX: Representation

1. Citizens in Kosovo shall have the right to participate in the election of:
   (a) At least 10 deputies in the House of Citizens of the Federal Assembly.
   (b) At least 20 deputies in the National Assembly of the Republic of Serbia.

2. The modalities of elections for the offices specified in paragraph 1 shall be determined by the Federal Republic of Yugoslavia and the Republic of Serbia respectively, under procedures to be agreed with the Head of the KVM.

3. The Chamber of Citizens shall have the opportunity to present to the appropriate authorities a list of candidates from which shall be drawn:
   (a) At least one citizen in Kosovo to serve in the Federal Government, and at least one citizen to serve in the Government of the Republic of Serbia.
   (b) At least one judge on the Federal Constitutional Court, one judge on the Federal Court, and three judges on the Supreme Court of Serbia.

Article X: Amendment

1. The Chamber of Citizens of the Assembly of Kosovo, after consulting with the Chamber of National Communities, may by a majority of two-thirds of its members, which majority must include a majority of those members elected from the national communities pursuant to Article II.2 (b) (ii), adopt amendments to this Constitution.

2. There shall, however, be no amendments to Article I.3-5 or to this Article, nor shall any amendment diminish the rights granted by Articles VI and VII.

Article XI: Entry into Force

This Constitution shall enter into force upon the signature of the Agreement.

Chapter 3; **Conduct and Supervision of Elections**

Article I: Conditions for Elections

1. The Parties shall ensure that conditions exist for the organisation of free and fair elections, which include but are not limited to:
   (a) freedom of movement for all citizens;
   (b) an open and free political environment;
   (c) an environment conducive to the return of displaced persons;
   (d) a safe and secure environment that ensures freedom of assembly, association, and expression;
   (e) an electoral legal framework of rules and regulations complying with OSCE commitments, which will be implemented by a Central Election Commission, as set forth in Article III of this Chapter, which is representative of the population of Kosovo in terms of national communities and political parties; and

(f) free media, effectively accessible to registered political parties and candidates, and available to voters throughout Kosovo.

2. The Parties request the OSCE to certify when elections will be effective under current conditions on Kosovo, and to provide assistance to the Parties to create conditions for free and fair elections.

3. The Parties shall comply fully with Paragraphs 7 and 8 of the OSCE Copenhagen Document, which are attached to this Chapter.

Article II: Role of the OSCE

1. The Parties request the OSCE to adopt and put in place an elections program for Kosovo and supervise elections as set forth in the Agreement.

2. The Parties request the OSCE to supervise, in a manner to be determined by the OSCE and in cooperation with other international organisations the OSCE deems necessary, the preparation and conduct of elections for:
   (a) Members of the Kosovo Assembly;
   (b) Members of Communal Assemblies;
   (c) other officials popularly elected in Kosovo under the Agreement and the laws and Constitution of Kosovo at the discretion of the OSCE.

3. The Parties request the OSCE to establish a Central Election Commission in Kosovo ("the Comission").

4. Consistent with Article [ ] of Chapter 5, the first elections shall be held within nine months of the entry into force of the Agreement. The President of the Commission shall decide, in consultation with the Parties, the exact timing and order of elections for Kosovo political offices.

Article III: Central Election Commission

1. The Commission shall adopt electoral Rules and Regulations on all matters necessary for the conduct of free and fair elections in Kosovo, including rules relating to: the eligibility and registration of candidates, parties, and voters, including displaced persons and refugees; ensuring a free and fair elections campaign; administrative and technical preparation for elections including the establishment, publication, and certification of election results; and the role of international and domestic election observers.

2. The responsibilities of the Commission, as provided in the electoral Rules and Regulations, shall include:
   (a) the preparation, conduct, and supervision of all aspects of the electoral process, including development and supervision of political party and voter registration, and creation of secure and transparent procedures for production and dissemination of ballots and sensitive election materials, vote counts, tabulations, and publication of elections results;
   (b) ensuring compliance with the electoral Rules and Regulations established pursuant to the Agreement, including establishing auxiliary bodies for this purpose as necessary;
   (c) ensuring that action is taken to remedy any violation of any provision of the Agreement, including imposing penalties such as removal from candidate or party lists, against any person, candidate, political party, or body that violates such provisions; and
   (d) accrediting observers, including personnel from international organisations and foreign and domestic non-governmental organisations, and ensuring that the Parties grant the accredited observers unimpeded access and movement.

3. The Commission shall consist of the head of the OSCE Kosovo Verification Mission or his representative, representatives of national communities as identified by the national communities and at the invitation of the President of the Commission, representatives of political parties n Kosovo invited by the President of the Commission, and any such other persons as the head of the President of the Commission may decide. The head of the Kosovo Verification Mission shall act as the President of the Commission. In the event of disputes within the Commission, the decision of the President shall be final and binding.

4. The Commission shall enjoy the right to establish communication facilities, and to engage local and administrative staff.

Chapter 4
Economic Issues
Article I

1. The economy of Kosovo shall function in accordance with free market principles.

2. The authorities established to levy and collect taxes and other charges are set forth in the Agreement. Except as otherwise expressly provided, all authorities have the right to keep all revenues from their own taxes or other charges consistent with the Agreement.

3. Certain revenue from Kosovo taxes and duties shall accrue to the Communes, taking into account the need for an equalisation of revenues between the Communes based on objective criteria. The Assembly of Kosovo shall enact appropriate non-discriminatory legislation for this purpose. The Communes may also levy local taxes in accordance with the Agreement.

4. The Federal Republic of Yugoslavia shall be responsible for the collection of all customs duties at international borders in Kosovo. There shall be no impediments to the free movement of persons, goods, services, and capital between Kosovo and other parts of the Federal Republic of Yugoslavia.

5. Federal authorities shall ensure that Kosovo receives a proportionate and equitable share of benefits that may be derived from international agreements concluded by the Federal Republic and of Federal resources.

6. Federal and other authorities shall within their respective powers and responsibilities ensure the free movement of persons, goods, services, and capital to Kosovo, including from international sources. They shall in particular allow access to Kosovo without discrimination for persons delivering such goods and services.

7. If expressly required by an international donor or lender, international contracts for reconstruction projects shall be concluded by the authorities of the Federal Republic of Yugoslavia which shall establish appropriate mechanisms to make such funds available to Kosovo authorities. Unless precluded by language in existing contracts, all reconstruction projects that exclusively concern Kosovo shall be managed and implemented by the appropriate Kosovo authority.

Article II

1. The Parties agree to reallocate ownership and resources in accordance insofar as possible with the distribution of powers and responsibilities set forth in the Agreement, in the following areas:
   (a) government-owned assets (including educational institutions, hospitals, natural resources, and production facilities);
   (b) pension and social insurance contributions;
   (c) revenues to be distributed under Article I.4 of this Chapter; and
   (d) any other matters relating to economic relations between the Parties not covered by the Agreement.

2. The Parties agree to the creation of a Claim Settlement Commission (CSC) to resolve all disputes between them on matters referred to in paragraph 1.
   (a) The CSC shall consist of three experts designated by Kosovo, three experts designated jointly by the Federal Republic of Yugoslavia and the Republic of Serbia, and three independent experts designated (by the Head of the KVM).
   (b) The decisions of the CSC shall be final and binding. The Parties shall implement them without delay.

3. Authorities receiving ownership of public facilities shall have the power to operate such facilities.

Chapter 4 A

Humanitarian Assistance, Reconstruction and Economic Development

1. In parallel with the continuing full implementation of this Agreement, urgent attention must be focused on meeting the real humanitarian and economic needs of Kosovo in order to help create the conditions for reconstruction and lasting economic recovery. International assistance will be provided without discrimination between national communities.

2. The parties welcome the willingness of the European Commission working with the international community to co-ordinate international support for the parties' effort. Specifically, the European Commission will be organising an international donors' conference within one month of signature of this Agreement.

3. The international community will provide immediate and unconditional humanitarian assistance, focusing primarily on refugees and internally displaced persons returning to their former homes. The parties welcome and endorse the UNHCR's lead role in co-ordination of this effort, and endorse its intention, in close co-operation with the KVM, to plan an early, peaceful, orderly and phased return of refugees and displaced persons in conditions of safety and dignity.

4. The international community will provide the means for the rapid improvement of living conditions for the population of Kosovo through the reconstruction and rehabilitation of housing and local infrastructure (including water, energy, health and local education infrastructure) based on damage assessment surveys.

5. Assistance will also be provided to support the establishment and development of the institutional and legislative framework laid down in the Agreement, including local governance and tax settlement, and to reinforce civil society, culture and education. Social welfare will also be addressed, with priority given to the protection of vulnerable social groups.

6. It will also be vital to lay the foundations for sustained development, based on a revival of the local economy. This must take account of the need to address unemployment, and to stimulate the economy by a range of mechanisms. The European Commission will be giving urgent attention to this.

7. International assistance, with the exception of Humanitarian aid, will be subject to full compliance with the Agreement as well as other conditionalities defined in advance by the donors and the absorptive capacity of Kosovo.

Chapter 6

The Ombudsman
Article I: General

1. There shall be an Ombudsman, who shall monitor the realisation of the rights of members of national communities and the protection of human rights and fundamental freedoms in Kosovo. The Ombudsman shall have unimpeded access to any person or place and shall have the right to appear and intervene before any domestic, Federal, or (consistent with the rules of such bodies) international authority upon his or her request. In carrying out its mandate, no person, institution, or entity of the Parties may interfere with the functions of the Ombudsman.

2. The Ombudsman shall be an eminent person of high moral standing who possesses a demonstrated commitment to human rights and the rights of the national communities. He or she shall be nominated by the President and shall be elected by the Assembly from a list of candidates prepared by the President of the European Court for Human Rights for a non-renewable three year term. The Ombudsman shall not be a citizen of any State or entity that was part of the Former Yugoslavia, or of any neighbouring State. Pending the election of the President and the Assembly, the Head of the KVM shall designate a person to serve as Ombudsman on an interim basis who shall be succeeded by a person selected pursuant to the procedure set forth in this paragraph.

3. The Ombudsman shall be independently responsible for choosing his or her own staff. He or she shall have two Deputies. The Deputies shall each be drawn from different national communities.
   (a) The salaries and expenses of the Ombudsman and his or her staff shall be determined and paid by the Kosovo Assembly. The salaries and expenses shall be fully adequate to implement the Ombudsman's mandate.
   (b) The ombudsman and members of his or her staff shall not be held criminally or civilly liable for any acts carried out within the scope of their duties.

Article II: Jurisdiction

1. The Ombudsman shall consider:
   (a) alleged or apparent violations of human rights and fundamental freedoms in Kosovo, as provided in the Constitutions of the Federal Republic of Yugolsavia and the Republic of Serbia, and the European Convention for the Protection of Human Rights and Fundamental Freedoms and the Protocols thereto; and
   (b) alleged or apparent violations of the rights of national communities specified in the Agreement.
2. All persons in Kosovo shall have the right to submit complaints to the Ombudsman. The Parties agree not to take any measures to punish persons who intend to submit or who have submitted such allegations, or in any other way to deter the exercise of this right.

Article III: Powers and Duties

1. The Ombudsman shall investigate alleged violations falling within the jurisdiction set forth in Article II.1. He may act either on his own initiative or in response to an allegation presented by any Party or person, non-governmental organisation, or group of individuals claiming to be the victim of a violation or acting on behalf of alleged victims who are deceased or missing. The work of the Ombudsman shall be free of charge to the person concerned.
2. The Ombudsman shall have complete, unimpeded, and immediate access to any person, place, or information upon his or her request.
   (a) He shall have access to and may examine all official documents, and he can require any person, including officials of Kosovo, to co-operate by providing relevant information, documents, and files.
   (b) The Ombudsman may attend administrative hearings and meetings of other Kosovo institutions in order to gather information.
   (c) He may examine facilities and places where persons deprived of their liberty are detained, work, or are otherwise located.
   (d) The Ombudsman and staff shall maintain the confidentiality of all confidential information obtained by them, unless the Ombudsman determines that such information is evidence of a violation of rights falling within his or her jurisdiction, in which case that information may be revealed in public reports or appropriate legal proceedings.
   (e) The Parties undertake to ensure cooperation with the Ombudsman's investigations. Willful and knowing failure to comply shall be a criminal offense prosecutable in any jurisdiction of the Parties. Where an official impedes an investigation by refusing to provide necessary information, the Ombudsman shall contact that official's superior or the public prosecutor for appropriate penal action to be taken in accordance with the law.
3. The Ombudsman shall issue findings and conclusions in the form of a published report promptly after concluding an investigation.
   (a) A Party, institution, or official identified by the Ombudsman as a violator shall, within a period specified by the Ombudsman, explain in writing how it will comply with any prescriptions the Ombudsman may put forth for remedial measures.
   (b) In the event that a person or entity does not comply with the conclusions and recommendations of the Ombudsman, the report shall be forwarded for further action to the Joint Commission set forth in Chapter 5 of the Agreement, to the President of the appropriate Party, and to any other officials or institutions that the Ombdusman deems proper.

Chapter 8
Amendment, Comprehensive Assessment, and Final Clauses

Article I: Amendment and Comprehensive Assessment

1. Amendments to the Agreement shall be adopted by agreement of all the Parties.
2. Each Party may propose amendments at any time and will consider and consult with the other Parties with regard to proposed amendments.

3. Three years after the entry into force of the Agreement, there shall be a comprehensive assessment of the Agreement under international auspices with the aim of improving its implementation and determining whether to implement proposals by any Party for additional steps.

Article II: Final Clauses

1. The Agreement is signed in the English language. After signature of the Agreement, translations will be made into Serbian, Albanian, and other languages of the national communities of Kosovo, and attached to the English text.
2. The Agreement shall enter into force upon signature.

Federal Republic of Yugoslavia; Republic of Serbia; Kosovo

16. Press Briefing by the Contact Group Negotiators, 18 February 1999

PHIL REEKER: We have the three negotiating ambassadors from the Rambouillet talks again this afternoon. We will follow the usual format; that will be, each Ambassador will give a short opening remark and then we will cut to your questions. As usual, when you ask a question, please give your name and your agency, and wait for the microphone. I am pleased once again to introduce Ambassador Wolfgang Petritsch of the European Union, Ambassador Boris Mayorskiy of the Russian Federation, and Ambassador Christopher Hill of the United States. We will let Ambassador Mayorskiy deliver the opening remarks today.

AMBASSADOR MAYORSKIY: Good evening... good late afternoon to you all. Ladies and gentlemen, here you are again... good news from the negotiations at Rambouillet. I will give you some idea as to how things are developing there although generally speaking our work continues to be very tough, very difficult, very burdensome in many ways, but I think it's beginning to start being rewarding. We have, within the days that we haven't seen you, quite a considerable number of miles passed by the conference. We have gone through a number of substantive stages, one being a finalization by the sides -- by the parties let's call them delegations, with the initial proposal of the three negotiators given to them on the basis of the political settlement; their preparation of written notes and remarks on those documents, and their proposals on how those can be improved; the presentation of these elements to us; our study of these proposals as negotiators, our assessment of them; and then finally discussing them in full with the parties before we proceeded to proposing to them a revised draft of our initial proposals which included quite a few ideas put forward by both of the sides. This onerous work was finished today about 3:00 in the morning. Two more hours went for the multiplication of texts produced. We had a chance already to meet with the two delegations. We passed them the newborn baby with the kind invitation to kindly consider it as a final version. This kind invitation is being kindly considered now by the parties while we sit here with you. So, I can say that it is not yet the end of the conference, but we are making substantive progress, and this time I think we should not be shy to report it and enjoy it. So then, this is what I would start [with], and we will be prepared... unless my colleagues want to add something to this laconic introduction. Chris? No? Then we are prepared to take your questions. I was trying to be as factual as I could.

QUESTION: BBC Russian Service. This morning we heard about President Yeltsin's statement where he invited President Clinton, so to speak, not to touch Kosovo. Does this mark an appearance of a rift in position of Russia and the other partners in the Contact Group?

AMBASSADOR MAYORSKIY: I wonder what kind of answer you expect to this question? Yes, no, maybe, perhaps, what?

QUESTION: No, if you briefly outline the Russian position in the case the talks fail, something like that.

AMBASSADOR MAYORSKIY: I don't think this is a correct question to be put to me.

QUESTION: (off mike) Why not?

AMBASSADOR MAYORSKIY: Because you are expecting me to deliver you a Russian position of a statement of a Russian president. Now this is the kind of logic that escapes me. I know about this statement exactly as much as you do, maybe less. We are here to discuss negotiations.

QUESTION: Paul Taylor, Reuters. It seems from some of your own travels that the key to this negotiation is in Belgrade, not just in Rambouillet. Firstly, Mr. Mayorskiy, could you tell us what you felt about your fellow mediator's mission to Belgrade? Secondly, could all OF you gentlemen tell us whether any further attempts are planned to go to Belgrade and seek a final agreement or whether the final agreement is to be sought here?

AMBASSADOR MAYORSKIY: My personal feeling regarding this trip was that my colleague got a commission from his Secretary of State to go there and to do certain things she told him to do. This is how I deeply felt about it, and when it comes to the trip, I think Chris will tell you himself.

AMBASSADOR HILL: Well, let me just say that we believe that the negotiations that were begun at Rambouillet need to be finished at Rambouillet. We believe the negotiating teams here are empowered to reach an agreement. It may have been that some of their instructions may have been inadequate for the task. I believe that the instructions are now very adequate to the task, and so we have to see if we can reach an agreement by noontime on Saturday. So, in terms of the trip to Belgrade, I had the opportunity to press the point that we expect to see a political agreement by Saturday and adequate mechanisms for ensuring that this political agreement is carried out, and we expect this to happen by noontime.

QUESTION: Are you going again to Belgrade?

AMBASSADOR HILL: I don't know.

AMBASSADOR MAYORSKIY: That is a good answer.

AMBASSADOR PETRITSCH: Let me just add that we are working as a team, basically. But of course there is also, there might be situations where some of us have bilateral chores to fulfill, so this is nothing extraordinary. The center of the negotiations is here in Rambouillet; it's going to be something that will be completed here or will fail here, but in many ways it is necessary that things will be done also some place else if we speak of some aspects of this. This is nothing special, I would say, and we consider it not as a breach of anything.

QUESTION: CNN. Could you just elaborate -- Are you going again to Belgrade?

AMBASSADOR HILL: I don't know if I am going again to Belgrade. I do not rule it out, but I am not ruling it in either. At this time, I don't know.

QUESTION: CNN. What would it be dependent on?

AMBASSADOR HILL: It would be dependent on instructions to go to Belgrade and agreement to receive me there.

QUESTION: CBS News. I just wanted to follow up with Ambassador Hill on the earlier question. What is the U.S. response to President Yeltsin's remarks earlier today?

AMBASSADOR HILL: Let me stress that we have worked very well together in the Contact Group. As someone who has spent a lot of time in the Contact Group in the Bosnian conflict, one of the striking aspects of this iteration of it is the degree to which we have pulled together and agreed on the need to find a solution, find a lasting solution in Kosovo, to find mechanisms for ensuring that political agreements are carried out. So we, I think, have a lot going for us as we go in. We would rather accent the issues where we agree, and there are a lot of those issues. The fact that some of us spent a lot time in the last few days putting together this political settlement -- Ambassador Mayorskiy himself was up until about 3 or 4 a.m. this morning working on that, working with teams of American lawyers, EU lawyers. We have had numerous Contact Group meetings within the Chateau. This morning we were with both parties together working as a team. We have been working very, very well as a team and we intend to do so... and we intend to continue that and again, we intend to get this agreement by noontime on Saturday.

QUESTION: Can you give us a sense, since you don't have the agreement yet, of what the major issues are yet?

AMBASSADOR HILL: Yes, let me say that I think that one of the major problems will be how this political settlement is enforced and how we ensure compliance, ensure implementation. And we do have some difference on how that is done. Certainly the United States -- and you should ask my colleague, Ambassador Petritsch from the EU -- but I think we are very clear on what we believe needs to be done to get this.

QUESTION: BBC. Do you intend to submit the military document to the parties at all? Will it be the subject of negotiations or will it be something to take or leave? And the second part, can you confirm that Mr. Thaci is going to Ljubljana to consult with (inaudible) Demaci? That is what the Albanian representatives of the KLA are saying today. What does it mean for the negotiation process?

AMBASSADOR HILL: I think the idea, first of all, with respect to travel outside of the actual conference area, this is up to the conference host, but the concept is that if travel is helpful to the process, no one wants to stand in the way of travel that could be helpful, and so we look upon ideas like that as ideas that are presumably attempting to get the arrangement done.

AMBASSADOR MAYORSKIY: And I can qualify that, by adding that still a travel from the site of the negotiation is treated as an exception if it

happens... It is not a general rule, if you feel like traveling you go. The negotiators and the delegations are in principle supposed to stay where they are in Rambouillet all the time.

AMBASSADOR HILL: I would rather put it, people are encouraged to remain at the Chateau.

AMBASSADOR MAYORSKIY: But there are no rules without exceptions, as you know (inaudible).

QUESTION: And the military document?

AMBASSADOR HILL: There has been very full discussion of the military aspects of this and I think, speaking from the point of view of the United States, we consider these military aspects essential to the completion of this settlement.

AMBASSADOR MAYORSKIY: I can add to this that there was no official presentation of any military annexes to the delegations up to now.

QUESTION: (off mike)

AMBASSADOR MAYORSKIY: This is the kind of question that we will not answer. «Que sera, sera.» I hope you know this song, and you know the name of the film from which it was taken. I think it was called «The Man Who Knew Too Much.» Doris Day and... And the second thing is that, if there were discussions on military -- active discussion on military aspects of the – Now, speaking as a Russian representative, I can assure you that we were not taking part in those discussions.

QUESTION: New York Times. From the Contact Group point of view, does Mr. Milutinovic, the Serbian President, have the power to sign the final document and agreement?

AMBASSADOR HILL: I think when someone signs, they will be signing on behalf of their government. When the United States has a negotiation, people have received authorization to sign on behalf of the United States Government. It is our belief that anyone signing the document will have adequate authorization to do so. I don't consider this a problem.

QUESTION: Kosovo Information Center. I would like to ask Ambassador Hill, as the most authoritative author of this paper from its early stages, that is, its inception, you described the paper earlier, or the drafts, rather, as a swinging pendulum between the ideas of the two parties. I would like to know how many of the Albanian principle remarks have been included in that paper, and is there an exit strategy to assure the Kosovar Albanians that this interim solution does not become a permanent one?

AMBASSADOR HILL: Look, we have been working on drafts over the past few months. I think Ambassador Mayorskiy gave you a pretty lengthy description of how the most recent draft was put together and how it was presented to the parties, that it was presented to them with the invitation that they consider this a final draft; meaning we are not at take it or leave it, but certainly people should consider this a final draft. If you are asking us what we think of this draft, whether we think it is a good draft, yes, we do. We feel that this draft meets the important concerns of both parties. It is indeed a compromise, and indeed there are people on both sides who are very unhappy with this draft. Believe me, I have heard a lot of that in the last few days.

QUESTION: Irish Times. As you know two members of the European Parliament today came to Rambouillet to give a report to Mr. Petritsch on war crimes in Kosovo. They asked that President Milosevic be indicted for war crimes, and they are very concerned that the Serb leadership may receive a form of amnesty or a guarantee of non-prosecution in exchange for an agreement. In fact, we are even told that this is contained in Article 7 of the final draft. Can you tell us with any certainty that there will be no amnesty for war crimes in this agreement?

AMBASSADOR PETRITSCH: I was asked to meet these two members of the European Parliament in my capacity as the European Union Special Envoy, which I did this afternoon, and they handed me over a study that they have conducted on the military activities during the summer of 1998. There was no talk about who was going to be indicted; there was no talk about anything. I have not read the report yet, understandably, but we had not discussed the details and of course, also, I was not in a capacity to discuss the details of the agreement.

QUESTION: (Off mike) AMBASSADOR PETRITSCH: This is something that we are not going to answer, but this was also, as I might stress again, not part of my meeting.

QUESTION: CNN. How significant is it that the KLA keep insisting that their ground commanders won't disarm?

AMBASSADOR MAYORSKIY: What is KLA?

QUESTION: CNN. Is that a trick question?

AMBASSADOR MAYORSKIY: No, it is not a trick question.

QUESTION: CNN. How significant is it, please, that elements of the KLA are saying that their commanders, their people on the ground, are not going to disarm?

AMBASSADOR HILL: I think you need to bear in mind that we don't have an agreement yet and we have a very busy few days ahead of us in order to reach an agreement. And then I think once we reach an agreement, then I think perhaps we can evaluate how significant it is when some people say they don't want to abide by the agreement. But as of today, we don't have an agreement.

QUESTION: (Off mike)

AMBASSADOR HILL: We have to see how it looks after the agreement is reached. We don't have an agreement, so it is very hard to evaluate people's comments in advance of any kind of agreement. They don't know what they would be asked to do, they don't know what the mechanisms are for safeguarding the people there in implementing the political settlement. I am not surprised they would take that view in the absence of an agreement.

QUESTION: Financial Times. Apparently one part of this political agreement, or what you hope would be a final text on a political agreement, is an addition of a second chamber for Kosovo. Apparently this is something the Serb side wanted in because it would reflect the other nationalities, the other minorities. The Albanian side apparently complains that this would dilute (inaudible) and possibly have a veto on the assembly. Can you comment on that?

AMBASSADOR HILL: Well, these are issues that are being discussed on the table, there is a difference of views on whether the assembly should have one house or two houses. There is a question that, if you make it two houses, how would you divide the powers between the two houses. These are just ongoing discussions, and if you would like to get a badge, you can come in and we can talk about it; you could join one of the delegations if you haven't already done so. (Laughter)

AMBASSADOR PETRITSCH: Can I just add something? We are not going to go into details as we have already stressed, but there should be a fair and balanced deal and it should be above all workable. So we are looking into all different aspects, in all the proposals that are being made, but it is not something that can be now isolated and said this is it and this we want.

QUESTION: BBC. Ambassador Hill, you said earlier that you were looking to get a political agreement signed by the deadline on Saturday.

AMBASSADOR HILL: That was half the sentence, but go ahead.

QUESTION: And that there would need to be mechanisms to make sure it is implemented. But as the military texts -- the annexes which deal with security and military matters -- we understand have not been presented to the delegation --

AMBASSADOR HILL: They have been briefed, fully discussed. The question was whether they were formally presented, but they have been absolutely, fully discussed and people are aware of what is in them.

QUESTION: My question is, is the achievement you are looking for for the deadline on Saturday, the agreement in order to sign just the political document, and discuss, or finish discussing the military implementation later?

AMBASSADOR HILL: Absolutely not.

QUESTION: Associated Press. Are there any circumstances under which these talks might go beyond Saturday?

AMBASSADOR PETRITSCH: Circumstances have to be judged when we are there, once we cross them. Then we will see what we have to (crosstalk). There is a cutoff date, Saturday noon, and this is it, full stop.

AMBASSADOR MAYORSKIY: By the way, what is the day today? Is it Thursday? Then we have two whole days to wait until the deadline comes.

QUESTION: (Off mike)

AMBASSADOR MAYORSKIY: No, this is my question.

AMBASSADOR HILL: Contact Group Ministers took a strong position that the cutoff date and time was noontime Saturday.

QUESTION: CNN. (Off mike) Do you have any idea whether (inaudible) going on in Washington and other places there may be an extension (inaudible)?

AMBASSADOR HILL: I haven't been in Washington or any other places, but I can assure you we are very firmly committed to getting this done by noontime on Saturday.

QUESTION: RIA-Novosti. Can you foresee whether or not there will be a Contact Group meeting after Saturday or Sunday? That's my first question and my second question is: Can you tell us whether or not there will be a press conference on Saturday with the journalists?

AMBASSADOR MAYORSKIY: I don't know. I think the response to both your questions is «maybe». But I don't know.Before you leave, let me tell

you one small thing as representative of Russia. I don't know about the sources, and of course we cannot cover everything that is being written about the negotiations in the world press, but what reaches us here and now sometimes contains articles -- hopefully at least one of the authors of these articles is here -- where it is suggested that the role of Russia in these negotiations is to convince Yugoslavia that they should accept NATO presence as implementation of the agreements we are working on. Now let me tell you this, that nothing of the kind is happening in the course of these negotiations. And if the authors of these articles refer to diplomatic sources and they say that one diplomat told us that, then they are listening to the diplomats who are telling them blatant lies. I am sorry to say that, but this is the way it is.(End press conference)

(Begin pull-aside)

QUESTION: When do you expect to get a reaction to the draft?

AMBASSADOR HILL: We expect pretty soon.

QUESTION: (Crosstalk)

AMBASSADOR HILL: They got the political parts of the draft this morning (crosstalk) and I think we will probably have some meetings this evening about it.

QUESTION: Have you gotten any reactions from both sides?

AMBASSADOR HILL: Yes, they both don't like it.

QUESTION: Can you give us a sense of what the atmosphere is like in there now?

AMBASSADOR HILL: Speaking personally, it is very busy and there is a real sense that we are getting to the end here, so it is a little more tense now.

QUESTION: You sound really upbeat.

AMBASSADOR HILL: I am not upbeat. You just don't know me. I am always like this.

QUESTION: You seem more confident.

AMBASSADOR HILL: Well, look, there is a real logic to getting this thing done for all parties concerned, and I hope that they will see their interest and get it done, but this is very difficult and I don't want to imply that it is in the bag by any means.

QUESTION: Are you still convinced that NATO will bomb if there is no agreement?

AMBASSADOR HILL: You know what our position is on that. I mean it is not for me to give you an ultimate view on that.

QUESTION: Is your feeling as one that was expressed by Secretary Albright last Sunday that the Albanian side is willing to sign the agreement? Or has the mood changed?

AMBASSADOR HILL: I think we have had good cooperation. Frankly, we, I mean the Albanian delegation I think has done well. They came in as a diverse group of people, they formed themselves well, they have responded well to drafts. I can't say what their reaction is to all the provisions of all the agreement. They need to look at the whole thing and they need to decide where their interests are. I think the entire agreement, including the annexes on implementation, are ones that should make them want to sign.

QUESTION: After the agreement is signed, do you think that Kosovo will have a self-government as you envisioned in the plan?

AMBASSADOR HILL: Absolutely. Absolutely.

QUESTION: There are some suggestions that Mr. Milosevic is just enjoying stringing this out and that he loves being the center of attention and in fact, your going there and possibly other officials going there, that there will be just more of this from him.

AMBASSADOR HILL: I cannot believe that he is really enjoying this. If he is enjoying this, he must be a real masochist. There is nothing much to enjoy.

Journalist: But he is getting a lot of attention.

AMBASSADOR HILL: Well, there is a lot of -- how to put it -- it is a very difficult period for him because we are forcing him to make some very harsh decisions that he is going to have to make.

QUESTION: The talks will just flounder on KLA refusal to disarm on the one side and...

AMBASSADOR HILL: We have a deadline here. It is Saturday noontime, and we think everyone understands that deadline. They are very clear what they have to do. They are going to have to make some tough choices. This isn't easy for anybody. It is certainly not easy for the Albanians, certainly not easy for people in the KLA who have been out in the woods fighting for something that they are not going to get in this agreement. They absolutely not going to get independence from this agreement. Not easy for them but not easy for the Serbs either. So, you bet it's tough and...

QUESTION: When will you go to Belgrade?

AMBASSADOR HILL: I don't know. I do not know.

PHIL REEKER: He answered that question before.

QUESTION: Are you glad you started this process, though? I mean, as you think about it now, you don't have any doubts that this was the right thing to do?

AMBASSADOR HILL: Speaking as someone who has spent a lot time in the Balkans, I mean anyone who has been there understands the problem of Kosovo. It is a very special problem in the Balkans. It has been around for at least a century. In many respects, here we are in 1999 and we are still dealing with the breakup of the Ottoman Empire. So anyone who has been involved with that, who understands it, you bet they want to be involved in finishing it up.

QUESTION: Is this tougher for you than Dayton?

AMBASSADOR HILL: Yes.

QUESTION: (inaudible) delegations were interested in the political structures have been incorporated (inaudible)?

AMBASSADOR HILL: Well, you know, this is a negotiating process.

QUESTION: I was just wondering if you could tell us some of the ways those structures have been modified?

AMBASSADOR HILL: No, I really can't. It is a negotiating process. What happens is you get comments from one side, you go in another room and you get comments from the other side. You try to incorporate the more sensible of the comments, and then you bring out a new draft and, lo and behold, they look and they say, «Where did this come from?» Well, it obviously came from the other side and they don't like that. And then they say, «Well, what happened to our idea?» and you say «Sorry, the other side couldn't allow that in there and neither could we.» And so it is a very painful difficult process and so any time you're putting a draft on the table, there is a certain exhilaration that you are moving forward; on the other hand, you wait for the blow-back, and that is what you get. Everyone gets very grouchy about it, they say «why are we here,» etc. Well, they need to calm down, think it through, and I think they will understand that we are doing something that does make sense.

QUESTION: CNN. (Inaudible) about the Belgrade issue?

AMBASSADOR HILL: If I am asked to go to Belgrade... If I am asked by the United States, by my boss, to go to Belgrade, and if that is accepted on the other side, I will go to Belgrade.

QUESTION: So is there a necessity, do you think, to go?

AMBASSADOR HILL: I think that is something that is being looked at, and if that decision is made I will certainly go. I do believe that the Serb delegation is senior enough and I think they understand what the issues are and I think they can see where their interests lie. They have communications back to Belgrade. If it is necessary to give another message there, to talk on those terms, we can certainly do that.

QUESTION: How would you describe your last meeting with Milosevic?

AMBASSADOR HILL: My last meeting with Milosevic was not easy, and frankly it was very tense, because the subject is a very difficult one. I know there is some speculation that he enjoys tense and difficult subjects. I am not sure I could bear that out by personal observation.

QUESTION: (Inaudible) the idea that there would be an arms implementation is not separable from this agreement. Are any of the details (inaudible) modifiable?

AMBASSADOR HILL: Well, look, the concept here is that we will handle the security. Now, you listen to the parties, you see if they have some ideas, but we are going to decide how we need to implement that agreement.

QUESTION: «We» being the Contact Group.

AMBASSADOR HILL: Well, we being the people who will be involved in the implementation mechanism.

QUESTION: Would you explain the comment «a novice like me» from your Russian colleague?

AMBASSADOR HILL: Well, the Russian Federation has a view that they believe, they are in favor of finding a political solution. They are working very hard on finding a political solution. They do not agree with the idea of a military aspect to the enforcement. On the other hand, we are working very well together in the Contact Group and we are not encountering obstacles in this. And what they have said is that if the two sides agree to have a military aspect to this, they will certainly support that. They are not standing in the way of the two sides agreeing to have a military implementation mechanism, and that is precisely what we are trying to get from the two parties.

QUESTION: Why was the military document not yet presented?

AMBASSADOR HILL: It has been fully presented and fully discussed.

17. Kosova Delegation Statement on New Proposal for a Settlement, 18 February 1999

The Kosova delegation has studied the revised proposals relating to a political settlement put forward by the Contact Group. This is a substantively new draft introduced after Kosova has negotiated constructively on the basis of the initial proposal put forward by the Contact Group. The Delegation of Kosova returns this document to the Contact Group as it is unacceptable for consideration at this late stage. In fact, it represents a breach of faith by the Contact Group. The reasons for this attitude are as follows:

The Conference Process

The delegation of Kosova notes that the 'non-negotiable principles' proposed by the Contact Group envision an interim agreement with a mechanism for a final settlement after an interim period of three years. On this basis, the delegation of Kosova has accepted to come to Rambouillet.

The delegation received, on 6 February, the principal draft documents on a political settlement from the Contact Group. Despite the difficulties and sacrifices this has entailed, the delegation of Kosova has negotiated in a constructive way on the basis of the drafts that were presented, and has indicated that, with some modifications that were proposed, these could be acceptable to it, provided the remaining issues relating, for example, to military matters and other issues, such as the referendum, could be addressed.

In this way, the Delegation of Kosova has contributed to the conference for some 12 days, basing its comments and attitude on these documents that were officially put forward. The Contact Group should have acted on these comments (in fact there was no response for days), and should have noted and acted upon the failure of the Federal Republic of Yugoslavia to exhibit any constructive attitude whatever. Instead, there has now suddenly been submitted a new draft which represents a breach of the principles which, both in terms of substance and in terms of procedure, underpin these talks. This new draft, in terms of matters of principle of the greatest importance and some other important substantive questions, is entirely directed against the position of Kosova and, indeed, the Contact Group's own proposals.

If the consent of the delegation of Kosova is sought, the unilateral changes imposed, apparently as a result of talks outside of the Conference, must be reversed. There cannot be a process of obtaining concessions from the Kosova delegation first, through the process of regular proximity talks which this delegation has constructively supported from the first day of the conference, and of then imposing a second set of unacceptable concessions as a result of separate negotiations between the Contact Group and Belgrade in which the Kosova delegation has no involvement.

It was agreed that changes to the first draft presented on 6 February would be obtained either on the basis of agreement of both delegations, or if the Contact Group were persuaded by arguments put forward by one side that a change would better facilitate the implementation of the agreement as outlined in the initial draft. There is no room for a unilateral alteration of the most fundamental principles which underpin the political agreement as a whole. Hence, the Delegation of Kosova returns the new draft on the political aspects of the settlement to the negotiators as a procedurally and substantially unacceptable document.

For the moment, it suffices to refer to two major new elements which render this new draft unreceivable.

The Issue of Sovereignty and Legal Status

The first point relates to the insertion of the word 'sovereignty' into the preamble of Annex 1 (where, in fact, there was no preambular section at all before). This is made even worse by the formal declaration that the authorities of governance set forth in the agreement originate from the Federal Republic of Yugoslavia. This action is fundamentally inconsistent with the understanding that a settlement would be without prejudice to the status of Kosova for the interim period.

The overall structure and concept of all of the texts presented thus far deliberately did not address the legal relationship or issues of hirarchy between the entities in the interim period. Hence, even the formulation in the preamble of the Framework Interim Agreement refers to 'sovereignty and terrritorial integrity of the Federal Republic of Yugoslavia' in a way which is consisstent with this basic approach. It notes the attachment of the international community to those two principles in relation to the Federal Republic of Yugoslavia, but does not purport to reflect the position of Kosova in the matter.

No reference to sovereignty was included in Annex 1, which has been the basis of intensive and constructive work of the delegation of Kosova for over ten days now. As opposed to the Framework Agreement's Preamble, there is merely a reference to territorial integrity in Annex 1. This formulation is used in the context of the exercise of federal authority, rather than as a matter of status for Kosova. And even that reference to territorial integrity in the first draft of that Annex was qualified in the comments of the delegation of Kosova by referring to the formulation in the Framework Interim Agreement which pointed to the attachment of the international community to that concept, and not necessarily of Kosova.

The Kosova delegation will not countenance a total change to the character of the agreement at the last moment, even if it is achieved through the insertion of a single word. Moreover, the proposal that the rights and powers of Kosva are derived from the Federal Republic of Yugoslavia is similarly conceptually incompatible with the approach that was taken by the Contact Group and the conference from the very beginning of the talks.

It is the position of the delegation of Kosova that a referendum on the further status of Kosova must be held after the expiry of an interim period. Again, a reference to sovereignty would constrain the delegation of Kosova to insist on a far clearer formulation of the obligation to hold a referendum in the concluding provisions of the Framework Interim Agreement than might have been contemplated otherwise. The delegation of Kosova notes in this context that the formal subordination of Kosova to the Federal Republic of Yugoslavia legal order, its sovereignty and territorial integrity which is now suddenly proposed would appear to be permanent (i.e., only possible to be reversed with the consent of the FRY), despite the firm decision in the 'non-negotiable principles' that clearly envisage a final settlement after an interim period of three years through an agreed mechansim.

If the wording to which objection is made here cannot be removed, and if no improvement can be made in relation to the arrangement at the time of expiry of the agreement after three years, there is not basis for agrrement. If this proposal is not acted upon, the only other option for the delegation of Kosvoa would be to insist, correspondingly, that the following provision also be included in the preamble:

> The people of Kosovo are entitled to exercise the right to self-determination. This right shall be exercised at the conclusion of the interim period of three years.

The issue of the second chamber

The Kosova delegation has great difficulty in accepting the concept of national communities and special rights. It believes this concept to be in conflict with the aim of a tolderant political system for Kosova with equal rights for all citizens. Instead, segregation and parallelism will be encouraged. Nevertheless, the Kosova delegation has responded constructively, not challenging the concept and instead proposing modalities for its implementation which will guarantee the rights of all and which will not lead to the risk of division and obstruction in the Kosova political system according to ethnic criteria.

There is ample provision for extra representation of groups through the system of reserved seats in the Kosova Assembly. In the new text, there has been retained the special representation of members of national communities in the Assembly. However, in addition, a very large body with membership almost as big as the Assembly has suddenly been invented, ensuring that there would exist an entirely disproportionate representation of the population of Kosova. This double or triple representation and the process of co-decision is a violation of the democratic principle and not acceptable.

While it is argued that the second chamber is largely symbolic and will not have 'real powers', this does not alleviate the concerns of the Kosova delegation. This is a new, substantial institution which will greatly increase the risk of Kosova politics being subordinated to ethnic divisions and obstruction. Moreover, its proposed powers are in fact more than symbolic. The Kosova delegation is also very concerned about further unilateral increases by the Contact Group, at the insistence of the Federal Republic of Yugoslavia, to the powers to be enjoyed by the second chamber. However, even as conceived now, there is no basis for agreement.

In sum, the sudden introduction of the entirely new concept of the second chamber is unwarranted and represents and affront against the very helpful, and for it painful, way in which the Kosova delegaiton has treated the issue of national communities. The Kosova delegation finds that such a unilateral change of the initial texts cannot be justified according to the rules of the conference and must be removed.

If there has to be a further layer of representation which is indeed of an advisory character, one might consider the creation of an advisory body attached to the Office of the President. It is, after all, the President who will first entertain representations by members of national communities under the proposal contained in Article II (4&5) of the original draft. In this way, constructive involvement and advice could be interjected with a view to fully representing again the views of members of national communities at the appropriate stage. Any proposal beyond this violates the basic framework on which all discussions have been conducted thus far.

Conclusion

In conclusion, the delegation of Kosva requires that these fundamental and unilateral changes be immediately reversed. Instead, the Contact Group must take into account the constructive proposals put forward by the delegation of Kosova throughout these talks, which throughout remained within the proposals contained in the initial draft.

18. Draft Chapter 5, Implementation I, 19 February 1999

[Note: The military draft chapter presented on the same date is not presented here again as it is identical to the one included in the final text of the agreement.]

Article I: Institutions, Implementation Mission

1. The Parties invite the OSCE, in cooperation with the European Union, to constitute an Implementation Mission in Kosovo. All responsibilities and powers previously vested in the Kosovo verification Mission and its Head by prior agreements shall be continued in the Implementation Mission and its Chief.

Joint Commission

2. A Joint Commission shall serve as the central mechanism for monitoring and coordinating the civilian implementation of the Agreement. It shall consist of the Chief of the Implementation Mission (CIM), one Federal and one Republic representative, one representative of each national community in Kosovo, the President of the Chamber of Citizens, and a representative of the President of Kosovo. Meetings of representatives of organisations specified in the Agreement or needed for its implementation.

3. The CIM shall serve as the Chair of the Joint Commission. The Chair shall coordinate and organise the work of the Joint Commission and decide the time and place of its meetings. The Parties shall abide by and fully implement the decisions of the Joint Commission. The Joint Commission shall operate on the basis of consensus, but in the event consensus cannot be reached, the Chair's decision shall be final.

4. The Chair shall have full and unimpeded access to all places, and information (including documents and other records) within Kosovo that in his judgment are necessary to his responsibilities with regard to the aspects described in Article V.

Joint Council and Local Councils

5. The CIM may, as necessary, establish a Kosovo Joint Council and Local Councils, for informal dispute resolution and cooperation. The Kosovo Joint Council would consist of one member from each of the national communities in Kosovo. Local Councils would consist of representatives of each national community living in the locality where the Local Council is established.

Article II: Responsibilities and Powers

1. The CIM shall:
   (a) supervise and direct the implementation of the aspects of the Agreement described in Article V pursuant to a schedule that he shall specify;

(b) maintain close contact with the Parties to promote full compliance with those aspects of the Agreement;

(c) facilitate, as he deems necessary, the resolution of difficulties arising in connection with such implementation;

(d) participate in meetings of donor organisations, including on issues of rehabilitation and reconstruction, in particular by putting forward proposals and identifying priorities for their consideration as appropriate;

(e) coordinate the activities of civilian organisations and agencies in Kosovo assisting in the implementation of the aspects of the Agreement described in Article V, respecting fully their specific organisational procedures;

(f) report periodically to the bodies responsible for constituting the Mission on progress in the implementation of the aspects of the Agreement described in Article V; and

(g) carry out the functions specified in the Agreement pertaining to police and security forces.

2. The CIM shall also carry out other responsibilities set forth in the Agreement or as may be later agreed.

Article III: Status of Implementation Mission

1. Implementation Mission personnel shall be allowed unrestricted movement and access into and throughout Kosovo at any time.

2. The Parties shall facilitate the operations of the Implementation Mission, including by the provision of assistance as requested with regard to transportation, subsistence, accommodation, communication, and other facilities.

3. The Implementation Mission shall enjoy such legal capacity as may be necessary for the exercise of its functions under the laws and regulations of Kosovo, the Federal Republic of Yugoslavia, and the Republic of Serbia. Such legal capacity shall include the capacity to contract, and to acquire and dispose of real ad personal property.

4. Privileges and immunities are hereby accorded as follows to the CIM and associated personnel:

(a) the Implementation Mission and its premises, archives, and other property shall enjoy the same privileges and immunities as a diplomatic mission under the Vienna Convention on Diplomatic Relations;

(b) the CIM and professional members of his staff and their families shall enjoy the same privileges and immunities as are enjoyed by diplomatic agents and their families under the Vienna Convention on Diplomatic Relations; and

(c) other members of the CIM staff and their families shall enjoy the same privileges and immunities as are enjoyed by members of the administrative and technical staff and their families under the Vienna Convention on Diplomatic Relations.

Article IV: Process of Implementation

General

1. The Parties acknowledge that complete implementation will require political acts and measures, and the election and establishment of institutions and bodies set forth in the Agreement. The Parties agree to proceed expeditiously with these tasks on a schedule set by the Joint Commission. The Parties shall provide active support, cooperation, and participation for the successful implementation of the Agreement.

Elections and Census

2. Within nine months of the entry into force of the Agreement, there shall be elections in accordance with and pursuant to procedures specified in Chapter 3 of the Agreement for authorities established herein, according to a voter list prepared to international standards by the Central Election Commission. The Organisation for Security and Cooperation in Europe (OSCE) shall supervise those elections to ensure that they are free and fair.

3. Under the supervision of the OSCE and with the participation of Kosovo authorities and experts nominated by and belonging to the national communities of Kosovo, Federal authorities shall conduct an objective and free census of the population in Kosovo under rules and regulations agreed with the OSCE in accordance with international standards. The census shall be carried out when the OSCE determines that conditions allow an objective and accurate enumeration.

(a) The first census shall be limited to name, place of birth, place of usual residence and address, gender, age, citizenship, national community, and religion.

(b) The authorities of the Parties shall provide each other and the OSCE with all records necessary to conduct the census, including data about places of residence, citizenship, voters' lists, and other information.

Transitional Provisions

4. All laws and regulations in effect in Kosovo when the Agreement enters into force shall remain in effect unless and until replaced by laws or regulations adopted by a competent body. All laws and regulations applicable in Kosovo that are incompatible with the Agreement shall be presumed to have been harmonised with the Agreement. In particular, martial law in Kosovo is hereby revoked.

5. Institutions currently in place in Kosovo shall remain until superseded by bodies created by or in accordance with the Agreement. The CIM may recommend to the appropriate authorities the removal and appointment of officials and the curtailment of operations of existing institutions in Kosovo if he deems it necessary for the effective implementation of the Agreement. If the action recommended is not taken in the time requested, the Joint Commission may decide to take the recommended action.

6. Prior to the election of Kosovo officials pursuant to the Agreement, the CIM shall take the measures necessary to ensure the development and functioning of independent media in keeping with international standards, including allocation of radio and television frequencies.

Article V: Authority to Interpret

The CIM shall be the final authority in theater regarding interpretation of [the Framework and the Chapters now distributed (1, 2, 3, 4, 4A, 5, 6, and 8)] of this Agreement, and the Parties agree to abide by his determinations as binding on all Parties and persons.

---

19.   President Clinton and President Chirac, Joint press conference, Washington, DC, 19 February 1999

PRESIDENT CLINTON: Please sit down. Good afternoon. President Chirac and I, as always, have had a very good meeting. We had a lot to discuss and we have a lot to do together. Most importantly today we are working together to end the fighting in Kosovo and to help the people there obtain the autonomy and self-government they deserve. We now call on both sides to make the tough decisions that are necessary to stop the conflict immediately, before more people are killed and the war spreads. The talks going on outside Paris are set to end on Saturday. The Kosovo Albanians have shown courage in moving forward the peace accord that we, our NATO allies, and Russia have proposed. Serbia's leaders now have a choice to make. They can join an agreement that meets their legitimate concerns and gives them a chance to show that an autonomous Kosovo can thrive as part of their country, or they can stonewall. But if they do, they will be held accountable. If there is an effective peace agreement, NATO stands ready to help implement it. We also stand united in our determination to use force if Serbia fails to meet its previous commitment to withdraw forces from Kosovo, and if it fails to accept the peace agreement. I have ordered our aircraft to be ready, to act as part of a NATO operation, and I will continue to consult very closely with Congress in the days ahead. ...

PRESIDENT CHIRAC: ...

The President has covered, more or less, all the subjects that were on the agenda of our talks, so I'm going to make two remarks only. The first is to say that our agreement on the present problems in Kosovo is an unqualified agreement, it's a complete agreement. We're almost at the end of the time allotted for trying to work things out at Rambouillet, and after President Clinton and I would like to say to the two parties, and in particular to President Milosevic -- who in fact holds more or less the key to the solution -- that the time has come to shoulder all his responsibilities and to choose the path of wisdom, and not the path of war, which would bear very serious consequences for people who would make that choice, for themselves and for their people. It's a very heavy responsibility that they would be taking, if they were to do that. I've already had occasion to say that, as far as the Europeans are concerned, it is our continent which is involved here, and we want our continent to be in peace, to be at peace, and we will not accept that situations such as the present situation in Kosovo should continue. ...

PRESIDENT CLINTON: -- French and American journalists, beginning with Mr. Hunt.

QUESTION: President Clinton, President Milosevic refused to meet with the U.S. Envoy today, Christopher Hill, and said that he would not give up Kosovo, even at the price of a bombing. Is there any possibility that NATO would extend the Saturday noon deadline for reaching an agreement? And what do you say to President Yeltsin of Russia when he said that, we will not allow Kosovo to be touched? And for President Chirac, did you and President Clinton find agreement today on the issue of Iraqi sanctions?

PRESIDENT CLINTON: First, let me say I think it would be a mistake to extend the deadline. And I respect the position of Russia and I thank the Russians for supporting the peace process, as well as the proposed agreement. We had many of the same tensions in Bosnia, where ultimately we wound up working together for peace. I believe that is what will happen.

I would like to go back to the -- just very briefly -- to the merits of the argument that Mr. Milosevic made. He says that if he accepts this multinational peacekeeping force it's like giving up Kosovo. I personally believe it's the only way he can preserve Kosovo as a part of Serbia. Under their laws, Kosovo is supposed to be autonomous, but a part of Serbia. Its autonomy was effectively stripped from it years ago. We are now trying to find some way to untangle the injuries and harms and arguments that have come from both sides, and permit a period of three years to develop within which the Serbian security forces can withdraw, a police force, civil institutions can be developed -- we can give them a chance to prove that they can function together. I don't think, unless we do this, there is any way for the integrity of Serbia ultimately to be preserved, because of the incredible hostility and the losses and the anger that's already there.

So I'm not trying to -- at least from our part, and I believe President Chirac and all the Europeans feel the same way -- we're trying to give this a chance to work, not trying to provide a wedge to undo Serbia.

Mr. President.

PRESIDENT CHIRAC: Well, I entirely share the position expressed by President Clinton. I would doubt that -- I'm convinced that the only possibility for Mr. Milosevic, the only way he can keep Kosovo within internationally recognized frontiers, as of course, planned in the Yugoslav constitution, a high degree of substantial autonomy, substantial autonomy -- the only way he can keep the situation is to accept the proposals that are made today. Any other solution, I repeat, would involve for Mr. Milosevic some very serious consequences, indeed.

QUESTION: If the failure is -- everything fails tomorrow, what could then prevent a military strike on the part of NATO? If there is no agreement tomorrow, what would then prevent --

PRESIDENT CLINTON: I think there would have to be an agreement before the strikes commence. I don't think there is an option. Because, keep in mind, part of what we have asked is that President Milosevic do things that he has already agreed to do, as I said in my opening statement. And we would -- the NATO nations have decided, and have given the Secretary General authority, to pursue a strategy which would at least reduce his capacity to take further aggressive military action against the Kosovar Albanians.

This assumes, of course, that he doesn't accept it and that they do, as we discussed. But that would be my position. I believe that is both our positions.

PRESIDENT CHIRAC: Without a shadow of a doubt.

...

QUESTION: Mr. President, if it appears that the Serbs -- they have to be sanctioned because they refuse the presence of NATO troops in Kosovo, have you the assurance that the Kosovo Liberation Army will renounce its demands on independence?

PRESIDENT CHIRAC: Well, as I said before, the pressure that we are exerting, legitimately, especially we're exercising on both parties, on both sides. And we replied to a question on Serbia because theQuestion was on Serbia, but let's be perfectly clear -- a lot will depend on the personal position adopted by Mr. Milosevic.

But it goes without saying that if the failure, the breakdown, was caused by the Kosovars, their responsibility, sanctions of a different kind, probably, but very firm sanctions would be applied against them. We haven't -- there's no choice. I mean, we don't have to choose. We want peace, that's all.

PRESIDENT CLINTON: First of all, I can entirely support what President Chirac said. But if I could just emphasize that the agreement requires that they accept autonomy, at least for three years, and sets in motion a three-year process to resolve all these outstanding questions. Three years would

give us time to stop the killing, cool the tempers. And it would also give time for the Serbs to argue that if they return to the original constitutional intent -- that is, to have genuine autonomy for Kosovo, as Kosovo once enjoyed -- that that would be the best thing for them, economically and politically. And people would have a chance to see and feel those things.

Right now -- after all that's gone on, and all the people that have died, and all the bloody fighting, and all the incredibly vicious things that have been said -- you know, we just need a timeout here. We need a process within which we can get the security forces out -- as Mr. Milosevic said he would do, before -- and build some internal institutions within Kosovo capable of functioning, and then see how it goes. I think that's the most important thing.

And so, yes -- to go back to what President Chirac said -- yes, both sides have responsibility. Their responsibility would be to acknowledge that that is the deal for the next three years, during which time we resolve the long-term, permanent questions.

Thank you very much.

20. Statement by the NATO Secretary General on behalf of the North Atlantic Council, 19 February 1999

The Alliance today recalls the demands set out in its statement of 30 January 1999, including the necessity of compliance by all parties involved with the appropriate UN Security Council Resolutions.

It expresses its full support to the efforts of the Contact Group to secure an interim political settlement for Kosovo at Rambouillet which provides for a substantially greater degree of autonomy for Kosovo, reaffirms the sovereignty and territorial integrity of the FRY, protects the rights of all national communities, and contains effective measures for its implementation including an international military presence.

The deadline set by the Contact Group for the parties to come to an agreement is approaching fast, underlining the urgency of finding a peaceful solution. They must therefore accept their responsibilities and show the maximum flexibility and political will to bring the negotiations to a successful conclusion.

The crisis in Kosovo remains a threat to peace and security in the region. NATO's strategy is to halt the violence and support the completion of negotiations on an interim political settlement for Kosovo, thus averting a humanitarian catastrophe.

A viable political settlement must be guaranteed by an international military presence. Accordingly, the Alliance is prepared, following acceptance by the parties, to lead a multinational peacekeeping force with broad participation, to implement and enforce the military aspects of an interim agreement, which include specific commitments by both parties, and to contribute to an environment which supports the OSCE and other organisations in the implementation of the civil aspects.

As clearly spelled out in the statement by the North Atlantic Council of 30 January and if no agreement is reached by the deadline set by the Contact Group, NATO is ready to take whatever measures are necessary - in the light of both parties' compliance with international commitments and requirements, including in particular assessment by the Contact Group of the response to its demands - to avert a humanitarian catastrophe by compelling compliance with the demands of the international community and the achievement of a political settlement. These include the use of air strikes as well as other appropriate measures.

NATO has taken appropriate steps to prepare its forces to ensure that they are ready in the event that military action is necessary

21. Department of State Spokesman Briefing on Kosovo peace talks, Rambouillet, 20 February 1999

MR. RUBIN: Right now, Secretary Albright is meeting with President Milutinovic and the Kosovo Albanians are working with some of our technical experts. The work is continuing. There has been no decision about the future because the work is continuing. We are aware of what time it is.

QUESTION: When you say future, you mean bombing --

MR. RUBIN: No, I was asked a question whether BBC is correct to say the deadline has been extended until Monday. No such decision has been made. There are various ideas on how to move from the current situation to an agreement and we may be hearing different peoples ideas of that, but right now, the focus is on achieving an agreement and Secretary Albright is having a one-on-one meeting with President Milutinovic in her hold room. She has held meetings with him with the other Ministers. She has met with the Ministers as a group. She has addressed the entire Kosovo Albanian delegation. She has met privately with three or four of the key Kosovo Albanian leaders and their work is very intense. Everyone has a sense of urgency and I don't think anyone who is telling you what the future will hold, knows the answer to the questions.

QUESTION: But is there a new deadline?

MR. RUBIN: Well, we are aware of what time it is.

QUESTION: OK, so, I mean is the deadline extended? How would you describe it?

MR. RUBIN: We are continuing our work at l:30 (p.m.)

QUESTION: There is a report that there has been a call for the Secretary and the Foreign Secretaries from London and Germany all to go and see Mr. Milosovic.

MR. RUBIN: Nobody is making any such plans right now. The work is focused here on Rambouillet, and that is what we are doing. And everybody who is speculating on the future is entitled to do that, but no decisions have been made.

QUESTION: Has Milosovic asked to see them?

MR. RUBIN: No, not to my knowledge

QUESTION: And is the NATO forces as you all have conceived it "take it or leave it," is that a deal-breaker still?

MR. RUBIN: We are not interested in a partial -- in an approach where the political and the military are separated in terms of the agreement because we believe that we have a lot of experience with agreements in this part of the world, and we think that agreements on paper are not nearly as important as agreements that are complied with through an implementation process.

QUESTION: Can there be a middle ground where it is not necessarily the force as you conceived. There may be a mixture of some military and KVM, a few less troops?

MR. RUBIN: You know NATO has worked on a military implementation plan and I have not heard anybody talking about making substantial adjustments in that implementation plan.

QUESTION: Has the Serb position on NATO deployment changed at all in the last day?

MR. RUBIN: Again, we are continuing the work. If everything were great, we would tell you that. If everything were terrible, we would tell you that too, and so what we are doing is working on it and I really don't want to speak for the delegations.

QUESTION: Does the fact that this is still continuing, does the fact that the talks continue, that the work continues mean that you are still hopeful at this point -- just now of getting an agreement?

MR. RUBIN: I wouldn't say anyone has a sense of clarity about where the future lies. Right now we are focused on trying to achieve a sense of both parties to the Contact Group plan.

QUESTION: Does that mean that you do expect to get an agreement or not? I am confused by that answer.

MR. RUBIN: That is on purpose.

QUESTION: Would you say that the majority of your effort or more of your effort is being focused on getting a political agreement right now with the parties inside or is more of your work focusing on getting NATO into Kosovo ?

MR. RUBIN: I think we are all focused on the idea that this cannot be separated because we have seen agreements, political agreements in the past, not the implemented and each aspect of the work may be at a different point, but the focus is on both questions.

QUESTION: Are you working on the NATO force? ...

MR. RUBIN: Yes, both parties understand what NATO's military implementation enforcement entails, and I am not going to negotiate out here while this work is going on.

QUESTION: Let's roll back. Yesterday, Milosovic would not speak to an American negotiator.

MR. RUBIN: I said that was not encouraging.

QUESTION: Right. Today are the Serbs speaking to Americans about the NATO force?

MR. RUBIN: Secretary Albright and President Milutinovic have been meeting for some time. They started about l:30 p.m. They are probably still talking. They just ended and I need to go back inside and they are not only talking about the political agreement.

QUESTION: Have there been any calls from Milosovic, Jamie?

MR. RUBIN: Not to my knowledge.

## 22.	James Rubin, US Press Briefing, Rambouillet, 20 February 1999

MR. RUBIN: ... Secretary Albright has finished meeting with President Milutinovic, met with most of the Contact Group Ministers and the experts, and Ambassador Hill continues to talk to the Kosovo Albanians. We are determined not to allow the political and military pieces of this to be separated and we will not do that because in the absence of the military implementation of an agreement, we have no reason to believe that it would in fact be implemented. So we are determined to keep those two pieces together and that is obviously one of the difficult hurdles that we are working on and no decisions have been made about precisely how the time will be dealt with, that is, extensions. There have been no decisions and you may have heard again, different delegations suggesting their specific ideas of the time question be addressed, but there have been no decisions.

QUESTION: What do you say about the comment Mr. Thaci made about threats from the Serbs that if he didn't sign the political agreement, that they would kill him or something like that?

MR. RUBIN: I understood that there were some pictures taken that he was concerned about inside, but you know, we know that the KLA and the Serbs have been fighting for a long time and so we are aware of that and that is the reason we are here. But certainly we don't support threats by anybody to kill anybody.

QUESTION: Jamie, a couple of questions about the NATO peacekeeping force. Does it matter to the United States indeed if it is under NATO as for instance, under UN supervision in some way? And must the whole issue be resolved here or would it be enough of an accomplishment to get the principle established and you know, fill in the pieces a bit later on?

MR. RUBIN: First of all, there is no consideration being given by the United States about a NATO implementation force, period. That doesn't mean it couldn't be endorsed by the United Nations, but as far as who would do the job and how it would operate, it is only a NATO force that's been considered. As far as when is an agreement an agreement, we are here trying to break the back of two main questions. Question one, the political arrangements by which the Kosovo Albanians can live with self-government for the next three years, and question number two, is the requirement that there be a military implementation of any such agreement. Those are the main questions. Those are the questions we are trying to get answered in the affirmative. Everyone knows that if one wrote those questions, you may still have technical things you work on, but those are the main questions.

QUESTION: Are there now divisions between the NATO allies and the question of separating or not separating the military and the political?

MR. RUBIN: No, I just wanted to make sure that everyone understood our views.

QUESTION: Not at all? No (inaudible).

MR. RUBIN: You will have to ask others for their views.

QUESTION: In which way is OSCE involved in this?

MR. RUBIN: The OSCE is obviously planning the key role in supervising the KVM and obviously their evacuation is something that is on people's minds, and if the agreement is struck, it is our view that the KVM, the OSCE will need to be involved in the monitoring process along with NATO.

QUESTION: Why should Milosovic take the United States and the other members of the Contact Group seriously in their threat to reach an agreement by a new deadline when quite clearly we've already past that deadline by three hours. Why should Milosovic take us at our word?

MR. RUBIN: The United States and the President of the United States have made clear our intentions. If the Serbs are responsible for a breakdown of these talks and whether or not it occurs at 3:01 or 4:01 or 12:01, doesn't change NATO's determination to act.

QUESTION: What has happened since the deadline past that has kept you talking? Has there been any actual progress or do you just keep talking about the same thing over and over again?

MR. RUBIN: My experience in these negotiations is until you have these types of negotiations and you will of course talk about the same subject over and over again until you either get an agreement or you conclude you can't.

QUESTION: Is there a benchmark you are using at which point you will say look, we are just not going to get it?

MR. RUBIN: Again, this is a judgment call. That is why diplomats are here, senior diplomats are here, senior ministers are here so that they can make these judgment calls and it is our view that we have to keep the political and military tracks moving and that we can't separate them and we are determined to do that, and if the Serbs are responsible for these discussions breaking down, they would be making a big mistake to think the fact that we continue to talk for a couple of hours is going to change NATO's determination to act.

QUESTION: Is it fair to say that a compromise may be emerging with two elements. One, your comment about the UN possibly blessing a NATO force and two --

MR. RUBIN: That's been part of this for a long time, there is nothing new about that.

QUESTION: It isn't. Well, I also heard there was some talk about the semantics, which is what exactly you would call this force that goes in?

MR. RUBIN: That's not what is the issue being debated right now in any serious way.

QUESTION: What about the placement of the NATO force? ...

MR. RUBIN: That is the level of detail I would prefer not to get into but the military preparations for NATO continue at NATO and they are doing that work and we are determined to keep the political and military tracks.

QUESTION: On the political side, can you confirm that some of the issues include the assembly, the judicial system?

MR. RUBIN: The political side? You know, this agreement has a number of complex components, but the basic points remain the same which is self-government for the Kosovo Albanians. You know this is a long document and the words continue to be discussed; meaning, I don't want to discuss out here what is being debated inside in any detail.

QUESTION: Have there been any phone calls by any of the Contact Group foreign ministers or Secretary Albright to Milosovic?

MR. RUBIN: The Secretary hasn't; I couldn't speak for the rest.

QUESTION: What does Secretary Albright bring, if anything with her, to the talks at Rambouillet or is it the same standard line that she is reiterating in the Chateau right now. Has she brought anything in addition to what she has said in the past?

MR. RUBIN: No, I mean we are here to try to -- you know everyone recognized that in the final 24 hours the discussions would become more intense and that decisions would have to be made. These are tough political decisions and what she brought is her presence to try to galvanize decision-making and the decisions are nearing the time when they will have to be made.

QUESTION: Has she conferred with President Clinton today during the course (inaudible).

MR. RUBIN: The delegation briefed the White House.

QUESTION: Have the Albanians accepted the political aspects of the deal?

MR. RUBIN: Again, I don't want to get in the middle of what is going on in there. There is obviously a couple of points I wanted to make, wanted to give you an update. You may be hearing a lot of to-ing and fro-ing from different people about what deadline, what has passed or not passed, and that no decisions have been made.

QUESTION: Has anyone talked about rehabilitation assistance?

MR. RUBIN: Yes, I think that the draft agreement envisages major reconstruction assistance for the Kosovo Albanians and that is certainly part of the reason why we think they should see their way clear to an agreement.

QUESTION: Surely to bring this to a close, you need some kind of a deadline or use some other word if you like, I mean, the end of today, tomorrow, otherwise it could just go on and on forever?

MR. RUBIN: We recognize the nature of diplomacy and the importance of using deadlines to bring decision-making. We think it is working, it is a few hours after 12:00 and there is a lot of intense discussion about real political decisions. And as far as what a further deadline would look like or could be, I just can't confirm for you what the intentions of the ministers are.

23. Conclusions of the Contact Group, Rambouillet, 20 February 1999

A fortnight ago, the FRY and Serb delegation and the Kosovar delegation, summoned by the Contact Group to meet, agreed to come to Rambouillet.The aim of these negotiations was to reach an interim agreement on substantial autonomy for Kosovo while respecting the FRY's national sovereignty and territorial integrity.

The purpose was to allow the inhabitants of Kosovo to live again in peace.Last week, in Paris, we decided to extend these negotiations by one additional week. They were to end at noon today.No effort has been spared either by the three negotiators or by the member states of the Contact Group to achieve this goal.

Today, Contact Group ministers heard the Parties and the report of the negotiators. Very substantial progress has been made in reaching

agreement on the Framework and Political Chapters of the Interim Agreement for Peace and Self-Government in Kosovo.

At the request of the Parties, we believe that this justifies an ultimate effort to finalise as a whole the Interim Agreement and the proposed arrangements for an international military and civilian presence in Kosovo, if so agreed by the Parties, to implement and guarantee the Interim Agreement. This work must be completed by 15.00 on Tuesday 23 February 1999.Ministers recalled that they had spelt out in London on 29 January and Paris on 14 February, that those responsible for the failure of the talks would be held accountable.

24. Secretary of State Albright, Press conference on the Kosovo, France, 20 February 1999

SECRETARY ALBRIGHT: (in progress) Ambassador Hill and his colleagues have bridged many major gaps and resolved most of the political issues which divided the parties. The Kosovar Albanians have negotiated with discipline and unity of purpose. They have not yet accepted every element of the interim political settlement, but it was my judgment and that of my Contact Group colleagues that the remaining issues can be resolved with a reasonable amount of effort.

Belgrade, in contrast, has taken every opportunity for evasion and delay. The Serb delegation bears the lion's share of responsibility for the difficulties we have experienced today. Belgrade has said that it can accept the political settlement although my sense is that this is not completely firm. However, the Serb refusal to even consider the presence of a NATO-led military implementation force in Kosovo is largely responsible for the failure to reach full agreement.

For this reason, we were extremely reluctant to offer the parties more time to reach an agreement, but the Contact Group believes the remaining differences can, with hard work and good will, be resolved, and the Contact Group has given them until 3 o'clock Tuesday afternoon to finalize the settlement.

Let me stress that we expect nothing less than a complete interim agreement including Belgrade's acceptance of a NATO-led force and a civilian mission building on the OSCE's Kosovo verification mission. Until the parties have accepted all provisions of the agreement, preparations for NATO military action will continue and if that agreement is not confirmed by Tuesday, Secretary General Solana will draw the appropriate conclusions. This is not the outcome any of us had hoped for, but our work is not over, and I haven't given up hope that faced with the bleak alternatives, both sides will agree to take yes for an answer on every element of this settlement.

The objectives of the United States, of our Contact Group partners remain unchanged. We seek a solution that offers Kosovo Albanians the rights that have so long been denied, while protecting the security of all of Kosovo's people. We will not permit Belgrade to conduct repressive operations against the people of Kosovo, or to create a new humanitarian catastrophe, and we will build on the hard work done here by the Contact Group negotiators, and by the co-chairs Robin Cook and Hubert Vedrine. Their determination will be needed even more in the days ahead. When I spoke to President Clinton earlier this afternoon, he and I agreed that the international community and the United States must stay the course, and we will.

QUESTION: Madam Secretary, if this is a fair construction, it would seem the Serbs gave enough on the political front to move the deadline, and keep you here, for instance, just short of a trip you have to make to Asia, that's an important trip. Given Milosevic's track record, given what's happened here, isn't it possible that he will give just enough on a NATO force to prevent a breakdown, but not enough to satisfy the United States and its partners? In a sense, I am asking you if he isn't, in a sense, playing you along a little bit?

SECRETARY ALBRIGHT: Well, I think that today was a little bit more complicated than that, Barry. I think that what we said -- and let me take a little time to explain this -- is that the Kosovar Albanians, I think, needed and felt that they needed additional clarification on some of the political aspects of the interim accord, and from my perspective, the reason for extending the deadline had to do with that. They felt that they needed more time and work -- and I am speaking only for myself in this, the others may have made different calculations -- but that there needed to be additional clarification and that they had not given an unqualified yes, but that they had as a whole understood what was needed, and clearly, this is a very difficult issue. We are dealing with how they see the future of how their people will be able to govern themselves.

As far as the Serbs were concerned, they basically, I think, were not focusing that much on the political agreement, and felt that on the whole, they could accept that. The problem was that they did not want to engage at all on the security part of it, and for us that is a complete non-starter, because a political agreement without the military annexes is just a piece of paper. The security annexes are needed in order to implement the political agreement, and be concerned about what we are concerned about, which is the security of the people and the ability of a lot of the aspects of the political agreement to take root -- all the local institutions that are supposed to take root -- and therefore, just making an agreement on the political part doesn't do any good.

So, the question is, I believe, that it will be possible to clarify some of the questions that the Kosovar Albanians have in the deadline given, but I do think that we are going to have to verify the bona fides and all of the Serbs as to whether they are willing to deal on the military annex.

QUESTION: Madam Secretary, have you been in touch, have you or any of your other Minister colleagues been in touch with Milosevic today; do you expect to be in touch with him in the next 48 hours, is anybody going to Belgrade to talk to him directly? And, do we interpret from all of what's gone on the last hour that you will stay through the deadline?

SECRETARY ALBRIGHT: First of all, let me say as far as I know, no one has been in touch with Milosevic today. It is unclear as to what plans are for people to or not to be in touch with him. I think my first order of business is to deal with the Kosovar Albanians to try to help in making and helping these explanations, helping them understand more what this document contains, so I have no plans to go to Belgrade. I think that there's a dynamic here that is a dynamic that develops in any kind of thing, so obviously, I don't rule anything in or rule anything out, as Jamie has taught me to say. But, there are no plans.

QUESTION: Is it fair to say that the last version that you have invited the parties to consider as the final one is more accommodating to the Serbian demands?

SECRETARY ALBRIGHT: I do not think that is fair to say. I think that in any negotiation, the negotiators try to work out something that works for both sides in terms of developing what I think will be a unique structure in terms of autonomy, and that I would hope that as the Kosovar group really understands fully the depth of self-government that they will be allowed as a result of this, that it will be seen as a prototype document of what an autonomous region, where the people will be able to have local elections, local police, etc. I think it's a very interesting document that is being worked out as carefully and neutrally and fairly as possible by excellent negotiators.

QUESTION: Madame Secretary, if I understand you correctly, it sounds as if you are somewhat optimistic that by Tuesday's deadline you will be able to clarify the remaining points on the Kosovar Albanian side, but you sound, or seem to sound, less optimistic that you will able to close the remaining gaps and convince Milosevic to accept a NATO-led force. Is that correct?

SECRETARY ALBRIGHT: I would say that is a fair assessment. I think that their lack of desire to engage at all today on that subject, I found unrealistic and unproductive, and since they fully have understood that it is impossible to have a political document without, if I can put it this way, the legs of the security aspect of it, otherwise it is just a table top with no legs, and it is impossible without it. So I would say that's it.

QUESTION: I just wanted to ask very quickly about whether there is unity among the Contact Group members for this NATO-led force as you see it.

SECRETARY ALBRIGHT: I think you know that the Russians do not favor such a force. However, they have in various conversations and letters made it clear that they had no objections in us passing, working the military annex.

QUESTION: Madame Secretary, given your statement just now that there has been no budging at all by the Serbs on the military question, and the repeated statements in past days and today by the U.S. that the two, the military and the political, must be part of the same agreement, what reason at all do you have to hope that there will be any change between now and Tuesday? Why extend the deadline at all?

SECRETARY ALBRIGHT: Well, first of all, I think that we have a responsibility as Contact Group members and the negotiators to try everything that we can. And today, as I made clear, was not clear-cut. There were questions by the Kosovo Albanians about the political document that I think are worth answering and dealing with, and also I think we have known in the past when dealings in negotiations that often the dynamics of pressures change, and it is my hope that in the next forty-eight hours that President Milosevic will understand that this agreement is one that will, I think, provide a way for the Kosovar Albanians to have a good and decent and autonomous life within Serbia and one that will be set up in a way to

protect the people, the ordinary people, who are suffering from the fighting. So I would hope that President Milosevic would wake up and smell the coffee.

QUESTION: Just to follow up on that, why, since there have been all of these extensions, should he believe that this time you really are serious? And also, you are saying that you still don't have complete agreement with the Kosovo Albanians, but knowing your famous persuasive powers, it seems likely that you might have been able to get that today, and there are reports that in fact some of the European allies said were really politically here, we need to give this extension, and I wonder if you could comment on both those things.

SECRETARY ALBRIGHT: Well, I think that, first of all, let me say that we are dealing with a very complicated document as far as the political issues are concerned, and the Kosovar Albanians as a delegation believe, and I agree with them, that they have a huge responsibility to make sure that they get what they can for their people and they want to be assured that this is an agreement that does provide, that it is an interim agreement, and that it does provide the best kind of ability for them to exercise their rights. And I think that, I thought we were pretty close today, but we weren't able to push it over the goal line. I think it's worth trying, and I think it's worth pushing again with Milosevic. I think that Milosevic would make a grave mistake to miscalculate about our intentions, and that we are not into endless extensions. As I said last time, as a professor I don't like to do that. But I did think that there have been, from the Kosovar side, it was really worth giving an extra couple of days.

QUESTION: Madame Secretary, do you believe that the international community can expect a just and long-standing solution for Kosovo while democracy still is, and I'm afraid is going to stay, persona non grata in Serbia?

SECRETARY ALBRIGHT: It is clearly part of the difficulty of the problem. I would think that at some stage the people of Yugoslavia and Serbia would see that their country keeps diminishing under this leadership, that it started out a fairly large country, and it is losing various pieces of it. We are very supportive of a free media and the possibilities for oppositions to function within Serbia, and I think our constant pressure on that line is something that is a part of what we are doing. I do think that it is possible for even this leadership to understand that it is in its interests to go forward with the kind of agreement that is being presented here. That the political aspect of it is a very carefully drawn-out document, as I have stated, and that the implementation, the military aspect, will provide security and the ability of not only Albanians but also the minorities in Kosovo to be able to pursue a normal life.

QUESTION: Secretary Albright, you mentioned before and have repeated today that you see this agreement as being part of a process of creating new forms of sovereignty and new kinds of political structures. You've also mentioned questions that the Kosovo Albanian side has had with the political aspects. Can you go into any more detail about that? Can you at least tell us anything about the themes that have come up in their concerns?

SECRETARY ALBRIGHT: I have not been part of all the deliberations with them, but I think that what is important here is that they wish to be able to have an identity that is respected, and that allows their people to have elections and local police and, as you know, one of the major issues in the last years has been the ability of Albanians to get an education in their own language, and to be able to have the kinds of schools and worship the way they want to. So that those are some of the themes within the political document, one that creates an ability, and this is my belief about how many groups or many entities may function in the future is, that there is a great deal of autonomy at the local level, allowing people to be able to live their lives according to their (inaudible.)

QUESTION: You express a great deal of confidence about getting Kosovar Albanian agreement by Tuesday, but apparently they are still insisting upon a referendum on independence after three years. Isn't that a pretty big obstacle?

SECRETARY ALBRIGHT: Well, they are definitely, that is the point that they are concerned about, but I think that the language as it is being developed, makes it very clear that this is an interim agreement, that at its termination would take into consideration a number of different factors in determining what the permanent status of Kosovo would be. Among those things, to use the diplomatic word "inter alia," there is, in fact, how to assess the views of the people. And I think that it is a matter of how it is all worded in this document, but I think what is very important for people to know is that this is an interim document, and this goes to the question the gentleman asked about Serbia. Three years in our very dynamic world can bring very different results, and after three years of people being able to elect their own officials, have their local police, their own schools, and relate differently to Belgrade, I think it is very hard to predict exactly what mechanisms would be the most useful for determining the status of Kosovo ultimately. This is an interim agreement that has a lot of dynamic aspects to it, and I am sure that there will be many changes both in Kosovo and in Serbia in the next three years. Thank you.

25. James Rubin, Press Briefing on the Kosovo peace talks, Rambouillet, France, 21 February 1999

MR. RUBIN: Secretary Albright has been at the Chateau for several hours. Secretary Albright met first over lunch with the four main leaders of the Kosovar Albanian delegation. They spent about an hour and a half together. Clearly what we are trying to do is help to push the Kosovar Albanians across the finish line so that they can agree to the combined political and military package that the Contact Group has put together. She is now meeting with the President of Serbia, Milutinovic. There, what she is hoping to do, is to see whether President Milotunovic will begin to see whether President Milutinovic will for the first time engage seriously on the requirement that the agreement be a political agreement combined with military implementation. I don't know what the outcome of that discussion is, but based on previous discussions, it's hard to be optimistic that the Serb President will engage seriously on that subject.

QUESTION: Why did she decide to meet him today? You had said yesterday, she had said yesterday the focus was going to be on the Kosovar side where she saw the problem being. Why did she decide to meet with Milotunovic?

MR. RUBIN: The Secretary is in the Chateau. She had a lengthy meeting with the four Kosovar Albanian leaders. She deputized Ambassador Dobbins, Ambassador Hill, the chief negotiator, to work with the Kosovar Albanians to try to work through their concerns and get the necessary clarifications that they would need in order to be able to move forward and agree to the combined military and political agreement.

President Milutinovic is in the castle. This is not simply a one-sided equation. What I'm suggesting to you is that it's perfectly appropriate for her to meet with President Milotunovic, again to see whether they will be able to or willing to engage seriously on the crucial military question, but given past practice, it is hard to be optimistic that they will. So, that is a proposition one wants to test regularly in order to see whether anything has changed.

QUESTION: The Kosovars have not agreed with the agreement?

MR. RUBIN: The Kosovar Albanians have moved in the direction that we want, have been doing so. We're working very hard at it. I'm not here to say that we've achieved that. That would be an extraordinarily difficult thing to achieve. Remember what we're dealing with here. We're dealing with the people who have to make fundamental life and death decisions. Anyone who thinks that this can happen in the snap of a finger doesn't understand what it is like to be a people who have been oppressed for so long.

QUESTION: But if the Albanians are moving the way they are, doesn't that put extra pressure on the Serbs? Doesn't it make their intransigence more likely to lead to military response?

MR. RUBIN: We believe it is extremely important to put pressure on the Serbs. We cannot put the full amount of pressure if we don't get an agreement from the Kosovar Albanians. Contrary to what many of you seem to believe, it has never been the view of NATO or the United States that a Serb refusal along with a Kosovar Albanian refusal would necessarily lead to NATO military action. All of the officials who have worked on this have made very clear that in order to move towards military action, it has to be clear that the Serbs were responsible. So the fact that yesterday we didn't move towards military action when neither party gave a full yes, should not have come as a surprise to any of you who have been watching or listening closely to what the Administration or NATO officials have been saying.

QUESTION: Well that's the point of the question. With the Albanians moving closer to agreement, doesn't that increase the likelihood that the Serbs will be the clear and only offender and subject to military force?

MR. RUBIN: It's very difficult to be half pregnant in a situation like this. One needs to decide whether one can achieve agreement, and know who's responsible, and gray makes it more difficult to put the kind of pressure that you've asked about.

QUESTION: (inaudible) the Serbs made some (inaudible) concession or not?

MR. RUBIN: The Serb side, as I've indicated, I don't know what the results of Secretary Albright's meeting with President Milotunovic will be. She's doing it right now. But based on previous meetings and discussions that Ambassador Hill has had with President Milotunovic, it is hard to be optimistic that they are going to engage seriously on the important question of the combination of a political agreement and a military agreement which in our view are inseparable.

QUESTION: So what will you do Tuesday afternoon after 3 o'clock?

MR. RUBIN: Well, today is Sunday about 5 o'clock, that gives us 46 hours in which to make that decision, and that decision will be made by more than one country, and all I can tell you is that we believe it's extremely important, as negotiators and leaders of this negotiation, to use deadlines to exert pressure so that political decisions are made. In the absence of political decisions being made, we can't move this process forward.

QUESTION: Then the Secretary will definitely stay till Tuesday?

MR. RUBIN: No decision about her future activities has been made.

QUESTION: Is there any room for negotiation on the military annex?

MR. RUBIN: The NATO view is clear. And that is that it has to be a NATO force with a NATO chain of command and sufficient size and authority to do the job. And I've heard no NATO countries make any serious changes in those basic objectives.

QUESTION: Considering the dissent within the Contact Group on air strikes, Russia saying it's needless and inadmissible yesterday, won't the U.S. go it alone?

MR. RUBIN: I don't accept the premise of your question. The Russians have never been part of NATO's decision making on air strikes. We have never expected Russia to be supportive of the possibility of air attacks and NATO Secretary General now has the authority to act based on an assessment of what goes on here at Rambouillet, and that assessment is not going to be affected by the description you have. If NATO were to act, that would be 16 countries, not the (inaudible).

NATO is an alliance with 16 countries. The fact that Russia doesn't support military action is not a surprise, but NATO's authority has been given to Secretary General Solana. He has that authority and he doesn't need to seek political authority from any other body.

QUESTION: Is Secretary Albright thinking of going to Belgrade at all for direct talks?

MR. RUBIN: No decisions on that.

QUESTION: Will NATO accept Russians along if there are going to be ground troops?

MR. RUBIN: We would welcome Russian participation in any peace keeping force along the lines the Russians participated in Bosnia. I think there have been some discussions to that effect, but I don't believe that decisions have been made, it would be up to Russia to describe its view, but we've certainly been welcoming of it.

QUESTION: (inaudible)

MR. RUBIN: Well, it depends on who you're talking to. NATO remember, is 16 countries, 14 of which come from Europe, all of whom have given Secretary General Solana this authority, so they've already made that decision.

26. James Rubin, Press Briefing on the Kosovo peace talks, Rambouillet, France, 21 February 1999

MR. RUBIN: Any suggestion that the Secretary of State has given the Kosovar Albanians a deadline of midnight tonight is false. What is not false is that Secretary Albright expressed a great sense of urgency in the meetings today and asked for the Kosovar Albanians to work closely with Ambassador Hill and other members of her delegation and the negotiating team to work their way through the texts as quickly as possible. She indicated that she wasn't sure of her schedule, and they talked about different problems that they wanted to work on. I do expect the Secretary to stay overnight in Paris, and she will be receiving an update in the next couple of hours from Ambassador Hill as to whether she should return to the Castle tonight, or whether she should proceed to further meetings tomorrow morning. No decisions have been made about that but she certainly expressed a sense of urgency.

QUESTION: So she may return tonight?

MR. RUBIN: It's possible. I wouldn't rule it out.

QUESTION: (Inaudible)

MR. RUBIN: I wouldn't say that either. The way negotiations work is that the lawyers and the detail people work through texts, they work on subjects, and they try to save big issues for the political decisions that often can be made with the assistance of the Secretary of State, so they may have worked themselves down to a couple of things they want to know, a couple of clarifications, a couple of assurances, at which point she could be involved. So the fact that she would be returning wouldn't necessarily mean that we were going to get to yes, but it could mean that we're getting closer.

QUESTION: Tell me why the Albanians think that there is a deadline. What is in her presentation could lead them to come away and think that there's a deadline?

MR. RUBIN: I think she expressed a sense of urgency to them.

QUESTION: And to the Serbs, too, by the way?

MR. RUBIN: I think that the focus, as I indicated to you, of her efforts today has been on the Kosovar Albanians. She met with President Milutinovic, with not high hopes that he was going to change his basic tune, and her hopes were not unrealized, if you can get all those double negatives.

QUESTION: How tough did she talk to the Albanians?

MR. RUBIN: She explained to them very clearly, as she explained to all of you, but maybe they didn't understand, that if one is to apply the military pressure on the Serbs that is necessary to get them to agree or that is the only way to get them to agree, that we need to work from the Kosovar Albanian yes, in order for Secretary General Solana to draw the appropriate conclusions. And so I think she explained very forcefully that reality. And, they, I think, sensed a sense of urgency on her part, and based on her schedule, which she might have told them, I don't know if I'm going to stay till tomorrow, they might have seen that as more than it was. She has told them about her schedule the same that she has told me, that I told you, which is she doesn't know how long she's going to stay.

QUESTION: Are any of the Albanians expressing any kind of concerns about if you pull out the --

MR. RUBIN: I'm sorry, let me just add to this that it doesn't rule out there may have been a misunderstanding about this, because, you know, that happens, but I'm confirming to all of you, and I suspect they may find out about this too, I will certainly let them know that they (inaudible) ... Yes, she expressed a sense of urgency, she said she wants to start as soon as possible, as early as tonight was basically her message.

QUESTION: Have any of the Albanians expressed concern about after you pull out the Kosovo verification mission and start dropping bombs on the Serbs, that the Serbs in Kosovo might become increasingly surly?

MR. RUBIN: No. No, I haven't heard them say that. I've been in most of the meetings, if they have those concerns they haven't expressed them.

QUESTION: They've indicated to you that they would not mind you bombing?

MR. RUBIN: They have not answered that question. Let me be very clear on that. What she has done is to explain to them certain realities, very much like she explained to all of you in the rain about what the different courses of action are. ...

27.   Draft for Chapter 8, Article 1 (3), 22 February 1999, 05.25 hrs, and proposed draft side-letter

Three years after entry into force of this agreement, an international meeting shall be convened to determine a mechanism for a Final Settlement for Kosovo on the basis of the expressed will of the people, opinions of relevant authorities, each Party's efforts regarding the implementation of this agreement, and the Helsinki Final Act, and to undertake a comprehensive assessment of the implementation of this Agreement and to consider proposals by any Party for additional measures.

Rambouillet, 22 February 1999

This letter concerns the formulation (attached) [*above*] proposed for Chapter 8, Article 1 (3) of the interim Framework Agreement. We will regard this proposal, or any other formulation of that Article that may be agreet at Rambouillet, as confirming a right for the people of Kosovo to hold a referendum on the final status of Kosovo after three years.

Sincerely,
Madeline Albright, Secretary of State

[Note: *This letter, possibly only seen by the US legal advisers who drafted it during that dramatic night, was not signed and only remained a draft. The US took the position that it would only be available should Kosovo sign the agreement by the deadline. Nevertheless, Kosovo communicated its understandings along the lines indicated in the letter to the US Secretary of State when making its declaration of acceptance in principle at the conclusion of the Rambouillet talks, see Document 14.B. 35.*]

28.   James Rubin, Department of State Briefing, Rambouillet, 23 March 1999

MR. RUBIN: Secretary Albright has been meeting with key members of the Kosovo Albanian delegation. Since we all last talked last night, she spoke on the phone with Secretary General Solana. She spoke in the middle of the night to President Clinton. She has consulted twice now with Foreign Minister Cook, last night and again this morning. She spoke also this morning to Foreign Minister Ivanov, and she just spoke to the Prime Minister of Albania, Prime Minister Majko and last night to Foreign Minister of Albania Milo, and obviously there it is to try to get the political support from the Albanian government for the emerging agreement. All I can say as far as the status of the two sides are concerned, is so far this morning she has not yet met with officials from the Serb side. We do expect Milutinovic here this morning or at some point today. She has been focused on the Kosovo Albanians. The negotiators worked all night until I believe 7:30, 8:00 in the morning on the documents, and Ambassador Hill called her very early and said that he thought it would be helpful if she came here this morning to try to advance the process. The Kosovo Albanians continue to move towards agreement with the plan put forward here at Rambouillet. The Serbian delegation, although working on the political side, still is not prepared to engage seriously on the military piece which is an integral part of the package..

QUESTION: You said the negotiations last night were with the Albanians exclusively.

MR. RUBIN: No, that was with both the Serbs and Albanians all night long by Ambassador Hill and his negotiating team.

QUESTION: What is the problem with the Albanians still? What is still the catch?

MR. RUBIN: Well, I'd rather not specify any specific wording other than to say that the main point remains and that is for them understanding that the Contact Group plan does envision an expression of the will of the people to be taken into account at the end of the three years, but not a situation where the international community is going to endorse a recognized referendum with respect to independence. That's the same point where we were yesterday, but the more we explain it to them that it is real progress to them to have the international community make clear that it is not precluded and that this agreement doesn't decide the future. It creates an interim agreement that gives them the self-government that they so desperately and justly deserve; a very high degree of self-government. It gets the Serb forces out that have been oppressing them, and it brings in the NATO forces. Those are the three pillars of the agreement and that is what has been focused on, but it is correct that the Kosovo Albanians are still seeking clarifications on the issue of the referendum and other relatively minor issues.

The text thing is long, there is a habit as one problem is solved, another problem pops up. And what we are trying to do is close the gaps where the problems pop up and get to a place where there is full agreement and that, in the final hours, can always be a big challenge.

QUESTION: Do you believe you can bring this to closure with the Kosovars today?

MR. RUBIN: I am not going to make any predictions. This is an extraordinarily difficult enterprise. We are asking people to make their decisions that will affect their lives for a long time. It is a life and death issue for them. We believe we are continuing to move in the right direction. We want to get across the finish line with the Kosovo Albanians as soon as possible, but I am not going to make any predictions.

QUESTION: As far as the Serbs are concerned, would the United States consider easing sanctions, either sanctions imposed last year or the outer wall of sanctions to get them to...?

MR. RUBIN: Our position on that is that there were sanctions imposed by the international community last year affecting privatization, affecting investment in Serbia, affecting visas for Serb officials, prohibiting airline flights. Those were all put into place because of the Serb crackdown on Kosovo, and if a peace agreement were signed and implemented that ended that crackdown, remove Serbian forces to a large extent and brought in NATO, the reasons for that set of sanctions would no longer be there and the United States and others would act accordingly.

With respect to the outer wall, that is, things like participation in international financial institutions, we have said that that is something that we would consider taking into account a number of factors including progress on Kosovo, but there has been no serious discussion by us of anything beyond that.

QUESTION: A little about her conversation with the President. Did China and her trip come up? It is an important trip, I take it. Is it going to be delayed? Did the President encourage her to keep at it endlessly, or tell us what you can about that conversation and about the rest of her world agenda which I think extends beyond Kosovo.

MR. RUBIN: Well, thank you for pointing out the obvious, Barry, that it does extend beyond Kosovo. However, America has important interests in Kosovo. The United States is prepared to commit, under the circumstances the President described, ground forces to a peace implementation force, and therefore, that by itself speaks volumes about the importance of this issue to the United States and therefore the appropriateness of the Secretary of State being here to try to advance it. And there are many other issues in the world.

... QUESTION: Jamie, is there any discussion, how do you move the Serbs forward on the military side? Any discussion of changing the composition, the leadership of the military force on the ground, any discussion of a trip to Belgrade by either the Secretary of State or any minister?

MR. RUBIN: I think that it has been our judgment all along that it is only the credible threat and the reality of military pressure that will bring President Milosevic to understand the need to move on the military portion of this integrated agreement. And, as I have indicated and the Secretary made very clear yesterday, the best way to get that pressure and the reality of military force is to get the Kosovo Albanians across the finish line, so that NATO can be in a position to act. So that is what she is focused on.

With respect to trips to Belgrade, I don't have anything to report to you about Secretary Albright's plans. I am not aware of anyone else at this point planning to travel. I have heard that the other ministers may be in telephone contact with President Milosevic shortly, but it would be up to those ministers to describe any such plans or any result from such calls. We all know who the decision maker is in Serbia and it is President Milosevic, but we don't believe that in the absence of the reality of military force which can only happen if we cross this extraordinarily difficult finish line and get the Kosovo Albanians to agree and that is when that pressure will be real in the mind of the leadership in Serbia.

QUESTION: What happens if you don't get the Kosovo Albanians across the finishing line, as you put it, by Tuesday's deadline? Do you stay here until you do?

MR. RUBIN: Well, that's one of those questions that is a totally legitimate question, but is not going to yield an answer that will be satisfied. We are determined to do what we can do to get the Kosovo Albanians to say "yes." If we don't, we will review the bidding at that time, but we don't want to see that happen and therefore, we don't want to speculate about what would happen if it did.

QUESTION: Serb forces (inaudible) on the move in Kosovo. There has been some shelling in the last couple of days. They seem to be taking advantage of the lull in pressure here. Do you have a message for Milosevic on that front?

MR. RUBIN: Secretary Albright in her conversation with President Milutinovic made very clear that there is another piece of this puzzle, and that is compliance with the October agreement and that the Serbs should not misunderstand or focus on negotiations as losing sight of the importance of their not breaking the agreement of last October and conducting military operations in Kosovo. There has been fighting, we have told the Serbs that this is precisely the wrong thing to do and we have tried to make sure that any activity in Kosovo does not spin out of control both through the work of the KVM on the ground and through discussion here. It would be a big mistake for the Serbs to escalate the fighting on the ground. They should remember that the credible reality of military pressure is coming to bear on them precisely because of the offensive operation conducted at Racak, which led the international community to this point.

QUESTION: Jamie, the German Foreign Minister said yesterday in Luxembourg there will be no more extension, no deadline extensions as far as he is concerned. Is that the Secretary's view too? Is tomorrow afternoon still a deadline?

MR. RUBIN: From now on, in order to avoid any misunderstandings from some of you, I am not going to speak about tomorrow and the next day and day after that. We need deadlines to concentrate the minds of decision-makers, and as far as we are concerned, we are not talking about extending the deadline at this point and that is where we are.

QUESTION: Are the Kosovars asking for, insisting on any movement by the Serbs on the NATO troop issue before they give their "yes"?

MR. RUBIN: No, the Kosovars are being asked the question of whether they can agree to the agreement that is on the table and they are focused on whether they can agree to the agreement, not whether the Serbs can agree to the agreement.

QUESTION: But before they are willing to finally put their name on their part of the agreement, does anyone on the Kosovar side ask that they get some kind of sign, some kind of a commitment from the Serb side on

whether --?

MR. RUBIN: I haven't heard that. That strikes me as self-defeating given the fact that I have just said the Serbs are not engaging seriously on the military piece of the puzzle, so I haven't heard anybody suggest that other than you, Michael.

29. James Rubin, Interview, Rambouillet, 23 February 1999

MR. RUBIN: The final text has been presented to the two sides. What we're doing now is hoping to get an answer from the two sides. We certainly hope that the Kosovar Albanians seize this historic opportunity not only for peace, but for them receiving an incredible amount of self-government, running their own lives, for a situation which Serb forces would be removed that have been threatening them, and a situation where NATO forces would come in to protect them. It's an historic opportunity for them; but only they can make this decision. We're awaiting that.

QUESTION: So you're still not confident that the Kosovar Albanians will accept this text, even after we're now up to the fourth day of trying to convince them?

MR. RUBIN: Well, again, people who are suffering from this kind of oppression have their own ways and their own decisions they have to make. Unfortunately for the people of Kosovo, this conflict is in an early stage. It's not like the conflict between the Israelis and the Palestinians; it's not even like the conflict in Bosnia, which was finally solved after many, many conferences at Dayton. This is at an early stage, and the parties may not be exhausted.

So we're hoping that they can move forward as far as they can move so that we can make this an important chapter in the Kosovo story where we move closer down the road to peace. But peace is a process, it's not an event.

QUESTION: We understand that this final text was worked on through the night by the negotiators. That means, obviously, final amendments. Is there not a danger now that the Serb delegation will come back in these final -- (inaudible) – before the deadline and say they, too, are no longer happy with it and then we have both sides, neither of them agreeing?

MR. RUBIN: Well, neither side has ever agreed to the text. So you can't lose one side when you're trying to gain the other, because you never had one side.

The job of negotiators is to work on texts; to take into account all the legitimate concerns of both sides; to try to close the gaps where they can; and ultimately, to lead the leaders to make the political decisions.

30. Interim Agreement for Peace and Self-Government in Kosovo, 23 February 1999

CONTENTS
Framework
Chapter 2: Police and Civil Public Security
Chapter 3: Conduct and Supervision of Elections
Chapter 4a: Economic Issues
Chapter 5: Implementation I
Chapter 6: Ombudsman
Chapter 7: Implementation
Appendices
Chapter 8: Amendment, Comprehensive Assessment, and Final Clauses

The Parties to the present Agreement,

<u>Convinced</u> of the need for a peaceful and political solution in Kosovo as a prerequisite for stability and democracy,

<u>Determined</u> to establish a peaceful environment in Kosovo,

<u>Reaffirming</u> their commitment to the Purposes and Principles of the United Nations, as well as to OSCE
principles, including the Helsinki Final Act and the Charter of Paris for a new Europe,

<u>Recalling</u> the commitment of the international community to the sovereignty and territorial integrity of the Federal Republic of Yugoslavia,

<u>Recalling</u> the basic elements/principles adopted by the Contact Group at its ministerial meeting in London on January 29, 1999,

Recognizing the need for democratic self-government in Kosovo, including full participation of the members of all national communities in political decision-making,

Desiring to ensure the protection of the human rights of all persons in Kosovo, as well as the rights of the members of all national communities,

Recognizing the ongoing contribution of the OSCE to peace and stability in Kosovo,

Noting that the present Agreement has been concluded under the auspices of the members of the Contact Group and the European Union and undertaking with respect to these members and the European Union to abide by this Agreement,

Aware that full respect for the present Agreement will be central for the development of relations with European institutions,

Have agreed as follows:

Framework

Article I: Principles

1. All citizens in Kosovo shall enjoy, without discrimination, the equal rights and freedoms set forth in this Agreement.

2. National communities and their members shall have additional rights specified in Chapter 1. Kosovo, Federal, and Republic authorities shall not interfere with the exercise of these additional rights. The national communities shall be legally equal as specified herein, and shall not use their additional rights to endanger the rights of other national communities or the rights of citizens, the sovereignty and territorial integrity of the Federal Republic of Yugoslavia, or the functioning of representative democratic government in Kosovo.

3. All authorities in Kosovo shall fully respect human
rights, democracy, and the equality of citizens and national communities.

4. Citizens in Kosovo shall have the right to democratic self-government through legislative, executive, judicial, and other institutions established in accordance with this Agreement. They shall have the opportunity to be represented in all institutions in Kosovo. The ri ght to democratic self-government shall include the right to participate in free and fair elections.

5. Every person in Kosovo may have access to international institutions for the protection of their rights in accordance with the procedures of such institutions.

6. The Parties accept that they will act only within their powers and responsibilities in Kosovo as specified by this Agreement. Acts outside those powers and responsibilities shall be null and void. Kosovo shall have all rights and powers set forth herein, including in particular as specified in the Constitution at Chapter 1. This Agreement shall prevail over any other legal provisions of the Parties and shall be directly applicable. The Parties shall harmonize their governing practices and documents with this Agreement.

7. The Parties agree to cooperate fully with all international organizations working in Kosovo on the implementation of this Agreement.

Article II: Confidence-Building Measures End of Use of Force

1. Use of force in Kosovo shall cease immediately. In accordance with this Agreement, alleged violations of the cease-fire shall be reported to international observers and shall not be used to justify use of force in response.

2. The status of police and security forces in Kosovo, including withdrawal of forces, shall be governed by the terms of this Agreement. Paramilitary and irregular forces in Kosovo are incompatible with the terms of this Agreement.

Return

3. The Parties recognize that all persons have the right to return to their homes. Appropriate authorities shall take all measures necessary to facilitate the safe return of persons, including issuing necessary documents. All persons shall have the right to reoccupy their real property, assert their occupancy rights in state-owned property, and recover their other property and personal possessions. The Parties shall take all measures necessary to readmit returning persons to Kosovo.

4. The Parties shall cooperate fully with all efforts by the United Nations High Commissioner for Refugees , (UNHCR) and other international and non-governmental organizations concerning the repatriation and return of persons, including those organizations, monitoring of the treatment of persons following their return.

Access for International Assistance

5. There shall be no impediments to the normal flow of goods into Kosovo, including materials for the reconstruction of homes and structures. The Federal Republic of Yugoslavia shall not require visas, customs, or licensing for persons or things for the Implementation Mission (IM), the UNHCR, and other international organizations, as well as for non-governmental organizations working in Kosovo as determined by the Chief of the Implementation Mission (CIM).

6. All staff, whether national or international, working with international or non-governmental organizations including with the Yugoslav Red Cross, shall be allowed unrestricted access to the Kosovo population for purposes of international assistance. All persons in Kosovo shall similarly have safe, unhindered, and direct access to the staff of such organizations.

Other Issues

7. Federal organs shall not take any decisions that have a differential, disproportionate, injurious, or discriminatory effect on Kosovo. Such decisions, if any, shall be void with regard to Kosovo.

8. Martial law shall not be declared in Kosovo.

9. The Parties shall immediately comply with all requests for support from the implementation Mission (IM). The IM shall have its own broadcast frequencies for radio and television programming in Kosovo. The Federal Republic of Yugoslavia shall provide all necessary facilities, including frequencies for radio communications, to all humanitarian organizations responsible for delivering aid in Kosovo.

Detention of Combatants and Justice Issues

10. All abducted persons or other persons held without charge shall be released. The Parties shall also release and transfer in accordance with this Agreement all persons held in connection with the conflict. The Parties shall cooperate fully with the International Committee of the Red Cross (ICRC) to facilitate its work in accordance with its mandate, including ensuring full access to all such persons, irrespective of their status, wherever they might be held, for visits in accordance with the ICRC's standard operating procedures.

11. The Parties shall provide information, through tracing mechanisms of the ICRC, to families of all persons who are unaccounted for. The Parties shall cooperate fully with the ICRC and the International Commission on Missing Persons in their efforts to determine the identity, whereabouts, and fate of those unaccounted for.

12. Each Party:

(a) shall not prosecute anyone for crimes related to the conflict in Kosovo, except for persons accused of having committed serious violations of international humanitarian law. In order to facilitate transparency, the Parties shall grant access to foreign experts (including forensics experts) along with state investigators;

(b) shall grant a general amnesty for all persons already convicted of committing politically motivated crimes related to the conflict in Kosovo. This amnesty shall not apply to those properly convicted of committing serious violations of international humanitarian law at a fair and open trial conducted pursuant to international standards.

13. All Parties shall comply with their obligation to cooperate in the investigation and prosecution of serious violations of international humanitarian law.

(a) As required by United Nations Security Council resolution 827 (1993) and subsequent resolutions, the Parties shall fully cooperate with the International Criminal Tribunal for the Former Yugoslavia in its investigations and prosecutions, including complying with its requests for assistance and its orders.

(b) The Parties shall also allow complete, unimpeded,and unfettered access to international experts-including forensics experts and investigators-to investigate allegations of serious violations of international humanitarian law.

Independent Media

14. Recognizing the importance of free and independent media for the development of a democratic political climate necessary for the reconstruction and development of Kosovo, the Parties shall ensure the widest possible press freedoms in Kosovo in all media, public and private, including print, television, radio, and Internet.

Chapter 1, Constitution

Affirming their belief in a peaceful society, justice, tolerance, and reconciliation,

Resolved to ensure respect for human rights and the equality of all citizens and national communities,

Recognizing that the preservation and promotion of the national, cultural, and linguistic identity of each national community in Kosovo are necessary for the harmonious development of a peaceful society,

Desiring through this interim Constitution to establish institutions of democratic self-government in Kosovo grounded in respect for the territorial integrity and sovereignty of the Federal Republic of Yugoslavia and from this Agreement, from which the authorities of governance set forth herein originate,

Recognizing that the institutions of Kosovo should fairly represent the national communities in Kosovo and foster the exercise of their rights and those of their members,

Recalling and endorsing the principles/basic elements adopted by the Contact Group at its ministerial meeting in London on January 29, 1999,

Article I: Principles of Democratic Self-Government in Kosovo

1. Kosovo shall govern itself democratically through the legislative, executive, judicial, and other organs and institutions specified herein. Organs and institutions of Kosovo shall exercise their authorities consistent with the terms of this Agreement.

2. All authorities in Kosovo shall fully respect human rights, democracy, and the equality of citizens and national communities.

3. The Federal Republic of Yugoslavia has competence in Kosovo over the following areas, except as specified elsewhere in this Agreement: (a) territorial integrity, (b) maintaining a common market within the Federal Republic of Yugoslavia, which power shall be exercised in a manner that does not discriminate against Kosovo, (c) monetary policy, (d) defense, (e) foreign policy, (f) customs services, (g) federal taxation, (h) federal elections, and (i) other areas specified in this Agreement.

4. The Republic of Serbia shall have competence in Kosovo as specified in this Agreement, including in relation to Republic elections.

5. Citizens in Kosovo-may continue to participate in areas in which the Federal Republic of Yugoslavia and the Republic of Serbia have competence through their representation in relevant institutions, without prejudice to the exercise of competence by Kosovo authorities set forth in this Agreement.

6. With respect to Kosovo:
(a) There shall be no changes to the borders of Kosovo;
(b) Deployment and use of police and security forces shall be governed by Chapters 2 and 7 of this Agreement; and
(c) Kosovo shall have authority to conduct foreign relations within its areas of responsibility equivalent to the power provided to Republics under Article 7 of the Constitution of the Federal Republic of Yugoslavia.

7. There shall be no interference with the right of citizens and national communities in Kosovo to call upon appropriate institutions of the Republic of Serbia for the following purposes:
(a) assistance in designing school curricula and standards;
(b) participation in social benefits programs, such as care for war veterans, pensioners, and disabled persons; and
(c) other voluntarily received services, provided that these services are not related to police and security matters governed by Chapters 2 and 7 of this Agreement, and that any Republic personnel serving in Kosovo pursuant to this paragraph shall be unarmed service providers acting at the invitation of a national community in Kosovo. The Republic shall have the authority to levy taxes or charges on those citizens requesting services pursuant to this paragraph, as necessary to support the provision of such services.

8. The basic territorial unit of local self-government in Kosovo shall be the commune. All responsibilities in Kosovo not expressly assigned elsewhere shall be the responsibility of the communes.

9. To preserve and promote democratic self-government in Kosovo, all candidates for appointed, elective, or other public office, and all office holders, shall meet the following criteria:

(a) No person who is serving a sentence imposed by the International Criminal Tribunal for the Former Yugoslavia, and no person who is under indictment by the Tribunal and who has failed to comply with an order to appear before the Tribunal, may stand as a candidate or hold any office; and

(b) All candidates and office holders shall renounce violence as a mechanism for achieving political goals; past political or resistance activities shall not be a bar to holding office in Kosovo.

Article II: The Assembly

General

1. Kosovo shall have an Assembly, which shall be comprised of 120 Members.
(a) Eighty members shall be directly elected.
(b) A further 40 Members shall be elected by the members of qualifying national communities.
(i) Communities whose members constitute more than 0.5 per cent of the Kosovo population but less than 5 per cent shall have ten of these seats, to be divided among them in accordance with their proportion of the overall population.
(ii) communities whose members constitute more than 5 per cent of the Kosovo population shall divide the remaining thirty seats equally. The Serb and Albanian national communities shall be presumed to meet the 5 per cent population threshold.

Other Provisions

2. Elections for all Members shall be conducted democratically, consistent with the provisions of Chapter 3 of this Agreement. Members shall be elected for a term of three years.

3. Allocation of seats in the Assembly shall be based on data gathered in the census referred to in Chapter 5 of this Agreement. Prior to the completion of the census, for purposes of this Article declarations of national community membership made during voter registration shall be used to determine the percentage of the Kosovo population that each national community represents.

4. Members of the Assembly shall be immune from all civil or criminal proceedings on the basis of words expressed or other acts performed in their capacity as Members of the Assembly.

Powers of the Assembly

5. The Assembly shall be responsible for enacting laws of Kosovo, including in political, security, economic, social, educational, scientific, and cultural areas as set out below and elsewhere in this Agreement. This Constitution and the laws of the Kosovo Assembly shall not be subject to change or modification by authorities of the Republics or the Federation.

(a) The Assembly shall be responsible for:
(i) Financing activities of Kosovo institutions, including by levying taxes and duties on sources within Kosovo;
(ii) Adopting budgets of the Administrative organs and other institutions of Kosovo, with the exception of communal and national community institutions unless otherwise specified herein;
(iii) Adopting regulations concerning the organization and procedures of the Administrative organs of Kosovo;
(iv) Approving the list of Ministers of the Government, including the Prime minister;
(v) Coordinating educational arrangements in Kosovo, with respect for the authorities of national communities and Communes;
(vi) Electing candidates for judicial office put forward by the President of Kosovo;
(vii) Enacting laws ensuring free movement of goods, services, and persons in Kosovo consistent with this Agreement;
(viii) Approving agreements concluded by the President within the areas of responsibility of Kosovo;
(ix) Cooperating with the Federal Assembly, and with the Assemblies of the Republics, and conducting relations with foreign legislative bodies;
(x) Establishing a framework for local self-government;
(xi) Enacting laws concerning inter-communal issues and relations between national communities, when necessary;
(xii) Enacting laws regulating the work of medical institutions and hospitals;

(xiii) Protecting the environment, where inter-communal issues are involved;

(xiv) Adopting programs of economic, scientific, technological, demographic, regional, and social development, as well as urban planning;

(xv) Adopting programs for the development of agriculture and of rural areas;

(xvi) Regulating elections consistent with Chapters 3 and 5;

(xvii) Regulating Kosovo-owned property; and (xviii) Regulating land registries.

(b) The Assembly shall also have authority to enact laws in areas within the responsibility of the Communes if the matter cannot be effectively regulated by the Communes or if regulation by individual Communes might prejudice the rights of other Communes. In the absence of a law enacted by the Assembly under this subparagraph that preempts communal action, the Communes shall retain their authority.

Procedure

6. Laws and other decisions of the Assembly shall be adopted by majority of Members present and voting.

7. A majority of the Members of a single national community elected to the Assembly pursuant to paragraph 1(b) may adopt a motion that a law or other decision adversely affects the vital interests of their national community. The challenged law or decision shall be suspended with regard to that national community until the dispute settlement procedure in paragraph 8 is completed.

8. The following procedure shall be used in the event of a motion under paragraph 7:

(a) The Members making the vital interest motion shall give reasons for their motion. The proposers of the legislation shall be given an opportunity to respond.

(b) The Members making the motion shall appoint within one day a mediator of their choice to assist in reaching an agreement with those proposing the legislation.

(c) If mediation-does not produce an agreement within seven days, the matter may be submitted for a binding ruling. The decision shall be rendered by a panel comprising three Members of the Assembly: one Albanian and one Serb, each appointed by his or her national community delegation; and a third Member, who will be of a third nationality and will be selected within two days by consensus of the Presidency of the Assembly.

(i) A vital interest motion shall be upheld if the legislation challenged adversely affects the community's fundamental constitutional rights, additional rights as set forth in Article VII, or the principle of fair treatment.

(ii) If the motion is not upheld, the challenged legislation shall enter into force for that community.

(d) Paragraph (c) shall not apply to the selection of Assembly officials.

(e) The Assembly may exclude other decisions from this procedure by means of a law enacted by a majority that includes a majority of each national community elected pursuant to paragraph 1(b).

9. A majority of the Members shall constitute a quorum. The Assembly shall otherwise decide its own rules of procedure.

Leadership

10. The Assembly shall elect from among its Members a Presidency, which shall consist of a President, two Vice-Presidents, and other leaders in accordance with the Assembly's rules of procedure. Each national community meeting the threshold specified in paragraph 1(b)(ii) shall, be represented in the leadership. The President of the Assembly shall not be from the same national community as the President of Kosovo.

11. The President of the Assembly shall represent it, call its sessions to order, chair its meetings, coordinate the work of any committees it may establish, and perform other tasks prescribed by the rules of procedure of the Assembly.

Article III: President of Kosovo

1. There shall be a President of Kosovo, who shall be elected by the Assembly by vote of a majority of its members. The President of Kosovo shall serve for a three-year term. No person may serve more than two terms as President of Kosovo.

2. The President of Kosovo shall be responsible for:

(i) Representing Kosovo, including before any international or Federal body or any body of the Republics;

(ii) Proposing to the Assembly candidates for Prime Minister, the Constitutional Court, the Supreme Court, and other Kosovo judicial offices;

(iii) Meeting regularly with the democratically elected representatives of the national communities;

(iv) Conducting foreign relations and concluding agreements within this power consistent with the authorities of Kosovo institutions under this Agreement. Such agreements shall only enter into force upon approval by the Assembly;

(v) Designating a representative to serve on the Joint Commission established by Article I.2 of Chapter 5 of this Agreement;

(vi) Meeting regularly with the Federal and Republic Presidents; and

vii) other functions specified herein or by law.

Article IV: Government and Administrative Organs

1. Executive power shall be exercised by the Government. The Government shall be responsible for implementing the laws of Kosovo, and of other government authorities when such responsibilities are devolved by those authorities. The Government shall also have competence to propose laws to the Assembly.

(a) The Government shall consist of a Prime Minister and Ministers, including at least one person from each national community meeting the threshold specified in paragraph 1(b)(ii) of Article II. Ministers shall head the Administrative Organs of Kosovo.

(b) The candidate for Prime Minister proposed by the President shall put forward a list of Ministers to the Assembly. The Prime Minister, together with the list of Ministers, shall be approved by a majority of those present and voting in the Assembly. In the event that the Prime Minister is not able to obtain a majority for the Government, the President shall propose a new candidate for Prime Minister within ten days.

(c) The Government shall resign if a no confidence motion is adopted by a vote of a majority of the members of the Assembly. If the Prime Minister or the Government resigns, the President shall select a new candidate for Prime Minister who shall seek to form a Government.

(d) The Prime Minister shall call meetings of the Government, represent it as appropriate, and coordinate its work. Decisions of the Government shall require a majority of Ministers present and voting. The Prime Minister shall cast the deciding vote in the event Ministers are equally divided. The Government shall otherwise decide its own rules of procedure.

2. Administrative organs shall be responsible for assisting the Government in carrying out its duties.

(a) National communities shall be fairly represented at all levels in the Administrative Organs.

(b) Any citizen in Kosovo claiming to have been directly and adversely affected by the decision of an executive or administrative body shall have the right to-judicial review of the legality of that decision after exhausting all avenues for administrative review. The Assembly shall enact a law to regulate this review.

3. There shall be a Chief Prosecutor who shall be responsible for prosecuting individuals who violate the criminal laws of Kosovo. He shall head an Office of the Prosecutor, which shall at all levels have staff representative of the population of Kosovo.

Article V: Judiciary

General

1. Kosovo shall have a Constitutional Court, a Supreme Court, District Courts, and Communal Courts.

2. The Kosovo courts shall have jurisdiction over all matters arising under this Constitution or the laws of Kosovo except as specified in paragraph 3. The Kosovo courts shall also have jurisdiction over questions of federal law, subject to appeal to the Federal courts on these questions after all appeals available under the Kosovo system have been exhausted.

3. Citizens in Kosovo may opt to have civil disputes to which they are party adjudicated by other courts in the Federal Republic of Yugoslavia, which shall apply the law applicable in Kosovo.

4. The following rules will apply to criminal cases:

(a) At the start of criminal proceedings, the defendant is entitled to have his or her trial transferred to another Kosovo court that he or she designates.

(b) In criminal cases in which all defendants and victims are members of the same national community, all members of the judicial council will be from a national community of their choice if any party so requests.

(c) A defendant in a criminal case tried in Kosovo courts is entitled to have at least one member of the judicial council hearing the case to be from his or her national community. Kosovo authorities will consider and allow judges of other courts in the Federal Republic of Yugoslavia to serve as Kosovo judges for these purposes.

Constitutional Court

5. The Constitutional Court shall consist of nine judges. There shall be at least one Constitutional Court judge from each national community meeting the threshold specified in paragraph 1(b)(ii) of Article II. Until such time as the Parties agree to discontinue this arrangement, 5 judges of the Constitutional Court shall be selected from a list drawn up by the President of the European Court of Human Rights.

6. The Constitutional Court shall have authority to resolve disputes relating to the meaning of this Constitution. That authority shall include, but is not limited to, determining whether laws applicable in Kosovo, decisions or acts of the President, the Assembly, the Government, the Communes, and the national communities are compatible with this Constitution.

(a) Matters may be referred to the Constitutional Court by the President of Kosovo, the President or Vice-Presidents of the Assembly, the Ombudsman, the communal assemblies and councils, and any national community acting according to its democratic procedures.

(b) Any court which finds in the course of adjudicating a matter that the dispute depends on the answer to a question within the Constitutional Court's jurisdiction shall refer the issue to the Constitutional Court for a preliminary decision.

7. Following the exhaustion of other legal remedies, the Constitutional Court shall at the request of any person claiming to be a victim have jurisdiction over complaints that human rights and fundamental freedoms and the rights of members of national communities set forth in this Constitution have been violated by a public authority.

8. The Constitutional Court shall have such other jurisdiction as may be specified elsewhere in this Agreement or by law.

Supreme Court

9. The Supreme Court shall consist of nine judges. There shall be at least one Supreme Court judge from each national community meeting the threshold specified in paragraph 1(b)(ii) of Article II.

10. The Supreme Court shall hear appeals from the District Courts and the Communal Courts. Except as otherwise provided in this Constitution, the Supreme Court shall be the court of final appeal for all cases arising under law applicable in Kosovo. Its decisions shall be recognized and executed by all authorities in the Federal Republic of Yugoslavia.

Functioning of the Courts

11. The Assembly shall determine the number of District and Communal Court judges necessary to meet current needs.

12. Judges of all courts in Kosovo shall be distinguished jurists of the highest moral character. They shall be broadly representative of the national communities of Kosovo.

13. Removal of a Kosovo judge shall require the consensus of the judges of the Constitutional Court. A Constitutional Court judge whose removal is in question shall not participate in the decision on his case.

14. The Constitutional Court shall adopt rules for itself and for other courts in Kosovo. The Constitutional and Supreme Courts shall each adopt decisions by majority vote of their members.

15. Except as otherwise specified in their rules, all Kosovo courts shall hold public proceedings. They shall issue published opinions setting forth the reasons for their decisions.

Article VI: Human Rights and Fundamental Freedoms

1. All authorities in Kosovo shall ensure internationally recognized human rights and fundamental freedoms.

2. The rights and freedoms set forth in the European Convention for the Protection of Human Rights and Fundamental Freedoms and its Protocols shall apply directly in Kosovo. Other internationally recognized human rights instruments enacted into law by the Kosovo Assembly shall also apply. These rights and freedoms shall have priority over all other law.

3. All courts, agencies, governmental institutions, and other public institutions of Kosovo or operating in relation to Kosovo shall conform to these human rights and fundamental freedoms.

Article VII: National Communities

1. National communities and their members shall have additional rights as set forth below in order to preserve and express their national, cultural, religious, and linguistic identities in accordance with international standards and the Helsinki Final Act. Such rights shall be exercised in conformity with human rights and fundamental freedoms.

2. Each national community may elect, through democratic means and in a manner consistent with the principles of Chapter 3 of this Agreement, institutions to administer its affairs in Kosovo.

3. The national communities shall be subject to the laws applicable in Kosovo, provided that any act or decision concerning national communities must be non-discriminatory. The Assembly shall decide upon a procedure for resolving disputes between national communities.

4. The additional rights of the national communities, acting through their democratically elected institutions, are to:

(a) preserve and protect their national, cultural, religious, and linguistic identities, including by:

(i) inscribing local names of towns and villages, of squares and streets, and of other topographic names in the language and alphabet of the national community in addition to signs in Albanian and Serbian, consistent with decisions about style made by the communal institutions;

(ii) providing information in the language and alphabet of the national community;

(iii) providing for education and establishing educational institutions, in particular for schooling in their own language and alphabet and in national culture and history, for which relevant authorities will provide financial assistance; curricula shall reflect a spirit of tolerance between national communities and respect for the rights of members of all national communities in accordance with international standards;

(iv) enjoying unhindered contacts with representatives of their respective national communities, within the Federal Republic of Yugoslavia and abroad;

(v) using and displaying national symbols, including symbols of the Federal Republic of Yugoslavia and the Republic of Serbia;

(vi) protecting national traditions on family law by, if the community decides, arranging rules in the field of inheritance; family and matrimonial relations; tutorship; and adoption;

(vii) the preservation of sites of religious, historical, or cultural importance to the national community in cooperation with other authorities;

(viii) implementing public health and social services on a non-discriminatory basis as to citizens and national communities;

(ix) operating religious institutions in cooperation with religious authorities; and

(x) participating in regional and international non-governmental organizations in accordance with procedures of these organizations;

(b) be guaranteed access to, and representation in, public broadcast media, including provisions for separate programming in relevant languages under the direction of those nominated by the respective national community on a fair and equitable basis; and

(c) finance their activities by collecting contributions the national communities may decide to levy on members of their own communities.

5. Members of national communities shall also be individually guaranteed:

(a) the right to enjoy unhindered contacts with members of their respective national communities elsewhere in the Federal Republic of Yugoslavia and abroad;

(b) equal access to employment in public services at all levels;

(c) the right to use their languages and alphabets;

(d) the right to use and display national community symbols;

(e) the right to participate in democratic institutions that will determine the national community's exercise of the collective rights set forth in this Article; and

(f) the right to establish cultural and religious associations, for which relevant authorities will provide financial assistance.

6. Each national community and, where appropriate, their members acting individually may exercise these additional rights through Federal institutions and institutions of the Republics, in accordance with the procedures of those institutions and without prejudice to the ability of Kosovo institutions to carry out their responsibilities.

7. Every person shall have the right freely to choose to be treated or not to be treated as belonging to a national community, and no disadvantage shall result from that choice or from the exercise of the rights connected to that choice.

Article VIII: Communes

1. Kosovo shall have the existing communes. Changes may be made to communal boundaries by act of the Kosovo Assembly after consultation with the authorities of the communes concerned.

2. Communes may develop relationships among themselves for their mutual benefit.

3. Each commune shall have an Assembly, an Executive Council, and such administrative bodies as the commune may establish.

(a) Each national community whose membership constitutes at least three percent of the population of the commune shall be represented on the Council in proportion to its share of the communal population or by one member, whichever is greater.

(b) Prior to the completion of a census, disputes over communal population percentages for purposes of this paragraph shall be resolved by reference to declarations of national community membership in the voter registry.

4. The communes shall have responsibility for:

(a) law enforcement, as specified in Chapter 2 of this Agreement;

(b) regulating and, when appropriate, providing child care;

(c) providing education, consistent with the rights and duties of national communities, and in a spirit of tolerance between national communities and respect for the rights of the members of all national communities in accordance with international standards;

(d) protecting the communal environment;

(e) regulating commerce and privately-owned stores;

(f) regulating hunting and fishing;

(g) planning and carrying out public works of communal importance, including roads and water supplies, and participating in the planning and carrying out of Kosovo-wide public works projects in coordination with other communes and Kosovo authorities;

(h) regulating land use, town planning, building regulations, and housing construction-

(i) developing programs for tourism, the hotel industry, catering, and sport;

(j) organizing fairs and local markets;

(k) organizing public services of communal importance, including fire, emergency response, and police consistent with Chapter 2 of this Agreement; and (1) financing the work of communal institutions, including raising revenues, taxes, and preparing budgets.

5. The communes shall also have responsibility for all other areas within Kosovo's authority not expressly assigned elsewhere herein, subject to the provisions of Article II.5(b) of this Constitution.

6. Each commune shall conduct its business in public and shall maintain publicly available records of its deliberations and decisions.

Article IX: Representation

l. Citizens in Kosovo shall have the right to participate in the election of:

(a) At least 10 deputies in the House of Citizens of the Federal Assembly; and

(b) At least 20 deputies in the National Assembly of the Republic of Serbia.

2. The modalities of elections for the deputies specified in paragraph 1 shall be determined by the Federal Republic of Yugoslavia and the Republic of Serbia respectively, under procedures to be agreed with the Chief of the Implementation Mission.

3. The Assembly shall have the opportunity to present to the appropriate authorities a list of candidates from which shall be drawn:

(a) At least one citizen in Kosovo to serve in the Federal Government, and at least one citizen in Kosovo to serve in the Government of the Republic of Serbia; and

(b) At least one judge on the Federal Constitutional Court, one judge on the Federal Court, and three judges on the Supreme Court of Serbia.

Article X: Amendment

1. The Assembly may by a majority of two-thirds of its Members, which majority must include a majority of the Members elected from each national community pursuant to Article II.1(b)(ii), adopt amendments to this Constitution.

2. There shall, however, be no amendments to Article I.3-8 or to this Article, nor shall any amendment diminish the rights granted by Articles VI and VII.

Article XI: Entry into Force

This Constitution shall enter into force upon signature of this Agreement.

Chapter 2, Police and Civil Public Security

Article I: General Principles

1. All law enforcement agencies, organizations and personnel of the Parties, which for purposes of this Chapter will include customs and border police operating in Kosovo, shall act in compliance with this Agreement and shall observe internationally recognized standards of human rights and due process. In exercising their functions, law enforcement personnel shall not discriminate on any ground, such as sex, race, color, language, religion, political or other opinion, national or social origin, association with a national community, property, birth or other status.

2. The Parties invite the organization for Security and Cooperation in Europe (OSCE) through its Implementation Mission (IM) to monitor and supervise implementation of this Chapter and related provisions of this Agreement. The Chief of the Implementation Mission (CIM) or his designee shall have the authority to issue binding directives to the Parties and subsidiary bodies on police and civil public security matters to obtain compliance by the Parties with the terms of this Chapter. The Parties agree to cooperate fully with the IM and to comply with its directives. Personnel assigned to police-related duties within the IM shall be permitted to wear a uniform while serving in this part of the mission.

3. In carrying out his responsibilities, the CIM will inform and consult KFOR as appropriate.

4. The IM shall have the authority to:

(a) Monitor, observe, and inspect law enforcement activities, personnel, and facilities, including border police and customs units, as well as associated judicial organizations, structures, and proceedings;

(b) Advise law enforcement personnel and forces, including border police and customs units, and, when necessary to bring them into compliance with this Agreement, including this Chapter, issue appropriate binding directions in coordination with KFOR;

(c) Participate in and guide the training of law enforcement personnel;

(d) In coordination with KFOR, assess threats to public order;

(e) Advise and provide guidance to governmental authorities on how to deal with threats to public order and on the organization of effective civilian law enforcement agencies;

(f) Accompany the Parties, law enforcement personnel as they carry out their responsibilities, as the IM deems appropriate;

(g) Dismiss or discipline public security personnel of the Parties for cause; and

(h) Request appropriate law enforcement support from the international community to enable IM to carry out the duties assigned in this Chapter.

5. All Kosovo, Republic and Federal law enforcement and Federal military authorities shall be obligated, in their respective areas of authority, to ensure freedom of movement and safe passage for all persons, vehicles and goods. This obligation includes a duty to permit the unobstructed passage into Kosovo of police equipment which has been approved by the CIM and COMKFOR for use by Kosovo police, and of any other support provided under subparagraph 4(h) above.

6. The Parties undertake to provide one another mutual assistance, when requested, in the surrender of those accused of committing criminal acts within a Party's jurisdiction, and in the investigation and prosecution of offenses across the boundary of Kosovo with other parts of the FRY. The Parties shall develop agreed procedures and mechanisms for responding to these requests. The CIM or his designee shall resolve disputes on these matters.

7. The IM shall aim to transfer law enforcement responsibilities described in Article II below to the law enforcement officials and organizations described in Article II at the earliest practical time consistent with civil public security.

Article II: Communal Police

1. As they build up, Communal police units, organized and stationed at the communal and municipal levels, shall assume primary responsibility for law enforcement in Kosovo. The specific responsibilities of the communal police will include police patrols and crime prevention, criminal investigations, arrest and detention of criminal suspects, crowd control, and traffic control.

2. Number and Composition. The total number of communal police established by this Agreement operating within Kosovo shall not exceed 3,000 active duty law enforcement officers. However, the CIM shall have the authority to increase or decrease this personnel coiling if he determines such action is necessary to meet operational needs. Prior to taking any such action, the CIM shall consult with the Criminal Justice Administration and other officials as appropriate. The national communities in each commune shall be fairly represented in the communal police unit.

3. Criminal Justice Administration.

a. A Criminal Justice Administration (CJA) shall be established. It shall be an Administrative Organ of Kosovo, reporting to an appropriate member of the Government of Kosovo as determined by the Government. The CJA shall provide general coordination of law enforcement operations in Kosovo. Specific functions of the CJA shall include general supervision over, and providing guidance to, communal police forces through their commanders, assisting in the coordination between separate communal police forces, and oversight of the operations of the police academy. In carrying out these responsibilities, the CJA may issue directives, which shall be binding on communal police commanders and personnel. In the exercise of its functions, the CJA shall be subject to any directions given by CIM.

b. Within twelve months of the establishment of the CJA, the CJA shall submit for review by the CIM a plan for the coordination and development of law enforcement bodies and personnel in Kosovo within its jurisdiction. This plan shall serve as the framework for law enforcement coordination and development in Kosovo and be subject to modification by the CIM.

c. The IM will endeavor to develop the capacities of the CJA as quickly as possible. Prior to the point when the CJA is able to properly carry out the functions described in the preceding paragraph, as determined by the CIM, the IM shall carry out these functions.

4. Communal Commanders. Subject to review by the CIM, each commune will appoint, and may remove for cause, by majority vote of the communal council, a communal police commander with responsibility for police operations within the commune.

5. Service in Police.

(a) Recruitment for public security personnel will be conducted primarily at the local level. Local and communal governments, upon consultation with communal Criminal Justice Commissions, will nominate officer candidates to attend the Kosovo Police Academy. Offers of employment will be made by communal police commanders, with the concurrence of the academy director, only after the candidate has successfully completed the academy basic recruit course.

(b) Recruitment, selection and training of communal police officers shall be conducted under the direction of the IM during the period of its operation.

(c) There shall be no bar to service in the communal police based on prior political activities. Members of the police shall not, however, be permitted while they hold this public office to participate in party political activities other than membership in such a party.

(d) Continued service in the police is dependent upon behavior consistent with the terms of this Agreement, including this Chapter. The IM shall supervise regular reviews of officer performance, which shall be conducted in accordance with international due process norms.

6. Uniforms and Equipment.

(a) All communal police officers, with the exception of officers participating in crowd control functions, shall wear a standard uniform. Uniforms shall include a badge, picture identification, and name tag.

(b) Communal police officers may be equipped with a sidearm, handcuffs, a baton, and a radio.

(c) Subject to authorization or modification by the CIM, each commune may maintain, either at the communal headquarters or at municipal stations, no more than one long-barreled weapon not to exceed 7.62 mm for every fifteen police officers assigned to the commune. Each such weapon must be approved by and registered with the IM and KFOR pursuant to procedures established by the CIM and COMKFOR. When not in use, all such weapons will be securely stored and each commune will keep a registry of these weapons.

(i) In the event of a serious law enforcement threat that would justify the use of these weapons, the communal police commander shall obtain IM approval before employing these weapons.

(ii) The communal police commander may authorize the use of these weapons without prior approval of the IM for the sole purpose of self-defense. In such cases, he must report the incident no later than one hour after it occurs to the IM and KFOR.

(iii) If the CIM determines that a weapon has been used by a member of a communal police force in a manner contrary to this Chapter, he may take appropriate corrective measures; such measures may include reducing the number of such weapons that the communal police force is allowed to possess or dismissing or disciplining the law enforcement personnel involved.

(d) Communal police officers engaged in crowd control functions will receive equipment appropriate to their task, including batons, helmets and shields, subject to IM approval.

Article III: Interim Police Academy

1. Under the supervision of the IM, the CJA shall establish an interim Police Academy that will offer mandatory and professional development training for all public security personnel, including border police. Until the interim police academy is established, IM will oversee a temporary training program for public security personnel including border police.

2. All public security personnel shall be required to complete a course of police studies successfully before serving as communal police officers.

3. The Academy shall be headed by a Director appointed and removed by the CJA in consultation with the Kosovo Criminal Justice Commission and the IM. The Director shall consult closely with the IM and comply fully with its recommendations and guidance.

4. All Republic and Federal police training facilities in Kosovo, including the academy at Vucitrn, will cease operations within 6 months of the entry into force of, this Agreement.

Article IV: Criminal Justice Commissions

1. The parties shall establish a Kosovo Criminal Justice Commission and Communal Criminal Justice Commissions. The CIM or his designee shall chair meetings of these Commissions. They shall be forums for cooperation, coordination and the resolution of disputes concerning law enforcement and civil public security in Kosovo.

2. The functions of the Commissions shall include the following:

(a) Monitor, review, and make recommendations regarding the operation of law enforcement personnel and policies in Kosovo, including communal police units;

(b) Review, and make recommendations regarding the recruitment, selection and training of communal police officers and commanders;

(c) Consider complaints regarding police practices filed by individuals or national communities, and provide information and recommendations to communal police commanders and the CIM for consideration in their reviews of officer performance; and

(d) In the Kosovo Criminal Justice Commission only: In consultation with designated local, Republic and Federal police liaisons, monitor jurisdiction sharing in cases of overlapping criminal jurisdiction between Kosovo, Republic and Federal authorities.

3. The membership of the Kosovo Criminal Justice Commission and each Communal Criminal Justice Commission shall be representative of the population and shall include:

(a) In the Kosovo Criminal Justice Commission:

(i) a representative of each commune;

(ii) the head of the Kosovo CJA;

(iii) a representative of each Republic and
Federal law enforcement component operating in Kosovo (for example, Customs police and Border police);

(iv) a representative of each national community;

(v) a representative of the IM, during its period of operation in Kosovo;

(vi) a representative of the VJ border guard, as appropriate;

(vii) a representative of the MUP, as appropriate, while present in Kosovo; and

(viii) A representative of KFOR, as appropriate.

(b) In the Communal Criminal Justice Commissions:

(i) the communal police commander;

(ii) a representative of any Republic and Federal law enforcement component operating in the commune;

(iii) a representative of each national community;

(iv) a civilian representative of the communal
government;

(v) a representative of the IM, during its period of operation in Kosovo;

(vi) a representative of the VJ border guard, who shall have observer status, as appropriate; and

(vii) A representative of KFOR, as appropriate.

4. Each Criminal Justice Commission shall meet at least monthly, or at the request of any Commission member.

Article V: Police Operations in Kosovo

1. The communal police established by this Agreement shall have exclusive law enforcement authority and jurisdiction and shall be the only police presence in Kosovo following the reduction and eventual withdrawal from Kosovo by the MUP, with the exception of border police as specified in Article VI and any support provided pursuant to Article I(3)(h).

(a) During the transition to communal police, the remaining MTJP shall carry out only normal policing duties, and shall draw down, pursuant to the schedule described in Chapter 7.

(b) During the period of the phased drawdown of the MUP, the MUP in Kosovo shall have authority to conduct only civil police functions and shall be under the supervision and control of the CIM. The IM may dismiss from service, or take other appropriate disciplinary action against, MUP personnel who obstruct implementation of this Agreement.

2. Concurrent Law Enforcement in Kosovo.

(a) Except as provided in Article V.1 and Article VI, Federal and Republic law enforcement officials may only act within Kosovo in cases of hot pursuit of a person suspected of committing a serious criminal offense.

(i) Federal and Republic authorities shall as soon as practicable, but in no event later than one hour after their entry into Kosovo while engaged in a hot pursuit, notify the nearest Kosovo law enforcement officials that the pursuit has crossed into Kosovo. Once notification has been made, further pursuit and apprehension shall be coordinated with Kosovo law enforcement. Following apprehension,

suspects shall be placed into the custody of the authorities originating the pursuit. If the suspect has not been apprehended within four hours, the original pursuing authorities shall cease their pursuit and immediately depart Kosovo unless invited to continue their pursuit by the CJA or the CIM.

(ii) In the event the pursuit is of such short duration as to preclude notification, Kosovo law enforcement officials shall be notified that an apprehension has been made and shall be given access to the detainee prior to his removal from Kosovo.

(iii) Personnel engaged in hot pursuit under the provisions of this Article may only be civilian police, may only carry weapons appropriate for normal civilian police duties (sidearms, and long-barreled weapons not to exceed 7.62mm), may only travel in officially marked police vehicles, and may not exceed a total of eight personnel at any one time. Travel in armored personnel carriers by police engaged in hot pursuit is strictly prohibited.

(iv) The same rules shall apply to hot pursuit of suspects by Kosovo law enforcement authorities to Federal territory outside of Kosovo.

(b) All Parties shall provide the highest degree of mutual assistance in law enforcement matters in response to reasonable requests.

Article VI: Security on International Borders

1. The Government of the FRY will maintain official border crossings on its international borders (Albania and FYROM).

2. Personnel from the organizations listed below may be present along Kosovo's international borders and at international border crossings, and may not act outside the scope of the authorities specified in this Chapter.

(a) Republic of Serbia Border Police

(i) The Border Police shall continue to exercise authority at Kosovo's international border crossings and in connection with the enforcement of Federal Republic of Yugoslavia immigration laws. The total number of border police shall be drawn down to 75 within 14 days of entry into force of this Agreement.

(ii) while maintaining the personnel threshold specified in subparagraph (i), the ranks of the existing Border Police units operating in Kosovo shall be supplemented by new recruits so that they are representative of the Kosovo population.

(iii) All Border Police stationed in Kosovo must attend police training at the Kosovo police academy within 18 months of the entry into force of this Agreement.

(b) Customs Officers

(i) The FRY Customs Service will continue to exercise customs jurisdiction at Kosovo's official international border crossings and in such customs warehouses as may be necessary within Kosovo. The total number of customs personnel shall be drawn down to 50 within 14 days of the entry into force of this Agreement.

(ii) Kosovar Albanian officers of the Customs Service shall be trained and compensated by the FRY.

(c) The CIM shall conduct a periodic review of customs and border police requirements and shall have the authority to increase or decrease the personnel ceilings described in paragraphs (a)(i) and (b)(i) above to reflect operational needs and to adjust the composition of individual customs units.

Article VII: Arrest and Detention

1. Except pursuant to Article V, Article I(3)(h), and sections (a)-(b) of this paragraph, only officers of the communal police shall have authority to arrest and detain individuals in Kosovo.

(a) Border Police officers shall have authority within Kosovo to arrest and detain individuals who have violated criminal provisions of the immigration laws.

(b) Officers of the Customs Service shall have authority within Kosovo to arrest and detain individuals for criminal violations of the customs laws.

2. Immediately upon making an arrest, the arresting officer shall notify the nearest Communal Criminal Justice Commission of the detention and the location of the detainee. He subsequently shall transfer the detainee to the nearest appropriate jail in Kosovo at the earliest opportunity.

3. Officers may use reasonable and necessary force proportionate to the circumstances to effect arrests and keep suspects in custody.

4. Kosovo and its constituent communes shall establish jails and prisons to accommodate the detention of criminal suspects and the imprisonment of individuals convicted of violating the laws applicable in Kosovo. Prisons shall be operated consistent with international standards. Access shall be provided to international personnel, including representatives of the International Committee of the Red Cross.

Article VIII: Administration of Justice

1. Criminal Jurisdiction over Persons Arrested within Kosovo.

(a) Except in accordance with Article V and subparagraph (b) of this paragraph, any person arrested within Kosovo shall be subject to the jurisdiction of the Kosovo courts.

(b) Any person arrested within Kosovo, in accordance with the law and with this Agreement, by the Border Police or Customs Police shall be subject to the jurisdiction of the FRY courts. If there is no applicable court of the FRY to hear the case, the Kosovo courts shall have jurisdiction.

2. Prosecution of Crimes.

(a) The CJA shall, in consultation with the CIM, appoint and have the authority to remove the Chief Prosecutor.

(b) The IM shall have the authority to monitor, observe, inspect, and when necessary, direct the operations of the office of the Prosecutor and any and all related staff.

Article IX: Final Authority to Interpret

The CIM is the final authority regarding interpretation of this Chapter and his determinations are binding on all Parties and persons.

Chapter 3, Conduct and Supervision of Elections

Article I: Conditions for Elections

1. The Parties shall ensure that conditions exist for the organization of free and fair elections, which include but are not limited to:

a) freedom of movement for all citizens;

b) an open and free political environment;

c) an environment conducive to the return of displaced persons;

d) a safe and secure environment that ensures freedom of assembly, association, and expression;

e) an electoral legal framework of rules and regulations complying with OSCE commitments, which will be implemented by a Central Election Commission, as set forth in Article III, which is representative of the population of Kosovo in terms of national communities and political parties; and

f) free media, effectively accessible to registered political parties and candidates, and available to voters throughout Kosovo.

2. The Parties request the OSCE to certify when elections will he effective under current conditions in Kosovo, and to provide assistance to the Parties to create conditions for free and fair elections.

3. The Parties shall comply fully with Paragraphs 7 and 8 of the OSCE Copenhagen Document, which are attached to this Chapter.

Article II: Role of the OSCE

1. The Parties request the OSCE to adopt and put in place an elections program for Kosovo and supervise elections as set forth in this Agreement.

2. The Parties request the OSCE to supervise, in a manner to be determined by the OSCE and in cooperation with other international organizations the OSCE deems necessary, the preparation and conduct of elections for:

a) Members of the Kosovo Assembly;

b) Members of Communal Assemblies;

c) other officials popularly elected in Kosovo under this Agreement and the laws and Constitution of Kosovo at the discretion of the OSCE.

3. The Parties request the OSCE to establish a Central Election Commission in Kosovo ("the Commission").

4. Consistent with Article IV of Chapter 5, the first elections shall be held within nine months of the entry into force of this Agreement. The President of the Commission shall decide, in consultation with the Parties, the exact timing and order of elections for Kosovo political offices.

Article III: Central Election Commission

1. The Commission shall adopt electoral Rules and Regulations on all matters necessary for the conduct of free and fair elections in Kosovo, including rules relating to: the eligibility and registration of candidates, parties, and voters, including displaced persons and refugees; ensuring a free and fair elections campaign; administrative and technical preparation for elections including the establishment, publication, and certification of election results; and the role of international and domestic election observers.

2. The responsibilities of the Commission, as provided in the electoral Rules and Regulations, shall include:

a) the preparation, conduct, and supervision of all aspects of the electoral process, including development and supervision of political party and voter registration, and creation of secure and transparent procedures for production and dissemination of ballots and sensitive election materials, vote counts, tabulations, and publication of elections results;

b) ensuring compliance with the electoral Rules and Regulations established pursuant to this Agreement, including establishing auxiliary bodies for this purpose as necessary;

c) ensuring that action is taken to remedy any violation of any provision of this Agreement, including imposing penalties such as removal from candidate or party lists, against any person, candidate, political party, or body that violates such provisions; and

d) accrediting observers, including personnel from international organizations and foreign and domestic non-governmental organizations, and ensuring that the Parties grant the accredited observers unimpeded access and movement.

3. The Commission shall consist of a person appointed by the Chairman-in-office (CIO) of the OSCE, representatives of all national communities, and representatives of political parties in Kosovo selected by criteria to be determined by the Commission. The person appointed by the CIO shall act as the President of the Commission. The rules of procedure of the Commission shall provide that in the exceptional circumstance of an unresolved dispute within the Commission, the decision of the President shall be final and binding.

4. The Commission shall enjoy the right to establish communication facilities, and to engage local and administrative staff.

Chapter 4a, Economic Issues

Article I

1. The economy of Kosovo shall function in accordance with free market principles.

2. The authorities established to levy and collect taxes and other charges are set forth in this Agreement. Except as otherwise expressly provided, all authorities have the right to keep all revenues from their own taxes or other charges consistent with this Agreement.

3. Certain revenue from Kosovo taxes and duties shall accrue to the Communes, taking into account the need for an equalization of revenues between the Communes based on objective criteria. The Assembly of Kosovo shall enact appropriate non-discriminatory legislation for this purpose. The Communes may also levy local taxes in accordance with this Agreement.

4. The Federal Republic of Yugoslavia shall be responsible for the collection of all customs duties at international borders in Kosovo. There shall be no impediments to the free movement of persons, goods, services, and capital to and from Kosovo.

5. Federal authorities shall ensure that Kosovo receives a proportionate and equitable share-of benefits that may be derived from international agreements concluded by the Federal Republic and of Federal resources.

6. Federal and other authorities shall within their respective powers and responsibilities ensure the free movement of persons, goods, services, and capital to Kosovo, including from international sources. They shall in particular allow access to Kosovo without discrimination for persons delivering such goods and services.

7. If expressly required by an international donor or lender, international contracts for reconstruction projects shall be concluded by the authorities of the Federal Republic of Yugoslavia, which shall establish appropriate mechanisms to make such funds available to

Kosovo authorities. Unless precluded by the terms of contracts, all reconstruction projects that exclusively concern Kosovo shall be managed and implemented by the appropriate Kosovo authority.

Article II

1. The Parties agree to reallocate ownership and resources in accordance insofar as possible with the distribution of powers and responsibilities set forth in this Agreement, in the following areas:

(a) government-owned assets (including educational institutions, hospitals, natural resources, and production facilities);

(b) pension and social insurance contributions;

(c) revenues to be distributed under Article I.5; and

(d) any other matters relating to economic relations between the Parties not covered by this Agreement.

2. The Parties agree to the creation of a Claim Settlement Commission (CSC) to resolve all disputes between them on matters referred to in paragraph 1.

(a) The CSC shall consist of three experts designated by Kosovo, three experts designated jointly by the Federal Republic of Yugoslavia and the Republic of Serbia, and three independent experts designated by the CIM.

(b) The decisions of the CSC, which shall be taken by majority vote, shall be final and binding. The Parties shall implement them without delay.

3. Authorities receiving ownership of public facilities shall have the power to operate such facilities.

Chapter 4b, Humanitarian Assistance, Reconstruction and Economic Development

1. In parallel with the continuing full implementation of this Agreement, urgent attention must be focused on meeting the real humanitarian and economic needs of Kosovo in order to help create the conditions for reconstruction and lasting economic recovery. International assistance will be provided without discrimination between national communities.

2. The Parties welcome the willingness of the European Commission working with the international community to co-ordinate international support for the parties' efforts. Specifically, the European Commission will organize an international donors, conference within one month of entry into force of this Agreement.

3. The international community will provide immediate and unconditional humanitarian assistance, focusing primarily on refugees and internally displaced persons returning to their former homes. The Parties welcome and endorse the UNHCR's lead role in co-ordination of this effort, and endorse its intention, in close co-operation with the Implementation Mission, to plan an early, peaceful, orderly and phased return of refugees and displaced persons in conditions of safety and dignity.

4. The international community will provide the means for the rapid improvement of living conditions for the population of Kosovo through the reconstruction and rehabilitation of housing and local infrastructure (including water, energy, health and local education infrastructure) based on damage assessment surveys.

5. Assistance will also be provided to support the establishment and development of the institutional and legislative framework laid down in this Agreement, including local governance and tax settlement, and to reinforce civil society, culture and education ' Social welfare will also be addressed, with priority given to the protection of vulnerable social groups.

6. It will also be vital to lay the foundations for sustained development, based on a revival of the local economy. This must take account of the need to address unemployment, and to stimulate the economy by a range of mechanisms. The European Commission will be giving urgent attention to this.

7. International assistance, with the exception of humanitarian aid, will be subject to full compliance with this Agreement as well as other conditionalities defined in advance by the donors and the absorptive capacity of Kosovo.

Chapter 5, Implementation I

Article I: Institutions

Implementation Mission

1. The Parties invite the OSCE, in cooperation with the European Union, to constitute an Implementation Mission in Kosovo. All responsibilities and powers previously vested in the Kosovo Verification Mission and its Head by prior agreements shall be continued in the Implementation Mission and its Chief.

Joint Commission

2. A Joint Commission shall serve as the central mechanism for monitoring and coordinating the civilian implementation of this Agreement. It shall consist of the Chief of the Implementation Mission (CIM), one Federal and one Republic representative, one representative of each national community in Kosovo, the President of the Assembly, and a representative of the President of Kosovo. Meetings of the Joint Commission may be attended by other representatives of organizations specified in this Agreement or needed for its implementation.

3. The CIM shall serve as the Chair of the Joint Commission. The Chair shall coordinate and organize the work of the Joint Commission and decide the time and place of its meetings. The Parties shall abide by and fully implement the decisions of the Joint Commission. The Joint Commission shall operate on the basis of consensus, but in the event consensus cannot be reached, the Chair's decision shall be final.

4. The Chair shall have full and unimpeded access to all places, persons, and information (including documents and other records) within Kosovo that in his judgment are necessary to his responsibilities with regard to the civilian aspects of this Agreement.

Joint Council and Local Councils

5. The CIM may, as necessary, establish a Kosovo Joint Council and Local Councils, for informal dispute resolution and cooperation. The Kosovo Joint Council would consist of one member from each of the national communities in Kosovo. Local Councils would consist of representatives of each national community living in the locality where the Local Council is established.

Article II: Responsibilities and Powers

1. The CIM shall:

(a) supervise and direct the implementation of the civilian aspects of this Agreement pursuant to a schedule that he shall specify;

(b) maintain close contact with the Parties to promote full compliance with those aspects of this Agreement;

(c) facilitate, as he deems necessary, the resolution of difficulties arising in connection with such implementation;

(d) participate in meetings of donor organizations, including on issues of rehabilitation and reconstruction, in particular by putting forward proposals and identifying priorities for their consideration as appropriate;

(e) coordinate the activities of civilian organizations and agencies in Kosovo assisting in the implementation of the civilian aspects of this Agreement, respecting fully their specific organizational procedures;

(f) report periodically to the bodies responsible for constituting the Mission on progress in the implementation of the civilian aspects of this Agreement; and

(g) carry out the functions specified in this Agreement pertaining to police and security forces.

2. The CIM shall also carry out other responsibilities set forth in this Agreement or as may he later agreed.

Article III: Status of Implementation Mission

1. Implementation Mission personnel shall be allowed unrestricted movement and access into and throughout Kosovo at any time.

2. The Parties shall facilitate the operations of the Implementation Mission, including by the provision of assistance as requested with regard to transportation, subsistence, accommodation, communication, and other facilities.

3. The Implementation Mission shall enjoy such legal capacity as may be necessary for the exercise of its functions under the laws and regulations of Kosovo, the Federal Republic of Yugoslavia, and the Republic of Serbia. Such legal capacity shall include the capacity to contract, and to acquire and dispose of real and personal property.

4. Privileges and immunities are hereby accorded as follows to the Implementation Mission and associated personnel:

(a) the Implementation Mission and its premises, archives, and other property shall enjoy the same privileges and immunities as a diplomatic mission under the Vienna Convention on Diplomatic Relations;

(b) the CIM and professional members of his staff and their families shall enjoy the same privileges and immunities as are enjoyed by diplomatic agents and their families under the Vienna Convention on Diplomatic Relations; and

(c) other members of the Implementation Mission staff and their families shall enjoy the same privileges and immunities as are enjoyed by members of the administrative and technical staff and their families under the Vienna Convention on Diplomatic Relations.

Article IV: Process of Implementation

General

1. The Parties acknowledge that complete implementation will require political acts and measures, and the election and establishment of institutions and bodies set forth in this Agreement. The Parties agree to proceed expeditiously with these tasks on a schedule set by the Joint Commission. The Parties shall provide active support, cooperation, and participation for the successful implementation of this Agreement.

Elections and Census

2. Within nine months of the entry into force of this Agreement, there shall be elections in accordance with and pursuant to procedures specified in Chapter 3 of this Agreement for authorities established herein, according to a voter list prepared to international standards by the Central Election Commission. The Organization for Security and Cooperation in Europe (OSCE) shall supervise those elections to ensure that they are free and fair.

3. Under the supervision of the OSCE and with the participation of Kosovo authorities and experts nominated by and belonging to the national communities of Kosovo, Federal authorities shall conduct an objective and free census of the population in Kosovo under rules and regulations agreed with the OSCE in accordance with international standards. The census shall be carried out when the OSCE determines that conditions allow an objective and accurate enumeration.

(a) The first census shall be limited to name, place of birth, place of usual residence and address, gender, age, citizenship, national community, and religion.

(b) The authorities of the Parties shall provide each other and the OSCE with all records necessary to conduct the census, including data about places of residence, citizenship, voters, lists, and other information.

Transitional Provisions

4. All laws and regulations in effect in Kosovo when this Agreement enters into force shall remain in effect unless and until replaced by laws or regulations adopted by a competent body. All laws and regulations applicable in Kosovo that are incompatible with this Agreement shall be presumed to have been harmonized with this Agreement. In particular, martial law in Kosovo is hereby revoked.

5. Institutions currently in place in Kosovo shall remain until superseded by bodies created by or in accordance with this Agreement. The CIM may recommend to the appropriate authorities the removal and appointment of officials and the curtailment of operations of existing institutions in Kosovo if he deems it necessary for the effective implementation of this Agreement. If the action recommended is not taken in the time requested, the Joint Commission may decide to take the recommended action.

6. Prior to the election of Kosovo officials pursuant to this Agreement, the CIM shall take the measures necessary to ensure the development and functioning of independent media in keeping with international standards, including allocation of radio and television frequencies.

Article V: Authority to Interpret

The CIM shall be the final authority in theater regarding interpretation of the civilian aspects of this Agreement, and the Parties agree to abide by his determinations as binding on all Parties and persons.

Chapter 6, The Ombudsman

Article I: General

1. There shall be an Ombudsman, who shall monitor the realization of the rights of members of national communities and the protection of human rights and fundamental freedoms in Kosovo. The Ombudsman shall have unimpeded access to any person or place and shall have the right to appear and intervene before any domestic, Federal, or (consistent with the rules of such bodies) international authority upon his or her request. No person, institution, or entity of the Parties may interfere with the functions of the Ombudsman.

2. The Ombudsman shall be an eminent person of high moral standing who possesses a demonstrated commitment to human rights and the rights of members of national communities. He or she shall be nominated by the President of Kosovo and shall be elected by the Assembly from a list of candidates prepared by the President of the European Court of Human Rights for a non-renewable three-year term. The Ombudsman shall not be a citizen of any State or entity that was a part of the former Yugoslavia, or of any neighboring State. Pending the election of the President and the Assembly, the CIM shall designate a person to serve as Ombudsman on an interim basis who shall be succeeded by a person selected pursuant to the procedure set forth in this paragraph.

3. The Ombudsman shall be independently responsible for choosing his or her own staff. He or she shall have two Deputies. The Deputies shall each be drawn from different national communities.

(a) The salaries and expenses of the Ombudsman and his or her staff shall be determined and paid by the Kosovo Assembly. The salaries and expenses shall be fully adequate to implement the Ombudsman's mandate.

(b) The Ombudsman and members of his or her staff shall not be held criminally or civilly liable for any acts carried out within the scope of their duties.

Article II: Jurisdiction

The Ombudsman shall consider:

(a) alleged or apparent violations of human rights and fundamental freedoms in Kosovo, as provided in the Constitutions of the Federal Republic of Yugoslavia and the Republic of Serbia, and the European Convention for the Protection of Human Rights and Fundamental Freedoms and the Protocols thereto; and

(b) alleged or apparent violations of the rights of members of national communities specified in this Agreement.

2. All persons in Kosovo shall have the right to submit complaints to the Ombudsman. The Parties agree not to take any measures to punish persons who intend to submit or who have submitted such allegations, or in any other way to deter the exercise of this right.

Article III: Powers and Duties

1. The Ombudsman shall investigate alleged violations falling within the jurisdiction set forth in Article II.1. He or she may act either on his or her own initiative or in response to an allegation presented by any Party or person, non-governmental organization, or group of individuals claiming to be the victim of a violation or acting on behalf of alleged victims who are deceased or missing. The work of the Ombudsman shall be free of charge to the person concerned.

2. The Ombudsman shall have complete, unimpeded, and immediate access to any person, place, or information upon his or her request.

(a) The Ombudsman shall have access to and may examine all official documents, and he or she can require any person, including officials of Kosovo, to cooperate by providing relevant information, documents, and files.

(b) The Ombudsman may attend administrative hearings and meetings of other Kosovo institutions in order to gather information.

(c) The Ombudsman may examine facilities and places where persons deprived of their liberty are detained, work, or are otherwise located.

(d) The Ombudsman and staff shall maintain the confidentiality of all confidential information obtained by them, unless the Ombudsman determines that such information is evidence of a violation of rights falling within his or her jurisdiction, in which case that information may be revealed in public reports or appropriate legal proceedings.

(e) The Parties undertake to ensure cooperation with the ombudsman's investigations. Willful and knowing failure to comply shall be a criminal offense prosecutable in any Jurisdiction of the Parties. Where an official impedes an investigation by refusing to provide necessary information, the Ombudsman shall contact that officials superior or the public prosecutor for appropriate penal action to be taken in accordance with the law.

3. The Ombudsman shall issue findings and conclusions in the form of a published report promptly after concluding an investigation.

(a) A Party, institution, or official identified by the Ombudsman as a violator shall, within a period specified by the Ombudsman, explain in writing how it will comply with any prescriptions the Ombudsman may put forth for remedial measures.

(b) In the event that a person or entity does not comply with the conclusions and recommendations of the Ombudsman, the report shall be forwarded for further action to the Joint Commission established by Chapter 5 of this Agreement, to the President of the appropriate Party, and to any other officials or institutions that the Ombudsman deems proper.

Chapter 7, Implementation II
Article I: General Obligations

1. The Parties undertake to recreate, as quickly as possible, normal conditions of life in Kosovo and to co- operate fully with each other and with all international organizations, agencies, and non-governmental organizations involved in the implementation of this Agreement. They welcome the willingness of the international community to send to the region a force to assist in the implementation of this Agreement. a. The United Nations Security Council is invited to pass a resolution under Chapter VII of the Charter endorsing and adopting the arrangements set forth in this Chapter, including the establishment of a multinational military implementation force in Kosovo. The Parties invite NATO to constitute and lead a military force to help ensure compliance with the provisions of this Chapter. They also reaffirm the sovereignty and territorial integrity of the Federal Republic of Yugoslavia (FRY).

b. The Parties agree that NATO will establish and deploy a force (hereinafter IIKFORII) which may be composed of ground, air, and maritime units from NATO and non-NATO nations, operating under the authority and subject to the direction and the political control of the North Atlantic Council (NAC) through the NATO chain of command. The Parties agree to facilitate the deployment and operations of this force and agree also to comply fully with all the obligations of this Chapter. c. it is agreed that other States may assist in implementing this Chapter. The Parties agree that the modalities of those States' participation will be the subject of agreement between such participating States and NATO. 2. The purposes of these obligations are as follows:

a. to establish a durable cessation of hostilities. Other than those Forces provided for in this Chapter, under no circumstances shall any armed Forces enter, reenter, or remain within Kosovo without the prior express consent of the KFOR Commander (COMKFOR). For the purposes of this Chapter, the term "Forces" includes all personnel and organizations with military capability, including regular army, armed civilian groups, paramilitary groups, air forces, national guards, border police, army reserves, military police, intelligence services, Ministry of Internal Affairs, Local, Special, Riot and Anti-Terrorist Police, and any other groups or individuals so designated by COMKFOP,. The only exception to the provisions of this paragraph is for civilian police engaged in hot pursuit of a person suspected of committing a serious criminal offense, as provided for in Chapter 2;

b. to provide for the support and authorization of the KFOR and in particular to authorize the KFOR to take such actions as are required, including the use of necessary force, to ensure compliance with this Chapter and the protection of the KFOR, Implementation Mission (IM), and other international organizations, agencies, and non-governmental organizations involved in the implementation of this Agreement, and to contribute to a secure environment;

c. to provide, at no cost, the use of all facilities and services required for the deployment, operations and support of the KFOR.

3. The Parties understand and agree that the obligations undertaken in this Chapter shall apply equally to each Party. Each Party shall be held individually responsible for compliance with its obligations, and each agrees that delay or failure to comply by one Party shall not constitute cause for any other Party to fail to carry out its own obligations. All Parties shall be equally subject to such enforcement action by the KFOR as may be necessary to ensure implementation of this Chapter in Kosovo and the protection of the KFOR, IM, and other international organizations, agencies, and non- governmental organizations involved in the implementation of this Agreement.

Article II: Cessation of Hostilities

1. The Parties shall, immediately upon entry into force of this Agreement (EIF), refrain from committing any hostile or provocative acts of any type against each other or against any person in Kosovo. They shall not encourage or organize hostile or provocative demonstrations.

2. In carrying out the obligations set forth in paragraph 1, the Parties undertake in particular to cease the firing of all weapons and explosive devices except as authorized by COMKFOR. They shall not place any mines, barriers, unauthorized checkpoints, observation posts (with the exception of COMKFOR-approved border observation posts and crossing points), or protective obstacles. Except as provided in Chapter 2, the Parties shall not engage in any military, security, or training-related activities, including ground, air, or air defense operations, in or over Kosovo, without the prior express approval of COMKFOR.

3. Except for Border Guard forces (as provided for in Article IV), no Party shall have Forces present within a 5 kilometer zone inward from the international border of the FRY that is also the border of Kosovo (hereinafter "the Border Zone") . The Border Zone will be marked on the ground by EIF + 14 days by VJ Border Guard personnel in accordance with direction from IM. COMKFOR may determine small scale reconfigurations for operational reasons.

4. a. With the exception of civilian police performing normal police duties as determined by the CIM, no Party shall have Forces present within 5 kilometers of the Kosovo side of the boundary of Kosovo with other parts of the FRY.

b. The presence of any Forces within 5 kilometers of the other side of that boundary shall be notified to COMKFOR; if, in the judgment of COMKFOR, such presence threatens or would threaten implementation of this Chapter in Kosovo, he shall contact the authorities responsible for the Forces in question and may require those Forces to withdraw from or remain outside that area.

5. No Party shall conduct any reprisals, counter-attacks, or any unilateral actions in response to violations of this Chapter by another Party. The Parties shall respond to alleged violations of this Chapter through the procedures provided in Article XI.

Article III: Redeployment, Withdrawal, and Demilitarization of Forces

In order to disengage their Forces and to avoid any further conflict, the Parties shall immediately upon EIF begin to re-deploy, withdraw, or demilitarize their Forces in accordance with Articles IV, V, and VI.

Article IV: VJ Forces

1. VJ Army Units

a. By K-Day + 5 days, all VJ Army units in Kosovo (with the exception of those Forces specified in paragraph 2 of this Article) shall have completed redeployment to the approved cantonment sites listed at Appendix A to this Chapter. The senior vi commander in Kosovo shall confirm in writing to COMKFOR by K-Day + 5 days that the VJ is in compliance and provide the information required in Article VII below to take account of withdrawals or other changes made during the redeployment. This information shall be updated weekly.

b. By K-Day + 30 days, the Chief of the VJ General Staff, through the senior VJ commander in Kosovo, shall provide for approval by COMKFOR a detailed plan for the phased withdrawal of Vi Forces from Kosovo to other locations in Serbia to ensure the following timelines are met:

1) By K-Day + 90 days, VJ authorities must, to the satisfaction of COMKFOR, withdraw from Kosovo to other locations in Serbia 50% of men and materiel and all designated offensive assets. Such assets are taken to be: main battle tanks; all other armored vehicles mounting weapons greater than 12.7mm; and, all heavy weapons (vehicle mounted or not) of over 82mm.

2) By K-Day + 180 days, all VJ Army personnel and equipment (with the exception of those Forces specified in paragraph 2 of this Article) shall be withdrawn from Kosovo to other locations in Serbia.

2. VJ Border Guard Forces

a. VJ Border Guard forces shall be permitted but limited to a structure of 1500 members at pre- February 1998 Border Guard Battalion facilities located in Djakovica, Prizren, and Urosevac and subordinate facilities within the 5 kilometer Border Zone, or at a limited number of existing facilities in the immediate proximity of the Border Zone subject to the prior approval of COMKFOR, with that number to be reached by K-Day + 14 days. An additional number of VJ personnel - - totaling no more than 1000 C2 and logistics forces -- will be permitted to remain in the approved cantonment sites listed at Appendix A to fulfill brigade-level functions related only to border security. After an initial 90 day period from K-Day, COMKFOR may at any time review the deployments of VJ personnel and may require further adjustments to force levels, with the objective of reaching the minimum force structure required for legitimate border security, as the security situation and the conduct of the Parties warrant.

b. VJ elements in Kosovo shall be limited to weapons of 82mm and below. They shall possess neither armored vehicles (other than wheeled vehicles mounting weapons of 12.7mm or less) nor air defense weapons.

C. VJ Border Guard units shall be permitted to patrol in Kosovo only within the Border Zone and solely for the purpose of defending the border against external attack and maintaining its integrity by preventing illicit border crossings. Geographic terrain considerations may require Border Guard maneuver inward of the Border Zone; any such maneuver shall be coordinated with and approved by COMKFOR.

d. With the exception of the Border Zone, VJ units may travel through Kosovo only to reach duty stations and garrisons in the Border Zone or approved cantonment sites. Such travel may only be along routes and in accordance with procedures that have been determined by COMKFOR after consultation with the CIM, VJ unit commanders, communal government authorities, and police commanders. These routes and procedures will be determined by K-Day + 14 days, subject to re- determination by COMKFOR at any time. VJ forces in Kosovo but outside the Border Zone shall be permitted to act only in self-defense in response to a hostile act pursuant to Rules of Engagement (ROE) which will be approved by COMKFOR in consultation with the CIM. When deployed in the Border Zone, they will act in accordance with ROE established under control of COMKFOR.

e. VJ Border Guard forces may conduct training activities only within the S kilometer Border Zone, and only with the prior express approval of COMKFOR.

3. Yugoslav Air and Air Defense Forces (YAADF) All aircraft, radars, surface-to-air missiles (including man-portable air defense systems (MANPADS) and anti-aircraft artillery in Kosovo shall immediately upon EIF begin withdrawing from Kosovo to other locations in Serbia outside the 25 kilometer Mutual Safety Zone as

defined in Article X. This withdrawal shall be completed and reported by the senior VJ commander in Kosovo to the appropriate NATO commander not more than 10 days after EIF. The appropriate NATO commander shall control and coordinate use of airspace over Kosovo commencing at EIF as further specified in Article X. No air defense systems, target tracking radars, or anti-aircraft artillery shall be positioned or operated within Kosovo or the 25 kilometer Mutual Safety Zone without the prior express approval of the appropriate NATO commander.

Article V: Other Forces

1. The actions of Forces in Kosovo other than KFOR, VJ, MUP, or local police forces provided for in Chapter 2 (hereinafter referred to as "Other Forces") shall be in accordance with this Article. Upon EIF, all Other Forces in Kosovo must immediately observe the provisions of Article I, paragraph 2, Article II, paragraph 1, and Article III and "in addition refrain from all hostile intent, military training and formations, organization of demonstrations, and any movement in either direction or smuggling across international borders or the boundary between

Kosovo and other parts of the FRY. Furthermore, upon EIF, all Other Forces in Kosovo must publicly commit themselves to demilitarize on terms to be determined by COMKFOR, renounce violence, guarantee security of international personnel, and respect the international borders of the FRY and all terms of this Chapter.

2. Except as approved by COMKFOR, from K-Day, all other Forces in Kosovo must not carry weapons:

a. within 1 kilometer of VJ and MUP cantonments listed at Appendix A;

b. within 1 kilometer of the main roads as follows:

1) Pec - Lapusnik - Pristina
2) border - Djakovica - Klina
3) border - Prizren - Suva Rika - Pristina
4) Djakovica - Orahovac - Lapusnik - Pristina
5) Pec-Djakovica - Prizren - Urosevac - border
6) border - Urosevac - Pristina - Podujevo - border
7) Pristina - Kosovska Mitrovica - border
8) Kosovka Mitrovica - (Rakos) - Pec
9) Pec - Border with Montenegro (through Pozaj)
10) Pristina - Lisica - border with Serbia
11) Pristina - Gnjilane - Urosevac
12) Gnjilane - Veliki Trnovac - border with Serbia;
13) Prizren - Doganovic

c. within 1 kilometer of the Border Zone;
d. in any other areas designated by COMKFOR.

3. By K-Day + 5 days, all Other Forces must abandon and close all fighting positions, entrenchments, and checkpoints.

4. By K-Day + 5 days, all Other Forces' commanders designated by COMKFOR shall report completion of the above requirements in the format at Article VII to COMKFOR and continue to provide weekly detailed status reports until demilitarization is complete.

5. COMKFOR will establish procedures for demilitarization and monitoring of Other Forces in Kosovo and for the further regulation-of their activities. These procedures will be established to facilitate a phased demilitarization program as follows:

a. By K-Day + 5 days, all Other Forces shall establish secure weapons storage sites, which shall be registered with and verified by the KFOR;

b. By K-Day + 30 days, all other Forces shall store all prohibited weapons (any weapon 12.7mm or larger, any anti-tank or anti-aircraft weapons, grenades, mines or explosives) and automatic weapons in the re gistered weapons storage sites. Other Forces commanders shall confirm completion of weapons storage to COMKFOR no later than K-Day + 30 days;

c. By K-Day + 30 days, all Other Forces shall cease wearing military uniforms and insignia, and cease carrying prohibited weapons and automatic weapons;

d. By K-Day + 90 days, authority for storage sites shall pass to the KFOR. After this date, it shall be illegal for Other Forces to possess prohibited weapons and automatic weapons, and such weapons shall be subject to confiscation by the KFOR;

e. By K-Day + 120 days, demilitarization of all Other Forces shall be completed.

6. By EIF + 30 days, subject to arrangements by COMKFOR if necessary, all Other Forces personnel who are not of local origin, whether or not they are legally within Kosovo, including individual advisors, freedom fighters, trainers, volunteers, and personnel from neighboring and other States, shall be withdrawn from Kosovo.

Article VI: MUP

1. Ministry of Interior Police (MUP) is defined as all police and public security units and personnel under the control of Federal or Republic authorities except for the border police referred to in Chapter 2 and police academy students and personnel at the training school in Vucitrn referred to in Chapter 2. The CIM, in consultation with COMKFOR, shall have the discretion to exempt any public security units from this definition if he determines that it is in the public interest (e.g. firefighters).

a. By K-Day + 5 days, all MUP units in Kosovo (with the exception of the border police referred to in Chapter 2) shall have completed redeployment to the approved cantonment sites listed at Appendix A to this Chapter or to garrisons outside Kosovo. The senior MUP commander in Kosovo or his representative shall confirm in writing by K-Day + 5 days to COMKFOR and the CIM that the MUP is in compliance and update the information required in Article VII to take account of withdrawals or other changes made during the redeployment. This information shall be updated weekly. Resumption of normal communal police patrolling will be permitted under the supervision and control of the IM and as specifically approved by the CIM in consultation with COMKFOR, and will be contingent on compliance with the terms of this Agreement.

b. Immediately upon EIF, the following withdrawals shall begin:
1) By K-Day + 5 days, those MUP units not assigned to Kosovo prior to 1 February 1998 shall withdraw all personnel and equipment from Kosovo to other locations in Serbia.
2) By K-Day + 20 days, all Special Police, including PJP, SAJ, and JSO forces, and their equipment shall be withdrawn from their cantonment sites out of Kosovo to other locations in Serbia. Additionally, all MUP offensive assets (designated as armored vehicles mounting weapons 12.7mm or larger, and all heavy weapons (vehicle mounted or not) of over 82mm) shall be withdrawn.

c. By K-Day + 30 days, the senior MUP commander shall provide for approval by COMKFOR, in consultation with the CIM, a detailed plan for the phased drawdown of the remainder of MUP forces. In the event that COMKFOR, in consultation with the CIM, does not approve the plan, he has the authority to issue his own binding plan for further MUPdrawdowns. The CIM will decide at the same time when the remaining MUP units will wear new insignia. In any case, the following time-table must be met:
1) by K-Day + 60 days, 50% drawdown of the remaining MUP units including reservists. The CIM after consultations with COMKFOR shall have the discretion to extend this deadline for up to K-Day + 90 days if he judges there to be a risk of a law enforcement vacuum;
2) by K-Day + 120 days, further drawdown to 2500 MUP. The CIM after consultations with COMKFOR shall have the discretion to extend this deadline for up to K-Day + 180 days to meet operational needs;
3) transition to communal police force shall begin as Kosovar police are trained and able to assume their duties. The CIM shall organize this transition between MUP and communal police;
4) in any event, by EIF + one year, all Ministry of Interior Civil Police shall be drawn down to zero. The CIM shall have the discretion to extend this deadline for up to an additional 12 months to meet operational needs.

d. The 2500 MUP allowed by this Chapter and referred to in Article V.1(a) of Chapter 2 shall have authority only for civil police functions and be under the supervision and control of the CIM.

Article VII: Notifications

1. By K-Day + 5 days, the Parties shall furnish the following specific information regarding the status of all conventional military; all police, including military police, Department of Public Security Police, special police; paramilitary; and all Other Forces in Kosovo, and shall update the COMKFOR weekly on changes in this information:
a. location, disposition, and strengths of all military and special police units referred to above;
b. quantity and type of weaponry of 12.7 mm and above, and ammunition for such weaponry, including location of cantonments and supply depots and storage sites;
c. positions and descriptions of any surface-to-air missiles/launchers, including mobile systems, anti-aircraft artillery, supporting radars, and associated command and control systems;
d. positions and descriptions of all mines, unexploded ordnance, explosive devices, demolitions, obstacles, booby traps, wire entanglements, physical or military hazards to the safe movement of any personnel in Kosovo, weapons systems, vehicles, or any other military equipment; and
e. any further information of a military or security nature requested by the COMKFOR.

Article VIII: Operations and Authority of the KFOR

1. Consistent with the general obligations of Article I, the Parties understand and agree that the KFOR will deploy and operate without hindrance and with the authority to take all necessary action to help ensure compliance with this Chapter.
2. The Parties understand and agree that the KFOR shall have the right:
a. to monitor and help ensure compliance by all Parties with this Chapter and to respond promptly to any violations and restore compliance, using military force if required. This includes necessary action to:
1) enforce VJ and MUP reductions;
2) enforce demilitarization of Other Forces;
3) enforce restrictions on all VJ, MUP and Other Forces' activities, movement and training in Kosovo;
b. to establish liaison arrangements with IM, and support IM as appropriate;
c. to establish liaison arrangements with local Kosovo authorities, with Other Forces, and with FRY and Serbian civil and military authorities;
d. to observe, monitor, and inspect any and all facilities or activities in Kosovo, including within the Border Zone, that the COMKFOR believes has or may have military capability, or are or may be associated with the employment of military or police capabilities, or are otherwise relevant to compliance with this Chapter;
e. to require the Parties to mark and clear minefields and obstacles and to monitor their performance;
f. to require the Parties to participate in the Joint Military Commission and its subordinate military commissions as described in Article XI.
3. The Parties understand and agree that the KFOR shall have the right to fulfill its supporting tasks, within the limits of its assigned principal tasks, its capabilities, and available resources, and as directed by the NAC, which include the following:
a. to help create secure conditions for the conduct by others of other tasks associated with this Agreement, including free and fair elections;
b. to assist the movement of organizations in the accomplishment of humanitarian missions;
c. to assist international agencies in fulfilling their responsibilities in Kosovo;
d. to observe and prevent interference with the movement of civilian populations, refugees, and displaced persons, and to respond appropriately to deliberate threat to life and person.
4. The Parties understand and agree that further directives from the NAC may establish additional duties and responsibilities for the KFOR in implementing this Chapter.
5. KFOR operations shall be governed by the following provisions:
a. KFOR and its personnel shall have the legal status, rights, and obligations specified in Appendix 13 to this Chapter;
b. The KFOR shall have the right to use all necessary means to ensure its full ability to communicate and shall have the right to the unrestricted use of the entire electromagnetic spectrum. In implementing this right, the KFOR shall make reasonable efforts to coordinate with the appropriate authorities of the Parties;
c. The KFOR shall have the right to control and regulate surface traffic throughout Kosovo including the movement of the Forces of the Parties. All military training activities and movements in Kosovo must be authorized in advance by COMKFOR;
d. The KFOR shall have complete and unimpeded freedom of movement by ground, air, and water into and throughout Kosovo. It shall in Kosovo have the right to bivouac, maneuver, billet, and utilize any areas or facilities to carry out its responsibilities as required for its support, training, and operations, with such advance notice as may be practicable. Neither the KFOR nor any of its personnel shall be liable for any damages to public or private property that they may cause in the course of duties related to the implementation of this Chapter. Roadblocks, checkpoints, or other impediments to KFOR freedom of movement shall constitute a breach of this Chapter and the violating Party shall be subject to military action by the KFOR, including the use of necessary force to ensure compliance with this Chapter.

6. The Parties understand and agree that COMKFOR shall have the authority, without interference or permission of any Party, to do all that he judges necessary and proper, including the use of military force, to protect the KFOR and the IM, and to carry out the responsibilities listed in this Chapter. The Parties shall comply in all respects with KFOR instructions and requirements.

7. Notwithstanding any other provisions of this Chapter, the Parties understand and agree that COMKFOR has the right and is authorized to compel the removal, withdrawal, or relocation of specific Forces and weapons, and to order the cessation of any activities whenever the COMKFOR determines such Forces, weapons, or activities to constitute a threat or potential threat to either the KFOR or its mission, or to another Party. Forces failing to redeploy, withdraw, relocate, or to cease threatening or potentially threatening activities following such a demand by the KFOR shall be subject to military action by the KFOR, including the use of necessary force, to ensure compliance, consistent with the terms set forth in Article I, paragraph 3.

Article IX: Border Control

The Parties understand and agree that, until other arrangements are established, and subject to provisions of this Chapter and Chapter 2, controls along the international border of the FRY that is also the border of Kosovo will be maintained by the existing institutions normally assigned to such tasks, subject to supervision by the KFOR and the IM, which shall have the right to review and approve all personnel and units, to monitor their performance, and to remove and replace any personnel for behavior inconsistent with this Chapter.

Article X: Control of Air Movements

The appropriate NATO commander shall have sole authority to establish-rules and procedures governing command and control of the airspace over Kosovo as well as within a 25 kilometer Mutual Safety Zone (MSZ). This MSZ shall consist of FRY airspace within 25 kilometers outward from the boundary of Kosovo with other parts of the FRY. This Chapter supersedes the NATO Kosovo Verification Mission Agreement of October 12, 1998 on any matter or area in which they may contradict each other. No military air traffic, fixed or rotary wing, of any Party shall be permitted to fly over Kosovo or in the MSZ without the prior express approval of the appropriate NATO commander. violations of any of the provisions above, including the appropriate NATO commander's rules and procedures governing the airspace over Kosovo, as well as unauthorized flight or activation of FRY Integrated Air Defense (IAE)S) within the MSZ, shall be subject to military action by the KFOR, including the use of necessary force. The KFOR shall have a liaison team at the FRY Air Force HQ and a YAADF liaison shall be established with the KFOR. The Parties understand and agree that the appropriate NATO commander may delegate control of normal civilian air activities to appropriate FRY institutions to monitor operations, deconflict KFOR air traffic movements, and ensure smooth and safe operation of the air traffic system.

Article XI: Establishment of a Joint Military Commission

1. A Joint Military Commission (JMC) shall be established with the deployment of the KFOR to Kosovo.

2. The JMC shall be chaired by COMKFOR or his representative and consist of the following members:

   a. the senior Yugoslav military commander of theForces of the FRY or his representative;

   b. the Ministers of Interior of the FRY and Republic of Serbia or their representatives;

   c. a senior military representative of all other Forces;

   d. a representative of the IM;

   e. other persons as COMKFOR shall determine, including one or more representatives of the Kosovo civilian leadership.

1. The JMC shall:

   a. serve as the central body for all Parties to address any military complaints, questions, or problems that require resolution by the COMKFOR, such as allegations of cease-fire violations or other allegations of non-compliance with this Chapter;

   b. receive reports and make recommendations for specific actions to COMKFOR to ensure compliance by the Parties with the provisions of this Chapter;

   c. assist COMKFOR in determining and implementing local transparency measures between the Parties.

4. The JMC shall not include any persons publicly indicted by the International Criminal Tribunal for the Former Yugoslavia.

5. The JMC shall function as a consultative body to advise COMKFOR. However, all final decisions shall be made by COMKFOR and shall be binding on the Parties.

6. The JMC shall meet at the call of COMKFOR. Any Party may request COMKFOR to convene a meeting.

7. The JMC shall establish subordinate military commissions for the purpose of providing assistance in carrying out the functions described above. Such commissions shall be at an appropriate level, as COMKFOR shall direct. Composition of such commissions shall be determined by COMKFOR.

Article XII: Prisoner Release

1. By EIF + 21 days, the Parties shall release and transfer, in accordance with international humanitarian standards, all persons held in connection with the conflict (hereinafter "prisoners"). In addition, the Parties shall cooperate fully with the International Committee of the Red Cross (ICRC) to facilitate its work, in accordance with its mandate, to implement and monitor a plan for the release and transfer of prisoners in accordance with the above deadline. In preparation for compliance with this requirement, the Parties shall:

   a. grant the ICRC full access to all persons, irrespective of their status, who are being held by them in connection with the conflict, for visits in accordance with the ICRC's standard operating procedures;

   b. provide to the ICRC any and all information concerning prisoners, as requested by the ICRC, by EIF + 14 days.

2. The Parties shall provide information, through the tracing mechanisms of the ICRC, to the families of all persons who are unaccounted for. The Parties shall cooperate fully with the ICRC in its efforts to determine the identity, whereabouts, and fate of those unaccounted for.

Article XIII: Cooperation

The Parties shall cooperate fully with all entities involved in implementation of this settlement, as described in the Framework Agreement, or which are otherwise authorized by the United Nations Security Council, including the International Criminal Tribunal for the former Yugoslavia.

Article XIV: Notification to Military Commands

Each Party shall ensure that the terms of this Chapter and written orders requiring compliance are immediately communicated to all of its Forces.

Article XV: Final Authority to Interpret

1. Subject to paragraph 2, the KFOR Commander is the final authority in theater regarding interpretation of this Chapter and his determinations are binding on all Parties and persons.

2. The CIM is the final authority in theater regarding interpretation of the references in this Chapter to his functions (directing the VJ Border Guards under Article II, paragraph 3; his functions concerning the MUP under Article VI) and his determinations are binding on all Parties and persons.

Article XVI: K-Day

The date of activation of KFOR--to be known as K-Day--shall be determined by NATO.

Appendices:

A. Approved VJ/MUP Cantonment Sites

B. Status of Multi-National Military Implementation Force

Appendix A: Approved VJ/MUP Cantonment Sites

1. There are 13 approved cantonment sites in Kosovo for all VJ units, weapons, equipment, and ammunition. Movement to cantonment sites, and subsequent withdrawal from Kosovo, will occur in accordance with this Chapter. As the phased withdrawal of VJ units progresses along the timeline as specified in this Chapter, COMKFOR will close selected cantonment sites.

2. Initial approved VJ cantonment sites:

   a) Pristina SW 423913NO210819E

   b) Pristina Airfield 423412NO210040E

c) Vuctrin North 424936NO20575SE
d) Kosovska Mitrovica 425315NO2OS227E
e) Gnjilane NE 422807NO21284SE
f) Urosevac 422233NO2107S3E
g) Prizren 421315NO204SO4E
h) Djakovica SW 422212NO202530E
i) Pec 4239ION020172SE
j) Pristina Explosive Storage Fac 423636NO211225E
k) Pristina Ammo Depot SW 423518NO205923E
l) Pristina Ammo Depot 510 424211NO211056E
m) Pristina Headquarters facility 423938NO210934E

3. Within each cantonment site, VJ units are required to canton all heavy weapons and vehicles outside of storage facilities.

4. After EIF + 180 days, the remaining 2500 VJ forces dedicated to border security functions provided for in this Agreement will be garrisoned and cantoned at the following locations: Djakovica, Prizren, and Ursoevac; subordinate border posts within the Border Zone; a limited number of existing facilities in the immediate proximity of the Border zone subject to the prior approval of COMKFOR; and headquarters/C2 and logistic support facilities in Pristina.

5. There are 37 approved cantonment sites for all MUP and Special Police force units in Kosovo. There are seven (7) approved regional SUPS. Each of the 37 approved cantonment sites will fall under the administrative control of one of the regional SUPS. Movement to cantonment sites, and subsequent withdrawal of MUP from Kosovo, will occur in accordance with this Chapter.

6. Approved MUP regional SUPs and cantonment sites:
    a) Kosovska Mitrovica SUP 42530ON0205200E
      1) Kosovska Mitrovica (2 locations)
      2) Leposavic
      3) Srbica
      4) Vucitrn
      5) Zubin Potok
    b) Pristina SUP 42400ON0211000E
      1) Pristina (6 locations)
      2) Glogovac
      3) Kosovo Polje
      4) Lipjan
      5) Obilic
      6) Podujevo
    c) Pec SUP 42390ON0201600E
      1) Pec (2 locations)
      2) Klina
      3) Istok
      4) Malisevo
    d) Djakovica SUP 42230ON0202600E
      1) Djakovica (2 locations)
      2) Decani
    e) Urosevac SUP 42220ON0211000E
      1) Urosevac (2 locations)
      2) Stimlje
      3) Strpce
      4) Kacanik
    f) Gnjilane SUP 42280ON0212900E
      1) Gnjilane (2 locations)
      2) Kamenica
      3) Vitina
      4) Kosovska
      5) Novo Brdo
    g) Prizren SUP 42130ON0204500E
      1) Prizren (2 locations)
      2) Orahovac
      3) Suva Reka
      4) Gora

7. Within each cantonment site, MUP units are required to canton all vehicles above 6 tons, including APCs and BOVs, and all heavy weapons outside of storage facilities.

8. KFOR will have the exclusive right to inspect any cantonment site or any other location, at any time, without interference from any Party.

Appendix B: Status of Multi-National Military Implementation Force

1. For the purposes of this Appendix, the following expressions shall have the meanings hereunder assigned to them:

a. "NATO" means the North Atlantic Treaty Organization (NATO), its subsidiary bodies, its military Headquarters, the NATO-led KFOR, and any elements/units forming any part of KFOR or supporting KFOR, whether or not they are from a NATO member country and whether or not they are under NATO or national command and control, when acting in furtherance of this Agreement.

b. "Authorities in the FRY" means appropriate authorities, whether Federal, Republic, Kosovo or other.

c. "NATO personnel" means the military, civilian, and contractor personnel assigned or attached to or employed by NATO, including the military, civilian, and contractor personnel from non-NATO states participating in the Operation, with the exception of personnel locally hired.

d. "the Operation" means the support, implementation, preparation, and participation by NATO and NATO personnel in furtherance of this Chapter.

e. "Military Headquarters" means any entity, whatever its denomination, consisting of or constituted in part by NATO military personnel established in order to fulfill the Operation.

f. "Authorities" means the appropriate responsible individual, agency, or organization of the Parties.

g. "Contractor personnel" means the technical experts or functional specialists whose services are required by NATO and who are in the territory of the FRY exclusively to serve NATO either in an advisory capacity in technical matters, or for the setting up, operation, or maintenance of equipment, unless they are:
    (1) nationals of the FRY; or
    (2) persons ordinarily resident in the FRY.

h. "Official use" means any use of goods purchased, or of the services received and intended for the performance of any function as required by the operation of the Headquarters.

i. "Facilities" means all buildings, structures, premises, and land required for conducting the operational, training, and administrative activities by NATO for the Operation as well as for accommodation-of NATO personnel.

2. Without prejudice to their privileges and immunities under this Appendix, all NATO personnel shall respect the laws applicable in the FRY, whether Federal, Republic, Kosovo, or other, insofar as compliance with those laws is compatible with the entrusted tasks/mandate and shall refrain from activities not compatible with the nature of the Operation.

3. The Parties recognize the need for expeditious departure and entry procedures for NATO personnel. Such personnel shall be exempt from passport and visa regulations and the registration requirements applicable to aliens. At all entry and exit points to/from the FRY, NATO personnel shall be permitted to enter/exit the FRY on production of a national identification (ID) card. NATO personnel shall carry identification which they may be requested to produce for the authorities in the FRY, but operations, training, and movement shall not be allowed to be impeded or delayed by such requests.

4. NATO military personnel shall normally wear uniforms, and NATO personnel may possess and carry arms if authorized to do so by their orders. The Parties shall accept as valid, without tax or fee, drivers, licenses and permits issued to NATO personnel by their respective national authorities.

5. NATO shall be permitted to display the NATO flag and/or national flags of its constituent national elements/units on any NATO uniform, means of transport, or facility.

6. a. NATO shall be immune from all legal process, whether civil, administrative, or criminal.

b. NATO personnel, under all circumstances and at all times, shall be immune from the Parties, jurisdiction in respect of any civil, administrative, criminal, or disciplinary offenses which may be committed by them in the FRY. The Parties shall assist States participating in the operation in the exercise of their jurisdiction over their own nationals.

c. Notwithstanding the above, and with the NATO Commander's express agreement in each case, the authorities in the FRY may exceptionally exercise jurisdiction in such matters, but only in respect of Contractor personnel who are not subject to the jurisdiction of their nation of citizenship.

7. NATO personnel shall be immune from any form of arrest, investigation, or detention by the authorities in the FRY. NATO personnel erroneously arrested or detained shall immediately be turned over to NATO authorities.

8. NATO personnel shall enjoy, together with their vehicles, vessels, aircraft, and equipment, free and unrestricted passage and unimpeded access throughout the FRY including associated airspace and territorial waters. This shall include, but not be limited to, the right of bivouac, maneuver, billet, and utilization of any areas or facilities as required for support, training, and operations. 9. NATO shall be exempt from duties, taxes, and other charges and inspections and custom regulations including providing inventories or other routine customs documentation, for personnel, vehicles, vessels, aircraft, equipment, supplies, and provisions entering, exiting, or transiting the territory of the FRY in support of the Operation.

10. The authorities in the FRY shall facilitate, on a priority basis and with all appropriate means, all movement of personnel, vehicles, vessels, aircraft, equipment, or supplies, through or in the airspace, ports, airports, or roads used. No charges may be assessed against NATO for air navigation, landing, or takeoff of aircraft, whether government-owned or chartered. Similarly, no duties, dues, tolls or charges may be assessed against NATO ships, whether government-owned or chartered, for the mere entry and exit of ports. Vehicles, vessels, and aircraft used in support of the operation shall not be subject to licensing or registration requirements, nor commercial insurance.

11. NATO is granted the use of airports, roads, rails, and ports without payment of fees, duties, dues, tolls, or charges occasioned by mere use. NATO shall not, however, claim exemption from reasonable charges for specific services requested and received, but operations/movement and access shall not be allowed to be impeded pending payment for such services.

12. NATO personnel shall be exempt from taxation by the Parties on the salaries and emoluments received from NATO and on any income received from outside the FRY. 13. NATO personnel and their tangible moveable property imported into, acquired in, or exported from the FRY shall be exempt from all duties, taxes, and other charges and inspections and custom regulations.

14. NATO shall be allowed to import and to export, free of duty, taxes and other charges, such equipment, provisions, and supplies as NATO shall require for the operation, provided such goods are for the official use of NATO or for sale to NATO personnel. Goods sold shall be solely for the use of NATO personnel and not transferable to unauthorized persons.

15. The Parties recognize that the use of communications channels is necessary for the Operation. NATO shall be allowed to operate its own internal mail services. The Parties shall, upon simple request, grant all telecommunications services, including broadcast services, needed for the Operation, as determined by NATO. This shall include the right to utilize such means and services as required to assure full ability to communicate, and the right to use all of the electromagnetic spectrum for this purpose, free of cost. In implementing this right, NATO shall make every reasonable effort to coordinate with and take into account the needs and requirements of appropriate authorities in the FRY.

16. The Parties shall provide, free of cost, such public facilities as NATO shall require to prepare for and execute the Operation. The Parties shall assist NATO in obtaining, at the lowest rate, the necessary utilities, such as electricity, water, gas and other resources, as NATO shall require for the Operation.

17. NATO and NATO personnel shall be immune from claims of any sort which arise out of activities in pursuance of the operation; however, NATO will entertain claims on an *ex gratia* basis.

18. NATO shall be allowed to contract directly for the acquisition of goods, services, and construction from any source within and outside the FRY. Such contracts, goods, services, and construction shall not be subject to the payment of duties, taxes, or other charges. NATO may also carry out construction works with their own personnel.

19. Commercial undertakings operating in the FRY only in the service of NATO shall be exempt from local laws and regulations with respect to the terms and conditions of their employment and licensing and registration of employees, businesses, and corporations.

20. NATO may hire local personnel who on an individual basis shall remain subject to local laws and regulations with the exception of labor/employment laws. However, local personnel hired by NATO shall:

a. be immune from legal process in respect of words spoken or written and all acts performed by them in their official capacity;

b. be immune from national services and/or national military service obligations;

c. be subject only to employment terms and conditions established by NATO; and

d. be exempt from taxation on the salaries and emoluments paid to them by NATO.

21. In carrying out its authorities under this Chapter, NATO is authorized to detain individuals and, as quickly as possible, turn them over to appropriate officials.

22. NATO may, in the conduct of the Operation, have need to make improvements or modifications to certain infrastructure in the FRY, such as roads, bridges, tunnels, buildings, and utility systems. Any such improvements or modifications of a non-temporary nature shall become part of and in the same ownership as that infrastructure. Temporary improvements or modifications may be removed at the discretion of the NATO Commander, and the infrastructure returned to as near its original condition as possible, fair wear and tear excepted.

23. Failing any prior settlement, disputes with the regard to the interpretation or application of this Appendix shall be settled between NATO and the appropriate authorities in the FRY.

24. Supplementary arrangements with any of the Parties may be concluded to facilitate any details connected with the Operation.

25. The provisions of this Appendix shall remain in force until completion of the Operation or as the Parties and NATO otherwise agree.

Chapter 8, Amendment, Comprehensive Assessment, and Final Clauses

Article I: Amendment and Comprehensive Assessment

1. Amendments to this Agreement shall be adopted by agreement of all the Parties, except as otherwise provided by Article X of Chapter 1.

2. Each Party may propose amendments at any time and will consider and consult with the other Parties with regard to proposed amendments.

3. Three years after the entry into force of this Agreement, an international meeting shall be convened to determine a mechanism for a final settlement for Kosovo, on the basis of the will of the people, opinions of relevant authorities, each Party's efforts regarding the implementation of this Agreement, and the Helsinki Final Act, and to undertake a comprehensive assessment of the implementation of this Agreement and to consider proposals by any Party for additional measures.

Article II: Final Clauses

1. This Agreement is signed in the English language. After signature of this Agreement, translations will be made into Serbian, Albanian, and other languages of the national communities of Kosovo, and attached to the English text.

2. This Agreement shall enter into force upon signature.

For the Federal Republic of Yugoslavia

For the Republic of Serbia

For Kosovo

Witnessed by:

For the European Union; For the Russian Federation; For the United States of America

[*Note: When the agreement was signed by Kosovo at the Paris Conference, only the US and European Union mediators witnessed the act of signature.*]

31.   Letter from the FRY/Serb Delegation to the Negotiators, 23 February 1999

Delegation of the Government of
the Republic of Serbia
Meeting in Rambouillet

Rambouillet, 23 February 1999

HE Mr Christopher Hill, Ambassador
HE Mr Wolfgang Petritsch, Ambassador
HE Mr Boris Maiorski, Ambassador

The Delegation of the Government of the Republic of Serbia wishes to emphasize that major progress has been achieved in the talks in Rambouillet in defining political solution on important issues related to substantial self-government of Kosovo and Metohija within the Republic of Serbia.

We are in agreement on the following issues in particular:

- the basic elements of the Contact Group;
- preambular part and basic principles of the framework political agreement defining political bases and obligations related to self-government, guaranteeing sovereignty and territorial integrity of the Republic of Serbia and the FR of Yugoslavia;
- the competencies and authorities that the Republic of Serbia, in accordance with its regulations, transfers to the Autonomous Province;
- the fact that the FR of Yugoslavia fully exercises its authority in Kosovo and Metohija;
- the the Assembly as well as its executive body has certain functions;
- the contents of the rights ensuring equality of all national communities--Albanians, Serbs, Muslims, turks, Romanies, Goranies and Egyptians--living in Kosovo and Metohija;
- additional rights of national communities affirming their national identity;
- the content of self-government functions of communes as a basic form of local self-governance;
- Ombudsman as a new additional institution for the protection of human, civil and minority rights.

In the talks, our delegation pointed to eight vital issues which at the same time ensure a substantial self-government and sovereignty and territorial integrity of the Republic of Serbia and of the FR of Yugoslavia.

In the talks, we did not reach an agreement on important elements concerning the method of functions of the organs, the existence of certain institutions and their competencies, the most important being: the term 'Constitution', decision-making in the Assembly; President of Kosovo and Metohija, judicial system, Constitutional Court, property and some other issues. In addition, there is a number of issues that have not been defined at all, the most important being the work of administrative organs, inspection, financing and other administrative control--while some solutions are unworkable in paractice. We are also of the opinion that some of the institutions are not necessary since they are not in line with character of autonomy.

We would particularly like to emphasize, the same as the Contact Group that there can be no independence of Kosovo and Metohija nor the third republic.

It is necessary to define the above issues precisely because this is a document with which all people and all national communities in Kosovo and Meohija should live in equality and have a certain future. Therefore, all elements of self-government at the time of defining of the Agreement have to be known and clearly defined. In further work, this should be adequately addressed and consistently resolved.

The FR of Yugoslavia and the Republic of Serbia are fully ready to continue the work, in line with the positive spirit of this meeting. We therefore consider that it would be extremely useful to set a reasonable deadline to create appropriate conditions and different approach to successfully resume the work and successffully address those questions. In that connection, we would like to point out that direct talks between the two delegations would be very useful.

Professor Dr Ratko Markovic, Head of the Delegation

32.   Letter from the FRY/Serb Delegation to the Negotiators, 23 February 1999

Delegation of the Government of
the Republic of Serbia
Meeting in Rambouillet

Rambouillet, 23 February 1999

HE Mr Christopher Hill, Ambassador
HE Mr Wolfgang Petritsch, Ambassador
HE Mr Boris Maiorski, Ambassador

The delegation of the Government of the Republic of Serbia wishes to emphasize that major progress has been achieved in the talks in Rambouillet in defining political solution on important issues related to substantial self-government of Kosovo and Metohija within the Republic of Serbia.

In the talks, our delegation pointed to eight vital issues which at the same time ensure a substantial self-government and sovereignty and territorial integrity of the Republic of Serbia and of the FR of Yugoslavia. We would particularly like to emphasize, the same as the Conact Group that there can be no independence of Kosovo and Metohija nor the third republic. Therefore, all elements of self-government at the time of defining of the Agreement have to be known and clearly defined. In further work, this should be adequately addressed and consistently resolved.

The FRY agreed to discuss the scope and character of international presence in Kosmet to implement the agreement to be accepted in Rambouillet. The FR of Yugoslavia and the Republic of Serbia are fully ready to continue the work, in line with the positive spirit of this meeting. We therefore consider that it would be extremely useful to set a reasonable deadline to create appropriate conditions and different approach to successfully resume the work and successfully address those questions. In that connection, we would like to point out that direct talks between the two delegations would be very useful.

Professor Dr Ratko Markovic, Head of the Delegation

33.   Letter from the FRY/Serb Delegation to the Negotiators, 23 February 1999, 16.00 hrs

Delegation of the Government of
the Republic of Serbia
Meeting in Rambouillet

Rambouillet, 23 February 1999

HE Mr Christopher Hill, Ambassador
HE Mr Wolfgang Petritsch, Ambassador
HE Mr Boris Maiorski, Ambassador

The delegation of the Government of the Republic of Serbia wishes to emphasize that major progress has been achieved in the talks in Rambouillet in defining political solution on substantial self-government of Kosovo and Metohija respectful of sovereignty and territorial integrity of the Republic of Serbia and of the FR of Yugoslavia.

We would particularly like to emphasize, the same as the Contact Group that there can be no independence of Kosovo and Methohija nor the third republic.

Therefore, all elements of self-government at the time of defining of the Agreement have to be known and clearly defined. In further work, this should be adequately addressed and consistently resolved. In that sense, we are ready to participate in the next meeting on the issue.

The FRY agreed to dicuss the scope and character of international presence in Kosmet to implement the agreement to be accepted in Rambouillet.

The FR of Yugoslavia and the Republic of Serbia are fully ready to continue the work, in line with the positive spirit of this meeting. We therefore consider that it would be extremely useful to set a reasonable deadline to create appropriate conditions and different approach to successfully resume the work and successfully address those questions. In that connection, we would like to point out that direct talks between the two delegations would be very useful.

Professor Dr Ratko Markovic, Head of the Delegation

34. Statement by the Delegation of Kosovo, 23 February 1999, 16.30hrs

The Delegation of Kosova

Rambouillet, 23 February

To the Co-Chairmen and Negotiators:

This declaration is given with full consensus.

The Delegation of Kosova with consensus understands that it can sign the agreement in two weeks after consultations with the people of Kosova, political and military institutions.

In order to do these consultations, the delegation has voted in favor of this agreement as presented in the negotiation of 23 February, which will undergo only technical review on the part of experts. In this context, the Delegation of Kosova invites and expects the rapid deployment of NATO on the ground as an essential part of the agreement.

The Delegation of Kosova understands and this will be confirmed again upon signature, that at the end of the interim period of three years, Kosova will hold a referendum to ascertain the will of the people as provided in Article I (3) of Chapter 8 of the agreement. The Delegation of Kosova also notes that the KLA intends to exercise the opportunity to engage in a process of transformation and welcomes also assurances as to cooperative bilateral work to carry out this process consistent with the agreement.

The Delegation of Kosova

35. Letter from the Delegation of Kosovo to US Secretary of State Albright, 23 February 1999

Madam Albright,

The Delegation of Kosovo has conveyed to the negotiators its acceptance of the Interim Agreement for Peace and Self-Government in Kosova as presented to the negotiators today, subject only to final technical review.

We want to convey to you our understanding on two points. First, we acknowledge your view that the Agreement allows and does not preclude a referendum in Kosova, which will demonstrate the will of the people in Kosova, and which will be conveyed to the international meeting to be convened to determine a mechanism for a final settlement for Kosova, as called for in Article I (3) of Chapter 8.

Second, we welcome the opportunity to work with the United States on the transformation of the KLA. We understand that Ambassador James Dobbins will serve as the Representative of the United States in the implemtation process of this agreement. We look forward to cooperating with him in this regard. We will convey the name of our representatives as soon as practical.

Thank you for your efforts on behalf of the people of Kosovo.

The delegation of Kosova

36. Co-chairmen's Conclusions on the Rambouillet Accords, 23 February 1999

1. Contact Group Ministers met in Rambouillet on 23 February at the end of more than two weeks of intensive efforts to reach an agreement on substantial autonomy for Kosovo, while respecting the national sovereignty and territorial integrity of the Federal Republic of Yugoslavia.

2. Ministers noted the historic nature of the Rambouillet Conference, which launched a process on the basis of the principles and basic elements adopted by the Contact Group in London on 29 January, bringing together those long divided by deep and bitter differences.

3. These have been complex and difficult negotiations, as we expected. The important efforts of the parties and the unstinting commitment of our negotiators Ambassadors Hill, Petritsch and Mayorsky, have led to a consensus on substantial autonomy for Kosovo, including on mechanisms for free and fair elections to democratic institutions, for the governance of Kosovo, for the protection of human rights and the rights of members of national communities ; and for the establishment of a fair judicial system.

4. A political framework is now in place, as set out in the Rambouillet Accords, and the groundwork has thereby been laid for finalising the implementation Chapters of the Agreement, including the modalities of the invited international civilian and military presence in Kosovo. It is essential that the agreement on the interim accord be completed and signed as a whole. In this spirit, the parties committed themselves to attend a conference, covering all aspects of implementation, in France on 15 March, following consultations with the parties and relevant international organisations. We are determined to monitor closely that this commitment is fully respected, in order to complete the Rambouillet process.

5. The parties must abstain from any action which would undermine the achievements of Rambouillet. In particular, we expect the parties to honour fully and immediately the cease-fire which should be in place throughout Kosovo, to abstain from all provocative actions and to abide fully by their commitments of October 1998 and to comply with the relevant Security Council Resolutions. We fully support the mission and personnel of the OSCE's Kosovo Verification Mission, and we insist that the parties provide for the security of KVM and other international personnel, for which they will be held responsible.

6. We pledge ourselves to work together to achieve a settlement meeting the legitimate aspirations of all the people of Kosovo. Only such a settlement can create the conditions in which a humanitarian catastrophe can be avoided. Those who prevent the completion of the interim agreement for Kosovo, or who provoke further hostilities or who threaten the security of KVM, will be held fully accountable for their actions.

37. Joint Press Conference by the two Co-Chairmen, Rambouillet, 23 February 1999

Foreign Minister Hubert Védrine: I want to emphasize the following point. A lot of progress has been made. Here for the first time, a process has been launched regarding Kosovo. Historically, there's never been a start on a solution before. But the work is not finished. That is why we decided on this new implementation conference to start March 15. We emphasize that the agreement on implementation will have to encompass all aspects without exception, civilian and military. Between now and then, we are ready to assist the two sides in explaining the agreement to their people. We are asking the co-negotiators to continue their work and under our guidance to prepare for this date with the two sides. No side should make any mistake as to our resolve. The commitments made in October 1998 must be kept in full. We're going to remain mobilized for success. We're going to remain completely vigilant and in constant contact. One last point: Each of the two sides addressed a letter to the co-negotiators and Contact Group in which they state their vision of things, their aspirations and their interpretation of the Rambouillet Accords.

Foreign Secretary Robin Cook: I'd like to join wholeheartedly in what Hubert Védrine has just said and in the joint statement of our conclusions which he has just presented. We've accomplished a great deal here even though we haven't done enough. What we've accomplished can be measured if you think back to the Contact Group meeting in London four weeks ago which was the starting point for the process. At the time, four weeks ago, there were no talks and no agreement on holding talks. At present, we have an agreement between the two sides for a democratic Kosovo, with its own assembly, its own courts, its own police. What we've created here at Rambouillet is a process, and today does not mark the end of the process but only the end of the first phase in the process. We will be using the next three weeks to try to convince both the Serbs and the Albanians that the documents that have been debated and approved here are a good solution for both sides. They provide autonomy for Kosovo and ensure the protection of the Serb community in Kosovo. On March 15, we will begin the second phase of the process. At that conference, we will be looking for an agreement on the complete implementation of the political texts we have negotiated here. That will require an agreement on an international civilian and military presence in Kosovo. I'd like to add that there have been reports recently on violence in Kosovo. All this is very disturbing. The two sides are responsible for this violence and we are watching them. But today I would tell Belgrade that the Holbrooke package they agreed to in October establishes the lines on which we will judge their military conduct and whether we have to take measures in response to it. I urge the authorities not to cross these red lines: use the next three weeks to strengthen the agreement for peace, not to break the cease-fire agreement we've already achieved.

Q. - Can you tell us about the political document and the military component of a NATO force in Kosovo?

Mr. Cook: First, the force will be led and commanded by NATO. NATO members are ready to provide an international force to offer stability, so that political stability can take root. We did not obtain an agreement on such a military force. That will be part of the discussions on implementation at the conference to start in France on March 15.

Q. - I've heard mention of a civilian and military system for the future peace in Kosovo. I didn't hear the word NATO used. Could you explain why the word NATO does not appear in the communiqué?

Mr. Cook: Because this a Contact Group meeting, not a NATO meeting, and the Contact Group includes a country which is not a NATO member. But there is no change in the NATO decisions.

Q. - So NATO would not be alone in leading these forces, so would there be U.N. monitoring?

Mr. Cook: It's not a NATO communiqué. I said--and this is something that's accepted by all the NATO countries--that if other countries want to participate, we'd agree and we'd explore the practical aspects. But the force will be NATO-commanded.

Mr. Védrine: I agree entirely with what Robin Cook has just said. The measures taken by NATO remain unchanged. But what we want to present to you today are the results achieved by the Contact Group at Rambouillet. It is very important to emphasize that we have achieved this agreement on the main aspects even if the Albanians tell us: "Yes, in principle, but we have to consult our base..."--that's why there's this 15-day period or a bit more--and even if the Serbs tell us: "Yes, but we have a number of points that still have to be discussed." We have the agreement on the essential principles, and that was the objective we set in London. That is why we are presenting this result to you today.

Q. - Two related questions. Mr. Cook said you were going to spend the three weeks urging the parties to reach an agreement on the points. Did you obtain something signed or not, especially on the political aspects? Mr. Cook says the two sides are responsible for the violence today. The document says you will hold them responsible. How are you going to do that?

Mr. Cook: The answer to your second question is that the NATO decisions taken after the "October package" remain in effect, and NATO preparations are more advanced than they were last October. That is still an integral part of the October decision, and I urge Belgrade to remember it.

As Hubert Védrine said, we received letters from both delegations here. The Kosovar delegation stipulates that the delegation understands that it may sign the declaration but wishes to consult its base for 15 days; the letter from the Serb side commits them to substantial autonomy for Kosovo and gives their consent to be present on March 15 in order to discuss the implementation of an international presence. Let's see how we can implement this accord. We have in fact received substantial agreement We do not have signatures. That should come before or during the March 15 conference. We are going to lean on the two delegations and tell them when they return that it is a good conclusion for both sides.

Q. - Does the document taken back by the two sides contain any idea of a referendum on the future of Kosovo, and a binding referendum?

Mr. Védrine: That is not in the interim draft agreement. There is a clause on a consultation at the end of three years but it does not use that term. We know that it is one of the aspects of the problem, that the Kosovo Albanians continue to aspire to a referendum. They have said so again moreover. It is one element of the problem but the solution put forward by the Contact Group, the document on the interim solution, does not include that aspect.

38.   Secretary of State Albright, Press Conference, Rambouillet, 23 February 1999

SECRETARY ALBRIGHT (In Progress): The work of the international mediators is intensely rewarding, for their good will and commitment can open paths of peace that were not visible before. At Rambouillet, the negotiators helped bring Kosovo Albanian factions together as a cohesive delegation, and they helped develop a vision of what a democratic Kosovo might look like. But their work has also been intensely frustrating, for ultimately, however skilled their efforts and pure their motives, they cannot take the place of political will and courage among the parties to a conflict. Because of their hesitation we have not reached full agreement today. But we have decisively broken the stalemate that hung over Kosovo for so long. We will leave Rambouillet with something that months of shuttle

negotiations and years of international concern have not achieved; a viable plan for alternative democracy in Kosovo through an interim political settlement. Today the Kosovo Albanian delegation undertook to sign the agreement after it is reviewed by technical experts and discussed with the people of Kosovo. The delegation invited NATO to deploy a force on the ground as part of this settlement. Kosovo would have its own constitution and government with full responsibility for all the issues that affect the daily lives of its people. Serbian police units would be rapidly withdrawn. The Yugoslav military would be restricted to patrolling a five-kilometer border zone. The Kosovo Liberation Army would also be de-militarized, and we are prepared to help retrain qualified members who wish to join Kosovo's new multi-ethnic police. This settlement is the best deal either side can hope to achieve. The Contact Group extended its deadline and kept working over the past few days because we are well aware that a collapse here risked igniting renewed conflict and a humanitarian catastrophe. Unfortunately, President Milosevic and his delegation failed to seize this opportunity for progress. The Serbs moved forward today as they saw the Kosovo Albanians getting close to 'yes.' This pressure pushed Belgrade to accept many of the basic elements of Kosovo self-government, but they continue to balk at decisions on critical security issues. We believe that the best way forward is to allow the parties time to reflect on the choices before them. That is why Foreign Ministers Vedrine and Cook and the Contact Group negotiators today brought the Rambouillet talks to a close. The Kosovo Albanians have requested two weeks for consideration. Belgrade must be ready to move by then as well, or prepare to face the consequences. This period of reflection should not be taken by either side as an excuse for military activities on the ground. We are particularly concerned by recent movements of Serb forces and by harassment of members of the Kosovo Verification Mission. The Mission security must be assured, and there should be no doubt that NATO's January 30th decision permitting Secretary General Solana to authorize air strikes remains in force. We also call on the Kosovo Liberation Army to refrain from provocations, and we will be looking at ways to bring greater pressure to bear on those who seek to block the coming of peace. The people of Kosovo held out high hopes for this conference, and they deserve to have those hopes realized. I would say to them, and to those around the world who care for peace, do not despair. Support those of your leaders who have supported peace and America will stand with you. Here at Rambouillet, we have come far, far down the field toward peace. Your courage and determination will help us cross the goal line. I now am ready to answer your questions.

QUESTION: Is the Serb acceptance of self-rule and the other political elements of this agreement unqualified, and secondly, because you said the Albanians do have two weeks for consideration, did they agree to this, or their qualified agreement to this, is it based on their understanding that there will be a referendum?

SECRETARY ALBRIGHT: Well, first of all, on the Serb question, I think that the Serbs have not given an unqualified yes. They have engaged on the political document and qualified some of their reactions to it, and they have not engaged at all on the security part, the security chapters, of the document.

What they have done, I think, to put it in the clearest possible way, is that in 1989 they stripped Kosovo of its autonomy. And what they have done in the last few days and then their response is to agree that Kosovo should have autonomy. And we want there to be not just autonomy, but autonomy and democracy. So they have restored some of what they had before but as you know the autonomy in 1989 was under a communist system, and it did not have democratic elements to it, and in the work as of today they have at least agreed that the area should have autonomy, but we are disagreeing or there are questions about parts of the text in which the structures of it are described. And, as I say, they have not engaged at all on the military aspects.

The Kosovar Albanians have said that they have, I guess in diplomatic parlance, what they've done is agree to this in principle, they would have, its the equivalent to having initialed the text, but they want to go back and consult with their people about it. You know, for the Serbs to agree, all they have to do is make one phone call. For the Kosovars, it means, really as they are learning about democracy and engaging with other people, it means consulting with them. I think from their perspective they have not given up what they consider their right to a referendum. But that is not something that is in the document.

QUESTION: But is it in the statement that they signed whereby they said they accepted the political document?

SECRETARY ALBRIGHT: First of all, the political document does say that when the time for review comes, there will be a conference and meeting, and a number of ways will be -- a number of factors will be taken into consideration by that meeting as to the permanent status of Kosovo, among them the view of the people. And the Kosovars interpret this, their interpretation of it is that it's a referendum.

QUESTION: Madame Secretary, you have the qualified agreement of half an agreement, which you said would only be a piece of paper without the other half, is that still your opinion?

SECRETARY ALBRIGHT: I do not believe that this is a full agreement without the military, that that is the agreement, it has a political part and the military part. What we have is a couple of weeks here for both sides to assess, and I believe that without full engagement by the Serbs on the military aspects of this, there is not a full agreement.

QUESTION: What incentive is there for them to come to a full agreement?

SECRETARY ALBRIGHT: Both the incentives are the same as they have been all along, which is the disincentive that there is the potential of military action, and the incentives are that they would in fact be part of what is an historic process of bringing Kosovo up into a new level of autonomy, and from their perspective, frankly, that Kosovo remains a part of Serbia.

QUESTION: Madame Secretary, I think you just answered my question, but let me ask it again to be absolutely sure that I understand it. If the Serbs do not accept the military chapters of this agreement when the conference resumes in three weeks, are they liable to be bombed?

SECRETARY ALBRIGHT: Let me just say this: That as we assess what is happening, you know, the way that I laid out the various scenarios, it was going to be, you know, if one side said no and the other side said yes, I think that as we look at what's going to be happening it's now to a great extent up to the Kosovar Albanians to create this black-or-white situation, the extent to which they now follow up on the political part and continue to make clear that a NATO implementation force is something that they want. But let me also say that I believe that the linkage of force and diplomacy, as we have described it now so many times, did in the end move this process forward. I think it's important to remember that the threat of the use of force is often useful in diplomacy and it is a tool and not an end in itself. We are going to make a judgement about how the process is going on, the level of engagement, but I maintain that if the Serbs do not follow through and engage on the military and security, the police parts of this document, that they are subject to the same disincentives as before, but also that the Kosovars have a responsibility in fulfilling their part to make their answer a clear and unequivocal 'yes.'

QUESTION: (In French) Madame Secretary, despite all the extraordinary energy that you spent here, don't you have the feeling even so this evening that Rambouillet is a failure?

SECRETARY ALBRIGHT: (In French.) Not at all. I believe that here was something that was very difficult and very complicated. I think that it's very important to remember that the Albanians are coming from a society which is not really accustomed to work like this, it was a very diverse delegation, composed of all kinds of people, who had not worked together before, and yet they worked together very well, and we knew before that it would be very difficult. We have worked a lot and I am very satisfied with all we have done.

QUESTION: I'd like to follow up on Barry's question a little bit. Christopher Hill has been describing the last couple of days as an effort, it's like when you're nailing down a floor board, you nail down one side and sometimes the other side pops up, in what looks like another three weeks extension of a deadline, of a negotiating deadline, is there a mechanism to prevent the things you feel you have nailed down from popping back up?

SECRETARY ALBRIGHT: Part of what the Albanians agreed to, was that they in fact had initialed, which means that they agreed in principle, and that they would be looking at what are known as some technical aspects of it. So, from their perspective, they have agreed in principle to this document which, I think, is one of the reasons on how to keep the floor boards from popping up.

QUESTION: All along the United States has been saying, you can't separate the two elements of this agreement, that the political and the military annexes really are one and the same together. Why now, are you in fact, in a way, separating the two elements of this agreement?

SECRETARY ALBRIGHT: No, we have not. We have not separated them at all. What we have done, is capture what we have agreed on, which is from the perspective of the Albanians, the full agreement, from the perspective of the Serbs, at least, a recognition that autonomy is something that needs to exist for Kosovo and we are mid-way or part-way in the process. I've been trying to figure out what yard line we're on, but I think that we have taken a long way, but we have not, absolutely not, given up the basic construct, which is that there is no agreement without the security, the

military and security aspects of it.

I think we may have -- let me just say this, I think we may have confused people by talking about it as if it were two agreements. It's not, it's one agreement with many chapters in it. And so, the chapters are, there are chapters that are devoted to military and security aspects. It's just that the Serbs have chosen to separate it, but from our perspective, it's one book.

QUESTION: Do you have any indication from the Serbs that they're ready to move at all on the military side, the implementation force?

SECRETARY ALBRIGHT: Well, they have said different words. They have talked about an international presence. They are using different words. It depends on whether you ask me in the middle of the night, or early in the morning, whether I think that's movement forward or not. But I think that they are accepting the fact that some kind of an international presence, after all, they did accept the KVM and OSCE mission, which is something that they had said they would not do before. It was asked earlier, when we were all together whether the force could be anything different then a NATO-led force. I can just tell you point blank from the perspective of the United States, absolutely not, it must be a NATO-led force. It can however cooperate with other kinds of forces, for instance, as we know in Bosnia, the Russians have in fact joined a NATO-led force.

QUESTION: Madam Secretary, is it your understanding that Adem Demaci endorses this accord, this agreement in principle to the extent that the delegation here does?

SECRETARY ALBRIGHT: I can't speak for him. I spoke with him today, but not recently, you have to ask him.

QUESTION: Do you think the delegation here would have done what they did today, offer this support in principle, had he not endorsed it?

SECRETARY ALBRIGHT: It's very hard for me to totally describe to you the dynamics of the group. I do think that they took a very bold step on behalf of democracy and their people. They, I think, worked incredibly hard to put their group together. You know, it's interesting, if you go back three weeks now, I guess, people were wondering whether there'd be an Albanian delegation, or whether they'd come here at all. And when they came here, who they were and how they would work together. I think that they have worked together in an exemplary way. Having been a part of delegations myself, I know that you go through days, periods when you agree and disagree and people test out things, and I think that the fact that they agreed in principle to this document is a sign of their boldness and vision and desire to have a Kosovo which reflects their hopes and aspirations. So, I believe that they worked together very well and in a remarkable way that people didn't expect, and I'm not myself very clear about the inner dynamics of it.

QUESTION: Madam Secretary, could you please qualify the Serb position on the military issue, if you would please perhaps by (inaudible) what they actually have signed in their letter of comment on the talks because when you opened these remarks, you said they have not engaged on the military issues, but you've said that they've agreed on some terminology at some moments, at different times of the day or night, to various military aspects. That would seem to be an absolute key (inaudible) on what you may or may have not got agreement on here, and reflect a little bit on whether they've been let off the hook or not?

SECRETARY ALBRIGHT: Well, I think in their latest iteration, they're talking about the possibility of discussing an international presence. They do not like to use the word "military." Well, something like that, I don't have the exact -- it's not their favorite subject.

QUESTION: Madam Secretary, if I can follow up on Barry's question earlier, can I also get a clarification. You have mentioned, regarding whether or not there would still be the threat of NATO air-strikes against the Serbs if you get a yes from the Kosovar Albanians three weeks from now. You said it's a black and white situation, and it's up to them. But if you get not just an agreement in principle, if you get a yes that they sign on to this document, and in fact do sign on the dotted line, is the threat of military force, NATO air-strikes still in effect as far as you are concerned?

SECRETARY ALBRIGHT: All I can tell you is the procedure that exists, is that Secretary General Solana has the authority to use force. I think that from my perspective, it's the parties themselves that have the opportunities to create the black or white situation. I think the marriage of force and diplomacy, as I've described it, continues to exist, and, to follow up on the metaphor here, Secretary General Solana has the ring, so I think that we can figure out where this is going to go. We're going to watch it very carefully. But let me just repeat here, you all get completely fixated about whether we're going to bomb, when we're going to bomb, rather than thinking about what has happened here, which is something quite remarkable, which is that there was no Kosovo process. There were brave negotiators, or shuttlers,

Chris Hill, I think, gets the shuttle award. Remember, I managed when I was here two weeks ago, to get them to meet at a table. These people have now engaged in a process, probably not as full as we would like it at the end, but they are moving forward, and I think that we should take, or the parties, more importantly, the parties should take a lot of satisfaction in what has happened here, and I think the Kosovar Albanians should take a lot of satisfaction in their ability to work through a very difficult situation.

So, I would hope that in the next two or three weeks, we can focus our attention on watching how the Albanians work to get the support of their people, how they begin the process of democratically getting support for an agreement, and that's going to be our focus while Secretary General Solana continues to have the ability to do what he needs to.

QUESTION: Madam Secretary, has the United States invited some members of the Albanian delegation to visit the U.S. within the upcoming two weeks, specifically the members of the KLA, representatives from KLA? And my second part of the question would be, does the United States recognize the right of the people of Kosovo to decide on their future status after the passage of the interim agreement?

SECRETARY ALBRIGHT: First of all, let me say that we did discuss the possibility of their coming to visit, and we agreed with what it says in the document that the views of the people of Kosovo need to be consulted.

That is our view. Thank you very much.

39.   Press Statement by Members of the Security Council, 23 February 1999

"Members of the Security Council took note of the conclusions of the co-chairmen of the Rambouillet Conference at the end of the two weeks of intensive efforts aimed at reaching an agreement on substantial autonomy for Kosovo, which respects the national sovereignty and territorial integrity of the FRY.

Members of the council noted with satisfaction that, with the Rambouillet Agreements, a political framework for substantial autonomy has been set out.

Members of the Coucil noted the commitment of the parties to attend a conference covering all aspects of the implementation of these agreements, in France on 15 March. Members of the council encouraged the parties to work constructively to this end.

Members of the Council underlined that it was essential for all the parties to refrain from any action which could jeopardise the achievements of the Rambouillet negotiations, and to fully comply with their commitments of October 1998 and the relevant security council resolutions.

Members of the Council will continue to follow closely the situation.".

40.   Statement by the Secretary General of NATO on the outcome of the Rambouillet talks, 23 February 1999

NATO welcomes the substantial progress made in the Kosovo Peace Talks in Rambouillet towards a political settlement which will give Kosovo a significant degree of autonomy and help bring stability to the region. However, a final agreement has not yet been reached. I appeal to the parties to accept rapidly the Contact Group Peace Plan in its entirety, including its military aspects, and at the very latest by the time of the implementation conference in France on 15th March. During the period until the 15th March, NATO expects the parties to work constructively to bring about a peace settlement. In particular they must respect the cease fire, refrain from all provocations and carry out all of the provisions of the UNSC Resolutions on Kosovo. The Federal Republic of Yugoslavia must comply fully with all of its commitments under its agreement of October 25th, 1998 with NATO. The OSCE Kosovo Verification Mission must be allowed to carry out its work and both parties must ensure the safety of its personnel. NATO will continue to watch the situation on the ground very closely. We are very concerned by the violence in Kosovo in recent days. We remain ready to use whatever means are necessary to bring about a peaceful solution to the crisis in Kosovo and to prevent further human suffering. Those who prevent the achievement of an interim agreement, provoke violent incidents or threaten the security of the Kosovo Verification Mission personnel will be held fully responsible for their actions. Since the beginning of the crisis, NATO has fully supported the efforts of the international community to bring peace to Kosovo and to help achieve a negotiated political solution. Our stance in putting the threat of force at the service of diplomacy has helped to create the conditions for the Rambouillet talks to make progress. The Alliance remains ready to lead an international military force in Kosovo which would guarantee the implementation of an interim political settlement. I call on both parties to build on the considerable progress that has been achieved at Rambouillet and to seize this opportunity to achieve a lasting settlement for the benefit of all the peoples of the region. NATO stands ready to help them in this endeavour.

Chapter 16: The Paris Conference and the Outbreak of Hostilities

In the days following upon the conclusion of the Rambouillet talks, an intensive effort was mounted to persuade Kosovo to sign. The United States launched an Albanian-language television programme, attempting to explain the advantages of the agreement. US Senator Dole, a long-standing supporter of the cause of the Kosovo Albanians, was dispatched to the region, to try and persuade the KLA leadership to accept. More crucially, Hashim Thaci, who had appeared to obstruct a decision to accept the agreement, apparently under instruction, now turned into a campaigner for acceptance. In a rather dangerous mission he travelled throughout Kosovo, visiting every KLA district leader in turn. It was said that he managed to obtain the signature of all of then under a piece of paper endorsing the accord. On several occasions it appeared as if Kosovo would sign, even in advance of the follow-on conference. However, no such signature took place.

The Contact Group negotiators and the delegations of the FRY/Serbia and of Kosovo assembled again at the Paris International Conference Centre on Avenue Kleber on 15 March 1999. As the attempt to isolate the delegations had not been successful before, they were no longer constrained in their movements. On the first day of the follow-on conference, the delegation of Kosovo presented to the co-chairmen of the Conference and others a formal letter, confirming its decision taken at Rambouillet to accept the interim agreement as presented on 23 February. 'We would be honoured to sign the Agreement in your presence at a time and place of your choosing,' the letter stated.

Rather than offering an immediate opportunity to sign, the negotiators strongly pressed Kosovo to delay such a step, to permit further discussions to take place with the FRY/Serb delegation. After all, at the conclusion of the Rambouillet session, the FRY/Serbia had appeared to embrace the political elements of the settlement at least in principle. It was hoped that there now would exist an opportunity to address FRY/Serb reluctance to consider implementation, including military implementation. That issue had not really been offered for discussion at Rambouillet. In a significant about-turn, the Contact Group was now willing to discuss the modalities for implementation in some detail.

However, the FRY/Serbia was not willing to exploit this opportunity to address its concerns in that respect. Instead, on the first day of the conference, it presented its own version of the political part of the agreement. Rather than focusing on limited changes, this counter-draft effectively sought to re-open the discussions on a political settlement as a whole and start again from the beginning. In fact, some of the proposed changes fell even outside of the non-negotiable principles. The draft proposed a formal subordination of Kosovo to Serbia, abolished restrictions on the exercise of Federal functions in Kosovo and correspondingly reduced the functions of the Kosovo assembly. The office of the President of Kosovo would be abolished and its government replaced by a weakened Council of Ministers. There would be no Kosovo Constitutional and Supreme Court. In addition, the entire implementation chapters, both military and civilian, had been simply struck out, with the exception of OSCE election monitoring and provisions for the Ombudsman, although even those provisions were significantly altered. Even Chapter 4 (a) on humanitarian assistance, reconstruction and economic development was deleted in its entirety.

The attitude of the FRY/Serbia infuriated the negotiators, including even Russian Ambassador Mayorski. All hopes for a settlement were now effectively dashed. The negotiators responded to the submission of the new draft by the FRY/Serbia by stating jointly in a formal letter 'the unanimous view of the Contact Group that only technical adjustments can be considered which, of course, must be accepted as such and approved by the other delegation".[1] Hence, it was confirmed that the exhausting process of seeking to tempt the FRY/Serb delegation into accepting the agreement by making concessions on the political settlement had now been concluded. Instead, the talks would indeed focus on implementation. Accordingly, over the days which followed, Kosovo was presented with the opportunity to discuss the issues of economic reconstruction, of civil implementation and of the holding of elections by the OSCE, and of military implementation in detail with the relevant implementing organizations. The FRY/Serb side did not take up this offer.

Clearly, over the weeks following upon the Rambouillet conference, the Belgrade government had changed its initially apparently moderately positive assessment of the Rambouillet accords. When it was evident that Kosovo would definitely sign, it seemed to go out of its way to provoke a breakdown of the peace process, without feeling it necessary to deploy any diplomatic subtleties. In fact, the negotiators emerged somewhat shaken from their sessions in the FRY/Serb delegation room, where they had been greeted with the words "have you come to fu*k us again"?

Essentially, Belgrade had decided to call NATO's bluff. In view of this attitude, subsequent claims that Rambouillet failed because the United States insisted inflexibly on the implementation chapters and offered no negotiations on the subject to Belgrade are misplaced. The entire follow-on conference had been called to address implementation, but there was no interest whatever in discussions on the part of the FRY/Serbia.

---

[1] Letter, 16 March 1999, Document 16.A.3.

Given this deadlock, the text of the agreement in its form of 23 February was opened for signature on 18 March. In a formal ceremony, Kosovo signed the agreement, witnessed by only two of the three negotiators. The flat refusal of Ambassador Mayorski to witness the signature of Kosovo to the outcome of the Rambouillet and Paris talks is somewhat startling. After all, up to that moment at least the pretence had been maintained that the negotiators were serving the Contact Group, rather than a particular government represented within it or even a particular party to the talks. In view of Belgrade's latest conduct, it had been hoped that unity in the Contact Group could now be restored. But with the implementation of the threat of the use of force looming, Moscow decided to dissociate itself from the conference result.

As is customary upon signature or ratification of legal instruments of this kind, the delegation of Kosovo issued an interpretative statement at the moment of signature.[2] In so doing, it communicated certain understandings. It indicated that the text was now definite and not subject to further modification, other than purely technical changes. Kosovo also indicated that it regarded NATO-led implementation according to the provisions of the interim agreement to constitute a condition essential to the overall package and to the consent given by Kosovo. It committed itself to full cooperation with all implementing organisations and invited their early deployment. Kosovo confirmed its intention, already indicated at the conclusion of the conference at Rambouillet, that at the termination of the interim period of three years the people of Kosovo would exercise their will through a referendum. This expression of the will of the people would be conveyed to the international meeting to determine the mechanism for a final settlement for Kosovo, consistent with the interim agreement, in particular Article I (3) of Chapter 8. Finally, the delegation noted again the intention of the KLA to exercise the opportunity to engage in a process of transformation and welcomed assurances as to cooperative bilateral contacts to carry out this process consistent with the interim agreement.

The following day, one last attempt was made to engage the FRY/Serb delegation in substantive discussions. As this attempt proved fruitless, the co-chairmen of the Conference, the Foreign Ministers of the United Kingdom and France, issued a statement which indicated that the Kosovo delegation had seized the opportunity of peace and committed itself to the accords as a whole. Far from seizing this opportunity, the Yugoslav delegation had tried to unravel the Rambouillet Accords, the statement continued.[3] The conference was, however, not terminated, but merely adjourned, pending an expression of acceptance by the FRY/Serbia.

The Belgrade government had used the break in talks since 23 February to deploy troop concentrations on the border with Kosovo and in Kosovo itself. These forces had already engaged in significant offensive operations during the Paris follow-on talks and now increased their activities even further, attacking again entire villages and other civilian installations. In view of this situation, the KVM was rapidly withdrawn from Kosovo on the day of the adjournment of the conference. Within a few days the number of displaced was again rising in very significant numbers.

On 22 March, the negotiators travelled to Belgrade, along with Richard Holbrooke, to make one final attempt to persuade the FRY/Serbia to cease offensive operations and to accept the Rambouillet accords. Again, no progress was achieved. Instead, the following day, the parliament in Belgrade voted to reject the interim agreement. Richard Holbrooke then returned to Brussels where NATO, upon having received a briefing on his discussions, authorized the launching of military operations against the FRY. The NATO Secretary General explained that this action had been taken in order to "avert a humanitarian catastrophe".[4] The attacks would be "directed towards disrupting the violent attacks being committed by the Serb Army and Special Police Forces and weakening their ability to cause [a] further humanitarian catastrophe".

The strong references to the unfolding humanitarian tragedy were meant to point to the legal justification for the operation, which remained one of humanitarian action. The three principal demands that were to be enforced militarily could be logically connected with that justification. In order to arrest the further deterioration of the humanitarian situation, the use of excessive and disproportionate force by the FRY/Serbia would need to stop, as this practice had caused the large-scale displacement of civilians in Kosovo. This requirement was rather a cautious one, inasmuch as it did not appear to insist on an immediate cease-fire by Belgrade. The ongoing FRY/Serb offensive against the KLA was therefore not necessarily rejected, but only the means through which it was being conducted was condemned and subjected to counter action.

In the absence of compliance with this demand, NATO would strike directly against the military infrastructure actually engaged in excessive and indiscriminate attacks. This aim would appear to fulfil the legal requirement of necessity, imminence of the threat to a civilian population and proportionality of the forcible counter measure.

There would also be included a prospective element of action, i.e. that of weakening the future potential of the FRY/Serbia to engage in such activities. This slightly broader aim was justified with reference to the past record of these forces, which

---

[2] Declaration of Kosovo, 18 March 1999, Document 16.B.5.
[3] Statement, 19 March 1999, Document 16.B.10.
[4] Press Statement by Dr Javier Solana, 23 March 1999, Document 16.C.2.

had extended from the involvement in probable genocide and ethnic cleansing in Croatia and Bosnia and Herzegovina, to causing the initial exodus from Kosovo in 1998. Through this measure, the demands of the Security Council for a troop withdrawal, and the FRY's own commitments in the Holbrooke agreements of October 1998, would be forcibly implemented. Again, as there existed no Security Council mandate towards this end, the use of force in this context would need to be justified with reference to an overwhelming humanitarian need.

The use of force in support of international efforts to secure Yugoslav agreement to an interim political settlement also mirrored an aim established by the United Nations Security Council to which no enforcement mandate was attached. It reflects a view that the humanitarian emergency could not be improved in the longer term in the absence of a settlement. However, the statement of the NATO Secretary-General was rather nuanced, inasmuch as it referred merely to the interim political settlement. The use of force by NATO was thus, at least according to this initial statement, not necessarily directed towards achieving an acceptance of the Rambouillet package in its entirety. Instead, the Secretary-General referred to the more flexible requirement that a "viable political settlement must be guaranteed by an international military presence". On the other hand, the UK Prime Minister stated that the operation would have as its minimum the objective to curb continued Serbian repression in Kosovo in order to avert a humanitarian disaster. It would therefore target the military capability of the Serb dictatorship. To avoid such action, "Milosevic must do what he promised to do last October. End the repression; withdraw his troops to barracks; get them down to the levels agree; and withdraw from Kosovo the tanks, heavy artillery and other weapons he brought into Kosovo early last year. He must agree to the proposals set out in the Rambouillet Accords, including a NATO led ground force."[5]

The initiation of hostilities was strongly criticised by Russia and China in the United Nations Security Council, presaging a controversy about the moral and legal justification of NATO's action over the weeks to come. The extraordinarily rapid outpouring of refugees as a result of a strategy of mass deportation employed by FRY/Serb forces in Kosovo also led to considerable soul-searching about the political wisdom and military effectiveness of the operation. These, and other questions, will be addressed in the next volume of this *Series*. For the moment, it may be sufficient to conclude that the episode as a whole cannot be seen to represent a new universal mechanism of collective security in action, although some modest developments can be discerned. Changes in the international system were sufficient to provide for the authoritative identification of the dreadful human rights situation in the territory. Yugoslavia could no longer invoke the armour state sovereignty to protect itself from international interest or criticism. There was also no shortage of mechanisms for preventative diplomacy, especially within the CSCE/OSCE, which were deployed. However, these were mainly dependent on the consent and cooperation of the FRY/Serbia. As Belgrade had declared the Kosovo issue to be the one core element of its construction of an ethnic politics, it was unlikely to relinquish this prize voluntarily. Faced with such deadlock, the Kosovo issue was permitted to simmer on, without significant international involvement, until limited violence on the part of the KLA triggered massive counter-action by FRY/Serb authorities. Although extermination to the point of genocide was avoided, in contrast to practices developed in relation to Croatia and Bosnia and Herzegovina, indiscriminate attacks against civilians were launched once more. Despite this 'moderation', massive displacement and civilian suffering occurred in a way which was internationally visible.

Despite the increasing urgency of the situation, classical tools of diplomacy were deployed again over the summer of 1998, after it had become clear that no strong collective security action would be forthcoming from the Security Council. When these had yielded no result other than a rise of the tally of the displaced to 300,000 by the end of the summer, NATO threatened the use of force. This was done in a state of legal and institutional ambiguity, which was quickly painted over by Belgrade's acceptance of the Holbrooke mission and the endorsement of this result of NATO's threat.

NATO's second threat of the use of force, in support of the Rambouillet talks, again was permitted to take place in a state of legal ambiguity. Few states objected, and the Security Council associated itself with the Rambouillet project. Obviously, it was hoped and perhaps assumed that a peaceful settlement would still be possible, obviating the need for a use of force by NATO. But when Rambouillet failed, a number of states were less keen to accept the consequence of the chain of events they had themselves in part set into motion. Rather than strengthening the concept of universal collective security, which may also include the vindication of the rights of a people threatened with forced displacement or extermination, the operation became identified with the position the NATO states, imposing a view upon the European region that governments cannot freely jeopardize the lives of entire populations they purport to represent.

Ironically, even this decisive action has in a sense masked the failure which underlies this entire episode at a deeper level: the unwillingness of the organized international community to involve itself effectively in disputes about self-determination of peoples. For, this issue, as yet unresolved, will gradually return to dominate the international agenda, both in general terms and also in relation to Kosovo.

---

[5] UK Prime Minister's Statement on Kosovo, 23 March 1999, Document 16.C.3.

A. Preparations for the Paris Conference

1. Cook-Vedrine Statement on Kosovo, 5 March 1999

The negotiators have briefed the British and French co-Chairmen on their discussions in Belgrade and Pristina following the Rambouillet Conference. The co-Chairmen note that the Rambouillet Accords have put in place the political framework for substantial autonomy for Kosovo, on which there was consensus at Rambouillet.

The aim of the follow-up Conference which will begin on 15 March is to reach full agreement on all the civilian and military aspects of implementation of the Accords.

The co-Chairmen emphasise that an invited international military force is an integral part of the package. The presence of such a force, to ensure successful implementation, is in the interest of the Parties.

The co-Chairmen expect the parties to come to the follow-up Conference ready to finalise the interim agreement, including the arrangements for an international military force. Those who put obstacles in the way of the successful realisation of the Rambouillet Accords will be held responsible.

The two co-Chairmen also note with concern the situation on the ground in Kosovo. Any who by recourse to violence contravene the commitments they have made to the international community will have to answer for their actions.

2. Press Statement by James P. Rubin, US Spokesman, 10 March 1999

Today, Secretary Albright and Senator Robert Dole addressed all Kosovo residents in a live broadcast transmitted on TV Tirana. They emphasized that the Rambouillet Agreement will provide self-government and security for the people of Kosovo and urged the people of Kosovo to call upon their leaders to sign the Agreement immediately. The Secretary stressed that signature by the Kosovo Albanians will allow the international community to increase pressure on Slobodan Milosevic. Senator Dole called for the leaders of the Kosovo Albanians to take a stand for the Agreement, which they indicate that they have accepted. He said that what is at issue is the safety of their mothers, friends, and families and this should not be delayed by a power struggle within the KLA. The broadcast reaches throughout Kosovo and is watched by approximately two-thirds of households there. The interviews were part of the "Agreement for Peace" program, a USIA-produced series which has aired nightly over Albanian television for the past two weeks. The program allows Albanian and Kosovar-Albanian journalists to interview senior United States Government officials live on prime time television.

3. US Envoy Senator Dole and Amb. Hill Press Conference, US Embassy London, 6 March 1999

SENATOR DOLE: Thank you very much. Let me introduce Ambassador Christopher Hill. He is here to answer all the tough questions. (Laughter.) We've just had a meeting with General Clark, and also met with Secretary of State Albright, and we discussed with both of them the meetings we had yesterday with the Kosovars in Skopje. We were unable to go to Pristina because I couldn't get a visa from Mr. Milosevic, which is not unusual conduct for him. But first I want to commend Secretary Albright for her continuing effort to bring this to a successful conclusion. I think we will be successful because of the work that she's done, the work that Ambassador Hill and others have done. We had long meetings yesterday for 4, 5, 6 hours, we met with most of the Albanian delegation. We made good progress. They promised to sign the agreement tomorrow, to sign the document tomorrow and Ambassador Hill will be meeting with them sometime around midday tomorrow.

I went to a Macedonia, Skopje, at the request of President Clinton and Secretary Albright. I've had a long relationship with the Albanian community having gone there in 1990, gone to Kosovo in 1990. And of course it was 1989 when Milosevic took away their autonomy and most everything else. I went there as a volunteer -- I'm not with the government, not employed by anybody -- I went there because I felt I had some credibility and they would listen to me. And I told them very frankly that many of their friends in the United States were disappointed they didn't sign the agreement in France. They should have signed the agreement a couple of weeks ago and everyday that they waited was another respite for

Milosevic, who has caused the problem in the first place.

We reaffirmed to them that NATO forces would provide the best possible protection for the people and that obviously the people should be the biggest priority of every Albanian leader. We think we made some progress. So I would just say that they indicated to us many times that they would keep their word. I think they will keep their word. That means they will sign the document tomorrow. That means from that moment on the pressure will be on Slobodan Milosevic to do the same. And I hope that all happens tomorrow. I know it's a difficult decision for the Albanians. It's made more difficult by some of the recent activities in Kosovo initiated by the Serbs. It takes courage, but in my view in must be done. It's not a perfect agreement, probably not the one they would draft, but I think it's the best possible agreement. And I hope they would do as they told us yesterday and sign it, let's get on with it. I'd be happy to respond to any questions or maybe if the Ambassador wanted to add to that, I'd like to offer anything.

AMBASSADOR HILL: Let me just say that I was with Senator Dole yesterday. We were both there at the request of Secretary Albright to follow up on the Rambouillet Conference. I think there has been a lot of progress made in getting the Albanians toward a "yes." Secretary Albright worked very hard on that in Rambouillet, as many of you know, and I think there was more progress yesterday and we're hoping in that the very near future we will have a 'yes' from the Albanians and we can go on and get a 'yes' from the Serbs and put this conflict behind us.

QUESTION: You sound as if you're saying in the future and Mr. Hill you're saying tomorrow?

SENATOR DOLE: Well that's the future. (Laughter.)

QUESTION: Is there a deal they will sign tomorrow?

SENATOR DOLE: That's what they told us, they promised us they would do it tomorrow.

QUESTION: In Pristina?

SENATOR DOLE: Wherever the Ambassador meets them.

AMBASSADOR HILL: Several of the groups are already ready to sign and the issue is that the KLA is going to make its decision and they've said they'll do that tomorrow.

SENATOR DOLE: They'll meet tomorrow and I think its fair to say 90% positive that it would be in the affirmative. And the next question is, "well, if its affirmative, when can you sign the agreement?" and they said immediately.

QUESTION: Will you be meeting with them tomorrow Ambassador?

AMBASSADOR HILL: Yes, I will be.

QUESTION: KLA commanders are saying last week at the first anniversary of the war that they would fight on until full independence. Previous agreement isn't the same as full independence is it? It would suggest there is a difference between the people in the field and on the delegation?

SENATOR DOLE: There are some differences, I mean you never get 100%, at least in my experience in any negotiation, you never get 100%. There are obviously some who would do as you suggest fight on for independence, but I think the KLA understands that they will be demilitarized, they will still have a role in the future in Kosovo, the political future, police force, whatever. But we were talking directly to people, heavily involved with the KLA. My view is they made a determination or will make that determination tomorrow that this is a good agreement for the people of Kosovo.

QUESTION: Could we be clear as to the scope of what it is they might sign tomorrow. Does this include both the political aspects and indeed the critical military bolstering of any peace accords? In other words the Kosovars sign the (inaudible) in France on the 15ᵗʰ with a done deal, merely then the pressure is on Belgrade?

AMBASSADOR HILL: We have stressed repeatedly that is a package deal and you cannot agree to part of it and not the other. So when the Albanians make a commitment to sign, they are referring to the entire package. Obviously there are parts of it they like less than other parts but they understand it's a total package.

QUESTION: Could we just be clear, is your aim and expectation that you will have signatures from all the people on the delegation from Rambouillet, or more, or roughly all of them or how exactly -- what is the critical sort of mass of Albanians?

SENATOR DOLE: The Ambassador will be there but I think we expect everyone in the delegation.

AMBASSADOR HILL: Yes, we expect that all the groups represented on that delegation will agree. And when we refer to the Albanians agreeing to the Rambouillet accords, we are referring to their representatives on the delegation.

QUESTION: Why did they change their minds. What were you able to do that they were not able to do in Rambouillet?

SENATOR DOLE: I'm not certain of the change in mind but of just getting everything back on track. I think there were so many rumors around the United States about certain things, about not changing the agreement -- there were other rumors about KLA representative coming to Washington before the agreement was signed. And I think our efforts yesterday were just to get it back on track. They did sign a letter addressed to the Secretary in Rambouillet that said they would do this within two weeks and they're going to get it done, maybe a couple of days ahead of time.

QUESTION: Can you say what -- detail anything about your discussion as to the future of KLA fighters? You just mentioned it briefly that there was, that they agreed they would be demilitarized but that there might be some way of them having a role?

SENATOR DOLE: I can't say much beyond that. I think they must understand there's no flexibility as far as demilitarization is concerned and I think they understand that. I think they also understand -- maybe Ambassador Hill is better prepared to respond -- but we're talking about an agreement and we believe the NATO forces will provide the protection for the people. There will not be a need for KLA activities and it's going to be a sharper reduced Serb presence too. So I think they do plan to come to Washington -- is that right Chris? --

AMBASSADOR HILL: They do, yes.

SENATOR DOLE: -- where there will be further discussions.

QUESTION: With the Kosovo side then on the verge of signing up, how worried are you about the military position on the ground? There's been a lot of troop build-ups by Belgrade. There's obviously been a fairly significant level of continuing violence day by day. Are you concerned at all that in the next 7 or 8 days that remain that we could see some very significant offensive by the Belgrade authorities?

AMBASSADOR HILL: There are two issues here: one is the issue of the Rambouillet accords where we do feel we're making significant progress with the Albanians. The second issue is the issue of compliance and what is going on on the ground. And you were very correct to point that there are a lot of troublesome developments on the ground. There are considerably more Yugoslav military than there should be, especially out of garrisons, and it's a situation that's deeply troublesome.

QUESTION: Senator Dole, can you give us a little detail of your meeting. How long were you on the ground there and who did you meet?

SENATOR DOLE: We started meeting about noon, I think we were still at it at seven o'clock. We had group meetings, one-on-one meetings, telephone calls, looking for Mr. Thaci -- never could find him, so if anyone locates him let us know. But in any event we were able to do what we hoped to do. We would have liked to have had the agreement signed yesterday, but since we couldn't get into Kosovo, that was not possible. And I don't know why Milosevic decided that that would not be a good day for me to visit.

QUESTION: Are you saying Hashim Thaci wasn't part of the delegation you met yesterday?

SENATOR DOLE: He wasn't there yesterday. We couldn't locate him. We've been trying for three days to find him. My understanding based on other conversations is that the decision will be made tomorrow and we hope to get it all signed up.

QUESTION: Can you have an agreement without Mr. Thaci's signature?

SENATOR DOLE: No, he'll be part of it.

QUESTION: So how can you have any confidence in a process where the main man doesn't turn up?

SENATOR DOLE: I don't know whether he is the main man or not, I mean he is the leader but --

AMBASSADOR HILL: Senator Dole had two very good discussions with Yacob Krasniqi yesterday and so the issue is the question of whether the general staff will give the order for someone from the KLA to sign. Obviously, a signature of the document has to include someone from the KLA. I don't know whether that will be Mr. Thaci or Mr. Krasniqi or someone else, but the issue is the general staff giving that permission.

SENATOR DOLE: And the impression we had was that even though there were parts they didn't like, that there was general agreement that this was the right thing to do and if something happens tomorrow, if somebody finds some glaring problem that we didn't know about, it could change things.

QUESTION: Ambassador Hill how would you characterize the behavior of the Serbs in this process? Generally have you any grounds for optimism in the sense of getting the Serbs to sign?

AMBASSADOR HILL: Well, I was in Belgrade the other day and the Yugoslav government has continued to take a position that while they are prepared to work with us on the political accords, and indeed there was a lot of progress on the political side, they are not prepared to accept a NATO-led force. And our view is that this is a package and the package includes a NATO-led force. And I must say in discussions in Belgrade not only with the Government, but in the opposition as well as the press and journalists, I think there was a real understanding that a NATO-led force is part of this.

QUESTION: Senator Dole, based on that, how can we proceed from here? We know that the ethnic Albanians have suggested that the Serbs have clearly since October said "no" to a NATO-led ground force. How can we possibly have peace without that?

SENATOR DOLE: That's the next step. I think the first step is getting the Albanians. We've tried to tell them we've already lost a couple of weeks where we could have been working on this -- not me, but others who have the responsibility -- and this is the first step. And when they sign, we can direct more attention to Milosevic, the Serbs. I'm not going to be involved in that but other people will be involved. Hopefully he will find some way to be able to sign the agreement. And I think one thing that came out of the meeting yesterday is that the Albanians understand that this all happens. They have a very serious responsibility to demonstrate they can govern and that they can treat minorities as they should be treated, Serbs and other minority groups in Kosovo.

So its going to be a real test because they hope that the end of three years, of course, to have some kind of referendum, that the international community will make a certain recommendation. My view was that they were very responsible, the next step will be up to Milosevic if the Albanians do as they say they'll do tomorrow.

QUESTION: Are you 100% confident?

SENATOR DOLE: Well, you are never 100%, but I've had a lot of experience with my colleagues in the Congress and generally it works out. If people give you their word they -- I'm looking at one of my witnesses George in the back, he was there when they pledged that we'd keep our word and this is what we're going to do. I told them very honestly, I said I don't know a lot about many things, but I know a lot about the U.S. Congress. And there's a lot of frustration now, even among their friends who wonder "Why are they doing this? How can you help your friends when they sort of push you away -- and that's what the Albanians have done for two weeks?" I believe they understand that this is something that must be resolved very quickly and they're prepared to do that.

QUESTION: Sir, can you tell us to what extent the threat of military force has concentrated minds in Belgrade?

SENATOR DOLE: One would hope that Belgrade would understand that this conflict in Kosovo has to end, all conflicts end, and that this one will also end. And they should, I believe, understand that the agreement we have is a fair agreement, which is to say that there is in that agreement that the Kosovo Albanian side doesn't like at all. And yet in its overall shape, it's an agreement that, I think, is fair to their interests and fair to the Yugoslav Serb interests. I think the issue of the NATO-led force is very much in everyone's interest. I cannot believe that any Serb can truly feel that an American soldier is his enemy. That is, I think, that even Serbs have to understand that this is in their interests, that this is the way to implement an agreement, whose purpose is to make sure that all national communities in Kosovo can now live together, and that they can begin to build political institutions which they lack very much now, and build an economy. And it's an interim agreement. That is, after three years, people can look at it again and see what additional steps can be made. So no one is being asked to give up their dreams, no one is being asked to make a permanent commitment, but they are being asked to make a very serious commitment to peace there. So I think it's in their interests. The question of what can propel the Serbs to understand this, what is the best way to exert leverage on them, obviously there are a number of issues there. But with regard to the compliance question, they are out of compliance now. This is deeply troubling, and I think they have to understand that this simply can't be allowed to go on.

QUESTION: (inaudible) you fly in tomorrow. They sign. If everything goes the way you expect it to be, then what happens? Are you taking this document someplace? What happens then?

AMBASSADOR HILL: Once we get the Albanians on board, then we want to work very hard to get the Serbs on board so that when they come to France for the so-called Rambouillet II, although it won't be at Rambouillet Chateau, both sides will be in a position to say "yes" and they will get on to the main purpose of that conference which is the implementation.

QUESTION: You're talking a little bit further down the line than I'm talking about. I'm talking about what are you going to do. Are they going to hand you the document and are you going to take it some place?

...

B.   The Paris Follow-on Conference

1.   Letter From Hashim Thaci, Chairman of the Presidency of the Kosova Delegation, 15 March 1999

To the Chairmen, Conference on the Interim Agreement for Peace and Self-government in Kosova

Dear Mr. Vedrine and Cook,

After the consultations of the Kosova delegation with political and military factors, as well as with the people of Kosova, concerning the Agreement for Peace and Self–governance (dated February 23, 1999) from the Rambouillet meeting, this delegation and I personally say „Yes" to this Agreement. We would be honored to sign the Agreement in your presence at a time and place of your choosing. The Agreement creates a chance and a perspective for Kosova and its people. Our consultations in Kosova were necessary and very important. Now that a positive mood on behalf of the Agreeement has been created within the political and military structures, the Kosova delegation is able to sign the Agreement. In this success of ours, your contribution as well as the contribution of the administration of your countries was great. The fate of the Albanian people of Kosova is at a historical turning point, and the Kosova delegation has a big responsibility. You have shown attention and patience concerning this fact. Our delegation, and I, are very thankful for this. We will expect your help, as well as the help of your Governments, in the future. The people of Kosova have been and will continue to be allies of your countries, and you can count on this. Kosova needs freedom and democracy. Your personal contribution and that of your countries are essential and respected.

Sincerely,

    The Kosova Delegation, Chairman, Hashim Thaçi

2.   FRY Revised Draft Agreement, 15 March 1999

~~Interim~~ Agreement for ~~Peace and~~ Self-Government in ~~Kosovo~~ Kosmet

The ~~parties~~ Signatories to the present Agreement,

Convinced of the need for a peaceful and political solution in ~~Kosovo~~ Kosmet as a prerequisite for stability and democracy,

Determined to establish a peaceful environment in ~~Kosovo~~ Kosmet,

Reaffirming their commitment to the Purposes and Principles of the United Nations as well as to the OSCE principles, including the Helsinki Final Act and the Charter of Paris for a new Europe,

Recalling the commitment of the international community to the sovereignty and territorial integrity of the Federal Republic of Yugoslavia,

Recalling the basic elements/principles adopted by the Contact Group at its ministerial meeting in London of January 29, 1999,

Recognizing the need for democratic self-government in ~~Kosovo~~ Kosmet, including full participation of the members of all national communities in political decision-making,

Desiring to ensure the protection of the human rights of all persons in ~~Kosovo~~ Kosmet, as well as the rights of the members of all national communities,

~~Recognizing the ongoing contribution of the OSCE to peace and stability in Kosovo,~~

Noting that the present Agreement has been concluded under the auspices of the members of the Contact Group and the European Union and undertaking with respect to these members and the European Union to abide by this Agreement,

Aware that full respect for the present Agreement will be central for the development of relations with European institutions,

Have agreed as follows:

Framework
Article 1: Principles

1.   All citizens in ~~Kosovo~~ Kosmet shall enjoy, without discrimination, the equal rights and freedoms set forth in this Agreement.

2.   National communities and their members shall have additional rights specified in Chapter 1. ~~Kosovo~~ Kosmet, Federal, and Republic authorities shall not interfere with the exercise of these additional rights. The national communities shall be legally equal as specified herein, and shall not use their additional rights to endanger the rights of other national communities or the rights of citizens, the sovereignty and territorial integrity of the Federal Republic of Yugoslavia, or the functioning of representative democratic government in ~~Kosovo~~ Kosmet.

3.   All authorities in ~~Kosovo~~ Kosmet shall fully respect human rights, democracy, and the equality of citizens and national communities.

4.   Citizens in ~~Kosovo~~ Kosmet shall have the right to democratic self-government through ~~legislative~~ normative, executive, judicial, and other institutions established in accordance with this Agreement. They shall have the opportunity to be represented in all institutions in ~~Kosovo~~ Kosmet. The right to democratic self-government shall include the right to participate in free and fair elections.

5.   Every person in ~~Kosovo~~ Kosmet may have access to international institutions for the protection of their rights in accordance with the procedures of such institutions.

6.   The ~~Parties~~ Signatories accept that they will act only within their powers and responsibilities in ~~Kosovo~~ Kosmet as specified by this Agreement. Acts outside those powers and responsibilities shall be null and void. ~~Kosovo~~ Kosmet shall have all rights and powers set forth herein, including in particular as specified in the ~~Constitution~~ Basic Act at Chapter 1. ~~This Agreement shall prevail over any other legal provisions of the Parties and shall be directly applicable. The Parties shall harmonize their governing practices and documents with this Agreement.~~

7.   The ~~Parties~~ Signatories agree to cooperate fully with all international organizations working in ~~Kosovo~~ Kosmet on the implementation of this Agreement.

Article ll: Confidence Building Measures
End of Use of Force

1.   Use of force in ~~Kosovo~~ Kosmet shall cease immediately. ~~In accordance with this Agreement, alleged violations of the cease-fire shall be reported to international observers and shall not be used to justify use of force in response.~~

2.   The status of police and security forces in ~~Kosovo~~ Kosmet, ~~including withdrawal of forces~~ shall be governed by the terms of this Agreement. Paramilitary and irregular forces in ~~Kosovo~~ Kosmet are incompatible with the terms of this Agreement.

Return

3.   The ~~Parties~~ Signatories recognize that all persons have the right to return to their homes. Appropriate authorities shall take all measures necessary to facilitate the safe return of persons, including issuing necessary documents **under the condition that they are the citizens of the FRY.** ~~All persons shall have the right to reoccupy their real property, assert their occupancy rights in state-owned property, and recover their other property and personal possessions.~~ The ~~parties~~ Signatories shall take all measures necessary to readmit returning persons to ~~Kosovo,~~ Kosmet.

4.   The ~~Parties~~ Signatories shall cooperate fully with all efforts by the United Nations High Commissioner for Refugees (UNHCR) and other international and non-governmental organizations acting under auspices of the UNHCR concerning the repatriation and return of persons, including those organizations' monitoring of the treatment of persons following their return.

Access for International Assistance

5.   There shall be no impediments to the normal flow of goods into Kosovo including materials for the reconstruction of homes and structures. ~~The Federal Republic of Yugoslavia shall not require visas, customs, or licensing for persons of things for the implementation Mission (IM), the UNHCR, and other international organizations, as well as for non governmental~~

~~organizations working in Kosovo as determined by the Chief of the Implementation Mission (CIM).~~

6. All staff, whether national or international, working with international or non-governmental organizations including with the Yugoslav Red Cross, shall be allowed unrestricted access to the ~~Kosovo~~ **Kosmet** population for purposes of international assistance. All persons in ~~Kosovo~~ **Kosmet** shall similarly have safe, unhindered, and direct access to the staff of such organizations.

~~Other issues~~

7. ~~Federal organs shall not take any decisions that have a different disproportionate, injurious, or discriminately effect on Kosovo. Such decisions, if any, shall be void with regard to Kosovo.~~

8. ~~Martial law shall not be declared in Kosovo.~~

9. ~~The Parties shall immediately comply with all requests for support from the Implementation Mission (IM). The IM shall have its own broadcast frequencies for radio and television programming in Kosovo.~~ The Federal Republic of Yugoslavia shall provide all necessary facilities, including frequencies for radio communications, to all humanitarian organizations responsible for delivering aid in Kosovo.

~~Detention of Combatants and Justice Issues~~

10. All abducted persons or other persons held without charge shall be released. ~~The Parties shall also release and transfer in accordance with this Agreement all persons held in connection with the conflict.~~ The ~~parties~~ **Signatories** shall cooperate fully with the International Committee of the Red Cross (ICRC) to facilitate its work in accordance with its mandate, including ensuring full access to all such persons, irrespective of their status, wherever they might be held, for visits in accordance with the ICRC's standard operating procedures.

11. All ~~Parties~~ **Signatories** shall provide information, through tracing mechanisms of the ICRC, to families of all persons who are unaccounted for. The ~~Parties~~ **Signatories** shall cooperate fully with the ICRC and the International Commission on Missing persons in their efforts to determine the identity, whereabouts, and fate of those unaccounted for.

12. Each ~~Party~~ **Signatory**:

    (a) shall not prosecute anyone for crimes related to the conflict in ~~Kosovo~~ **Kosmet**, except for persons accused of ~~serious violations of international humanitarian law~~ **crimes against humanity and international law.** The **Signatories** shall grant access to foreign experts (including forensics experts) along with state investigators;

    (b) shall grant a general amnesty for all persons already convicted of committing politically motivated crimes related to the conflict in ~~Kosovo~~ **Kosmet**. This amnesty shall not apply to those properly convicted of committing ~~serious violations of international humanitarian law~~ **crimes against humanity and international law** at a fair and open trial conducted pursuant to international standards.

13. ~~All Parties shall comply with their obligation to cooperate in the investigation and prosecution of serious violations of international humanitarian law.~~

    (a) ~~As required by United Nations Security Council resolution 827 (1993) and subsequent resolutions, the Parties shall fully cooperate with the International Criminal Tribunal for the Former Yugoslavia in its investigations and prosecutions, including complying with its requests for assistance and its orders.~~

    (b) ~~The Parties shall also allow complete, unimpeded, and unfettered access to international experts including forensic experts and investigators to investigate allegations of serious violations of international humanitarian law.~~

Independent Media

14. Recognizing the importance of free and independent media for the development of a democratic political climate necessary for the reconstruction and development of Kosovo, the Parties shall ensure the widest possible press freedoms in Kosovo in all media, public and private, including print, television, radio and Internet.

Chapter 1, ~~Constitution~~ Basic Act

Affirming their belief in a peaceful society, justice, tolerance, and reconciliation.

Resolved to ensure respect for human rights and the equality of all citizens and national communities.

Recognizing that the preservation and promotion of the national, cultural, and linguistic identity of each national community in ~~Kosovo~~ **Kosmet** are necessary for the harmonious development of a peaceful society,

Desiring through this ~~interim Constitution~~ **Basic Act** to establish institutions of democratic self-government in ~~Kosovo~~ **Kosmet** grounded in respect for the territorial integrity and sovereignty of the Federal Republic of Yugoslavia and from this Agreement, from which the authorities of governance set forth herein originate,

Recognizing that the institutions of ~~Kosovo~~ **Kosmet** should fairly represent the national communities in ~~Kosovo~~ **Kosmet** and foster the exercise of their rights and those of their members.

Recalling and endorsing the principles/basic elements adopted by the Contact group at its ministerial meeting in London on January 29, 1999.

Article 1: Principles of Democratic Self-Government in Kosovo

1. **Recognizing multi-ethnic character of Kosmet, substantial self-government shall be based on self-government of citizens in Kosmet and self-government of national communities in Kosmet.**

2. **Respecting the sovereignty and territorial integrity of the Federal Republic of Yugoslavia and of the Republic of Serbia, substantial self-government in Kosmet shall be based on broadest powers and rights of Kosmet organs and national communities in Kosmet. However, federal organs and organs of the Republic of Serbia shall also exercise their powers and rights in Kosmet.**

3. **All federal laws shall be valid and implemented, in accordance with the Constitution of the FRY, in the entire territory of the FRY, including the territory of Kosmet.**

4. **All republican laws enacted in accordance with the Constitution of the Republic of Serbia, whose validity and implementation are possible in line with personal principle, shall be valid and implemented in Kosmet for those physical and legal persons who chose to have these regulations implemented in the institutions, services and organizations founded by the Republic of Serbia, or whose functioning it regulated or whose work it finances (for example the laws in the field of education, science, culture, health-care, marital and family relations, adoption, tutorship, child and youth care, veterans' and disabled persons' protection, heritage, labour relations, social protection, social insurance and other).**

   In the fields listed above, the Assembly of Kosmet shall enact its regulations with legal force which shall be valid and implemented for those physical and legal persons in Kosmet who opt for them. They shall also be valid and implemented in the institutions, services and organizations founded by Kosmet, or whose work it regulated or finances.

5. **In the fields in which validity and implementation of republican laws are not possible along the personal principle, the Assembly of Kosmet shall enact its regulations with legal effect which will be valid for all physical and legal persons in Kosmet. However, decision-making within each national community shall ensure protection from discrimination or endangering on the basis of nationality (for example, agriculture, environment, protection of plants and animals, hunting and fishing, use and management of land, public information, urban planning and construction, organization and work of the organs of Kosmet, public services of importance for Kosmet and other fields).**

6. **Each national community may enact separate rules for its members, in order to protect their specific national**

characteristics, subject to their approval (for example in the field of matrimonial and family relations, adoption, tutorship and heritage).

7. Federal laws, in the entire territory of the FRY, including in Kosmet, in accordance with the Constitution of the FRY, shall be directly enforced by the federal organs through their regional organs (they shall enact enforcement regulations, individual legal acts and carry out administration control and inspection duties);

8. Republican laws, which on the basis of personal principle, are valid and implemented in Kosmet, shall be enforced, as in the entire territory of the Republic of Serbia, including in Kosmet, by republican organs (they shall enact enforcement regulations, individual legal acts, carry out administration control and inspection duties).

9. Provincial regulations with legal effect implemented on the basis of personal principle, as well as provincial regulations with legal effect which are valid and implemented for all physical and legal persons in Kosmet, shall be enforced by the organs of Kosmet (they shall enact enforcement regulations, individual legal acts, carry out administration control and inspection duties).

10. Individual regulations of national communities shall be enforced by the organs of that national community.

1. ~~Kosovo~~ Kosmet shall govern itself democratically through the ~~legislative~~ normative, executive, judicial, and other organs and institutions specified herein. Organs and institutions of ~~Kosovo~~ Kosmet shall exercise their authorities consistent with the terms of this Agreement.

2. All authorities in ~~Kosovo~~ Kosmet shall fully respect human rights, democracy, and the equality of citizens and national communities.

3. ~~The Federal Republic of Yugoslavia has competence in Kosovo over the following areas, except as specified elsewhere in this Agreement: (a) territorial integrity, (b) maintaining a common market within the Federal Republic of Yugoslavia, which power shall be exercised in a manner that does not discriminate against Kosovo, (c) monetary policy, (d) defence, (e) foreign policy, (f) customs service, (g) federal taxation, (h) federal elections, and (i) other areas specified in this Agreement.~~

4. ~~The Republic of Serbia shall have competence in Kosovo as specified in this Agreement, including in relation to Republic elections.~~

5. ~~Citizens in Kosovo may continue to participate in areas in which the Federal Republic of Yugoslavia and the Republic of Serbia have competence through their representation in relevant institutions, without prejudice to the exercise of competence by Kosovo authorities set forth in this Agreement.~~

6. ~~With respect to Kosovo.~~
    (a) ~~There shall be no changes to the borders of Kosovo;~~
    (b) ~~Deployment and use of police and security forces shall be governed by Chapter 2 and 7 of this Agreement; and~~
    (c) ~~Kosovo shall have authority to conduct foreign relations within its areas of responsibility equivalent to the power provided to Republics under Article 7 of the Constitution of the Federal Republic of Yugoslavia.~~

7. ~~There shall be no interference with the right of citizens and national communities in Kosovo to call upon appropriate institutions of the Republic of Serbia for the following purposes:~~
    (a) ~~assistance in designing school curricula and standards;~~
    (b) ~~participation in social benefits programs, such as care for war veterans, pensioners, and disabled persons; and~~
    (c) ~~other voluntary received services, provided that these services are not related to police and security matters governed by Chapter 2 and 7 of this Agreement, and that any Republic personnel serving in Kosovo pursuant to this paragraph shall be unarmed service providers acting at the invitation of a national community in Kosovo.~~
    ~~The Republic shall have the authority to levy taxes or charges on those citizens requesting services pursuant to this paragraph, as necessary to support the provision of such services.~~

8. The basic territorial unit of local self-government in ~~Kosovo~~ Kosmet shall be the commune. All responsibilities in ~~Kosovo~~ Kosmet not expressly assigned elsewhere shall be the responsibility of the communes.

9. To preserve and promote democratic self-government in ~~Kosovo~~ Kosmet, all candidates for appointed, elective, or other public office, and all office holders, shall meet the following criteria:
    (a) ~~No person who is serving a sentence imposed by the International Criminal Tribunal for the Former Yugoslavia, and no person who is under indictment by the Tribunal and who has failed to comply with an order to appear before the Tribunal, may stand as a candidate or hold any office; and~~
    (b) All candidates and office holders shall renounce violence as a mechanism for achieving political goals; past political ~~or resistance~~ activities shall not be a bar to holding office in ~~Kosovo~~ Kosmet.

Article ll: The Assembly

1. Kosmet shall have an Assembly which shall comprise 130 members, Ninety-five members shall be elected directly by citizens, through the system of proportionate representation. Kosmet shall be one electoral unit and thirty-five shall be elected by the national communities of Albanians, Serbs, Turks, Romanies, Egyptians, Goranies and Muslims, five members each.

   The Assembly of Kosmet shall make decisions from its competencies by majority vote of those present and voting, unless otherwise stipulated by this Basic Act.

   When the Assembly of Kosovo enacts regulations which are valid and implemented in relation to all physical and legal persons in Kosmet (when no option exists for the regulations of the Republic of Serbia), such regulations shall be enacted by majority vote of those members present and voting. At least three members from the same national community, elected by the national community, may in relation to the proposed regulation initiate a separate procedure for the protection of their vital national interests in the following cases:
   - regarding the election of organs of Kosmet and equal representation of all national communities in them;
   - regarding resettlement of population;
   - regarding impediments to the exercise of rights;
   - regarding endangering security;
   - regarding worsening of conditions of life;
   - regarding the adoption of the Kosmet budget.

   In a separate proceeding managed by the President of the Assembly of Kosmet, together with the Vice-Presidents of the Assembly of Kosmet, those proposing the regulations and the representatives of national communities elected by the national community, shall endeavour to eliminate the causes affecting vital national interests. Those taking part in this proceeding have to take account equally of the protection of general interests and vital national interests. Should this procedure prove to be unsuccessful (within 30 days of its initiation) and the regulation is not enacted, a proposal for its adoption may again be placed on the agenda of the Assembly of Kosmet, if at least six months have elapsed since it was asserted that the causes affecting vital national interests have not been eliminated.

2. The Assembly of Kosmet shall enact President and 6 Vice-Presidents, at least one from each national community, at the proposal of the members elected by national communities, for a four-year term. No one shall be elected as President or Vice-Presidents of the Assembly of Kosmet for more than two terms.

   The President and Vice-Presidents shall decide among themselves who will exercise which competency of the President of the Assembly of Kosmet.

The President of the Assembly promulgates the regulations enacted by the Assembly of Kosmet, represents the Assembly of Kosmet, proposes agenda for the meetings of the Assembly of Kosmet and chairs its meetings, holds regular meetings with the President of the National Assembly of Serbia and Presidents of the Chambers of the Federal Assembly, maintains contacts with the organs of national communities, proposes candidates for the President of the Council of Minister, proposes candidates for judges of courts in Kosmet and performs other duties set forth in the Basic Act and other regulations.

~~General~~

1. ~~Kosovo shall have an Assembly, which shall be comprised of 120 Members.~~

    (a) ~~Eighty Members shall be directly elected.~~

    (b) ~~A further forty Members shall be elected by the members of qualifying national communities.~~

        (I) ~~Communicate whose members constitute more than 0.5 per cent of the Kosovo population but less than 5 per cent shall have ten of these seats, to be divided among them in accordance with their proportion of the overall population.~~

        (II) ~~Communities whose members constitute more than 5 per cent of the Kosovo population shall divide the remaining thirty seats equally. The Serb and Albanian national communities shall be presumed to meet the 5 per cent population threshold.~~

~~Other Provisions~~

2. ~~Elections for all Members shall be conducted democratically, consistent with the provisions of Chapter 3 of this Agreement. Members shall be elected for a term of three years.~~

3. ~~Allocation of seats in the Assembly shall be based on data gathered in the census referred to in Chapter 5 of this Agreement. Prior to the completion of the census, for purposes of this Article declarations of national community membership made during voter registration shall be used to determine the percentage of the Kosovo population that each national community represents.~~

4. ~~Members of the Assembly shall be immune from all civil or criminal proceedings on the basis of words expressed or other acts performed in their capacity as members of the Assembly.~~

Powers of the Assembly

5. The Assembly shall be responsible for enacting ~~laws~~ **decisions and regulations with legal force** of ~~Kosovo~~ **Kosmet**, including in political, ~~security,~~ economic, social, educational, scientific and cultural areas as set out below and elsewhere in this Agreement. ~~This Constitution and the laws of the Kosovo Assembly shall not be subject to change or modification by authorities of the Republic or the Federation.~~

    (a) The Assembly shall be responsible for:

        (i) Financing activities of ~~Kosovo~~ **Kosmet** institutions, including by levying taxes and duties of sources within ~~Kosovo~~ **Kosmet**;

        (ii) Adopting of budgets of the Administrative organs and other institutions of ~~Kosovo~~ **Kosmet**, with the exception of communal and national community institutions unless otherwise specified herein;

        (iii) Adopting regulations concerning the organization and procedures of the Administrative organs of ~~Kosovo~~ **Kosmet**;

        (iv) Approving the list of Ministers of the ~~Government~~ **Council of Ministers**, including the Prime Minister;

        (v) Coordinating educational arrangements in ~~Kosovo~~ **Kosmet,** with respect for the authorities of national communities and Communes;

        (vi) Electing candidates for judicial office put forward by the President of **Assembly of** ~~Kosovo~~ **Kosmet**;

        (vii) ~~Enacting laws ensuring free movement of goods, services, and persons in Kosovo consistent with this Agreement;~~

        (viii) ~~Approving agreements concluded by the President within the areas of responsibility of Kosovo;~~

        (ix) ~~Cooperating with the Federal Assembly, and with the Assemblies of the Republic, and conducting relations with foreign legislative bodies;~~

        (x) Establishing a framework for local self-government;

        (xi) Enacting ~~laws~~ **regulations** concerning inter-communal issues and relations between national communities when necessary;

        (xii) Enacting ~~laws~~ **regulations** regulating the work of medical institutions and hospitals;

        (xiii) Protecting the environment, where intercommunal issues are involved;

        (xiv) Adopting programs or economic, scientific, technological, demographic, regional, and social development, as well as urban planning;

        (xv) Adopting programs for the development of agriculture and of rural areas;

        (xvi) Regulating elections ~~consistent with Chapters 3 and 5~~;

        (xvii) Regulating ~~Kosovo~~ **Kosmet**-owned property; and

        (xviii) Regulating land registries.

    (b) The Assembly shall also have authority to enact ~~laws~~ **decisions and regulations with force of law** in areas within the responsibility of the Communes if the matter cannot be effectively regulated by the Communes or if regulation by individual Communes might prejudice the rights of other Communes **on the basis of the agreement of these communes.** In the absence of ~~a law~~ **decisions** enacted by the Assembly under this subparagraph that preempts communal action, the Communes shall retain their authority.

Procedure

6. ~~Laws and other decisions of the Assembly shall be adopted by majority of members present and voting.~~

7. ~~A majority of the Members of a single national community elected to the Assembly pursuant to paragraph 1(b) may adopt a motion that a law or other decision adversely affects the vital interests of their national community. The challenged law or decision shall be suspended with regard to that national community until the dispute settlement in paragraph 8 is completed.~~

8. ~~The following procedure shall be used in the event of a motion under paragraph 7:~~

    (a) ~~The Members making the vital interest motion shall give reasons for their motion. The proposers of the legislation shall be given an opportunity to respond.~~

    (b) ~~The Members making the motion shall appoint within one day a mediator of their choice to assist in reaching an agreement with those proposing the legislation.~~

    (c) ~~If mediation does not produce an agreement within seven days, the matter may be submitted for a binding ruling. The decision shall be rendered by a panel comprising three Members of the Assembly; one Albanian and one Serb, each appointed by his or her national community delegation; and a third Member, who will be of a third nationality and will be selected within two days by consensus of the Presidency of the Assembly.~~

        (i) ~~A vital interest motion shall be upheld if the legislation challenged adversely affects the community's fundamental constitutional rights, additional rights as set forth in Article VII, or the principle of fair treatment.~~

        (ii) ~~If the motion is not upheld, the challenged legislation shall enter into force for that community.~~

    (d) ~~Paragraph (c) shall not apply to the selection of Assembly officials.~~

    (e) ~~The Assembly may exclude other decisions from this procedure by means of a law enacted by a majority that includes a majority of each national community elected pursuant to paragraph 1(b).~~

9. ~~A majority of the Members shall constitute a quorum. The Assembly shall otherwise decide its own rules of procedure.~~

Leadership

10. ~~The Assembly shall elect from among its Members a Presidency, which shall consist of a President, two Vice Presidents, and other leaders in accordance with the Assembly's rules of procedure. Each national community meeting the threshold specified in paragraph 1(b)(ii) shall be represented in the leadership. The President of the Assembly shall not be from the same national community as the President of Kosovo.~~

11. ~~The President of the Assembly shall represent it, call its sessions to order, chair its meetings, coordinate the work of any committees it may establish, and perform other tasks prescribed by the rules of the procedure of the Assembly.~~

~~Article III: President of Kosovo~~

1. ~~There shall be a President of Kosovo, who shall be elected by the Assembly by vote of a majority of its members. The President of Kosovo shall serve for a three year term. No person may serve more than two terms as President of Kosovo.~~

2. ~~The President of Kosovo shall be responsible for:~~

    (i) ~~Representing Kosovo, including before any international or Federal body, or anybody of the Republics.~~

    (ii) ~~Proposing to the Assembly candidates for Prime Minister, the Constitutional Court, the Supreme Court, and other Kosovo judicial offices.~~

    (iii) ~~Meeting regularly with the democratically elected representatives of the national communities.~~

    (iv) ~~Conducting foreign relations and concluding agreements within his power consistent with the authorities of Kosovo institutions under this Agreement. Such agreements shall only enter into force upon approval by the Assembly.~~

    (v) ~~Designating a representative to serve on the Joint Commission established by Article 1.2 of Chapter 5 of this Agreement;~~

    (vi) ~~Meeting regularly with the Federal and Republic Presidents; and~~

    (vii) ~~Other functions specified herein or by law.~~

Article IV: ~~The Government~~ **Council of Ministers** and Administrative organs

The Council of Ministers shall perform executive functions. It shall be responsible for the enforcement of the regulations of Kosmet and shall make proposals for their adoption to the Assembly of Kosmet.

The Council of Ministers shall be composed of the President and Ministers. The candidate for the President of the Council of Ministers shall be proposed by the President of the Assembly of Kosmet. The candidate for the President of the Council of Ministers shall make a list of candidates for Ministers make sure that each national community is represented with at least one candidate and shall submit it to the Assembly for adoption. The President of the Council of Ministers cannot be from the same national community as the President of the Assembly of Kosmet. The Council of Ministers shall be elected when it receives majority of the total number of the members of the Assembly of Kosmet, i.e. when it receives majority by representatives of each individual national community.

1. ~~Executive power shall be exercised by the Government. The Government shall be responsible for implementing the laws of Kosovo, and of the government authorities when such responsibilities are devolved by those authorities. The Government shall also have competence to propose laws to the Assembly of Kosovo.~~

    (a) ~~The Government shall consist of a Prime Minister and Ministers including at least one person from each national community meeting the threshold specified in paragraph 1(b)(ii) of Article II. Ministers shall head the Administrative Organs of Kosovo.~~

    (b) ~~The candidate for Prime Minister proposed by the President shall put forward a list of Ministers to the Assembly. The Prime Minister, together with the list of Ministers shall be approved by a majority of those present and voting in the Assembly. In the event that the Prime Minister is not able to~~ ~~obtain a majority for the Government, the President shall propose a new candidate for Prime Minster within ten days.~~

    (c) ~~The Government shall resign if a no confidence motion is adopted by a vote of a majority of the members of the Assembly. If the Prime Minister or the Government resigns, the President shall select a new candidate for Prime Minister who shall seek to form a Government.~~

    (d) ~~The Prime Minister shall call meetings of the Government, represent it as appropriate, and coordinate its work. Decisions of the Government shall require a majority of Ministers present and voting. The Prime Minister shall cast the deciding vote in the event Ministers are equally divided. The Government shall otherwise decide its own rules of procedure.~~

2. Administrative Organs shall be responsible for assisting the ~~Government~~ **Council of Ministers** in carrying out its duties.

    The administration organs of Kosmet shall be responsible for direct implementation of laws and decision-making in administration matters. Public officials working in the administration organs shall be fairly representative of each national community.

    (a) ~~National communities shall be fairly represented at all levels in the Administrative Organs.~~

    (b) ~~Any citizen of Kosovo claiming to have been directly and adversely affected by the decision of an executive or administrative body shall have the right to judicial review of the legality of that decision after exhausting all avenues for administrative review. The Assembly shall enact law to regulate this review.~~

3. ~~There shall be a Chief Prosecutor who shall be responsible for prosecuting individuals who violate the criminal laws of Kosovo. He shall head an Office of the Prosecutor, which shall at all levels have staff representative of the population of Kosovo.~~

Article V: ~~Judiciary~~ Courts and enforcement

1. **The functions of the courts in Kosmet shall be performed by the courts of the Republic of Serbia, Kosmet courts and the courts of national communities.**

    The courts in Kosmet, except the courts of national communities, shall implement the federal and republican laws, and provincial decisions and regulations with legal force.

2. **Citizens and legal persons in Kosmet shall have the right to choose the court which will try their case. Any citizen or legal person in Kosmet may, at the start of court proceedings (litigation, out-of-court proceedings and criminal) as a plaintiff, petitioner or accused, choose to be tried either by the Court of the Republic of Serbia or Kosmet court.**

    If other participants in the proceedings (defendant or the wronged party) are not members of the same national community judges as plaintiff or the defendant, they may request that the members of the panel be chosen from their national community. They are also entitled to other rights in the proceedings, specified by the laws on proceedings.

    The courts of national communities may be established by those national communities which established the separate rules for the settlement of disputes among the members of that national community, who accepted those rules and who agreed to the competencies of these courts.

3. **The Kosmet courts shall be established, organized and their judges and jurors elected by the Assembly of Kosmet. The Kosmet courts shall be established as first instance, second instance and the High Court of Kosmet.**

    The High Court of Kosmet, in addition to the competencies related to trials according to regular and extraordinary legal means, in a separate permanent council composed of five judges, shall ensure that all regulations enacted by the organs of Kosmet are in line with the Basic Act of Kosmet, as well as that other regulations and general acts of Kosmet are in line with the regulations with legal force enacted by the Assembly of Kosmet. In exercising this authority, this council may revoke any regulation or general act of the organs of Kosmet.

All regulations and general acts of Kosmet enacted from the competencies of the federal and republican organs set forth in the Constitution of the Federal Republic of Yugoslavia and the Constitution of the Republic of Serbia, shall be null and void. The federal and republican laws and other general acts of the federal and republican organs enacted in the fields in which Kosmet enacts regulations with legal force, implemented for all citizens and legal persons in Kosmet, shall be null and void.

4. The function of the Public Prosecutor in Kosmet shall be performed by the Federal, Republican and Kosmet Public Prosecutor. The Federal and republican prosecutor shall act before the republican and Kosmet courts, whereas the Kosmet prosecutor shall act before the Kosmet courts. The establishment, organization and competencies or Kosmet Public Prosecutor shall be specified by the regulation adopted by the Assembly of Kosmet.

5. A citizen in Kosmet who, by legally effective and enforceable ruling of the court of the Republic of Serbia or the Kosmet court, is sentenced to an unconditional prison term in a prison set up by the Republic of Serbia according to enforcement regulations of the Republic of Serbia, if he is convicted by the republican court in the prison set up by the Assembly of Kosmet and according to enforcement regulations enacted by it, if he is sentenced by the Kosmet court.

General

1. Kosovo shall have a Constitutional Court, a Supreme Court, District Courts, and Communal Courts.

2. The Kosovo courts shall have jurisdiction over all matters arising under this Constitution or the laws of Kosovo except as specified in paragraph 3. The Kosovo courts shall also have jurisdiction over questions of federal law, subject to appeal to the Federal courts on these questions after all appeals available under the Kosovo system have been exhausted.

3. Citizens in Kosovo may opt to have civil disputes to which they are partly adjudicated by other courts in the Federal Republic of Yugoslavia, which shall apply the law applicable in Kosovo.

4. The following rules will apply to criminal cases:

   (a) At the start of criminal proceedings, the defendant is entitled to have his or her trial transferred to another Kosovo court that he or she designates.

   (b) In criminal cases in which all defendants and victims are members of the same national community, all members of the judicial council will be from a national community of their choice if any party so requests.

   (c) A defendant in a criminal case tried in Kosovo courts is entitled to have at least one member of the judicial council hearing the case to be from his or her national community. Kosovo authorities will consider and allow judges or other courts in the Federal Republic of Yugoslavia to serve as Kosovo judges for these purposes.

Constitutional Court

5. The Constitutional Court shall consist of nine judges. There shall be at least one constitutional court judge from each national community qualifying court judge from each national community meeting the threshold specified under paragraph 1(b)(ii) of Article ll. Until such time as the Parties agree to discontinue this arrangement, 5 judges of the Constitutional Court shall be selected from a list drawn up by the President of the European Court of Human Rights.

6. The Constitutional Court shall have authority to resolve disputes relating to the meaning of this Constitution. That authority shall include, but is not limited to, determining whether laws applicable in Kosovo, decisions or acts of the President, the Assembly, the Government, the Communes, and the national communities are compatible with this Constitution.

   (a) Matters may be referred to the Constitutional Court by the President of Kosovo, the President or Vice Presidents of the Assembly, the Ombudsman, the communal assemblies and councils, and any national community acting according to its democratic procedures.

   (b) Any court which finds in the course of adjudicating a matter that the dispute depends on the answer to a question within the Constitutional Court's jurisdiction shall refer the issue to the Constitutional Court for a preliminary decision.

7. Following the exhaustion of other legal remedies, the Constitutional Court shall at the request of any person claiming to be a victim have jurisdiction over complaints that human rights and fundamental freedoms and the rights of members of national communities set forth in this Constitution have been violated by a public authority.

8. The Constitutional Court shall have such other jurisdiction, as may be specified elsewhere in this Agreement or by law.

Supreme Court

9. The Supreme Court shall consist of nine judges. There shall be at least one Supreme Court judge from each national community meeting the threshold specified in paragraph 1(b)(ii) of Article ll.

10. The Supreme court shall hear appeals from the District Courts and the Communal Courts. Except as otherwise provided in this Constitution, the Supreme court shall be the court of final appeal for all cases arising under law applicable in Kosovo. Its decisions shall be recognized and executed by all authorities in the Federal Republic of Yugoslavia.

Functioning of the Courts

11. The Assembly shall determine the number of District and Communal court judges necessary to meet current needs.

12. Judges of all courts in Kosovo shall be distinguished jurists of the highest moral character. They shall be broadly representative of the national communities of Kosovo.

13. Removal of a Kosovo judge shall require the consensus of the judges of the Constitutional Court. A Constitutional Court judge whose removal is in question shall not participate in the decision on his case.

14. The Constitutional Court shall adopt rules for itself and for other courts in Kosovo. The Constitutional and Supreme Courts shall each adopt decisions by majority vote of their members.

15. Except as otherwise specified in their rules, all Kosovo courts shall hold public proceedings. They shall issue published opinions setting forth the reasons for their decision.

Local Police

1. In the communes in Kosmet, local police may be established as an organ performing certain police duties in the territory of a commune.

   Heads and chiefs of departments of local police shall be appointed by an organ of communal government in charge of internal affairs with the approval of all national communities living in that commune.

   Local police shall be representative of the national composition of the residents of the commune.

   In communes with mixed population, local police departments shall be set up comprising police officers, members of the same national community. These departments shall carry out the tasks of local police in relation to members of the same national community.

   In relation to members of different national communities, the duties of local police shall be jointly performed by local police officers from each department of local police.

2. Local police shall be responsible for preventing smaller violations of public order, investigation and other functions of police related to offences, traffic and patrol activities, fire protection, safety of traffic in local roads, prevention and suppression of offences, recording and controlling residence of citizens, establishment of a unique identification number and issuance of identity cards.

   Other duties of police (State security, aliens, borders, serious criminal acts, arms, ammunition, explosives and other hazardous substances, traffic in regional main roads, passports, etc) in the communes where local police has been set up and all police duties in the communes where local police has not been set up, shall be performed by the state police. In larger places with mixed population traffic and patrol duties, in addition to local police, shall be performed by the State police, comprising police officers of different nationalities.

Relations between local and state police shall be based on mutual cooperation and they shall provide information to each other on all issues of importance to the performance of their duties.

3. The members of the local police may use, as means of coercion, guns, rubber truncheons, handcuffs and passenger transport vehicles as well as appropriate communications means.

Local police shall be trained in appropriate police schools and its members shall be specifically trained to perform police duties in areas with mixed population.

The commune where local police has been established shall set up a commission to oversee its work. It will be composed of the representatives of all national communities living in the commune.

Article Vl: Human Rights and Fundamental Freedoms

1. All authorities in ~~Kosovo~~ **Kosmet** shall ensure internationally recognized human rights and fundamental freedoms in ~~Kosovo~~ **Kosmet**.

2. The rights and freedoms set forth in the European Convention for the Protection of Human Rights and Fundamental Freedoms and its Protocols shall apply directly in ~~Kosovo~~ **Kosmet**. Other internationally recognized human rights instruments enacted into ~~laws~~ **its regulations** by the ~~Kosovo~~ **Kosmet** Assembly shall also apply. These rights and freedoms shall have priority over all other law.

3. All courts, agencies, government institutions, and other public institutions of ~~Kosovo~~ **Kosmet** or operating in relation to ~~Kosovo~~ **Kosmet** shall conform to these human rights and fundamental freedoms.

Article Vll: National Communities

1. National communities and their members shall have additional rights as set forth below in order to preserve and express their national, cultural, religious, and linguistic identities in accordance with international standards and the Helsinki Final Act. Such rights shall be exercised in conformity with human rights and fundamental freedoms.

2. Each national community may elect through democratic means ~~and in a manner consistent with the principles of Chapter 3,~~ institutions to administer its affairs in ~~Kosovo~~ **Kosmet**.

3. ~~The national communities shall be subject to the laws applicable in Kosovo, provided that any act or decision concerning national communities must be non discriminatory. The Assembly shall decide upon a procedure for resolving disputes between national communities.~~

4. The additional rights of the national communities, ~~acting through their democratically elected institutions,~~ are to:
   (a) preserve and protect their national, cultural, religious, and linguistic identities, including by:
      (i) inscribing local names of towns and villages, of squares and streets, and of other topographic names in the language and alphabet of the national community in addition to signs in Albanian and Serbian, consistent with decisions about style made by the communal institutions.
      (ii) providing information in the language and alphabet of the national community.
      (iii) providing for education and establishing educational institutions, in particular for schooling in their own language and alphabet and in national culture and history, for which relevant authorities will provide financial assistance; curricula shall reflect a spirit of tolerance between national communities and respect for

the rights of members of all national communities in accordance with international standards.
      (iv) enjoying unhindered contacts with representatives of their respective national communities, within the Federal Republic of Yugoslavia and abroad.
      (v) using and displaying national symbols, including symbols of the Federal Republic of Yugoslavia and the Republic of Serbia;
      (vi) protecting national traditions on family law by, if the community decides, arranging rules in the field of inheritance, family and matrimonial relations; tutorship; and adoption.
      (vii) the preservation of sites of religious, historical, or cultural importance to the national community, in cooperation with other authorities.
      (viii) ~~implementing public health and social services on a non discriminatory basis as to citizens and national communities.~~
      (ix) operating religious institutions in cooperation with religious authorities; and
      (x) participating in regional and international non-governmental organizations in accordance with procedures of these organizations.
   (a) be guaranteed access to, and representation in, public broadcast media, including provisions for separate programming in relevant languages under the direction of those nominated by the respective national community on a fair and equitable basis; and
   (b) finance their activities by collecting contributions the national communities may decide on levy on members of their own communities.

5. ~~Members of national communities shall also be individually guaranteed:~~
   (a) the right to enjoy unhindered contacts with members of their respective national communities elsewhere in the Federal Republic of Yugoslavia and abroad.
   (b) equal access to employment in public services at all levels.
   (c) the right to use their languages and alphabets.
   (d) ~~the right to use and display national community symbols.~~
   (e) ~~The right to participate in democratic institutions that will determine the national community's exercise of the collective rights set forth in this Article; and~~
   (f) ~~The right to establish cultural and religious associations, for which relevant authorities will provide financial assistance.~~

6. Each national community and, where appropriate, their members acting individually may exercise these additional rights through Federal institutions and institutions of the Republics, in accordance with the procedures of those institutions and without prejudice to the ability of Kosovo institutions to carry out their responsibilities.

7. Every person shall have the right freely to choose to be treated or not to be treated as belonging to a national community, and no disadvantage shall result from that choice or from the exercise of the rights connected to that choice.

Article Vlll: Communes

1. **Communes shall be units of local self-government.**

2. **The Assembly of Kosmet may change the present borders of the existing communes only with their prior consent.**

3. **Each commune shall have an Assembly, Executive Board and administration authorities. The organs of commune shall be set up in accordance with the principles that the organs of Kosmet have been set up.**

   Through its organs, in accordance with the legal powers of the Assembly of Kosmet, a commune shall be responsible for:
   - **making development plans, town planning, budget and annual accounts**
   - **regulating and ensuring and development of communal activities;**
   - **regulating and ensuring the use of city construction land and business space;**

- taking care of construction, maintenance and use of local roads and streets and other public facilities of communal importance;
- establishing organs, organizations and services for communal needs and regulating their work.

The Assembly of Kosmet may devolve some of the duties from its competencies to a certain commune and transfer the funds to it to carry out that work.

1. ~~Kosovo shall have the existing communes. Changes may be made to communal boundaries by act of the Kosovo Assembly after consultation with the authorities of the communes concerned.~~
2. ~~Communes may develop relationships among themselves for their mutual benefit.~~
3. ~~Each commune shall have an Assembly, an Executive Council, and such administrative bodies as the commune may establish:~~
   - (a) ~~Each national community whose membership constitutes at least three per cent of the population of the commune shall be represented on the Council in proportion to its share of the communal population or by one member, whichever is greater.~~
   - (b) ~~Prior to the completion of a census, disputes over communal population percentages for purposes of this paragraph shall be resolved by reference to declarations of national community membership in the voter registry.~~
4. ~~The communes shall have responsibility for:~~
   - (a) ~~Law enforcement, as specified in Chapter 2 of this Agreement.~~
   - (b) ~~Regulating and, when appropriate, providing child care.~~
   - (c) ~~Providing education, consistent with the rights and duties of national communities, and in a spirit of tolerance between national communities and respect for the rights of the members of all national communities in accordance with international standards.~~
   - (d) ~~Protecting the communal environment.~~
   - (e) ~~Regulating commerce and privately-owned stores.~~
   - (f) ~~Regulating hunting and fishing.~~
   - (g) ~~Planning and carrying out public works of communal importance, including roads and water supplies, and participating in the planning and carrying out of Kosovo-wide public works projects in coordination with other communes and Kosovo authorities.~~
   - (h) ~~Regulating land use, town planning, building regulations, and housing construction.~~
   - (i) ~~Developing programs for tourism, the hotel industry, catering, and sport.~~
   - (j) ~~Organizing fairs and local markets.~~
   - (k) ~~Organizing public services of communal importance, including fire, emergency response, and police consistent with Chapter 2 of this Agreement; and~~
   - (l) ~~Financing the work of communal institutions, including raising revenues, taxes and preparing budgets.~~
5. ~~The communes shall also have responsibility for all other areas within Kosovo's authority not expressly assigned elsewhere herein, subject to the provisions of Article ll 5(b) of this Constitution.~~
6. ~~Each commune shall conduct its business in public and shall maintain publicly available records of its deliberations and decisions.~~

<u>Article IX: Representation</u>

1. **The citizens in Kosmet shall be represented by at least 10 representatives in the Chamber of Citizens of the Federal Assembly and at least 20 representatives in the National Assembly of the Republic of Serbia.**
2. **At least one citizen in Kosmet shall be elected to the Federal Government and to the Government of the Republic of Serbia.**
3. **At least one citizen in Kosmet shall be elected as judge of the Federal Court and three judges in the Supreme Court of Serbia.**
1. ~~Citizens in Kosovo shall have the right to participate in the election of:~~
   - (a) ~~At least 10 deputies in the House of Citizens of the Federal Assembly; and~~
   - (b) ~~At least 20 deputies in the National Assembly of the Republic of Serbia.~~
2. ~~The modalities of elections for the deputies specified in paragraph 1 shall be determined by the Federal Republic of Yugoslavia and the Republic of Serbia respectively, under procedures to be agreed with the Chief of the Implementation Mission.~~
3. ~~The Assembly shall have the opportunity to present to the appropriate authorities a list of candidates from which shall be drawn:~~
   - (a) ~~at least one citizen in Kosovo to serve in the Federal Government, and at least one citizen in Kosovo to serve in the Government of the Republic of Serbia; and~~
   - (b) ~~At least one judge on the Federal Constitution Court, one judge on the Federal court, and three judges on the Supreme court of Serbia.~~

<u>Article X: Amendment</u>

1. The Assembly may by a majority of two-thirds of its members, which majority must include a majority of the Members elected ~~from~~ **by** the national community pursuant ~~to Article ll, 1(b) (ii),~~ adopt amendments to this ~~Constitution~~ **Basic Act**.
2. There shall, however, be no amendments to Article 1.3 **8** or to this Article, nor shall any amendment diminish the rights granted by Articles Vl and Vll.

<u>Article Xl: Entry into force</u>

This ~~Constitution~~ **Basic Act** shall enter into force upon ~~signature~~ **entering into force** of this Agreement.

Chapter 3, Conduct and Supervision of Elections
Census and the first Parliamentary elections

1. **The competent state authorities shall organise, together with the OSCE, as soon as possible, an objective and free census of the population in Kosmet. The census shall include information on places of residence, citizenship, nationality and other data relevant to the conduct of elections.**
2. **Free and fair elections for organs of Kosmet shall be held within nine months of the signing of the Agreement on Kosmet, under the supervision of OSCE.**
3. **The rules for the first elections for the Assembly of Kosmet, communal assemblies in Kosmet, harmonization of candidates on the basis of the OSCE electoral standards, shall be determined by the representatives of all national communities and all political parties in Kosmet.**

<u>Article l: Conditions for Elections</u>

1. ~~The Parties shall ensure that conditions exist for the organization of free and fair elections, which include but are not limited to:~~
   - (a) ~~freedom of movement for all citizens;~~
   - (b) ~~an open and free political environment;~~
   - (c) ~~an environment conducive to the return of displaced persons;~~
   - (e) ~~a safe and secure environment that ensure freedom of assembly, association, and expression;~~
   - (f) ~~an electoral legal framework of rules and regulations complying with OSCE commitments, which will be implemented by a Central Election Commission, as set forth in Article lll of this Chapter, which is representative of the population of Kosovo in terms of national communities and political parties; and~~
   - (g) ~~free media, effectively accessible to all registered political parties and candidates, and available to voters throughout Kosovo.~~
2. ~~The Parties request the OSCE to certify when elections will be effective under current conditions in Kosovo, and to provide assistance to the Parties to create conditions for free and fair elections.~~
3. ~~The Parties shall comply fully with Paragraphs 7 and 8 of the OSCE Copenhagen Document, which are attached to this Chapter.~~

<u>Article ll: Role of the OSCE</u>

1. ~~The Parties request the OSCE to adopt and put in place an elections program for Kosovo and supervise elections as set forth in the Agreement.~~

2. ~~The Parties request the OSCE to supervise, in a manner to be determined by the OSCE and in co-operation with other international organizations the OSCE deems necessary, the preparation and conduct of elections for:~~
   (a) ~~Members of the Kosovo Assembly;~~
   (b) ~~Members of the Communal Assemblies;~~
   (c) ~~other officials popularly elected in Kosovo under the Agreement and the laws and Constitution of Kosovo at the discretion of the OSCE.~~
3. ~~The Parties request the OSCE to establish a Central Election Commission in Kosovo ("the Commission").~~
4. ~~Consistent with Article IV of Chapter 5, the first elections shall be held within nine months of the entry into force of the Agreement. The President of the Commission shall decide, in consultation with the Parties, the exact timing and order of elections for Kosovo political offices.~~

~~Article III: Central Election Commission~~
1. ~~The Commission shall adopt electoral Rules and Regulations on all matters necessary for the conduct of free and fair elections in Kosovo, including rules relating to: the eligibility and registration of candidates, parties, and voters, including displaced persons and refugees; ensuring a free and fair elections campaign; administrative and technical preparation for elections including the establishment, publication, and certification of election results; and the role of international and domestic election observers.~~
2. ~~The responsibilities of the Commission, as provided in the electoral Rules and Regulations, shall include:~~
   (a) ~~the preparation, conduct, and supervision of all aspect of the electoral process, including development and supervision of political party and voter registration, and creation of secure and transparent procedures for production and dissemination of ballots and sensitive election materials, vote counts, tabulations, and publication of elections results;~~
   (b) ~~ensuring compliance with the electoral Rules and Regulations, established pursuant to the Agreement, including establishing auxiliary bodies for this purpose as necessary;~~
   (c) ~~ensuring that action is taken to remedy any violation of any provision of the Agreement, including imposing penalties such as removal from candidate or party lists, against any person, candidate, political party, or body that violates such provisions; and~~
   (d) ~~accrediting observers, including personnel from international organisations, and ensuring that the Parties grant the accredited observers unimpeded access and movement.~~
3. ~~The Commission shall consist of a person appointed by the Chairman in Office (CIO) of the OSCE, representatives of all national communities, and representatives of political parties in Kosovo selected by criteria to be determined by the Commission. The person appointed by the CIO shall act as the President of the Commission. The rules of procedure of the Commission shall provide that in the exceptional circumstance of an unresolved dispute within the Commission, the decision of the President shall be final and binding.~~
4. ~~The Commission shall enjoy the right to establish communication facilities, and to engage local and administrative staff.~~

Chapter 4, **Economic Issues**
Article 1
1. The economy of ~~Kosovo~~ **Kosmet** shall function in accordance with free market principles.
2. The authorities established to levy and collect taxes and other charges are set forth in the Agreement. Except as otherwise expressly provided, all authorities have the right to keep all revenues from their own taxes or other charges consistent with the Agreement.
3. Certain revenue from ~~Kosovo~~ **Kosmet** taxes and duties shall accrue to the Communes, taking into account the need for an equalization of revenues between the Communes based on objective criteria. The Assembly of ~~Kosovo~~ **Kosmet** shall enact appropriate non-

discriminatory ~~laws~~ **regulations** for this purpose. The Communes may also levy taxes in accordance with the Agreement.
4. ~~The Federal Republic of Yugoslavia shall be responsible for the collection of all customs duties at international borders in Kosovo. There shall be no impediments to the free movement of persons, goods, services, and capital to and from Kosovo.~~
5. ~~Federal authorities shall ensure that Kosovo receives a proportionate and equitable share of benefits that may be derived from international agreements concluded by the Federal Republic and of Federal resources.~~
6. ~~Federal and other authorities shall within their respective powers and responsibilities ensure the free movement of persons, goods, services, and capital to Kosovo, including from international sources. They shall in particular allow access to Kosovo without discrimination for persons delivering such goods and services.~~
7. If expressly required by an international donor or lender, international contracts for reconstruction projects shall be concluded by the authorities of the Federal Republic of Yugoslavia which shall establish appropriate mechanisms to make such funds available to ~~Kosovo~~ **Kosmet** authorities. Unless precluded by the terms of contracts, all reconstruction projects that exclusively concern ~~Kosovo~~ **Kosmet** shall be managed and implemented by the appropriate ~~Kosovo~~ **Kosmet** authority.

Article II
1. ~~The Parties agree to reallocate ownership and resources in accordance insofar as possible with the distribution of powers and responsibilities set forth in the Agreement, in the following areas:~~
   (a) ~~government owned assets (including educational institutions, hospitals, natural resources, and production facilities);~~
   (b) ~~pension and social insurance contributions;~~
   (c) ~~revenues to be distributed under Article 1.5 of this chapter; and~~
   (d) ~~any other matters relating to economic relations between the Parties not covered by the Agreement.~~
2. ~~The Parties agree to the creation of a Claim Settlement Commission (CSC) to resolve all disputes between them on matters referred to in paragraph 1.~~
   (a) ~~The CSC shall consist of three experts designated by Kosovo, three experts designated jointly by the Federal Republic of Yugoslavia and the Republic of Serbia, and three independent experts designated by the CIM.~~
   (b) ~~The decisions of the CSC which shall be taken by majority vote, shall be final and binding. The Parties shall implement them without delay.~~
3. ~~Authorities receiving ownership of public facilities shall have the power to operate such facilities.~~

~~Chapter 4-A, Humanitarian Assistance, Reconstruction and Economic Development~~
1. ~~In parallel with the continuing full implementation of this Agreement, urgent attention must be focused on meeting the real humanitarian and economic needs of Kosovo in order to help create the conditions for reconstruction and lasting economic recovery. International assistance will be provided without discrimination between national communities.~~
2. ~~The parties welcome the willingness of the European Commission working with the international community to co-ordinate international support for the parties' effort. Specifically, the European Commission will be organizing an international donors' conference within one month of signature of this Agreement.~~
3. ~~The international community will provide immediate and unconditional humanitarian assistance, focusing primarily on refugees and internally displaced persons returning to their former homes. The parties welcome and endorse the UNHCR's lead role in co ordination of this effort, and endorse its intention, in close co operation with the IM, to plan an early, peaceful, orderly and phased return of refugees and displaced persons in conditions of safety and dignity.~~
4. ~~The international community will provide the means for the rapid improvement of living conditions for the population of Kosovo~~

~~through the reconstruction and rehabilitation of housing and local infrastructure (including water, energy, health and local education infrastructure) based on damage assessment surveys.~~

5. ~~Assistance will also be provided to support the establishment and development of the institutional and legislative framework laid down in the Agreement, including local governance and tax settlement, and to reinforce civil society, culture and education. Social welfare will also be addressed, with priority given to the protection of vulnerable social groups.~~

6. ~~It will also be vital to lay the foundations for sustained development, based on a revival of the local economy. This must take account of the need to address unemployment, and to stimulate the economy by a range of mechanisms. The European Commission will be giving urgent attention to this.~~

7. ~~International assistance, with the exception of Humanitarian aid, will be subject to full compliance with this Agreement as well as other conditionalities defined in advance by the donors and the absorptive capacity of Kosovo.~~

Chapter 6, The Ombudsman

Article 1: General

1. There shall be an Ombudsman, who shall monitor the realization of the rights of members of national communities and the protection of human rights and fundamental freedoms in ~~Kosovo~~ **Kosmet**. The Ombudsman shall have unimpeded access to any person or place and shall have the right to appear and intervene before any domestic, Federal, or (consistent with the rules of such bodies) international authority upon his or her request. No person, institution, or entity of the ~~Parties~~ **Signatories** may interfere with the functions of the Ombudsman.

2. The Ombudsman shall be an eminent person of high moral standing who possessed a demonstrated commitment to human rights and the rights of members of national communities. He or she shall be nominated by the President of the **Assembly of** ~~Kosovo~~ **Kosmet** and be elected by the Assembly ~~from a list of candidates prepared by the President of the European Court for Human Rights for a non renewable three year term. The Ombudsman shall not be a citizen of any State or entity that was a part of the Former Yugoslavia, or of any neighboring State. Pending the election of the President and the Assembly, the CIM shall designate a person to serve as Ombudsman on an interim basis who shall be succeeded by a person selected pursuant to the procedure set forth in this paragraph.~~

3. The Ombudsman shall be independently responsible for choosing his or her own staff. He or she shall have ~~two~~ **six** Deputies. ~~The deputies~~ **One deputy** shall ~~each~~ be ~~drawn~~ **elected** from ~~different~~ **each** national communities.

   (a) The salaries and expenses of the Ombudsman and his or her staff shall be determined and paid by the Kosovo Assembly. The salaries and expenses shall be fully adequate to implement the Ombudsman's mandate.

   (b) ~~The Ombudsman and members of his or her staff shall not be held criminally or civilly liable for any acts carried out within the scope of their duties.~~

~~**The Ombudsman and his or her deputies shall have immunity equal to the immunity of the members of the Assembly.**~~

Article 11: Jurisdiction

1. The Ombudsman shall consider:

   (a) alleged or apparent violations of human rights and fundamental freedoms in ~~Kosovo~~ **Kosmet**, as provided in the Constitutions of the Federal Republic of Yugoslavia and the Republic of Serbia, and the European Convention for the Protection of Human Rights and Fundamental Freedoms and the Protocols thereto; and

   (b) alleged or apparent violations of the rights of members of national communities specified in this Agreement.

2. All persons in ~~Kosovo~~ **Kosmet** shall have the right to submit complaints to the Ombudsman. The ~~Parties~~ **Signatories** agree not to take any measures to punish persons who intend to submit or who have submitted such allegations, or in any other way to deter the exercise of this right.

Article lll: Powers and Duties

1. The Ombudsman shall investigate alleged violations falling within the jurisdiction set forth in Article ll.1. He or she may act either on his or her own initiative or in response to an allegation presented by any Party or person, non-governmental organization, or group of individuals claiming to be the victim of a violation or acting on behalf of alleged victims who are deceased or missing. The work of the Ombudsman shall be free of charge to the person concerned.

1. The Ombudsman shall have complete, unimpeded, and immediate access to any person, place, or information upon his or her request.

   (a) The Ombudsman shall have access to and may examine all official documents, and he or she can require any person, including officials of ~~Kosovo~~ **Kosmet** to cooperate by providing relevant information, documents, and files.

   (b) The Ombudsman may attend administrative hearings and meetings of other ~~Kosovo~~ **Kosmet** institutions in order to gather information.

   (c) The Ombudsman may examine facilities and places where persons deprived of their liberty are detained, work, or are otherwise located.

   (d) The Ombudsman and staff shall maintain the confidentiality of all confidential information obtained by them, unless the Ombudsman determines that such information is evidence of a violation of rights falling within his or her jurisdiction, in which case that information may be revealed in public reports or appropriate legal proceedings.

   (e) The ~~Parties~~ **Signatories** undertake to ensure cooperation with the Ombudsman's investigations. ~~Willful and knowing failure to comply shall be a criminal offense prosecutable in any jurisdiction of the Parties. Where an official impedes an investigation by refusing to provide necessary information, the Ombudsman shall contact that officials superior or the public prosecutor for appropriate penal action to be taken in accordance with the law.~~

3. The Ombudsman shall issue findings and conclusions in the form of a published report promptly after concluding an investigation.

   (a) ~~A Party, institution, or official identified by the Ombudsman as a violator shall, within a period specified by the Ombudsman, explain in writing how it will comply with any prescriptions the Ombudsman may put forth for remedial measures.~~

   (b) ~~In the event that a person or entity does not comply with the conclusions and recommendations of the Ombudsman, the report shall be forwarded for further action to the Joint Commission established by Chapter 5 of this Agreement, to the President of the appropriate Party, and to any other officials or institutions that the Ombudsman deems proper.~~

Chapter 8, Amendment, Comprehensive Assessment, and Final Clauses

Article 1: Amendment and Comprehensive Assessment

1. Amendments to this Agreement shall be adopted by agreement of all the ~~Parties~~ **Signatories**, except as otherwise provided by Article X of Chapter 1.

2. Each ~~Party~~ **Signatory** may propose amendments at any time and will consider and consult with the other ~~Parties~~ **Signatories** with regard to proposed amendments.

3. ~~Three years after the entry into force of this Agreement, an international meeting shall be convened to determine a mechanism for a final settlement for Kosovo, on the basis of the will of the people, opinions of relevant authorities, each Party's efforts regarding the implementation of this Agreement, and the Helsinki Final Act, and to undertake a comprehensive assessment of the implementation of this Agreement and to consider proposals by any Party for additional measures.~~

4. **After three years, the signatories shall comprehensively review this Agreement with a view to improving its implementation and shall consider the proposals of any signatory for additional**

measures, whose adoption shall require the consent of all signatories.

Article ll: Final Clauses

1. This Agreement is signed in the **Albanian, English, Romany, Serbian and Turkish language.** ~~English language. After signature of this Agreement, translations will be made into Serbian, Albanian, and other languages of the national communities of Kosovo, and attached to the English text.~~

2. This Agreement shall enter into forces ~~upon signature~~ **after each signatory informs the other that it completed its internal procedure.**

[*A listing of members of delegations has been omitted.*]

3. Letter from the three Negotiators to Head of Republic of Serbia Delegation, 16 March 1999

To Professor Dr Ratko MARKOVIC
Head of the Delegation
of the Government of the
Republic of Serbia

Paris, 16 March 1999

Dear Professor Markovic,
Thank you for your letter of 15 March 1999.

We are surprised by your statement that you did not receive a written response to your proposal concerning the rules of procedure. We enclose a copy of the Verbal Note submitted by the French Embassy in Belgrade to the Federal Ministry of Foreign Affairs of the Federal Republic of Yugoslavia dated 10 March 1999. As you know, the meeting of experts decided upon in our meeting of 15 March took place. We understand further consultations are planned, but would like to emphasise the unanimous view of the Contact Group that only technical adjustements can be considered which, of course, must be accepted as such and approved by the other delegation. We note your comments on the security measures at the hotel and name plates displayed in the Kleber center. We have forwarded a copy of your letter to the French authorities with the request to take any action they consider appropriate.

Yours sincerely

[signed] Ambassador Christopher HILL; Ambassador Wolfgang PETRITSCH; Ambassador Boris Majorsky

4. NATO-Russia Permanent Joint Council Meeting at Ambassadorial Level, 17 March 1999

The NATO-Russia Permanent Joint Council (PJC) at Ambassadorial level met on Wednesday, 17 March 1999 at NATO Headquarters. NATO and Russia continued their regular consultations on the crisis in Kosovo. They will continue their efforts aimed at peace and stability in the region. They underscored the urgency and importance of the ongoing talks in Paris. Ambassadors received a briefing on the meeting of Chiefs of Staff under the auspices of the PJC held on 10 March 1999. NATO and Russia reviewed Russia's participation in Partnership for Peace. They discussed ongoing activities and exchanged views and information on further activities later this year. NATO briefed on ongoing work with regard to the Defence Capabilities Initiatives to be adopted at the Washington Summit with the aim to support the ability of the Alliance to undertake the full range of its missions. ...

5. Declaration submitted by Kosovo to Negotiators upon Signature of the Rambouillet Accords, 18 March 1999

THE DELEGATION OF KOSOVA,

Acting on behalf of the people of Kosova and of its legitimate and lawful political and military institutions and after full consultation,

Committed to the political and economic development of Kosova according to the principles of democracy, a free market economy, human rights and the equal treatment of all,

Determined to promote peace and stability in Kosova, and the exercise by the legitimate authorities of Kosova and the people of Kosova of self-government, permanent sovereignty over natural resources and self-determination,

Recognizing with appreciation the contribution made to this end by the members of the Contact Group, the Co-Chairmen, Negotiators and hosts of the conference, the international institutions involved in the negotiating and implementation process, and especially the tireless efforts for peace made by US Secretary of State Albright,

Stressing the need for an immediate cessation of hostilities in Kosova, the withdrawal of FRY/Serb military, paramilitary and police forces and full compliance with mandatory demands of the United Nations Security Council by all parties, including the duty to cooperate fully and unconditionally with the International Criminal Tribunal for the former Yugoslavia,

Noting the grave humanitarian situation in Kosova and the need for immediate acceptance of the Interim Agreement by all parties in order to avoid a humanitarian catastrophe, which is already well on the way,

Noting also that this present situation has been found by the United Nations Security Council to constitute a threat to international peace and security and respectfully but urgently *reminding* NATO in this context of its humanitarian responsibilities and of the firm determination to hold those preventing the completion of the interim agreement or provoking further hostilities 'fully accountable'.

UNANIMOUSLY DECLARES AND CONFIRMS THE FOLLOWING:

In formally affixing the signatures of the authorized representatives of the Delegation of Kosova to the Interim Agreement for Peace and Self-government in Kosova of 23 February 1999, Kosova confirms its acceptance of said Interim Agreement as indicated in the Declaration mady by the Kosova Delegation on 23 February 1999 at the conclusion of the international conference on Kosova held at Rambouillet and expresses its consent.

In so doing, the Delegation of Kosova registers its understanding of certain points as follows:

The Delegation of Kosova confirms that its consent relates to the text as presented and accepted on 23 February 1999 as an integrated whole. This text is definite and not subject to further negotiations or modifications other than purely technical changes. As provided in the rules of procedure of the Conference, such technical changes shall not be introduced without the approval of Kosova. The interpretation and application of the text shall be subject to the established rules of treaty interpretation, consistent with Article II of Chapter 8 of the Interim Agreement.

As already expressed on 23 February 1999, Kosova invites and expects the rapid deployment of NATO and the full and effective exercise of the functions provided for it and others charged with the implementation of the Interim Agreement strictly in accordance with the modalities for command and control and the time-table established in the Interim Agreement. Full implementation also of this aspect of the Interim Agreement constitutes a condition essential to the overall package and to the consent given by Kosova. Kosova looks forward to being consulted about the precise pattern of NATO deployments.

In addition to the rapid implementation of the military aspects of the Interim Agreement through the NATO presence, Kosova also invites and expects the rapid deployment and full and effective exercise of the functions of the civilian elements of implementation. It looks forward to the establishment of an accelerated time-table for the taking up of these functions by the relevant international bodies and their representatives and pleges its full support also for this task. In this context, Kosova notes with gratitude the undertaking given by the European Union and others to contribute rapidly and significantly to the reconstruction of Kosova on the basis of full equality of all segments of the Kosova population supporting the implementation of the Interim Agreement.

The Delegation of Kosova confirms again that at the termination of the interim period of three years the people of Kosova will exercise their will through a referendum, conducted freely and fairly. The expressed will of the people of Kosova will be conveyed to the international meeting to determine the mechanism for a final settlement for Kosova, consistent with the Interim Agreement, in particular Article I (3) of Chapter 8.

The Delegation of Kosova again notes the intention of the KLA to exercise the opportunity to engage in a process of transformation and welcomes assurances also as to cooperative bilateral contacts to carry out this process consistent with the Interim Agreement.

Hashim Thaci, Chairman of the Presidency of the Delegation of Kosova

6. Kosovo Statement on Formal Signing of Interim Agreement for Peace and Self-government, 18 March 1999

Today, a new chapter has been opened in the history of Kosova. The people of Kosova, acting through their delegation, have committed themselves to the Interim Agreement for Peace and Self-government in Kosova. In so doing, the people of Kosova have opted for the path of peace and reconciliation on the basis of tolerance, democracy and economic development according to free market principles in Kosova, where self-government will now, finally, be established.

The decision to sign the Interim Agreement was not an easy one. Even at the time of this momentous occasion in the history of Kosova, civilians in the villages and towns are suffering from direct military attacks by FRY forces. Once more, entire villages are being burnt to the ground. Civilians are being subjected to executions, torture and beatings. Once more, thousands have been driven from their homes.

Kosova has made clear upon signature that it expects the international community to deliver the implementation of the interim agreement in accordance with all its provisions, which are now no longer open to modification of any sort. In particular, Kosova has welcomed and expects the rapid deployment of the NATO implementation force, and of the other elements of implementation.

The delegation of Kosova has also drawn to the attention of NATO the unambiguous determination of the Contact Group, made at the outset of the Rambouillet process and consistently reiterated since, that those who prevent the completion of the interim agreement or provoke further hostilities will be held 'fully accountable'. Some forty days have passed since commencement of negotiations at Rambouillet. While Kosova has had to take difficult decisions and accept compromize in the interest of achieving a peaceful interim settlement, the FRY has been given opportunity after opportunity to join the process of peace and reconciliation. Instead of embracing these opportunities, they have once again resorted to violence and oppression. The situation in the region has already been characterized as a threat to international peace and security by the UN Security Council. In view of the grave and overwhelming humanitarian emergency which has been created by the FRY in Kosova, the people of Kosva now expect that decisive steps be taken by NATO to address this increasingly desperate situation and to turn the vision of Rambouillet, to which the international community has committed itself along with the people of Kosova, into reality.

7. Identical Letters from Kosova, 18 March 1999

HE Hubert Vedrine, Co-Chairman
HE Robin Cook, Co-Chairman
HE Secretary of State M. Albright
HE Javier Solana, Secretary-General of NATO
18 March 1999

Your Excellencies

The Delegation of Kosova has just embraced the Rambouillet Interim Agreement for Peace and Self-government. While the Delegation of Kosova has confidence in the success of this agreement and in the commitments made by the international community in relation to it, it feels constrained to bring to your attention the following.

Even at this moment, while the Paris Conference is concluding, the Belgrade regime is engaged in a brutal offensive against the people of Kosova and, through this action, also against the peace process. The Belgrade regime has again launched widespead offensive operations creating a very difficult and dangerous situation. These operations include the use of heavy weapons and personnel in clear violation of the binding undertakings given to Ambassador Holbrooke and the international community in October of last year. These acts also include terrorist operations in cities.

Once again, the victims of these operations are principally innocent civilians who are being recklessly and directly targeted. Once again, entire villages are subjected to wholesale destruction. Once again, there is uncontrolled looting. This is happening at the precise moment of the publication of the authoritative report by the international community on the FRY/Serb practices in this respect, relating to the example of the tragedy of Racak.

The Delegation of Kosova is aware, as you must be, that such further atrocities and provocations are intended to deflect all those assembled here in Paris from the path of peace to be achieved through the Rambouillet process. In spite of these provocations, the Delegation of Kosova stands by this process as is evidenced in its decision to sign and bring into force immediately the Interim Agreement, including NATO implementation according to the arrangements for command and control that have been established and fixed in Chapter 7 of the Interim Agreement.

The hour of peace is now, and this moment must not be wasted at the expense of the civilian population of Kosova. The United Nations Security Council and other authoritative agencies have already determined that the situation in the region constitutes a threat to international peace and security. The latest onslaught represents not only a cynical attack and grave affront against the organizers of the Paris conference, the negotiators and the members of the contact group and all others committed to the peace process. In violating the terms of the October agreement so flagrantly, in seeking to ruin the chance of peace and reconciliation and in attacking a civilian population, a humanitarian disaster is now being created which requires an unambiguous response.

The Delegation of Kosova respectfully reminds you of your humanitarian responsibilities and of the determination unanimously and repeatedly stated by the Contact Group to hold those preventing the completion of the interim agreement or provoking further hostilities 'fully accountable'.

The Delegation of Kosova uses this opportunity to assure you once again of its highest consideration.

Hashim Thaci, Chairman of the Delegation

8. Department of State Daily Press Briefing, Washington, DC, 18 March 1999

QUESTION: The status of the planning for evacuation in -

MR. FOLEY: I have nothing to update since yesterday. As I said yesterday, we are looking closely at those plans. We want to be in a position to implement withdrawal of our personnel in Belgrade, of our personnel in Kosovo as necessary. I have nothing to announce in terms of implementation, but it's something that we will do as soon as we see the need.

QUESTION: Any plans for last minute shuttle diplomacy? I think there was a Reuters story about European diplomats expected to go to Belgrade this weekend.

MR. FOLEY: You may have seen Jamie Rubin spoke to that on television earlier. He said that we weren't ruling out any particular steps. There's nothing that I'm aware of. I think this will be a matter for the co-chairmen to decide. Certainly, we don't - let me put it this way, we are really at the crunch point now. We have a Serb no, so far, to the peace plan. We have Serb actions on the ground -- and I will describe them in further detail in a minute -- which constitute non-compliance with the October commitments. In other words, the Serbs, on the two triggers for the NATO decision, are out of compliance and the NATO decision is becoming more and more relevant, given that Serb behavior.

But in terms of what precisely happens next, it's up to the co-chairs, first of all, to decide that this round of negotiations has come to an end. I would anticipate that decision shortly; I don't know exactly when. It will be up to the co-chairs to decide if they wish to pursue a further diplomatic effort. Secretary Albright has been in touch with Foreign Minister Vedrine, Foreign Secretary Cook today. I wouldn't rule that out. But I think President Milosevic already knows where things stand, and we already know where things stand with him. Unless we see quickly a reversal on his part, then, as Mr. Rubin indicated earlier, really, the NATO Act-Ord being in effect will be - NATO will be the decision maker in the next instance.

But in terms of further diplomatic moves, we don't seek military action for the sake of military action. We would like to see President Milosevic reverse course. But again, we don't see signs that he's about to do so.

QUESTION: What is it that you're not ruling out?

MR. FOLEY: She asked if there were going to be any diplomatic efforts -

QUESTION: She used the word shuttling. Let's re-rack and try it this way. I didn't get her statement and I wasn't watching television, so I'm operating a little blind; I come to the State Department for these things. Secretary Albright yesterday had no plans. Is she beginning to have plans to do some traveling on behalf of a last diplomatic effort? Is that what you're not ruling out?

MR. FOLEY: No, I think the question was more generally whether anyone was planning diplomatic efforts because you and I have seen the same press reports that perhaps, some of our European friends may be considering trips to Belgrade or what not. I don't rule that out. They will decide themselves. We will be in touch with them.

But really, the critical factor here is not whether someone makes a visit to Belgrade or not, it's whether President Milosevic reverses course. We are seeing quite the opposite. He's digging in his heels; he's digging in his forces; he's refusing to negotiate. He's putting himself in a position where he will bear the consequences of his obstinacy.

Everyone knows that the NATO Act-Ord is in effect, that NATO is prepared to act. I think we have solidarity on the part of our allies. The conditions are clear. President Milosevic does not have much time to reverse course. Whether he needs to hear that message again in person or not is not a terribly important detail. If a visit produced a change of course, change of opinion on his part, that's a good thing. I don't think we would hold out exceptional hopes in that regard.

QUESTION: I think people know that NATO has been prepared to act for a long time; but the question has been, is NATO really serious about acting on the terms that NATO sets for itself? The fact that you're talking now about the possibility of an extension of time -

MR. FOLEY: I'm sorry, where did you - in any sense I talked about an extension of any kind?

QUESTION: To the extent that you raise the issue yourself about, well, maybe another visit.

MR. FOLEY: Let me, if I can, interject something. We had a very similar debate - maybe you and I or Mr. Rubin and other journalists in December. We were asked, because the United States had indicated in that situation, whether if Saddam did not cooperate with UNSCOM and once it was clear he had not cooperated, you were asking us a question involving military timing and you were questioning our credibility and willingness. You waited a few more days, and the result was Operation Desert Fox.

Then others raised questions of a different nature after that. That's the nature of journalism is that you ask tough, skeptical questions. We will do our business. We will not, through you, let President Milosevic know the timing of what may follow. That's a matter of national security, and I'm not in a position to talk about that. But for you to conclude that we are extending something or that we are delaying something is erroneous. We will act - we and our NATO allies - when it's the right moment, when it's in our interest to act.

QUESTION: I'm not really concluding anything. I'm trying to actually understand what message you're trying to send. I got the impression through some of the things that you were saying, including, well, if another mission has to go to Belgrade and we get a yes out of Milosevic, then that's great. I mean, you're leaving open yourself the possibility that there will be another mission to Belgrade, which of course would require more time to execute. So I'm just trying to understand how serious that possibility is. It sounds like there may be a difference of opinion between the United States and its European allies.

MR. FOLEY:I'm not suggesting that. I don't believe decisions have been made yet in that regard. We'll let the - whether the Europeans are planning another visit or not to Belgrade; I'm just saying I wouldn't rule it out. I'm not saying that I'm criticizing that in any way.

NATO is fully capable of acting at a moment of its own choosing. The signs are not good for President Milosevic. He is way out of compliance on the ground. He has refused to engage seriously, let alone sign the peace accords. The writing for him is on the wall, unless he completely reverses course.

As to when something might happen, what might happen before that action takes place are details; they're not fundamentally important.

QUESTION: Jim, one thing the Secretary did say on the Hill is that the Serbs are building up their security forces in and around Kosovo, and that

alone would be a violation. Can you give us those figures?

MR. FOLEY: Serb, VJ and MUPP operations, apparently designed to root out the KLA, destroy villages and displace the Albanian population, continue. KLA units have been withdrawing from the Cicavica Mountains, north of Vucitrn, in the wake of the recent Serb offensive there.

A new offensive about five kilometers northwest of Prizren has also been reported. An estimated 200 MUPP and VJ tank and armored armed truck support are involved in this operation, which has produced an additional 1,500 internally displaced persons.

In a village northeast of Pec, three Kosovar Albanian brothers, who disappeared two days ago, were found. All, tragically, had been shot at close range, one with his throat slit, another handcuffed. In a village east of Orahovac, there was a large funeral for nine KLA fighters, killed on March 15.

According to KVM observers, the VJ is conducting last minute training drills and call up of reservists and regulars in apparent or possible preparation for possible NATO action. The KVN confirms four tanks are in position at Podujevo air field and six large concrete barriers have been pre-positioned along the roadway near Gnjilane. The barriers could be designed to cut off KVM departure routes or to deter entry of NATO forces.

I gave figures yesterday, Jim, on our estimates of the numbers of Serb, VJ and MUT forces either outside or in Kosovo. I'd refer you to those figures; I don't have them before me today. They were in the 18,000 to 21,000 range. But obviously, the situation on the ground is very alarming.

QUESTION: Can I just follow up? This air field, is that central to the evacuation planning?

MR. FOLEY: Which evacuation plan - of the KVM monitors?

QUESTION: The KVM.

MR. FOLEY: I'm not in a position to talk publicly about evacuation plans; that's a security matter.

QUESTION: And one more thing - the nine bodies found and the three others, do you now believe that the humanitarian catastrophe that some people have been talking about has already begun?

MR. FOLEY: Well, that's a judgment call. The situation is worsening there. The numbers of internally displaced persons are going up. I can give you some figures on that. We have increasing numbers of people being forced from their homes, mostly as a result of the VJ offensive in the Cicavica Mountains. The UN High Commissioner for Refugees estimates over 80,000 people have been displaced since December 24. Now, that's an update; a few weeks ago I gave you a figure, I think, in the 50,000 neighborhood. So that continues to go up.

QUESTION: (Inaudible.)

MR. FOLEY: Since December 24 - 45,000 since the close of the first round of negotiations at Rambouillet on February 23. UNHCR and about 50 or so non-governmental organizations are still operating in Kosovo, continuing to do really heroic work in spite of obstacles. They've increased emergency convoys that go into the countryside in search of displaced persons. They've had their vehicles stopped; they've been searched; they've been stoned; they've had their access to displaced people blocked by Serbian police, VJ also, in one case, the KLA. So these are very difficult conditions, but they are still there on the ground looking for people who are displaced.

The fact is that most of these people are not facing the elements. The numbers of displaced people that we give you mean these are people who are not living in their homes. In most cases, they are able to - thanks to the work of these humanitarian workers - able to get shelter of some kind and food.

QUESTION: When you began your military description, you spoke of an offensive. By the time you ended it, you were describing steps - by your description - being taken to defend against the possibility of a NATO attack.

MR. FOLEY: Right.

QUESTION: Is this a mixture of things, or are they, plausibly enough, digging in, preparing to be bombed by NATO and wouldn't you expect a country about to bombed to take steps? Or are they moving independently against civilians, killing people, taking towns, rooting people from their homes? Is it a combination of these things?

MR. FOLEY: It's a combination. Of course, people are fleeing because of the heightened military activity, as well as the attacks on some villages. That is happening. They are also positioning themselves in such a way that one could infer that they are anticipating NATO military action. It's a combination.

Now I don't know if you're a mind reader, Barry, but the ability to read Mr. Milosevic's mind is a hazardous endeavor, and he may not know his mind either. I tried to make the point yesterday that he's making the gamble of a lifetime, gambling with the fate of his country, because he cannot predict what will happen if it comes to military action. On the other hand, if the Serbs reverse course and embrace the peace plan, he can count on a stable future and one that's better for the people of Kosovo and the people of his own country.

QUESTION: Just a quick one -- I didn't know, when you said offenses, if you meant they're on the move, or you literally meant offensive in military terms. Apparently, you mean they're on the move and you can't --

MR. FOLEY: They're on the move, but they have been undertaking military actions, though, against the KLA in Kosovo in recent weeks.

QUESTION: Also when you were describing, you talked about these barriers - some sort of barriers they're erecting that you said could be designed to hinder the withdrawal of KVM? What did you mean by that?

MR. FOLEY: Yes, well I can just repeat. I'd have to check further for you in terms of what's behind it. But four tanks are in a position; six large concrete barriers pre-positioned along the roadway that might be designed to cut off KVM departure routes or deter entry of NATO forces.

QUESTION: Is this along a road where the NATO forces would be coming in, or why -

MR. FOLEY: Well, I'm not able to specify where these roads are and what there purpose might be in the mind of military planners. I'm just pointing out to you that they're engaged in provocative activity.

QUESTION: So you're raising the possibility of the Serbs using the KVM as human shields?

MR. FOLEY: Well, you're saying that; I'm not suggesting that. Now that you raise the point, let's remember that President Milosevic made a commitment, first of all, to invite the KVM monitors into Kosovo; secondly, to guarantee their safety. We hold him responsible for living up to that commitment. Certainly, at a moment when the Serb authorities are saying they don't want a NATO force but they do want the OSCE monitors to play a role, it would be very ironic and self-defeating were there to be any threats or impediments to the KVM monitors.

QUESTION: Is there just one place where you see this happening?

MR. FOLEY: I'm only aware of that one instance.

QUESTION: And this offensive that you're talking about in such stark terms today, when exactly did this become - I mean, I realize there's been some talk about moving troops for weeks and some US officials were sort of discounting it as a real problem.

MR. FOLEY: I'm not sure they were discounting it. The fact is there was a build-up along the borders.

QUESTION: And when did it become a critical mass, though? I mean, it just seems that it's convenient that it all comes to a point at the same time.

MR. FOLEY: I don't know if it's convenient, but you're able to watch your television screens as we are. All of us have seen a significant up-tick in military action. We've seen villages burning in the last couple of days. It seems to me - and I don't have a studied answer for you, I'd have to check and see what our analysts see as a threshold day, if there was such one, when military activity increased. But anecdotally, it seems to have been in the last number of days that they've really stepped up the military action on the ground.

QUESTION: The last week, you would say?

MR. FOLEY: Anecdotally, in about the last week, I would say.

QUESTION: The visit by the Kosovar Albanians - the Rubin-Thaci show. Is that on for Saturday?

MR. FOLEY: I don't have the exact date. Ambassador Hill talked this morning with the Kosovar Albanian delegation about their visit. We have no announcement to make today about who's coming and when. Maybe we'll be in a position to do that tomorrow; I'll let you know.

9. Secretary of State Albright, Remarks on Developments in Kosovo, Washington, DC, 18 March 1999

SECRETARY ALBRIGHT: Good afternoon. I have come up here today, and will be joined by Secretary Cohen, Chairman Shelton and Sandy Berger, to brief Congress on developments in Kosovo and to discuss current plans and options. This morning I spoke with the Kosovo Albanian leaders in France and I congratulated them for their courage and vision in signing the agreement negotiated in Paris.

Their signature shows their commitment to a peaceful settlement and to a future of democratic self-government for all the people of Kosovo. The Kosovar Albanians have shown that they are willing to work as partners with the international community. Unfortunately, the Serbian negotiators have gone backwards. They have refused to engage in

discussions of civilian and military implementation, while attempting to reopen issues previously settled at Rambouillet. Obviously, there can be no agreement if the Serbs do not sign. Right now there is no sign that the Serbs will agree. So the situation is as clear as it could be: the Albanians have said yes to the accords and the Serbs are saying no. At the same time, Belgrade security forces are stepping up their unjustified and aggressive actions in Kosovo. If Belgrade doesn't reverse course, the Serbs alone will be responsible for the consequences. I would just like to remind President Milosevic that NATO stands ready to take whatever measures are necessary.

10. Statement by the Co-Chairs of the Contact Group, France, 19 March 1999

1. The Rambouillet Accords are the only peaceful solution to the Kosovo problem.

2. In Paris, the Kosovo delegation seized this opportunity and, by their signature, have committed themselves to the Accords as a whole.

3. Far from seizing this opportunity, the Yugoslav delegation has tried to unravel the Rambouillet Accords.

4. Therefore, after consultation with our partners in the Contact Group (Germany, Italy, the Russian Federation, the United States, the European Union, the Chairman-in-Office of the OSCE) we consider there is no purpose in extending the talks any further. The negotiations are adjourned. The talks will not resume unless the Serbs express their acceptance of the Accords.

5. We will immediately engage in consultations with our partners and allies to he ready to act We will be in contact with the Secretary General of NATO. We ask the Chairman-in-Office of the OSCE to take all appropriate measures for the safety of the KVM- The Contact Group will remain seized of the issue.

6. We solemnly warn the authorities in Belgrade against any military offensive on the ground and any impediment to the freedom of movement and of action of the KVM, which would contravene their commitments. Such violations would have the gravest consequences.

11. President Clinton, Excerpt from Press Conference, Washington, DC, 19 March 1999

PRESIDENT CLINTON: Ladies and gentlemen, as all of you know, we have been involved in an intensive effort to end the conflict in Kosovo for many weeks now. With our NATO allies and with Russia, we proposed a peace agreement to stop the killing and give the people of Kosovo the self-determination and government they need and to which they are entitled under the constitution of their government. Yesterday, the Kosovar Albanians signed that agreement. Even though they have not obtained all they seek, even as their people remain under attack, they've had the vision to see that a just peace is better than an unwinnable war. Now only President Milosevic stands in the way of peace. Today the peace talks were adjourned because the Serbian negotiators refused even to discuss key elements of the peace plan. NATO has warned President Milosevic to end his intransigence and repression, or face military action. Our allies are strongly united behind this course. We are prepared, and so are they, to carry it out. Today I reviewed our planning with my senior advisors and met with many members of Congress. As we prepare to act we need to remember the lessons we have learned in the Balkans. We should remember the horror of the war in Bosnia, the sounds of sniper fire aimed at children, the faces of young men behind barbed wire, the despairing voices of those who thought nothing could be done. It took precious time to achieve allied unity there, but when we did, our firmness ended all that. Bosnia is now at peace. We should remember the thousands of people facing cold and hunger in the hills of Kosovo last fall. Firmness ended that as well. We should remember what happened in the village of Racak back in January -- innocent men, women and children taken from their homes to a gully, forced to kneel in the dirt, sprayed with gunfire -- not because of anything they had done, but because of who they were. Now, roughly 40,000 Serbian troops and police are massing in and around Kosovo. Our firmness is the only thing standing between them and countless more villages like Racak -- full of people without protection, even though they have now chosen peace. Make no mistake, if we and our allies do not have the will to act, there will be more massacres. In dealing with aggressors in the Balkans, hesitation is a license to kill. But action and resolve can stop armies, and save lives. We must also understand our stake in peace in the Balkans, and in Kosovo. This is a humanitarian crisis, but it is much more. This is a conflict with no natural boundaries. It threatens our national interests. If it continues, it will push refugees across borders, and draw in neighboring countries. It will undermine the credibility of NATO, on which stability in Europe and our own credibility depend. It will likely reignite the historical animosities, including those that can embrace Albania, Macedonia, Greece, even Turkey. These divisions still have the potential to make the next century a truly violent one for that part of the world that straddles Europe, Asia and the Middle East. Unquestionably, there are risks in military action, if that becomes necessary. U.S. and other NATO pilots will be in harm's way. The Serbs have a strong air defense system. But we must weigh those risks against the risks of inaction. If we don't act, the war will spread. If it spreads, we will not be able to contain it without far greater risk and cost. I believe the real challenge of our foreign policy today is to deal with problems before they do permanent harm to our vital interests. That is what we must do in Kosovo. Let me just make one other statement about this. One of the things that I wanted to do when I became President is to take advantage of this moment in history to build an alliance with Europe for the 21st century, with a Europe undivided, strong, secure, prosperous and at peace. That's why I have supported the unification of Europe financially, politically, economically. That is why I've supported the expansion of NATO and a redefinition of its missions. What are the challenges to our realizing that dream? The challenge of a successful partnership with Russia that succeeds in its own mission; the challenge of a resolution of the difficulties between Greece and Turkey so that Turkey becomes an ally of Europe in the West for the long-term; and the challenge of instability in the Balkans -- in different ways, all those things are at stake here. I honestly believe that by acting now we can help to give our children and our grandchildren a Europe that is more united, more democratic, more peaceful, more prosperous, and a better partner for the United States for a long time to come. I will say again to Mr. Milosevic, as I did in Bosnia, I do not want to put a single American pilot into the air; I do not want anyone else to die in the Balkans; I do not want a conflict. I would give anything to be here talking about something else today. But a part of my responsibility is to try to leave to my successors, and to our country in the 21st century, an environment in Europe that is stable, humane and secure. It will be a big part of America's future. Thank you very much. Mr. Hunt?

QUESTION: Mr. President, as you mentioned, Yugoslav forces seem to be mobilizing for war in Kosovo, despite the warnings of NATO air strikes. After so many threats in the past, why should President Milosevic take this one seriously? And is there a deadline for him to comply? And is it your intention to keep pounding Serb targets until he agrees to your peace terms?

PRESIDENT CLINTON: Well, there are several questions there, but let me say, I think he should take this seriously, because we meant -- we were serious in Bosnia. And it was the combined impact of NATO's action in Bosnia, plus the reversals they sustained on the ground in fighting, plus the economic embargo, that led them to conclude that peace was the better course. Now, he says here that this is not like what happened last fall, that this threatens Serbia's sovereignty to have a multinational force on the ground in Kosovo. But he has put that at risk by his decade -- and I want to reemphasize that -- his decade of denial of the autonomy to which the Kosovars are legally entitled as a part of Serbia. My intention would be to do whatever is possible, first of all, to weaken his ability to massacre them, to have another Bosnia; and secondly, to do all that I can to induce him to take -- it is not my peace agreement. It was an agreement worked out, and negotiated, and argued over, with all the parties' concerns being taken into account. I will say again -- for the longest time, we did not believe that either side would take this agreement. And the fact that the Kosovar Albanians did it I think reflects foresight and wisdom on their part. They did not get everything they wanted. And in a peace agreement, nobody ever gets everything they want. We've seen it in the Middle East, in Northern Ireland, everywhere else. So it is not my agreement. It is the best agreement that all the parties can get to give us a chance to go forward without bloodshed. I

believe, also, as I have said publicly to Mr. Milosevic and to the Serbs, it is their best chance to keep Kosovo as a part of Serbia and as a part of Yugoslavia. And so I would hope that the agreement could be accepted, and I'll do what I can to see that it is.

QUESTION: And the deadline, sir -- is there one?

PRESIDENT CLINTON: I don't want to discuss that. We're working on that. I expect to be working on this all weekend.

QUESTION: Mr. President, you met this morning with members of Congress. And afterward, some of them came out and said that they had trouble imagining how you could justify air strikes in Kosovo unless the Serbs launched a new offensive first. In fact, Senator Nickles actually suggested that it might take a significant massacre before such a move would get public support. In your mind, does the mere fact that the Serbs refused to sign a peace treaty justify air strikes? Or do you think they need to -- if they took military action, only then you could act?

PRESIDENT CLINTON: Well, first, I believe they have already taken provocative actions. And there was, in the very recent past, the massacre at the village that I mentioned in my opening statement. Plus, there is the long unquestioned record of atrocity in Bosnia. So what we have tried to do along -- and, frankly, the Russians have been with us in this; I don't mean that they support military action, but they've been with us in the peace process -- is we could see that the same thing that happened in Bosnia and that had happened to some extent in Kosovo already, and had already produced tens of thousands of refugees in Kosovo, was going to happen there. And it seems to me that if we know that, and if we have a NATO action order predicated on the implementation of the peace process, and the failure to do it triggering reaction, that we ought to do what we can to prevent further atrocities. I understand what Senator Nickles was saying -- I think he was saying that the American public has not seen the sort of atrocities there they saw in Bosnia, that that is not fresh in people's minds. But with all the troops that have been massed, and what we know about their plans and what they have publicly said about them, I would hate to think that we'd have to see a lot of other little children die before we could do what seems to be, to me, clearly the right thing to do to prevent it.

QUESTION: So you would act first then? I mean --

PRESIDENT CLINTON: I don't think it's accurate to say we're acting first. I think they have acted first. They have massed their troops, they have continued to take aggressive action. They have already leveled one village in the recent past and killed a lot of innocent people. I do not believe that we ought to have to have thousands more people slaughtered and buried in open soccer fields before we do something. I think that would be unfortunate if we had said we have to have a lot more victims before we can stop what we know is about to happen.

QUESTION: Mr. President, it seems you're on the verge of committing U.S. forces to combat without a clear definition of your threshold for doing so. In January, Serb troops massacred 44 civilians. You called it murder and demanded that the Serb forces withdraw. They did not. Last month, you said it would be a mistake to extend the deadline, but the deadline passed. Last week, your administration said atrocities would be punished, and then after that a bomb went off in a Kosovo market and killed numerous children. What level of atrocities, sir, is a sufficient trigger? What is your threshold?

PRESIDENT CLINTON: Well, you've just made my case. I think that the threshold has been crossed. But when I said that the deadline should not be extended, Mr. Pelley, what I said was that those of us who were trying to shepherd the process should not extend the deadline. When the parties themselves asked for a delay, that's an entirely different kettle of fish. The rest of us can't be so patronizing that we can't say to both sides they had no right to ask for a delay. They asked, themselves, for a delay, and I thought it was the right thing to do. I still believe that it was the right thing to do. And it did lead to one side accepting the agreement. You have made another point, which I did not make in my remarks, but I would like to make, based on the factual statements you made -- everything you said was right, all the factual things you've cited -- which is that there are, basically, two grounds on which, in my judgment, NATO could properly take action. One is the fact that we have already said that if the peace agreement were accepted by the Kosovars, but not by the Serbs, we would take action to try to minimize the ability of the Serbs just to overrun and slaughter the Kosovars. That's the first thing I said. The second thing, what you said is quite right. While our threat of force last year did result in the drastic reduction of the tension and a lot of the refugees going home, it is absolutely true that there have been actions taken since then and forced movements since then that would trigger the other NATO action order to use force. The reason that has not been done, frankly, is because the peace process was going on and we knew that if we could just get an agreement from both sides that we could end the violence and we wouldn't have to act under either ground. So from my point of view, as I made clear to the Congress today, I think the threshold for their conduct has already been crossed. John?

QUESTION: Sir, if I might follow up -- with the OSCE monitors leaving tonight, if Serbian forces move into Kosovo, will that trigger NATO strikes?

PRESIDENT CLINTON: I've already said, I do not believe that -- I think that whatever threshold they need to cross has been crossed. I think that, in view of the present state of things, it would be better if I did not say any more about any particular plans we might have.

QUESTION: Sir, you said on Kosovo that if we don't act, the war will spread. That's very similar to what we said when we went into Bosnia several years ago. Our troops are still there. How can you assure the American people that we're not getting into a quagmire in Bosnia?

PRESIDENT CLINTON: Well, first of all, in Bosnia we have brought about 70 percent of our troops home. It has not been a quagmire. I told the American people we might well have some loss of life there, but I was convinced we would lose fewer lives and do more good over the long run if we intervened when we did. I feel the same way about Kosovo. The argument that I tried to make for our putting troops there, if we could reach a peace agreement, was that we were moving in the right direction, the Europeans had been willing to shoulder a much bigger share of the responsibility, we were only going to be asked to put up about, oh, 15 percent of the troops. But I don't want to get in the position in Kosovo that I was in in Bosnia, where the Pentagon came to me with a very honest estimate of when they thought we could finish. And we turned out to be wrong about that. We were not able to stabilize the situation as quickly as we thought we could. And this business in Kosovo is not helping any. Keep in mind, there could be some ramifications in Bosnia, as well as in Macedonia, where we have troops. So I can just tell you that I think that we have tried to limit our involvement, we have tried to limit our mission, and we will conclude it as quickly as we can. I think that in all these cases, you have to ask yourself, what will be the cost and the duration of involvement and the consequences if we do not move. And I have asked myself that question as well. Again, I would say to you, I would not be doing this if I did not think, number one, whenever we can stop a humanitarian disaster at an acceptable price, we ought to do it. Two, I'm convinced we'll be dragged into this thing under worse circumstances at greater cost if we don't act. And three, this is, to me, a critical part of the objective I brought to the presidency of trying to leave office with an alliance between the United States and a more unified, more prosperous, more peaceful, more stable Europe. And this is one of the big three questions still hanging out there, as I said in my opening remarks, and I'm trying to resolve this.

C. The Initiation of Hostilities

1. Statement by the North Atlantic Council on the Situation in Kosovo, 22 March 1999

In response to Belgrade's continued intransigence and repression, the Secretary General of NATO, to whom the North Atlantic Council had delegated on 30 January the authority to decide on air operations, is completing his consultations with the Allies to this end. In view of the evolution of the situation on the ground in Kosovo, the North Atlantic Council has also authorised today the Secretary General to decide, subject to further consultations, on a broader range of air operations if necessary.

2. Press Statement by Dr Javier Solana, Secretary General of NATO, 23 March 1999

Good evening, ladies and gentlemen,

I have just directed SACEUR, General Clark, to initiate air operations in the Federal Republic of Yugoslavia. I have taken this decision after extensive consultations in recent days with all the Allies, and after it became clear that the final diplomatic effort of Ambassador Holbrooke in Belgrade has not met with success. All efforts to achieve a negotiated, political solution to the Kosovo crisis having failed, no alternative is open but to take military action.

We are taking action following the Federal Republic of Yugoslavia Government's refusal of the International Community's demands:

- Acceptance of the interim political settlement which has been negotiated at Rambouillet;
- Full observance of limits on the Serb Army and Special Police Forces agreed on 25 October;
- Ending of excessive and disproportionate use of force in Kosovo.

As we warned on the 30 January, failure to meet these demands would lead NATO to take whatever measures were necessary to avert a humanitarian catastrophe. NATO has fully supported all relevant UN Security Council resolutions, the efforts of the OSCE, and those of the Contact Group. We deeply regret that these efforts did not succeed, due entirely to the intransigence of the FRY Government. This military action is intended to support the political aims of the international community. It will be directed towards disrupting the violent attacks being committed by the Serb Army and Special Police Forces and weakening their ability to cause further humanitarian catastrophe.

We wish thereby to support international efforts to secure Yugoslav agreement to an interim political settlement. As we have stated, a viable political settlement must be guaranteed by an international military presence. It remains open to the Yugoslav Government to show at any time that it is ready to meet the demands of the international community. I hope it will have the wisdom to do so.

At the same time, we are appealing to the Kosovar Albanians to remain firmly committed to the road to peace which they have chosen in Paris. We urge in particular Kosovar armed elements to refrain from provocative military action.

Let me be clear: NATO is not waging war against Yugoslavia.

We have no quarrel with the people of Yugoslavia who for too long have been isolated in Europe because of the policies of their government. Our objective is to prevent more human suffering and more repression and violence against the civilian population of Kosovo. We must also act to prevent instability spreading in the region. NATO is united behind this course of action. We must halt the violence and bring an end to the humanitarian catastrophe now unfolding in Kosovo. We know the risks of action but we have all agreed that inaction brings even greater dangers. We will do what is necessary to bring stability to the region. We must stop an authoritarian regime from repressing its people in Europe at the end of the 20th century. We have a moral duty to do so.

The responsibility is on our shoulders and we will fulfil it.

3. Statement by the Prime Minister, Tony Blair, in the House of Commons, Tuesday, 23 March 1999

Madam Speaker, with your permission I will make a statement on Kosovo. As I speak, it is still unclear what the outcome of Mr Holbrooke's talks in Belgrade will be, but there is little cause to be optimistic. On the assumption they produce no change in President Milosevic's position and the repression in Kosovo by Serb forces continues, Britain stands ready with our NATO allies to take military action. We do so for very clear reasons. We do so primarily to avert what would otherwise be a humanitarian disaster in Kosovo.

Let me give the House an indication of the scale of what is happening: a quarter of a million Kosovars, more than 10 per cent of the population, are now homeless as a result of repression by Serb forces. 65,000 people have been forced from their homes in the last month, and no less than 25,000 in the four days since peace talks broke down. Only yesterday, 5,000 people in the Srbica area were forcibly evicted from their villages. Much of the Drenica region of northern Kosovo is being cleared of ethnic Albanians. Every single village the UNHCR observers could see in the Glogovac and Srbica region yesterday were on fire. Families are being uprooted and driven from their homes. There are reports of masked irregulars separating out the men: we don't know what has happened to them. The House will recall that at Srebrenica, they were killed. Since last summer 2000 people have died. Without the international verification force, there is no doubt the numbers would have been vastly higher.

We act also because we know from bitter experience throughout this century, most recently in Bosnia, that instability and civil war in one part of the Balkans inevitably spills over into the whole of it, and affects the rest of Europe too. Let me remind the House. There are now over 1 million refugees from the former Yugoslavia in the EU. If Kosovo was left to the mercy of Serbian repression, there is not merely a risk but a probability of re-igniting unrest in Albania; Macedonia de-stabilised; almost certain knock-on effects in Bosnia; and further tension between Greece and Turkey. There are strategic interests for the whole of Europe at stake. We cannot contemplate, on the doorstep of the EU, a disintegration into chaos and disorder. And thirdly Madam Speaker, we have made a very plain promise to the Kosovar people. Thousands of them returned to their homes as a result of the ceasefire we negotiated last October. We have said to them and to Mr Milosevic we would not tolerate the brutal suppression of the civilian population. After the massacre at Racak, these threats to Milosevic were repeated. To walk away now would not merely destroy NATO's credibility, more importantly it would be a breach of faith with thousands of innocent civilians. whose only desire is to live in peace and who took us at our word. I say this to the British people. There is a heavy responsibility on a government when putting our forces into battle, to justify such action. I warn: the potential consequences of military action are serious, both for NATO forces and the people in the region. Their suffering cannot be ended overnight. But in my judgement the consequences of not acting are more serious still for human life and for peace in the long term. We must act: to save thousands of innocent men, women and children from humanitarian catastrophe, from death, barbarism and ethnic cleansing by a brutal dictatorship; to save the stability of the Balkan region, where we know chaos can engulf all of Europe. We have no alternative but to act and act we will, unless Milosevic even now chooses the path of peace.

Let me recap briefly on the last few months. Last October, NATO threatened to use force to secure Milosevic's agreement to a cease-fire and an end to the repression that was then in hand. This was successful - at least for a while. Diplomatic efforts, backed by NATO's threat, led to the creation of the 1500 strong Kosovo Verification Mission. A NATO extraction force was established in neighbouring Macedonia in case the monitors got into difficulty. At the same time, Milosevic gave an undertaking to the US envoy Mr Holbrooke that he would withdraw Serb forces so that their numbers returned to the level before February 1998 – roughly 10,000 internal security troops and 12,000 Yugoslav army troops. Milosevic never fulfilled that commitment, indeed the numbers have gone up. We believe there are some 16,000 internal security and 20,000 Yugoslav army troops now in Kosovo, with a further 8,000 army reinforcements poised just over the border. In January, NATO warned Milosevic that it would respond if he failed to come into compliance with the October agreements: if the repression continued; and if he frustrated the peace process. Milosevic has failed to meet any of these requirements.

Even then, intense diplomatic efforts have been under way. My Rt Hon Friend the Foreign Secretary, and his French colleague Mr Vedrine, have co-chaired the peace talks in France. There is an agreement now on the table. Autonomy for Kosovo would be guaranteed, with a democratically-elected Assembly, accountable institutions and locally controlled police forces. After three years Kosovo's status would be reviewed. The rights of all its inhabitants – including Serbs – would be protected, regardless of their ethnic background. And the awful conflict that has been a blight on the lives of its peoples could come to an end. The Kosovo Albanians have signed the peace agreement. The Serbs have not. They have reneged on the commitments they made on the political texts at Rambouillet. And they refuse to allow a peace-keeping force in Kosovo under NATO command to underpin implementation. It takes two sides to make peace. So far only one side has shown itself willing to make the commitment. It was Milosevic who stripped Kosovo of its autonomy in 1989. It is Milosevic who is now refusing to tackle a political problem by political means. NATO action would be in the form of air strikes. It will involve many NATO countries. It has the full support of NATO. It will have as its minimum objective to curb continued

Serbian repression in Kosovo in order to avert a humanitarian disaster. It would therefore target the military capability of the Serb dictatorship. To avoid such action, Milosevic must do what he promised to do last October. End the repression; withdraw his troops to

barracks; get them down to the levels agreed; and withdraw from Kosovo the tanks, heavy artillery and other weapons he brought into Kosovo early last year. He must agree to the proposals set out in the Rambouillet Accords, including a NATO led ground force. Any attack by Serbian forces against NATO personnel engaged in peace-keeping missions elsewhere in the region would be completely unjustified and would be met with a swift and severe response in self-defence. President Milosevic should be in no doubt about our determination to protect our forces and to deal appropriately with any threats to them. Mr Holbrooke has made the position of the international community crystal clear to Milosevic. There can be no doubt about what is at stake. The choice is now his. Milosevic can choose peace for the peoples of Kosovo and an end to the Federal Republic of Yugoslavia's isolation in Europe. Or he can choose continued conflict and the serious consequences that would follow. I hope the House will join with me in urging President Milosevic to choose the path of peace; and support NATO and the international community in action should he fail to do so.

4.   NATO Press Release: Political and Military Objectives of Action with Regard to in Kosovo, 23 March 1999

NATO's overall political objectives remain to help achieve a peaceful solution to the crisis in Kosovo by contributing to the response of the international community. More particularly, the Alliance made it clear in its statement of 30th January 1999 that its strategy was to halt the violence and support the completion of negotiations on an interim political solution. Alliance military action is intended to support its political aims. To do so, NATO's military action will be directed towards halting the violent attacks being committed by the VJ and MUP and disrupting their ability to conduct future attacks against the population of Kosovo, thereby supporting international efforts to secure FRY agreement to an interim political settlement

5.   Ambassador Holbrooke, Interview on ABC's Nightline, March 24, 1999

MR. KOPPEL: And joining us now from Budapest, U.S. Special Envoy Richard Holbrooke. Ambassador Holbrooke, give us a little bit of an understanding of Milosevic. He becomes more and more interesting with each passing day to an American audience. What was it that went on between the two of you -- because after all, you did engage in fairly protracted talks? Was it just no win from the beginning?

AMBASSADOR HOLBROOKE: I've been negotiating with him and meeting -- and met with him now for 3 1/2 years since the summer of 1995, and the sessions in the last 2 days were the most bleak and the least engaged that we've ever had. As a person, he is very agile, he's adept. He can make rapid mood changes, but I believe they're controlled. I do not buy the theory that he does not have control of himself; I see no evidence of that. But I do believe that he's quite isolated. A tremendous amount of our non-negotiating exchanges -- and it isn't continuous negotiating, a lot of it is a discussion -- a lot of it concerns what is wrong with the Western press; how it's being used and abused and tricked by now the Albanians -- once it used to be the Muslims. I remember when the bomb fell in the marketplace in Sarajevo in August of 1995. He actively argued that it was Muslims killing themselves in order to lure us into an air war. We got exactly the same version of more recent events in the last 2 days.

MR. KOPPEL: Do you think he actually believes that autonomy is inevitably in 3 years going to lead to independence?

AMBASSADOR HOLBROOKE: His answer to that was that he is offering the Albanians autonomy; we are covertly supporting their independence. He made this statement not withstanding the fact that the United States, every member of the European Union, and every other major country in the world has stated repeatedly that we do not support independence of Kosovo and that we do not support involuntary changing of borders through violent means.

MR. KOPPEL: When you were talking before about Milosevic's mood swings, you left me with a clear impression that he does it for effect, either to distract you, break off a certain part of the conversation. Get into that a little bit; what's he after?

AMBASSADOR HOLBROOKE: It has been said of Slobodan Milosevic two things, which I think are worth repeating here -- neither of them are original insights of mine -- that he is not an ultra-extremist nationalist like some of the wilder men of Bosnia like Karadzic, Mladic, and Sesilj, in Belgrade; that he is really a former communist with a business background, an apparatchik whose primary goal is simply to obtain power, whatever the costs. But he does not have a sustaining ideology or a grand design.

The second thing that's been said of him, which is very relevant to your question, was said by a Yugoslav journalist, who observed of him once, that he is both the arsonist and the fireman of these crises. At this point in time, of course, he is only the arsonist.

MR. KOPPEL: Do you have any instincts as to how long it will be before we get some sort of a diplomatic feeler from Milosevic?

AMBASSADOR HOLBROOKE: None at all, Ted. If I did, I would certainly shape my recommendations to the President and Secretary Albright accordingly. But when I left the presidential palace yesterday morning -- with President Milosevic's final comment to me being, will I ever see you again, and my response being, that's up to you, Mr. President -- I could not tell where we were going, except that we were crossing a decisive and possibly historic watershed.

MR. KOPPEL: ... Ambassador Holbrooke, you had probably as much opportunity to speak with President Milosevic as any American diplomat. What is it that ultimately will cause him to change his mind, do you think?

AMBASSADOR HOLBROOKE: I can't answer that question, Ted. All I can tell you -- and I want to be very clear on this -- is that when I left his office yesterday morning -- actually early afternoon -- I did not leave until I was absolutely sure that President Milosevic understood the full consequences that would follow from the positions he had taken on the two key issues which we were focused on: the continuation of the offensive, which he first said was not taking place at all, and then said he wouldn't stop -- even though it wasn't taking place; and secondly, his adamant refusal to even discuss the question of an international NATO-led peacekeeping force in Kosovo. That force has been portrayed in the Serb media as an anti-Serb, pro-Albanian force but, in fact, it was designed to bring peace to an area where the two ethnic groups have such deep-seated animosity that an outside presence is necessary under the Rambouillet agreements for some interim period.

MR. KOPPEL: Isn't it inevitable that the Yugoslav Government will now depict the NATO air force as being, in effect, an arm of the Kosovar Albanians?

AMBASSADOR HOLBROOKE: For sure; they're doing that already.

MR. KOPPEL: And given that, isn't it going to be extremely difficult then for him to back away from where he is right now? In other words, when I ask you what will cause him finally to reach some kind of an agreement, he's in a bit of a corner here himself, isn't he?

AMBASSADOR HOLBROOKE: I can't see inside his mind, despite the amount of time I've spent with him. He has put himself in a box. He triggered the military actions that are now taking place and which will lead to the destruction of his military establishment by swift, severe and sustained military action. At what point he will ask us to stop is something none of us can answer. But he will know how serious the damage is and how accurate it is.

MR. KOPPEL: You better than anyone alive know what Milosevic's customary pattern is. When the pain threshold gets a little bit too high, when he is beginning to feel real pain, inevitably then he tends to come back and say, all right, let's talk. Is a "let's talk" enough to end the bombing?

AMBASSADOR HOLBROOKE: That's a very good question. You know, today his brother, who is the Yugoslav Ambassador in Moscow, said we're ready to continue talking on political issues and immediately the world press said there's a new offer from Belgrade; but in fact, it was an old offer. If President Milosevic is willing to discuss the international peacekeeping force led by NATO, as envisaged in the military part of the Rambouillet agreements, within the framework of the agreements that bring autonomy and self-governing to Kosovo, if that's what he means by let's talk, then that is the basis for a resumption of the diplomatic dialogue. But what his brother said in Moscow today was really, frankly, just the same old stuff.

MR. KOPPEL: Well, let me ask you to focus on what you have just defined as being enough, then, to stop the bombing. In the past what he has done is said let's talk, but in the time that it takes to get the talks started he tends to continue his military operations. What guarantees will we have that he doesn't do that?

AMBASSADOR HOLBROOKE: Well, let me be very clear on this. My previous answer should not be misunderstood. If the offensive is continuing, "let's talk" turns into a talk-talk/fight-fight strategy. You and I both grew up some 30 years ago when that happened in Vietnam -- you covering the Paris peace talks and I as junior member of the American delegation to the American talks with the North Vietnamese. That was talk-talk/fight-fight, and it went on for 3 or 4 years. We're not going to get into something like that, not even for 3 or 4 weeks or 3 or 4 days. The on-the-ground military situation must also dramatically change. The enormous offensive, which the Yugoslav security and military forces are now undertaking, which is causing tens of thousands of new refugees -- people who had been able to return to their homes after the October cease-fire agreements and now are being driven out again by their flagrant violation -- must come to an end.

MR. KOPPEL: President Milosevic, Ambassador, has probably been led to believe that certainly not the United States and probably not any of the other NATO governments would be inclined to send ground troops into Yugoslavia or Kosovo for any other purpose than peacekeeping after a cease-fire. Doesn't that give him a tremendous advantage, knowing that no ground troops will come in to force his hand?

AMBASSADOR HOLBROOKE: The United States and its allies have said that what we're talking about is an invited -- that is a permissive -- peacekeeping force, not an army of invasion.

MR. KOPPEL: Let me see if I can get you to focus a little more precisely on my question, because he seems to be under the impression that all he has to survive is air attacks, that he does not face any danger of ground troops coming in.

AMBASSADOR HOLBROOKE: Well, you said "all he has to survive" -- that minimizes what damage -- and the damage is substantial and will be more substantial -- that he is going to suffer. I don't think now is the time to discuss a ground troop option. It has been ruled out at this time by the President and the Secretary of Defense. The Congress is debating it. It's not my authority to discuss this issue. I want to be clear simply on what my mission was and the consequences that flowed from President Milosevic's continuing refusal to deal with the two issues I put on the table before him.

6. Last Appeal to President Milosevic by the Chairman-in-Office of the OSCE, 24 March 1999

The OSCE Chairman-in-Office, Norwegian Foreign Minister Knut Vollebaek, strongly urges Yugoslav authorities to seize the opportunity to find a peaceful solution to the Kosovo conflict. "This is absolutely necessary to prevent a further deterioration of the humanitarian situation in Kosovo", says Foreign Minister Vollebæk. In a telephone conversation today the Chairman-in-Office appealed to President Slobodan Milosevic to accept the Rambouillet Agreement and to put an immediate end to the excessive use of force by Yugoslav and Serbian forces in Kosovo. President Milosevic, however, showed no willingness to back down. The OSCE stands ready to assist in implementing the Rambouillet Accord. The OSCE Kosovo Verification Mission, which for security reasons temporarily has been evacuated to the former Yugoslav Republic of Macedonia, will be prepared to start this work at very short notice. Yugoslav authorities must look to the future of their country and the well being of its citizens. "They must now give peace a chance", says the Chairman-in-Office.

7. Press Statement by the NATO Secretary General following the Commencement of Air Operations, 24 March 1999

I have been informed by SACEUR, General Clark, that at this moment NATO Air Operations against targets in the Federal Republic of Yugoslavia have commenced. In the last months the international community has spared no efforts to achieve a negotiated solution in Kosovo. But it has not been possible. Clear responsibility for the air strikes lies with President Milosevic who has refused to stop his violent action in Kosovo and has refused to negotiate in good faith. The time has now come for action. Let me reiterate: NATO is not waging war against Yugoslavia. We have no quarrel with the people of Yugoslavia who for too long have been isolated in Europe because of the policies of their government. Our actions are directed against the repressive policy of the Yugoslav leadership. We must stop the violence and bring an end to the humanitarian catastrophe now taking place in Kosovo. We have a moral duty to do so. NATO's men and women in uniform, who are carrying out this important mission, are among the best in the world. I am confident that they will be successful.

8. Statement made by the UN Secretary-General on NATO military action against Yugoslavia, 24 March 1999

I speak to you at a grave moment for the international community. Throughout the last year, I have appealed on many occasions to the Yugoslav authorities and the Kosovo Albanians to seek peace over war, compromise over conflict. I deeply regret that, in spite of all the efforts made by the international community, the Yugoslav authorities have persisted in their rejection of a political settlement, which would have halted the bloodshed in Kosovo and secured an equitable peace for the population there. It is indeed tragic that diplomacy has failed, but there are times when the use of force may be legitimate in the pursuit of peace. In helping maintain international peace and security, Chapter VIII of the United Nations Charter assigns an important role to regional organizations. But as Secretary-General I have many times pointed out, not just in relation to Kosovo, that under the Charter the Security Council has primary responsibility for maintaining international peace and security -- and this is explicitly acknowledged in the North Atlantic Treaty. Therefore the Council should be involved in any decision to resort to the use of force.

9. President Clinton, Address to the Nation, Washington, DC, 24 March 1999

My fellow Americans, today our Armed Forces joined our NATO allies in air strikes against Serbian forces responsible for the brutality in Kosovo. We have acted with resolve for several reasons. We act to protect thousands of innocent people in Kosovo from a mounting military offensive. We act to prevent a wider war; to diffuse a powder keg at the heart of Europe that has exploded twice before in this century with catastrophic results. And we act to stand united with our allies for peace. By acting now we are upholding our values, protecting our interests and advancing the cause of peace. Tonight I want to speak to you about the tragedy in Kosovo and why it matters to America that we work with our allies to end it. First, let me explain what it is we are responding to. Kosovo is a province of Serbia, in the middle of southeastern Europe, about 160 miles east of Italy. That's less than the distance between Washington and New York, and only about 70 miles north of Greece. Its people are mostly ethnic Albanian and mostly Muslim. In 1989, Serbia's leader, Slobadan Milosevic, the same leader who started the wars in Bosnia and Croatia, and moved against Slovenia in the last decade, stripped Kosovo of the constitutional autonomy its people enjoyed; thus denying them their right to speak their language, run their schools, shape their daily lives. For years, Kosovars struggled peacefully to get their rights back. When President Milosevic sent his troops and police to crush them, the struggle grew violent.

Last fall our diplomacy, backed by the threat of force from our NATO Alliance, stopped the fighting for a while, and rescued tens of thousands of people from freezing and starvation in the hills wherethey had fled to save their lives. And last month, with out allies and Russia, we proposed a peace agreement to end the fighting for good. The Kosovar leaders signed that agreement last week. Even though it does not give them all the want, even though their people were still being savaged, they saw that a just peace is better than a long and unwinnable war. The Serbian leaders, on the other hand, refused even to discuss key elements of the peace agreement. As the Kosovars were saying "yes" topeace, Serbia stationed 40,000 troops in and around Kosovo in preparation for a major offensive -- and in clear violation of the commitments they had made. Now, they've started moving from village to village, shelling civilians and torching their houses. We've seen innocent people taken from their homes, forced to kneel in the dirt and sprayed with bullets; Kosovar men dragged from their families, fathers and sons together, lined up and shot in cold blood. This is not war in the traditional sense. It is an attack by tanks and artillery on a largely defenseless people, whose leaders already have agreed topeace. Ending this tragedy is a moral imperative. It is also importantto America's national interest. Take a look at this map. Kosovo is a small place, but it sits on a major fault line between Europe, Asia and the Middle East, at the meeting place of Islam and both the Western and Orthodox branches of Christianity. To the south are our allies, Greece and Turkey; to the north, our new democratic allies in Central Europe. And all around Kosovo there are other small countries, struggling with their own economic and political challenges -- countries that could be overwhelmed by a large, new wave of refugees from Kosovo. All the ingredients for a major war are there: ancient grievances, struggling democracies, and in the center of it all a dictator in Serbia who has done nothing since the Cold War ended but start new wars and pour gasoline on the flames of ethnic and religious division. Sarajevo, the capital of neighboring Bosnia, is where World War I began. World War II and the Holocaust engulfed this region. In both wars Europe was slow to recognize the dangers, and the United States waited even longer to enter the conflicts. Just imagine if leaders back then had acted wisely and early enough, how many lives could have been saved, how many Americans would not have had to die. We learned some of the same lessons in Bosnia just a few years ago. The world did not act early enough to stop that war, either. And let's not forget what happened -- innocent people herded into concentration camps, children gunned down by snipers on their way to school, soccer fields and parks turned into cemeteries; a quarter of a million people killed, not because of anything they have done, but because of who they were. Two million Bosnians became refugees. This was genocide in the heart of Europe -- not in 1945, but in 1995. Not in some grainy newsreel from our parents' and grandparents' time, but in our own time, testing our humanity and our resolve. At the time, many people believed nothing could be done to end the bloodshed in Bosnia. They said, well, that's just the way those people in the Balkans are. But when we and our allies joined with courageous Bosnians to stand up to the aggressors, we helped to end the war. We learned that in the Balkans, inaction in the face of brutality simply invites more brutality. But firmness can stop armies and save lives. We must apply that lesson in Kosovo before what happened in Bosnia happens there, too. Over the last few months we have done everything we possibly could to solve this problem peacefully. Secretary Albright has worked tirelessly for a negotiated agreement. Mr. Milosevic has refused.

On Sunday I sent Ambassador Dick Holbrooke to Serbia to make clear to him again, on behalf of the United States and our NATO allies, that he must honor his own commitments and stop his repression, or face military action. Again, he refused. Today, we and our 18 NATO allies agreed to do what we said we would do, what we must do to restore the peace. Our mission is clear: to demonstrate the seriousness of NATO's purpose so that the Serbian leaders understand the imperative of reversing course. To deter an even bloodier offensive against innocent civilians in Kosovo and, if necessary, to seriously damage the Serbian military's capacity to harm the people of Kosovo. In short, if President Milosevic will not make peace, we will limit his ability to make war. Now, I want to be clear with you, there are risks in this military action -- risks to our pilots and the people on the ground. Serbia's air defenses are strong. It could decide to intensify its assault on Kosovo, or to seek to harm us or our allies elsewhere. If it does, we will deliver a forceful response. Hopefully, Mr. Milosevic will realize his present course is self-destructive and unsustainable. If he decides to accept the peace agreement and demilitarize Kosovo, NATO has agreed to help to implement it with a peace-keeping force. If NATO is invited to do so, our troops should take part in that mission to keep the peace. But I do not intend to put our troops in Kosovo to fight a war. Do our interests in Kosovo justify the dangers to our Armed Forces? I've thought long and hard about that question. I am convinced that the dangers of acting are far outweighed by the dangers of not acting -- dangers to defenseless people and to our national interests. If we and our allies were to allow this war to continue with no response, President Milosevic would read our hesitation as a license to kill. There would be many more massacres, tens of thousands more refugees, more victims crying out for revenge. Right now our firmness is the only hope the people of Kosovo have to be able to live in their own country without having to fear for their own lives. Remember: We asked them to accept peace, and they did. We asked them to promise to lay down their arms, and they agreed. We pledged that we, the United States and the other 18 nations of NATO, would stick by them if they did the right thing. We cannot let them down now. Imagine what would happen if we and our allies instead decided just to look the other way, as these people were massacred on NATO's doorstep. That would discredit NATO, the cornerstone on which our security has rested for 50 years now. We must also remember that this is a conflict with no natural national boundaries. Let me ask you to look again at a map. The red dots are towns the Serbs have attacked. The arrows show the movement of refugees -- north, east and south. Already, this movement is threatening the young democracy in Macedonia, which has its own Albanian minority and a Turkish minority. Already, Serbian forces have made forays into Albania from which Kosovars have drawn support. Albania is a Greek minority. Let a fire burn here in this area and the flames will spread. Eventually, key U.S. allies could be drawn into a wider conflict, a war we would be forced to confront later -- only at far greater risk and greater cost.

I have a responsibility as President to deal with problems such as this before they do permanent harm to our national interests. America has a responsibility to stand with our allies when they are trying to save innocent lives and preserve peace, freedom and stability in Europe. That is what we are doing in Kosovo. If we've learned anything from the century drawing to a close, it is that if America is going to be prosperous and secure, we need a Europe that is prosperous, secure undivided and free. We need a Europe that is coming together, not falling apart; a Europe that shares our values and shares the burdens of leadership. That is the foundation on which the security of our children will depend. That is why I have supported the political and economic unification of Europe. That is why we brought Poland, Hungary and the Czech Republic into NATO, and redefined its missions, and reached out to Russia and Ukraine for new partnerships. Now, what are the challenges to that vision of a peaceful, secure, united, stable Europe? The challenge of strengthening a partnership with a democratic Russia, that, despite our disagreements, is a constructive partner in the work of building peace. The challenge of resolving the tension between Greece and Turkey and building bridges with the Islamic world. And, finally, the challenge of ending instability in the Balkans so that these bitter ethnic problems in Europe are resolved the force of argument, not the force of arms; so that future generations of Americans do not have to cross the Atlantic to fight another terrible war. It is this challenge that we and our allies are facing in Kosovo. That is why we have acted now -- because we care about saving innocent lives; because we have an interest in avoiding an even crueler and costlier war; and because our children need and deserve a peaceful, stable, free Europe. Our thoughts and prayers tonight must be with the men and women of our Armed Forces who are undertaking this mission for the sake of our values and our children's future. May God bless them and may God bless America.

10. Edited Transcript of Press Conference by Prime Minister Tony Blair, Berlin, 24 March 1999

I can confirm that NATO air strikes against Serb forces have begun and that UK forces are engaged in this action. Any political leader thinks long and hard before committing forces to action and the inevitable risks that are attached to it. I would not take this course if I did not think it was the right thing to do. I want to pay tribute at the outset to our Armed Forces. We owe a huge debt to them for their courage and their professionalism. Tonight there are families in Britain who will be feeling a real sense of anxiety. They can feel too however a real sense of pride at the contribution their loved ones are making to peace and stability in Europe. We are taking this action for one very simple reason: to damage Serb forces sufficiently to prevent Milosevic from continuing to perpetrate his vile oppression against the Kosovo Albanian people. Already 400,000 people have been displaced, over 250,000 remain homeless. In the last week alone 25,000 people have been driven from their homes. These are the harsh and real facts. Kosovo is right on Europe's doorstep. As previous Balkan crises have shown, the effects are felt far and wide. And as I said yesterday, there are now more than one million refugees from former Yugoslavia in European Union countries. Let me set out too some of the background to the story about the region and the man who has brought it so much death and barbarism. Milosevic came to power in 1987 by exploiting Serb nationalism. He threw aside the ethnically balanced

arrangements which held Yugoslavia together for 45 years. In 1989 he stripped Kosovo of the autonomy it had enjoyed for 40 years and imposed direct control from Belgrade. In 1991, in the face of revolt from Slovenia and Croatia, his army laid siege to the Croatian city of Vukovar and the following summer shelled the historic port city of Dubrovnik. In 1992 he helped trigger the Bosnian war in which some 250,000 Bosnians were killed. He gave to the world the hideous term 'ethnic cleansing' as over 2 million people were driven from their homes, mainly by the Serbs. The Bosnian war went on until 1995 and only ended when NATO summoned the resolve to use force. Events on the ground finally turned against the Serb forces and Milosevic was forced to sign up to the Dayton Agreement. In Kosovo the conflict has smouldered for years as Kosovo Albanians, 90 per cent of the population there, tried to regain self-rule. Last March Serb forces massacred 60 – 80 Kosovars in and around the village of Precaz (phon), triggering a sharp worsening of the conflict. Hundreds then died as Serb forces and the Kosovo Liberation Army battled it out. Hundreds of thousands of people were, as I have described, made homeless. Many returned, however, after a cease-fire last October negotiated by the US envoy, Richard Holbrooke. Again, only when NATO threatened force unless the killing stopped did Milosevic back down. He agreed then for the 2,000 strong Kosovo Verification Mission, backed by air verification through NATO. He also agreed to reduce Serb forces to the pre-February 1998 levels and withdraw his heavy weapons, so that was the agreement he made last October. But he broke his word again. The cease-fire broke down again, the killing resumed again. Serb force levels went back to where they had started. In January, following the massacre of 45 civilians at Racak, we demanded that Milosevic cease the repression and take a constructive part in peace talks. He pretended to comply but in reality, as we know, he did not do so. Still, even then, we tried to get him to walk the path of peace. In talks, chaired jointly by the UK and by France, we constructed an agreement. It was difficult to do, but we did it. The Kosovo Albanians signed it; Milosevic rejected it, again. Nobody in the light of this history can say either that we have not tried to find a peaceful resolution to this conflict, or that Milosevic has not been warned of the consequences of continuing to repress the civilian population in Kosovo. As I said yesterday, there are serious consequences for our forces and for the people of the region in the action we are taking. Tonight's attack alone will not bring the curtain down on the scenes you have been witnessing of families fleeing their homes and trudging towards as yet undiscovered sanctuary. Nor can we be sure about how Milosevic will respond. But I repeat this warning, just as we have made good the threat to attack if he did not comply with the agreement he had entered into, so if there is retaliation against NATO forces elsewhere in the region, our response will be swift and severe. The forces ranged against Milosevic are truly international. NATO is united. Of the 13 nations who have made aircraft available, 8 are in action tonight. Britain is a peaceful nation, we are a peaceful people who take no joy in war. But we know from our own history and from our own character that there are times when we have to stand up and fight for peace, when force is the final resort of those who know that the only peace that ever lasts is a just peace, a peace based on justice. Justice is all that those poor people, driven from their homes in their thousands in Kosovo, are asking for, the chance to live free from fear. We have in our power the means to help them secure justice and we have a duty to see that justice is now done.

11. Security Council Provisional Record, 3988th Meeting, 24 March 1999, 5.35 p.m. (NY time), Extract

Mr. Lavrov (Russian Federation) (*spoke in Russian*): The Russian Federation is profoundly outraged at the use by the North Atlantic Treaty Organization (NATO) of military force against the Federal Republic of Yugoslavia. In recent weeks, when we were constantly hearing threats - detrimental to the negotiating process - that there would be missile strikes against Serbian positions in Kosovo and other parts of Serbia, the Russian Government strongly proclaimed its categorical rejection of the use of force in contravention of decisions of the Security Council and issued repeated warnings about the long- term harmful consequences of this action not only for the prospects of a settlement of the Kosovo situation and for safeguarding security in the Balkans, but also for the stability of the entire modern multi-polar system of international relations. Those who are involved in this unilateral use of force against the sovereign Federal Republic of Yugoslavia - carried out in violation of the Charter of the United Nations and without the authorization of the Security Council - must realize the heavy responsibility they bear for subverting the Charter and other norms of international law and for attempting to establish in the world, de facto, the primacy of force and unilateral diktat. The members of NATO are not entitled to decide the date of other sovereign and independent States. They must not forget that they are not only members of their alliance but also Members of the United Nations, and that it is their obligation to be guided by the United Nations Charter, in particular its Article 103, which clearly establishes the absolute priority for Members of the Organization of Charter obligations over any other international obligations. Attempts to justify the NATO strikes with arguments about preventing a humanitarian catastrophe in Kosovo are completely untenable. Not only are these attempts in no way based on the Charter or other generally recognized rules of international law, but the unilateral use of force will lead precisely to a situation with truly devastating humanitarian consequences. Moreover, by the terms of the definition of aggression adopted by the General Assembly in 1974,

"No consideration of whatever nature, whether political, economic, military or otherwise, may serve as a justification for aggression".
(General Assembly resolution 3314 (XXIX), annex, article 5. Para.1)

We certainly do not seek to defend violations of international humanitarian law by any party. But it is possible to combat violations of the law only with clean hands and only on the solid basis of the law. Otherwise lawlessness would spawn lawlessness. It would be unthinkable for a national court in a civilized democratic country to uphold illegal methods to combat crime. Attempts to apply a different standard to international law and to disregard its basic norms and principles create a dangerous precedent that could cause acute destabilization and chaos on the regional and global level. If we do not put an end to this very dangerous trend, the virus of illegal unilateral approaches could spread not merely to other geographical regions but to spheres of international relations other than questions of peace and security. The fact that NATO has opted to use force in Kosovo raises very serious questions about the sincerity of the repeated assurances that that alliance was not claiming the role of the world's policeman and was prepared to cooperate in the interests of common European security. In the light of this turn of events, we shall draw the appropriate conclusions in our relations and contacts with that organization. NATO's decision to use military force is particularly unacceptable from any point of view because the potential of political and diplomatic methods to yield a settlement in Kosovo has certainly not been exhausted. The enormous quantity of complicated work done by the international community has now been dealt a very powerful, a very grave and probably an irrevocable blow. The Russian Federation vehemently demands the immediate cessation of this illegal military action against the Federal Republic of Yugoslavia. We reserve the right to raise in the Security Council the question of the adoption by the Council, under the United Nations Charter, of appropriate measures with respect to this situation, which has arisen as a result of NATO's illegal actions and which poses a clear threat to international peace and security. Today, the President of the Russian Federation, Boris N. Yeltsin, issued the following statement:

"Russia is profoundly outraged by NATO's military action against sovereign Yugoslavia, which is nothing less than an act of open aggression. Only the Security Council can decide on what measures, including the use of force, should be taken to maintain or restore international peace and security. The Security Council did not take such decisions with regard to Yugoslavia. Not only the Charter of the United Nations has been violated; the Founding Act on Mutual Relations, Cooperation and Security Between NATO and The Russian Federation has been violated as well. A dangerous precedent has been created regarding the policy of diktat and force, and the whole of the international rule of law has been threatened. We are basically talking about an attempt by NATO to enter the twenty-first century in the uniform of the world's policeman. Russian will never agree to that.

The Security Council must discuss the situation that has emerged and demand the immediate cessation of NATO's use of force. For its part, the leadership of the Russian Federation will review its relationship with NATO as an organization, which has shown disrespect for the fundamental basis of the system of international relations. As President and Supreme Commander, I have already given the following instructions: to cut short the visit of the United States of the Chairman of the Government of the Russian Federation, Yevgeny Primakov; to demand an urgent convening of a meeting of the Security Council of the United Nations and to seek an immediate cessation of NATO's military action; to recall to Moscow the chief military representative of the Russian Federation to NATO; to suspend our participation in the Partnership for Peace programme and to end the carrying out of the programme on Russia-NATO partnership; and to postpone talks for the opening of a NATO liaison mission in Moscow. "I have already appealed to the President of the United States, Bill Clinton, and to the leaders of other NATO member countries to put an immediate end to this military adventure, which threatens the lives of peaceful people and could lead to an explosion of the situation in the Balkans. A settlement of the situation in Kosovo, as the settlement of other similar problems, is only possible through negotiations. The quicker they are resumed, the greater the possibility for the international community to find a political settlement to the situation. Russia is prepared to interact with other members of the Contact Group in order to reach that goal. Those who decided upon military adventure bear the full responsibility to their peoples and to the world community for the dire consequences of this for international stability. If the military conflict increases, then Russian reserves the right to take adequate measures, including military measures, to ensure its own and common European security". ...

Mr. Burleigh (United States of America): The current situation in Kosovo is of grave concern to all of us. We and our allies have begun military action only with the greatest reluctance. But we believe that such action is necessary to respond to Belgrade's brutal persecution of Kosovar Albanians, violations of international law, excessive and indiscriminate use of force, refusal to negotiate to resolve the issue peacefully and recent military build-up in Kosovo - all of which foreshadow a humanitarian catastrophe of immense proportions. We have begun today's action to avert this humanitarian catastrophe and to deter further aggression and repression in Kosovo. Serb forces numbering 40,000 are now in action in and around Kosovo. Thirty thousand Kosovars have fled their homes just since 19 March. As a result of Serb action in the last five weeks, there are more than 60,000 new refugees and displaced persons. The total number of displaced persons is approaching a quarter of a million. The continuing offensive by the Federal Republic of Yugoslavia is generating refugees and creating pressures on neighbouring countries, threatening the stability of the region. Repressive Serb action in Kosovo has already resulted in cross-border activity in Albania, Bosnia and the former Yugoslav Republic of Macedonia. Recent actions by Belgrade also constitute a threat to the safety of international observers and humanitarian workers in Kosovo. Security Council resolutions 1199 (1998) and 1203 (1998) recognized that the situation in Kosovo constitutes a threat to peace and security in the region and invoked Chapter VII of the Charter. In resolution 1199 (1998), the Council demanded that Serbian forces take immediate steps to improve the humanitarian situation and avert the impending humanitarian catastrophe. In October 1998, Belgrade entered into agreements and understandings with the North Atlantic Treaty Organization (NATO) and the Organization for Security and Cooperation in Europe (OSCE) to verify its compliance with Security Council demands, particularly on reduction of security forces, cooperation with international observers, cooperation with humanitarian relief agencies and negotiations on a political settlement for substantial autonomy. Belgrade has refused to comply. The actions of the Federal Republic of Yugoslavia also violate its commitments under the Helsinki Final Act, as well as its obligations under the international law of human rights. Belgrade's actions in Kosovo cannot be dismissed as an internal matter. For months, Serb actions have led to escalating explosions of violence. It is imperative that the international community take quick measures to avoid humanitarian suffering and widespread destruction, which could exceed that of the 1998 offensive.

I reiterate that we have initiated action today with the greatest reluctance. Our preference has been to achieve our objectives in the Balkans through peaceful means. Since fighting erupted in February 1998, we have been actively engaged in seeking resolution of the conflict through diplomacy under the auspices of the Contact Group backed by NATO. These efforts led to talks in Rambouillet and Paris, which produced a fair, just and balanced agreement. The Kosovar Albanians signed that agreement, but Belgrade rejected all efforts to achieve a peaceful resolution. We are mindful that violations of the ceasefire and provocations by the Kosovo Liberation Army have also contributed to this situation. However, it is Belgrade's systematic policy of undermining last October's agreements and thwarting all diplomatic efforts to resolve the situation which have prevented a peaceful solution and have led us to today's action. In this context, we believe that action by NATO is justified and necessary to stop the violence and prevent an even greater humanitarian disaster. As President Clinton said today, "We and our allies have a chance to leave our children a Europe that is free, peaceful and stable. But we must act now to do that". ...

The President (spoke in Chinese): I shall now make a statement in my capacity as the representative of China. Today, 24 March, the North Atlantic Treaty Organization (NATO), with the United States in the lead, mobilized its airborne military forces and launched military strikes against the Federal Republic of Yugoslavia, seriously exacerbating the situation in the Balkan region. This act amounts to a blatant violation of the United Nations Charter and of the accepted norms of international law. The Chinese Government strongly opposes this act. The question of Kosovo, as an internal matter of the Federal Republic of Yugoslavia, should be resolved among the parties concerned in the Federal Republic of Yugoslavia themselves. Settlement of the Kosovo issue should be based on respect for the sovereignty and territorial integrity of the Federal Republic of Yugoslavia and on guaranteeing the legitimate rights and interests of all ethnic groups in the Kosovo region. Recently, the parties concerned have been working actively towards a political settlement of the crisis. We have always stood for the peaceful settlement of disputes through negotiations, and are opposed to the use or threat of use of force in international affairs and to power politics whereby the strong bully the weak. We oppose interference in the internal affairs of other States, under whatever pretext or in whatever form. It has always been our position that under the Charter it is the Security Council that bears primary responsibility for the maintenance of international peace and security. And it is only the Security Council that can determine whether a given situation threatens international peace and security and can take appropriate action. We are firmly opposed to any act that violates this principle and that challenges the authority of the Security Council. The Chinese Government vigorously calls for an immediate cessation of the military attacks by NATO against the Federal Republic of Yugoslavia. China calls on the international community and on the parties concerned in the Federal Republic of Yugoslavia to make concerted efforts to stabilize the situation as soon as possible and to defuse the crisis so as to bring peace back to the Balkan region at an early date. I now resume my functions as President of the Security Council. ...

Mr. Lavrov (Russian Federation) (spoke in Russian): I have already said what my position is. Nothing of what I have heard here has changed that position. In any case, the assertion that the traditional basis for the use of force lies beyond the confines of the United Nations Charter is something that I cannot take seriously. I have set forth my position, and it has absolutely not changed. But I have taken the floor just to make two factual clarifications, as some of my colleagues have mentioned by way or argument certain events that were not quite presented correctly. I would like to make the facts known, particularly given that this is an open, public meeting at which Members of the United Nations that are not members of the Security Council are present. I must therefore clarify two points. The first point has to do with some colleagues' mention of the fact that Russia is a member of the Contact Group. That is quite correct, but they went on to say that Russia was a co-sponsor of the package of documents of the Contact Group. That is only partially true. The Contact Group adopted a document in London that is the basis of the draft political settlement. It is also true that that document enjoys the full co-sponsorship of the Russian Federation. With regard to the military implementation, the Contact Group never discussed that documents, not because the Russian Federation did not want it to be discussed but because our partners in the Contact Group decided to discuss the military aspects of the implementation of the agreement behind our backs, in the North Atlantic Treaty Organization (NATO) and not in the Contact Group. We were discussing this with our partners in the Contact group and made offers so that questions about the implementation of the agreement would be the subject of co-sponsorship within the Contact Group. That was not done. So when they say that Russia is a co-sponsor of everything that was rejected by Belgrade, that is not the true situation. Now, I repeat: our Western partners in the Contact Group decided to prepare and discuss the military aspects behind our backs, and Russia had nothing to do with that proposal. It was the choice of our Western partners to do this. The second clarification that I wanted to make has to do with the statement made by some of our colleagues to the effect that NATO's actions became inevitable because one or two of the permanent members of the Security Council had blocked action in the Council. That is simply not correct, for one simple reason: no proposals on this topic were introduced in the Security Council by anyone. There was never any draft resolution; there were no informal discussions, not even in the corridors - at least not with one permanent member of the Security Council, namely, Russia. Those discussions never took place. I am not saying what the results of those discussions were, but to state now that one or two permanent members of the Security Council blocked action in the Council is simply, diplomatically speaking, not true. These are the clarifications I wanted to make so that everyone knows what the facts are.

[*A full record of this meeting, and of the second meeting on this issue held on 26 March, along with the draft resolution introduced by Belarus, India and the Russian Federation of that date, will be featured in the second volume of this series.*]

12. Press Statement by Dr Javier Solana, NATO Secretary General, 25 March 1999

Yesterday evening around 8 p.m., Operation Allied Force began. Last night's operation was carried out with a broad participation by Allies. This demonstrates NATO solidarity, unity and resolve in carrying out this action. Let me stress that strikes were conducted against carefully chosen military targets focussed on the air defence network of the Federal Republic of Yugoslavia. Our initial reports indicate that these first strikes were successful. All NATO aircraft returned safely to their bases. I express on behalf of the North Atlantic Council our gratitude to the men and women in our Allied armed services who were involved. ... Let me reiterate we are determined to continue until we have achieved our objectives: to halt the violence and to stop further humanitarian catastrophe. Let me emphasise once again that we have no quarrel with the people of Yugoslavia. Our actions are directed against the repressive policies of the Yugoslav government, which is refusing to respect civilized norms of behaviour in this Europe at the end of the 20th century. The responsibility for the current crisis rests with President Milosevic. It is up to him to comply with the demands of the international community. I strongly urge him to do so.

Summary Index

This summary index attempts to link together documents across chapters according to principal themes. Documents and decisions of particular international institutions or organisations or specific governments can be best identified through the detailed table of contents

Carrington Conference, *see* Peaceful Settlement

Conference for Security and Cooperation in Europe, *see* Organization for Security and Cooperation in Europe

Constitutional Issues
Chapter 4, 45-73
Introduction, 25-26
Memoranda of the Parties, 48-49
Opinions of the Badinter Commission, 81-81

History of the Region
Chronology, 15-23
Introduction, 24-33
Memoranda by the Parties, 48-49
Chapter 4, Introduction and Section 4.A, 45-58

Holbrooke Agreement
NATO action, Chapter 12, 272-286
Kosovo Verification Mission, Chapter 13, 287-346

Human Rights
Introduction, 25-26.
Carrington drafts, 80
Badinter opinions, 81-83
OSCE reports, Section 5.D, 97-119
Chapter 6, 120-184
Hill drafts, Chapter 14, 347-391
Rambouillet drafts, Section 15.B, 419-474

Humanitarian Situation
UN Secretary-General's reports, Chapter 8, 193-218
ICRC and UNHCR reports, Chapter 11, 250-270
OSCE and Kosovo Diplomatic Observer Mission verification, Section 13.B, 300-342

KLA (UCK), *see* military situation.

Kosovo Government
Chapter 4, Introduction, 48-49
Chapter 4.C, 64-73

Military Situation
CSCE CPC Mission, 102-104
UN Secretary-General's reports, including OSCE, NATO and other submissions, Chapter 8, 193-218
NATO activities, Chapter 12, 272-286
Holbrooke Agreement, NATO aerial verification, Chapter 12, 272-286
OSCE and Kosovo Diplomatic Observer Mission verification, Chapter 13, 287-342
NATO and Rambouillet, 414, 416, 417
NATO and the initiation of hostilities, Section 16.C, 495-501

Minority Rights, *see* Human Rights

Organisation for Security and Cooperation in Europe
CSCE Monitoring Mission, 77-79, Sections 5.B-C, 94-119
Holbrooke Agreement, NATO aerial verification, Chapter 12, 272-286
OSCE and Kosovo Diplomatic Observer Mission verification, Chapter 13, 287-342

Peaceful Settlement
Carrington Conference, 74-76, Section 4.A, 80
London Conference, 76
Special Group, 76, Section 5.B, 89-93
St Egidio Agreement, 93
Contact Group, Section 9.A, 234-238, 415, 417
Secretary-General's reports, Chapter 8, 193-218
Holbrooke Agreement, Chapter 12, 272-286
OSCE and Kosovo Diplomatic Observer Mission verification, Chapter 13, 287-342
Russian settlement, 292
Hill process, Chapter 14, 347-383

Rambouillet Conference, Chapter 15, 392-474
Paris Conference, Chapter 16, 475-502

Sanctions
SC Resolution 1160, 188
SC Resolution 1199, 190
Secretary-General's Reports, Chapter 8, 195-218
EC/EU sanctions, Section 9.A, 219-228

Secession/Self-determination
Introduction, 26-28
FRY memorandum, 39-40
SFRY Constitution, 54
Serbia Constitution, 56
Kosovo decisions, 72-78
EPC decisions, 80-81
Kosovo memoranda, 83-85, 86-88, 90-91, 100-102
Badinter opinions, 81-82

Succession of States
FRY declaration, 63-64
SC Resolution 777, 89
OSCE action, 95

Territorial Integrity/Unity, see Secession/Self-determination

War Crimes
International Criminal Tribunal, Chapter 10, 239-250
Further Security Council resolutions and statement, Chapter 7, 185-191
Secretary-General's Reports, Chapter 8, 193-218
ICRC and UNHCR reports, Chapter 11, 252-279
OSCE, KDOM, NATO, UN reports, Section 13.B, 300-342
Hill drafts, Chapter 14, 347-391
Rambouillet drafts, Section 15.B, 419-474